Fundamentals of Investments

Valuation and Management

The McGraw-Hill/Irwin Series in Finance, Insurance, and Real Estate

Stephen A. Ross
Franco Modigliani Professor of Finance and Economics
Sloan School of Management
Massachusetts Institute of Technology
Consulting Editor

Financial Management

Adair
Excel Applications for Corporate Finance
Second Edition

Benninga and Sarig
Corporate Finance: A Valuation Approach

Block and Hirt
Foundations of Financial Management
Twelfth Edition

Brealey, Myers, and Allen
Principles of Corporate Finance
Eighth Edition

Brealey, Myers, and Marcus
Fundamentals of Corporate Finance
Fifth Edition

Brooks
FinGame Online 4.0

Bruner
Case Studies in Finance: Managing
for Corporate Value Creation
Fifth Edition

Chew
The New Corporate Finance: Where Theory
Meets Practice
Third Edition

Chew and Gillan
Corporate Governance at the Crossroads:
A Book of Readings

DeMello
Cases in Finance
Second Edition

Grinblatt and Titman
Financial Markets and Corporate Strategy
Second Edition

Helfert
Techniques of Financial Analysis: A Guide to Value
Creation
Eleventh Edition

Higgins
Analysis for Financial Management
Eighth Edition

Kester, Ruback, and Tufano
Case Problems in Finance
Twelfth Edition

Ross, Westerfield, and Jaffe
Corporate Finance
Eighth Edition

Ross, Westerfield, Jaffe, and Jordan
Corporate Finance: Core Principles and Applications

Ross, Westerfield, and Jordan
Essentials of Corporate Finance
Fifth Edition

Ross, Westerfield, and Jordan
Fundamentals of Corporate Finance
Eighth Edition

Shefrin
Behavioral Corporate Finance: Decisions
That Create Value

White
Financial Analysis with an Electronic Calculator
Sixth Edition

Investments

Adair
Excel Applications for Investments

Bodie, Kane, and Marcus
Essentials of Investments
Sixth Edition

Bodie, Kane, and Marcus
Investments
Seventh Edition

Hirschey and Nofsinger
Investments: Analysis and Behavior

Hirt and Block
Fundamentals of Investment Management
Eighth Edition

Jordan and Miller
Fundamentals of Investments: Valuation and
Management
Fourth Edition

Financial Institutions and Markets

Rose and Hudgins
Bank Management and Financial Services
Seventh Edition

Rose and Marquis
Money and Capital Markets: Financial Institutions
and Instruments in a Global Marketplace
Ninth Edition

Saunders and Cornett
Financial Institutions Management: A Risk
Management Approach
Fifth Edition

Saunders and Cornett
Financial Markets and Institutions: An Introduction
to the Risk Management Approach
Third Edition

International Finance

Eun and Resnick
International Financial Management
Fourth Edition

Kuemmerle
Case Studies in International Entrepreneurship:
Managing and Financing Ventures in the Global
Economy

Real Estate

Brueggeman and Fisher
Real Estate Finance and Investments
Thirteenth Edition

Corgel, Ling, and Smith
Real Estate Perspectives: An Introduction
to Real Estate
Fourth Edition

Ling and Archer
Real Estate Principles: A Value Approach
Second Edition

Financial Planning and Insurance

Allen, Melone, Rosenbloom, and Mahoney
Pension Planning: Pension, Profit-Sharing, and Other
Deferred Compensation Plans
Ninth Edition

Altfest
Personal Financial Planning

Harrington and Niehaus
Risk Management and Insurance
Second Edition

Kapoor, Dlabay, and Hughes
Focus on Personal Finance: An Active Approach
to Help You Develop Successful Financial Skills

Kapoor, Dlabay, and Hughes
Personal Finance
Eighth Edition

Fundamentals of Investments
Valuation and Management

Fourth Edition

Bradford D. Jordan
University of Kentucky

Thomas W. Miller, Jr.
Saint Louis University

McGraw-Hill
Irwin

Boston   Burr Ridge, IL   Dubuque, IA   New York   San Francisco   St. Louis
Bangkok   Bogotá   Caracas   Kuala Lumpur   Lisbon   London   Madrid   Mexico City
Milan   Montreal   New Delhi   Santiago   Seoul   Singapore   Sydney   Taipei   Toronto

McGraw-Hill
Irwin

FUNDAMENTALS OF INVESTMENTS: VALUATION AND MANAGEMENT Published by McGraw-Hill/Irwin, a business unit of The McGraw-Hill Companies, Inc., 1221 Avenue of the Americas, New York, NY, 10020. Copyright © 2008 by The McGraw-Hill Companies, Inc. All rights reserved. No part of this publication may be reproduced or distributed in any form or by any means, or stored in a database or retrieval system, without the prior written consent of The McGraw-Hill Companies, Inc., including, but not limited to, in any network or other electronic storage or transmission, or broadcast for distance learning.

Some ancillaries, including electronic and print components, may not be available to customers outside the United States.

This book is printed on acid-free paper.

1 2 3 4 5 6 7 8 9 0 DOW/DOW 0 9 8 7 6

ISBN: 978-0-07-302721-0
MHID: 0-07-302721-9

Editorial director: *Brent Gordon*
Executive editor: *Michele Janicek*
Developmental editor II: *Jennifer V. Rizzi*
Marketing manager: *Julie Phifer*
Project manager: *Bruce Gin*
Lead production supervisor: *Michael R. McCormick*
Designer: *Cara David*
Lead media project manager: *Cathy L. Tepper*
Cover design: *Eric Kass,* Funnel
Interior design: *Amanda Kavanagh,* Art Design
Typeface: *10/12 Times Roman*
Compositor: *Interactive Composition Corporation*
Printer: *R. R. Donnelley*

Library of Congress Cataloging-in-Publication Data

Jordan, Bradford D.
    Fundamentals of investments : valuation and management / Bradford D. Jordan, Thomas W. Miller, Jr.--4th ed.
        p. cm.--(The McGraw-Hill/Irwin series in finance, insurance, and real estate)
    ISBN-13: 978-0-07-302721-0 (alk. paper)
    ISBN-10: 0-07-302721-9 (alk. paper)
    1. Investments. I. Miller, Thomas W. II. Title. III. Series.
HG4521.C66 2008
332.6--dc22

                                                                2006017644

www.mhhe.com

To my late father, S. Kelly Jordan Sr., a great stock picker.

BDJ

To my parents, Tom and Kathy Miller, my wife Carolyn, and #21—Thomas W. Miller, III.

TWM, Jr.

About the Authors

Bradford D. Jordan
Gatton College of Business and Economics, University of Kentucky

Bradford D. Jordan is Professor of Finance and holder of the Richard W. and Janis H. Furst Endowed Chair in Finance at the University of Kentucky. He has a long-standing interest in both applied and theoretical issues in investments, and he has extensive experience teaching all levels of investments. Professor Jordan has published numerous research articles on issues such as valuation of fixed-income securities, tax effects in investments analysis, the behavior of security prices, IPO valuation, and pricing of exotic options. He is co-author of *Fundamentals of Corporate Finance* and *Essentials of Corporate Finance*, two of the most widely used finance textbooks in the world.

Thomas W. Miller, Jr.
John Cook School of Business, Saint Louis University

Tom Miller is the Associate Dean for Academic Programs and Professor of Finance at the John Cook School of Business at Saint Louis University. Professor Miller has a long-standing interest in derivative securities and investments and has published numerous articles on various topics in these areas. Professor Miller has been honored with many research and teaching awards. Professor Miller is a co-author (with David Dubofsky) of *Derivatives: Valuation and Risk Management* (Oxford University Press). Professor Miller's interests include golf, skiing, and American saddlebred horses.

So why *did* we write this book?

As we toiled away, we asked ourselves this question many times, and the answer was always the same: *Our students made us.*

Traditionally, investments textbooks tend to fall into one of two camps. The first type has a greater focus on portfolio management and covers a significant amount of portfolio theory. The second type is more concerned with security analysis and generally contains fairly detailed coverage of fundamental analysis as a tool for equity valuation. Today, most texts try to cover all the bases by including some chapters drawn from one camp and some from another.

The result of trying to cover everything is either a very long book or one that forces the instructor to bounce back and forth between chapters. This frequently leads to a noticeable lack of consistency in treatment. Different chapters have completely different approaches: Some are computational, some are theoretical, and some are descriptive. Some do macroeconomic forecasting, some do mean-variance portfolio theory and beta estimation, and some do financial statements analysis. Options and futures are often essentially tacked on the back to round out this disconnected assortment.

The goal of these books is different from the goal of our students. Our students told us they come into an investments course wanting to learn how to make investment decisions. As time went by, we found ourselves supplying more and more supplemental materials to the texts we were using and constantly varying chapter sequences while chasing this elusive goal. We finally came to realize that the financial world had changed tremendously, and investments textbooks had fallen far behind in content and relevance.

What we really wanted, and what our students really needed, was a book that would do several key things:

- Focus on the students as investment managers by giving them information they can act on instead of concentrating on theories and research without the proper context.
- Offer strong, consistent pedagogy, including a balanced, unified treatment of the main types of financial investments as mirrored in the investment world.
- Organize topics in a way that would make them easy to apply—whether to a portfolio simulation or to real life—and support these topics with hands-on activities.

We made these three goals the guiding principles in writing this book. The next several sections explain our approach to each and why we think they are so important.

Who Is This Book For?

This book is aimed at introductory investments classes with students who have relatively little familiarity with investments. A typical student may have taken a principles of finance class and had some exposure to stocks and bonds, but not much beyond the basics. The introductory investments class is often a required course for finance majors, but students from other areas often take it as an elective. One fact of which we are acutely aware is that this may be the only investments class many students will ever take.

We intentionally wrote this book in a relaxed, informal style that engages the student and treats him or her as an active participant rather than a passive information absorber. We think the world of investments is exciting and fascinating, and we hope to share our considerable enthusiasm for investing with the student. We appeal to intuition and basic principles whenever possible because we have found that this approach effectively promotes understanding. We also make extensive use of examples throughout, drawing on "real world" material and familiar companies wherever appropriate.

By design, the text is not encyclopedic. As the table of contents indicates, we have a total of 20 chapters. Chapter length is about 30 to 40 pages, so the text is aimed at a single-term course; most of the book can be covered in a typical quarter or semester.

Aiming the book at a one-semester course necessarily means some picking and choosing, with regard to both topics and depth of coverage. Throughout, we strike a balance by introducing and covering the essentials while leaving some of the details to follow-up courses in security analysis, portfolio management, and options and futures.

How Does the Fourth Edition of This Book Expand upon the Goals Described Above?

Based on user feedback, we have made numerous improvements and refinements in the fourth edition of *Fundamentals of Investments: Valuation and Management.* We updated every chapter to reflect current market practices and conditions, and we significantly expanded and improved the end-of-chapter material. Also, in a notable change, we now have a chapter devoted to market efficiency and a chapter devoted to behavioral finance.

To give some examples of our additional new content:

- Chapter 3 introduces a detailed presentation of the NASD's new TRACE system and methods to obtain futures contract and option contract price quotes using the Internet.

- Chapter 6 contains a new section covering the residual income model (RIM).

- Chapter 7 has been expanded to include event studies, informed traders, insider trading, and illegal insider trading. New material includes the performance of professional money managers and stock market anomalies.

- Chapter 8 contains a substantial amount of new material on behavioral finance. In addition to a greatly expanded section on technical analysis, new material in this chapter includes prospect theory, overconfidence, misperceiving randomness, overreacting to chance events, sentiment-based risk, and limits to arbitrage.

- Chapter 10 discusses bond risk measures based on duration.

- Chapter 11 now illustrates the importance of asset allocation using three securities.

- Chapter 12 extends the CAPM with a discussion of the Fama-French three-factor model.

- Chapter 14 contains a new example of how to change the beta of a stock portfolio using stock index futures.

- Chapter 15 now includes a discussion of option "moneyness."

- Chapter 16 covers using an online calculator to value stock options and it now has a section about hedging stock with stock options.

- Chapter 17 (which was Chapter 7) now includes a section about financial statement forecasting using the percentage of sales approach with a detailed case study that values Starbucks Corporation.

- Chapter 18 covers make-whole call provisions.

- Chapter 19 has some enhanced material on U.S. Savings Bonds and updated material on the size of bid-ask spreads in municipal bond markets.

For the fourth edition, we significantly expanded and improved the end-of-chapter material. We added new problems throughout, and we increased the number of CFA questions. We created new questions that test understanding of concepts with no calculations involved. In addition, our *What's on the Web?* questions give students assignments to perform based on information they retrieve from various Web sites. Our *Standard & Poor's* Problems require the use of the educational version of Market Insight, which provides access to S&P's well-known Compustat database, and they provide instructors with an easy way to incorporate current, real-world data. Finally, in selected chapters, we have created spreadsheet assignments, which ask students to create certain types of spreadsheets to solve problems.

We continue to emphasize the use of the Web in investments analysis, and we integrate Web-based content in several ways. First, wherever appropriate, we provide a commented link in the margin. These links send readers to selected, particularly relevant Web sites. Second, our *Work the Web* feature, expanded and completely updated for this edition, appears in most chapters. These boxed readings use screen shots to show students how to access, use, and interpret various types of key financial and market data. Finally, as previously noted, new end-of-chapter problems rely on data retrieved from the Web.

We continue to provide *Spreadsheet Analysis* exhibits, which we have enhanced for this edition. These exhibits illustrate directly how to use spreadsheets to do certain types of important problems, including such computationally intensive tasks as calculating Macaulay duration, finding Black-Scholes-Merton option prices, and determining optimal portfolios based on Sharpe ratios. We also continue to provide, where relevant, readings from *The Wall Street Journal*, which have been thoroughly updated for this edition.

How Is This Book Relevant to the Student?

Fundamental changes in the investments universe drive our attention to relevance. The first major change is that individuals are being asked to make investment decisions for their own portfolios more often than ever before. There is, thankfully, a growing recognition that traditional "savings account" approaches to investing are decidedly inferior. At the same time, the use of employer-sponsored "investment accounts" has expanded enormously. The second major change is that the investments universe has exploded with an ever-increasing number of investment vehicles available to individual investors. As a result, investors must choose from an array of products, many of which are very complex, and they must strive to choose wisely.

Beyond this, students are more interested in subjects that affect them directly (aren't we all). By taking the point of view of the student as an investor, we are better able to illustrate and emphasize the relevance and importance of the material.

Our approach is evident in the table of contents. Our first chapter is motivational; we have found that this material effectively "hooks" students and even motivates a semester-long discourse on risk and return. Our second chapter answers the student's next natural question: "How do I get started investing and how do I buy and sell securities?" The third chapter surveys the different types of investments available. After only three chapters, very early in the term, students have learned something about the risks and rewards from investing, how to get started investing, and what investment choices are available.

We close the first part of the text with a detailed examination of mutual funds. Without a doubt, mutual funds have become the most popular investment vehicles for individual investors. There are now more mutual funds than there are stocks on the NYSE! Given the size and enormous growth in the mutual fund industry, this material is important for investors. Even so, investments texts typically cover mutual funds in a cursory way, often banishing the material to a back chapter under the obscure (and obsolete) heading of "investment companies." Our early placement lets students quickly explore a topic they have heard a lot about and are typically very interested in.

How Does This Book Allow Students to Apply the Investments Knowledge They Learn?

After studying this text, students will have the basic knowledge needed to move forward and actually act on what they have learned. We have developed two features to encourage students in making decisions as an investment manager. Learning to make good investment decisions comes with experience, while experience (regrettably) comes from making bad investment decisions. As much as possible, we press our students to get those bad decisions out of their systems before they start managing real money!

Not surprisingly, most students don't know how to get started in buying and selling securities. We have learned that providing some structure, especially with a portfolio simulation, greatly enhances the experience. Therefore, we have a series of *Get Real!* boxes. These boxes (at the end of each chapter) usually describe actual trades for students to explore. The intention is to show students how to gain real experience with the principles and instruments covered in the chapter. The second feature is a series of *Stock-Trak* exercises that take students through specific trading situations using *Stock-Trak Portfolio Simulations,* which can be found in the book's Web site, www.mhhe.com/jm4e.

Because we feel that portfolio simulations are so valuable, we have taken steps to assist instructors who, like us, plan to integrate portfolio simulations into their courses. Beyond the features mentioned above, we have organized the text so that the essential material needed before participating in a simulation is covered at the front of the book. Most notably, with every book, we have included a *free* subscription to *Stock-Trak Portfolio Simulations. Stock-Trak* is the leading provider of investment simulation services to the academic community; providing *Stock-Trak* free represents a significant cost savings to students. To our knowledge, ours is the first (and only) investments text to directly offer a full-featured online brokerage account simulation with the book at no incremental cost.

How Does This Book Maintain a Consistent, Unified Treatment?

In most investments texts, depth of treatment and presentation vary dramatically from instrument to instrument, which leaves the student without an overall framework for understanding the many types of investments. We stress early on that there are essentially only four basic types of financial investments—stocks, bonds, options, and futures. In parts 2 through 6, our simple goal is to take a closer look at each of these instruments. We take a unified approach to each by answering these basic questions:

1. What are the essential features of the instrument?
2. What are the possible rewards?
3. What are the risks?
4. What are the basic determinants of investment value?
5. For whom is the investment appropriate and under what circumstances?
6. How is the instrument bought and sold, and how does the market for the instrument operate?

By covering investment instruments in this way, we teach the students what questions to ask when looking at any potential investment.

Unlike other introductory investments texts, we devote several chapters beyond the basics to the different types of fixed-income investments. Students are often surprised to learn that the fixed-income markets are so much bigger than the equity markets and that money management opportunities are much more common in the fixed-income arena.

Possibly the best way to see this is to look at recent CFA exams and materials and note the extensive coverage of fixed-income topics. We have placed these chapters toward the back of the text because we recognize not everyone will want to cover all this material. We have also separated the subject into several shorter chapters to make it more digestible for students and to allow instructors more control over what is covered.

Acknowledgments

We have received extensive feedback from reviewers at each step along the way, and we are very grateful to the following dedicated scholars and teachers for their time and expertise:

Ann Hackert, Idaho State University

Allan Zebedee, San Diego State University

Carl R. Chen, University of Dayton

Charles Appeadu, University of Wisconsin–Madison

Christos Giannikos, Bernard M. Baruch College

David Dubofsky, University of Louisville

David Louton, Bryant College

David Loy, Illinois State University

David Peterson, Florida State University

Deborah Murphy, University of Tennessee–Knoxville

Donald Wort, California State University–East Bay

David Stewart, Winston-Salem State University

Edward Miller, University of New Orleans

Felix Ayadi, Fayetteville State University

Gioia Bales, Hofstra University

Gay B. Hatfield, University of Mississippi

Howard Van Auken, Iowa State University

Howard W. Bohnen, St. Cloud State University

Joe Brocato, Tarleton State University

John Paul Broussard, Rutgers, The State University of New Jersey

Jorge Omar R. Brusa, University of Arkansas

Ji Chen, University of Colorado

Johnny Chan, University of Dayton

John Clinebell, University of Northern Colorado

John Romps, St. Anselm College

Jim Tipton, Baylor University

Joe Walker, University of Alabama–Birmingham

John Wingender, Creighton University

Jeff Edwards, Portland Community College

Jeff Manzi, Ohio University

Kerri McMillan, Clemson University

Lalatendu Misra, University of Texas at San Antonio

Lisa Schwartz, Wingate University

Linda Martin, Arizona State University

Michael C. Ehrhardt, University of Tennessee–Knoxville

Matthew Fung, Saint Peter's College

M. J. Murray, Winona State University

Michael Nugent, SUNY–Stony Brook

Nozar Hashemzadeh, Radford University

Paul Bolster, Northeastern University

Percy S. Poon, University of Nevada, Las Vegas

Patricia Clarke, Simmons College

Richard W. Taylor, Arkansas State University

Ronald Christner, Loyola University–New Orleans

Scott Barnhart, Clemson University

Scott Beyer, University of Wisconsin–Oshkosh

Samira Hussein, Johnson County Community College

Stuart Michelson, University of Central Florida

Steven Lifland, High Point University

Stephen Chambers, Johnson County Community College

Steve Meyer, Saint Louis University

Samuel H. Penkar, University of Houston

Thomas M. Krueger, University of Wisconsin–La Crosse

William Compton, University of North Carolina–Wilmington

William Lepley, University of Wisconsin–Green Bay

William Elliott, Oklahoma State University

Yvette Harman, Miami University of Ohio

Zekeriah Eser, Eastern Kentucky University

We'd like to thank Kay Johnson, Penn State University–Erie, for developing the Test Bank and the self-study questions.

The following doctoral and MBA students did outstanding work on this text: Pankaj Maskara, John Gonas, Hinh Khieu, Luke Johnson, Steve Kelemen, and Janell Nelson; to them fell the unenviable task of technical proofreading and, in particular, careful checking of each calculation throughout the text and supplements.

We are deeply grateful to the select group of professionals who served as our development team on this edition: Michele Janicek, Executive Sponsoring Editor; Jen Rizzi, Development Editor II; Julie Phifer, Marketing Manager; Bruce Gin, Project Manager; Cara David, Designer; and Michael McCormick, Production Supervisor.

Bradford D. Jordan

Thomas W. Miller, Jr.

Coverage

This book was designed and developed explicitly for a first course in investments taken by either finance majors or nonfinance majors. In terms of background or prerequisites, the book is nearly self-contained, but some familiarity with basic algebra and accounting is assumed. The organization of the text has been designed to give instructors the flexibility they need to teach a quarter-long or semester-long course.

To present an idea of the breadth of coverage in the fourth edition of *Fundamentals of investments,* the following grid is presented chapter by chapter. This grid contains some of the most significant new features and a few selected chapter highlights. Of course, for each chapter, features like opening vignettes, *Work the Web, Spreadsheet Analyses, Get Real, Investment Updates,* and end-of-chapter material have been thoroughly reviewed and updated.

Chapters	Selected Topics of Interest	Learning Objective/Comment
>> PART ONE Introduction		
Chapter 1 A Brief History of Risk and Return	Dollar returns and percentage returns.	Average returns differ by asset class.
	Return variability and calculating variance and standard deviation.	Return variability also differs by asset class.
	Arithmetic versus geometric returns.	Geometric average tells you what you actually earned per year, compounded annually. Arithmetic returns tell you what you earned in a typical year.
	The risk-return trade-off.	Historically, higher returns are associated with higher risk.
Chapter 2 Buying and Selling Securities	Brokerage accounts and choosing a broker.	Discussion of the different types of brokers and accounts available to an individual investor.
	Short sales.	Description of the process of short-selling stock.
	Investor objectives, constraints, and strategies.	Presentation of issues like risk and return, resource constraints, market timing, and asset allocation.
Chapter 3 Overview of Security Types	Classifying securities.	Interest-bearing, equity, and derivative securities.
	New Material: NASD's new TRACE system and transparency in the corporate bond market.	Up-to-date discussion of new developments in fixed income markets with respect to price, volume, and transactions reporting.
	Equity securities.	Obtain price quotes for equity securities.
	Derivative securities. *New Material:* Obtaining futures contract and option contract price quotes using the Internet.	Define the types of derivative securities, interpreting their price quotes, and calculating gains and losses from these securities.

Coverage (cont.)

Chapters	Selected Topics of Interest	Learning Objective/Comment
Chapter 4 Mutual Funds	Investment companies and types of funds.	Covers concepts like open-end versus closed-end funds and net asset value.
	Mutual fund organization, creation, costs, and fees.	Present types of expenses and fees, like front-end loads, 12b-1 fees, management fees, and turnover.
	Short-term funds, long-term funds, and fund performance.	Discussion of money market mutual funds versus the variety of available stock and bond funds and how to find their performance.
	Special funds like closed-end funds, exchange-traded funds, and hedge funds.	The closed-end fund discount mystery and a discussion of exchange-traded funds (ETFs).

Chapters	Selected Topics of Interest	Learning Objective/Comment
Chapter 7 Stock Price Behavior and Market Efficiency	Forms of market efficiency.	The effects of information on stock prices with respect to market efficiency.
	New Material: Event studies using actual events surrounding Elan Corporation.	Explains how new information gets into stock prices and how researchers measure it.
	New Material: Informed traders, insider trading, and illegal insider trading.	*New Example*: Martha Stewart and ImClone.
	Expanded Material: Market efficiency and the performance of professional money managers.	Discusses the performance of professional money managers versus static benchmarks.
	Expanded Material: Anomalies.	Presentation of the day-of-the-week effect, the amazing January effect, the turn-of-the-year effect, and the turn-of-the-month effect.
	New Material: Bubbles and crashes.	Shows the extent of famous events like the crash of 1929, the crash of October 1987, the Asian market crash, and the "dot-com" bubble and crash.
Chapter 8 *New Chapter* Behavioral Finance and the Psychology of Investing	*New Material*: Introduction to behavioral finance.	The influence of reasoning errors on investor decisions.
	New Material: Prospect theory.	How investors tend to behave differently when faced with prospective gains and losses.
	New Material: Overconfidence, misperceiving randomness, and overreacting to chance events.	Examines the consequences of these serious errors in judgment.
	New Material: Sentiment-based risk and limits to arbitrage.	*New Examples*: 3Com/Palm mispricing, the Royal Dutch/Shell price ratio.
	Expanded Material: Technical analysis.	*New Material*: Elliott waves, expanded discussions of charting, moving averages, MACD, money flow, and Fibonacci numbers.

>> PART THREE   Interest Rates and Bond Valuation

Chapter 9 Interest Rates	Interest rate history, *New Example*: A quick review of the time value of money.	A graphical presentation of the long-term history of interest rates.
	Money market rates and their prices.	Important money market concepts including pricing U.S. Treasury bills, bank discount yields versus bond equivalent yields, annual percentage rates, and effective annual returns.
	Rates and yields on fixed-income securities.	The Treasury yield curve, the term structure of interest rates, and Treasury STRIPS.
	Nominal versus real interest rates.	The Fisher hypothesis.
	Determinants of nominal interest rates.	Problems with traditional theories and modern term structure theory.

Coverage (cont.)

Chapters	Selected Topics of Interest	Learning Objective/Comment
Chapter 10 Bond Prices and Yields	Straight bond prices and yield to maturity (YTM).	Calculate straight bond prices and yield to maturity.
	Duration. *New Material*: Bond risk measures based on duration.	Calculate and interpret a bond's duration. The dollar value of an 01, yield value of a 32nd.
	Immunization.	Minimize the uncertainty concerning the value of a bond portfolio at its target date.

>> PART FOUR   Portfolio Management

Chapters	Selected Topics of Interest	Learning Objective/Comment
Chapter 11 Diversification and Risky Asset Allocation	Expected returns and variances.	Calculate expected returns and variances using equal and unequal probabilities.
	Portfolios and the effect of diversification on portfolio risk.	Compute portfolio weights, expected returns, variances, and why diversification works.
	The importance of asset allocation.	The effect of correlation on the risk-return trade-off.
	The Markowitz efficient frontier. *New Material*: Illustrating the importance of asset allocation using three securities.	Compute risk-return combinations using various portfolio weights for three assets.
Chapter 12 Return, Risk, and the Security Market Line	Diversification, systematic and unsystematic risk.	Total risk is comprised of unsystematic and systematic risk and only unsystematic risk can be reduced through diversification.
	Measuring systematic risk with beta.	The average beta is 1.00. Assets with a beta greater than 1.00 have more than average systematic risk.
	The security market line and the reward-to-risk ratio.	The security market line describes how the market rewards risk. All assets will have the same reward-to-risk ratio in a competitive financial market.
	The capital asset pricing model (CAPM).	Expected return depends on the reward for bearing systematic risk as well as the pure time value of money.
	New Material: Extending CAPM.	One of the most important extensions of the CAPM is the Fama-French three-factor model.

Chapters	Selected Topics of Interest	Learning Objective/Comment
Chapter 13 Performance Evaluation and Risk Management	Performance evaluation measures.	Calculate and interpret the Sharpe ratio, the Treynor ratio, and Jensen's alpha.
	Sharpe optimal portfolios.	The portfolio with the highest possible Sharpe ratio given the assets comprising the portfolio is Sharpe optimal.
	Value-at-Risk (VaR).	VaR is the evaluation of the probability of a significant loss.
	Enhanced Example: VaR for a Sharpe optimal portfolio.	Combine the concepts of a Sharpe ratio, a Sharpe optimal portfolio, and VaR.

>> PART FIVE   Futures and Options

Chapters	Selected Topics of Interest	Learning Objective/Comment
Chapter 14 Futures Contracts	The basics of futures contracts and using them to hedge price risk.	Futures quotes from the Internet and financial press, short and long hedging, futures accounts.
	Spot-futures parity.	Basis, cash markets, and cash-futures arbitrage.
	Stock index futures. *New Example*: Changing the beta of a stock portfolio using stock index futures.	Index arbitrage, speculating with stock index futures, and hedging stock market risk with stock index futures.
	Hedging interest rate risk with futures.	Show how to use portfolio duration when deciding how many futures contracts to use to hedge a bond portfolio.
Chapter 15 Stock Options	Option basics and option quotes. *New Material*: Stock option ticker symbols.	The difference between call and put options, European and American options, online option price quotes, and option chains.
	Option payoffs and profits. *New Material*: Option "moneyness."	Diagram long and short option payoffs and profits for calls and puts.
	Option strategies.	Protective puts, covered calls, and straddles.
	Employee stock options (ESOs).	Features of ESOs and repricing ESOs.
	Put-call parity.	Show how a call option price equals a put option price, the price of an underlying share of stock, and appropriate borrowing.

Coverage (cont.)

Features

Pedagogical Features

From your feedback, we have included many pedagogical features in this text that will be valuable learning tools for your students. This walkthrough highlights some of the most important elements.

Chapter Openers ———→

These one-paragraph introductions for each chapter present facts and misconceptions that may surprise you. An explanation is more fully developed in the chapter.

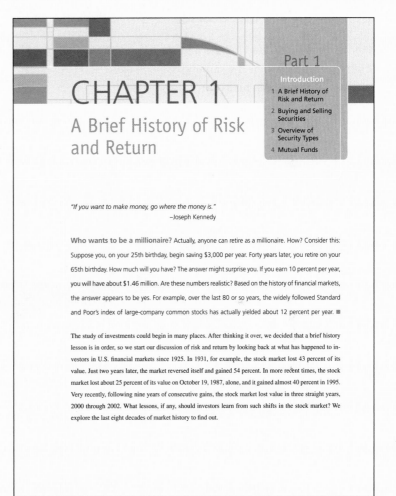

CHAPTER 1

A Brief History of Risk and Return

Part 1

Introduction

1 A Brief History of Risk and Return

2 Buying and Selling Securities

3 Overview of Security Types

4 Mutual Funds

"If you want to make money, go where the money is."
–Joseph Kennedy

Who wants to be a millionaire? Actually, anyone can retire as a millionaire. How? Consider this: Suppose you, on your 25th birthday, begin saving $3,000 per year. Forty years later, you retire on your 65th birthday. How much will you have? The answer might surprise you. If you earn 10 percent per year, you will have about $1.46 million. Are these numbers realistic? Based on the history of financial markets, the answer appears to be yes. For example, over the last 80 or so years, the widely followed Standard and Poor's index of large-company common stocks has actually yielded about 12 percent per year. ∎

The study of investments could begin in many places. After thinking it over, we decided that a brief history lesson is in order, so we start our discussion of risk and return by looking back at what has happened to investors in U.S. financial markets since 1925. In 1931, for example, the stock market lost 43 percent of its value. Just two years later, the market reversed itself and gained 54 percent. In more recent times, the stock market lost about 25 percent of its value on October 19, 1987, alone, and it gained almost 40 percent in 1995. Very recently, following nine years of consecutive gains, the stock market lost value in three straight years, 2000 through 2002. What lessons, if any, should investors learn from such shifts in the stock market? We explore the last eight decades of market history to find out.

Web Addresses

Web sites are called out in the margins, along with a notation of how they relate to the chapter material.

	Case 1	Case 2
Ending Stock Price	$40.33	$34.78
January 1 value	$3,700	$3,700
December 31 value	4,033	3,478
Dividend income	185	185
Capital gain or loss	333	−222

At the beginning of the year, on January 1, the stock is selling for $37 per share, and, as we calculated above, your total outlay for 100 shares is $3,700. Over the year, Harley pays dividends of $1.85 per share. By the end of the year, then, you received dividend income of

$$\text{Dividend income} = \$1.85 \times 100 = \$185$$

As in Case 1, suppose that as of December 31, Harley was selling for $40.33, meaning that the value of your stock increased by $3.33 per share. Your 100 shares are now worth $4,033, so you have a capital gain of

$$\text{Capital gain} = (\$40.33 - \$37) \times 100 = \$333$$

On the other hand, if the price had dropped to, say, $34.78 (Case 2), you would have a capital loss of

$$\text{Capital loss} = (\$34.78 - \$37) \times 100 = -\$222$$

Notice that a capital loss is the same thing as a negative capital gain.

The **total dollar return** on your investment is the sum of the dividend and the capital gain (or loss):

$$\text{Total dollar return} = \text{Dividend income} + \text{Capital gain (or loss)}$$

In our first example here, the total dollar return is thus given by

$$\text{Total dollar return} = \$185 + \$333 = \$518$$

Key Terms

Key terms are indicated in bold and defined in the margin. The running glossary in the margin helps students quickly review the basic terminology for the chapter.

total dollar return
The return on an investment measured in dollars that accounts for all cash flows and capital gains or losses.

Now that you know how to calculate returns on a hypothetical stock, you should begin looking at real stocks. The nearby *Work the Web* box describes how to get going. Meanwhile, in the next several sections, we will take a look at the returns that some common types of investments have earned over the last 80 years.

Check This!

Every major section in each chapter ends with questions for review. This feature helps students test their understanding of the material before moving on to the next section.

CHECK THIS

1.1a What are the two parts of total return?
1.1b Why are unrealized capital gains or losses included in the calculation of returns?
1.1c What is the difference between a dollar return and a percentage return? Why are percentage returns usually more convenient?

Investment Updates

These boxed readings, reprinted from various business press sources, provide additional real-world events and examples to illustrate the material in the chapter. Some articles are from the past two years to highlight very recent events, and others present events of more historical significance.

INVESTMENT UPDATES

AFTER 30 YEARS OF INVESTING, MARKET HAS NO SURE THING

The stock market exists to enrich investors, while utterly humiliating them. With great regularity, I receive e-mails from readers who are convinced that you should own only blue-chip companies, or only high-dividend stocks, or only technology companies. And all I can think about is the market's litany of once-sure things. It happens again and again. Hot stocks turn cold. Highflying stock funds crash and burn. Time-tested stock-picking strategies suddenly falter. To understand just how capricious the market can be, consider results from the past three decades.

As the Decades Turn

Take a look at the accompanying table (Swings and Roundabouts), which shows returns calculated by Baltimore's T. Rowe Price Associates using data from Chicago's Ibbotson Associates. In particular, focus on the performance of large, small and foreign stocks in each of the past three decades. I think of these as the three key stock-market sectors.

As you will see, large-company stocks—which are so beloved after their dazzling gains in the 1990s—didn't fare quite so well in the prior two decades. They ranked second behind foreign stocks in the 1980s and they lagged behind both small and foreign stocks in the 1970s. Similarly, small stocks ranked first in the 1970s, second in the 1990s and third in the 1980s. Meanwhile, foreign stocks were first in the 1980s, second in the 1970s and third in the 1990s.

In other words, none of the sectors consistently ranked as the top performer and all had periods of dreadful performance. Moreover, if you look at results for the 30 years through December 2001, there isn't a huge difference between the average annual returns for large, small and foreign stocks. Of course, if you were really clever, you would figure out which sector was going to be the decade's top performer,

and then invest everything in that sector. But I am not smart enough to make that sort of market call, and I don't think anybody else is, either.

Gerald Perritt, a money manager in Largo, Fla., and editor of the Mutual Fund Letter, a monthly newsletter, says he has lately met many investors who got themselves into financial trouble. All have one thing in common: They failed to diversify and instead made big investment bets that turned sour. "Diversification is good," Mr. Perritt says. "But if it's so good, why don't more people practice it? Return is the most visible element in the investing process. The least visible is risk. People see the return they miss by diversifying. We don't think about what will happen if a big bet goes in the wrong direction."

My hunch is that the current decade will be a lackluster one for blue-chip shares. Large-company stocks have been dazzling performers over the past two decades, and now they are burdened by lofty share price-to-earnings multiples and boast only skimpy dividend yields. Indeed, I suspect foreign and small stocks will prove to be the market's new darlings. But I am unwilling to invest based on such hunches. So what should an investor do? Owning a little bit of everything that has worked well in the past, and it still seems like a mighty fine strategy to me.

Glancing at the performance of narrower market sectors strengthens the case for humility. In the past two years, three of the market's best-performing segments have been gold, bargain-priced "value" stocks and realestate investment trusts, or REITs. Meanwhile, "growth" stocks, including once-sparkling technology shares, have been crushed. But look at the accompanying table to see results from earlier decades. Unfortunately, data aren't available for all time periods. Still, there are enough results to see how unpredictable market returns can be. Sure, value stocks were strong performers in 2000

Work the Web

Various actual screenshots are showcased throughout the text to illustrate how to access specific features of selected Web sites.

Numbered Examples

Separate numbered and titled examples are integrated throughout the chapters. Each example illustrates an intuitive or mathematical application in a step-by-step format. There is enough detail in the explanations so that the student doesn't have to look elsewhere for additional information.

EXAMPLE 1.1   Calculating Percentage Returns

Suppose you buy some stock for $25 per share. After one year, the price is $35 per share. During the year, you received a $2 dividend per share. What is the dividend yield? The capital gains yield? The percentage return? If your total investment was $1,000, how much do you have at the end of the year?

Your $2 dividend per share works out to a dividend yield of

$$\text{Dividend yield} = D_{t+1} / P_t$$
$$= \$2/\$25$$
$$= 8\%$$

(continued)

Chapter 1 ■ A Brief History of Risk and Return   5

Spreadsheet Analysis

Self-contained spreadsheet examples show students how to set up spreadsheets to solve problems—a vital part of every business student's education.

Now that you know how to calculate and, more importantly, interpret average returns and standard deviations, the nearby *Spreadsheet Analysis* box shows how to do the calculations using Excel, which can really speed up things when we have a lot of data.

SPREADSHEET ANALYSIS

Using a Spreadsheet to Calculate Average Returns and Volatilities

Here is an Excel spreadsheet summarizing the formulas and analysis needed to calculate average returns and standard deviations using the 1990s as an example:

	A	B	C	D	E	F	G	H
1								
2		Using a spreadsheet to calculate average returns and standard deviations						
3								
4	Looking back in the chapter, the data suggest that the 1990s were one							
5	of the best decades for stock market investors. We will find out just how good by							
6	calculating the average returns and standard deviations for this period. Here are the							
7	year-by-year returns on the large company S&P 500 index:							
8								
9		Year	Return(%)	Year	Return(%)			
10		1990	−3.10	1995	37.58			
11		1991	30.46	1996	22.96			
12		1992	7.62	1997	33.36			
13		1993	10.08	1998	28.58			
14		1994	1.32	1999	21.04			
15								
16		Average return (%):	18.99					
17		Standard deviation (%):	14.16					
18								
19	The formulas we used to do the calculations are just =AVERAGE(C10:C14;E10:E14)							
20	and =STDEV(C10:C14;E10:E14). Notice that the average return in the 1990s was 18.99							
21	percent per year, which is larger than the long-run average of 12.3 percent. At the same							
22	time, the standard deviation, 14.16 percent, was smaller than the 20.2 percent long-run value.							

Numbered Equations →

Key equations are highlighted and numbered sequentially in each chapter for easy reference.

dividend yield
The annual stock dividend as a percentage of the initial stock price.

capital gains yield
The change in stock price as a percentage of the initial stock price.

total percent return
The return on an investment measured as a percentage that accounts for all cash flows and capital gains or losses.

In our example, the price at the beginning of the year was $37 per share and the dividend paid during the year on each share was $1.85. If we express this dividend as a percentage of the beginning stock price, the result is the **dividend yield**:

$$\text{Dividend yield} = D_{t+1} / P_t \qquad (1.1)$$
$$= \$1.85 / \$37 = .05 = 5\%$$

This says that for each dollar we invested we received 5 cents in dividends.

The second component of our percentage return is the **capital gains yield**. This yield is calculated as the change in the price during the year (the capital gain) divided by the beginning price. With the $40.33 ending price, we get:

$$\text{Capital gains yield} = (P_{t+1} - P_t) / P_t \qquad (1.2)$$
$$= (\$40.33 - \$37) / \$37$$
$$= \$3.33 / \$37 = .09 = 9\%$$

This 9 percent yield means that for each dollar invested we got 9 cents in capital gains.

Putting it all together, per dollar invested, we get 5 cents in dividends and 9 cents in capital gains for a total of 14 cents. Our **total percent return** is 14 cents on the dollar, or 14 percent. When a return is expressed on a percentage basis, we often refer to it as the *rate of return,* or just "return," on the investment. Notice that if we combine the formulas for the dividend yield and capital gains yield, we get a single formula for the total percentage return:

$$\text{Percentage return} = \text{Dividend yield} + \text{Capital gains yield} \qquad (1.3)$$
$$= D_{t+1} / P_t + (P_{t+1} - P_t) / P_t$$
$$= (D_{t+1} + P_{t+1} - P_t) / P_t$$

Figures and Tables →

This text makes extensive use of real data and presents them in various figures and tables. Explanations in the narrative, examples, and end-of-chapter problems will refer to many of these exhibits.

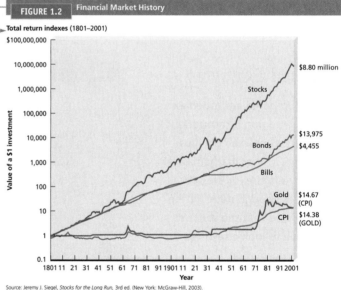

FIGURE 1.2   Financial Market History

Total return indexes (1801–2001)

Source: Jeremy J. Siegel, *Stocks for the Long Run,* 3rd ed. (New York: McGraw-Hill, 2003).

Summary and Conclusions ⟶

Each chapter ends with a summary that highlights the important points of the chapter. This provides a handy checklist for students when they review the chapter.

4.8 Summary and Conclusions

We have covered many aspects of mutual fund investing in this chapter. We have seen that there are thousands of mutual funds and dozens of types. A few of the more important distinctions we made can be summarized as follows:

1. Some funds are open-end and some are closed-end. Open-end funds stand ready to buy or sell shares. Closed-end funds do not; instead, their shares trade on the stock exchanges.

2. Some open-end funds have front-end loads, meaning that there is a fee tacked on to the fund's net asset value when you buy. Other funds are no-load. Various costs and fees exist, including back-end loads and 12b-1 fees.

3. Funds have very different objectives and, as a result, very different risk and return potentials. Furthermore, funds with similar-sounding objectives can, in fact, be quite different. It is important to consider a fund's actual holdings and investment policies, not just read its stated objective.

4. Mutual fund information is widely available, but performance information should be used with caution. The best performing funds are often the ones with the greatest risks or the ones that just happened to be in the right investment at the right time.

Get Real!

For instructors looking to give their students a taste of what it means to be an investment manager, this feature (at the end of each chapter) acts as a first step by explaining to students how they can actually apply the material they just learned. The *Get Real* boxes encourage students—whether for practice in a trading simulation, or with real money—to make investment decisions, and they also give some helpful tips to keep in mind.

Chapter Review Problems and Self-Test

Students are provided with one to three practice problems per chapter with worked-out solutions to test their abilities in solving key problems related to the content of the chapter.

Test Your IQ

An average of 15 multiple-choice questions are included for each chapter, many of which are taken from past CFA exams. This text is unique in that it is the only text that presents CFA questions in multiple-choice format—which is how they appear on the actual exam. Answers to these questions appear in Appendix A.

GET REAL

This chapter covered the basics of brokerage accounts, some important trade types, and, finally, some big-picture issues regarding investment strategies and objectives. How should you, as an investor or investment manager, put this information to work?

The answer is that you need to open a brokerage account! Investing is like many activities; the best way to learn is by making mistakes. Unfortunately, making mistakes with real money is an expensive way to learn, so we don't recommend trying things like short sales with real money, at least not at first.

Instead, to learn about how to trade and gain some experience with making (and losing) money, you should open a Stock-Trak account (or a similar simulated brokerage account). Take it seriously. Try various trade types and strategies and see how they turn out. The important thing to do is to follow your trades and try to understand why you made or lost money and also why you made or lost the amount you did.

In a similar vein, you should carefully review your account statements to make sure you understand exactly what each item means and how your account equity is calculated.

After you have gained some experience trading "on paper," you should open a real account as soon as you can pull together enough money. Try visiting some on-line brokers such as Ameritrade to find out the minimum amount you need to open an account. The amount has been declining. In 2005, you could open a cash account for as little as $500, but to open a margin account, you need in the area of $2,000. Or, you can visit www.sharebuilder.com and www.buyandhold.com to open accounts with no money at all!

Looking back at Chapter 1, you know that it's important to get started early. Once you have a real account, however, it's still a good idea to keep a separate "play money" account to test trading ideas to make sure you really understand them before committing your precious real money.

Chapter Review Problems and Self-Test

1. **The Account Balance Sheet** Suppose you want to buy 10,000 shares of Intel Corporation at a price of $30 per share. You put up $200,000 and borrow the rest. What does your account balance sheet look like? What is your margin?

2. **Short Sales** Suppose that in the previous problem you shorted 10,000 shares instead of buying. The initial margin is 60 percent. What does the account balance sheet look like following the short?

3. **Margin Calls** You purchased 500 shares of stock at a price of $56 per share on 50 percent margin. If the maintenance margin is 30 percent, what is the critical stock price?

Answers to Self-Test Problems

1. The 10,000 shares of Intel cost $300,000. You supply $200,000, so you must borrow $100,000. The account balance sheet looks like this:

Assets		Liabilities and Account Equity	
10,000 shares of Intel	$300,000	Margin loan	$100,000
		Account equity	200,000
Total	$300,000	Total	$300,000

Your margin is the account equity divided by the value of the stock owned:

Margin = $200,000/$300,000
= .666 . . .
= 67%

2. Following the short, your account is as follows:

Assets		Liabilities and Account Equity	
Proceeds from sale	$300,000	Short position	$300,000
Initial margin deposit	180,000	Account equity	180,000
Total	$480,000	Total	$480,000

Notice that you shorted $300,000 worth of stock, so, with a 60 percent margin requirement, you deposited $180,000.

Chapter 2 ■ Buying and Selling Securities   65

Test Your Investment Quotient

1. **Investment Objectives** An individual investor's investment objectives should be expressed in terms of:
   a. Risk and return.
   b. Capital market expectations.
   c. Liquidity needs and time horizon.
   d. Tax factors and legal and regulatory constraints.

2. **Asset Allocation** Which of the following best reflects the importance of the asset allocation decision to the investment process? The asset allocation decision:
   a. Helps the investor decide on realistic investment goals.
   b. Identifies the specific securities to include in a portfolio.
   c. Determines most of the portfolio's returns and volatility over time.
   d. Creates a standard by which to establish an appropriate investment horizon.

3. **Leverage** You deposit $100,000 cash in a brokerage account and purchase $200,000 of stocks on margin by borrowing $100,000 from your broker. Later, the value of your stock holdings falls to $150,000, whereupon you get nervous and close your account. What is the percentage return on your investment (ignore interest paid)?
   a. 0 percent
   b. −25 percent
   c. −50 percent
   d. −75 percent

4. **Leverage** You deposit $100,000 cash in a brokerage account and short sell $200,000 of stocks. Later, the value of the stocks held short rises to $250,000, whereupon you get nervous and close your account. What is the percentage return on your investment?
   a. 0 percent
   b. −25 percent
   c. −50 percent
   d. −75 percent

5. **Account Margin** You deposit $100,000 cash in a brokerage account and purchase $200,000 of stocks on margin by borrowing $100,000 from your broker. Later, the value of your stock holdings falls to $175,000. What is your account margin in dollars?
   a. $50,000
   b. $75,000
   c. $100,000
   d. $150,000

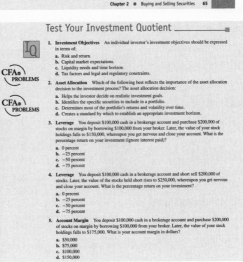

www.mhhe.com/jm4e

Concept Questions

At the end of every chapter are 10 to 15 concept questions that further reinforce key concepts found throughout the chapter.

Questions and Problems

A variety of problems (average of 20 per chapter) are included in each chapter to test students' understanding of the conceptual and mathematical elements. Each problem is labeled with the subject and the level—core or intermediate. Selected answers appear in Appendix B, and complete solutions are included in the Instructor's Manual.

www.mhhe.com/jm4e

Concept Questions

1. **Margin** What does it mean to purchase a security on margin? Why might you do it?
2. **Short Sales** What does it mean to sell a security short? Why might you do it?
3. **Margin Requirements** What is the reason margin requirements exist?
4. **Allocation versus Selection** What is the difference between asset allocation and security selection?
5. **Allocation versus Timing** Are market timing and active asset allocation similar? Why or why not?
6. **Street Name Registration** Why is street name registration advantageous to investors? Under what circumstances is it required?
7. **Broker–Customer Relations** Suppose your broker tips you on a hot stock. You invest heavily, but, to your considerable dismay, the stock plummets in value. What recourse do you have against your broker?
8. **Long Profits** An important difference between a long position in stock and a short position concerns the potential gains and losses. Suppose a stock sells for $18 per share, and you buy 500 shares. What are your potential gains and losses?
9. **Liquidity** The liquidity of an asset directly affects the risk of buying or selling that asset during adverse market conditions. Describe the liquidity risk you face with a short stock position during a market rally, and a long stock position during a market decline.
10. **Short Sale Profits** Suppose you sell short 1,000 shares of a stock at $60 per share. Ignoring borrowing costs and fees, what is the maximum profit you can earn from this investment? What is the potential maximum loss?

Questions and Problems

Core Questions

1. **Calculating Margin** Simmons Corporation stock sells for $83 per share, and you've decided to purchase as many shares as you possibly can. You have $13,000 available to invest. What is the maximum number of shares you can buy if the initial margin is 50 percent?
2. **Margin** You purchase 400 shares of Omni Co. stock on margin at a price of $65. Your broker requires you to deposit $15,000. What is your margin loan amount? What is the initial margin requirement?
3. **Margin Return** In the previous problem, suppose you sell the stock at a price of $75. What is your return? What would your return have been had you purchased the stock without margin? What if the stock price is $65 when you sell the stock?
4. **Margin** Repeat the previous two problems assuming the initial margin requirement is 40 percent. Does this suggest a relationship between the initial margin and returns?

S&P Problems

Now included in the end-of-chapter material are problems directly incorporating the Educational Version of Market Insight, a service based on Standard & Poor's renowned Compustat database. These problems provide an easy method of including current real-world data into the course.

What's on the Web?

These three to five end-of-chapter activities show students how to use and learn from the vast amount of financial resources available on the Internet.

www.mhhe.com/jm4e

STANDARD
&POOR'S

S&P Problems

www.mhhe.com/edumarketinsight

1. **Margin** Download the historical stock prices for Tootsie Roll Industries (TR) under the "Mthly. Adj. Prices" link. Assume you purchased 400 shares of Tootsie Roll stock at the closing price six months ago. The initial margin requirement is 50 percent and the maintenance margin is 30 percent. Show the account balance sheet based on monthly closing prices for the last five months. At what stock price will you receive a margin call? Are any margin deposits required over this period? What is your return on this investment?
2. **Short Sales** Download the historical stock prices for Ford (F) under the "Mthly. Adj. Prices" link. Assume you short sold 200 shares of Ford stock at the closing price six months ago. The initial margin requirement is 50 percent and the maintenance margin is 30 percent. Show the account balance sheet based on monthly closing prices for the last five months. At what stock price will you receive a margin call? Are any margin deposits required over this period? What is your return on this investment?

What's on the Web?

1. **Risk Tolerance** As we discussed in the chapter, risk tolerance is based on an individual's personality and investment goals. There are numerous risk tolerance questionnaires on the Web. One, provided by Merrill Lynch, is located at individual.ml.com. Go to the Web site, locate the questionnaire, and take the quiz. How conservative or aggressive are you?
2. **Short Interest** You can find the number of short sales on a particular stock at finance.yahoo.com. Go to the site and find the number of shares short sold for ExxonMobil (XOM) under the "Profile" link. How many shares are sold short in the current month? What about the previous month? What do the "Percent of Float" and "Short Ratio" mean?

Stock-Trak Exercises ⟶

Unique to this text! This text is the only book that incorporates Stock-Trak Portfolio Simulations® exercises. Stock-Trak is one of the most successful trading simulations with over 30,000 college students having trading accounts each semester (see Supplements for more information). Go to the next level in teaching your students about investments management by encouraging your students to use this product. Chapters with Stock-Trak Exercises will have the logo and the URL for the book's Web site. The actual exercise and questions related to the chapter will be presented in both the Student and Instructor portions of the Web site. Instructors and Students must be registered for Stock-Trak in order to make trades (see the Supplement Section of the Preface or the insert card for more information.)

Stock-Trak Exercises

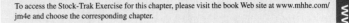

STOCK|TRAK
GLOBAL PORTFOLIO SIMULATIONS

To access the Stock-Trak Exercise for this chapter, please visit the book Web site at www.mhhe.com/jm4e and choose the corresponding chapter.

STOCK|TRAK
GLOBAL PORTFOLIO SIMULATIONS

Trading Mutual Funds and ETFs with Stock-Trak

Stock-Trak allows you to trade mutual funds and ETFs as simply as it allows you to trade common stocks. There are restrictions: You cannot use margin to buy mutual fund shares and fund shares cannot be sold short. You should consult the most recent rules at the Stock-Trak Web site (www.stocktrak.com) for other restrictions that might apply.

To trade mutual funds with Stock-Trak, you must know the ticker symbol of the fund whose shares you wish to buy or sell. Unfortunately, you cannot find ticker symbols in *The Wall Street Journal*. Mutual fund symbols can be conveniently obtained through many quote servers on the Internet, such as finance.yahoo.com. To find even more information on mutual funds, the Morningstar Web site (www.morningstar.com) is one of the best. You simply type the name of the mutual fund into the look-up box and submit it to the server. After you have the ticker symbol for the fund of interest, you can use it just like a stock ticker. On the Morningstar Web site, you can also find detailed information such as the asset allocation, loads, 12b-1 fees, the largest holdings of the fund, and more.

Mutual fund tickers normally have five letters, where the last letter is an X. For example, FMAGX is the ticker for the Fidelity Magellan Fund, VFINX is the ticker for the Vanguard Index Trust 500 Fund, and SNXFX is the ticker for the Schwab 1000 Equity Fund.

When buying mutual fund shares, you are taking a long position, hoping the fund's share price will increase. Suppose you want to invest $10,000 in Scudder Dreman Small Cap Value A shares, which has the ticker symbol KDSAX. You would place the following order:

Transaction	Amount ⑦	Symbol ⑦	Order Type	Price	Term
◉ Buy	10000	KDSAX	◉ Market		GTC
○ Sell	Enter 99999 to close your entire position				

My Buying Power   Preview >

Later, suppose you wanted to sell $4,000 in KDSAX shares. You would submit this order:

Transaction	Amount ⑦	Symbol ⑦	Order Type	Price	Term
○ Buy	4000	KDSAX	◉ Market		GTC
◉ Sell	Enter 99999 to close your entire position				

My Buying Power   Preview >

Since you are selling dollar amounts, not shares, and the mutual fund may have paid a dividend that was reinvested, you should enter 99999 in the dollar amount for the sell order to sell your entire position in the mutual fund.

With ETFs, unlike mutual funds, margin can be used, and short selling is allowed. To trade ETFs, you must look up the ticker. As of 2005 all available ETFs are listed on the American Stock Exchange, so an easy way to get an ETF ticker (and learn more about ETFs) is to go to www.amex.com.

Stock-Trak Exercises

1. **Mutual Fund Purchases**   Find a bond fund on Morningstar that interests you and invest $25,000 in the fund.
2. **Stock Fund Purchases**   Find a stock fund on Morningstar that interests you and invest $20,000 in the fund.

Resources

Teaching and Learning Supplements

We have developed a number of supplements for both teaching and learning to accompany this text. Each product has been significantly revised for the fourth edition.

For Instructors

Instructor's Resource CD-ROM

ISBN 0-07-325740-0

The Instructor's Resource CD-ROM contains the following assets:

Instructor's Manual, *prepared by Thomas W. Miller Jr.,* Saint Louis University

Developed to clearly outline the chapter material as well as provide extra teaching support, the first section of the Instructor's Manual includes an annotated outline of each chapter with suggested Web sites, references to PowerPoint slides, teaching tips, additional examples, and current events references. The second section contains complete worked-out solutions for the end-of-chapter questions and problems, prepared by Joe Smolira, Belmont University.

Test Bank, *prepared by Kay Johnson*, Penn State University–Erie

With almost 1,500 questions, this Test Bank, in Microsoft Word, provides a variety of question formats (true-false, multiple-choice, fill-in-the-blank, and problems) and levels of difficulty to meet any instructor's testing needs.

Computerized Test Bank (Windows) This computerized version of the Test Bank utilizes McGraw-Hill's EZ Test testing software to quickly create customized exams. This user-friendly program allows instructors to sort questions by format; edit existing questions or add new ones; and scramble questions for multiple versions of the same test.

PowerPoint Presentation, *prepared by Thomas W. Miller Jr.*, Saint Louis University

More than 300 full-color slides of images and tables from the text, lecture outlines, and additional examples and data are available with this product.

Videos ISBN 0-07-326175-0 (DVD format)

The McGraw-Hill/Irwin series of finance videos are 10-minute case studies on topics such as Financial Markets, Stocks, Bonds, Portfolio Management, Derivatives, and Going Public.

Digital Solutions

Online Learning Center (OLC):

Online Support at www.mhhe.com/jm4e

The Online Learning Center (OLC) contains FREE access to additional Web-based study and teaching aids created for this text, such as:

Student Support

Updated! Self-Study Software

With the new self-study program, students can test their knowledge of one chapter or a number of chapters by using self-grading questions written specifically for this text. There are at least 100 questions per chapter. Students can set a timer function to simulate a test environment, or they can choose to have answers pop up as they finish each question. Questions were prepared by Kay Johnson, Penn State University–Erie.

Excel Templates

Corresponding to most end-of-chapter problems, each template allows the student to work through the problem using Excel, reinforcing each concept. Each end-of-chapter problem with a template is indicated by an Excel icon in the margin beside it.

Other Features

Be sure to check out the other helpful features found on the OLC including key-term flashcards, links to Corporate Finance Online study problems, and Finance around the World.

Teaching Support

Along with having access to all of the same material your students can view on the book's OLC, you also have password-protected access to the Instructor's Manual, Solutions to end-of-chapter problems, Instructor's PowerPoint, Excel Template Solutions, Video clips, Video projects and questions, and teaching notes to Investments Online.

OLCs can be delivered in multiple ways—through the textbook Web site (www.mhhe.com/jm4e), through PageOut (see Packages below), or within a course management system like Blackboard, WebCT, TopClass, or eCollege. Ask your campus representative for more details.

Investments Online

As part of the OLC, instructors and students will also have access to Investments Online, found on the opening page. Investments Online is an exclusive Web tool from McGraw-Hill/Irwin. For each of the 18 key investment topics, students can complete challenging exercises and discussion questions that draw on recent articles, company reports, government data, and other Web-based resources. For instructors, there are password-protected teaching notes to assist with classroom integration of the material.

PageOut at www.pageout.net

Free to adopters, this Web page generation software is designed to help you create your own course Web site, without all of the hassle. In just a few minutes, even the most novice computer user can have a functioning course Web site.

Simply type your material into the template provided and PageOut instantly converts it to HTML. Next, choose your favorite of three easy-to-navigate designs and your class Web home page is created, complete with online syllabus, lecture notes, and bookmarks. You can even include a separate instructor page and an assignment page.

PageOut offers enhanced point-and-click features, including a Syllabus Page that applies a real-world link to original text material, an automatic grade book, and a discussion board where you and your students can exchange questions and post announcements. Ask your campus representative to show you a demo.

Options Available for Purchase and Packaging

You may also package either version of the text with a variety of other learning tools that are available for your students.

Stock-Trak Portfolio Stimulation

Give your students investment management experience! McGraw-Hill/Irwin has partnered with *Stock-Trak* and is providing a **free** subscription to the *Stock-Trak Portfolio Simulation* for one semester with the purchase of every new copy of *Fundamentals of Investments: Valuation and Management, Fourth Edition* by Jordan and Miller. *Stock-Trak* gives students $500,000 and allows them to trade stocks, options, futures, bonds, mutual funds, and international stocks—no other simulation offers all these types of securities! More than 600 professors have used this service, and around 30,000 college students each semester participate. All trades are done on the Web at www.stocktrak.com/cj. See this site for more information or use the Stock-Trak card bound into this text. Stock-Trak exercises are available on the book Web site, www.mhhe.com/jm4e.

Standard & Poor's Educational Version of Market Insight

McGraw-Hill/Irwin and the Institutional Market Services division of Standard & Poor's are pleased to announce an exclusive partnership that offers instructors and students **free** access to the educational version of Standard & Poor's Market Insight with each new textbook. The Educational Version of Market Insight is a rich online resource that provides six years of fundamental financial data for more than 1,000 companies in the database. S&P-specific problems can be found at the end of almost all chapters in this text. For more details, please see the bound-in card inside the front cover of this text, or visit www.mhhe.com/edumarketinsight.

The Wall Street Journal

If you order this package, your students can subscribe to *The Wall Street Journal*—both print and online versions—for 15 weeks at a specially priced rate of $20.00 in addition to the price of the text. Students will receive a "How to Use the *WSJ*" handbook plus a card explaining how to start the subscription to both versions.

BusinessWeek

Your students can subscribe to 15 weeks of *BusinessWeek* for a specially priced rate of $8.25 in addition to the price of the text. Students will receive a pass-code card shrink-wrapped with their new text. The card directs students to a Web site where they enter the code and then gain access to *BusinessWeek's* registration page to enter address info and set up their print and online subscription.

Financial Times

Your students can subscribe to the *Financial Times* for 15 weeks at a specially priced rate of $10 in addition to the price of the text by ordering this special package. Students will receive a subscription card shrink-wrapped with their new text to fill in and send to the *Financial Times* to start receiving their subscription. Instructors, once you order, make sure you contact your sales representative to receive a complimentary one-year subscription.

Brief Contents

Contents

CHAPTER 1

A Brief History of Risk and Return

"If you want to make money, go where the money is."
–Joseph Kennedy

Who wants to be a millionaire? Actually, anyone can retire as a millionaire. How? Consider this: Suppose you, on your 25th birthday, begin saving $3,000 per year. Forty years later, you retire on your 65th birthday. How much will you have? The answer might surprise you. If you earn 10 percent per year, you will have about $1.46 million. Are these numbers realistic? Based on the history of financial markets, the answer appears to be yes. For example, over the last 80 or so years, the widely followed Standard and Poor's index of large-company common stocks has actually yielded about 12 percent per year. ■

The study of investments could begin in many places. After thinking it over, we decided that a brief history lesson is in order, so we start our discussion of risk and return by looking back at what has happened to investors in U.S. financial markets since 1925. In 1931, for example, the stock market lost 43 percent of its value. Just two years later, the market reversed itself and gained 54 percent. In more recent times, the stock market lost about 25 percent of its value on October 19, 1987, alone, and it gained almost 40 percent in 1995. Very recently, following nine years of consecutive gains, the stock market lost value in three straight years, 2000 through 2002. What lessons, if any, should investors learn from such shifts in the stock market? We explore the last eight decades of market history to find out.

Our primary goal in this chapter is to see what financial market history can tell us about risk and return. One of the most important things to get out of this discussion is a perspective on the numbers. What is a high return? What is a low return? More generally, what returns should we expect from financial assets such as stocks and bonds, and what are the risks from such investments? Beyond this, we hope that by studying what *did* happen in the past, we will at least gain some insight into what *can* happen in the future.

The history of risk and return is made day by day in global financial markets. The Internet is an excellent source of information on financial markets. Visit our Web site (at www.mhhe.com/jm4e) for suggestions on where to find information on recent financial market events. We will suggest other sites later in the chapter.

Not everyone agrees on the value of studying history. On the one hand, there is philosopher George Santayana's famous comment, "Those who do not remember the past are condemned to repeat it." On the other hand, there is industrialist Henry Ford's equally famous comment, "History is more or less bunk." These extremes aside, perhaps everyone would agree with Mark Twain, who observed, with remarkable foresight (and poor grammar), that "October. This is one of the peculiarly dangerous months to speculate in stocks in. The others are July, January, September, April, November, May, March, June, December, August, and February."

Two key observations emerge from a study of financial market history. First, there is a reward for bearing risk, and, at least on average, that reward has been substantial. That's the good news. The bad news is that greater rewards are accompanied by greater risks. The fact that risk and return go together is probably the single most important fact to understand about investments, and it is a point to which we will return many times.

1.1 Returns

We wish to discuss historical returns on different types of financial assets. First, we need to know how to compute the return from an investment. We will consider buying shares of stock in this section, but the basic calculations are the same for any investment.

DOLLAR RETURNS

If you buy an asset of any type, your gain (or loss) from that investment is called the *return* on your investment. This return will usually have two components. First, you may receive some cash directly while you own the investment. Second, the value of the asset you purchase may change. In this case, you have a capital gain or capital loss on your investment.[1]

To illustrate, suppose you purchased 100 shares of stock in Harley-Davidson on January 1. At that time, Harley was selling for $37 per share, so your 100 shares cost you $3,700. At the end of the year, you want to see how you did with your investment.

The first thing to consider is that over the year, a company may pay cash dividends to its shareholders. As a stockholder in Harley, you are a part owner of the company, and you are entitled to a portion of any money distributed. So if Harley chooses to pay a dividend, you will receive some cash for every share you own.

[1]As a practical matter, what is and what is not a capital gain (or loss) is determined by the Internal Revenue Service. Even so, as is commonly done, we use these terms to refer to a change in value.

In addition to the dividend, the other part of your return is the capital gain or loss on the stock. This part arises from changes in the value of your investment. For example, consider these cash flows:

	Case 1	Case 2
Ending Stock Price	$40.33	$34.78
January 1 value	$3,700	$3,700
December 31 value	4,033	3,478
Dividend income	185	185
Capital gain or loss	333	−222

Our favorite investments Web site is Finance Yahoo! at

Our favorite investments Web site is Finance Yahoo! at finance.yahoo.com Visit this site and look around!

At the beginning of the year, on January 1, the stock is selling for $37 per share, and, as we calculated above, your total outlay for 100 shares is $3,700. Over the year, Harley pays dividends of $1.85 per share. By the end of the year, then, you received dividend income of

$$\text{Dividend income} = \$1.85 \times 100 = \$185$$

As in Case 1, suppose that as of December 31, Harley was selling for $40.33, meaning that the value of your stock increased by $3.33 per share. Your 100 shares are now worth $4,033, so you have a capital gain of

$$\text{Capital gain} = (\$40.33 - \$37) \times 100 = \$333$$

On the other hand, if the price had dropped to, say, $34.78 (Case 2), you would have a capital loss of

$$\text{Capital loss} = (\$34.78 - \$37) \times 100 = -\$222$$

Notice that a capital loss is the same thing as a negative capital gain.

total dollar return
The return on an investment measured in dollars that accounts for all cash flows and capital gains or losses.

The **total dollar return** on your investment is the sum of the dividend and the capital gain (or loss):

$$\text{Total dollar return} = \text{Dividend income} + \text{Capital gain (or loss)}$$

In case 1, the total dollar return is thus given by

$$\text{Total dollar return} = \$185 + \$333 = \$518$$

Overall, between the dividends you received and the increase in the price of the stock, the value of your investment increased from $3,700 to $3,700 + $518 = $4,218.

A common misconception often arises in this context. Suppose you hold on to your Harley-Davidson stock and don't sell it at the end of the year. Should you still consider the capital gain as part of your return? Isn't this only a "paper" gain and not really a cash gain if you don't sell it?

The answer to the first question is a strong yes, and the answer to the second is an equally strong no. The capital gain is every bit as much a part of your return as the dividend, and you should certainly count it as part of your return. The fact that you decide to keep the stock and don't sell (you don't "realize" the gain) is irrelevant because you could have converted it to cash if you had wanted to. Whether you choose to do so is up to you.

After all, if you insist on converting your gain to cash, you could always sell the stock and immediately reinvest by buying the stock back. There is no difference between doing this and just not selling (assuming, of course, that there are no transaction costs or tax consequences from selling the stock). Again, the point is that whether you actually cash out and buy pizzas (or whatever) or continue to hold the investment doesn't affect the return you actually earn.

PERCENTAGE RETURNS

It is usually more convenient to summarize information about returns in percentage terms than in dollar terms, because that way your return doesn't depend on how much you actually invested. With percentage returns the question we want to answer is: How much do we get *for each dollar* we invest?

To answer this question, let P_t be the price of the stock at the beginning of the year and let D_{t+1} be the dividend paid on the stock during the year. The following cash flows are the same as those shown earlier, except that we have now expressed everything on a per-share basis:

	Case 1	Case 2
Ending Stock Price	$40.33	$34.78
January 1 value	$37.00	$37.00
December 31 value	40.33	34.78
Dividend income	1.85	1.85
Capital gain or loss	3.33	−2.22

In our example, the price at the beginning of the year was $37 per share and the dividend paid during the year on each share was $1.85. If we express this dividend as a percentage of the beginning stock price, the result is the **dividend yield**:

dividend yield
The annual stock dividend as a percentage of the initial stock price.

$$\text{Dividend yield} = D_{t+1} / P_t \qquad (1.1)$$
$$= \$1.85 / \$37 = .05 = 5\%$$

This says that for each dollar we invested we received 5 cents in dividends.

The second component of our percentage return is the **capital gains yield**. This yield is calculated as the change in the price during the year (the capital gain) divided by the beginning price. With the $40.33 ending price, we get:

capital gains yield
The change in stock price as a percentage of the initial stock price.

$$\text{Capital gains yield} = (P_{t+1} - P_t) / P_t \qquad (1.2)$$
$$= (\$40.33 - \$37) / \$37$$
$$= \$3.33 / \$37 = .09 = 9\%$$

This 9 percent yield means that for each dollar invested we got 9 cents in capital gains.

Putting it all together, per dollar invested, we get 5 cents in dividends and 9 cents in capital gains for a total of 14 cents. Our **total percent return** is 14 cents on the dollar, or 14 percent. When a return is expressed on a percentage basis, we often refer to it as the *rate of return,* or just "return," on the investment. Notice that if we combine the formulas for the dividend yield and capital gains yield, we get a single formula for the total percentage return:

total percent return
The return on an investment measured as a percentage that accounts for all cash flows and capital gains or losses.

$$\text{Percentage return} = \text{Dividend yield} + \text{Capital gains yield} \qquad (1.3)$$
$$= D_{t+1} / P_t + (P_{t+1} - P_t) / P_t$$
$$= (D_{t+1} + P_{t+1} - P_t) / P_t$$

WORK THE WEB

To look up information on common stocks using the Web, you need to know the "ticker" symbol for the stocks in which you are interested. You can look up ticker symbols in many places, including one of our favorite sites, finance.yahoo.com. Here we have looked up (using the "Symbol Lookup" link) and entered ticker symbols for some well-known "tech" stocks.

YAHOO! FINANCE Sign In
New User? Sign Up   Finance Home - Help

Tuesday, May 9, 2006, 4:21PM ET - **U.S. Markets Closed.**

Home | Investing | News & Commentary | Retirement & Planning | Banking & Credit | Loans | Taxes | My Portfolios ▾

Get Quotes dell csco intc msft   **GO**   Symbol Lookup | Finance Search

Once we hit "Get Quotes," this is what we got:

View: Summary | Real-Time ECN | **Columnar** [New View]

Columnar   Edit

Symbol	Time	Trade	Change	% Chg	Volume	Intraday	Related Info
DELL	4:00PM ET	25.20	↓ 1.23	-4.65%	82,866,074		Chart, Messages, Key Stats, More
CSCO	4:00PM ET	21.68	↓ 0.08	-0.37%	67,926,951		Chart, Messages, Key Stats, More
INTC	4:00PM ET	19.90	↓ 0.21	-1.04%	65,640,787		Chart, Messages, Key Stats, More
MSFT	4:01PM ET	23.62	↓ 0.11	-0.46%	68,913,383		Chart, Messages, Key Stats, More

As you can see, we get the price for each stock, along with information about the change in price and volume (number of shares traded). You will find a lot of links to hit and learn more, so have at it!

To check our calculations, notice that we invested $3,700 and ended up with $4,218. By what percentage did our $3,700 increase? As we saw, we picked up $4,218 − $3,700 = $518. This is an increase of $518 / $3,700, or 14 percent.

EXAMPLE 1.1	Calculating Percentage Returns

Suppose you buy some stock for $25 per share. After one year, the price is $35 per share. During the year, you received a $2 dividend per share. What is the dividend yield? The capital gains yield? The percentage return? If your total investment was $1,000, how much do you have at the end of the year?

Your $2 dividend per share works out to a dividend yield of

$$\text{Dividend yield} = D_{t+1} / P_t$$
$$= \$2/\$25$$
$$= 8\%$$

(continued)

Chapter 1 ■ A Brief History of Risk and Return   **5**

The per-share capital gain is $10, so the capital gains yield is

$$\text{Capital gains yield} = (P_{t+1} - P_t) / P_t$$
$$= (\$35 - \$25) / \$25$$
$$= \$10 / \$25$$
$$= 40\%$$

The total percentage return is thus 8% + 40% = 48%.

If you had invested $1,000, you would have $1,480 at the end of the year. To check this, note that your $1,000 would have bought you $1,000 / $25 = 40 shares. Your 40 shares would then have paid you a total of 40 × $2 = $80 in cash dividends. Your $10 per share gain would give you a total capital gain of $10 × 40 = $400. Add these together and you get $480, which is a 48 percent total return on your $1,000 investment.

Now that you know how to calculate returns on a hypothetical stock, you should begin looking at real stocks. The nearby *Work the Web* box describes how to get going. Meanwhile, in the next several sections, we will take a look at the returns that some common types of investments have earned over the last 80 years.

CHECK THIS

1.1a What are the two parts of total return?

1.1b Why are unrealized capital gains or losses included in the calculation of returns?

1.1c What is the difference between a dollar return and a percentage return? Why are percentage returns usually more convenient?

1.2 The Historical Record

We now examine year-to-year historical rates of return on five important categories of financial investments. These returns can be interpreted as what you would have earned if you had invested in portfolios of the following asset categories:

WWW

Annual historical financial market data can be downloaded (but not for free) at www.globalfindata.com

1. **Large-company stocks.** The large-company stock portfolio is based on the Standard and Poor's (S&P's) 500 index, which contains 500 of the largest companies (in terms of total market value of outstanding stock) in the United States.

2. **Small-company stocks.** This is a portfolio composed of stock of smaller companies, where "small" corresponds to the smallest 20 percent of the companies listed on the New York Stock Exchange, again as measured by market value of outstanding stock.

3. **Long-term corporate bonds.** This is a portfolio of high-quality bonds with 20 years to maturity.

4. **Long-term U.S. government bonds.** This is a portfolio of U.S. government bonds with 20 years to maturity.

5. **U.S. Treasury bills.** This is a portfolio of Treasury bills (T-bills for short) with a three-month maturity.

If you are not entirely certain what these investments are, don't be overly concerned. We will have much more to say about each in later chapters. For now, just take as given that these are some of the things that you could have put your money into in years gone by. In addition to the year-to-year returns on these financial instruments, the year-to-year percentage changes in the Consumer Price Index (CPI) are also computed. The CPI is a standard measure of consumer goods price inflation.

Here is a bit of market jargon for you. A company's *total market capitalization* (or market "cap" for short) is equal to its stock price multiplied by the number of shares of stock. In other words, it's the total value of the company's stock. Large companies are often called "large-cap" stocks, and small companies are called "small-cap" stocks. We'll use these terms frequently.

A FIRST LOOK

Before examining the different portfolio returns, we first take a look at the "big picture." Figure 1.1 shows what happened to $1 invested in these different portfolios at the beginning of 1926 and held over the 80-year period ending in 2005 (for clarity, the long-term

FIGURE 1.1 — A $1 Investment in Different Types of Portfolios: 1926–2005 (Year-end 1925 = $1)

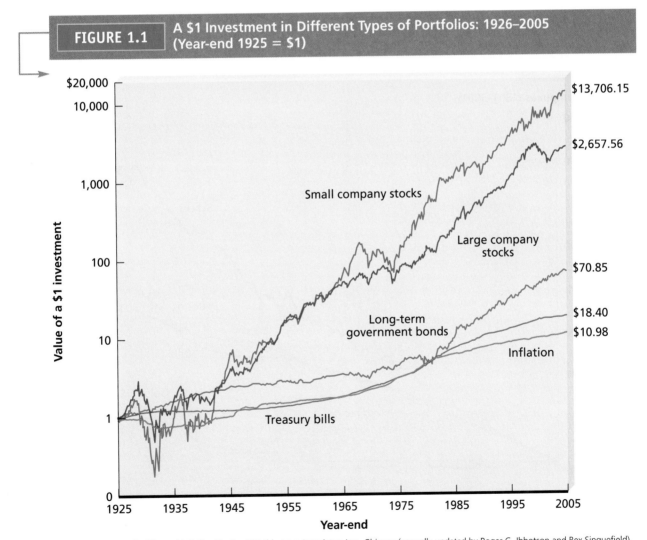

Source: *Stocks, Bonds, Bills, and Inflation Yearbook™*, Ibbotson Associates, Inc., Chicago (annually updated by Roger G. Ibbotson and Rex Sinquefield). All rights reserved.

corporate bonds are omitted). To fit all the information on a single graph, some modification in scaling is used. As is commonly done with financial time series, the vertical axis is scaled so that equal distances measure equal percentage (as opposed to dollar) changes in value. Thus, the distance between $10 and $100 is the same as that between $100 and $1,000, since both distances represent the same 900 percent increases.

Looking at Figure 1.1, we see that the small-company investment did the best overall. Every dollar invested grew to a remarkable $13,706 over the 80 years. The larger common stock portfolio did less well; a dollar invested in it grew to $2,657.

At the other end, the T-bill portfolio grew to only $18.40. This is even less impressive when we consider the inflation over this period. As illustrated, the increase in the price level was such that $10.98 is needed just to replace the original $1.

Given the historical record, why would anybody buy anything other than small-company stocks? If you look closely at Figure 1.1, you will probably see the answer—risk. The T-bill portfolio and the long-term government bond portfolio grew more slowly than did the stock portfolios, but they also grew much more steadily. The small stocks ended up on top, but, as you can see, they grew quite erratically at times. For example, the small stocks

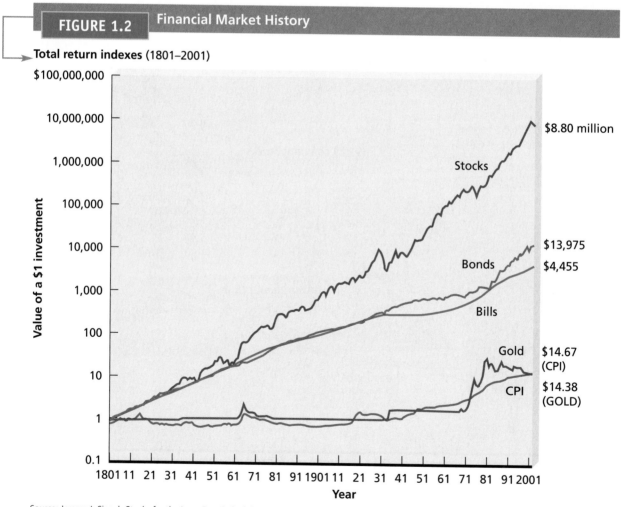

FIGURE 1.2 **Financial Market History**

Total return indexes (1801–2001)

Source: Jeremy J. Siegel, *Stocks for the Long Run,* 3rd ed. (New York: McGraw-Hill, 2003).

were the worst performers for about the first 10 years and had a smaller return than long-term government bonds for almost 15 years.

A LONGER RANGE LOOK

The data available on the stock returns before 1925 are not comprehensive, but it is nonetheless possible to trace reasonably accurate returns in U.S. financial markets as far back as 1802. Figure 1.2 shows the values, in 2001, of $1 invested in stocks, long-term bonds, short-term bills, and gold. The CPI is also included for reference.

Inspecting Figure 1.2, we see that $1 invested in stocks grew to an astounding $8.80 million over this 200-year period. During this time, the returns from investing in stocks dwarf those earned on other investments. Notice also in Figure 1.2 that, after two centuries, gold has managed to keep up with inflation, but that is about it.

What we see thus far is that there has been a powerful financial incentive for long-term investing. The real moral of the story is this: Get an early start!

A CLOSER LOOK

To illustrate the variability of the different investments, Figures 1.3 through 1.6 plot the year-to-year percentage returns in the form of vertical bars drawn from the horizontal axis. The height of a bar tells us the return for the particular year. For example, looking at the long-term government bonds (Figure 1.5), we see that the largest historical return (40.35 percent) occurred in 1982. This was a good year for bonds. In comparing these

| FIGURE 1.3 | Year-to-Year Total Returns on Large-Company Stocks: 1926–2005 |

Large company stocks
Return indices, returns, and dividend yields

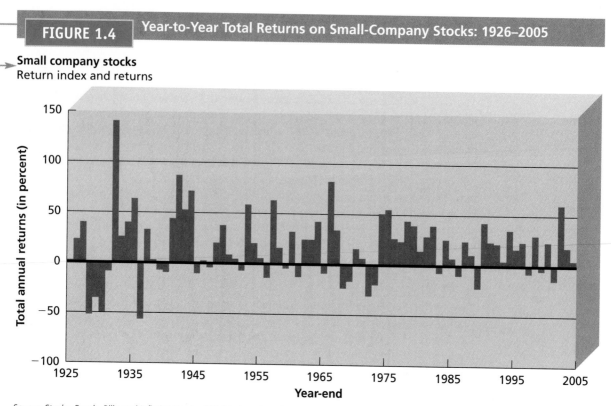

FIGURE 1.4 — Year-to-Year Total Returns on Small-Company Stocks: 1926–2005

Small company stocks
Return index and returns

Source: *Stocks, Bonds, Bills, and Inflation Yearbook*™, Ibbotson Associates, Inc., Chicago (annually updated by Roger G. Ibbotson and Rex A. Sinquefield). All rights reserved.

charts, notice the differences in the vertical axis scales. With these differences in mind, you can see how predictably the Treasury bills (bottom of Figure 1.5) behaved compared to the small stocks (Figure 1.4).

The returns shown in these bar graphs are sometimes very large. Looking at the graphs, we see, for example, that the largest single-year return was a remarkable 143 percent for the small-cap stocks in 1933. In the same year, the large-company stocks returned "only" 53 percent. In contrast, the largest Treasury bill return was 15 percent, in 1981. For future reference, the actual year-to-year returns for the S&P 500, long-term government bonds, Treasury bills, and the CPI are shown in Table 1.1 on pages 13 and 14.

CHECK THIS

1.2a   With 20-20 hindsight, what was the best investment for the period 1926–35?

1.2b   Why doesn't everyone just buy small stocks as investments?

1.2c   What was the smallest return observed over the 80 years for each of these investments? Approximately when did it occur?

1.2d   About how many times did large stocks (common stocks) return more than 30 percent? How many times did they return less than –20 percent?

1.2e   What was the longest "winning streak" (years without a negative return) for large stocks? For long-term government bonds?

1.2f   How often did the T-bill portfolio have a negative return?

FIGURE 1.5   Year-to-Year Total Returns on Bonds and Bills: 1926–2005

Long-term government bonds
Return indices, returns, and yields

U.S. Treasury bills
Return index and returns

Source: *Stocks, Bonds, Bills, and Inflation Yearbook™*, Ibbotson Associates, Inc., Chicago (annually updated by Roger G. Ibbotson and Rex A. Sinquefield). All rights reserved.

FIGURE 1.6   Year-to-Year Inflation: 1926–2005

Inflation
Cumulative index and rates of change

1.3   Average Returns: The First Lesson

As you've probably begun to notice, the history of financial market returns in an undigested form is complicated. What we need are simple measures to accurately summarize and describe all these numbers. Accordingly, we discuss how to go about condensing detailed numerical data. We start by calculating average returns.

CALCULATING AVERAGE RETURNS

The obvious way to calculate average returns on the different investments in Figures 1.3 to 1.6 is to simply add up the yearly returns and divide by 80. The result is the historical average of the individual values. For example, if you add the returns for large common stocks for the 80 years, you will get about 984 percent. The average annual return is thus 984/80 = 12.3%. You can interpret this 12.3 percent just like any other average. If you picked a year at random from the 80-year history and you had to guess the return in that year, the best guess is 12.3 percent.

AVERAGE RETURNS: THE HISTORICAL RECORD

Table 1.2 shows the average returns for the investments we have discussed. These averages don't reflect the impact of inflation. Notice that over this 80-year period the average inflation rate was 3.1 percent per year while the average return on U.S. Treasury bills was 3.8 percent per year. Thus, the average return on Treasury bills exceeded the average rate of inflation by only .7 percent per year. At the other extreme, the return on large-cap common stocks exceeded the rate of inflation by a whopping 12.3% − 3.1% = 9.2%.

Our analysis thus far has covered market history going back to 1925. You might be wondering about the more recent past. The nearby *Investment Updates* box provides more detail on the stock market's ups and downs since 1970.

| TABLE 1.1 | Year-to-Year Total Returns: 1926–2005 | | | |

Year	Large-Company Stocks	Long-Term Government Bonds	U.S. Treasury Bills	Consumer Price Index
1926	13.75%	5.69%	3.30%	−1.12%
1927	35.70	6.58	3.15	−2.26
1928	45.08	1.15	4.05	−1.16
1929	−8.80	4.39	4.47	0.58
1930	−25.13	4.47	2.27	−6.40
1931	−43.60	−2.15	1.15	−9.32
1932	−8.75	8.51	0.88	−10.27
1933	52.95	1.92	0.52	0.76
1934	−2.31	7.59	0.27	1.52
1935	46.79	4.20	0.17	2.99
1936	32.49	5.13	0.17	1.45
1937	−35.45	1.44	0.27	2.86
1938	31.63	4.21	0.06	−2.78
1939	−1.43	3.84	0.04	0.00
1940	−10.36	5.70	0.04	0.71
1941	−12.02	0.47	0.14	9.93
1942	20.75	1.80	0.34	9.03
1943	25.38	2.01	0.38	2.96
1944	19.49	2.27	0.38	2.30
1945	36.21	5.29	0.38	2.25
1946	−8.42	0.54	0.38	18.13
1947	5.05	−1.02	0.62	8.84
1948	4.99	2.66	1.06	2.99
1949	17.81	4.58	1.12	−2.07
1950	30.05	−0.98	1.22	5.93
1951	23.79	−0.20	1.56	6.00
1952	18.39	2.43	1.75	0.75
1953	−1.07	2.28	1.87	0.75
1954	52.23	3.08	0.93	−0.74
1955	31.62	−0.73	1.80	0.37
1956	6.91	−1.72	2.66	2.99
1957	−10.50	6.82	3.28	2.90
1958	43.57	−1.72	1.71	1.76
1959	12.01	−2.02	3.48	1.73
1960	0.47	11.21	2.81	1.36
1961	26.84	2.20	2.40	0.67
1962	−8.75	5.72	2.82	1.33

(continued)

TABLE 1.1   (continued)

Year	Large-Company Stocks	Long-Term Government Bonds	U.S. Treasury Bills	Consumer Price Index
1963	22.70%	1.79%	3.23%	1.64%
1964	16.43	3.71	3.62	0.97
1965	12.38	0.93	4.06	1.92
1966	−10.06	5.12	4.94	3.46
1967	23.98	−2.86	4.39	3.04
1968	11.03	2.25	5.49	4.72
1969	−8.43	−5.63	6.90	6.20
1970	3.94	18.92	6.50	5.57
1971	14.30	11.24	4.36	3.27
1972	18.99	2.39	4.23	3.41
1973	−14.69	3.30	7.29	8.71
1974	−26.47	4.00	7.99	12.34
1975	37.23	5.52	5.87	6.94
1976	23.93	15.56	5.07	4.86
1977	−7.16	0.38	5.45	6.70
1978	6.57	−1.26	7.64	9.02
1979	18.61	1.26	10.56	13.29
1980	32.50	−2.48	12.10	12.52
1981	−4.92	4.04	14.60	8.92
1982	21.55	44.28	10.94	3.83
1983	22.56	1.29	8.99	3.79
1984	6.27	15.29	9.90	3.95
1985	31.73	32.27	7.71	3.80
1986	18.67	22.39	6.09	1.10
1987	5.25	−3.03	5.88	4.43
1988	16.61	6.84	6.94	4.42
1989	31.69	18.54	8.44	4.65
1990	−3.10	7.74	7.69	6.11
1991	30.46	19.36	5.43	3.06
1992	7.62	7.34	3.48	2.90
1993	10.08	13.06	3.03	2.75
1994	1.32	−7.32	4.39	2.67
1995	37.58	25.94	5.61	2.54
1996	22.96	0.13	5.14	3.32
1997	33.36	12.02	5.19	1.70
1998	28.58	14.45	4.86	1.61
1999	21.04	−7.51	4.80	2.68
2000	−9.10	17.22	5.98	3.39
2001	−11.89	5.51	3.33	1.55
2002	−22.10	15.15	1.61	2.4
2003	28.69	2.01	0.94	1.9
2004	10.88	8.12	1.14	3.3
2005	4.91	6.89	2.79	3.4

Source: Author calculations based on data obtained from *Global Financial Data*, Bloomberg, Standard and Poor's, and other sources.

TABLE 1.2 — Average Annual Returns: 1926–2005

Investment	Average Return	Maximum	Minimum
Large stocks	12.3	53.99%	−43.34%
Small stocks	17.4	142.87	−58.01
Long-term corporate bonds	6.2	43.79	−8.09
Long-term government bonds	5.8	40.35	−9.19
U.S. Treasury bills	3.8	14.71	−0.02
Inflation	3.1	13.31	−10.30

Source: *Stocks, Bonds, Bills, and Inflation Yearbook™*, Ibbotson Associates, Inc., Chicago (annually updated by Roger G. Ibbotson and Rex A. Sinquefield). All rights reserved.

TABLE 1.3 — Average Annual Returns and Risk Premiums: 1926–2005

Investment	Average Return	Risk Premium
Large stocks	12.3%	8.5%
Small stocks	17.4	13.6
Long-term corporate bonds	6.2	2.8
Long-term government bonds	5.8	2.0
U.S. Treasury bills	3.8	0.0

Source: *Stocks, Bonds, Bills, and Inflation Yearbook™*, Ibbotson Associates, Inc., Chicago (annually updated by Roger G. Ibbotson and Rex A. Sinquefield). All rights reserved.

RISK PREMIUMS

Now that we have computed some average returns, it seems logical to see how they compare with each other. Based on our discussion above, one such comparison involves government-issued securities. These are free of much of the variability we see in, for example, the stock market.

The government borrows money by issuing debt securities, which come in different forms. The ones we focus on here are Treasury bills. Because these instruments have a very short investment life and because the government can always raise taxes or print money to pay its bills, at least in the short run, there is essentially no risk associated with buying them. Thus, we call the rate of return on such debt the **risk-free rate**, and we will use it as a kind of investing benchmark.

A particularly interesting comparison involves the virtually risk-free return on T-bills and the risky return on common stocks. The difference between these two returns can be interpreted as a measure of the **risk premium** on the average risky asset (assuming that the stock of a large U.S. corporation has about average risk compared to all risky assets). We call this the risk premium because it is the additional return we earn by moving from a risk-free investment to a typical risky one, and we interpret it as a reward for bearing risk.

THE FIRST LESSON

From the data in Table 1.2, we can calculate risk premiums for the five different categories of investments. The results are shown in Table 1.3. Notice that the risk premium on T-bills is shown as zero in the table because they are our riskless benchmark. Looking at Table 1.3, we see that the average risk premium earned by the large-cap common stock portfolio is 12.3 − 3.8 = 8.5%. This is a significant reward. The fact that it exists historically is an

risk-free rate
The rate of return on a riskless investment.

risk premium
The extra return on a risky asset over the risk-free rate; the reward for bearing risk.

AFTER 30 YEARS OF INVESTING, MARKET HAS NO SURE THING

The stock market exists to enrich investors, while utterly humiliating them. With great regularity, I receive e-mails from readers who are convinced that you should own only blue-chip companies, or only high-dividend stocks, or only technology companies. And all I can think about is the market's litany of once-sure things. It happens again and again. Hot stocks turn cold. Highflying stock funds crash and burn. Time-tested stock-picking strategies suddenly falter. To understand just how capricious the market can be, consider results from the past three decades.

As the Decades Turn

Take a look at the accompanying table (Swings and Roundabouts), which shows returns calculated by Baltimore's T. Rowe Price Associates using data from Chicago's Ibbotson Associates. In particular, focus on the performance of large, small and foreign stocks in each of the past three decades. I think of these as the three key stock-market sectors.

As you will see, large-company stocks—which are so beloved after their dazzling gains in the 1990s—didn't fare quite so well in the prior two decades. They ranked second behind foreign stocks in the 1980s and they lagged behind both small and foreign stocks in the 1970s. Similarly, small stocks ranked first in the 1970s, second in the 1990s and third in the 1980s. Meanwhile, foreign stocks were first in the 1980s, second in the 1970s and third in the 1990s.

In other words, none of the sectors consistently ranked as the top performer and all had periods of dreadful performance. Moreover, if you look at results for the 30 years through December 2001, there isn't a huge difference between the average annual returns for large, small and foreign stocks. Of course, if you were really clever, you would figure out which sector was going to be the decade's top performer,

and then invest everything in that sector. But I am not smart enough to make that sort of market call, and I don't think anybody else is, either.

Gerald Perritt, a money manager in Largo, Fla., and editor of the Mutual Fund Letter, a monthly newsletter, says he has lately met many investors who got themselves into financial trouble. All have one thing in common: They failed to diversify and instead made big investment bets that turned sour. "Diversification is good," Mr. Perritt says. "But if it's so good, why don't more people practice it? Return is the most visible element in the investing process. The least visible is risk. People see the return they miss by diversifying. We don't think about what will happen if a big bet goes in the wrong direction."

My hunch is that the current decade will be a lackluster one for blue-chip shares. Large-company stocks have been dazzling performers over the past two decades, and now they are burdened by lofty share price-to-earnings multiples and boast only skimpy dividend yields. Indeed, I suspect foreign and small stocks will prove to be the market's new darlings. But I am unwilling to invest based on such hunches. So what should an investor do? Owning a little bit of everything has worked well in the past, and it still seems like a mighty fine strategy to me.

Glancing at the performance of narrower market sectors strengthens the case for humility. In the past two years, three of the market's best-performing segments have been gold, bargain-priced "value" stocks and real estate investment trusts, or REITs. Meanwhile, "growth" stocks, including once-sparkling technology shares, have been crushed. But look at the accompanying table to see results from earlier decades. Unfortunately, data aren't available for all time periods. Still, there are enough results to see how unpredictable market returns can be. Sure, value stocks were strong performers in 2000

important observation, and it is the basis for our first lesson: Risky assets, on average, earn a risk premium. Put another way, there is a reward, on average, for bearing risk.

Why is this so? Why, for example, is the risk premium for stocks so much larger than the risk premium for bonds? More generally, what determines the relative sizes of the risk premiums for the different assets? These questions speak to the heart of the modern theory of investments, and we will discuss the issues involved many times in the chapters ahead. For now, part of the answer can be found by looking at the historical variability of returns of these different investments. So, to get started, we now turn our attention to measuring variability in returns.

Swings and Roundabouts
All market sectors enjoy periods of dazzling gains. But none performs well all the time.

	Bear Markets		Long-Run Annual Performance			
	1973–74	2000–01	1970s	1980s	1990s	30 Years*
Large-company stocks	−42.6%	−29.3%	5.9%	17.6%	18.2%	12.2%
Small-company stocks	−43.2	−19.4	11.5	15.8	15.1	14.9
Foreign markets	−35.2	−36.6	10.1	22.8	7.3	11.2
Growth stocks	NA	−42.2	NA	16.3	20.6	NA
Value stocks	NA	−13.4	NA	18.3	15.4	NA
Real-estate Trusts	−52.6	35.2	NA	12.5	8.1	9.4
Intermediate bonds	4.9	19.4	7.0	11.9	7.2	8.5
Treasury bills	13.5	7.9	6.3	8.9	4.9	6.7
Gold	133.1	5.9	30.7	−2.5	−3.1	6.4

*Through December 31, 2001.

Note: All returns are annualized, except for the two bear markets, for which cumulative performance is shown.

NA: Not available.

and 2001. But they lagged behind growth stocks in the 1990s. True, REITs have generated great results recently. But they didn't do much better than intermediate-term government bonds in the 1990s. And gold? You have to go back to the 1970s to find a decent decade for the yellow metal.

When the Bear Growls

To get a handle on down-market performance, I had T. Rowe Price calculate returns for the two most-searing bear markets of recent decades, the 1973–74 debacle and the 2000–01 tech wreck. In both stock-market declines, gold, bonds, and Treasury bills posted gains, even as other sectors were crushed. Clearly, if you want a little bear-market protection, these are good assets to own.

But how did different stock-market sectors fare? Consider the 1973–74 crash. The two hardest-hit sectors were REITs and small-company stocks. If you were worried about a bear market and you had taken your cues from the 1973–74 crash, you would have avoided both sectors. Yet REITs, the hardest-hit sector in the 1973–74 crash, were the biggest winners in the recent bear market. Small-company stocks, meanwhile, didn't perform quite so impressively in the 2000–01 market decline. Nonetheless, they lost far less money than large-company stocks.

As the data make clear, there aren't many sure things in investing. But that doesn't mean you can't make good money over time. If you simply build a well-diversified portfolio and hang on for the long haul, history suggests you will be handsomely rewarded. "Here's a 30-year period that includes two grueling bear markets and one awful decade, the 1970s," notes Steven Norwitz, a T. Rowe Price vice president. "But if you invested through the whole period, you got pretty attractive returns."

Source: Jonathan Clements, *The Wall Street Journal,* April 28, 2002. © 2002 Dow Jones & Company, Inc. All Rights Reserved Worldwide.

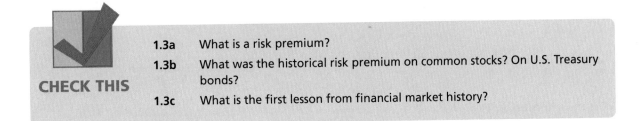

CHECK THIS

1.3a What is a risk premium?

1.3b What was the historical risk premium on common stocks? On U.S. Treasury bonds?

1.3c What is the first lesson from financial market history?

1.4 Return Variability: The Second Lesson

We have already seen that year-to-year returns on common stocks tend to be more volatile than returns on, say, long-term government bonds. We now discuss how to measure this variability so we can begin examining the important subject of risk.

FREQUENCY DISTRIBUTIONS AND VARIABILITY

To get started, we can draw a *frequency distribution* for large-company stock returns like the one in Figure 1.7. What we have done here is to count the number of times that an annual return on the large-company stock portfolio falls within each 10 percent range. For example, in Figure 1.7, the height of 14 for the bar within the interval 10 percent to 20 percent means that 14 of the 80 annual returns are in that range. Notice also that most of the returns are in the –10 to 40 percent range.

variance
A common measure of volatility.

standard deviation
The square root of the variance.

What we need to do now is to actually measure the spread in these returns. We know, for example, that the return on the S&P 500 index of common stocks in a typical year was 12.3 percent. We now want to know by how much the actual return differs from this average in a typical year. In other words, we need a measure of returns volatility. The **variance** and its square root, the **standard deviation**, are the most commonly used measures of volatility. We briefly review how to calculate these next. If you've already studied basic statistics, you should notice that we are simply calculating an ordinary sample variance and standard deviation, just as you may have done many times before.

THE HISTORICAL VARIANCE AND STANDARD DEVIATION

Variance measures the average squared difference between the actual returns and the average return. The bigger this number is, the more the actual returns tend to differ from the average return. To illustrate how we calculate historical variance, suppose a particular investment had returns of 10 percent, 12 percent, 3 percent, and –9 percent over the last four years. The average return is (10% + 12% + 3% – 9%) / 4 = 4%.

FIGURE 1.7 — Frequency Distribution of Returns on Common Stocks: 1926–2005

Large company stocks

						2004			
		2000		1988	2003	1997			
		1990	2005	1986	1999	1995			
		1981	1994	1979	1998	1991			
		1977	1993	1972	1996	1989			
		1969	1992	1971	1983	1985			
		1962	1987	1968	1982	1980			
		1953	1984	1965	1976	1975			
		1946	1978	1964	1967	1955			
	2001	1940	1970	1959	1963	1950			
	1973	1939	1960	1952	1961	1945			
2002	1966	1934	1956	1949	1951	1938	1958		
1974	1957	1932	1948	1944	1943	1936	1935	1954	
1931 1937	1930	1941	1929	1947	1926	1942	1927	1928	1933

Percent axis: –80 –70 –60 –50 –40 –30 –20 –10 0 10 20 30 40 50 60 70 80 90

Percent

Notice that the return is never actually equal to 4 percent. Instead, the first return deviates from the average by $10\% - 4\% = 6\%$, the second return deviates from the average by $12\% - 4\% = 8\%$, and so on. To compute the variance, we square each of these deviations, add them up, and divide the result by the number of returns less one, or three in this case.[2] These calculations are summarized immediately below.

$$(10 - 4)^2 = 36$$
$$(12 - 4)^2 = 64$$
$$(3 - 4)^2 = 1$$
$$(-9 - 4)^2 = \underline{169}$$
$$270 \rightarrow \rightarrow 270/3 = 90$$

www

For an easy-to-read
review of basic
statistics, see
www.robertniles.
com/stats/

To recap, we first calculate the differences between actual returns and their average by subtracting out 4 percent. Second, we square each difference. Third, we sum all squared deviations to get 270. Finally, we divide the sum of the squared deviations by $4 - 1 = 3$.

By these calculations we get $Var(R)$ or σ^2 (read this as "sigma squared"), which is the variance of the return:

$$Var(R) = \sigma^2 = 270/(4 - 1) = 90$$

The standard deviation is the square root of the variance. So, if $SD(R)$ or σ stands for the standard deviation of return:

$$SD(R) = \sigma = \sqrt{90} = 9.487\%$$

The square root of the variance is used because the variance is measured in "squared" percentages and is hard to interpret. The standard deviation is an ordinary percentage, which here is 9.487 percent.

In general, if we have N historical returns, where N is some number, we can write the historical variance as:

$$Var(R) = [(R_1 - \bar{R})^2 + (R_2 - \bar{R})^2 + \cdots + (R_N - \bar{R})^2] / (N - 1) \quad \text{(1.4)}$$

This formula tells us to do just what we did above: Take each of the N individual returns $(R_1, R_2, \ldots, R_N)$ and subtract the average return, $\bar{R}$; then square the results, and add them all up; finally, divide this total by the number of returns less one $(N - 1)$. The standard deviation is always the square root of $Var(R)$.

[2]The reason for dividing by $N - 1$ rather than simply N is based on statistical sampling theory, which is beyond the scope of this book. Just remember that to calculate a variance about a sample average, you need to divide the sum of squared deviations from the average by $N - 1$.

EXAMPLE 1.2   Calculating the Variance and Standard Deviation

Calculate return averages, variances, and standard deviations for S&P 500 large-cap stocks and Treasury bonds (T-bonds) using data for the first five years in Table 1.1, 1926–1930.
First, calculate return averages as follows:

S&P 500 Large-Company Stocks	T-Bonds
13.75	5.69
35.70	6.58
45.08	1.15
−8.80	4.39
−25.13	4.47
60.60	22.28
Average return: 60.60 / 5 = 12.12	22.28 / 5 = 4.46

(continued)

Using the averages above, calculate the squared deviations from the average returns and sum the squared deviations as follows:

S&P 500 Large-Company Stocks	T-Bonds
$(13.75 - 12.12)^2 =$ 2.66	$(5.69 - 4.46)^2 =$ 1.51
$(35.70 - 12.12)^2 =$ 556.02	$(6.58 - 4.46)^2 =$ 4.49
$(45.08 - 12.12)^2 =$ 1,086.36	$(1.15 - 4.46)^2 =$ 10.96
$(-8.80 - 12.12)^2 =$ 437.65	$(4.39 - 4.46)^2 =$ 0.00
$(-25.13 - 12.12)^2 =$ 1,387.56	$(4.47 - 4.46)^2 =$ 0.00
3,470.25	16.96

Calculate return variances by dividing the sums of squared deviations by four, the number of returns less one.

$$\text{S\&P 500: } 3{,}470.24/4 = 867.56 \quad \text{T-bonds: } 16.97/4 = 4.24$$

Standard deviations are then calculated as the square root of the variance:

$$\text{S\&P 500: } \sqrt{867.56} = 29.45 \quad \text{T-bonds: } \sqrt{4.24} = 2.06$$

Notice that the large-company stock portfolio had a volatility almost 10 times greater than the T-bond portfolio, which is not unusual during periods of market turbulence.

THE HISTORICAL RECORD

Figure 1.8 summarizes much of our discussion of capital market history so far. It displays average returns, standard deviations, and frequency distributions of annual returns on a common scale. In Figure 1.8, notice, for example, that the standard deviation for the small-stock portfolio (32.9 percent per year) is more than 10 times larger than the T-bill portfolio's standard deviation (3.1 percent per year). We will return to these figures momentarily.

NORMAL DISTRIBUTION

normal distribution

A symmetric, bell-shaped frequency distribution that is completely defined by its average and standard deviation.

For many different random events in nature, a particular frequency distribution, the **normal distribution** (or *bell curve*) is useful for describing the probability of ending up in a given range. For example, the idea behind "grading on a curve" comes from the fact that exam scores often resemble a bell curve.

Figure 1.9 illustrates a normal distribution and its distinctive bell shape. As you can see, this distribution has a much cleaner appearance than the actual return distributions illustrated in Figure 1.7. Even so, like the normal distribution, the actual distributions do appear to be at least roughly mound shaped and symmetric. When this is true, the normal distribution is often a very good approximation.

Also, keep in mind that the distributions in Figure 1.8 are based on only 80 yearly observations, while Figure 1.9 is, in principle, based on an infinite number. So, if we had been able to observe returns for, say, 1,000 years, we might have filled in a lot of the irregularities and ended up with a much smoother picture. For our purposes, it is enough to observe that the returns are at least roughly normally distributed.

The usefulness of the normal distribution stems from the fact that it is completely described by the average and the standard deviation. If you have these two numbers, then there is nothing else to know. For example, with a normal distribution, the probability that we end up within one standard deviation of the average is about 2/3. The probability that we end up within two standard deviations is about 95 percent. Finally, the probability of being more than three standard deviations away from the average is less than 1 percent. These ranges and the probabilities are illustrated in Figure 1.9.

FIGURE 1.8

Historical Returns, Standard Deviations, and Frequency Distributions: 1926–2005

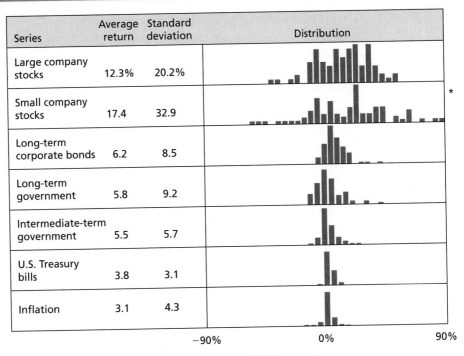

Series	Average return	Standard deviation	Distribution
Large company stocks	12.3%	20.2%	
Small company stocks	17.4	32.9	
Long-term corporate bonds	6.2	8.5	
Long-term government	5.8	9.2	
Intermediate-term government	5.5	5.7	
U.S. Treasury bills	3.8	3.1	
Inflation	3.1	4.3	

−90%   0%   90%

*The 1933 small company stocks total return was 142.9 percent.

Source: *Stocks, Bonds, Bills, and Inflation Yearbook*™, Ibbotson Associates, Inc., Chicago (annually updated by Roger G. Ibbotson and Rex A. Sinquefield). All rights reserved.

FIGURE 1.9

The Normal Distribution: Illustrated Returns Based on the Historical Return and Standard Deviation for a Portfolio of Large Common Stocks

Probability

68%

95%

99%

Return on large common stocks

-3σ	-2σ	-1σ	0	$+1\sigma$	$+2\sigma$	$+3\sigma$
−48.3%	−28.1%	−7.9%	12.3%	32.5%	52.7%	72.9%

To see why this is useful, recall from Figure 1.8 that the standard deviation of returns on the large common stocks is 20.2 percent. The average return is 12.3 percent. So, assuming that the frequency distribution is at least approximately normal, the probability that the return in a given year is in the range of −7.9 percent to 32.5 percent (12.3 percent plus or minus one standard deviation, 20.2 percent) is about 2/3. This range is illustrated in Figure 1.9. In other words, there is about one chance in three that the return will be *outside* this range. This literally tells you that, if you buy stocks in large companies, you should expect to be outside this range in one year out of every three. This reinforces our earlier observations about stock market volatility. However, there is only a 5 percent chance (approximately) that we would end up outside the range of −28.1 percent to 52.7 percent (12.3 percent plus or minus 2 × 20.2%). These points are also illustrated in Figure 1.9.

THE SECOND LESSON

Our observations concerning the year-to-year variability in returns are the basis for our second lesson from capital market history. On average, bearing risk is handsomely rewarded, but, in a given year, there is a significant chance of a dramatic change in value. Thus, our second lesson is this: The greater the potential reward, the greater is the risk.

Thus far in this chapter, we have emphasized the year-to-year variability in returns. We should note that even day-to-day movements can exhibit considerable volatility. For example, not long ago, on September 17, 2001, the Dow Jones Industrial Average (DJIA) plummeted 684.81 points, or 7.13 percent. By historical standards, it was a bad day for the 30 stocks that comprise the DJIA (as well as for a majority of stocks in the market). Still, while the drop was the largest one-day decrease in the DJIA ever in terms of points, it actually wasn't quite in the top 12 largest one-day percentage decreases in history, as illustrated in the following table:

Top 12 One-Day Percentage Declines in the Dow-Jones Industrial Average			
December 12, 1914	−24.4%	August 12, 1932	−8.4%
October 19, 1987	−22.6	March 14, 1907	−8.3
October 28, 1929	−12.8	October 26, 1987	−8.0
October 29, 1929	−11.7	July 21, 1933	−7.8
November 6, 1929	− 9.9	October 18, 1937	−7.7
December 18, 1899	− 8.7	February 1, 1917	−7.2

Source: *Dow Jones.*

This discussion highlights the importance of looking at returns in terms of percentages rather than dollar amounts or index points. For example, before 2001, the biggest one-day loss in terms of points was on April 14, 2000, when the DJIA declined by 618 points. The second worst was the 554-point drop of October 27, 1987. By contrast, the 5.57-point drop in the DJIA on December 18, 1899, marked the fifth worst day in the history of the index, but a 5.6-point loss in the DJIA in today's market would hardly be noticed. This is precisely why we relied on percentage returns when we examined market history in this chapter.[3]

[3]By the way, as you may have noticed, what's kind of weird is that 6 of the 12 worst days in the history of the DJIA occurred in October, including the top 3. We have no clue as to why. Furthermore, looking back at the Mark Twain quote near the beginning of the chapter, how do you suppose he knew? Sounds like a case for CSI: Wall Street.

EXAMPLE 1.3   Investing in Growth Stocks

As a practical matter, the phrase *growth stock* is frequently a euphemism for small-company stock. Are such investments suitable for "widows and orphans"? Before answering, you should consider historical volatility. For example, from the historical record, what is the approximate probability that you will actually lose 16 percent or more of your money in a single year if you buy stocks from a group of such companies?

The historical average return on a small-company stock portfolio is about 17 percent, with an annual standard deviation of about 33 percent. From our rule of

(continued)

thumb, there is about a 1/3 probability that you will experience a return outside the range −16 percent to 50 percent (17% ± 33%).

The odds of being above or below this range are about equal. There is thus about a 1/6 chance (half of 1/3) that you will lose more than 16 percent. So you should expect this to happen once in every six years, on average. Such investments can thus be *very* volatile, and they are not well-suited for those who cannot afford to bear the risk.

Now that you know how to calculate and, more importantly, interpret average returns and standard deviations, the nearby *Spreadsheet Analysis* box shows how to do the calculations using Excel, which can really speed up things when we have a lot of data.

SPREADSHEET ANALYSIS

Using a Spreadsheet to Calculate Average Returns and Volatilities

Here is an Excel spreadsheet summarizing the formulas and analysis needed to calculate average returns and standard deviations using the 1990s as an example:

	A	B	C	D	E	F	G	H
1								
2		Using a spreadsheet to calculate average returns and standard deviations						
3								
4	Looking back in the chapter, the data suggest that the 1990s were one							
5	of the best decades for stock market investors. We will find out just how good by							
6	calculating the average returns and standard deviations for this period. Here are the							
7	year-by-year returns on the large company S&P 500 index:							
8								
9		Year	Return(%)	Year	Return(%)			
10		1990	−3.10	1995	37.58			
11		1991	30.46	1996	22.96			
12		1992	7.62	1997	33.36			
13		1993	10.08	1998	28.58			
14		1994	1.32	1999	21.04			
15								
16		Average return (%):		18.99				
17		Standard deviation (%):		14.16				
18								
19	The formulas we used to do the calculations are just =AVERAGE(C10:C14;E10:E14)							
20	and =STDEV(C10:C14;E10:E14). Notice that the average return in the 1990s was 18.99							
21	percent per year, which is larger than the long-run average of 12.3 percent. At the same							
22	time, the standard deviation, 14.16 percent, was smaller than the 20.2 percent long-run value.							

CHECK THIS

1.4a In words, how do we calculate a variance? A standard deviation?

1.4b What is the first lesson from financial market history? The second lesson?

1.5 More on Average Returns

Thus far in this chapter, we have looked closely at simple average returns. But there is another way of computing an average return. The fact that average returns are calculated two different ways leads to some confusion, so our goal in this section is to explain the two approaches and also the circumstances under which each is appropriate.

ARITHMETIC VERSUS GEOMETRIC AVERAGES

Let's start with a simple example. Suppose you buy a particular stock for $100. Unfortunately, the first year you own it, it falls to $50. The second year you own it, it rises back to $100, leaving you where you started (no dividends were paid).

What was your average return on this investment? Common sense seems to say that your average return must be exactly zero since you started with $100 and ended with $100. But if we calculate the returns year-by-year, we see that you lost 50 percent the first year (you lost half of your money). The second year, you made 100 percent (you doubled your money). Your average return over the two years was thus $(-50\% + 100\%)/2 = 25\%$!

So which is correct, 0 percent or 25 percent? The answer is that both are correct; they just answer different questions. The 0 percent is called the **geometric average return**. The 25 percent is called the **arithmetic average return**. The geometric average return answers the question *"What was your average compound return per year over a particular period?"* The arithmetic average return answers the question *"What was your return in an average year over a particular period?"*

Notice that, in previous sections, the average returns we calculated were all arithmetic averages, so we already know how to calculate them. What we need to do now is (1) learn how to calculate geometric averages and (2) learn the circumstances under which one average is more meaningful than the other.

geometric average return

The average compound return earned per year over a multiyear period.

arithmetic average return

The return earned in an average year over a multi-year period.

CALCULATING GEOMETRIC AVERAGE RETURNS

First, to illustrate how we calculate a geometric average return, suppose a particular investment had annual returns of 10 percent, 12 percent, 3 percent, and –9 percent over the last four years. The geometric average return over this four-year period is calculated as $(1.10 \times 1.12 \times 1.03 \times .91)^{1/4} - 1 = 3.66\%$. In contrast, the average arithmetic return we have been calculating is $(.10 + .12 + .03 - .09)/4 = 4.0\%$.

In general, if we have N years of returns, the geometric average return over these N years is calculated using this formula:

$$\text{Geometric average return} = [(1 + R_1) \times (1 + R_2) \times \cdots \times (1 + R_N)]^{1/N} - 1 \qquad (1.5)$$

This formula tells us that four steps are required:

1. Take each of the N annual returns $R_1, R_2, \ldots, R_N$ and add a one to each (after converting them to decimals!).

2. Multiply all the numbers from step 1 together.

3. Take the result from step 2 and raise it to the power of $1/N$.

4. Finally, subtract one from the result of step 3. The result is the geometric average return.

One thing you may have noticed in our examples thus far is that the geometric average returns seem to be smaller. It turns out that this will always be true (as long as the returns

EXAMPLE 1.4

Calculating the Geometric Average Return

Calculate the geometric average return for S&P 500 large-cap stocks for the first five years in Table 1.1, 1926–1930.

First, convert percentages to decimal returns, add one, and then calculate their product.

S&P 500 Returns	Product
13.75	1.1375
35.70	× 1.3570
45.08	× 1.4508
–8.80	× 0.9120
–25.13	× 0.7487
	1.5291

Notice that the number 1.5291 is what our investment is worth after five years if we started with a one-dollar investment. The geometric average return is then calculated as

$$\text{Geometric average return} = 1.5291^{1/5} - 1 = 0.0886, \text{ or } 8.86\%$$

Thus the geometric average return is about 8.86 percent in this example. In contrast, in Example 1.2, the average arithmetic return was calculated as 12.12 percent. Here is a tip: If you are using a financial calculator, you can put $1 in as the present value, $1.5291 as the future value, and 5 as the number of periods. Then, solve for the unknown rate. You should get the same answer we did.

are not all identical, in which case the two "averages" would be the same). To illustrate, Table 1.4 shows the arithmetic averages and standard deviations from Figure 1.8, along with the geometric average returns.

As shown in Table 1.4, the geometric averages are all smaller, but the magnitude of the difference varies quite a bit. The reason is that the difference is greater for more volatile investments. In fact, there is useful approximation. Assuming all the numbers are expressed in decimals (as opposed to percentages), the geometric average return is approximately equal to the arithmetic average return minus half the variance. For example, looking at the large-company stocks, the arithmetic average is .123 and the standard deviation is .202,

TABLE 1.4

Geometric versus Arithmetic Average Returns: 1926–2005

Series	Geometric Mean	Arithmetic Mean	Standard Deviation
Large-company stocks	10.4%	12.3%	20.2%
Small-company stocks	12.6	17.4	32.9
Long-term corporate bonds	5.9	6.2	8.5
Long-term government bonds	5.5	5.8	9.2
Intermediate-term government bonds	5.3	5.5	5.7
U.S. Treasury bills	3.7	3.8	3.1
Inflation	3.0	3.1	4.3

implying that the variance is .040804. The approximate geometric average is thus .123 − .040804/2 = .1026, which is quite close to the actual value.

EXAMPLE 1.5 | **More Geometric Averages**

Take a look back at Figure 1.1. There, we showed the value of a $1 investment after 80 years. Use the value for the large-company stock investment to check the geometric average in Table 1.4.

In Figure 1.1, the large-company investment grew to $2,657.56 over 80 years. The geometric average return is thus

$$\text{Geometric average return} = 2{,}657.56^{1/80} - 1 = .1036, \text{ or } 10.4\%$$

This 10.4% is the value shown in Table 1.4. For practice, check some of the other numbers in Table 1.4 the same way.

ARITHMETIC AVERAGE RETURN OR GEOMETRIC AVERAGE RETURN?

When we look at historical returns, the difference between the geometric and arithmetic average returns isn't too hard to understand. To put it slightly differently, the geometric average tells you what you actually earned per year on average, compounded annually. The arithmetic average tells you what you earned in a typical year. You should use whichever one answers the question you want answered.

A somewhat trickier question concerns forecasting the future, and there is a lot of confusion about this point among analysts and financial planners. The problem is this. If we have *estimates* of both the arithmetic and geometric average returns, then the arithmetic average is probably too high for longer periods and the geometric average is probably too low for shorter periods.

The good news is that there is a simple way of combining the two averages, which we will call *Blume's formula*.[4] Suppose we calculated geometric and arithmetic return averages from N years of data and we wish to use these averages to form a T-year average return forecast, $R(T)$, where T is less than N. Here's how we do it:

$$R(T) = \frac{T-1}{N-1} \times \text{Geometric average} + \frac{N-T}{N-1} \times \text{Arithmetic average}$$

For example, suppose that, from 25 years of annual returns data, we calculate an arithmetic average return of 12 percent and a geometric average return of 9 percent. From these averages, we wish to make 1-year, 5-year, and 10-year average return forecasts. These three average return forecasts are calculated as follows:

$$R(1) = \frac{1-1}{24} \times 9\% + \frac{25-1}{24} \times 12\% = 12\%$$

$$R(5) = \frac{5-1}{24} \times 9\% + \frac{25-5}{24} \times 12\% = 11.5\%$$

$$R(10) = \frac{10-1}{24} \times 9\% + \frac{25-10}{24} \times 12\% = 10.875\%$$

Thus, we see that 1-year, 5-year, and 10-year forecasts are 12 percent, 11.5 percent, and 10.875 percent, respectively.

[4]This elegant result is due to Marshal Blume. ("Unbiased Estimates of Long-Run Expected Rates of Return," *Journal of the American Statistical Association,* September 1974, pp. 634–638.)

EXAMPLE 1.6

Forecasting Average Returns

Over the 80-year period 1926–2005, the geometric average return for the S&P 500 index was 10.4 percent and the arithmetic average return was 12.3 percent. Calculate average return forecasts for 1, 5, 10, and 25 years into the future.

In this case, we would use Blume's formula with values of $T = 1, 5, 10,$ and 25 and $N = 80$:

$$R(T) = \frac{T-1}{79} \times 10.4\% + \frac{80-T}{79} \times 12.3\%$$

T	R(T)
1	12.3%
5	12.2
10	12.1
25	11.7
80	10.4

Notice that short-term forecasts are closer to the arithmetic average return and long-term forecasts are closer to the geometric average return.

This concludes our discussion of geometric versus arithmetic averages. One last note: In the future, when we say "average return," we mean arithmetic average unless we explicitly say otherwise.

CHECK THIS

1.5a Over a five-year period, an investment in a broad market index yielded annual returns of 10, 16, –5, –8, and 7 percent. What were the arithmetic and geometric average annual returns for this index?

1.5b Over a 25-year period, an investment in a broad market index yielded an arithmetic average return of 4 percent and a geometric average return of 3.6 percent. Using Blume's formula, what would be the 5-year and 10-year average return forecasts?

1.6 Risk and Return

In previous sections we explored financial market history to see what we could learn about risk and return. In this section we summarize our findings and then conclude our discussion by looking ahead at the subjects we will be examining in later chapters.

THE RISK-RETURN TRADE-OFF

Figure 1.10 is a way of putting together our findings on risk and return. What it shows is that there is a risk-return trade-off. At one extreme, if we are unwilling to bear any risk at all, but we are willing to forgo the use of our money for a while, then we can earn the

FIGURE 1.10   Risk-Return Trade-Off

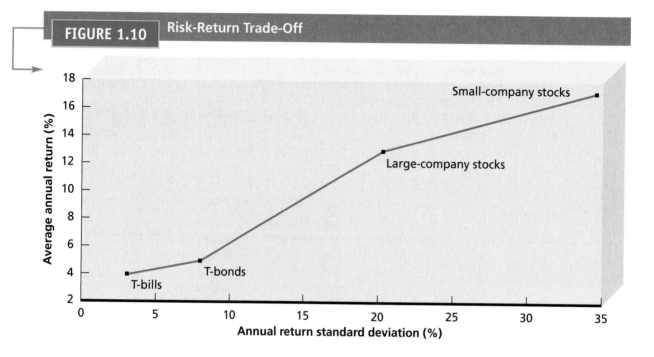

risk-free rate. Because the risk-free rate represents compensation for just waiting, it is often called the *time value of money.*

If we are willing to bear risk, then we can expect to earn a risk premium, at least on average. Further, the more risk we are willing to bear, the greater is the risk premium. Investment advisers like to say that an investment has a "wait" component and a "worry" component. In our figure, the time value of money is the compensation for waiting, and the risk premium is the compensation for worrying.

There are two important caveats to this discussion. First, risky investments do not *always* pay more than risk-free investments. Indeed, that is precisely what makes them risky. In other words, there is a risk premium *on average,* but, over any particular time interval, there is no guarantee. Second, we have intentionally been a little imprecise about what we mean exactly by risk. As we will discuss in the chapters ahead, not all risks are compensated. Some risks are cheaply and easily avoidable, and there is no expected reward for bearing them. It is only those risks that cannot be easily avoided that are compensated (on average).

A LOOK AHEAD

In the remainder of this text, we focus exclusively on financial assets. An advantage of this approach is that it is limited to four major types: stocks, bonds, futures, and options, in the order that we cover them. This means that we won't be discussing collectibles such as classic automobiles, baseball cards, coins, fine art, or stamps. We also won't be discussing real estate or precious metals such as gold and platinum. It's not that these are unimportant; rather, they are very specialized. So, instead of treating them superficially, we leave a discussion of them for another day (and another book).

As we've indicated, to understand the potential reward from an investment, it is critical to first understand the risk involved. There is an old saying that goes like this: It's easy to make a small fortune investing in_____ (put your favorite investment here)—just start with a large fortune! The moral is that the key to successful investing is to make informed, intelligent decisions about risk. For this reason, we are going to pay particular attention to the things that determine the value of the different assets we discuss and the nature of the associated risks.

One common characteristic that these assets have is that they are bought and sold around the clock and around the world in vast quantities. The way they are traded can be very different, however. We think it is important and interesting to understand exactly what happens when you buy or sell one of these assets, so we will be discussing the different trading mechanisms and the way the different markets function. We will also describe actual buying and selling at various points along the way to show you the steps involved and the results of placing buy and sell orders and having them executed.

1.7 Summary and Conclusions

This chapter explores financial market history. Such a history lesson is useful because it tells us what to expect in the way of returns from risky assets. We summarized our study of market history with two key lessons:

1. Risky assets, on average, earn a risk premium. There is a reward for bearing risk.
2. The greater the potential reward from a risky investment, the greater is the risk.

When we put these two lessons together, we concluded that there is a risk-return trade-off: The only way to earn a higher return is to take on greater risk.

GET REAL

This chapter took you through some basic, but important, investment-related calculations. We then walked through the modern history of risk and return. How should you, as an investor or investment manager, put this information to work?

The answer is that you now have a rational, objective basis for thinking about what you stand to make from investing in some important broad asset classes. For the stock market as a whole, as measured by the performance of large-company stocks, you know that you might realistically expect to make 12 percent or so per year on average.

Equally important, you know that you won't make 12 percent in any one year; instead, you'll make more or less. You know that the standard deviation is about 20 percent per year, and you should know what that means in terms of risk. In particular, you need to understand that in one year out of every six, you should expect to lose more than 8 percent (12 percent minus one standard deviation), so this will be a relatively common event. The good news is that in one year out of six, you can realistically expect to earn more than 32 percent (12 percent plus one standard deviation).

The other important, practical thing to understand from this chapter is that a strategy of investing in very low risk assets (such as T-bills) has historically barely kept up with inflation. This might be sufficient for some investors, but if your goal is to do better than that, then you will have to bear some amount of risk to achieve it.

arithmetic average return 24
capital gains yield 4
dividend yield 4
geometric average return 24
normal distribution 20
risk-free rate 15

risk premium 15
standard deviation 18
total dollar return 3
total percent return 4
variance 18

Chapter Review Problems and Self-Test _____

1. **Calculating Returns**   You bought 400 shares of Metallica Heavy Metal, Inc., at $30 per share. Over the year, you received $.75 per share in dividends. If the stock sold for $33 at the end of the year, what was your dollar return? Your percentage return?

2. **Calculating Returns and Variability**   Using the following returns, calculate the arithmetic average returns, the variances, the standard deviations, and the geometric returns for the following stocks:

Year	Michele, Inc.	Janicek Co.
1	12%	5%
2	−4	−15
3	0	10
4	20	38
5	2	17

3. **Forecasting Returns**   Over a 30-year period an asset had an arithmetic return of 12.8 percent and a geometric return of 10.7 percent. Using Blume's formula, what is your best estimate of the future annual returns over the next 5 years? 10 years? 20 years?

Answers to Self-Test Problems

1. Your dollar return is just your gain or loss in dollars. Here, we receive $.75 in dividends on each of our 400 shares, for a total of $300. In addition, each share rose from $30 to $33, so we make $3 × 400 shares = $1,200. Our total dollar return is thus $300 + $1,200 = $1,500.

   Our percentage return (or just "return" for short) is equal to the $1,500 we made divided by our initial outlay of $30 × 400 shares = $12,000; so $1,500/12,000 = .125 = 12.5%. Equivalently, we could have just noted that each share paid a $.75 dividend and each share gained $3, so the total dollar gain per share was $3.75. As a percentage of the cost of one share ($30), we get $3.75/30 = .125 = 12.5%.

2. First, calculate arithmetic averages as follows:

Michele, Inc.	Janicek Co.
12%	5%
−4	−15
0	10
20	38
2	17
30%	55%
Average return: 30/5 = 6%	55/5 = 11%

www.mhhe.com/jm4e

Using the arithmetic averages above, calculate the squared deviations from the arithmetic average returns and sum the squared deviations as follows:

Michele, Inc.	Janicek Co.
$(12 - 6)^2 = 36$	$(5 - 11)^2 = 36$
$(-4 - 6)^2 = 100$	$(-15 - 11)^2 = 676$
$(0 - 6)^2 = 36$	$(10 - 11)^2 = 1$
$(20 - 6)^2 = 196$	$(38 - 11)^2 = 729$
$(2 - 6)^2 = 16$	$(17 - 11)^2 = 36$
384	1,478

Calculate return variances by dividing the sums of squared deviations by four, which is the number of returns less one.

$$\text{Michele: } 384/4 = 96 \quad \text{Janicek: } 1{,}478/4 = 369.5$$

Standard deviations are then calculated as the square root of the variance.

$$\text{Michele: } \sqrt{96} = 9.8\% \quad \text{Janicek: } \sqrt{369.5} = 19.22\%$$

Geometric returns are then calculated as:

$$\text{Michele: } [(1 + .12)(1 - .04)(1 + .00)(1 + .20)(1 + .02)]^{1/5} - 1 = 5.65\%$$

$$\text{Janicek: } [(1 + .05)(1 - .15)(1 + .10)(1 + .38)(1 + .17)]^{1/5} - 1 = 9.65\%$$

3. To find the best forecast, we apply Blume's formula as follows:

$$R(5) = \frac{5 - 1}{29} \times 10.7\% + \frac{30 - 5}{29} \times 12.8\% = 12.51\%$$

$$R(10) = \frac{10 - 1}{29} \times 10.7\% + \frac{30 - 10}{29} \times 12.8\% = 12.15\%$$

$$R(20) = \frac{20 - 1}{29} \times 10.7\% + \frac{30 - 20}{29} \times 12.8\% = 11.42\%$$

Test Your Investment Quotient

1. **Prices and Returns** You plan to buy a common stock and hold it for one year. You expect to receive both $1.50 from dividends and $26 from the sale of the stock at the end of the year. If you wanted to earn a 15 percent rate of return, what is the maximum price you would pay for the stock today?

    a. $22.61
    b. $23.91
    c. $24.50
    d. $27.50

2. **Returns** A portfolio of non-dividend-paying stocks earned a geometric mean return of 5 percent between January 1, 1994, and December 31, 2000. The arithmetic mean return for the same period was 6 percent. If the market value of the portfolio at the beginning of 1994 was $100,000, the market value of the portfolio at the end of 2000 was *closest* to:

    a. $135,000
    b. $140,710
    c. $142,000
    d. $150,363

Chapter 1 ■ A Brief History of Risk and Return **31**

3. **Standard Deviation** Which of the following statements about standard deviation is true? Standard deviation

a. Is the square of the variance.
b. Can be a positive or negative number.
c. Is denominated in the same units as the original data.
d. Is the arithmetic mean of the squared deviations from the mean.

4. **Normal Distribution** An investment strategy has an expected return of 12 percent and a standard deviation of 10 percent. If the investment returns are normally distributed, the probability of earning a return less than 2 percent is closest to:

a. 10 percent
b. 16 percent
c. 32 percent
d. 34 percent

5. **Normal Distribution** What are the mean and standard deviation of a standard normal distribution?

	Mean	Standard Deviation
a.	0	0
b.	0	1
c.	1	0
d.	1	1

6. **Normal Distribution** Given a data series that is normally distributed with a mean of 100 and a standard deviation of 10, about 95 percent of the numbers in the series will fall within which of the following ranges?

a. 60 to 140
b. 70 to 130
c. 80 to 120
d. 90 to 110

7. **Asset Types** Stocks, bonds, options, and futures are the four major types of

a. Debt
b. Real assets
c. Equity
d. Financial assets

8. **Investment Returns** Suppose the value of an investment doubles in a one-year period. In this case, the rate of return on this investment over that one-year period is what amount?

a. 100 percent even if the gain is not actually realized.
b. 200 percent even if the gain is not actually realized.
c. 100 percent only if the gain is actually realized.
d. 200 percent only if the gain is actually realized.

9. **Historical Returns** Which of the following asset categories has an annual returns history most closely linked to historical annual rates of inflation?

a. U.S. Treasury bills
b. Corporate bonds
c. Large-company stocks
d. Small-company stocks

10. **Historical Returns** Based on the annual returns history since 1926, which asset category, on average, has yielded the highest risk premium?

a. U.S. government bonds
b. Corporate bonds
c. Large-company stocks
d. Small-company stocks

11. **Stat 101** Over a four-year period, an investment in Outa' Synch common stock yields returns of —10, 40, 0, and 20. What is the arithmetic return over this period?
   a. 5 percent
   b. 7.5 percent
   c. 10 percent
   d. 12.5 percent

12. **Stat 101** You calculate an average historical return of 20 percent and a standard deviation of return of 10 percent for an investment in Stonehenge Construction Co. You believe these values well represent the future distribution of returns. Assuming that returns are normally distributed, what is the probability that Stonehenge Construction will yield a negative return?
   a. 17 percent
   b. 33 percent
   c. 5 percent
   d. 2.5 percent

13. **Stat 101** Which of the following statements about a normal distribution is incorrect?
   a. A normal distribution is symmetrically centered on its mean.
   b. The probability of being within one standard deviation from the mean is about 68 percent.
   c. The probability of being within two standard deviations from the mean is about 95 percent.
   d. The probability of a negative value is always one-half.

14. **Normal Distribution** Based on a normal distribution with a mean of 500 and a standard deviation of 150, the z-value for an observation of 200 is closest to:
   a. —2.00
   b. —1.75
   c. 1.75
   d. 2.00

15. **Normal Distribution** A normal distribution would least likely be described as:
   a. Asymptotic.
   b. A discrete probability distribution.
   c. A symmetrical or bell-shaped distribution.
   d. A curve that theoretically extends from negative infinity to positive infinity.

Concept Questions

1. **Risk versus Return** Based on the historical record, rank the following investments in increasing order of risk. Rank the investments in increasing order of average returns. What do you conclude about the relationship between the risk of an investment and the return you expect to earn on it?
   a. Large stocks
   b. Treasury bills
   c. Long-term government bonds
   d. Small stocks

2. **Return Calculations** A particular stock had a return last year of 4 percent. However, you look at the stock price and notice that it actually didn't change at all last year. How is this possible?

3. **Returns Distributions** What is the probability that the return on small stocks will be less than —100 percent in a single year (think about it)? What are the implications for the distribution of returns?

4. **Arithmetic versus Geometric Returns** What is the difference between arithmetic and geometric returns? Suppose you have invested in a stock for the last 10 years. Which number is more important to you, the arithmetic or geometric return?

5. **Blume's Formula**   What is Blume's formula? When would you want to use it in practice?

6. **Inflation and Returns**   Look at Table 1.1 and Figures 1.5 and 1.6. When were T-bill rates at their highest? Why do you think they were so high during this period?

7. **Inflation and Returns**   The returns we have examined are not adjusted for inflation. What do you suppose would happen to our estimated risk premiums if we did account for inflation?

8. **Taxes and Returns**   The returns we have examined are not adjusted for taxes. What do you suppose would happen to our estimated returns and risk premiums if we did account for taxes? What would happen to our volatility measures?

9. **Taxes and Treasury Bills**   As a practical matter, most of the return you earn from investing in Treasury bills is taxed right away as ordinary income. Thus, if you are in a 40 percent tax bracket and you earn 5 percent on a Treasury bill, your aftertax return is only $.05 \times (1 - .40) = .03$, or 3 percent. In other words, 40 percent of your return goes to pay taxes, leaving you with just 3 percent. Once you consider inflation and taxes, how does the long-term return from Treasury bills look?

10. **The Long Run**   Given your answer to the last question and the discussion in the chapter, why would any rational person do anything other than load up on 100 percent small stocks?

Questions and Problems _____

■

Core Questions

1. **Calculating Returns**   Suppose you bought 100 shares of stock at an initial price of $89 per share. The stock paid a dividend of $1.20 per share during the following year, and the share price at the end of the year was $97. Compute your total dollar return on this investment. Does your answer change if you keep the stock instead of selling it? Why or why not?

2. **Calculating Yields**   In the previous problem, what is the capital gains yield? The dividend yield? What is the total rate of return on the investment?

3. **Calculating Returns**   Rework Problems 1 and 2 assuming that you buy 750 shares of the stock and the ending share price is $81.50.

4. **Historical Returns**   What is the historical rate of return on each of the following investments? What is the historical risk premium on these investments?
   a. Long-term government bonds
   b. Treasury bills
   c. Large stocks
   d. Small stocks

5. **Calculating Average Returns**   The rate of return on Jurassic Jalopies, Inc., stock over the last five years was –8 percent, 34 percent, –16 percent, 8 percent, and 19 percent. Over the same period, the return on Stonehenge Construction Company's stock was –18 percent, 27 percent, –9 percent, 24 percent, and 17 percent. What was the arithmetic average return on each stock over this period?

6. **Calculating Returns and Variability**   Using the following returns, calculate the arithmetic average returns, the variances, and the standard deviations for stocks A and B.

Year	A	B
1	24%	32%
2	6	2
3	–8	–15
4	19	21
5	15	11

7. **Return Calculations**   A particular stock has a dividend yield of 2.4 percent. Last year, the stock price fell from $74 to $66. What was the return for the year?

34   **Part 1**   ■   Introduction

www.mhhe.com/jm4e

8. **Geometric Returns** A stock has had returns of 11 percent, −6 percent, −12 percent, 19 percent, and 37 percent over the last five years. What is the geometric return for the stock?

9. **Arithmetic and Geometric Returns** A stock has had returns of 29 percent, 11 percent, 18 percent, −6 percent, −19 percent, and 34 percent over the last six years. What are the arithmetic and geometric returns for the stock?

Intermediate Questions

10. **Returns and the Bell Curve** An investment has an expected return of 12 percent per year with a standard deviation of 28 percent. Assuming that the returns on this investment are at least roughly normally distributed, how frequently do you expect to earn between −16 percent and 40 percent? How often do you expect to earn less than −16 percent?

11. **Returns and the Bell Curve** An investment has an expected return of 8 percent per year with a standard deviation of 4 percent. Assuming that the returns on this investment are at least roughly normally distributed, how frequently do you expect to lose money?

12. **Using Returns Distributions** Based on the historical record, if you invest in long-term U.S. Treasury bonds, what is the approximate probability that your return will be less than −3.4 percent in a given year? What range of returns would you expect to see 95 percent of the time? 99 percent of the time?

13. **Using Returns Distributions** Based on the historical record, what is the approximate probability that an investment in small stocks will double in value in a single year? How about triple in a single year?

14. **Risk Premiums** Refer to Table 1.1 for large-stock and T-bill returns for the period 1973–1977:
    a. Calculate the observed risk premium in each year for the common stocks.
    b. Calculate the average returns and the average risk premium over this period.
    c. Calculate the standard deviation of returns and the standard deviation of the risk premium.
    d. Is it possible that the observed risk premium can be negative? Explain how this can happen and what it means.

15. **Geometric Return** Your grandfather invested $1,000 in a stock 48 years ago. Currently the value of his account is $197,000. What is his geometric return over this period?

16. **Forecasting Returns** You have found an asset with a 12.60 percent arithmetic average return and a 10.15 percent geometric return. Your observation period is 40 years. What is your best estimate of the return of the asset over the next 5 years? 10 years? 20 years?

17. **Geometric Averages** Look back to Figure 1.1 and find the value of $1 invested in each asset class over this 80-year period. Calculate the geometric return for small-company stocks, long-term government bonds, Treasury bills, and inflation.

18. **Arithmetic and Geometric Returns** A stock has returns of 21 percent, 7 percent, −19 percent, 16 percent, and 13 percent. What are the arithmetic and geometric returns?

19. **Arithmetic and Geometric Returns** A stock has had the following year-end prices and dividends:

Year	Price	Dividend
0	$58.12	$ –
1	61.56	0.55
2	54.32	0.60
3	64.19	0.63
4	74.13	0.72
5	79.32	0.81

What are the arithmetic and geometric returns for the stock?

20. Arithmetic versus Geometric Returns   You are given the returns for the following three stocks:

Year	Stock A	Stock B	Stock C
1	11%	8%	−15%
2	11	15	34
3	11	10	16
4	11	9	8
5	11	13	12

Calculate the arithmetic return, geometric return, and standard deviation for each stock. Do you notice anything about the relationship between an asset's arithmetic return, standard deviation, and geometric return? Do you think this relationship will always hold?

Spreadsheet Problems

21. Return and Standard Deviation   The 1980s was a good decade for investors in S&P 500 stocks. To find out how good, construct a spreadsheet that calculates the arithmetic average return, variance, and standard deviation for the S&P 500 returns during the 1980s using spreadsheet functions.

S&P Problems

www.mhhe.com/edumarketinsight

STANDARD &POOR'S

1. Industry Comparison   On the Market Insight Home Page, follow the "Industry" link to go to the industry home page. The drop down menu allows you to select different industries. Answer the following questions for these industries: Air Freight & Logistics, Apparel Retail, Department Stores, Electric Utilities, Home Improvement Retail, Investment Banking & Brokerage, and Regional Banks.

   a. How many companies are in each industry?
   b. What are the total sales in each industry?
   c. Do the industries with the largest total sales have the most companies in the industry? What does this tell you about competition in the various industries?

2. Calculating Returns   Download the historical stock prices for Boeing (BA) under the "Mthly. Adj. Prices" link. Use the closing stock prices to calculate the monthly return each month for the last twelve months. Do your calculations match the return calculations given in the file? Why or why not? Now calculate the dividends paid each month.

3. Calculating Standard Deviation   Download the historical stock prices for Canon (CAJ) under the "Mthly. Adj. Prices" link. Using the monthly returns in the file, calculate the monthly standard deviation of Canon stock for the past 12 months.

What's on the Web?

1. Ticker Symbols   Go to finance.yahoo.com and look up the ticker symbols for the following companies: 3M Company, International Business Machines, Dell Computer, Advanced Micro Devices, American Standard Company, and Bed, Bath & Beyond.

2. Average Return and Standard Deviation   Go to finance.yahoo.com and enter the ticker symbol for your favorite stock. Now, look for the historical prices and find the monthly closing stock price for the last six years. Calculate the annual arithmetic average return, the standard deviation, and the geometric return for this period.

3. Stock Performance   What are the best-performing stocks over the past year? Go to finance.yahoo.com and select the "Stock Screener" link. You will see a "Performance" category and a pull-down menu labeled "1 Yr Stock Perf." Select "Up more than 200%" and "Find Stocks." How many stocks have increased more than 200 percent over the past year? Now go back and select "Down more than 90%." How many stocks have dropped more than 90 percent in value over the past year?

Stock-Trak Exercises

To access the Stock-Trak Exercise for this chapter, please visit the book Web site at www.mhhe.com/jm4e and choose the corresponding chapter.

CHAPTER 2

Buying and Selling Securities

"Don't gamble! Take all your savings and buy some good stock and hold it till it goes up. If it don't go up, don't buy it."

–Will Rogers

You might wish to try Will Rogers's well-known stock market advice, but first you must know the basics of securities trading. Fortunately, trading is a relatively simple task, as attested to by the billions of shares of stocks that trade among investors on a typical day. Essentially, you begin the process by opening a trading account with a brokerage firm and then submitting trading orders. But you should know about some important details beforehand. ■

We hope reading about the history of risk and return in our previous chapter generated some interest in investing on your own. To help you get started, this chapter covers the basics of the investing process. We begin by describing how you go about buying and selling securities such as stocks and bonds. We then outline some of the most important considerations and constraints to keep in mind as you get more involved in the investing process.

2.1 Getting Started

Suppose you have some money that you want to invest. One way to get started is to open an account with a securities broker, such as A.G. Edwards or Merrill Lynch. Such accounts are often called *brokerage* or *trading accounts*. Opening a trading account is straightforward and really much like opening a bank account. You will be asked to supply some basic information about yourself and to sign an agreement (often simply called a customer's agreement) that spells out your rights and obligations and those of your broker. You then give your broker a check and instructions on how you want the money invested.

To illustrate, suppose that instead of going to Disneyland, you would rather own part of it. You therefore open an account with $10,000. You instruct your broker to purchase 100 shares of Walt Disney stock and to retain any remaining funds in your account. Your broker will locate a seller and purchase the stock on your behalf. Say shares of stock in Walt Disney Corporation are selling for about $60 per share, so your 100 shares will cost $6,000. In addition, for providing this service, your broker will charge you a commission. How much depends on a number of things, including the type of broker and the size of your order, but on this order, $50 wouldn't be an unusual commission charge. After paying for the stock and paying the commission, you would have $3,950 left in your account. Your broker will hold your stock for you or deliver the shares to you, whichever you wish. At a later date, you can sell your stock by instructing your broker to do so. You would receive the proceeds from the sale, less another commission charge. You can always add money to your account and purchase additional securities, and you can withdraw money from your account or even close it altogether.

In broad terms, this basic explanation is really all there is to it. As we begin to discuss in the next section, however, there is a range of services available to you, and there are important considerations that you need to take into account before you actually begin investing.

CHOOSING A BROKER

The first step in opening an account is choosing a broker. Brokers are traditionally divided into three groups: full-service brokers, discount brokers, and deep-discount brokers. What distinguishes the three groups is the level of service they provide and the resulting commissions they charge.

With a deep-discount broker, essentially the only services provided are account maintenance and order execution—that is, buying and selling. You generally deal with a deep-discount broker over the telephone or, increasingly, using a Web browser (see the next section on online brokers).

At the other extreme, a full-service broker will provide investment advice regarding the types of securities and investment strategies that might be appropriate for you to consider (or avoid). The larger brokerage firms do extensive research on individual companies and securities and maintain lists of recommended (and not recommended) securities. They maintain offices throughout the country, so, depending on where you live, you can actually stop in and speak to the person assigned to your account. A full-service broker will even manage your account for you if you wish.

Discount brokers fall somewhere between the two cases we have discussed so far, offering more investment counseling than the deep-discounters and lower commissions than the full-service brokers. Which type of broker should you choose? It depends on how much advice and service you need or want. If you are the do-it-yourself type, then you may seek out the lower commissions. If you are not, then a full-service broker might be more suitable. Often investors begin with a full-service broker, and then, as they gain experience and confidence, move on to a discount broker.

We should note that the brokerage industry is very competitive, and differences between broker types seem to be blurring. Full-service brokers frequently discount commissions to attract new customers (particularly those with large accounts), and you should not hesitate to ask about commission rates. Similarly, discount brokers have begun to offer securities research and extensive account management services. Basic brokerage services have become almost commodity-like, and, more and more, brokerage firms are competing by offering financial services such as retirement planning, credit cards, and check-writing privileges, to name a few.

ONLINE BROKERS

The most important recent change in the brokerage industry is the rapid growth of online brokers, also known as e-brokers or cyberbrokers. With an online broker, you place buy and sell orders over the Internet using a Web browser.

Before 1995, online accounts essentially did not exist; by 2005, many millions of investors were buying and selling securities online. Online investing has fundamentally changed the discount and deep-discount brokerage industry by slashing costs dramatically. In a typical online trade, no human intervention is needed by the broker as the entire process is handled electronically, so operating costs are held to a minimum. As costs have fallen, so have commissions. Even for relatively large trades, online brokers typically charge less than $20 per trade. For budget-minded investors and active stock traders, the attraction is clear.

Competition among online brokers is fierce. Some take a no-frills approach, offering only basic services and very low commission rates. Others, particularly the larger ones, charge a little more but offer a variety of services, including research and various banking services such as check-writing privileges, credit cards, debit cards, and even mortgages. As technology continues to improve and investors become more comfortable using it, online brokerages will almost surely become the dominant form because of their enormous convenience—and the low commission rates.

SECURITY INVESTORS PROTECTION CORPORATION

As you are probably aware, when you deposit money in a bank, your account is normally protected (up to $100,000) by the Federal Deposit Insurance Corporation, or FDIC, which is an agency of the U.S. government. However, brokerage firms, even though they are often called investment banks, cannot offer FDIC coverage. Most brokerage firms do belong to the **Security Investors Protection Corporation**, or **SIPC**, which was created in 1970. The SIPC insures your account for up to $500,000 in cash and securities, with a $100,000 cash maximum. Some brokers carry additional insurance beyond SIPC minimums. Unlike the FDIC, the SIPC is not a government agency; it is a private insurance fund supported by the securities industry. However, by government regulations, almost all brokerage firms operating in the United States are required to be members of the SIPC.

There is a very important difference between SIPC coverage and FDIC coverage. Up to the maximum coverage, the value of whatever you deposit in a bank is fully guaranteed by the FDIC; you will not lose a cent under any circumstances with FDIC coverage. In contrast, the SIPC ensures only that you will receive whatever cash and securities were held for you by your broker in the event of fraud or other failure. The value of any securities, however, is not guaranteed. In other words, you can lose everything in an SIPC-covered account if the value of your securities falls to zero.

Security Investors Protection Corporation (SIPC)
Insurance fund covering investors' brokerage accounts with member firms.

BROKER–CUSTOMER RELATIONS

There are several other important things to keep in mind when dealing with a broker. First, any advice you receive is *not* guaranteed. Far from it—buy and sell recommendations carry the explicit warning that you rely on them at your own risk. Your broker does have a duty to exercise reasonable care in formulating recommendations and not recommend anything grossly unsuitable, but that is essentially the extent of it.

Second, your broker works as your agent and has a legal duty to act in your best interest; however, brokerage firms are in the business of generating brokerage commissions. This fact will probably be spelled out in the account agreement that you sign. There is, therefore, the potential for a conflict of interest. On rare occasions, a broker is accused of "churning" an account, which refers to extensive trading for the sole purpose of generating commissions. In general, you are responsible for checking your account statements and notifying your broker in the event of any problems, and you should certainly do so.

Finally, in the unlikely event of a significant problem, your account agreement will probably specify very clearly that you must waive your right to sue and/or seek a jury trial. Instead, you agree that any disputes will be settled by arbitration and that arbitration is final and binding. Arbitration is not a legal proceeding, and the rules are much less formal. In essence, a panel is appointed by a self-regulatory body of the securities industry to review the case. The panel will be composed of a small number of individuals who are knowledgeable about the securities industry, but a majority of them will not be associated with the industry. The panel makes a finding, and, absent extraordinary circumstances, its findings cannot be appealed. The panel does not have to disclose factual findings or legal reasoning.

To learn more about dispute resolution, visit www.nasd.com

CHECK THIS

2.1a	What are the differences between full-service and deep-discount brokers?
2.1b	What is the SIPC? How does SIPC coverage differ from FDIC coverage?

2.2 Brokerage Accounts

The account agreement that you sign has a number of important provisions and details specifying the types of trades that can be made and who can make them. Another important concern is whether the broker will extend credit and, if so, the terms under which credit will be extended. We discuss these issues next.

CASH ACCOUNTS

cash account
A brokerage account in which all transactions are made on a strictly cash basis.

A **cash account** is the simplest arrangement. Securities can be purchased to the extent that sufficient cash is available in the account. If additional purchases are desired, then the needed funds must be promptly supplied.

MARGIN ACCOUNTS

margin account
A brokerage account in which, subject to limits, securities can be bought and sold on credit.

call money rate
The interest rate brokers pay to borrow bank funds for lending to customer margin accounts.

With a **margin account**, you can, subject to limits, purchase securities on credit using money loaned to you by your broker. Such a purchase is called a *margin purchase*. The interest rate you pay on the money you borrow is based on the broker's **call money rate**, which is, loosely, the rate the broker pays to borrow the money. You pay some amount over the call money rate, called the *spread;* the exact spread depends on your broker and the size of the loan. Suppose the call money rate has been hovering around 7 percent. If a brokerage firm charges a 2.5 percent spread above this rate on loan amounts under $10,000, then you would pay a total of about 9.5 percent. However, this is usually reduced for larger loan amounts. For example, the spread may decline to .75 percent for amounts over $100,000.

Several important concepts and rules are involved in a margin purchase. For concreteness, we focus on stocks in our discussion. The specific margin rules for other investments can be quite different, but the principles and terminology are usually similar.

In general, when you purchase securities on credit, some of the money is yours and the rest is borrowed. The amount that is yours is called the **margin**. Margin is usually expressed as a percentage. For example, if you take $7,000 of your own money and borrow an additional $3,000 from your broker, your total investment will be $10,000. Of this $10,000, $7,000 is yours, so the margin is $7,000 / $10,000 = .70, or 70 percent.

margin
The portion of the value of an investment that is *not* borrowed.

It is useful to create an account balance sheet when thinking about margin purchases (and some other issues we'll get to in just a moment). To illustrate, suppose you open a margin account with $5,000. You tell your broker to buy 100 shares of Microsoft. Microsoft is selling for $80 per share, so the total cost will be $8,000. Since you have only $5,000 in the account, you borrow the remaining $3,000. Immediately following the purchase, your account balance sheet would look like this:

Assets		Liabilities and Account Equity	
100 shares of Microsoft	$8,000	Margin loan	$3,000
		Account equity	5,000
Total	$8,000	Total	$8,000

On the left-hand side of this balance sheet, we list the account assets, which, in this case, consist of the $8,000 in Microsoft stock you purchased. On the right-hand side, we first list the $3,000 loan you took out to partially pay for the stock; this is a liability because, at some point, the loan must be repaid. The difference between the value of the assets held in the account and the loan amount is $5,000. This amount is your *account equity*, that is, the net value of your investment. Notice that your margin is equal to the account equity divided by the value of the stock owned and held in the account: $5,000 / $8,000 = .625, or 62.5 percent.

EXAMPLE 2.1 | **The Account Balance Sheet**

You want to buy 1,000 shares of Wal-Mart at a price of $24 per share. You put up $18,000 and borrow the rest. What does your account balance sheet look like? What is your margin?

The 1,000 shares of Wal-Mart cost $24,000. You supply $18,000, so you must borrow $6,000. The account balance sheet looks like this:

Assets		Liabilities and Account Equity	
1,000 shares of Wal-Mart	$24,000	Margin loan	$ 6,000
		Account equity	18,000
Total	$24,000	Total	$24,000

Your margin is the account equity divided by the value of the stock owned:

$$\text{Margin} = \$18,000 / \$24,000$$
$$= .75 = 75 \text{ percent}$$

initial margin

The minimum margin that must be supplied on a securities purchase.

INITIAL MARGIN When you first purchase securities on credit, there is a minimum margin that you must supply. This percentage is called the **initial margin**. The minimum percentage (for stock purchases) is set by the Federal Reserve (the "Fed"), but the exchanges and individual brokerage firms may require higher amounts.

The Fed's power to set initial margin requirements was established in the Securities Exchange Act of 1934. In subsequent years, initial margin requirements ranged from a low of 45 percent to a high of 100 percent. Since 1974, the minimum has been 50 percent (for stock purchases). In other words, if you have $10,000 in cash that is not borrowed, you can borrow up to an additional $10,000, but no more.

We emphasize that these initial margin requirements apply to stocks. In contrast, for the most part, there is little initial margin requirement for government bonds. On the other hand, margin is not allowed at all on certain other types of securities.

EXAMPLE 2.2 | **Calculating Initial Margin**

Suppose you have $6,000 in cash in a trading account with a 50 percent initial margin requirement. What is the largest order you can place (ignoring commissions)? If the initial margin were 60 percent, how would your answer change?

When the initial margin is 50 percent, you must supply half of the total, so $12,000 is the largest order you could place. When the initial margin is 60 percent, your $6,000 must equal 60 percent of the total. In other words, it must be the case that

$$\$6{,}000 = 0.60 \times \text{Total order}$$
$$\text{Total order} = \$6{,}000/.60$$
$$= \$10{,}000$$

As this example illustrates, the higher the initial margin required, the less you can borrow.

---

maintenance margin

The minimum margin that must be present at all times in a margin account.

MAINTENANCE MARGIN In addition to the initial margin requirement set by the Fed, brokerage firms and exchanges generally have a **maintenance margin** requirement. For example, the New York Stock Exchange (NYSE) requires a minimum of 25 percent maintenance margin. This amount is the minimum margin required at all times after the purchase.

The maintenance margin set by your broker is sometimes called the "house" margin requirement. The level is established by your broker, who may vary it depending on what you are buying. For low-priced and very volatile stocks, the house margin can be as high as 100 percent, meaning no margin at all.

margin call

A demand for more funds that occurs when the margin in an account drops below the maintenance margin.

A typical maintenance margin would be 30 percent. If your margin falls below 30 percent, then you may be subject to a **margin call**, which is a demand by your broker to add to your account, pay off part of the loan, or sell enough securities to bring your margin back up to an acceptable level. If you do not or cannot comply, your securities may be sold. The loan will be repaid out of the proceeds, and any remaining amounts will be credited to your account.

To illustrate, suppose your account has a 50 percent initial margin requirement and a 30 percent maintenance margin. A particular stock is selling for $50 per share. You have $20,000, and you want to buy as much of this stock as you possibly can. With a 50 percent initial margin, you can buy up to $40,000 worth, or 800 shares. The account balance sheet looks like this:

Assets		Liabilities and Account Equity	
800 shares @$50/share	$40,000	Margin loan	$20,000
		Account equity	20,000
Total	$40,000	Total	$40,000

Unfortunately, right after you buy it, the company reveals that it has been artificially inflating earnings for the last three years (this is not good), and the share price falls to $35 per share. What does the account balance sheet look like when this happens? Are you subject to a margin call?

To create the new account balance sheet, we recalculate the total value of the stock. The margin loan stays the same, so the account equity is adjusted as needed:

Assets		Liabilities and Account Equity	
800 shares @$35/share	$28,000	Margin loan	$20,000
		Account equity	8,000
Total	$28,000	Total	$28,000

As shown, the total value of your "position" (i.e., the stock you hold) falls to $28,000, a $12,000 loss. You still owe $20,000 to your broker, so your account equity is $28,000 − $20,000 = $8,000. Your margin is therefore $8,000/$28,000 = .286, or 28.6 percent. You are below the 30 percent minimum, so you are subject to a margin call.

THE EFFECTS OF MARGIN Margin is a form of *financial leverage*. Any time you borrow money to make an investment, the impact is to magnify both your gains and losses, hence the use of the term "leverage." The easiest way to see this is through an example. Imagine that you have $30,000 in an account with a 60 percent initial margin. You now know that you can borrow up to an additional $20,000 and buy $50,000 worth of stock (why?). The call money rate is 5.50 percent; you must pay this rate plus a .50 percent spread. Suppose you buy 1,000 shares of IBM at $50 per share. One year later, IBM is selling for $60 per share. Assuming the call money rate does not change and ignoring dividends, what is your return on this investment?

At the end of the year, your 1,000 shares are worth $60,000. You owe 6 percent interest on the $20,000 you borrowed, or $1,200. If you pay off the loan with interest, you will have $60,000 − $21,200 = $38,800. You started with $30,000 and ended with $38,800, so your net gain is $8,800. In percentage terms, your return was $8,800/$30,000 = .2933, or 29.33 percent.

How would you have done without the financial leverage created from the margin purchase? In this case, you would have invested just $30,000. At $50 per share, you would have purchased 600 shares. At the end of the year, your 600 shares would be worth $60 apiece, or $36,000 total. Your dollar profit is $6,000, so your percentage return would be $6,000/$30,000 = .20, or 20 percent. If we compare this to the 29.33 percent that you made above, it's clear that you did substantially better by leveraging.

The downside is that you would do much worse if IBM's stock price fell (or didn't rise very much). For example, if IBM had fallen to $40 a share, you would have lost (check these calculations for practice) $11,200, or 37.33 percent on your margin investment, compared to $6,000, or 20 percent on the unmargined investment. This example illustrates how leveraging an investment through a margin account can cut both ways.

EXAMPLE 2.3 A Marginal Investment?

A year ago, you bought 300 shares of Ford at $55 per share. You put up the 60 percent initial margin. The call money rate plus the spread you paid was 8 percent. What is your return if the price today is $50? Compare this to the return you would have earned if you had not invested on margin.

Your total investment was 300 shares at $55 per share, or $16,500. You supplied 60 percent, or $9,900, and you borrowed the remaining $6,600. At the end of the year, you owe $6,600 plus 8 percent interest, or $7,128. If the stock sells for $50, then your position is worth 300 × $50 = $15,000. Deducting the $7,128 leaves $7,872 for you. Since you originally invested $9,900, your dollar loss is $9,900 −$7,872 = $2,028. Your percentage return is −$2,028/$9,900 = −20.48 percent.

If you had not leveraged your investment, you would have purchased $9,900/$55 = 180 shares. These would have been worth 180 × $50 = $9,000. You therefore would have lost $900; your percentage return would have been −$900/$9,900 = −9.09 percent, compared to the −20.48 percent that you lost on your leveraged position.

EXAMPLE 2.4 How Low Can It Go?

In our previous example (Example 2.3), suppose the maintenance margin was 40 percent. At what price per share would you have been subject to a margin call? To answer, let P^* be the critical price. You own 300 shares, so, at that price, your stock is worth 300 × P^*. You borrowed $6,600, so your account equity is equal to the value of your stock less the $6,600 you owe, or 300 × P^* − $6,600. We can summarize this information as follows:

$$\text{Amount borrowed} = \$6,600$$

$$\text{Value of stock} = 300 \times P^*$$

$$\text{Account equity} = 300 \times P^* - \$6,600$$

From our preceding discussion, your percentage margin is your dollar margin (or account equity) divided by the value of the stock:

$$\text{Margin} = \frac{\text{Account equity}}{\text{Value of stock}}$$

$$= \frac{300 \times P^* - \$6,600}{300 \times P^*}$$

To find the critical price, we will set this margin to the maintenance margin and solve for P^*:

$$\text{Maintenance margin} = \frac{\text{Number of shares} \times P^* - \text{Amount borrowed}}{\text{Number of shares} \times P^*}$$

Solving for P^* yields

$$P^* = \frac{\text{Amount borrowed/Number of shares}}{1 - \text{Maintenance margin}}$$

(continued)

Finally, setting the maintenance margin equal to 40 percent, we obtain this critical price, $P*$:

$$P* = \frac{\$6,600/300}{1 - .40}$$

$$= \frac{\$6,600}{180} = \$36.67$$

At any price below $36.67, your margin will be less than 40 percent, and you will be subject to a margin call. So, $36.67 is the lowest possible price that could be reached before you are subject to a margin call.

As Example 2.4 shows, you can calculate the critical price (the lowest price before you get a margin call) as follows:

$$P* = \frac{\text{Amount borrowed/Number of shares}}{1 - \text{Maintenance margin}} \tag{2.1}$$

For example, suppose you had a margin loan of $40,000, which you used to purchase, in part, 1,000 shares. The maintenance margin is 37.5 percent. What's the critical stock price, and how do you interpret it?

See if you don't agree that the critical stock price, $P*$, is $40/.625 = $64. The interpretation is straightforward: If the stock price falls below $64, you're subject to a margin call.

A NOTE ON ANNUALIZING RETURNS

In Chapter 1, we talked about the need to compute percentage returns, but, so far, we've only considered annual returns. Of course, the actual length of time you own an investment will almost never be exactly a year. To compare investments, however, we will usually need to express returns on a per-year or "annualized" basis, so we need to do a little bit more work.

For example, suppose you bought 200 shares of Cisco at a price of $80 per share. In three months, you sell your stock for $85. You didn't receive any dividends. What is your return for the three months? What is your annualized return?

In this case, we say that your *holding period,* which is the length of time you own the stock, is three months. From our discussion in Chapter 1, with a zero dividend, you know that the percentage return can be calculated as:

$$\text{Percentage return} = (P_{t+1} - P_t)/P_t = (\$85 - \$80)/\$80 = .0625 = 6.25\%$$

This 6.25 percent is your return for the three-month holding period, but what does this return amount to on a per-year basis? To find out, we need to convert this to an annualized return, meaning a return expressed on a per-year basis. Such a return is often called an **effective annual return**, or **EAR** for short. The general formula is this:

effective annual return (EAR)
The return on an investment expressed on a per-year, or "annualized," basis.

$$1 + EAR = (1 + \text{holding period percentage return})^m \tag{2.2}$$

where m is the number of holding periods in a year.

In our example, the holding period percentage return is 6.25 percent, or .0625. The holding period is three months, so there are four (12 months/3 months) periods in a year. The annualized return, or *EAR*, is thus calculated as:

$$1 + EAR = (1 + \text{holding period percentage return})^m$$
$$= (1 + .0625)^4$$
$$= 1.2744$$

So, your annualized return is 27.44 percent.

A "QWEST" for Returns

Suppose you buy some stock in Qwest (no, that's not a typo, that's how the company spells it) at a price of $60 per share. Four months later, you sell it for $63. No dividend is paid. What is your annualized return on this investment?

For the four-month holding period, your return is:

$$\text{Percentage return} = (P_{t+1} - P_t)/P_t = (\$63 - \$60)/\$60 = .05 = 5\%$$

There are three four-month periods in a year, so the annualized return is:

$$1 + EAR = (1 + \text{holding period percentage return})^m = (1 + .05)^3 = 1.1576$$

Subtracting the one, we get an annualized return of .1576, or 15.76 percent.

More Annualized Returns

Suppose you buy some stock in Apple Computer at a price of $80 per share. Three *years* later, you sell it for $100. No dividends were paid. What is your annualized return on this investment?

The situation here is a bit different because your holding period is now longer than a year, but the calculation is basically the same. For the three-year holding period, your return is:

$$\text{Percentage return} = (P_{t+1} - P_t)/P_t = (\$100 - \$80)/\$80 = .25 = 25\%$$

How many three-year holding periods are there in a single year? The answer is one-third, so *m* in this case is 1/3. The annualized return is:

$$1 + EAR = (1 + \text{holding period percentage return})^m$$
$$= (1 + .25)^{1/3}$$
$$= 1.0772$$

Subtracting the one, we get an annualized return of .0772, or 7.72 percent.

Things get a little more complicated when we consider holding periods different from a year on a margin purchase. For example, suppose the call money rate is 9 percent, and you pay a spread of 2 percent over that. You buy 1,000 shares of Costco at $40 per share, but you only put up half the money. In three months, Costco is selling for $42 per share, and you close out your position. What is your annualized return assuming no dividends are paid?

In this case, you invested $40,000, half of which, $20,000, is borrowed. How much do you have to repay in three months? Here we have to adjust for the fact that the interest rate is 11 percent per year, but you only borrowed the money for three months. In this case, the amount you repay is equal to:

$$\text{Amount repaid} = \text{Amount borrowed} \times (1 + \text{interest rate year})^t$$

where *t* is the fraction of a year. In our case, *t* would be 3 months/12 months, or .25. So, plugging in our numbers, we get:

$$\text{Amount repaid} = \text{Amount borrowed} \times (1 + \text{interest rate per year})^t$$
$$= \$20,000 \times (1 + .11)^{.25}$$
$$= \$20,000 \times 1.02643$$
$$= \$20,528.67$$

So, when you sell your stock, you get $42,000, of which $20,528.67 is used to pay off the loan, leaving you with $21,471.33. You invested $20,000, so your dollar gain is $1,471.33, and your percentage return for your three-month holding period is $1,471.33/$20,000 = .0736, or 7.36 percent.

Finally, we have to convert this 7.36 percent to an annualized return. There are four three-month periods in a year, so:

$$1 + EAR = (1 + \text{holding period percentage return})^m$$
$$= (1 + .0736)^4$$
$$= 1.3285$$

So, your annualized return is 32.85 percent.

HYPOTHECATION AND STREET NAME REGISTRATION

As part of your margin account agreement, you must agree to various conditions. We discuss two of the most important next.

HYPOTHECATION Any securities you purchase in your margin account will be held by your broker as collateral against the loan made to you. This practice protects the broker because the securities can be sold by the broker if the customer is unwilling or unable to meet a margin call. Putting securities up as collateral against a loan is called **hypothecation**. In fact, a margin agreement is sometimes called a hypothecation agreement. In addition, to borrow the money that it loans to you, your broker will often *re*-hypothecate your securities, meaning that your broker will pledge them as collateral with its lender, normally a bank.

hypothecation
Pledging securities as collateral against a loan.

STREET NAME REGISTRATION Securities in a margin account are normally held in **street name**. This means that the brokerage firm is actually the registered owner. If this were not the case, the brokerage firm could not legally sell the securities should a customer refuse to meet a margin call or otherwise fail to live up to the terms of the margin agreement. With this arrangement, the brokerage firm is the "owner of record," but the account holder is the "beneficial owner."

street name
An arrangement under which a broker is the registered owner of a security.

When a security is held in street name, anything mailed to the security owner, such as an annual report or a dividend check, goes to the brokerage firm. The brokerage firm then passes these on to the account holder. Street name ownership is actually a great convenience to the owner. In fact, because it is usually a free service, even customers with cash accounts generally choose street name ownership. Some of the benefits are:

1. Since the broker holds the security, there is no danger of theft or other loss of the security. This is important because a stolen or lost security cannot be easily or cheaply replaced.

2. Any dividends or interest payments are automatically credited, and they are often credited more quickly (and conveniently) than they would be if the owner received the check in the mail.

3. The broker provides regular account statements showing the value of securities held in the account and any payments received. Also, for tax purposes, the broker will provide all the needed information on a single form at the end of the year, greatly reducing the owner's record-keeping requirements.

OTHER ACCOUNT ISSUES

If you do not wish to manage your account yourself, you can set up an *advisory account*. In this case, you pay someone else to make buy and sell decisions on your behalf. You are responsible for paying any commissions or other costs, as well as a management fee.

In a relatively recent innovation, brokerage firms have begun to offer *wrap accounts*. In such an account, you choose a money manager or a set of money managers from a group offered by the brokerage firm. All of the costs, commissions, and expenses associated with your account are "wrapped" into a single fee that you pay, hence the name. If you simply authorize your broker to trade for you, then there is no management fee, but you are still responsible for any commissions. This arrangement is termed a *discretionary account*.

Most of the large brokerage firms offer accounts that provide for complete money management, including check-writing privileges, credit cards, and margin loans, especially for larger investors. Such accounts are generally called *asset management accounts*. The terms of these accounts differ from broker to broker, and the services provided frequently change in response to competition.

Finally, if you want to buy and sell a broad variety of individual securities, then a brokerage account is almost a requirement. It is true that some companies and other entities (such as the U.S. government) do sell directly to the public, at least at certain times and subject to various restrictions, so you can buy securities directly in some cases. In fact, you could buy and sell through the want ads in your local paper if you were so inclined, but given the modest commissions charged by deep-discount brokers, this hardly seems worth the trouble.

However, you should be aware that if you do not wish to actively buy and sell securities, but you do want to own stocks, bonds, or other financial assets, there is an alternative to a brokerage account: a *mutual fund*. Mutual funds are a means of combining or pooling the funds of a large group of investors. The buy and sell decisions for the resulting pool are then made by a fund manager, who is compensated for the service. Mutual funds have become so important that we will devote an entire chapter to them (Chapter 4) rather than give them short shrift here.

CHECK THIS

2.2a	What is the difference between a cash and margin account?
2.2b	What is the effect of a margin purchase on gains and losses?
2.2c	What is a margin call?

2.3 Short Sales

An investor who buys and owns shares of stock is said to be *long* in the stock or to have a *long position*. An investor with a long position will make money if the price of the stock increases and lose money if it goes down. In other words, a long investor hopes that the price will increase.

Now consider a different situation. Suppose you thought, for some reason, that the stock in a particular company was likely to *decrease* in value. You obviously wouldn't want to buy any of it. If you already owned some, you might choose to sell it.

short sale
A sale in which the seller does not actually own the security that is sold.

Beyond this, you might decide to engage in a **short sale**. In a short sale, you actually sell a security that you do not own. This is referred to as *shorting* the stock. After the short sale, the investor is said to have a *short position* in the security.

Financial assets of all kinds are sold short, not just shares of stock, and the terms "long" and "short" are universal. However, the mechanics of a short sale differ quite a bit across security types. Even so, regardless of how the short sale is executed, the essence is the same. An investor with a long position benefits from price increases, and, as we will see, an investor with a short position benefits from price decreases. For the sake of illustration, we focus here on shorting shares of stock. Procedures for shorting other types of securities are discussed in later chapters.

BASICS OF A SHORT SALE

How can you sell stock you don't own? It is easier than you might think: You borrow the shares of stock from your broker and then you sell them. At some future date, you will buy the same number of shares that you originally borrowed and return them, thereby eliminating the short position. Eliminating the short position is often called *covering the position* or, less commonly, *curing the short*.

You might wonder where your broker will get the stock to loan you. Normally, it will simply come from other margin accounts. Often, when you open a margin account, you are asked to sign a loan-consent agreement, which gives your broker the right to loan shares held in the account. If shares you own are loaned out, you still receive any dividends or other distributions and you can sell the stock if you wish. In other words, the fact that some of your stock may have been loaned out is of little or no consequence as far as you are concerned.

An investor with a short position will profit if the security declines in value. For example, assume that you short 1,000 shares of Liz Claiborne at a price of $10 per share. You receive $10,000 from the sale (more on this in a moment). A month later, the stock is selling for $6 per share. You buy 1,000 shares for $6,000 and return the stock to your broker, thereby covering your position. Because you received $10,000 from the sale and it cost you only $6,000 to cover, you made $4,000.

Conventional Wall Street wisdom states that the way to make money is to "buy low, sell high." With a short sale, we hope to do exactly that, just in opposite order—sell high, buy low. If a short sale strikes you as a little confusing, it might help to think about the everyday use of the terms. Whenever we say that we are "running short" on something, we mean we don't have enough of it. Similarly, when someone says "don't sell me short," they mean don't bet on them not to succeed.

EXAMPLE 2.7 | **The Long and Short of It**

Suppose you short 2,000 shares of Lucent at $35 per share. Six months later you cover your short. If Lucent is selling for $30 per share at that time, did you make money or lose money? How much? What if you covered at $40?

If you shorted at $35 per share and covered at $30, you originally sold 2,000 shares at $35 and later bought them back at $30, so you made $5 per share, or $10,000. If you covered at $40, you lost $10,000.

SHORT SALES: SOME DETAILS

When you short a stock, you must borrow it from your broker, so there are various requirements you must fulfill. First, there is an initial margin and a maintenance margin. Second, after you sell the borrowed stock, the proceeds from the sale are credited to your account, but you cannot use them. They are, in effect, frozen until you return the stock. Finally, if any dividends are paid on the stock while you have a short position, you must pay them.

To illustrate, we will again create an account balance sheet. Suppose you want to short 100 shares of Sears when the price is $30 per share. This means you will borrow shares of stock worth a total of $30 \times 100 = \$3,000$. Your broker has a 50 percent initial margin and a 40 percent maintenance margin on short sales.

An important thing to keep in mind with a margin purchase of securities is that margin is calculated as the value of your account equity relative to the value of the securities purchased. With a short sale, margin is calculated as the value of your account equity relative to the value of the securities sold short. Thus, in both cases, margin is equal to equity value divided by security value.

In our example here, the initial value of the securities sold short is $3,000 and the initial margin is 50 percent, so you must deposit at least half of $3,000, or $1,500, in your account. With this in mind, after the short sale, your account balance sheet is as follows:

Assets		Liabilities and Account Equity	
Proceeds from sale	$3,000	Short position	$3,000
Initial margin deposit	1,500	Account equity	1,500
Total	$4,500	Total	$4,500

WWW

There are many sites devoted to the fine art of short selling. Try www.bearmarket central.com

As shown, four items appear on the account balance sheet:

1. *Proceeds from sale.* This is the $3,000 you received when you sold the stock. This amount will remain in your account until you cover your position. Note that you will not earn interest on this amount—it will just sit there as far as you are concerned.
2. *Margin deposit.* This is the 50 percent margin that you had to post. This amount will not change unless there is a margin call. Depending on the circumstances and your particular account agreement, you may earn interest on the initial margin deposit.
3. *Short position.* Because you must eventually buy back the stock and return it, you have a liability. The current cost of eliminating that liability is $3,000.
4. *Account equity.* As always, the account equity is the difference between the total account value ($4,500) and the total liabilities ($3,000).

We now examine two scenarios: (1) the stock price falls to $20 per share, and (2) the stock price rises to $40 per share.

If the stock price falls to $20 per share, then you are still liable for 100 shares, but the cost of those shares is now just $2,000. Your account balance sheet becomes:

Assets		Liabilities and Account Equity	
Proceeds from sale	$3,000	Short position	$2,000
Initial margin deposit	1,500	Account equity	2,500
Total	$4,500	Total	$4,500

Notice that the left-hand side doesn't change. The same $3,000 you originally received is still held, and the $1,500 margin you deposited is still there also. On the right-hand side, the short position is now a $2,000 liability, down from $3,000. Finally, the good news is that the account equity rises by $1,000, so this is your gain. Your margin is equal to account equity divided by the security value (the value of the short position), $2,500/$2,000 = 1.25, or 125 percent.

However, if the stock price rises to $40, things are not so rosy. Now, the 100 shares for which you are liable are worth $4,000:

Assets		Liabilities and Account Equity	
Proceeds from sale	$3,000	Short position	$4,000
Initial margin deposit	1,500	Account equity	500
Total	$4,500	Total	$4,500

Again, the left-hand side doesn't change. The short liability rises by $1,000, and, unfortunately for you, the account equity declines by $1,000, the amount of your loss.

To make matters worse, when the stock price rises to $40, you are severely undermargined. The account equity is $500, but the value of the stock sold short is $4,000. Your margin is $500 / $4,000 = 12.5 percent. Since this is well below the 40 percent maintenance margin, you are subject to a margin call. You have two options: (1) buy back some or all of the stock and return it, or (2) add funds to your account.

EXAMPLE 2.8 **A Case of The Shorts**

You shorted 5,000 shares of a particular stock at a price of $30 per share. The initial margin is 50 percent, and the maintenance margin is 40 percent. What does your account balance sheet look like following the short?

Following the short, your account becomes:

Assets		Liabilities and Account Equity	
Proceeds from sale	$150,000	Short position	$150,000
Initial margin deposit	75,000	Account equity	75,000
Total	$225,000	Total	$225,000

Notice that you shorted $150,000 worth of stock, so, with a 50 percent margin requirement, you deposited $75,000.

EXAMPLE 2.9 **Margin Calls**

In our previous example (Example 2.8), at what price per share would you be subject to a margin call?

To answer this one, let P^* be the critical price. The short liability then is 5,000 shares at a price of P^*, or $5,000 \times P^*$. The total account value is $225,000, so the account equity is $225,000 - 5,000 \times P^*$. We can summarize this information as follows:

$$\text{Short position} = 5,000 \times P^*$$

$$\text{Account equity} = \$225,000 - 5,000 \times P^*$$

(continued)

Notice that the total account value, $225,000, is the sum of your initial margin deposit plus the proceeds from the sale, and this amount does not change. Your margin is the account equity relative to the short liability:

$$\text{Margin} = \frac{\text{Account equity}}{\text{Value of stock}}$$

$$= \frac{\text{Initial margin deposit} + \text{Short proceeds} - \text{Number of shares} \times P^*}{\text{Number of shares} \times P^*}$$

$$= \frac{\$150,000 + 75,000 - 5,000 \times P^*}{5,000 \times P^*}$$

To find the critical price, we will set this margin equal to the maintenance margin and solve for P^*:

$$\text{Maintenance margin} =$$
$$\frac{\text{Initial margin deposit} + \text{Short proceeds} - \text{Number of shares} \times P^*}{\text{Number of shares} \times P^*}$$

Solving for P^* yields:

$$P^* = \frac{(\text{Initial margin deposit} + \text{Short proceeds})/\text{Number of shares}}{1 + \text{Maintenance margin}}$$

Finally, setting the maintenance margin equal to 40 percent, we obtain this critical price, P^*:

$$P^* = \frac{\$225,000/5,000}{1.40} = \$32.14$$

At any price *above* $32.14, your margin will be less than 40 percent, so you will be subject to a margin call. So $32.14 is the highest possible price that could be reached before you are subject to a margin call.

As Example 2.9 shows, you can calculate the critical price on a short sale (the highest price before you get a margin call) as follows:

$$P^* = \frac{(\text{Initial margin deposit} + \text{Short proceeds})/\text{Number of shares}}{1 + \text{Maintenance margin}}$$

For example, suppose you shorted 1,000 shares at $50. The initial margin is 50 percent, and the maintenance margin is 40 percent. What's the critical stock price, and how do you interpret it?

Noting that the initial margin deposit is $25,000 (50 percent of the short proceeds), see if you don't agree that the critical stock price, P^*, is $75/1.4 = $53.57. So, if the stock price rises above $53.57, you're subject to a margin call.

At this point, you might wonder whether short selling is a common practice among investors. Actually, it is quite common and a substantial volume of stock sales are initiated by short sellers. The nearby *Investment Updates* box is a sample *Wall Street Journal* box reporting **short interest**. Short interest is the amount of common stock held in short positions. As shown, the amount of stock held short for some companies can be several tens of millions of shares, and the total number of shares held short across all companies can be several billion shares. A nearby *Work the Web* box shows how to find short interest for a particular company.

short interest
The amount of common stock held in short positions.

SHORT POSITIONS FALL ON NASDAQ BUT BEARS PROFIT

Short interest edged lower on the NASDAQ Stock Market, but bearish bets are still doing relatively well so far this year.

For the monthly period ending Sept. 15, the number of short-selling positions not yet closed out at NASDAQ, including all issues, fell 0.2% to 5,811,842,432 from 5,821,353,067 in mid-August.

Marketwide, the short ratio, or number of days' average volume represented by the outstanding short positions at the exchange, rose to 4.0 compared with 3.6.

Investors who sell securities "short" borrow stock and sell it, betting the stock's price will fall and they will be able to buy the shares back later at a lower price for return to the lender. Short interest often is considered an indication of the level of skepticism in the market. Short interest reflects the number of shares that have yet to be repurchased to give back to lenders. In general, the higher the short interest, the more people are expecting a downturn. Short positions rise in value as stocks fall, and vice versa.

Despite recent declines in short interest at both NASDAQ and the rival New York Stock Exchange, the average short portfolio has gained 4.4% this year, according to the hedge-fund consulting firm Treflie Capital Management. That means short sellers have beaten major stock indexes like the Dow Jones Industrial Average, NASDAQ Composite, and Standard & Poor's 500.

NASDAQ SHORT SELLING HIGHLIGHTS

LARGEST SHORT POSITIONS

RANK		SEP 15	AUG 15	CHANGE
1	Nasdaq-100 Trust	207,213,982	221,879,299	-14,665,317
2	Microsoft Corp	119,257,228	98,872,718	20,384,510
3	Level 3 Communicat	94,756,643	99,105,127	-4,348,484
4	Sirius Satellite	94,371,328	102,938,137	-8,566,809
5	Charter Comm A	88,887,252	86,203,619	2,683,633
6	Yahoo! Inc	79,475,645	83,281,872	-3,806,227
7	Sun Microsystems	59,903,586	48,971,356	10,932,230
8	Intel Corp	54,908,923	51,950,213	2,958,710
9	Cisco Systems	53,941,817	49,600,636	4,341,181
10	XM Satellite Radio	50,798,786	56,318,009	-5,519,223
11	JDS Uniphase	44,139,730	58,425,157	-14,285,427
12	Oracle Corp	42,454,791	40,330,055	2,124,736
13	Applied Materials	41,767,225	44,479,425	-2,712,200
14	eBay Inc	38,664,986	40,664,898	-1,999,912
15	Amazon.com	34,834,058	37,836,056	-3,001,998
16	Comcast Corp A	34,239,277	36,230,682	-1,991,405
17	Adobe Systems	31,272,274	29,446,511	1,825,763
18	Qualcomm Inc	30,421,006	25,170,118	5,250,888
19	Apple Computer Inc	29,176,423	28,722,965	453,458
20	Dell Inc	26,475,186	34,432,630	-7,957,444
21	Amylin Pharma	25,826,727	27,091,332	-1,264,605
22	Amgen Inc	23,447,767	24,213,972	-766,205
23	Juniper Networks	21,448,128	21,711,508	-263,380
24	OmniVision Technol	20,697,728	18,334,878	2,362,850
25	Symantec Corp	20,617,318	21,566,505	-949,187
26	Nextel Partners	19,895,895	19,797,342	98,553
27	Atmel Corp	19,315,692	18,033,572	1,282,120
28	RF Micro Devices	18,832,586	16,665,138	2,167,448
29	Ciena Corp	18,575,106	17,873,831	701,275
30	Millennium Pharma	18,099,455	19,892,324	-1,792,869

LARGEST CHANGES

RANK		SEP 15	AUG 15	CHANGE
INCREASES (in shares)				
1	Microsoft Corp	119,257,228	98,872,718	20,384,510
2	Sun Microsystems	59,903,586	48,971,356	10,932,230
3	Capstone Turbine	6,990,160	866,247	6,123,913
4	Qualcomm Inc	30,421,006	25,170,118	5,250,888
5	Cisco Systems	53,941,817	49,600,636	4,341,181
6	ValueClick Inc	6,728,382	3,110,011	3,618,371
7	Discovery Hldg A	10,735,934	7,174,419	3,561,515
8	Intel Corp	54,908,923	51,950,213	2,958,710
9	Hudson City Bncp	14,389,382	11,484,804	2,904,578
10	Charter Comm A	88,887,252	86,203,619	2,683,633
11	WebMD Inc	8,797,734	6,211,156	2,586,578
12	Align Technology	10,999,360	8,583,788	2,415,572
13	OmniVision Technol	20,697,728	18,334,878	2,362,850
14	Integrated Device	16,370,108	14,014,192	2,355,916
15	Nvidia Corp	13,500,120	11,277,403	2,222,717
16	RF Micro Devices	18,832,586	16,665,138	2,167,448
17	Oracle Corp	42,454,791	40,330,055	2,124,736
18	Redback Networks Inc	4,672,278	2,634,068	2,038,210
19	JetBlue Airways	18,082,751	16,070,302	2,012,449
20	Applebee's Int'l	3,287,277	1,358,077	1,929,200
DECREASES (in shares)				
1	Nasdaq-100 Trust	207,213,982	221,879,299	-14,665,317
2	JDS Uniphase	44,139,730	58,425,157	-14,285,427
3	Sirius Satellite	94,371,328	102,938,137	-8,566,809
4	Dell Inc	26,475,186	34,432,630	-7,957,444
5	Sanmina-SCI Corp	7,403,829	14,104,377	-6,700,548
6	Zhone Technol	3,232,560	9,391,463	-6,158,903
7	XM Satellite Radio	50,798,786	56,318,009	-5,519,223
8	Dobson Comm A	17,584,697	22,879,634	-5,294,937
9	IAC/InterActiveCorp	10,096,934	15,309,935	-5,213,001
10	Level 3 Communicat	94,756,643	99,105,127	-4,348,484
11	Expedia Inc	17,746,848	22,051,156	-4,304,308
12	Siebel Systems Inc	12,399,459	16,523,607	-4,124,148
13	Yahoo! Inc	79,475,645	83,281,872	-3,806,227
14	Altera Corp	12,663,099	16,058,908	-3,395,809
15	Human Genome Sciences	10,531,378	13,856,157	-3,324,779
16	Eyetech Pharmas Inc	6,938,042	10,145,821	-3,207,779
17	Network Appliance	14,061,154	17,120,595	-3,059,441
18	PMC-Sierra Inc	11,934,010	14,974,738	-3,040,728
19	Amazon.com	34,834,058	37,836,056	-3,001,998
20	Applied Materials	41,767,225	44,479,425	-2,712,200
21	Novell Inc	17,003,081	19,701,331	-2,698,250
22	Ameritrade Hldg A	8,915,081	11,568,138	-2,653,057
23	MCI Inc	6,563,561	9,111,976	-2,548,415
24	Andrew Corp	8,615,403	10,994,852	-2,379,449
25	Bed Bath & Beyond	6,659,610	8,854,709	-2,195,099

Nasdaq Short Interest

Billions of shares

Short Interest Ratio

Short Interest Ratio (4.0) is the number of trading days at average daily volume required to cover total short interest position.

LARGEST SHORT INTEREST RATIOS

The short interest ratio is the number of days it would take to cover the short interest if trading continued at the average daily volume for the month.

RANK		SEP 15 SHORT INT	AVG DLY VOL-a	DAYS TO COVER
1	Aksys Ltd	2,185,529	17,123	128
2	Integrated Alarm	4,599,466	40,821	113
3	SCO Group Inc	4,013,342	37,030	108
4	1-800 Contacts	1,302,658	15,294	85
5	Planar Systems	2,616,414	35,253	74
6	BUCA Inc	1,313,600	18,281	72
7	ParkerVision Inc	2,280,831	32,204	71
8	Global Crossing Ltd	5,490,641	77,916	70
9	Mair Holdings Inc	1,513,619	23,712	64
10	Medis Technol	4,691,976	93,204	50
11	KVH Industries	1,982,084	45,850	43
12	Learning Tree Int'l	1,221,667	28,371	43
13	Bank of the Ozarks	2,013,703	47,903	42
14	Antigenics Inc	7,472,167	179,836	42
15	Introgen Therapeut	6,070,529	146,202	42
16	Navarre Corp	10,102,418	249,370	41
17	Biolase Technology	5,036,799	125,001	40
18	FalconStor Sftware	4,424,668	110,574	40
19	Multimedia Games	9,271,304	247,411	37
20	DTS Inc	2,070,145	58,835	35

Issues that split in the latest month are excluded.
The largest percentage increase and decrease sections are limited to issues with previously established short positions in both months.

WORK THE WEB

You can find the short interest for the current month in many financial publications. But what if you want a longer history of the shares sold short for a particular company? At www.nasdaq.com, you can find the short interest for companies listed on the NASDAQ for the previous 12 months. We went to the site and looked up Yahoo!, and this is what we found:

YHOO - Yahoo! Inc. - Common Stock

Month	Short Interest	Percent Change	Average Daily Share Volume	Days to Cover
March 2006	73,504,478	(5.44)	19,773,403	3.72
February 2006	77,733,246	(5.67)	35,735,179	2.18
January 2006	82,408,380	3.05	17,052,680	4.83
December 2005	79,969,085	(7.78)	21,970,649	3.64
November 2005	86,717,343	9.55	20,807,599	4.17
October 2005	79,159,966	(0.40)	16,222,850	4.88
September 2005	79,475,645	(4.57)	14,150,721	5.62
August 2005	83,281,872	10.00	21,326,788	3.91
July 2005	75,713,736	(1.55)	15,053,534	5.03
June 2005	76,903,469	(2.30)	16,894,098	4.55
May 2005	78,710,903	2.06	21,136,816	3.72
April 2005	77,123,611	2.71	20,931,176	3.68

As you can see, the short interest in Yahoo! has risen from about 17 million shares in September 2004 to about 21 million shares in August 2005. Why would you want a history of short sales? Some investors use short sales as a technical indicator, which we discuss in a later chapter. Here's a question for you: What do you think "Days to Cover" means?

We conclude our discussion of short sales with a *very* important observation. With a long position, the most you can ever lose is your total investment. In other words, if you buy $10,000 worth of stock, $10,000 is the most you can lose because the worst that can happen is the stock price drops to zero. However, if you short $10,000 in stock, you can lose *much more* than $10,000 because the stock price can keep rising without any particular limit. In fact, as our previous chapter showed, stock prices do tend to rise, at least on average. With this in mind, potential short sellers should remember the following classic bit of Wall Street wisdom: "He that sells what isn't his'n, must buy it back or go to prison!"[1]

CHECK THIS	**2.3a**	What is a short sale?
	2.3b	Why might an investor choose to short a stock?
	2.3c	What is the maximum possible loss on a short sale? Explain.

[1]Of course, the same is true for "she that sells what isn't hers'n"; it just doesn't rhyme as well.

BUMPY MARKET REMINDS INVESTORS TO ASSESS THEIR RISK TOLERANCE

Do-It-Yourself Crowd Has Quizzes to Rate Courage on Finances

Risk

For many investors, it's a word that has all but disappeared from the lexicon. Throughout much of the 1990s, stocks mostly went up. And even when they went down, many investors saw the slump as just another buying opportunity because stocks soon would go up again.

But the bumpy ride of the past six months finally has woken investors up to the fact that, with stocks more volatile these days than anytime in history, risk is playing an increasingly significant role in their lives.

Did you root the NASDAQ Composite Index higher when it bested 5000 earlier this year, but secretly fear for your overbloated technology shares? Did you panic when the NASDAQ subsequently plummeted in March and April, then kick yourself for not investing more when the market rebounded days later?

These dueling visions of fear and greed reflect the fact that many of today's do-it-yourself investors haven't assessed their own tolerance for risk, captivated instead by the lure of what seems to be easy, almost riskless, riches.

The current, and often myopic, quest for market wealth has spawned "a willingness to take risks that [average investors] haven't had in the past," says Robert J. Shiller, an economics professor at Yale University and author of a new market tome, "Irrational Exuberance." In the process, he says, "investors haven't stopped to think about what risk is at all."

Until the recent market drop, "people had no clue what [risk] is about," agrees Joanna Bickel, a project manager at TIAA-CREF, the big New York provider of retirement services, which is working to bring a more sophisticated risk-assessment tool to its Web site later this year so that its investors can better gauge their own risk profile.

There once was a time when risk assessment was the duty of stockbrokers or financial planners, who questioned clients to gauge their comfort level for volatility and potential losses. But with the explosion of online trading, investors have taken control of their own finances. In the process, they have cast aside the mental due diligence that ultimately determines whether they're sleepless in Cisco or bored by Boeing.

It's an age-old quest for balance. Investors who structure their portfolios so that they are comfortable with both the rewards and risks are the ones who sleep best when market downdrafts keep others awake at night. Moreover, they aren't the ones berating themselves for missing out on big gains when the market rebounds.

To help investors determine the level of risk they're most comfortable with, here's a statistically based risk-tolerance quiz constructed with the help of Investment Technologies Inc., a New York firm that provides investment tools and risk-assessment instruments to financial institutions such as banks and investment firms.

Financial companies increasingly rely on risk quizzes similar to this one, though often far more detailed, to better assess a client's true tolerance for market vicissitudes. As investors continue to take on increasing responsibility for their own money—through online trading or in self-managed 401(k) and IRA retirement accounts —"the issue of how individual investors make investment decisions is becoming a huge issue," says Brian Rom, president of Investment Technologies.

All manner of risk-assessment quizzes are available. Some are posted on financial Web sites, others are available from financial planners and investment companies. Some are relatively simple and are designed to match an investor with particular mutual funds or annuities.

The more sophisticated quizzes are based on statistical research that quantifies the psychological behavior of people and their money habits. Such "behavioral finance" studies have determined that many people typically aren't rational but are irrational when it comes to money and risk.

For example, research has shown that most people fear loss more than they value comparable gain. Offer someone a sure $50 or, on the flip of a coin, the possibility of winning $100 or winning nothing, and chances are they'll pocket the sure thing. Conversely, penalize them $50 to start, then offer a flip of a coin to lose $100 or lose nothing, and they'll invariably take the coin toss. Both scenarios are statistically equivalent, yet people tend to view "the possibility of recouping a loss as more important than the possibility of greater gain," even though the coin flip could mean an even greater loss, says James Corter, associate professor of statistics and education at New York's Columbia University.

The accompanying quiz is based on research done by Mr. Corter. At just eight questions, it is short, but it is backed by empirical studies and "has adequate reliability and validity," says Mr. Corter.

The quiz is designed to reveal where an individual falls along the risk spectrum. It is accompanied by a chart detailing where a variety of stock and bond investments, based on historical performance and volatility, fall along the risk spectrum, to give quiz takers an idea of the class of investments most likely to match an investor's temperament.

Certainly, no risk quiz can tell you everything about your financial courage, and your score here doesn't mean that if you fall into a more conservative category that you can't stomach a little exposure to volatile tech stocks. "But if you answer the questions candidly," says Ms. Bickel at TIAA-CREF, "and don't worry about whether you come out conservative or a swinger, you'll have an accurate portrayal of your risk level that you can use when building your portfolio."

Risk Advisor

Do you know your risk tolerance? This short questionnaire can help you gain a better understanding of your tolerance for market vicissitudes. Answer the questions, tally the results and match the score to the Suitable Investments.*

1. Choose the statement that best describes your interests in an investment program.

   A My primary aim is to achieve high long-term return in the value of my portfolio, even if that means accepting some significant short-term swings in values.

   B My primary interest is in stable growth in the value of my portfolio, even if that means somewhat lower returns over time.

   C I attach equal value to maximizing long-term returns and minimizing fluctuations in value.

2. How important are the following factors when you decide to purchase a stock or mutual fund?

   a) Short-term potential for the price to appreciate.

   b) Long-term potential for the price to appreciate.

   c) If a stock, the potential that the company will be bought or taken over.

   d) Gain or loss in the price over the past six months.

   e) Gain or loss in the price over the past five years.

   f) Stock was recommended by a friend or coworker.

   g) Risk that the price could drop.

   h) Potential that the investment will pay dividends.

Very Important	Somewhat Important	Not At All Important
A	B	C
A	B	C
A	B	C
A	B	C
A	B	C
A	B	C
A	B	C
A	B	C

3. a) Would you put $5,000 of your assets into an investment where you have a 70% chance of doubling your money (to $10,000) and a 30% chance of losing the entire $5,000?

   Yes_____ No_____

   b) How about an 80% chance of doubling to $10,000 and a 20% chance of losing the entire $5,000?

   Yes_____ No_____

   c) How about a 60% chance of doubling to $10,000 and a 40% chance of losing the entire $5,000?

   Yes_____ No_____

(continued)

4. Suppose you have a choice between two mutual funds, both of which are broadly diversified into 6 asset classes (e.g., stocks, bonds, real estate, etc.). The charts below show the changes in value over the past 12 months for

One-year returns for assets in portfolio A

One-year returns for assets in portfolio B

the assets in each portfolio. Which portfolio of assets do you prefer to invest in?

5. Assume that you have made an investment that has dropped in value by $2,000 and you find yourself faced with the following choice (please circle only one option):

   A Sell and take the immediate $2,000 loss (a 100% chance of loss).

   B Hold on to it with a 50% chance of recouping the $2,000 and a 50% chance of losing an additional $2,000.

   C No preference.

6. Assume that you have recently invested $10,000 in a stock and that the value of this stock has dropped 15% in value in one week. You can discover no reason for this decline, and the broader market has not dipped accordingly. Which of the following actions would you be most likely to take? (Circle one answer only.)

   A Buy more.

   B Sell all your holdings in the fund immediately and put the money into a less volatile investment.

   C Sell half of your holdings in the fund immediately and put the money elsewhere.

   D Wait for the price to recover and then sell all your holdings in the fund.

   E Do nothing (occasional dips in price are to be expected).

7. The following charts show quarterly performance of two equity mutual funds over the past two years. Which do you prefer to invest in?

Fund A quarterly returns

Fund B quarterly returns

2.4 Investor Objectives, Constraints, and Strategies

Different investors will have very different investment objectives and strategies. For example, some will be very active, buying and selling frequently; others will be relatively inactive, buying and holding for long periods of time. Some will be willing to bear substantial risk in seeking out returns; for others, safety is a primary concern. In this section, we describe, in general terms, some strategies that are commonly pursued and their relationship to investor constraints and objectives.

8. As an investor in stock and bond markets, how would you rate your degree of experience relative to other individual investors? (Please circle one.)

 A Extremely experienced

 B More than average experience

 C Average experience

 D Less than average experience

 E Little or no experience

Source: Investment Technologies Inc.

Scoring

1 – A. 15; B. 0; C. 7

FOR EACH QUESTION:

2a) – A. 0; B. 1; C. 2

2b) through 2e)

 A. 2; B. 1; C. 0

FOR EACH QUESTION:

2f) through 2h)

 A. 0: B. 1; C. 2

FOR EACH QUESTION:

3a) through 3c)

 Yes. 5; No. 0

4 – A. 10; B. 0

5 – A. 0; B. 10; C. 10

6 – A. 15; B. 0; C. 5; D. 0; E. 10

7 – A. 10; B. 0

8 – A. 20; B. 15; C. 10; D. 5; E. 0

Score In Points	Suitable Investments*
0–11	Avoid risk! Open a money-market account—or buy a bigger mattress.
12–33	Gentlemen (and ladies) prefer bonds, and are most at home with high-grade corporate and government bonds of an intermediate duration.
34–55	You're still a bond buyer. But you're willing to live a bit closer to the edge with interest-only U.S. Treasury STRIPS.
56–77	Mix it up. Convertible bonds and stocks are to your liking. But safer utilities and large blue chips are as risky as you go. Real-estate investment trusts fit too.
78–99	Stock up on stocks. At the low end, you're comfortable with larger value stocks; at the high end, riskier midcap and growth stocks work.
100+	Viva Las Vegas, baby! Place your bets on 'Net stocks and new-tech issues. Risks are high, but so are the payoffs.

*Suitable investments are based upon an analysis of the volatility of 75 various bond and stock indices, and apply to investment horizons of between 10 and 15 years.

Source: Jeff D. Opdyke, *The Wall Street Journal*, © 2003 Dow Jones & Company. All Rights Reserved Worldwide.

In thinking about investor objectives, the most fundamental question is: Why invest at all? For the most part, the only sensible answer is that we invest today to have more tomorrow. In other words, investment is simply deferred consumption; instead of spending today, we choose to wait because we wish to have (or need to have) more to spend later. There is no difference, really, between investing and saving.

Given that we invest now to have more later, the particular investment strategy chosen will depend on, among other things, willingness to bear risk, the time horizon, and taxes. We discuss these and other issues next.

RISK AND RETURN

Probably the most fundamental decision that an investor must make concerns the amount of risk that she is willing to bear. Most investors are *risk-averse*, meaning that, all other

WWW

How risk-averse are you? Take a test at moneycentral.msn.com

Look for "Prepare to Invest" under "Investing Insight."

things the same, they dislike risk and want to expose themselves to the minimum risk level possible. However, as our previous chapter indicated, larger returns are generally associated with larger risks, so there is a trade-off. In formulating investment objectives, the individual must therefore balance return objectives with risk tolerance.

Attitudes toward risk are strictly personal preferences, and individuals with very similar economic circumstances can have very different degrees of risk aversion. For this reason, the first thing that must be assessed in evaluating the suitability of an investment strategy is risk tolerance. Unfortunately, this is not an easy thing to do. Most individuals have a difficult time articulating in any precise way their attitude toward risk (what's yours?). One reason is that risk is not a simple concept; it is not easily defined or measured. Nevertheless, the nearby *Investment Updates* box contains an article from *The Wall Street Journal* about risk tolerance that has a short quiz that might help you assess your attitude toward risk. When you take the quiz, remember there are no right or wrong answers. Afterwards, score your risk tolerance as shown at the end of the article.

INVESTOR CONSTRAINTS

In addition to attitude toward risk, an investor's investment strategy will be affected by various constraints. We discuss five of the most common and important constraints next.

WWW

Can you open a brokerage account with no money? See www.sharebuilder.com and www.buyandhold.com

RESOURCES Probably the most obvious constraint, and the one to which many students can most easily relate, is *resources*. Obviously, if you have no money, you cannot invest at all! Beyond that, certain types of investments and investment strategies either explicitly or effectively have minimum requirements. For example, a margin account must normally have a minimum of $2,000 when it is established.

What is the minimum resource level needed? It depends on the investment strategy, and there is no precise answer. Through mutual funds, investments in the stock market can be made for as little as $500 to start, with subsequent investments as small as $100 or less. However, since there are frequently minimum commission levels, account fees, and other costs associated with buying and selling securities, an investor interested in actively trading on her own would probably need more like $5,000 to $50,000.

HORIZON The investment *horizon* refers to the planned life of the investment. For example, individuals frequently save for retirement, where the investment horizon, depending on your age, can be very long. On the other hand, you might be saving to buy a house in the near future, implying a relatively short horizon.

The reason that horizon is important is evident in our previous chapter. It is true that stocks outperformed the other investments in the long run, but there were short periods over which they did much worse. Consequently, if you have to pay tuition in 30 days, stocks are probably not the best investment for that money. Thus, in thinking about the riskiness of an investment, one important consideration is when the money will be needed.

LIQUIDITY Some investors may need to sell an asset quickly. In such cases, the asset's *liquidity* is particularly important. An asset with a high degree of liquidity is one that can be sold quickly without a significant price concession. Such an asset is said to be liquid.

Notice that liquidity has two related dimensions. After all, any asset can be sold quickly and easily if the price is cut sufficiently, so it's not just a question of the ease with which an asset can be sold. Liquidity is difficult to measure precisely, but some assets are clearly much more liquid than others. A good way to think about liquidity is to imagine buying an asset and then immediately reselling it. The less you would lose on this "round-trip" transaction, the more liquid is the asset.

TAXES Different types of investments are taxed very differently. When we talk about the return on an investment, what is really relevant is the *aftertax* return. As a result, taxes are a vital consideration. Higher tax bracket investors will naturally seek investment strategies with favorable tax treatments, while lower tax bracket (or tax-exempt) investors will focus more on pretax returns.

In addition, the way in which an investment is held can dramatically affect its tax status. The tax laws and other rules are in a constant state of flux, so we will stick to broad principles. The general idea is that certain types of accounts, particularly retirement savings accounts, receive preferential tax treatment. The tax break can be enormous, and, as a result, the amount you can invest each year in these accounts is strictly limited. There are also lots of rules regarding when you can withdraw the money, and it is important to pay careful attention to them.

In terms of tax treatment, there are basically two types of retirement savings accounts. With the first type, you pay taxes today on money you earn, but, if you then invest the after-tax dollars in a retirement savings account, you pay no taxes at all when you take the money out later. This means that dividends, interest, and capital gains are not taxed, a big break. Currently, this type of account is called a Roth Individual Retirement Account (Roth IRA).

With the second type of account, you don't pay taxes on the money you earn today if you invest it. Such accounts are "tax-deferred" and are the way most employer-sponsored retirement accounts (such as so-called 401(k) plans) are set up. Later, when you retire, you owe income taxes on whatever you take out of the account. So, the two types of accounts really come down to this: You either pay taxes today and don't pay taxes later, or vice versa.

SPECIAL CIRCUMSTANCES Beyond the general constraints we have discussed, essentially everyone will have some special or unique requirements or opportunities. For example, many companies will match certain types of investments made by employees on a dollar-for-dollar basis (typically up to some maximum per year). In other words, you double your money immediately with complete certainty. Since it is difficult to envision any other investment with such a favorable payoff, such an opportunity should probably be taken even though there may be some undesirable liquidity, tax, or horizon considerations.

A list of possible special circumstances would be essentially endless, so we make no attempt to produce one here. Just to give a few examples, however, the number of dependents and their needs will vary from investor to investor, and the need to provide for dependents will be an important constraint. Some investors want to invest only in companies whose products and activities they consider to be socially or politically suitable, and some investors want to invest primarily in their own community or state. Finally, some investors, such as corporate insiders, face regulatory and legal restrictions on their investing, and others, such as political officeholders, may have to avoid (or at least ethically *should* avoid) some types of investments out of concern for conflicts of interest.

STRATEGIES AND POLICIES

In formulating an investment strategy or policy, the four key areas that must be addressed are investment management, market timing, asset allocation, and security selection. We discuss each of these next.

INVESTMENT MANAGEMENT A basic decision that you and every other investor must make is whether you will manage your investments yourself or hire someone else to do it. At the one extreme, you can open an account with a broker and make all of the buy and sell decisions yourself. At the other extreme, you can invest all of your money in a managed account, such as a wrap account, and make no buy and sell decisions at all.

Often investors partially manage their investments themselves and partially use professional managers. For example, you might divide your money between, say, four different mutual funds. In this case, you have hired four different money managers. However, you decided what types of funds to buy, you chose the particular funds within each type, and you decided how to divide your money between the funds.

Managing your money by yourself might seem to be the cheapest way to go because you save on the management fees. Appearances can be deceiving, however. First of all, you should consider the value of your time. For some, researching investments and making investment decisions is something of a hobby; for many of us, however, it is too time-consuming, and this is a powerful incentive to hire professional management. Also, for some strategies, the costs of doing it yourself can exceed those of hiring someone, even after considering fees, simply because of the higher commissions and other fees that individual investors frequently pay. For example, it might not be a bad idea for some of your investment to be in real estate, but a small investor will find it very difficult to directly acquire a sound real estate investment at reasonable cost.

An interesting question regarding professional management concerns the possibility of generating superior returns. It would seem logical to argue that by hiring a professional investor to manage your money, you would earn more, at least on average. Surely the pros make better investment decisions than the amateurs! Surprisingly, this isn't necessarily true. We will return to this subject in later chapters, but, for now, we simply note that the possibility of a superior return may not be a compelling reason to prefer professional management.

MARKET TIMING A second basic investment decision you must make is whether you will try to buy and sell in anticipation of the future direction of the overall market. For example, you might move money into the stock market when you think it is going to rise, and move money out when you think it is going to fall. This activity is called **market timing**. Some investors very actively move money around to try to time short-term market movements; others are less active but still try to time longer-term movements. A fully passive strategy is one in which no attempt is made to time the market.

Market timing certainly seems like a reasonable thing to do; after all, why leave money in an investment if you expect it to decrease in value? You might be surprised that a common recommendation is that investors *not* try to time the market. As we discuss in more detail in a later chapter, the reason is that successful market timing is, to put it mildly, very difficult. To outperform a completely passive strategy, you must be able to very accurately predict the future; if you make even a small number of bad calls, it is likely that you will never catch up.

ASSET ALLOCATION Another fundamental decision that must be made concerns the distribution of your investment across different types of assets. We saw in Chapter 1 that different asset types—small stocks, large stocks, bonds—have very different risk and return characteristics. In formulating your investment strategy, you must decide what percentage of your money will be placed in each of these broad categories. This decision is called **asset allocation**.

An important asset allocation decision for many investors is how much to invest in common stocks and how much to invest in bonds. There are some basic rules of thumb for this decision, one of the simplest being to split the portfolio into 60 percent stocks and 40 percent bonds. A slightly more sophisticated rule of thumb is that your equity percentage should be equal to your age subtracted from 100 (or 110, depending on the source). Under this rule, a 22-year-old college student should have $100 - 22 = 78$ percent (or $110 - 22 = 88$ percent) of her portfolio in stocks. This approach gradually reduces your exposure to stocks as you get older. Most of the major investment firms and many Web sites maintain

market timing
Buying and selling in anticipation of the overall direction of a market.

asset allocation
The distribution of investment funds among broad classes of assets.

recommended asset allocation schemes, which can be custom-tailored for individuals depending on their risk tolerance, wealth, and retirement goals.

security selection
Selection of specific securities within a particular class.

SECURITY SELECTION Finally, after deciding who will manage your investment, whether you will try to time the market, and the various asset classes you wish to hold, you must decide which specific securities to buy within each class. This is termed **security selection**.

For example, you might decide that you want 30 percent of your money in small stocks. This is an asset allocation decision. Next, however, you must decide *which* small stocks to buy. Here again there is an active strategy and a passive strategy. With an active strategy, we try to identify those small stocks that we think will do the best in the future; in other words, we try to pick "winners." Investigating particular securities within a broad class in an attempt to identify superior performers is often called *security analysis*.

With a passive security selection strategy, we might just acquire a diverse group of small stocks, perhaps by buying a mutual fund that holds shares in hundreds of small companies (such funds are discussed in detail in Chapter 4).

A useful way to distinguish asset allocation from security selection is to note that asset allocation is essentially a macro-level activity because the focus is on whole markets or classes of assets. Security selection is a much more micro-level activity because the focus is on individual securities.

If we simultaneously consider the active versus passive aspects of asset allocation and security selection, four distinct investment strategies emerge, which we summarize in the following two-by-two table:

	Security Selection	
Asset Allocation	**Active**	**Passive**
Active	I	II
Passive	III	IV

With strategy I, we actively move money between asset classes based on our beliefs and expectations about future performance and we also try to pick the best performers in each class. This is a fully active strategy. At the other extreme, strategy IV, we follow a fully passive strategy, neither changing asset allocation very much nor choosing individual securities in an attempt to identify the likely best performers.

With strategy II, we actively vary our holdings by class, but we don't try to choose particular securities within each class. With this strategy, we might move back and forth between short-term government bonds and small stocks in an attempt to time the market. Finally, with strategy III, we don't vary our asset allocations, but we do select individual securities. A diehard stock picker would fall into this category; such an investor holds 100 percent stocks and concentrates solely on buying and selling individual stocks.

CHECK THIS

2.4a   What does the term "risk-averse" mean?

2.4b   What are some of the constraints investors face in making investment decisions?

2.4c   What is asset allocation?

2.5 Summary and Conclusions

This chapter explores the investing process. We discuss how to choose a broker and various aspects of broker–customer relations, including hypothecation and street name registration. The use of margin to purchase securities is covered, and the financial leverage effect of a margin purchase is emphasized. We describe short sales in some detail and stress the potentially unlimited losses that can arise from a short position. Finally, we cover some of the constraints faced by investors, and we briefly describe some basic investment strategy considerations, including market timing, asset allocation, and security selection.

GET REAL

This chapter covered the basics of brokerage accounts, some important trade types, and, finally, some big-picture issues regarding investment strategies and objectives. How should you, as an investor or investment manager, put this information to work?

The answer is that you need to open a brokerage account! Investing is like many activities; the best way to learn is by making mistakes. Unfortunately, making mistakes with real money is an expensive way to learn, so we don't recommend trying things like short sales with real money, at least not at first.

Instead, to learn about how to trade and gain some experience with making (and losing) money, you should open a Stock-Trak account (or a similar simulated brokerage account). Take it seriously. Try various trade types and strategies and see how they turn out. The important thing to do is to follow your trades and try to understand why you made or lost money and also why you made or lost the amount you did.

In a similar vein, you should carefully review your account statements to make sure you understand exactly what each item means and how your account equity is calculated.

After you have gained some experience trading "on paper," you should open a real account as soon as you can pull together enough money. Try visiting some online brokers such as Ameritrade to find out the minimum amount you need to open an account. The amount has been declining. In 2005, you could open a cash account for as little as $500, but to open a margin account, you need in the area of $2,000. Or, you can visit www.sharebuilder.com and www.buyandhold.com to open accounts with no money at all!

Looking back at Chapter 1, you know that it's important to get started early. Once you have a real account, however, it's still a good idea to keep a separate "play money" account to test trading ideas to make sure you really understand them before committing your precious real money.

Key Terms

Chapter Review Problems and Self-Test

1. **The Account Balance Sheet**   Suppose you want to buy 10,000 shares of Intel Corporation at a price of $30 per share. You put up $200,000 and borrow the rest. What does your account balance sheet look like? What is your margin?

2. **Short Sales**   Suppose that in the previous problem you shorted 10,000 shares instead of buying. The initial margin is 60 percent. What does the account balance sheet look like following the short?

3. **Margin Calls**   You purchased 500 shares of stock at a price of $56 per share on 50 percent margin. If the maintenance margin is 30 percent, what is the critical stock price?

Answers to Self-Test Problems

1. The 10,000 shares of Intel cost $300,000. You supply $200,000, so you must borrow $100,000. The account balance sheet looks like this:

Assets		Liabilities and Account Equity	
10,000 shares of Intel	$300,000	Margin loan	$100,000
		Account equity	200,000
Total	$300,000	Total	$300,000

Your margin is the account equity divided by the value of the stock owned:

$$\text{Margin} = \$200,000/\$300,000$$
$$= .666 \dots$$
$$= 67\%$$

2. Following the short, your account is as follows:

Assets		Liabilities and Account Equity	
Proceeds from sale	$300,000	Short position	$300,000
Initial margin deposit	180,000	Account equity	180,000
Total	$480,000	Total	$480,000

Notice that you shorted $300,000 worth of stock, so, with a 60 percent margin requirement, you deposited $180,000.

3. The lowest price the stock can drop before you receive a margin call is:

$$P* = \frac{\text{Amount borrowed/Number of shares}}{1 - \text{Maintenance margin}}$$

You borrowed $500 \times \$56 \times .50 = \$14,000$. Therefore:

$$P* = \frac{14,000/500}{1 - .30} = \$40.00$$

You will receive a margin call if the stock drops below $40.00.

Test Your Investment Quotient

1. Investment Objectives An individual investor's investment objectives should be expressed in terms of:

   a. Risk and return.
   b. Capital market expectations.
   c. Liquidity needs and time horizon.
   d. Tax factors and legal and regulatory constraints.

2. Asset Allocation Which of the following best reflects the importance of the asset allocation decision to the investment process? The asset allocation decision:

   a. Helps the investor decide on realistic investment goals.
   b. Identifies the specific securities to include in a portfolio.
   c. Determines most of the portfolio's returns and volatility over time.
   d. Creates a standard by which to establish an appropriate investment horizon.

3. Leverage You deposit $100,000 cash in a brokerage account and purchase $200,000 of stocks on margin by borrowing $100,000 from your broker. Later, the value of your stock holdings falls to $150,000, whereupon you get nervous and close your account. What is the percentage return on your investment (ignore interest paid)?

   a. 0 percent
   b. −25 percent
   c. −50 percent
   d. −75 percent

4. Leverage You deposit $100,000 cash in a brokerage account and short sell $200,000 of stocks. Later, the value of the stocks held short rises to $250,000, whereupon you get nervous and close your account. What is the percentage return on your investment?

   a. 0 percent
   b. −25 percent
   c. −50 percent
   d. −75 percent

5. Account Margin You deposit $100,000 cash in a brokerage account and purchase $200,000 of stocks on margin by borrowing $100,000 from your broker. Later, the value of your stock holdings falls to $175,000. What is your account margin in dollars?

   a. $50,000
   b. $75,000
   c. $100,000
   d. $150,000

6. Account Margin You deposit $100,000 cash in a brokerage account and purchase $200,000 of stocks on margin by borrowing $100,000 from your broker. Later, the value of your stock holdings falls to $150,000. What is your account margin in percent?

   a. 25 percent
   b. 33 percent

    c. 50 percent

    d. 75 percent

7. **Account Margin**   You deposit $100,000 cash in a brokerage account and short sell $200,000 of stocks on margin. Later, the value of the stocks held short rises to $225,000. What is your account margin in dollars?

    a. $50,000

    b. $75,000

    c. $100,000

    d. $150,000

8. **Account Margin**   You deposit $100,000 cash in a brokerage account and short sell $200,000 of stocks on margin. Later, the value of the stocks held short rises to $250,000. What is your account margin in percent?

    a. 20 percent

    b. 25 percent

    c. 33 percent

    d. 50 percent

9. **Margin Calls**   You deposit $100,000 cash in a brokerage account and purchase $200,000 of stocks on margin by borrowing $100,000 from your broker, who requires a maintenance margin of 30 percent. Which of the following is the largest value for your stock holdings for which you will still receive a margin call?

    a. $200,000

    b. $160,000

    c. $140,000

    d. $120,000

10. **Margin Calls**   You deposit $100,000 cash in a brokerage account and short sell $200,000 of stocks. Your broker requires a maintenance margin of 30 percent. Which of the following is the lowest value for the stocks you are holding short for which you will still receive a margin call?

    a. $260,000

    b. $240,000

    c. $220,000

    d. $200,000

11. **Investment Decisions**   Which of the following investment factors, strategies, or tactics is the least relevant to a passive investment policy?

    a. Market timing

    b. Asset allocation

    c. Political environment

    d. Tax status

12. **Investment Decisions**   Which of the following investment factors, strategies, or tactics is most associated with an active investment policy?

    a. Market timing

    b. Asset allocation

    c. Security selection

    d. Tax status

13. **Investment Decisions**   Which of the following investment strategies or tactics will likely consume the greatest amount of resources, time, effort, and so on, when implementing an active investment policy?

    a. Market timing

    b. Asset allocation

    c. Security selection

    d. Tax strategy

14. **Investment Decisions** Which of the following investment strategies or tactics is likely the most relevant in the decision to short sell a particular stock?

   a. Market timing
   b. Asset allocation
   c. Security selection
   d. Tax strategy

15. **Investment Constraints** Which of the following investment constraints is expected to have the most fundamental impact on the investment decision process for a typical investor?

   a. Investor's tax status
   b. Investor's time horizon
   c. Investor's need for liquidity
   d. Investor's attitude toward risk

Concept Questions

1. **Margin** What does it mean to purchase a security on margin? Why might you do it?

2. **Short Sales** What does it mean to sell a security short? Why might you do it?

3. **Margin Requirements** What is the reason margin requirements exist?

4. **Allocation versus Selection** What is the difference between asset allocation and security selection?

5. **Allocation versus Timing** Are market timing and active asset allocation similar? Why or why not?

6. **Street Name Registration** Why is street name registration advantageous to investors? Under what circumstances is it required?

7. **Broker–Customer Relations** Suppose your broker tips you on a hot stock. You invest heavily, but, to your considerable dismay, the stock plummets in value. What recourse do you have against your broker?

8. **Long Profits** An important difference between a long position in stock and a short position concerns the potential gains and losses. Suppose a stock sells for $18 per share, and you buy 500 shares. What are your potential gains and losses?

9. **Liquidity** The liquidity of an asset directly affects the risk of buying or selling that asset during adverse market conditions. Describe the liquidity risk you face with a short stock position during a market rally, and a long stock position during a market decline.

10. **Short Sale Profits** Suppose you sell short 1,000 shares of a stock at $60 per share. Ignoring borrowing costs and fees, what is the maximum profit you can earn from this investment? What is the potential maximum loss?

Questions and Problems

Core Questions

1. **Calculating Margin** Simmons Corporation stock sells for $83 per share, and you've decided to purchase as many shares as you possibly can. You have $13,000 available to invest. What is the maximum number of shares you can buy if the initial margin is 50 percent?

2. **Margin** You purchase 400 shares of Omni Co. stock on margin at a price of $65. Your broker requires you to deposit $15,000. What is your margin loan amount? What is the initial margin requirement?

3. **Margin Return** In the previous problem, suppose you sell the stock at a price of $75. What is your return? What would your return have been had you purchased the stock without margin? What if the stock price is $65 when you sell the stock?

4. **Margin** Repeat the previous two problems assuming the initial margin requirement is 40 percent. Does this suggest a relationship between the initial margin and returns?

5. **Margin Purchases**   You have $13,000 and decide to invest on margin. If the initial margin requirement is 60 percent, what is the maximum dollar purchase you can make?

6. **Margin Calls**   You buy 900 shares of stock at a price of $85 and an initial margin of 60 percent. If the maintenance margin is 35 percent, at what price will you receive a margin call?

7. **Margin Calls**   You decide to buy 400 shares of stock at a price of $49 and an initial margin of 50 percent. What is the maximum percentage decline in the stock before you will receive a margin call if the maintenance margin is 25 percent?

8. **Margin Calls on Short Sales**   The stock of Cruize Industries is trading at $64. You feel the stock price will decline, so you short 900 shares at an initial margin of 50 percent. If the maintenance margin is 30 percent, at what share price will you receive a margin call?

9. **Margin Calls on Short Sales**   You short sold 1,000 shares of stock at a price of $56 and an initial margin of 50 percent. If the maintenance margin is 30 percent, at what share price will you receive a margin call? What is your account equity at this stock price?

10. **Taxes and Returns**   You purchase a stock at the beginning of the year at a price of $86. At the end of the year the stock pays a dividend of $1.40 and you sell the stock for $98. What is your return for the year? Now suppose that dividends are taxed at your marginal tax rate of 31 percent and long-term capital gains (over 11 months) are taxed at 20 percent. What is your aftertax return for the year?

Intermediate Questions

11. **Calculating Margin**   Using the information in Problem 1, construct your equity account balance sheet at the time of your purchase. What does your balance sheet look like if the share price rises to $90? What if it falls to $65 per share? What is your margin in both cases? Round the number of shares down to the nearest number of whole shares.

12. **Calculating Margin**   You've just opened a margin account with $10,000 at your local brokerage firm. You instruct your broker to purchase 450 shares of Smolira Golf stock, which currently sells for $41 per share. What is your initial margin? Construct the equity account balance sheet for this position.

13. **Margin Call**   Suppose you purchase 400 shares of stock at $72 per share with an initial cash investment of $15,000. If your broker requires a 30 percent maintenance margin, at what share price will you be subject to a margin call? If you want to keep your position open despite the stock price plunge, what alternatives do you have?

14. **Margin and Leverage**   In the previous problem, suppose the call money rate is 5 percent and you are charged a 1.5 percent premium over this rate. Calculate your return on investment for each of the following share prices one year later. What would your rate of return be in each case if you purchased $15,000 of stock with no margin? Ignore dividends.
    a. $96
    b. $72
    c. $64

15. **Margin and Leverage**   Suppose the call money rate is 6.8 percent, and you pay a spread of 1.9 percent over that. You buy 1,000 shares at $46 per share with an initial margin of 50 percent. One year later, the stock is selling for $53 per share, and you close out your position. What is your return assuming no dividends are paid?

16. **Margin and Leverage**   Suppose the call money rate is 5.8 percent, and you pay a spread of 2.5 percent over that. You buy 800 shares of stock at $32 per share. You put up $15,000. One year later, the stock is selling for $37 per share, and you close out your position. What is your return assuming a dividend of $.64 per share is paid?

17. **Margin Interest**   Suppose you take out a margin loan for $45,000. The rate you pay is an 8.7 percent effective rate. If you repay the loan in six months, how much interest will you pay?

18. **Margin Interest**   Suppose you take out a margin loan for $32,000. You pay a 6.9 percent effective rate. If you repay the loan in two months, how much interest will you pay?

19. **Annualized Returns**   Suppose you hold a particular investment for 7 months. You calculate that your holding-period return is 15 percent. What is your annualized return?

20. **Annualized Returns**   In the previous question, suppose your holding period was 5 months instead of 7. What is your annualized return? What do you conclude in general about the length of your holding period and your annualized return?

21. **Annualized Returns**   Suppose you buy stock at a price of $48 per share. Five months later, you sell it for $41. You also received a dividend of $.15 per share. What is your annualized return on this investment?

22. **Calculating Returns**   Looking back at Problem 12, suppose the call money rate is 6 percent and your broker charges you a spread of 1.25 percent over this rate. You hold the stock for six months and sell at a price of $46 per share. The company paid a dividend of $.25 per share the day before you sold your stock. What is your total dollar return from this investment? What is your effective annual rate of return?

23. **Short Sales**   You believe that Culligan, Inc., stock is going to fall and you've decided to sell 2,000 shares short. If the current share price is $54, construct the equity account balance sheet for this trade. Assume the initial margin is 100 percent.

24. **Short Sales**   Repeat the previous problem assuming you short the 2,000 shares on 75 percent margin.

25. **Calculating Short Sale Returns**   You just sold short 1,200 shares of Wetscope, Inc., a fledgling software firm, at $86 per share. You cover your short when the price hits $73 per share one year later. If the company paid $1.20 per share in dividends over this period, what is your rate of return on the investment? Assume an initial margin of 50 percent.

26. **Short Sales**   You believe the stock in Freeze Frame Co. is going to fall, so you short 1,600 shares at a price of $83. The initial margin is 50 percent. Construct the equity balance sheet for the original trade. Now construct an equity balance sheet for a stock price of $73 and a stock price of $93. What is your margin at each of these stock prices? What is your effective annual return if you cover your short position at each of these prices in five months?

S&P Problems

www.mhhe.com/edumarketinsight

1. **Margin**   Download the historical stock prices for Tootsie Roll Industries (TR) under the "Mthly. Adj. Prices" link. Assume you purchased 400 shares of Tootsie Roll stock at the closing price six months ago. The initial margin requirement is 50 percent and the maintenance margin is 30 percent. Show the account balance sheet based on monthly closing prices for the last five months. At what stock price will you receive a margin call? Are any margin deposits required over this period? What is your return on this investment?

2. **Short Sales**   Download the historical stock prices for Ford (F) under the "Mthly. Adj. Prices" link. Assume you short sold 200 shares of Ford stock at the closing price six months ago. The initial margin requirement is 50 percent and the maintenance margin is 30 percent. Show the account balance sheet based on monthly closing prices for the last five months. At what stock price will you receive a margin call? Are any margin deposits required over this period? What is your return on this investment?

What's on the Web?

1. **Risk Tolerance**   As we discussed in the chapter, risk tolerance is based on an individual's personality and investment goals. There are numerous risk tolerance questionnaires on the Web. One, provided by Merrill Lynch, is located at individual.ml.com. Go to the Web site, locate the questionnaire, and take the quiz. How conservative or aggressive are you?

2. **Short Interest**   You can find the number of short sales on a particular stock at finance.yahoo.com. Go to the site and find the number of shares short sold for ExxonMobil (XOM) under the "Profile" link. How many shares are sold short in the current month? What about the previous month? What do the "Percent of Float" and "Short Ratio" mean?

3. **Broker Call Money Rate** What is the current broker call money rate? To find out, go to www.money-rates.com and look up "Key Interest Rates."

4. **Margin Purchases** Suppose you have a margin account with TDWaterhouse. You purchase 1,000 shares of IBM stock on 50 percent margin at today's price. Go to finance.yahoo.com to find your purchase price. Ignoring transaction costs, how much will you borrow? Next, go to www.money-rates.com to find the current broker call money rate. Finally, go to www.tdwaterhouse.com to find out how much above the current broker call money rate you will pay. Hint: Do a search for "margin rates" on this site. If you keep your investment for one year, how much will you pay in interest assuming the margin rate stays the same? What does the stock price have to be in one year for you to break even on your investment?

Stock-Trak Exercises

To access the Stock-Trak Exercise for this chapter, please visit the book Web site at www.mhhe.com/jm4e and choose the corresponding chapter.

CHAPTER 3

Overview of Security Types

"An investment operation is one which upon thorough analysis promises safety of principal and an adequate return. Operations not meeting these requirements are speculative."

–Benjamin Graham

You invest $5,000 in Yahoo! common stock and just months later sell the shares for $7,500, realizing a 50 percent return. Not bad! At the same time, your neighbor invests $5,000 in Yahoo! stock options, which are worth $25,000 at expiration—a 400 percent return. Yahoo! Alternatively, your Yahoo! shares fall in value to $2,500, and you realize a 50 percent loss. Too bad! But at the same time your neighbor's Yahoo! stock options are now worthless. Clearly, there is a big difference between stock shares and stock options. Security type matters. ∎

Our goal in this chapter is to introduce you to some of the different types of securities that are routinely bought and sold in financial markets around the world. As we mentioned in Chapter 1, we will be focusing on financial assets such as bonds, stocks, options, and futures in this book, so these are the securities we briefly describe here. The securities we discuss are covered in much greater detail in the chapters ahead, so we touch on only some of their most essential features in this chapter.

For each of the securities we examine, we ask three questions. First, what is its basic nature and what are its distinguishing characteristics? Second, what are the potential gains and losses from owning it? Third, how are its prices quoted in the financial press?

3.1 Classifying Securities

To begin our overview of security types, we first develop a classification scheme for the different securities. As shown in Table 3.1, financial assets can be grouped into three broad categories, and each of these categories can be further subdivided into a few major subtypes. This classification is not exhaustive, but it covers the major types of financial assets. In the sections that follow, we describe these assets in the order they appear in Table 3.1.

When we examine some of these security types in more detail, we will see that the distinctions can become a little blurred, particularly with some recently created financial instruments; as a result, some financial assets are hard to classify. The primary reason is that some instruments are hybrids, meaning that they are combinations of the basic types.

As you may have noticed in our discussion, financial assets, such as bonds and stocks, are often called securities. They are often called financial "instruments" as well. In certain contexts, there are distinctions between these terms, but they are used more or less interchangeably in everyday discussion, so we will stick with common usage.

3.1a	What are the three basic types of financial assets?
3.1b	Why are some financial assets hard to classify?

CHECK THIS

3.2 Interest-Bearing Assets

Broadly speaking, interest-bearing assets (as the name suggests) pay interest. Some pay interest implicitly and some pay it explicitly, but the common denominator is that the value of these assets depends, at least for the most part, on interest rates. The reason that these assets pay interest is that they all begin life as a loan of some sort, so they are all debt obligations of some issuer.

There are many types of interest-bearing assets. They range from the relatively simple to the astoundingly complex. We discuss some basic types and their features next. The more complex types are discussed in later chapters.

TABLE 3.1   **Classification of Financial Assets**

Basic Types	Major Subtypes
Interest-bearing	Money market instruments
	Fixed-income securities
Equities	Common stock
	Preferred stock
Derivatives	Futures
	Options

MONEY MARKET INSTRUMENTS

money market instruments

Debt obligations of large corporations and governments with an original maturity of one year or less.

For the most part, **money market instruments** are the simplest form of interest-bearing asset. Money market instruments generally have the following two properties:

1. They are essentially IOUs sold by large corporations or governments to borrow money.

2. They mature in less than one year from the time they are sold, meaning that the loan must be repaid within one year.

Most money market instruments trade in very large denominations, and most, but not all, are quite liquid.

The most familiar example of a money market instrument is a Treasury bill, or T-bill for short. Every week, the U.S. Treasury borrows billions of dollars by selling T-bills to the public. Like many (but not all) money market instruments, T-bills are sold on a *discount basis.* This simply means that T-bills are sold at a price that is less than their stated face value. In other words, an investor buys a T-bill at one price and later, when the bill matures, receives the full face value. The difference is the interest earned.

U.S. Treasury bills are the most liquid type of money market instrument—that is, the type with the largest and most active market. Other types of money market instruments traded in active markets include bank certificates of deposit (or CDs) and corporate and municipal money market instruments.

The potential gain from buying a money market instrument is fixed because the owner is promised a fixed future payment. The most important risk is the risk of default, which is the possibility that the borrower will not repay the loan as promised. With a T-bill, there is no possibility of default, so, as we saw in Chapter 1, T-bills are essentially risk-free. In fact, most money market instruments have relatively low risk, but there are exceptions, and a few spectacular defaults have occurred in the past.

Prices for different money market instruments are quoted in the financial press in different ways. In fact, usually interest rates are quoted, not prices, so some calculation is necessary to convert rates to prices. The procedures are not complicated, but they involve a fair amount of detail, so we save them for another chapter.

FIXED-INCOME SECURITIES

fixed-income securities

Longer-term debt obligations, often of corporations and governments, that promise to make fixed payments according to a preset schedule.

Fixed-income securities are exactly what the name suggests: securities that promise to make fixed payments according to some preset schedule. The other key characteristic of a fixed-income security is that, like a money market instrument, it begins life as a loan of some sort. Fixed-income securities are therefore debt obligations. They are typically issued by corporations and governments. Unlike money market instruments, fixed-income securities have lives that exceed 12 months at the time they are issued.

The words "note" and "bond" are generic terms for fixed-income securities, but "fixed income" is more accurate. This term is being used more frequently as securities are increasingly being created that don't fit within traditional note or bond frameworks but are nonetheless fixed-income securities.

EXAMPLES OF FIXED-INCOME SECURITIES To give one particularly simple example of a fixed-income security, near the end of every month, the U.S. Treasury sells between $25 billion and $35 billion of two-year notes to the public. If you buy a two-year note when it is issued, you will receive a check every six months for two years for a fixed amount, called the bond's *coupon,* and in two years you will receive the face amount on the note.

Suppose you buy $1 million in face amount of a 4 percent, two-year note. The 4 percent is called the *coupon rate,* and it tells you that you will receive 4 percent of the $1 million

Corporate bond quotes have become more available with the rise of the Internet. One site where you can find current corporate bond prices is www.nasdbondinfo.com. We went there and looked for bonds issued by Minnesota Mining and Manufacturing (3M, stock symbol MMM). Here is a look at one of these bonds:

Issue: MMM.GB MINNESOTA MINING AND MANUFACTURING COMPANY 6.375 02/15/2028			Time and Sales			Descriptive Data		
In Portfolio	Rating Moody's/S&P/Fitch	---- Last Sale ----			---- Most Recent ----			
		Date	Price	Yield	Date	Price	Yield	
☐	Aa1 / AA /	03/30/2006	107.583	5.760015	03/30/2006	107.58	5.760015	

The bond has a coupon rate of 6.375 percent and matures on February 2028. The last sale price of this bond was 107.583, which gives a yield to maturity of about 5.76 percent. Then, by clicking on the "Descriptive Data" link for this bond, we obtained this detailed information for this bond:

Detailed Bond Information   Call Schedule

Symbol: MMM.GB
Issue: MMM 6.375 02/15/28
Cusip: 604059AE5
Bond Type: DEBENTURE
Moody's/S&P/Fitch Rating Aa1 / AA /
Payment Frequency: Semiannually
Industry: MANUFACTURING
Industry Subsector: Conglomerate/Diversified Mfg
Coupon Type: Fixed:Plain Vanilla Fixed Coupon
Callable: N
Other Features:

Composite Trade Information

	Last Sale						Most Recent			Net Change
Date	Price	Yield	High Price	Low Price	High Yield	Low Yield	Date	Price	Yield	Price
03/30/2006	107.583	5.760015	107.583	107.583	5.760015	5.760015	03/30/2006	107.583	5.760015	-1.68

Not only does the site provide the most recent price and yield information, we also find out that the fixed coupon rate is paid semiannually, and the bond is not callable. The credit rating for this bond is Aa1 from Moody's and AA from Standard and Poor's.

face value each year, or $40,000, in two $20,000 semiannual "coupon" payments. In two years, in addition to your final $20,000 coupon payment, you will receive the $1 million face value. The price you would pay for this note depends on market conditions. U.S. government security prices are discussed in detail in a later chapter.

current yield

Annual coupon divided by the current bond price.

You must be careful not to confuse the *coupon rate* with **current yield**. The current yield is the annual coupon divided by the current bond price. For most bonds, the coupon rate never changes. But the current yield fluctuates with the price of the bond.

Suppose you buy $100,000 in face amount of a just-issued five-year U.S. Treasury note. If the coupon rate is 5 percent, what will you receive over the next five years if you hold on to your investment?

You will receive 5 percent of $100,000, or $5,000, per year, paid in two semiannual coupons of $2,500. In five years, in addition to the final $2,500 coupon payment, you will receive the $100,000 face amount.

Check out bond basics at www.investing inbonds.com

To give a slightly different example, suppose you take out a 48-month car loan. Under the terms of the loan, you promise to make 48 payments of $400 per month. It may not look like it to you, but in taking out this loan, you have issued a fixed-income security to your bank. In fact, your bank may turn around and sell your car loan (perhaps bundled with a large number of other loans) to an investor. Actually, car loans are not sold all that often, but there is a very active market in student loans, which are routinely bought and sold in huge quantities.

To learn more about TRACE, visit www.nasd.com and select TRACE.

FIXED-INCOME PRICE QUOTES Corporate bond dealers now report trade information through what is known as the Transactions Report and Compliance Engine (TRACE). As this is written, daily transaction prices are reported on thousands of bonds. A nearby *Work the Web* box shows you how to get data from TRACE.

As shown in Figure 3.1, *The Wall Street Journal* provides a daily snapshot of the data from TRACE by reporting information on the 40 most active issues. Most of the information is self-explanatory. Of note, however, is the column labeled "EST SPREAD." The Est spread is the estimated yield spread over a particular U.S. Treasury issue (a yield spread is just the difference in yields). The spread is reported in basis points, where 1 basis point is equal to .01 percent. The selected U.S. Treasury issue's maturity (in years) is given in the column labeled "UST" (the standard abbreviation for U.S. Treasury). You will note that all the numbers in the column are positive, which indicates that the market views these corporate bonds as riskier than U.S. Treasury bonds.

In Figure 3.1, which bond has the longest maturity? Assuming a face value of $1,000 each, how much would you have to pay for 100 of these? Verify that the reported current yield is correct.

The bond with the longest maturity is the Key Corp Capital Vii bond with a 5.700% coupon. It matures June 15, 2035. Based on the reported closing price, the price you would pay is 97.308 percent of face value per bond. Assuming a $1,000 face value, this is $973.08 per bond, or $97,308 for 100 bonds. The current yield is the annual coupon divided by the price, which, in this case, would be 5.70/97.308 = 5.86 percent.

The potential gains from owning a fixed-income security come in two forms. First, there are the fixed payments promised and the final payment at maturity. In addition, the prices of most fixed-income securities rise when interest rates fall, so there is the possibility of a gain from a favorable movement in rates. An unfavorable change in interest rates will produce a loss.

FIGURE 3.1   NYSE Corporate Bond Trading

Corporate Bonds

Monday, July 18, 2005

Forty most active fixed-coupon corporate bonds

COMPANY (TICKER)	COUPON	MATURITY	LAST PRICE	LAST YIELD	*EST SPREAD	UST†	EST $ VOL (000's)
New Cingular Wireless Services Inc (CNG)	8.750	Mar 01, 2031	137.264	5.908	144	30	108,520
Dominion Resources Inc (D)	5.150	Jul 15, 2015	99.960	5.155	93	10	96,925
Ford Motor Co (F)	7.450	Jul 16, 2031	83.500	9.119	466	30	83,040
Albertson's Inc (ABS)	7.500	Feb 15, 2011	111.393	5.121	111	5	59,085
Ford Motor Credit Co (F)	5.800	Jan 12, 2009	96.001	7.118	312	5	50,522
Alltel (AT)	4.656	May 17, 2007	100.649	4.306	43	2	50,400
Sprint Capital Corp (FON)	6.875	Nov 15, 2028	111.844	5.930	147	30	47,981
Sempra Energy (SRE)	4.621	May 17, 2007	100.309	4.467	59	2	45,200
Koninklijke KPN (KPN)	8.000	Oct 01, 2010	115.008	4.707	71	5	43,200
Health Care Property Investors (HCP)	6.875	Jun 08, 2015	111.287	5.570	135	10	42,800
Lehman Brothers Holdings (LEH)	4.800	Mar 13, 2014	99.469	4.875	65	10	41,650
Viacom Inc (VIA)	4.625	May 15, 2018	88.869	5.872	170	10	41,300
Credit Suisse First Boston (CRDSUI)	4.875	Jan 15, 2015	99.721	4.912	69	10	40,939
Wal-Mart Stores Inc (WMT)	4.125	Jul 01, 2010	98.556	4.452	43	5	39,335
AstraZeneca PLC (AZN)	5.400	Jun 01, 2014	104.732	4.739	52	10	38,928
Ford Motor Credit Co (F)	7.000	Oct 01, 2013	97.250	7.452	324	10	38,817
Boeing Capital Corp (BA)	5.800	Jan 15, 2013	107.080	4.668	45	10	38,780
Kraft Foods (KFT)	6.250	Jun 01, 2012	108.396	4.798	59	10	38,623
Ford Motor Credit Co (F)	7.875	Jun 15, 2010	100.125	7.841	384	5	38,154
Wal-Mart Stores Inc (WMT)	4.500	Jul 01, 2015	97.974	4.757	58	10	38,005
Bank of America (BAC)	3.850	Feb 15, 2008	98.968	4.278	35	3	37,871
Barrick Gold Finance Inc (ABX)	4.875	Nov 15, 2014	98.903	5.023	84	10	37,800
KeyCorp Capital Vii (KEY)	5.700	Jun 15, 2035	97.308	5.892	149	30	37,800
HSBC Finance Corp (HSBC)	6.500	Jan 24, 2006	101.283	3.925	n.a.	n.a.	37,468
BellSouth Corp (BLS)	4.750	Nov 15, 2012	99.778	4.785	60	10	36,901
Kroger Co (KR)	7.450	Mar 01, 2008	106.971	4.584	65	3	36,742
DaimlerChrysler North America Holding Corp (DCX)	4.875	Jun 15, 2010	98.773	5.160	116	5	36,571
CIT Group Inc (CIT)	5.000	Feb 01, 2015	99.423	5.077	90	10	36,460
Dell Inc (DELL)	7.100	Apr 15, 2028	122.965	5.342	88	30	35,936
Kroger Co (KR)	6.200	Jun 15, 2012	106.379	5.091	88	10	35,200
Citigroup (C)	5.000	Sep 15, 2014	100.710	4.902	68	10	32,126
Dow Chemical Co (DOW)	6.000	Oct 01, 2012	108.160	4.652	47	10	31,242
General Electric Capital (GE)	4.250	Jan 15, 2008	99.936	4.277	34	3	30,855
Royal Bank of Scotland Group PLC (RBS)	5.000	Nov 12, 2013	101.254	4.810	59	10	30,700
Goldman Sachs Group Inc (GS)	4.500	Jun 15, 2010	99.249	4.673	66	5	30,155
Viacom Inc (VIA)	7.700	Jul 30, 2010	110.477	5.297	130	5	29,260
Time Warner Inc (TWX)	7.700	May 01, 2032	123.483	5.937	147	30	28,723
Sprint Capital (FON)	8.375	Mar 15, 2012	118.978	4.985	79	10	28,662
International Lease Finance Corp (AIG)	5.750	Oct 15, 2006	101.793	4.236	36	2	28,660
JPMorgan Chase and Co (JPM)	5.625	Aug 15, 2006	101.573	4.100	n.a.	n.a.	28,295
General Electric Capital (GE)	4.875	Mar 04, 2015	100.751	4.776	55	10	27,638

Volume represents total volume for each issue; price/yield data are for trades of $1 million and greater. * Estimated spreads, in basis points (100 basis points is one percentage point), over the 2, 3, 5, 10 or 30-year hot run Treasury note/bond. 2-year: 3.625 06/07; 3-year: 3.750 05/08; 5-year: 3.875 07/10; 10-year: 4.125 05/15; 30-year: 5.375 02/31. †Comparable U.S. Treasury issue.

Source: MarketAxess Corporate BondTicker

Another significant risk for many fixed-income securities is the possibility that the issuer will not make the promised payments. This risk depends on the issuer. It doesn't exist for U.S. government bonds, but for many other issuers the possibility is very real. Finally, unlike most money market instruments, fixed-income securities are often quite illiquid, again depending on the issuer and the specific type.

CHECK THIS

3.2a   What are the two basic types of interest-bearing assets?

3.2b   What are the two basic features of a fixed-income security?

3.3 Equities

Equities are probably the most familiar type of security. They come in two forms: common stock and preferred stock. Of these, common stock is much more important, so we discuss it first.

COMMON STOCK

WWW

Are you a Foolish investor? Go to "Fool's School" at www.fool.com

Common stock represents ownership in a corporation. If you own 1,000 shares of IBM, for example, then you own about .00006 percent of IBM (IBM has roughly 1.55 billion shares outstanding). It's really that simple. As a part owner, you are entitled to your pro rata share of anything paid out by IBM, and you have the right to vote on important matters regarding IBM. If IBM were to be sold or liquidated, you would receive your share of whatever was left over after all of IBM's debts and other obligations (such as wages) were paid.

The potential benefits from owning common stock come primarily in two forms. First, many companies (but not all) pay cash dividends to their shareholders. However, neither the timing nor the amount of any dividend is guaranteed. At any time, it can be increased, decreased, or omitted altogether. Dividends are paid strictly at the discretion of a company's board of directors, which is elected by the shareholders.

The second potential benefit from owning stock is that the value of your stock may rise because share values in general increase or because the future prospects for your particular company improve (or both). The downside is just the reverse: your shares may lose value if either the economy or your particular company falters. As we saw back in Chapter 1, both the potential rewards and the risks from owning common stock have been substantial, particularly shares of stock in smaller companies.

PREFERRED STOCK

The other type of equity security, preferred stock, differs from common stock in several important ways. First, the dividend on a preferred share is usually fixed at some amount and never changed. Further, in the event of liquidation, preferred shares have a particular face value. The reason that preferred stock (or preference stock, as it is sometimes termed) is called "preferred" is that a company must pay the fixed dividend on its preferred stock before any dividends can be paid to common shareholders. In other words, preferred shareholders must be paid first.

The dividend on a preferred stock can be omitted at the discretion of the board of directors, so, unlike a debt obligation, there is no legal requirement that the dividend be paid (as long as the common dividend is also skipped). However, some preferred stock is *cumulative,* meaning that any and all skipped dividends must be paid in full (although without interest) before common shareholders can receive a dividend.

Potential gains from owning preferred stock consist of the promised dividend plus any gains from price increases. The potential losses are just the reverse: the dividend may be skipped, and the value of your preferred shares may decline from either marketwide decreases in value or diminished prospects for your particular company's future business (or both).

Preferred stock issues are not rare, but they are much less frequently encountered than common stock issues. Most preferred stock is issued by large companies, particularly banks and public utilities.

In many ways, preferred stock resembles a fixed-income security; in fact, it is sometimes classified that way. In particular, preferred stocks usually have a fixed payment and a fixed liquidation value (but no fixed maturity date). The main difference is that preferred stock is not a debt obligation. Also, for accounting and tax purposes, preferred stock is treated as equity.

Having said this, preferred stock is a good example of why it is sometimes difficult to neatly and precisely classify every security type. To further complicate matters, some preferred stock issues have dividends that are not fixed, so it seems clear that these are not fixed-income securities, but there are also bond issues that do not make fixed payments and allow the issuer to skip payments under certain circumstances. As we mentioned earlier, these are examples of hybrid securities.

To give a more difficult example, consider a *convertible bond.* Such a bond is an ordinary bond in every way except that it can be exchanged for a fixed number of shares of stock anytime at the bondholder's discretion. Whether this is really a debt or equity instrument is difficult (or even impossible) to say.

COMMON STOCK PRICE QUOTES

Unlike fixed-income securities, the price quotes on common and preferred stock are fairly uniform. Part of the common stock page from *The Wall Street Journal* can be seen in Figure 3.2. Locate the entry for Lowe's Companies.

FIGURE 3.2   NYSE Trading

THE WALL STREET JOURNAL.

NEW YORK STOCK EXCHANGE COMPOSITE TRANSACTIONS

TUESDAY, JULY 19, 2005

52-WEEK HI	LO	STOCK (DIV)	YLD %	PE	VOL 100s	CLOSE	NET CHG
65.46	51.20	LockhdMartin 1.00	1.6	20	17819	61.47	-0.28
81.18	53.35	LoewsCp .60	.7	11	3558	80.26	-0.22
49.84	24.86	LoneStarTch	...	11	7323	47	1.17
46.50	20.45	LongsDrg .56	1.3	42	3028	44.80	0.15
21.98	11.65	LongvwFibr .11e	.5	36	2780	20.22	0.09
28.73	21.05	LA Pac .50f	2.1	6	5669	24.34	-0.11
↓ 63.99	45.90	Lowes Cos .24f	.4	22	38035	64.56	0.91
44.51	32.12	Lubrizol 1.04	2.4	25	1968	42.91	0.16
14	5.75	Lubys	...	42	2966	13.53	-0.02
4.16	2.35	LucentTch	...	8	515097	3.13	0.01
12.88	9.53	LmntMtgCap 1.08m	10.2	6	3991	10.61	-0.25
22.96	16.23	LuxottGp .28e	1.2	28	325	22.60	-0.24
12.22	7.94	Lydall	...	dd	45	9.02	0.07
35.65	17.04	Lyondell .90	3.2	21	18619	27.91	-0.08

M

52-WEEK HI	LO	STOCK (DIV)	YLD %	PE	VOL 100s	CLOSE	NET CHG
14.80	12.21	M&F Wrldwd	...	10	50	13.24	0.02
111.40	92.04	M&T Bnk 1.80f	1.6	17	2376	109.44	-0.68
65.21	49.07	MBIA 1.12	1.8	11	6537	61.45	-0.75
29.01	18.28	MBNA Cp .56	2.2	15	109003	25.85	-0.37
89.63	48.88	MDC Hldgs s .72f	.8	8	4548	87.35	-0.25
17.10	12.53	MDS .13g	...	...	84	16.17	0.20
↓ 30	23.79	MDU Res .72	2.4	16	2103	29.90	0.04
18.46	7.33	MEMC Elec	...	15	11860	17.49	-0.01

52-WEEK HI	LO	STOCK (DIV)	YLD %	PE	VOL 100s	CLOSE	NET CHG
29.31	21.51	NoEuroOil 1.93e	6.8	15	107	28.18	-0.17
30.81	25.24	NoForkBcp s .88	3.0	14	19558	29.47	-0.23
21.74	17.17	NE Util .70f	3.3	dd	4327	21.45	-0.07
52.99	38.61✦	NorthnBrdr 3.20	6.2	18	736	51.95	0.70
58.15	49.54✦	NorthrpGrum 1.04f	1.9	16	7615	54.92	-0.77
11.65	8.50	NostrRltyFin n .15p	...	...	125	10.63	-0.16
39.20	28.84	NowestNG 1.30	3.4	19	1703	38.32	-0.06
52.20	28.40	NOVA Chem .40g	...	...	2478	34.45	0.70
50.99	43.21	Novartis ADS .86e	1.8	21	23013	49.05	0.61
58.04	31.10	NovstrFnl 6.80e	16.9	9	2850	40.34	0.28
↓ 27.34	20.75	Novelis n .18e	.7	...	915	27.42	0.37
60.10	49.09	NovoNordisk .86e	1.7	...	300	51.15	0.10
31.46	23.01	NSTAR s 1.16	3.8	18	1434	30.84	-0.09
19.43	14.43	NTT DoCoMo .19e	1.2	...	395	15.36	0.02
28.15	16.26	NuSkin A .36	1.4	23	2866	25.44	-0.16
65.26	37.36	Nucor s .60a	1.2	6	21887	49.90	0.17
42.52	24.52	NuveenInv .72	1.9	22	2353	37.43	0.19
25.86	19.53	NYMagic .24	1.0	15	15	23.99	0.46

O

52-WEEK HI	LO	STOCK (DIV)	YLD %	PE	VOL 100s	CLOSE	NET CHG
7.35	1.26	OCA lf	...	6	3600	1.81	-0.03
29.76	24.10	OGE Engy 1.33	4.6	17	1531	29.07	-0.07
37.76	19.35	OM Group lf	...	dd	1580	23.82	-0.27
22.05	12.26	OMI Cp .32	1.7	6	7430	19.03	0.08

THE TALE OF THE TAPE

The on-air "ticker tape" is a familiar sight on television, particularly on financially oriented shows and networks. The most widely watched such channel is CNBC. All day long, at the bottom of the screen, two rolls of information scroll by.

On CNBC, the upper band shows trading on the New York Stock Exchange, and the lower band shows trading on the NASDAQ Stock Market. A lot of other information (too much, in fact, for us to cover here) will also scroll by.

To learn more, go to moneycentral.msn.com/investor and link to CNBC TV. As you will see, you can create your own ticker for display on your computer screen just by following the directions given. A personalized ticker allows you to track just the stocks that interest you the most. We created our own ticker:

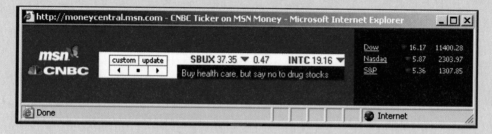

If you click on "custom," you can add your own list of ticker symbols. You can pause the ticker and make it run forward and backward if you wish.

The display is called a "ticker" because, at one time, it was printed on a thin strip of "ticker tape" (paper) by a "ticker" machine (so named because of the sound it made while printing). In fact, the reason for ticker symbols in the first place was to make information quicker and easier to print. Perhaps you have seen old film footage of a "ticker tape parade" in New York. The paper that rains down on the celebrities and dignitaries is ticker tape.

Ticker machines date to an era before television (if you can imagine such a time). The first one was introduced in 1867 and was later improved upon by none other than Thomas Edison. To learn more, visit the Web site www.stocktickercompany.com.

The first two numbers (labeled "52 WEEK HI" and "LO") are the highest and lowest price per share that the stock has sold for over the past 52 weeks. Thus, Lowe's sold for as high as $63.99 per share and as low as $45.90 per share. The next piece of information is the company name, often abbreviated.

Following the company name is the dividend, labeled "(DIV)" and the dividend yield, labeled "YLD %." Like most dividend-paying companies, Lowe's pays dividends on a quarterly basis; the dividend number reported here, $.24, is actually four times the most recent quarterly dividend. The dividend yield is this annualized dividend divided by the closing price (discussed just below). Next, the price-earnings ratio, or "PE," is reported. This ratio, as the name suggests, is equal to the price per share divided by earnings per share. Earnings per share is calculated as the sum of earnings per share over the last four quarters. We will discuss dividends, dividend yields, and price-earnings ratios in detail in a later chapter.

The next piece of information, "VOL 100s," is the trading volume for the day, measured in hundreds. Stocks are usually traded in multiples of 100 called "round lots." Anything that is not a multiple of 100 is called an "odd lot." On this particular day, then, 38,035 round lots, or about 3.8 million shares, were traded.

INVESTMENT UPDATES

REBALANCING YOUR PORTFOLIO

A year of major shifts in the world's financial markets is forcing investment advisers to overhaul some of their basic advice on asset allocation.

As a result, this fall as individual investors gear up for the ritual end-of-year reassessment and rebalancing of their portfolios, they might find they need to make bigger changes than in the past.

For instance, the longstanding 60%-in-stocks-and-40%-in-bonds rule for a medium-risk Baby Boomer portfolio is being tossed out the window at some firms. Instead, financial planners say, they are increasingly advising clients to test the waters of foreign investments, especially in Europe and Japan, as well as alternative investments such as hedge funds.

Portfolios that haven't been rebalanced this year most likely drifted toward U.S. real-estate related holdings, intermediate-term bonds, value stocks and small-capitalization stocks, all of which should be reined in, advisers say.

The shifting advice is the result of a range of the sometimes surprising changes in the investing landscape over the past year to 18 months. The federal-funds target rate has climbed to 4% from its nearly half-century low of 1% as recently as mid-2004, guiding short-term interest rates higher. That steady climb in itself is rapidly turning investors off debt investments, especially the riskiest so-called junk bonds, and instead increasing the appeal of cash-like investments such as money-market funds.

At the same time, the dollar has staged an unexpected surge. U.S. stocks, meanwhile, have been relatively flat this year, which has sent investors looking for better returns abroad.

Complicating matters: Energy prices remain high, an immediate concern that throws a wrench into investment planning because it is still unclear what the longer-term impact will be on the economy and the stock market. And real-estate prices have showed signs of softening in the past few months, perhaps signaling that the decade-long real-estate boom is cooling off. As a result, some once-popular real-estate investment trust stocks are now increasingly viewed as having topped out and run their course in recent months.

All this upheaval signals what some financial advisers believe is a turning point for investors. Namely, the changed landscape means people might need to make more than the usual small tune-up this year and possibly further down the road. "I think we're about to enter a multi-year shift," says David Darst, chief investment strategist at Morgan Stanley's individual investor group. "People should question how much their portfolios are returning," in a market in transition.

Investors need to be cautious about rebalancing. It is generally unwise to make significant changes to an investment strategy based on short-term market movements. And the current environment of relatively low returns across the board means it is crucial to minimize transaction costs and taxes, for example, taxes on capital-gains distributions from mutual funds at year-end.

One way to limit costs like these is to start rebalancing with a 401 (k) or other tax-deferred account, and use new money, like individual retirement account contributions, stock dividends and bond interest payments, to adjust existing holdings. Rebalancing now could also mean selling off stocks at a loss to offset gains, reducing year-end taxes in the process.

Interviews with 21 strategists nationwide indicated that there are a number of adjustments that investors should consider. Here is their advice on where the smart money may be headed.

Stocks

Many strategists now favor high-quality stocks over the lower-quality names that have led the market in recent years. Low-quality stocks are often smaller companies with substantial debt—but today, many have lofty stock valuations because investors were willing to make aggressive bets on them during the earlier stages of the bull market. For instance, many advisers recommend trimming holdings in energy and utilities, which are two lower-quality sectors that have been the S&P 500's top performers this year.

Instead, some advisers say that higher-quality sectors like health-care and consumer staples are set to take the lead. The reason: Rising interest rates, inflation fears, and other market jitters will make investors look for surer bets, says Sam Stovall, chief investment strategist at Standard & Poor's. High-quality

(continued)

stocks, which normally command higher valuations, are now trading at a 10% discount to lower-quality stocks, says Mr. Stovall.

Strategists are especially bullish on health care and technology—areas that, like the broader market, have barely budged this year. Health-care companies stand to benefit from an aging population. And while the current wave of high energy prices might cause consumers to cut back on, say, new clothes or vacations, they will always spend money on medicine. "It's not a discretionary item," says Bryan Olson, vice president at Schwab's Center for Investment Research.

Thanks to strong performance in overseas markets, many investors may find their international-stock allocation has grown over the past year. Rather than cutting back, many strategists are raising their recommended foreign-stock allocations. They see a number of headwinds facing the U.S. stock market, including slowing profit growth and high energy prices, and good prospects for continued growth in emerging markets and Japan.

Bonds and Cash

One message rings loud and clear right now: Anything but bonds.

Many advisers say the expectation of rising interest rates and corresponding lower bond prices suggest investors aren't being rewarded to take on longer-term bond risk heading into next year.

That is why advisers are suggesting shorter-term U.S. bonds for medium-risk investors next year, with more-conservative investors being led into shorter-term U.S. municipal bonds. Some planners are calling for a mix that reduces bond holdings to as little as 15% of holdings, down from the more common 25% to 30% for a medium-risk and size portfolio. This might include more Treasury Inflation-Protected Securities, which offer investors upside with rising inflation.

"Fixed income as a whole is just not that attractive," and hasn't been for a while, says Nic Richard, head of asset allocation at Citigroup Private Bank.

In the five years ended 2004, cash or short-term fixed income investments held by U.S. households rose more than 41% to a record $5.7 trillion, while bond holdings declined, according to a Citigroup Private Bank investment-outlook bulletin released this month. While Citigroup cautions against "the risk of risk aversion," in the report, the trend mirrors many public companies hoarding cash these days amid restrained spending.

Cash was once seen as a place-holder: an idle bet that didn't generate returns but offered security. It is now being bumped up to 10% of holdings or more, especially as yields on some money-market accounts close in on the 4.57% yield on a 10-year Treasury note.

Alternative Investments

Alternative investments are taking up an ever-growing chunk of the pie even in medium-risk portfolios. Both Morgan Stanley and Citibank recommend 10% to 12% allocations to hedge funds, with another 4% or 5% devoted to private-equity, managed-futures funds and other, more opaque, items. The figure could ramp up to as much as 40% of a portfolio for more risk-friendly clients.

Upping holdings in alternative investments remains a more likely option for wealthier investors since categories like hedge funds often require $1 million of investable assets from the get-go.

Source: Diya Gullapalli and Eleanor Laise. *The Wall Street Journal*, November 12, 2005. © 2005 Dow Jones & Company, Inc. All Rights Reserved Worldwide.

The column labeled "CLOSE" is the closing price, meaning the last price at which a trade occurred before regular trading hours ended at 4:00 P.M. EST. Finally, the "NET CHG" is the change in the closing price from the previous trading day. So, on this particular day, Lowe's closed at $64.56, up $0.91 from the day before.

The information contained in *The Wall Street Journal* can be obtained online in many places, of course. The nearby *Work the Web* box describes one way. You can also get preferred stock quotes in *The Wall Street Journal*. They appear in a separate section with a relatively simple format.

Throughout this chapter, we have looked at information from *The Wall Street Journal*. One problem is that prices reported in the financial press are always from the previous day. Before you trade, you'll want more up-to-date pricing, particularly in fast-moving markets. Using an Internet server, such as Yahoo!, let's do this. Here, as in Chapter 1, we have entered a ticker symbol ("Dell" for Dell Computer).

To track stocks & more, **Register**

Quotes & Info	Enter Symbol(s): e.g. YHOO, ^DJI	DELL	GO	Symbol Lookup	Finance Search

Dell Inc. (DELL)   At 1:07PM ET: **35.13** ↑0.10 (0.29%)

Here is what we get:

DELL INC (NasdaqNM:DELL) Delayed quote data   [Edit]

Last Trade:	**35.13**	Day's Range:	35.03 - 35.36
Trade Time:	1:07PM ET	52wk Range:	33.85 - 42.57
Change:	↑0.10 (0.29%)	Volume:	7,286,078
Prev Close:	35.03	Avg Vol (3m):	15,403,400
Open:	35.20	Market Cap:	85.05B
Bid:	35.12 × 6900	P/E (ttm):	25.59
Ask:	35.13 × 1500	EPS (ttm):	1.37
1y Target Est:	45.52	Div & Yield:	N/A (N/A)

DELL 2-Sep 1:07pm (C)Yahoo!
1d 5d 3m 6m 1y 2y 5y max

Annual Report for DELL

Add DELL to Portfolio   Set Alert   Download Data

Most of the information here is self-explanatory. The abbreviation "Market Cap" is short for "market capitalization," which is the total value of all outstanding shares. Notice, on this particular day, Dell was up .29 percent, compared to the $35.03 ("Prev Close") that you would see in *The Wall Street Journal*. We'll discuss other unfamiliar terms, such as "Bid" and "Ask," a little later in the book. For now, a good exercise is to select a detailed quote yourself and find out what information is in the links below the stock quote.

These days, you can also see "real-time" quotes. If you click on the real-time market link or the "Real-Time ECN" link that appears left of the detailed view, you will get:

DELL INC (RT-ECN)

Symbol:	**DELL**
Last Trade:	**35.06** 1:20PM ET
After Hours Change:	N/A
Today's Change:	↑0.03 (0.09%)
Bid:	35.06
Ask:	35.07

This is a free Real-Time ECN quote.

Each Real-Time ECN quote is from INET and does not necessarily represent the best bid or ask in the marketplace.

To interpret this information, you will need to know the company's ticker symbol. The ticker symbol is a unique combination of letters assigned to each company. Lowe's ticker symbol, for example, is LOW. Stock price information is also available all day long on television and on the Web. Our nearby *Investment Updates* box explains how to interpret a very common site on television, the on-air ticker. As explained there, once you understand the display, you can actually create your own ticker to track the investments that interest you the most.

CHECK THIS

3.3a   What are the two types of equity securities?

3.3b   Why is preferred stock sometimes classified as a fixed-income security?

3.4 Derivatives

There is a clear distinction between real assets, which are essentially tangible items, and financial assets, which are pieces of paper describing legal claims. Financial assets can be further subdivided into primary and derivative assets. A **primary asset** (sometimes called a *primitive asset*) is a security that was originally sold by a business or government to raise money, and a primary asset represents a claim on the assets of the issuer. Thus, stocks and bonds are primary financial assets.

In contrast, as the name suggests, a **derivative asset** is a financial asset that is derived from an existing primary asset rather than issued by a business or government to raise capital. As we will see, derivative assets usually represent claims either on other financial assets, such as shares of stock or even other derivative assets, or on the future price of a real asset such as gold. Beyond this, it is difficult to give a general definition of the term "derivative asset" because there are so many different types, and new ones are created almost every day. On the most basic level, however, any financial asset that is not a primary asset is a derivative asset.

To give a simple example of a derivative asset, imagine that you and a friend buy 1,000 shares of a dividend-paying stock, perhaps the Lowe's stock we discussed. You each put up half the money, and you agree to sell your stock in one year. Furthermore, the two of you agree that you will get all the dividends paid while your friend gets all the gains or absorbs all the losses on the 1,000 shares.

This simple arrangement takes a primary asset, shares of Lowe's stock, and creates two derivative assets, the dividend-only shares that you hold and the no-dividend shares held by your friend. Derivative assets such as these actually exist, and there are many variations on this basic theme.

Two types of derivative assets, futures and options, are particularly important. Many other types exist, but they can usually be built up from these two basic types, possibly by combining them with other primary assets. Futures are the simpler of the two, so we discuss them first.

primary asset
Security originally sold by a business or government to raise money.

derivative asset
A financial asset that is derived from an existing traded asset rather than issued by a business or government to raise capital. More generally, any financial asset that is not a primary asset.

FUTURES CONTRACTS

In many ways, a futures contract is the simplest of all financial assets. A **futures contract** is just an agreement made today regarding the terms of a trade that will take place later. For example, suppose you know that you will want to buy 100 ounces of gold in six months. One thing you could do is to strike a deal today with a seller in which you promise to pay, say, $400 per ounce in six months for the 100 ounces of gold. In other words, you and the seller agree that six months from now, you will exchange $40,000 for 100 ounces of gold. The agreement that you have created is a futures contract.

With your futures contract, you have locked in the price of gold six months from now. Suppose that gold is actually selling for $450 per ounce in six months. If this occurs, then

futures contract
An agreement made today regarding the terms of a trade that will take place later.

you benefit from having entered into the futures contract because you have to pay only $400 per ounce. However, if gold is selling for $350, you lose because you are forced to pay $400 per ounce. Thus, a futures contract is essentially a bet on the future price of whatever is being bought or sold. Notice that with your futures contract, no money changes hands today.

After entering into the futures contract, what happens if you change your mind in, say, four months, and you want out of the contract? The answer is that you can sell your contract to someone else. You would generally have a gain or a loss when you sell. The contract still has two months to run. If market participants generally believe that gold will be worth more than $400 when the contract matures in two months, then your contract is valuable, and you would have a gain if you sold it. If, on the other hand, market participants think gold will not be worth $400, then you would have a loss on the contract if you sold it because you would have to pay someone else to take it off your hands.

Futures contracts are traded all over the world on many types of assets, and futures contracts can be traced back to ancient civilizations. As we discuss in detail in a later chapter, there are two broad categories of futures contracts: *financial futures* and *commodity futures*. The difference is that, with financial futures, the underlying asset is intangible, usually stocks, bonds, currencies, or money market instruments. With commodity futures, the underlying asset is a real asset, typically either an agricultural product (such as cattle or wheat) or a natural resource product (such as gold or oil).

FUTURES PRICE QUOTES

An important feature of traded futures contracts is that they are *standardized*, meaning that one contract calls for the purchase of a specific quantity of the underlying asset. Further, the contract specifies in detail what the underlying asset is and where it is to be delivered. For example, with a wheat contract, one contract specifies that 5,000 bushels of a particular type of wheat will be delivered at one of a few approved locations on a particular date in exchange for the agreed-upon futures price.

In Figure 3.3, futures price quotations for U.S. Treasury bonds (or "T-bonds" for short) are seen as they appear in *The Wall Street Journal*. (A nearby *Work the Web* contains links for futures price quotes.) Looking at Figure 3.3, we see these are quotes for delivery of T-bonds with a total par, or face, value of $100,000. The letters CBT indicate to us where

---

FIGURE 3.3   Futures Trading

THE WALL STREET JOURNAL.

FUTURES

TUESDAY, JULY 19, 2005

Interest Rate Futures

	OPEN	HIGH	LOW	SETTLE	CHG	LIFETIME HIGH	LIFETIME LOW	OPEN INT
Sept	116-15	116-20	115-14	115-22	−23	119-23	108-15	560,897
Dec	115-28	116-05	115-03	115-09	−23	119-07	108-23	15,697

Treasury Bonds (CBT)-$100,000; pts 32nds of 100%
Est vol 162,922; vol Fri 198,479; open int 576,644, +686.

Source: Reprinted by permission from *The Wall Street Journal*, July 19, 2005. © 2005 Dow Jones & Company, Inc. All Rights Reserved Worldwide.

Futures price quotes have also become more available with the rise of the Internet. Sites where you can find futures price quotes include www.cbot.com, www.cme.com, and www.nymex.com.

At the Chicago Board of Trade (CBOT), futures contracts for grains (e.g., corn, wheat,

soybeans), interest rates (U.S. Treasury notes and bonds, German bonds), and Dow Jones Index Futures are listed.

There are some unique aspects to each futures contract. For example, here is a sample soybean futures screen from the CBOT's Web site.

Soybeans Futures (S)

Delayed 10 minute data as of April 25, 2006 17:00 CDT

| Quotes | Settlement | Daily Vol | Time & Sales | Volatility | Historical Data | Spreads |

| Open Auction | Electronic | Combinations | Real-Time Quotes |

Exp	Last 1 / Last 2	Net Chg	Open	High	Low	Close	Settle	Prev Settle	Hi/Lo Limit
06May	579'4 13:18 580'0 13:18	+5'2	574'4 575'4 9:35	580'0 13:03	571'4 10:14	579'0 580'0 13:18	579'4	574'2	629'4 529'4
06Jul	593'2 13:18 593'4 13:18	+5'0	588'0 589'4 9:33	594'0 13:03	584'6 10:14	593'0 593'4 13:18	593'2	588'2	643'2 543'2

Locate the line that starts with 06Jul. This is a very active futures contract that calls for July delivery of 5,000 bushels of soybeans. Note that these quotes are obtained at the end of the day's trading. By convention, soybean prices are still quoted in cents and eighths of a cent even though the minimum price change is one-fourth cent, or 2/8th of a cent. Under the **Settle** column, you can see an entry of 593'2, which is 593 and 2/8th cents, or $5.93¼. The daily low was 584'6, which is 584 and 6/8th cents, or $5.84¾.

At the Chicago Mercantile Exchange (CME), trading exists in a wide variety of markets including agricultural futures (live cattle, feeder

cattle, lean hogs, frozen pork bellies), foreign exchange rate futures, S&P 500 futures, and interest rate futures (LIBOR, Eurodollar). At the New York Mercantile Exchange (NYMEX), futures contracts for metals (copper, silver, gold, platinum) and energy (crude oil, heating oil, unleaded gasoline) are traded.

A complete list of all the contracts traded at each commodity exchange can be found at the respective exchange's Web site. You should understand that it takes a great deal of study to understand futures markets, their usage, and their quoting conventions. Your school might even offer a course where you can study futures markets in depth.

this contract is traded; in this case, it is the Chicago Board of Trade, the largest futures exchange in the world.

The first column in Figure 3.3 tells us the delivery date for the bond specified by the contract. For example, the "Sept" indicates that the first contract listed is for T-bond delivery in September. The second is for delivery in December. Following the delivery month, we have a series of prices. In order, we have the open price, the high price, the low price, and the settle price. The open price is the price at the start of the trading day, the high and low are highest and lowest prices for the day, and the settle is the price on the final trade of the day. The "CHG" is the change in the settle price from the previous trading day.

The columns labeled "LIFETIME HIGH" and "LIFETIME LOW" refer to the highest and lowest prices over the life of this contract. Finally, the "OPEN INT" tells us how many contracts are currently outstanding.

To get a better idea of how futures contracts work, suppose you buy one September contract at the settle price. What you have done is agree to buy T-bonds with a total par value of $100,000 in September at a price of 115-22 per $100 of par value, where the "22" represents $^{22}/_{32}$. Thus 115-22 can also be written as $115^{22}/_{32}$, which represents a price of $115,687.50 per $100,000 face value. No money changes hands today. However, if you take no further action, when September rolls around your T-bonds will be delivered, and you must pay for them at that time.

Actually, most futures contracts don't result in delivery. Most buyers and sellers close out their contracts before the delivery date. To close out a contract, you take the opposite side. For example, suppose that with your one T-bond contract, you later decide you no longer wish to be in it. To get out, you simply sell one contract, thereby canceling your position.

GAINS AND LOSSES ON FUTURES CONTRACTS

Futures contracts have the potential for enormous gains and losses. To see why, let's consider again buying T-bond contracts based on the settle prices in Figure 3.3. To make matters somewhat more interesting, suppose you buy 20 September contracts at the settle price of 115 $^{22}/_{32}$ per $100 of par value.

One month later, because of falling inflation, the futures price of T-bonds for September delivery rises five dollars to $120^{22}/_{32}$. This may not seem like a huge increase, but it generates a substantial profit for you. You have locked in a price of $115^{22}/_{32}$ per $100 par value. The price has risen to $120^{22}/_{32}$, so you make a profit of $5 per $100 of par value, or $5,000 per $100,000 face value. With 20 contracts, each of which calls for delivery of $100,000 in face value of T-bonds, you make $20 \times \$5,000 = \$100,000$, so your profit is a tidy $100,000. Of course, if the price had decreased by five dollars, you would have lost $100,000 on your 20-contract position.

EXAMPLE 3.3 **Future Shock**

It is July. Suppose you purchase five September T-bond contracts at a settle price of 115-22. How much will you pay today? Suppose in one month you close your position and the September futures price at that time is 110-21. Did you make or lose money? How much?

When you purchase the five contracts, you pay nothing today because the transaction is for September. However, you have agreed to pay 115-22 per $100 par value. If, when you close your position in a month, the futures price is 110-21, you have a loss of 115–22 − 110–21 = $5^{1}/_{32}$ per $100 par value, or $5^{1}/_{32} \times 1,000 = \$5,031.25$ per contract. Your total loss is thus $5,031.25 \times 5$ contracts, or $25,156.25 in all (ouch!).

CHECK THIS

3.4a   What is a futures contract?

3.4b   What are the general types of futures contracts?

3.4c   Explain how you make or lose money on a futures contract.

option contract

An agreement that gives the owner the right, but not the obligation, to buy or sell a specific asset at a specified price for a set period of time.

An **option contract** is an agreement that gives the owner the right, but not the obligation, to buy or sell (depending on the type of option) a specific asset at a specific price for a specific period of time. The most familiar options are stock options. These are options to buy or sell shares of stock, and they are the focus of our discussion here. Options are a very flexible investment tool, and a great deal is known about them. We present some of the most important concepts here; our detailed coverage begins in a later chapter.

OPTION TERMINOLOGY

call option

An option that gives the owner the right, but not the obligation, to buy an asset.

put option

An option that gives the owner the right, but not the obligation, to sell an asset.

Options come in two flavors, calls and puts. The owner of a **call option** has the right, but not the obligation, to *buy* an underlying asset at a fixed price for a specified time. The owner of a **put option** has the right, but not the obligation, to *sell* an underlying asset at a fixed price for a specified time.

Options occur frequently in everyday life. Suppose, for example, that you are interested in buying a used car. You and the seller agree that the price will be $3,000. You give the seller $100 to hold the car for one week, meaning that you have one week to come up with the $3,000 purchase price, or else you lose your $100.

This agreement is a call option. You paid the seller $100 for the right, but not the obligation, to buy the car for $3,000. If you change your mind because, for example, you find a better deal elsewhere, you can just walk away. You'll lose your $100, but that is the price you paid for the right, but not the obligation, to buy. The price you pay to purchase an option, the $100 in this example, is called the **option premium**.

option premium

The price you pay to buy an option.

strike price

The price specified in an option contract at which the underlying asset can be bought (for a call option) or sold (for a put option). Also called the striking price or exercise price.

A few other definitions will be useful. First, the specified price at which the underlying asset can be bought or sold with an option contract is called the **strike price**, the *striking price,* or the *exercise price*. Using an option to buy or sell an asset is called *exercising* the option.

The *last trading day* for all listed stock options in the United States is the third Friday of the option's expiration month (except when Friday falls on a holiday, in which case the last trading day is the third Thursday). The *expiration day* for stock options is the Saturday immediately following the last trading day. The expiration day is the last day (in the case of *American-style* options) or the only day (in the case of *European-style* options) on which an option may be *exercised*.

OPTIONS VERSUS FUTURES

Our discussion thus far illustrates the two crucial differences between an option contract and a futures contract. The first is that the purchaser of a futures contract is *obligated* to buy the underlying asset at the specified price (and the seller of a futures contract is obligated to sell). The owner of a call option has the right, but not the obligation, to buy.

The second important difference is that when you buy a futures contract, you pay no money, at the time of purchase (and you receive none if you sell). However, if you buy an option contract, you pay the premium; if you sell an option contract, you receive the premium.

OPTION PRICE QUOTES

To learn more about options visit the Learning Center at www.cboe.com

Like futures contracts, most option contracts are standardized. One call option contract, for example, gives the owner the right to buy 100 shares (one round lot) of stock. Similarly, one put option contract gives the owner the right to sell 100 shares.

Figure 3.4 presents intraday 20-minute delay quotes for call and put options on Home Depot common stock. The data is from finance.yahoo.com. To obtain these option quotes, enter a ticker symbol (here: HD), then find and click the option link. At the time these quotes were obtained, Home Depot stock was trading at $40.33.

The first column in Figure 3.4 lists strike prices for options with September expiration. More precisely, these options expire at the close of trading on September 16,

FIGURE 3.4 | Options Trading

View By Expiration: **Sep 05** | Oct 05 | Nov 05 | Jan 06 | Feb 06 | Jan 07 | Jan 08

CALL OPTIONS   Expire at close Fri, Sep 16, 2005

Strike	Symbol	Last	Chg	Bid	Ask	Vol	Open Int
30.00	HDIF.X	**10.00**	**0.00**	10.30	10.50	46	46
32.50	HDIZ.X	**8.40**	**0.00**	7.90	8.00	1	68
35.00	HDIG.X	**5.70**	**0.00**	5.40	5.50	20	215
37.50	HDIU.X	**3.50**	**↑0.30**	2.95	3.10	4	1,317
40.00	HDIH.X	**0.95**	**↓0.15**	0.90	0.95	476	10,027
42.50	HDIV.X	**0.10**	**↓0.05**	0.10	0.15	435	11,550
45.00	HDII.X	**0.05**	**0.00**	N/A	0.05	10	7,643
47.50	HDIS.X	**0.05**	**0.00**	N/A	0.05	10	1,217
50.00	HDIJ.X	**0.05**	**0.00**	N/A	0.05	1	1

PUT OPTIONS   Expire at close Fri, Sep 16, 2005

Strike	Symbol	Last	Chg	Bid	Ask	Vol	Open Int
32.50	HDUZ.X	**0.05**	**0.00**	N/A	0.05	0	10
35.00	HDUG.X	**0.05**	**0.00**	N/A	0.05	20	540
37.50	HDUU.X	**0.05**	**0.00**	N/A	0.10	10	8,072
40.00	HDUH.X	**0.45**	**0.00**	0.45	0.50	747	9,363
42.50	HDUV.X	**2.20**	**↑0.15**	2.10	2.25	22	2,312
45.00	HDUI.X	**4.50**	**0.00**	4.50	4.70	2	310
47.50	HDUS.X	**7.50**	**0.00**	7.00	7.20	20	177

Highlighted options are in-the-money.

2005. Option data for other expiration months can be obtained by clicking on other views.

The second column is the unique symbol for each option. For example, the symbol for the Home Depot September 40 call option is "HDIH.X." The "HD" stands for Home Depot; the "I" represents September (for calls, expiration months correspond to the letters A through L, so, for calls, the ninth month gets the ninth letter of the alphabet, I); the "H" refers to the strike (H can be 40, 140, 240, etc.); and the "X" is the symbol Yahoo! uses for U.S. options. Note that the symbol for the Home Depot September 40 put option is "HDUH.X." For puts, expiration months correspond to the letters M through X. So, for puts, the ninth month gets the twenty-first letter of the alphabet, U.

Columns three and four list last sale prices and the change from the previous close. Current bid and ask prices appear in the next two columns. The bid price is the price *you* will receive if you want to sell an option at the prevailing market price; the ask price is the price *you* will pay if you want to buy an option at the prevailing market price. Volume and open interest numbers appear in the last two columns. Volume is the number of contracts traded that day. Open interest is the number of contracts outstanding.

Referring to the Home Depot September 35 call options, we see that 20 call option contracts have been traded so far in this trading day, and the last transaction price for this option was $5.70 per share. Because each listed option contract actually involves 100 shares, the price per contract was $5.70 × 100 = $570.

The bid and ask prices reflect current market conditions, not the market conditions that prevailed at the time of the last transaction price. Based on the bid and ask prices, what price would you pay now for one of these call options? Remember, the ask price is the price *you* pay, so you would pay $5.50 per share, or $550 for the contract. (If you were selling, you would sell at the bid price of $5.40 per share, or $540 for the contract.)

Suppose you wanted the right to buy 500 shares of Home Depot for $40 sometime between now and September 16. What would you buy? Based on the information in Figure 3.4, how much would you have to pay?

You want the right to buy, so you want to purchase call options. Because each contract is for 100 shares, and you want the right to buy 500 shares, you need five contracts. The contract you want would be described as the Home Depot September 40 call option. From Figure 3.4, the option premium for the contract with a $40 strike and a September expiration is $0.95, so one contract would cost $0.95 × 100 = $95. The cost for five contracts would therefore be 5 × $95 = $475.

EXAMPLE 3.4   **Put Options**

Suppose you want the right to sell 200 shares of Home Depot between now and September 16 at a price of $40. In light of the information in Figure 3.4, what contract should you buy? How much will it cost you?

You want the right to sell stock at a fixed price, so you want to buy put options. Specifically, you want to buy two September 40 put contracts. In Figure 3.4, the last-sale premium for this contract is given as $0.45. Recalling that this is the premium per share, one contract will cost you $45; so two contracts would cost $90.

GAINS AND LOSSES ON OPTION CONTRACTS

As with futures contracts, option contracts have the potential for large gains and losses. To examine this, let's consider our previous example in which you paid $475 for five Home Depot September 40 call contracts. Suppose you hold on to your contracts until September rolls around, and they are just about to expire. What are your gains (or losses) if Home Depot is selling for $55 per share? $30 per share?

If Home Depot is selling for $55 per share, you will profit handsomely. You have the right to buy 500 shares at a price of $40 per share. Because the stock is worth $55, your options are worth $15 per share, or $7,500 in all. So you invested $475 and ended up with more than 15 times that in just about three months. Not bad.

If the stock ends up at $30 per share, however, the result is not so pretty. You have the right to buy the stock for $40 when it is selling for $30, so your call options expire worthless. You lose the entire $475 you originally invested. In fact, if the stock price is anything less than $40, you lose $475.

EXAMPLE 3.5   **More on Puts**

In Example 3.4, you bought two Home Depot September 40 put contracts for $90. Suppose that September arrives, and Home Depot is selling for $15 per share. How did you do? What's the break-even stock price, that is, the price at which you just make enough to cover your $90 cost?

Your put contracts give you the right to sell 200 shares of Home Depot at a price of $40 per share. If the stock is worth only $15 per share, your put options are worth $25 per share, or $5,000 in all. To determine the break-even stock price, notice that you paid $0.45 per share for the option, so this is what you must make per share to break even. The break-even stock price is thus $40 − $0.45 = $39.55.

INVESTING IN STOCKS VERSUS OPTIONS

To get a better idea of the potential gains and losses from investing in stocks compared to investing in options, let's suppose you have $10,000 to invest. You're looking at Macron Technology, which is currently selling for $50 per share. You also notice that a call option with a $50 strike price and three months to maturity is available. The premium is $4. Macron pays no dividends.

You're considering investing all $10,000 either in the stock or in the call options. What is your return from these two investments, if, in three months, Macron is selling for $55 per share? What about $45 per share?

First, if you buy the stock, your $10,000 will purchase two round lots, meaning 200 shares. A call contract costs $400 (why?), so you can buy 25 of them. Notice that your 25 contracts give you the right to buy 2,500 shares at $50 per share.

If, in three months, Macron is selling for $55, your stock will be worth 200 shares × $55 = $11,000. Your dollar gain will be $11,000 less the $10,000 you invested, or $1,000. Because you invested $10,000, your return for the three-month period is $1,000/$10,000 = 10%. If Macron is selling for $45 per share, then you lose $1,000, and your return is −10 percent.

If Macron is selling for $55, your call options are worth $55 − $50 = $5 each, but now you control 2,500 shares, so your options are worth 2,500 shares × $5 = $12,500 total. You invested $10,000, so your dollar return is $12,500 − $10,000 = $2,500, and your percentage return is $2,500/$10,000 = 25%, compared to 10 percent on the stock investment. However, if Macron is selling for $45 when your options mature, then you lose everything, and your return is −100 percent.

EXAMPLE 3.6 | **Put Returns**

In our example for Macron Technology, suppose a put option is also available with a premium of $2.50. Calculate your percentage return for the three-month holding period if the stock price declines to $47 per share. What is your annualized return?

One put contract costs $250, so you can buy 40 of them. Notice that your 40 contracts give you the right to *sell* 4,000 shares at $50 per share.

If, in three months, Macron is selling for $47, your put options are worth $50 − $47 = $3 each. You control 4,000 shares, so your options are worth 4,000 shares × $3 = $12,000 total. You invested $10,000, so your dollar return is $12,000 − $10,000 = $2,000, and your percentage return is $2,000/$10,000 = 20%.

To annualize your return, we need to compute the effective annual return, recognizing that there are 4 three-month periods in a year:

$$1 + EAR = 1.20^4$$
$$1 + EAR = 2.0736$$
$$EAR = 1.0736 = 107.36\%$$

Your annualized return is thus about 107 percent.

CHECK THIS

3.5a What is a call option? A put option?

3.5b If you buy a call option, what do you hope will happen to the underlying stock? What if you buy a put option?

3.5c What are the two key differences between a futures contract and an option contract?

3.6 Summary and Conclusions

In this chapter we examine the basic types of financial assets. We discuss three broad classes: interest-bearing assets, equities, and derivative assets. Each of these major groups can be further subdivided. Interest-bearing assets include money market instruments and fixed-income securities. The two major equity types are common stock and preferred stock. The two most important types of derivative assets are futures and options.

For each of the major types of financial assets, we cover three topics. We first describe the basic nature of the asset with an emphasis on what the owner of the asset is entitled to receive. We then illustrate how prices are quoted in the financial press, and we show how to interpret information presented online as well as in *The Wall Street Journal*. Finally, we indicate, in fairly broad terms, the potential gains and losses from buying and selling each type of asset.

GET REAL

This chapter covered the basics of the four main types of financial assets: stocks, bonds, futures, and options. In addition to discussing basic features, we alerted you to some of the risks associated with these instruments. We particularly stressed the large potential gains and losses possible with derivative assets. How should you, as an investor or investment manager, put this information to work?

Following up on our previous chapter, you need to execute each of the possible transaction types suggested by this chapter in a simulated brokerage account. Your goal is to experience some of the large gains (and losses) to understand them on a personal level. Try to do at least the following:

1. Buy a corporate or government bond.
2. Buy agriculture, natural resource, and financial futures contracts.
3. Sell agriculture, natural resource, and financial futures contracts.
4. Buy put and call option contracts.
5. Sell put and call option contracts.

In each case, once you have created the position, be sure to monitor it regularly by checking prices, trading activity, and relevant news using *The Wall Street Journal* or an online information service to understand why it changes in value.

One thing you will discover if you execute these trades is that some of these investments carry relatively low risk and some carry relatively high risk. Which are which? Under what circumstances is each of these investments appropriate? We will have more to say about these investments later, but you'll get a lot more out of our discussion (and have some fun stories to tell) if you already have some personal experience. As always, it's better to become educated about these things with play money before you commit real money.

Key Terms

call option 88
current yield 75
derivative asset 84
fixed-income securities 74
futures contract 84
money market instruments 74

option contract 88
option premium 88
primary asset 84
put option 88
strike price 88

Chapter Review Problems and Self-Test

1. **Corporate Bond Quotes**   In Figure 3.1, locate the "Boeing Capital Corp" bond that matures in the year 2013. What is the coupon rate on this issue? Suppose you purchase $100,000 in face value. How much will this cost? Assuming semiannual payments, what will you receive in coupon payments?

2. **Call Options**   In Figure 3.4, locate the Home Depot September 37.50 call option. If you buy 10 contracts, how much will you pay? Suppose that in September, just as the option is about to expire, Home Depot is selling for $42.50 per share. What are your options worth? What is your net profit?

Answers to Self-Test Problems

1. Based on Figure 3.1, the Boeing Capital Corp bond that matures in 2013 has a 5.8 percent coupon rate. The price, as a percentage of face value, is 107.08, or 107.08 percent. If you buy $100,000 in face value, you would thus pay $107,080. You will receive 5.8 percent of $100,000, or $5,800, in coupon payments every year, paid in two $2,900 semiannual installments.

2. From Figure 3.4, the September 37.50 call premium is 3.50, or $3.50. Because one contract involves 100 shares, the cost of a contract is $350, and 10 contracts would cost $3,500. In September, if Home Depot is selling for $42.50, then you have the right to buy 10 contracts × 100 shares = 1,000 shares at $37.50. Your contracts are thus worth $42.50 − $37.50 = $5 per share, or $5,000 total. Because they cost you $3,500, your net profit is $1,500.

Test Your Investment Quotient

1. **Money Market Securities**   Which of the following is not a common characteristic of money market securities?
   a. Sold on a discount basis.
   b. Mature in less than one year.
   c. Most important risk is default risk.
   d. All of the above are characteristics.

2. **Money Market Securities**   Which of the following money market securities is the most liquid?
   a. U.S. Treasury bills.
   b. Bank certificates of deposit.
   c. Corporate money market debt.
   d. Municipality money market debt.

3. **Options**   A European option can be exercised
   a. Only after American options.
   b. Anytime up to and including the expiration date.
   c. Only on the day before the expiration date.
   d. Only on a European exchange.

4. **Fixed-Income Securities** Your friend told you she just received her semiannual coupon payment on a U.S. Treasury note with a $100,000 face value that pays a 6 percent annual coupon. How much money did she receive from this coupon payment?

   a. $3,000
   b. $6,000
   c. $30,000
   d. $60,000

5. **Common Stock** A corporation with common stock issued to the public pays dividends

   a. At the discretion of management, who are elected by the shareholders.
   b. At the discretion of shareholders, since they own the corporation.
   c. At the discretion of the company's board of directors, who are elected by shareholders.
   d. At the discretion of the company's board of directors, who are appointed by management.

6. **Futures Contracts** You buy (go long) five copper futures contracts at 100 cents per pound, where the contract size is 25,000 pounds. At contract maturity, copper is selling for 102 cents per pound. What is your profit (+) or loss (−) on the transaction?

   a. −$2,500
   b. +$2,500
   c. −$25,000
   d. +$25,000

7. **Futures Contracts** You sell (go short) 10 gold futures contracts at $400 per ounce, where the contract size is 100 ounces. At contract maturity, gold is selling for $410 per ounce. What is your profit (+) or loss (−) on the transaction?

   a. −$1,000
   b. +$1,000
   c. −$10,000
   d. +$10,000

8. **Option Contracts** You buy 100 CJC call option contracts with a strike price of 95 at a quoted price of $1. At option expiration, CJC sells for $97. What is your net profit on the transaction?

   a. $2,000
   b. $5,000
   c. $10,000
   d. $20,000

9. **Option Contracts** You buy 100 CJC put option contracts with a strike price of 92 at a quoted price of $8. At option expiration, CJC sells for $83.80. What is your net profit on the transaction?

   a. $200
   b. $1,000
   c. $2,000
   d. $10,000

CFA® PROBLEMS

10. **Short Sales** Which of the following statements about short selling is true?

   a. A short position may be hedged by writing call options.
   b. A short position may be hedged by purchasing put options.
   c. Short sellers may be subject to margin calls if the stock price increases.
   d. Stocks that pay large dividends should be sold short before the ex-dividend date and bought afterward to take advantage of the large price declines in a short time period.

Concept Questions

1. **Money Market Instruments** What are the distinguishing features of a money market instrument?

2. **Preferred Stock** Why is preferred stock "preferred"?

3. **WSJ Stock Quotes** What is the PE ratio reported for stocks in *The Wall Street Journal?* In particular, how is it computed?

4. **Yields** The current yield on a bond is the coupon rate divided by the price. Thus, it is very similar to what number reported for common and preferred stocks?

5. **Volume Quotations** Explain how volume is quoted for stocks, corporate bonds, futures, and options.

6. **Futures Contracts** Changes in what price lead to gains and/or losses in futures contracts?

7. **Futures Contracts** What is the open interest on a futures contract? What do you think will usually happen to open interest as maturity approaches?

8. **Futures versus Options** What is the difference between a futures contract and an option contract? Do the buyer of a futures contract and the buyer of an option contract have the same rights? What about the seller?

9. **Asset Types** What is the distinction between a real asset and a financial asset? What are the two basic types of financial assets, and what does each represent?

10. **Puts versus Calls** Suppose a share of stock is selling for $100. A put and a call are offered, both with $100 strike prices and nine months to maturity. Intuitively, which do you think is more valuable?

Questions and Problems

Core Questions

1. **Stock Quotations** You found the following stock quote for DRK Enterprises, Inc., at your favorite Web site. What was the closing price for this stock yesterday? How many round lots of stock were traded yesterday?

YTD	52 Weeks						Yld		Vol		Net
%Chg	Hi	Lo	Stock	(SYM)	Div	%	PE	100s	Close	Chg
−16.7	32.37	18.90	DRK	(DRK)	.30	1.30	16	2855	??	0.26

2. **Stock Quotations** In the previous problem, assume the company has 25 million shares of stock outstanding. What was net income for the most recent four quarters?

3. **Dividend Yields** The following stock quote for Ehrhardt-Daves Corporation (EDC) appeared on an online quote server:

YTD	52 Weeks						Yld		Vol		Net
%Chg	Hi	Lo	Stock	(SYM)	Div	%	PE	100s	Close	Chg
14.8	91.12	64.13	Ehrdt-Daves	(EDC)	??	3.8	21	3186	84.12	−0.86

What was the last quarterly dividend paid by EDC?

4. **Earnings per Share** In the previous problem, what is the earnings per share (EPS) for the company?

5. **Bonds** You purchase 4,000 bonds with a par value of $1,000 for $920 each. The bonds have a coupon rate of 8.4 percent paid semiannually, and mature in 10 years. How much will you receive on the next coupon date? How much will you receive when the bonds mature?

6. **Futures Profits**   The contract size for platinum futures is 50 troy ounces. Suppose you need 700 troy ounces of platinum and the current futures price is $860 per ounce. How many contracts do you need to purchase? How much will you pay for your platinum? What is your dollar profit if platinum sells for $895 a troy ounce when the futures contract expires? What if the price is $840 at expiration?

7. **Option Profits**   You purchase 10 call option contracts with a strike price of $70 and a premium of $3.20. If the stock price at expiration is $78.14, what is your dollar profit? What if the stock price is $67.56?

8. **Stock Quotations**   You found the following stock quote for Gigantus Corporation in today's newspaper. What was the stock selling for on January 1?

YTD % Chg	52 Weeks Hi	52 Weeks Lo	Stock	(SYM)	Div	Yld %	PE	Vol 100s	Close	Net Chg
−1.5	55.66	44.94	Gigantus	(GIG)	1.30	2.5	16	12690	51.80	0.13

Use the following bond quote for the next two questions:

Company (Ticker)	Coupon	Maturity	Last Price	Last Yield	EST Spread	UST	EST $ Vol (000's)
Int'l Systems (ISU)	7.700	May 1, 2032	126.326	5.768	141	30	46,206

9. **Bond Quotations**   What is the current yield of the bond? What is the yield to maturity of the comparable U.S. Treasury bond?

10. **Bond Quotations**   If you currently own 25 of the bonds, how much will you receive on the next coupon date?

Use the following cotton futures quote for the next three problems:

Cotton (NYBOT) 50,000 lbs.; cents per lb.	Open	High	Low	Settle	Chg	Lifetime High	Lifetime Low	Open Int
Mar	49.61	49.95	48.50	48.64	−1.79	72.00	42.60	64,967
May	51.30	51.50	50.83	51.10	−0.88	67.00	45.00	2,541
July	52.50	52.70	51.50	51.62	−1.43	68.50	46.25	24,867
Dec	54.38	54.38	53.28	53.45	−1.30	69.00	48.30	3,201
Est. vol 21,683; vol Fri. 17,485; open int. 95,576, +72								

11. **Futures Quotations**   How many of the March contracts are currently open? How many of these contracts should you sell if you wish to deliver 400,000 pounds of cotton in March? If you actually make delivery, how much will you receive? Assume you locked in the settle price.

12. **Futures Quotations**   Approximately how many cotton futures contracts of all maturities were traded yesterday? The day before yesterday?

13. **Using Futures Quotations**   Suppose you buy 15 of the December cotton futures contracts at the last price of the day. One month from now, the futures price of this contract is 57.94, and you close out your position. Calculate your dollar profit on this investment.

www.mhhe.com/jm4e

Use the following option quote for the next three problems:

GNR Option/Strike		Exp.	Call Vol.	Call Last	Put Vol.	Put Last
75.25	65	June	3	10.40	1	0.15
75.25	70	June	21	5.30	16	0.25
75.25	70	July	42	6.00	67	0.45
75.25	75	June	85	1.11	89	0.85
75.25	75	July	8	2.30	124	1.65
75.25	75	Oct	160	3.80	193	2.80
75.25	75	Jan	35	5.10	68	3.70
75.25	80	June	28	0.10	19	9.90
75.25	80	July	9	0.50	4	5.05
75.25	85	June	2	0.05	7	9.95

14. **Options Quotations**   What was the closing share price of the underlying stock? If you wanted to purchase the right to sell 2,000 shares of GNR stock in July at a strike price of $75 per share, how much would this cost you?

15. **Options Quotations**   Which put contract sells for the lowest price? Which one sells for the highest price? Explain why these respective options trade at such extreme prices.

16. **Using Options Quotations**   In Problem 14, suppose GNR stock sells for $71.85 per share immediately prior to your options' expiration. What is the rate of return on your investment? What is your rate of return if the stock sells for $78.45 per share (think about it)? Assume your holding period for this investment is exactly three months.

17. **Options versus Stock**   You've located the following option quote for Eric-Cartman, Inc. (ECI):

ECI Option/Strike		Exp.	Call Vol.	Call Last	Put Vol.	Put Last
20.25	10	Sep	29	5.50	...	...
20.25	15	Sep	333	7	69	1
20.25	25	Dec	5	2	...	...
20.25	30	Sep	76	2	188	8.75
20.25	35	Oct	89	0.50	...	...

Two of the premiums shown can't possibly be correct. Which two? Why?

18. **Annualized Returns**   Suppose you have $20,000 to invest. You're considering Miller-Moore Equine Enterprises (MMEE), which is currently selling for $40 per share. You also notice that a call option with a $40 strike price and six months to maturity is available. The premium is $4.00. MMEE pays no dividends. What is your annualized return from these two investments if, in six months, MMEE is selling for $46 per share? What about $35 per share?

19. **Annualized Returns**   In the previous question, suppose a dividend of $.50 per share is paid. Comment on how the returns would be affected.

20. **Option Returns**   In Problem 18, suppose a put option with a $40 strike is also available with a premium of $2.50. Calculate your percentage return for the six-month holding period if the stock price declines to $36.40 per share.

What's on the Web?

1. **Option Prices**   You want to find the option prices for ConAgra Foods (CAG). Go to finance.yahoo.com, get a stock quote, and follow the "Options" link. What is the option premium and strike price for the highest and lowest strike price options that are nearest to expiring? What are the option premium and strike price for the highest and lowest strike price options expiring next month?

2. **Futures Quotes**   Go to www.cbot.com and find the contract specifications for corn futures. What is the size of the corn futures contract? On the CBOT Web site, find the settle price for the corn futures contract that will expire the soonest. If you go long 10 contracts, how much will the corn cost at the current price?

3. **LEAPS**   Go to www.cboe.com, highlight the "Products" tab, then follow the "LEAPS" link. What are LEAPS? What are the two types of LEAPS? What are the benefits of equity LEAPS? What are the benefits of index LEAPS?

4. **FLEX Options**   Go to www.cboe.com, highlight the "Institutional" tab, then follow the "FLEX Options" link. What is a FLEX option? When do FLEX options expire? What is the minimum size of a FLEX option?

Stock-Trak Exercises

STOCK | TRAK
GLOBAL PORTFOLIO SIMULATIONS

To access the Stock-Trak Exercise for this chapter, please visit the book Web site at www.mhhe.com/jm4e and choose the corresponding chapter.

CHAPTER 4

Mutual Funds

"Take calculated risks. That is quite different from being rash."
–George S. Patton

With only $2,000 to invest, you can easily own shares in Microsoft, GM, McDonald's, IBM, Coke, and many more stocks through a mutual fund. Or, you can invest in a portfolio of government bonds or other investments. Indeed, many thousands of different mutual funds are available to investors. In fact, there are about as many mutual funds as there are different stocks traded on the NASDAQ and the New York Stock Exchange combined. There are funds for aggressive investors, conservative investors, short-term investors, and long-term investors. There are bond funds, stock funds, international funds, and you-name-it funds. Is there a right fund for you? This chapter will help you find out. ■

As we discussed in an earlier chapter, if you do not wish to actively buy and sell individual securities on your own, you can invest in stocks, bonds, or other financial assets through a *mutual fund*. Mutual funds are simply a means of combining or pooling the funds of a large group of investors. The buy and sell decisions for the resulting pool are then made by a fund manager, who is compensated for the service provided.

Because mutual funds provide indirect access to financial markets for individual investors, they are a form of financial intermediary. In fact, mutual funds are now the largest type of intermediary in the United States, followed by commercial banks and life insurance companies.

For mutual fund facts
and figures, visit
www.ici.org

Mutual funds have become so important that we devote this entire chapter to them. The number of funds and the different fund types available have grown tremendously in recent years. As of the beginning of 2005, an estimated 92 million Americans in 54 million households owned mutual funds, up from just 5 million households in 1980. Investors contributed $288 billion to mutual funds in 2004, and, by the end of the year, mutual fund assets totaled $8 *trillion.*

One of the reasons for the proliferation of mutual funds and fund types is that mutual funds have become, on a very basic level, consumer products. They are created and marketed to the public in ways that are intended to promote buyer appeal. As every business student knows, product differentiation is a basic marketing tactic, and in recent years mutual funds have become increasingly adept at practicing this common marketing technique.

In fact, if you are not already a mutual fund investor, it is very likely that you will be in the near future. The reason has to do with a fundamental change in the way businesses of all types provide retirement benefits for employees. It used to be that most large employers offered so-called defined benefit pensions. With such a plan, when you retire, your employer pays you a pension typically based on years of service and salary. The key is that the pension benefit you receive is based on a predefined formula, hence the name.

Defined benefit plans are rapidly being replaced by "defined contribution" plans. With a defined contribution plan, your employer will contribute money each pay period to a retirement account on your behalf, but you have to select where the funds go. With this arrangement, the benefit you ultimately receive depends entirely on how your investments do; your employer only makes contributions. Most commonly, you must choose from a group of mutual funds for your investments, so it is very important that you understand the different types of mutual funds, as well as their risk and return characteristics.

4.1 Investment Companies and Fund Types

investment company
A business that specializes in pooling funds from individual investors and investing them.

At the most basic level, a company that pools funds obtained from individual investors and invests them is called an **investment company**. In other words, an investment company is a business that specializes in managing financial assets for individual investors. All mutual funds are, in fact, investment companies. As we will see, however, not all investment companies are mutual funds.

In the sections that follow, we will be discussing various aspects of mutual funds and related entities. Figure 4.1 is a big-picture overview of some of the different types of funds and how they are classified. It will serve as a guide for the next several sections. We will define the various terms that appear as we go along.

OPEN-END VERSUS CLOSED-END FUNDS

As Figure 4.1 shows, there are two fundamental types of investment companies, *open-end funds* and *closed-end funds.* The difference is very important. Whenever you invest in a mutual fund, you do so by buying shares in the fund. However, how shares are bought and sold depends on which type of fund you are considering.

open-end fund
An investment company that stands ready to buy and sell shares at any time.

With an **open-end fund**, the fund itself will sell new shares to anyone wishing to buy and will redeem (i.e., buy back) shares from anyone wishing to sell. When an investor wishes to buy open-end fund shares, the fund simply issues them and then invests the money received. When someone wishes to sell open-end fund shares, the fund sells some of its assets and uses the cash to redeem the shares. As a result, with an open-end fund, the number of shares outstanding fluctuates through time.

closed-end fund
An investment company with a fixed number of shares that are bought and sold only in the open stock market.

With a **closed-end fund**, the number of shares is fixed and never changes. If you want to buy shares, you must buy them from another investor. Similarly, if you wish to sell shares that you own, you must sell them to another investor.

FIGURE 4.1 Fund Types

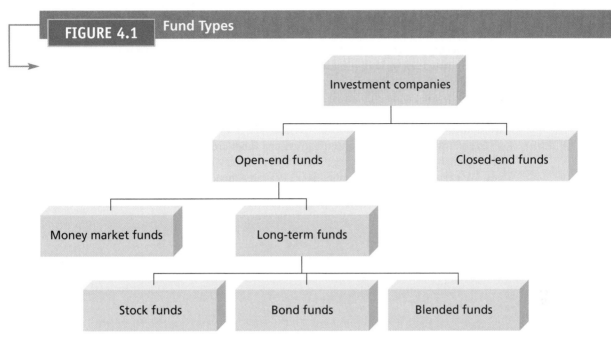

Thus, the key difference between an open-end fund and a closed-end fund is that, with a closed-end fund, the fund itself does not buy or sell shares. In fact, as we discuss below, shares in closed-end funds are listed on stock exchanges just like ordinary shares of stock, where their shares are bought and sold in the same way. Open-end funds are more popular among individual investors than closed-end funds.

Strictly speaking, the term "mutual fund" actually refers only to an open-end investment company. Thus, the phrase "closed-end fund" is a bit of an oxymoron, kind of like jumbo shrimp, and the phrase "open-end mutual fund" is a redundancy, an unnecessary repetition, or restatement. Nonetheless, particularly in recent years, the term "investment company" has all but disappeared from common use, and investment companies are now generically called mutual funds. We will stick with this common terminology to avoid any confusion.

NET ASSET VALUE

net asset value
The value of assets less liabilities held by a mutual fund, divided by the number of shares outstanding. Abbreviated NAV.

A mutual fund's **net asset value** is an important consideration. Net asset value is calculated by taking the total value of the assets held by the fund less any liabilities and then dividing by the number of outstanding shares. For example, suppose a mutual fund has $105 million in assets and $5 million in liabilities based on current market values and a total of 5 million shares outstanding. Based on the value of net assets held by the fund, $100 million, each share has a value of $100 million/5 million = $20. This $20 is the fund's net asset value, often abbreviated as NAV.

EXAMPLE 4.1 Net Asset Value

The Fidelity Magellan Fund is one of the largest mutual funds in the United States with about $54 billion invested and approximately 509 million shares outstanding (as of late 2005). What is its net asset value?

The net asset value is simply the asset value per share, or $54 billion/509 million = $106.

With one important exception, the net asset value of a mutual fund will change essentially every day simply because the value of the assets held by the fund fluctuates. The one exception concerns money market mutual funds, which we discuss in a later section.

As we noted, an open-end fund will generally redeem or buy back shares at any time. The price you will receive for shares you sell is the net asset value. Thus, in our example just above, you could sell your shares back to the fund and receive $20 each. Because the fund stands ready to redeem shares at any time, shares in an open-end fund are always worth their net asset value.

In contrast, because the shares of closed-end funds are bought and sold in the stock markets, their share prices at any point in time may or may not be equal to their net asset values. We examine this issue in more detail in a later section.

CHECK THIS

4.1a   What is an investment company?

4.1b   What is the difference between an open-end fund and a closed-end fund?

4.2 Mutual Fund Operations

In this section, we discuss some essentials of mutual fund operations. We focus on how mutual funds are created, marketed, regulated, and taxed. Our discussion here deals primarily with open-end funds, but much of it applies to closed-end funds as well. Further details on closed-end funds are provided in a later section.

MUTUAL FUND ORGANIZATION AND CREATION

A mutual fund is simply a corporation. Like a corporation, a mutual fund is owned by its shareholders. The shareholders elect a board of directors; the board of directors is responsible for hiring a manager to oversee the fund's operations. Although mutual funds often belong to a larger "family" of funds, every fund is a separate company owned by its shareholders.

WWW

All the major fund families have Web sites. Try, e.g., www.vanguard.com

Most mutual funds are created by investment advisory firms, which are businesses that specialize in managing mutual funds. Investment advisory firms are also called mutual fund companies. Increasingly, such firms have additional operations such as discount brokerages and other financial services.

There are hundreds of investment advisory firms in the United States. The largest, and probably best known, is Fidelity Investments, with 350 mutual funds, about $1.1 trillion in assets under management, and 19 million customers. Dreyfus, Franklin, and Vanguard are some other well-known examples. Many brokerage firms, such as Merrill Lynch and Charles Schwab, also have large investment advisory operations.

Investment advisory firms create mutual funds simply because they wish to manage them to earn fees. A typical management fee might be .75 percent of the total assets in the fund per year. A fund with $200 million in assets would not be especially large, but could nonetheless generate management fees of about $1.5 million per year. Thus, there is a significant economic incentive to create funds and attract investors to them.

For example, a company like Fidelity might one day decide that there is a demand for a fund that buys stock in companies that grow and process citrus fruits. Fidelity could form a mutual fund that specializes in such companies and call it something like the Fidelity Lemon Fund.[1] A fund manager would be appointed, and shares in the fund would be

---

[1]Fidelity would probably come up with a better name.

offered to the public. As shares are sold, the money received is invested. If the fund is a success, a large amount of money will be attracted and Fidelity would benefit from the fees it earns. If the fund is not a success, the board can vote to liquidate it and return shareholders' money or merge it with another fund.

As our hypothetical example illustrates, an investment advisory firm such as Fidelity can (and often will) create new funds from time to time. Through time, this process leads to a family of funds all managed by the same advisory firm. Each fund in the family will have its own fund manager, but the advisory firm will generally handle the record keeping, marketing, and much of the research that underlies the fund's investment decisions.

In principle, the directors of a mutual fund in a particular family, acting on behalf of the fund shareholders, could vote to fire the investment advisory firm and hire a different one. As a practical matter, this rarely, if ever, occurs. At least part of the reason is that the directors are originally appointed by the fund's founder, and they are routinely reelected. Unhappy shareholders generally "vote with their feet"—that is, sell their shares and invest elsewhere.

TAXATION OF INVESTMENT COMPANIES

As long as an investment company meets certain rules set by the Internal Revenue Service, it is treated as a "regulated investment company" for tax purposes. This is important because a regulated investment company does not pay taxes on its investment income. Instead, the fund passes through all realized investment income to fund shareholders, who then pay taxes on these distributions as though they owned the securities directly. Essentially, the fund simply acts as a conduit, funneling gains and losses to fund owners.

To qualify as a regulated investment company, the fund must follow three basic rules. The first rule is that it must in fact be an investment company holding almost all of its assets as investments in stocks, bonds, and other securities. The second rule limits the fund to using no more than 5 percent of its assets when acquiring a particular security. This is a diversification rule. The third rule is that the fund must pass through all realized investment income to fund shareholders.

THE FUND PROSPECTUS AND ANNUAL REPORT

Mutual funds are required by law to produce a document known as a *prospectus*. The prospectus must be supplied to any investor wishing to purchase shares. Mutual funds must also provide an annual report to their shareholders. The annual report and the prospectus, which are sometimes combined, contain financial statements along with specific information concerning the fund's expenses, gains and losses, holdings, objectives, and management. We discuss many of these items in the next few sections.

CHECK THIS

4.2a   How do mutual funds usually get started?

4.2b   How are mutual funds taxed?

4.3   Mutual Fund Costs and Fees

All mutual funds have various expenses that are paid by the fund's shareholders. These expenses can vary considerably from fund to fund, however, and one of the most important considerations in evaluating a fund is its expense structure. All else the same, lower expenses are preferred, of course, but, as we discuss, matters are not quite that cut-and-dried.

TYPES OF EXPENSES AND FEES

Basically, there are four types of expenses or fees associated with buying and owning mutual fund shares:

1. Sales charges or "loads."
2. 12b-1 fees.
3. Management fees.
4. Trading costs.

We discuss each of these in turn.

SALES CHARGES Many mutual funds charge a fee whenever shares are purchased. These fees are generally called **front-end loads**. Funds that charge loads are called *load funds*. Funds that have no such charges are called *no-load funds*.

front-end load
A sales charge levied on purchases of shares in some mutual funds.

When you purchase shares in a load fund, you pay a price in excess of the net asset value, called the *offering price*. The difference between the offering price and the net asset value is the *load*. Shares in no-load funds are sold at net asset value.

Front-end loads can range as high as 8.5 percent, but 5 percent or so would be more typical. Some funds, with front-end loads in the 2 percent to 3 percent range, are described as *low-load funds*.

Front-end loads are expressed as a percentage of the offering price, not the net asset value. For example, suppose a load fund has an offering price of $100 and a net asset value of $98. The front-end load is $2, which, as a percentage of the $100 offering price, is $2/$100 = 2$ percent. The way front-end loads are calculated understates the load slightly. In our example here, you are paying $100 for something worth only $98, so the load is really $2/$98 = 2.04$ percent.

EXAMPLE 4.2 | **Front-End Loads**

On a particular day, according to *The Wall Street Journal,* the Common Sense Growth fund had a net asset value of $13.91. The offering price was $15.20. Is this a load fund? What is the front-end load?

Because the offering price, which is the price you must pay to purchase shares, exceeds the net asset value, this is definitely a load fund. The load can be calculated by taking the difference between the offering price and the net asset value, $1.29, and dividing by the $15.20 offering price. The result is a hefty front-end load of 8.5 percent.

Some funds have "back-end" loads, which are charges levied on redemptions. These loads are often called *contingent deferred sales charges* and abbreviated CDSC. The CDSC usually declines through time. It might start out at 6 percent for shares held less than one year, then drop to 3 percent for shares held for two years, and disappear altogether on shares held for three or more years.

12b-1 fees
Named for SEC Rule 12b-1, which allows funds to spend up to 1 percent of fund assets annually to cover distribution and marketing costs.

12B-1 FEES So-called **12b-1 fees** are named after the Securities and Exchange Commission (SEC) rule that permits them. Mutual funds are allowed to use a portion of the fund's assets to cover distribution and marketing costs. Funds that market directly to the public may use 12b-1 fees to pay for advertising and direct mailing costs. Funds that rely on brokers and other sales force personnel often use 12b-1 fees to provide compensation for their services. The total amount of these fees could be .75 percent to 1.0 percent of the fund's assets per year.

Frequently, 12b-1 fees are used in conjunction with a CDSC. Such funds will often have no front-end load, but they effectively make it up through these other costs. Such funds may look like no-load funds, but they are really disguised load funds. Mutual funds with no front-end or back-end loads and no or minimal 12b-1 fees are often called "pure" no-load funds to distinguish them from the "not-so-pure" funds that may have no loads but still charge hefty 12b-1 fees.

MANAGEMENT FEES We briefly discussed management fees in an earlier section. Fees are usually based first on the size of the fund. Beyond this, there is often an incentive provision that increases the fee if the fund outperforms some benchmark, often the S&P 500 index. Management fees generally range from .25 percent to 1.0 percent of total fund assets every year.

TRADING COSTS Mutual funds have brokerage expenses from trading just like individuals do. As a result, mutual funds that do a lot of trading will have relatively high trading costs.

Trading costs can be difficult to get a handle on because they are not reported directly. However, in the prospectus, funds are required to report something known as **turnover**. A fund's turnover is a measure of how much trading a fund does. It is calculated as the lesser of a fund's total purchases or sales during a year, divided by average daily assets.[2]

turnover
A measure of how much trading a fund does, calculated as the lesser of total purchases or sales during a year divided by average daily assets.

EXAMPLE 4.3	Turnover

Suppose a fund had average daily assets of $50 million during a particular year. It bought $80 million worth of stock and sold $70 million during the year. What is its turnover?

The lesser of purchases or sales is $70 million, and average daily assets are $50 million. Turnover is thus $70/$50 = 1.4 times.

A fund with a turnover of 1.0 has, in effect, sold off its entire portfolio and replaced it once during the year. Similarly, a turnover of .50 indicates that, loosely speaking, the fund replaced half of its holdings during the year. All else the same, a higher turnover indicates more frequent trading and higher trading costs.

EXPENSE REPORTING

Mutual funds are required to report expenses in a fairly standardized way in the prospectus. The exact format varies, but the information reported is generally the same. There are three parts to an expense statement. Figure 4.2 shows this information as it was reported for the Fidelity Low-Priced Stock Fund.

The first part of the statement shows shareholder transaction expenses, which are generally loads and deferred sales charges. As indicated, for this fund, there is a 3 percent front-end load on shares purchased, but none on dividends received that are reinvested in the fund (it's common for mutual fund shareholders to simply reinvest any dividends received from the fund). The next item shows that there is no CDSC. The fourth item, labeled "redemption fee," refers to a back-end load that is applied under certain circumstances.

---

[2]Purchases and sales for a fund are usually different because of purchases and redemptions of fund shares by shareholders. For example, if a fund is growing, purchases will exceed sales.

FIGURE 4.2 Mutual Fund Expenses

Fidelity®
Low-Priced Stock
Fund

Prospectus

Fee Table

The following table describes the fees and expenses that are incurred when you buy, hold, or sell shares of the fund.

The annual fund operating expenses provided below for the fund do not reflect the effect of any reduction of certain expenses during the period.

Shareholder fees (paid by the investor directly)

Maximum sales charge (load) on purchases (as a % of offering price)[A]	3.00%
Sales charge (load) on reinvested distributions	None
Deferred sales charge (load) on redemptions	None
Redemption fee on shares held less than 90 days (as a % of amount redeemed)[B]	1.50%

[A] Lower sales charges may be available for fund balances over $250,000.

[B] A redemption fee may be charged when you sell your shares or if your fund balance falls below the balance minimum for any reason, including solely due to declines in the fund's net asset value per share (NAV).

Annual fund operating expenses (paid from fund assets)

Management fee	0.75%
Distribution and/or Service (12b-1) fees	None
Other expenses	0.24%
Total annual fund operating expenses	0.99%

A portion of the brokerage commissions that the fund pays is used to reduce the fund's expenses. In addition, through arrangements with the fund's custodian and transfer agent, credits realized as a result of uninvested cash balances are used to reduce custodian and transfer agent expenses. Including these reductions, the total fund operating expenses would have been 0.97%.

This **example** helps you compare the cost of investing in the fund with the cost of investing in other mutual funds.

Let's say, hypothetically, that the fund's annual return is 5% and that your shareholder fees and the fund's annual operating expenses are exactly as described in the fee table. This example illustrates the effect of fees and expenses, but is not meant to suggest actual or expected fees and expenses or returns, all of which may vary. For every $10,000 you invested, here's how much you would pay in total expenses if you sell all of your shares at the end of each time period indicated:

1 year	$ 398
3 years	$ 606
5 years	$ 831
10 years	$ 1,477

The second part of the statement, "Annual fund operating expenses," includes the management and 12b-1 fees. This fund's management fee was .75 percent of assets. There was no 12b-1 fee. The other expenses include things like legal, accounting, and reporting costs along with director fees. At .24 percent of assets, these costs are not trivial. The sum of these three items is the fund's total operating expense expressed as a percentage of assets, .99 percent in this case. To put this in perspective, this fund has about $15 billion in assets, so operating costs were about $150 million, of which about $112.5 million was paid to the fund manager.

The third part of the expense report gives a hypothetical example showing the total expense you would incur over time per $10,000 invested. The example is strictly hypothetical, however, and is only a rough guide. As shown here, your costs would amount to $1,477 after 10 years per $10,000 invested, assuming a return of 5 percent per year. This third part of the expense statement is not all that useful, really. What matters for this fund is that expenses appear to run about .99 percent per year, so that is what you pay in addition to loads.

One thing to watch out for is that funds may have 12b-1 fees but may choose not to incur any distribution or marketing costs. Similarly, the fund manager can choose to rebate some of the management fee in a particular year (especially if the fund has done poorly). These actions create a low expense figure for a given year, but this does not mean that expenses won't be higher in the future.

WHY PAY LOADS AND FEES?

Given that pure no-load funds exist, you might wonder why anyone would buy load funds or funds with substantial CDSC or 12b-1 fees. It is becoming increasingly difficult to give a good answer to this question. At one time, there simply weren't many no-load funds, and those that existed weren't widely known. Today, there are many good no-load funds, and competition among funds is forcing many funds to lower or do away with loads and other fees.

Having said this, there are basically two reasons that you might want to consider a load fund or a fund with above-average fees. First, you may simply want a fund run by a particular manager. A good example of this is the Fidelity Magellan Fund we mentioned earlier. For many years, it was run by Peter Lynch, who is widely regarded as one of the most successful managers in the history of the business. The Magellan Fund was a load fund, leaving you no choice but to pay the load to obtain Lynch's expertise.

The other reason to consider paying a load is that you want a specialized type of fund. For example, you might be interested in investing in a fund that invests only in a particular foreign country, such as Brazil. We'll discuss such specialty funds in a later section, but for now we note that there is little competition among specialty funds, and, as a result, loads and fees tend to be higher.

CHECK THIS

4.3a   What is the difference between a load fund and a no-load fund?

4.3b   What are 12b-1 fees?

4.4 Short-Term Funds

Mutual funds are usually divided into two major groups, short-term funds and long-term funds. Short-term funds are collectively known as *money market mutual funds*. Long-term funds essentially include everything that is not a money market fund. We discuss long-term funds in our next section; here we focus on money market funds.

MONEY MARKET MUTUAL FUNDS

money market mutual fund

A mutual fund specializing in money market instruments.

As the name suggests, **money market mutual funds**, or MMMFs, specialize in money market instruments. As we describe elsewhere, these are short-term debt obligations issued by governments and corporations. Money market funds were introduced in the early 1970s and have grown tremendously. By 2005, about 1,000 money market funds managed almost $2 trillion in assets. All money market funds are open-end funds.

Most money market funds invest in high-quality, low-risk instruments with maturities of less than 90 days. As a result, they have relatively little risk. However, some buy riskier assets or have longer maturities than others, so they do not all carry equally low risk. For example, some buy only very short-term U.S. government securities and are therefore essentially risk-free. Others buy mostly securities issued by corporations which entail some risk. We discuss the different types of money market instruments and their relative risks elsewhere in the book.

WWW

Visit
www.mfea.com
for info on thousands of
funds, including MMMFs.

MONEY MARKET FUND ACCOUNTING A unique feature of money market funds is that their net asset values are always $1 per share. This is purely an accounting gimmick, however. A money market fund simply sets the number of shares equal to the fund's assets. In other words, if the fund has $100 million in assets, then it has 100 million shares. As the fund earns interest on its investments, the fund owners are simply given more shares.

The reason money market mutual funds always maintain a $1 net asset value is to make them resemble bank accounts. As long as a money market fund invests in very safe, interest-bearing, short-maturity assets, its net asset value will not drop below $1 per share. However, there is no guarantee that this will not happen, and the term "breaking the buck" is used to describe dropping below $1 in net asset value. This is a very rare occurrence, but, in 1994, several large money market funds experienced substantial losses because they purchased relatively risky derivative assets and broke the buck, so it definitely can happen.

TAXES AND MONEY MARKET FUNDS Money market funds are either taxable or tax-exempt. Taxable funds are more common; of the $2 trillion in total money market fund assets in 2005, taxable funds accounted for about 84 percent. As the name suggests, the difference in the two fund types lies in their tax treatment. As a general rule, interest earned on state and local government (or "municipal") securities is exempt from federal income tax. Nontaxable money market funds therefore buy only these types of tax-exempt securities.

Some tax-exempt funds go even further. Interest paid by one state is often subject to state taxes in another. Some tax-exempt funds therefore buy only securities issued by a single state. For residents of that state, the interest earned is free of both federal and state taxes. For beleaguered New York City residents, there are even "triple-tax-free" funds that invest only in New York City obligations, thereby allowing residents to escape federal, state, and local income taxes on the interest received.

Because of their favorable tax treatment, tax-exempt money market instruments have much lower interest rates, or *yields*.[3] For example, in early 2006, taxable money funds offered about 4.01 percent interest, whereas tax-exempt funds offered only 2.62 percent interest. Which is better depends on your individual tax bracket. If you're in a 40 percent bracket, then the taxable fund is paying only $.0401 \times (1 - .40) = .0241$, or 2.41 percent, on an aftertax basis, so you're better off with the tax-exempt fund.

---

[3]We discuss how yields on money market instruments are calculated in another chapter.

EXAMPLE 4.4 | Taxes and Money Market Fund Yields

In our discussion just above, suppose you were in a 20 percent tax bracket. Which type of fund is more attractive?

On an aftertax basis, the taxable fund is offering $.012 \times (1 - .20) = .0096$, or .96 percent, so the taxable fund is more attractive.

MONEY MARKET DEPOSIT ACCOUNTS

Most banks offer what are called "money market" deposit accounts, or MMDAs, which are much like money market mutual funds. For example, both money market funds and money market deposit accounts generally have limited check-writing privileges.

There is a very important distinction between such a bank-offered money market account and a money market fund, however. A bank money market account is a bank deposit and offers FDIC protection, whereas a money market fund does not. A money market fund will generally offer SIPC protection, but this is not a perfect substitute. Confusingly, some banks offer both money market accounts and, through a separate, affiliated entity, money market funds.

CHECK THIS

4.4a   What is a money market mutual fund? What are the two types?

4.4b   How do money market mutual funds maintain a constant net asset value?

4.5 Long-Term Funds

www

One of the best mutual fund sites is

www.morningstar.com

There are many different types of long-term funds. Historically, mutual funds were classified as stock, bond, or income funds. As a part of the rapid growth in mutual funds, however, it is becoming increasingly difficult to place all funds into these three categories. Also, providers of mutual fund information do not use the same classification schemes.

Mutual funds have different goals, and a fund's objective is the major determinant of the fund type. All mutual funds must state the fund's objective in the prospectus. For example, the Fidelity Independence Fund states:

> The fund's objective is capital appreciation. Normally, the fund's strategy is to invest primarily in common stocks of domestic and foreign issuers. The fund strategy may result in the realization of capital gains without considering the tax consequences to shareholders. Fidelity Management & Research Company (FMR) is not constrained by any particular investment style and may invest in "growth" stocks, "value" stocks, or both, at any given time.

Thus, this fund invests in different types of stocks with the goal of capital appreciation. This is clearly a stock fund, and it might further be classified as a "capital appreciation" fund or "aggressive growth" fund, depending on whose classification scheme is used.

Mutual fund objectives are an important consideration; unfortunately, the truth is they frequently are too vague to provide useful information. For example, a very common objective reads like this: "The Big Bucks Fund seeks capital appreciation, income, and capital preservation." Translation: The fund seeks to (1) increase the value of its shares,

(2) generate income for its shareholders, and (3) not lose money. Well, don't we all! More to the point, funds with very similar-sounding objectives can have very different portfolios and, consequently, very different risks. As a result, it is a mistake to look only at a fund's stated objective: Actual portfolio holdings speak louder than prospectus promises.

STOCK FUNDS

Stock funds exist in great variety. We consider nine separate general types and some subtypes. We also consider some new varieties that don't fit in any category.

CAPITAL APPRECIATION VERSUS INCOME The first four types of stock funds trade off capital appreciation and dividend income.

1. *Capital appreciation.* As in our example just above, these funds seek maximum capital appreciation. They generally invest in companies that have, in the opinion of the fund manager, the best prospects for share price appreciation without regard to dividends, company size, or, for some funds, country. Often this means investing in unproven companies or companies perceived to be out-of-favor.

2. *Growth.* These funds also seek capital appreciation, but they tend to invest in larger, more established companies. Such funds may be somewhat less volatile as a result. Dividends are not an important consideration.

3. *Growth and income.* Capital appreciation is still the main goal, but at least part of the focus is on dividend-paying companies.

4. *Equity income.* These funds focus almost exclusively on stocks with relatively high dividend yields, thereby maximizing the current income on the portfolio.

Among these four fund types, the greater the emphasis on growth, the greater the risk, at least as a general matter. Again, however, these are only rough classifications. Equity income funds, for example, frequently invest heavily in public utility stocks; such stocks had heavy losses in the first part of the 1990s.

COMPANY SIZE-BASED FUNDS These next two fund types focus on companies in a particular size range.

1. *Small company.* As the name suggests, these funds focus on stocks in small companies, where "small" refers to the total market value of the stock. Such funds are often called "small-cap" funds, where "cap" is short for total market value or capitalization. In Chapter 1, we saw that small stocks have traditionally performed very well, at least over the long run, hence the demand for funds that specialize in such stocks. With small-company mutual funds, what constitutes small is variable, ranging from perhaps $10 million up to $1 billion or so in total market value, and some funds specialize in smaller companies than others. Since most small companies don't pay dividends, these funds necessarily emphasize capital appreciation.

2. *Midcap.* These funds usually specialize in stocks that are too small to be in the S&P 500 index but too large to be considered small cap stocks.

INTERNATIONAL FUNDS The next two fund groups invest internationally. Research has shown that diversifying internationally can significantly improve the risk-return trade off for investors, and international funds have been among the most rapidly growing funds. However, that growth slowed sharply in the late 1990s.

1. *Global.* These funds have substantial international holdings but also maintain significant investments in U.S. stocks.

2. *International.* These funds are like global funds, except they focus on non-U.S. equities.

Among international funds, some specialize in specific regions of the world, such as Europe, the Pacific Rim, or South America. Others specialize in individual countries. Today, there is at least one mutual fund specializing in essentially every country in the world that has a stock market, however small.

International funds that specialize in countries with small or recently established stock markets are often called *emerging markets funds.* Almost all single-country funds, and especially emerging markets funds, are not well-diversified and have historically been extremely volatile.

Many funds that are not classified as international funds may actually have substantial overseas investments, so this is one thing to watch out for. It is not unusual for a fund to call itself a "growth" fund and actually invest heavily outside the United States.

SECTOR FUNDS Sector funds specialize in specific sectors of the economy and often focus on particular industries or particular commodities. There are far too many different types to list here. There are funds that only buy software companies, and funds that only buy hardware companies. There are funds that specialize in natural gas producers, oil producers, and precious metals producers. In fact, essentially every major industry in the U.S. economy is covered by at least one fund.

One thing to notice about sector funds is that, like single-country funds, they are obviously not well-diversified. Every year, many of the best performing mutual funds (in terms of total return) are sector funds simply because whatever sector of the economy is hottest will generally have the largest stock price increases. Funds specializing in that sector will do well. In the same vein, and for the same reason, the worst performing funds are also almost always some type of sector fund. When it comes to mutual funds, past performance is almost always an unreliable guide to future performance; nowhere is this more true than with sector funds.

OTHER FUND TYPES AND ISSUES Three other types of stock funds that don't fit easily into one of the above categories bear discussing: *index funds*, so-called *social conscience funds*, and *tax-managed funds.*

   1. *Index funds.* Index funds simply hold the stocks that make up a particular index in the same relative proportions as the index. The most important index funds are S&P 500 funds, which are intended to track the performance of the S&P 500, the large stock index we discussed in Chapter 1. By their nature, index funds are passively managed, meaning that the fund manager trades only as necessary to match the index. Such funds are appealing in part because they are generally characterized by low turnover and low operating expenses. Another reason index funds have grown rapidly is that there is considerable debate over whether mutual fund managers can consistently beat the averages. If they can't, the argument runs, why pay loads and management fees when it's cheaper just to buy the averages by indexing? To put the importance of index funds into perspective, as of late 2005, the largest single stock mutual fund in the United States was the Vanguard 500 Index Fund, with $74 billion in assets. This fund, as the name suggests, is an S&P 500 index fund.

   2. *Social conscience funds.* These funds are a relatively new creation. They invest only in companies whose products, policies, or politics are viewed as socially desirable. The specific social objectives range from environmental issues to personnel policies. The Parnassus Fund is a well-known example, avoiding the

To learn more about
"social conscience"
funds, visit
www.socialinvest.org
and
www.domini.com

Is vice nice? Visit
www.vicefund.com
to find out.

WWW

alcoholic beverage, tobacco, gambling, weapons, and nuclear power industries. Of course, consensus on what is socially desirable or responsible is hard to find. In fact, there are so-called sin funds (and sector funds) that specialize in these very industries!

3. *Tax-managed funds.* Taxable mutual funds are generally managed without regard for the tax liabilities of fund owners. Fund managers focus on (and are frequently rewarded based on) total pretax returns. However, recent research has shown that some fairly simple strategies can greatly improve the aftertax returns to shareholders and that focusing just on pretax returns is not a good idea for taxable investors. Tax-managed funds try to hold down turnover to minimize realized capital gains, and they try to match realized gains with realized losses. Such strategies work particularly well for index funds. For example, the Schwab 1000 Fund is a fund that tracks the Russell 1000 Index, a widely followed 1,000-stock index. However, the fund will deviate from strictly following the index to a certain extent to avoid realizing taxable gains, and, as a result, the fund holds turnover to a minimum. Fund shareholders have largely escaped taxes as a result. We predict funds promoting such strategies will become increasingly common as investors become more aware of the tax consequences of fund ownership.

TAXABLE AND MUNICIPAL BOND FUNDS

Most bond funds invest in domestic corporate and government securities, although some invest in foreign government and non-U.S. corporate bonds as well. As we will see, there are a relatively small number of bond fund types. Basically, five characteristics distinguish bond funds:

1. Maturity range. Different funds hold bonds of different maturities, ranging from quite short (2 years) to quite long (25–30 years).

2. Credit quality. Some bonds are much safer than others in terms of the possibility of default. United States government bonds have no default risk, while so-called junk bonds have significant default risk.

3. Taxability. Municipal bond funds buy only bonds that are free from federal income tax. Taxable funds buy only taxable issues.

4. Type of bond. Some funds specialize in particular types of fixed-income instruments such as mortgages.

5. Country. Most bond funds buy only domestic issues, but some buy foreign company and government issues.

SHORT-TERM AND INTERMEDIATE-TERM FUNDS As the names suggest, these two fund types focus on bonds in a specific maturity range. Short-term maturities are generally considered to be less than five years. Intermediate-term would be less than 10 years. There are both taxable and municipal bond funds with these maturity targets.

One thing to be careful of with these types of funds is that the credit quality of the issues can vary from fund to fund. One fund could hold very risky intermediate-term bonds, while another might hold only U.S. government issues with similar maturities.

GENERAL FUNDS For both taxable and municipal bonds, this fund category is kind of a catch-all. Funds in this category simply don't specialize in any particular way. Our warning just above concerning varied credit quality applies here. Maturities can differ substantially as well.

HIGH-YIELD FUNDS High-yield municipal and taxable funds specialize in low-credit quality issues. Such issues have higher yields because of their greater risks. As a result, high-yield bond funds can be quite volatile.

MORTGAGE FUNDS A number of funds specialize in so-called mortgage-backed securities such as GNMA (Government National Mortgage Association, referred to as "Ginnie Mae") issues. We discuss this important type of security in detail in a later chapter. There are no municipal mortgage-backed securities (yet), so these are all taxable bond funds.

WORLD FUNDS A relatively limited number of taxable funds invest worldwide. Some specialize in only government issues; others buy a variety of non-U.S. issues. These are all taxable funds.

INSURED FUNDS This is a type of municipal bond fund. Municipal bond issuers frequently purchase insurance that guarantees the bond's payments will be made. Such bonds have very little possibility of default, so some funds specialize in them.

SINGLE-STATE MUNICIPAL FUNDS Earlier we discussed how some money market funds specialize in issues from a single state. The same is true for some bond funds. Such funds are especially important in large states such as California and other high-tax states. Confusingly, this classification refers only to long-term funds. Short and intermediate single-state funds are classified with other maturity-based municipal funds.

STOCK AND BOND FUNDS

This last major fund group includes a variety of funds. The only common feature is that these funds don't invest exclusively in either stocks or bonds. For this reason, they are often called "blended" or "hybrid" funds. We discuss a few of the main types.

BALANCED FUNDS Balanced funds maintain a relatively fixed split between stocks and bonds. They emphasize relatively safe, high-quality investments. Such funds provide a kind of "one-stop" shopping for fund investors, particularly smaller investors, because they diversify into both stocks and bonds.

ASSET ALLOCATION FUNDS Two types of funds carry this label. The first is an extended version of a balanced fund. Such a fund holds relatively fixed proportional investments in stocks, bonds, money market instruments, and perhaps real estate or some other investment class. The target proportions may be updated or modified periodically.

The other type of asset allocation fund is often called a *flexible portfolio fund*. Here, the fund manager may hold up to 100 percent in stocks, bonds, or money market instruments, depending on her views about the likely performance of these investments. These funds essentially try to time the market, guessing which general type of investment will do well (or least poorly) over the months ahead.

CONVERTIBLE FUNDS Some bonds are convertible, meaning they can be swapped for a fixed number of shares of stock at the option of the bondholder. Some mutual funds specialize in these bonds.

INCOME FUNDS An income fund emphasizes generating dividend and coupon income on its investments, so it would hold a variety of dividend-paying common, as well as preferred, stocks and bonds of various maturities.

FIGURE 4.3   Mutual Fund Objectives

MUTUAL-FUND OBJECTIVES

Categories compiled by The Wall Street Journal, based on classifications by Lipper Inc.

STOCK FUNDS

Emerging Markets (EM): Funds that invest in emerging-market equity securities, where the "emerging market" is defined by a country's GNP per capita and other economic measures.

Equity Income (EI): Funds that seek high current income and growth of income through investment in equities.

European Region (EU): Funds that invest in markets or operations concentrated in the European region.

Global Stock (GL): Funds that invest in securities traded outside of the U.S. and may own U.S. securities as well.

Gold Oriented (AU): Funds that invest in gold mines, gold-oriented mining finance houses, gold coins or bullion.

Health/Biotech (HB): Funds that invest in companies related to health care, medicine and biotechnology.

International Stock (IL) (non-U.S.): Canadian; International; International Small Cap.

Latin American (LT): Funds that invest in markets or operations concentrated in the Latin American region.

Large-Cap Growth (LG): Funds that invest in large companies with long-term earnings that are expected to grow significantly faster than the earnings of stocks in major indexes. Funds normally have above-average price-to-earnings ratios, price-to-book ratios and three-year earnings growth.

Large-Cap Core (LC): Funds that invest in large companies, with wide latitude in the type of shares they buy. On average, the price-to-earnings ratios, price-to-book ratios, and three-year earnings growth are in line with those of the U.S. diversified large-cap funds' universe average.

Large-Cap Value (LV): Funds that invest in large companies that are considered undervalued relative to major stock indexes based on price-to-earnings ratios, price-to-book ratios or other factors.

Midcap Growth (MG): Funds that invest in midsize companies with long-term earnings that are expected to grow significantly faster than the earnings of stocks in major indexes. Funds normally have above-average price-to-earnings ratios, price-to-book ratios and three-year earnings growth.

Midcap Core (MC): Funds that invest in midsize companies, with wide latitude in the type of shares they buy. On average, the price-to-earnings ratios, price-to-book ratios, and three-year earnings growth are in line with those of the U.S. diversified midcap funds' universe average.

Midcap Value (MV): Funds that invest in midsize companies that are considered undervalued relative to major stock indexes based on price-to-earnings ratios, price-to-book ratios or other factors.

Multicap Growth (XG): Funds that invest in companies of various sizes, with long-term earnings that are expected to grow significantly faster than the earnings of stocks in major indexes. Funds normally have above-average price-to-earnings ratios, price-to-book ratios, and three-year earnings growth.

Multicap Core (XC): Funds that invest in companies of various sizes with average price-to-earnings ratios, price-to-book ratios and earnings growth.

Multicap Value (XV): Funds that invest in companies of various size, normally those that are considered undervalued relative to major stock indexes based on price-to-earnings ratios, price-to-book ratios or other factors.

Natural Resources (NR): Funds that invest in natural-resource stocks.

Pacific Region (PR): Funds that invest in China Region; Japan; Pacific Ex-Japan; Pacific Region.

Science & Technology (TK): Funds that invest in science and technology stocks. Includes Telecommunication funds.

Sector (SE): Funds that invest in financial services; real estate; specialty & miscellaneous.

S&P 500 Index (SP): Funds that are passively managed, and are designed to replicate the performance of the Standard & Poor's 500-stock Index on a reinvested basis.

Small-Cap Growth (SG): Funds that invest in small companies with long-term earnings that are expected to grow significantly faster than the earnings of stocks in major indexes. Funds normally have above-average price-to-earnings ratios, price-to-book ratios, and three-year earnings growth.

Small-Cap Core (SC): Funds that invest in small companies, with wide latitude in the type of shares they buy. On average, the price-to-earnings ratios, price-to-book ratios, and three-year earnings growth are in line with those of the U.S. diversified small-cap funds' universe average.

Small-Cap Value (SV): Funds that invest in small companies that are considered undervalued relative to major stock indexes based on price-to-earnings ratios, price-to-book ratios or other factors.

Specialty Equity (SQ): Funds that invest in all market capitalization ranges, with no restrictions for any one range. May have strategies that are distinctly different from other diversified stock funds.

Utility (UT): Funds that invest in utility stocks.

TAXABLE BOND FUNDS

Short-Term Bond (SB): Ultra-short Obligation; Short Investment Grade Debt; Short-Intermediate Investment Grade Debt.

Short-Term U.S. (SU): Short U.S. Treasury; Short U.S. Government; Short-Intermediate U.S. Government debt.

Intermediate Bond (IB): Funds that invest in investment-grade debt issues (rated in the top four grades) with dollar-weighted average maturities of five to 10 years.

Intermediate U.S. (IG): Intermediate U.S. Government; Intermediate U.S. Treasury.

Long-Term Bond (AB): Funds that invest in corporate and government debt issues in the top grades.

Long-Term U.S. (LU): General U.S. Government; General U.S. Treasury; Target Maturity.

General U.S. Taxable (GT): Funds that invest in general bonds.

High-Yield Taxable (HC): Funds that aim for high current yields from fixed-income securities and tend to invest in lower-grade debt.

Mortgage (MT): Adjustable Rate Mortgage; GNMA; U.S. Mortgage.

World Bond (WB): Emerging Markets Debt; Global Income; International Income; Short World Multi-Market Income.

MUNICIPAL DEBT FUNDS

Short-Term Muni (SM): California Short-Intermediate Muni Debt; Other States Short-Intermediate Muni Debt; Short-Intermediate Muni Debt; Short Muni Debt.

Intermediate Muni (IM): Intermediate-term Muni Debt including single states.

General Muni (GM): Funds investing in muni-debt issues in the top four credit ratings.

Single-State Municipal (SS): Funds that invest in debt of individual states.

High-Yield Municipal (HM): Funds that invest in lower rated muni debt.

Insured Muni (NM): California Insured Muni Debt; Florida Insured Muni Debt; Insured Muni Debt; New York Insured Muni Debt.

STOCK & BOND FUNDS

Balanced (BL): Primary objective is to conserve principal, by maintaining a balanced portfolio of both stocks and bonds.

Stock/Bond Blend (MP): Multipurpose funds such as Balanced Target Maturity; Convertible Securities; Flexible Income; Flexible Portfolio; Global Flexible and Income funds, that invest in both stocks and bonds.

Source: Reprinted by permission of *The Wall Street Journal*, October 4, 2005. © 2005 Dow Jones & Company, Inc. All Rights Reserved Worldwide.

MUTUAL FUND OBJECTIVES: RECENT DEVELOPMENTS

As we mentioned earlier, a mutual fund's stated objective may not be all that informative. In recent years, there has been a trend toward classifying a mutual fund's objective based on its actual holdings. For example, Figure 4.3 illustrates the classifications used by *The Wall Street Journal.*

A key thing to notice in Figure 4.3 is that most general-purpose funds (as opposed to specialized types such as sector funds) are classified based on the market "cap" of the stocks they hold (small, midsize, or large) and also on whether the fund tends to invest in either "growth" or "value" stocks (or both). We will discuss growth versus value stocks in a later chapter; for now, it is enough to know that "growth" stocks are those considered more likely to grow rapidly. "Value" stocks are those that look to be relatively undervalued and thus may be attractive for that reason. Notice that, in this scheme, *all* stocks are "growth," "value," or a blend of the two, a classic example of the Lake Wobegon effect.[4]

[4]Lake Wobegon is a mystical place in Minnesota made famous by Garrison Keillor where "the men are strong, the women are beautiful, and all the children are above average." See www.phc.mpr.org for more.

As we have discussed in the chapter, there are many thousands of mutual funds, so how do you pick one? One answer is to visit one of the many mutual fund sites on the Web and use a fund selector. Here is an example of how they are used. We went to www.morningstar.com and clicked on the "Fund Selector." We then indicated that we were interested in a domestic stock fund that invests in small capitalization growth stocks with relatively low expenses and several other features. Out of a database of more than 15,000 funds, here is what was returned:

| Change Criteria | Results of Search | New Search | Analyst Insights | Instructions |

View: Snapshot   Results: 1-25 of 83 Previous 25 | Next 25

Check boxes to: **Test in a Portfolio** | **Add to my Portfolio**   **Score These Results**

▲ Fund Name	Morningstar Category	Morningstar Rating	YTD Return (%)	Expense Ratio (%)	Total Assets ($ mil)
ABN AMRO/Veredus Aggressi	Small Growth	★★★	-0.43	1.43	723
AFBA Five Star Small Cap	Small Growth	★★★	-0.63	1.53	180
AFBA Five Star Small Cap	Small Growth	★★★★	-0.39	1.28	180
AllianceBernstein Small C	Small Growth	★★★	1.50	1.59	386
American Funds Smallcap W	Small Growth	★★★★	11.40	1.14	14,189
American Funds Smallcap W	Small Growth	★★★★	11.14	1.49	14,189
American Funds Smallcap W	Small Growth	★★★	11.44	1.12	14,189
American Funds Smallcap W	Small Growth	★★★★★	11.40	1.14	14,189
American Funds Smallcap W	Small Growth	★★★★	11.12	1.49	14,189
American Funds Smallcap W	Small Growth	★★★★★	11.67	0.81	14,189
AmSouth Small Cap I	Small Growth	★★★	--	1.43	266
Artisan Small Cap	Small Growth	★★★★	7.10	1.27	1,014
Atlas Emerging Growth A	Small Growth	★★★	5.56	1.53	58
Baron Capital Asset Ins	Small Growth	★★★★	-1.07	1.36	310
Baron Growth	Small Growth	★★★★★	2.43	1.33	4,906
Baron Small Cap	Small Growth	★★★★	4.53	1.33	2,716
BNY Hamilton Small Cap Gr	Small Growth	★★★	-0.44	1.23	724
Bridgeway Ultra-Small Com	Small Growth	★★★★★	3.83	1.12	114
Buffalo Small Cap	Small Growth	★★★★★	0.87	1.01	1,958
Century Small Cap Select	Small Growth	★★★★★	4.21	1.50	978
Columbia Acorn A	Small Growth	★★★★★	9.49	1.20	15,426
Columbia Acorn USA A	Small Growth	★★★★	9.84	1.51	1,087
Evergreen Growth A	Small Growth	★★★	6.49	1.27	1,024
Evergreen Special Equity	Small Growth	★★★	1.56	1.57	283
FBR Small Cap	Small Growth	★★★★★	0.40	1.59	896
Small Growth Avg			**4.17**	**1.73**	**764**
S&P 500			**2.65**		

Check boxes to: **Test in a Portfolio** | **Add to my Portfolio**   **Score These Results**

View: Snapshot   Results: 1-25 of 83 Previous 25 | Next 25

This search narrowed things down in a hurry! Now we have a list of 83 funds, the first 25 of which are shown here in alphabetical order. Clicking on the name of the fund takes you to the Morningstar Web page on the fund, where you can learn more about the fund.

The mutual fund "style" box is an increasingly common sight. A style box is a way of visually representing a fund's investment focus by placing the fund into one of nine boxes like this:

As shown, this particular fund focuses on large-cap, value stocks.

These newer mutual fund objectives are also useful for screening mutual funds. As our nearby *Work the Web* box shows, many Web sites have mutual fund selectors that allow you to find funds with particular characteristics.

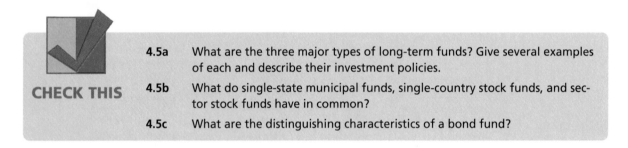

CHECK THIS

4.5a What are the three major types of long-term funds? Give several examples of each and describe their investment policies.

4.5b What do single-state municipal funds, single-country stock funds, and sector stock funds have in common?

4.5c What are the distinguishing characteristics of a bond fund?

4.6 Mutual Fund Performance

We close our discussion of open-end mutual funds by looking at some of the performance information reported in the financial press. We then discuss the usefulness of such information for selecting mutual funds.

MUTUAL FUND PERFORMANCE INFORMATION

Mutual fund performance is very closely tracked by a number of organizations. Financial publications of all types periodically provide mutual fund data, and many provide lists of recommended funds. We examine *Wall Street Journal* information in this section, but by no means is this the only source or the most comprehensive.[5] However, *The Wall Street Journal* is a particularly timely source because it reports mutual fund year-to-date returns on a daily basis, and it provides a summary of average investment performance by fund category on a regular basis. The information we consider here applies only to open-end funds.

---

[5]For more detailed information, publications from companies such as Morningstar, Weisenberger, and Value Line are often available in the library or online. Of course, a mutual fund's prospectus and annual report contain a great deal of information as well.

FIGURE 4.4   Mutual-Fund Yardsticks

Mutual-Fund Yardsticks: How Fund Categories Stack Up

All returns are for periods ended Sept. 30. Fund-category abbreviations used in performance tables appear in parentheses after category name. All performance numbers are preliminary.

INVESTMENT OBJECTIVE	SEPTEMBER	3RD QTR	12 MONTHS	3 YEARS*	5 YEARS*
DIVERSIFIED STOCK and STOCK/BOND FUNDS					
Large-Cap Core (LC)	+0.92%	+3.70%	+11.55%	+14.28%	– 2.90%
Large-Cap Growth (LG)	+1.00	+4.46	+12.56	+13.36	– 7.84
Large-Cap Value (LV)	+1.04	+3.75	+13.35	+17.39	+ 3.40
Midcap Core (MC)	+1.05	+5.22	+20.21	+21.05	+ 4.63
Midcap Growth (MG)	+1.40	+6.24	+20.65	+19.37	– 4.69
Midcap Value (MV)	+0.47	+4.66	+20.19	+24.14	+11.73
Small-Cap Core (SC)	+0.70	+5.26	+18.87	+23.39	+ 8.59
Small-Cap Growth (SG)	+1.03	+5.66	+18.55	+20.41	– 2.42
Small-Cap Value (SV)	+0.25	+4.40	+18.45	+24.04	+14.61
Multicap Core (XC)	+0.94	+4.44	+14.68	+17.01	+ 0.20
Multicap Growth (XG)	+1.78	+6.75	+17.70	+18.78	– 7.75
Multicap Value (XV)	+0.88	+3.69	+15.13	+18.97	+ 5.81
Equity Income (EI)	+0.84	+3.42	+13.69	+16.69	+ 4.10
S&P 500 Funds (SP)	+0.76	+3.46	+11.64	+16.04	– 2.03
Specialty Divers. Equity (SQ)	+0.52	+2.32	+ 0.84	– 3.97	+ 3.40
Balanced (BL)	+0.38	+2.71	+ 9.74	+11.60	+ 2.05
Stock/Bond Blend (MP)	+0.71	+3.14	+10.08	+12.73	+ 2.86
Avg. U.S. Stock Fund [1]	+0.97	+4.65	+15.57	+17.94	+ 0.01
SECTOR STOCK FUNDS					
Science & Technology (TK)	+2.06%	+ 7.60%	+18.17%	+25.66%	–16.79%
Telecommunication	+1.85	+ 7.90	+23.88	+32.81	–13.00
Health/Biotechnology (HB)	+0.46	+ 7.00	+15.80	+16.26	– 0.83
Utility (UT)	+3.38	+ 8.12	+33.26	+25.38	+ 1.18
Natural Resources (NR)	+6.35	+22.51	+52.00	+38.09	+16.97
Sector (SE)	+0.31	+ 2.49	+18.56	+21.19	+12.39
Real Estate	+0.35	+ 3.22	+26.05	+26.02	+18.56

INVESTMENT OBJECTIVE	SEPTEMBER	3RD QTR	12 MONTHS	3 YEARS*	5 YEARS*
WORLD STOCK FUNDS					
Global (GL)	+ 2.44%	+ 7.59%	+19.68%	+19.72%	+ 0.38%
International (IL)	+ 3.77	+10.96	+25.19	+22.84	+ 2.03
European Region (EU)	+ 1.66	+ 9.12	+27.54	+27.10	+ 4.93
Emerging Markets (EM)	+ 8.56	+17.52	+44.21	+37.18	+14.71
Latin American (LT)	+15.48	+29.30	+76.84	+56.87	+17.46
Pacific Region (PR)	+ 6.16	+12.63	+27.98	+23.48	+ 4.91
Gold Oriented (AU)	+16.60	+20.65	+13.76	+23.40	+27.48
TAXABLE-BOND FUNDS					
Short-Term (SB)	–0.27%	+0.09%	+1.45%	+ 2.25%	+4.17%
Long-Term (AB)	–1.15	–0.67	+2.88	+ 5.23	+6.51
Intermediate Bond (IB)	–0.96	–0.61	+2.41	+ 3.97	+5.99
Intermediate U.S. (IG)	–0.50	–0.37	+3.01	+ 2.91	+5.67
Short-Term U.S. (SU)	–0.38	–0.14	+0.99	+ 1.42	+4.02
Long-Term U.S. (LU)	–1.35	–1.19	+2.70	+ 2.56	+5.74
General U.S. Taxable (GT)	–0.64	+0.09	+3.36	+ 5.41	+5.73
High-Yield Taxable (HC)	–0.75	+1.27	+6.05	+13.89	+5.81
Mortgage (MT)	–0.50	–0.16	+2.31	+ 2.72	+5.11
World Bond (WB)	–0.30	+0.91	+7.65	+11.89	+9.74
Avg. Taxable-Bond Fund [2]	–0.72	–0.06	+3.06	+ 5.44	+5.53
MUNICIPAL-BOND FUNDS					
Short-Term Muni (SM)	...	+0.23%	+1.41%	+1.79%	+3.54%
Intermediate Muni (IM)	–0.55%	–0.33	+1.68	+2.44	+4.70
General Muni (GM)	–0.72	–0.17	+3.49	+3.50	+5.50
Single-State Muni (SS)	–0.66	–0.23	+3.07	+3.13	+5.25
High-Yield Muni (HM)	–0.72	+0.44	+7.19	+5.91	+6.22
Insured Muni (NM)	–0.86	–0.44	+3.13	+3.11	+5.44

Figure 4.4 reproduces "Mutual-Fund Yardsticks," a feature appearing in the *Journal*. This table compares the recent investment performance of the major fund categories, including equity funds, bond funds, and balanced stock and bond funds.

Figure 4.5 is a small section of the mutual fund price quotations regularly reported in *The Wall Street Journal*. All of the funds listed in Figure 4.5 belong to the very large family of funds managed by Fidelity Investments. The Blue Chip Growth Fund (abbreviated BluCh) is highlighted. The first piece of information given is the net asset value, NAV, for the fund. Following the fund name is the fund objective based on the categories shown in Figure 4.3. As its name suggests, the Blue Chip Fund has a large cap focus.[6]

---

[6]A blue chip stock is a well-established, profitable, very-well regarded company. A good example might be GE. The term "blue chip" refers to the game of poker, in which chips are used for betting. The blue chips are the most valuable.

FIGURE 4.5   Mutual Funds

NAV$ 8/31	FUND NAME	INV OBJ	TOTAL RETURN & RANK AUG	YR	3 YR	5 YR	10 YR	MAX INIT CHRG	EXP RAT
10.00	HiIncAdvT p	HC	0.0	16.0 A	24.8 A	8.5 A	7.9 A	3.50	1.06
11.08	IntBdT p	SB	1.0	2.7 A	4.5 A	6.3 A	5.8 A	2.75	0.95
17.39	IntCpApT p	IL	2.5	22.3 D	14.6 D	-0.7 C	NS..	3.50	1.74
15.37	LgeCapT p	LC	-1.1	13.3 B	8.6 D	-7.0 E	NS..	3.50	1.41
26.37	MidCapT p	MC	2.8	27.7 B	20.8 A	4.7 C	NS..	3.50	1.32
13.27	MunIncT p	GM	1.1	5.4 B	5.3 B	6.5 A	6.1 A	3.50	0.79
15.41	NwInsghtT p	XG	1.0	28.3 A	NS..	NS..	NS..	3.50	1.43
18.62	OvseaT p	IL	2.9	22.9 D	16.2 C	-1.3 D	6.1 C	3.50	1.48
26.23	SmllCapT p	SC	-1.8	30.5 A	21.7 B	2.2 E	NS..	3.50	1.58
9.48	STFIT p	SB	0.6	1.6 D	3.0 B	4.6 B	5.0 C	1.50	0.83
11.77	StrInT p	GT	1.2	9.4 A	12.3 A	9.1 A	8.6 A	3.50	1.07
35.15	ValStraT p	MV	-2.3	19.4 D	19.4 C	7.8 E	10.6 D	3.50	1.38
Fidelity Adv Focus B									
21.82	HthCarB p	HB	1.3	20.0 B	11.1 D	0.7 C	NS..	0.00	2.06
15.12	TechB t	TK	-0.8	23.3 B	17.2 C	-17.1 B	NS..	0.00	2.21
Fidelity Adv Focus T									
22.78	HthCarT p	HB	1.2	20.5 B	11.6 D	1.2 C	NS..	3.50	1.56
44.68	NatRecT p	NR	7.8	55.8 D	29.5 D	12.8 D	12.8 E	3.50	1.48
15.75	TechT p	TK	-0.8	23.9 B	17.8 B	-16.7 B	NS..	3.50	1.62
Fidelity Freedom									
12.30	FF2000	MP	0.4	6.1 E	5.7 E	2.2 C	NS..	0.00	0.08
11.07	FF2005	MP	0.4	9.6 C	NS..	NS..	NS..	0.00	0.08
13.95	FF2010	BL	0.4	10.0 C	9.2 C	1.6 C	NS..	0.00	0.08
11.37	FF2015	BL	0.4	12.2 B	NS..	NS..	NS..	0.00	0.08
14.38	FF2020	XC	0.2	13.9 D	12.0 D	0.0 C	NS..	0.00	0.08
12.03	FF2020T p	MP	0.3	12.0 B	NS..	NS..	NS..	3.50	0.58
11.66	FF2025 p	BL	0.2	14.7 A	NS..	NS..	NS..	0.00	0.08
14.55	FF2030	XC	0.1	15.7 C	13.2 C	-1.0 C	NS..	0.00	0.08
11.84	FF2035	XC	0.0	16.3 C	NS..	NS..	NS..	0.00	0.08
8.55	FF2040	XC	0.1	16.8 B	14.1 B	NS..	NS..	0.00	0.08
11.40	Income	MP	0.4	5.5 E	4.8 E	3.1 B	NS..	0.00	0.08
Fidelity Invest									
16.23	A Mgr	MP	-0.3	6.8 D	8.0 B	0.7 D	8.0 C	0.00	0.74
17.23	AggrGr r	XG	0.2	18.5 D	17.1 B	-20.7 E	2.8 E	0.00	0.83
17.37	AggrInt	IL	2.4	23.1 D	15.5 D	0.2 C	7.1 C	0.00	1.24
11.53	AMgrAggr	MP	-0.3	16.7 A	15.9 A	-4.8 E	NS..	0.00	0.94
14.87	AMgrGr	MP	-0.8	7.8 D	9.0 D	-1.5 E	7.7 C	0.00	0.83
12.90	AMgrIn	MP	0.8	9.2 C	8.4 D	4.6 B	6.9 D	0.00	0.63
18.81	Balanc	BL	0.4	18.1 A	14.8 A	7.1 A	10.7 A	0.00	0.67
42.04	BluCh	LC	-1.3	9.9 D	8.7 D	-7.2 E	6.3 E	0.00	0.68
12.65	CAMun	SS	1.1	5.7 B	5.1 B	6.0 B	6.3 A	0.00	0.48
39.93	Canad r	IL	5.6	43.3 A	29.9 A	10.5 A	12.8 A	0.00	1.20
26.64	CapAp	XC	-0.2	18.3 B	20.1 A	0.3 C	9.8 C	0.00	0.94
18.22	ChinaReg	PR	-2.3	19.9 C	18.0 C	2.4 C	NS..	0.00	1.22
8.51	CpInc r	HC	0.5	14.0 A	21.7 A	6.9 B	8.0 A	0.00	0.78
61.72	Contra	XG	0.8	23.6 B	15.8 B	3.0 A	11.7 A	0.00	0.94
22.21	CnvSc	MP	1.8	15.5 A	14.6 A	2.3 C	12.0 A	0.00	0.67
11.67	CTMun r	SS	1.0	3.7 E	4.3 D	5.9 B	5.8 A	0.00	0.49
13.28	Destl	LC	-1.0	14.5 B	9.8 C	-6.1 D	4.7 E	8.24	0.49
11.69	DestII	LC	-0.5	9.7 D	9.4 C	-3.6 C	8.7 B	8.24	0.61
11.46	DestIIA p	LC	-0.5	9.1 D	8.6 D	-4.4 D	NS..	8.24	1.34
10.99	Discovery	LC	-0.5	9.5 D	9.1 D	-4.0 C	NS..	0.00	0.91
26.87	DisEq	LC	-0.6	19.9 A	13.0 A	-1.5 B	9.2 B	0.00	0.89
28.36	DivGth	LC	-1.7	7.4 E	8.3 D	-0.1 A	11.2 A	0.00	0.90
30.85	DivIntl	IL	3.4	27.1 B	21.2 B	6.3 A	12.6 A	0.00	1.15
15.18	EmrMkt r	EM	1.9	48.1 A	27.5 B	8.5 D	0.4 E	0.00	1.23
52.70	Eq Inc	EI	-0.7	11.7 D	12.4 C	3.9 D	10.0 B	0.00	0.70
24.02	EQII	EI	-1.0	12.3 D	13.5 B	4.2 C	9.9 C	0.00	0.68
38.19	Europ r	EU	3.1	42.2 A	26.7 B	3.0 C	10.8 B	0.00	1.11
23.77	ErCapAp r	EU	3.2	33.2 B	17.9 D	5.1 C	11.4 B	0.00	1.22
274.47	Exch	LC	0.3	13.9 B	11.9 B	0.9 A	9.8 A	0.00	0.63
20.95	Export	XC	-0.9	20.4 A	17.7 A	4.6 B	14.2 A	0.00	0.86
30.37	Fidel	LC	-1.0	10.5 D	11.0 B	-3.5 C	9.2 B	0.00	0.61
21.16	Fifty	XC	-0.2	17.4 B	9.6 E	3.8 B	10.8 B	0.00	1.05
11.75	FLMu r	SS	1.0	4.5 C	4.7 C	6.1 A	5.8 A	0.00	0.49
9.97	FltRateHi r	HC	0.4	4.6 E	NS..	NS..	NS..	0.00	0.84
25.94	FournOne	XV	0.0	14.8 D	13.2 D	0.0 E	NS..	0.00	0.08
11.06	GNMA	MT	0.9	3.7 A	3.7 B	5.8 B	6.1 A	0.00	0.60
10.31	GovtInc	LU	1.4	3.7 B	3.8 B	6.3 B	6.1 B	0.00	0.63
58.24	GroCo	XG	-0.5	22.1 C	18.0 B	-7.9 C	9.7 B	0.00	0.84
37.86	GroInc	LC	-1.5	8.5 E	7.6 E	-1.9 B	8.9 B	0.00	0.70
8.91	HighInc r	HC	0.3	8.8 B	15.0 B	4.3 D	6.3 B	0.00	0.77
18.52	Indepndnc	XC	-0.4	19.8 B	10.8 E	-6.0 E	9.3 C	0.00	0.76
11.48	InProBnd	IG	2.1	5.1 B	7.1 A	NS..	NS..	0.00	0.50
10.45	IntBd	SB	1.1	2.7 A	4.5 A	6.5 A	6.1 A	0.00	0.61
10.19	IntGov	SU	1.1	2.0 A	2.9 A	5.8 A	5.8 A	0.00	0.60
30.38	IntlDisc	IL	3.3	28.8 B	20.5 B	4.0 B	9.5 B	0.00	1.10
27.22	IntlSmCap r	IL	4.9	43.3 A	NS..	NS..	NS..	0.00	1.30
10.12	IntMu	IM	0.9	3.6 A	4.4 A	5.8 A	5.6 A	0.00	0.43
7.51	InvGB	IB	1.1	4.3 B	5.3 B	6.9 B	6.5 B	0.00	0.61
13.67	Japan r	PR	10.2	15.5 E	14.9 E	-6.1 E	3.8 C	0.00	1.04
13.53	JpnSmCo r	PR	3.9	14.2 E	21.6 B	3.6 C	NS..	0.00	1.04
14.79	LargeCap	LC	-0.4	12.0 C	8.8 D	-6.9 E	7.8 C	0.00	0.78
26.59	LatinAm r	LT	6.2	65.8 E	43.0 D	13.3 D	11.1 E	0.00	1.19
12.93	LcpVl	XV	-0.4	19.3 B	14.8 B	NS..	NS..	0.00	1.07
25.95	LevCoSt	MC	1.8	41.4 A	48.8 A	NS..	NS..	0.00	0.88
42.64	LowP r	MV	-0.1	25.6 B	21.0 A	18.1 A	16.2 A	0.00	0.98
105.13	MagIn	LC	-1.1	10.9 C	9.4 C	-4.7 D	7.0 D	0.00	0.63
12.23	MAMun	SS	1.3	5.8 B	5.3 A	6.4 A	6.1 A	0.00	0.47
15.34	McpVl	MV	-1.2	26.6 B	18.3 D	NS..	NS..	0.00	0.90
25.57	MidCap	MG	0.6	27.5 B	16.8 C	0.2 A	12.7 A	0.00	0.71
12.08	MIMun	SS	1.0	4.2 D	4.9 B	6.2 A	5.8 A	0.00	0.50
11.61	MNMun	SS	0.9	4.3 D	4.6 C	5.8 B	5.6 B	0.00	0.51
11.23	MtgSec	MT	0.9	3.7 A	4.3 A	6.4 A	6.5 A	0.00	0.62
13.15	MuniInc	GM	1.1	5.7 B	5.6 A	6.8 A	6.4 A	0.00	0.47
14.43	NewMkt r	WB	1.6	15.6 A	19.8 A	13.5 A	15.8 A	0.00	0.94
32.86	NewMill	XG	2.0	19.9 C	14.1 C	-4.8 B	15.4 A	0.00	0.96
11.82	NJMun r	SS	1.1	5.6 B	5.1 B	6.2 A	5.9 A	0.00	0.49
13.11	NYMun	SS	1.1	5.1 C	5.2 A	6.6 A	6.3 A	0.00	0.48
11.99	OHMun	SS	1.0	4.9 C	5.1 B	6.3 A	5.9 A	0.00	0.50
35.66	OTC	XG	-0.9	22.6 B	15.4 C	-11.2 D	8.0 C	0.00	0.91
37.21	Ovrse	IL	2.9	23.3 C	16.8 C	-0.8 D	6.6 C	0.00	1.05
11.02	PAMun r	SS	1.1	4.6 D	4.7 C	6.0 B	5.8 A	0.00	0.50
21.47	PcBas r	PR	3.5	24.3 C	16.8 D	-0.2 D	4.6 B	0.00	1.20
19.11	Puritn	BL	-0.1	9.3 D	10.7 B	5.1 A	9.1 B	0.00	0.65
32.29	RealE	SE	-4.1	28.5 A	24.6 B	19.9 A	15.5 B	0.00	0.86
12.13	RealEstInc r	SE	-0.3	9.9 D	NS..	NS..	NS..	0.00	0.85
18.44	SE Asia r	PR	-3.2	32.9 A	19.8 C	5.3 B	3.8 C	0.00	1.21
18.38	SmallCap r	SC	-0.4	21.8 D	20.2 C	7.8 C	NS..	0.00	1.07
21.50	SmCapInd	SC	0.7	27.8 A	16.6 E	5.9 D	8.2 E	0.00	0.95
12.74	SmlCpVal r	SC	-0.7	NS..	NS..	NS..	NS..	0.00	NA
8.93	STBF	SB	0.7	2.1 B	3.3 B	5.0 B	5.2 B	0.00	0.56
10.27	StIntMu	SM	0.5	1.3 B	2.4 B	4.0 B	4.2 A	0.00	0.49
23.59	StkSlc	LC	-0.7	14.6 B	12.3 A	-3.5 C	7.5 D	0.00	0.85
11.96	StratDivInc	EI	-0.1	17.6 A	NS..	NS..	NS..	0.00	0.90
10.66	StratInc	GT	1.2	9.7 A	12.4 A	9.4 A	NS..	0.00	0.76
10.91	TaxFrB r	GM	1.3	5.8 B	5.8 A	NS..	NS..	0.00	0.25
10.65	TotalBond	IB	1.1	4.7 A	NS..	NS..	NS..	0.00	0.65
55.04	Trend	LC	-0.6	13.5 B	12.3 A	-2.7 B	5.7 E	0.00	0.84
10.03	UltShortBd r	SB	0.3	2.2 B	2.0 D	NS..	NS..	0.00	0.55
11.11	USBI	IB	1.2	4.0 C	5.2 B	7.0 A	6.7 A	0.00	0.32
14.84	Utility	UT	1.4	27.0 D	19.0 C	-4.6 E	7.8 E	0.00	0.89
77.69	Value	MV	-0.9	26.4 B	20.4 B	14.4 A	12.6 C	0.00	0.95
19.02	Wrldw	GL	1.2	19.2 C	15.6 C	2.2 B	7.7 C	0.00	1.23
Fidelity Selects									
37.49	Banking r	SE	-1.9	4.3 E	9.0 E	7.8 D	13.1 C	0.00	0.95
59.97	Biotech r	HB	0.7	14.0 D	17.6 B	-9.3 E	11.6 C	0.00	0.99
62.30	Broker r	SE	-0.4	32.4 A	19.3 C	3.5 E	17.9 A	0.00	0.98
66.14	Chem r	SE	-4.4	18.8 D	17.3 C	14.8 C	10.4 E	0.00	1.08
35.60	Comp r	TK	-1.3	24.6 B	16.9 C	-18.2 C	7.4 B	0.00	1.05
47.82	CstHou r	SE	-4.9	33.5 A	24.7 B	21.2 A	15.4 B	0.00	1.09
74.61	DfAero r	SE	0.6	28.8 A	21.0 C	12.4 C	15.2 B	0.00	1.02
18.88	DevCom r	TK	0.1	22.4 C	24.9 A	-18.3 C	6.0 C	0.00	1.07
42.02	Electr r	TK	-1.5	34.6 A	16.2 C	-16.6 B	10.6 A	0.00	0.96
47.07	Energy r	NR	8.1	71.2 A	33.1 C	14.0 C	16.1 C	0.00	0.97
61.25	EngSvc r	NR	6.9	65.9 B	30.3 D	10.0 E	18.0 B	0.00	0.98

Source: Reprinted by permission of *The Wall Street Journal*, September 6, 2005. © 2005 Dow Jones & Company, Inc. All Rights Reserved Worldwide.

After the fund objective comes a series of performance measures. The first number is the return for the month just ended. So, in this case, the Blue Chip Fund was down 1.3 percent for the month. Next, we have returns for the previous 1, 3, 5, and 10 years. The returns for the periods longer than a year are annualized. Thus, the Blue Chip Fund averaged 6.3 percent per year over the previous 10 years. An "NS" for a performance number just means that the fund did not exist at the start of the period.

A letter grade is assigned to each of the 1-, 3-, 5-, and 10-year returns. A grade of "A" means that the fund's return is in the top 20 percent of all funds in the same category. A grade of "B" means the next 20 percent, and so on. Notice that the grades are strictly relative, so mutual funds, in effect, are graded on the curve!

Finally, the last two columns report the maximum front-end load ("MAX INIT CHRG") and the fund's annual expenses ("EXP RAT"). The expense figure includes management fees, 12b-1 fees, and any other fees. Many of the funds in Figure 4.5, such as the Aggressive Growth Fund ("AggGr"), have a small letter after the name, indicating a footnote. These footnotes generally alert you to back-end loads and similar charges; a small "r," for example, indicates a redemption charge, which is similar to a back-end load.

HOW USEFUL ARE FUND PERFORMANCE RATINGS?

If you look at the performance ratings reported in Figure 4.5, you might wonder why anyone would buy a fund in a category other than those with the highest returns. Well, the lessons learned in Chapter 1 suggest the answer is these historical returns do not consider the riskiness of the various fund categories. For example, if the market has done well, the best ranked funds may simply be the riskiest funds, since the riskiest funds normally perform the best in a rising market. In a market downturn, however, these best ranked funds are most likely to become the worst ranked funds, since the riskiest funds normally perform the worst in a falling market.

These problems with performance measures deal with the evaluation of historical performance. However, there is an even more fundamental criterion. Ultimately, we don't care about historical performance; we care about *future* performance. Whether historical performance is useful in predicting future performance is the subject of ongoing debate. However, one thing we can say is that some of the poorest-performing funds are those with very high costs. These costs act as a constant drag on performance, and such funds tend to have persistently poorer returns than otherwise similar funds.

CLOSED FUNDS

Sometimes, an open-end fund will choose to close, meaning that the fund will no longer sell shares to new investors. The use of the word "close" here should not be confused with "closed-end," because the number of shares can still fluctuate as existing owners buy and sell. Why would a fund choose to close? It usually happens when a fund grows so rapidly (due to good past performance) that the fund manager feels that the incoming cash is more than the fund can invest profitably. When this occurs, the fund in question is usually a small-cap fund, but large-cap funds have also closed on occasion. Funds that close often reopen at a later date. A nearby *Investment Updates* box has more on the issues surrounding closed funds.

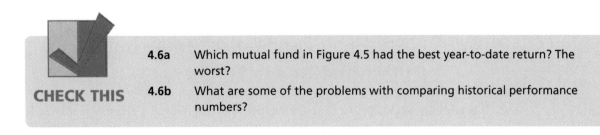

CHECK THIS

4.6a   Which mutual fund in Figure 4.5 had the best year-to-date return? The worst?

4.6b   What are some of the problems with comparing historical performance numbers?

TO CLOSE OR NOT TO CLOSE A FUND?

Turning Away Potential Investors Can Help Performance, but Letting Everyone In Could Boost Profits

"Go away" isn't what you want to hear from a company with which you'd like to do business.

But in the case of mutual-fund managers who are turning away potential investors in their funds, that message may be a signal to consider a firm's other offerings or watch for future reopenings.

Closing funds to prospective buyers can be a good thing for existing investors, fund researchers and financial advisers say, because performance can slip when funds grow so large that managers have trouble executing their strategies. Fund-management companies, however, have a financial incentive to keep the doors open even as portfolios swell: Their fees are figured as a percentage of those growing assets.

"Closing funds is one of the better indicators that a fund company is putting fund investors' long-term interests ahead of its own short-term profit goals," says Russel Kinnel, director of fund research at Morningstar Inc. in Chicago.

Turning away new investors is particularly critical with small-stock funds—since the limited supply of shares in small companies limits the dollars a manager can invest in a single stock. Some managers who invest in the tiniest stocks close their portfolios to new investors at $50 million or $100 million. When funds choose not to close, the managers usually end up buying a larger number of stocks or buying more and more larger stocks, thus changing the fund's profile.

Fund managers say there are no hard and fast rules about when to close; that depends on factors including whether the managers tend to trade frequently and how much money they are running outside of a particular mutual fund but in the same style.

A number of highly regarded fund families currently have at least half of their portfolios closed to most new investors. The largest such groups in total fund assets: Dodge & Cox, Artisan, Longleaf Partners, Third Avenue, and Hotchkis & Wiley. The fund managers generally say the closed funds are approaching capacity for their style or that they aren't finding sufficient opportunities to put new cash to work. (Some "closed" funds remain open to certain retirement-plan participants or to clients of financial planners who have relationships with the funds.)

"We manage money for the benefit of our existing clients," says Ken Olivier, a spokesman for Dodge & Cox, which closed two of its four funds to new investors last year. The San Francisco firm doesn't feel its Dodge & Cox Stock Fund and Dodge & Cox Balanced Fund are too large, at $46.3 billion and $22.5 billion, respectively, but wanted to slow the flow of new money to avoid realizing too late that that point had been reached. There are no current plans to reopen, Mr. Olivier says.

Dodge & Cox and other large firms with numerous closed funds are generally companies that are "focused on a few defined approaches to investing and not on being an asset-gathering operation," notes Tim Medley, a financial adviser in Jackson, Mississippi. Most of the firms are also privately owned. In contrast, "publicly owned management firms may have a quarterly earnings agenda" that makes them more reluctant to turn off the spigot of new investor cash, Mr. Medley says.

A willingness of fund managers to close portfolios before they become too bloated is one factor Morningstar considers in assigning what it calls

4.7 Closed-End Funds, Exchange-Traded Funds, and Hedge Funds

It is probably fitting that we close our mutual fund chapter with a discussion of closed-end funds and exchange-traded funds. As we will see, such funds have some unusual aspects.

stewardship ratings that are intended to reflect how well a fund serves shareholders. At the 10 largest fund firms with at least half of their funds closed to new investors, all the funds that have been assigned those relatively new ratings are rated A or B on the A-to-F scale.

Morningstar has often criticized fund firms, including the nation's largest, for not closing funds as promptly as it believes they should. Mr. Kinnel points to Fidelity Magellan Fund and Fidelity Low-Priced Stock Fund, currently with $53.9 billion and $37.3 billion, respectively, in assets, as "good examples of funds that should have closed much sooner" than they did.

He names $53.4 billion Fidelity Contrafund and American Funds' $111 billion Growth Fund of America as two funds that are still delivering great performance but that he believes should close because ballooning assets are a growing handicap.

Fidelity Investments spokesman John Brockelman says the firm has "closed quite a number of funds" over the years, based on what is appropriate for each fund. "The decision of when to close is not a marketing decision. It is not a decision that is based on Fidelity's bottom line. It is a decision on what is in the best long-term interests of our shareholders," he says.

At American Funds, spokesman Chuck Freadhoff says closing Growth Fund is something that the firm looks at but "at this point, we don't see that shareholders are being disadvantaged by the size of the fund." The fund's portfolio is divided into portions that are managed independently by eight individual managers and a team of analysts.

Closing a fund is no guarantee of stellar future performance, of course. And while many funds close after a great run, others do so after less-thrilling results. A case in point: Tweedy, Browne Global Value Fund and Tweedy, Browne American Value Fund, which closed to new investors in May. The funds, with $7.2 billion and $628 million, respectively, in assets, rank in the bottom 10 percent of their Morningstar peer groups for the past three and five years.

In closing the funds, Tweedy cited a shortage of attractive investment opportunities and a desire not to dilute the existing investors' stakes in portfolio holdings. In a mid-July update to fund investors, the managers said cash positions in the funds are rising because "bargains remain scarce around the globe" and the managers are doing more selling than buying. Cash reserves at mid-year were about 21 percent of assets in the global fund and 18 percent in the U.S.-stock fund.

Tweedy officials could not be reached for comment.

While small-stock funds have always been among those most apt to close, such closures are particularly common these days, after several years in which small stocks have gained more than large ones. Seven of 11 funds are closed at small-stock specialist Wasatch Funds, for example, and six of those even bar new investments from existing shareholders. Wasatch Micro Cap Fund, now closed for the third time since its 1995 launch, had the best return among stock funds for the 10 years through August— up an average of 24.15 percent a year, according to Morningstar.

The firm has a policy of closing its small-stock funds at small sizes and "we will take what some may consider drastic measures to maintain that performance," says Eric Johnson, director of mutual funds.

Source: Karen Damato, *The Wall Street Journal*, September 9, 2005. © 2005 Reprinted with permission of *The Wall Street Journal*, Dow Jones & Company, Inc. All Rights Reserved Worldwide.

CLOSED-END FUNDS PERFORMANCE INFORMATION

As we described earlier, the major difference between a closed-end fund and an open-end fund is that closed-end funds don't buy and sell shares. Instead, there is a fixed number of shares in the fund, and these shares are bought and sold on the open market. About 600 closed-end funds have their shares traded on U.S. stock exchanges, which is far fewer than the roughly 8,000 long-term, open-end mutual funds available to investors.

Figure 4.6 shows some quotes for a particular type of closed-end fund, "World Equity Funds." As the name suggests, these funds generally invest outside the United States, and

FIGURE 4.6 | Closed-End Funds

CLOSED-END FUNDS

Explanatory Notes

Closed-end funds sell a limited number of shares and invest the proceeds in securities. Unlike open-end funds, closed-ends generally do not buy their shares back from investors who wish to cash in their holdings. Instead, fund shares trade on a stock exchange. The data also include the fund's most recent net asset value, its closing share price on the day NAV was calculated, and the percentage difference between the market price and the NAV (often called the premium or discount).

Source: Lipper

Exchange abbreviations:
A: American; **C:** Chicago; **N:** NYSE; **O:** Nasdaq; **T:** Toronto;
z: does not trade on an exchange.
Footnotes appear after a fund's name.
f: Rights offering in process.
g: Rights offering announced.
h: Lipper data have been adjusted for rights offering.
J: Rights offering expired, but Lipper data have not yet adjusted.

m: Convertible note — NAV not market conversion value.
o: Tender offer in process.
t: The Fund's yield is overstated due to a change in dividend payout frequency.
v: NAV is converted at the commercial rand rate.
x: Leveraged fund.
y: NAV and market price are in Canadian dollars.
N/A: Not available or not applicable.
*: Fund not in existence for entire period.

Friday, September 30, 2005

FUND NAME	STOCK EXCH/ TICKER	NAV	MKT PRICE	8/31 ASSETS	TOTAL EXP	3-MO MKT RET	1-YR MKT RET	3-YR AVG MKT RET	1-YR AVG NAV RET	9/30 PREM DISC	6/30 PREM DISC
World Equity Funds											
AbrdnAusEq	A/IAF	12.30	13.43	192.1	1.8	12.9	59.6	44.3	34.1	9.2	6.2
AsiaPacFd	N/APB	17.89	16.21	182.7	2.0	6.3	21.9	25.9	23.9	-9.4	-8.6
Asia Tigers	N/GRR	14.44	13.77	83.7	2.0	14.5	37.7	28.7	33.3	-4.6	-6.7
BlackRock Gl Opps Equity	N/BOE	24.63	23.44	295.2	0.0	-4.1	*	*	*	-4.8	4.2
Brazil	N/BZF	52.10	49.60	669.4	1.3	30.9	93.2	83.3	73.6	-4.8	-5.9
Cdn Genl Inv-y	T/CGI	25.35	22.33	450.2	1.3	21.1	75.9	43.3	43.4	-11.9	-16.8
Cdn Wrld Fd Ltd-y	T/CWF	5.53	4.69	19.2	1.8	13.0	20.6	21.7	17.7	-15.2	-23.7
Central Europe & Russia-x	N/CEE	46.44	49.10	381.1	1.3	59.9	109.3	60.1	72.0	5.7	-9.8
Chile	N/CH	18.54	17.74	188.0	1.9	29.3	58.3	53.4	46.8	-4.3	-13.2
China	N/CHN	24.90	25.96	257.9	1.4	-8.6	-0.2	39.9	9.0	4.3	11.3
CloughGlobAlloc	A/GLV	24.57	27.34	216.9	0.0	21.5	42.4	*	33.2	11.3	6.2
CloughGlobalEquity	A/GLQ	22.43	23.10	350.5	0.0	17.0	*	*	*	3.0	2.1
EV TxAdvGlbDivInc	N/ETG	23.05	20.02	1713.0	1.1	3.5	16.6	*	24.7	-13.1	-10.4
EtnVncTxAdvOpp	N/ETO	27.33	23.42	366.6	1.1	12.6	29.7	*	40.0	-14.3	-12.7
Economic Inv Tr-xy	T/EVT.T	92.04	65.00	405.5	0.0	-1.9	21.0	19.7	17.1	-29.4	-23.6
Emer Mkts Tel	N/ETF	13.18	11.26	105.0	1.8	12.9	39.7	26.9	38.7	-14.6	-14.5
Europe Fd	N/EF	12.78	11.61	124.0	1.2	9.9	26.9	27.4	25.1	-9.2	-11.1
First Israel	N/ISL	18.26	16.21	73.0	1.9	16.2	34.1	31.3	27.6	-11.2	-14.2
Germany Fund-x	N/GER	9.59	8.65	139.4	1.6	10.6	27.4	24.8	24.2	-9.8	-11.6
Greater China	N/GCH	18.76	16.73	238.5	2.3	2.6	11.9	30.2	18.3	-10.8	-11.0
Herzfeld Caribb	O/CUBA	7.98	7.00	13.1	3.7	11.1	44.6	27.5	45.4	-12.3	-14.0
India Fund	N/IFN	36.95	39.80	1036.3	1.6	33.3	76.5	66.0	67.2	7.7	-1.1
Indonesia	A/IF	5.46	5.75	52.0	2.0	-1.5	41.5	53.6	28.8	5.3	-1.5
ING Gl Eq Div & Prem Opp	N/IGD	18.92	19.97	1797.9	0.0	2.2	*	*	*	5.5	6.8
Japan Equity-c	N/JEQ	7.88	8.64	94.6	1.1	42.8	43.3	30.5	29.6	9.6	-6.9
Japan Smaller Cap	N/JOF	13.07	17.58	187.5	1.5	62.8	58.5	47.3	28.0	34.5	-6.8
JF China Region Fund	N/JFC	15.70	13.74	70.8	2.2	6.3	16.3	33.2	20.5	-12.5	-11.9
Korea Equity	N/KEF	8.72	8.45	67.9	2.7	19.4	55.6	31.9	52.5	-3.1	-3.1
Korea	N/KF	34.94	33.34	1404.9	1.3	21.9	66.0	40.0	62.8	-4.6	-6.0
Latin Amer Eq-x	N/LAQ	34.53	31.00	180.0	1.4	32.6	85.0	55.0	72.9	-10.2	-13.9
Latin Amer Disc	N/LDF	30.02	27.24	197.4	1.5	36.2	90.4	61.8	76.5	-9.3	-13.4
Lazard Gl Tot Ret & Inc	N/LGI	20.98	19.20	198.4	1.1	5.5	13.5	*	17.0	-8.5	-9.0
Malaysia	N/MF	5.98	5.86	59.0	1.5	3.9	3.3	18.3	4.7	-2.0	-0.8
Mexico Eqty&Inc	N/MXE	23.24	20.57	52.6	2.1	17.6	58.2	41.0	53.0	-11.5	-12.8
Mexico	N/MXF	32.62	28.44	529.7	1.6	18.5	56.8	37.7	58.2	-12.8	-12.3
Mrg Stn Asia-Pac	N/APF	16.19	14.72	538.4	1.2	12.2	31.6	27.7	26.6	-9.1	-10.1
MS E Europe	N/RNE	34.34	36.77	112.9	1.9	31.5	77.1	60.6	44.2	7.1	-4.0
Mrg Stn Emg Mkts	N/MSF	24.38	21.57	391.0	1.5	18.8	40.1	41.2	47.5	-11.5	-11.7
Mrg Stn India	N/IIF	38.44	43.06	536.6	1.4	34.1	90.3	72.3	70.9	12.0	2.4
New Germany-x	N/GF	11.85	10.47	283.4	1.2	12.3	44.8	50.7	34.1	-11.6	-13.1
New Ireland	N/IRL	25.76	23.25	118.3	1.8	7.4	39.4	39.7	29.4	-9.7	-12.5
Nich-App Intl & Prem Str	N/NAI	25.81	24.25	232.3	0.0	5.8	*	*	*	-6.0	-0.7
PIMCO Gl StksPLUS & Inc	N/PGP	25.38	24.10	228.0	0.0	-2.2	*	*	*	-5.0	4.3
S&P QualRnksGlEqMgd	A/BQY	16.44	14.50	99.0	0.0	4.5	10.6	*	16.3	-11.8	-13.0
Scudder New Asia-x	N/SAF	19.71	19.03	162.2	1.8	18.8	45.4	36.4	30.8	-3.5	-9.4
Singapore	N/SGF	10.86	9.39	103.6	1.7	6.0	13.6	27.6	10.1	-13.5	-12.3
Spain	N/SNF	10.38	13.20	88.4	2.0	9.1	28.5	41.6	29.9	27.2	27.7
Swiss Helvetia	N/SWZ	17.71	14.89	414.5	1.1	8.6	22.7	25.1	20.6	-15.9	-14.5
Taiwan	N/TWN	15.10	13.52	260.8	2.1	-0.2	21.2	19.4	18.2	-10.5	-10.6
Taiwan Greater China	N/TFC	5.26	4.88	109.8	2.8	-4.5	13.5	11.7	10.0	-7.2	-6.4
Templeton Dragon	N/TDF	21.83	19.55	787.4	1.5	8.1	27.5	41.5	26.6	-10.4	-7.9
Templeton Em Mkt	N/EMF	19.50	19.82	319.6	1.6	13.5	39.2	43.4	40.6	1.6	2.0
Templeton Russia & E Eur	N/TRF	48.32	56.30	225.0	1.8	42.4	72.1	69.6	48.9	16.5	4.5
Thai Capital-c	A/TF	9.12	9.12	26.3	2.3	2.6	18.1	44.6	13.5	0.0	5.4
Thai	N/TTF	8.70	9.83	106.0	1.7	3.3	24.1	47.8	15.4	13.0	18.7
Third Canadian-xy	T/THD	43.11	34.80	162.3	1.2	20.2	59.6	40.2	62.0	-19.3	-21.5

they are a relatively common type (single-state municipal funds are the most common). The entry for the single-country Korea Fund is highlighted.

Examining the entry for the Korea Fund, the first entry after the name is the exchange where the shares are traded (N is NYSE, O is NASDAQ, A is American, T is Toronto) followed by the ticker symbol. Next, we have the NAV, the market price per share, the fund's total assets, and the fund's expense ratio. The several columns that follow report returns over various intervals based on the fund's market price and also the one-year return based on the fund's NAV.

An important thing to notice is that the Korea Fund's NAV, $34.94, does not equal its market price, $33.34. The percentage difference is ($33.34 − $34.94)/$34.94 = −.046 = −4.6 percent, which is the number shown in the second to last column. The last column shows this same calculation from the previous quarter. We will say more about this discount in a moment, but notice that (1) essentially all the closed-end funds have either premiums or discounts, (2) the premiums and discounts can be relatively large, and (3) the premiums and discounts fluctuate (compare the last two columns).

THE CLOSED-END FUND DISCOUNT MYSTERY

Wall Street has many unsolved puzzles, and one of the most famous and enduring has to do with prices of shares in closed-end funds. As we noted earlier, shares in closed-end funds trade in the marketplace. Furthermore, as the Korea Fund shows, share prices can differ from net asset values. In fact, many closed-end funds sell at a discount relative to their net asset values, and the discount is sometimes substantial.

For example, suppose a closed-end fund owns $100 million worth of stock. It has 10 million shares outstanding, so the NAV is clearly $10. It would not be at all unusual, however, for the share price to be only $9, indicating a 10 percent discount. What is puzzling about this discount is that you can apparently buy $10 worth of stock for only $9!

To make matters even more perplexing, as we have noted, the typical discount fluctuates over time. Sometimes, the discount is very wide; at other times, it almost disappears. Despite a great deal of research, the closed-end fund discount phenomenon remains largely unexplained.

Because of the discount available on closed-end funds, it is often argued that funds with the largest discounts are attractive investments. The problem with this argument is that it assumes that the discount will narrow or disappear. Unfortunately, this may or may not happen; the discount might get even wider.

Sometimes, certain closed-end funds sell at a premium, implying that investors are willing to pay more than the NAV for shares. This case is not quite as perplexing; however, after all, investors in load funds do the same thing. The reasons we discussed for paying loads might apply to these cases.

One last comment on closed-end funds seems appropriate. When a closed-end fund is first created, its shares are offered for sale to the public. For example, a closed-end fund might raise $50 million by selling 5 million shares to the public at $10 per share (the original offer price is almost always $10), which is the fund's NAV.

If you pay $10, then you are very likely to shortly discover two unpleasant facts. First, the fund promoter will be paid, say, 7 percent of the proceeds right off the top, or about $3.5 million (this will be disclosed in the prospectus). This fee will come out of the fund, leaving a total value of $46.5 million and a NAV of $9.30. Further, as we have seen, the shares will probably trade at a discount relative to NAV in the market, so you would lose another piece of your investment almost immediately. In short, newly offered closed-end funds are generally very poor investments.

EXCHANGE-TRADED FUNDS

Exchange-traded funds, or ETFs, are a relatively recent innovation. Although they have been around since 1993, they really began to grow in the late 1990s. As of 2005, there were about 150 traded ETFs. Basically, an ETF is an index fund, and, when you buy an ETF, you are buying the particular basket of stocks in the index. For example, the best known ETF is a "Standard and Poor's Depositary Receipt," or SPDR (pronounced "spider"), which is simply the S&P 500 index.

What makes an ETF different from an index fund is that, as the name suggests, an ETF actually trades like a closed-end fund. ETFs can be bought and sold during the day, and they can be sold short. They generally have very low expenses, lower even than index funds, but you must pay a commission when you buy and sell shares.

The fact that ETFs trade like shares in closed-end funds raises the possibility that they too could sell at a discount to their net asset values, but this probably won't happen. The reason is a little complicated, but, in essence, the fund will buy and sell directly like an open-end fund, but there is usually a minimum size of, say, 50,000 shares. Furthermore, an ETF will redeem shares in kind, meaning that if you sell a block of 50,000 shares to the fund, you actually receive the underlying stock instead of cash. So, if an ETF were to sell for a discount, big investors would buy up shares, redeem them in exchange for stock, and then sell the stock, thereby capturing the discount.

Which is better, an ETF or a more traditional index fund? It's hard to say. For an index like the S&P 500, it probably doesn't make much difference. However, one place where ETFs seem to have an edge is with some of the more specialized indexes. For example, ETFs provide a very cheap way of purchasing non-U.S. indexes. Similarly, there are ETFs that track industry indexes for which few ordinary index funds are available. A nearby *Investment Updates* box provides more information on the index fund versus ETF debate.

HEDGE FUNDS

hedge fund
An investment company not accessible by the general public.

Hedge funds are a special type of investment company. They are like mutual funds in that a fund manager invests a pool of money obtained from investors. Traditionally, hedge funds were only lightly regulated. As of 2005, however, like mutual funds, most hedge funds are required to file regular reports with the Securities and Exchange Commission (SEC). Hedge funds are generally free to pursue almost any investment style they wish. In contrast, as we have discussed, mutual funds are relatively limited in their permitted investment strategies. For example, mutual funds are usually not allowed to do things like sell short or use large degrees of leverage.

Hedge funds are also not required to maintain any particular degree of diversification or liquidity. They don't have to redeem shares on demand, and historically, they had minimal disclosure requirements. The reason that hedge funds historically avoided many of the restrictions placed on mutual funds is that they only accept "financially sophisticated" investors, and they do not offer their securities for sale to the public. A financially sophisticated investor is, as a practical matter, usually either an institution or a high net worth (i.e., rich) individual. Some types of hedge funds are limited to no more than 50 to 100 investors.

Extensive information about hedge funds is available on the Internet. Try Hedge World www.hedgeworld.com and Hedge Fund Center www.hedgefund center.com

HEDGE FUND FEES Hedge funds typically have a special fee structure, where, in addition to a general management fee of 1 to 2 percent of fund assets, the manager is paid a special performance fee. This special performance fee is often in the range from 20 to 40 percent of profits realized by the fund's investment strategy. A modest fee structure might be one that charges an annual management fee of 1 percent of the fund's assets plus 20 percent of any profits realized; however, more elaborate fee structures are common.

HEDGE FUND STYLES Worldwide there are thousands of hedge funds, and the number keeps growing. Big hedge funds may require a minimum investment of $1 million or more. Small hedge funds may only require a minimum investment of $50,000 or less. Whether large or small, each fund develops its own investment style or niche.

Information about starting your own hedge fund is available at Turn Key Hedge Funds www.turnkeyhedge funds.com

For example, a hedge fund may focus on a particular sector, like technology, or a particular global region, like Asia or eastern Europe. Alternatively, a hedge fund may pursue a particular investment strategy, like the "market-neutral strategy" in which the fund maintains a portfolio approximately equally split between long and short positions. By being long in some securities and short in others, the portfolio is hedged against market risk and hence the term "market neutral." Incidentally, this is often thought to be the source of the term "hedge fund," originally referring to funds that were hedged against market risk.

MAKING CASE FOR ETFs, INDEX FUNDS

Both Vehicles Help Create More-Diversified Portfolios with Low Overall Expenses

Exchange-traded funds and traditional mutual funds that track indexes are close cousins, not identical twins.

Both ETFs and index funds represent baskets of securities that track the performance of specific indexes. However, because ETFs are bought and sold through a broker and trade on an exchange like stocks, they are more advantageous in some situations while index funds win out in others. So, instead of poring over which to include in your portfolio, using both can help you create a well-diversified portfolio, with low overall expenses.

"ETFs and index funds, collectively, are a wonderful way to build a portfolio … [together] they cover all the asset classes; they're both really cheap; they both track really well," said Chip Roame, managing principal of Tiburon Strategic Advisors.

"In certain instances, ETFs make more sense. In certain instances, index funds make more sense," he added.

Index funds may be a better bet than ETFs in automatic-investment plans such as 401(k)s, where you regularly invest small increments of money. That's because investors who trade ETFs have to pay commissions. Investors who buy index funds don't. So by making several periodic investments an investor will pay commissions of as much as $25 each time they trade. That can significantly erode an investment.

Some firms have devised ways to include ETFs in 401 (k) plans without passing the costs on to plan participants by bundling trades together. And online broker ShareBuilder Securities Corp. has an automatic investment plan that lets investors trade for as low as $1 to $4 per trade.

ETFs are a good option for buy-and-hold investors with large lump sums to invest. One reason is that ETF fees are generally lower than index funds. According to Morningstar, ETFs charge an average fee of 0.42 percent of assets annually, while index funds charge 0.77 percent on average. Of course, you'll still end up paying the initial commission to buy the ETF, but if you hold onto it long enough, you will recoup that cost.

Another reason ETFs may be a better pick than index funds is their tax efficiency. When a large investor exits from a mutual fund, the fund has to sell some of the underlying securities to generate the money. That triggers a capital-gain distribution for all fund shareholders. With ETFs, though, the shares are sold on the open market, so if one investor cashes out, it doesn't affect others.

Specialists or very large shareholders can opt to get rid of their ETFs by exchanging them for the underlying stocks. But, because the transaction is done "in-kind" (no cash payment is being made), there are no distributable capital gains to other shareholders. Also, when that swap occurs, the ETF can purge its lowest-cost shares, which reduces the possibility that the ETF will realize capital gains in the future if the holdings are changed when the index rebalances.

While many experts say ETFs are also the way to go for active traders, commission costs are still a big issue. While many active traders use ETFs because they are transparent and allow for intraday trading, each time a trade is made the investor has to pay a commission, which will eat into profits, said Noel Archard, principal with Vanguard VIPERs. "Beating the market is tough, and if your trading costs go up, you're making a hard thing impossible," he said.

A few other points to consider: Because ETFs trade like stocks, ETF investors are able to execute limit and stop-loss orders, bet against an index by selling the shares short, and use hedging strategies just as they would with stocks. Also, ETFs track nearly twice as many benchmarks as index funds.

But index funds have the ability to reinvest quarterly dividends, which can add to performance, and they can lend out securities to earn additional income, something ETFs can't do. There also are more bond-index funds than bond ETFs.

Today, however, the term "hedge fund" mainly refers to an investment company free to pursue a wide range of investment styles.

FUNDS OF FUNDS A significant portion of the money invested in hedge funds is funneled through "funds of funds." A fund of funds is just what the name suggests: An investment company that invests in hedge funds. For an investor, a fund of funds has the advantage that the fund manager may have expertise in selecting hedge funds; moreover, having multiple hedge funds offers a diversification benefit. However, a fund of funds charges fees of its own, on top of the already hefty hedge fund fees, so these advantages come with a cost.

STARTING YOUR OWN HEDGE FUND Ever dreamed about becoming an investment portfolio manager? You can by starting your own hedge fund. It may be easier than you think. A hedge fund is typically structured as a limited partnership in which the manager is a general partner and the investors are limited partners. Rather than stumble through the legal details, we simply advise that you will need the services of a lawyer familiar with investment companies, but the bottom line is that it's not difficult to do. Actually, the hardest part about setting up your own hedge fund is finding willing investors. Essentially, you need to find well-to-do individuals who have faith in your investment ideas. Bear in mind, however, that you will have to register your hedge fund if you have more than 15 investors. There are other requirements, too, and you should make sure you know them all.

CHECK THIS

4.7a What is a closed-end fund and how does it differ from a mutual fund?

4.7b What is meant by the Net Asset Value (NAV) of a closed-end fund?

4.7c What is a hedge fund? What are the important differences between a hedge fund and a mutual fund?

4.7d What is a market neutral investment strategy? Why is this strategy available to hedge funds but not to mutual funds?

4.8 Summary and Conclusions

We have covered many aspects of mutual fund investing in this chapter. We have seen that there are thousands of mutual funds and dozens of types. A few of the more important distinctions we made can be summarized as follows:

1. Some funds are open-end and some are closed-end. Open-end funds stand ready to buy or sell shares. Closed-end funds do not; instead, their shares trade on the stock exchanges.

2. Some open-end funds have front-end loads, meaning that there is a fee tacked on to the fund's net asset value when you buy. Other funds are no-load. Various costs and fees exist, including back-end loads and 12b-1 fees.

3. Funds have very different objectives and, as a result, very different risk and return potentials. Furthermore, funds with similar-sounding objectives can, in fact, be quite different. It is important to consider a fund's actual holdings and investment policies, not just read its stated objective.

4. Mutual fund information is widely available, but performance information should be used with caution. The best performing funds are often the ones with the greatest risks or the ones that just happened to be in the right investment at the right time.

This chapter covered the essentials of mutual funds. How should you, as an investor or investment manager, put this information to work?

The first thing to do is to start looking at mutual fund prospectuses. These are written to be accessible to novice investors (or, at least, they are *supposed* to be written that way). The best way to begin exploring is to visit Web sites. Almost any large mutual fund company will have extensive online information available. Links to some of the better known families are available at our Web page. It is important to look at different funds within a given family and also to look across families. Compare growth funds to growth funds, for example. This adventure will give you some of the real-life background you need to select the types of funds most suitable for you or someone else.

Once you have examined prospectuses on different funds, it's time to invest. Beginning with your simulated account, pick a few funds, invest, and observe the outcomes. Open-end mutual funds are probably the place most of you will begin investing real dollars. An initial purchase can be made with a relatively small amount, perhaps $500, and subsequent purchases can be made in amounts of as little as $100 or less.

Most important of all, as we discussed to start the chapter, most employers now provide employees with retirement plans. The way these work is that, typically, your employer will make a contribution to a mutual fund you select (often from a fairly limited set). Your employer may even match, or more than match, a contribution you make. Such plans may be the only retirement benefit offered, but they can be an extraordinary opportunity for those who take full advantage of them by getting the largest possible match and then investing in a suitable fund. It's an important choice, so the more knowledge you have regarding mutual funds, the better your outcome is likely to be.

Key Terms

12b-1 fees 104
closed-end fund 100
front-end load 104
hedge fund 124
investment company 100

money market mutual fund 108
net asset value 101
open-end fund 100
turnover 105

Chapter Review Problems and Self-Test

1. **Front-End Loads**   The Madura HiGro Fund has a net asset value of $50 per share. It charges a 3 percent load. How much will you pay for 100 shares?

2. **Turnover**   The Starks Income Fund's average daily total assets were $100 million for the year just completed. Its stock purchases for the year were $20 million, while its sales were $12.5 million. What was its turnover?

1. You will pay 100 times the offering price. Since the load is computed as a percentage of the offering price, we can compute the offering price as follows:

$$\text{Net asset value} = (1 - \text{Front-end load}) \times \text{Offering price}$$

In other words, the NAV is 97 percent of the offering price. Since the NAV is $50, the offering price is $50/.97 = $51.55. You will pay $5,155 in all, of which $155 is a load.

2. Turnover is the lesser of purchases or sales divided by average daily assets. In this case, sales are smaller at $12.5, so turnover is $12.5/$100 = .125 times.

Test Your Investment Quotient _____

1. **Investment Companies**   Which of the following statements typically does not characterize the structure of an investment company?

   a. An investment company adopts a corporate form of organization.
   b. An investment company invests a pool of funds belonging to many investors in a portfolio of individual investments.
   c. An investment company receives an annual management fee ranging from 3 to 5 percent of the total value of the fund.
   d. The board of directors of an investment company hires a separate investment management company to manage the portfolio of securities and handle other administrative duties.

2. **Expense Statement**   Which of the following is *not* part of the expense statement?

   a. Shareholder transactions expenses
   b. Shareholder demographic profile
   c. Annual operating expenses
   d. A hypothetical example of expenses

3. **Mutual Fund Investing**   Which of the following is the least likely advantage of mutual fund investing?

   a. Diversification
   b. Professional management
   c. Convenience
   d. Mutual fund returns are normally higher than market average returns

4. **Open-End Funds**   An open-end mutual fund is owned by which of the following?

   a. An investment company
   b. An investment advisory firm
   c. A "family of funds" mutual fund company
   d. Its shareholders

5. **Closed-End Funds**   Which of the following is most true of a closed-end investment company?

   a. The fund's share price is usually greater than net asset value.
   b. The fund's share price is set equal to net asset value.
   c. Fund shares outstanding vary with purchases and redemptions by shareholders.
   d. Fund shares outstanding are fixed at the issue date.

6. **Closed-End Funds**   A closed-end fund is owned by which of the following?

   a. An investment company
   b. An investment advisory firm
   c. A "family of funds" mutual fund company
   d. Its shareholders

7. **Investment Advisory Firms**   Which of the following is not true about the typical relationship between a mutual fund and an investment advisory firm? The investment advisory firm
   a. Owns the mutual fund.
   b. Manages the mutual fund's assets.
   c. Manages shareholder purchase and redemption operations.
   d. Receives a management fee for services rendered.

8. **Fund Types**   Which mutual fund type is most likely to own stocks paying the highest dividend yields?
   a. Capital appreciation fund
   b. Equity income fund
   c. Growth and income fund
   d. Growth fund

9. **Fund Types**   Which mutual fund type is most likely to own stocks paying the lowest dividend yields?
   a. Capital appreciation fund
   b. Equity income fund
   c. Growth and income fund
   d. Growth fund

10. **Fund Types**   Which mutual fund type will most likely incur the greatest tax liability for its investors?
    a. Index fund
    b. Municipal bond fund
    c. Income fund
    d. Growth fund

11. **Fund Types**   Which mutual fund type will most likely incur the smallest tax liability for its investors?
    a. Index fund
    b. Municipal bond fund
    c. Income fund
    d. Growth fund

12. **Fund Types**   Which mutual fund type will most likely incur the greatest overall risk levels for its investors?
    a. Large-cap index fund
    b. Insured municipal bond fund
    c. Money market mutual fund
    d. Small-cap growth fund

13. **Mutual Fund Fees**   Which of the following mutual fund fees is assessed on an annual basis?
    a. 12b-1 fees
    b. Front-end load
    c. Back-end load
    d. Contingent deferred sales charge (CDSC)

14. **Mutual Fund Fees**   Which of the following mutual fund fees will most likely be the biggest expense for a long-term fund investor?
    a. 12b-1 fees
    b. Front-end load
    c. Back-end load
    d. Contingent deferred sales charge (CDSC)

15. **Mutual Fund Fees**   Which of the following mutual fund fees and expenses is the most difficult for investors to assess?
    a. Sales charges or "loads"
    b. 12b-1 fees
    c. Management fees
    d. Trading costs

Chapter 4 ■ Mutual Funds   **129**

Concept Questions

1. **Fund Ownership**   Who actually owns a mutual fund? Who runs it?

2. **Loads**   Given that no-load funds are widely available, why would a rational investor pay a front-end load? More generally, why don't fund investors always seek out funds with the lowest loads, management fees, and other fees?

3. **Money Market Funds**   Is it true that the NAV of a money market mutual fund never changes? How is this possible?

4. **Money Market Deposit Accounts**   What is the difference between a money market deposit account and a money market mutual fund? Which is riskier?

5. **Front-End Loads**   You are interested in investing in a mutual fund that charges a front-end load of 5 percent. If the length of your investment is one year, would you invest in this fund? Suppose the length of your investment is 20 years? How are the length of your investment and front-end loads related?

6. **Open versus Closed-End Funds**   An open-end mutual fund typically keeps a percentage, often around 5 percent, of its assets in cash or liquid money market assets. How does this affect the fund's return in a year in which the market increases in value? How about during a bad year? Closed-end funds do not typically hold cash. What is it about the structure of open-end and closed-end funds that would influence this difference?

7. **12b-1 Fees**   What are 12b-1 fees? What expenses are 12b-1 fees intended to cover? Many closed-end mutual funds charge a 12b-1 fee. Does this make sense to you? Why or why not?

8. **Open versus Closed-End Funds**   If you were concerned about the liquidity of mutual funds shares that you held, would you rather hold shares in a closed-end fund or an open-end fund? Why?

9. **Performance**   Refer to Figure 4.5. Look at the 10-year performance for the funds listed. Why do you suppose there are so few poor performers? Hint: Think about the hit TV show *Survivor*.

10. **Mutual Fund Fees**   Suppose you want to invest in a mutual fund and are given the choice of two share classes. Class U shares charge a fee as a percentage of the initial investment upfront. Class B shares charge the same fee, but the fee is taken out of the total assets at the end of the year. Which share class would provide you with the highest total return? Assume the fund makes no distributions prior to the fee assessment at the end of the year.

Questions and Problems

Core Questions

1. **Net Asset Value**   The World Income Appreciation Fund has current assets with a market value of $4.5 billion and has 130 million shares outstanding. What is the net asset value (NAV) for this mutual fund?

2. **Front-End Loads**   Suppose the mutual fund in the previous problem has a current market price quotation of $34.10. Is this a load fund? If so, calculate the front-end load.

3. **Calculating NAV**   The Tiki Growth and Equity Fund is a "low-load" fund. The current offer price quotation for this mutual fund is $48.65, and the front-end load is 1.5 percent. What is the NAV? If there are 13.4 million shares outstanding, what is the current market value of assets owned by the Tiki fund?

4. **Money Market Funds**   The Hydro Liquid Assets Money Market Mutual Fund has a NAV of $1 per share. During the year, the assets held by this fund appreciated by 4.6 percent. If you had invested $15,000 in this fund at the start of the year, how many shares would you own at the end of the year? What will the NAV of this fund be at the end of the year? Why?

5. **NAV**   An open-end mutual fund has the following stocks:

Stock	Shares	Stock Price
A	4,000	$68
B	9,000	32
C	6,500	44
D	8,400	56

If there are 50,000 shares of this mutual fund, what is its NAV?

6. **NAV**   Suppose the fund in the previous problem has liabilities of $75,000. What is the NAV of the fund now?

7. **Front-End Load**   In the previous problem, assume the fund is sold with a 5 percent front-end load. What is the offering price of the fund?

8. **Turnover**   A mutual fund sold $75 million of assets during the year and purchased $68 million in assets. If the average daily assets of the fund was $120 million, what was the fund turnover?

9. **Closed-End Funds**   A closed-end fund has total assets of $350 million and liabilities of $800,000. Currently, 20 million shares are outstanding. What is the NAV of the fund? If the shares currently sell for $15.27, what is the premium or discount on the fund?

10. **Mutual Fund Returns**   You invested $10,000 in a mutual fund at the beginning of the year when the NAV was $41.86. At the end of the year the fund paid $.34 in short-term distributions and $1.25 in long-term distributions. If the NAV of the fund at the end of the year was $43.51, what was your return for the year?

Intermediate Questions

11. **Calculating Turnover**   A sector fund specializing in commercial bank stocks had average daily assets of $2.7 billion during the year. This fund sold $1.45 billion worth of stock during the year, and its turnover ratio was .47. How much stock did this mutual fund purchase during the year?

12. **Calculating Fees**   In the previous problem, suppose the annual operating expense ratio for the mutual fund is 1.25 percent, and the management fee is .85 percent. How much money did the fund's management earn during the year? If the fund doesn't charge any 12b-1 fees, how much were miscellaneous and administrative expenses during the year?

13. **Calculating Fees**   You purchased 2,000 shares in the New Pacific Growth Fund on January 2, 2006, at an offering price of $41.20 per share. The front-end load for this fund is 5 percent, and the back-end load for redemptions within one year is 2 percent. The underlying assets in this mutual fund appreciate (including reinvested dividends) by 12 percent during 2006, and you sell back your shares at the end of the year. If the operating expense ratio for the New Pacific Fund is 1.65 percent, what is your total return from this investment? What do you conclude about the impact of fees in evaluating mutual fund performance?

14. **Calculating Fees**   Suppose in the previous problem that the mutual fund has no front-end load or back-end load. Further suppose that the operating expense ratio for the fund is .95 percent. What is your return on investment now?

Refer to Figure 4.5 to answer Questions 15–18.

15. **Fund Objectives**   Locate the OTC Portfolio Fund. What is its objective? What is its one-year return? How does this compare to other mutual funds with the same objective?

16. **Fund Loads**   Of the funds listed, what is the highest load?

17. **Fund Costs**   Of the funds listed, what types have the lowest costs? The highest?

18. **Purchase Prices**   Locate the Destiny 1 Fund. If you buy 1,000 shares, what would you pay?

19. **Front-End Loads and Returns**   You are considering an investment in a mutual fund with a 5 percent front-end load. Assuming the fund return is 12 percent per year, what is your return in 1 year? 2 years? 5 years? 10 years? 20 years? 30 years? Graph and explain your answers.

20. **Expenses and Returns**   The Bruin Stock Fund sells Class A shares that have a front-end load of 5.75 percent, a 12b-1 fee of .23 percent, and other fees of .73 percent. There are also Class B shares with a 5 percent CDSC that declines 1 percent per year, a 12b-1 fee of 1.00 percent, and other fees of .73 percent. If the portfolio return is 11 percent per year and you plan to sell after the third year, should you invest in Class A or Class B shares? What if your investment horizon is 20 years?

21. **Expenses and Returns**   You are going to invest in a stock mutual fund with a 5 percent front-end load and a 1.40 percent expense ratio. You also can invest in a money market mutual fund with a 4 percent return and an expense ratio of .20 percent. If you plan to keep your investment for two years, what annual return must the stock mutual fund earn to exceed an investment in the money market fund? What if your investment horizon is 10 years?

22. **Taxes and MMMFs**   Suppose you're evaluating three alternative MMMF investments. The first fund buys a diversified portfolio of municipal securities from across the country and yields 3.9 percent. The second fund buys only taxable, short-term commercial paper and yields 6.1 percent. The third fund specializes in the municipal debt from the state of New Jersey and yields 3.6 percent. If you are a New Jersey resident, your federal tax bracket is 35 percent, and your state tax bracket is 8 percent, which of these three MMMFs offers you the highest aftertax yield?

23. **Taxes and MMMFs**   In the previous problem, which MMMF offers you the highest yield if you are a resident of Texas, which has no state income tax?

24. **Closed-End Funds**   The Argentina Fund has $360 million in assets and sells at a 12.8 percent discount to NAV. If the quoted share price for this closed-end fund is $18.43, how many shares are outstanding? If you purchase 1,000 shares of this fund, what will the total shares outstanding be now?

25. **Closed-End Fund Discounts**   Suppose you purchase 5,000 shares of a closed-end mutual fund at its initial public offering; the offer price is $25 per share. The offering prospectus discloses that the fund promoter gets an 8 percent fee from the offering. If this fund sells at a 10 percent discount to NAV the day after the initial public offering, what is the value of your investment?

What's on the Web?

1. **Bond Funds**   One of the best Internet sites for information on mutual funds is www.morningstar.com. Go to the Web site and find the ticker symbol for the Harbor Bond Fund. Find all of the following information on the Web site for this fund: loads, expense ratio, top five holdings, bond quality ratings, the fund's rank in its category for the last seven years, and the Morningstar rating. Next, find out how the Morningstar star ranking system works.

2. **Stock Funds**   Go to www.morningstar.com and find the ticker symbol for a domestic stock fund. Enter the ticker symbol and find the following information for the fund: manager and manager start date, year-to-date return, three-year return, five-year return, front-end or back-end loads, actual and maximum 12b-l fees, management fees, expense ratio, the top 25 holdings, and the fund address and phone number.

3. **Morningstar Fund Selector**   Find the Mutual Fund Selector on the Morningstar Web site. How many funds fit the following criteria: domestic stock fund, minimum initial purchase equal to or less than $500, expense ratio less than or equal to category average, and turnover less than 75 percent?

4. **ETFs**   Go to www.amex.com. Once there, find out the advantages Amex lists for individuals buying ETFs. Now, find out how many ETFs AMEX lists. How many ETFs are international? What are Diamonds, Spyders, and Cubes (QQQ)? What does each of these three invest in?

Stock-Trak Exercises

To access the Stock-Trak Exercise for this chapter, please visit the book Web site at www.mhhe.com/jm4e and choose the corresponding chapter.

www.mhhe.com/jm4e

CHAPTER 5

The Stock Market

"One of the funny things about the stock market is that every time one man buys, another sells, and both think they are astute."

–William Feather

"If you don't know who you are, the stock market is an expensive place to find out."

–Adam Smith (pseud. for George J. W. Goodman)

On May 17, 1792, a group of commodity brokers met and signed the now famous Buttonwood Tree Agreement, thereby establishing the forerunner of what soon became the New York Stock Exchange. Today, the NYSE is the world's largest and best known stock market. On a typical day, the NYSE executes buy and sell transactions in well over a billion shares. Established in 1971, and now famous as an arena for "tech" stock investing, the NASDAQ daily executes trades for a similar number of stock shares. Together, the NYSE and NASDAQ account for the vast majority of stock trading in the United States. ∎

With this chapter, we begin in earnest our study of stock markets. This chapter presents a "big picture" overview of how a stock market works and how to read and understand stock market information reported in the financial press.

5.1 The Primary and Secondary Stock Markets

primary market
The market in which new securities are originally sold to investors.

secondary market
The market in which previously issued securities trade among investors.

The stock market consists of a **primary market** and a **secondary market**. In the primary, or new-issue market, shares of stock are first brought to the market and sold to investors. In the secondary market, existing shares are traded among investors.

In the primary market, companies issue new securities to raise money. In the secondary market, investors are constantly appraising the values of companies by buying and selling shares previously issued by these companies. We next discuss the operation of the primary market for common stocks, and then we turn our attention to the secondary market for stocks.

THE PRIMARY MARKET FOR COMMON STOCK

initial public offering (IPO)
An initial public offering occurs when a company offers stock for sale to the public for the first time.

The primary market for common stock is how new securities are first brought to market. It is best known as the market for **initial public offerings (IPOs)**. An IPO occurs when a company offers stock for sale to the public for the first time. Typically, the company is small and growing, and it needs to raise capital for further expansion.

To illustrate how an IPO occurs, suppose that several years ago you started a software company. Your company was initially set up as a privately held corporation with 100,000 shares of stock, all sold for one dollar per share. The reason your company is privately held is that shares were not offered for sale to the general public. Instead, you bought 50,000 shares for yourself and sold the remaining 50,000 shares to a few supportive friends and relatives.

Fortunately, your company has prospered beyond all expectations. However, company growth is now hampered by a lack of capital. At an informal stockholders' meeting, it is agreed to take the company public. Not really knowing how to do this, you consult your ac-

investment banking firm
A firm specializing in arranging financing for companies.

countant, who recommends an **investment banking firm**. An investment banking firm, among other things, specializes in arranging financing for companies by finding investors to buy newly issued securities.

After lengthy negotiations, including an examination of your company's current financial condition and plans for future growth, your investment banker suggests an issue of 4 million shares of common stock. Two million shares will be distributed to the original stockholders (you and your original investors) in exchange for their old shares. These 2 million shares distributed to the original stockholders ensure that effective control of the corporation will remain in their hands.

underwrite
To assume the risk of buying newly issued securities from a company and reselling them to investors.

After much haggling, your investment banker agrees to **underwrite** the stock issue by purchasing the other 2 million shares from your company for $10 per share. The net effect of this transaction is that you have sold half the company to the underwriter for $20 million. The proceeds from the sale will allow your company to construct its own headquarters building and to double its staff of programmers and sales consultants.

Your investment banker will not keep the 2 million shares but instead will resell them in the primary market. She thinks the stock can probably be sold for $12 per share in an IPO. The difference between the $12 the underwriter sells the stock for and the $10 per share you received is called the *underwriter spread* and is a basic part of the underwriter's compensation.

fixed commitment
Underwriting arrangement in which the investment banker guarantees the firm a fixed amount for its securities.

best effort
Arrangement in which the investment banker does not guarantee the firm a fixed amount for its securities.

This agreement, under which the underwriter pays the firm a fixed amount, is called a **fixed commitment**. With a fixed (or firm) commitment, the underwriter assumes the risk that investors cannot be persuaded to buy the stock at a price above $10 per share. The other major type of arrangement, called a **best effort**, is just that. Here, the investment banker devotes a best effort to sell as many shares of the issue as possible at the stated fixed offering price. Strictly speaking, a best-effort arrangement is therefore *not* underwritten, but the phrase "best-effort underwriting" is often used nonetheless. Fixed commitment is, by far, the more common type.

For more on IPOs, check
out IPO Central at
www.hoovers.com

**Securities and
Exchange
Commission (SEC)**
Federal regulatory agency
charged with enforcing
U.S. securities laws and
regulations.

prospectus
Document prepared as
part of a security offering
detailing a company's
financial position, its operations, and investment
plans for the future.

red herring
A preliminary prospectus
not yet approved by the
SEC.

As is common with an IPO, some restrictions are imposed on you as part of the under-writing contract. Most important, you and the other original stockholders agree not to sell any of your personal stockholdings for six months after the underwriting (this is called the "lock-up" period). This ties most of your wealth to the company's success and makes sell-ing the stock to investors a more credible undertaking by the underwriter. Essentially, in-vestors are assured that you will be working hard to expand the company and increase its earnings.

After the underwriting terms are decided, much of your time will be devoted to the me-chanics of the offering. In particular, before shares can be sold to the public, the issue must obtain an approved registration with the **Securities and Exchange Commission (SEC)**. The SEC is the federal regulatory agency charged with regulating U.S. securities markets.

SEC regulations governing IPOs are especially strict. To gain SEC approval, you must prepare a **prospectus**, normally with the help of outside accounting, auditing, and legal ex-perts. The prospectus contains a detailed account of your company's financial position, its operations, and its investment plans for the future. Once the prospectus is prepared, it is submitted to the SEC for approval. The SEC makes no judgment about the quality of your company or the value of your stock. Instead, it only checks to make sure that various rules regarding full disclosure and other issues have been satisfied.

While awaiting SEC approval, your investment banker will circulate a preliminary prospectus among investors to generate interest in the stock offering. This document is commonly called a **red herring** because the cover page is stamped in red ink, indicating that final approval for the stock issue has not yet been obtained. The preliminary prospec-tus is essentially complete except for the final offering price and a few other pieces of in-formation. These are not set because market conditions might change while SEC approval is being sought. Upon obtaining SEC approval, the prospectus will be updated and com-pleted, and your underwriter can begin selling your company's shares to investors.

To publicize an offering, the underwriter will usually place announcements in newspa-pers and other outlets. Because of their appearance, these announcements are known as *tombstones,* and they are a familiar sight in the financial press. A sample tombstone as it ap-peared in *The Wall Street Journal* is shown in Figure 5.1.

As Figure 5.1 shows, a typical tombstone states the name of the company, some infor-mation about the stock issue being sold, and the underwriters for the issue. All but very small issues generally involve more than one underwriter, and the names of the participat-ing underwriters are usually listed at the bottom of the tombstone. Those listed first are the "lead" underwriters, who are primarily responsible for managing the issue process.

Initial public stock offerings vary in size a great deal. The 2 million share issue for your hypothetical software company discussed above is a fairly small issue. One of the largest public offerings in the United States was AT&T Wireless, a subsidiary of AT&T. The new shares were offered at $29.50 per share to create a $70 billion public offering.

THE SECONDARY MARKET FOR COMMON STOCK

In the secondary market for common stock, investors buy and sell shares with other in-vestors. If you think of the primary market as the new-car showroom at an automotive dealer, where cars are first sold to the public, then the secondary market is just the used-car lot.

Secondary market stock trading among investors is directed through three channels. An investor may trade:

1. Directly with other investors.

2. Indirectly through a broker who arranges transactions for others.

3. Directly with a dealer who buys and sells securities from inventory.

FIGURE 5.1 IPO Tombstone

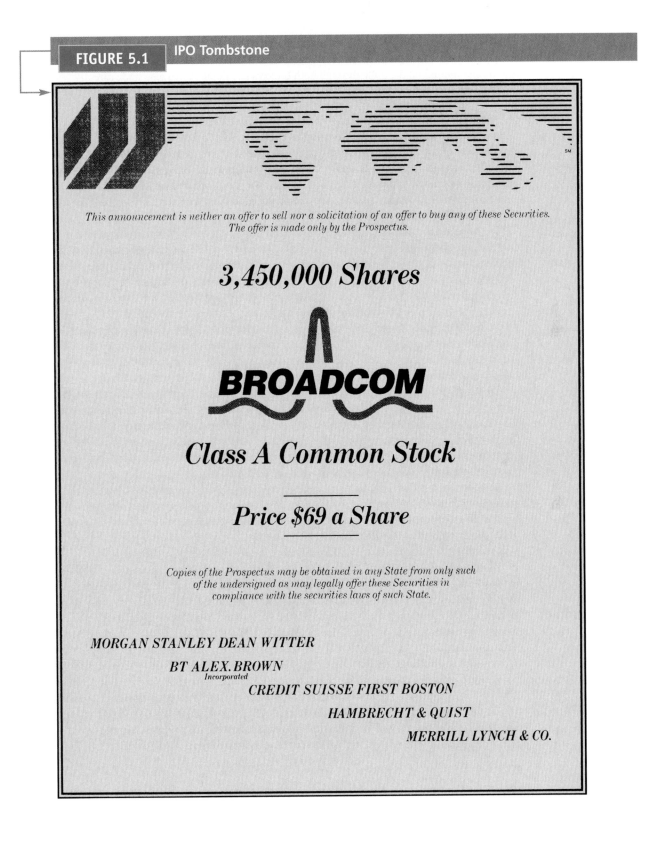

This announcement is neither an offer to sell nor a solicitation of an offer to buy any of these Securities.
The offer is made only by the Prospectus.

3,450,000 Shares

BROADCOM

Class A Common Stock

Price $69 a Share

Copies of the Prospectus may be obtained in any State from only such
of the undersigned as may legally offer these Securities in
compliance with the securities laws of such State.

MORGAN STANLEY DEAN WITTER

BT ALEX. BROWN
Incorporated

CREDIT SUISSE FIRST BOSTON

HAMBRECHT & QUIST

MERRILL LYNCH & CO.

As we discussed in Chapter 2, for individual investors, almost all common stock transactions are made through a broker. However, large institutional investors, such as pension funds and mutual funds, trade through both brokers and dealers, and also trade directly with other institutional investors.

DEALERS AND BROKERS

Because most securities transactions involve dealers and brokers, it is important that you understand exactly what these terms mean. A **dealer** maintains an inventory and stands ready to buy and sell at any time. By contrast, a **broker** brings buyers and sellers together but does not maintain an inventory. Thus, when we speak of used-car dealers and real estate brokers, we recognize that the used-car dealer maintains an inventory, whereas the real estate broker normally does not.

In the securities markets, a dealer stands ready to buy securities from investors wishing to sell them and to sell securities to investors wishing to buy them. An important part of the dealer function involves maintaining an inventory to accommodate temporary buy and sell order imbalances. The price a dealer is willing to pay is called the **bid price**. The price at which a dealer will sell is called the **ask price** (sometimes called the offer or offering price). The difference between the bid and ask prices is called the **spread**.

A dealer attempts to profit by selling securities at a price higher than the average price paid for them. Of course, this is a goal for all investors, but the distinguishing characteristic of securities dealers is that they hold securities in inventory only until the first opportunity to resell them. Essentially, trading from inventory is their business.

Dealers exist in all areas of the economy, of course, not just in the stock markets. For example, your local university bookstore is both a primary and secondary market textbook dealer. If you buy a new book, then this is a primary market transaction. If you buy a used book, this is a secondary market transaction, and you pay the store's ask price. If you sell the book back, you receive the store's bid price, often half the ask price. The bookstore's spread is the difference between the bid and the ask price.

In contrast, a securities broker arranges transactions between investors, matching investors wishing to buy securities with investors wishing to sell securities. Brokers may match investors with other investors, investors with dealers, and sometimes even dealers with dealers. The distinctive characteristic of securities brokers is that they do not buy or sell securities for their own account. Facilitating trades by others is their business.

Most common stock trading is directed through an organized stock exchange or a trading network. Whether on a stock exchange or through a trading network, the goal is to match investors wishing to buy stocks with investors wishing to sell stocks. The largest, most active organized stock exchange in the United States is the New York Stock Exchange (NYSE). Second and third in size are the Chicago Stock Exchange (CHX) and the American Stock Exchange (AMEX), respectively. These are followed by four regional exchanges: the Boston Stock Exchange (BSE), the Cincinnati Stock Exchange (CSE) (which is actually located in Chicago!), the Pacific Stock Exchange (PSE) in Los Angeles, and the Philadelphia Stock Exchange (PHLX). The major competitor to the organized stock exchanges is the vast trading network known as NASDAQ. In 1998, NASDAQ and the AMEX merged to form a single company, but the two organizations retained their original features. We next discuss the organization of the NYSE, and then we turn to a discussion of NASDAQ.

dealer
A trader who buys and sells securities from inventory.

broker
An intermediary who arranges security transactions among investors.

bid price
The price a dealer is willing to pay.

ask price
The price at which a dealer is willing to sell. Also called the *offer* or *offering* price.

spread
The difference between the bid and ask prices.

CHECK THIS

5.1a Is an IPO a primary or a secondary market transaction?

5.1b Which is bigger, the bid price or the ask price? Why?

5.1c What is the difference between a securities broker and a securities dealer?

5.2 The New York Stock Exchange

The New York Stock Exchange (NYSE, pronounced "Ny-see"), popularly known as the Big Board, celebrated its bicentennial in 1992. It has occupied its current building on Wall Street since the turn of the twentieth century. For more than 200 years, the NYSE operated as a not-for-profit corporation. However, by the time you read this, the NYSE will almost certainly be a publicly owned, for-profit corporation. Our subsequent discussion in this chapter concerning the NYSE reflects the structure of the exchange as it exists at the time of this writing. How this structure will change as a result of the NYSE's decision to become publicly owned has not been announced at the time this is written.

NYSE MEMBERSHIP

The NYSE has 1,366 exchange **members**, who are said to own "seats" on the exchange. Technically, a seat is the personal property of the individual purchasing it. Typically, however, the individual who is the registered owner of a seat is an employee of a securities firm such as Merrill Lynch. The securities firm has actually paid for the seat and is effectively the owner. The firm is said to be a member organization (or member firm), and some member organizations own numerous seats on the exchange in this way.

Exchange seat owners can buy and sell securities on the exchange floor without paying commissions. For this and other reasons, exchange seats are valuable assets and are regularly bought and sold. Interestingly, prior to 1986, the highest seat price paid was $625,000 just before the 1929 market crash. Since then, the lowest seat price paid was $55,000 in 1977. As it turns out, that was a very good price for the buyer. In 2005, seat prices reached a new record high, $3 million.

In addition to paying the price of a seat, a prospective NYSE member must be sponsored by two current members and possess a clean record with regard to security laws violations or felony convictions of any kind. However, it is not necessary to actually own a seat to trade commission-free on the exchange floor, since seats can be leased. Leasing is common, and about half of all NYSE seats are leased. Even if you only wish to lease a seat on the exchange, you must pass the same close scrutiny as someone wishing to buy a seat.

Exchange members elect 24 members of a 27-member board of directors. The three additional board members—the chairman of the board, the executive vice chairman, and the president—are *ex officio* members selected by the Board. "*Ex officio*" means that they are members of the board of directors by virtue of their positions as appointed professional managers of the exchange. While the board sets exchange policy, actual management is performed by a professional staff. Technically, NYSE members collectively own the exchange, but the NYSE is organized to insulate professional staff from undue pressure from exchange members.

TYPES OF MEMBERS

The largest number of NYSE members are registered as **floor brokers**. The business of a floor broker is to execute customer orders to buy and sell stocks. A floor broker's primary responsibility to customers is to get the best possible price for their orders. Their number varies, but over 500 NYSE members are floor brokers.

NYSE floor brokers typically are employees of brokerage companies that are NYSE member firms, in which case they are called "house" or "commission" brokers. Member firms operating as brokerage companies accept customer orders to buy and sell securities and relay these orders to their floor brokers for execution. Member firm activities represent the most vital functions of the NYSE, simply because their business is the original reason the exchange exists.

In contrast to house brokers, independent brokers are individuals who essentially make money by executing orders on a freelance basis. At one time, independent brokers were known as "$2 brokers," reflecting a standard fee for their services. Today, they help house brokers manage orders on busy days, and they may also execute orders directly for individual customers, particularly those with specialized needs.

Second in number of NYSE members are **specialists**, so named because each acts as an assigned dealer for a small set of securities. With a few exceptions, each security listed for trading on the NYSE is assigned to a single specialist. Specialists are also called *market makers* because they are obligated to maintain a fair and orderly market for the securities assigned to them.

As market makers, specialists post bid prices and ask prices for securities assigned to them. The bid price is the price at which a specialist is obligated to buy a security from a seller, and an ask price is the price at which a specialist is obligated to sell a security to a buyer. As we have discussed elsewhere, the difference between the bid price and the ask price is called the bid-ask spread, or simply the spread.

Specialists make a market by standing ready to buy at bid prices and to sell at ask prices when there is a temporary disparity between the flow of buy and sell orders for a security. In this capacity, they act as dealers for their own accounts. In so doing, they provide liquidity to the market. Their function is vital, since the work of commission brokers would be quite difficult without the specialists. As we discuss in the next section, specialists also act as brokers.

Almost 500 NYSE members are specialists. These specialists work for one of eleven (as of 2005) specialist firms, and over half of all NYSE trading is concentrated in stocks managed by the three largest specialist firms. These three largest specialist firms and the number of stocks for which they act as specialists as of 2005 are shown immediately below.

Specialist Firm	Number of Stocks
LaBranche & Co.	570
Spear, Leeds & Kellogg Specialists	552
Banc of America Specialist, Inc.	426

In recent years, floor brokers have become less important on the exchange floor because of the efficient **SuperDOT system** (the "DOT" stands for designated order turnaround), which allows orders to be transmitted electronically directly to the specialist. SuperDOT trading now accounts for a substantial percentage of all trading on the NYSE, particularly on small orders.

Finally, a small number of NYSE members are **floor traders**, who independently trade for their own accounts. Floor traders try to anticipate temporary price fluctuations and profit from them by buying low and selling high. In recent decades, the number of floor traders has declined substantially, suggesting that it has become increasingly difficult to profit from short-term trading on the exchange floor.

NYSE-LISTED STOCKS

A company is said to be "listed" on the NYSE if its stock is traded there. In 2005, stocks from about 2,800 companies were listed on the Big Board, with a market value of about $13 trillion. This total includes many large companies so well known that we easily recognize them by their initials—for example, IBM, GE, and GM. This total also includes many companies that are not so readily recognized. For example, relatively few would instantly recognize AEP as American Electric Power, but AEX might be recognized as American Express.

U.S. companies that wish to have their stock listed for trading on the Big Board must apply for the privilege. If the application is approved, the company must pay an initial listing fee. In 2005, this fee was $36,800, plus a per-share charge that ranged from $14,750 per million shares for the first 2 million shares, to $1,900 for each million shares above 300 million. In addition to an initial listing fee, the NYSE assesses an annual listing fee. In 2005, the annual listing fee was $930 per million (subject to a $35,000 minimum fee).

The NYSE has minimum requirements for companies wishing to apply for listing on the Big Board. Although the requirements might change from time to time, some example minimum requirements in effect in 2005 included:

1. The company's total number of shareholders must be at least 2,200, and stock trading in the previous six months must have been at least 100,000 shares a month on average.

2. At least 1.1 million stock shares must be held in public hands.

3. Publicly held shares must have at least $100 million in market value ($60 million for IPOs).

4. The company must have aggregate earnings of $10 million before taxes in the previous three years and $2 million pretax earnings in each of the preceding two years.

In practice, most companies with stock listed on the NYSE easily exceed these minimum listing requirements.

CHECK THIS

5.2a   What are the types of members of the New York Stock Exchange?

5.2b   Which NYSE member type is the most numerous? Which type is the second most numerous?

5.3 Operation of the New York Stock Exchange

Now that we have a basic idea of how the NYSE is organized and who the major players are, we turn to the question of how trading actually takes place. Fundamentally, the business of the NYSE is to attract and process *order flow*—the flow of customer orders to buy and sell stocks. Customers of the NYSE are the millions of individual investors and tens of thousands of institutional investors who place their orders to buy and sell NYSE-listed stock shares with member-firm brokers.

The NYSE has been quite successful in attracting order flow. In 2005, the average stock trading volume on the NYSE was well over 1 billion shares per day. About one-third of all NYSE stock trading volume is attributable to individual investors, and almost half is derived from institutional investors. The remainder represents NYSE member trading, which is largely attributed to specialists acting as market makers.

NYSE FLOOR ACTIVITY

Quite likely you have seen film footage of the NYSE trading floor on television, or you may have visited the NYSE and viewed exchange floor activity from the gallery (when it is open). Either way, you saw a big room, about the size of a small basketball gym. This big room is aptly called "the big room." There are several other, smaller rooms that you normally do not see. One is called "the garage" because that is what it was before it was taken over for securities trading, and the other is called the "blue room" because, well, the room is painted blue.

On the floor of the exchange are a number of stations, each with a roughly figure-eight shape. These stations have multiple counters with numerous computer terminal screens above and on the sides. People operate behind and in front of the counters in relatively stationary positions.

Other people move around on the exchange floor, frequently returning to the many telephone booths positioned along the exchange walls. In all, you may have been reminded of worker ants moving around an ant colony. It is natural to wonder: What are all those people doing down there (and why are so many wearing funny-looking coats)?

As an overview of exchange floor activity, here is a quick look at what goes on. Each of the counters at the figure-eight shaped stations is a **specialist's post**. Specialists normally operate in front of their posts to monitor and manage trading in the stocks assigned to them. Clerical employees working for the specialists operate behind the counters. Moving from the many telephone booths out to the exchange floor and back again are swarms of floor brokers, receiving relayed customer orders, walking out to specialist posts where the orders can be executed, and returning to confirm order executions and receive new customer orders.

To better understand activity on the NYSE trading floor, imagine yourself as a floor broker. Your phone clerk has just handed you an order to sell 3,000 shares of KO (the ticker symbol for Coca-Cola common stock) for a customer of the brokerage company that employs you. The order is a **market order**, meaning that the customer wants to sell the stock at the best possible price as soon as possible. You immediately walk (running violates exchange rules) to the specialist's post where KO stock is traded.

Upon approaching the specialist's post where KO is traded, you check the terminal screen for information on the current market price for KO stock. The screen reveals that the last executed trade for KO was at 70.63 and that the specialist is bidding 70.50 per share. You could immediately sell to the specialist at 70.50, but that would be too easy.

Instead, as the customer's representative, you are obligated to get the best possible price. It is your job to "work" the order, and your job depends on providing satisfactory order execution service. So you look around for another broker who represents a customer who wants to buy KO stock. Luckily, you quickly find another broker at the specialist's post with a market order to buy 3,000 shares of KO. Noticing that the specialist is asking 70.75 per share, you both agree to execute your orders with each other at a price of 70.63. This price, about halfway between the specialist's bid and ask prices, saves each of your customers approximately $.13 \times 3,000 = \$390$ compared to the specialist's prices.

In a trade of this type, in which one floor broker buys from another, the specialist acts only as a broker assisting in matching buy orders and sell orders. On an actively traded stock, many floor brokers can be buying and selling. In such cases, trading is said to occur "in the crowd." Thus, the specialist functions as a broker as long as buyers and sellers are available. The specialist steps in as a dealer only when necessary to fill an order that would otherwise go unfilled.

In reality, not all orders are executed so easily. For example, suppose you are unable to quickly find another broker with an order to buy 3,000 shares of KO. Because you have a market order, you may have no choice but to sell to the specialist at the bid price of 70.50. In this case, the need to execute an order quickly takes priority, and the specialist provides the necessary liquidity to allow immediate order execution.

In this situation, the specialist is often able to help floor brokers by agreeing to "stop" the stock. By stopping stock for a sell order, the specialist agrees to try to help you get a better price while also guaranteeing a minimum price. For your sell order, the specialist might guarantee a minimum price of 70.50 but try to get a better price, say, 70.63. So agreed, you leave the order with the specialist. If the next offer to buy KO is at a price of 70.63, the specialist will fill your order at that price. But if no better offer appears forthcoming, the specialist will execute the order at the guaranteed price of 70.50—if necessary, from the specialist's own inventory.

specialist's post
Fixed place on the exchange floor where the specialist operates.

market order
A customer order to buy or sell securities marked for immediate execution at the current market price.

Stopping stock is also a goodwill gesture. The NYSE places great emphasis on the quality of performance by specialists, which is evaluated regularly through surveys of floor brokers' satisfaction. Specialists are expected to assist brokers in getting the best prices for customer orders, to provide liquidity to the market, and to maintain an orderly market for all securities assigned to them. Stopping stock helps accomplish these objectives.

Note an important caveat concerning this discussion of NYSE floor operations. If you think about it, there's no way that the NYSE could trade more than a billion shares a day using this system. It's just not physically possible. What actually happens is that over 99 percent of orders are processed electronically using the SuperDOT. Based on volume of orders submitted, however, that number drops to about 75 percent. The implication is that larger orders are handled by floor brokers, but smaller orders are not.

SPECIAL ORDER TYPES

limit order
Customer order to buy or sell securities with a specified "limit" price. The order can be executed only at the limit price or better.

Many orders are transmitted to the NYSE floor as **limit orders**. A limit order is an order to buy or sell stock, where the customer specifies a maximum price he is willing to pay in the case of a buy order, or a minimum price he will accept in the case of a sell order. For example, suppose that as a NYSE floor broker, you receive a limit order to sell 3,000 shares of KO stock at 70.75. This means that the customer is not willing to accept any price below 70.75 per share, even if it means missing the trade.

One strategy for handling limit orders is to hold the order and frequently check for potential buyers at the specialist post for KO stock. However, this is unnecessary because you can leave a limit order with the specialist. As a service to brokers, NYSE specialists display unfilled limit orders on the terminal screens at their posts for all approaching brokers to see. If another broker wants to buy KO at 70.75, the specialist will execute the sale for you. This service saves considerable time and energy for busy floor brokers. Indeed, monitoring and executing unfilled limit orders is a very important function of the NYSE specialist.

stop order
Customer order to buy or sell securities when a preset "stop" price is reached.

A **stop order** may appear similar to a limit order, but there is an important difference. With a stop order, the customer specifies a "stop" price. This stop price serves as a trigger point. No trade can occur until the stock price reaches this stop price. When the stock price reaches the stop price, the stop order is immediately converted into a market order. Since the order is now a market order, the customer may get a price that is better or worse than the stop price. Thus, the stop price only serves as a trigger point for conversion into a market order. Unlike a limit price, the stop price places no limit on the price at which a trade can occur. Once converted to a market order, the trade is executed just like any other market order.

The most common type of stop order is a *stop-sell* order, which is an order to sell shares if the stock price falls to a specified stop price below the current stock price. This type of order is generally called a *stop-loss* because it is usually intended to limit losses on a long position. The other type is a *stop-buy* order, which is an order to buy shares if the price rises to a specified stop price above the current stock price. Stop-buy orders are often placed in conjunction with short sales, again as means of limiting losses.

Placing stop-loss orders is frequently touted as a smart trading strategy, but there are a couple of issues we should mention. For concreteness, suppose you buy 1,000 shares of GoGo Corp. at $20. You simultaneously place a stop-sell order at $15. Thus you seem to have limited your potential loss to $5 per share.

Unfortunately, after the market closes, a rumor circulates that GoGo has uncovered a significant accounting fraud. The next morning, the stock opens at $8, meaning the first trade occurs at $8 per share. Because this price is below your $15 stop price, a market order to sell your stock will be placed and executed, and you'll lose much more than $5 per share. What you discover is that your stop-loss guarantees only that a market order to sell will be placed as soon as the stock trades at $15 *or below*.

Adding insult to injury, after your stock is sold, a creditable announcement is made indicating that the rumor is false. GoGo shares promptly bounce back to $20, but you were

Order Type	Buy	Sell
Market order	Buy at best price available for immediate execution.	Sell at best price available for immediate execution.
Limit order	Buy at best price available, but not more than the preset limit price. Forgo purchase if limit is not met.	Sell at best price available, but not less than the preset limit price. Forgo sale if limit is not met.
Stop order	Convert to a market order to buy when the stock price crosses the stop price from below.	Convert to a market order to sell when the stock price crosses the stop price from above. Also known as a "stop-loss."
Stop-limit order	Convert to a limit order to buy when the stock price crosses the stop price from below.	Convert to a limit order to sell when the stock price crosses the stop price from above.

TABLE 5.1 Stock Market Order Types

sold out at a big loss. Thus, a second danger in blindly using stop-loss orders is that volatile conditions can lead to an unfavorable stop sale. Table 5.1 summarizes the characteristics of limit and stop orders.

A limit price can be attached to a stop order to create a *stop-limit order*. This is different from a simple stop order in that once the stock price reaches the preset stop price the order is converted into a limit order. By contrast, a simple stop order is converted into a market order. At this point, the limit order is just like any other limit order. Notice that with a stop-limit order you must specify two prices, the stop and the limit. The two prices can be the same, or they can be different. In our GoGo Corp. example, you could place a stop-limit sell order at $15 stop, $12 limit. This order converts to a limit order to sell at $12 or better if the price ever hits $15 or below. Thus you will never sell below $12. Of course, you may never sell at all unless your limit price is reached! Our nearby *Work the Web* box shows how these orders are entered in an actual online brokerage account.

Another type of order that requires special attention is the *short-sale order*. As explained elsewhere, a short sale involves borrowing stock shares and then selling the borrowed shares in the hope of buying them back later at a lower price. Short-sale loans are normally arranged through the customer's broker. New York Stock Exchange rules require that when shares are sold as part of a short-sale transaction, the order must be marked as a short-sale transaction when it is transmitted to the NYSE floor.

NYSE uptick rule

Rule for short sales requiring that before a short sale can be executed, the last price change must be an uptick.

Sell orders marked as short sales are subject to the **NYSE uptick rule**.[1] According to the NYSE uptick rule, a short sale can be executed only if the last price change was an uptick. For example, suppose the last two trades were executed at 55.50 and then 55.63. The last price change was an uptick of .13, and a short sale can be executed at a price of 55.63 or higher. Alternatively, suppose the last two trades were executed at 55.50 and 55.25, where the last price change was a downtick of .25. In this case, a short sale can be executed only at a price higher than 55.25.

The NYSE enacted the uptick rule to make it more difficult for speculators to drive down a stock's price by repeated short sales. Interestingly, the uptick rule is a NYSE rule only and does not necessarily apply to short-sale transactions executed elsewhere. Since many NYSE-listed stocks are now traded elsewhere, the uptick rule is less of a constraint than it once was. The NASDAQ has a similar rule.

Finally, colored coats are worn by many of the people on the floor of the exchange. The color of the coat indicates the person's job or position. Clerks, runners, visitors, exchange

[1]In 2004, the SEC adopted Regulation SHO, which includes a temporary rule that establishes a procedure to suspend the uptick rule for specified securities. The NYSE is a strong proponent to keep the uptick rule.

To illustrate the importance of getting order types straight, we have captured the actual trading screen from one of the largest online brokers, Ameritrade. On the screen below, the stock entered is GE, which is conglomerate giant General Electric. The order being placed is a limit order to buy 100 shares at $34.11.

The limit order is good for the day only. Under "Special Instructions" you will notice "AON," which stands for "all or none." This means we want the full 100 shares, or no shares at all. The routing selection actually allows us to choose the market on which the trade will take place.

Review your order (place within 90 sec.)   <u>Edit time limit</u>

Buy 100 shares of **GE (GENERAL ELEC CO COM)**
Last: 34.16, Bid: 34.15, Ask: 34.16, Bid/Ask size: 5400X1500
Real Time Quote Provided by NYSE @ 3:07:37 PM EDT

Limit at $34.11

Expiration:	Day
Routing:	Auto Routing
Sp. Instructions:	AON

Estimated Total*: $-3,411.00

[Place Order] [Change Order] [Do Not Place Order]

Clicking on the "Review Order" button allows you to double-check your order before you submit it for transaction. Here is our review screen:

Review your order (place within 90 sec.)   <u>Edit time limit</u>

Buy 100 shares of **GE (GENERAL ELEC CO COM)**
Last: 34.16, Bid: 34.15, Ask: 34.16, Bid/Ask size: 5400X1500
Real Time Quote Provided by NYSE @ 3:07:37 PM EDT

Limit at $34.11

Expiration:	Day
Routing:	Auto Routing
Sp. Instructions:	AON

Estimated Total*: $-3,411.00

[Place Order] [Change Order] [Do Not Place Order]

After checking to make sure we have entered everything correctly, we just hit the "Place Order" button to submit our order.

officials, and so on, wear particular colors to identify themselves. Also, since things can get a little hectic on a busy day with the result that good clothing may not last long, the cheap coats offer some protection. Nevertheless, many specialists and floor brokers wear a good business suit every day simply out of habit and pride.

CHECK THIS

5.3a What are the four main types of orders to buy and sell common stocks?

5.3b What do specialists do?

5.3c What is a limit order? How do limit and stop orders differ?

5.4 NASDAQ

In terms of total dollar volume of trading, the second largest stock market in the United States is NASDAQ (say "Naz-dak"). In fact, in terms of companies listed and, on most days recently, number of shares traded, NASDAQ is bigger than the NYSE. The somewhat odd name is derived from the acronym NASDAQ, which stands for National Association of Securities Dealers Automated Quotations system. But NASDAQ is now a proper name in its own right.

NASDAQ OPERATIONS

NASDAQ's Web site is
www.nasdaq.com
Click on "NASDAQ
Corporate."

Introduced in 1971, the NASDAQ market is a computer network of securities dealers who disseminate timely security price quotes to NASDAQ subscribers. These dealers act as market makers for securities listed on NASDAQ. As market makers, NASDAQ dealers post bid and ask prices at which they accept sell and buy orders, respectively. With each price quote, they also post the number of stock shares that they obligate themselves to trade at their quoted prices.

Like NYSE specialists, NASDAQ market makers trade on an inventory basis, using their inventory as a buffer to absorb buy and sell order imbalances. Unlike the NYSE specialist system, NASDAQ features multiple market makers for actively traded stocks. Thus, there are two key differences between the NYSE and NASDAQ:

1. NASDAQ is a computer network and has no physical location where trading takes place.

2. NASDAQ has a multiple market maker system rather than a specialist system.

over-the-counter (OTC) market
Securities market in which trading is almost exclusively done through dealers who buy and sell for their own inventories.

Traditionally, a securities market largely characterized by dealers who buy and sell securities for their own inventories is called an **over-the-counter (OTC) market**. Consequently, NASDAQ is often referred to as an OTC market. However, in their efforts to promote a distinct image, NASDAQ officials prefer that the term OTC not be used when referring to the NASDAQ market. Nevertheless, old habits die hard, and many people still refer to NASDAQ as an OTC market.

The NASDAQ is actually made up of two separate markets, the NASDAQ National Market (NNM) and the NASDAQ Capital Market. The Capital Market was previously known as the Smallcap Market. As the market for NASDAQ's larger and more actively traded securities, the NASDAQ National Market lists about 4,000 securities, including some of the best-known companies in the world. The NASDAQ Capital Market is for small companies and lists about 1,000 individual securities. As you might guess, an important difference in the two markets is that the National Market has more stringent listing

You can actually watch trading take place on the Web by visiting one of the biggest ECNs, INET at www.island.com. (INET used to be called Island.) INET is somewhat unusual in that the "order book," meaning the list of buy and sell orders, is public in real time.

As shown, we have captured a sample of orders for Intel Corporation. On the left-hand side are the buy orders. On the right-hand side are sell orders. All orders are limit orders, and both the limit price and quantity are shown. The inside quotes (the highest bid, or buy, and the lowest ask, or sell, order) in this market are at the top, so we sometimes hear the expression "top of the book" quotes.

If you visit the site, you can see trading take place as limit orders are entered and executed. Notice that on this particular day, by 5:16 P.M., Island had traded more than 21 million shares of Intel. At that time, the inside quotes were a bid price of $23.75 and an ask price of $23.82. In addition to the orders shown, there were also 19 more buy orders and one more sell order.

INET home	system stats	help

GET STOCK

INTC go

☐ Aggregate by Price

INTC

INTC

LAST MATCH		TODAY'S ACTIVITY	
Price	23.7600	Orders	261,945
Time	17:08:09	Volume	21,357,760

BUY ORDERS		SELL ORDERS	
SHARES	PRICE	SHARES	PRICE
752	23.7500	3,750	23.8200
7,000	23.7200	4,000	23.8500
1,000	23.7100	1,000	23.8700
300	23.7000	500	23.8700
2,400	23.6800	1,000	23.8800
2,400	23.6800	100	24.2900
500	23.6800	1,000	24.3500
2,000	23.6700	300	24.4300
2,000	23.6600	500	24.4900
600	23.6600	2,000	24.6800
1,000	23.6500	500	24.7000
2,000	23.6400	300	24.8500
1,000	23.6400	81	26.0000
100	23.6200	100	27.0000
300	23.5700	300	29.9000
(19 more)		(1 more)	

As of 17:16:53

requirements. Of course, as Capital Market companies become more established, they may move up to the National Market.

NASDAQ PARTICIPANTS

As we mentioned previously, the NASDAQ has historically been a dealer market, characterized by competing market makers. In 2005, there were about 300 such market makers, which amounts to about 15 stocks per market maker.

In a very important development, in the late 1990s, the NASDAQ system was opened to so-called **electronic communications networks (ECNs)**. ECNs are basically Web sites that allow investors to trade directly with one another. Our nearby *Work the Web* box describes one of the biggest ECNs, Island (www.island.com), and contains important information about ECN "order books."

electronic communications network (ECN)
A Web site that allows investors to trade directly with each other.

Investor buy and sell orders placed on ECNs are transmitted to the NASDAQ and displayed along with market maker bid and ask prices. As a result, the ECNs open up the NASDAQ by essentially allowing individual investors to enter orders, not just market makers. As a result, the ECNs act to increase liquidity and competition.

If you check prices on the Web for both NASDAQ- and NYSE-listed stocks, you'll notice an interesting difference. For NASDAQ stocks, you can actually see the bid and ask prices as well as recent transactions information. The bid and ask prices for the NASDAQ listings you see represent **inside quotes**, that is, the highest bid and the lowest ask prices. For a relatively small fee (or possibly even free from your broker), you can even have access to "Level II" quotes, which show all of the posted bid and ask prices and, frequently, the identity of the market maker. Of course, NYSE specialists post bid and ask prices as well; they are just not disclosed to the general public (they are available by subscription at a cost substantially higher than that for Level II NASDAQ quotes).

The success of the NASDAQ National Market as a competitor to NYSE and other organized exchanges can be judged by its ability to attract stock listings by companies that traditionally might have chosen to be listed on the NYSE. Such well-known companies as Microsoft, Apple Computer, Intel, Dell, Yahoo!, and Starbucks list their securities on NASDAQ.

inside quotes
Highest bid quotes and the lowest ask quotes offered by dealers for a security.

CHECK THIS

5.4a   How does NASDAQ differ from the NYSE?
5.4b   What are the different levels of access to the NASDAQ network?

5.5 NYSE and NASDAQ Competitors

third market
Off-exchange market for securities listed on an organized exchange.

The NYSE and NASDAQ face strong competition in the market for order execution services from securities trading firms operating in the **third market**. The phrase "third market" refers to trading in exchange-listed securities that occurs off the exchange on which the security is listed. For example, a substantial volume of NYSE-listed stock trading is executed through independent securities trading firms.

fourth market
Market for exchange-listed securities in which investors trade directly with other investors, usually through a computer network.

NASDAQ and NYSE also face substantial competition from the **fourth market**. The term "fourth market" refers to direct trading of exchange-listed securities among investors. A good example of fourth-market trading activity is Instinet, an ECN (and one of the oldest) that facilitates trading among its subscribers, particularly after-hours trading. However, as we discussed in our previous section, these fourth-market ECNs are increasingly becoming integrated into the NASDAQ system.

The third and fourth markets are not the only NYSE and NASDAQ competitors. Regional exchanges also attract substantial trading volume away from NYSE and NASDAQ. For example, thousands of stocks are dually listed on NYSE and either on NASDAQ or on at least one regional exchange.

CHECK THIS

5.5a   What is the third market for securities?
5.5b   What is the fourth market for securities?

5.6 Stock Market Information

Many newspapers publish current price information for a selection of stocks. In the United States, the newspaper best known for reporting stock price information is *The Wall Street Journal*. Investors interested in an overview of stock market activity refer to daily summaries. Among other things, these summaries contain information regarding several stock market indexes. Immediately below, we describe the most important stock market indexes.

THE DOW JONES INDUSTRIAL AVERAGE

WWW

For more on the Dow, visit

averages.dowjones. com

Look for "Averages" under "Blue Chip Indexes."

The most widely followed barometer of day-to-day stock market activity is the Dow Jones Industrial Average (DJIA), often called the "Dow" for short. The DJIA is an index of the stock prices of 30 large companies representative of American industry. There are two more specialized Dow Jones averages, a utilities average and a transportation average. We will focus on the industrial average. Figure 5.2 reproduces a chart of the DJIA from "The Dow Jones Averages" column, which is published every day in *The Wall Street Journal*.

Figure 5.2 shows daily high, low, and closing prices for the DJIA from April 2005 through September 2005. As indicated in the upper right-hand portion, the vertical bars in the chart indicate the range of index high and low values on each trading day. The tick mark

FIGURE 5.2 Dow Jones Industrial Average

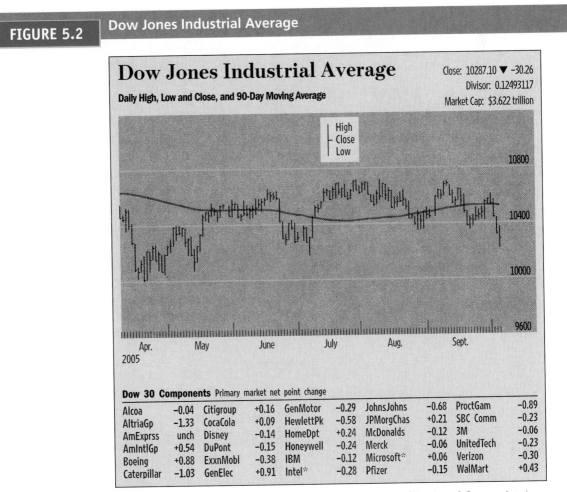

Source: *The Wall Street Journal*, October 7, 2005. Reprinted by permission of Dow Jones & Company, Inc. via Copyright Clearance Center, Inc. © 2005 Dow Jones & Company, Inc. All Rights Reserved Worldwide.

on the right side of each day's bar marks the closing value of the index on that day. We therefore see that, based on closing prices, the Dow reached a high of about 10,700 during this period compared to a low of about 10,000. Figure 5.2 also contains a box that lists the 30 well-known companies in the index.

Although the Dow is the most familiar stock market index, a number of other indexes are widely followed. In fact, as we begin to discuss next, the Dow is not the most representative index by any means, and the way it is computed presents various problems that can make it difficult to interpret.

STOCK MARKET INDEXES

What are the Russell indexes? Visit www.russell.com to find out.

The "Dow Jones Averages" column is informative, but a serious market watcher may be interested in more detail regarding recent stock market activity. A more comprehensive view of stock market trading is contained in Figure 5.3, which is also published daily in *The Wall Street Journal.*

The excerpt we examine here, "Major Stock Indexes," reports information about a variety of stock market indexes in addition to the Dow Jones averages. Of the non–Dow Jones

---

FIGURE 5.3 Stock Market Major Indexes

Major Stock Indexes

	DAILY					52-WEEK			YTD
Dow Jones Averages	HIGH	LOW	CLOSE	NET CHG	% CHG	HIGH	LOW	% CHG	% CHG
30 Industrials	10369.55	10218.09	10287.10	−30.26	−0.29	10940.55	9749.99	+ 1.60	− 4.60
20 Transportations	3697.58	3618.12	3650.21	+26.69	+0.74	3876.13	3282.43	+ 9.23	− 3.89
15 Utilities	416.22	401.86	408.68	− 6.49	−1.56	437.63	299.07	+36.65	+22.01
65 Composite	3457.65	3390.53	3423.56	− 9.52	−0.28	3542.87	3051.58	+10.46	+ 0.82
Dow Jones Indexes									
Wilshire 5000	12012.58	11811.17	11904.11	−64.04	−0.54	12469.86	10748.01	+ 7.75	− 0.56
US Total Market	290.26	285.35	287.66	− 1.51	−0.52	300.65	260.08	+ 7.40	− 0.59
US Large-Cap	256.94	252.71	254.75	− 0.88	−0.34	265.80	235.14	+ 4.74	− 1.91
US Mid-Cap	390.84	383.55	386.62	− 4.17	−1.07	404.65	323.22	+16.56	+ 4.31
US Small-Cap	421.37	412.49	416.13	− 3.99	−0.95	442.84	362.30	+11.81	+ 0.43
US Growth	1082.50	1063.14	1071.65	− 6.61	−0.61	1125.96	979.87	+ 6.38	− 1.75
US Value	1524.57	1499.69	1511.98	− 5.86	−0.39	1580.88	1375.59	+ 6.57	− 0.63
Global Titans 50	194.17	191.74	193.20	− 0.38	−0.20	199.75	179.07	+ 5.03	− 0.93
Asian Titans 50	133.13	129.25	129.62	− 3.54	−2.66	135.59	106.04	+19.90	+ 7.78
DJ STOXX 50	3252.07	3204.46	3215.77	−40.60	−1.25	3296.04	2638.92	+16.97	+15.89
Nasdaq Stock Market									
Nasdaq Comp	2110.83	2069.04	2084.08	−18.94	−0.90	2218.15	1903.02	+ 6.96	− 4.20
Nasdaq 100	1576.36	1540.34	1552.94	−18.58	−1.18	1627.46	1406.85	+ 6.67	− 4.21
Biotech	769.33	741.69	748.96	−20.73	−2.69	803.76	641.35	+ 6.28	− 2.55
Computer	933.35	913.75	920.75	− 8.79	−0.95	989.32	839.02	+ 6.83	− 4.61
Standard & Poor's Indexes									
500 Index	1202.14	1181.92	1191.49	− 4.90	−0.41	1245.04	1094.81	+ 5.38	− 1.69
MidCap 400	696.48	684.00	689.85	− 6.33	−0.91	725.02	583.00	+15.30	+ 4.00
SmallCap 600	339.79	332.36	335.52	− 2.90	−0.86	357.86	286.80	+13.27	+ 2.04
SuperComp 1500	271.52	266.89	269.07	− 1.27	−0.47	281.41	245.07	+ 6.50	− 1.06
New York Stock Exchange and Others									
NYSE Comp	7459.94	7349.95	7399.66	−36.70	−0.49	7663.82	6516.10	+11.20	+ 2.06
NYSE Financial	7392.89	7314.18	7350.53	− 3.76	−0.05	7512.69	6639.74	+ 7.20	− 1.91
Russell 2000	648.54	633.38	639.45	− 5.53	−0.86	688.51	564.88	+ 9.76	− 1.86
Value Line	400.21	392.80	395.89	− 2.71	−0.68	420.30	354.47	+ 8.46	− 2.11
Amex Comp	1684.14	1643.48	1651.64	−32.41	−1.92	1738.76	1273.40	+29.19	+15.15

Source: Reuters

indexes shown, by far the best known and most widely followed is the Standard and Poor's Index of 500 stocks, commonly abbreviated as the S&P 500, or often just the S&P. We have seen this index before. In Chapter 1, we used it as a benchmark to track the performance of large common stocks for the last eight decades.

If you were to scrutinize the various indexes in Figure 5.3, you would quickly find that there are essentially four differences between them: (1) the market covered; (2) the types of stocks included; (3) how many stocks are included; and (4) how the index is calculated.

The first three of these differences are straightforward. Some indexes listed in Figure 5.3, such as the Dow Jones Utilities, focus on specific industries. Others, such as the NASDAQ Composite, focus on particular markets. Some have a small number of stocks; others, such as the Wilshire 5000 (which actually has over 6,000!), have a huge number.

How stock market indexes are computed is not quite so straightforward, but it is important to understand. There are two major types of stock market index: price-weighted and value-weighted. With a **price-weighted index**, stocks are held in the index in proportion to their share prices. With a **value-weighted index**, stocks are held in proportion to their total company market values.

The best way to understand the difference between price and value weighting is to consider an example. To keep things relatively simple, we suppose that there are only two companies in the entire market. We have the following information about their shares outstanding, share prices, and total market values:

	Shares Outstanding	Price per Share		Total Market Value	
		Beginning of Year	End of Year	Beginning of Year	End of Year
Company A	50 million	$10	$14	$500 million	$700 million
Company B	1 million	$50	$40	$ 50 million	$ 40 million

As shown, Company A has a lower share price but many more shares outstanding. Ignoring dividends, notice that Company A's stock price rose by 40 percent ($10 to $14) while Company B's stock price fell by 20 percent ($50 to $40).

The question we want to answer here is simply: How did the market do for the year? There are several ways we could answer this question. We could first focus on what happened to the average share price. The average share price was ($10 + $50)/2 = $30 at the beginning of the year, and ($14 + $40)/2 = $27 at the end, so the average share price fell. If we take the average share price as our index, then our index fell from 30 to 27, for a change of −3 points. Because the index began at 30, this is a −3/30 = −10% decrease. We might therefore say that the market was "off" by 10 percent.

This is an example of a price-weighted index. Because Company B's stock price is five times bigger than Company A's, it carries five times as much weight in the index. This explains why the index was down even though Company A's stock gained 40 percent whereas Company B's stock only lost 20 percent. The Dow Jones indexes are price weighted.

Alternatively, instead of focusing on the price of a typical share, we could look at what happened to the total value of a typical company. Here we notice that the average total value, in millions, rose from ($500 + $50)/2 = $275 to ($700 + $40)/2 = $370. If we take average total company value as our index, then our index rose from 275 to 370, a 35 percent *increase*.

This is an example of a value-weighted index. The influence a company has in this case depends on its overall change in total market value, not just its stock price change. Because Company A has a much larger total value, it carries a much larger weight in the index. With the exception of the Dow Jones indexes, most of the other indexes in Figure 5.3, including the Standard & Poor's, are value weighted.

price-weighted index
Stock market index in which stocks are held in proportion to their share price.

value-weighted index
Stock market index in which stocks are held in proportion to their total company market value.

Take a look at the "value" and "growth" indexes at
www.barra.com
Click on "S&P/Barra Indexes."

Now we have a problem. One index tells us the market was down by 10 percent, while the other tells us it was up by 35 percent. Which one is correct? The answer seems fairly obvious. The total value of the market as a whole grew from $550 million to $740 million, so the market as a whole increased in value. Put differently, investors as a whole owned stock worth $550 million at the beginning of the year and $740 million at the end of the year. So, on the whole, stock market investors earned 35 percent, even though the average share price went down.

This example shows that a price-weighted index can be misleading as an indicator of total market value. The basic flaw in a price-weighted index is that the effect a company has on the index depends on the price of a single share. However, the price of a single share is only part of the story. Unless the number of shares is also considered, the true impact on the overall market isn't known, and a distorted picture can emerge.

EXAMPLE 5.1 **Caution: Indexes Under Construction**

Suppose there are only two stocks in the market and the following information is given:

	Shares Outstanding	Price per Share Beginning of Year	End of Year
Quark Co.	10 million	$10	$11
Bashir, Inc.	20 million	$20	$25

Construct price- and value-weighted indexes and calculate the percentage changes in each.

The average share price rose from $15 to $18, or $3, so the price-weighted index would be up by 3/15 = 20 percent. Average total market value, in millions, rose from $250 to $305, so the value-weighted index rose by 55/250 = 22 percent.

MORE ON PRICE-WEIGHTED INDEXES

Earlier we indicated that the Dow Jones averages are price weighted. Given this, you may wonder why the Dow Jones Industrial Average has such a high value when the stock prices used to calculate the average are much smaller. To answer this question, we must explain one last detail about price-weighted indexes.

The extra detail concerns the effects of stock splits on price-weighted indexes. For example, in a 2-for-1 stock split, all current shareholders receive two new shares in exchange for each old share that they own. However, the total value of the company does not change because it is still the same company after the stock split. There are just twice as many shares, each worth half as much.

A stock split has no effect on a value-weighted index since the total value of the company does not change. But it can have a dramatic effect on a price-weighted index. To see this, consider what happens to the price-weighted and value-weighted indexes we created above when Company B enacts a 2-for-1 stock split. Based on beginning prices, with a 2-for-1 split, Company B's shares fall to $25. The price-weighted index falls to $(10 + 25)/2 = 17.50$ from 30, even though nothing really happened.

For a price-weighted index, the problem of stock splits can be addressed by adjusting the divisor each time a split occurs. Once again, an example is the best way to illustrate. In the case stated just above, suppose we wanted the index value to stay at 30 even though B's price per share fell to $25 as a result of the split. The only way to accomplish this is to add together the new stock prices and divide by something less than 2.

This new number is called the *index divisor,* and it is adjusted as needed to remove the effect of stock splits. To find the new divisor in our case, the stock prices are $25 and $10, and we want the index to equal 30. We solve for the new divisor, *d,* as follows:

$$\text{Index level} = \frac{\text{Sum of stock prices}}{\text{Divisor}}$$

$$30 = \frac{25 + 10}{d}$$

$$d = \frac{35}{30} = 1.16666\ldots$$

The new divisor is thus approximately 1.17.

Adjusting the divisor takes care of the problem in one sense, but it creates another problem. Because we are no longer dividing the sum of the share prices by the number of companies in the index, we can no longer interpret the change in the index as the change in price of an average share.

EXAMPLE 5.2   **Adjusting the Divisor**

Take a look back at Example 5.1. Suppose that Bashir splits 5-for-1. Based on beginning information, what is the new divisor?

Following a 5-for-1 split, Bashir's share price will fall from $20 to $4. With no adjustment to the divisor, the price-weighted index would drop from 15 to (10 + 4)/2 = 7. To keep the index at its old level of 15, we need to solve for a new divisor such that (10 + 4)/d = 15. In this case, the new divisor would be 14/15 = .93333 . . ., illustrating that the divisor can drop below 1.0.

THE DOW JONES DIVISORS

The method we described of adjusting the divisor on a price-weighted index for stock splits is the method used to adjust the Dow Jones averages. Through time, with repeated adjustments for stock splits, the divisor becomes smaller and smaller. As Figure 5.2 shows, as of October 7, 2005, the divisor was a nice, round .12493117. Since there are 30 stocks in the index, the divisor on the DJIA would be 30 if it were never adjusted, so it has declined substantially. Divisors for the other Dow Jones averages have similarly odd values.

Given its shortcomings, you might wonder why the financial press continues to report the Dow Jones averages. The reason is tradition; the Dow Jones averages have been around for more than 100 years, and each new generation of investors becomes accustomed to its quirks.

MORE ON INDEX FORMATION: BASE-YEAR VALUES

We next discuss one or two more details about indexes. First, to ease interpretation, the starting value of an index is usually set equal to some simple base number, like 100 or 1,000. For example, if you were to create a value-weighted index for the NYSE, the actual value of the index would be very large and cumbersome, so adjusting it makes sense.

To illustrate, suppose we have a value-weighted index with a starting value of 1.4 million. If we want the starting value to be 100, we just divide the starting value, and every

You've calculated values for an index over a four-year period as follows:

Year 1:   1,687 million
Year 2:   1,789 million
Year 3:   1,800 million
Year 4:   1,700 million

Suppose you wanted the index to start at 1,000. What would the reindexed values be?

To reindex these numbers, we need to (1) divide each of them by the starting value, 1,687 million, and then (2) multiply each by 1,000. Thus, we have:

Year 1:   1,687 million/1,687 million × 1,000 = 1,000.00
Year 2:   1,789 million/1,687 million × 1,000 = 1,060.46
Year 3:   1,800 million/1,687 million × 1,000 = 1,066.98
Year 4:   1,700 million/1,687 million × 1,000 = 1,007.71

subsequent value, by 1.4 million and then multiply by 100. So, if the next value of the index is 1.6 million, the "reindexed" value would be 1.6 million/1.4 million × 100 = 114.29, which is easily interpreted as a 14.29 percent increase over a base of 100.

Finally, an important consideration in looking at indexes is whether dividends are included. Most indexes don't include them. As a result, the change in an index measures only the capital gain (or loss) component of your return. When you're trying to evaluate how a particular type of stock market investment has done over time, dividends have to be included to get an accurate picture.

So which index is the best? The most popular alternative to the DJIA is the value-weighted S&P 500. You might further wonder, however, why this popular index limits itself to 500 stocks. The answer is timeliness and accuracy. Almost all stocks in the S&P 500 index trade every day, and therefore accurate daily updates of market prices are available each day. Stocks that do not trade every day can cause **index staleness**. Index staleness occurs when an index does not reflect all current price information because some of the stocks in the index have not traded recently. Also, as a practical matter, the largest 500 companies account for a very large portion of the value of the overall stock market.

index staleness
Condition that occurs when an index does not reflect all current price information because some of the stocks in the index have not traded recently.

CHECK THIS

5.6a   What is the difference between price- and value-weighting in the construction of stock market indexes? Give an example of a well-known index of each type.

5.6b   Which is better, price or value weighting? Why?

5.6c   Which stock market index is likely to contain the greater degree of index staleness, the S&P 500 or the Wilshire 5000 index?

5.7 Summary and Conclusions

This chapter introduced you to stock markets. We discussed who owns stocks, how the stock exchanges operate, and how stock market indexes are constructed and interpreted. Along the way we saw that:

1. Individual investors, directly or through mutual funds, own over half of all traded stocks. The rest are owned mostly by financial institutions such as pension funds and insurance companies.

2. The stock market is composed of a primary market, where stock shares are first sold, and a secondary market, where investors trade shares among themselves. In the primary market, companies raise money for investment projects. Investment bankers specialize in arranging financing for companies in the primary market. Investment bankers often act as underwriters, buying newly issued stock from the company and then reselling the stock to the public. The primary market is best known as the market for initial public offerings (IPOs).

3. In the secondary market, investors trade securities with other investors. Secondary market transactions are directed through three channels: directly with other investors, indirectly through a broker, or directly with a dealer. We saw that a broker matches buyers and sellers; a dealer buys and sells out of inventory.

4. Most common stock trading is directed through an organized stock exchange or through a trading network. The largest organized stock exchange in the United States is the New York Stock Exchange (NYSE). Popularly known as the Big Board, NYSE is owned by its members. There are three major types of NYSE members: floor brokers, specialists, and floor traders. We discussed the role of each in the functioning of the exchange.

GET REAL

This chapter covered the operations and organization of the major stock markets. It also covered some of the most important order types and the construction of stock market indexes. How should you, as an investor or investment manager, put this information to work?

First, as in some previous chapters, you need to submit as many as possible of the different order types suggested by this chapter in a simulated brokerage account (note that not all simulated brokerage accounts allow all trade types). Your goal is to gain experience with the different order types and what they mean and accomplish for you as an investor or investment manager.

In each case, once you have placed the order, be sure to monitor the price of the stock in question to see if any of your orders should be executed. When an order is executed, compare the result to the stop or limit price to see how you did.

The second thing to do is to start observing the different indexes and learning how they are computed, what's in them, and what they are intended to cover. For example, the NASDAQ 100 is made up of the largest NASDAQ stocks. Is this index broadly representative of big stocks in general? Of NASDAQ stocks in general? Why is the Russell 2000 index widely followed (note that it *does not* contain 2,000 big stocks)? Visit www.russell.com to learn more.

5. The second largest stock market in the United States is NASDAQ. NASDAQ is a computer network of securities dealers and electronic communications networks (ECNs).

6. The NYSE and NASDAQ face strong competition from securities trading firms operating in the third and fourth markets. The third market refers to off-exchange trading of exchange-listed securities by securities firms. The fourth market refers to direct trading among investors. The regional stock exchanges also attract substantial trading volume away from NYSE and NASDAQ.

7. The most widely followed barometer of day-to-day stock market activity is the Dow Jones Industrial Average (DJIA). The DJIA is an index of the stock prices of 30 large companies representative of American industry. Other indexes are also common. Among these, the best known is the Standard & Poor's Index of 500 stocks, abbreviated as the S&P 500. We described how these indexes are computed, with particular attention to some of the problems encountered.

Key Terms

ask price 138
best effort 135
bid price 138
broker 138
dealer 138
electronic communications network
  (ECN) 147
fixed commitment 135
floor broker 139
floor traders 140
fourth market 148
index staleness 154
initial public offering (IPO) 135
inside quotes 148
investment banking firm 135
limit order 143
market order 142
NYSE member 139

NYSE uptick rule 144
over-the-counter (OTC) market 146
price-weighted index 151
primary market 135
prospectus 136
red herring 136
secondary market 135
Securities and Exchange Commission
  (SEC) 136
specialist 140
specialist's post 142
spread 138
stop order 143
SuperDOT system 140
third market 148
underwrite 135
value-weighted index 151

Chapter Review Problems and Self-Test

1. **Index Construction**   Suppose there are only two stocks in the market and the following information is given:

		Price per Share	
	Shares Outstanding	Beginning of Year	End of Year
Ally Co.	100 million	$ 60	$ 66
McBeal, Inc.	400 million	$120	$100

Construct price- and value-weighted indexes and calculate the percentage changes in each.

2. **Stock Splits** In the previous problem, suppose that McBeal splits 3-for-1. Based on beginning information, what is the new divisor?

Answers to Self-Test Problems

1. The average share price at the beginning of the year is ($60 + 120)/2 = $90. At the end of the year, the average price is $83. Thus, the average price declined by $7 from $90, a percentage drop of –$7/$90 = –7.78%. Total market cap at the beginning of the year is $60 × 100 + $120 × 400 = $54 billion. It falls to $46.6 billion, a decline of $7.4 billion. The percentage decline is –$7.4 billion/$54 billion = –13.7%, or almost twice as much as the price-weighted index.

2. Following a 3-for-1 split, McBeal's share price falls from $120 to $40. To keep the price-weighted index at its old level of 90, we need a new divisor such that (60 + 40)/d = 90. In this case, the new divisor would be 100/90 = 1.1111.

Test Your Investment Quotient

1. **Stop-Loss Order** If you place a stop-loss order to sell 100 shares of stock at $55 when the current price is $62, how much will you receive for each share if the price drops to $52?
   a. $50
   b. $55
   c. $54.87
   d. Cannot tell from the information given.

2. **Uptick Rule** You wish to sell short 100 shares of XYZ Corporation stock. If the last two transactions were $34.12 followed by $34.25, you can short on the next transaction only at a price of
   a. $34.12 or higher
   b. $34.25 or higher
   c. $34.25 or lower
   d. $34.12 or lower

3. **Uptick Rule** Which of the following is false regarding the NYSE uptick rule?
   a. The rule does not apply to short sales executed on other exchanges.
   b. The NYSE enacted the rule to make it more difficult for speculators to drive down a stock's price by repeated short sales.
   c. The rule has become less of a constraint than it once was.
   d. The rule applies when shorting a stock or when covering a short.

4. **Value-Weighted Index** An analyst gathered the following data about stocks J, K, and L, which together form a value-weighted index:

	December 31, Year 1		December 31, Year 2	
Stock	Price	Shares Outstanding	Price	Shares Outstanding
J	$40	10,000	$50	10,000
K	$30	6,000	$20	12,000*
L	$50	9,000	$40	9,000

*2-for-1 stock split.

The ending value-weighted index (base index = 100) is closest to:
   a. 92.31
   b. 93.64
   c. 106.80
   d. 108.33

5. **Dow Jones Index**   The divisor for the Dow Jones Industrial Average (DJIA) is most likely to decrease when a stock in the DJIA

   a. Has a stock split.
   b. Has a reverse split.
   c. Pays a cash dividend.
   d. Is removed and replaced.

6. **New York Stock Exchange**   Which of the following activities are *not* conducted by specialists on the NYSE?

   a. Acting as dealers for their own accounts.
   b. Monitoring compliance with margin requirements.
   c. Providing liquidity to the market.
   d. Monitoring and executing unfilled limit orders.

7. **Stock Markets**   What is a securities market characterized by dealers who buy and sell securities for their own inventories called?

   a. A primary market
   b. A secondary market
   c. An over-the-counter market
   d. An institutional market

8. **Stock Markets**   What is the over-the-counter market for exchange-listed securities called?

   a. Third market
   b. Fourth market
   c. After-market
   d. Block market

9. **Stock Indexes**   If the market price of each of the 30 stocks in the Dow Jones Industrial Average changes by the same percentage amount during a given day, which stock will have the greatest impact on the DJIA?

   a. The one whose stock trades at the highest dollar price per share.
   b. The one whose total equity has the highest market value.
   c. The one having the greatest amount of equity in its capital structure.
   d. The one having the lowest volatility.

10. **Stock Indexes**   In calculating the Standard & Poor's stock price indexes, how are adjustments for stock splits made?

    a. By adjusting the divisor.
    b. Automatically, due to the manner in which the index is calculated.
    c. By adjusting the numerator.
    d. Quarterly, on the last trading day of each quarter.

11. **Stock Indexes**   Which of the following indexes includes the largest number of actively traded stocks?

    a. The NASDAQ Composite Index
    b. The NYSE Composite Index
    c. The Wilshire 5000 Index
    d. The Value Line Composite Index

12. **New York Stock Exchange**   The largest number of NYSE members are registered as:

    a. Stockholders
    b. Floor brokers
    c. Specialists
    d. Floor traders

13. **New York Stock Exchange**   The second largest number of NYSE members are registered as:

    a. Stockholders
    b. Floor brokers
    c. Specialists
    d. Floor traders

14. **Stock Trading**   An institutional investor wishing to sell a very large block of stock, say, 10,000 shares or more, is most likely to get the best price in which market?

   a. The primary market
   b. The secondary market
   c. The third market
   d. The fourth market

15. **Stock Indexes**   Which one of the following statements regarding the Dow Jones Industrial Average is false?

   a. The DJIA contains 30 well-known large-company stocks.
   b. The DJIA is affected equally by dollar changes in low- and high-priced stocks.
   c. The DJIA is affected equally by percentage changes in low- and high-priced stocks.
   d. The DJIA divisor must be adjusted for stock splits.

Concept Questions

1. **Primary and Secondary Markets**   If you were to visit your local Chevrolet retailer, there is both a primary and a secondary market in action. Explain. Is the Chevy retailer a dealer or a broker?

2. **Specialists**   On the NYSE, does a specialist act as a dealer or a broker? Or both?

3. **Market and Limit Orders**   What is the difference between a market order and a limit order? What is the potential downside to each type of order?

4. **Stop That!**   What is a stop-loss order? Why might it be used? Is it sure to stop a loss?

5. **Order Types**   Suppose Microsoft is currently trading at $100. You want to buy it if it reaches $120. What type of order should you submit?

6. **Order Types**   Suppose Dell is currently trading at $65. You think that if it reaches $70, it will continue to climb, so you want to buy it if and when it gets there. Should you submit a limit order to buy at $70?

7. **NASDAQ Quotes**   With regard to the NASDAQ, what are inside quotes?

8. **Index Composition**   There are basically four factors that differentiate stock market indexes. What are they? Comment on each.

9. **Index Composition**   Is it necessarily true that, all else the same, an index with more stocks is better? What is the issue here?

10. **Upticks**   What is the uptick rule? Where does it apply? Why does it exist?

Questions and Problems

Core Questions

1. **Price-Weighted Divisor**   Able, Baker, and Charlie are the only three stocks in an index. The stocks sell for $46, $128, and $75, respectively. If Baker undergoes a 2-for-1 stock split, what is the new divisor for the price-weighted index?

2. **Price-Weighted Divisor**   In the previous problem, assume that Baker undergoes a 3-for-1 stock split. What is the new divisor now?

3. **Order Books**   You find the following order book on a particular stock. The last trade on the stock was at $70.54.

Buy Orders		Sell Orders	
Shares	**Price**	**Shares**	**Price**
250	$70.53	100	$70.56
100	70.52	400	70.57
900	70.51	1,000	70.59
75	70.49	700	70.60
		900	70.61

a. If you place a market buy order for 100 shares, at what price will it be filled?

b. If you place a market sell order for 100 shares, at what price will it be filled?

c. Suppose you place a market order to buy 400 shares. At what price will it be filled?

4. **Price-Weighted Index** You are given the following information concerning two stocks that make up an index. What is the price-weighted return for the index?

	Shares Outstanding	Price per Share Beginning of Year	Price per Share End of Year
Kirk, Inc.	45,000	$84	$93
Picard Co.	60,000	41	49

5. **Value-Weighted Index** Calculate the index return for the information in the previous problem using a value-weighted index.

6. **Reindexing** In Problem 5, assume that you want to reindex with the index value at the beginning of the year equal to 100. What is the index level at the end of the year?

7. **Index Level** In Problem 5, assume the value-weighted index level was 408.16 at the beginning of the year. What is the index level at the end of the year?

8. **Reindexing** You have calculated the following values for an index over a five-year period:

Year 1: 6,251 million
Year 2: 6,483 million
Year 3: 6,124 million
Year 4: 6,503 million
Year 5: 6,698 million

Suppose you wanted the index to start at 500. What would the reindexed values be?

Intermediate
Questions

9. **Price-Weighted Divisor** Look back at Problem 1. Assume that Able undergoes a 1-for-3 reverse stock split. What is the new divisor?

10. **DJIA** On August 30, 2005, the DJIA closed at 10,412.82. The divisor at that time was 0.12560864. Suppose the next day the prices for 29 of the stocks remained unchanged and one stock increased by $5.00. What would the DJIA level be the next day?

11. **DJIA** In August 2005, IBM was one of the highest priced stocks in the DJIA and Disney was one of the lowest. The closing price for IBM on August 30, 2005, was $80.54 and the closing price for Disney was $25.29. Suppose the next day the other 29 stock prices remained unchanged and IBM increased 5 percent. What would the new DJIA level be? Now assume Disney increased by 5 percent and find the new DJIA level.

12. **DJIA** Looking back at the previous problems, what would the new index level be if all stocks on the DJIA increased by $1.00 per share on August 30, 2005?

13. **Price-Weighted Divisor** You construct a price-weighted index of 40 stocks. At the beginning of the day the index is 3,487.25. During the day, 39 stock prices remain the same, and one stock price increases by $5.00. At the end of the day, your index value is 3,502.18. What is the divisor on your index?

14. **Price-Weighted Indexes** Suppose the following three defense stocks are to be combined into a stock index in January 2003 (perhaps a portfolio manager believes these stocks are an appropriate benchmark for his or her performance):

	Shares (millions)	Price 1/1/04	Price 1/1/05	Price 1/1/06
Douglas McDonnell	220	$119	$123	$132
Dynamics General	400	35	31	39
International Rockwell	350	62	54	68

a. Calculate the initial value of the index if a price-weighting scheme is used.

b. What is the rate of return on this index for the year ending December 31, 2004? For the year ending December 31, 2005?

15. **Price-Weighted Indexes**   In the previous problem, suppose that Douglas McDonnell shareholders approve a 3-for-1 stock split on January 1, 2005. What is the new divisor for the index? Calculate the rate of return on the index for the year ending December 31, 2005, if Douglas McDonnell's share price on January 1, 2006, is $44.00 per share.

16. **Value-Weighted Indexes**   Repeat Problem 14 if a value-weighted index is used. Assume the index is scaled by a factor of 10 million; that is, if the average firm's market value is $5 billion, the index would be quoted as 500.

17. **Value-Weighted Indexes**   In the previous problem, will your answers change if Douglas McDonnell stock splits? Why or why not?

18. **Equally Weighted Indexes**   In addition to price-weighted and value-weighted indexes, an equally weighted index is one in which the index value is computed from the average rate of return of the stocks comprising the index. Equally weighted indexes are frequently used by financial researchers to measure portfolio performance.

    a. Using the information in Problem 14, compute the rate of return on an equally weighted index of the three defense stocks for the year ending December 31, 2004.

    b. If the index value is set to 100 on January 1, 2004, what will the index value be on January 1, 2005? What is the rate of return on the index for 2005?

19. **Equally Weighted versus Value-Weighted Indexes**   Historically there have been periods where a value-weighted index has a higher return than an equally weighted index and other periods where the opposite has occurred. Why do you suppose this would happen? Hint: Look back to Chapter 1.

20. **Geometric Indexes**   Another type of index is the geometric index. The calculation of a geometric index is similar to the calculation of a geometric return:

$$1 + R_G = [(1 + R_1)(1 + R_2) \ldots (1 + R_N)]^{1/N}$$

    The difference in the geometric index construction is the returns used are the returns for the different stocks in the index for a particular period, such as a day or year. Construct the geometric index returns for Problem 14 over each of the two years. Assume the beginning index level is 100.

21. **Geometric Indexes**   We have seen the importance of geometric returns through time. A geometric index is across different stocks at a particular point in time, such as a day. Constructing a portfolio that exactly replicates a geometric index is thus impossible. Given this, why would you want to use a geometric index? In other words, what does a geometric index measure? Now consider the Value Line Arithmetic Index (VLA), which is equally weighted, and the Value Line Geometric Index (VLG). On February 1, 1988, both indexes were set to a value of 210.75. As of the close of the market on August 30, 2005, the VLA was at 1,848.80 and the VLG was at 404.67. Why would you expect to see such a disparity in the two index levels?

22. **Interpreting Index Values**   Suppose you want to replicate the performance of several stock indexes, some of which are price-weighted, others value-weighted, and still others equally weighted. Describe the investment strategy you need for each of the index types. Are any of the three strategies passive, in that no portfolio rebalancing need be performed to perfectly replicate the index (assuming no stock splits or cash distributions)? Which of the three strategies do you think is most often followed by small investors? Which strategy is the most difficult to implement?

S&P Problems

www.mhhe.com/edumarketinsight

1. **Index Construction**   You have decided that you want a stock market index that tracks publishing companies. The three constituent companies you have decided to use are McGraw-Hill

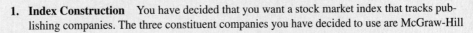

Companies (MHP), Dow Jones & Company (DJ), and Value Line Inc. (VALU). For each company, download the monthly stock prices. Under the "Financial Hlts" link you can find the number of shares outstanding. Construct a price-weighted and a value-weighted index for the publishing industry for the last six months. Use a beginning index value of 100 where appropriate. What are the monthly returns for each index?

What's on the Web?

1. **Specialists** Go to www.nyse.com and find the discussion of NYSE members. What are the five essential functions of the specialist according to the Web site?

2. **DJIA** As you have seen, in a price-weighted index, a stock with a higher price has a higher weight in the index return. To find out the weight of the stocks in the DJIA, go to www.djindexes.com. Which stock in the DJIA has the highest weight? The lowest weight?

3. **DJIA** You want to find the current divisor for the DJIA. Go to www.djindexes.com and look up the current divisor.

4. **S&P 500** To find out the most recent changes in the S&P 500, go to www2.standardandpoors.com. Once at the Web site, find the 10 most recent additions and deletions to the stocks in the index.

5. **Nikkei 225** The Nikkei 225 Index is a highly followed index that measures the performance of the Japanese stock market. Go to www.nni.nikkei.co.jp and find out if the Nikkei 225 is a price-weighted or value-weighted index. What is the divisor for this index? When was the latest reconstitution of the index? Which stocks were added? Which stocks were deleted?

Stock-Trak Exercises

STOCK|TRAK
GLOBAL PORTFOLIO SIMULATIONS

To access the Stock-Trak Exercise for this chapter, please visit the book Web site at www.mhhe.com/jm4e and choose the corresponding chapter.

CHAPTER 6

Common Stock Valuation

"Ignore the stock market, ignore the economy and buy a business you understand."

–Warren Buffett

"Prediction is difficult, especially about the future."

–Niels Bohr[1]

Common stock valuation is one of the most challenging tasks in financial analysis. A fundamental assertion of finance holds that the value of an asset is based on the present value of its future cash flows. Accordingly, common stock valuation attempts the difficult task of predicting the future. Consider that the dividend yield for a typical large-company stock might be about 2 percent. This implies that the present value of dividends to be paid over the next 10 years constitutes only a portion of the current stock price. Thus, much of the value of a typical stock is derived from dividends to be paid more than 10 years away! ■

In this chapter, we examine several methods commonly used by financial analysts to assess the economic value of common stocks. These methods are grouped into two categories: dividend discount models and price ratio models. After studying these models, we provide an analysis of a real company to illustrate the use of the methods discussed in this chapter.

[1]This quote has also been attributed to Yogi Berra, Samuel Goldwyn, and Mark Twain.

6.1 Security Analysis: Be Careful Out There

It may seem odd that we start our discussion with an admonition to be careful, but in this case, we think it is a good idea. The methods we discuss in this chapter are examples of those used by many investors and security analysts to assist in making buy and sell decisions for individual stocks. The basic idea is to identify both "undervalued" or "cheap" stocks to buy and "overvalued" or "rich" stocks to sell. In practice, however, many stocks that look cheap may in fact be correctly priced for reasons not immediately apparent to the analyst. Indeed, the hallmark of a good analyst is a cautious attitude and a willingness to probe further and deeper before committing to a final investment recommendation.

The type of security analysis we describe in this chapter falls under the heading of **fundamental analysis**. Numbers such as a company's earnings per share, cash flow, book equity value, and sales are often called *fundamentals* because they describe, on a basic level, a specific firm's operations and profits (or lack of profits).

Fundamental analysis represents the examination of these and other accounting statement-based company data used to assess the value of a company's stock. Information regarding such things as management quality, products, and product markets is often examined as well.

We urge you to be cautious when you apply these techniques. Further, the simpler the technique, the more cautious you should be. As our later chapter on market efficiency explains, there is good reason to believe that too-simple techniques that rely on widely available information are not likely to yield systematically superior investment results. In fact, they could lead to unnecessarily risky investment decisions. This is especially true for ordinary investors (like most of us) who do not have timely access to the information that a professional security analyst working for a major securities firm would possess.

As a result, our goal here is not to teach you how to "pick" stocks with a promise that you will become rich. Certainly, one chapter in an investments text is not likely to be sufficient to acquire that level of investment savvy. Still, an appreciation of the techniques in this chapter is important simply because buy and sell recommendations made by securities firms are frequently couched in the terms we introduce here. Much of the discussion of individual companies in the financial press relies on these concepts as well, so some background is necessary just to interpret commonly presented investment information. In essence, you must learn both the jargon and the concepts of security analysis.

fundamental analysis
Examination of a firm's accounting statements and other financial and economic information to assess the economic value of a company's stock.

WWW

Visit the New York Society of Security Analysts Web site at
www.nyssa.org

CHECK THIS

6.1a   What is fundamental analysis?

6.1b   What is a "rich" stock? What is a "cheap" stock?

6.1c   Why does valuing a stock necessarily involve predicting the future?

6.2 The Dividend Discount Model

A fundamental principle of finance holds that the economic value of a security is properly measured by the sum of its future cash flows, where the cash flows are adjusted for risk and the time value of money. For example, suppose a risky security will pay either $100 or $200 with equal probability one year from today. The expected payoff of the security in one year is $150 = 0.5 \times \$100 + 0.5 \times \$200$.

The security's value today is the $150 expected future value discounted for a one-year waiting period. If the appropriate discount rate for this security is, say, 5 percent, then the present value of the expected future value is $150 / 1.05 = $142.86. If instead the appropriate discount rate is 15 percent, then the present value is $150 / 1.15 = $130.43. As this example illustrates, the choice of a discount rate can have a substantial impact on what investors will pay for a security.

dividend discount model (DDM)
Method of estimating the value of a share of stock as the present value of all expected future dividend payments.

A popular model used to value common stock is the **dividend discount model**, or **DDM**. The dividend discount model values a share of stock as the sum of all expected future dividend payments, where the dividends are adjusted for risk and the time value of money.

For example, suppose a company pays a dividend at the end of each year. Let $D(t)$ denote a dividend to be paid t years from now, and let $V(0)$ represent the present value of the future dividend stream. Also, let k denote the appropriate risk-adjusted discount rate. Using the dividend discount model, the present value of a share of this company's stock is measured as this sum of discounted future dividends:

$$V(0) = \frac{D(1)}{(1+k)} + \frac{D(2)}{(1+k)^2} + \frac{D(3)}{(1+k)^3} + \cdots + \frac{D(T)}{(1+k)^T}$$ (6.1)

In equation 6.1, we assume that the last dividend is paid T years from now. The value of T depends on the time of the *terminal,* or last, dividend. Thus, if $T = 3$ years and $D(1) = D(2) = D(3) = \$100$, the present value, $V(0)$, is stated as:

$$V(0) = \frac{\$100}{(1+k)} + \frac{\$100}{(1+k)^2} + \frac{\$100}{(1+k)^3}$$

WWW

Check out the American Association of Individual Investors Web site at
www.aaii.com

If the discount rate is $k = 10$ percent, then a quick calculation yields $V(0) = \$248.69$. Thus, the stock price should be about $250 per share.

EXAMPLE 6.1 | **Using the Dividend Discount Model**

Suppose again that a stock pays three annual dividends of $100 per year and the discount rate is $k = 15$ percent. In this case, what is the present value $V(0)$ of the stock?

With a 15 percent discount rate, we have:

$$V(0) = \frac{\$100}{(1.15)} + \frac{\$100}{(1.15)^2} + \frac{\$100}{(1.15)^3}$$

Check that the answer is $V(0) = \$228.32$.

EXAMPLE 6.2 | **More Dividend Discount Model**

Suppose instead that the stock pays three annual dividends of $10, $20, and $30 in years 1, 2, and 3, respectively, and the discount rate is $k = 10$ percent. What is the present value $V(0)$ of the stock?

In this case, we have:

$$V(0) = \frac{\$10}{(1.10)} + \frac{\$20}{(1.10)^2} + \frac{\$30}{(1.10)^3}$$

Check that the answer is $V(0) = \$48.16$.

CONSTANT DIVIDEND GROWTH RATE MODEL

constant growth rate model

A version of the dividend discount model that assumes a constant dividend growth rate.

For many applications, the dividend discount model is greatly simplified by assuming that dividends will grow at a constant growth rate. This is called a **constant growth rate model**. Letting a constant growth rate be denoted by g, then successive annual dividends are stated as $D(t + 1) = D(t)(1 + g)$.

For example, suppose the next dividend is $D(1) = \$100$, and the dividend growth rate is $g = 10$ percent. This growth rate yields a second annual dividend of $D(2) = \$100 \times 1.10 = \$110$ and a third annual dividend of $D(3) = \$100 \times 1.10 \times 1.10 = \$100 \times (1.10)^2 = \$121$. If the discount rate is $k = 12$ percent, the present value of these three sequential dividend payments is the sum of their separate present values:

$$V(0) = \frac{\$100}{(1.12)} + \frac{\$110}{(1.12)^2} + \frac{\$121}{(1.12)^3}$$

$$= \$263.10$$

If the number of dividends to be paid is large, calculating the present value of each dividend separately is tedious and possibly prone to error. Fortunately, if the growth rate is constant, some simplified expressions are available to handle certain special cases. For example, suppose a stock will pay annual dividends over the next T years and these dividends will grow at a constant growth rate g and be discounted at the rate k. The current dividend is $D(0)$, the next dividend is $D(1) = D(0)(1 + g)$, the following dividend is $D(2) = D(1)(1 + g) = D(0)(1 + g)^2$, and so forth. The present value of the next T dividends, that is, $D(1)$ through $D(T)$, can be calculated using this formula:

WWW

Try surfing to the Association for Investment Management and Research Web site at www.cfainstitute.org

$$V(0) = \frac{D(0)(1 + g)}{k - g}\left[1 - \left(\frac{1 + g}{1 + k}\right)^T\right] \qquad g \neq k \qquad (6.2)$$

Notice that this expression requires that the growth rate and the discount rate not be equal to each other, that is, $k \neq g$, because $k = g$ would imply division by zero. Actually, when the growth rate is equal to the discount rate, that is, $k = g$, the effects of growth and discounting cancel exactly, and the present value $V(0)$ is simply the number of payments T times the current dividend $D(0)$:

$$V(0) = T \times D(0)$$

The constant growth rate model is easy to use. Suppose that the growth rate is $g = 8$ percent, the discount rate is $k = 10$ percent, the number of future annual dividends is $T = 20$ years, and the current dividend is $D(0) = \$10$. In this case, the constant growth rate model provides a present value of:

$$V(0) = \frac{\$10(1.08)}{.10 - .08}\left[1 - \left(\frac{1.08}{1.10}\right)^{20}\right]$$

$$= \$165.88$$

EXAMPLE 6.3 | **Using the Constant Growth Model**

Suppose that the dividend growth rate is 10 percent, the discount rate is 8 percent, there are 20 years of dividends to be paid, and the current dividend is $10. What is the value of the stock based on the constant growth model?

Plugging in the relevant numbers, we have:

$$V(0) = \frac{\$10(1.10)}{.08 - .10}\left[1 - \left(\frac{1.10}{1.08}\right)^{20}\right]$$

$$= \$243.86$$

Thus, the price should be $V(0) = \$243.86$.

CONSTANT PERPETUAL GROWTH

constant perpetual growth model
A version of the dividend discount model in which dividends grow forever at a constant rate, and the growth rate is strictly less than the discount rate.

A particularly simple form of the dividend discount model occurs in the case in which a firm will pay dividends that grow at the constant rate g forever. This case is called the **constant perpetual growth model**. In the constant perpetual growth model, present values are calculated using this formula:

$$V(0) = \frac{D(0)(1 + g)}{k - g} \qquad (g < k) \qquad (6.3)$$

Because $D(0)(1 + g) = D(1)$, we can also write the constant perpetual growth model as:

$$V(0) = \frac{D(1)}{k - g} \qquad (g < k) \qquad (6.4)$$

Either way, we have a very simple, and very widely used, formula for the value of a share of stock based on future dividend payments.

Notice that the constant perpetual growth model requires that the growth rate be strictly less than the discount rate, that is, $g < k$. It looks as if the share value would be negative if this were not true. Actually, the formula is simply not valid in this case. The reason is that a perpetual dividend growth rate greater than the discount rate implies an *infinite* value because the present value of the dividends keeps getting bigger and bigger. Because no security can have infinite value, the requirement that $g < k$ simply makes good economic sense.

To illustrate the constant perpetual growth model, suppose that the growth rate is $g = 4$ percent, the discount rate is $k = 9$ percent, and the current dividend is $D(0) = \$10$. In this case, a simple calculation yields:

$$V(0) = \frac{\$10(1.04)}{.09 - .04} = \$208$$

EXAMPLE 6.4 | **Using the Constant Perpetual Growth Model**

Suppose dividends for a particular company are projected to grow at 5 percent forever. If the discount rate is 15 percent and the current dividend is $10, what is the value of the stock?

$$V(0) = \frac{\$10(1.05)}{.15 - .05} = \$105$$

As shown, the stock should sell for $105.

APPLICATIONS OF THE CONSTANT PERPETUAL GROWTH MODEL

Visit the AEP and DTE Web sites at
www.aep.com
www.dteenergy.com

In practice, the constant perpetual growth model is the most popular dividend discount model because it is so simple to use. Certainly, the model satisfies Einstein's famous dictum: "Simplify as much as possible, but no more." However, experienced financial analysts are keenly aware that the constant perpetual growth model can be usefully applied only to companies with a history of relatively stable earnings and if dividend growth is expected to continue into the distant future.

A standard example of an industry for which the constant perpetual growth model can often be usefully applied is the electric utility industry. Consider American Electric Power, which is traded on the New York Stock Exchange under the ticker symbol AEP. In 2005, AEP was paying an annual dividend of $1.40; thus we set $D(0) = \$1.40$.

To use the constant perpetual growth model, we also need a discount rate and a growth rate. An old quick and dirty rule of thumb for a risk-adjusted discount rate for electric utility companies is the yield to maturity on 20-year maturity U.S. Treasury bonds, plus 2 percent. At the time this example was written, the yield on 20-year maturity T-bonds was about 5.3 percent. Adding 2 percent, we get a discount rate of $k = 7.3$ percent.

In 2005, AEP had not increased its dividend in over a decade. However, a future growth rate of zero percent for AEP might be unduly pessimistic because earnings growth in the electric utilities industry was projected to be about 2 percent per year. Thus, a rate of, say, 1.5 percent might be more realistic as an estimate of future growth for AEP.

Putting it all together, we have $k = 7.3$ percent, $g = 1.5$ percent, and $D(0) = \$1.40$. Using these numbers, we obtain this estimate for the value of a share of AEP stock:

$$V(0) = \frac{\$1.40\,(1.015)}{.073 - .015} = \$24.50$$

This estimate is somewhat below the mid-2005 AEP stock price of $38.80, possibly suggesting that AEP stock was overvalued.

We emphasize the word "possibly" here because we made several assumptions in the process of coming up with this estimate. A change in any of these assumptions could easily lead us to a different conclusion. We will return to this point several times in future discussions.

EXAMPLE 6.5	Valuing Detroit ED

In 2005, the utility company Detroit Edison (DTE) paid a $2.06 dividend. Using $D(0) = \$2.06$, $k = 7.3$ percent, and an industry average growth rate of $g = 2$ percent, calculate a present value estimate for DTE. Compare this with the mid-2005 DTE stock price of $47.56.

Plugging in the relevant numbers, we immediately have:

$$V(0) = \frac{\$2.06(1.02)}{.073 - .02} = \$39.65$$

This estimate is below the mid-2005 DTE stock price of $47.56, suggesting that DTE stock was overvalued.

HISTORICAL GROWTH RATES

geometric average dividend growth rate
A dividend growth rate based on a geometric average of historical dividends.

arithmetic average dividend growth rate
A dividend growth rate based on an arithmetic average of historical dividends.

In the constant growth model, a company's historical average dividend growth rate is frequently taken as an estimate of future dividend growth. Sometimes historical growth rates are provided in published information about the company. Other times it is necessary to calculate a historical growth rate yourself. There are two ways to do this: (1) using a **geometric average dividend growth rate** or (2) using an **arithmetic average dividend growth rate**. Both methods are relatively easy to implement, as we will now illustrate.

To illustrate the difference between a geometric average and an arithmetic average of historical dividend growth, suppose that the Kwik Kiwi Company paid the following dividends at the end of each of the years indicated immediately below.

2005:	$2.20	2002:	$1.75
2004:	2.00	2001:	1.70
2003:	1.80	2000:	1.50

We begin with a geometric average growth rate because it is the easiest to calculate. Notice that five years elapsed between the $1.50 dividend paid at the end of 2000 and the $2.20 dividend paid at the end of 2005. A geometric average growth rate is equivalent to a constant rate of growth over the five-year period that would grow the dividend from $1.50 to $2.20. That is, it is the growth rate that solves this growth equation:

$$\$2.20 = \$1.50(1 + g)^5$$

$$g = \left(\frac{\$2.20}{\$1.50}\right)^{1/5} - 1 = .08$$

Thus, in this case, the five-year geometric average dividend growth rate is 8 percent. Notice that this calculation is similar to our calculation of the geometric average return in Chapter 1.

In general, if $D(0)$ is the earliest dividend used and $D(N)$ is the latest dividend used to calculate a geometric average dividend growth rate over N years, the general equation used is:

$$g = \left[\frac{D(N)}{D(0)}\right]^{1/N} - 1 \qquad (6.5)$$

In the above example, $D(0) = \$1.50$, $D(N) = \$2.20$, and $N = 5$, which yields $g = 8\%$.

An arithmetic average growth rate takes a little more effort to calculate, because it requires that we first calculate each year's dividend growth rate separately and then calculate an arithmetic average of these annual growth rates. For our Kwik Kiwi example, the arithmetic average of five years of dividend growth is calculated as follows:

Year	Dividend	Yearly Growth Rates
2005	$2.20	10.00% = (2.20 − 2.00)/2.00
2004	2.00	11.11% = (2.00 − 1.80)/1.80
2003	1.80	2.86% = (1.80 − 1.75)/1.75
2002	1.75	2.94% = (1.75 − 1.70)/1.70
2001	1.70	13.33% = (1.70 − 1.50)/1.50
2000	1.50	
		SUM/N = 40.24%/5 = 8.05%

Summing the five yearly growth rates yields 40.24%, and dividing by five yields an arithmetic average growth rate of 40.24%/5 = 8.05%. Notice that this arithmetic average growth rate is close to the geometric average growth rate of 8.0 percent that we first calculated. This is usually the case for dividend growth rates, but not always. A large difference between the two means that the dividend grew erratically, which makes the use of the constant growth formula a little questionable in the first place.

EXAMPLE 6.6 Erratic Dividend Growth

To illustrate how the geometric average and the arithmetic average of historical dividend growth can differ, consider the following dividends paid by the Kwerky Kiwi Company:

2005:	$2.20	2002:	$2.00
2004:	2.00	2001:	1.50
2003:	1.80	2000:	1.50

(continued)

For Kwerky Kiwi, the arithmetic average of five years of dividend growth is calculated as follows:

Year	Dividend	Yearly Growth Rates
2005	$2.20	10.00% = (2.20 − 2.00)/2.00
2004	2.00	11.11% = (2.00 − 1.80)/1.80
2003	1.80	−10.00% = (1.80 − 2.00)/2.00
2002	2.00	33.33% = (2.00 − 1.50)/1.50
2001	1.50	0.00% = (1.50 − 1.50)/1.50
2000	1.50	
		44.44/5 = 8.89%

In this case, summing the five yearly growth rates yields 44.44, and dividing by five yields an arithmetic average growth rate of 44.44/5 = 8.89%. Notice that this arithmetic average growth rate is somewhat larger than the geometric average growth rate of 8.0 percent.

As this example shows, sometimes the arithmetic and geometric growth rate averages can yield rather different results. In practice, most analysts prefer to use a geometric average when calculating an average historical dividend growth rate. In any case, a historical average growth rate may or may not be a reasonable estimate of future dividend growth. Many analysts adjust their estimates to reflect other information available to them, for example, whether the growth rate appears to be sustainable.

THE SUSTAINABLE GROWTH RATE

As we have seen, when using the constant perpetual growth model, it is necessary to come up with an estimate of g, the growth rate of dividends. In our previous discussions, we described two ways to do this: (1) using the company's historical average growth rate or (2) using an industry median or average growth rate. We now describe a third way, known as the **sustainable growth rate**, which involves using a company's earnings to estimate g.

As we have discussed, a limitation of the constant perpetual growth model is that it should be applied only to companies with stable dividend and earnings growth. Essentially, a company's earnings can be paid out as dividends to its stockholders or kept as **retained earnings** within the firm to finance future growth. The proportion of earnings paid to stockholders as dividends is called the **payout ratio**. The proportion of earnings retained for reinvestment is called the **retention ratio**.

If we let D stand for dividends and EPS stand for earnings per share, then the payout ratio is simply D/EPS. Because anything not paid out is retained, the retention ratio is just one minus the payout ratio. For example, if a company's current dividend is $4 per share, and its earnings per share are currently $10, then the payout ratio is $4 / $10 = .40, or 40 percent, and the retention ratio is 1 − .40 = .60, or 60 percent.

A firm's sustainable growth rate is equal to its return on equity (ROE) times its retention ratio.[2]

$$\text{Sustainable growth rate} = \text{ROE} \times \text{Retention ratio} \qquad (6.6)$$
$$= \text{ROE} \times (1 - \text{Payout ratio})$$

Return on equity is commonly computed using an accounting-based performance measure and is calculated as a firm's net income divided by shareholders' equity:

$$\text{Return on equity (ROE)} = \text{Net Income / Equity} \qquad (6.7)$$

sustainable growth rate
A dividend growth rate that can be sustained by a company's earnings.

retained earnings
Earnings retained within the firm to finance growth.

payout ratio
Proportion of earnings paid out as dividends.

retention ratio
Proportion of earnings retained for reinvestment.

[2]Strictly speaking, this formula is correct only if ROE is calculated using beginning-of-period shareholders' equity. If ending figures are used, then the precise formula is ROE × Retention ratio / [1 − (ROE × Retention ratio)]. However, the error from not using the precise formula is usually small, so most analysts do not bother with it.

Calculating Sustainable Growth

In 2005, American Electric Power (AEP) had a return on equity (ROE) of 14.59 percent, earnings per share (EPS) of $2.94, and paid dividends of $D(0) = \$1.40$. What was AEP's retention rate? Its sustainable growth rate?

AEP's dividend payout was $1.40/$2.94 = .476, or 47.6 percent. Its retention ratio was thus $1 - .476 = .524$, or 52.4 percent. Finally, AEP's sustainable growth rate was $.1459 \times 52.4\% = 7.645\%$.

Valuing American Electric Power (AEP)

Using AEP's sustainable growth rate of 7.645 percent (see Example 6.7) as an estimate of perpetual dividend growth and its current dividend of $1.40, what is the value of AEP's stock assuming a discount rate of 7.3 percent?

If we plug the various numbers into the perpetual growth model, we obtain a value of $V(0) = \$1.40(1.07645)/(.073 - .07645) = -\$436.82$! Clearly, something is wrong because we have a negative price. The problem is that the estimate of the sustainable growth rate (7.645%) is greater than the discount rate (7.3%). So, if the discount rate is appropriate, we conclude the estimate of the sustainable growth rate is too high.

Valuing Detroit Edison (DTE)

In 2005, DTE had a return on equity (ROE) of 6.64 percent, earnings per share (EPS) of $2.08, and a per-share dividend of $D(0) = \$2.06$. Assuming a 7.3 percent discount rate, what is the value of DTE's stock?

DTE's payout ratio was $2.06/$2.08 = .990, or 99 percent. Thus, DTE's retention ratio was $1 - .990 = .01$, or just 1 percent. DTE's sustainable growth rate is thus $6.64\% \times .01 = .0664\%$. Finally, using the constant growth model, we obtain a value of $\$2.06(1.00664)/(.073 - .00664) = \$31.25$, which is quite a bit less than the mid-2005 DTE share price of $47.56. This suggests that DTE stock was overvalued, or perhaps the sustainable growth estimate is too low.

A common problem with sustainable growth rates is that they are sensitive to year-to-year fluctuations in earnings. As a result, security analysts routinely adjust sustainable growth rate estimates to smooth out the effects of earnings variations. Unfortunately, there is no universally standard method to adjust a sustainable growth rate, and analysts depend a great deal on personal experience and their own subjective judgment. Our nearby *Work the Web* box contains more information on analyst-estimated growth rates.

CHECK THIS

6.2a Compare the dividend discount model, the constant growth model, and the constant perpetual growth model. How are they alike? How do they differ?

6.2b What is a geometric average growth rate? How is it calculated?

6.2c What is a sustainable growth rate? How is it calculated?

We discussed use of the sustainable growth formula to estimate a company's growth rate; however, the formula is not foolproof. Changes in the variables of the model can have a dramatic effect on growth rates. One of the most important tasks of an equity analyst is estimating future growth rates. These estimates entail a detailed analysis of the company. One place to find earnings and sales growth rates on the Web is Yahoo! Finance at finance.yahoo.com. Here, we pulled up a quote for Coca-Cola (KO) and followed the "Analysts Estimates" link. Below you will see an abbreviated look at the results.

Earnings Estimates	Current Qtr Sep-05	Next Qtr Dec-05	Current Year Dec-05	Next Year Dec-06
Avg. Estimate	0.53	0.46	2.12	2.29
No. of Analysts	15	14	18	18
Low Estimate	0.50	0.44	2.05	2.15
High Estimate	0.56	0.49	2.17	2.41
Year Ago EPS	0.50	0.46	2.06	2.12
Revenue Estimates	**Current Qtr Sep-05**	**Next Qtr Dec-05**	**Current Year Dec-05**	**Next Year Dec-06**
Avg. Estimate	6.06B	5.58B	23.27B	24.48B
No. of Analysts	7	7	13	11
Low Estimate	5.94B	5.49B	22.90B	24.06B
High Estimate	6.20B	5.79B	23.81B	25.15B
Year Ago Sales	5.66B	N/A	N/A	23.27B
Sales Growth	7.0%	N/A	N/A	5.2%

As shown, analysts expect revenue (sales) of $23.27 billion in 2005, growing to $24.48 billion in 2006, an increase of 5.20 percent.

We also have the following table comparing Coca-Cola to some benchmarks:

Growth Estimates	KO	Industry	S&P 500
Current Qtr.	6.0%	7.9%	15.7%
Next Qtr.	0.0%	7.8%	13.3%
This Year	2.9%	5.6%	12.7%
Next Year	8.0%	9.0%	10.7%
Past 5 Years	8.9%	N/A	N/A
Next 5 Years	8.0%	9.02%	10.62%
Price/Earnings	20.80	19.68	16.40
PEG Ratio	2.60	2.18	1.54

As you can see, estimated earnings growth for KO is slightly lower than estimates for the industry and quite a bit less than the S&P 500 estimate. Here is an assignment for you: What is the PEG ratio? Locate a financial glossary on the Web (there are lots of them) to find out.

6.3 The Two-Stage Dividend Growth Model

In the previous section, we examined dividend discount models based on a single growth rate. You may have already thought that a single growth rate is often unrealistic, because companies experience temporary periods of unusually high or low growth, with growth eventually converging to an industry average or an economywide average. In these cases, financial analysts frequently use a **two-stage dividend growth model**.

A two-stage dividend growth model assumes that a firm will initially grow at a rate g_1 during a first stage of growth lasting T years and thereafter grow at a rate g_2 during a perpetual second stage of growth. The present value formula for the two-stage dividend growth model is stated as follows:

two-stage dividend growth model
Dividend model that assumes a firm will temporarily grow at a rate different from its long-term growth rate.

$$V(0) = \frac{D(0)(1 + g_1)}{k - g_1}\left[1 - \left(\frac{1 + g_1}{1 + k}\right)^T\right] + \left(\frac{1 + g_1}{1 + k}\right)^T \frac{D(0)(1 + g_2)}{k - g_2} \qquad (6.8)$$

At first glance, this expression looks a little complicated. However, it simplifies if we look at its two distinct parts individually. The first term on the right-hand side measures the present value of the first T dividends and is the same expression we used earlier for the constant growth model. The second term then measures the present value of all subsequent dividends.

Using the formula is mostly a matter of "plug and chug" with a calculator. For example, suppose a firm has a current dividend of $2, and dividends are expected to grow at the rate $g_1 = 20$ percent for $T = 5$ years, and thereafter grow at the rate $g_2 = 5$ percent. With a discount rate of $k = 12$ percent, the present value $V(0)$ is calculated as:

$$V(0) = \frac{\$2(1.20)}{.12 - .20}\left[1 - \left(\frac{1.20}{1.12}\right)^5\right] + \left(\frac{1.20}{1.12}\right)^5 \frac{\$2(1.05)}{.12 - .05}$$

$$= \$12.36 + \$42.36$$

$$= \$54.72$$

In this calculation, the total present value of $54.72 is the sum of a $12.36 present value for the first five dividends plus a $42.36 present value for all subsequent dividends.

EXAMPLE 6.10   Using the Two-Stage Model

Suppose a firm has a current dividend of $D(0) = \$5$, which is expected to "shrink" at the rate $g_1 = -10$ percent for $T = 5$ years and thereafter grow at the rate $g_2 = 4$ percent. With a discount rate of $k = 10$ percent, what is the value of the stock? Using the two-stage model, present value, $V(0)$, is calculated as:

$$V(0) = \frac{\$5(.90)}{.10 - (-.10)}\left[1 - \left(\frac{.90}{1.10}\right)^5\right] + \left(\frac{.90}{1.10}\right)^5 \frac{\$5(1.04)}{.10 - 0.4}$$

$$= \$14.25 + \$31.78$$

$$= \$46.03$$

The total present value of $46.03 is the sum of a $14.25 present value of the first five dividends plus a $31.78 present value of all subsequent dividends.

The two-stage growth formula requires that the second-stage growth rate be strictly less than the discount rate, that is, $g_2 < k$. However, the first-stage growth rate g_1 can be greater than, less than, or equal to the discount rate. In the special case where the first-stage growth rate is equal to the discount rate, that is, $g_1 = k$, the two-stage formula reduces to this form:

$$V(0) = D(0) \times T + \frac{D(0)(1 + g_2)}{k - g_2}$$

You may notice with satisfaction that this two-stage formula is much simpler than the general two-stage formula. However, a first-stage growth rate is rarely exactly equal to a risk-adjusted discount rate, so this simplified formula sees little use.

EXAMPLE 6.11 | **Valuing American Express (AXP)**

American Express trades on the New York Stock Exchange under the ticker symbol AXP. In 2005, AXP was paying a dividend of $.48 and analysts forecast five-year growth rates of 13.3 percent for AXP and 11.65 percent for the financial services industry. Assume the growth rate for the financial services industry will remain constant. Then, assuming AXP's growth rate will revert to the industry average after five years, what value would we place on AXP, if we use a discount rate of 13 percent?

$$V(0) = \frac{\$.48 \times 1.133}{.13 - .133}\left[1 - \left(\frac{1.133}{1.13}\right)^5\right] + \left(\frac{1.133}{1.13}\right)^5 \frac{\$.48 \times 1.1165}{.13 - .1165}$$

$$= (-\$181.28) \times (-.013345) + 1.013345 \times \frac{\$.48 \times 1.1165}{.13 - .1165}$$

$$= \$2.42 + \$40.23$$

$$= \$42.65$$

This present value estimate is less than AXP's mid-2005 share price of $53.40. Is AXP overvalued? What other factors could explain the difference?

EXAMPLE 6.12 | **Have a Pepsi? (PEP)**

Pepsi shares trade on the New York Stock Exchange under the ticker symbol PEP. In 2005, Pepsi was paying a dividend of $.95 and analysts forecast a five-year growth rate of 10 percent for Pepsi and a 9 percent growth rate for the soft-drink industry. Suppose Pepsi grows at 10 percent for five years and then at 9 percent thereafter. Assuming a 10.5 percent discount rate, what value would we place on PEP?

Plugging this information into the two-stage dividend growth model, we get:

$$V(0) = \frac{\$.95 \times 1.10}{.105 - .10}\left[1 - \left(\frac{1.10}{1.105}\right)^5\right] + \left(\frac{1.10}{1.105}\right)^5 \frac{\$.95 \times 1.09}{.105 - .09}$$

$$= \$4.69 + \$67.49$$

$$= \$72.18$$

This estimate is about 30 percent higher than PEP's mid-2005 share price of $55.54. Suppose we try a second-stage growth rate of 8.50 percent. Then, we get:

$$V(0) = \frac{\$.95 \times 1.10}{.105 - .10}\left[1 - \left(\frac{1.10}{1.105}\right)^5\right] + \left(\frac{1.10}{1.105}\right)^5 \frac{\$.95 \times 1.085}{.105 - .085}$$

$$= \$4.69 + \$50.38$$

$$= \$55.07$$

This yields a much more realistic stock price estimate and illustrates how sensitive dividend growth price formulas can be to small changes in estimated growth rates.

The last case we consider is nonconstant growth in the first stage. As a simple example of nonconstant growth, consider the case of a company that is currently not paying dividends. You predict that, in five years, the company will pay a dividend for the first time. The dividend will be $.50 per share. You expect that this dividend will then grow at a rate of 10 percent per year indefinitely. The required return on companies such as this one is 20 percent. What is the price of the stock today?

To see what the stock is worth today, we first find out what it will be worth once dividends are paid. We can then calculate the present value of that future price to get today's price. The first dividend will be paid in five years, and the dividend will grow steadily from then on. Using the dividend growth model, we can say that the price in four years will be:

$$V(4) = D(4) \times (1 + g)/(k - g)$$
$$= D(5)/(k - g)$$
$$= \$.50/(.20 - .10)$$
$$= \$5$$

If the stock will be worth $5 in four years, then we can get the current value by discounting this price back four years at 20 percent:

$$V(0) = \$5/1.20^4 = \$5/2.0736 = \$2.41$$

The stock is therefore worth $2.41 today.

The problem of nonconstant growth is only slightly more complicated if the dividends are not zero for the first several years. For example, suppose that you have come up with the following dividend forecasts for the next three years:

Year	Expected Dividend
1	$1.00
2	2.00
3	2.50

After the third year, the dividend will grow at a constant rate of 5 percent per year. The required return is 10 percent. What is the value of the stock today?

In dealing with nonconstant growth, a time line can be very helpful. Figure 6.1 illustrates one for this problem. The important thing to notice is when constant growth starts. As we've shown, for this problem, constant growth starts at Time 3. This means that we can use our constant growth model to determine the stock price at Time 3, $V(3)$. By far the most common mistake in this situation is to incorrectly identify the start of the constant growth phase and, as a result, calculate the future stock price at the wrong time.

As always, the value of the stock is the present value of all future dividends. To calculate this present value, we first have to compute the present value of the stock price three

FIGURE 6.1   Time Line

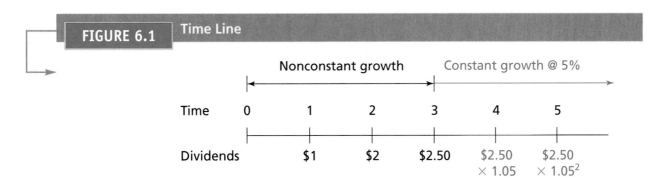

years down the road, just as we did before. We then have to add in the present value of the dividends that will be paid between now and then. So, the price in three years is:

$$V(3) = D(3) \times (1 + g)/(k - g)$$
$$= \$2.50 \times 1.05/(.10 - .05)$$
$$= \$52.50$$

We can now calculate the total value of the stock as the present value of the first three dividends plus the present value of the price at Time 3, $V(3)$.

$$V(0) = \frac{D(1)}{(1+k)^1} + \frac{D(2)}{(1+k)^2} + \frac{D(3)}{(1+k)^3} + \frac{V(3)}{(1+k)^3}$$
$$= \frac{\$1}{1.10} + \frac{2}{1.10^2} + \frac{2.50}{1.10^3} + \frac{52.50}{1.10^3}$$
$$= \$.91 + 1.65 + 1.88 + 39.44$$
$$= \$43.88$$

The value of the stock today is thus $43.88.

EXAMPLE 6.13 | **"Supernormal" Growth**

Chain Reaction, Inc., has been growing at a phenomenal rate of 30 percent per year because of its rapid expansion and explosive sales. You believe that this growth rate will last for three more years and that the rate will then drop to 10 percent per year. If the growth rate then remains at 10 percent indefinitely, what is the total value of the stock? Total dividends just paid were $5 million, and the required return is 20 percent.

Chain Reaction's situation is an example of supernormal growth. It is unlikely that a 30 percent growth rate can be sustained for any extended length of time. To value the equity in this company, we first need to calculate the total dividends over the supernormal growth period:

Year	Total Dividends (in millions)
1	$5.00 × 1.3 = $ 6.500
2	6.50 × 1.3 = 8.450
3	8.45 × 1.3 = 10.985

The price at Time 3 can be calculated as:

$$V(3) = D(3) \times (1 + g)/(k - g)$$

where g is the long-run growth rate. So we have:

$$V(3) = \$10.985 \times 1.10/(.20 - .10) = \$120.835 \text{ million}$$

To determine the value today, we need the present value of this amount plus the present value of the total dividends:

$$V(0) = \frac{D(1)}{(1+k)^1} + \frac{D(2)}{(1+k)^2} + \frac{D(3)}{(1+k)^3} + \frac{V(3)}{(1+k)^3}$$
$$= \frac{\$6.50}{1.20} + \frac{8.45}{1.20^2} + \frac{10.985}{1.20^3} + \frac{120.835}{1.20^3}$$
$$= \$5.42 + 5.87 + 6.36 + 69.93$$
$$= \$87.58$$

The total value of the stock today is thus $87.58 million. If there were, for example, 20 million shares, then the stock would be worth $87.58/20 = $4.38 per share.

DISCOUNT RATES FOR DIVIDEND DISCOUNT MODELS

You may wonder where the discount rates used in the preceding examples come from. The answer is that they come from the *capital asset pricing model* (CAPM). Although a detailed discussion of the CAPM is deferred to a later chapter, we can point out here that, based on the CAPM, the discount rate for a stock can be estimated using this formula:

$$\text{Discount rate} = \text{U.S. T-bill rate} + (\text{Stock beta} \times \text{Stock market risk premium}) \quad (6.9)$$

The components of this formula, as we use it here, are defined as follows:

U.S. T-bill rate:	Return on 90-day U.S. T-bills
Stock beta:	Risk relative to an average stock
Stock market risk premium:	Risk premium for an average stock

The basic intuition for this approach can be traced back to Chapter 1. There we saw that the return we expect to earn on a risky asset had two parts, a "wait" component and a "worry" component. We labeled the wait component as the *time value of money,* and we noted that it can be measured as the return we earn from an essentially riskless investment. Here we use the return on a 90-day Treasury bill as the riskless return.

We called the worry component the *risk premium,* and we noted that the greater the risk, the greater the risk premium. Depending on the exact period studied, the risk premium for the market as a whole over the past 75 or so years has averaged about 9.0 percent. This 9.0 percent can be interpreted as the risk premium for bearing an average amount of stock market risk, and we use it as the stock market risk premium.

beta
Measure of a stock's risk relative to the stock market average.

Finally, when we look at a particular stock, we recognize that it may be more or less risky than an average stock. A stock's **beta** is a measure of a single stock's risk relative to an average stock, and we discuss beta at length in a later chapter. For now, it suffices to know that the market average beta is 1.0. A beta of 1.5 indicates that a stock has 50 percent more risk than the average stock, so its risk premium is 50 percent higher. A beta of .50 indicates that a stock is 50 percent less risky than average and has a smaller risk premium.

When this chapter was written, the T-bill rate was about 3.1 percent. Taking the concept of stock beta as given for now, a stock beta of .8 yields an estimated discount rate of 3.1% + (.8 × 9%) = 10.3%. Similarly, a stock beta of 1.2 yields the discount rate of 3.1% + (1.2 × 9%) = 13.9%. For the remainder of this chapter, we will use discount rates calculated according to this CAPM formula.

OBSERVATIONS ON DIVIDEND DISCOUNT MODELS

We have examined three dividend discount models: the constant perpetual growth model, the two-stage dividend growth model, and the nonconstant growth model. Each model has advantages and disadvantages. Certainly, the main advantage of the constant perpetual growth model is that it is simple to compute. However, it has several disadvantages: (1) it is not usable for firms not paying dividends, (2) it is not usable when the growth rate is greater than the discount rate, (3) it is sensitive to the choice of growth rate and discount rate, (4) discount rates and growth rates may be difficult to estimate accurately, and (5) constant perpetual growth is often an unrealistic assumption.

The two-stage dividend growth model offers several improvements: (1) it is more realistic, since it accounts for low, high, or zero growth in the first stage, followed by constant long-term growth in the second stage, and (2) it is usable when the first-stage growth rate is greater than the discount rate. However, the two-stage model is also sensitive to the choice of discount rate and growth rates, and it is not useful for companies that don't pay dividends. The nonconstant growth model is more flexible in this regard, but it still remains sensitive to the discount and growth rates assumed.

Financial analysts readily acknowledge the limitations of dividend discount models. Consequently, they also turn to other valuation methods to expand their analyses. In the next two sections, we discuss some popular stock valuation methods based on the residual income model and based on price ratios.

CHECK THIS

6.3a   What are the three parts of a CAPM-determined discount rate?

6.3b   Under what circumstances is a two-stage dividend discount model appropriate?

6.4   The Residual Income Model

To this point, we have been valuing only firms that pay dividends. What about the many companies that don't pay dividends? As it turns out, there is an elegant and simple model that we can use.

RESIDUAL INCOME

At the beginning of any period, we can think of the book, or the accounting, equity in a firm as representing the total amount that stockholders have tied up in the company. Let B_{t-1} stand for the book equity per share at the beginning of a period that ends at time t. Over the period, the stockholders have a required return on that investment of k. Thus, the required return in dollars, or required earnings per share (EPS), during the period that ends at time t, or $REPS_t$, is just:

$$REPS_t = B_{t-1} \times k$$

The difference between actual earnings, EPS_t, and required earnings, $REPS_t$, during a period is called the *residual income, RI*, and is given by:

$$RI_t = EPS_t - REPS_t = EPS_t - B_{t-1} \times k$$

Economic Value Added (EVA)
A financial performance measure based on the difference between a firm's actual earnings and required earnings.

Residual income is sometimes called **Economic Value Added**, or **EVA** for short. It is also called "abnormal" earnings. Whatever it is called, it is the excess of actual earnings over required earnings. We can also think of it as the value created by a firm in period t.

Next, we can write the value of a share of stock as the sum of two parts. The first part is the current book value of the firm (i.e., what is currently invested). The second part is the present value of all future residual earnings. That is,

$$P_0 = B_0 + \frac{EPS_1 - B_0 \times k}{(1+k)^1} + \frac{EPS_2 - B_1 \times k}{(1+k)^2} + \frac{EPS_3 - B_2 \times k}{(1+k)^3} + \cdots \qquad (6.10)$$

WWW
To learn more above Economic Value Added (EVA) visit
www.eva.com

When we developed the constant perpetual growth model for dividend-paying stocks, we made the simplifying assumption that *dividends* grow at a constant rate of g. Here we make the similar assumption that *earnings* grow at a constant rate of g. With this assumption, we can simplify equation (6.10) to:

$$P_0 = B_0 + \frac{EPS_0(1+g) - B_0 \times k}{k - g} \qquad (6.11)$$

residual income model (RIM)
A method for valuing stock in a company that does not pay dividends.

Equation (6.11) is known as the **residual income model**, or **RIM**. If we write both terms in equation (6.11) with a common denominator, we get another way to write the residual income model:

$$P_0 = \frac{EPS_1 - B_0 \times g}{k - g} \qquad (6.12)$$

THE RIM VERSUS THE CONSTANT GROWTH DDM

clean surplus relationship (CSR)
An accounting relationship in which earnings minus dividends equals the change in book value per share.

The RIM is closely related to the constant perpetual growth dividend model. To see the connection, assume that the change in book value per share on a stock is equal to earnings per share minus dividends. This is known as the **clean surplus relationship (CSR)**, written as:

$$EPS_1 - D_1 = B_1 - B_0 \quad \text{or} \quad D_1 = EPS_1 + B_0 - B_1$$

Note that in practice the CSR does not exactly hold because various "dirty" surplus changes to book equity are allowed. But it is usually a good approximation, particularly over the long run.

Assuming that earnings and dividends per share grow at rate g, the CSR shows that book value per share must also grow at rate g, so we can write:

$$D_1 = EPS_1 + B_0 - B_1 = EPS_1 + B_0 - B_0(1 + g) = EPS_1 - B_0 \times g \qquad (6.13)$$

Plugging the expression for D_1 in equation (6.13) into equation (6.12), we see right away that the residual income model is mathematically the same as the constant perpetual growth model:

$$P_0 = \frac{EPS_1 - B_0 \times g}{k - g} = \frac{D_1}{k - g}$$

So these two approaches are really the same, but the RIM is more flexible because we can apply it to any stock, not just dividend payers.

Although we do not present them, there are other forms of the RIM. For example, a two-stage residual income model incorporates two different periods of growth. And the assumption of nonconstant growth for a number of years followed by constant growth can be handled by another form of the residual income model.

EXAMPLE 6.14 | **The Price of FIZ**

Shares of National Beverage Corporation trade on the American Stock Exchange with the ticker symbol FIZ. National Beverage Corporation does not pay dividends. It is July 1, 2005, and shares of FIZ are trading at $7.98. We have the following data:

	July 1, 2005 (time 0)
EPS_0	$0.47
DIV	$0
Book value, B_0	$4.271

Assume $g = 9$ percent and $k = 10.3$ percent. Using the residual income model,

$$P_0 = B_0 + \frac{EPS_0(1 + g) - B_0 \times k}{k - g}$$

$$= \$4.271 + \frac{\$.47(1 + .09) - \$4.271 \times .103}{.103 - .09}$$

$$= \$4.271 + \frac{\$.5123 - \$.4399}{\$.013} = \$9.84.$$

Verify this price using equation (6.12). Be careful to use g, not $(1 + g)$. Is the market price for FIZ shares too low? If you say yes, what are you saying about the assumed values for g and k?

EXAMPLE 6.15 | The Growth of FIZ

Using the relevant data in Example 6.14 and the residual income model, what growth rate g results in a price of $7.98?

$$P_0 = B_0 + \frac{EPS_0(1 + g) - B_0 \times k}{k - g}$$

$$\$7.98 = 4.271 + \frac{.47(1 + g) - 4.271 \times .103}{.103 - g}$$

$$\$3.709 \times (.103 - g) = .47 + .47g - .4399$$

$$\$.3820 - 3.709g = .47g + .0301$$

$$.3519 = 4.179 \, g$$

$$g = .0842, \text{ or } 8.42\%$$

CHECK THIS

6.4a What does the residual income model do that the perpetual constant growth model cannot do?

6.4b What is the critical assumption that makes the residual income model mathematically equal to the perpetual constant growth model?

6.5 Price Ratio Analysis

Price ratios are widely used by financial analysts, more so even than dividend discount models. Of course, all valuation methods try to accomplish the same thing, which is to appraise the economic value of a company's stock. However, analysts readily agree that no single method can adequately handle this task on all occasions. In this section, we therefore examine several of the most popular price ratio methods and provide examples of their use in financial analysis.

PRICE-EARNINGS RATIOS

price-earnings (P/E) ratio
Current stock price divided by annual earnings per share (EPS).

earnings yield (E/P)
Inverse of the P/E ratio: earnings per share divided by price per share.

The most popular price ratio used to assess the value of common stock is a company's **price-earnings ratio**, abbreviated as **P/E ratio**. In fact, as we saw in Chapter 3, P/E ratios are reported in the financial press every day. As we discussed, a price-earnings ratio is calculated as the ratio of a firm's current stock price divided by its annual earnings per share (EPS).

The inverse of a P/E ratio is called an **earnings yield**, and it is measured as earnings per share divided by the current stock price (E/P). Clearly, an earnings yield and a price-earnings ratio are simply two ways to measure the same thing. In practice, earnings yields are less commonly stated and used than P/E ratios.

Because most companies report earnings each quarter, annual earnings per share can be calculated either as the most recent quarterly earnings per share times four or as the sum of the last four quarterly earnings per share figures. Most analysts prefer the first method of multiplying the latest quarterly earnings per share value times four. However, some published data sources, including *The Wall Street Journal,* report annual earnings per share as the sum of the last four quarters' figures. The difference is usually small, but it can sometimes be a source of confusion.

growth stocks
A term often used to describe high-P/E stocks.

Visit the Starbucks and Ford
Web sites at
www.starbucks.com
and
www.ford.com

value stocks
A term often used to describe low-P/E stocks.

price-cash flow (P/CF) ratio
Current stock price divided by current cash flow per share.

cash flow
In the context of the price-cash flow ratio, usually taken to be net income plus depreciation.

Financial analysts often refer to high-P/E stocks as **growth stocks**. To see why, notice that a P/E ratio is measured as the *current* stock price over *current* earnings per share. Now, consider two companies with the same current earnings per share, where one company is a high-growth company and the other is a low-growth company. Which company do you think should have a higher stock price, the high-growth company or the low-growth company?

This question is a no-brainer. All else equal, we would be surprised if the high-growth company did not have a higher stock price, and therefore a higher P/E ratio. In general, companies with higher expected earnings growth will have higher P/E ratios, which is why high-P/E stocks are often referred to as growth stocks.

To give an example, Starbucks Corporation is a specialty coffee retailer with a history of aggressive sales growth. Its stock trades on NASDAQ under the ticker symbol SBUX. In mid-2005, SBUX stock traded at $51.61 with earnings per share (EPS) of $1.08, and so had a P/E ratio of $51.61/$1.08 = 47.79. This P/E ratio is well above the average P/E ratio of about 16.5 for the S&P 500 (of which SBUX is a member). SBUX has never paid a dividend. Instead, Starbucks reinvests all earnings. So far this strategy has been successful, as the firm has grown at an average rate of 24 percent over the preceding five years.

The reason high-P/E stocks are called growth stocks seems obvious enough; however, in a seeming defiance of logic, low-P/E stocks are often referred to as **value stocks**. The reason is that low-P/E stocks are often viewed as "cheap" relative to *current* earnings. (Notice again the emphasis on "current.") This suggests that these stocks may represent good investment values, and hence the term value stocks.

In mid-2005, shares of the well-known S&P 500 auto company Ford (F) were trading at a price of $10.84. With earnings per share of EPS = $1.39, the P/E ratio is $10.84/$1.39 = 7.80. This is well below the S&P 500 average, and so Ford might be considered a value stock.

Having said all this, we want to emphasize that the terms "growth stock" and "value stock" are mostly just commonly used labels. Of course, only time will tell whether a high-P/E stock actually turns out to be a high-growth stock, or whether a low-P/E stock is really a good value. The nearby *Investment Updates* box contains additional discussion of P/E ratios.

PRICE-CASH FLOW RATIOS

Instead of price-earnings (P/E) ratios, many analysts prefer to look at price-cash flow (P/CF) ratios. A **price-cash flow (P/CF) ratio** is measured as a company's current stock price divided by its current annual cash flow per share. Like earnings, cash flow is normally reported quarterly and most analysts multiply the last quarterly cash flow figure by four to obtain annual cash flow. Again, like earnings, many published data sources report annual cash flow as a sum of the latest four quarterly cash flows.

There are a variety of definitions of **cash flow**. In this context, the most common measure is simply calculated as net income plus depreciation, so this is the one we use here. In a later chapter, we examine in detail how cash flow is calculated in a firm's financial statements. Cash flow is usually reported in a firm's financial statements and labeled as cash flow from operations (or operating cash flow).

The difference between earnings and cash flow is often confusing, largely because of the way that standard accounting practice defines net income. Essentially, net income is measured as revenues minus expenses. Obviously, this is logical. However, not all expenses are actually cash expenses. The most important exception is depreciation.

When a firm acquires a long-lived asset such as a new factory facility, standard accounting practice does not deduct the cost of the factory all at once, even though it is actually paid for all at once. Instead, the cost is deducted over time. These deductions do not represent actual cash payments, however. The actual cash payment occurred when the

INVESTMENT UPDATES

ONCE A RUST BELT RELIC, U.S. STEEL IS NOW PROFITABLE, EFFICIENT . . . AND UNDERVALUED

Regardless of whether Pittsburgh-based U.S. Steel begins a major buyback program soon, its shares now look attractive, trading around $40. The current price is less than six times projected 2004 profits of $7.35 and six times the Wall Street consensus estimate for 2005 of $6.47 a share.

Bulls note that the 2005 consensus assumes a marked decline in domestic steel prices, which have more than doubled this year to about $650 a ton for benchmark hot-rolled products, up from $300 in late 2003. If steel prices hold around current levels, U.S. Steel could earn $10 or more a share in 2005. That may sound outlandish, but the company netted $2.56 a share from operations in the third quarter and could earn $3 in the current one.

"U.S. Steel is very undervalued," says Alan Fournier, a principal at Pennant Capital Management, a Chatham, N.J., investment firm. "The company is worth 50 percent more than where it's trading."

David Tepper, the head of Appaloosa Management, the company's second-largest shareholder, recently told management on its earnings conference call that U.S. Steel "has the lowest valuation" among the world's major steel makers. The latest publicly disclosed data shows that Tepper's Chatham, N.J.-based firm, a distressed-debt specialist that manages $3 billion, owns 5 percent of the company's 130 million outstanding shares.

Fournier and Tepper want U.S. Steel to buy back stock with its strong earnings and cash flow. Management has resisted those requests, preferring to use free cash to pay down debt, fund pension obligations, and make acquisitions.

Many investors still view U.S. Steel as a rusting relic of a bygone era when steel producers ruled American industry. But the company is now one of the globe's leading steel makers at a time when the industry may be on the brink of years of prosperity. U.S. Steel has world-class mills in the United States and central Europe. It also controls a vast supply of iron ore, a critical steel input in tight supply.

Indeed, U.S. Steel's integrated structure, which made it the industry leader in the early 20th century, is also a major advantage in the early 21st century.

"Our position has never been better in my 20-plus years at the company," says John Surma, U.S. Steel's chief executive. "World appetite for steel is strong, and I don't see why that should change. Supply is constrained."

U.S. Steel is the biggest U.S.-based producer, with total expected 2004 production of 22 million tons, but it ranks sixth globally and accounts for just 2 percent of total world production. U.S. Steel generally is viewed as an asset acquirer—last year, it bought a steel outfit in Serbia—but it's conceivable the company could be taken over. One potential buyer is Arcelor, Europe's largest steel manufacturer.

The steel market's strength is being driven by rising demand from China, which now consumes 30 percent of the world's annual output of 1 billion tons. Chinese demand has doubled in the past four years. India, Eastern Europe, and the states of the former Soviet Union are sources of significant steel demand. Domestic steel consumption also has been high. U.S. Steel has a highly profitable steel plant in Slovakia, which is turning into a center of European auto production.

The Street worries that the sharp increase in steel prices will reverse, as it often has in the past. The cycle last turned down—in brutal fashion—in 2001, leading to bankruptcies of nearly half the U.S. steel industry. Given the importance of Chinese demand, steel stocks have been vulnerable to any sign of a slowdown in China's economy. U.S. Steel shares dipped last month when spot prices fell about $100 a ton from their peak summer level of $750.

U.S. Steel stock (with its famed ticker symbol X) rose over $3 last week amid some positive analyst comments. Goldman Sachs' Aldo Mazzaferro raised his rating to Outperform from In-Line, telling clients that the company "appears to be on the verge of a major breakout in earnings power." He lifted his 2005 profit projection to $8.25 a share from $7.90 and boosted his price target to $58 from $49.

factory was purchased. At this point you may be a little confused about why the difference is important, but hang in there for a few more paragraphs.

Most analysts agree that in examining a company's financial performance, cash flow can be more informative than net income. To see why, consider the hypothetical example of two identical companies: Twiddle-Dee Co. and Twiddle-Dum Co. Suppose that both companies have the same constant revenues and expenses in each year over a three-year period. These constant revenues and cash expenses (excluding depreciation) yield the same constant annual cash flows, and they are stated as follows:

	Twiddle-Dee	Twiddle-Dum
Revenues	$5,000	$5,000
Cash expenses	– 3,000	– 3,000
Cash flow	$2,000	$2,000

Thus, both companies have the same $2,000 cash flow in each of the three years of this hypothetical example.

Next, suppose that both companies incur total depreciation of $3,000 spread out over the three-year period. Standard accounting practices sometimes allows a manager to choose among several depreciation schedules. Twiddle-Dee Co. chooses straight-line depreciation, and Twiddle-Dum Co. chooses accelerated depreciation. These two depreciation schedules are tabulated below:

	Twiddle-Dee	Twiddle-Dum
Year 1	$1,000	$1,500
Year 2	1,000	1,000
Year 3	1,000	500
Total	$3,000	$3,000

Note that total depreciation over the three-year period is the same for both companies. However, Twiddle-Dee Co. has the same $1,000 depreciation in each year, while Twiddle-Dum Co. has accelerated depreciation of $1,500 in the first year, $1,000 in the second year, and $500 depreciation in the third year.

Now, let's look at the resulting annual cash flows and net income figures for the two companies, recalling that in each year, Cash flow = Net income + Depreciation:

	Twiddle-Dee		Twiddle-Dum	
	Cash Flow	Net Income	Cash Flow	Net Income
Year 1	$2,000	$1,000	$2,000	$ 500
Year 2	2,000	1,000	2,000	1,000
Year 3	2,000	1,000	2,000	1,500
Total	$6,000	$3,000	$6,000	$3,000

Note that Twiddle-Dum Co.'s net income is lower in the first year and higher in the third year than Twiddle-Dee Co.'s net income. This is purely a result of Twiddle-Dum Co.'s accelerated depreciation schedule, and has nothing to do with Twiddle-Dum Co.'s actual profitability. However, an inexperienced analyst observing Twiddle-Dum Co.'s rapidly rising annual earnings figures might incorrectly label Twiddle-Dum as a growth company. An experienced analyst would observe that there was no cash flow growth to support this naive conclusion.

Financial analysts typically use both price-earnings ratios and price-cash flow ratios. They point out that when a company's earnings per share is not significantly larger than its cash flow per share (CFPS), this is a signal, at least potentially, of good-quality earnings. The term "quality" means that the accounting earnings mostly reflect actual cash flow, not just accounting numbers. When earnings are bigger than cash flow, this may be a signal of poor quality earnings.

Going back to some of our earlier examples, Starbucks Corporation had cash flow per share of CFPS = $2.10, yielding a P/CF ratio of $51.61/$2.10 = 24.58. Notice that cash flow per share was close to double that of earnings per share, suggesting high-quality earnings. Ford had cash flow per share of CFPS = $11.98, yielding a P/CF ratio of $10.84/$11.98 = .90. Ford cash flow per share is an unusually large 8.6 times its earnings per share, suggesting high-quality earnings.

PRICE-SALES RATIOS

price-sales (P/S) ratio
Current stock price divided by annual sales per share.

An alternative view of a company's performance is provided by its **price-sales (P/S) ratio**. A price-sales ratio is calculated as the current price of a company's stock divided by its current annual sales revenue per share. A price-sales ratio focuses on a company's ability to generate sales growth. Essentially, a high P/S ratio would suggest high sales growth, while a low P/S ratio might indicate sluggish sales growth.

For example, Starbucks Corporation had sales per share of $14.87 to yield a price-sales ratio of P/S = $51.61/$14.87 = 3.47. Ford had sales per share of $90.42 for a price-sales ratio of P/S = $10.84/$90.42 = .12. Notice the large variation in price-sales ratios for the two companies. The main reason for this difference is that the two companies are in very different kinds of businesses. Security analysts recognize that price-sales ratios cannot be compared in isolation from other important information.

PRICE-BOOK RATIOS

price-book (P/B) ratio
Market value of a company's common stock divided by its book (or accounting) value of equity.

A very basic price ratio for a company is its **price-book (P/B) ratio**, sometimes called the market-book ratio. A price-book ratio is measured as the market value of a company's outstanding common stock divided by its book value of equity.

Price-book ratios are appealing because book values represent, in principle, historical cost. The stock price is an indicator of current value, so a price-book ratio simply measures what the equity is worth today relative to what it cost. A ratio bigger than 1.0 indicates that the firm has been successful in creating value for its stockholders. A ratio smaller than 1.0 indicates that the company is actually worth less than it cost.

This interpretation of the price-book ratio seems simple enough, but the truth is that because of varied and changing accounting standards, book values are difficult to interpret. For this and other reasons, price-book ratios may not have as much information value as they once did.

APPLICATIONS OF PRICE RATIO ANALYSIS

Check out the Intel
Web site at
www.intel.com

Price-earnings ratios, price-cash flow ratios, and price-sales ratios are commonly used to calculate estimates of expected future stock prices. This is done by multiplying a historical average price ratio by an expected future value for the price-ratio denominator variable. For example, Table 6.1 summarizes such a price ratio analysis for Intel Corporation (INTC) based on mid-2005 information.

In Table 6.1, the five-year average ratio row contains five-year average P/E, P/CF, and P/S ratios. The current value row contains values for earnings per share, cash flow per share, and sales per share; and the growth rate row contains five-year projected growth rates for EPS, CFPS, and SPS.

The expected price row contains expected stock prices one year hence. The basic idea is this. Because Intel had an average P/E ratio of 37.30, we will assume that Intel's stock price will be 37.30 times its earnings per share one year from now. To estimate Intel's earnings one year from now, we note that Intel's earnings are projected to grow at a rate of 17.5 percent per

	Earnings	Cash Flow	Sales
Five-year average price ratio	37.30(P/E)	19.75 (P/CF)	6.77(P/S)
Current value per share	$ 1.16 (EPS)	$ 1.94 (CFPS)	$ 5.47(SPS)
Growth rate	17.5%	13.5%	10.5%
Expected stock price	$50.84	$43.49	$40.92

year. If earnings continue to grow at this rate, next year's earnings will be equal to this year's earnings times 1.175. Putting it all together, we have:

$$\text{Expected price} = \text{Historical P/E ratio} \times \text{Projected EPS}$$
$$= \text{Historical P/E ratio} \times \text{Current EPS}$$
$$\times (1 + \text{Projected EPS growth rate})$$
$$= 37.30 \times \$1.16 \times 1.175$$
$$= \$50.84$$

The same procedure is used to calculate an expected price based on cash flow per share:

$$\text{Expected price} = \text{Historical P/CF ratio} \times \text{Projected CFPS}$$
$$= \text{Historical P/CF ratio} \times \text{Current CFPS}$$
$$\times (1 + \text{Projected CFPS growth rate})$$
$$= 19.75 \times \$1.94 \times 1.135$$
$$= \$43.49$$

Finally, an expected price based on sales per share is calculated as:

$$\text{Expected price} = \text{Historical P/S ratio} \times \text{Projected SPS}$$
$$= \text{Historical P/S ratio} \times \text{Current SPS}$$
$$\times (1 + \text{Projected SPS growth rate})$$
$$= 6.77 \times \$5.47 \times 1.105$$
$$= \$40.92$$

See Mickey's Web site at
www.disney.go.com

Notice that in the case of Intel, the price ratio methods yield prices ranging from about $41 to about $51. However, when this analysis was made in mid-2005 Intel's stock price was around $26.50. This difference may be explained by the fact that price ratios for Intel have fallen sharply in recent years. For example, Intel's P/E ratio fell from a high of 55 in 2001 to just 22.1 in 2004. With such a large price-ratio decline, a historical average price ratio may be inaccurate.

	Earnings	Cash Flow	Sales
Five-year average price ratio	31.38 (P/E)	16.51 (P/CF)	1.99(P/S)
Current value per share	$ 1.09 (EPS)	$ 1.70 (CFPS)	$15.05 (SPS)
Growth rate	18.0%	14.0%	7.0%
Expected stock price	$40.36	$31.99	$32.05

EXAMPLE 6.16 Going to Disneyland

Table 6.2 contains information about Walt Disney Corporation. Calculate expected share prices using each of the three price ratio approaches we have discussed.

For example, using the P/E approach, we come up with the following estimates of the price of Walt Disney stock in one year:

$$\text{Expected price} = \text{Historical P/E ratio} \times \text{Current EPS}$$
$$\times (1 + \text{projected EPS growth})$$
$$= 31.38 \times \$1.09 \times 1.18$$
$$= \$40.36$$

CHECK THIS

6.5a Why are high-P/E stocks sometimes called growth stocks?

6.5b Why might an analyst prefer a price-cash flow ratio to a price-earnings ratio?

6.6 An Analysis of the McGraw-Hill Company

Stock market investors have available to them many sources of information about the financial performance of companies with publicly traded stock shares. Indeed, the sheer volume of information available can often be overwhelming. For this reason, several sources publish reference summaries for individual companies.

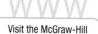

Visit the McGraw-Hill
Web site at
www.mcgraw-hill.com

One well-known example is the *Value Line Investment Survey,* a published reference with frequent updates. *Value Line* provides what many investors consider to be the best one-page company summaries available. Current updates to the *Value Line Investment Survey* are available at most stock brokerage offices and many public libraries. Figure 6.2 presents a one-page summary for the McGraw-Hill Corporation published by *Value Line* in August 2005. We will make frequent reference to information found in the *Value Line* summary in the discussion of McGraw-Hill.

As shown in the title bar of Figure 6.2, McGraw-Hill stock trades on the New York Stock Exchange (NYSE) under the ticker symbol MHP. When this survey went to press in August 2005, McGraw-Hill's stock price was $47.04, with a P/E ratio of 20.9. *Value Line* calculates a P/E ratio as the most recent stock price divided by the latest six months' earnings per share plus earnings per share estimated for the next six months. McGraw-Hill's relative P/E ratio of 1.11 is obtained by dividing its current P/E by the median P/E ratio of all stocks under review by *Value Line.* The dividend yield of 1.4 percent is calculated by dividing estimated dividends for the coming year by the current stock price.

Check out Value-Line's
Web site at
www.valueline.com

At this point, as you look over *Value Line*'s summary in Figure 6.2, you will realize that *Value Line* has packed a considerable amount of information onto a single page. We acknowledge the efficiency of the *Value Line* one-page surveys by not trying to cover all items on the entire page. Most items are well-explained in Figure 6.3, which contains a

FIGURE 6.2 *Value Line* Analysis Chart

McGRAW-HILL NYSE-MHP

RECENT PRICE **47.04**	P/E RATIO **20.9** (Trailing: 22.9 Median: 21.0)	RELATIVE P/E RATIO **1.11**	DIV'D YLD **1.4%**	**VALUE LINE**

TIMELINESS 3 Lowered 9/3/04
SAFETY 1 Raised 6/4/93
TECHNICAL 4 Lowered 8/12/05
BETA .80 (1.00 = Market)

High: 9.7 11.0 12.3 18.8 25.8 31.6 33.8 35.4 34.8 35.0 46.1 48.0
Low: 7.8 8.0 9.3 11.2 17.1 23.6 20.9 24.3 25.4 25.9 34.6 40.5

LEGENDS
— 14.0 x "Cash Flow" p sh
···· Relative Price Strength
2-for-1 split 4/96
2-for-1 split 3/99
2-for-1 split 5/05
Options: Yes
Shaded area indicates recession

Target Price Range 2008 | 2009 | 2010

2008-10 PROJECTIONS

	Price	Gain	Ann'l Total Return
High	85	(+80%)	17%
Low	70	(+50%)	12%

Insider Decisions

	S	O	N	D	J	F	M	A	M
to Buy	0	0	0	0	0	0	0	0	0
Options	1	0	0	5	0	0	0	1	0
to Sell	1	0	0	2	1	1	0	1	0

Institutional Decisions

	3Q2004	4Q2004	1Q2005
to Buy	234	250	250
to Sell	209	227	250
Hld's(000)	284654	283422	280256

Percent shares traded 12 8 4

% TOT. RETURN 7/05
	THIS STOCK	VL ARITH. INDEX
1 yr.	24.4	23.2
3 yr.	54.5	86.2
5 yr.	67.9	75.6

© VALUE LINE PUB., INC. 08-10

1989	1990	1991	1992	1993	1994	1995	1996	1997	1998	1999	2000	2001	2002	2003	2004	2005	2006		08-10	
4.59	4.95	4.95	5.22	5.55	6.95	7.33	7.72	8.92	9.46	10.20	11.02	12.02	12.48	12.68	13.83	15.45	16.65	Sales per sh A	36.85
.60	.61	.50	.52	.57	1.09	1.14	1.23	1.47	1.63	1.81	2.12	2.33	2.57	2.71	2.97	3.30	3.75	"Cash Flow" per sh	5.25
.43	.44	.38	.39	.44	.51	.57	.63	.73	.86	1.01	1.18	1.23	1.48	1.64	1.91	2.25	2.65	Earnings per sh B	3.75
.25	.27	.28	.28	.29	.29	.30	.33	.36	.39	.43	.47	.49	.51	.54	.60	.66	.66	Div'ds Decl'd per sh D■	.72
.15	.24	.13	.13	.13	.19	.15	.16	.20	.45	.39	.25	.30	.18	.30	.37	.40	.40	Cap'l Spending per sh	.50
2.26	2.44	2.55	2.31	2.08	2.30	2.58	3.42	3.62	3.94	4.32	4.53	4.80	5.65	6.72	7.86	9.45	11.50	Book Value per sh E	17.30
389.48	391.42	392.37	393.07	395.31	397.38	400.57	398.12	396.41	394.22	391.42	388.57	386.44	383.67	380.79	379.63	375.00	375.00	Common Shs Outst'g C	370.00
20.4	14.8	18.6	19.1	18.2	16.7	16.7	17.7	20.6	23.6	26.8	23.6	24.6	21.1	18.7	20.6	Bold figures Value Line estimates		Avg Ann'l P/E Ratio	21.0
1.54	1.10	1.19	1.16	1.08	1.11	1.12	1.11	1.19	1.23	1.53	1.53	1.26	1.15	1.07	1.10			Relative P/E Ratio	1.40
2.9%	4.1%	3.7%	3.6%	3.4%	3.2%	3.3%	2.4%	1.9%	1.6%	1.7%	1.6%	1.6%	1.8%	1.5%				Avg Ann'l Div'd Yield	1.5%

CAPITAL STRUCTURE as of 6/30/05
Total Debt $389.6 mill. Due in 5 Yrs $389.2 mill.
LT Debt $.4 mill. LT Interest Nil
(Less than 1% of Cap'l)
Leases, Uncapitalized Annual rentals $180.6 mill.
Pension Assets-12/04 $1126 mill.
Oblig. $1026 mill.

Pfd Stock None

Common Stock 373,800,000 shs.
as of 7/15/05

MARKET CAP: $17.6 billion (Large Cap)

1995	1996	1997	1998	1999	2000	2001	2002	2003	2004	2005	2006		08-10
2935.3	3074.7	3534.1	3729.1	3992.0	4281.0	4645.5	4787.7	4827.9	5250.5	5800	6250	Sales ($mill)	7800
21.6%	21.5%	22.0%	22.8%	24.7%	26.3%	22.5%	27.5%	28.4%	29.9%	30.0%	31.5%	Operating Margin	33.5%
231.4	238.6	293.5	299.2	308.4	362.3	420.6	408.8	403.2	392.7	400	415	Depreciation ($mill)	475
227.1	250.1	290.7	341.9	401.6	461.7	480.4	576.8	629.4	736.4	835	995	Net Profit ($mill)	1385
41.2%	36.8%	38.3%	39.0%	39.0%	38.5%	38.5%	36.3%	37.0%	37.0%	37.0%	37.0%	Income Tax Rate	37.0%
7.7%	8.1%	8.2%	9.2%	10.1%	10.8%	10.3%	12.0%	13.0%	14.0%	14.5%	16.0%	Net Profit Margin	17.7%
193.3	130.9	258.2	137.3	28.2	20.9	d63.4	d101.0	262.5	479.1	300	350	Working Cap'l ($mill)	600
557.4	556.9	607.0	452.1	354.8	817.5	833.6	458.9	.4	.5	Nil	Nil	Long-Term Debt ($mill)	Nil
1035.1	1361.1	1434.7	1551.8	1691.5	1761.0	1853.9	2165.9	2557.1	2984.5	3570	4315	Shr. Equity ($mill)	6400
15.9%	14.2%	15.4%	18.1%	20.6%	18.9%	18.9%	22.4%	24.7%	24.8%	23.5%	23.0%	Return on Total Cap'l	21.5%
21.9%	18.4%	18.3%	22.0%	23.7%	25.2%	25.9%	26.6%	24.6%	24.7%	23.5%	23.0%	Return on Shr. Equity	21.5%
10.4%	8.7%	10.3%	12.1%	13.7%	15.9%	15.7%	17.5%	16.5%	17.0%	16.5%	17.5%	Retained to Com Eq	17.5%
53%	53%	49%	45%	42%	40%	40%	34%	33%	31%	30%	25%	All Div'ds to Net Prof	19%

CURRENT POSITION ($MILL.)

	2003	2004	6/30/05
Cash Assets	695.6	680.6	245.9
Receivables	956.4	1051.4	1121.1
Inventory (FIFO)	301.2	300.5	433.9
Other	303.0	415.3	415.9
Current Assets	2256.2	2447.8	2216.8
Accts Payable	306.2	318.3	285.5
Debt Due	26.0	5.1	389.2
Other	1661.5	1645.3	1671.1
Current Liab.	1993.7	1968.7	2345.8

ANNUAL RATES

of change (per sh)	Past 10 Yrs.	Past 5 Yrs.	Est'd '02-'04 to '08-'10
Sales	8.0%	6.5%	17.0%
"Cash Flow"	14.0%	11.0%	11.0%
Earnings	14.0%	14.0%	13.0%
Dividends	7.0%	7.0%	4.5%
Book Value	15.0%	11.0%	18.5%

QUARTERLY SALES ($ mill.) B

Calendar	Mar.31	Jun.30	Sep.30	Dec.31	Full Year
2002	846.7	1191	1577	1172	4787.7
2003	830.8	1172	1602	1222	4827.9
2004	919.9	1245	1722	1361	5250.5
2005	1029	1456	1840	1475	5800
2006	1050	1555	2010	1635	6250

EARNINGS PER SHARE B

Calendar	Mar.31	Jun.30	Sep.30	Dec.31	Full Year
2002	.08	.35	.71	.34	1.48
2003	.11	.37	.76	.40	1.64
2004	.14	.43	.85	.49	1.91
2005	.21	.51	.95	.58	2.25
2006	.30	.60	1.05	.70	2.65

QUARTERLY DIVIDENDS PAID D■

Calendar	Mar.31	Jun.30	Sep.30	Dec.31	Full Year
2001	.245	.245	.245	.245	.98
2002	.255	.255	.255	.255	1.02
2003	.270	.270	.270	.270	1.08
2004	.300	.300	.300	.300	1.20
2005	.165	.165			

BUSINESS: The McGraw-Hill Companies, Inc. is a global information provider serving financial, education, and business information markets through brands such as *Standard & Poors, McGraw-Hill Education, Business Week, Aviation Week,* and *Platts.* 2004 sales and oper. profit by bus. seg.: Educ., 46%, 26%; Fin'l Svcs., 39%, 65%; Media, 15%, 9%. Has active acquisition program, incl. Mac-millan/McGraw-Hill Sch. Pub. joint vent. in '89; purchased remaining 50%, 10/93; divested S&P ComStock, 2/03; Juvenile Retail Publishing, 1/04. Owns 4 TV stations. Has 16,070 emplys. Off./dir. own 1.2% of shrs. (3/05 Proxy). Chrmn., Pres. and CEO: Harold (Terry) McGraw III. Inc.: NY. Addr.: 1221 Ave. of the Americas, NY, NY 10020. Tel.: 212-512-2000. Internet: www.mcgraw-hill.com.

McGraw-Hill's shares are a decent long-term investment choice. The company's share earnings have been advancing steadily over the past several years. We anticipate that given McGraw's brand recognition, market share, and access to the financial markets, this growth is likely to continue. Indeed, the company has implemented several strategies that should enhance sales over the next 3 to 5 years. Too, we expect management to remain focused on effective cost management and widening operating margins, which we believe ought to expand 3 or 4 percentage points over the pull to 2008–2010. Accordingly, at the current quotation, the stock offers worthwhile 3-to-5-year price appreciation potential.

The company's education segment (43% of revenues) continues to perform well. This is the result of sales advances supplemented by effective cost control. These factors should further enhance McGraw's bottom line through the end of the year. In particular, the company awaits a pending decision from lawmakers in Texas regarding how much of $295 million in educational funding will be used for instructional materials. We think McGraw benefit from the resolution of this matter.

Meanwhile, the Financial Services segment (41%) is also showing margin growth. Strength there has been largely attributable to healthy revenue gains. Management notes that the flagship entity in that segment, Standard & Poor's, has been capitalizing on issuer and investor demand for securitized debt. The company's exposure to international regions, including Europe, Asia, Latin America, and Canada has been the key of late. In particular, mortgage-backed securities and Collateralized Debt Obligations are benefiting from high demand for attractive yields, firm credit quality, and asset protection. Given the improving global economic climate, these trends should continue over the next several quarters.
Simon R. Shoucair   August 19, 2005

Sales (and Operating Margins) by Business Line

	2003	2004	2005	2006
Education	2286(14.1%)	2395(14.2%)	2600(14.3%)	2750(14.5%)
Financial Svcs.	1769(37.8%)	2055(41.8%)	2250(43.0%)	2450(45.0%)
Info./Media Svc.	773(14.2%)	800(14.9%)	900(15.0%)	1050(15.5%)
Segment Total	4828(28.4%)	5250(29.9%)	5750(30.0%)	6250(31.5%)
After depreciation; before corporate and interest expenses.

(A) Incl. Macmillan/McGraw-Hill Pub. Co. from 10/93. (B) Dil. egs., beg. 1997. Excl. nonrecur. gains, (losses): '88, 10¢; '89, (61¢); '93, (82¢); '96, $1.23; '98, (5¢); '99, (12¢); '00, 5¢; '01, (53¢); '03, 30¢; '04, 10¢. Excl. charge for acctg. change: '00, (35¢). Next egs. report due late Oct. Egs. and rev. may not sum due to rounding. (C) In millions, adjusted for splits.

(D) Div. hist. paid in Mar., June, Sept., & Dec. Div. reinv. plan available. (E) Incl. intgbls., at 12/31/04: $1,660 million, $8.72/share.

Company's Financial Strength	A+
Stock's Price Stability	95
Price Growth Persistence	100
Earnings Predictability	100

To subscribe call 1-800-833-0046.

Source: *Value Line* Investment Survey, 2006.

FIGURE 6.3   *Value Line* Analysis Chart

Getting the Most from the Value Line Page

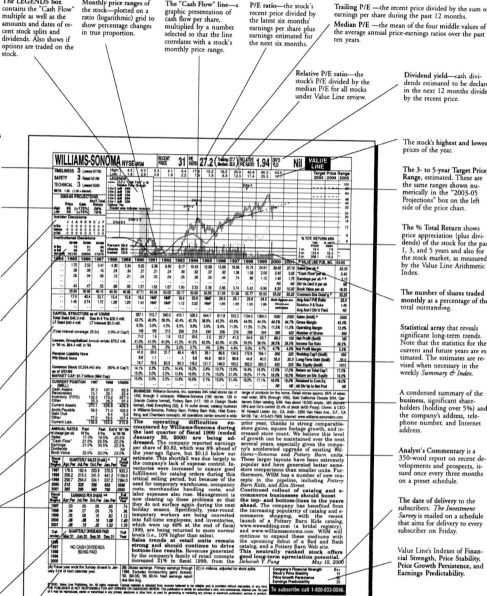

The LEGENDS box contains the "Cash Flow" multiple as well as the amounts and dates of recent stock splits and dividends. Also shows if options are traded on the stock.

Monthly price ranges of the stock—plotted on a ratio (logarithmic) grid to show percentage changes in true proportion.

The "Cash Flow" line—a graphic presentation of cash flow per share, multiplied by a number selected so that the line correlates with a stock's monthly price range.

P/E ratio—the stock's recent price divided by the latest six months' earnings per share plus earnings estimated for the next six months.

Trailing P/E —the recent price divided by the sum of earnings per share during the past 12 months.

Median P/E —the mean of the four middle values of the average annual price-earnings ratios over the past ten years.

Relative P/E ratio—the stock's P/E divided by the median P/E for all stocks under Value Line review.

Dividend yield—cash dividends estimated to be declared in the next 12 months divided by the recent price.

Here is the core of Value Line's advice—the rank for Timeliness; the rank for Safety; the Technical rank. And next to each is normally the date each last changed. Beta shows the stock's sensitivity to fluctuations in the market as a whole.

Projected stock price returns to 2003-05, both absolute (gain/loss without dividends) and total (annual, including dividends).

The record of insider decisions—decisions by officers and directors to buy or sell as reported to the SEC.

The number of large institutions —including banks, insurance companies, mutual funds—buying or selling during the past three quarters and the total number of shares owned.

The capital structure as of recent date showing the percentage of capital in long-term debt and shareholders' equity. Also, Market Capitalization.

Current position—current assets and current liabilities, the components of working capital.

Annual rates of change (on a per-share basis). Actual past, estimated future.

Sales and earnings are shown for each quarter, with earnings on a per share basis.

Quarterly dividends paid are actual payments. The total of dividends paid in four quarters may not equal the figure shown in the annual series on dividends declared. (Sometimes a dividend declared at the end of the year will be paid in the first quarter of the following year.)

Footnotes explain a number of things, such as the way earnings are reported, and the net effect of nonrecurring items.

The stock's highest and lowest prices of the year.

The 3- to 5-year Target Price Range, estimated. These are the same ranges shown numerically in the "2003-05 Projections" box on the left side of the price chart.

The % Total Return shows price appreciation (plus dividends) of the stock for the past 1, 3, and 5 years and also for the stock market, as measured by the Value Line Arithmetic Index.

The number of shares traded monthly as a percentage of the total outstanding.

Statistical array that reveals significant long-term trends. Note that the statistics for the current and future years are estimated. The estimates are revised when necessary in the weekly *Summary & Index*.

A condensed summary of the business, significant shareholders (holding over 5%) and the company's address, telephone number, and Internet address.

Analyst's Commentary is a 350-word report on recent developments and prospects, issued once every three months on a preset schedule.

The date of delivery to the subscribers. *The Investment Survey* is mailed on a schedule that aims for delivery to every subscriber on Friday.

Value Line's Indexes of Financial Strength, Price Stability, Price Growth Persistence, and Earnings Predictability.

Source: *Value Line*, "How to Invest in Common Stocks: A Guide to Using the Value Line Investment Survey," 2003.

complete sample explanation page. However, some items in Figure 6.2 may differ from those in Figure 6.3 reflecting changes made by *Value Line*. In the following discussion, we refer only to information needed to illustrate the analytic methods discussed previously in this chapter.

USING THE DIVIDEND DISCOUNT MODEL

Our first task is to estimate a discount rate for McGraw-Hill. The *Value Line Investment Survey* reports a beta of .80 for McGraw-Hill stock. Using a current Treasury bill rate of 3.1 percent and a historical stock market risk premium of 9 percent, we obtain a CAPM discount rate estimate for McGraw-Hill of $3.1\% + .80 \times 9\% = 10.3\%$.

Our next task is to calculate a sustainable growth rate. *Value Line* reports projected 2006 earnings per share of $2.65 and projected 2006 dividends per share of $.66, implying a retention ratio of $1 - \$.66/\$2.65 = .751$. *Value Line* also reports a projected 2006 return on equity of ROE = 23.0 percent (reported as "Return on Shr. Equity"). Putting these together yields a sustainable growth rate of $.751 \times 23.0\% = 17.27\%$, which may be somewhat high for a mature company like McGraw-Hill.

Finally, with a discount rate and sustainable growth rate we can calculate a share price for McGraw-Hill. Using a constant dividend growth rate model with the 2005 dividend of $D(0) = \$.66$, a discount rate of $k = 10.3$ percent, and a growth rate of 17.27 percent, we get:

$$V(0) = \frac{\$0.66 \times 1.1727}{.103 - .1727}$$
$$= -\$11.10$$

which cannot be. The negative price is due to a growth rate greater than the discount rate, indicating we cannot use the constant dividend growth rate model. As a good analyst would, we'll try something else.

USING THE RESIDUAL INCOME MODEL

In reality, a sustainable growth rate of over 17 percent is not feasible. *Value Line* reports that the actual dividend growth rate over the previous five years was 7 percent (from the box labeled "Annual Rates"). You can audit this number by calculating a simple or geometric average dividend growth rate using dividends per share from 2000 through 2005. (Which one rounds to 7 percent?)

Let's assume that "today" is January 1, 2005. Also, let's keep the 7 percent growth rate and 10.3 percent discount rate. From the *Value Line Investment Survey* (VL), we can fill in columns two and three of the table below:

	2005 (time 0)	2006 (VL)	2006 (CSR)
Beginning BV per share	NA	$9.45	$9.45
EPS	2.25	2.65	2.4075*
DIV	0.66	0.66	1.7460**
Ending BV per share	9.45	11.50	10.1115*

*2.25 × 1.07; 9.45 × 1.07.
**"Plug" = 2.4075 − (10.1115 − 9.45).

The fourth column comes from using the clean surplus relationship (CSR). Here, we grow EPS and book value per share using a growth rate of 7 percent. Then we calculate the dividend "plug" that makes the change in book value equal to EPS minus dividends.

Now we can estimate two prices for McGraw-Hill shares using the RIM—one from data provided by *Value Line* and one from data using the clean surplus relationship. In addition, we can compare these values using a constant dividend growth rate model that uses a dividend growth rate of 7 percent. Using the RIM, we get:

$$P_0 = 9.45 + \frac{2.4075 - 9.45 \times .103}{.103 - .07} = \$52.91 \quad \text{(CSR)}$$

$$P_0 = 9.45 + \frac{2.65 - (11.50 - 9.45)}{.103 - .07} = \$27.63 \quad \text{(VL)}$$

Using the DDM, we get:

$$P_0 = \frac{1.7460}{.103 - .07} = \$52.91 \quad (CSR)$$

$$P_0 = \frac{.66}{.103 - .07} = \$20.00 \quad (VL)$$

The \$.66 used is *Value Line*'s estimate of next year's dividend, D_1, because *Value Line* forecasts no dividend growth between 2005 and 2006. As you would expect, both the RIM and the DDM indicate a price of \$52.91 for McGraw-Hill when we use the CSR. This share value is reasonably close to McGraw-Hill's recently reported stock price of \$47.04. RIM and DDM prices using data from *Value Line* differ, however, because of "dirty surplus."

USING PRICE RATIO ANALYSIS

Value Line reports annual growth rates for sales, cash flow, earnings, dividends, and book values in the box labeled "Annual Rates." These include historical five-year and ten-year growth rates, along with expected growth rates for the next three to five years. We will estimate expected future stock prices using five-year average price ratios that we will calculate along with expected growth rates supplied by *Value Line*.

The *Value Line* survey reports annual average price-earnings ratios, but it does not report average price to cash flow per share ratios, P/CF, or average price to sales per share ratios, P/S. In this case, because all these numbers are on a per-share basis, a quick way to calculate an average P/CF ratio is to multiply an average P/E ratio by the ratio of earnings per share to cash flow per share. That is, P/CFPS = P/E × EPS/CFPS (recall that the "E" in P/E stands for EPS, so they cancel).

For example, McGraw-Hill's 2004 average P/E was 20.60, EPS was \$1.91, CFPS was \$2.97, and SPS was \$13.83. Thus, a quick calculation of McGraw-Hill's 2004 average P/CF ratio is 20.60 × \$1.91/\$2.97 = 13.25. Similarly, the average P/S ratio is 20.60 × \$1.91/\$13.83 = 2.84. In Table 6.3, we provide average price ratio calculations for P/CF and P/S ratios for the years 2000 through 2004, along with five-year averages for each price ratio.

We use the five-year average price ratios calculated in Table 6.3 in the price ratio analysis presented in Table 6.4. We use the expected growth rates for earnings, cash flow, and

| TABLE 6.3 | Price Ratio Calculations for McGraw-Hill Co. (MHP) |

	2000	2001	2002	2003	2004	Average
EPS	1.18	1.23	1.48	1.64	1.91	1.49
P/E	23.60	24.60	21.10	18.70	20.60	21.72
CFPS	2.12	2.33	2.57	2.71	2.97	2.54
P/CF	13.14	12.99	12.15	11.32	13.25	12.57
SPS	11.02	12.02	12.48	12.68	13.83	12.41
P/S	2.53	2.52	2.50	2.42	2.84	2.56

TABLE 6.4

TABLE 6.4 Price Ratio Analysis for McGraw-Hill Co. (MHP) August 2005
Stock Price: $47.04

	Earnings	Cash Flow	Sales
Five-year average price ratio	21.72 (P/E)	12.57 (P/CF)	2.56 (P/S)
Current value per share	$ 1.91 (EPS)	$ 2.97 (CFPS)	$13.83 (SPS)
Growth rate	13.0%	11.0%	17.0%
Expected share price	$46.88	$41.44	$41.42

sales provided by *Value Line* (from the "Annual Rates" box) to calculate expected share prices for McGraw-Hill *one year from now*. For ease, we restate the three formulas used to calculate expected prices below. As an exercise, you should verify the expected share prices in Table 6.4.

$$\text{Expected share price} = \text{P/E ratio} \times \text{EPS} \times (1 + \text{EPS growth rate})$$

$$\text{Expected share price} = \text{P/CF ratio} \times \text{CFPS} \times (1 + \text{CFPS growth rate})$$

$$\text{Expected share price} = \text{P/S ratio} \times \text{SPS} \times (1 + \text{SPS growth rate})$$

We can now summarize our analysis by listing the stock prices obtained by the different ways we have described in this chapter, along with the model used to derive them.

DDM, with calculated sustainable growth rate:	Not defined
DDM, historical growth rate, *Value Line* input:	$20.00
DDM, historical growth rate, CSR:	$52.91
RIM, historical growth rate, *Value Line* input:	$27.63
RIM, historical growth rate, CSR:	$52.91
Price-earnings model:	$46.88
Price-cash flow model:	$41.44
Price-sales model:	$41.42

Notice the wide range of share values we obtained by our various ways. This is not uncommon in security analysis, and it suggests how daunting a task security analysis sometimes can be. In this case, the price-earnings model yields a value closest to the observed stock price of $47.04. However, the goal is not to find a model that yields a value closest to the current price. Rather, the goal is to find a model about which we are confident, For example, if we were confident in the RIM and assumed the clean surplus relationship, then we would conclude that McGraw-Hill stock is fairly priced. But if we use the RIM but did not assume the clean surplus relationship holds, then we would conclude that McGraw-Hill shares are somewhat overpriced.

CHECK THIS

6.6a Locate *Value Line*'s projected growth rate in dividends. How does it compare to the sustainable growth rate we estimated? The historical growth rates? Revalue the stock using the constant perpetual dividend model and this growth rate.

6.6b Assume that the sustainable growth rate we calculated is the growth rate for the next five years only and that dividends will grow thereafter at the rate projected by *Value Line* analysts. Using these growth rates, revalue the stock using the two-stage dividend growth model.

6.7 Summary and Conclusions

In this chapter, we examined several methods of fundamental analysis used by financial analysts to value common stocks. The methods examined were various dividend discount models, residual income models, and price ratio models. We saw that:

1. Dividend discount models value common stock as the sum of all expected future dividend payments, where the dividends are adjusted for risk and the time value of money.

2. The dividend discount model is often simplified by assuming that dividends will grow at a constant growth rate. A particularly simple form of the dividend discount model is the case in which dividends grow at a constant perpetual growth rate. The simplicity of the constant perpetual growth model makes it the most popular dividend discount model. However, it should be applied only to companies with stable earnings and dividend growth.

3. Dividend models require an estimate of future growth. We described the sustainable growth rate, which is measured as a firm's return on equity times its retention ratio, and illustrated its use.

4. Companies often experience temporary periods of unusually high or low growth, where growth eventually converges to an industry average. In such cases, analysts frequently use a two-stage dividend growth model.

5. The difference between actual and required earnings in any period is called residual income. Residual income is sometimes called Economic Value Added or, sometimes, abnormal earnings.

6. The residual income model is a method that can be used to value a share of stock in a company that does not pay dividends. To derive the residual income model, a series of constant growth assumptions are made for EPS, assets, liabilities, and equity. Together, these growth assumptions result in a sustainable growth rate.

7. The residual income model breaks the value of a share of stock into two parts: the current book value of the firm and the present value of all residual earnings (i.e., income).

8. The clean surplus relationship is an accounting relationship that says earnings minus dividends equals the change in book value per share. The clean surplus relationship might not hold in actual practice. But if the clean surplus relationship is true, then the residual income model is mathematically equivalent to the constant perpetual growth model.

9. Price ratios are widely used by financial analysts. The most popular price ratio is a company's price-earnings ratio. A P/E ratio is calculated as the ratio of a firm's stock price divided by its earnings per share (EPS).

10. Financial analysts often refer to high-P/E stocks as growth stocks and low-P/E stocks as value stocks. In general, companies with high expected earnings growth will have high P/E ratios, which is why high-P/E stocks are referred to as growth stocks. Low-P/E stocks are referred to as value stocks because they are viewed as cheap relative to current earnings.

11. Instead of price-earnings ratios, many analysts prefer to look at price-cash flow (P/CF) ratios. A price-cash flow ratio is measured as a company's stock

price divided by its cash flow per share. Most analysts agree that cash flow can provide more information than net income about a company's financial performance.

12. An alternative view of a company's performance is provided by its price-sales (P/S) ratio. A price-sales ratio is calculated as the price of a company's stock divided by its annual sales revenue per share. A price-sales ratio focuses on a company's ability to generate sales growth. A high P/S ratio suggests high sales growth, while a low P/S ratio suggests low sales growth.

13. A basic price ratio for a company is its price-book (P/B) ratio. A price-book ratio is measured as the market value of a company's outstanding common stock divided by its book value of equity. A high P/B ratio suggests that a company is potentially expensive, while a low P/B value suggests that a company may be cheap.

14. A common procedure using price-earnings ratios, price-cash flow ratios, and price-sales ratios is to calculate estimates of expected future stock prices. However, each price ratio method yields a different expected future stock price. Since each method uses different information, each makes a different prediction.

GET REAL

This chapter introduced you to some of the basics of common stock valuation and fundamental analysis. It focused on three important tools used by stock analysts in the real world to assess whether a particular stock is "rich" or "cheap": dividend discount models, residual income models, and price ratio analysis. How should you, as an investor or investment manager, put this information to use?

The answer is that you need to pick some stocks and get to work! As we discussed in the chapter, experience and judgment are needed to use these models, and the only way to obtain these is through practice. Try to identify a few stocks that look cheap and buy them in a simulated brokerage account such as Stock-Trak. At the same time, find a few that look rich and short them. Start studying P/E ratios. Scan *The Wall Street Journal* (or a similar source of market information) and look at the range of P/Es. What's a low P/E? What's a high one? Do they really correspond to what you would call growth and value stocks?

The Internet is a copious source for information on valuing companies. Try, for example, Stock Sheet (www.stocksheet.com), Market Watch (www.marketwatch.com), Hoovers Online (www.hoovers.com), and Zacks (www.zacks.com). Don't forget to check out the Motley Fool (www.fool.com).

Several trade associations have informative Web sites that can be helpful. For individual investors there is the American Association of Individual Investors (www.aaii.com) and for professional security analysts there is the New York Society of Security Analysts (www.nyssa.org). The Association for Investment Management and Research (www.aimr.com) provides a financial analyst's certification that is highly respected among security analysts.

Key Terms

Chapter Review Problems and Self-Test

1. **The Perpetual Growth Model**   Suppose dividends for Tony's Pizza Company are projected to grow at 6 percent forever. If the discount rate is 16 percent and the current dividend is $2, what is the value of the stock?

2. **The Two-Stage Growth Model**   Suppose the Titanic Ice Cube Co.'s dividend grows at a 20 percent rate for the next three years. Thereafter, it grows at a 12 percent rate. What value would we place on Titanic assuming a 15 percent discount rate? Titanic's most recent dividend was $3.

3. **Residual Income Model**   Suppose Al's Infrared Sandwich Company has a current book value of $10.85 per share. The most recent earnings per share were $2.96 per share, and earnings are expected to grow at 6 percent forever. The appropriate discount rate is 8.2 percent. Assume the clean surplus relationship is true. Assuming the company maintains a constant retention ratio, what is the value of the company according to the residual income model if (a) there are no dividends, and (b) there are dividends of $1.00 per share?

4. **Price Ratio Analysis**   The table below contains some information about the Jordan Air Co. Provide expected share prices using each of the three price ratio approaches we have discussed.

PRICE RATIO ANALYSIS FOR JORDAN AIR (CURRENT STOCK PRICE: $40)			
	Earnings	Cash Flow	Sales
Five-year average price ratio	25 (P/E)	7 (P/CF)	1.5 (P/S)
Current value per share	$2.00 (EPS)	$6.00 (CFPS)	$30.00 (SPS)
Growth rate	10%	16%	14%

Answers to Self-Test Problems

1. Plugging the relevant numbers into the constant perpetual growth formula results in:

$$V(0) = \frac{\$2(1.06)}{.16 - .06} = \$21.20$$

As shown, the stock should sell for $21.20.

2. Plugging all the relevant numbers into the two-stage formula gets us:

$$V(0) = \frac{\$3(1.20)}{.15 - .20}\left[1 - \left(\frac{1.20}{1.15}\right)^3\right] + \left(\frac{1.20}{1.15}\right)^3 \frac{\$3(1.12)}{.15 - .12}$$

$$= \$9.81 + \$127.25$$

$$= \$137.06$$

Thus, the stock should sell for about $137.

3. Recall the formula for the residual income model when the clean surplus relationship is true:

$$P_0 = B_0 + \frac{EPS_0(1+g) - B_0 \times k}{k - g}$$

Next, make a table of all the information that you need to put into the formula:

Al's Infrared Sandwich Company	Time 0, i.e., Now
Beginning book value, B_0	10.85
Earnings per share, EPS_0	2.96
Growth rate, g	6%
Discount rate, k	8.2%

We can now solve the problem.

$$P_0 = 10.85 + \frac{2.96(1 + .06) - 10.85 \times .082}{.082 - .06}$$

$$P_0 = \$113.03$$

4. Using the P/E approach, we come up with the following estimate of the price of Jordan Air in one year:

$$\text{Estimated price} = \text{Average P/E} \times \text{Current EPS} \times (1 + \text{Growth rate})$$

$$= 25 \times \$2 \times 1.10$$

$$= \$55$$

Using the P/CF approach, we get:

$$\text{Estimated price} = \text{Average P/CF} \times \text{Current CFPS} \times (1 + \text{Growth rate})$$

$$= 7 \times \$6 \times 1.16$$

$$= \$48.72$$

Finally, using the P/S approach, we get:

$$\text{Estimated price} = \text{Average P/S} \times \text{Current SPS} \times (1 + \text{Growth rate})$$

$$= 1.5 \times \$30 \times 1.14$$

$$= \$51.30$$

Test Your Investment Quotient

1. **Sustainable Growth** A company has a return on equity of ROE = 20 percent, and from earnings per share of EPS = $5, it pays a $2 dividend. What is the company's sustainable growth rate?

    a. 8 percent
    b. 10 percent
    c. 12 percent
    d. 20 percent

2. **Sustainable Growth** If the return on equity for a firm is 15 percent and the retention ratio is 40 percent, the sustainable growth rate of earnings and dividends is which of the following?

    a. 6 percent
    b. 9 percent
    c. 15 percent
    d. 40 percent

3. Dividend Discount Model A common stock pays an annual dividend per share of $2.10. The risk-free rate is 7 percent and the risk premium for this stock is 4 percent. If the annual dividend is expected to remain at $2.10, the value of the stock is closest to:

a. $19.09
b. $30.00
c. $52.50
d. $70.00

4. Dividend Discount Model The constant-growth dividend discount model will not produce a finite value if the dividend growth rate is which of the following?

a. Above its historical average.
b. Above the required rate of return.
c. Below its historical average.
d. Below the required rate of return.

5. Dividend Discount Model In applying the constant-growth dividend discount model, a stock's intrinsic value will do which of the following when the required rate of return is lowered?

a. Decrease
b. Increase
c. Remain unchanged
d. Decrease or increase, depending on other factors.

6. Dividend Discount Model The constant-growth dividend discount model would typically be most appropriate for valuing the stock of which of the following?

a. New venture expected to retain all earnings for several years.
b. Rapidly growing company.
c. Moderate growth, mature company.
d. Company with valuable assets not yet generating profits.

7. Dividend Discount Model A stock has a required return of 15 percent, a constant growth rate of 10 percent, and a dividend payout ratio of 50 percent. What should the stock's P/E ratio be?

a. 3.0
b. 4.5
c. 9.0
d. 11.0

8. Dividend Discount Model Which of the following assumptions does the constant growth dividend discount model require?

I. Dividends grow at a constant rate.
II. The dividend growth rate continues indefinitely.
III. The required rate of return is less than the dividend growth rate.

a. I only
b. III only
c. I and II only
d. I, II, and III

9. Dividend Discount Model A stock will not pay dividends until three years from now. The dividend then will be $2.00 per share, the dividend payout ratio will be 40 percent, and return on equity will be 15 percent. If the required rate of return is 12 percent, which of the following is closest to the value of the stock?

a. $27
b. $33
c. $53
d. $67

10. Dividend Discount Model Assume that at the end of the next year, Company A will pay a $2.00 dividend per share, an increase from the current dividend of $1.50 per share. After that, the dividend is expected to increase at a constant rate of 5 percent. If you require a 12 percent return on the stock, what is the value of the stock?

   a. $28.57
   b. $28.79
   c. $30.00
   d. $31.78

11. **Dividend Discount Model**   A share of stock will pay a dividend of $1.00 one year from now, with dividend growth of 5 percent thereafter. In the context of a dividend discount model, the stock is correctly priced at $10 today. According to the constant dividend growth model, if the required return is 15 percent, what should the value of the stock be two years from now?

   a. $11.03
   b. $12.10
   c. $13.23
   d. $14.40

12. **Cash Flow**   Which of the following implies the highest quality earnings?

   a. Cash flow less than earnings.
   b. Cash flow greater than depreciation.
   c. Cash flow less than earnings minus depreciation.
   d. Cash flow greater than earnings.

13. **Price Ratios**   Two similar companies have the same price-sales and price-earnings ratios. However, company A has a lower price-cash flow ratio than company B. This most likely indicates that

   a. A has lower quality earnings than B.
   b. A has lower quality cash flow than B.
   c. A uses straight-line depreciation, while B uses accelerated depreciation.
   d. A uses accelerated depreciation, while B uses straight-line depreciation.

14. **Price Ratios**   Two similar companies acquire substantial new production facilities, which they both will depreciate over a 10-year period. However, Company A uses accelerated depreciation while Company B uses straight-line depreciation. In the first year that the assets are depreciated, which of the following is most likely to occur?

   a. A's P/CF ratio will be higher than B's.
   b. A's P/CF ratio will be lower than B's.
   c. A's P/E ratio will be higher than B's.
   d. A's P/E ratio will be lower than B's.

15. **Price Ratios**   An analyst estimates the earnings per share and price-to-earnings ratio for a stock market series to be $43.50 and 26 times, respectively. The dividend payout ratio for the series is 65 percent. The value of the stock market series is closest to

   a. 396
   b. 735
   c. 1131
   d. 1866

16. **P/E Ratio**   An analyst gathered the following information about a stock market index:

Required rate of return:	16%
Expected dividend payout ratio:	30%
Expected return on equity investment:	20%

The expected price-earnings (P/E) ratio of the index is closest to

   a. 3.5
   b. 7.0
   c. 15.0
   d. 35.00

www.mhhe.com/jm4e

17. **P/E Ratio**   A company's return on equity is greater than its required return on equity. The earnings multiplier (P/E) for that company's stock is most likely to be positively related to the

   a. Risk-free rate
   b. Market risk premium
   c. Earnings retention ratio
   d. Stock's capital asset pricing model beta

18. **Residual Income Model**   The residual income model separates the value of the firm into two basic components. What are these two components?

   a. The current book value and the present value of future earnings.
   b. The value of earnings per share and the value of cash flow per share.
   c. The current value of the firm's shares and the future value of its shares.
   d. The time value of money and the value of bearing risk.

19. **Residual Income**   Residual income is the difference between

   a. Actual earnings less expected earnings.
   b. Any increase in the value of the firm.
   c. The value of profitable investment projects.
   d. The value added by economical use of assets.

20. **Clean Surplus Relation**   The clean surplus relation says that

   a. Assets minus liabilities minus shareholder's equity equals the change in current assets plus debt payments.
   b. The difference between earnings and dividends equals the change in book value.
   c. Dividends minus earnings equals one minus the payout ratio.
   d. The difference between earnings and dividends equals the change in surplus inventory.

Concept Questions

1. **Dividend Discount Model**   What is the basic principle behind dividend discount models?

2. **P/E Ratios**   Why do growth stocks tend to have higher P/E ratios than value stocks?

3. **Residual Income Model**   What happens in the residual income model when EPS is negative?

4. **Cash Flow**   In computing the price-cash flow ratio, how is cash flow per share usually measured?

5. **Stock Valuation**   Why does the value of a share of stock depend on dividends?

6. **Stock Valuation**   A substantial percentage of the companies listed on the NYSE and the NASDAQ don't pay dividends, but investors are nonetheless willing to buy shares in them. How is this possible given your answer to the previous question?

7. **Dividends**   Referring to the previous two questions, under what circumstances might a company choose not to pay dividends?

8. **Constant Perpetual Growth Model**   Under what two assumptions can we use the constant perpetual growth model presented in the chapter to determine the value of a share of stock? Comment on the reasonableness of these assumptions.

9. **Dividend Growth Models**   Based on the dividend growth models presented in the chapter, what are the two components of the total return of a share of stock? Which do you think is typically larger?

10. **Constant Perpetual Growth Model**   In the context of the constant perpetual growth model, is it true that the growth rate in dividends and the growth rate in the price of the stock are identical?

Questions and Problems _____

1. **Dividend Valuation** CJ Industries will pay a regular dividend of $3.25 per share for each of the next four years. At the end of the four years, the company will also pay out a $50 per share liquidating dividend, and the company will cease operations. If the discount rate is 11 percent, what is the current value of the company's stock?

2. **Dividend Valuation** In the previous problem, suppose the current share price is $50. If all other information remains the same, what must the liquidating dividend be?

3. **Dividend Discount Model** Trust Bankers just paid an annual dividend of $2 per share. The expected dividend growth rate is 6 percent, the discount rate is 12 percent, and the dividends will last for 5 more years. What is the value of the stock? What if the dividends last for 10 more years? 30 years? 100 years?

4. **Dividend Discount Model** Apple Grove, Inc., will pay dividends for the next 10 years. The expected dividend growth rate for this firm is 7 percent, the discount rate is 14 percent, and the stock currently sells for $30 per share. How much must the most recent dividend payment have been?

5. **Dividend Growth Model** Suppose that McKenzie, Inc., just paid a dividend of $4.00 per share. The company will continue to pay dividends for the next 25 years, and then go out of business. If the discount rate is 10 percent per year, what is the value of the stock for a dividend growth rate of 20 percent? 12 percent? 6 percent? 0 percent? −5 percent?

6. **Perpetual Dividend Growth** A company just paid a dividend of $1.80. If the dividends will grow at 6.2 percent per year and you require a return of 11.8 percent, what is the most you should be willing to pay for the stock?

7. **Perpetual Dividend Growth** Atlantis Seafood Company stock currently sells for $60 per share. The company is expected to pay a dividend of $4.10 per share next year, and analysts project that dividends should increase at 4 percent per year for the indefinite future. What must the relevant discount rate be for Atlantis stock?

8. **Perpetual Dividend Growth** Xytex Products just paid a dividend of $1.80 per share, and the stock currently sells for $35. If the discount rate is 12 percent, what is the dividend growth rate?

9. **Perpetual Dividend Growth** Star Light & Power increases its dividend 4.5 percent per year every year. This utility is valued using a discount rate of 9 percent, and the stock currently sells for $48 per share. If you buy a share of stock today and hold on to it for at least three years, what do you expect the value of your dividend check to be three years from today?

10. **Sustainable Growth** Johnson Products earned $2.20 per share last year and paid a $.75 per share dividend. If ROE was 18 percent, what is the sustainable growth rate?

11. **Sustainable Growth** Joker stock has a sustainable growth rate of 6 percent, ROE of 17 percent, and dividends per share of $1.40. If the P/E ratio is 23, what is the value of a share of stock?

12. **Capital Asset Pricing Model** A certain stock has a beta of .7. If the risk-free rate of return is 4.5 percent and the market risk premium is 8.5 percent, what is the expected return of the stock? What is the expected return of a stock with a beta of 1.25?

13. **Residual Income Model** Bill's Bakery expects *earnings* per share of $EPS = 5 next year. Current book value is $4.50 per share. The appropriate discount rate for Bill's Bakery is 12 percent. Calculate the share price for Bill's Bakery if earnings grow at 4 percent forever.

14. **Residual Income Model** For Bill's Bakery described in the previous question, suppose instead that current earnings per share are $5. Calculate the share price for Bill's Bakery if earnings grow at 4 percent forever.

15. **Two-Stage Dividend Growth Model** Underwood Industries just paid a dividend of $1.45 per share. The dividends are expected to grow at a 25 percent rate for the next eight years and then level off to a 7 percent growth rate indefinitely. If the required return is 14 percent, what is the value of the stock today?

16. **Two-Stage Dividend Growth Model** The dividend for Weaver, Inc., is expected to grow at 21 percent for the next 12 years before leveling off at a 6 percent rate indefinitely. If the firm just paid a dividend of $1.34 and you require a return of 12 percent on the stock, what is the most you should pay per share?

17. **Multiple Growth Rates** Netscape Communications does not currently pay a dividend. You expect the company to begin paying a $5 per share dividend in 10 years, and you expect dividends to grow perpetually at 7 percent per year thereafter. If the discount rate is 15 percent, how much is the stock currently worth?

18. **Multiple Growth Rates** PerfectlySoft Corp. is experiencing rapid growth. Dividends are expected to grow at 25 percent per year during the next three years, 20 percent over the following year, and then 7 percent per year thereafter indefinitely. The required return on this stock is 13 percent, and the stock currently sells for $62.10 per share. What is the projected dividend for the coming year?

19. **Multiple Growth Rates** Callaway Corporation is expected to pay the following dividends over the next four years: $9.00, $11.00, $7.00, $1.50. Afterwards, the company pledges to maintain a constant 7 percent growth rate in dividends forever. If the required return on the stock is 14 percent, what is the current share price?

20. **Multiple Required Returns** My Money, Inc., just paid a dividend of $3.50 per share on its stock. The growth rate in dividends is expected to be a constant 6.5 percent per year indefinitely. Investors require a 19 percent return on the stock for the first three years, then a 14 percent return for the next three years, and then an 11 percent return thereafter. What is the current share price for My Money?

21. **Price Ratio Analysis** Given the information below for Seger Corporation, compute the expected share price at the end of 2006 using price ratio analysis.

Year:	2000	2001	2002	2003	2004	2005
Price	$64.00	$72.00	$77.00	$89.00	$86.00	$108.00
EPS	2.55	2.70	2.80	2.90	3.40	3.75
CFPS	5.20	5.75	6.12	6.53	6.75	7.14
SPS	47.00	50.80	55.43	60.27	64.96	67.85

22. **Dividend Growth Analysis** In the previous problem, suppose the dividends per share over the same period were $.77, $.82, $.89, $.94, $1.01, and $1.09, respectively. Compute the expected share price for 2006 using the perpetual growth method. Assume the market risk premium is 8.5 percent, Treasury bills yield 5 percent, and the projected beta of the firm is .85.

23. **Price Ratio Analysis for Internet Companies** Given the information below for HooYah! Corporation, compute the expected share price at the end of 2006 using price ratio analysis.

Year:	2000	2001	2002	2003	2004	2005
Price	$18.00	$53.00	$143.00	$208.00	$101.00	$9.00
EPS	−6.00	−3.20	−2.10	−1.40	0.03	0.05
CFPS	−8.00	−5.20	−2.60	−0.85	0.04	0.08
SPS	8.00	13.00	17.00	19.40	20.50	17.45

24. **Price Ratio Analysis for Internet Companies** Given the information below for StartUp.Com, compute the expected share price at the end of 2006 using price ratio analysis.

Year:	2002	2003	2004	2005
Price	N/A	$93.12	$43.05	$11.50
EPS	N/A	−8.10	−6.50	−5.20
CFPS	N/A	−10.20	−7.10	−5.05
SPS	N/A	3.60	7.10	10.20

25. **Price Ratio Analysis** The current price of Parador Industries stock is $70 per share. Current earnings per share are $4.50, the earnings growth rate is 10 percent, and Parador does not pay a dividend. The expected return on Parador stock is 14 percent. What one-year ahead P/E ratio is consistent with Parador's expected return and earnings growth rate?

26. **Price Ratio Analysis** The current price of Parador Industries stock is $70 per share. Current sales per share are $23, the sales growth rate is 9 percent, and Parador does not pay a dividend. The expected return on Parador stock is 14 percent. What one-year ahead P/S ratio is consistent with Parador's expected return and sales growth rate?

Use the following information to answer Problems 27–31.

Abbott Laboratories (ABT) engages in the discovery, development, manufacture, and sale of a line of health care and pharmaceutical products. Below you will find selected information from *Value Line*. Use the *Value Line* estimated 2005 figures as the actual year-end figures for the company. The beta reported was 0.85 and the risk-free rate was 3.79 percent. Assume a market risk premium of 8 percent.

2001	2002	2003	2004	2005	2006	©VALUE LINE PUB., INC.
10.48	11.31	12.45	12.49	14.45		Sales per sh
2.65	2.83	3.01	3.05	3.40		"Cash Flow" per sh
1.88	2.06	2.21	2.27	2.50		Earnings per sh[A]
.84	.94	.98	1.04	1.10		Div'ds Decl'd per sh[B]
.75	.83	.79	.82	.85		Cap'l Spending per sh
5.83	6.82	8.27	9.09	9.50		Book Value per sh[C]
1554.5	1563.1	1580.2	1575.1	1550.0		Common Shs Outst'g[D]
26.6	22.3	18.7	18.7	*Bold figures are*	Avg Ann'l P/E Ratio
1.36	1.22	1.07	1.00	*Value Line*	Relative P/E Ratio
1.6%	2.0%	2.3%	2.4%	*estimates*	Avg Ann'l Div'd Yield
16285	17683	19678	19678	22400		Sales ($mill)
27.0%	28.9%	27.0%	28.2%	28.0%		Operating Margin
1168.0	1177.3	1274.0	1288.7	1375		Depreciation ($mill)
2944.1	3242.4	3479.2	3522.8	3925		Net Profit ($mill)
8.4%	24.5%	22.0%	21.4%	24.0%		Income Tax Rate
18.1%	18.3%	17.7%	17.9%	17.5%		Net Profit Margin
492.4	2119.6	2650.9	3908.9	2595		Working Cap'l ($mill)
4335.5	4274.0	3452.3	4787.9	3050		Long-Term Debt ($mill)
9059.4	10665	13072	14326	14700		Shr. Equity ($mill)
22.8%	22.3%	21.5%	18.8%	22.5%		Return on Total Cap'l
32.5%	30.4%	26.6%	24.6%	26.5%		Return on Shr. Equity
18.5%	17.0%	15.0%	13.4%	15.0%		Retained to Com Eq
43%	44%	44%	45%	43%		All Div'ds to Net Prof

The high and low share price each year were:

	2001	2002	2003	2004	2005
High	$57.20	$58.00	$47.20	$47.60	$50.00
Low	42.00	29.80	33.80	38.30	38.10

27. **Constant Perpetual Growth Model**   What is the sustainable growth rate and required return for Abbott Laboratories? Using these values, calculate the 2006 share price of Abbott Laboratories Industries stock according to the constant dividend growth model.

28. **Price Ratios**   Using the P/E, P/CF, and P/S ratios, estimate the 2006 share price for Abbott Laboratories. Use the average stock price each year to calculate the price ratios.

29. **Residual Income Model**   Assume the sustainable growth rate and required return you calculated in Problem 27 are valid. Use the clean surplus relationship to calculate the share price for Abbott Laboratories with the residual income model.

30. **Clean Surplus Dividend**   Use the information from the previous problem and calculate the stock price with the clean surplus dividend. Do you get the same stock price as in the previous problem? Why or why not?

31. **Stock Valuation**   Given your answers in the previous questions, do you feel Abbott Laboratories is overvalued or undervalued at its current price of around $40? At what price do you feel the stock should sell?

32. **Residual Income Model and Nonconstant Growth**   When a stock is going through a period of nonconstant growth for T periods, followed by constant growth forever, the residual income model can be modified as follows:

$$V(0) = \sum_{t=1}^{T} \frac{EPS_T + B_{t-1} - B_1}{(1+k)^t} + \frac{V(T)}{(1+k)^T}$$

where:

$$V(T) = B_T + \frac{EPS_T(1+g) - B_T \times k}{k-g}$$

Al's Infrared Sandwich Company had a book value of $10.85 at the beginning of the year, and the earnings per share for the past year were $2.88. Molly Miller, a research analyst at Miller, Moore & Associates, estimates that the book value and earnings per share will grow at 12.5 and 11 percent per year for the next four years, respectively. After four years, the growth rate is expected to be 6 percent. Molly believes the required return for the company is 8.2 percent. What is the value per share?

The following questions are from the 2000 Level II CFA® Exam. Use this information to answer Problems 33–38.

The management of Telluride, an international diversified conglomerate based in the United States, believes the recent strong performance of its wholly owned medical supply subsidiary, Sundanci, has gone unnoticed. In order to realize Sundanci's full value, Telluride has announced that it will divest Sundanci in a tax-free spinoff.

Sue Carroll, CFA, is the Director of Research at Kesson and Associates. In developing an investment recommendation for Sundanci, Carroll has directed her analysts to determine a valuation of Sundanci using various disciplines. To assist her analysis, Carroll has gathered the information shown on the next page.

Sundanci Actual 1999 and 2000 Financial Statements for Fiscal Years Ending May 31		
($ in millions except per-share data)		
Income Statement	**1999**	**2000**
Revenue	$474	$598
Depreciation	20	23
Other operating expenses	368	460
Income before taxes	86	115
Taxes	26	35
Net income	60	80
Dividends	18	24
Earnings per share	$0.714	$0.952
Dividend per share	$0.214	$0.286
Common shares outstanding	84.0	84.0
Balance sheet		
Current assets	$201	$326
Net property, plant and equipment	474	489
Total assets	675	815
Current liabilities	57	141
Long-term debt	0	0
Total liabilities	57	141
Shareholder equity	618	674
Total liabilities and equity	675	815
Capital expenditures	34	38
Selected Financial Information		
Required rate of return on equity	14%	
Growth rate of industry	13%	
Industry P/E ratio	26	

33. Sustainable Growth Rate   Calculate the ROE for 2000. What is the sustainable growth rate?

34. Sustainable Growth Rate   Carroll learns that Sundanci's Board of Directors is considering the following policy changes that will affect Sundanci's sustainable growth rate:

Director A proposes an increase in the quarterly dividend to $.15 per share. This would increase the annual dividend to $.60.

Director B proposes a two-for-one stock split.

Would each of these changes increase, decrease, or not affect Sundanci's sustainable growth rate, given that the other factors remain unchanged? Identify which component of the sustainable growth rate model, if any, is affected by each proposal.

35. Two-Stage Dividend Growth Model   Helen Morgan, CFA, has been asked by Carroll to determine the potential valuation for Sundanci using the dividend discount model. Morgan anticipates that Sundanci's earnings and dividends will grow at 32 percent for two years and 13 percent thereafter. Calculate the current value of a share of Sundanci stock using the two-stage dividend discount model.

36. P/E Ratio Valuation   Christie Johnson, CFA, has been assigned by Carroll to analyze Sundanci using the constant dividend growth price-earnings ratio model. Johnson assumes that Sundanci's earnings and dividends will grow at a constant rate of 13 percent. Note: The constant dividend growth price-earnings ratio using next year's earnings is P/E ratio = Payout ratio/$(k - g)$. Calculate the P/E ratio based on the information given and Johnson's assumptions.

37. **P/E Ratio**   Identify, within the context of the constant dividend growth model, how each of the following factors will affect the P/E ratio of Sundanci. In other words, will each of the following factors increase, decrease, or possibly increase or decrease the P/E ratio? Assume all other factors remain constant.

   a. The beta of Sundanci increases substantially.
   b. The estimated growth rate of Sundanci's earnings and dividends increases.
   c. The dividend payout ratio of Sundanci increases.
   d. The market risk premium increases.

38. **Payout Ratio and P/E**   Explain why an increase in the dividend payout ratio may not have the effect that the constant dividend growth P/E model suggests.

S&P Problems

www.mhhe.com/edumarketinsight

**STANDARD
&POOR'S**

1. **Constant Perpetual Growth Model**   Locate the information for American Electric Power (AEP). If you follow the "Financial Hlts" link you will find the current stock price, most recent dividend, and the five-year growth rate for dividends. Assuming the five-year dividend growth rate is equal to the perpetual growth rate, what is the implied required return for AEP shareholders? Does this number make sense?

2. **Sustainable Growth**   What is the sustainable growth rate for AutoZone (AZO)? Under "Excel Analytics" you will find a link for annual ratios. This report shows return on equity and the payout ratio. Calculate the sustainable growth rate for AutoZone each year for the past five years. Is the sustainable growth rate the same every year? Why or why not?

3. **Price Ratio Analysis**   Locate the information for Walgreen Co. (WAG). All of the information used in this problem is found under "Excel Analytics." Use the "Mthly. Adj. Prices" link and find the year-end stock price for Walgreen Co. for all available years. Next, find the earnings per share for the last five years using EPS Basic from Operations. Locate the balance sheet for each of the past five years and record the Common Equity and Common Shares Outstanding. Use the Annual Cash Flow Statement to find the Net Cash Flow from Operating Activities. Divide both common equity and cash flow by the shares outstanding each year to find the annual book value per share and cash flow per share. Record these numbers. Calculate the price-earnings ratio, price-cash flow ratio, and price-book value ratio for each year. Using this information, compute the expected share price for Walgreen Co. at the end of the next year using price ratio analysis.

What's on the Web

1. **Sustainable Growth Rate**   You can find the home page for Caterpillar, Inc., at www.caterpillar.com. Go to this page and find the most recent annual report for Caterpillar. Calculate the sustainable growth rate for each of the past two years. Are these values the same? Why or why not?

2. **Sustainable Growth Rate**   Go to finance.yahoo.com and find the analysts' estimates for DuPont's (DD) growth rate over the next five years. How does this compare to the industry, sector, and S&P 500 growth rates? Now find the EPS and dividends per share for DuPont and calculate the sustainable growth rate. How does your number compare to analysts' estimates for the company? Why might these estimates differ?

3. **Perpetual Dividend Growth Model**   Go to finance.yahoo.com and find the following information: the beta, the most recent annual dividend, and analysts' estimated growth rate for Johnson & Johnson (JNJ). Next, find the three-month Treasury bill yield on finance.yahoo.com. Assuming the market risk premium is 9 percent, what is the required

www.mhhe.com/jm4e

return for JNJ? What is the value of JNJ stock using the perpetual dividend growth model? Does JNJ appear overpriced, underpriced, or correctly priced? Why might this analysis be inappropriate, or at least misleading?

Stock-Trak Exercises ———————————————— ∎

STOCK | TRAK
GLOBAL PORTFOLIO SIMULATIONS

To access the Stock-Trak Exercise for this chapter, please visit the book Web site at www.mhhe.com/jm4e and choose the corresponding chapter.

CHAPTER 7

Stock Price Behavior and Market Efficiency

"A market is the combined behavior of thousands of people responding to information, misinformation, and whim."

–Kenneth Chang

"If you want to know what's happening in the market, ask the market."

–Japanese Proverb

Controversial, intriguing, and baffling issues are at the heart of this chapter. We begin by investigating a very basic question: Can you, as an investor, consistently "beat the market"? You may be surprised to learn that evidence strongly suggests that the answer to this question is probably not. We show that even professional money managers have trouble beating the market. At the end of the chapter, we describe some market phenomena that sound more like carnival side shows, such as the "amazing January effect." ∎

7.1 Introduction to Market Efficiency

efficient markets hypothesis (EMH)
The hypothesis stating that, as a practical matter, investors cannot consistently "beat the market."

For more on market efficiency, go to
http://www.e-m-h.org

Market efficiency is probably the most controversial and intriguing issue in investments. The debate that has raged around market efficiency for decades shows few signs of abating. The central issue in the market efficiency debates is: Can you (or anyone else) consistently "beat the market"?

If the answer to this question is no, then the market is said to be efficient. The **efficient markets hypothesis (EMH)** asserts that, as a practical matter, organized financial markets like the New York Stock Exchange are efficient. The controversy surrounding the EMH centers on this assertion.

In the sections that follow, we discuss many issues surrounding the EMH. You will notice that we focus our discussion on stock markets. The reason is that the debate on the EMH and the associated research have largely centered on these markets. However, the same principles and arguments would also apply to any organized financial market, such as the markets for government bonds, corporate bonds, commodity futures, and options.

CHECK THIS

7.1a What is the central issue in the market efficiency debate?

7.1b How would you state the efficient market hypothesis?

7.2 What Does "Beat the Market" Mean?

Good question. As we discussed in Chapter 1 and elsewhere, there is a risk-return trade-off. On average at least, we expect riskier investments to have larger returns than less risky assets. So the fact that an investment appears to have a high or low return doesn't tell us much. We need to know if the return was high or low relative to the risk involved.

excess return
A return in excess of that earned by other investments having the same risk.

Instead, to determine if an investment is superior to another, we need to compare **excess returns**. The excess return on an investment is the difference between what that investment earned and what other investments with the same risk earned. A positive excess return means that an investment has outperformed other investments of the same risk. Thus, *consistently earning a positive excess return* is what we mean by "beating the market."

CHECK THIS

7.2a What is an excess return?

7.2b What does it mean to "beat the market"?

7.3 Foundations of Market Efficiency

Three economic forces can lead to market efficiency: (1) investor rationality, (2) independent deviations from rationality, and (3) arbitrage. These conditions are so powerful that any one of them can result in market efficiency. We discuss aspects of these conditions in detail throughout this chapter. Given their importance, however, we briefly introduce each of them here. In our discussions, we use the term "rational" to mean only that investors do not systematically overvalue or undervalue financial assets in light of the information that they possess.

If every investor always made perfectly rational investment decisions, earning an excess return would be difficult, if not impossible. The reason is simple: If everyone is fully rational, equivalent risk assets would all have the same expected returns. Put differently, no bargains would be there to be had, because relative prices would all be correct.

However, even if the investor rationality condition does not hold, the market could still be efficient. Suppose that many investors are irrational, and a company makes a relevant announcement about a new product. Some investors will be overly optimistic, some will be overly pessimistic, but the net effect might be that these investors cancel each other out. In a sense, the irrationality is just noise that is diversified away. As a result, the market could still be efficient (or nearly efficient). What is important here is that irrational investors don't all (or mostly all) have similar beliefs. However, even under this condition, called "independent deviations from rationality," the market still may be efficient.

Let us now think of a market with many irrational traders and further suppose that their collective irrationality does not balance out. In this case, observed market prices can be too high or too low relative to their risk. Now suppose there are some well-capitalized, intelligent, and rational investors. This group of traders would see these high or low market prices as a profit opportunity and engage in arbitrage—buying relatively inexpensive stocks and selling relatively expensive stocks.

If these rational arbitrage traders dominate irrational traders, the market will still be efficient. We sometimes hear the expression "Market efficiency doesn't require that *everybody* be rational, just that *somebody* is." In our next section, we look more closely at market efficiency and discuss several different forms.

CHECK THIS

7.3a What three economic conditions cause market efficiency?

7.3b How would well-capitalized, intelligent, and rational investors profit from market inefficiency?

7.4 Forms of Market Efficiency

Now that we have a little more precise notion of what beating the market means, we can be a little more precise about market efficiency. A market is efficient *with respect to some particular information* if that information is not useful in earning a positive excess return. Notice the emphasis we place on "with respect to some particular information."

For example, it seems unlikely that knowledge of Shaquille O'Neal's free-throw shooting percentage (low) would be of any use in beating the market. If so, we would say that the market is efficient with respect to the information in Shaq's free-throw percentage. On the other hand, if you have prior knowledge concerning impending takeover offers, you could most definitely use that information to earn a positive excess return. Thus, the market is not efficient with regard to this information. We hasten to add that such information is probably "insider" information, and insider trading is generally, though not always, illegal (in the United States, at least). As we discuss later in the

FIGURE 7.1 | Information Sets for Market Efficiency

Strong-form information set:
all information of any kind, public or private.

Semistrong-form information set:
all publicly available information.

Weak-form information set:
past price and volume.

chapter, using insider information illegally might well earn you a stay in a jail cell and a stiff financial penalty.

Thus, the question of whether a market is efficient is meaningful only relative to some type of information. Put differently, if you are asked whether a particular market is efficient, you should always reply, "With respect to what information?" Three general types of information are particularly interesting in this context, and it is traditional to define three forms of market efficiency: weak, semistrong, and strong.

The particular sets of information used in the three forms of market efficiency are *nested*. That is, the information set in the strong form includes the information set in the semistrong form, which in turn includes the information set in the weak form. Figure 7.1 shows the relationships among the information sets.

A weak-form efficient market is one in which the information reflected in past prices and volume figures is of no value in beating the market. As we discuss in our next chapter, one form of stock market analysis, called "technical analysis," is based on using past prices and volume to predict future prices. If a market is weak-form efficient, however, then technical analysis is of no use whatsoever. You might as well read tea leaves as stock price charts if the market is weak-form efficient.

In a semistrong-form efficient market, publicly available information of any and all kinds is of no use in beating the market. If a market is semistrong-form efficient, then the fundamental analysis techniques we described in a previous chapter are useless. Also, notice that past prices and volume data are publicly available information, so if a market is semistrong-form efficient, it is also weak-form efficient.

The implications of semistrong-form efficiency are, at a minimum, semistaggering. What it literally means is that nothing in the library, for example, is of any value in earning a positive excess return. How about a firm's financial statement? Useless. How about information in the financial press? Worthless. This book? Sad to say, if the market is semistrong-form efficient, there is nothing in this book that will be of any use in beating the market. You can imagine that this form of market efficiency is hotly disputed.

Finally, in a strong-form efficient market no information of any kind, public or private, is useful in beating the market. Notice that if a market is strong-form efficient, it is necessarily weak- and semistrong-form efficient as well. Ignoring the issue of legality, possession of nonpublic inside information of many types clearly would enable you to earn essentially unlimited returns, so this case is not particularly interesting. Instead, the market efficiency debate focuses on the first two forms.

CHECK THIS

7.4a What role does information play in determining whether markets are efficient?

7.4b What are the forms of market efficiency?

7.5 Why Would a Market Be Efficient?

The driving force toward market efficiency is simply competition and the profit motive. Investors constantly try to identify superior-performing investments. Using the most advanced information processing tools available, investors and security analysts constantly appraise stock values, buying those stocks that look even slightly undervalued and selling those that look even slightly overvalued. This constant appraisal and subsequent trading activity (as well as all the research behind these activities) act to ensure that prices never differ much from their efficient market price.

To give you an idea of how strong the incentive is to identify superior investments, consider a large mutual fund such as the Fidelity Magellan Fund. As we mentioned in Chapter 4, this is one of the largest equity funds in the United States, with about $51 billion under management (as of early 2006). Suppose Fidelity was able through its research to improve the performance of this fund by 20 basis points for one year only (recall that a basis point is 1 percent of 1 percent, i.e., 0.0001). How much would this one-time 20-basis point improvement be worth?

The answer is 0.0020 times $51 billion, or $102 million. Thus, Fidelity would be willing to spend up to $102 million to boost the performance of this one fund by as little as one-fifth of one percent for a single year only. As this example shows, even relatively small performance enhancements are worth tremendous amounts of money and thereby create the incentive to unearth relevant information and use it.

Because of this incentive, the fundamental characteristic of an efficient market is that prices are correct in the sense that they fully reflect relevant information. If and when new information comes to light, prices may change, and they may change by a lot. It just depends on the nature of the new information. However, in an efficient market, right here, right now, price is a consensus opinion of value, where that consensus is based on the information and intellect of hundreds of thousands, or even millions, of investors around the world.

CHECK THIS

7.5a What is the driving force behind market efficiency?

7.5b Why does this driving force work?

7.6 Some Implications of Market Efficiency

DOES OLD INFORMATION HELP PREDICT FUTURE STOCK PRICES?

In its weakest form, the efficient market hypothesis is the simple statement that stock prices fully reflect all past information. If this is true, this means that studying past price movements in the hopes of predicting future stock price movements is really a waste of time.

In addition, a very subtle prediction is at work here. That is, no matter how often a particular stock price path has related to subsequent stock price changes in the past, there is no assurance that this relationship will occur again in the future.

Researchers have used sophisticated statistical techniques to test whether past stock price movements are of any value in predicting future stock price movements. This turns out to be a surprisingly difficult question to answer clearly and without qualification.

In short, although some researchers have been able to show that future returns are partly predictable by past returns, the predicted returns are not *economically* important, which means that predictability is not sufficient to earn an excess return. In addition, trading costs generally swamp attempts to build a profitable trading system on the basis of past returns. Researchers have been unable to provide evidence of a superior trading strategy that uses only past returns. That is, trading costs matter, and buy-and-hold strategies involving broad market indexes are extremely difficult to outperform. (If you know how to outperform a broad market index after accounting for trading costs, please share it with us.)

RANDOM WALKS AND STOCK PRICES

If you were to ask people you know whether stock market prices are predictable, many of them would say yes. To their surprise, and perhaps yours, it is very difficult to predict stock market prices. In fact, considerable research has shown that stock prices change through time as if they are random. That is, stock price increases are about as likely as stock price decreases. When the path that a stock price follows shows no discernible pattern, then the stock's price behavior is largely consistent with the notion of a **random walk**. A random walk is related to the weak-form version of the efficient market hypothesis because past knowledge of the stock price is not useful in predicting future stock prices.

random walk
No discernible pattern to the path that a stock price follows through time.

Figure 7.2 illustrates daily price changes for Intel stock from April 1, 2004, through April 1, 2005. To qualify as a true random walk, Intel stock price changes would have to be truly independent from day to day. In addition, the distribution of possible stock prices each day must be the same. Even so, the graph of daily price changes for Intel stock is essentially what a random walk looks like. It is certainly hard to see any pattern in the daily price changes of Intel.

HOW DOES NEW INFORMATION GET INTO STOCK PRICES?

In its semistrong form, the efficient market hypothesis is the simple statement that stock prices fully reflect publicly available information. Stock prices change when traders buy and sell shares based on their view of the future prospects for the stock. The future prospects for the stock are influenced by unexpected news announcements. Examples of unexpected news announcements might include an increase or decrease in the dividend paid by a stock, an increase or decrease in the forecast for future earnings, lawsuits over company practices, or changes in the leadership team. As shown in Figure 7.3, prices could adjust to a positive news announcement in three basic ways.

- *Efficient market reaction:* The price instantaneously adjusts to, and fully reflects, new information. There is no tendency for subsequent increases or decreases to occur.

FIGURE 7.2 Daily Price Change for Intel Common Stock, April 1, 2004 to April 1, 2005

FIGURE 7.3 Possible Market Price Reactions to a News Announcement

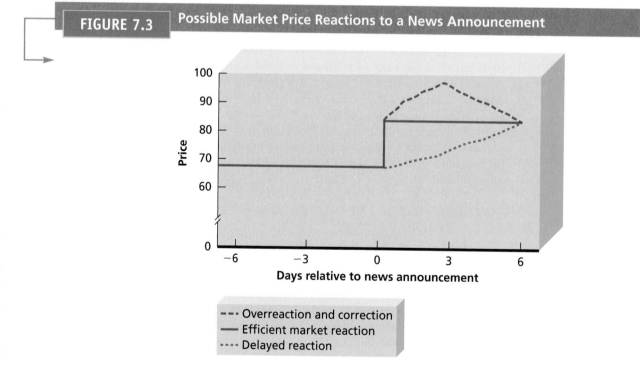

--- Overreaction and correction
— Efficient market reaction
····· Delayed reaction

- *Delayed reaction:* The price partially adjusts to the new information, but days elapse before the price completely reflects new information.
- *Overreaction and correction:* The price overadjusts to the new information; it overshoots the appropriate new price but eventually falls to the new price.

EVENT STUDIES

event study
A research method designed to help study the effects of news on stock prices.

Researchers have examined the effects of many types of news announcements on stock prices. Such researchers are interested in the adjustment process itself as well as the size of the stock price reaction to a news announcement. To test for the effects of new information on stock prices, researchers use an approach called an **event study**. As an illustration of the implications of market efficiency, let us look at how researchers use this method.

On Friday, February 25, 2005, executives of Elan Corporation, one of the makers of a new drug used to treat multiple sclerosis, announced that the company was voluntarily halting the supply and marketing of the drug. In addition, the company advised doctors to stop prescribing the drug. Even though the drug had approval from the U.S. Food and Drug Administration, executives of Elan Corporation felt that potentially serious side effects of the drug meant that sales of the drug should be suspended. On Monday, February 28, 2005, Elan shares plummeted $18.10, or more than 69 percent, to $8.00. Figure 7.4 is a graph of the price per share of Elan Corporation in the days surrounding this news announcement.

When researchers look for effects of news on stock prices, however, they must make sure that overall market news is accounted for in their analysis. The reason is simple. Suppose the whole market had fallen drastically on February 28, 2005. How would you be able to separate the overall market decline from the isolated news concerning Elan Corporation?

abnormal returns
The remaining return on a stock after overall market returns have been removed.

To answer this question, researchers calculate **abnormal returns**. The equation to calculate an abnormal return is simply:

$$\text{Abnormal return} = \text{Observed return} - \text{Expected return} \qquad (7.1)$$

FIGURE 7.4 The Price of Shares in Elan Corporation, February 11, 2005 through March 14, 2005

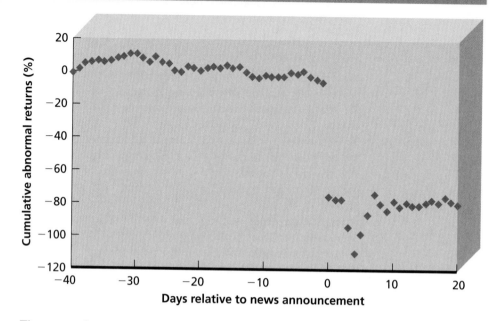

The expected return can be calculated using a market index (like the NASDAQ 100 Index or the S&P 500 Index) or by using a long-term average return on the stock. Researchers then align the abnormal return on a stock to the days relative to the news announcement. Usually, researchers assign the value of zero to the day a news announcement is made. One day after the news announcement is assigned a value of +1, two days after the news announcement is assigned a value of +2, and so on. Similarly, one day before the news announcement is assigned the value of −1.

According to the efficient market hypothesis, the abnormal return today should relate only to information released on that day. Any previously released information should have no effect on abnormal returns because this information has been available to all traders. Also, the return today cannot be influenced by information that traders do not yet know.

To evaluate abnormal returns, researchers usually accumulate them over some period. Figure 7.5 is a plot of the cumulative abnormal returns for Elan beginning 40 days before the announcement. The first cumulative abnormal return, or CAR, is just equal to the abnormal return on day −40. The CAR on day −39 is the sum of the first two abnormal returns, the CAR on day −38 is the sum of the first three, and so on. By examining CARs, we can see if there was an over- or under-reaction to an announcement.

As you can see in Figure 7.5, Elan's cumulative abnormal return hovered around zero before the announcement. After the news was released, there was a large, sharp downward movement in the CAR. The stock price gyrated as additional news was released, but the overall pattern of cumulative abnormal returns is essentially what the efficient market hypothesis would predict. That is, there is a flat area of cumulative abnormal returns, a sharp break in cumulative abnormal returns, and another flat area of cumulative abnormal returns.

CHECK THIS

7.6a How is a random walk affiliated with the efficient market hypothesis?

7.6b What are the possible market price reactions to a news announcement?

7.6c How do researchers use event studies to examine the effects of news announcements on stock prices?

7.7 Informed Traders and Insider Trading

Recall that if a market is strong-form efficient, no information of any kind, public or private, is useful in beating the market. However, inside information of many types clearly would enable you to earn essentially unlimited returns. This fact generates an interesting question: Should any of us be able to earn returns based on information that is not known to the public?

In the United States (and in many other countries, though not all), making profits on nonpublic information is illegal. This ban is said to be necessary if investors are to have trust in U.S. stock markets. The United States Securities and Exchange Commission (SEC) is charged with enforcing laws concerning illegal trading activities. As a result, it is important for you to be able to distinguish between informed trading, insider trading, and legal insider trading.

INFORMED TRADING

informed trader
An investor who makes a buy or sell decision based on public information and analysis.

When an investor makes a decision to buy or sell a stock based on publicly available information and analysis, this investor is said to be an **informed trader**. The information that an informed trader possesses might come from reading *The Wall Street Journal,* reading quarterly reports issued by a company, gathering financial information from the Internet, talking to other traders, or a host of other sources.

INSIDER TRADING

Some informed traders are also insider traders. When you hear the term *insider trading,* you most likely think that such activity is illegal. However, as you will see at the end of this section, not all insider trading is illegal.

material nonpublic information
Private knowledge that can substantially influence the share price of a stock.

WHO IS AN INSIDER? For the purposes of defining illegal insider trading, an insider is someone who has **material nonpublic information**. Such information is both not known to the public and, if it were known, would impact the stock price. A person can be charged with insider trading when he or she acts on such information in an attempt to make a profit.

Frequently, when an illegal insider trade occurs, there is a *tipper* and a *tippee.* The tipper is the person who has, on purpose, divulged material nonpublic information. The tippee is the person who has knowingly used such information in an attempt to make a profit. For example, a tipper could be a CEO who spills some inside information to a friend who does not work for the company. If the friend then knowingly uses this inside information to make a trade, this tippee is guilty of insider trading.

Proving that a trader is a tippee is difficult for the SEC, because keeping track of insider information flows and subsequent trades is difficult. For example, suppose a person makes a trade based on the advice of a stockbroker. Even if the broker based this advice on material nonpublic information, the trader might not have been aware of the broker's knowledge. The SEC must prove that the trader was, in fact, aware that the broker's information was based on material nonpublic information.

Sometimes, people accused of insider trading claim that they just "overheard" someone talking. Suppose, for example, you are at a restaurant and overhear a conversation between Bill Gates and his CFO concerning some potentially explosive news regarding Microsoft, Inc. If you then go out and make a trade in an attempt to profit from what you overheard, you would be violating the law (even though the information was "innocently obtained"). When you take possession of material nonpublic information, you become an insider and are bound to obey insider trading laws. Note that in this case, Bill Gates and his CFO, although careless, are not necessarily in violation of insider trading laws.

LEGAL INSIDER TRADING A company's corporate insiders can make perfectly legal trades in the stock of their company. To do so, they must comply with the reporting rules made by the U.S. Securities and Exchange Commission. When they make a trade and report it to the SEC, these trades are reported to the public. In addition, corporate insiders must declare that trades that they made were based on public information about the company, rather than "inside" information. Most public companies also have guidelines that must be followed. For example, companies commonly allow insiders to trade only during certain windows throughout the year, often sometime after earnings have been announced.

IT'S NOT A GOOD THING: WHAT DID MARTHA DO? Martha Stewart became one of America's most successful entrepreneurs by telling people how to entertain, cook, and decorate their homes. She built her superhomemaker personality into a far-flung international enterprise. When her company went public in 1999, the initial public offering raised $873 million. Today, Martha Stewart Living Omnimedia, Inc. (MSO), has a market capitalization of well over $1 billion and employs about 500 people (including interns). Stewart owns more than 10 percent of the shares in the company.

Stewart was in the legal news because the U.S. Securities and Exchange Commission believed that Martha Stewart was told by her friend Sam Waksal, who founded a company called ImClone, that a cancer drug being developed by ImClone had been rejected by the Food and Drug Administration. This development was bad news for ImClone. Martha Stewart sold her 3,928 shares in ImClone on December 27, 2001. On that day, ImClone traded below $60 per share, a level that Stewart claimed triggered an existing stop-loss order. However, the SEC believed that Stewart illegally sold her shares because she had information concerning FDA rejection before it became public.

The FDA rejection was announced after the market closed on Friday, December 28, 2001. This news was a huge blow to ImClone shares, which closed at about $46 per share on the following Monday (the first trading day after the information became public). Shares in ImClone subsequently fell to under $10 per share about six months later, in mid-2002. Ironically, shares of ImClone rallied to sell for more than $80 per share in mid-2004.

In June 2003, Stewart and her stockbroker, Peter Bacanovic, were indicted on nine federal counts. They both pleaded not guilty. Stewart's trial began in January 2004. Just days before the jury began to deliberate, however, Judge Miriam Cedarbaum dismissed the most serious charge—securities fraud. Stewart, however, was convicted on all four counts of obstructing justice and lying to investigators.

Judge Cedarbaum fined Stewart $30,000 and sentenced her to five months in prison, two years of probation, and five months of home confinement after her release. The fine was the maximum allowed under federal rules; the sentence was the minimum the judge could impose. Peter Bacanovic, Stewart's broker, was fined $4,000 and was sentenced to five months in prison and two years of probation.

So, to summarize, Martha Stewart was accused, but not convicted, of insider trading. She was accused, and convicted, of obstructing justice and lying to investigators. Although her conviction bars her from taking on the duties of an executive officer, MSO still paid Martha over $5 million in 2005 (base pay plus perks).

CHECK THIS

7.7a What makes a stock trader an informed trader?

7.7b What traders are considered to be insiders?

7.7c What is the difference between legal insider trading and illegal insider trading?

7.8 How Efficient Are Markets?

ARE FINANCIAL MARKETS EFFICIENT?

Financial markets are one of the most extensively documented human endeavors. Colossal amounts of financial market data are collected and reported every day. These data, particularly stock market data, have been exhaustively analyzed to test market efficiency.

You would think that with all this analysis going on, we would know whether markets are efficient, but really we don't. Instead, what we seem to have, at least in the minds of many researchers, is a growing realization that beyond a point, we just can't tell.

For example, it is not difficult to program a computer to test trading strategies that are based solely on historic prices and volume figures. Many such strategies have been tested, and the bulk of the evidence indicates that such strategies are not useful.

More generally, market efficiency is difficult to test for four basic reasons:

1. The risk-adjustment problem.
2. The relevant information problem.
3. The dumb luck problem.
4. The data snooping problem.

We briefly discuss each in turn.

The first issue, the risk-adjustment problem, is the easiest to understand. Earlier, we noted that beating the market means consistently earning a positive excess return. To determine whether an investment has a positive excess return, we have to adjust for its risk. As we discuss elsewhere in this book, the truth is that we are not even certain exactly what we mean by risk, much less how to measure it precisely and then adjust for it. Thus, what appears to be a positive excess return may just be the result of a faulty risk-adjustment procedure.

The second issue, the relevant information problem, is even more troublesome. Remember that the concept of market efficiency is meaningful only relative to some particular information. As we look back in time and try to assess whether some particular market behavior was inefficient, we have to recognize that we cannot possibly know all the information that may have been underlying that market behavior.

For example, suppose we see that 10 years ago the price of a stock shot up by 100 percent over a short period of time, and then subsequently collapsed. We dig through all the historical information we can find, but we can find no reason for this behavior. What can we conclude? Nothing, really. For all we know, an undocumented rumor existed of a takeover that never materialized, and relative to this information, the price behavior was perfectly efficient.

In general, there is no way to tell whether we have all the relevant information. Without *all* the relevant information, we cannot tell if some observed price behavior is inefficient. Put differently, any price behavior, no matter how bizarre, might be efficient, and therefore explainable, with respect to *some* information.

The third problem has to do with evaluating investors and money managers. One type of evidence frequently cited to prove that markets can be beaten is the enviable track record of certain legendary investors. For example, *The Wall Street Journal* article reproduced in the nearby *Investment Updates* box gives some information on the track record of superstar investor Warren Buffett.

A hidden argument in the *Investment Updates* box is that because some investors seem to be able to beat the market, it must be the case that there are market inefficiencies. Is this correct? Maybe yes, maybe no. You may be familiar with the following expression: "If you put an immortal monkey in front of a typewriter, this monkey will eventually produce

WARREN BUFFETT, UNPLUGGED

Warren Buffett, the billionaire investor and insurance executive, was in his office here this summer when he received a faxed letter about a company he'd never heard of.

The letter was from an adviser to Forest River Inc., an Elkhart, Ind., recreational vehicle maker. He proposed that Mr. Buffett buy the company for $800 million.

Mr. Buffett liked what he saw: The company had a big market share and little debt.

The next day, Mr. Buffett offered to buy Forest River and to let its founder, Peter Liegl, continue running it. He sealed the deal, at an undisclosed price, in a 20-minute meeting one week later. As the meeting wrapped up, Mr. Buffett told Mr. Liegl not to expect to hear from him more than once a year. Says Mr. Liegl: "It was easier to sell my business than to renew my driver's license."

Mr. Buffett says he knows an attractive acquisition candidate when he sees it. "If I don't know it in five to 10 minutes," Mr. Buffett says, "then I'm not going to know it in 10 weeks."

Mr. Buffett, an Omaha native, learned about investing under the tutelage of the classic "value" investor Benjamin Graham, who preached buying beaten-down stocks with good underlying value. He became a broker in 1951 at Buffett-Falk & Co., his father's stock-brokerage firm in Omaha, before going

to work for Mr. Graham in New York three years later. In 1965, Mr. Buffett bought control of Berkshire, a foundering New Bedford, Mass., fabric mill. He soon purchased National Indemnity Cos., an Omaha insurer, which gave Berkshire $20 million of assets.

Mr. Buffett calculates that since 1951, he has generated an average annual return of about 31%. The average return for the Standard & Poor's 500 over that period is 11% a year. A $1,000 investment in Berkshire in 1965 would be worth about $5.5 million today. Over the past decade, Berkshire shares have tripled in price, returning twice as much, in percentage terms, as the S&P 500.

Mr. Buffett, with a personal net worth of $43 billion, is the nation's second-richest man, after Bill Gates. His nearly 55-year record has brought him recognition as one of the best investors ever, earned him fierce loyalty from Berkshire shareholders, and inspired legions of investors who attempt to ape his moves.

Though his empire has grown, Mr. Buffett says his routine has changed little over the years. He says he spends the better part of most workdays thinking and reading. He fields a handful of phone calls, and on most days, he confers with the chiefs of a few Berkshire subsidiaries. He seldom holds meetings. "There isn't much going on here," he says of his office on a typical day.

Hamlet." In a similar manner, suppose we have thousands of monkeys who are tasked with picking stocks for a portfolio. We would find that some of these monkeys would appear to be amazingly talented and rack up extraordinary gains. As you surely recognize, however, this is just caused by random chance.

Similarly, if we track the performance of thousands of money managers over some period of time, some managers will accumulate remarkable track records and a lot of publicity. Are they good or are they lucky? If we could track them for many decades, we might be able to tell, but for the most part, money managers are not around long enough for us to accumulate sufficient data. We discuss the performance of money managers as a group later in the chapter.

Our final problem has to do with what is known as "data snooping." Instead of monkeys at typewriters, think of what can happen if thousands of finance researchers with thousands of computers are all studying the same data and are looking for inefficiencies. Apparent patterns, or anomalies, will surely be found.

In fact, researchers *have* discovered extremely simple patterns that, at least historically, have been both highly successful and very hard to explain. We discuss some of these later

Around midday, a call came in from David Sokol, chief executive of Berkshire's MidAmerican Energy subsidiary. Mr. Buffett put his hands behind his head and cradled the phone against his shoulder, nodding when Mr. Sokol told him that MidAmerican had received a government approval for its pending acquisition of PacificCorp (a utility) for $5.1 billion in cash, plus $4.3 billion of assumed debt. Mr. Buffett, sipping a Coke from a Styrofoam cup, soon ended the conversation.

Mr. Buffett tends to stick to investments for the long haul, even when the going gets bumpy. Mr. Sokol recalls bracing for an August 2004 meeting at which he planned to break the news to Mr. Buffett that the Iowa utility needed to write off about $360 million for a soured zinc project. Mr. Sokol says he was stunned by Mr. Buffett's response: "David, we all make mistakes." Their meeting lasted only 10 minutes.

"I would have fired me if I was him," Mr. Sokol says.

"If you don't make mistakes, you can't make decisions," Mr. Buffett says. "You can't dwell on them."

Mr. Buffett has relied on gut instinct for decades to run Berkshire Hathaway Inc. Watch him at work inside his $136 billion investment behemoth, and what you see resembles no other modern financial titan. He spends most of his day alone in an office with no computer, no stock-quote machine or stock-data terminal. He keeps a muted television set tuned to CNBC, the financial-news network. Although he occasionally carries a cell phone on the road, he does not use one in Omaha. He keeps no calculator on his desk, preferring to do most calculations in his head. "I deplore false precision in math," he says, explaining that he does not need exact numbers for most investment decisions. On the cabinet behind his desk are two black phones with direct lines to his brokers on Wall Street.

On a recent Wednesday morning, Mr. Buffett had barely settled into his seat when one of them rang. It was John Freund, his longtime broker from Citigroup Inc.'s investment-banking unit. Mr. Freund briefed Mr. Buffett on a stock position he had been building for Berkshire. "If we bought a couple million, that would be fine," Mr. Buffett said, giving Mr. Freund a parameter for how many shares he wanted to buy that day. (Mr. Buffett declines to identify the stock.)

By the end of the day, Mr. Buffett had bought $140 million of the stock for Berkshire's investment portfolio—equal to the entire asset value of many mutual funds.

Even with such heavy trading, Mr. Buffett's desk isn't littered with stock research. "I don't use analysts or fortune tellers," he says. "If I had to pick one, I don't know which it would be."

Source: Susan Pulliam and Karen Richardson, *The Wall Street Journal*, November 12, 2005. Reprinted by permission of Dow Jones & Company, Inc. © 2005 Dow Jones & Company, Inc. All Rights Reserved Worldwide.

in the chapter. These discoveries raise another problem: ghosts in the data. If we look long enough and hard enough at any data, we are bound to find some apparent patterns by sheer chance. But are these patterns real? Only time will tell.

Notwithstanding the four problems we have discussed, based on the last 20 to 30 years of scientific research, three generalities about market efficiency seem in order. First, short-term stock price and market movements appear to be very difficult, or even impossible, to predict with any accuracy (at least with any objective method of which we are aware). Second, the market reacts quickly and sharply to new (i.e., unanticipated) information, and the vast majority of studies of the impact of new information find little or no evidence that the market underreacts or overreacts to new information in a way that can be profitably exploited. Third, *if* the stock market can be beaten, the way to do it is at least not *obvious*, so the implication is that the market is not grossly inefficient.

SOME IMPLICATIONS OF MARKET EFFICIENCY

To the extent that you think a market is efficient, there are some important investment implications. Going back to Chapter 2, we saw that the investment process can be viewed as having two parts: asset allocation and security selection. Even if all markets are efficient, asset allocation is still important because the way you divide your money among the various types of investments will strongly influence your overall risk-return relation.

However, if markets are efficient, then security selection is less important, and you do not have to worry too much about overpaying or underpaying for any particular security. In fact, if markets are efficient, you would probably be better off just buying a large basket of stocks and following a passive investment strategy. Your main goal would be to hold your costs to a minimum while maintaining a broadly diversified portfolio. We discussed index funds, which exist for just this purpose, in Chapter 4.

In broader terms, if markets are efficient, then little role exists for professional money managers. You should not pay load fees to buy mutual fund shares, and you should shop for low management fees. You should not work with full-service brokers, and so on.

If markets are efficient, there is one other thing that you should not do: You should not try to time the market. Recall that market timing amounts to moving money in and out of the market based on your expectations of future market direction. By trying to time the market, all you will accomplish is to guarantee that you will, on average, underperform the market.

In fact, market efficiency aside, market timing is hard to recommend. Historically, most of the gains earned in the stock market have tended to occur over relatively short periods of time. If you miss even a single one of these short market runups, you will likely never catch up. Put differently, successful market timing requires phenomenal accuracy to be of any benefit, and anything less than that will, based on the historical record, result in underperforming the market.

CHECK THIS

7.8a   What are the four basic reasons market efficiency is difficult to test?

7.8b   What are the implications to investors if markets are efficient?

7.9 Market Efficiency and the Performance of Professional Money Managers

Let's have a stock market investment contest in which you are going to take on professional money managers. Of course, the professional money managers have at their disposal their skill, banks of computers, and scores of analysts to help pick their stocks. Does this sound like an unfair match? Well, it is—you have a terrific advantage.

It's true. You can become an expert investor by using the following investment strategy: Hold a broad-based market index. One such index that you can easily buy is a mutual fund called the Vanguard 500 Index Fund (there are other market index mutual funds, too). This low-fee mutual find is designed to produce investment results that correspond to the price and yield performance of the S&P 500 Index. The fund tracks the performance of the S&P 500 Index by investing its assets in the stocks that make up the S&P 500 Index. By the way, this fund is popular—as of April 2006, the Vanguard 500 Index Fund was the largest stock mutual fund in the United States, with over $111 billion in assets.

As discussed in a previous chapter, a general equity mutual fund (GEF) is simply a pool of money invested in stocks that is overseen by a professional money manager. The number

FIGURE 7.6　The Growth of Actively Managed Equity Funds, 1986–2003

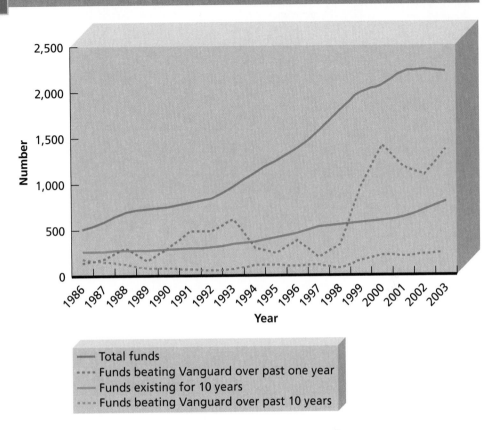

Legend:
— Total funds
···· Funds beating Vanguard over past one year
— Funds existing for 10 years
···· Funds beating Vanguard over past 10 years

of GEFs has grown substantially during the past 20 years. Figure 7.6 shows the growth in the number of GEFs from 1986 through 2003. The solid blue line shows the total number of funds that have existed for at least one year, while the solid red line shows the number of funds that have existed for at least 10 years. From Figure 7.6, you can see that it is diffi-cult for professional money managers to keep their funds in existence for 10 years (if it were easy, there would not be much difference between the solid blue line and the solid red line).

Figure 7.6 also shows the number of these funds that beat the performance of the Van-guard 500 Index Fund. You can see that there is much more variation in the dashed blue line than in the dashed red line. What this means is that in any given year, it is hard to predict how many professional money managers will beat the Vanguard 500 Index Fund. But the low level and low variation of the dashed red line means that the percentage of professional money managers who can beat the Vanguard 500 Index Fund over a 10-year investment period is low and stable.

Figures 7.7 and 7.8 are bar charts that show the percentage of managed equity funds that beat the Vanguard 500 Index Fund. Figure 7.7 uses return data for the previous year only, while Figure 7.8 uses return data for the previous 10 years. As you can see from Figure 7.7, in only 6 of the 18 years spanning 1986 through 2003 did more than half the professional money managers beat the Vanguard 500 Index Fund. The performance is worse when it comes to 10-year investment periods (1977–1986 through 1994–2003). As shown in Figure 7.8, in only 2 of these 18 investment periods did more than half the professional money managers beat the Vanguard 500 Index Fund.

FIGURE 7.7

The Percentage of Managed Equity Funds Beating the Vanguard 500 Index Fund, One-Year Returns

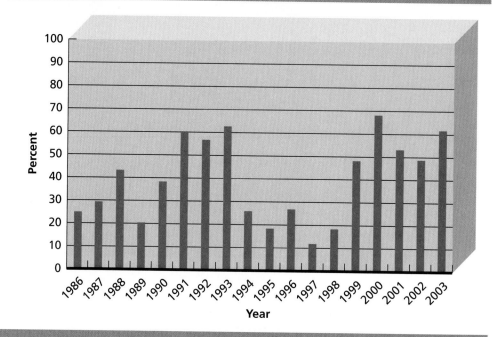

FIGURE 7.8

Percentage of Managed Equity Funds Beating the Vanguard 500 Index Fund, 10-Year Returns

Table 7.1 presents more evidence concerning the performance of professional money managers. Using data from 1977 through 2003, we divide this time period into 1-year investment periods, rolling 3-year investment periods, rolling 5-year investment periods, and rolling 10-year investment periods. Then, after we calculate the number of investment periods, we ask two questions: (1) what percentage of the time did half the

Length of Each Investment Period (Years)	Span	Number of Investment Periods	Number of Investment Periods Half the Funds Beat Vanguard	Percent	Number of Investment Periods Three-Fourths of the Funds Beat Vanguard	Percent
1	1977–2003	27	12	44.4%	3	11.1%
3	1979–2003	25	11	44.0	3	12.0
5	1981–2003	23	6	26.1	3	13.0
10	1986–2003	18	2	11.1	0	0.0

Source: Author calculations.

professionally managed funds beat the Vanguard 500 Index Fund? and (2) what percentage of the time did three-fourths of the professionally managed funds beat the Vanguard 500 Index Fund?

As you see in Table 7.1, the performance of professional money managers is generally quite poor relative to the Vanguard Index 500 Fund. In addition, the performance of professional money managers declines the longer the investment period.

The figures and table in this section raise some difficult and uncomfortable questions for security analysts and other investment professionals. If markets are inefficient, and tools like fundamental analysis are valuable, why don't mutual fund managers do better? Why can't mutual fund managers even beat a broad market index?

The performance of professional money managers is especially troublesome when we consider the enormous resources at their disposal and the substantial survivorship bias that exists. The survivorship bias comes into being because managers and funds that do especially poorly disappear. If beating the market was possible, then this Darwinian process of elimination should lead to a situation in which the survivors, as a group, are capable of doing so. The fact that professional money managers seem to lack the ability to outperform a broad market index is consistent with the notion that, overall, the equity market is efficient.

So if the market is this efficient, what is the role for portfolio managers? The role of a portfolio manager in an efficient market is to build a portfolio to meet the specific needs of individual investors. You have learned that a basic principle of investing is to hold a well-diversified portfolio. However, exactly which diversified portfolio is optimal varies by investor.

Some factors that influence portfolio choice include the investor's age, tax bracket, risk aversion, and even employer. Employer? Sure, suppose you work for Starbucks and part of your compensation is stock options. Like many companies, Starbucks offers its employees the opportunity to purchase company stock at less than market value. Of course, you would take advantage of this opportunity. You can imagine that you could wind up with a lot of Starbucks stock in your portfolio, which means you are not holding a diversified portfolio. The role of your portfolio manager would be to help you add other assets to your portfolio so that it is once again well diversified.

CHECK THIS

7.9a How well do professional money mangers perform, on average, against a broad market index?

7.9b What are the implications of this performance to investors?

7.10 Anomalies

In this section, we discuss some aspects of stock price behavior that are both baffling and potentially hard to reconcile with market efficiency. Researchers call these *market anomalies*. Keep three facts in mind as you read about market anomalies. First, anomalies are generally "small," in that they do not involve many dollars relative to the overall size of the stock market. Second, many anomalies are fleeting and tend to disappear when discovered. Finally, anomalies are not easily used as the basis for a trading strategy, because transaction costs render many of them unprofitable.

THE DAY-OF-THE-WEEK EFFECT

In the stock market, which day of the week has, on average, the biggest return? The question might strike you as silly; after all, what would make one day different from any other on average? On further reflection, though, you might realize that one day is different: Monday.

When we calculate a daily return for the stock market, we take the percentage change in closing prices from one trading day to the next. For every day except Monday this is a 24-hour period. However, because the markets are closed on the weekends, the average return on Monday is based on the percentage change from Friday's close to Monday's close, a 72-hour period. Thus, the average Monday return would be computed over a three-day period, not just a one-day period. Therefore, because of this longer time period, we would predict that Monday should have the highest return; in fact Monday's average return should be three times as large.

day-of-the-week effect

The tendency for Monday to have a negative average return.

Given this reasoning, it may come as a surprise to you to learn that Monday has the lowest average return. In fact, Monday is the only day with a *negative* average return. This is the **day-of-the-week effect**. Table 7.2 shows the average return by day of the week for the S&P 500 for the period January 1950 through December 2004.

In the 54 years spanning 1950 to 2004, the negative return on Monday is significant, both in a statistical sense and in an economic sense. This day-of-the-week effect appears not to be a fluke; it exists in other markets, such as the bond market, and it exists in stock markets outside the United States. It has defied explanation since it was first documented in the early 1980s. Interestingly, the effect is much stronger in the 1950–1979 time period than in the 1980–2004 time period.

Still, critics of the efficient markets hypothesis point to this strange return behavior as evidence of market inefficiency. While this return behavior is odd, exploiting it presents a problem. That is, how this return behavior can be used to earn a positive excess return is not clear. This is especially true in the 1980–2004 time period (i.e., in the period following the time when the effect was first documented). So whether this strange return behavior points to inefficiency is hard to say.

TABLE 7.2 Average Daily S&P 500 Returns, by Day of the Week (Dividends Included)

Time Period	Monday	Tuesday	Weekday Wednesday	Thursday	Friday
1950–2004	−0.072%	0.032%	0.089%	0.041%	0.080%
1950–1979	−0.137	0.001	0.094	0.061	0.115
1980–2004	0.006	0.069	0.083	0.018	0.039

Source: Author calculations.

THE AMAZING JANUARY EFFECT

We saw in Chapter 1 that returns from small-cap common stocks have significantly outdistanced the returns from large-cap common stocks. Beginning in the early 1980s, researchers reported that the difference was too large even to be explained by differences in risk. In other words, small stocks appeared to earn positive excess returns.

Further research found that, in fact, a substantial percentage of the return on small stocks has historically occurred early in the month of January, particularly in the few days surrounding the turn of the year. Even closer research documents that this peculiar phenomenon is more pronounced for stocks that have experienced significant declines in value, or "losers."

Thus, we have the famous "small-stock-in-January-especially-around-the-turn-of-the-year-for-losers effect," or SSIJEATTOTYFLE for short. For obvious reasons, this phenomenon is usually just dubbed the **January effect**. To give you an idea of how big this effect is, we first plotted average returns by month going back to 1926 for large stocks in Figure 7.9A. As shown, the average return per month has been just under 1 percent.

January effect
Tendency for small stocks to have large returns in January.

In Figure 7.9A, there is nothing remarkable about January; the largest average monthly return for large stocks occurred in July (followed closely by December); the lowest in September. From a statistical standpoint, there is nothing too exceptional about these large stock returns. After all, some month has to be the highest, and some month has to be the lowest.

Figure 7.9B, however, shows average returns by month for small stocks (notice the difference in vertical axis scaling between Figures 7.9A and 7.9B). The month of January definitely jumps out. Over the 79 years covered, small stocks gained, on average, about 6.5 percent in the month of January alone! Comparing Figures 7.9A and 7.9B, we see, outside the month of January, small stocks have not done especially well relative to large stocks. To a lesser extent, we see that small stocks have done better than large stocks in February, but large stocks have done better than small stocks by about the same amount in October.

The January effect appears to exist in many major markets around the world, so it's not unique to the United States (it's actually more pronounced in some other markets). It also

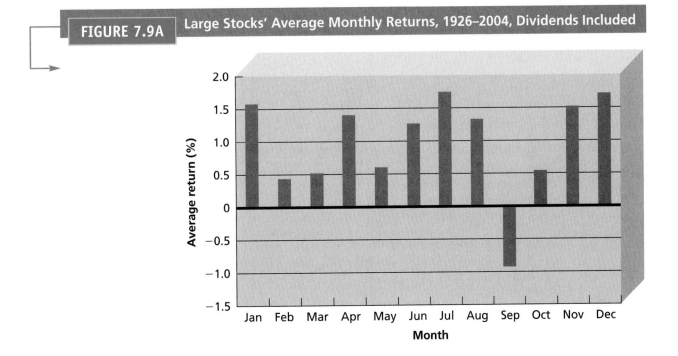

FIGURE 7.9A Large Stocks' Average Monthly Returns, 1926–2004, Dividends Included

FIGURE 7.9B Small Stocks' Average Monthly Returns, 1926–2004, Dividends Included

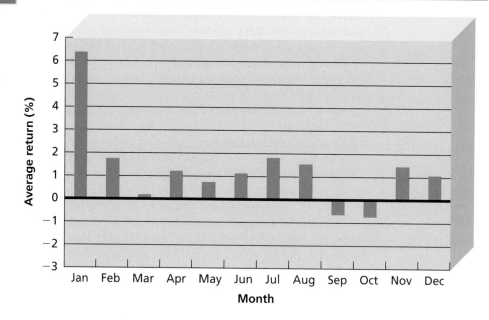

exists in some markets other than stock markets. Critics of market efficiency point to enormous gains to be had from simply investing in January and ask: How can an efficient market have such unusual behavior? Why don't investors take advantage of this opportunity and thereby drive it out of existence?

In Table 7.3, you can see that, on average, small stock returns were 4.84 percent higher than large stock returns in the 1926–2004 time period. The next best month in this period (February) is essentially canceled out by the worst month (October). When we break the 1926–2004 time period into smaller time intervals, you can see that the January effect has diminished over time. In fact, in the 1978–2004 time period, the *best* monthly difference of 2.46 percent (January) is essentially canceled out by the worst monthly difference of −2.47 percent (October).

Unlike the day-of-the-week effect, the January effect is at least partially understood. Two factors are thought to be important. The first is tax-loss selling. Investors have a strong tax incentive to sell stocks that have gone down in value to realize the loss for tax purposes. This trading leads to a pattern of selling in these stocks near the end of the year and buying after the turn of the year. In large stocks, this activity wouldn't have much effect, but in the smaller stocks, it could.

TABLE 7.3 Monthly Returns of Small Stocks Minus Monthly Returns of Large Stocks, by Various Time Periods, 1926–2004

Time Period	Best Difference (%) Month		Next Best Difference (%) Month		Worst Difference (%) Month	
1926–2004	4.84%	January	1.35%	February	−1.26%	October
1926–1951	6.73	January	1.51	February	−1.64	December
1952–1977	5.42	January	0.87	February	−1.37	October
1978–2004	2.46	January	1.67	February	−2.47	October

Source: Author calculations.

The tax-loss selling argument is plausible because researchers have looked to see whether the January effect existed in the United States before there was an income tax—and they found no January effect. However, the January effect has been found in other countries that didn't (or don't) have calendar tax years or didn't (or don't) have capital gains taxes. However, foreign investors in those markets (such as U.S. investors) did (or do). So, debate continues about the tax-loss selling explanation.

The second factor has to do with institutional investors. The argument here has several pieces, but the gist of it is that these large investors compensate portfolio managers based on their performance over the calendar year. Portfolio managers therefore pile into small stocks at the beginning of the year because of their growth potential, bidding up prices. Over the course of the year, they shed the stocks that do poorly because they don't want to be seen as having a bunch of "losers" in their portfolio (this is called "window dressing"). Also, because performance is typically measured relative to the S&P 500, portfolio managers who begin to lag because of losses in small stocks have an incentive to sell them and buy S&P 500 stocks to make sure they don't end up too far behind the S&P 500. Managers who are well ahead late in the year also have an incentive to move into S&P 500 stocks to preserve their leads (this is called "bonus lock-in").

In evaluating the oddity that is known as the January effect, keep in mind that, unlike the day-of-the-week effect, the January effect does not even exist for the market as a whole, so, in big-picture terms, it is not all that important. Also, it doesn't happen every year, so attempts to exploit it will occasionally result in substantial losses.

TURN-OF-THE-YEAR EFFECT

Researchers have delved deeply into the January effect to see whether the effect is due to returns during the whole month of January or to returns bracketing the end of the year. Researchers look at returns over a specific three-week period and compare these returns to the returns for the rest of the year. In Table 7.4, we calculated daily market returns from 1962 through 2004. The specific three-week period we call "Turn-of-the-Year Days" is the last week of daily returns in a calendar year and the first two weeks of daily returns in the next calendar year. Any daily return that does not fall into this three-week period is put into the "Rest-of-the-Days" category.

As you can see in Table 7.4, the returns in the "Turn-of-the-Year Days" category are higher than returns in the "Rest-of-the-Days" category. Further, the difference is apparent in the 1984–2004 period. However, the difference was more than twice as large in the 1962–1983 period.

TURN-OF-THE-MONTH EFFECT

Financial market researchers have also investigated whether a turn-of-the-month effect exists. In Table 7.5, we took daily stock market returns and separated them into two categories. If the daily return is from the last day of any month or the following three days of

TABLE 7.4	The Turn-of-the-Year Effect

	Market Return on the:	
Time Period	Turn-of-the-Year Days (%)	Rest-of-the-Days (%)
1962–2004	0.144%	0.039%
1962–1983	0.172	0.031
1984–2004	0.116	0.047

Source: Author calculations.

TABLE 7.5   The Turn-of-the-Month Effect

Time Period	Market Return on the:	
	Turn-of-the-Month Days (%)	Rest-of-the-Days (%)
1962–2004	0.138%	0.024%
1962–1983	0.126	0.020
1984–2004	0.151	0.028

Source: Author calculations.

the following month, it is put into the "Turn-of-the-Month-Days" category. All other daily returns are put into the "Rest-of-the-Days" category.

As you can see in Table 7.5, the returns in the "Turn-of-the-Month" category are higher than the returns in the "Rest-of-the-Days" category. As with the turn-of-the-year anomaly, the turn-of-the-month effect is apparent in each of the three time periods we report. Interestingly, the effect appears to be stronger in the 1984–2004 period than in the 1962–1983 period. Again, the fact that this effect exists is puzzling to proponents of the EMH.

The day-of-the-week, turn-of-the-month, turn-of-the-year, and the January effect are examples of calendar anomalies. There are noncalendar anomalies as well. Two well-known noncalendar anomalies have to do with earnings announcements and price/earnings ratios.

THE EARNINGS ANNOUNCEMENT PUZZLE

As you saw earlier in this chapter, unexpected news releases can have a dramatic impact on the price of a stock. One news item that is particularly important to investors is an earnings announcement. These announcements contain information about past earnings and future earnings potential.

Researchers have shown that substantial price adjustments do occur in anticipation of the actual earnings. According to the EMH, stock prices should then respond very quickly to unanticipated news, or the earnings "surprise." However, researchers have found that it takes days (or even longer) for the market price to adjust fully. In addition, some researchers have found that buying stocks after positive earnings surprises is a profitable investment strategy.

THE PRICE/EARNINGS (P/E) PUZZLE

As we have discussed elsewhere, the P/E ratio is widely followed by investors and is used in stock valuation. Researchers have found that, on average, stocks with relatively low P/E ratios outperform stocks with relatively high P/E ratios, even after adjusting for other factors, like risk. Because a P/E ratio is publicly available information, according to the EMH, it should already be reflected in stock prices. However, purchasing stocks with relatively low P/E ratios appears to be a potentially profitable investment strategy.

There are many other noncalendar anomalies. For example, the market appears to do worse on cloudy days than sunny days. But rather than continuing with a laundry list of anomalies—however much fun they might provide—we will instead turn to some spectacular events in market history.

CHECK THIS

7.10a What is the day-of-the-week effect?

7.10b What is the amazing January effect?

7.10c What is the turn-of-the-year effect?

7.11   Bubbles and Crashes

As a famous songwriter penned, "History shows again and again, how nature points up the folly of men." Nowhere is this statement seemingly more appropriate in finance than in a discussion of bubbles and crashes.[1]

bubble

A situation where observed prices soar far higher than fundamentals and rational analysis would suggest.

crash

A situation where market prices collapse significantly and suddenly.

A **bubble** occurs when market prices soar far in excess of what normal and rational analysis would suggest. Investment bubbles eventually pop because they are not based on fundamental values. When a bubble does pop, investors find themselves holding assets with plummeting values.

A **crash** is a significant and sudden drop in marketwide values. Crashes are generally associated with a bubble. Typically, a bubble lasts much longer than a crash. A bubble can form over weeks, months, or even years. Crashes, on the other hand, are sudden, generally lasting less than a week. However, the disastrous financial aftermath of a crash can last for years.

THE CRASH OF 1929

During the Roaring Twenties, the stock market was supposed to be the place where everyone could get rich. The market was widely believed to be a no-risk situation. Many people invested their life savings without learning about the potential pitfalls of investing. At the time, investors could purchase stocks by putting up 10 percent of the purchase price and borrowing the remainder from a broker. This level of leverage was one factor that led to the sudden market downdraft in October 1929.

As you can see in Figure 7.10, on Friday, October 25, the Dow Jones Industrial Average closed up about a point, at 301.22. On Monday, October 28, it closed at 260.64, down

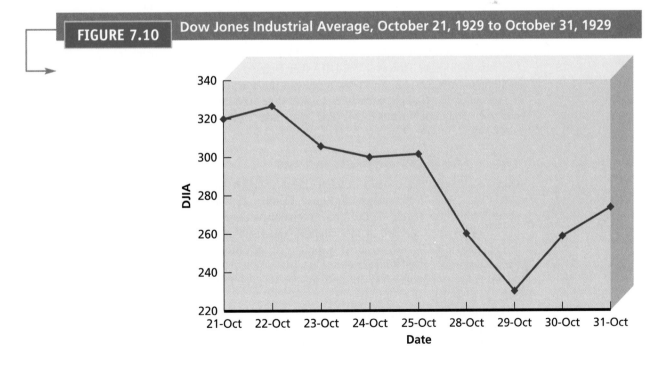

FIGURE 7.10   Dow Jones Industrial Average, October 21, 1929 to October 31, 1929

[1]Lyrics from "Godzilla," by Donald "Buck Dharma" Roeser (as performed by Blue Oyster Cult).

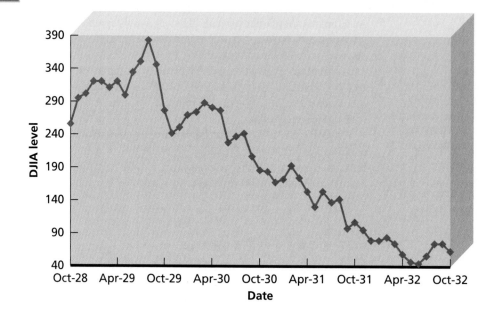

13.5 percent. On Tuesday, October 29, the Dow closed at 230.07, with an interday low of 212.33, which is about 30 percent lower than the closing level on the previous Friday. On this day, known as "Black Tuesday," NYSE volume of 16.4 million shares was more than four times normal levels.

Although the Crash of 1929 was a large decline, it pales with respect to the ensuing bear market. As shown in Figure 7.11, the DJIA rebounded about 20 percent following the October 1929 crash. However, the DJIA then began a protracted fall, reaching the bottom at 40.56 on July 8, 1932. This level represents about a 90 percent decline from the record high level of 386.10 on September 3, 1929. By the way, the DJIA did not surpass its previous high level until November 24, 1954, more than 25 years later.

THE CRASH OF OCTOBER 1987

Once, when we spoke of *the* Crash, we meant October 29, 1929. That was until October 1987. The Crash of 1987 began on Friday, October 16. On huge volume (at the time) of about 338 million shares, the DJIA fell 108 points to close at 2,246.73. It was the first time in history that the DJIA fell by more than 100 points in one day.

October 19, 1987, now wears the mantle of "Black Monday," and this day was indeed a dark and stormy one on Wall Street; the market lost about 22.6 percent of its value on a new record volume of about 600 million shares traded. The DJIA plummeted 508.32 points to close at 1,738.74.

During the day on Tuesday, October 20, the DJIA continued to plunge in value, reaching an intraday low of 1,616.21. But the market rallied and closed at 1,841.01, up 102 points. From the then market high on August 25, 1987, of 2,746.65 to the intraday low on October 20, 1987, the market had fallen over 40 percent.

FIGURE 7.12   Dow Jones Industrial Average, October 1986 to October 1990

After the Crash of 1987, however, there was no protracted depression. In fact, as you can see in Figure 7.12, the DJIA took only two years to surpass its previous market high made in August 1987.

What happened? It's not exactly ancient history, but, here again, debate rages. One faction says that irrational investors had bid up stock prices to ridiculous levels until Black Monday, when the bubble burst, leading to panic selling as investors dumped their stocks. The other faction says that before Black Monday, markets were volatile, volume was heavy, and some ominous signs about the economy were filtering in. From the close on October 13 to the close on October 16, 1987, for example, the market fell by over 10 percent, the largest three-day drop since May 1940 (when German troops broke through French lines near the start of World War II). To top it all off, market values had risen sharply because of a dramatic increase in takeover activity, but Congress was in session and was actively considering antitakeover legislation.

Another factor is that beginning a few years before the Crash of 1987, large investors had developed techniques known as *program trading* designed for very rapid selling of enormous quantities of shares of stock following a market decline. These techniques were still largely untested because the market had been strong for years. However, following the huge sell-off on October 16, 1987, sell orders came pouring in on Monday at a pace never before seen. In fact, these program trades were (and are) blamed by some for much of what happened.

One of the few things we know for certain about the Crash of 1987 is that the stock exchanges suffered a meltdown. The NYSE simply could not handle the volume. Posting of prices was delayed by hours, so investors had no idea what their positions were worth. The specialists couldn't handle the flow of orders, and some specialists actually began selling. NASDAQ went off-line when it became impossible to get through to market makers. It has even been alleged that many stopped answering the phone.

On the two days following the crash, prices *rose* by about 14 percent, one of the biggest short-term gains ever. Prices remained volatile for some time, but as antitakeover talk in Congress died down, the market recovered.

The Crash of 1987 led to some significant market changes. Upgrades have made it possible to handle much heavier trading volume, for example. One of the most interesting changes was the introduction of **NYSE circuit breakers**. Different circuit breakers are triggered if the DJIA drops by 10, 20, or 30 percent. These 10, 20, and 30 percent decline levels in the DJIA, respectively, will result in the following actions:

1. A 10 percent drop in the DJIA will halt trading for one hour if the decline occurs before 2 P.M.; for one half hour if the decline occurs between 2 and 2:30 P.M.; and it will have no effect if the decline occurs between 2:30 and 4:00 P.M.

2. A 20 percent drop in the DJIA will halt trading for two hours if the decline occurs before 1 P.M.; for one hour if the decline occurs between 1 and 2 P.M.; and for the remainder of the day if it occurs between 2 and 4 P.M.

3. A 30 percent drop will halt trading for the remainder of the day regardless of when the decline occurs.

These specific circuit breaker trigger levels were implemented in 1998. Because circuit breakers are designed to slow a market decline, they are often called "speed bumps." Naturally, how well they work is a matter of debate.

One of the most remarkable things about the crash is how little impact it seems to have had. If you look back at the data in Chapter 1, you will see that the market was actually up slightly in 1987. The postcrash period was one of the better times to be in the market, and the Crash of 1987 increasingly looks like a blip in one of the most spectacular market increases that U.S. investors have ever seen. One thing is clearly true: October is the cruelest month for market investors. Indeed two years after the Crash of 1987, a minicrash occurred on October 13, 1989, as the DJIA fell 190 points in the afternoon (following the collapse of a proposed buyout of United Airlines).

THE ASIAN CRASH

The crash of the Nikkei Index, which began in 1990, lengthened into a particularly long bear market. It is quite like the Crash of 1929 in that respect.

The Asian crash started with a booming bull market in the 1980s. Japan and emerging Asian economies seemed to be forming a powerful economic force. The "Asian economy" became an investor outlet for those wary of the U.S. market after the Crash of 1987.

To give you some idea of the bubble that was forming in Japan between 1955 and 1989, real estate prices in Japan increased by 70 times, and stock prices increased 100 times over. In 1989, price-earnings ratios of Japanese stocks climbed to unheard of levels as the Nikkei index soared past 39,000. In retrospect, there were numerous warning signals about the Japanese market. At the time, however, optimism about the continued growth in the Japanese market remained high. Crashes never seem to occur when the outlook is poor, so, as with other crashes, many people did not see the impending Nikkei crash.

As you can see in Figure 7.13, in three years from December 1986 to the peak in December 1989, the Nikkei 225 Index rose 115 percent. Over the next three years, the index lost 57 percent of its value. In April 2003, the Nikkei Index stood at a level that was 80 percent off its peak in December 1989.

THE "DOT-COM" BUBBLE AND CRASH

How many Web sites do you think existed at the end of 1994? Would you believe only about 10,000? By the end of 1999, the number of Web sites stood at about 9,500,000 and at the end of 2004, there were about 57,000,000 Web sites.

FIGURE 7.13   Nikkei 225 Index, January 1984 to June 2005

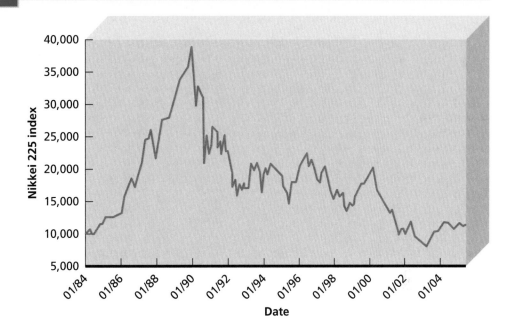

By the mid-1990s, the rise in Internet use and its international growth potential fueled widespread excitement over the "new economy." Investors did not seem to care about solid business plans—only big ideas. Investor euphoria led to a surge in Internet IPOs, which were commonly referred to as "dot-coms" because so many of their names ended in ".com." Of course, the lack of solid business models doomed many of the newly formed companies. Many of them suffered huge losses and some folded relatively shortly after their IPOs.

The extent of the dot-com bubble and subsequent crash is presented in Table 7.6 and Figure 7.14, which compare the Amex Internet Index and the S&P 500 Index. As shown in Table 7.6, the Amex Internet Index soared from a level of 114.60 on October 1, 1998, to its peak of 688.52 in late March 2000, an increase of 500 percent. The Amex Internet Index

TABLE 7.6   Values of the Amex Internet Index and the S&P 500 Index

Date	Amex Internet Index Value	Gain to Peak from Oct. 1, 1998 (%)	Loss from Peak to Trough (%)	S&P 500 Index Value	Gain to Peak from Oct. 1, 1998 (%)	Loss from Peak to Trough (%)
October 1, 1998	114.68			986.39		
Late March 2000 (peak)	688.52	500%		1,293.72	31%	
Early October 2002 (trough)	58.59		−91%	776.76		−40%

Source: Author calculations.

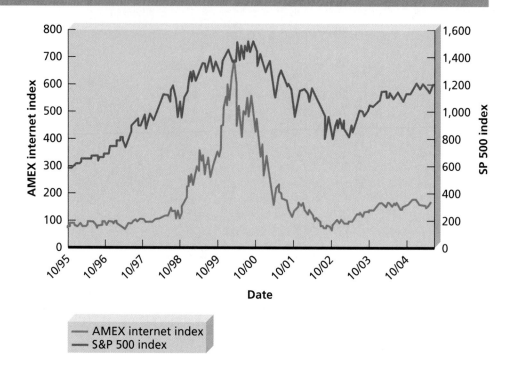

FIGURE 7.14 — Values of the AMEX Internet Index and the S&P 500 Index, October 1995 through May 2005

then fell to a level of 58.59 in early October 2002, a drop of 91 percent. By contrast, the S&P 500 Index rallied about 31 percent in the same 1998–2000 time period and fell 40 percent during the 2000–2002 time period.

CHECK THIS

7.11a   What is a stock market bubble? A stock market crash?

7.11b   What is a major difference between the Crash of October 1929 and the Crash of October 1987?

7.11c   What are NYSE circuit breakers? What are they intended to do?

7.12 Summary and Conclusions

In this chapter, we examined market price behavior and market efficiency. The efficient markets hypothesis (EMH) asserts that, as a practical matter, organized financial markets like the New York Stock Exchange are efficient. Researchers who study efficient markets often ask whether it is possible to "beat the market." We say that you beat the market if you can consistently earn returns in excess of those earned by other investments having the same risk. If a market is efficient, earning these excess returns is not possible, except by luck. The controversy surrounding the EMH centers on this assertion.

The EMH states that the market is efficient with respect to some particular information if that information is not useful in earning a positive excess return. The forms of market efficiency and their information sets are:

1. *Weak Form*: past price and volume information.

2. *Semistrong Form*: all publicly available information.

3. *Strong Form*: all information of any kind, public or private.

You learned how information affects market prices by influencing traders to act on the arrival of information. You then learned how to distinguish among informed trading, illegal insider trading, and legal insider trading.

Testing market efficiency is difficult. We discussed four reasons for this: (1) the risk-adjustment problem, (2) the relevant information problem, (3) the dumb luck problem, and (4) the data-snooping problem.

We then presented evidence concerning tests of market efficiency. One lesson you should learn is that professional money managers have been unable to beat the market consistently. This is true despite their tremendous resources, experience, opportunities, and incentives. Also, this is true despite patterns and other oddities that have occurred historically in the stock market. The fact that professional money managers have been unable to beat the market supports the notion that markets are generally rather efficient.

We close the chapter by discussing some aspects of stock price behavior that are both baffling and hard to reconcile with market efficiency. We discussed the day-of-the-week effect, the amazing January effect, the turn-of-the-year effect, the turn-of-the-month effect, the earnings announcement puzzle, and the price/earnings (P/E) puzzle. Finally, we talked about some famous bubbles and crashes, including the Crash of October 1929, the Crash of October 1987, the Asian crisis, and the dot-com bubble and crash.

GET REAL

This chapter covered market efficiency. In it, we raised a significant question: Can you, or indeed anyone, consistently beat the market? In other words, is the market efficient? This is a question that every investor needs to think about because it has direct, practical implications for investing and portfolio management.

If you think the market is relatively efficient, then your investment strategy should focus on minimizing costs and taxes. Asset allocation is your primary concern, and you will still need to establish the risk level you are comfortable with. But beyond this, you should be a buy-and-hold investor, transacting only when absolutely necessary. Investments such as low-cost, low-turnover mutual funds make a lot of sense. Tools for analyzing the market are irrelevant at best. Thus, in some ways, the appropriate investment strategy is kind of boring, but it's the one that will pay off over the long haul in an efficient market.

In contrast, if you think the market is not particularly efficient, then you've got to be a security picker. You also have to decide what market analyzing tools will be the ones you use. This is also true if you are in the money management business; you have to decide which specific stocks or bonds to hold.

In the end, the only way to find out if you've got what it takes to beat the market is to try, and the best way to try is with a simulated brokerage account such as Stock-Trak. Be honest with yourself: You think you can beat the market; most novice investors do. Some change their minds and some don't. As to which tools to use, you will just have to find out which ones work (or don't work) for you.

Key Terms

abnormal returns 213
bubble 229
crash 229
day-of-the-week effect 224
efficient markets hypothesis (EMH) 207
event study 213

excess return 207
informed trader 215
January effect 225
material nonpublic information 215
NYSE circuit breakers 232
random walk 211

Chapter Review Problems and Self-Test

1. **Market Research**   Smolira Investment Trust (SIT) runs a retirement account for college professors, with a current market value of $2 billion. Alchemy, Inc., offers to conduct market research in an attempt to sift through the market data to find a way to increase the return to SIT's portfolio by 30 basis points per year. Alchemy is offering to conduct the research for the sum of $9 million. Is this price too high or too low?

2. **Picking a Money Manager**   You are helping your very rich aunt Molly to decide where to invest her portfolio. She is planning to take a 10-year world tour after she invests the bulk of her portfolio. She thinks that picking a money manager is unimportant because she believes any professional money manager must be able to beat the market. She's just planning to pick a professional money manager at random. What do you tell her?

Answers to Self-Test Problems

1. Assuming that Alchemy, Inc., actually can conduct research that allows Smolira Investment Trust (SIT) to increase its portfolio return by 30 basis points, SIT would be willing to pay up to $2,000,000,000 times 0.0030 = $6,000,000 for this research. So the price of $9 million is too high.

2. You could show her Figure 7.8. In this figure, it is clear that picking a professional manager at random gives her about a 25 to 30 percent chance of beating a market fund like the Vanguard 500 Index Fund. If she invests her sizable portfolio in the Vanguard 500 Index Fund, she has about a 70 to 75 percent chance of beating a professional money manager picked at random.

Test Your Investment Quotient

1. **Efficient Markets Hypothesis**   A market anomaly refers to
   a. An exogenous shock to the market that is sharp but not persistent.
   b. A price or volume event that is inconsistent with historical price or volume trends.
   c. A trading or pricing structure that interferes with efficient buying or selling of securities.
   d. Price behavior that differs from the behavior predicted by the efficient markets hypothesis.

2. **Efficient Markets Hypothesis**   Which of the following assumptions does not imply an informationally efficient market?
   a. Security prices adjust rapidly to reflect new information.
   b. The timing of one news announcement is independent of other news announcements.
   c. The risk-free rate exists, and investors can borrow and lend unlimited amounts at the risk-free rate.
   d. Many profit-maximizing participants, each acting independently of the others, analyze and value securities.

3. **Efficient Markets Hypothesis**   After lengthy trial and error, you discover a trading system that would have doubled the value of your investment every six months if applied over the last

three years. Which of the following problems makes it difficult to conclude that this is an example of market inefficiency?

a. Risk-adjustment problem
b. Relevant information problem
c. Dumb luck problem
d. Data snooping problem

4. **Efficient Markets Hypothesis** In discussions of financial market efficiency, which of the following is not one of the stylized forms of market efficiency?

a. Strong form
b. Semistrong form
c. Weak form
d. Economic form

5. **Beating the Market** Which of the following is not considered a problem when evaluating the ability of a trading system to "beat the market"?

a. Risk-adjustment problem
b. Relevant information problem
c. Data measurement problem
d. Data snooping problem

6. **Calendar Anomalies** Which month of the year, on average, has had the highest stock market returns as measured by a small-stock portfolio?

a. January
b. March
c. June
d. December

7. **Circuit Breakers** Which of the following intraday changes in the Dow Jones Industrial Average (DJIA) will trigger a circuit breaker halting NYSE trading for one hour?

a. 10 percent drop before 2 P.M.
b. 10 percent drop after 2 P.M.
c. 10 percent rise before 2 P.M.
d. 10 percent rise after 2 P.M.

8. **Efficient Markets Hypothesis** The SEC has regulations that prohibit trading on inside information. If the market is _____ -form efficient, such regulation is not needed.

a. weak
b. semistrong
c. technical
d. strong

9. **The January Effect** Which of the following is a possible explanation of the January effect?

    I. Institutional window dressing
   II. Bonus demand
  III. Tax-loss selling

a. I only
b. I and II only
c. I and III only
d. I, II, and III

10. **NYSE Circuit Breakers** Circuit breakers implemented by the NYSE were designed to

a. Reduce the January effect.
b. Reduce the effect of technical trading.
c. Eliminate program trading.
d. Slow a market decline.

11. **Market Efficiency Implications**   Assume the market is semistrong-form efficient. The best investment strategy is to

    a. Examine the past prices of a stock to determine the trend.

    b. Invest in an actively managed mutual fund whose manager searches for underpriced stocks.

    c. Invest in an index fund.

    d. Examine the financial statements for a company to find stocks that are not selling at intrinsic value.

12. **Market Efficiency Implications**   Assume the market is weak-form efficient. If this is true, technical analysts _____ earn excess returns and fundamental analysts _____ earn excess returns.

    a. could; could

    b. could; could not

    c. could not; could not

    d. could not; could

13. **Efficient Markets Hypothesis**   Which of the following is *not* true concerning the efficient markets hypothesis?

    a. Markets that are less organized are not as likely to be efficient.

    b. Markets with wide fluctuations in prices cannot be efficient.

    c. The efficient markets hypothesis deals only with the stock market.

    d. Prices in an efficient market are fair on average.

14. **Efficient Markets Hypothesis**   You purchase a stock that you expect to increase in value over the next year. One year later, after the discovery that the CEO embezzled funds and the company is close to bankruptcy, the stock has fallen in price. Which of the following statements is true?

    a. This is a violation of weak-form efficiency.

    b. This is a violation of semistrong-form efficiency

    c. This is a violation of all forms of market efficiency.

    d. This is not a violation of market efficiency.

15. **Efficient Markets Hypothesis**   Which of the following statements concerning market efficiency is true?

    a. If the market is weak-form efficient, it is also semistrong-form efficient.

    b. If the market is semistrong-form efficient, it is also strong-form efficient.

    c. If the market is weak-form efficient, it is also strong-form efficient.

    d. If the market is semistrong-form efficient, it is also weak-form efficient.

Concept Questions

1. **Efficient Markets**   A stock market analyst is able to identify mispriced stocks by comparing the average price for the last 10 days to the average price for the last 60 days. If this is true, what do you know about the market?

2. **Efficient Markets**   Critically evaluate the following statement: "Playing the stock market is like gambling. Such speculative investing has no social value, other than the pleasure people get from this form of gambling."

3. **Misconceptions about Efficient Markets**   Several celebrated investors and stock pickers have recorded huge returns on their investments over the past two decades. Is the success of these particular investors an invalidation of an efficient stock market? Explain.

4. **Interpreting Efficient Markets**   For each of the following scenarios, discuss whether profit opportunities exist from trading in the stock of the firm under the conditions that (1) the market is not weak-form efficient, (2) the market is weak-form but not semistrong-form

efficient, (3) the market is semistrong-form but not strong-form efficient, and (4) the market is strong-form efficient.

   a. The stock price has risen steadily each day for the past 30 days.
   b. The financial statements for a company were released three days ago, and you believe you've uncovered some anomalies in the company's inventory and cost control reporting techniques that are understating the firm's true liquidity strength.
   c. You observe that the senior management of a company has been buying a lot of the company's stock on the open market over the past week.
   d. Your next-door neighbor, who happens to be a computer analyst at the local steel plant, casually mentions that a German steel conglomerate hinted yesterday that it might try to acquire the local firm in a hostile takeover.

5. **Performance of the Pros**   In the mid- to late-1990s, the performance of the pros was unusually poor—on the order of 90 percent of all equity mutual funds underperformed a passively managed index fund. How does this bear on the issue of market efficiency?

6. **Efficient Markets**   A hundred years ago or so, companies did not compile annual reports. Even if you owned stock in a particular company, you were unlikely to be allowed to see the balance sheet and income statement for the company. Assuming the market is semistrong-form efficient, what does this say about market efficiency then compared to now?

7. **Efficient Markets Hypothesis**   You invest $10,000 in the market at the beginning of the year, and by the end of the year your account is worth $15,000. During the year the market return was 10 percent. Does this mean that the market is inefficient?

8. **Efficient Markets Hypothesis**   Which of the following statements are true about the efficient market hypothesis?

   a. It implies perfect forecasting ability.
   b. It implies that prices reflect all available information.
   c. It implies an irrational market.
   d. It implies that prices do not fluctuate.
   e. It results from keen competition among investors.

9. **Semistrong Efficiency**   If a market is semistrong-form efficient, is it also weak-form efficient? Explain.

10. **Efficient Markets Hypothesis**   What are the implications of the efficient markets hypothesis for investors who buy and sell stocks in an attempt to "beat the market"?

11. **Efficient Markets Hypothesis**   Aerotech, an aerospace technology research firm, announced this morning that it hired the world's most knowledgeable and prolific space researchers. Before today, Aerotech's stock had been selling for $100. Assume that no other information is received over the next week and the stock market as a whole does not move.

   a. What do you expect will happen to Aerotech's stock?
   b. Consider the following scenarios:

      i. The stock price jumps to $118 on the day of the announcement. In subsequent days it floats up to $123, then falls back to $116.
      ii. The stock price jumps to $116 and remains at that level.
      iii. The stock price gradually climbs to $116 over the next week.

   Which scenario(s) indicate market efficiency? Which do not? Why?

12. **Efficient Markets Hypothesis**   When the 56-year-old founder of Gulf & Western, Inc., died of a heart attack, the stock price immediately jumped from $18.00 a share to $20.25, a 12.5 percent increase. This is evidence of market inefficiency, because an efficient stock market would have anticipated his death and adjusted the price beforehand. Assume that no other information is received and the stock market as a whole does not move. Is this statement about market efficiency true or false? Explain.

13. **Efficient Markets Hypothesis**   Today, the following announcement was made: "Early today the Justice Department reached a decision in the Universal Product Care (UPC) case. UPC has

been found guilty of discriminatory practices in hiring. For the next five years, UPC must pay $2 million each year to a fund representing victims of UPC's policies." Assuming the market is efficient, should investors not buy UPC stock after the announcement because the litigation will cause an abnormally low rate of return? Explain.

14. **Efficient Markets Hypothesis**   Newtech Corp. is going to adopt a new chip-testing device that can greatly improve its production efficiency. Do you think the lead engineer can profit from purchasing the firm's stock before the news release on the device? After reading the announcement in *The Wall Street Journal,* should you be able to earn an abnormal return from purchasing the stock if the market is efficient?

15. **Efficient Markets Hypothesis**   TransTrust Corp. has changed how it accounts for inventory. Taxes are unaffected, although the resulting earnings report released this quarter is 20 percent higher than what it would have been under the old accounting system. There is no other surprise in the earnings report and the change in the accounting treatment was publicly announced. If the market is efficient, will the stock price be higher when the market learns that the reported earnings are higher?

16. **Efficient Markets Hypothesis**   The Durkin Investing Agency has been the best stock picker in the country for the past two years. Before this rise to fame occurred, the Durkin newsletter had 200 subscribers. Those subscribers beat the market consistently, earning substantially higher returns after adjustment for risk end transaction costs. Subscriptions have skyrocketed to 10,000. Now, when the Durkin Investing Agency recommends a stock, the price instantly rises several points. The subscribers currently earn only a normal return when they buy recommended stock because the price rises before anybody can act on the information. Briefly explain this phenomenon. Is Durkin's ability to pick stocks consistent with market efficiency?

17. **Efficient Markets Hypothesis**   Your broker commented that well-managed firms are better investments than poorly managed firms. As evidence, your broker cited a recent study examining 100 small manufacturing firms that eight years earlier had been listed in an industry magazine as the best-managed small manufacturers in the country. In the ensuing eight years, the 100 firms listed have not earned more than the normal market return. Your broker continued to say that if the firms were well managed, they should have produced better-than-average returns. If the market is efficient, do you agree with your broker?

18. **Efficient Markets Hypothesis**   A famous economist just announced in *The Wall Street Journal* his findings that the recession is over and the economy is again entering an expansion. Assume market efficiency. Can you profit from investing in the stock market after you read this announcement?

19. **Efficient Markets Hypothesis**   Suppose the market is semistrong-form efficient. Can you expect to earn excess returns if you make trades based on

   a. Your broker's information about record earnings for a stock?
   b. Rumors about a merger of a firm?
   c. Yesterday's announcement of a successful new product test?

20. **Efficient Markets Hypothesis**   The efficient markets hypothesis implies that all mutual funds should obtain the same expected risk-adjusted returns. Therefore, we can simply pick mutual funds at random. Is this statement true or false? Explain.

21. **Efficient Markets Hypothesis**   Assume that markets are efficient. During a trading day, American Golf, Inc., announces that it has lost a contract for a large golfing project, which, prior to the news, it was widely believed to have secured. If the market is efficient, how should the stock price react to this information if no additional information is released?

22. **Efficient Markets Hypothesis**   Prospectors, Inc., is a publicly traded gold prospecting company in Alaska. Although the firm's searches for gold usually fail, the prospectors occasionally find a rich vein of ore. What pattern would you expect to observe for Prospector's cumulative abnormal returns if the market is efficient?

Questions and Problems

1. **Cumulative Abnormal Returns**   On November 14, Thorogood Enterprises announced that the public and acrimonious battle with its current CEO had been resolved. Under the terms of the deal, the CEO would step down from his position immediately. In exchange, he was given a generous severance package. Given the information below, calculate the cumulative abnormal return (CAR) around this announcement. Assume the company has an expected return equal to the market return. Graph and interpret your results. Do your results support market efficiency?

Date	Market Return (%)	Company Return (%)
11/7	0.3%	0.2%
11/8	−0.2	0.0
11/9	0.2	0.3
11/10	0.9	0.7
11/11	0.1	0.1
11/14	−0.1	1.8
11/15	1.3	1.1
11/16	−0.6	−0.5
11/17	−0.2	−0.3
11/18	0.3	0.4
11/21	0.5	0.4

2. **Cumulative Abnormal Returns**   The following diagram shows the cumulative abnormal returns (CAR) for oil exploration companies announcing oil discoveries over a 30-year period. Month 0 in the diagram is the announcement month. Assume that no other information is received and the stock market as a whole does not move. Is the diagram consistent with market efficiency? Why or why not?

Time in months relative to event month

3. **Cumulative Abnormal Returns**   The following figures present the results of four cumulative abnormal returns (CAR) studies. Indicate whether the results of each study support, reject, or are inconclusive about the semistrong form of the efficient market hypothesis. In each figure, time 0 is the date of an event.

(a)   (b)

(c)   (d)

4. **Cumulative Abnormal Returns**   A study analyzed the behavior of the stock prices of firms that had lost antitrust cases. Included in the diagram are all firms that lost the initial court decision, even if the decision was later overturned on appeal. The event at time 0 is the initial, pre-appeal court decision. Assume no other information was released, aside from that disclosed in the initial trial. The stock prices all have a beta of 1. Is the diagram consistent with market efficiency? Why or why not?

Time in months relative to event month

Intermediate Questions

5. **Cumulative Abnormal Returns**   Ross Co., Westerfield, Inc., and Jaffe Company announced a new agreement to market their respective products in China on July 18 (7/18), February 12 (2/12), and October 7 (10/7), respectively. Given the information below, calculate the cumulative abnormal return (CAR) for these stocks as a group. Assume all companies have an expected return equal to the market return. Graph and interpret your results. Do your results support market efficiency?

	Ross Co.			Westerfield, Inc.			Jaffe Company	
Date	Market Return (%)	Company Return (%)	Date	Market Return (%)	Company Return (%)	Date	Market Return (%)	Company Return (%)
7/12	−0.3%	−0.5%	2/8	−0.9%	−1.1%	10/1	0.5%	0.3%
7/13	0.0	0.2	2/9	−1.0	−1.1	10/2	0.4	0.6
7/16	0.5	0.7	2/10	0.4	0.2	10/3	1.1	1.1
7/17	−0.5	−0.3	2/11	0.6	0.8	10/6	0.1	−0.3
7/18	−2.2	1.1	2/12	−0.3	−0.1	10/7	−2.2	−0.3
7/19	−0.9	−0.7	2/15	1.1	1.2	10/8	0.5	0.5
7/20	−1.0	−1.1	2/16	0.5	0.5	10/9	−0.3	−0.2
7/23	0.7	0.5	2/17	−0.3	−0.2	10/10	0.3	0.1
7/24	0.2	0.1	2/18	0.3	0.2	10/13	0.0	−0.1

CHAPTER 8

Behavioral Finance and the Psychology of Investing

"The investor's chief problem, and even his worst enemy, is likely to be himself."

–Benjamin Graham

"There are three factors that influence the market: Fear, Greed, and Greed."

–Market folklore

Be honest: Do you think of yourself as a better than average driver? If you do, you are not alone. About 80 percent of the people who are asked this question will say yes. Evidently, we tend to overestimate our abilities behind the wheel. Is the same thing true when it comes to making investment decisions? ■

You will probably not be surprised when we say that human beings sometimes make errors in judgment. How these errors, and other aspects of human behavior, affect investors and asset prices falls under the general heading of "behavioral finance." In the first part of this chapter, our goal is to acquaint you with some common types of mistakes investors make and their financial implications. As you will see, researchers have identified a wide variety of potentially damaging behaviors. In the second part of the chapter, we describe a trading strategy known as "technical analysis." Some investors use technical analysis as a tool to try to exploit patterns in prices. These patterns are thought to exist (by advocates of technical analysis) because of predictable behavior by investors.

8.1 Introduction to Behavioral Finance

Sooner or later, you are going to make an investment decision that winds up costing you a lot of money. Why is this going to happen? You already know the answer. Sometimes you make sound decisions, but you just get unlucky when something happens that you could not have reasonably anticipated. At other times (and painful to admit) you just make a bad decision, one that could have (and should have) been avoided. The beginning of investment wisdom is to recognize the circumstances that lead to poor decisions and thereby cut down on the damage done by investment blunders.

behavioral finance
The area of finance dealing with the implications of investor reasoning errors on investment decisions and market prices.

As we previously noted, the area of research known as **behavioral finance** attempts to understand and explain how reasoning errors influence investor decisions and market prices. Much of the research done in the area of behavioral finance stems from work in the area of cognitive psychology, which is the study of how people, including investors, think, reason, and make decisions. Errors in reasoning are often called *cognitive errors*.

Some proponents of behavioral finance believe that cognitive errors by investors will cause market inefficiencies. Recall that in a previous chapter, we identified three economic conditions that lead to market efficiency: (1) investor rationality, (2) independent deviations from rationality, and (3) arbitrage. For a market to be inefficient, all three of these conditions must be absent. That is, it must be the case that a substantial portion of investors make irrational investment decisions, and the collective irrationality of these investors then must lead to an overly optimistic or pessimistic market situation that cannot be corrected via arbitrage by rational, well-capitalized investors. Whether this actually occurs in financial markets is the subject of a raging debate, and we are not going to take sides. Instead, our goal is to introduce you to the ideas and issues.

CHECK THIS

8.1a   What is behavioral finance?

8.1b   What three conditions must be absent for a market to be inefficient?

8.2 Prospect Theory

prospect theory
An alternative theory to classical, rational economic decision making, which emphasizes, among other things, that investors tend to behave differently when they face prospective gains and losses.

Prospect theory, developed in the late 1970s, is a collection of ideas that provides an alternative to classical, rational economic decision making. The foundation of prospect theory rests on the idea that investors are much more distressed by prospective losses than they are happy about prospective gains. Researchers have found that a typical investor considers the pain of a $1 loss to be about twice as great as the pleasure received from the gain of $1. Also, researchers have found that investors respond in different ways to identical situations. The difference depends on whether the situation is presented in terms of losses or in terms of gains.

Investors seem to be willing to take more risk to avoid the loss of a dollar than they are to make a dollar profit. Also, if an investor has the choice between a sure gain and a gamble that could increase or decrease the sure gain, the investor is likely to choose the sure gain. Choosing a sure gain over a gamble is called *risk-averse behavior.* If the same investor is faced with a sure loss and a gamble that could increase or decrease the sure loss, the investor is likely to take the gamble. Choosing the gamble over the sure loss is called *risk-taking behavior.*

This focus on gains and losses and the tendency of investors to be risk-averse with regard to gains, but risk-taking when it comes to losses, is the essence of prospect theory. In contrast, a fully rational investor (in an economic sense) is presumed to care only about his or her overall wealth, not the gains and losses associated with individual pieces of that wealth.

To give a simple example, suppose you own just two stocks (which is, of course, a bad idea from a diversification standpoint). On a particular day, one stock goes up sharply, but the other goes down so that your total wealth in unchanged. On another day, neither stock changes price at all. In both cases, your total wealth was unaffected, but in the first case you would probably be upset that your big gain was canceled out. If you are, you are focusing on the individual pieces, not the big picture. As we will see in the next few subsections, this kind of thinking can lead to potentially damaging errors in judgment.

FRAME DEPENDENCE

If an investment problem is presented in two different (but really equivalent) ways, investors often make inconsistent choices. That is, how a problem is described, or framed, seems to matter to people. Some people believe that frames are transparent; that is, investors should be able to see through the way the question is asked. Do they? Do you? Try this: Jot down your answers in the following two scenarios.

Scenario One. Suppose we give you $1,000. You have the following choice:

A. You can receive another $500 for sure.

B. You can flip a fair coin. If the coin-flip comes up heads, you get another $1,000, but if it comes up tails, you get nothing.

Scenario Two. Suppose we give you $2,000. You have the following choice:

A. You can lose $500 for sure.

B. You can flip a fair coin. If the coin-flip comes up heads, you lose $1,000, but if it comes up tails, you lose nothing.

What were your answers? Did you choose option A in the first scenario and option B in the second? If that's what you did, you are guilty of just focusing on gains and losses, and not paying attention to what really matters, namely, the impact on your wealth. However, you are not alone. About 85 percent of the people who are presented with the first scenario choose option A, and about 70 percent of the people who are presented with the second scenario choose option B.

If you look closely at the two scenarios, you will see that they are actually identical. You end up with $1,500 for sure if you pick option A, or else you end up with a 50-50 chance of either $1,000 or $2,000 if you pick option B. So you should pick the same option in both scenarios. Which option you prefer is up to you, but the point is that you should never pick option A in one scenario and option B in the other. But people do this because the phrasing, or framing, of the question leads people to answer the questions differently. This phenomenon is known as *frame dependence*.

Our frame dependence example offers several important investment lessons. First, an investor can always frame a decision problem in broad terms (like wealth) or in narrow terms (like gains and losses). Second, broad and narrow frames often lead the investor to make different choices. Although using a narrow frame (like gains and losses) is human nature, doing so can lead to irrational decisions. Therefore, using broad frames, like overall wealth, results in better investment decisions.

MENTAL ACCOUNTS AND LOSS AVERSION

When you add a new stock to your portfolio, it is human nature for you to associate the stock with its purchase price. As the price of the stock changes through time, you will have unrealized gains or losses when you compare the current price to the purchase price.

mental accounting
Associating a stock with its purchase price.

Through time, you will mentally account for these gains and losses, and how you feel about the investment depends on whether you are ahead or behind. This behavior is known as **mental accounting**.

When you engage in mental accounting, you unknowingly have a personal relationship with each of your stocks. As a result, selling one of them becomes more difficult. It is as if you have to "break up" with this stock, or "fire" it from your portfolio. As with personal relationships, these "stock relationships" can be complicated and, believe it or not, make selling stocks difficult at times.

In fact, you may have particular difficulty selling a stock at a price lower than your purchase price. If you sell a stock at a loss, you may have a hard time thinking that purchasing the stock in the first place was correct. You may feel this way even if the decision to buy was actually a very good decision. A further complication is that you will also think that if you can just somehow "get even," you will be able to sell the stock without any hard feelings. This phenomenon is known as **loss aversion**, which is the reluctance to sell investments such as shares of stock after they have fallen in value. Loss aversion is also called the "break-even" or "disposition effect," and those suffering from it are sometimes said to have "get-evenitis." Legendary investor Warren Buffett offers the following advice: "The stock doesn't know you own it. You have feelings about it, but it has no feelings about you. The stock doesn't know what you paid. People shouldn't get emotionally involved with their stocks."

loss aversion
A reluctance to sell investments after they have fallen in value. Also known as the *breakeven or disposition effect.*

To see if you are likely to suffer from loss aversion, consider the following two investments:

Investment One. A year ago, you bought shares in Fama Enterprises for $40 per share. Today, these shares are worth $20 each.

Investment Two. A year ago, you bought shares in French Company for $5 per share. Today, these shares are worth $20 each.

What will you do? Will you (1) sell one of these stocks; (2) sell both of these stocks; (3) hold one of these stocks; or (4) hold both of these stocks?

Because you are reading about loss aversion, you will undoubtedly recognize that if you choose to keep the shares in Fama Enterprises, you might be suffering from loss aversion. Why do we say might? Well, consider this. Suppose you are considering a new investment in Fama Enterprises. Does your rational analysis say that it is reasonable to purchase shares at $20? If the rational answer is no, then you should sell. If the rational answer is yes, then you do not suffer from loss aversion. However, if you argued to yourself that if shares in Fama Enterprises were a good buy at $40, then they must be a steal at $20, you probably have a raging case of loss aversion. So, to summarize, there are two important lessons from this example:

- **Lesson One**: The market says that shares in Fama Enterprises are worth $20. The market does not care that you paid $40 a year ago.
- **Lesson Two**: You should not care about your purchase price of Fama Enterprises either. You must evaluate your shares at their current price.

How about the shares in French Company? Do you sell them and take the profit? Once again, the lessons are the same. The market says that shares in French Company are worth $20 per share today. The fact that you paid $5 a year ago is not relevant. Note that selling either of these stocks has tax consequences. Your careful analysis should acknowledge the existence of taxes and transaction fees, and their impact on the net proceeds available to you after you sell a security.

How destructive is loss aversion? Perhaps the most famous case of loss aversion, or "get-evenitis," occurred in 1995, when 28-year-old Nicholas Leeson caused the collapse of his employer, the 233-year-old Barings Bank. At the end of 1992, Leeson had lost about £2 million, which he hid in a secret account. By the end of 1993, his losses were about £23 million, and they mushroomed to £208 million at the end of 1994 (at the time, this was $512 million). Instead of admitting to these losses, Leeson gambled more of the bank's money in an attempt to "double-up and catch-up." On February 23, 1995, Leeson's losses were about £827 million ($1.3 billion) and his trading irregularities were uncovered. Although he attempted to flee from prosecution, he was caught, arrested, tried, convicted, and imprisoned. Also, his wife divorced him.

It is unlikely that you will suffer from a case of loss aversion as severe as Nicholas Leeson's, but loss aversion does affect everyday investors. For example, we know that individual investors sell "winners" more frequently than they sell "losers." If a typical individual investor had 100 stocks with unrealized gains, the investor might sell 15 of them and keep 85. If the same investor had 100 stocks with unrealized losses, the investor would tend to sell 10 of them and keep 90. That is, individual investors are typically about 1.5 times more likely to sell a stock that has gone up in price than they are to sell a stock that has fallen in price.

This effect is worse when investors hold mutual funds. With mutual funds, when investors choose to sell, they are more than 2.5 times as likely to sell a winning fund than a losing fund. How about professional money managers who manage the mutual funds? They also suffer from loss aversion.

HOUSE MONEY

Casinos in Las Vegas (and elsewhere) know all about a concept called "playing with house money." The casinos have found that gamblers are far more likely to take big risks with money that they have won from the casino (i.e., the "house money"). Also, casinos have found that gamblers are not as upset about losing house money as they are about losing the money they brought with them to gamble.

It may seem natural for you to feel that some money is precious because you earned it through hard work, sweat, and sacrifice, whereas other money is less precious because it came to you as a windfall. But these feelings are plainly irrational because any dollar you have buys the same amount of goods and services no matter how you obtained that dollar. The lessons are:

- **Lesson One**. There are no "paper profits." Your profits are yours.

- **Lesson Two**. All your money is your money. That is, you should not separate your money into bundles labeled "house money" and "my money."

Let us return to the shares of Fama Enterprises and French Company. Suppose both were to decline to $15. You might feel very differently about the decline depending on which stock you looked at. With Fama Enterprises, the decline makes a bad situation even worse. Now you are down $25 per share on your investment. On the other hand, with French Company, you only "give back" some of your "paper profit." You are still way ahead. This kind of thinking is playing with house money. Whether you lose from your original investment or from your investment gains is irrelevant.

Frame dependence, mental accounting, and the house money effect are all consistent with the predictions of prospect theory. Many other types of judgment errors have been documented. Here are a few examples:

- **Myopic loss aversion**: This behavior is the tendency to focus on avoiding short-term losses, even at the expense of long-term gains. For example, you might fail to invest "retirement" money into stocks because you have a fear of loss in the near term.

- **Regret aversion**: This aversion is the tendency to avoid making a decision because you fear that, in hindsight, the decision would have been less than optimal. Regret aversion relates to myopic loss aversion.

- **Sunk cost fallacy**: This mistake is the tendency to "throw good money after bad." An example is to keep buying a stock or mutual fund in the face of unfavorable developments.
- **Endowment effect**: This effect is the tendency to consider something that you own to be worth more than it would be if you did not own it. Because of the endowment effect, people sometimes demand more money to give up something than they would be willing to pay to acquire it.
- **Money illusion**: If you suffer from a money illusion, you are confused between real buying power and nominal buying power (i.e., you do not account for the effects of inflation).

CHECK THIS

8.2a	What is the basic prediction of prospect theory?
8.2b	What is frame dependence?
8.2c	How are mental accounting and loss aversion related?

8.3 Overconfidence

A serious error in judgment you can make as an investor is to be overconfident. We are all overconfident about our abilities in many areas (recall our question about your driving ability at the beginning of the chapter). Here is another example. Ask yourself: What grade will I receive in this course (in spite of the arbitrary and capricious nature of the professor)? In our experience, almost everyone will either say A or, at worst, B. Sadly, when we ask our students this question, we always feel confident (but not overconfident) that at least some of our students are going to be disappointed.

Concerning investment behavior, overconfidence appears in several ways. The classic example is diversification, or the lack of it. Investors tend to invest too heavily in the company for which they work. When you think about it, this loyalty can be very bad financially. This is because both your earning power (your income) and your retirement nest egg depend on one company.

Other examples of the lack of diversification include investing too heavily in the stocks of local companies. You might also do this because you read about them in the local news or you know someone who works there. That is, you might be unduly confident that you have a high degree of knowledge about local companies versus distant companies.

OVERCONFIDENCE AND TRADING FREQUENCY

If you are overconfident about your investment skill, you are likely to trade too much. You should know that researchers have found that investors who make relatively more trades have lower returns than investors who trade less frequently. Based on brokerage account activity over a particular period, researchers found that the average household earned an annual return of 16.4 percent. However, those households that traded the most earned an annual return of only 11.4 percent. The moral is clear: Excessive trading is hazardous to your wealth.

OVERTRADING AND GENDER: "IT'S (BASICALLY) A GUY THING"

In a study published in 2001, Professors Brad Barber and Terrance Odean examined the effects of overconfidence. Two possible effects of overconfidence are that it leads to more trading and more trading leads to lower returns. If investors could be divided into groups that differed in overconfidence, then these effects could be examined.

Barber and Odean use the fact that psychologists have found that men are more overconfident than women in the area of finance. So, do men trade more than women? Do portfolios of men underperform the portfolios of women? Barber and Odean show that the answer to both questions is yes.

Barber and Odean examine the trading accounts of men and women and find that men trade about 50 percent more than women. They find that both men and women reduce their portfolio returns through excessive trading. However, men do so by 94 basis points more per year than women. The difference is even bigger between single men and single women. Single men trade 67 percent more than single women, and single men reduce their return by 144 basis points compared to single women.

Using four risk measures, and accounting for the effects of marital status, age, and income, Professors Barber and Odean also find that men invested in riskier positions than women. Young and single people held portfolios that displayed more return volatility and contained a higher percentage of stocks in small companies. Investors with higher incomes also accepted more market risk. These results are comforting because it seems to make sense that the relatively young and the relatively wealthy should be willing to take more investment risk, particularly if they do not have dependents.

WHAT IS A DIVERSIFIED PORTFOLIO TO THE EVERYDAY INVESTOR?

It is clear to researchers that most investors have a poor understanding of what constitutes a well-diversified portfolio. Researchers have discovered that the average number of stocks in a household portfolio is about four, and the median is about three.

Ask yourself: What percentage of these households beat the market? If you are like most people, your answer is too low. Researchers have found, however, that even when accounting for trading costs, about 43 percent of the households outperformed the market. Surprised? The lack of diversification is the source of your surprise.

Think about it like this. Suppose all investors held just one stock in their account. If there are many stocks, about half the individual stock returns outperform the market average. Therefore, about half the investors will beat the market. Quickly: Did you think that you would certainly be in that half that would beat the market? If you did, this should show you that you might be prone to overconfidence.

CHECK THIS

8.3a   How does overconfidence appear in investment behavior?

8.3b   What are the effects of trading frequency on portfolio performance?

8.4 Misperceiving Randomness and Overreacting to Chance Events

Cognitive psychologists have discovered that the human mind is a pattern-seeking device. As a result, we can conclude that causal factors or patterns are at work behind sequences of events even when the events are truly random. In behavioral finance, this is known as the

representativeness heuristic

Concluding that causal factors are at work behind random sequences.

representativeness heuristic, which says that if something is random, it should look random. But what does random look like?

Suppose we flip a coin 20 times and write down whether we get a head or a tail. Then we do it again. The results of our two sets of 20 flips are:

First 20:   T T T H T T T H T T H H H T H H T H H H

Second 20:   T H T H H T T H T H T H T H T T H T H T H H

Do these sequences of heads and tails both look random to you? Most people would say that the first 20 and the second 20 somehow look "different," even though both are random sequences and both have 10 heads and 10 tails.

Let's look at this a bit differently by graphing the results. We'll start at zero. If a head occurs, we will subtract one; if a tail occurs, we will add one. Table 8.1 lists the results. Suppose we graph the two sets of 20 flips in Figure 8.1. Do the two series look different to you? Do you think the line labeled First 20 has a pattern to it, but the line labeled Second 20 appears to be random? If you do, your mind saw a pattern in a random sequence of coin flips, even though both patterns are the result of random coin flips with 10 heads and 10 tails.

TABLE 8.1	The Results of Two Sets of 20 Coin Flips

Flip Number	First 20 Flips Result	+1/−1	Accumulated Sum	Second 20 Flips Result	+1/−1	Accumulated Sum
			0			0
1	T	1	1	T	1	1
2	T	1	2	H	−1	0
3	T	1	3	T	1	1
4	H	−1	2	H	−1	0
5	T	1	3	H	−1	−1
6	T	1	4	T	1	0
7	T	1	5	T	1	1
8	H	−1	4	H	−1	0
9	T	1	5	T	1	1
10	T	1	6	H	−1	0
11	H	−1	5	T	1	1
12	H	−1	4	H	−1	0
13	H	−1	3	T	1	1
14	T	1	4	T	1	2
15	H	−1	3	H	−1	1
16	H	−1	2	T	1	2
17	T	1	3	H	−1	1
18	H	−1	2	T	1	2
19	H	−1	1	H	−1	1
20	H	−1	0	H	−1	0
Number of heads	10			10		
Number of tails	10			10		

FIGURE 8.1   The Pattern of Two Different Sets of 20 Coin Flips

THE "HOT-HAND" FALLACY

Basketball fans generally believe that success breeds success. Suppose we look at the recent performance of two basketball players named LeBron and Shaquille. Both of these players make half of their shots. But LeBron just made two shots in a row, while Shaquille just missed two shots in a row. Researchers have found that if they ask 100 basketball fans which player has the better chance of making the next shot, 91 of them will say LeBron, because he has a "hot hand." Further, 84 of these fans believe that it is important for teammates to pass the ball to LeBron after he has made two or three shots in a row.

But—and the sports fans among you will have a hard time with this—researchers have found that the hot hand is an illusion. That is, players really do not deviate much from their long-run shooting averages, although fans, players, announcers, and coaches think they do. Cognitive psychologists actually studied the shooting percentage of one professional basketball team for a season. The findings are presented in Table 8.2. Detailed analysis of shooting data failed to show that players make or miss shots more or less frequently than what would be expected by chance. That is, statistically speaking, all the shooting percentages in Table 8.2 are the "same."

The shooting percentages in Table 8.2 may suggest that teams will try harder to stop a shooter who has made the last two or three shots. To take this into account, researchers have also studied free throw percentages. Researchers told fans that a certain player was a 70 percent free throw shooter and was about to shoot two foul shots. They asked fans to predict what would happen on the second shot if the player

1. Made the first free throw.

2. Missed the first free throw.

Fans thought that this 70 percent free throw shooter would make 74 percent of the second free throws after making the first free throw, but would only make 66 percent of the second

TABLE 8.2 | Shooting Percentages and the History of Previous Attempts

Shooting Percentage on Next Shot	History of Previous Attempts
46%	Made 3 in a row
50	Made 2 in a row
51	Made 1
52	First shot of the game
54	Missed 1
53	Missed 2 in a row
56	Missed 3 in a row

free throws after missing the first free throw. Researchers studied free throw data from a professional basketball team over two seasons. They found that the result of the first free throw does not matter when it comes to making or missing the second free throw. On average, the shooting percentage on the second free throw was 75 percent when the player made the first free throw. On average, the shooting percentage on the second free throw was also 75 percent when the player missed the first free throw.

It is true that basketball players shoot in streaks. But these steaks are within the bounds of long-run shooting percentages. So it is an illusion that players are either "hot" or "cold." If you are a believer in the "hot hand," however, you are likely to reject these facts because you "know better" from watching your favorite teams over the years. You are being fooled by randomness, because randomness often appears in clusters.

clustering illusion
Human belief that random events that occur in clusters are not really random.

The **clustering illusion** is our human belief that random events that occur in clusters are not really random. For example, it strikes most people as very unusual if heads comes up four times in a row during a series of coin flips. However, if a fair coin is flipped 20 times, there is about a 50 percent chance of getting four heads in a row. Ask yourself, if you flip four heads in a row, do you think you have a "hot hand" at coin flipping?

Mutual fund investing is one area where investors seem to fall prey to the clustering illusion. Every year, funds that have had exceptionally good performance receive large inflows of investor money. Despite the universal disclaimer that "past performance is no guarantee of future results," investors nonetheless clearly chase past returns.

THE GAMBLER'S FALLACY

People commit the gambler's fallacy when they assume that a departure from what occurs on average, or in the long run, will be corrected in the short run. Another way to think about the gambler's fallacy is that because an event has not happened recently, it has become "overdue" and is more likely to occur. People sometimes refer (wrongly) to the "law of averages" in such cases.

Roulette is a random gambling game where gamblers can make various bets on the spin of the wheel. There are 38 numbers on an American roulette table, two green ones, 18 red ones, and 18 black ones. One possible bet is to bet whether the spin will result in a red number or in a black number. Suppose a red number has appeared five times in a row. Gamblers will often become confident that the next spin will be black, when the true chance remains at about 50 percent (of course, it is exactly 18 in 38).

The misconception arises from the human intuition that the overall odds of the wheel must be reflected in a small number of spins. That is, gamblers often become convinced that the wheel is "due" to hit a black number after a series of red numbers. Gamblers do know that the odds of a black number appearing are always unchanged: 18 in 38. But

OTHERS' BAD BEHAVIOR CAN BE GOOD FOR YOU

Behavioral finance is clearly working its way from academia into the nitty-gritty business of running mutual-fund portfolios.

Lewis Sanders, chief executive of Alliance Capital Management, held forth on the subject at Morningstar's annual investment conference in June, and JP Morgan Asset Management has launched a stable of funds whose investment framework exploits the concept. Basically, behavioral finance looks at why investors make bad, irrational decisions—whether it's holding on to losing stocks for too long or selling winners too early. These poor decisions create market inefficiencies that savvy investors can capitalize on.

"Chasing strong investment performance, whether through asset classes or investment managers, seems to be a permanent feature of investor decision-making," Sanders pointed out. He walked the audience through a number of blind spots, one being that investors tend to focus disproportionately on the part of their portfolio that's not performing well.

Sanders concluded that investors "systematically buy high and sell low" — adding that in most cases, they are unaware of their biases. There's no doubt that irrational investment decisions are common,

but does behavioral finance form the underpinning of a worthy portfolio management style?

There are some skeptics. "I'm not personally aware of any models that would allow analysts to scientifically or precisely choose their entry points based on behavioral finance," says Don Cassidy, senior research analyst at Lipper, who is a student of the discipline. What's more, many money-management shops already watch for behavioral-finance moves. Value investing, for example, holds that the market can become too pessimistic about certain stocks, creating buying opportunities.

JPMorgan Asset Management, which is trying to raise its profile as a fund manager, insists that behavioral finance is a sound investment framework, having launched four of its Intrepid funds in February 2003. It has run similar portfolios in Europe for about a decade.

Silvio Tarca, who heads the U.S. behavioral-finance team at JPMorgan Asset Management, says the funds look for "securities that have been mispriced by irrational investor behavior. We're looking for securities with attractive valuations and improving earnings expectations where the investment sentiment has turned favorable."

gamblers cannot help but feel that after a long series of red numbers, a black one must appear to restore the "balance" between red and black numbers over time. Thousands of betting systems exist that claim to be able to generate money by betting opposite to recent outcomes. One simple example in roulette is to wait until four red numbers in a row appear—then bet on black. Internet hucksters sell "guaranteed" betting systems that are basically based on the gambler's fallacy. None of them work. Think about it. If these betting systems actually worked, why would they be for sale?

Of course, there are many other related investor errors and biases. Here is a partial list:

- **Law of small numbers**: If you believe in the law of small numbers, you believe that a small sample of outcomes always resembles the long-run distribution of outcomes. If your investment guru has been right five out of seven times recently, you might believe that his long-run average of being correct is also five out of seven. The law of small numbers is related to recency bias and to the gambler's fallacy.

- **Recency bias**: Humans tend to give recent events more importance than less recent events. For example, during the great bull market that occurred from 1995 to 1999,

Intrepid managers focus on three behavioral patterns:

- Investors are too optimistic about past winners and too pessimistic about past losers.
- Analysts tend to underreact to earnings information when they revise their forecasts, thereby underestimating a stock's intrinsic worth.
- Investors tend to hold recent losing stocks for too long and sell their winners too quickly.

The combination of value and momentum investing should balance each other. Emphasizing valuation provides some downside protection, notes Morningstar's Dan McNeela.

Tarca acknowledges that there are other portfolio managers incorporating behavioral-finance tenets into their strategies. But many managers "spend a good deal of their time meeting with company management and sell-side analysts trying to make qualitative assessments about a company's business prospects, as opposed to [our] more quantitative approach," he says.

The JPMorgan Intrepid Mid Cap (PECAX), previously under the BancOne fund stable until it was acquired, came into the fold late last year. So far this year the portfolio has gained 14.51%, placing it in

the top 5% of Morningstar's mid-cap blend category. The other funds are off to a good start, for the most part. Intrepid Value Fund (JPIVX) gained 17.5% last year, besting 90% of its Morningstar peers. Intrepid Contrarian Fund (JIISX) was up 16% last year, landing it in the bottom half of its group. Intrepid Growth Fund (JPGSX) gained 10.50% last year, surpassing 74% of its peers. Intrepid American Fund (JPIAX) notched a 12.7% gain, placing it in the top 17% of its group. Intrepid European (VEUAX), launched in 2000, has a five-year return of 7.77%, ranking it in the top 27% of its group.

Other firms have tried to incorporate behavioral finance. Take **AllianceBernstein Wealth Appreciation Strategies** (AWAAX), which automatically rebalances the portfolio if it strays five percentage points from the targeted 50-50 split between growth and value stocks.

"We're really trimming from the outperforming asset class and buying the underperforming asset class, which is exactly the thing people can't do by themselves," says Tom Fontaine, senior portfolio manager at AllianceBernstein Investment Research and Management.

Source: Lawrence C. Strauss, *Barron's Online*, September 19, 2005.

many investors thought the market would continue its big gains for a long time—forgetting that bear markets also occur (which happened from 2000 to 2002). Recency bias is related to the law of small numbers.

- **Self-attribution bias**: This bias occurs when you attribute good outcomes to your own skill, but blame bad outcomes on luck.
- **Wishful thinking bias**: You suffer from wishful thinking bias when you believe what you want to believe. Wishful thinking bias relates to self-attribution bias.
- **False consensus**: This is the tendency to think that other people are thinking the same thing about a stock we own (or are going to buy). False consensus relates to overconfidence and loss aversion.
- **Availability bias**: You suffer from availability bias when you put too much weight on information that is easily available and place too little weight on information that is hard to attain. Your financial decisions will suffer if you consider only information that is easy to obtain.

WWW

Visit
www.behavioural
finance.net
for many other terms and
concepts of behavioral
finance.

CHECK THIS

8.4a	What is the representativeness heuristic?
8.4b	What is the hot-hand fallacy? How could it affect investor decisions?
8.4c	What is the gambler's fallacy? How could it affect investor decisions?

8.5 Sentiment-Based Risk and Limits to Arbitrage

It is important to realize that the efficient markets hypothesis does not require every investor to be rational. As we have noted, all that is required for a market to be efficient is that at least some investors are smart and well-financed. These investors are prepared to buy and sell to take advantage of any mispricing in the marketplace. This activity is what keeps markets efficient. Sometimes, however, a problem arises in this context.

LIMITS TO ARBITRAGE

limits to arbitrage
The notion that the price of an asset may not equal its correct value because of barriers to arbitrage.

The term **limits to arbitrage** refers to the notion that under certain circumstances, rational, well-capitalized traders may be unable to correct a mispricing, at least not quickly. The reason is that strategies designed to eliminate mispricings are often risky, costly, or somehow restricted. Three important impediments are:

- *Firm-specific risk*: This issue is the most obvious risk facing a would-be arbitrageur. Suppose that you believe that observed price on General Motors stock is too low, so you purchase many, many shares. Then, some unanticipated negative news drives the price of General Motors stock even lower. Of course, you could try to hedge some firm-specific risk by shorting shares in another stock, say, Ford. But there is no guarantee that the price of Ford will fall if some firm-specific event triggers a decline in the price of General Motors. It might even rise, leaving you even worse off. Furthermore, in many, if not most, cases there might not even be a stock that could be considered a close substitute.

noise trader
A trader whose trades are not based on information or meaningful financial analysis.

- *Noise trader risk*: A **noise trader** is someone whose trades are not based on information or financially meaningful analysis. Noise traders could, in principle, act together to worsen a mispricing in the short run. Noise trader risk is important because the worsening of a mispricing could force the arbitrageur to liquidate early and sustain steep losses. As Keynes once famously observed, "Markets can remain irrational longer than you can remain solvent."[1]

sentiment-based risk
A source of risk to investors above and beyond firm-specific risk and overall market risk.

  Noise trader risk is also called **sentiment-based risk**, meaning the risk that an asset's price is being influenced by sentiment (or irrational belief) rather than fact-based financial analysis. If sentiment-based risk exists, then it is another source of risk beyond the systematic and unsystematic risks we discussed in an earlier chapter.

- *Implementation costs*: These costs include transaction costs such as bid-ask spreads, brokerage commissions, and margin interest. In addition, there might be some short-sale constraints. One short-sale constraint arises when there are not enough shares of the security to borrow so that the arbitrageur can take a large short position. Another short-sale constraint stems from legal restrictions. Many money managers, especially pension fund and mutual fund managers, are not allowed to sell short.

---

[1]This remark is generally attributed to Keynes, but whether he actually said it is not known.

When these or other risks and costs are present, a mispricing may persist because arbitrage is too risky or too costly. Collectively, these risks and costs create barriers or limits to arbitrage. How important these limits are is difficult to say, but we do know that mispricings occur, at least on occasion. To illustrate, we next consider two well-known examples.

THE 3COM/PALM MISPRICING

On March 2, 2000, a profitable provider of computer networking products and services, 3Com, sold 5 percent of one of its subsidiaries to the public via an initial public offering (IPO). At the time, the subsidiary was known as Palm (now it is known as palmOne).

3Com planned to distribute the remaining Palm shares to 3Com shareholders at a later date. Under the plan, if you owned 1 share of 3Com, you would receive 1.5 shares of Palm. So, after 3Com sold part of Palm via the IPO, investors could buy Palm shares directly, or they could buy them indirectly by purchasing shares of 3Com.

What makes this case interesting is what happened in the days that followed the Palm IPO. If you owned one 3Com share, you would be entitled, eventually, to 1.5 shares of Palm. Therefore, each 3Com share should be worth *at least* 1.5 times the value of each Palm share. We say "at least" because the other parts of 3Com were profitable. As a result, each 3Com share should have been worth much more than 1.5 times the value of one Palm share. But, as you might guess, things did not work out this way.

The day before the Palm IPO, shares in 3Com sold for $104.13. After the first day of trading, Palm closed at $95.06 per share. Multiplying $95.06 by 1.5 results in $142.59, which is the minimum value one would expect to pay for 3Com. But the day Palm closed at $95.06, 3Com shares closed at $81.81, more than $60 lower than the price implied by Palm. It gets stranger.

A 3Com price of $81.81 when Palm is selling for $95.06 implies that the market values the rest of 3Com's businesses (per share) at $81.81 − $142.59 = − $60.88. Given the number of 3Com shares outstanding at the time, this means the market placed a *negative* value of about −$22 billion for the rest of 3Com's businesses. Of course, a stock price cannot be negative. This means, then, that the price of Palm relative to 3Com was much too high.

To profit from this mispricing, investors would purchase shares of 3Com and short shares of Palm. In a well-functioning market, this action would force the prices into alignment quite quickly. What happened?

As you can see in Figure 8.2, the market valued 3Com and Palm shares in such a way that the non-Palm part of 3Com had a negative value for about two months, from March 2, 2000, until May 8, 2000. Even then, it took approval by the IRS for 3Com to proceed with the planned distribution of Palm shares before the non-Palm part of 3Com once again had a positive value.

THE ROYAL DUTCH/SHELL PRICE RATIO

Another fairly well known example of a mispricing involves two large oil companies. In 1907, Royal Dutch of the Netherlands and Shell of the United Kingdom agreed to merge their business enterprises and pay dividends on a 60-40 basis. So, whenever the stock prices of Royal Dutch and Shell are not in a 60-40 ratio, there is a potential opportunity to make an arbitrage profit. If, for example, the ratio were 50-50, you would buy Royal Dutch, and short sell Shell.

Figure 8.3 plots the daily deviations from the 60-40 ratio of the Royal Dutch price to the Shell price. If the prices of Royal Dutch and Shell are in a 60-40 ratio, there is a zero percentage deviation. If the price of Royal Dutch is too high compared to the Shell price, there is a positive deviation. If the price of Royal Dutch is too low compared to the price of Shell, there is a negative deviation. As you can see in Figure 8.3, there have been large and persistent deviations from the 60-40 ratio. In fact, the ratio is seldom at 60-40 for most of the time from 1962 through 2004.

FIGURE 8.2

The Percentage Difference between 1 Share of 3Com and 1.5 Shares of Palm, March 2, 2000 to July 27, 2000

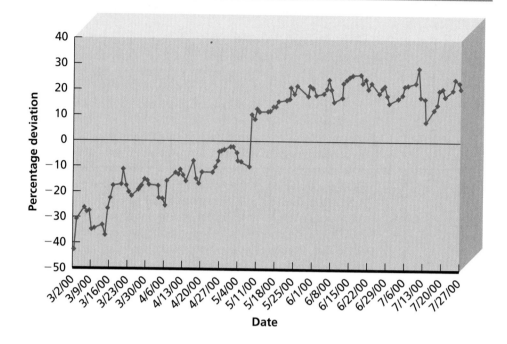

FIGURE 8.3

Royal Dutch and Shell 60–40 Price Ratio Deviations, 1962 to 2004

CHECK THIS

8.5a What does the term limits to arbitrage mean?

8.5b If there were no limits to arbitrage, what would have been the relationship between 1 share of 3Com and 1.5 shares of Palm?

8.5c If there were no limits to arbitrage, what would have been the relationship between the prices of Royal Dutch and Shell?

8.6 Technical Analysis

technical analysis
Using past price data and other nonfinancial data to identify future trading opportunities.

Many investors try to predict future stock price movements based on investor sentiment, errors in judgment, and/or historical price movements. These investors are using **technical analysis**. Unlike fundamental analysis, technical analysis does not rely on traditional valuation techniques like those presented in our earlier chapters.

WHY DOES TECHNICAL ANALYSIS CONTINUE TO THRIVE?

Proponents of the efficient markets hypothesis do not believe that technical analysis can assist investors in predicting future stock price movements. If that is the case, why is technical analysis still used? In fact, in this Internet and computer age, technical analysis is actually thriving. Why?

One possible reason that technical analysis still exists is that an investor can derive thousands of successful technical analysis systems by using historical security prices. Past movements of security prices are easy to fit into a wide variety of technical analysis systems. As a result, proponents of technical analysis can continuously tinker with their systems and find methods that fit historical prices. This process is known as "backtesting." Alas, successful investment is all about future prices.

Another possible reason that technical analysis still exists is simply that it sometimes works. Again, given a large number of possible technical analysis systems, it is possible that many of them will work (or appear to work) in the short run.

To give an example of a technical analysis tool, or a technical "indicator," consider trying to analyze market sentiment. The term "market sentiment" refers to the prevailing mood among investors about the future outlook of an individual security or the market. Market sentiment is generally classified as optimistic (bullish), neutral (undecided), or pessimistic (bearish).

Market sentiment usually takes time to change. That is, it takes time for, say, 80 percent of the investors to become bullish if only 50 percent of the investors are currently bullish. Investors who rely on market sentiment often believe that once 80 percent of the investors are bullish or bearish, a consensus has been reached. Further, once a consensus is reached, investors take this as a sign of an impending turn in the direction of the market. One way to measure market sentiment is to ask investors whether they think the market is going up or down. Suppose you ask 50 investors whether they are "bullish" or "bearish" on the market over the next month. Twenty say that they are bearish. The market sentiment index (MSI) can then be calculated as:

$$\text{MSI} = \frac{\text{Number of bearish investors}}{\text{Number of bullish investors} + \text{Number of bearish investors}}$$

$$\text{MSI} = \frac{20}{30 + 20} = 0.40$$

The MSI has a maximum value of 1.00, which occurs when every investor you ask is bearish on the market. The MSI has a minimum value of 0.00, which occurs when every investor you ask is bullish on the market. Note that if you are constructing a sentiment index, you will have to decide how many investors to ask, the identity of these investors, and their investment time frame, that is, daily, weekly, monthly, quarterly, or longer. You can construct a sentiment index for any financial asset for any investment time interval you choose.

People who calculate and use sentiment indexes often view them as "contrarian indicators." This means that if most other investors are bearish, perhaps the market is "oversold" and prices are due to rebound. Or if most other investors are bullish, perhaps the market is "overbought" and prices will be heading down.

The following saying is useful when you are trying to remember how to interpret the MSI: "When the MSI is high, it is time to buy; when the MSI is low, it is time to go." Note that there is no theory to guide investors as to what level of the MSI is "high" and what level is "low." This lack of precise guidance is a common problem with a technical indicator like the MSI.

Technical analysis techniques are centuries old, and their number is enormous. Many, many books on the subject have been written. For this reason, we only touch on the subject and introduce some of its key ideas in the next few sections. Although we focus on the use of technical analysis in the stock market, you should be aware that it is very widely used in commodity markets, and most comments herein apply to those markets as well.

Recall that investors with a positive outlook on the market are often called "bulls," and their outlook is characterized as "bullish." A rising market is called a "bull market." In contrast, pessimistic investors are called "bears," and their dismal outlook is characterized as "bearish." A falling market is called a "bear market." Technical analysts essentially search for bullish or bearish signals, meaning positive or negative indicators about stock prices or market direction.

DOW THEORY

Dow theory
A method for predicting market direction that relies on the Dow Industrial and the Dow Transportation averages.

Dow theory is a method of analyzing and interpreting stock market movements that dates back to the turn of the twentieth century. The theory is named after Charles Dow, a cofounder of the Dow Jones Company and an editor of the Dow Jones–owned newspaper, *The Wall Street Journal.*

The essence of Dow theory is that there are, at all times, three forces at work in the stock market: (1) a primary direction or trend, (2) a secondary reaction or trend, and (3) daily fluctuations. According to the theory, the primary direction is either bullish (up) or bearish (down), and it reflects the long-run direction of the market.

However, the market can, for limited periods of time, depart from its primary direction. These departures are called secondary reactions or trends and may last for several weeks or months. These are eliminated by *corrections,* which are reversions to the primary direction. Daily fluctuations are essentially noise and are of no real importance.

Learn more about Dow theory at
www.dowtheory.com
and
www.thedowtheory.com

The basic purpose of the Dow theory is to signal changes in the primary direction. To do this, two stock market averages, the Dow Jones Industrial Average (DJIA) and the Dow Jones Transportation Average (DJTA), are monitored. If one of these departs from the primary trend, the movement is viewed as secondary. However, if a departure in one is followed by a departure in the other, then this is viewed as a *confirmation* that the primary trend has changed. The Dow theory was, at one time, very well known and widely followed. It is less popular today, but its basic principles underlie more contemporary approaches to technical analysis.

ELLIOTT WAVES

Elliott wave theory
A method for predicting market direction that relies on a series of past market price swings (i.e., waves).

In the early 1930s, an accountant named Ralph Nelson Elliott developed the **Elliott wave theory**. While recuperating from life-threatening anemia (as well as his disastrous losses in the Crash of October 1929), Elliott read a book on Dow theory and began to study patterns

| FIGURE 8.4 | Basic Elliott Wave Pattern |

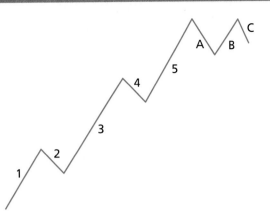

of market price movements. Elliott discovered what he believed to be a persistent and recurring pattern that operated between market tops and bottoms. His theory was that these patterns, which he called "waves," collectively expressed investor sentiment. Through use of sophisticated measurements that he called "wave counting," a wave theorist could forecast market turns with a high degree of accuracy.

In 1935, Elliott published his theory in his book called *The Wave Principle*. His main theory was that there was a repeating eight-wave sequence. The first five waves, which he called "impulsive," were followed by a three-wave "corrective" sequence. Figure 8.4 shows the basic Elliott wave pattern. The impulse waves are labeled numerically, 1 through 5, while the corrective waves are labeled A, B, and C.

The basic Elliott wave theory gets very complicated because, under the theory, each wave can subdivide into finer wave patterns that are classified into a multitude of structures. Notwithstanding the complex nature of the Elliott wave theory, it is still a widely followed indicator.

Learn more about the
Elliott wave at
www.elliottwave.com

SUPPORT AND RESISTANCE LEVELS

A key concept in technical analysis is the identification of support and resistance levels. A **support level** is a price or level below which a stock or the market as a whole is unlikely to fall. A **resistance level** is a price or level above which a stock or the market as a whole is unlikely to rise.

The idea behind these levels is straightforward. As a stock's price (or the market as a whole) falls, it reaches a point where investors increasingly believe that it can fall no further—the point at which it "bottoms out." Essentially, purchases by bargain-hungry investors ("bottom feeders") pick up at that point, thereby "supporting" the price. A resistance level is formed by reverse logic. As a stock's price (or the market as a whole) rises, it reaches a point where investors increasingly believe that it can go no higher—the point at which it "tops out." Once it does, sales by profit-hungry investors ("profit takers") pick up, thereby "resisting" further advances.

Resistance and support areas are usually viewed as psychological barriers. As the DJIA approaches levels with three zeros, such as 11,000, increased talk of "psychologically important" prices appears in the financial press. A "breakout" occurs when a stock (or the market as a whole) closes below a support level or above a resistance level. A breakout is usually interpreted to mean that the price move will continue in that direction.

As this discussion illustrates, much colorful language is used under the heading of technical analysis. We will see many more examples just ahead.

support level
Price or level below which a stock or the market as a whole is unlikely to fall.

resistance level
Price or level above which a stock or the market as a whole is unlikely to rise.

TECHNICAL INDICATORS

Learn more about charting at www.stockcharts.com **Select "Chart School."**

Technical analysts rely on a variety of technical indicators to forecast the direction of the market. Every day, *The Wall Street Journal* publishes a variety of such indicators. An excerpt of the "Diaries" section (from www.wsj.com) appears in Figure 8.5.

Much, but not all, of the information presented is self-explanatory. The first item listed in Figure 8.5 is the number of issues traded. This number fluctuates because, on any given

---

FIGURE 8.5   **Market Diaries**

Closing Stock Market Diaries
Wednesday, November 23, 2005

For Market Close of November 23, 2005

NYSE Market Diary	Latest Close	Previous Close	Week Ago
Issues Traded	3,430	3,453	3,448
Advances	1,955	1,950	1,599
Declines	1,312	1,338	1,720
Unchanged	163	165	129
New Highs	236	201	40
New Lows	80	143	195
Advancing Volume	938,942,910	1,102,865,020	808,539,860
Declining Volume	495,620,060	546,612,000	744,862,480
Volume Traded	1,447,470,320	1,678,437,020	1,579,886,720
Closing Tick	+ 654	+ 943	+ 662
Closing Arms (trin)	0.79	0.72	0.86
Block Trades	20,596	23,418	22,766
Nasdaq Market Diary	**Latest Close**	**Previous Close**	**Week Ago**
Issues Traded	3,183	3,193	3,170
Advances	1,601	1,672	1,225
Declines	1,416	1,372	1,800
Unchanged	166	149	145
New Highs	142	161	52
New Lows	25	33	78
Advancing Volume	1,077,429,015	1,070,311,832	839,076,463
Declining Volume	460,689,254	710,504,244	808,822,029
Volume Traded	1,570,548,436	1,855,457,769	1,676,645,732
Block Trades	n.a.	12,049	10,912
Amex Market Diary	**Latest Close**	**Previous Close**	**Week Ago**
Issues Traded	1,058	1,083	1,060
Advances	583	609	495
Declines	376	381	474
Unchanged	99	93	91
New Highs	119	127	15
New Lows	22	24	40
Advancing Volume	40,576,191	41,857,230	42,132,876
Declining Volume	25,913,140	30,073,405	18,187,670
Volume Traded	70,009,331	76,180,535	62,719,046
Block Trades	n.a.	1,022	865

Closing Tick = The net difference of the number of stocks closing higher than their previous trade from those closing lower; NYSE trading only.

Closing Arms = A comparison of the number of advancing and declining issues with the volume of shares rising and falling. Generally, an Arms of less than 1.00 indicates buying demand; above 1.00 indicates selling pressure.

Advancing, Declining, and Volume Traded and Block Trades reflect volume and trades on the NYSE or Amex exchanges only, not composite numbers.

Source: *The Wall Street Journal*, via www.wsj.com, August 5, 2005.

TABLE 8.3	Advance/Decline Line Calculation			
Weekday	**Issues Advancing**	**Issues Declining**	**Difference**	**Cumulative Difference**
Monday	1,777	1,475	+302	+302
Tuesday	2,192	1,067	+1,125	1,427
Wednesday	1,546	1,724	−178	1,249
Thursday	1,079	2,207	−1,128	+121
Friday	738	2,532	−1,794	−1,673

For a trader's glossary, check out
www.traders.com/
Documentation/
RESource_docs/
Glossary/glossary.html

day, there may be zero trading volume in some stocks listed on the NYSE. In the rows that follow, we see the number of price advances, the number of price declines, and the number of unchanged prices. The number of stock prices reaching new highs and new lows as of that day is also listed.

One popular technical indicator is called the *advance/decline line*. This indicator shows, for some given period, the cumulative difference between advancing issues and declining issues. For example, Table 8.3 contains advance and decline information for the August 1, 2005, to August 5, 2005, trading week.

In Table 8.3, notice how we take the difference between the number of issues advancing and declining on each day and then cumulate the difference through time. For example, on Monday, 302 more issues advanced than declined. On Tuesday, 1,125 more issues advanced than declined. Over the two days, the cumulative advance/decline is thus 302 + 1,125 = 1,427.

This cumulative advance/decline number, once plotted, is the advance/decline line. A downward-sloping advance/decline line would be considered a bearish signal, whereas an upward-sloping advance/decline line is a bullish signal. The advance/decline line is often used to measure market "breadth." If the market is going up, for example, then technical analysts view it as a good sign if there is market breadth. That is, the signal is more bullish if the advance is accompanied by a steeply upwardly sloping advance/decline line.

The next few rows in Figure 8.5 deal with trading volume. These rows represent trading volume for advancing issues, declining issues, and unchanged issues (which is calculated by subtracting advancing volume and declining volume from volume traded). For a technical analyst, heavy advancing volume is generally viewed as a bullish signal of buyer interest. This is particularly true if more issues are up than down and if a lot of new highs appear as well.

The last three numbers in Figure 8.5, found in the footnotes, are also of interest to technicians. The first, labeled "Closing Tick," is the difference between the number of issues that closed on an uptick and those that closed on a downtick. From our discussion of the NYSE short sale rule in a previous chapter, you know that an uptick occurs when the last price change was positive; a downtick is just the reverse. The tick gives an indication of where the market was heading as it closed.

The entry labeled "Closing Arms" is the ratio of average trading volume in declining issues to average trading volume in advancing issues. It is calculated as follows:

$$\text{Arms} = \frac{\text{Declining Volume/Declining Issue}}{\text{Advancing Volume/Advancing Issues}} \tag{8.1}$$

The ratio is named after its inventor, Richard Arms; it is often called the "trin," which is an acronym for "tr(ading) in(dex)." Notice that the numerator in this ratio is just the average volume for issues that declined on that day. The denominator is the average volume for advancing issues. Values greater than 1.00 are considered bearish because the indication is that declining shares had heavier volume. Using the number from Figure 8.5 for Wednesday, we can calculate the Arms value as follows:

$$\text{Arms} = \frac{495,620,060/1,312}{938,942,910/1,955} = \frac{377,759}{480,278} = 0.79$$

which rounds to the value shown in Figure 8.5. A caveat: Some sources reverse the numerator and the denominator when they calculate this ratio.

The final piece of information in Figure 8.5, "Block Trades," refers to trades in excess of 10,000 shares. At one time, these trades were taken to be indicators of buying or selling by large institutional investors. However, today these trades are routine, and it is difficult to see how this information is particularly useful.

RELATIVE STRENGTH CHARTS

relative strength
A measure of the performance of one investment relative to another.

Relative strength charts illustrate the performance of one company, industry, or market relative to another. If you look back at the *Value Line* exhibit in Chapter 6, you will see a plot labeled "relative strength." Very commonly, such plots are created to analyze how a stock has done relative to its industry or the market as a whole.

To illustrate how such plots are constructed, suppose that on some particular day, we invest equal amounts, say $100, in both Ford and GM (the amount does not matter; what matters is that the original investment is the same for both). On every subsequent day, we take the ratio of the value of our Ford investment to the value of our GM investment, and we plot it. A ratio bigger than 1.0 indicates that, on a relative basis, Ford has outperformed GM, and vice versa. Thus, a value of 1.20 indicates that Ford has done 20 percent better than GM over the period studied. Notice that if both stocks are down, a ratio bigger than 1.0 indicates that Ford is down by less than GM.

EXAMPLE 8.1	Relative Strength

Consider the following series of monthly stock prices for two hypothetical companies:

Month	Stock A	Stock B
1	$25	$50
2	24	48
3	22	45
4	22	40
5	20	39
6	19	38

On a relative basis, how has stock A done compared to stock B?

To answer, suppose we had purchased four shares of A and two shares of B for an investment of $100 in each. We can calculate the value of our investment in each month and then take the ratio of A to B as follows:

	Investment Value		
Month	Stock A (4 shares)	Stock B (2 shares)	Relative Strength
1	$100	$100	1.00
2	96	96	1.00
3	88	90	0.98
4	88	80	1.10
5	80	78	1.03
6	76	76	1.00

What we see is that over the first four months both stocks were down, but A outperformed B by 10 percent. However, after six months the two had done equally well (or equally poorly).

CHARTING

Technical analysts rely heavily on charts showing recent market activity in terms of either prices or, less frequently, volume. In fact, technical analysis is sometimes called "charting," and technical analysts are often called "chartists." There are many types of charts, but the basic idea is that by studying charts of past market prices (or other information), the chartist identifies particular patterns that signal the direction of a stock or the market as a whole. We briefly describe some charting techniques next.

OPEN-HIGH-LOW-CLOSE CHARTS (OHLC) Perhaps the most popular charting method is the bar chart. The most basic bar chart uses the stock's opening, high, low, and closing prices for the period covered by each bar. If the technician is constructing a daily bar chart, the technician will use the daily opening high, daily low, and daily closing prices of the stock. The high and low prices are represented by the top and bottom of the vertical bar and the opening and closing prices are shown by short horizontal lines crossing the vertical bar. The example of a bar chart in Figure 8.6 for Sun Microsystems is from www.stockcharts.com.

PRICE CHANNEL A price channel is a chart pattern using OHLC data that can slope upward, downward, or sideways. Price channels belong to the group of price patterns known as *continuation patterns*. A continuation pattern is a pattern where the price of the stock is expected to continue along its main direction. A price channel has two boundaries, an upper trendline and a lower trendline. The upper trendline marks resistance and the lower trendline marks support. If the overall price movement of the stock is downward, the upper trendline is called the main trendline, and the lower trendline is called the channel line. The example of a price channel for ChevronTexaco in Figure 8.7 is from the Web site www.stockcharts.com.

HEAD AND SHOULDERS A head and shoulders chart pattern belongs to a group of price charts known as *reversal patterns*. Reversal pattern charts also use OHLC data. These chart patterns signal that a reversal from the main trendline is possibly going to occur. Because it belongs to the reversal pattern group, a head and shoulders pattern is

FIGURE 8.6	Open-High-Low-Close Bar Chart for Sun Microsystems

FIGURE 8.7 Price Channel Chart for ChevronTexaco

ChevronTexaco (CVX) NYSE
10-Apr-2000 **Open** 80.91 **High** 82.80 **Low** 80.61 **Close** 81.50 **Volume** 1.3M **Chg** -0.36 (-0.43%) ▼
© StockCharts.com

FIGURE 8.8 Head and Shoulders Chart for CNET Networks, Inc.

CNET Networks, Inc. (CNET) Nasdaq Nat. Mkt
9-Jun-2000 **Open** 34.62 **High** 35.00 **Low** 33.75 **Close** 34.50 **Volume** 610.5K **Chg** +0.75 (+2.22%) ▲
© StockCharts.com

identified as either a *head and shoulders top* or a *head and shoulders bottom.* The example of a head and shoulders top for CNET Networks in Figure 8.8 is also from the Web site www.stockcharts.com.

As you can see, the head and shoulders top formation has three components: the *left shoulder,* the *head,* and the *right shoulder.* To qualify as a head and shoulders top pattern, the shoulders must be lower than the head. Then, a *neckline support* is drawn between the valleys formed by the left and right shoulders. The reversal signal is generated when the neckline is *pierced.* In the case of CNET, once the stock price fell below $45, the stock plunged to $25. Of course, there are *false piercings,* which do not result in a sudden down-draft of the stock.

WWW

For more technical analysis charts and explanations, visit
www.bigcharts.com
www.stockcharts.com
www.incredible charts.com

MOVING AVERAGES Moving averages are used to generate price reversal signals. As the name implies, a moving average is simply the average closing price of a stock over a fixed length of time, say 20 days. Each day, the new closing price is added to the calculation, and the oldest closing price is dropped from the calculation.

Moving averages are either simple or exponential. In a *simple moving average,* all days are given equal weighting. In an *exponential moving average,* more weight is given to the most recently observed price. Market technicians, like many investors, often believe that the latest price observed for a stock is the most important piece of information about the stock. In Example 8.2, we present data for a three-day simple moving average and data for a three-day exponential moving average, where two-thirds of the average weight is placed on the most recent price.

EXAMPLE 8.2	Three-Day Simple Moving Average and Three-Day Exponential Moving Average

Day	Closing Price	Three-Day Simple Moving Average	Three-Day Exponential Moving Average
1	$89.00		
2	88.44		$88.72
3	87.60	$88.35	87.97
4	86.20	87.41	86.79
5	85.75	86.52	86.10
6	84.57	85.51	85.08
7	83.64	84.65	84.12
8	76.70	81.64	79.17
9	76.65	79.00	77.49
10	75.48	76.28	76.15

To calculate the first three-day simple moving average, we need three closing prices. The first simple moving average entry is simply:

$$(\$89.00 + \$88.44 + \$87.60)/3 = \$88.35$$

The second simple moving average entry is:

$$(\$88.44 + \$87.60 + \$86.20)/3 = \$87.41$$

To calculate a three-day exponential moving average, we begin by averaging the first two days:

$$(\$89.00 + \$88.44)/2 = \$88.72$$

This is the first number that appears in the exponential moving average column. To obtain the next one, you must decide how much weight is placed on the latest price. As noted above, we selected a 2/3, or 0.667, weight. To calculate the next exponential moving average entry, we multiply the latest closing price by 0.667 and the previous exponential moving average entry by 0.333:

$$(0.667)(\$87.60) + (0.333)(\$88.72) = \$87.97$$

(continued)

The next exponential moving average entry is:

$$(0.667)(\$86.20) + (0.333)(\$87.97) = \$86.79$$

You can see that the simple moving average and the exponential moving average generate different numbers. The exponential moving average responds more quickly to the latest price information than does the simple moving average.

WWW

For a description of many technical indicators, including other moving average indicators, see www.incredible charts.com.

In practice, 50-day moving averages are frequently compared to 200-day moving averages. The 200-day moving average might be thought of as indicative of the long-run trend, while the 50-day average might be thought of as a short-run trend. If the 200-day average was rising while the 50-day average was falling, the indication might be that price declines are expected in the short term, but the long-term outlook is favorable. Alternatively, the indication might be that there is a danger of a change in the long-term trend. Our nearby *Work the Web* box gives an example.

PUTTING IT ALL TOGETHER Quite often, a market technician will be using multiple chart indicators to help in making trading decisions. Let's examine the collection of technical information available from the Web site www.bigcharts.com. We set the Web site controls to give us three months of daily data for General Motors (GM). In addition, we asked the Web site to provide us with 9-day and 18-day exponential moving averages, Bollinger bands, volume, *MACD*, and *money flow*. The results appear in Figure 8.9.

FIGURE 8.9   Technical Analysis Data for General Motors

Charts are easy to draw online. Two of the best sites are stockcharts.com and www.bigcharts.com. Here is an example from finance.yahoo.com:

As illustrated, we have drawn a moving average chart for Microsoft. The jagged line tracks Microsoft's daily stock price over the past year. The two smoother lines are the 50-day and 200-day moving averages. Notice the 50-day average crosses the 200-day average in August from below. Such a crossing is sometimes interpreted as a signal to buy. In this case, the signal was false in the short run because the stock subsequently fell in price. Despite the fall, the 50-day moving average remained above the 200-day moving average. Investors who stayed in have made a profit.

BOLLINGER BANDS John Bollinger created Bollinger bands in the early 1980s. The purpose of Bollinger bands is to provide *relative* levels of high and low prices. Bollinger bands represent a 2-standard deviation bound calculated from the moving average (this is why Bollinger bands do not remain constant). In Figure 8.9, the Bollinger bands surround a 20-day moving average. The Bollinger bands are the maroon bands that appear in the top chart. Bollinger bands have been interpreted in many ways by their users. For example, when the stock price is relatively quiet, the Bollinger bands are tight, which indicates a possible pent-up tension that must be released by a subsequent price movement.

MACD MACD stands for moving average convergence divergence. The MACD indicator shows the relationship between two moving averages of prices. The MACD is derived by dividing one moving average by another and then comparing this ratio to a third moving average, the signal line. In the GM example, the MACD uses a 12-day and a 26-day moving average and a 9-day signal line. The convergence/divergence of these three averages is represented by the solid black bars in the third chart of Figure 8.9. The basic MACD trading rule is to sell when the MACD falls below its signal line and to buy when the MACD rises above its signal line.

MONEY FLOW The idea behind money flow is to identify whether buyers are more eager to buy the stock than sellers are to sell it. In its purest form, money flow looks at each trade. To calculate the money flow indicator, the technician multiplies price and volume for the trades that occur at a price higher than the previous trade price. The technician then sums this money flow. From this sum, the technician subtracts another money flow: the accumulated total of price times volume for trades that occur at prices lower than the previous trade. Example 8.3 shows how to calculate money flow.

Traders using money flow look for a divergence between money flow and price. If price remains stable but money flow becomes highly positive, this is taken as an indicator that the stock price will soon increase. Similarly, if the stock price remains stable but the money flow becomes quite negative, this is taken as an indicator that the stock price will soon decrease. In Figure 8.9, the negative accumulation of money flow for GM signals to followers of money flow that further price declines for GM are in order.

EXAMPLE 8.3	Calculating Money Flow

Price	Up (+); Down (−); Unchanged (0)	Volume	Price × Volume	Money Flow (+)	Money Flow (−)	Net Money Flow
10						
11	+	1,000	11,000	11,000		
12	+	100	1,200	12,200		
12	0	500	6,000			
11	−	500	5,500		5,500	
10	−	50	500		6,000	
At the end of the day:						6,200

FIBONACCI NUMBERS

Traders using technical analysis are interested in timing their purchase or sale of a stock. As you know by now, these traders look for support or resistance stock price levels. As strange as it may seem, one source that traders use is known as the *golden mean.* The golden mean is sometimes abbreviated by the greek letter phi (ϕ). The golden mean, ϕ, is approximately equal to 1.618 (it is precisely equal to ($\sqrt{5} + 1$)/2). The golden mean is mathematically interesting, because, among other things, $\phi^2 = \phi + 1$.

The golden mean also results from a series of numbers known as *Fibonacci numbers.* The infinite Fibonacci series grows as follows:

$$1,1,2,3,5,8,13,21,34,55,89,144,233,377,610,987\ldots$$

Note that the series begins with 1,1 and grows by adding the two previous numbers together (for example, $21 + 34 = 55$). Let's look at the ratio of some number to their predecessor in the series:

$$21/13 = 1.6154$$
$$34/21 = 1.6190$$
$$55/34 = 1.6176$$
$$89/55 = 1.6182$$

The ratio converges to 1.618, or ϕ. Market technicians are interested in ϕ because:

$$(\phi - 1)/\phi = 0.618/1.618 = 0.382$$
$$1/\phi = 1.000/1.618 = 0.618 = \phi - 1$$

Market technicians use these numbers to predict support and resistance levels. For example, as a stock increases in value over time, it will occasionally pull back in value. Suppose a stock has increased from $40 to $60, and has recently begun to fall a bit in value. Using the $(\phi - 1) / \phi$ ratio, market technicians would predict the primary support area would occur at $52.36 ($60 − $40 = $20; $20 × 0.382 = $7.64; $60 − $7.64 = $52.36). A similar calculation that uses the $1 / \phi$ ratio of 0.618 instead of 0.382 results in the secondary support area of $47.64. If the stock were to pierce this secondary support level and close below it, the rally would be declared over. Market technicians would then begin to look for opportunities to sell the stock short if it subsequently rallied.

Nature provides many instances involving Fibonacci numbers. The number of petals on a flower is often a Fibonacci number. For example, black-eyed susans have 13 petals and ordinary daisies have 34. Also, pinecones and pineapples have spirals containing 8 or 13 scales. There are so many other examples that some observers classify Fibonacci numbers as a "law of nature." Because of this, some market technicians believe that the Fibonacci numbers should also apply to market prices.

OTHER TECHNICAL INDICATORS

We close our discussion of technical analysis by describing a few additional technical indicators. The "odd-lot" indicator looks at whether odd-lot purchases (purchases of fewer than 100 shares) are up or down. One argument is that odd-lot purchases represent the activities of smaller, unsophisticated investors, so when they start buying, it's time to sell. This is a good example of a "contrarian" indicator. In contrast, some argue that because short selling is a fairly sophisticated tactic, increases in short selling are a negative signal.

Some indicators can seem a little silly. For example, there is the "hemline" indicator, which is also known as the "bull markets and bare knees" indicator. Through much of the nineteenth century, long skirts dominated women's fashion and the stock market experienced many bear markets. In the 1920s, flappers revealed their knees and the stock market boomed. Even the stock market crash of October 1987 was predicted by hemlines. During the 1980s, miniskirts flourished, but by October 1987, a fashion shift had women wearing longer skirts.

One of the more famous (or fatuous, depending on how you look at it) indicators is the Super Bowl indicator, which forecasts the direction of the market based on whether the National Football Conference or the American Football Conference wins. A Super Bowl win by a National Football Conference team or an American Football Conference team that used to be in the old National Football League (i.e., Pittsburgh Steelers, Baltimore Colts) is bullish. This probably strikes you as absurd, so you might be surprised to learn that for the period 1967–1988, the Super Bowl indicator forecast the direction of the stock market with more than 90 percent accuracy. A nearby *Investment Updates* box contains more details about this indicator.

CHECK THIS

8.6a   What is technical analysis?

8.6b   What is the purpose of charting a stock's past price?

8.6c   What is the purpose of using technical indicators?

THE SUPER GUIDE TO INVESTING

Every January, about 90 million people in the United States watch television for a prediction of how well the stock market is going to do in the upcoming year. So you missed it this year? Maybe not. The stock market predictor we are talking about is the Super Bowl!

The Super Bowl indicator has become one of the more famous (or infamous) technical indicators of stock market performance. Here's how it works. In the 1960s, the original National Football League (NFL) and the upstart American Football League (AFL) were fighting for dominance. The Super Bowl indicator says that if a team from the original AFL wins the Super Bowl, the market posts a negative return for the year, and if a team from the original NFL wins, the market will post a gain for the year.

So how has the Super Bowl predictor performed? Take a look at the chart we obtained from www.cnn.com.

For the first 31 Super Bowls, the indicator was correct 28 out of 31 times! The Miami Dolphins are perhaps the best market predictor. When Miami won the Super Bowl in 1973, the market proceeded to drop by 14.7 percent. The next year was an even better indicator. The next year, the Dolphins beat the Minnesota Vikings and the S&P 500 lost 26.5 percent, the worst one-year performance in its history. When the Dolphins lost the Super Bowl in 1972, 1983, and 1985, the S&P 500 posted double-digit gains in each of those years.

So you are not ready to bet the ranch on the Super Bowl indicator? It's probably a good thing. Since 1997, the Super Bowl indicator has been right only twice, in 2002 and 2005. The New England Patriots, an AFL team, won the Super Bowl in both of these years and the S&P 500 dropped 30 percent in 2002 (but only 0.6 percent in 2005). The performance

in 2001 is not as clear. The Baltimore Ravens won the Super Bowl that year and the market lost 7.6 percent. The Ravens are the descendants of the original Cleveland Browns, a member of the original NFL. In this case, the Super Bowl indicator was incorrect. However, purists (especially in Cleveland) argue that since the Browns have been revived, the Ravens cannot be considered a member of the original NFL. But the Ravens did beat the New York Giants, an old NFL team. In 2003, the expansion Tampa Bay Buccaneers beat an original AFL team, the Oakland Raiders, and the market went up about 28 percent.

The Predictor (30-7-2)

Bullish years (22)
49ers - '82, '85, '89, '95
Bears- '86
Colts - '71
Cowboys - '72, '93, '94, '96
Giants - '87, '91
Packers, '67, '68, '97
Redskins - '83, '88, '92
Steelers - '75, '76, '79, '80

Bearish years (8)
Dolphins - '73, '74
Jets, '69
Patriots, '02, '05
Raiders - '77, '81, '84

Indicator missed (7)
Broncos - '98, '99
Chiefs - '70
49ers - '90
Cowboys - '78
Rams -'00
Patriots - '04

Inconclusive (2)
Ravens - '01*
Buccaneers - '03**

*Created when the old NFL Cleveland Browns moved to Baltimore, the NFL says the Ravens started life as an AFC team in 1996, which would mean the predictor was accurate.
**Expansion team

There are lots of other technical trading rules. How seriously should you take them? That's up to you, but our advice is to keep in mind that life is full of odd coincidences. Just because a bizarre stock market predictor seems to have worked well in the past doesn't mean that it's going to work in the future.

8.7 Summary and Conclusions

In this chapter, we examined behavioral finance and technical analysis. We learned that a key to becoming a wise investor is to avoid certain types of behavior. By studying behavioral finance, you can see the potential damage to your (or your client's) portfolio from overconfidence and psychologically induced errors.

The evidence is relatively clear on one point: Investors probably make mistakes. A much more difficult question, and one where the evidence is not at all clear, is whether risks stemming from errors in judgment by investors can influence market prices and lead to market inefficiencies. Market efficiency does not require that all investors behave in a rational fashion. It just requires that some do.

Nonetheless, many investors try to predict future stock price movements based on investor sentiment, errors in judgment, or historical price movements. Such investors rely on the tools of technical analysis, and we present numerous specific methods used by technical analysts. Whether these tools or methods work is much debated. We close this chapter by noting that it is possible that market prices are influenced by factors like errors in judgment by investors, sentiment, emotion, and irrationality. If they are, however, we are unaware of any scientifically proven method investors such as you can use to profit from these influences.

GET REAL

This chapter deals with various aspects of behavioral finance. How do you go about incorporating these concepts into the management of your portfolio? First, recall that one of the major lessons from this chapter is that, at times, you may be your own worst enemy when you are investing.

But suppose that you are able to harness your own psychological flaws that unduly influence your investment decisions. To profit from insights from behavioral finance, you might try to shift your portfolio to take advantage of situations where you perceive other market participants have incorrectly valued certain stocks, bonds, derivatives, market sectors, or even countries. Shifting portfolio weights to take advantage of these opportunities is called a "dynamic" trading strategy.

Here is one example of using a dynamic trading strategy. Consider a typical value/growth portfolio weight-shifting scheme. When there is a great deal of market overreaction, perhaps signaled by high market volatility, you would increase, or tilt, your relative portfolio weight toward value stocks. When there is a great deal of market underreaction, perhaps signaled by low market volatility, you would increase your relative weighting in growth stocks. The problem, of course, is knowing when and how to tilt your portfolio to take advantage of what you perceive to be market overreactions and underreactions. At times, you can do very well when you tilt your portfolio. Other times, to use an old commodity market saying, "you get your head handed to you."

There is a great amount of information available on the Internet about behavioral finance and building portfolios. One interesting place to start is the research section at www.psychonomics.com. Make sure that the money that you are using to test any trading scheme is only a small portion of your investment portfolio.

Key Terms

behavioral finance 245
clustering illusion 253
Dow theory 260
Elliott wave theory 260
limits to arbitrage 256
loss aversion 247
mental accounting 247
noise trader 256

prospect theory 245
relative strength 264
representativeness heuristic 251
resistance level 261
sentiment-based risk 256
support level 261
technical analysis 259

Chapter Review Problems and Self-Test

1. **It's All Relative**   Consider the following series of monthly stock prices for two companies:

Week	Phat Co	GRRL Power
1	$10	$80
2	12	82
3	16	80
4	15	84
5	14	85
6	12	88

On a relative basis, how has Phat done compared to GRRL Power?

2. **Simple Moving Averages**   Using the prices from the previous problem, calculate the three-month simple moving average prices for both companies.

Answers to Self-Test Problems

1. Suppose we had purchased eight shares of Phat and one share of GRRL Power. We can calculate the value of our investment in each month and then take the ratio of Phat to GRRL Power as follows:

Week	Investment Value Phat Co (8 shares)	GRRL Power (1 share)	Relative Strength
1	$80	$80	1.00
2	96	82	1.17
3	128	80	1.60
4	120	84	1.43
5	112	85	1.32
6	96	88	1.09

Phat Co. has significantly outperformed GRRL Power over much of this period; however, after six weeks, the margin has fallen to about 9 percent from as high as 60 percent.

2. The moving averages must be calculated relative to the share price; also note that results cannot be computed for the first two weeks because of insufficient data.

Week	Phat Co.	Phat Co Moving Average	GRRL Power	GRRL Power Moving Average
1	$10	—	$80	—
2	12	—	82	—
3	16	$12.67	80	$80.67
4	15	14.33	84	82.00
5	14	15.00	85	83.00
6	12	13.67	88	85.67

Test Your Investment Quotient

CFA® PROBLEMS

1. **Technical Analysis**   Which of the following is a basic assumption of technical analysis in contrast to fundamental analysis?

   a. Financial statements provide information crucial in valuing a stock.
   b. A stock's market price will approach its intrinsic value over time.
   c. Aggregate supply and demand for goods and services are key determinants of stock value.
   d. Security prices move in patterns, which repeat over long periods.

2. **Technical Analysis**   Which of the following is least likely to be of interest to a technical analyst?

   a. A 15-day moving average of trading volume.
   b. A relative strength analysis of stock price momentum.
   c. Company earnings and cash flow growth.
   d. A daily history of the ratio of advancing issues over declining issues.

3. **Dow Theory**   Dow theory asserts that three forces are at work in the stock market at any time. Which of the following is not one of these Dow theory forces?

   a. Daily price fluctuations
   b. A secondary reaction or trend
   c. A primary direction or trend
   d. Reversals or overreactions

4. **Technical Indicators**   The advance/decline line is typically used to

   a. Measure psychological barriers.
   b. Measure market breadth.
   c. Assess bull market sentiment.
   d. Assess bear market sentiment.

5. **Technical Indicators**   The Closing Arms (trin) ratio is the ratio of

   a. Average trading volume in declining issues to advancing issues.
   b. Average trading volume in NYSE issues to NASDAQ issues.
   c. The number of advancing issues to the number of declining issues.
   d. The number of declining issues to the number of advancing issues.

6. **Technical Indicators**   Resistance and support areas for a stock market index are viewed as technical indicators of

   a. Economic barriers
   b. Psychological barriers
   c. Circuit breakers
   d. Holding patterns

7. **Technical Analysis**   Which of the following are used by technical analysts?

   I. Historical prices
   II. Financial statements
   III. Historical volume
   IV. Investor sentiment

a. I and II only
b. I and III only
c. I, III, and IV only
d. I, II, III, and IV

8. **Technical Analysis** Which of the following technical measures has the effect of smoothing out day-to-day price fluctuations?

a. Moving average charts
b. Advance/decline lines
c. Candlestick charts
d. Point-and-figure charts

9. **Technical Analysis** Which of the following statements would a technical analyst agree with?

a. Financial statements provide invaluable information concerning a company's stock price.
b. The value of a share of stock should always be the present value of future dividends.
c. The stock market is at least weak-form efficient.
d. Stock prices follow patterns which repeat over time.

10. **Technical Analysis** Suppose a stock breaks through a support level. According to technical analysis, you should

a. Buy the stock.
b. Sell the stock.
c. Do nothing since this is a congestion area.
d. Buy the stock on margin.

11. **Advance/Decline Lines** An upward-sloping advance/decline line is considered_____, and a heavy advancing volume is considered _____.

a. bearish; bearish
b. bearish; bullish
c. bullish; bullish
d. bullish; bearish

12. **Behavioral Finance Concepts** Which of the following topics related to behavioral finance deals with the idea that investors experience more pain from a loss than pleasure from a comparable gain?

a. Frame dependence
b. Prospect theory
c. Loss aversion
d. Mental accounting

13. **Limits to Arbitrage** Which of the following is not a reason that rational, well-capitalized investors can correct a mispricing, at least not immediately?

a. Firm-specific risk
b. Implementation costs
c. Aversion risk
d. Noise trader risk

14. **Technical Indicators** Which of the following techniques deals with the breadth of the market?

a. Price channels
b. Advance/decline lines
c. Bollinger bands
d. Support and resistance lines

15. **Technical Indicators** Which of the following techniques does not assume there are psychologically important barriers in stock prices?

a. Price channels
b. Advance/decline lines
c. Bollinger bands
d. Support and resistance lines

Concept Questions

1. **Dow Theory** In the context of Dow theory, what are the three forces at work at all times? Which is the most important?

2. **Technical Analysis** To a technical analyst, what are support and resistance areas?

3. **Dow Theory** In the context of Dow theory, what are corrections and confirmations?

4. **Bad Breadth?** On a particular day, the stock market as a whole is up; however, losers outnumber gainers by 2,000 to 1,600. What might a technical analyst conclude?

5. **A Call to Arms** How is the Arms ratio computed? What is it designed to capture?

6. **Bad Timing?** A key concern in technical analysis such as the Dow theory is to identify turning points in market direction and thereby time the market. What are the implications of market efficiency for market timing?

7. **Dow Theory** Why do you think the industrial and transportation averages are the two that underlie Dow theory?

8. **Limits to Arbitrage** In the chapter, we discussed the 3Com/Palm and Royal Dutch/Shell mispricings. Which of the limits to arbitrage would least likely be the main reason for these mispricings? Explain.

9. **Contrarian Investing** What does it mean to be a contrarian investor? How would a contrarian investor use technical analysis?

10. **Technical Analysis** A frequent argument against the usefulness of technical analysis is that trading on a pattern has the effect of destroying the pattern. Explain what this means.

11. **Gaps** Gaps are another technical analysis tool used in conjunction with open-high-low-close charts. A gap occurs when either the low price for a particular day is higher than the high price from the previous day, or the high price for a day is lower than the low price from the previous day. Do you think gaps are a bullish or bearish signal? Why?

12. **Probabilities** Suppose you are flipping a fair coin in a coin-flipping contest and have flipped eight heads in a row. What is the probability of flipping a head on your next coin flip? Suppose you flipped a head on your ninth toss. What is the probability of flipping a head on your tenth toss?

13. **Prospect Theory** How do prospect theory and the concept of a rational investor differ?

14. **Frame Dependence** How can frame dependence lead to irrational investment decisions?

15. **Noise Trader Risk** What is noise trader risk? How can noise trader risk lead to market inefficiencies?

Questions and Problems

Core Questions

1. **Advance/Decline Lines** Use the data below to construct the advance/decline line for the stock market. Volume figures are in thousands of shares.

	Advancing	Adv. Vol.	Declining	Dec. Vol.
Monday	1,893	1,077,176	1,159	542,400
Tuesday	1,833	1,172,094	1,211	733,082
Wednesday	1,705	987,314	1,411	845,305
Thursday	1,821	1,042,316	1,305	750,318
Friday	1,784	1,258,634	1,187	645,847

2. **Calculating Arms Ratio** Using the data in the previous problem, construct the Arms ratio on each of the five trading days.

3. **Simple Moving Averages**   The table below shows the closing monthly stock prices for Amazon.com and Walt Disney. Calculate the simple three-month moving average for each month for both companies.

	AMZN	DIS
February	$35.18	$27.94
March	34.27	28.73
April	32.36	26.40
May	35.51	27.44
June	33.09	25.18
July	45.15	25.64
August	42.70	25.19
September	45.30	24.13
October	39.86	24.37
November	47.99	25.05

4. **Exponential Moving Averages**   Using the stock prices in the previous problem, calculate the exponential three-month moving average for both stocks where two-thirds of the average weight is placed on the most recent price.

5. **Exponential Moving Averages**   Calculate the exponential three-month moving average for Amazon.com and Walt Disney where 50 percent of the average weight is placed on the most recent price. How does this exponential moving average compare to your result from the previous problem?

6. **Market Sentiment Index**   A group of investors was polled each week for the last five weeks about whether they were bullish or bearish concerning the market. Construct the market sentiment index for each week based on these polls. Assuming the market sentiment index is being used as a contrarian indicator, which direction would you say the market is headed?

Week	Bulls	Bears
1	72	78
2	70	80
3	79	71
4	68	82
4	63	87

7. **Money Flow**   You are given the following information concerning the trades made on a particular stock. Calculate the money flow for the stock based on these trades. Is the money flow a positive or negative signal in this case?

Price	Volume
$84.12	
84.16	5,000
84.15	2,400
84.17	1,800
84.19	3,400
84.23	1,700
84.20	4,600

8. **Moving Averages** Suppose you are given the following information on the S&P 500:

Date	Close
8-Nov-05	1218.59
9-Nov-05	1220.65
10-Nov-05	1230.96
11-Nov-05	1234.72
14-Nov-05	1233.76
15-Nov-05	1229.01
16-Nov-05	1231.21
17-Nov-05	1242.80
18-Nov-05	1248.27
21-Nov-05	1254.85

Calculate the simple three-day moving average for the S&P 500 and the exponential three-day moving average where two-thirds of the weight is placed on the most recent close. Why would you want to know the moving average for an index? If the close on November 22, 2005, was above the three-day moving average, would it be a buy or sell signal?

9. **Support and Resistance Levels.** Below you will see a stock price chart for Cisco Systems from finance.yahoo.com. Do you see any resistance or support levels? What do support and resistance levels mean for the stock price?

10. **Advance/Decline Lines and Arms Ratio** Use the data below to construct the advance/decline line and Arms ratio for the market. Volume is in thousands of shares.

	Advancing	Advancing Vol.	Declining	Declining Vol.
Monday	1,132	987,064	2,205	1,203,543
Tuesday	1,287	843,456	2,103	1,356,406
Wednesday	1,451	864,056	1,978	1,135,056
Thursday	1,682	1,013,168	1,796	980,673
Friday	1,508	990,731	1,834	1,206,650

11. **Money Flow**   A stock had the following trades during a particular period. What was the money flow for the stock? Is the money flow a positive or negative signal in this case?

Price	Volume
$43.87	
43.89	1,600
43.88	1,200
43.90	600
43.90	1,400
43.88	1,100
43.86	800
43.84	1,300
43.83	1,400
43.82	1,000

Intermediate Questions

12. **Fibonacci Numbers**   A stock recently increased in price from $78 to $95. Using ϕ, what are the primary and secondary support areas for the stock?

13. **Simple Moving Averages**   Below you will find the closing stock prices for eBay over a three-week period. Calculate the simple three-day and five-day moving averages for the stock and graph your results. Are there any technical indications of the future direction of the stock price?

Date	Close
31-Oct-05	$39.61
1-Nov-05	40.27
2-Nov-05	41.08
3-Nov-05	41.55
4-Nov-05	41.58
7-Nov-05	41.87
8-Nov-05	42.30
9-Nov-05	42.08
10-Nov-05	43.31
11-Nov-05	43.89
14-Nov-05	43.53
15-Nov-05	43.05
16-Nov-05	42.54
17-Nov-05	43.80
18-Nov-05	44.67

14. **Exponential Moving Averages**   Use the information from the previous problem to calculate the three-day and five-day exponential moving averages for eBay and graph your results. Place two-thirds of the average weight on the most recent stock price. Are there any technical indications of the future direction of the stock price?

15. **Put/Call Ratio.**   Another technical indicator is the put/call ratio. The put/call ratio is the number of put options traded divided by the number of call options traded. The put/call ratio can be constructed on the market or an individual stock. Below you will find the number of puts and calls traded over a four-week period for all stocks:

Week	Puts	Calls
1	467,152	645,132
2	508,612	497,163
3	498,344	532,628
4	520,197	625,981

How would you interpret the put/call ratio? Calculate the put/call ratio for each week. From this analysis, does it appear the market is expected to be upward trending or downward trending?

What's on the Web? ■

1. **Bollinger Bands**   You can learn more about Bollinger bands at www.chartsmart.com. What does the site say about using Bollinger bands in technical analysis? Now go to finance.yahoo.com, and enter your favorite stock. Find the technical analysis section and view the Bollinger band for your stock. What does the chart tell you about this stock?

2. **Relative Strength**   Relative strength measures the performance of a stock against a "bogey," which is either another stock or suitable index. Pick your favorite stock and go to the technical analysis area of finance.yahoo.com. Compare the relative strength of your stock against a close competitor and the S&P 500 Index. How is this stock performing relative to these bogeys?

3. **Triangles**   Go to www.borsanaliz.com/eng. How many different types of triangles are listed on the site? What does each type of triangle mean to a technical analyst?

4. **Market Volume**   An important tool for most technical traders is market volume. Go to www.marketvolume.com. Look on the site to find the reasons market volume is considered important.

Stock-Trak Exercises ■

To access the Stock-Trak Exercise for this chapter, please visit the book Web site at www.mhhe.com/jm4e and choose the corresponding chapter.

CHAPTER 9

Interest Rates

"Remember that time is money."

–Benjamin Franklin

Benjamin Franklin stated a fundamental truth of commerce when he sagely advised young tradesmen that time is money. In finance, we call this the time value of money. But how much time corresponds to how much money? Interest constitutes a rental payment for money, and an interest rate tells us how much money for how much time. But there are many interest rates, each corresponding to a particular money market. Interest rates state money prices in each of these markets. ■

This chapter is the first dealing specifically with interest-bearing assets. As we discussed in a previous chapter, there are two basic types of interest-bearing assets, money market instruments and fixed-income securities. For both types of asset, interest rates are a key determinant of asset values. Furthermore, because trillions of dollars in interest-bearing assets are outstanding, interest rates play a pivotal role in financial markets and the economy.

Because interest rates are one of the most closely watched financial market indicators, we devote this entire chapter to them. We first discuss the many different interest rates that are commonly reported in the financial press, along with some of the different ways interest rates are calculated and quoted. We then go on to describe the basic determinants and separable components of interest rates.

9.1 Interest Rate History and Money Market Rates

Recall from Chapter 3 that money market instruments are debt obligations that have a maturity of less than one year at the time they are originally issued. Each business day, *The Wall Street Journal* publishes a list of current interest rates for several categories of money market securities in its "Money Rates" report. We will discuss each of these interest rates and the securities they represent immediately below. First, however, we take a quick look at the history of interest rates.

INTEREST RATE HISTORY

In Chapter 1, we saw how looking back at the history of returns on various types of investments gave us a useful perspective on rates of return. Similar insights are available from interest rate history. For example, in May 2006, short-term interest rates were about 4.8 percent and long-term rates were about 5.1 percent. We might ask, "Are these rates unusually high or low?" To find out, we examine Figure 9.1, which graphically illustrates 205 years of interest rates in the United States.

Two interest rates are plotted in Figure 9.1, one for bills and one for bonds. Both rates are based on U.S. Treasury securities, or close substitutes. We discuss bills and bonds in detail in this chapter and the next chapter. For now, it is enough to know that bills are short term and bonds are long term, so what is plotted in Figure 9.1 are short- and long-term interest rates.

FIGURE 9.1 Interest Rate History (U.S. Interest Rates, 1800–2005)

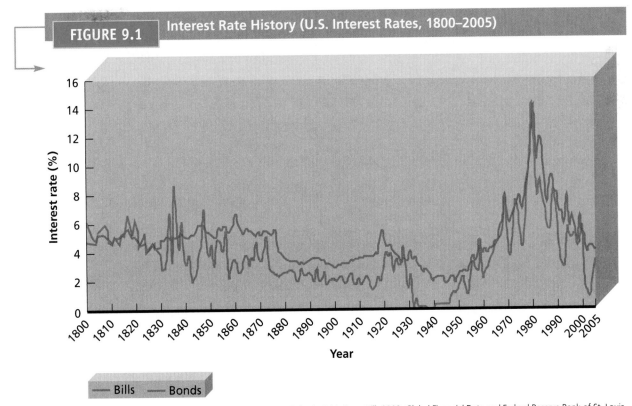

Source: Adapted from Jeremy J. Siegel, *Stocks for the Long Run*, 3rd ed., © McGraw-Hill, 2002; Global Financial Data and Federal Reserve Bank of St. Louis.

EXAMPLE 9.1

A Quick Review of the Time Value of Money

Undoubtedly, your instincts tell you that $1,000 received in three years is not the same as $1,000 received today. But if you are going to receive $1,000 today, what is an equivalent amount of money received in three years?

Fortunately, an equation tells us exactly what this is:

$$\text{Future value} = \text{Present value} \times (1 + r)^N \qquad (9.1)$$

In this equation, the r represents a periodic interest rate (expressed as a decimal), and the N represents the number of periods (expressed as an integer). Although the periods could be weeks, months, or years, the important thing to remember is that the interest rate must be expressed as an interest rate *per period*.

Suppose you have $1,000 to invest and you can invest at an annual rate of 3.5 percent per year. In Equation 9.1 the per period interest rate enters as 0.035. If you invest for three years ($N = 3$), the amount you will have in three years is:

$$\$1,108.718 = \$1,000 \times (1 + 0.035)^3 \qquad (9.2)$$

which would be rounded to $1,108.72.

You can also use Equation 9.1 to tell you how much a future amount is worth today. If we divide both sides of Equation 9.1 by $(1 + r)^N$ and rearrange terms, we get:

$$\text{Present value} = \frac{\text{Future value}}{(1 + r)^N} \qquad (9.3)$$

which, by the rules of exponents, can be written as:

$$\text{Present value} = \text{Future value} \times (1 + r)^{-N} \qquad (9.4)$$

That is, $(1 + r)^{-N}$ is just another way to write $1/(1 + r)^N$.

If you remember the relationship between Equations 9.1 and 9.4, you will soon become very comfortable with *compounding*, which is Equation 9.1, and *discounting*, which is Equation 9.4.

To continue with our numerical example, first note that $(1 + 0.035)^3 = 1.108718$. Therefore, using Equation 9.3,

$$\text{Present value} = \frac{\text{Future value}}{(1 + r)^N}$$

$$\$1,000 = \frac{\$1,081.718}{1.081718}$$

Suppose you invest $500 for 4 percent for six years. How much money will you have at the end of six years?

$$\text{Future value} = \text{Present value} \times (1 + r)^N$$

$$\$632.66 = \$500 \times (1.04)^6$$

Now suppose you will be getting $800 in four years. What is an equivalent amount today if you discount at 3.7 percent?

$$\text{Present value} = \text{Future value} \times (1 + r)^{-N}$$

$$\$691.79 = \$800 \times (1 + 0.037)^{-4}$$

Probably the most striking feature in Figure 9.1 is the fact that the highest interest rates in U.S. history occurred in the not-too-distant past. Rates began rising sharply in the 1970s, and then peaked at extraordinary levels in the early 1980s. They have generally declined since then. The other striking aspect of U.S. interest rate history is the very low short-term interest rates that prevailed from the 1930s to the 1960s. This was the result, in large part, of deliberate actions by the Federal Reserve Board to keep short-term rates low—a policy that ultimately proved unsustainable and even disastrous. Much was learned by the experience, however, and now the Fed is more concerned with controlling inflation.

With long-term rates around 5.1 percent as this chapter was written, many market observers have commented that these interest rate levels are extraordinarily low. Based on the history of interest rates illustrated in Figure 9.1, however, 5.1 percent may be low relative to the last 30 years, but it is not at all low compared to rates during the 170-year period from 1800 to 1970. Indeed, long-term rates would have to fall well below 4 percent to be considered low by historical standards. Example 9.1 shows how investors use interest rates.

MONEY MARKET RATES

Figure 9.2 reproduces a *Wall Street Journal* "Money Rates" report of interest rates for the most important money market instruments. A commonly quoted interest rate is the **prime rate**. The prime rate is a key short-term interest rate since it is the basis for interest rates that large commercial banks charge on short-term loans (rates are quoted as prime plus or minus a spread). The prime rate is well known as a **bellwether rate** of bank lending to business.

prime rate
The basic interest rate on short-term loans that the largest commercial banks charge to their most creditworthy corporate customers.

bellwether rate
Interest rate that serves as a leader or as a leading indicator of future trends, e.g., interest rates as a bellwether of inflation.

FIGURE 9.2	Money Market Interest Rates

Money Rates

Tuesday, September 6, 2005

The key U. S. and foreign annual interest rates· below are a guide to general levels but don't always represent actual transactions.

Commercial Paper

Yields paid by corporations for short-term financing, typically for daily operation

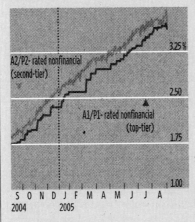

S O N D J F M A M J J A
2004   2005

Source: Federal Reserve

Prime Rate: 6.50% (effective 08/09/05). The base rate on corporate loans posted by at least 75% of the nation's 30 largest banks.
Discount Rate (Primary): 4.50% (effective 08/09/05).
Federal Funds: 3.875% high, 3.438% low, 3.500% near closing bid, 3.563% offered. Effective rate: 3.57%. Source: Tullett Prebon Information, Ltd. Federal-funds target rate: 3.500% (effective 08/09/05).
Call Money: 5.25% (effective 08/09/05).
Commercial Paper: Placed directly by General Electric Capital Corp.: 3.60% 30 to 45 days; 3.61% 46 to 59 days; 3.64% 60 to 89 days; 3.68% 90 to 119 days; 3.71% 120 to 149 days; 3.73% 150 to 179 days; 3.76% 180 to 209 days; 3.78% 210 to 239 days; 3.79% 240 to 267 days; 3.80% 268 to 270 days.

Euro Commercial Paper: Placed directly by General Electric Capital Corp.: 2.08% 30 days; 2.09% two months; 2.10% three months; 2.10% four months; 2.10% five months; 2.11% six months.
Dealer Commercial Paper: High-grade unsecured notes sold through dealers by major corporations: 3.63% 30 days; 3.65% 60 days; 3.69% 90 days.
Certificates of Deposit: 3.65% one month; 3.71% three months; 3.79% six months.
Bankers Acceptances: 3.66% 30 days; 3.69% 60 days; 3.74% 90 days; 3.79% 120 days; 3.83% 150 days; 3.87% 180 days. Source: Tullett Prebon Information, Ltd.
Eurodollars: 3.66% - 3.64% one month; 3.72% - 3.70% two months; 3.77% - 3.75% three months; 3.84% - 3.80% four months; 3.87% - 3.83% five months; 3.90% - 3.86% six months. Source: Tullett Prebon Information, Ltd.
London Interbank Offered Rates (Libor): 3.7025% one month; 3.7900% three months; 3.9100% six months; 4.05563% one year. Effective rate for contracts entered into two days from date appearing at top of this column.
Euro Libor: 2.11213% one month; 2.13000% three months; 2.14338% six months; 2.17438% one year. Effective rate for contracts entered into two days from date appearing at top of this column.
Euro Interbank Offered Rates (Euribor): 2.113% one month; 2.132% three months; 2.146% six months; 2.174% one year. Source: Reuters.
Foreign Prime Rates: Canada 4.25%; European Central Bank 2.00%; Japan 1.375%; Switzerland 2.62%; Britain 4.50%.
Treasury Bills: Results of the Tuesday, September 6, 2005, auction of short-term U.S. government bills, sold at a discount from face value in units of $1,000 to $1 million: 3.435% 13 weeks; 3.570% 26 weeks. Tuesday, August 30, 2005 auction: 3.470% 4 weeks.
Overnight Repurchase Rate: 3.50%. Source: Garban Intercapital.
Freddie Mac: Posted yields on 30-year mortgage commitments. Delivery within 30 days 5.53%, 60 days 5.56%, standard conventional fixed-rate mortgages: 3.375%, 2% rate capped one-year adjustable rate mortgages.
Fannie Mae: Posted yields on 30 year mortgage commitments (priced at par) for delivery within 30 days 5.556%, 60 days 5.591%, standard conventional fixed-rate mortgages. Constant Maturity Debt Index: 3.697% three months; 3.839% six months; 3.945% one year.
Merrill Lynch Ready Assets Trust: 2.83%.
Consumer Price Index: July, 195.4, up 3.2% from a year ago. Bureau of Labor Statistics.

Besides a prime rate for the United States, the "Money Rates" report also lists foreign prime rates for Canada, the European Central Bank, Japan, Switzerland, and Great Britain.

The **Federal funds rate** (or just "Fed funds") is a fundamental interest rate for commercial bank activity. The Fed funds rate is the interest rate that banks charge each other for overnight loans of $1 million or more. This interbank rate is set by continuous bidding among banks, where banks wishing to lend funds quote "offer rates" (rates at which they are willing to lend), and banks wishing to borrow funds quote "bid rates" (rates they are willing to pay). Notice that four different rates are stated: *high* is the highest rate offered and *low* is the lowest rate bid during a day's trading; *near closing bid* is a bid rate to borrow and *near closing offered* is an offered rate to lend near the end of the day's trading.

The Federal Reserve's **discount rate** is another pivotal interest rate for commercial banks. The discount rate is the interest rate that the Fed offers to commercial banks for overnight reserve loans. You might recall from your Money and Banking class that banks are required to maintain reserves equal to some fraction of their deposit liabilities. When a bank cannot supply sufficient reserves from internal sources, it must borrow reserves from other banks through the Federal funds market. Therefore, the Fed discount rate and the Fed funds rate are usually closely linked.

The Federal Reserve Bank is the central bank of the United States. It is charged with the responsibility of managing interest rates and the money supply to control inflation and promote stable economic growth. The discount rate is a basic tool of monetary policy for the Federal Reserve Bank. An announced change in the discount rate is often interpreted as a signal of the Federal Reserve's intentions regarding future monetary policy. For example, by increasing the discount rate, the Federal Reserve may be signaling that it intends to pursue a tight-money policy, most likely to control budding inflationary pressures. Similarly, by decreasing the discount rate, the Federal Reserve may be signaling an intent to pursue a loose-money policy to stimulate economic activity. Of course, many times a discount rate change is simply a case of the Federal Reserve catching up to financial market conditions rather than leading them. Indeed, the Federal Reserve often acts like the lead goose, who, upon looking back and seeing the flock heading in another direction, quickly flies over to resume its position as "leader" of the flock.

The next interest rate reported is the **call money rate**, or simply the call rate. "Call money" refers to loans from banks to security brokerage firms, and the call rate is the interest rate that brokerage firms pay on call money loans. As we discussed in Chapter 2, brokers use funds raised through call money loans to make margin loans to customers to finance leveraged stock and bond purchases. The call money rate is the basic rate that brokers use to set interest rates on customer call money loans. Brokers typically charge their customers the call money rate plus a premium, where the broker and the customer may negotiate the premium. For example, a broker may charge a customer the basic call money rate plus 1 percent for a margin loan to purchase common stock.

Commercial paper is short-term, unsecured debt issued by the largest corporations. The commercial paper market is dominated by financial corporations, such as banks and insurance companies, or financial subsidiaries of large corporations. As shown in Figure 9.2, a leading commercial paper rate is the rate that General Electric Capital Corporation (the finance arm of General Electric) pays on short-term debt issues. This commercial paper rate is a benchmark for this market because General Electric Capital is one of the largest single issuers of commercial paper. Most other corporations issuing commercial paper will pay a slightly higher interest rate than this benchmark rate. Commercial paper is a popular investment vehicle for portfolio managers and corporate treasurers with excess funds on hand that they wish to invest on a short-term basis. Euro commercial paper refers to commercial paper denominated in euros rather than dollars.

Certificates of deposit, or **CDs**, represent large-denomination deposits of $100,000 or more at commercial banks for a specified term. The interest rate paid on CDs usually varies

---

Federal funds rate
Interest rate that banks charge each other for overnight loans of $1 million or more.

discount rate
The interest rate that the Fed offers to commercial banks for overnight reserve loans.

call money rate
The interest rate brokerage firms pay for call money loans, which are bank loans to brokerage firms. This rate is used as the basis for customer rates on margin loans.

commercial paper
Short-term, unsecured debt issued by the largest corporations.

certificate of deposit (CD)
Large-denomination deposits of $100,000 or more at commercial banks for a specified term.

according to the term of the deposit. For example, a one-year CD may pay a higher interest rate than a six-month CD, which in turn may pay a higher interest rate than a three-month CD.

Large-denomination certificates of deposit are generally negotiable instruments, meaning that they can be bought and sold among investors. Consequently, they are often called negotiable certificates of deposit, or negotiable CDs. Negotiable CDs can be bought and sold through a broker. The large-denomination CDs described here should not be confused with the small-denomination CDs that banks offer retail customers. These small-denomination CDs are simply bank time deposits. They normally pay a lower interest rate than large-denomination CDs and are not negotiable instruments.

banker's acceptance
A postdated check on which a bank has guaranteed payment; commonly used to finance international trade transactions.

A **banker's acceptance** is essentially a postdated check upon which a commercial bank has guaranteed payment. Banker's acceptances are normally used to finance international trade transactions. For example, as an importer, you wish to purchase computer components from a company in Singapore and pay for the goods three months after delivery, so you write a postdated check. You and the exporter agree, however, that once the goods are shipped, your bank will guarantee payment on the date specified on the check.

After your goods are shipped, the exporter presents the relevant documentation, and, if all is in order, your bank stamps the word *ACCEPTED* on your check. At this point your bank has created an acceptance, which means it has promised to pay the acceptance's face value (the amount of the check) at maturity (the date on the check). The exporter can then hold on to the acceptance or sell it in the money market. The banker's acceptance rate published in "Money Rates" is the interest rate for acceptances issued by the largest commercial banks.

Eurodollars
U.S. dollar denominated deposits at foreign banks or foreign branches of U.S. banks.

Eurodollars are U.S. dollar denominated deposits at foreign banks or foreign branches of U.S. banks. Eurodollar rates are interest rates paid for large-denomination eurodollar certificates of deposit. Eurodollar CDs are negotiable and are traded in a large, very active Eurodollar money market. The "Money Rates" report lists Eurodollar rates for various maturities obtained from transactions occurring late in the day.

London Interbank Offered Rate (LIBOR)
Interest rate that international banks charge one another for overnight Eurodollar loans.

The **London Interbank Offered Rate (LIBOR)** is the interest rate offered by London commercial banks for dollar deposits from other banks. The LIBOR rate is perhaps the most frequently cited rate used to represent the London money market. Bank lending rates are often stated as LIBOR plus a premium, where the premium is negotiated between the bank and its customer. For example, a corporation may be quoted a loan rate from a London bank at LIBOR plus 2 percent. Euro LIBOR refers to deposits denominated in euros—the common currency of 12 European Union countries. Like LIBOR, the Euro LIBOR rate is calculated by the British Bankers Association (BBA) from quotes provided by London banks. The EURIBOR is an interest rate that also refers to deposits denominated in euros. However, the EURIBOR is based largely on interest rates from banks in the European Union interbank market.

U.S. Treasury bill (T-bill)
A short-term U.S. government debt instrument issued by the U.S. Treasury.

U.S. Treasury bills, or just **T-bills**, represent short-term U.S. government debt issued through the U.S. Treasury. The Treasury bill market is the world's largest market for new debt securities with one year or less to maturity. As such, the Treasury bill market leads all other credit markets in determining the general level of short-term interest rates. "Money Rates" reports Treasury bill interest rates set during the most recent weekly Treasury bill auction. Interest rates determined at each Treasury bill auction are closely watched by professional money managers throughout the world. The overnight repurchase, or "repo," rate is essentially the rate charged on overnight loans that are collateralized by U.S. Treasury securities.

The Federal Home Loan Mortgage Corporation (FHLMC), commonly called "Freddie Mac," and the Federal National Mortgage Association (FNMA), commonly called "Fannie Mae," are government-sponsored agencies that purchase large blocks of home mortgages and combine them into mortgage pools, where each pool may represent several tens of millions of dollars of home mortgages. We will discuss mortgage pools in depth in a later chapter. The interest rates reported in "Money Rates" are an indicator of rates on

For more on LIBOR, visit
www.bba.org.uk

newly created home mortgages. Because home mortgages are long-term obligations, these are not actually money market rates. However, with several trillion dollars of mortgages outstanding, the mortgage market has a considerable influence on money market activity.

The Merrill Lynch Ready Assets Trust is a money market fund for customer accounts with the brokerage firm of Merrill Lynch. Recall from Chapter 4 that money market funds are mutual funds that invest in money market instruments. The interest rate reported in the "Money Rates" report is an average of interest rates paid on fund accounts over the previous month.

CHECK THIS

9.1a Which money market interest rates are most important to commercial banks?

9.1b Which money market interest rates are most important to nonbank corporations?

9.2 Money Market Prices and Rates

pure discount security

An interest-bearing asset that makes a single payment of face value at maturity with no payments before maturity.

Money market securities typically make a single payment of face value at maturity and make no payments before maturity. Such securities are called **pure discount securities** because they sell at a discount relative to their face value. In this section, we discuss the relationship between the price of a money market instrument and the interest rate quoted on it.

One of the things you will notice in this section is that market participants quote interest rates in several different ways. This presents a problem when we wish to compare rates on different investments. But before we can do this, we must put them on a common footing.

After going through the various interest rate conventions and conversions needed to compare them, you might wonder why everybody doesn't just agree to compute interest rates and prices in some uniform way. Well perhaps they should, but they definitely do not. As a result, we must review some of the various procedures actually used in money markets. We hope you come to recognize that the calculations are neither mysterious nor even especially difficult, although they are rooted in centuries-old procedures and may sometimes be tedious. However, given the billions of dollars of securities traded every day based on these numbers, it is important to understand them.

One other thing to notice is that the word "yield" appears frequently. For now, you can take it as given that the yield on an interest-bearing asset is simply a measure of the interest rate being offered by the asset. We will discuss the topic of yields in greater detail in the next chapter.

basis point

With regard to interest rates or bond yields, one basis point is 1 percent of 1 percent.

Bond yields and many interest rates are quoted as a percentage with two decimal places, such as 11.82 percent. With this quote, the smallest possible change would be .01 percent, or .0001. This amount, which is 1 percent of 1 percent, is called a **basis point**. So, if our 11.82 percent rose to 11.94 percent, we would say rates rose by $94 - 82 = 12$ basis points. The quantity to the left of the decimal point (the "11") is called the "handle." Traders frequently omit the handle when quoting or discussing rates since, presumably, anyone actively trading would know it.

bank discount basis

A method for quoting interest rates on money market instruments.

BANK DISCOUNT RATE QUOTES

Interest rates for some key money market securities, including Treasury bills and banker's acceptances, are quoted on a **bank discount basis**, or simply discount basis. An interest rate quoted on a discount basis is often called a discount yield. If we are given an interest rate quoted on a bank discount basis for a particular money market instrument, then we calculate the price of that instrument as follows:

$$\text{Current price} = \text{Face value} \times \left(1 - \frac{\text{Days to maturity}}{360} \times \text{Discount yield}\right) \qquad (9.5)$$

The term "discount yield" here simply refers to the quoted interest rate. It should not be confused with the Federal Reserve's discount rate discussed earlier.

To give an example, suppose a banker's acceptance has a face value of $1 million that will be paid in 90 days. If the interest rate, quoted on a discount basis, is 5 percent, what is the current price of the acceptance?

As the following calculation shows, a discount yield of 5 percent and maturity of 90 days gives a current price of $987,500.

$$\$987,500 = \$1,000,000 \times \left(1 - \frac{90}{360} \times .05\right)$$

The difference between the face value of $1 million and the price of $987,500 is $12,500 and is called the "discount." This discount is the interest earned over the 90-day period until the acceptance matures.

Notice that the formula used to calculate the acceptance price assumes a 360-day business year. This practice dates back to a time when calculations were performed manually. Assuming a 360-day business year, with exactly four 90-day quarters rather than a true 365-day calendar year, made manual discount calculations simpler and less subject to error. Consequently, if $1 million is discounted over a full calendar year of 365 days using a bank discount yield of 5 percent and an assumed 360-day business year, the resulting price of $949,305.56 is calculated as follows:

$$\$949,305.56 = \$1,000,000 \times \left(1 - \frac{365}{360} \times .05\right)$$

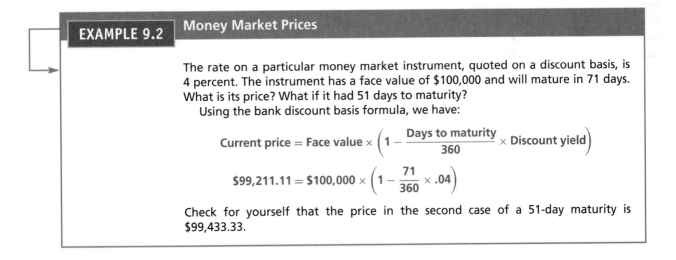

EXAMPLE 9.2   **Money Market Prices**

The rate on a particular money market instrument, quoted on a discount basis, is 4 percent. The instrument has a face value of $100,000 and will mature in 71 days. What is its price? What if it had 51 days to maturity?
Using the bank discount basis formula, we have:

$$\text{Current price} = \text{Face value} \times \left(1 - \frac{\text{Days to maturity}}{360} \times \text{Discount yield}\right)$$

$$\$99,211.11 = \$100,000 \times \left(1 - \frac{71}{360} \times .04\right)$$

Check for yourself that the price in the second case of a 51-day maturity is $99,433.33.

TREASURY BILL QUOTES

The Wall Street Journal reports current interest rates on U.S. Treasury bills each business day. Figure 9.3 reproduces a "Treasury Bills" interest rate report. The maturity of each bill issue is stated in month-day-year format, followed by the number of days remaining until the bill matures. The two columns following the days to maturity give the bid and asked

FIGURE 9.3   U.S. Treasury Bills

Treasury Bills

MATURITY	DAYS TO MAT	BID	ASKED	CHG	ASK YLD
Sep 08 05	1	3.26	3.25	0.01	3.30
Sep 15 05	8	3.45	3.44	−0.01	3.49
Sep 22 05	15	3.32	3.31	...	3.36
Sep 29 05	22	3.32	3.31	...	3.36
Oct 06 05	29	3.29	3.28	0.02	3.33
Oct 13 05	36	3.26	3.25	−0.01	3.31
Oct 20 05	43	3.27	3.26	...	3.32
Oct 27 05	50	3.27	3.26	0.01	3.32
Nov 03 05	57	3.33	3.32	0.02	3.38
Nov 10 05	64	3.34	3.33	0.02	3.40
Nov 17 05	71	3.36	3.35	0.02	3.42
Nov 25 05	79	3.40	3.39	0.04	3.46
Dec 01 05	85	3.42	3.41	0.04	3.49
Dec 08 05	92	3.43	3.42	0.02	3.50
Dec 15 05	99	3.39	3.38	−0.02	3.46
Dec 22 05	106	3.42	3.41	0.03	3.49
Dec 29 05	113	3.45	3.44	0.03	3.53
Jan 05 06	120	3.48	3.47	0.04	3.56
Jan 12 06	127	3.49	3.48	0.04	3.57
Jan 19 06	134	3.50	3.49	0.04	3.59
Jan 26 06	141	3.51	3.50	0.04	3.60
Feb 02 06	148	3.53	3.52	0.05	3.62
Feb 09 06	155	3.52	3.51	0.04	3.61
Feb 16 06	162	3.54	3.53	0.04	3.64
Feb 23 06	169	3.55	3.54	0.06	3.65
Mar 02 06	176	3.57	3.56	0.06	3.67

Source: *The Wall Street Journal*, September 7, 2005. Reprinted by permission of Dow Jones, Inc. via Copyright Clearance Center, Inc., © 2005 Dow Jones and Company, Inc. All Rights Reserved Worldwide.

WWW

For price and yield data on U.S. Treasury securities visit

www.govpx.com

discounts for each bill issue. The bid discount is used by Treasury bill dealers to state what they are willing to pay for a Treasury bill, and the asked discount is used to state what price a dealer will accept to sell a Treasury bill. The next column shows the change in the asked discount from the previous day.

For example, consider the bill issue with 155 days to maturity, with a bid discount rate of 3.52 percent and an asked discount rate of 3.51 percent. For a $1 million face value Treasury bill, the corresponding bid and asked prices can be calculated by using the discounts shown along with our bank discount basis pricing formula. For example, the bid price would be:

$$\text{Bid price} = \$984,844.44 = \$1,000,000 \times \left(1 - \frac{155}{360} \times .0352\right)$$

Check that the ask price would be $984,887.50.

EXAMPLE 9.3   T-Bill Prices

Suppose you wanted to buy a T-bill with 85 days to maturity and a face value of $5,000,000. How much would you have to pay if the asked discount is 3.41 percent?

Because you are buying, you must pay the asked price. To calculate the asked price, we use the asked discount in the bank discount basis formula:

$$\text{Asked price} = \$4,959,743.06 = \$5,000,000 \times \left(1 - \frac{85}{360} \times .0341\right)$$

Calculate a bid price for this T-bill assuming a bid discount of 3.42 percent. Notice that the asked price is higher than the bid price even though the asked discount is lower than the bid discount. The reason is that a bigger discount produces a lower price.

Treasury bill prices may be calculated using a built-in spreadsheet function. An example of how to use an Excel™ spreadsheet to calculate a Treasury bill price is shown in the nearby *Spreadsheet Analysis* box.

The last column in Figure 9.3 lists the asked yield ("ASK YLD") for each Treasury bill issue. It is important to realize that the asked yield is *not* quoted on a discount basis. Instead, it is a "bond equivalent yield." Unlike a discount rate, a bond equivalent yield assumes a 365-day calendar year. Bond equivalent yields are principally used to compare yields on Treasury bills with yields on other money market instruments as well as Treasury bonds and other bonds (we discuss these long-term yields in the next chapter).

BANK DISCOUNT YIELDS VERSUS BOND EQUIVALENT YIELDS

A bank discount yield is converted to a bond equivalent yield using the following formula:

$$\text{Bond equivalent yield} = \frac{365 \times \text{Discount yield}}{360 - \text{Days to maturity} \times \text{Discount yield}} \quad (9.6)$$

This conversion formula is correct for maturities of six months or less. Calculation of bond equivalent yields for maturities greater than six months is a little more complicated, and we will not discuss it here, particularly because T-bills with maturities greater than six months are no longer sold.

For example, suppose the asked discount rate on a T-bill with 170 days to maturity is 3.22 percent. What is the bond equivalent yield? Plugging into the conversion formula, a 3.22 percent discount is converted into a bond equivalent yield as follows:

$$3.315\% = \frac{365 \times .0322}{360 - 170 \times .0322}$$

The bond equivalent yield is thus 3.315 percent.

SPREADSHEET ANALYSIS

	A	B	C	D	E	F	G	H
1								
2			**Treasury Bill Price and Yield Calculations**					
3								
4	A Treasury bill traded on March 14, 2006, pays $100 on June 1, 2006. Assuming a							
5	discount rate of 6 percent, what are its price and bond equivalent yield?							
6	Hint: Use the Excel function TBILLPRICE and TBILLEQ.							
7								
8		$98.6833	= TBILLPRICE("3/14/2006","6/1/2006",0.06)					
9								
10		6.164%	= TBILLEQ("3/14/2006","6/1/2006",0.06)					
11								
12								
13	A credit card charges a nominal annual interest rate of 15 percent. With interest							
14	charged monthly, what is the effective annual rate (EAR) on this credit card?							
15	Hint: Use the Excel function EFFECT.							
16								
17		16.075%	= EFFECT(0.15,12)					
18								

EXAMPLE 9.4 — Bond Equivalent Yields

Suppose a T-bill has 45 days to maturity and an asked discount of 5 percent. What is the bond equivalent yield?

Using the bond equivalent yield conversion formulas, we have:

$$5.101\% = \frac{365 \times .05}{360 - 45 \times .05}$$

The bond equivalent yield is thus 5.101 percent.

Bond equivalent yields may be calculated using a built-in spreadsheet function. An example of how to use an Excel™ spreadsheet to calculate a bond equivalent yield is shown in the nearby *Spreadsheet Analysis* box.

One common cause of confusion about bond equivalent yield calculations is the way that leap years are handled. The rule is that we must use 366 days if February 29 occurs within the next 12 months. For example, 2008 will be a leap year. So, beginning on March 1, 2007, we must use 366 days in the numerator of Equation 9.6. Then beginning on March 1, 2008, we must revert to using 365 days.

EXAMPLE 9.5 — Back To The Future: Leap Year Bond Equivalent Yields

Calculate the asked yield (bond equivalent yield) for a T-bill price quoted in December 2007 with 119 days to maturity and an asked discount of 5.41 percent.

Because the 12-month period following the date of the price quote includes February 29, we must use 366 days. Plugging this into the conversion formula, we get:

$$5.60\% = \frac{366 \times .0541}{360 - 119 \times .0541}$$

This 5.60 percent is the ask yield stated as a bond equivalent yield.

We can calculate a Treasury bill asked price using the asked yield, which is a bond equivalent yield, as follows:

$$\text{Bill price} = \frac{\text{Face value}}{1 + \text{Bond equivalent yield} \times \text{Days to maturity}/365} \tag{9.7}$$

For example, just above we calculated the 3.315 percent bond equivalent yield on a T-bill with 170 days to maturity and a 3.22 percent asked discount rate. If we calculate its price using this bond equivalent yield, we get:

$$\$984,795 = \frac{\$1,000,000}{1 + .03315 \times 170/365}$$

Check that, ignoring a small rounding error, you get the same price using the bank discount formula.

BOND EQUIVALENT YIELDS, APRs, AND EARs

Money market rates not quoted on a discount basis are generally quoted on a "simple" interest basis. Simple interest rates are calculated just like the annual percentage rate (APR) on a consumer loan. So, for the most part, money market rates are either bank discount rates or APRs. For example, CD rates are APRs.

In fact, the bond equivalent yield on a T-bill with less than six months to maturity is also an APR. As a result, like any APR, it understates the true interest rate, which is usually called the *effective annual rate,* or EAR. In the context of the money market, EARs are sometimes referred to as effective annual yields, effective yields, or annualized yields. Whatever it is called, to find out what a T-bill, or any other money market instrument, is *really* going to pay you, yet another conversion is needed. We will get to the needed conversion in a moment.

First, however, recall that an APR is equal to the interest rate per period multiplied by the number of periods in a year. For example, if the rate on a car loan is 1 percent per month, then the APR is $1\% \times 12 = 12\%$. In general, if we let m be the number of periods in a year, an APR is converted to an EAR as follows:

$$1 + EAR = \left(1 + \frac{APR}{m}\right)^m \qquad (9.8)$$

For example, on our 12 percent APR car loan, the EAR can be determined by:

$$1 + EAR = \left(1 + \frac{.12}{12}\right)^{12}$$
$$= 1.01^{12}$$
$$= 1.126825$$
$$EAR = 12.6825\%$$

Thus, the rate on the car loan is really 12.6825 percent per year.

EXAMPLE 9.6	APRs and EARs

A typical credit card may quote an APR of 18 percent. On closer inspection, you will find that the rate is actually 1.5 percent per month. What annual interest rate are you *really* paying on such a credit card?

With 12 periods in a year, an APR of 18 percent is converted to an EAR as follows:

$$1 + EAR = \left(1 + \frac{.18}{12}\right)^{12}$$
$$= 1.015^{12}$$
$$= 1.1956$$
$$EAR = 19.56\%$$

Thus, the rate on this credit card is really 19.56 percent per year.

Effective annual rates may be calculated using a built-in spreadsheet function. An example of how to use an Excel™ spreadsheet to calculate an effective annual rate is shown in a previous *Spreadsheet Analysis* box.

Now, to see that the bond equivalent yield on a T-bill is just an APR, we can first calculate the price on the bill we considered earlier (3.22 percent asked discount, 170 days to maturity). Using the bank discount formula, the asked price, for $1 million in face value, is:

$$\text{Asked price} = \$984{,}794 = 1{,}000{,}000 \times \left(1 - \frac{170}{360} \times .0322\right)$$

The discount is $15,206. Thus, on this 170-day investment, you earn $15,206 in interest on an investment of $984,794. On a percentage basis, you earned:

$$1.544\% = \frac{\$15{,}206}{\$984{,}794}$$

In a 365-day year, there are $365/170 = 2.147$ periods of 170-day length. So if we multiply what you earned over the 170-day period by the number of 170-day periods in a year, we get:

$$3.315\% = 2.147 \times 1.544\%$$

This is the bond equivalent yield we calculated earlier.

Finally, for this T-bill we can calculate the EAR using this 3.315 percent:

$$1 + EAR = \left(1 + \frac{.03315}{2.147}\right)^{2.147}$$
$$= 1.03344$$
$$EAR = 3.344\%$$

In the end, we have three different rates for this simple T-bill. The last one, the EAR, finally tells us what we really want to know: What are we actually going to earn?

EXAMPLE 9.7 | **Discounts, APRs, and EARs**

A money market instrument with 60 days to maturity has a quoted ask price of 99, meaning $99 per $100 face value. What are the banker's discount yield, the bond equivalent yield, and the effective annual return?

First, to get the discount yield, we have to use the bank discount formula and solve for the discount yield:

$$\$99 = \$100 \times \left(1 - \frac{60}{360} \times \text{Discount yield}\right)$$

With a little algebra, we see that the discount yield is 6 percent.

We convert this to a bond equivalent yield as follows:

$$6.145\% = \frac{365 \times .06}{360 - 60 \times .06}$$

The bond equivalent yield is thus 6.145 percent.

Finally, to get the EAR, note that there are $365/60 = 6.0833$ sixty-day periods in a year, so:

$$1 + EAR = \left(1 + \frac{.06145}{6.0833}\right)^{6.0833}$$
$$= 1.06305$$
$$EAR = 6.305\%$$

This example illustrates the general result that the discount rate is lower than the bond equivalent yield, which in turn is less than the EAR.

CHECK THIS

9.2a   What are the three different types of interest rate quotes that are important for money market instruments?

9.2b   How are T-bill rates quoted? How are CD rates quoted?

9.2c   Of the three different types of interest rate quotes, which is the largest?
Which is the smallest? Which is the most relevant?

9.3   Rates and Yields on Fixed-Income Securities

Thus far, we have focused on short-term interest rates, where "short-term" means one year
or less. Of course, these are not the only interest rates we are interested in, so we now begin
to discuss longer-term rates by looking at fixed-income securities. To keep this discussion to
a manageable length, we defer the details of how some longer-term rates are computed to
another chapter.

Fixed-income securities include long-term debt contracts from a wide variety of issuers.
The largest single category of fixed-income securities is debt issued by the U.S. government. The second largest category of fixed-income securities is mortgage debt issued to
finance real estate purchases. The two other large categories of fixed-income securities are
debt issued by corporations and debt issued by municipal governments. Each of these categories represents several trillion dollars of outstanding debt. Corporate bonds and municipal government bonds are covered in later chapters.

Because of its sheer size, the leading world market for debt securities is the market for
U.S. Treasury securities. Interest rates for U.S. Treasury debt are closely watched through-
out the world, and daily reports can be found in most major newspapers. *The Wall Street
Journal* provides a daily summary of activity in the U.S. Treasury market in its "Credit
Markets" column, as seen in the nearby *Investment Updates* box.

For more information
on fixed-income
securities visit
www.bondmarkets.com

For the latest U.S.
Treasury rates, check
www.bloomberg.com

THE TREASURY YIELD CURVE

**Treasury yield
curve**
A graph of Treasury yields
plotted against maturities.

Every day, *The Wall Street Journal* contains a graphical display of a current **Treasury yield
curve**, which is a plot of Treasury yields against maturities. Yields are measured along the
vertical axis, and maturities are measured along the horizontal axis. The light gray line represents the most current yield curve, while the background lines represent recent yield
curves. Thus, the "Treasury Yield Curve" box illustrates both where Treasury interest rates
are now and where they were recently.

The Treasury yield curve is fundamental to bond market analysis because it represents
the interest rates that financial markets are charging to the world's largest debtor with the
world's highest credit rating—the U.S. government. In essence, the Treasury yield curve
represents interest rates for default-free lending across the maturity spectrum. As such, almost all other domestic interest rates are determined with respect to U.S. Treasury interest
rates. Our nearby *Work the Web* box shows how to get yield curves online.

Check out the "living
yield curve" at
www.smartmoney.
com/bonds

RATES ON OTHER FIXED-INCOME INVESTMENTS

The "Yield Comparisons" table beside the Treasury yield curve in the *Investment Updates*
box gives interest rates based on bond market indexes constructed by the securities firm
Merrill Lynch. Current interest rates and the highest and lowest interest rates over the

CREDIT MARKETS

Bonds Will Take Cue from Gas Prices, Fed

Katrina Fallout May Pause Interest-Rate Increases and Fuel Treasury Buying

Gasoline prices and the Federal Reserve's assessment of economic conditions will drive Treasury prices this week as investors continue to factor in the devastation of states around the Gulf of Mexico.

Last week, Treasurys rallied, with the bulk of the buying targeted at shorter-dated securities amid growing speculation the catastrophe in New Orleans and surrounding areas would stay the Fed's hand when policy makers meet later this month. The central bank has raised its federal-funds target rate a quarter percentage point at each meeting of the Federal Open Market Committee since June 2001, bringing the fed-funds target rate to its current 3.5%.

"If the Fed is going to do anything as a result of what's happening, obviously what they will do is skip," said Richard Gilhooly, an interest-rate strategist at BNP Paribas in New York. "It won't cost them anything to skip." The surge in gasoline prices alone is reason for the central bank to consider taking a break when it holds its policy meeting Sept. 20, he said.

The drop in the two-year note's yield—more than 0.3 percentage point on the week—helped steepen the benchmark-yield curve, which plots the yields between the two- and 10-year notes, to 0.29 percentage point from 0.11 percentage point in the beginning of the week. This brought an abrupt halt to the popular flattening trades that have dominated investment strategies for more than a year and dealt a fair amount of pain to those who favored such positions. More unwinding of these trades is expected this week.

Before last week, the bond market took its cue from crude-oil futures. But the more immediate effect of gasoline on consumers' wallets now has the undivided attention of fixed-income investors.

"The question now is whether the U.S. economy is merely going through another 'soft patch' or

previous 52-week period are reported for a number of bond indexes. These bond market indexes provide yield information on many different types of bonds. Since we will be discussing these in much more detail in several subsequent chapters, we touch on them only briefly here.

The first two indexes represent U.S. Treasury securities with 1- to 10-year maturities and 10- to 30-year maturities. The next two indexes represent U.S. government agency debt with 1- to 10-year maturities and debt with more than 10 years to maturity. A variety of government agencies borrow money in financial markets. The Tennessee Valley Authority (TVA) is an example.

In recent years, U.S. government agencies have issued debt with maturities as long as 50 years. U.S. government agency debt does not carry the same credit guarantee as U.S. Treasury debt, and therefore interest rates on agency debt reflect a premium over interest rates on Treasury debt. Also, agency securities are often subject to state taxes, whereas Treasury securities are not.

The next four indexes represent debt issued by domestic corporations according to their maturity and credit rating. Notice that corporate debt with a high credit quality pays a higher interest rate than U.S. government agency debt, which in turn pays a higher interest rate than U.S. Treasury debt. As expected, medium credit quality corporate debt pays a higher interest rate than high credit quality corporate debt.

Treasury Yield Curve

Yield to maturity of current bills, notes and bonds.

1 Month Ago

Yesterday

1 Year Ago

5.0%
4.0
3.0
2.0
1.0
0.0

1 3 6   2   5   10   30
month(s)   years
——— maturity ———

Source: Reuters

Yield Comparisons				
Based on Merrill Lynch Bond Indexes, priced as of midafternoon Eastern time.				
			52-WEEK	
	9/2	9/1	HIGH	LOW
Corp. Govt. Master	4.32%	4.30%	4.70%	3.73%
Treasury				
1-10 yr	3.81	3.79	4.22	2.83
10+ yr	4.29	4.28	4.93	4.18
Agencies				
1-10 yr	4.08	4.07	4.48	3.11
10+ yr	4.66	4.65	5.35	4.49
Corporate				
1-10 yr High Quality	4.40	4.39	4.78	3.53
Medium Quality	4.76	4.74	5.14	4.06
10+ yr High Quality	5.27	5.26	5.76	5.08
Medium Quality	5.54	5.53	6.17	5.48
Yankee bonds (1)	4.69	4.68	5.08	4.07
Current-coupon mortgages (2)				
GNMA 4.99% (3)	4.95	4.94	5.38	4.74
FNMA 5.49%	5.17	5.16	5.49	4.83
FHLMC 5.49%	5.21	5.20	5.51	4.89
High-yield corporates	7.66	7.64	8.51	6.76
Tax-Exempt Bonds				
7-12 yr G.O. (AA)	3.57	3.57	3.90	3.33
12-22 yr G.O. (AA)	3.92	3.92	4.29	3.63
22+ yr revenue (A)	4.26	4.26	4.93	4.22

Note: High quality rated AAA-AA; medium quality A-BBB/Baa; high yield, BB/Ba-C.
(1) Dollar-denominated, SEC-registered bonds of foreign issuers sold in the U.S. (2) Reflects the 52-week high and low of mortgage-backed securities indexes rather than the individual securities shown. (3) Government guaranteed.

whether this is the beginning of a more-protracted period of weakness," said Mark Cliffe, an economist at ING Financial Markets in London. He wasn't ready to come down on either side of the debate, but added. "The challenges facing the oil market mean that the risk of the latter is substantial."

Treasurys ended trading early Friday, and the market was closed yesterday. At 2 p.m. Friday, the benchmark 10-year note was down 2/32 point at 101 24/32. Its yield rose to 4.036% from 4.031% Thursday. The 30-year bond was up 6/32 point at 116 20/32 to yield 4.295% down from 4.305% Thursday.

Source: Agnes T. Crane, *The Wall Street Journal*, September 6, 2005. Reprinted by permission of Dow Jones, Inc., via Copyright Clearance Center, Inc. © 2005 Dow Jones & Company, Inc. All Rights Reserved Worldwide.

www

Visit these mortgage security Web sites:
www.fanniemae.com
www.ginniemae.gov
www.freddiemac.com

"Yankee bonds" are issued by foreign corporations for sale in the United States. These bonds are denominated in U.S. dollars so investors do not have to worry that changing foreign exchange rates will affect debt values.

As we noted previously, the Federal Home Loan Mortgage Corporation (FHLMC), or Freddie Mac, and the Federal National Mortgage Association (FNMA), or Fannie Mae, are government-sponsored agencies that repackage home mortgages into mortgage pools, where each pool represents several tens of millions of dollars of home mortgages. A third agency, the Government National Mortgage Association (GNMA), better known as "Ginnie Mae," is also an active mortgage repackager. The interest rates reported for these agencies correspond to indexes constructed from many mortgage pools.

"High-yield corporates" refers to corporate bonds with above-average default risk. These bonds are usually avoided by conservative investors, but they may be attractive to investors who understand and are willing to accept the risks involved. Because of their much higher credit risk, the interest rates for these bonds are significantly higher than those for even medium-quality corporate bonds.

"Tax-exempts" are bonds issued by municipal governments. Coupon interest payments on most municipal bonds are exempt from federal income taxes, and they are often exempt from state income taxes as well. The tax-exempt interest rates reported in the "Yield Comparisons" table are based on indexes for high-quality municipal bonds corresponding

What does the current Treasury yield curve look like? You can find the answer on the Web many different places. We went to www.bloomberg.com, and here is what we found after the market close on September 9, 2005:

As you can see, Bloomberg shows you the yield curve for today and yesterday. For this day, the yield curve shifted upward, as can be seen from the increase in the yield (or decrease in price) for each maturity. This yield curve would be considered a normal, upward-sloping yield curve. The short-term rates are about 3.6 percent, and the six-month rate is about 4.0 percent. Here's a question for you: This yield curve is from September 9, 2005. The 2-, 5- and 10-year maturity notes are dated 2, 5, and 10 years from this date. However the 30-year maturity is actually only 26 years. Why would the 26-year maturity Treasury bond be used for the 30-year interest rate?

U.S. TREASURIES

Bills

	COUPON	MATURITY DATE	CURRENT PRICE/YIELD	PRICE/YIELD CHANGE	TIME
3-Month	N.A.	12/08/2005	3.40/3.48	0.02/.020	09/09
6-Month	N.A.	03/09/2006	3.60/3.72	0.03/.004	09/09

Notes/Bonds

	COUPON	MATURITY DATE	CURRENT PRICE/YIELD	PRICE/YIELD CHANGE	TIME
2-Year	4.000	08/31/2007	100-07/3.87	0-00/-.001	09/09
3-Year	4.125	08/15/2008	100-20/3.88	0-00/-.004	09/09
5-Year	3.875	09/15/2010	99-24/3.93	0-02/-.019	09/09
10-Year	4.250	08/15/2015	101-01/4.12	0-06/-.025	09/09
30-Year	5.375	02/15/2031	114-27/4.40	0-18/-.034	09/09

© Bloomberg L.P.

to 10-year maturity and 20-year maturity general obligation bonds (GOs) and 30-year maturity revenue bonds.

General obligation bonds are secured by the general taxing power of the issuing municipality. Revenue bonds are secured by revenues generated from specific projects, for example, toll roads, airports, or user fees for services. As shown, because of their tax-exempt status, interest rates on high-quality municipal bonds are lower than interest rates on comparable U.S. Treasury securities.

CHECK THIS

9.3a What is the yield curve? Why is it important?

9.3b Why are corporate bond yields higher than Treasury bond yields?

9.3c Why are municipal bond yields lower than Treasury bond yields?

9.3d What are Yankee bonds?

9.4 The Term Structure of Interest Rates

term structure of interest rates

Relationship between time to maturity and interest rates for default-free, pure discount instruments.

The yield curve tells us the relationship between Treasury bond yields and time to maturity. The **term structure of interest rates** (or just "term structure") is a similar, but not identical, relationship. Recall that a pure discount instrument has a single payment of face value at maturity with no other payments until then. Treasury bonds are *not* pure discount instruments because they pay coupons every six months. Pure discount instruments with more than a year to maturity are often called "zero coupon bonds," or just "zeroes," because they are, in effect, bonds with a zero coupon rate.

The term structure of interest rates is the relationship between time to maturity and interest rates for default-free, pure discount instruments. So, the difference between the yield curve and the term structure is that the yield curve is based on coupon bonds, whereas the term structure is based on pure discount instruments. The term structure is sometimes called the "zero coupon yield curve" to distinguish it from the Treasury yield curve.

TREASURY STRIPS

U.S. Treasury STRIPS

Pure discount securities created by stripping coupons and principal payments of Treasury notes and bonds. Stands for Separate Trading of Registered Interest and Principal of Securities.

Until about 1987, the term structure of interest rates was not directly observable simply because default-free, pure discount instruments with maturities greater than one year did not exist or reliable data on them were not available. Today, however, the term structure of interest rates can be easily seen by examining yields on **U.S. Treasury STRIPS**.

STRIPS are pure discount instruments created by "stripping" the coupons and principal payments of U.S. Treasury notes and bonds into separate parts and then selling the parts separately. The term STRIPS stands for Separate Trading of Registered Interest and Principal of Securities. For example, a Treasury note with 10 years to maturity will make 20 semiannual coupon payments during its life and will also make a principal payment at maturity. This note can therefore be separated, or stripped, into 21 separate parts, and each part can be bought and sold separately. The Treasury originally allowed notes and bonds with 10 years or more to maturity (at the time they are issued) to be stripped. Today, any note or bond is strippable.

Figure 9.4 is a sample "U.S. Treasury STRIPS" daily report of individual STRIPS prices and yields as it appeared in *The Wall Street Journal*. Only maturities of 10 years or less are reported, but longer maturities exist. The first column of Figure 9.4 gives the maturity of each STRIPS listed. The second column reports whether the STRIPS were created from a coupon payment or a principal payment. There are three possible symbols in column 2: *ci* stands for coupon interest, *np* stands for note principal, and *bp* stands for bond principal.

FIGURE 9.4 Treasury STRIPS

U.S. Treasury Strips

MATURITY	TYPE	BID	ASKED	CHG	ASK YLD	MATURITY	TYPE	BID	ASKED	CHG	ASK YLD
Oct 05	ci	99:22	99:22	...	2.94	May 09	np	87:00	87:01	−5	3.81
Nov 05	ci	99:13	99:14	...	3.06	May 09	np	86:27	86:28	−5	3.85
Nov 05	np	99:12	99:12	...	3.28	Aug 09	ci	86:03	86:04	−5	3.83
Nov 05	np	99:12	99:12	...	3.27	Aug 09	np	86:00	86:01	−5	3.86
Jan 06	ci	98:29	98:30	...	3.07	Nov 09	ci	85:11	85:11	−5	3.82
Feb 06	ci	98:17	98:18	−1	3.36	Nov 09	bp	85:02	85:03	−5	3.89
Feb 06	bp	98:23	98:24	...	2.92	Feb 10	ci	84:16	84:17	−6	3.82
Feb 06	np	98:15	98:15	...	3.54	Feb 10	np	84:08	84:09	−6	3.89
Apr 06	ci	97:29	97:30	−1	3.48	May 10	ci	83:30	83:30	−6	3.77
May 06	ci	97:19	97:20	−1	3.52	Aug 10	ci	83:07	83:08	−6	3.75
May 06	np	97:17	97:17	−1	3.65	Aug 10	np	82:21	82:22	−6	3.89
May 06	np	97:16	97:17	−2	3.67	Nov 10	ci	82:17	82:18	−7	3.73
Jul 06	ci	97:07	97:07	−1	3.32	Feb 11	ci	81:00	81:01	−8	3.91
Aug 06	ci	96:22	96:22	−1	3.61	Feb 11	np	81:01	81:01	−8	3.90
Aug 06	np	96:19	96:19	−1	3.72	May 11	ci	80:07	80:07	−8	3.91
Oct 06	ci	96:02	96:02	−2	3.66	Aug 11	ci	79:11	79:12	−8	3.93
Nov 06	ci	95:23	95:24	−2	3.69	Aug 11	np	79:11	79:12	−8	3.93
Nov 06	np	95:22	95:22	−2	3.74	Nov 11	ci	78:16	78:17	−8	3.95
Nov 06	np	95:22	95:22	−1	3.74	Feb 12	ci	77:20	77:21	−7	3.97
Feb 07	ci	94:28	94:29	−2	3.68	Feb 12	np	77:21	77:22	−7	3.96
Feb 07	np	94:27	94:28	−2	3.70	May 12	ci	76:27	76:27	−7	3.98
May 07	ci	93:30	93:30	−3	3.73	Aug 12	ci	75:30	75:30	−7	4.01
May 07	np	93:29	93:30	−2	3.74	Aug 12	np	76:13	76:14	−7	3.91
May 07	np	93:28	93:29	−3	3.77	Nov 12	ci	75:03	75:03	−8	4.02
Aug 07	ci	93:01	93:02	−3	3.75	Nov 12	np	75:13	75:13	−8	3.96
Aug 07	ci	92:31	93:00	−3	3.78	Feb 13	ci	74:02	74:03	−8	4.07
Aug 07	np	92:31	93:00	−3	3.78	Feb 13	np	74:15	74:15	−8	4.00
Nov 07	ci	92:05	92:05	−4	3.76	May 13	ci	73:05	73:06	−8	4.10
Nov 07	np	92:03	92:04	−4	3.78	May 13	np	73:26	73:26	−8	3.99
Feb 08	ci	91:11	91:11	−3	3.75	Nov 13	np	72:01	72:01	−8	4.05
Feb 08	np	91:09	91:10	−3	3.77	Feb 14	ci	70:18	70:18	−9	4.17
Feb 08	np	91:07	91:08	−3	3.79	Feb 14	np	71:05	71:06	−9	4.07
May 08	ci	90:14	90:14	−4	3.77	May 14	ci	69:25	69:25	−10	4.18
May 08	np	90:11	90:11	−4	3.81	May 14	np	70:12	70:13	−10	4.08
May 08	np	90:11	90:12	−4	3.80	Aug 14	ci	68:31	68:31	−10	4.20
Aug 08	ci	89:17	89:18	−4	3.79	Nov 14	ci	68:07	68:07	−10	4.20
Aug 08	np	89:15	89:16	−4	3.81	Feb 15	ci	67:13	67:14	−10	4.22
Nov 08	ci	88:21	88:22	−4	3.80	Feb 15	bp	67:23	67:24	−10	4.17
Nov 08	np	88:19	88:20	−4	3.82	May 15	ci	66:23	66:24	−10	4.22
Nov 08	np	88:19	88:19	−4	3.83	Aug 15	ci	65:29	65:30	−10	4.24
Feb 09	ci	87:21	87:22	−4	3.86	Aug 15	bp	66:08	66:08	−10	4.18
Feb 09	np	87:22	87:23	−4	3.85	Nov 15	ci	65:04	65:05	−10	4.25
May 09	ci	86:28	86:29	−5	3.84	Nov 15	bp	65:12	65:13	−11	4.21

Source: *The Wall Street Journal*, September 7, 2005. Reprinted by permission of Dow Jones and Company, Inc., via Copyright Clearance Center, Inc. © 2005 Dow Jones and Company, Inc. All Rights Reserved Worldwide.

The next two columns contain bid and asked prices for each STRIPS. As always, the bid price is a quote of what dealers were willing to pay to buy the STRIPS, and the asked price is a quote of what dealers were willing to accept to sell the STRIPS.

STRIPS prices are stated as a price per $100 of face value. For example, suppose a coupon interest STRIPS has an asked price quote of 74:08. This means that the price per $100 face value is $74.25, because the 08 to the right of the colon in the stated price of 74:08 stands for thirty-seconds of a dollar. Thus, 74:08 stands for 74⁸⁄₃₂. The next-to-the-last column in Figure 9.4 reports the change in the asked price quote from the previous day. Price changes are also reported in thirty-seconds of a dollar. A −1 means −¹⁄₃₂ of a dollar, or −3.125 cents per $100 face value (an increase would have a positive sign).

Why are STRIPS prices quoted in thirty-seconds? Nobody really knows. That's the way they have been quoted historically, and the tradition continues. Why don't traders go to decimal quotes? They probably will someday, but financial market convention evolves slowly.

The last column in Figure 9.4 lists asked yields, which are yields on the STRIPS based on their asked price quotes. Notice that there is a different asked yield, or interest rate, for each maturity. This shows us that interest rates determined in financial markets generally differ according to the maturity of a security.

Read more about
STRIPS at
www.publicdebt.treas.
gov

YIELDS FOR U.S. TREASURY STRIPS

An asked yield for a U.S. Treasury STRIPS is an APR (APRs were discussed earlier in this chapter). It is calculated as two times the true semiannual rate. Calculation of the yield on a STRIPS is a standard time value of money calculation. The price today of the STRIPS is the *present value*; the face value received at maturity is the *future value*. As shown in Example 9.1, the relationship between present value and future value is:

$$\text{Present value} = \frac{\text{Future value}}{(1+r)^N}$$

In this equation, r is the rate per period and N is the number of periods. Notice that a period is not necessarily one year long.[1] For Treasury STRIPS, the number of periods is two times the number of years to maturity, here denoted by $2M$, and the interest rate is the "yield to maturity" (*YTM*) divided by 2:

$$\textbf{STRIPS price} = \frac{\textbf{Face value}}{(1 + \textbf{YTM}/2)^{2M}} \qquad (9.9)$$

Consider a STRIPS with an asked price of 55:18, a reported yield of 4.40, and 13.5 years to maturity. The actual semiannual rate is $4.40\%/2 = 2.20\%$. Also, 13.5 years to maturity converts to 2×13.5, or 27, semiannual periods. To check that the reported price is correct given the reported yield, we plug in future value, rate per period, and number of periods:

$$\text{STRIPS price} = \frac{\$100}{(1 + .022)^{27}}$$

$$55.568 = 55\tfrac{18}{32} = 55:18$$

The price shown is rounded to the nearest thirty-second.

If we need to go the other way and calculate the asked yield on a STRIPS given its price, we can rearrange the basic present value equation to solve it for r:

$$r = \left(\frac{\text{Future value}}{\text{Present value}}\right)^{\frac{1}{N}} - 1$$

For STRIPS, $N = 2M$ is the number of semiannual periods, and $r = YTM/2$ is the semiannual interest rate, so the formula is:

$$\textbf{YTM} = \textbf{2} \times \left[\left(\frac{\textbf{Face value}}{\textbf{STRIPS price}}\right)^{\frac{1}{2M}} - \textbf{1}\right] \qquad (9.10)$$

Consider a STRIPS maturing in six years with an asked price of 73:01. Its yield to maturity of 5.3072 percent as calculated immediately below becomes 5.31 percent after rounding to two decimal places.

$$5.3072\% = 2 \times \left[\left(\frac{100}{73.03125}\right)^{\frac{1}{12}} - 1\right]$$

As another example, consider a STRIPS maturing in 20 years with an asked price of 26:06. As calculated immediately below, its yield to maturity of 6.8129 percent becomes 6.81 percent after rounding to two decimal places.

$$6.8129\% = 2 \times \left[\left(\frac{100}{26.1875}\right)^{\frac{1}{40}} - 1\right]$$

---

[1] Any financial calculator can perform these calculations, but we will work them the hard way so that you can learn how to do them with any calculator.

9.4a What is the yield to maturity (YTM) on a STRIPS maturing in five years if its asked price quote is 77:24?

9.4b What is the YTM of a STRIPS maturing in 15 years if its asked price quote is 38:26?

9.4c What is the YTM of a STRIPS maturing in 25 years if its asked price quote is 18:21?

9.5 Nominal versus Real Interest Rates

nominal interest rates
Interest rates as they are normally observed and quoted, with no adjustment for inflation.

There is a fundamental distinction between *nominal* and *real* interest rates. **Nominal interest rates** are interest rates as we ordinarily observe them, for example, as they are reported in *The Wall Street Journal*. Thus, all the money market rates we discussed earlier in this chapter and the STRIPS yields we discussed just above are nominal rates.

REAL INTEREST RATES

real interest rates
Interest rates adjusted for the effect of inflation, calculated as the nominal rate less the rate of inflation.

Real interest rates are nominal rates adjusted for the effects of price inflation. To obtain a real interest rate, simply subtract an inflation rate from a nominal interest rate:

$$\text{Real interest rate} = \text{Nominal interest rate} - \text{Inflation rate} \qquad (9.11)$$

The real interest rate is so-called because it measures the real change in the purchasing power of an investment. For example, if the nominal interest rate for a one-year certificate of deposit is 7 percent, then a one-year deposit of $100,000 will grow to $107,000. But if the inflation rate over the same year is 4 percent, you would need $104,000 after one year passes to buy what cost $100,000 today. Thus, the real increase in purchasing power for your investment is only $3,000, and, therefore, the real interest rate is only 3 percent.

Figure 9.5 displays real interest rates based on annual rates of return on U.S. Treasury bills and inflation rates over the 55-year period 1950 through 2005. As shown in Figure 9.5, following a negative spike at the beginning of the Korean War in 1950, real interest rates for Treasury bills were generally positive until the Organization of Petroleum-Exporting Countries' (OPEC) oil embargo in 1973. After this, real rates were generally negative until the Federal Reserve Board initiated a tight-money policy to fight an inflationary spiral in the late 1970s. The tight-money policy caused the 1980s to begin with historically high real interest rates. Throughout the 1980s, real Treasury bill rates were falling as inflation subsided. During this 50-year period the average real Treasury bill interest rate was slightly less than 1 percent.

THE FISHER HYPOTHESIS

Fisher hypothesis
Assertion that the general level of nominal interest rates follows the general level of inflation.

The relationship between nominal interest rates and the rate of inflation is often couched in terms of the *Fisher hypothesis,* which is named for the famous economist Irving Fisher, who formally proposed it in 1930. The **Fisher hypothesis** simply asserts that the general level of nominal interest rates follows the general level of inflation.

According to the Fisher hypothesis, interest rates are on average higher than the rate of inflation. Therefore, it logically follows that short-term interest rates reflect current inflation, while long-term interest rates reflect investor expectations of future inflation. Figure 9.6 graphs nominal interest rates and inflation rates used to create Figure 9.5. Notice that when inflation rates were high, Treasury bill returns tended to be high also, as predicted by the Fisher hypothesis.

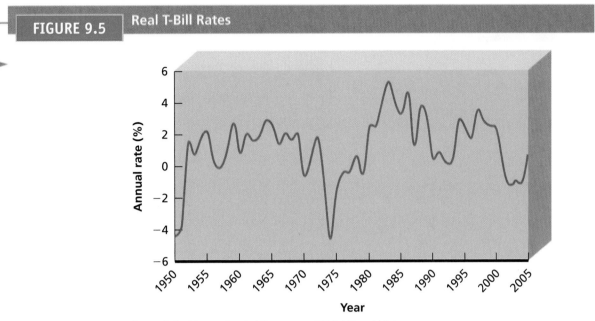

FIGURE 9.5   Real T-Bill Rates

Source: Federal Reserve Board of Governors and Global Financial Data.

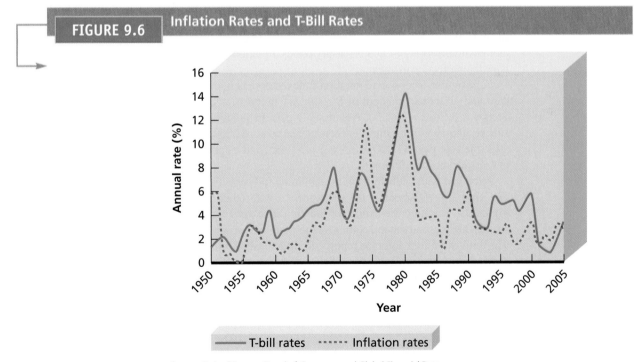

FIGURE 9.6   Inflation Rates and T-Bill Rates

Source: Federal Reserve Board of Governors and Global Financial Data.

FIGURE 9.7 Inflation-Indexed Treasury Securities

Inflation-Indexed Treasury Securities

RATE	MAT	BID/ASKED	CHG	*YLD	ACCR PRIN
3.375	01/07	103-25/26	−6	0.549	1228
3.625	01/08	106-07/08	−8	0.936	1204
3.875	01/09	108-29/30	−9	1.152	1186
4.250	01/10	112-11/12	−11	1.317	1156
0.875	04/10	97-25/26	−10	1.366	1027
3.500	01/11	110-25/26	−10	1.397	1118
3.375	01/12	111-14/15	−16	1.478	1096
3.000	07/12	109-17/18	−16	1.525	1082
1.875	07/13	102-08/09	−17	1.565	1060
2.000	01/14	103-04/05	−18	1.595	1051
2.000	07/14	103-07/08	−19	1.605	1032
1.625	01/15	99-28/29	−19	1.636	1019
1.875	07/15	102-03/04	−20	1.640	1000
2.375	01/25	107-24/25	−37	1.893	1032
3.625	04/28	131-25/26	−49	1.889	1203
3.875	04/29	137-27/28	−50	1.881	1183
3.375	04/32	133-08/09	−56	1.796	1096

*Yield to maturity on accrued principal.

Source: *The Wall Street Journal*, September 6, 2005. Reprinted by permission of Dow Jones, Inc., via Copyright Clearance Center, Inc. © 2005 Dow Jones & Company, Inc. All Rights Reserved Worldwide.

INFLATION-INDEXED TREASURY SECURITIES

In recent years, the U.S. Treasury has issued securities that guarantee a fixed rate of return in excess of realized inflation rates. These inflation-indexed Treasury securities pay a fixed coupon rate on their current principal and adjust their principal semiannually according to the most recent inflation rate. For investors wanting long-term protection against inflation along with the safety of U.S. Treasury bonds, inflation-indexed Treasury securities are perhaps the perfect investment.

For example, suppose an inflation-indexed note is issued with a coupon rate of 3.5 percent and an initial principal of $1,000. Six months later, the note will pay a coupon of $1,000 × 3.5%/2 = $17.50. Assuming 2 percent inflation over the six months since issuance, the note's principal is then increased to $1,000 × 102% = $1,020. Six months later, the note pays $1,020 × 3.5%/2 = $17.85, and its principal is again adjusted to compensate for recent inflation.

Price and yield information for inflation-indexed Treasury securities is reported in *The Wall Street Journal* in the same section with other Treasury securities, as shown in Figure 9.7. Locating the listing for inflation-indexed Treasury securities in Figure 9.7, we see that the first and second columns report the fixed coupon rate and maturity, respectively. The third and fourth columns report current bid/asked prices and the price change from the previous trading day. Prices for inflation-indexed securities are reported as a percentage of current accrued principal. The fifth and sixth columns list an inflation-adjusted yield to maturity and current accrued principal reflecting all cumulative inflation adjustments.

CHECK THIS

9.5a What is the difference between a nominal interest rate and a real interest rate?

9.5b What does the Fisher hypothesis assert?

9.5c What is the distinguishing feature of inflation-indexed Treasury securities?

INVESTMENT UPDATES

FED SEES BOND MARKET HAMPERING ITS STEPS TO KEEP INFLATION IN CHECK

As the Federal Reserve prepares to raise short-term interest rates again next week, officials there increasingly believe the bond market, which sets long-term rates, is diluting their efforts to tighten credit and contain inflation.

The result: The longer the bond market keeps long-term rates unusually low, the further the Fed is likely to raise the short-term rates it controls in an effort to keep the economy from overheating. Conversely, sharply higher bond yields would encourage the Fed to stop raising short-term rates.

This dynamic marks a striking break from the past when the Fed typically saw sharply higher bond yields as a reason to lift short-term rates further and low yields as a reason to worry about the economy.

Fed officials say future rate moves mostly depend on what data indicate about growth and inflation. With inflation low but the economy steadily using up unused capacity, officials plan to keep raising short-term rates to "neutral," a level thought to be between 3% and 5% that neither stimulates nor restrains economic growth. The bond market's unusual behavior is complicating that strategy by making it harder to know where neutral is.

Some policy makers worry that bond yields are being kept in check by overly complacent investor sentiment which could rapidly dissipate, pushing up mortgage rates and shaking the housing market. Indeed, some Fed officials see similarities between the attitudes of bond investors today and of stock investors in the late 1990s.

The Fed influences economic conditions by changing the target for the federal-funds rate, which is the rate charged on overnight loans between banks. That affects short-term consumer and business loans, including adjustable-rate mortgages. But longer-term rates, such as those for fixed-rate 30-year mortgages, are set by bond-market investors and have a bigger impact on the economy.

Low bond yields "are telling the Fed their job isn't done and they have to keep going," said Laurence Meyer, a former Fed governor and now an analyst at forecasting firm Macroeconomic Advisers. Mr. Meyer thinks the Fed eventually will raise its short-term rate to 4% from today's 3.25%, if bond yields rise significantly. If long-term rates don't rise, the Fed will have to raise short-term rates above 4.5%, he said.

The Fed is expected to raise the short-term rate to 3.5% on Tuesday. Since June of last year, the Fed has raised the Fed funds rate target from a 46-year low of 1% to 3.25%.

Yet, over the same period, the yield on the benchmark 10-year Treasury bond has declined. It fell from 4.7% to below 4% a month ago, although it has bounced back up to 4.3%. Yields have remained low even as the economy has been strong, inflation has drifted up, and the Fed has steadily raised short-term rates.

For months, Fed officials have debated the reasons long-term rates have declined. In February, Chairman Alan Greenspan labeled it a "conundrum." In a speech last week, Federal Reserve Bank of San Francisco President Janet Yellen said the debate "boils down to whether the [drop] is due to various 'special factors' operating independently of the current business cycle, or instead augurs bad economic news on the horizon."

If "special factors," such as increased investor confidence that inflation will remain low, or purchases of bonds by foreign central banks, are the reason for low bond yields, "the federal-funds rate probably needs to be somewhat higher than would otherwise be appropriate," Ms. Yellen said. But if the market is anticipating hard economic times, "a somewhat easier policy may be appropriate," she said.

In the past month, other key Fed policy makers have come to view special factors as the likelier explanation for low long-term rates than economic weakness. Many factors influence bond yields: expected inflation, which erodes an investor's purchasing power; the worldwide supply and demand for credit; what economists call a "term premium," the extra yield that investors demand for the many risks of lending money over a longer term, including fluctuations in economic growth and inflation; and Fed actions.

9.6 Traditional Theories of the Term Structure

Yield curves have been studied by financial economists for well over a century. During this period a number of different theories have been proposed to explain why yield curves may be upward sloping at one point in time and then downward sloping or flat at another point in time. We discuss three of the most popular traditional theories of the term structure in this section. We then present a modern perspective on the term structure in the following section.

EXPECTATIONS THEORY

expectations theory
The term structure of interest rates is a reflection of financial market beliefs regarding future interest rates.

According to the **expectations theory** of the term structure of interest rates, the shape of a yield curve expresses financial market expectations regarding future interest rates. Essentially, an upward-sloping yield curve predicts an increase in interest rates, and a downward-sloping yield curve predicts a decrease in interest rates. A flat yield curve expresses the sentiment that interest rates are not expected to change in the near future.

EXPECTATIONS AND FORWARD RATES The basic principles of the expectations theory can be explained with a two-period example. Let r_1 stand for the current market interest rate on a one-year investment, and let r_2 be the current market interest rate on a two-year investment. Also, let $r_{1,1}$ be the market interest rate on a one-year investment that will be available in one year. Of course, this rate is not known today.

For a two-year investment, you have two strategies available. First, you can invest for two years at the rate r_2. In this case, $1 invested today will become $$(1 + r_2)^2$ in two years. For example, if $r_2 = 10$ percent, you would have $1 \times (1.10)^2 = \$1.21$ in two years for every dollar you invest.

Alternatively, you can invest for one year at the rate r_1, and, at the end of one year, you can reinvest the proceeds at the rate $r_{1,1}$. In this case, $1 invested today will become $$(1 + r_1)(1 + r_{1,1})$ in two years. For example, suppose $r_1 = 10$ percent and, after a year passes, it turns out that $r_{1,1} = 8$ percent. Then you would end up with $1 \times 1.10 \times 1.08 = \$1.19$. Alternatively, suppose that after a year passes it turns out that $r_{1,1} = 12$ percent; then you would have $1 \times 1.10 \times 1.12 = \$1.232$. Notice that this second strategy entails some uncertainty since the next year's interest rate, $r_{1,1}$, is not known when you originally select your investment strategy.

The expectations theory of the term structure of interest rates asserts that, on average, the two-year investment proceeds, $$(1 + r_2)^2$ and $$(1 + r_1)(1 + r_{1,1})$, will be equal. In fact, we can obtain what is known as the implied **forward rate**, $f_{1,1}$, by setting the two total proceeds equal to each other:

forward rate
An expected future interest rate implied by current interest rates.

$$(1 + r_2)^2 = (1 + r_1)(1 + f_{1,1})$$

Solving for the forward rate, $f_{1,1}$, we see that:

$$f_{1,1} = \frac{(1 + r_2)^2}{1 + r_1} - 1$$

Notice that this forward interest rate is simply a future interest rate implied by current interest rates.

According to expectations theory, the forward rate $f_{1,1}$ is an accurate predictor of the rate $r_{1,1}$ to be realized one year in the future. Thus, if $r_2 = 10$ percent and $r_1 = 8$ percent, then $f_{1,1} = 12$ percent, approximately, which predicts that the one-year interest rate will increase from its current value of 10 percent to 12 percent. Alternatively, if $r_2 = 10$ percent and $r_1 = 12$ percent, then $f_{1,1} = 8$ percent, approximately, which predicts that the one-year interest rate will decrease from its current value of 10 percent to 8 percent.

In general, if $r_2 > r_1$, such that the term structure is upward sloping, then expectations theory predicts an interest rate increase. Similarly, if $r_2 < r_1$, indicating a downward-sloping term structure, then expectations theory predicts an interest rate decrease. Thus, the slope of the term structure points in the predicted direction of future interest rate changes.

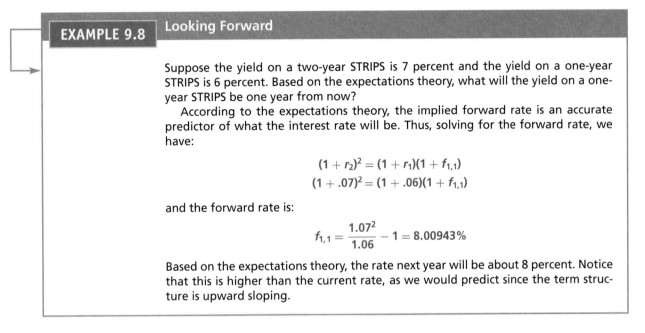

EXAMPLE 9.8 — Looking Forward

Suppose the yield on a two-year STRIPS is 7 percent and the yield on a one-year STRIPS is 6 percent. Based on the expectations theory, what will the yield on a one-year STRIPS be one year from now?

According to the expectations theory, the implied forward rate is an accurate predictor of what the interest rate will be. Thus, solving for the forward rate, we have:

$$(1 + r_2)^2 = (1 + r_1)(1 + f_{1,1})$$
$$(1 + .07)^2 = (1 + .06)(1 + f_{1,1})$$

and the forward rate is:

$$f_{1,1} = \frac{1.07^2}{1.06} - 1 = 8.00943\%$$

Based on the expectations theory, the rate next year will be about 8 percent. Notice that this is higher than the current rate, as we would predict since the term structure is upward sloping.

EXPECTATIONS THEORY AND THE FISHER HYPOTHESIS The expectations theory is closely related to the Fisher hypothesis we discussed earlier. The relationship between the expectations theory of interest rates and the Fisher hypothesis is stated as follows. If expected future inflation is higher than current inflation, then we are likely to see an upward-sloping term structure where long-term interest rates are higher than short-term interest rates. Similarly, if future inflation is expected to be lower than its current level, we would then be likely to see a downward-sloping term structure where long rates are lower than short rates.

In other words, taken together, the expectations theory and the Fisher hypothesis assert that an upward-sloping term structure tells us that the market expects that nominal interest rates and inflation are likely to be higher in the future.

MATURITY PREFERENCE THEORY

Another traditional theory of the term structure asserts that lenders prefer to lend short-term to avoid tying up funds for long periods of time. In other words, they have a preference for shorter maturities. At the same time, borrowers prefer to borrow long-term to lock in secure financing for long periods of time.

According to the **maturity preference theory**, then, borrowers have to pay a higher rate to borrow long-term rather than short-term to essentially bribe lenders into loaning funds for longer maturities. The extra interest is called a *maturity premium.*[2]

The Fisher hypothesis, maturity preference theory, and expectations theory can coexist without problem. For example, suppose the shape of a yield curve is basically determined

maturity preference theory
Long-term interest rates contain a maturity premium necessary to induce lenders into making longer-term loans.

[2]Traditionally, maturity preference theory has been known as "liquidity" preference theory and the maturity premium was termed a "liquidity" premium. However, as we discussed in a previous chapter, the term "liquidity" is universally used to indicate the relative ease with which an asset can be sold. Also, the term "liquidity premium" now has a different meaning. To avoid confusion and to make this theory more consistent with modern views of liquidity, interest rates, and the term structure, we have adopted the more descriptive name of maturity premium.

by expected future interest rates according to expectations theory. But where do expected future interest rates come from? According to the Fisher hypothesis, expectations regarding future interest rates are based on expected future rates of inflation. Thus, expectations theory and the Fisher hypothesis mesh quite nicely.

Furthermore, a basic yield curve determined by inflationary expectations could also accommodate maturity preference theory. All we need to do is add a maturity premium to longer term interest rates. In this view, long-term, default-free interest rates have three components: a real rate, an anticipated future inflation rate, and a maturity premium.

MARKET SEGMENTATION THEORY

market segmentation theory
Debt markets are segmented by maturity, with the result that interest rates for various maturities are determined separately in each segment.

An alternative theory of the term structure of interest rates is the **market segmentation theory**, which asserts that debt markets are segmented according to the various maturities of debt instruments available for investment. By this theory, each maturity represents a separate, distinct market. For example, one group of lenders and borrowers may prefer to lend and borrow using securities with a maturity of 10 years, while another group may prefer to lend and borrow using securities with a maturity of 5 years. Segmentation theory simply states that interest rates corresponding to each maturity are determined separately by supply and demand conditions in each market segment.

Another theory of the term structure, known as the *preferred habitat theory,* is essentially a compromise between market segmentation and maturity preference. In the preferred habitat theory, as in the market segmentation theory, different investors have different preferred maturities. The difference is that they can be induced to move to less preferred maturities by a higher interest rate. In the maturity preference theory, the preferred habitat is always toward shorter maturities rather than longer maturities.

CHECK THIS

9.6a   According to the expectations theory, what does an upward-sloping term structure indicate?

9.6b   What basic assertion does maturity preference theory make about investor preferences? If this assertion is correct, how does it affect the term structure of interest rates?

9.6c   What is a maturity premium?

9.7 Determinants of Nominal Interest Rates: A Modern Perspective

Our understanding of the term structure of interest rates has increased significantly in the last few decades. Also, the evolution of fixed-income markets has shown us that, at least to some extent, traditional theories discussed in our previous section may be inadequate to explain the term structure. We discuss some problems with these theories next and then move on to a modern perspective.

PROBLEMS WITH TRADITIONAL THEORIES

To illustrate some problems with traditional theories, we could examine the behavior of the term structure in the last two decades. What we would find is that the term structure is almost always upward sloping. But contrary to the expectations hypothesis, interest rates have not always risen. Furthermore, as we saw with STRIPS term structure, it is often the case that the term structure turns down at very long maturities. According to the expectations hypothesis, market participants apparently expect rates to rise for 20 or so years and then decline. This seems to be stretching things a bit.

In terms of maturity preference, the world's biggest borrower, the U.S. government, borrows much more heavily short term than long term. Furthermore, many of the biggest buyers of fixed-income securities, such as pension funds, have a strong preference for *long* maturities. It is hard to square these facts with the behavioral assumptions underlying the maturity preference theory.

Finally, in terms of market segmentation, the U.S. government borrows at all maturities. Many institutional investors, such as mutual funds, are more than willing to move among maturities to obtain more favorable rates. At the same time, some bond trading operations do nothing other than buy and sell various maturity issues to exploit even very small perceived premiums. In short, in the modern fixed-income market, market segmentation does not seem to be a powerful force.

MODERN TERM STRUCTURE THEORY

Going back to Chapter 1, we saw that long-term government bonds had higher returns, on average, than short-term T-bills. They had substantially more risk as well. In other words, there appears to be a risk-return trade-off for default-free bonds as well, and long-term bonds appear to have a risk premium.

Notice that this risk premium doesn't result from the possibility of default since it exists on default-free U.S. government debt. Instead, it exists because longer-term bond prices are more volatile than shorter-term prices. As we discuss in detail in the next chapter, the reason is that, for a given change in interest rates, long-term bond prices change more than short-term bonds. Put differently, long-term bond prices are much more sensitive to interest rate changes than short-term bonds. This is called *interest rate risk,* and the risk premium on longer-term bonds is called the *interest rate risk premium.*

The interest rate risk premium carried by long-term bonds leads us to a modern reinterpretation of the maturity preference hypothesis. All other things the same, investors do prefer short-term bonds to long-term bonds. The reason is simply that short-term bonds are less risky. As a result, long-term bonds have to offer higher yields to compensate investors for the extra interest rate risk.

Putting it together, the modern view of the term structure suggests that nominal interest rates on default-free securities can be stated as follows:

$$NI = RI + IP + RP \qquad (9.12)$$

where: NI = Nominal interest rate
RI = Real interest rate
IP = Inflation premium
RP = Interest rate risk premium

In Equation 9.12, the real rate of interest is assumed to be the same for all securities, and, on average, the real interest rate is positive, as predicted by the Fisher hypothesis.

As we discussed above, the inflation premium (IP) reflects investor expectations of future price inflation. The inflation premium may be different for securities with different maturities because expected inflation may be different over different future horizons. For example, the expected average rate of inflation over the next two years may be different from the expected average rate of inflation over the next five years.

In addition to the real rate and the inflation premium, nominal rates reflect an interest rate risk premium (RP) which increases with the maturity of the security being considered. As a result, if interest rates are expected to remain constant through time, the term structure would have a positive slope. This is consistent with maturity preference theory. Indeed, for zero coupon bonds the interest rate risk premium and the maturity premium are the same thing.

FIGURE 9.8   The Term Structure of Interest Rates

(a) Upward-sloping term structure

(b) Downward-sloping term structure

The separate effects of the inflation premium and the interest rate risk premium are difficult to distinguish. For example, the yields for U.S. Treasury STRIPS in Figure 9.4 reveal a substantial yield premium for long-maturity STRIPS over short-term STRIPS. This yield premium for long-maturity STRIPS reflects the combined effects of the inflation premium and the risk premium. However, it is unclear how much of the total premium is caused by an inflation premium and how much is caused by a risk premium. Figure 9.8 shows how nominal interest rates can be separated into the real interest rate, the inflation premium, and the interest rate risk premium.

LIQUIDITY AND DEFAULT RISK

Thus far we have examined the components of interest rates on default-free, highly liquid securities such as Treasury STRIPS. We now expand our coverage to securities that are less liquid, not default-free, or both, to present a more detailed decomposition of nominal interest rates. When we are finished, what we will see is that nominal interest rates for individual securities can be decomposed into five basic components as follows:

$$NI = RI + IP + RP + LP + DP \qquad (9.13)$$

where: NI = Nominal interest rate
RI = Real interest rate
IP = Inflation premium
RP = Interest rate risk premium
LP = Liquidity premium
DP = Default premium

We have already discussed the first three components of the nominal interest rate. We now consider the two new ones on our list, the default and liquidity premiums.

The *liquidity premium* (LP) is a reflection of the fact that two otherwise identical securities may have very different degrees of liquidity. All else the same, the one with less liquidity would have to offer a higher yield as compensation.

The fifth, and final, component of a nominal interest rate is a *default premium* (DP). Investors demand a default premium to assume the risk of holding a security that might default on its promised payments. Naturally, the greater is the risk of default for a particular bond issue, the larger is the default premium required by investors. The topic of default risk is discussed in detail for corporate bonds and municipal bonds in later chapters.

In addition to the five basic components we have discussed, there is one more important determinant of nominal interest rates, namely, tax status. As we briefly discussed in an earlier chapter, municipal bonds are not taxed at the federal level, but all other bonds are (including Treasury bonds). All else the same, taxable bonds must pay higher rates than nontaxable bonds. As a result, the rate on a high-quality municipal issue will normally be less than the rate on a Treasury issue, even though the Treasury is more liquid and has no default risk.

9.8 Summary and Conclusions

The time value of money is arguably the most important principle of finance. Interest rates are a convenient way to measure and state the time value of money. Furthermore, understanding interest rates is essential for understanding money market and fixed-income securities. In this chapter, we covered a number of topics relating to interest rates, including:

1. Important short-term money market rates include the prime rate, the Federal funds rate, and the Federal Reserve's discount rate. The prime rate is a bellwether of bank lending to business, while the Federal funds rate and the Federal Reserve's discount rate are indicators of the availability of money and credit within the banking system.

2. A Treasury yield curve graphs the relationship between yields on U.S. Treasury securities and their maturities. The Treasury yield curve is fundamental to bond market analysis because it represents the interest rates that financial markets are charging to the world's largest debtor with the world's highest credit rating—the U.S. government.

3. The term structure of interest rates is the fundamental relationship between time to maturity and interest rates for default-free, pure discount instruments such as U.S. Treasury STRIPS.

4. A number of different theories—including the expectations theory, the maturity preference theory, and the market segmentation theory—have been proposed to

explain why the term structure of interest rates and yield curves may be upward sloping at one point in time and then downward sloping or flat at another time. In a modern view of the term structure, yields on default-free, pure discount bonds are determined by the real rate of interest, expectations of future inflation, and an interest rate risk premium.

5. Interest rates have five basic components: the real rate, an inflation premium, an interest rate risk premium, a liquidity premium, and a default premium. U.S. Treasury securities are free of default risk and are very liquid, so the last two components are absent from such instruments. For other issues, however, these components are very important. Tax status is also an important determinant.

GET REAL

This chapter covered the essentials of interest rates. How should you, as an investor or investment manager, put this information to work?

The best thing to do is to buy a variety of instruments discussed in this chapter. STRIPS, in particular, are an important investment vehicle for both institutional and individual investors. To gain some practical experience with the risks and rewards from STRIPS investing, you should invest equal dollar amounts in several different STRIPS with different maturities. Pick short-term (a few years), intermediate-term (10 or so years), and long-term (25 years or longer), for example. Once you make these investments, monitor their yields and prices.

A good place to start with a study of interest rates is to visit some federal government Web sites. Try the U.S. Treasury (www.ustreas.gov), the Bureau of Public Debt (www.publicdebt.treas.gov), the Federal Reserve Board of Governors (www.federalreserve.gov), and the New York (www.ny.frb.org) and St. Louis (www.stls.frb.org) Federal Reserve banks. For the latest money market rates see Money Rates (www.money-rates.com), and for bank lending rates check out Banx (www.banx.com) or Bankrate (www.bankrate.com). Price and yield data for U.S. Treasury securities can be found at GovPX (www.govpx.com).

Key Terms

banker's acceptance 287
bank discount basis 288
basis point 288
bellwether rate 285
call money rate 286
certificate of deposit (CD) 286
commercial paper 286
discount rate 286
Eurodollars 287
expectations theory 306
Federal funds rate 286
Fisher hypothesis 302

forward rate 306
London Interbank Offered Rate (LIBOR) 287
market segmentation theory 308
maturity preference theory 307
nominal interest rates 302
prime rate 285
pure discount security 288
real interest rates 302
term structure of interest rates 299
Treasury yield curve 295
U.S. Treasury bill (T-bill) 287
U.S. Treasury STRIPS 299

Chapter Review Problems and Self-Test

1. **Money Market Prices** The rate on a particular money market instrument, quoted on a discount basis, is 5 percent. The instrument has a face value of $100,000 and will mature in 40 days. What is its price?

2. **Bond Equivalent Yields** Suppose a T-bill has 75 days to maturity and an asked discount of 4 percent. What is the bond equivalent yield?

Answers to Self-Test Problems

1. Using the bank discount basis formula, we have:

$$\text{Current price} = \text{Face value} \times \left(1 - \frac{\text{Days to maturity}}{360} \times \text{Discount yield}\right)$$

$$\$99,444.44 = \$100,000 \times \left(1 - \frac{40}{360} \times .05\right)$$

You would pay $99,444.44.

2. Using the bond equivalent yield conversion formula, we have:

$$4.09\% = \frac{365 \times .04}{360 - 75 \times .04}$$

The bond equivalent yield is thus 4.09 percent.

Test Your Investment Quotient

1. **Interest Rates** Which of the following interest rates is a bellwether (leading indicator) rate of bank lending to business?
   a. Unsecured business loan rate.
   b. Prime rate.
   c. Commercial paper rate.
   d. Banker's acceptance rate.

2. **Interest Rates** Among the following interest rates, which is normally the highest rate?
   a. Commercial paper rate.
   b. U.S. Treasury bill rate.
   c. Federal funds rate.
   d. Federal Reserve discount rate.

3. **T-Bill Yields** A U.S. Treasury bill with 180 days to maturity has a discount yield of 5 percent and a face value of $100,000. What is its current price?
   a. $97,500
   b. $95,000
   c. $92,500
   d. $90,000

4. **T-Bill Yields** A U.S. Treasury bill with 90 days to maturity has a price of $95,000. What is its discount yield?
   a. 5 percent
   b. 10 percent
   c. 15 percent
   d. 20 percent

5. **T-Bill Yields** A 30-day U.S. Treasury bill is selling at a 12 percent yield on a discount basis. Which of the following is the approximate bond equivalent yield?
   a. 6.0 percent
   b. 11.7 percent

CFA® PROBLEMS

c. 12.0 percent

d. 12.3 percent

6. **Effective Annual Rates**   A credit card company states an annual percentage rate (APR) of 12 percent, which is actually a rate of 1 percent per month. What is the EAR?

a. 12 percent

b. 12.68 percent

c. 13.08 percent

d. 13.76 percent

7. **STRIPS Yields**   A U.S. Treasury STRIPS maturing in 10 years has a current price of $502.57 for $1,000 of face value. What is the yield to maturity of this STRIPS?

a. 7.0 percent

b. 7.12 percent

c. 8.0 percent

d. 8.12 percent

8. **STRIPS Yields**   A U.S. Treasury STRIPS with $1,000 face value maturing in five years has a yield to maturity of 7 percent. What is the current price of this STRIPS?

a. $930

b. $712.99

c. $708.92

d. $650

9. **Bond Yields**   An analyst finds that the semiannual interest rate that equates the present value of the bond's cash flow to its current market price is 3.85 percent. Consider the following possible alternatives:

I. The bond equivalent yield on this security is 7.70 percent.

II. The effective annual yield on the bond is 7.85 percent.

III. The bond's yield-to-maturity is 7.70 percent.

IV. The bond's horizon return is 8.35 percent.

Which of these alternatives are true?

a. I and II only

b. II, III, and IV only

c. I, II, and III only

d. III only

10. **Forward Rates**   An analyst gathered the following spot rates:

Time (years)	Annual Spot Rate
1	15.0%
2	12.5
3	10.0
4	7.5

The one-year forward rate two years from now is closest to

a. −4.91 percent

b. 5.17 percent

c. 10.05 percent

d. 7.5 percent

11. **Zeroes**   If an investor's required return is 12 percent, the value of a 10-year maturity zero coupon bond with a maturity value of $1,000 is closest to:

a. $312

b. $688

c. $1,000

d. $1,312

12. **Fisher Hypothesis**   The Fisher hypothesis essentially asserts which of the following?

   a. Nominal interest rates follow inflation.
   b. Real interest rates follow inflation.
   c. Inflation follows real interest rates.
   d. Inflation follows nominal interest rates.

13. **Term Structure Theory**   Which one of the following statements about the term structure of interest rates is true?

   a. The expectations hypothesis indicates a flat yield curve if anticipated future short-term rates exceed current short-term rates.
   b. The expectations hypothesis contends that the long-term rate is equal to the anticipated short-term rate.
   c. The liquidity premium theory indicates that, all else being equal, longer maturities will have lower yields.
   d. The market segmentation theory contends that borrowers and lenders prefer particular segments of the yield curve.

14. **Term Structure Theory**   Which one of the following is not an explanation of the relationship between a bond's interest rate and its term to maturity?

   a. Default (credit) risk hypothesis
   b. Expectations hypothesis
   c. Liquidity preference hypothesis
   d. Segmentation hypothesis

15. **Term Structure Theory**   Which theory explains the shape of the yield curve by considering the relative demands for various maturities?

   a. Relative strength theory
   b. Segmentation theory
   c. Unbiased expectations theory
   d. Liquidity premium theory

16. **Term Structure Theory**   The concepts of spot and forward rates are most closely associated with which one of the following explanations of the term structure of interest rates?

   a. Expectations hypothesis
   b. Liquidity premium theory
   c. Preferred habitat hypothesis
   d. Segmented market theory

17. **Forward Rates**   The current one-year interest rate is 6 percent and the current two-year interest rate is 7 percent. What is the implied forward rate for next year's one-year rate?

   a. 9 percent
   b. 8 percent
   c. 7 percent
   d. 6 percent

18. **Forward Rates**   The current one-year interest rate is 7 percent and the current two-year interest rate is 6 percent. What is the implied forward rate for next year's one-year rate?

   a. 7 percent
   b. 6 percent
   c. 5 percent
   d. 4 percent

19. **Forward Rates**   The 6-month Treasury bill spot rate is 4 percent, and the 1-year Treasury bill spot rate is 5 percent. The implied 6-month forward rate 6 months from now is which of the following?

   a. 3.0 percent
   b. 4.5 percent
   c. 5.5 percent
   d. 5.9 percent

www.mhhe.com/jm4e

20. Forward Rates   An analyst gathers the following information:

Years to Maturity	Spot Rate
1	5.00%
2	6.00
3	6.50

Based on the data above, the one-year implied forward rate two years from now is *closest* to:

  a. 6.25 percent
  b. 7.01 percent
  c. 7.26 percent
  d. 7.51 percent

Concept Questions

1. **Interest Rate History**   Based on the history of interest rates, what is the range of short-term rates that has occurred in the United States? The range of long-term rates? What is a typical value for each?

2. **Discount Securities**   What are pure discount securities? Give two examples.

3. **Fed Funds versus the Discount Rate**   Compare and contrast the Fed funds rate and the discount rate. Which do you think is more volatile? Which market do you think is more active? Why?

4. **Commercial Paper**   Compare and contrast commercial paper and Treasury bills. Which would typically offer a higher interest rate? Why?

5. **LIBOR**   What is LIBOR? Why is it important?

6. **Bank Discount Rates**   Why do you suppose rates on some money market instruments are quoted on a bank discount basis? (*Hint:* Why use a 360-day year?)

7. **STRIPS**   With regard to STRIPS, what do "ci," "np," and "bp" represent?

8. **Nominal and Real Rates**   When we observe interest rates in the financial press, do we see nominal or real rates? Which are more relevant to investors?

9. **Munis versus Treasuries**   Which would have a higher yield, a municipal bond or a Treasury bond of the same maturity?

10. **Term Structure**   Discuss how each of the following theories for the term structure of interest rates could account for a downward-sloping term structure of interest rates:

  a. Pure expectations
  b. Liquidity preference
  c. Market segmentation

Questions and Problems

Core Questions

1. **STRIPS**   What is the price of a Treasury STRIPS with a face value of $100 that matures in seven years and has a yield to maturity of 5.6 percent?

2. **STRIPS**   A Treasury STRIPS matures in 7.5 years and has a yield to maturity of 6.9 percent. If the par value is $100,000, what is the price of the STRIPS? What is the quoted price?

3. **STRIPS**   A Treasury STRIPS is quoted at 78:24 and has six years until maturity. What is the yield to maturity?

4. **STRIPS**   What is the yield to maturity on a Treasury STRIPS with 10 years to maturity and a quoted price of 54:27?

5. **Fisher Effect**   A stock had a return of 12.2 percent last year. If the inflation rate was 4.3 percent, what was the approximate real return?

6. **Fisher Effect**   Your investments increased in value by 11.4 percent last year but your purchasing power increased by only 5.8 percent. What was the inflation rate?

7. **Treasury Bill Prices**   What is the price of a U.S. Treasury bill with 84 days to maturity quoted at a discount yield of 4.70 percent? Assume a $1 million face value.

8. **Treasury Bill Prices**   In the previous problem, what is the bond-equivalent yield?

9. **Treasury Bill Prices**   How much would you pay for a U.S. Treasury bill with 27 days to maturity quoted at a discount yield of 3.85 percent? Assume a $1 million face value.

10. **Treasury Bill Prices**   In the previous problem, what is the bond-equivalent yield?

Intermediate
Questions

11. **Treasury Bills**   A Treasury bill with 35 days to maturity is quoted at 99.43. What is the bank discount yield, the bond equivalent yield, and the effective annual return?

12. **Treasury Bills**   A Treasury bill purchased in December 2007 has 49 days until maturity and a bank discount yield of 4.68 percent. What is the price of the bill as a percentage of face value? What is the bond equivalent yield?

13. **Money Market Prices**   The treasurer of a large corporation wants to invest $20 million in excess short-term cash in a particular money market investment. The prospectus quotes the instrument at a true yield of 6.70 percent; that is, the EAR for this investment is 6.70 percent. However, the treasurer wants to know the money market yield on this instrument to make it comparable to the T-bills and CDs she has already bought. If the term of the instrument is 120 days, what are the bond-equivalent and discount yields on this investment?

Use the following information to answer the next six questions:
U.S. Treasury STRIPS, close of business February 15, 2006:

Maturity	Price	Maturity	Price
Feb07	95:21	Feb10	81:10
Feb08	90:27	Feb11	76:05
Feb09	85:24	Feb12	71:18

14. **Zero Coupon Bonds**   Calculate the quoted yield for each of the STRIPS given in the table above. Does the market expect interest rates to go up or down in the future?

15. **Zero Coupon Bonds**   What is the yield of the two-year STRIPS expressed as an EAR?

16. **Forward Interest Rates**   According to the pure expectations theory of interest rates, how much do you expect to pay for a one-year STRIPS on February 15, 2007? What is the corresponding implied forward rate? How does your answer compare to the current yield on a one-year STRIPS? What does this tell you about the relationship between implied forward rates, the shape of the zero coupon yield curve, and market expectations about future spot interest rates?

17. **Forward Interest Rates**   According to the pure expectations theory of interest rates, how much do you expect to pay for a five-year STRIPS on February 15, 2007? How much do you expect to pay for a two-year STRIPS on February 15, 2009?

18. **Forward Interest Rates**   This problem is a little harder. Suppose the term structure is set according to pure expectations and the maturity preference theory. To be specific, investors require no compensation for holding investments with a maturity of one year, but they demand a premium of .30 percent for holding investments with a maturity of two years. Given this information, how much would you pay for a one-year STRIPS on February 15, 2007? What is the corresponding implied forward rate? Compare your answer to the solutions you found in Problem 16. What does this tell you about the effect of a maturity premium on implied forward rates?

19. **Bond Price Changes**   Suppose the (quoted) yield on each of the six STRIPS increases by .25 percent. Calculate the percentage change in price for the one-year, three-year, and six-year STRIPS. Which one has the largest price change? Now suppose that the quoted price on each STRIPS decreases by 16/32. Calculate the percentage change in (quoted) yield for the one-year, three-year, and six-year STRIPS. Which one has the largest yield change? What do your answers tell you about the relationship between prices, yields, and maturity for discount bonds?

20. **Inflation and Returns**   You observe that the current interest rate on short-term U.S. Treasury bills is 4.24 percent. You also read in the newspaper that the GDP deflator, which is a common

www.mhhe.com/jm4e

macroeconomic indicator used by market analysts to gauge the inflation rate, currently implies that inflation is 3.5 percent. Given this information, what is the approximate real rate of interest on short-term Treasury bills? Is it likely that your answer would change if you used some alternative measure for the inflation rate, such as the CPI? What does this tell you about the observability and accuracy of real interest rates compared to nominal interest rates?

21. **Forward Interest Rates**   Consider the following spot interest rates for maturities of one, two, three, and four years.

$$r_1 = 4.9\% \qquad r_2 = 5.7\% \quad r_3 = 6.4\% \qquad r_4 = 7.1\%$$

What are the following forward rates, where $f_{1,k}$ refers to a forward rate for the period beginning in one year and extending for k years?

$$f_{1,1} = \qquad ; \quad f_{1,2} = \qquad ; \quad f_{1,3} =$$

Hint: Use the equation $(1 + r_1)(1 + f_{1,k})^k = (1 + r_{k+1})^{k+1}$ to solve for $f_{1,k}$.

22. **Forward Interest Rates**   Based on the spot interest rates in the previous question, what are the following forward rates, where $f_{k,1}$ refers to a forward rate beginning in k years and extending for 1 year?

$$f_{2,1} = \qquad ; \quad f_{3,1} =$$

Hint: Use the equation $(1 + r_k)^k(1 + f_{k,1}) = (1 + r_{k+1})^{k+1}$ to solve for $f_{k,1}$.

23. **Expected Inflation Rates**   Based on the spot rates in Question 21, and assuming a constant real interest rate of 2 percent, what are the expected inflation rates for the next four years?

Hint: Use the Fisher hypothesis and the unbiased expectations theory.

24. **Treasury Bills**   A Treasury bill that settles on July 17, 2006, pays $100,000 on August 16, 2006. Assuming a discount rate of 4.98 percent, what is the price and bond equivalent yield?

25. **Effective Annual Rate**   You have a car loan with a nominal rate of 7.2 percent. With interest charged monthly, what is the effective annual rate (EAR) on this loan?

What's on the Web

1. **Yield Curve**   What is the shape of the Treasury yield curve today? Go to www.bloomberg.com and find out. Is the yield curve upward sloping or downward sloping? According to the expectations theory, are interest rates in the future expected to be higher or lower than they are today?

2. **STRIPS**   Go to www.publicdebt.treas.gov and follow the "Treasury Securities at a Glance" link to find information on Treasury STRIPS. Answer the following questions: Which Treasury securities are eligible to be stripped? What are minimum par amounts for stripping? How do I buy STRIPS? Why do investors hold STRIPS?

3. **STRIPS**   Go to www.bondsonline.com and find the quotes for STRIPS that are offered for sale on the site. How many STRIPS are offered for sale? What is the lowest and highest yield to maturity? Are there STRIPS with the same maturity that have different prices? How could this happen?

CHAPTER 10

Bond Prices and Yields

"More money has been lost reaching for yield than at the point of a gun."

–Raymond Devoe

Interest rates go up and bond prices go down. But which bonds go down the most and which go down the least? Interest rates go down and bond prices go up. But which bonds go up the most and which go up the least? For bond portfolio managers, these are important questions about interest rate risk. For anyone managing a bond portfolio, an understanding of interest rate risk rests on an understanding of the relationship between bond prices and yields. ■

In the preceding chapter on interest rates, we introduced the subject of bond yields. As we promised there, we now return to this subject and discuss bond prices and yields in some detail. We first describe how bond yields are determined and how they are interpreted. We then go on to examine what happens to bond prices as yields change. Finally, once we have a good understanding of the relation between bond prices and yields, we examine some of the fundamental tools of bond risk analysis used by fixed-income portfolio managers.

10.1 Bond Basics

A bond essentially is a security that offers the investor a series of fixed interest payments during its life, along with a fixed payment of principal when it matures. So long as the bond issuer does not default, the schedule of payments does not change. When originally issued, bonds normally have maturities ranging from 2 years to 30 years, but bonds with maturities of 50 or 100 years also exist. Bonds issued with maturities of less than 10 years are usually called notes. A very small number of bond issues have no stated maturity, and these are referred to as perpetuities or consols.

STRAIGHT BONDS

The most common type of bond is the so-called straight bond. By definition, a straight bond is an IOU that obligates the issuer to pay the bondholder a fixed sum of money at the bond's maturity along with constant, periodic interest payments during the life of the bond. The fixed sum paid at maturity is referred to as bond principal, par value, stated value, or face value. The periodic interest payments are called coupons. Perhaps the best example of straight bonds are U.S. Treasury bonds issued by the federal government to finance the national debt. However, business corporations and municipal governments also routinely issue debt in the form of straight bonds.

In addition to a straight bond component, many bonds have additional special features. These features are sometimes designed to enhance a bond's appeal to investors. For example, convertible bonds have a conversion feature that grants bondholders the right to convert their bonds into shares of common stock of the issuing corporation. As another example, "putable" bonds have a put feature that grants bondholders the right to sell their bonds back to the issuer at a special put price.

These and other special features are attached to many bond issues, but we defer discussion of special bond features until later chapters. For now, it is only important to know that when a bond is issued with one or more special features, strictly speaking, it is no longer a straight bond. However, bonds with attached special features will normally have a straight bond component, namely, the periodic coupon payments and fixed principal payment at maturity. For this reason, straight bonds are important as the basic unit of bond analysis.

The prototypical example of a straight bond pays a series of constant semiannual coupons, along with a face value of $1,000 payable at maturity. This example is used in this chapter because it is common and realistic. For example, most corporate bonds are sold with a face value of $1,000 per bond, and most bonds (in the United States at least) pay constant semiannual coupons.

Check out the bonds section at www.bondmarkets.com

COUPON RATE AND CURRENT YIELD

A familiarity with bond yield measures is important for understanding the financial characteristics of bonds. As we briefly discussed in Chapter 3, two basic yield measures for a bond are its coupon rate and current yield.

coupon rate
A bond's annual coupon divided by its par value. Also called *coupon yield* or *nominal yield*.

A bond's **coupon rate** is defined as its annual coupon amount divided by its par value, or, in other words, its annual coupon expressed as a percentage of face value:

$$\text{Coupon rate} = \frac{\text{Annual coupon}}{\text{Par value}} \tag{10.1}$$

For example, suppose a $1,000 par value bond pays semiannual coupons of $40. The annual coupon is then $80, and, stated as a percentage of par value, the bond's coupon rate is $80/$1,000 = 8\%. A coupon rate is often referred to as the *coupon yield* or the *nominal yield*. Notice that the word "nominal" here has nothing to do with inflation.

current yield

A bond's annual coupon divided by its market price.

A bond's **current yield** is its annual coupon payment divided by its current market price:

$$\text{Current yield} = \frac{\text{Annual coupon}}{\text{Bond price}} \qquad (10.2)$$

For example, suppose a $1,000 par value bond paying an $80 annual coupon has a price of $1,032.25. The current yield is $80/$1,032.25 = 7.75%. Similarly, a price of $969.75 implies a current yield of $80/$969.75 = 8.25%. Notice that whenever there is a change in the bond's price, the coupon rate remains constant. However, a bond's current yield is inversely related to its price, and it changes whenever the bond's price changes.

CHECK THIS

10.1a What is a straight bond?

10.1b What is a bond's coupon rate? Its current yield?

10.2 Straight Bond Prices and Yield to Maturity

yield to maturity (YTM)

The discount rate that equates a bond's price with the present value of its future cash flows. Also called *promised yield* or just *yield*.

The single most important yield measure for a bond is its **yield to maturity**, commonly abbreviated as **YTM**. By definition, a bond's yield to maturity is the discount rate that equates the bond's price with the computed present value of its future cash flows. A bond's yield to maturity is sometimes called its *promised yield*, but, more commonly, the yield to maturity of a bond is simply referred to as its *yield*. In general, if the term "yield" is being used with no qualification, it means yield to maturity.

STRAIGHT BOND PRICES

For straight bonds, the following standard formula is used to calculate a bond's price given its yield:

$$\text{Bond price} = \frac{C/2}{YTM/2}\left[1 - \frac{1}{(1 + YTM/2)^{2M}}\right] + \frac{FV}{(1 + YTM/2)^{2M}}$$

This formula can be simplified just a bit as follows:

$$= \frac{C}{YTM}\left[1 - \frac{1}{(1 + YTM/2)^{2M}}\right] + \frac{FV}{(1 + YTM/2)^{2M}} \qquad (10.3)$$

where: C = Annual coupon, the sum of two semiannual coupons
FV = Face value
M = Maturity in years
YTM = Yield to maturity

In this formula, the coupon used is the annual coupon, which is the sum of the two semiannual coupons. As discussed in our previous chapter for U.S. Treasury STRIPS, the yield on a bond is an annual percentage rate (APR), calculated as twice the true semiannual yield. As a result, the yield on a bond somewhat understates its effective annual rate (EAR).

The straight bond pricing formula has two separate components. The first component is the present value of all the coupon payments. Since the coupons are fixed and paid on a regular basis, you may recognize that they form an ordinary annuity, and the first piece of the bond pricing formula is a standard calculation for the present value of an annuity. The other component represents the present value of the principal payment at maturity, and it is a standard calculation for the present value of a single lump sum.

Calculating bond prices is mostly "plug and chug" with a calculator. In fact, a good financial calculator or spreadsheet should have this formula built into it. In any case, we will work through a few examples the long way just to illustrate the calculations.

Suppose a bond has a $1,000 face value, 20 years to maturity, an 8 percent coupon rate, and a yield of 9 percent. What's the price? Using the straight bond pricing formula, the price of this bond is calculated as follows:

1. Present value of semiannual coupons:

$$\frac{\$80}{.09}\left[1 - \frac{1}{(1.045)^{40}}\right] = \$736.06337$$

2. Present value of $1,000 principal:

$$\frac{\$1,000}{(1.045)^{40}} = \$171.92871$$

The price of the bond is the sum of the present values of coupons and principal:

$$\text{Bond price} = \$736.06 + \$171.93 = \$907.99$$

So, this bond sells for $907.99.

EXAMPLE 10.1 **Calculating Straight Bond Prices**

Suppose a bond has 20 years to maturity and a coupon rate of 8 percent. The bond's yield to maturity is 7 percent. What's the price?

In this case, the coupon rate is 8 percent and the face value is $1,000, so the annual coupon is $80. The bond's price is calculated as follows:

1. Present value of semiannual coupons:

$$\frac{\$80}{.07}\left[1 - \frac{1}{(1.035)^{40}}\right] = \$854.20289$$

2. Present value of $1,000 principal:

$$\frac{\$1,000}{(1.035)^{40}} = \$252.57247$$

The bond's price is the sum of coupon and principal present values:

$$\text{Bond price} = \$854.20 + \$252.57 = \$1,106.77$$

This bond sells for $1,106.77.

Straight bond prices may be calculated using a built-in spreadsheet function. An example of how to use an Excel™ spreadsheet to calculate a bond price is shown in the nearby *Spreadsheet Analysis* box.

	A	B	C	D	E	F	G	H
1								
2			Calculating the Price of a Coupon Bond					
3								
4	A Treasury bond traded on March 30, 2006 matures in 20 years on March 30, 2026.							
5	Assuming an 8 percent coupon rate and a 7 percent yield to maturity, what is the							
6	price of this bond?							
7	Hint: Use the Excel function PRICE.							
8								
9		$110.6775	= PRICE("3/30/2006","3/30/2026",0.08,0.07,100,2,3)					
10								
11	For a bond with $1,000 face value, multiply the price by 10 to get $1,106.78.							
12								
13	This function uses the following arguments:							
14								
15		=PRICE("Now","Maturity", Coupon,Yield,100,2,3)						
16								
17	The 100 indicates redemption value as a percent of face value.							
18	The 2 indicates semi-annual coupons.							
19	The 3 specifies an actual day count with 365 days per year.							
20								
21								

PREMIUM AND DISCOUNT BONDS

Bonds are commonly distinguished according to whether they are selling at par value or at a discount or premium relative to par value. These three relative price descriptions— premium, discount, and par bonds—are defined as follows:

1. **Premium bonds**: Bonds with a price greater than par value are said to be selling at a premium. The yield to maturity of a premium bond is less than its coupon rate.

2. **Discount bonds**: Bonds with a price less than par value are said to be selling at a discount. The yield to maturity of a discount bond is greater than its coupon rate.

3. **Par bonds**: Bonds with a price equal to par value are said to be selling at par. The yield to maturity of a par bond is equal to its coupon rate.

The important thing to notice is that whether a bond sells at a premium or discount depends on the relation between its coupon rate and its yield. If the coupon rate exceeds the yield, the bond will sell at a premium. If the coupon is less than the yield, the bond will sell at a discount.

EXAMPLE 10.2 | **Premium and Discount Bonds**

Consider two bonds, both with eight years to maturity and a 7 percent coupon. One bond has a yield to maturity of 5 percent while the other has a yield to maturity of 9 percent. Which of these bonds is selling at a premium and which is selling at a discount? Verify your answer by calculating each bond's price.

(continued)

For the bond with a 9 percent yield to maturity, the coupon rate of 7 percent is less than the yield, indicating a discount bond. The bond's price is calculated as follows:

$$\frac{\$70}{.09}\left[1 - \frac{1}{(1.045)^{16}}\right] + \frac{\$1,000}{(1.045)^{16}} = \$887.66$$

For the bond with a 5 percent yield to maturity, the coupon rate of 7 percent is greater than the yield, indicating a premium bond. The bond's price is calculated as follows:

$$\frac{\$70}{.05}\left[1 - \frac{1}{(1.025)^{16}}\right] + \frac{\$1,000}{(1.025)^{16}} = \$1,130.55$$

The relationship between bond prices and bond maturities for premium and discount bonds is graphically illustrated in Figure 10.1 for bonds with an 8 percent coupon rate. The vertical axis measures bond prices, and the horizontal axis measures bond maturities.

Figure 10.1 also describes the paths of premium and discount bond prices as their maturities shorten with the passage of time, assuming no changes in yield to maturity. As shown, the time paths of premium and discount bond prices follow smooth curves. Over time, the price of a premium bond declines and the price of a discount bond rises. At maturity, the price of each bond converges to its par value.

Figure 10.1 illustrates the general result that, for discount bonds, holding the coupon rate and yield to maturity constant, the longer the term to maturity of the bond the greater is the discount from par value. For premium bonds, holding the coupon rate and yield to maturity constant, the longer the term to maturity of the bond the greater is the premium over par value.

FIGURE 10.1 Premium, Par, and Discount Bond Prices

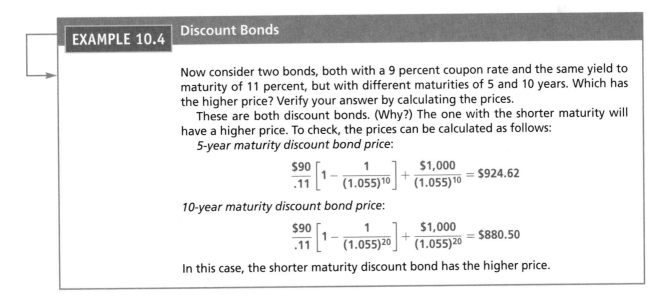

EXAMPLE 10.3 | **Premium Bonds**

Consider two bonds, both with a 9 percent coupon rate and the same yield to maturity of 7 percent, but with different maturities of 5 and 10 years. Which has the higher price? Verify your answer by calculating the prices.

First, since both bonds have a 9 percent coupon and a 7 percent yield, both bonds sell at a premium. Based on what we know, the one with the longer maturity will have a higher price. We can check these conclusions by calculating the prices as follows:

5-year maturity premium bond price:

$$\frac{\$90}{.07}\left[1 - \frac{1}{(1.035)^{10}}\right] + \frac{\$1,000}{(1.035)^{10}} = \$1,083.17$$

10-year maturity premium bond price:

$$\frac{\$90}{.07}\left[1 - \frac{1}{(1.035)^{20}}\right] + \frac{\$1,000}{(1.035)^{20}} = \$1,142.12$$

Notice that the longer maturity premium bond has a higher price, as we predicted.

EXAMPLE 10.4 | **Discount Bonds**

Now consider two bonds, both with a 9 percent coupon rate and the same yield to maturity of 11 percent, but with different maturities of 5 and 10 years. Which has the higher price? Verify your answer by calculating the prices.

These are both discount bonds. (Why?) The one with the shorter maturity will have a higher price. To check, the prices can be calculated as follows:

5-year maturity discount bond price:

$$\frac{\$90}{.11}\left[1 - \frac{1}{(1.055)^{10}}\right] + \frac{\$1,000}{(1.055)^{10}} = \$924.62$$

10-year maturity discount bond price:

$$\frac{\$90}{.11}\left[1 - \frac{1}{(1.055)^{20}}\right] + \frac{\$1,000}{(1.055)^{20}} = \$880.50$$

In this case, the shorter maturity discount bond has the higher price.

RELATIONSHIPS AMONG YIELD MEASURES

We have discussed three different bond rates or yields in this chapter—the coupon rate, the current yield, and the yield to maturity. We've seen the relationship between coupon rates and yields for discount and premium bonds. We can extend this to include current yields by simply noting that the current yield is always between the coupon rate and the yield to maturity (unless the bond is selling at par, in which case all three are equal).

Putting together our observations about yield measures, we have the following:

Premium bonds: Coupon rate > Current yield > Yield to maturity

Discount bonds: Coupon rate < Current yield < Yield to maturity

Par value bonds: Coupon rate = Current yield = Yield to maturity

Thus, when a premium bond and a discount bond both have the same yield to maturity, the premium bond has a higher current yield than the discount bond. However, as shown in Figure 10.1, the advantage of a high current yield for a premium bond is offset by the fact that the price of a premium bond must ultimately fall to its face value when the bond matures. Similarly, the disadvantage of a low current yield for a discount bond is offset by the fact that the price of a discount bond must ultimately rise to its face value at maturity. For these reasons, current yield is not a reliable guide to what an actual yield will be.

If you wish to get current price and yield information for Treasury note and bond issues, try the Internet. The nearby *Work the Web* box displays a typical search query and the search results from a popular Web site.

A NOTE ON BOND PRICE QUOTES

clean price
The price of a bond net of accrued interest; this is the price that is typically quoted.

dirty price
The price of a bond including accrued interest, also known as the *full* or *invoice price*. This is the price the buyer actually pays.

If you buy a bond between coupon payment dates, the price you pay will usually be more than the price you are quoted. The reason is that standard convention in the bond market is to quote prices net of "accrued interest," meaning that accrued interest is deducted to arrive at the quoted price. This quoted price is called the **clean price**. The price you actually pay, however, includes the accrued interest. This price is the **dirty price**, also known as the "full" or "invoice" price.

An example is the easiest way to understand these issues. Suppose you buy a bond with a 12 percent annual coupon, payable semiannually. You actually pay $1,080 for this bond, so $1,080 is the dirty, or invoice, price. Further, on the day you buy it, the next coupon is due in four months, so you are between coupon dates. Notice that the next coupon will be $60.

The accrued interest on a bond is calculated by taking the fraction of the coupon period that has passed, in this case two months out of six, and multiplying this fraction by the next coupon, $60. So, the accrued interest in this example is 2/6 × $60 = $20. The bond's quoted price (i.e., its clean price) would be $1,080 − $20 = $1,060.[1]

Keep in mind that clean prices and accrued interest are purely a quoting convention. The price that matters to you is the invoice price, because that is what you will actually pay for the bond. The only thing that's important about accrued interest on a bond is that it may impact the taxes you owe on the first coupon you receive.

CHECK THIS

10.2a A straight bond's price has two components. What are they?

10.2b What do you call a bond that sells for more than its face value?

10.2c What is the relationship between a bond's price and its term to maturity when the bond's coupon rate is equal to its yield to maturity?

10.2d Does current yield more strongly overstate yield to maturity for long-maturity or short-maturity premium bonds?

[1]The way accrued interest is calculated actually depends on the type of bond being quoted, for example, Treasury or corporate. The difference has to do with exactly how the fractional coupon period is calculated. In our example just above, we implicitly treated the months as having exactly the same length (i.e., 30 days each, 360 days in a year), which is consistent with the way corporate bonds are quoted. In contrast, for Treasury bonds, actual day counts are used. If you look back at our *Spreadsheet Analysis* exhibit, you'll see that we had to specify this treatment to value our Treasury bond.

Current information on Treasury bond prices and yields is available at the search tool at Bondpage.com (www.bondpage.com). An example query definition and the search results is shown below.

Treasury *Query Definition*

Express Search

Issue: _____

CUSIP List: _____

Ranges

	Minimum	Maximum
Maturity	2011	2012
Coupon		
Yield		
Price		
Call Prot		

Coupon Payments

Use Ctrl-Click to select multiple months.

- - - - - - - -
All Months
January
February
March

☑ **Exclude at maturity**

Constraints

	Yes	No
Callable	☐	☐
Active	☐	☐

Display Properties

Sort by: [Maturity ▼]

Rows per page: [100 ▼]

Updated Since: (Eastern) _____

[Find Bonds] [Clear Form]

Treasury *Query Result*

For more details, click on the Issue Description   1 - 11 of 11

Qty	Min	Issue	Coupon	Maturity Pmt Months	Price	YTM
500	20	T-NOTE Non Callable	3.500	01-15-2011 Jan,Jul	108.250	1.834
4968	20	T-NOTE Non Callable	5.000	02-15-2011 Feb,Aug	102.409	4.483
5000	20	T-BOND Callable	13.875	05-15-2011C May,Nov	105.360	12.502
5000	20	T-NOTE Non Callable	5.000	08-15-2011 Feb,Aug	102.534	4.498
5000	20	T-BOND Callable	14.000	11-15-2011C May,Nov	109.965	11.655
500	20	T-NOTE Non Callable	3.375	01-15-2012 Jan,Jul	108.704	1.885
5000	20	T-NOTE Non Callable	4.875	02-15-2012 Feb,Aug	101.869	4.530
500	20	T-NOTE Non Callable	3.000	07-15-2012 Jan,Jul	106.750	1.924
5000	20	T-NOTE Non Callable	4.375	08-15-2012 Feb,Aug	99.039	4.540
5000	20	T-BOND Callable	10.375	11-15-2012C May,Nov	111.795	8.142
5000	20	T-NOTE Non Callable	4.000	11-15-2012 May,Nov	96.772	4.540

Export All To Excel

C=Callable   LY=Lowest Yield   Rating=Moody's/S&P   MBR=Min Balance Remaining

Notice that three of the bonds have a much higher yield to maturity than the rest. The reason is that these bonds are the "Callable" bonds (also note the "C" after the maturity date). We will have more to say about callable bonds later.

10.3 More on Yields

In the previous section, we focused on finding a straight bond's price given its yield. In this section, we reverse direction to find a bond's yield given its price. We then discuss the relationship among the various yield measures we have seen. We finish the section with some additional yield calculations.

Before we begin the process of calculating yields, you should be aware of an important assumption made when yield is calculated. This assumption is that an investor will be able to reinvest the coupon interest payments at a rate equal to the yield to maturity of the bond. Therefore, an investor will earn the bond's yield to maturity only if the investor holds the bond to maturity and if all the coupon interest payments received are reinvested at a rate equal to the bond's yield to maturity. The actual rate earned on the bond can be lower or higher than the yield to maturity—it depends on how long the investor holds the bond and the rate at which the coupon payments are reinvested.

CALCULATING YIELDS

To calculate a bond's yield given its price, we use the same straight bond formula used previously. The only way to find the yield is by trial and error. Financial calculators and spreadsheets do it this way at very high speed.

To illustrate, suppose we have a 6 percent bond with 10 years to maturity. Its price is 90, meaning 90 percent of face value. Assuming a $1,000 face value, the price is $900 and the coupon is $60 per year. What's the yield?

To find out, all we can do is try different yields until we come across the one that produces a price of $900. However, we can speed things up quite a bit by making an educated guess using what we know about bond prices and yields. We know the yield on this bond

SPREADSHEET ANALYSIS

	A	B	C	D	E	F	G	H
1								
2			Calculating the Yield to Maturity of a Coupon Bond					
3								
4	A Treasury bond traded on March 30, 2006, matures in 8 years on March 30, 2014.							
5	Assuming an 8 percent coupon rate and a price of 110, what is this bond's yield							
6	to maturity?							
7	Hint: Use the Excel function YIELD.							
8								
9		6.3843%	= YIELD("3/30/2006","3/30/2014",0.08,110,100,2,3)					
10								
11	This function uses the following arguments:							
12								
13			= YIELD("Now","Maturity",Coupon,Price,100,2,3)					
14								
15	Price is entered as a percent of face value.							
16	The 100 indicates redemption value as a percent of face value.							
17	The 2 indicates semi-annual coupons.							
18	The 3 specifies an actual day count with 365 days per year.							
19								
20								

is greater than its 6 percent coupon rate because it is a discount bond. So let's first try 8 percent in the straight bond pricing formula:

$$\frac{\$60}{.08}\left[1 - \frac{1}{(1.04)^{20}}\right] + \frac{\$1,000}{(1.04)^{20}} = \$864.10$$

The price with an 8 percent yield is $864.10, which is somewhat less than the $900 price, but not too far off.

To finish, we need to ask whether the 8 percent we used was too high or too low. We know that the higher the yield, the lower is the price, thus 8 percent is a little too high. So let's try 7.5 percent:

$$\frac{\$60}{.075}\left[1 - \frac{1}{(1.0375)^{20}}\right] + \frac{\$1,000}{(1.0375)^{20}} = \$895.78$$

Now we're very close. We're still a little too high on the yield (since the price is a little low). If you try 7.4 percent, you'll see that the resulting price is $902.29, so the yield is between 7.4 and 7.5 percent (it's actually 7.435 percent).

EXAMPLE 10.5 **Calculating YTM**

Suppose a bond has eight years to maturity, a price of 110, and a coupon rate of 8 percent. What is its yield?

This is a premium bond, so its yield is less than the 8 percent coupon. If we try 6 percent, we get (check this) $1,125.61. The yield is therefore a little bigger than 6 percent. If we try 6.5 percent, we get (check this) $1,092.43, so the answer is slightly less than 6.5 percent. Check that 6.4 percent is almost exact (the exact yield is 6.3843 percent).

Yields to maturity may be calculated using a built-in spreadsheet function. An example of how to use an Excel™ spreadsheet to calculate a yield to maturity is shown in the nearby *Spreadsheet Analysis* box.

callable bond
A bond is callable if the issuer can buy it back before it matures.

call price
The price the issuer of a callable bond must pay to buy it back.

make-whole call price
The present value of the bond's remaining cash flows.

call protection period
The period during which a callable bond cannot be called. Also called a *call deferment period*.

YIELD TO CALL

The discussion in this chapter so far has assumed that a bond will have an actual maturity equal to its originally stated maturity. However, this is not always so since most bonds are **callable bonds**. When a bond issue is callable, the issuer can buy back outstanding bonds before the bonds mature. In exchange, bondholders receive a special **call price**, which is often equal to face value, although it may be slightly higher. When a call price is equal to face value, the bond is said to be *callable at par*.

When a bond is called, the bondholder does not receive any more coupon payments. Therefore, some callable bonds are issued with a provision known as a **make-whole call price**. The make-whole call price is calculated as the present value of the bond's remaining cash flows. The discount rate used to calculate the present value is often the yield of a comparable maturity treasury bond plus a prespecified premium. The first bonds issued to the investment public with a make-whole call provision were the Quaker State Corporation bonds issued in 1995. Since then, callable bonds issues with make-whole call provisions have become common.

Bonds are called at the convenience of the issuer, and a call usually occurs after a fall in market interest rates allows issuers to refinance outstanding debt with new bonds paying lower coupons. However, an issuer's call privilege is often restricted so that outstanding bonds cannot be called until the end of a specified **call protection period**, also termed a *call deferment period.* As a typical example, a bond issued with a 20-year maturity may be sold to investors subject to the restriction that it is callable anytime after an initial five-year call protection period.

yield to call (YTC)
Measure of return that assumes a bond will be redeemed at the earliest call date.

If a bond is callable, its yield to maturity may no longer be a useful number. Instead, the **yield to call**, commonly abbreviated **YTC**, may be more meaningful. Yield to call is a yield measure that assumes a bond issue will be called at its earliest possible call date.

We calculate a bond's yield to call using the straight bond pricing formula we have been using with two changes. First, instead of time to maturity, we use time to the first possible call date. Second, instead of face value, we use the call price. The resulting formula is thus:

$$\text{Callable bond price} = \frac{C}{YTC}\left[1 - \frac{1}{(1 + YTC/2)^{2T}}\right] + \frac{CP}{(1 + YTC/2)^{2T}} \qquad (10.4)$$

where:
$$C = \text{Constant annual coupon}$$
$$CP = \text{Call price of the bond}$$
$$T = \text{Time in years until earliest possible call date}$$
$$YTC = \text{Yield to call assuming semiannual coupons}$$

Calculating a yield to call requires the same trial-and-error procedure as calculating a yield to maturity. Most financial calculators will either handle the calculation directly or can be tricked into it by just changing the face value to the call price and the time to maturity to time to call.

To give a trial-and-error example, suppose a 20-year bond has a coupon of 8 percent, a price of 98, and is callable in 10 years. The call price is 105. What are its yield to maturity and yield to call?

Based on our earlier discussion, we know the yield to maturity is slightly bigger than the coupon rate. (Why?) After some calculation, we find it to be 8.2 percent.

To find the bond's yield to call, we pretend it has a face value of 105 instead of 100 ($1,050 versus $1,000) and will mature in 10 years. With these two changes, the procedure

SPREADSHEET ANALYSIS

	A	B	C	D	E	F	G	H
1								
2				Calculating Yield to Call				
3								
4	A bond traded on March 30, 2006 matures in 15 years on March 30, 2021 and may							
5	be called anytime after March 30, 2011 at a call price of 105. The bond pays an							
6	8.5 percent coupon and currently trades at par. What are the yield to maturity							
7	and yield to call for this bond?							
8								
9	Yield to maturity is based on the 2021 maturity and the current price of 100.							
10								
11		8.500%		= YIELD("3/30/2006","3/30/2021",0.085,100,100,2,3)				
12								
13	Yield to call is based on the 2011 call date and the call price of 105.							
14								
15		9.308%		= YIELD("3/30/2006","3/30/2011",0.085,100,105,2,3)				
16								
17								

is exactly the same. We can try 8.5 percent, for example:

$$\frac{\$80}{.085}\left[1 - \frac{1}{(1.0425)^{20}}\right] + \frac{\$1,050}{(1.0425)^{20}} = \$988.51$$

Because $988.51 is a little too high, the yield to call is slightly bigger than 8.5 percent. If we try 8.6, we find that the price is $981.83, so the yield to call is about 8.6 percent (it's 8.6276 percent).

A natural question comes up in this context. Which is bigger, the yield to maturity or the yield to call? The answer depends on the call price. However, if the bond is callable at par (as many are), then, for a premium bond, the yield to maturity is greater. For a discount bond, the reverse is true.

EXAMPLE 10.6 — **Yield to Call**

An 8.5 percent coupon bond maturing in 15 years is callable at 105 in 5 years. If the price is 100, which is bigger, the yield to call or the yield to maturity?

Since this is a par bond callable at a premium, the yield to call is bigger. We can verify this by calculating both yields. Check that the yield to maturity is 8.50 percent, whereas the yield to call is 9.308 percent.

Yields to call may be calculated using a built-in spreadsheet function. An example of how to use an Excel™ spreadsheet to calculate a yield to call is shown in the nearby *Spreadsheet Analysis* box.

CHECK THIS

10.3a What does it mean for a bond to be callable?

10.3b What is the difference between yield to maturity and yield to call?

10.3c Yield to call is calculated just like yield to maturity except for two changes. What are the changes?

10.4 Interest Rate Risk and Malkiel's Theorems

Bond yields are essentially interest rates, and, like interest rates, they fluctuate through time. When interest rates change, bond prices change. This is called **interest rate risk**. The term "interest rate risk" refers to the possibility of losses on a bond from changes in interest rates.

interest rate risk
The possibility that changes in interest rates will result in losses in a bond's value.

PROMISED YIELD AND REALIZED YIELD

The terms *yield to maturity* and *promised yield* both seem to imply that the yield originally stated when a bond is purchased is what you will actually earn if you hold the bond until it matures. Actually, this is not generally correct. The return or yield you actually earn on a bond is called the **realized yield**, and an originally stated yield to maturity is almost never exactly equal to the realized yield.

realized yield
The yield actually earned or "realized" on a bond.

The reason a realized yield will almost always differ from a promised yield is that interest rates fluctuate, causing bond prices to rise or fall. One consequence is that if a bond is sold before maturity, its price may be higher or lower than originally anticipated, and, as a result, the actually realized yield will be different from the promised yield.

FIGURE 10.2 | Bond Prices and Yields

Another important reason why realized yields generally differ from promised yields relates to the bond's coupons. We will get to this in the next section. For now, you should know that, for the most part, a bond's realized yield will equal its promised yield only if its yield doesn't change at all over the life of the bond, an unlikely event.

INTEREST RATE RISK AND MATURITY

While changing interest rates systematically affect all bond prices, it is important to realize that the impact of changing interest rates is not the same for all bonds. Some bonds are more sensitive to interest rate changes than others. To illustrate, Figure 10.2 shows how two bonds with different maturities can have different price sensitivities to changes in bond yields.

In Figure 10.2, bond prices are measured on the vertical axis, and bond yields are measured on the horizontal axis. Both bonds have the same 8 percent coupon rate, but one bond has a 5-year maturity while the other bond has a 20-year maturity. Both bonds display the inverse relationship between bond prices and bond yields. Since both bonds have the same 8 percent coupon rate, and both sell for par, their yields are 8 percent.

However, when bond yields are greater than 8 percent, the 20-year maturity bond has a lower price than the 5-year maturity bond. In contrast, when bond yields are less than 8 percent, the 20-year maturity bond has a higher price than the 5-year maturity bond. Essentially, falling yields cause both bond prices to rise, but the longer maturity bond experiences a larger price increase than the shorter maturity bond. Similarly, rising yields cause both bond prices to fall, but the price of the longer maturity bond falls by more than the price of the shorter maturity bond.

MALKIEL'S THEOREMS

The effect illustrated in Figure 10.2, along with some other important relationships among bond prices, maturities, coupon rates, and yields, is succinctly described by Burton Malkiel's five bond price theorems.[2] These five theorems are:

1. Bond prices and bond yields move in opposite directions. As a bond's yield increases, its price decreases. Conversely, as a bond's yield decreases, its price increases.

[2]Burton C. Malkiel, "Expectations, Bond Prices, and the Term Structure of Interest Rates," *Quarterly Journal of Economics*, May 1962, pp. 197–218.

2. For a given change in a bond's yield to maturity, the longer the term to maturity of the bond, the greater will be the magnitude of the change in the bond's price.

3. For a given change in a bond's yield to maturity, the size of the change in the bond's price increases at a diminishing rate as the bond's term to maturity lengthens.

4. For a given change in a bond's yield to maturity, the absolute magnitude of the resulting change in the bond's price is inversely related to the bond's coupon rate.

5. For a given absolute change in a bond's yield to maturity, the magnitude of the price increase caused by a decrease in yield is greater than the price decrease caused by an increase in yield.

The first, second, and fourth of these theorems are the simplest and most important. The first one says that bond prices and yields move in opposite directions. The second one says that longer-term bonds are more sensitive to changes in yields than shorter-term bonds. The fourth one says that lower coupon bonds are more sensitive to changes in yields than higher coupon bonds.

The third theorem says that a bond's sensitivity to interest rate changes increases as its maturity grows, but at a diminishing rate. In other words, a 10-year bond is much more sensitive to changes in yield than a 1-year bond. However, a 30-year bond is only slightly more sensitive than a 20-year bond. Finally, the fifth theorem says essentially that the loss you would suffer from, say, a 1 percent increase in yields is less than the gain you would enjoy from a 1 percent decrease in yields.

Table 10.1 illustrates the first three of these theorems by providing prices for 8 percent coupon bonds with maturities of 5, 10, and 20 years and yields to maturity of 7 percent and 9 percent. Be sure to check these for practice. As the first theorem says, bond prices are lower when yields are higher (9 percent versus 7 percent). As the second theorem indicates, the differences in bond prices between yields of 7 percent and 9 percent are greater for bonds with a longer term to maturity. However, as the third theorem states, the effect increases at a diminishing rate as the maturity lengthens. To see this, notice that $136.10 is 67.7 percent larger than $81.14, while $198.79 is only 46.1 percent larger than $136.10.

To illustrate the last two theorems, we present prices for 20-year maturity bonds with coupon rates and yields to maturity of 6 percent, 8 percent, and 10 percent (again, calculate these for practice) in Table 10.2. To illustrate the fourth theorem, compare the loss on the

TABLE 10.1 Bond Prices and Yields

Yields	Time to Maturity		
	5 Years	10 Years	20 Years
7%	$1,041.58	$1,071.06	$1,106.78
9%	960.44	934.96	907.99
Price difference	$ 81.14	$ 136.10	$ 198.79

TABLE 10.2 Twenty-Year Bond Prices and Yields

Yields	Coupon Rates		
	6 Percent	8 Percent	10 Percent
6%	$1,000.00	$1,231.15	$1,462.30
8%	802.07	1,000.00	1,197.93
10%	656.82	828.41	1,000.00

INVESTMENT UPDATES

GET A FRESH ANGLE ON YOUR FINANCES

Not sure whether you're saving enough or whether you have the right investment mix? To get a better handle on your portfolio, it sometimes helps to look at your finances from another angle.

1 How Much Do You Need in Conservative Investments to Feel Safe?

Investment advisers and Wall Street firms constantly exhort investors to consider their risk tolerance. For instance, we are often prodded to fill out those irritating questionnaires where we are asked whether our goal is "growth" or "capital preservation."

The answer, of course, is that we want both. Even retirees need growth from their portfolios. Even freshly minted college graduates hanker after some stability.

My advice: Forget risk tolerance. Instead, divide your portfolio into two parts. Designate one portion for "getting rich" and the other for "making sure I'm not poor."

How should you split your savings between the two? That brings us to our first question. Think about how much you need in conservative investments, like high-quality bonds, certificates of deposit, and savings accounts, to cover expected costs, pay for financial emergencies, and have a general sense of financial security.

If you are retired, this stash of safe money might be equal to your living expenses for the next three or five years. If you are still hauling in a paycheck, your conservative investments could amount to just three months' living expenses.

Once you have enough in conservative investments to soothe your fears, that will free you up to be more aggressive with the rest of your portfolio. You might invest your "getting rich" money in a mix of U.S. shares, foreign stocks, real-estate investment trusts, high-yield "junk" bonds and foreign bonds.

What if these investments hit a rough patch? With any luck, you won't be too unnerved, thanks to the financial cushion provided by your safe money.

2 How Much Do You Really Have in Bonds?

When you tote up your holdings of conservative investments, you probably count CDs, Treasury bonds,

high-quality corporate bonds, municipals, money-market funds, and savings accounts. But don't stop there.

I would expand the list to include Social Security retirement benefits, pension income, mortgage debt, and any other loans you have. After all, you regularly receive income from Social Security and your pension, just as you would from a bond. Meanwhile, your debts involve making regular payments to other folks.

All these dealings affect your sense of financial security, and they should influence how you structure your portfolio. For instance, if you expect a traditional company pension when you retire, you effectively have a huge position in bonds and thus you might want to load up on stocks in your investment portfolio.

On the other hand, if you have a heap of debts, your financial position is much more precarious and you may want to take less risk with your investments. On that score, consider your mortgage, which probably is your biggest debt. Let's say you have a $300,000 home and a $200,000 mortgage. The temptation is to deduct your mortgage from your home's value and declare that your total real-estate investment is $100,000.

But in truth, your real-estate exposure is equal to your home's full $300,000 value. Think about it: Whether you are mortgaged to the hilt or you are debt-free, you still benefit from every dollar of home-price appreciation and suffer every dollar of loss.

Meanwhile, I would view your $200,000 mortgage as a "negative bond" because, instead of earning interest, you are paying it. Suppose you also have $75,000 in government bonds, which means you have lent money to Uncle Sam. Overall, you owe a lot more money than you are owed—to the tune of $125,000.

In fact, your financial position may be more perilous than a couple whose portfolio is 100% in stocks but who own their home free and clear. The implication: You may want to tamp down risk, either by buying more bonds or by making extra principal payments on your mortgage.

Source: Jonathan Clements, *The Wall Street Journal*, October 16, 2005. © 2005 Dow Jones & Company, Inc. All Rights Reserved Worldwide.

6 percent and the 8 percent bonds as yields move from 8 percent to 10 percent. The 6 percent bond loses ($656.82 − $802.07)/$802.07 = −18.1%. The 8 percent bond loses ($828.41 − $1,000)/$1,000 = −17.2%, showing that the bond with the lower coupon is more sensitive to a change in yields. You can (and should) verify that the same is true for a yield increase.

Finally, to illustrate the fifth theorem, take a look at the 8 percent coupon bond in Table 10.2. As yields decrease by 2 percent from 8 percent to 6 percent, its price climbs by $231.15. As yields rise by 2 percent, the bond's price falls by $171.59.

As we have discussed, bond maturity is an important factor determining the sensitivity of a bond's price to changes in interest rates. However, bond maturity is an incomplete measure of bond price sensitivity to yield changes. For example, we have seen that a bond's coupon rate is also important. An improved measure of interest rate risk for bonds that accounts for both differences in maturity and differences in coupon rates is our next subject. A nearby *Investment Updates* box discusses the importance of bonds in an investment portfolio.

CHECK THIS

10.4a True or false: A bond price's sensitivity to interest rate changes increases at an increasing rate as maturity lengthens.

10.4b Which is more sensitive to an interest rate shift: a low-coupon bond or a high-coupon bond?

10.5 Duration

duration
A widely used measure of a bond's sensitivity to changes in bond yields.

To account for differences in interest rate risk across bonds with different coupon rates and maturities, the concept of **duration** is widely applied. As we will explore in some detail, duration measures a bond's sensitivity to interest rate changes. The idea behind duration was first presented by Frederick Macaulay in an early study of U.S. financial markets.[3] Today, duration is a very widely used measure of a bond's price sensitivity to changes in bond yields.

MACAULAY DURATION

There are several duration measures. The original version is called *Macaulay duration*. The usefulness of Macaulay duration stems from the fact that it satisfies the following approximate relationship between percentage changes in bond prices and changes in bond yields:

$$\text{Percentage change in bond price} \approx -\text{Duration} \times \frac{\text{Change in } YTM}{(1 + YTM/2)} \quad (10.5)$$

As a consequence, two bonds with the same duration, but not necessarily the same maturity, have approximately the same price sensitivity to a change in bond yields. This approximation is quite accurate for relatively small changes in yields, but it becomes less accurate when large changes are considered.

[3]Frederick Macaulay, *Some Theoretical Problems Suggested by the Movements of Interest Rates, Bond Yields, and Stock Prices in the United States since 1856* (New York: National Bureau of Economic Research, 1938).

To see how we use this result, suppose a bond has a Macaulay duration of six years, and its yield decreases from 10 percent to 9.5 percent. The resulting percentage change in the price of the bond is calculated as follows:

$$-6 \times \frac{.095 - .10}{1.05} = 2.86\%$$

Thus, the bond's price rises by 2.86 percent in response to a yield decrease of 50 basis points.

EXAMPLE 10.7 **Macaulay Duration**

A bond has a Macaulay duration of 11 years, and its yield increases from 8 percent to 8.5 percent. What will happen to the price of the bond?

The resulting percentage change in the price of the bond can be calculated as follows:

$$-11 \times \frac{.085 - .08}{1.04} = -5.29\%$$

The bond's price declines by approximately 5.29 percent in response to a 50 basis point increase in yields.

MODIFIED DURATION

Some analysts prefer to use a variation of Macaulay duration called *modified duration*. The relationship between Macaulay duration and modified duration for bonds paying semiannual coupons is simply:

$$\text{Modified duration} = \frac{\text{Macaulay duration}}{(1 + YTM/2)} \tag{10.6}$$

As a result, based on modified duration, the approximate relationship between percentage changes in bond prices and changes in bond yields is just:

$$\text{Percentage change in bond price} \approx -\text{Modified duration} \times \text{Change in } YTM \tag{10.7}$$

In other words, to calculate the percentage change in the bond's price, we just multiply the modified duration by the change in yields.

EXAMPLE 10.8 **Modified Duration**

A bond has a Macaulay duration of 8.5 years and a yield to maturity of 9 percent. What is its modified duration?

The bond's modified duration is calculated as follows:

$$\frac{8.5}{1.045} = 8.134$$

Notice that we divided the yield by 2 to get the semiannual yield.

EXAMPLE 10.9 | Modified Duration

A bond has a modified duration of seven years. Suppose its yield increases from 8 percent to 8.5 percent. What happens to its price?

We can very easily determine the resulting percentage change in the price of the bond using its modified duration:

$$-7 \times (.085 - .08) = -3.5\%$$

The bond's price declines by about 3.5 percent.

CALCULATING MACAULAY DURATION

Macaulay duration is often described as a bond's *effective maturity*. For this reason, duration values are conventionally stated in years. The first fundamental principle for calculating the duration of a bond concerns the duration of a zero coupon bond. Specifically, the duration of a zero coupon bond is equal to its maturity. Thus, on a pure discount instrument, such as the U.S. Treasury STRIPS, no calculation is necessary to come up with Macaulay duration.

The second fundamental principle for calculating duration concerns the duration of a coupon bond with multiple cash flows. The duration of a coupon bond is a weighted average of individual maturities of all the bond's separate cash flows. The weights attached to the maturity of each cash flow are proportionate to the present values of each cash flow.

A sample duration calculation for a bond with three years until maturity is illustrated in Table 10.3. The bond sells at par value. It has an 8 percent coupon rate and an 8 percent yield to maturity.

As shown in Table 10.3, calculating a bond's duration can be laborious—especially if the bond has a large number of separate cash flows. Fortunately, relatively simple formulas are available for many of the important cases. For example, if a bond is selling for par value, its duration can be calculated easily using the following formula:

$$\text{Par value bond duration} = \frac{(1 + YTM/2)}{YTM}\left[1 - \frac{1}{(1 + YTM/2)^{2M}}\right] \qquad (10.8)$$

where: M = Bond maturity in years
YTM = Yield to maturity assuming semiannual coupons

For example, using $YTM = 8\%$ and $M = 3$ years we obtain the same duration value (2.7259 years) computed in Table 10.3.

TABLE 10.3 | Calculating Bond Duration

Years	Cash Flow	Discount Factor	Present Value	Years × Present Value ÷ Bond Price
0.5	$ 40	.96154	$ 38.4615	.0192 years
1	40	.92456	36.9822	.0370
1.5	40	.88900	35.5599	.0533
2	40	.85480	34.1922	.0684
2.5	40	.82193	32.8771	.0822
3	1,040	.79031	821.9271	2.4658
			$1,000.00	2.7259 years
			Bond Price	Bond Duration

Chapter 10 ■ Bond Prices and Yields 337

EXAMPLE 10.10 **Duration for a Par Value Bond**

Suppose a par value bond has a 6 percent coupon and 10 years to maturity. What is its duration?

Since the bond sells for par, its yield is equal to its coupon rate, 6 percent. Plugging this into the par value bond duration formula, we have:

$$\text{Par value bond duration} = \frac{(1 + .06/2)}{.06}\left[1 - \frac{1}{(1 + .06/2)^{20}}\right]$$

After a little work on a calculator, we find that the duration is 7.66 years.

The par value bond duration formula (Equation 10.8) is useful for calculating the duration of a bond that is actually selling at par value. Unfortunately, the general formula for bonds not necessarily selling at par value is somewhat more complicated. The general duration formula for a bond paying constant semiannual coupons is:

$$\text{Duration} = \frac{1 + YTM/2}{YTM} - \frac{(1 + YTM/2) + M(CPR - YTM)}{YTM + CPR[(1 + YTM/2)^{2M} - 1]} \qquad (10.9)$$

where: CPR = Constant annual coupon rate
  M = Bond maturity in years
  YTM = Yield to maturity assuming semiannual coupons

Although somewhat tedious for manual calculations, this formula is used in many computer programs that calculate bond durations. Some popular personal computer spreadsheet packages also have a built-in function to perform this calculation.

EXAMPLE 10.11 **Duration for a Discount Bond**

A bond has a yield to maturity of 7 percent. It matures in 12 years. Its coupon rate is 6 percent. What is its modified duration?

We first must calculate the Macaulay duration using the unpleasant-looking formula just above. We finish by converting the Macaulay duration to modified duration. Plugging into the duration formula, we have:

$$\text{Duration} = \frac{1 + .07/2}{.07} - \frac{(1 + .07/2) + 12(.06 - .07)}{.07 + .06[(1 + .07/2)^{24} - 1]}$$

$$= \frac{1.035}{.07} - \frac{1.035 + 12(-.01)}{.07 + .06(1.035^{24} - 1)}$$

After a little button pushing, we find that the duration is 8.56 years. Finally, converting to modified duration, we find that the modified duration is equal to $8.56/1.035 = 8.27$ years.

Bond durations may be calculated using a built-in spreadsheet function. An example of how to use an Excel™ spreadsheet to calculate a Macaulay duration and modified duration are shown in the nearby *Spreadsheet Analysis* box.

	A	B	C	D	E	F	G	H
1								
2			**Calculating Macaulay and Modified Durations**					
3								
4	A Treasury bond traded on March 30, 2006, matures in 12 years on March 30, 2018.							
5	Assuming a 6 percent coupon rate and a 7 percent yield to maturity, what are the							
6	Macaulay and Modified durations of this bond?							
7	Hint: Use the Excel functions DURATION and MDURATION.							
8								
9		8.561	= DURATION("3/30/2006","3/30/2018",0.06,0.07,2,3)					
10								
11		8.272	= MDURATION("3/30/2006","3/30/2018",0.06,0.07,2,3)					
12								
13	These functions use the following arguments convention:							
14								
15		= DURATION("Now","Maturity",Coupon,Yield,2,3)						
16								
17	The 2 indicates semi-annual coupons.							
18	The 3 specifies an actual day count with 365 days per year.							
19								
20								

PROPERTIES OF DURATION

Macaulay duration has a number of important properties. For straight bonds, the basic properties of Macaulay duration can be summarized as follows:

1. All else the same, the longer a bond's maturity, the longer is its duration.
2. All else the same, a bond's duration increases at a decreasing rate as maturity lengthens.
3. All else the same, the higher a bond's coupon, the shorter is its duration.
4. All else the same, a higher yield to maturity implies a shorter duration, and a lower yield to maturity implies a longer duration.

As we saw earlier, a zero coupon bond has a duration equal to its maturity. The duration on a bond with coupons is always less than its maturity. Because of the second principle, durations much longer than 10 or 15 years are rarely seen. An exception to some of these principles involves very long maturity bonds selling at a very steep discount. This exception rarely occurs in practice, so these principles are generally correct.

A graphical illustration of the relationship between duration and maturity is presented in Figure 10.3, where duration is measured on the vertical axis and maturity is measured on the horizontal axis. In Figure 10.3, the yield to maturity for all bonds is 10 percent. Bonds with coupon rates of 0 percent, 5 percent, 10 percent, and 15 percent are presented. As the figure shows, the duration of a zero coupon bond rises step for step with maturity. For the coupon bonds, however, the duration initially moves closely with maturity, as our first duration principle suggests, but, consistent with the second principle, the lines begin to flatten out after four or five years. Also, consistent with our third principle, the lower coupon bonds have higher durations.

FIGURE 10.3 | Bond Duration and Maturity

10.5a What does duration measure?

10.5b What is the duration of a zero coupon bond?

10.5c What happens to a bond's duration as its maturity grows?

10.6 Bond Risk Measures Based on Duration

In this section, we examine some risk measures that are either based on duration or closely related to it. These measures are commonly used by bond traders and other fixed-income professionals.

DOLLAR VALUE OF AN 01

dollar value of an 01
Change in bond price resulting from a change in yield to maturity of one basis point.

A popular measure of interest rate risk among bond professionals is the **dollar value of an 01** (say "dollar value of an oh-one"), which measures the change in bond price resulting from a one basis point change in yield to maturity, where one basis point is 1 percent of 1 percent, that is, .01 percent. The dollar value of an 01 is also known as the *value of a basis point.* The dollar value of an 01 can be stated through the modified duration of a bond as follows:

$$\text{Dollar value of an 01} \approx \text{Modified duration} \times \text{Bond price} \times 0.01 \qquad (10.10)$$

YIELD VALUE OF A 32nd

yield value of a 32nd
Change in yield to maturity that would lead to a 1/32 change in bond price.

When bond prices are quoted in 1/32's of a point, as they are, for example, with U.S. Treasury notes and bonds, the **yield value of a 32nd** is often used by bond professionals as an additional or alternative measure of interest rate risk. The yield value of a 32nd is the change in yield to maturity that would lead to a 1/32 change in bond price. A simple way to obtain the yield value of a 32nd is to multiply the dollar value of an 01 by 32 and then invert the result:

$$\text{Yield value of a 32nd} \approx \frac{1}{32 \times \text{Dollar value of an 01}} \qquad (10.11)$$

EXAMPLE 10.12

Bond Risk Measures Based on Duration

The bond in Example 10.11 has a modified duration of 8.27 years, which represents 8.27 percent, or 0.0827 in decimal form. What is its dollar value of an 01? What is its yield value of a 32nd?

We must first calculate the price of this bond using the bond pricing formula provided earlier in this chapter:

$$\text{Bond·price} = \frac{6}{.07}\left[1 - \frac{1}{(1+.035)^{24}}\right] + \frac{100}{(1+.035)^{24}}$$

$$= \$91.971$$

Then, plugging the modified duration in decimal form, .0827, and the bond price as a percentage of par value, 91.971, into Equation 10.10, we obtain the dollar value of an 01:

$$\text{Dollar value of an 01} \approx .0827 \times 91.971 \times 0.01 = .07606$$

Thus, a one basis point change in yield will change the bond price by about $0.076, or 7.6 cents (in the opposite direction).

Next we multiply by 32 and invert to obtain the yield value of a 32nd:

$$\text{Yield value of a 32nd} \approx \frac{1}{32 \times .07606} = .41086$$

Now we see that a change in yield of .41 basis point, or .0041 percent, would lead to a change in bond price of about 1/32. As a check, we calculate a bond price obtained by changing the yield from 7 percent to 7.0041 percent:

$$\text{Bond price} = \frac{6}{.070041}\left[1 - \frac{1}{(1+.03500205)^{24}}\right] + \frac{100}{(1+.03500205)^{24}}$$

$$= \$91.94$$

The resulting price change is $0.0314 \approx \$91.97 - \$91.94$. Because 1/32 of a point corresponds to $0.03125, we see that our computed yield value of a 32nd is quite accurate.

CHECK THIS

10.6a What is the relationship between modified duration and the dollar value of an 01?

10.6b What is the relationship between the dollar value of an 01 and the yield value of a 32nd?

10.7 Dedicated Portfolios and Reinvestment Risk

Duration has another property that makes it a vital tool in bond portfolio management. To explore this subject, we first need to introduce two important concepts, dedicated portfolios and reinvestment risk.

DEDICATED PORTFOLIOS

dedicated portfolio

A bond portfolio created to prepare for a future cash outlay.

Bond portfolios are often created for the purpose of preparing for a future liability payment or other cash outlay. A portfolio formed for such a specific purpose is called a **dedicated portfolio**. When the future liability payment of a dedicated portfolio is due on a known date, that date is commonly called the portfolio's *target date*.

Pension funds provide a good example of dedicated portfolio management. A pension fund normally knows years in advance the amount of benefit payments it must make to its beneficiaries. The fund then purchases bonds in the amount needed to prepare for these payments.

For a practical view of bond portfolio management visit
www.jamesbaker.com

To illustrate, suppose the Safety First pension fund estimates that it must pay benefits of about $100 million in five years. Using semiannual discounting, and assuming that bonds currently yield 8 percent, the present value of Safety First's future liability is calculated as follows:

$$\frac{\$100,000,000}{(1.04)^{10}} \approx \$67,556,417$$

This amount, about $67.5 million, represents the investment necessary for Safety First to construct a dedicated bond portfolio to fund a future liability of $100 million.

Next, suppose the Safety First pension fund creates a dedicated portfolio by investing exactly $67.5 million in bonds selling at par value with a coupon rate of 8 percent to prepare for the $100 million payout in five years. The Safety First fund decides to follow a maturity matching strategy whereby it invests only in bonds with maturities that match the portfolio's five-year target date.

Since Safety First is investing $67.5 million in bonds that pay an 8 percent annual coupon, the fund receives $5.4 million in coupons each year, along with $67.5 million of principal at the bonds' five-year maturity. As the coupons come in, Safety First reinvests them. If all coupons are reinvested at an 8 percent yield, the fund's portfolio will grow to about $99.916 million on its target date. This is the future value of $67.5 million compounded at 4 percent semiannually for five years:

$$\$67.5 \text{ million} \times (1.04)^{10} \approx \$100 \text{ million}$$

This amount is also equal to the future value of all coupons reinvested at 8 percent, plus the $67.5 million of bond principal received at maturity. To see this, we calculate the future value of the coupons (using the standard formula for the future value of an annuity) and then add the $67.5 million:

$$\frac{\$5.4 \text{ million}}{.08}[(1.04)^{10} - 1] + \$67.5 \text{ million} \approx \$100 \text{ million}$$

Thus, as long as the annual coupons are reinvested at 8 percent, Safety First's bond fund will grow to the amount needed.

REINVESTMENT RISK

As we have seen, the bond investment strategy of the Safety First pension fund will be successful if all coupons received during the life of the investment can be reinvested at a constant 8 percent yield. However, in reality, yields at which coupons can be reinvested are uncertain, and a target date surplus or shortfall is therefore likely to occur.

reinvestment rate risk

The uncertainty about future or target date portfolio value that results from the need to reinvest bond coupons at yields not known in advance.

The uncertainty about future or target date portfolio value that results from the need to reinvest bond coupons at yields that cannot be predicted in advance is called **reinvestment rate risk**. Thus, the uncertain portfolio value on the target date represents reinvestment risk. In general, more distant target dates entail greater uncertainty and reinvestment risk.

To examine the impact of reinvestment risk, we continue with the example of the Safety First pension fund's dedicated bond portfolio. We will consider two cases, one in which all bond coupons are reinvested at a higher 9 percent yield, and one in which all coupons are reinvested at a lower 7 percent yield. In this case, the payment of the fixed $67.5 million principal plus the future value of the 10 semiannual coupons compounded at an uncertain rate, either 9 percent or 7 percent, comprises the total five-year target date portfolio value.

For 9 percent and 7 percent yields, these target date portfolio values are calculated as follows:

$$\frac{\$5.4 \text{ million}}{.09}[(1.045)^{10} - 1] + \$67.5 \text{ million} = \$100.678 \text{ million}$$

and

$$\frac{\$5.4 \text{ million}}{.07}[(1.035)^{10} - 1] + \$67.5 \text{ million} = \$99.175 \text{ million}$$

As shown, a target date portfolio value of $100.678 million is realized through a 9 percent reinvestment rate, and a value of $99.175 million is realized by a 7 percent reinvestment rate. The difference between these two amounts, about $1.5 million, represents reinvestment risk.

As this example illustrates, a maturity matching strategy for a dedicated bond portfolio entails substantial reinvestment risk. Indeed, this example understates a pension fund's total reinvestment risk since it considers only a single target date. In reality, pension funds have a series of target dates, and a shortfall at one target date typically coincides with shortfalls at other target dates as well.

A simple solution for reinvestment risk is to purchase zero coupon bonds that pay a fixed principal at a maturity chosen to match a dedicated portfolio's target date. Because there are no coupons to reinvest, there is no reinvestment risk! However, a zero coupon bond strategy has its drawbacks. As a practical matter, U.S. Treasury STRIPS are the only zero coupon bonds issued in sufficient quantity to even begin to satisfy the dedicated portfolio needs of pension funds, insurance companies, and other institutional investors. However, U.S. Treasury securities have lower yields than even the highest quality corporate bonds. A yield difference of only .25 percent between Treasury securities and corporate bonds can make a substantial difference in the initial cost of a dedicated bond portfolio.

For example, suppose that Treasury STRIPS have a yield of 7.75 percent. Using semiannual compounding, the present value of these zero coupon bonds providing a principal payment of $100 million at a five-year maturity is calculated as follows:

$$\frac{\$100 \text{ million}}{(1.03875)^{10}} \approx \$68.374 \text{ million}$$

This cost of $68.374 million based on a 7.75 percent yield is significantly higher than the previously stated cost of $67.556 million based on an 8 percent yield. From the perspective of the Safety First pension fund, this represents a hefty premium to pay to eliminate reinvestment risk. Fortunately, as we discuss in the next section, other methods are available at lower cost.

CHECK THIS

10.7a   What is a dedicated portfolio?

10.7b   What is reinvestment rate risk?

10.8 Immunization

immunization

Constructing a portfolio to minimize the uncertainty surrounding its target date value.

Constructing a dedicated portfolio to minimize the uncertainty in its target date value is called **immunization**. In this section, we show how duration can be used to immunize a bond portfolio against reinvestment risk.

PRICE RISK VERSUS REINVESTMENT RATE RISK

To understand how immunization is accomplished, suppose you own a bond with eight years to maturity. However, your target date is actually just six years from now. If interest rates rise, are you happy or unhappy?

Your initial reaction is probably "unhappy" because you know that as interest rates rise, bond values fall. However, things are not so simple. Clearly, if interest rates rise, then, in six years, your bond will be worth less than it would have been at a lower rate. This is called **price risk**. However, it is also true that you will be able to reinvest the coupons you receive at a higher interest rate. As a result, your reinvested coupons will be worth more. In fact, the net effect of an interest rate increase might be to make you *better* off.

price risk

The risk that bond prices will decrease, which arises in dedicated portfolios when the target date value of a bond or bond portfolio is not known with certainty.

As our simple example illustrates, for a dedicated portfolio, interest rate changes have two effects. Interest rate increases act to decrease bond prices (price risk) but increase the future value of reinvested coupons (reinvestment rate risk). In the other direction, interest rate decreases act to increase bond values but decrease the future value of reinvested coupons. The key observation is that these two effects—price risk and reinvestment rate risk—tend to offset each other.

You might wonder if it is possible to engineer a portfolio in which these two effects offset each other more or less precisely. As we illustrate next, the answer is most definitely yes.

IMMUNIZATION BY DURATION MATCHING

The key to immunizing a dedicated portfolio is to match its duration to its target date. If this is done, then the impacts of price and reinvestment rate risk will almost exactly offset, and interest rate changes will have a minimal impact on the target date value of the portfolio. In fact, immunization is often simply referred to as duration matching.

To see how a duration matching strategy can be applied to reduce target date uncertainty, suppose the Safety First pension fund initially purchases $67.5 million of par value bonds paying 8 percent coupons with a maturity of 6.2 years. From the par value duration formula we discussed earlier, a maturity of 6.2 years corresponds to a duration of 5 years. Thus, the duration of Safety First's dedicated bond portfolio is now matched to its five-year portfolio target date.

Suppose that immediately after the bonds are purchased, a one-time shock causes bond yields to either jump up to 10 percent or jump down to 6 percent. As a result, all coupons are reinvested at either a 10 percent yield or a 6 percent yield, depending on which way rates jump.

This example is illustrated in Figure 10.4, where the left vertical axis measures initial bond portfolio values, and the right vertical axis measures bond portfolio values realized by holding the portfolio until the bonds mature in 6.2 years. The horizontal axis measures the passage of time from initial investment to bond maturity. The positively sloped lines plot bond portfolio values through time for bond yields that have jumped to either 10 percent or 6 percent immediately after the initial investment of $67.5 million in par value 8 percent coupon bonds. This example assumes that after their initial jump, bond yields remain unchanged.

FIGURE 10.4 | Bond Price and Reinvestment Rate Risk

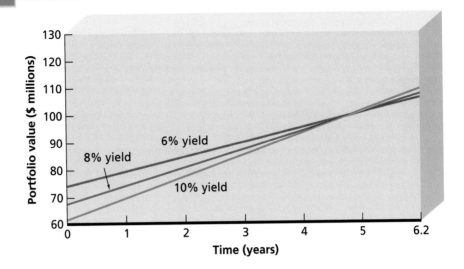

As shown in Figure 10.4, the initial jump in yields causes the value of Safety First's bond portfolio to jump in the opposite direction. If yields increase, bond prices fall, but coupons are reinvested at a higher interest rate, thereby leading to a higher portfolio value at maturity. In contrast, if yields decrease, bond prices rise, but a lower reinvestment rate reduces the value of the portfolio at maturity.

However, what is remarkable is that regardless of whether yields rise or fall, there is almost no difference in Safety First's portfolio value at the duration-matched five-year target date. Thus, the immunization strategy of matching the duration of Safety First's dedicated portfolio to its portfolio target date has almost entirely eliminated reinvestment risk.

DYNAMIC IMMUNIZATION

The example of the Safety First pension fund immunizing a dedicated bond portfolio by a duration matching strategy assumed that the bond portfolio was subject to a single yield shock. In reality, bond yields change constantly. Therefore, successful immunization requires that a dedicated portfolio be rebalanced frequently to maintain a portfolio duration equal to the portfolio's target date.

For example, by purchasing bonds with a maturity of 6.2 years, the Safety First pension fund had matched the duration of the dedicated portfolio to the fund's 5-year target date. One year later, however, the target date is four years away, and bonds with a duration of four years are required to maintain a duration matching strategy. Assuming interest rates haven't changed, the par value duration formula shows that a maturity of 4.7 years corresponds to a duration of 4 years. Thus, to maintain a duration-matched target date, the Safety First fund must sell its originally purchased bonds now with a maturity of 5.2 years and replace them with bonds having a maturity of 4.7 years.

dynamic immunization

Periodic rebalancing of a dedicated bond portfolio to maintain a duration that matches the target maturity date.

The strategy of periodically rebalancing a dedicated bond portfolio to maintain a portfolio duration matched to a specific target date is called **dynamic immunization**. The advantage of dynamic immunization is that reinvestment risk caused by continually changing bond yields is greatly reduced. The drawback of dynamic immunization is that each portfolio rebalancing incurs management and transaction costs. Therefore, portfolios should not be rebalanced too frequently. In practice, rebalancing on an intermittent basis, say, each quarter, is a reasonable compromise between the costs of rebalancing and the benefits of dynamic immunization.

CHECK THIS

10.8a   What are the two effects on the target date value of a dedicated portfolio of a shift in yields? Explain why they tend to offset.

10.8b   How can a dedicated portfolio be immunized against shifts in yields?

10.8c   Why is rebalancing necessary to maintain immunization?

10.9   Summary and Conclusions

This chapter covers the basics of bonds, bond yields, duration, and immunization. In this chapter we saw that:

1. Bonds are commonly distinguished according to whether they are selling at par value or at a discount or premium relative to par value. Bonds with a price greater than par value are said to be selling at a premium; bonds with a price less than par value are said to be selling at a discount.

2. There are three different yield measures: coupon yield or rate, current yield, and yield to maturity. Each is calculated using a specific equation, and which is the biggest or smallest depends on whether the bond is selling at a discount or premium.

3. Important relationships among bond prices, maturities, coupon rates, and yields are described by Malkiel's five bond price theorems.

4. A stated yield to maturity is almost never equal to an actually realized yield because yields are subject to bond price risk and coupon reinvestment rate risk. Bond price risk is the risk that a bond sold before maturity must be sold at a price different from the price predicted by an originally stated yield to maturity. Coupon reinvestment risk is the risk that bond coupons must be reinvested at yields different from an originally stated yield to maturity.

5. To account for differences in interest rate risk across bonds with different coupon rates and maturities, the concept of duration is widely applied. Duration is a direct measure of a bond's price sensitivity to changes in bond yields.

6. Bond portfolios are often created for the purpose of preparing for a future liability payment. Portfolios formed for such a specific purpose are called dedicated portfolios. When the future liability payment of a dedicated portfolio is due on a known date, that date is called the portfolio's target date.

7. Minimizing the uncertainty of the value of a dedicated portfolio's future target date value is called immunization. A strategy of matching a bond portfolio's duration to the target maturity date accomplishes this goal.

GET REAL

This chapter covered bond basics. How should you, as an investor or investment manager, put this information to work?

Now that you've been exposed to basic facts about bonds, their prices, and their yields, you might try applying the various principles we have discussed. Do this by buying some bonds and then observing the behavior of their prices and yields. Buying Treasury bonds is the best place to start.

With a simulated brokerage account (such as Stock-Trak), buy two Treasury bonds with the same maturity but different coupons. This will let you see the impact of coupon rates on price volatility. Similarly, buy two bonds with very different maturities but similar coupon rates. You'll see firsthand how maturity determines the risk of a bond.

While you're at it, calculate the durations of the bonds you buy. As their yields fluctuate, check that the percentage change in price is very close to what your calculated duration suggests it should be.

To learn more about bond prices and yields, visit some interesting Web sites such as Bonds Online (www.bondsonline.com), Investing in Bonds (www.investinginbonds.com), and James Baker & Assoc. (www.jamesbaker.com).

Key Terms

callable bond 329
call price 329
call protection period 329
clean price 326
coupon rate 320
current yield 321
dedicated portfolio 342
dirty price 326
dollar value of an 01 340
duration 335

dynamic immunization 345
immunization 344
interest rate risk 331
make-whole call price 329
price risk 344
realized yield 331
reinvestment rate risk 342
yield to call (YTC) 330
yield to maturity (YTM) 321
yield value of a 32nd 340

Chapter Review Problems and Self-Test

1. **Straight Bond Prices**   Suppose a bond has 10 years to maturity and a coupon rate of 6 percent. The bond's yield to maturity is 8 percent. What's the price?

2. **Premium Bonds**   Suppose we have two bonds, both with a 6 percent coupon rate and the same yield to maturity of 4 percent, but with different maturities of 5 and 15 years. Which has the higher price? Verify your answer by calculating the prices.

3. **Macaulay Duration**   A bond has a Macaulay duration of nine years, and its yield increases from 6 percent to 6.25 percent. What will happen to the price of the bond?

Answers to Self-Test Problems

1. Here, the coupon rate is 6 percent and the face value is $1,000, so the annual coupon is $60. The bond's price is calculated as follows:

Present value of semiannual coupons:

$$\frac{\$60}{.08}\left[1 - \frac{1}{(1.04)^{20}}\right] = \$407.70979$$

Present value of $1,000 principal:

$$\frac{\$1,000}{(1.04)^{20}} = \$456.38695$$

The bond's price is the sum of coupon and principal present values:

$$\text{Bond price} = \$407.71 + \$456.39 = \$864.10$$

2. Because both bonds have a 6 percent coupon and a 4 percent yield, both bonds sell at a premium, and the one with the longer maturity will have a higher price. We can verify these conclusions by calculating the prices as follows:

5-year maturity premium bond price:

$$\frac{\$60}{.04}\left[1 - \frac{1}{(1.02)^{10}}\right] + \frac{\$1,000}{(1.02)^{10}} = \$1,089.83$$

15-year maturity premium bond price:

$$\frac{\$60}{.04}\left[1 - \frac{1}{(1.02)^{30}}\right] + \frac{\$1,000}{(1.02)^{30}} = \$1,223.96$$

Notice that the longer maturity premium bond has a higher price, just as we thought.

3. The resulting percentage change in the price of the bond can be calculated as follows:

$$-9 \times \frac{.0625 - .06}{1.03} = -2.18\%$$

The bond's price declines by approximately 2.18 percent in response to a 25 basis point increase in yields.

Test Your Investment Quotient

1. **Yield to Maturity**   The yield to maturity on a bond is
   a. Below the coupon rate when the bond sells at a discount and above the coupon rate when the bond sells at a premium.
   b. The interest rate that makes the present value of the payments equal to the bond price.
   c. Based on the assumption that all future payments received are reinvested at the coupon rate.
   d. Based on the assumption that all future payments received are reinvested at future market rates.

2. **Bond Yields**   In which one of the following cases is the bond selling at a discount?
   a. Coupon rate is greater than current yield, which is greater than yield to maturity.
   b. Coupon rate, current yield, and yield to maturity are all the same.
   c. Coupon rate is less than current yield, which is less than yield to maturity.
   d. Coupon rate is less than current yield, which is greater than yield to maturity.

3. **Bond Yields**   When are yield to maturity and current yield on a bond equal?
   a. When market interest rates begin to level off.
   b. If the bond sells at a price in excess of its par value.
   c. When the expected holding period is greater than one year.
   d. If the coupon and market interest rate are equal.

4. **Bond Yields** Which of the following states the correct relationship among yield measures for discount bonds?

a. Coupon rate < Current yield < Yield to maturity
b. Current yield < Coupon rate < Yield to maturity
c. Coupon rate < Yield to maturity < Current yield
d. Yield to maturity < Coupon rate < Current yield

5. **Bond Yields** Which of the following states the correct relationship among yield measures for premium bonds?

a. Coupon rate > Current yield > Yield to maturity
b. Current yield > Coupon rate > Yield to maturity
c. Coupon rate > Yield to maturity > Current yield
d. Yield to maturity > Coupon rate > Current yield

6. **Bond Prices** Consider a five-year bond with a 10 percent coupon that is presently trading at a yield to maturity of 8 percent. If market interest rates do not change, one year from now the price of this bond

a. Will be higher
b. Will be lower
c. Will be the same
d. Cannot be determined

7. **Bond Prices** Using semiannual compounding, what would the price of a 15-year, zero coupon bond that has a par value of $1,000 and a required return of 8 percent be?

a. $308
b. $315
c. $464
d. $555

8. **Bond Prices** If an investor's required return is 12 percent, the value of a 10-year maturity zero coupon bond with a maturity value of $1,000 is *closest* to

a. $312
b. $688
c. $1,000
d. $1,312

9. **Duration** Another term for bond duration is

a. Actual maturity
b. Effective maturity
c. Calculated maturity
d. Near-term maturity

10. **Duration** Which of the following is not a property of duration?

a. A longer maturity generally yields a longer duration.
b. Duration generally increases at a decreasing rate as maturity lengthens.
c. A bigger coupon generally yields a longer duration.
d. A higher yield to maturity generally yields a shorter duration.

11. **Duration** Which statement is true for the Macaulay duration of a zero coupon bond?

a. It is equal to the bond's maturity in years.
b. It is equal to one-half the bond's maturity in years.
c. It is equal to the bond's maturity in years divided by its yield to maturity.
d. It cannot be calculated because of the lack of coupons.

12. **Duration** Which of the following states the correct relationship between Macaulay duration and modified duration?

a. Modified duration = Macaulay duration/$(1 + YTM/2)$
b. Modified duration = Macaulay duration $\times$ $(1 + YTM/2)$
c. Modified duration = Macaulay duration/YTM
d. Modified duration = Macaulay duration $\times$ YTM

13. **Duration** Which one of the following bonds has the shortest duration?
    a. Zero coupon, 10-year maturity
    b. Zero coupon, 13-year maturity
    c. 8 percent coupon, 10-year maturity
    d. 8 percent coupon, 13-year maturity

14. **Duration** Identify the bond that has the longest duration (no calculations necessary).
    a. 20-year maturity with an 8 percent coupon
    b. 20-year maturity with a 12 percent coupon
    c. 15-year maturity with a 0 percent coupon
    d. 10-year maturity with a 15 percent coupon

15. **Duration** Which bond has the longest duration?
    a. 8-year maturity, 6 percent coupon
    b. 8-year maturity, 11 percent coupon
    c. 15-year maturity, 6 percent coupon
    d. 15-year maturity, 11 percent coupon

16. **Duration** The duration of a bond normally increases with an increase in
    a. Term to maturity
    b. Yield to maturity
    c. Coupon rate
    d. All of the above

17. **Duration** When interest rates decline, what happens to the duration of a 30-year bond selling at a premium?
    a. It increases
    b. It decreases
    c. It remains the same
    d. It increases at first, then declines

18. **Duration** An 8 percent, 20-year corporate bond is priced to yield 9 percent. The Macaulay duration for this bond is 8.85 years. Given this information, how many years is the bond's modified duration?
    a. 8.12
    b. 8.47
    c. 8.51
    d. 9.25

19. **Using Duration** A 9-year bond has a yield to maturity of 10 percent and a modified duration of 6.54 years. If the market yield changes by 50 basis points, what is the change in the bond's price?
    a. 3.27 percent
    b. 3.66 percent
    c. 6.54 percent
    d. 7.21 percent

20. **Using Duration** A 6 percent coupon bond paying interest semiannually has a modified duration of 10 years, sells for $800, and is priced at a yield to maturity (YTM) of 8 percent. If the YTM increases to 9 percent, the predicted change in price, using the duration concept, is which of the following amounts?
    a. $76.56
    b. $76.92
    c. $77.67
    d. $80.00

21. **Immunization** Which of the following strategies is most likely to yield the best interest rate risk immunization results for a bond portfolio?
    a. Maturity matching
    b. Duration matching
    c. Buy and hold
    d. Investing in interest rate-sensitive stocks

22. **Immunization**   Consider two dedicated bond portfolios both with the same 10-year target dates. One is managed using a buy-and-hold strategy with reinvested coupons. The other is managed using a dynamic immunization strategy. The buy-and-hold portfolio is most likely to outperform the immunized portfolio under what kind of interest rate environment?

   a. Steadily rising interest rates.
   b. Steadily falling interest rates.
   c. Constant interest rates.
   d. Performance will be the same under any environment.

23. **Bond Yields**   A zero coupon bond paying $100 at maturity 10 years from now has a current price of $50. Its yield to maturity is *closest* to which of the following?

   a. 5 percent
   b. 6 percent
   c. 7 percent
   d. 8 percent

24. **Bond Price**   A newly issued 10-year option-free bond is valued at par on June 1, 2000. The bond has an annual coupon of 8.0 percent. On June 1, 2003, the bond has a yield to maturity of 7.1 percent. The first coupon is reinvested at 8.0 percent and the second coupon is reinvested at 7.0 percent. The price of the bond on June 1, 2003, is closest to

   a. 100.0 percent of par
   b. 102.5 percent of par
   c. 104.8 percent of par
   d. 105.4 percent of par

25. **Interest Rate Risk**   The interest rate risk of a noncallable bond is most likely to be positively related to the

   a. Risk-free rate
   b. Bond's coupon rate
   c. Bond's time to maturity
   d. Bond's yield to maturity

Concept Questions

1. **Bond Prices**   What are premium, discount, and par bonds?

2. **Bond Features**   In the United States, what is the normal face value for corporate and U.S. government bonds? How are coupons calculated? How often are coupons paid?

3. **Coupon Rates and Current Yields**   What are the coupon rate and current yield on a bond? What happens to these if a bond's price rises?

4. **Interest Rate Risk**   What is interest rate risk? What are the roles of a bond's coupon and maturity in determining its level of interest rate risk?

5. **Bond Yields**   For a premium bond, which is greater, the coupon rate or the yield to maturity? Why? For a discount bond? Why?

6. **Bond Yields**   What is the difference between a bond's promised yield and its realized yield? Which is more relevant? When we calculate a bond's yield to maturity, which of these are we calculating?

7. **Interpreting Bond Yields**   Is the yield to maturity (YTM) on a bond the same thing as the required return? Is YTM the same thing as the coupon rate? Suppose that today a 10 percent coupon bond sells at par. Two years from now, the required return on the same bond is 8 percent. What is the coupon rate on the bond now? The YTM?

8. **Interpreting Bond Yields**   Suppose you buy a 9 percent coupon, 15-year bond today when it's first issued. If interest rates suddenly rise to 15 percent, what happens to the value of your bond? Why?

9. **Bond Prices versus Yields**   (a) What is the relationship between the price of a bond and its YTM? (b) Explain why some bonds sell at a premium to par value, and other bonds sell at a

discount. What do you know about the relationship between the coupon rate and the YTM for premium bonds? What about discount bonds? For bonds selling at par value? (c) What is the relationship between the current yield and YTM for premium bonds? For discount bonds? For bonds selling at par value?

10. **Yield to Call**   For callable bonds, the financial press generally reports either the yield to maturity or the yield to call. Often yield to call is reported for premium bonds, and yield to maturity is reported for discount bonds. What is the reasoning behind this convention?

Questions and Problems _____

Core Questions

1. **Bond Prices**   Reynolds Inc. has 9 percent coupon bonds on the market that have 15 years left to maturity. If the YTM on these bonds is 8.2 percent, what is the current bond price?

2. **Bond Yields**   Corpstein Company bonds have a coupon rate of 8 percent, 19 years to maturity, and a current price of $904. What is the YTM? The current yield?

3. **Bond Prices**   A bond has a coupon rate of 7.5 percent and 13 years until maturity. If the yield to maturity is 6.3 percent, what is the price of the bond?

4. **Bond Prices**   A bond with 25 years until maturity has a coupon rate of 9 percent and a yield to maturity of 6.5 percent. What is the price of the bond?

5. **Yield to Maturity**   A bond sells for $864.50 and has a coupon rate of 8 percent. If the bond has 16 years until maturity, what is the yield to maturity of the bond?

6. **Yield to Maturity**   A bond with a maturity of 19.5 years sells for $913. If the coupon rate is 6 percent, what is the yield to maturity of the bond?

7. **Yield to Maturity**   Shane Industries has a bond outstanding that sells for $1,118. The bond has coupon rate of 7.5 percent and nine years until maturity. What is the yield to maturity of the bond?

8. **Yield to Maturity**   Sealord Fisheries issues zero coupon bonds on the market at a price of $180 per bond. Each bond has a face value of $1,000 payable at maturity in 20 years. What is the yield to maturity for these bonds?

9. **Yield to Call**   Sealord Fisheries zero coupon bonds referred to above are callable in 10 years at a call price of $500. Using semiannual compounding, what is the yield to call for these bonds?

10. **Yield to Call**   If instead the Sealord Fisheries zero coupon bonds referred to above are callable in 10 years at a call price of $475, what is their yield to call?

Intermediate Questions

11. **Coupon Rates**   Raider Corporation has bonds on the market with 13 years to maturity, a YTM of 7.5 percent, and a current price of $1,082.20. What must the coupon rate be on the company's bonds?

12. **Bond Prices**   Perry's Pizzeria issued 20-year bonds one year ago at a coupon rate of 9.40 percent. If the YTM on these bonds is 9.02 percent, what is the current bond price?

13. **Bond Yields**   Soprano's Spaghetti Factory issued 30-year bonds two years ago at a coupon rate of 8.5 percent. If these bonds currently sell for 78 percent of par value, what is the YTM?

14. **Bond Price Movements**   A zero coupon bond with an 8 percent YTM has 20 years to maturity. Two years later, the price of the bond remains the same. What's going on here?

15. **Realized Yield**   For the bond referred to in the previous question, what would be the realized yield if it were held to maturity?

16. **Bond Price Movements**   Bond P is a premium bond with a 9 percent coupon, a YTM of 7 percent, and 15 years to maturity. Bond D is a discount bond with a 9 percent coupon, a YTM of 11 percent, and also 15 years to maturity. If interest rates remain unchanged, what do you expect the price of these bonds to be 1 year from now? In 5 years? In 10 years? In 14 years? In 15 years? What's going on here?

17. **Interest Rate Risk**   Both bond A and bond B have 8 percent coupons and are priced at par value. Bond A has 2 years to maturity, while bond B has 15 years to maturity. If interest

352   Part 3   ■   Interest Rates and Bond Valuation

rates suddenly rise by 2 percent, what is the percentage change in price of bond A? Of bond B? If rates were to suddenly fall by 2 percent instead, what would the percentage change in price of bond A be now? Of bond B? Illustrate your answers by graphing bond prices versus YTM. What does this problem tell you about the interest rate risk of longer term bonds?

18. **Interest Rate Risk**   Bond J is a 5 percent coupon bond. Bond K is a 9 percent coupon bond. Both bonds have 10 years to maturity and have a YTM of 7 percent. If interest rates suddenly rise by 2 percent, what is the percentage price change of these bonds? What if rates suddenly fall by 2 percent instead? What does this problem tell you about the interest rate risk of lower-coupon bonds?

19. **Finding the Bond Maturity**   Crosby Co. has 7.5 percent coupon bonds with a YTM of 6.98 percent. The current yield on these bonds is 7.22 percent. How many years do these bonds have left until they mature?

20. **Finding the Bond Maturity**   You've just found a 10 percent coupon bond on the market that sells for par value. What is the maturity on this bond?

21. **Realized Yields**   Suppose you buy a 9 percent coupon bond today for $1,080. The bond has 15 years to maturity. What rate of return do you expect to earn on your investment? Two years from now, the YTM on your bond has increased by 2 percent, and you decide to sell. What price will your bond sell for? What is the realized yield on your investment? Compare this yield to the YTM when you first bought the bond. Why are they different? Assume interest payments are reinvested at the original YTM.

22. **Yield to Call**   Fooling Company has a 12 percent callable bond outstanding on the market with 20 years to maturity, call protection for the next 5 years, and a call premium of $80. What is the yield to call (YTC) for this bond if the current price is 118 percent of par value?

23. **Calculating Duration**   What is the Macaulay duration of a 7 percent coupon bond with nine years to maturity and a current price of $1,130.60? What is the modified duration?

24. **Using Duration**   In the previous problem, suppose the yield on the bond suddenly increases by 2 percent. Use duration to estimate the new price of the bond. Compare your answer to the new bond price calculated from the usual bond pricing formula. What do your results tell you about the accuracy of duration?

25. **Dollar Value of an 01**   What is the dollar value of an 01 for the bond in Problem 23?

26. **Yield Value of a 32nd**   A Treasury bond with 12 years to maturity is currently quoted at 105:13. The bond has a coupon rate of 8 percent. What is the yield value of a 32nd for this bond?

27. **Calculating Duration**   A bond with a coupon rate of 9 percent sells at a yield to maturity of 10 percent. If the bond matures in 17 years, what is the Macaulay duration of the bond? What is the modified duration?

28. **Calculating Duration**   Assume the bond in the previous problem has a yield to maturity of 8 percent. What is the Macaulay duration now? What does this tell you about the relationship between duration and yield to maturity?

29. **Calculating Duration**   You find a bond with 25 years until maturity that has a coupon rate of 8 percent and a yield to maturity of 7 percent. What is the Macaulay duration? The modified duration?

30. **Using Duration**   Suppose the yield to maturity on the bond in the previous problem increases by .25 percent. What is the new price of the bond using duration? What is the new price of the bond using the bond pricing formula? What if the yield to maturity increases by 1 percent? By 2 percent? By 5 percent? What does this tell you about using duration to estimate bond price changes for large interest rate changes?

31. **Using Duration**   Noah Kramer, a fixed-income portfolio manager based in the country of Sevista, is considering the purchase of Sevista government bonds. Sevista currently has government bonds evenly distributed among 5-, 10-, and 25-year maturities. Noah decides to evaluate two strategies for investing in Sevista bonds. The following table shows the details of the two strategies.

Strategy	5-Year Maturity Modified Duration = 4.83	15-Year Maturity Modified Duration = 14.35	25-Year Maturity Modified Duration = 23.81
I	$5 million	$0	$5 million
II	$0	$10 million	$0

The market value of the bonds purchased will be $10 million and the target modified duration is 15 years. Before choosing one of the two bond investment strategies, Kramer wants to study how the market value of the bonds will change if an instantaneous interest rate shift occurs immediately after his investment. The details of the interest rate shift are shown below.

Interest Rate Maturity (years)	Interest Rate Change (basis points)
5	Down 75
15	Up 25
25	Up 50

Calculate, for this instantaneous interest rate shift, the percentage change in the market value of the bonds that will occur under each investment strategy.

32. **Bootstrapping**   One method of obtaining an estimate of the term structure of interest rates is called bootstrapping. Suppose you have a one-year zero coupon bond with a rate of r_1 and a two-year bond with an annual coupon payment of C. To bootstrap the two-year rate, you can set up the following equation for the price (P) of the coupon bond:

$$P = \frac{C_1}{1 + r_1} + \frac{C_2 + \text{Par value}}{(1 + r_2)^2}$$

Since you can observe all of the variables except r_2, the spot rate for two years, you can solve for this interest rate. Suppose there is a zero coupon bond with one year to maturity that sells for $952 and a two-year bond with a 7 percent coupon paid annually that sells for $1,032. What is the interest rate for two years? Suppose a bond with three years until maturity and an 8 percent annual coupon sells for $1,060. What is the interest rate for three years?

33. **Bootstrapping**   You find that the one-, two-, three-, and four-year interest rates are 5.20 percent, 5.85 percent, 6.15 percent, and 6.75 percent. What is the yield to maturity of a four-year bond with an annual coupon rate of 8 percent? *Hint*: Use the bootstrapping technique in the previous problem to find the price of the bond.

Spreadsheet Problems

34. **Yield to Maturity**   A Treasury bond that settles on August 10, 2006, matures on April 15, 2011. The coupon rate is 5.6 percent and the quoted price is 106:17. What is the bond's yield to maturity? Use an actual day count with 365 days per year.

35. **Bond Yields**   A bond that settles on June 7, 2006, matures on July 1, 2030, and may be called at any time after July 1, 2010, at a price of 108. The coupon rate on the bond is 8 percent and the price is 111.50. What is the yield to maturity and yield to call on this bond? Use the NASD 30/360-day count basis.

36. **Duration**   A Treasury bond that settles on October 18, 2006, matures on March 30, 2021. The coupon rate is 8.2 percent and the bond has a 6.85 yield to maturity. What are the Macaulay duration and modified duration?

What's on the Web? ────────────────── ■

1. **Bond Markets**   Go to www.bondsonline.com. What is the outlook for the bond market today? What are the major news items today that are expected to influence the bond market?

www.mhhe.com/jm4e

2. **Government Bonds**   Go to www.bloomberg.com and look up the yields for U.S. government bonds. You should also find a listing for foreign government bonds. Are the yields on all government bonds the same? Why or why not?

Stock-Trak Exercises ⬛

STOCK|TRAK

GLOBAL PORTFOLIO SIMULATIONS

To access the Stock-Trak Exercise for this chapter, please visit the book Web site at www.mhhe.com/jm4e and choose the corresponding chapter.

CHAPTER 11

Diversification and Risky Asset Allocation

"Out of this nettle, danger,
We pluck this flower, safety."

–Shakespeare, *Henry IV*

Intuitively, we all know that diversification is important for managing investment risk. But how exactly does diversification work, and how can we be sure we have an efficiently diversified portfolio? Insightful answers can be gleaned from the modern theory of diversification and asset allocation. ∎

In this chapter, we examine the role of diversification and asset allocation in investing. Most of us have a strong sense that diversification is important. After all, "Don't put all your eggs in one basket" is a bit of folk wisdom that seems to have stood the test of time quite well. Even so, the importance of diversification has not always been well understood. Diversification is important because portfolios with many investments usually produce a more consistent and stable total return than portfolios with just one investment. When you own many stocks, even if some of them decline in price, others are likely to increase in price (or stay at the same price).

The role and impact of diversification on portfolio risk and return were first formally explained in the early 1950s by financial pioneer Harry Markowitz. These aspects of portfolio diversification were an important discovery—Professor Markowitz shared the 1986 Nobel Prize in Economics for his insights on the value of diversification.

Surprisingly, Professor Markowitz's insights are not related to how investors care about risk or return. In fact, we can talk about the benefits of diversification without having to know how investors care about risk. Realistically, however, it is investors who care about the benefits of diversification. Therefore, to help you understand Professor Markowitz's insights, we make two assumptions. First, we assume that investors prefer more return to less return, and second, we assume that investors prefer less risk to more risk. In this chapter, variance and standard deviation are measures of risk.

11.1 Expected Returns and Variances

In Chapter 1, we discussed how to calculate average returns and variances using historical data. We begin this chapter with a discussion of how to analyze returns and variances when the information we have concerns future possible returns and their probabilities. We do this because the notion of diversification involves future returns and variances of future returns.

EXPECTED RETURNS

We start with a straightforward case. Consider a period of time such as a year. We have two stocks, say, Starcents and Jpod. Starcents is expected to have a return of 25 percent in the coming year; Jpod is expected to have a return of 20 percent during the same period.

Find expected returns at
www.411stocks.com

In a situation such as this, if all investors agreed on these expected return values, why would anyone want to hold Jpod? After all, why invest in one stock when the expectation is that another will do better? Clearly, the answer must depend on the different risks of the two investments. The return on Starcents, although it is *expected* to be 25 percent, could turn out to be significantly higher or lower. Similarly, Jpod's *realized* return could be significantly higher or lower than expected.

For example, suppose the economy booms. In this case, we think Starcents will have a 70 percent return. But if the economy tanks and enters a recession, we think the return will be –20 percent. In this case, we say that there are *two states of the economy,* which means that there are two possible outcomes. This scenario is oversimplified, of course, but it allows us to illustrate some key ideas without a lot of computational complexity.

Suppose we think boom and recession are equally likely to happen, that is, a 50–50 chance of each outcome. Table 11.1 illustrates the basic information we have described and some additional information about Jpod. Notice that Jpod earns 30 percent if there is a recession and 10 percent if there is a boom.

Obviously, if you buy one of these stocks, say, Jpod, what you earn in any particular year depends on what the economy does during that year. Suppose these probabilities stay the same through time. If you hold Jpod for a number of years, you'll earn 30 percent about half the time and 10 percent the other half. In this case, we say your **expected return** on Jpod, $E(R_J)$, is 20 percent:

expected return
Average return on a risky asset expected in the future.

$$E(R_J) = .50 \times 30\% + .50 \times 10\% = 20\%$$

In other words, you should expect to earn 20 percent from this stock, on average.

TABLE 11.1 States of the Economy and Stock Returns

State of Economy	Probability of State of Economy	Security Returns If State Occurs	
		Starcents	Jpod
Recession	.50	–20%	30%
Boom	.50	70	10
	1.00		

TABLE 11.2   Calculating Expected Returns

		Starcents		Jpod	
(1) **State of Economy**	**(2)** **Probability of State of Economy**	**(3)** **Return If State Occurs**	**(4)** **Product (2) × (3)**	**(5)** **Return If State Occurs**	**(6)** **Product (2) × (5)**
Recession	.50	−20%	−10%	30%	15%
Boom	.50	70	35	10	05
	1.00		$E(R_S) = 25\%$		$E(R_J) = 20\%$

For Starcents, the probabilities are the same, but the possible returns are different. Here we lose 20 percent half the time, and we gain 70 percent the other half. The expected return on Starcents, $E(R_S)$, is thus 25 percent:

$$E(R_s) = .50 \times -20\% + .50 \times 70\% = 25\%$$

Table 11.2 illustrates these calculations.

In Chapter 1, we defined a risk premium as the difference between the returns on a risky investment and a risk-free investment, and we calculated the historical risk premiums on some different investments. Using our projected returns, we can calculate the *projected* or *expected risk premium* as the difference between the expected return on a risky investment and the certain return on a risk-free investment.

For example, suppose risk-free investments are currently offering an 8 percent return. We will say that the risk-free rate, which we label R_f, is 8 percent. Given this, what is the projected risk premium on Jpod? On Starcents? Because the expected return on Jpod, $E(R_J)$, is 20 percent, the projected risk premium is:

$$\begin{aligned} \textbf{Risk premium} &= \textbf{Expected return} - \textbf{Risk-free rate} \qquad \textbf{(11.1)}\\ &= E(R_J) - R_f \\ &= 20\% - 8\% \\ &= 12\% \end{aligned}$$

Similarly, the risk premium on Starcents is $25\% - 8\% = 17\%$.

In general, the expected return on a security or other asset is simply equal to the sum of the possible returns multiplied by their probabilities. So, if we have 100 possible returns, we would multiply each one by its probability and then add up the results. The sum would be the expected return. The risk premium would then be the difference between this expected return and the risk-free rate.

EXAMPLE 11.1   Unequal Probabilities

Look again at Tables 11.1 and 11.2. Suppose you thought a boom would occur 20 percent of the time instead of 50 percent. What are the expected returns on Starcents and Jpod in this case? If the risk-free rate is 10 percent, what are the risk premiums?

The first thing to notice is that a recession must occur 80 percent of the time (1 − .20 = .80) because there are only two possibilities. With this in mind, Jpod has a 30 percent return in 80 percent of the years and a 10 percent return in 20 percent of the years. To calculate the expected return, we just multiply the possibilities by the probabilities and add up the results:

$$E(R_J) = .80 \times 30\% + .20 \times 10\% = 26\%$$

(continued)

TABLE 11.3

Calculating Expected Returns

(1) State of Economy	(2) Probability of State of Economy	Starcents		Jpod	
		(3) Return If State Occurs	(4) Product (2) × (3)	(5) Return If State Occurs	(6) Product (2) × (5)
Recession	.80	−20%	−16%	30%	24%
Boom	.20	70	14	10	2
	1.00		$E(R_S) = -2\%$		$E(R_J) = 26\%$

If the returns are written as decimals:

$$E(R_J) = .80 \times .30 + .20 \times .10 = .26$$

Table 11.3 summarizes the calculations for both stocks. Notice that the expected return on Starcents is −2 percent.

The risk premium for Jpod is 26% − 10% = 16% in this case. The risk premium for Starcents is negative: −2% − 10% = −12%. This is a little unusual, but, as we will see, it's not impossible.

CALCULATING THE VARIANCE

There's more on risk measures at www.investopedia.com and www.teachmefinance.com

To calculate the variances of the returns on our two stocks, we first determine the squared deviations from the expected return. We then multiply each possible squared deviation by its probability. Next we add these up, and the result is the variance.

To illustrate, one of our stocks in Table 11.2, Jpod, has an expected return of 20 percent. In a given year, the return will actually be either 30 percent or 10 percent. The possible deviations are thus 30% − 20% = 10% or 10% − 20% = −10%. In this case, the variance is:

$$\text{Variance} = \sigma^2 = .50 \times (10\%)^2 + .50 \times (-10\%)^2$$
$$= .50 \times (.10)^2 + .50 \times (-.10)^2 = .01$$

Notice that we used decimals to calculate the variance. The standard deviation is the square root of the variance:

$$\text{Standard deviation} = \sigma = \sqrt{.01} = .10 = 10\%$$

Table 11.4 summarizes these calculations and the expected return for both stocks. Notice that Starcents has a much larger variance. Starcents has the higher expected return, but Jpod has less risk. You could get a 70 percent return on your investment in Starcents, but you could also lose 20 percent. However, an investment in Jpod will always pay at least 10 percent.

Which of these stocks should you buy? We can't really say; it depends on your personal preferences regarding risk and return. We can be reasonably sure, however, that some investors would prefer one and some would prefer the other.

TABLE 11.4

Expected Returns and Variances

	Starcents	Jpod
Expected return, $E(R)$	.25, or 25%	.20, or 20%
Variance, σ^2	.2025	.0100
Standard deviation, σ	.45, or 45%	.10, or 10%

You've probably noticed that the way we calculated expected returns and variances here is somewhat different from the way we did it in Chapter 1 (and, probably, different from the way you learned it in your statistics course). The reason is that we were examining historical returns in Chapter 1, so we estimated the average return and the variance based on some actual events. Here, we have projected *future* returns and their associated probabilities, so this is the information with which we must work.

EXAMPLE 11.2   More Unequal Probabilities

Going back to Table 11.3 in Example 11.1, what are the variances on our two stocks once we have unequal probabilities? What are the standard deviations?

Converting all returns to decimals, we can summarize the needed calculations as follows:

(1) State of Economy	(2) Probability of State of Economy	(3) Return Deviation from Expected Return	(4) Squared Return Deviation	(5) Product (2) × (4)
Starcents				
Recession	.80	$-.20 - (-.02) = -.18$	.0324	.02592
Boom	.20	$.70 - (-.02) = .72$	.5184	.10368
				$\sigma_S^2 = .12960$
Jpod				
Recession	.80	$.30 - .26 = .04$	.0016	.00128
Boom	.20	$.10 - .26 = -.16$	.0256	.00512
				$\sigma_J^2 = .00640$

Based on these calculations, the standard deviation for Starcents is $\sigma_S = \sqrt{.1296} = 36\%$. The standard deviation for Jpod is much smaller, $\sigma_J = \sqrt{.0064}$, or 8%.

CHECK THIS

11.1a   How do we calculate the expected return on a security?

11.1b   In words, how do we calculate the variance of an expected return?

11.2   Portfolios

portfolio
Group of assets such as stocks and bonds held by an investor.

Thus far in this chapter, we have concentrated on individual assets considered separately. However, most investors actually hold a **portfolio** of assets. All we mean by this is that investors tend to own more than just a single stock, bond, or other asset. Given that this is so, portfolio return and portfolio risk are of obvious relevance. Accordingly, we now discuss portfolio expected returns and variances.

PORTFOLIO WEIGHTS

portfolio weight
Percentage of a portfolio's total value invested in a particular asset.

There are many equivalent ways of describing a portfolio. The most convenient approach is to list the percentages of the total portfolio's value that are invested in each portfolio asset. We call these percentages the **portfolio weights**.

For example, if we have $50 in one asset and $150 in another, then our total portfolio is worth $200. The percentage of our portfolio in the first asset is $50/$200 = .25, or 25%. The percentage of our portfolio in the second asset is $150/$200 = .75, or 75%. Notice that the weights sum up to 1.00 (100%) because all of our money is invested somewhere.[1]

PORTFOLIO EXPECTED RETURNS

Let's go back to Starcents and Jpod. You put half your money in each. The portfolio weights are obviously .50 and .50. What is the pattern of returns on this portfolio? The expected return?

To answer these questions, suppose the economy actually enters a recession. In this case, half your money (the half in Starcents) loses 20 percent. The other half (the half in Jpod) gains 30 percent. Your portfolio return, R_P, in a recession will thus be:

$$R_P = .50 \times -20\% + .50 \times 30\% = 5\%$$

Table 11.5 summarizes the remaining calculations. Notice that when a boom occurs, your portfolio would return 40 percent:

$$R_P = .50 \times 70\% + .50 \times 10\% = 40\%$$

As indicated in Table 11.5, the expected return on your portfolio, $E(R_P)$, is 22.5 percent.

We can save ourselves some work by calculating the expected return more directly. Given these portfolio weights, we could have reasoned that we expect half our money to earn 25 percent (the half in Starcents) and half of our money to earn 20 percent (the half in Jpod). Our portfolio expected return is thus:

$$
\begin{aligned}
E(R_P) &= .50 \times E(R_S) + .50 \times E(R_J) \\
&= .50 \times 25\% + .50 \times 20\% \\
&= 22.5\%
\end{aligned}
$$

This is the same portfolio return that we calculated in Table 11.5.

This method of calculating the expected return on a portfolio works no matter how many assets there are in the portfolio. Suppose we had n assets in our portfolio, where n is any number at all. If we let x_1 stand for the percentage of our money in Asset i, then the expected return is:

$$E(R_P) = x_1 \times E(R_1) + x_2 \times E(R_2) + \cdots + x_n \times E(R_n) \qquad (11.2)$$

This says that the expected return on a portfolio is a straightforward combination of the expected returns on the assets in that portfolio. This seems somewhat obvious, but, as we will examine next, the obvious approach is not always the right one.

TABLE 11.5 — **Expected Portfolio Return**

(1) State of Economy	(2) Probability of State of Economy	(3) Portfolio Return If State Occurs	(4) Product (2) × (3)
Recession	.50	$.50 \times -20\% + .50 \times 30\% = 5\%$	2.5
Boom	.50	$.50 \times 70\% + .50 \times 10\% = 40\%$	20.0
			$E(R_P) = 22.5\%$

[1] Some of it could be in cash, of course, but we would then just consider cash to be another of the portfolio assets.

EXAMPLE 11.3 **More Unequal Probabilities**

Suppose we had the following projections on three stocks:

State of Economy	Probability of State of Economy	Returns Stock A	Returns Stock B	Returns Stock C
Boom	.50	10%	15%	20%
Bust	.50	8	4	0

We want to calculate portfolio expected returns in two cases. First, what would be the expected return on a portfolio with equal amounts invested in each of the three stocks? Second, what would be the expected return if half of the portfolio were in A, with the remainder equally divided between B and C?

From our earlier discussion, the expected returns on the individual stocks are:

$$E(R_A) = 9.0\% \quad E(R_B) = 9.5\% \quad E(R_C) = 10.0\%$$

(Check these for practice.) If a portfolio has equal investments in each asset, the portfolio weights are all the same. Such a portfolio is said to be *equally weighted*. Since there are three stocks in this case, the weights are all equal to 1/3. The portfolio expected return is thus:

$$E(R_P) = 1/3 \times 9.0\% + 1/3 \times 9.5\% + 1/3 \times 10.0\% = 9.5\%$$

In the second case, check that the portfolio expected return is 9.375%.

PORTFOLIO VARIANCE

From the preceding discussion, the expected return on a portfolio that contains equal investments in Starcents and Jpod is 22.5 percent. What is the standard deviation of return on this portfolio? Simple intuition might suggest that half of our money has a standard deviation of 45 percent, and the other half has a standard deviation of 10 percent. So the portfolio's standard deviation might be calculated as follows:

$$\sigma_P = .50 \times 45\% + .50 \times 10\% = 27.5\%$$

Unfortunately, this approach is *completely incorrect!*

Let's see what the standard deviation really is. Table 11.6 summarizes the relevant calculations. As we see, the portfolio's standard deviation is much less than 27.5 percent—it's only 17.5 percent. What is illustrated here is that the variance on a portfolio is *not* generally a simple combination of the variances of the assets in the portfolio.

TABLE 11.6 **Calculating Portfolio Variance and Standard Deviation**

(1) State of Economy	(2) Probability of State of Economy	(3) Portfolio Returns If State Occurs	(4) Squared Deviation from Expected Return*	(5) Product (2) × (4)
Recession	.50	5%	$(5 - 22.5)^2 = 306.25$	153.125
Boom	.50	40	$(40 - 22.5)^2 = 306.25$	153.125
			Variance, $\sigma_P^2 = 306.25$	
			Standard deviation, $\sigma_P = \sqrt{306.25} = 17.5\%$	

*Notice that we used percents for all returns. Verify that if we wrote returns as decimals, we would get a variance of .030625 and a standard deviation of .175, or 17.5%.

We can illustrate this point a little more dramatically by considering a slightly different set of portfolio weights. Suppose we put 2/11 (about 18 percent) in Starcents and the other 9/11 (about 82 percent) in Jpod. If a recession occurs, this portfolio will have a return of:

$$R_P = 2/11 \times -20\% + 9/11 \times 30\% = 20.91\%$$

If a boom occurs, this portfolio will have a return of:

$$R_P = 2/11 \times 70\% + 9/11 \times 10\% = 20.91\%$$

Notice that the return is the same no matter what happens. No further calculation is needed: This portfolio has a *zero* variance and no risk!

This is a nice bit of financial alchemy. We take two quite risky assets and, by mixing them just right, we create a riskless portfolio. It seems very clear that combining assets into portfolios can substantially alter the risks faced by an investor. This is a crucial observation, and we will begin to explore its implications in the next section.[2]

EXAMPLE 11.4 — Portfolio Variance and Standard Deviations

In Example 11.3, what are the standard deviations of the two portfolios?

To answer, we first have to calculate the portfolio returns in the two states. We will work with the second portfolio, which has 50 percent in Stock A and 25 percent in each of stocks B and C. The relevant calculations are summarized as follows:

State of Economy	Probability of State of Economy	Returns Stock A	Stock B	Stock C	Portfolio
Boom	.50	10%	15%	20%	13.75%
Bust	.50	8	4	0	5.00

The portfolio return when the economy booms is calculated as:

$$R_P = .50 \times 10\% + .25 \times 15\% + .25 \times 20\% = 13.75\%$$

The return when the economy goes bust is calculated the same way. Check that it's 5 percent and also check that the expected return on the portfolio is 9.375 percent. Expressing returns in decimals, the variance is thus:

$$\sigma_P^2 = .50 \times (.1375 - .09375)^2 + .50 \times (.05 - .09375)^2 = .0019141$$

The standard deviation is:

$$\sigma_P = \sqrt{.0019141} = 0.04375, \text{ or } 4.375\%$$

Check: Using equal weights, verify that the portfolio standard deviation is 5.5 percent.

Note: If the standard deviation in 4.375 percent, the variance should be somewhere between 16 and 25 (the squares of 4 and 5, respectively). If we square 4.375, we get 19.141. To express a variance in percentage, we must move the decimal *four* places to the right. That is, we must multiply 0.0019141 by 10,000—which is the square of 100.

---

[2]Earlier, we had a risk-free rate of 8 percent. Now we have, in effect, a 20.91 percent risk-free rate. If this situation actually existed, there would be a very profitable opportunity! In reality, we expect that all riskless investments would have the same return.

11.2a What is a portfolio weight?

11.2b How do we calculate the variance of an expected return?

11.3 Diversification and Portfolio Risk

Our discussion to this point has focused on some hypothetical securities. We've seen that portfolio risks can, in principle, be quite different from the risks of the assets that make up the portfolio. We now look more closely at the risk of an individual asset versus the risk of a portfolio of many different assets. As we did in Chapter 1, we will examine some stock market history to get an idea of what happens with actual investments in U.S. capital markets.

THE EFFECT OF DIVERSIFICATION: ANOTHER LESSON FROM MARKET HISTORY

In Chapter 1, we saw that the standard deviation of the annual return on a portfolio of large common stocks was about 20 percent per year. Does this mean that the standard deviation of the annual return on a typical stock in that group is about 20 percent? As you might suspect by now, the answer is no. This is an extremely important observation.

| TABLE 11.7 | Portfolio Standard Deviations |

(1) Number of Stocks in Portfolio	(2) Average Standard Deviation of Annual Portfolio Returns	(3) Ratio of Portfolio Standard Deviation to Standard Deviation of a Single Stock
1	49.24%	1.00
2	37.36	.76
4	29.69	.60
6	26.64	.54
8	24.98	.51
10	23.93	.49
20	21.68	.44
30	20.87	.42
40	20.46	.42
50	20.20	.41
100	19.69	.40
200	19.42	.39
300	19.34	.39
400	19.29	.39
500	19.27	.39
1,000	19.21	.39

Source: These figures are from Table 1 in Meir Statman, "How Many Stocks Make a Diversified Portfolio?" *Journal of Financial and Quantitative Analysis* 22 (September 1987), pp. 353–64. They were derived from E. J. Elton and M. J. Gruber, "Risk Reduction and Portfolio Size: An Analytic Solution," *Journal of Business* 50 (October 1977), pp. 415–37.

To examine the relationship between portfolio size and portfolio risk, Table 11.7 illustrates typical average annual standard deviations for equally weighted portfolios that contain different numbers of randomly selected NYSE securities.

In column 2 of Table 11.7, we see that the standard deviation for a "portfolio" of one security is just under 50 percent per year at 49.24 percent. What this means is that if you randomly select a single NYSE stock and put all your money into it, your standard deviation of return would typically have been about 50 percent per year. Obviously, such a strategy has significant risk! If you were to randomly select two NYSE securities and put half your money in each, your average annual standard deviation would have been about 37 percent.

The important thing to notice in Table 11.7 is that the standard deviation declines as the number of securities is increased. By the time we have 100 randomly chosen stocks (and 1 percent invested in each), the portfolio's volatility has declined by 60 percent, from 50 percent per year to 20 percent per year. With 500 securities, the standard deviation is 19.27 percent per year, similar to the 20 percent per year we saw in Chapter 1 for large common stocks. The small difference exists because the portfolio securities, portfolio weights, and the time periods covered are not identical. The nearby *Investment Updates* box offers further historical perspective on the need for diversification.

THE PRINCIPLE OF DIVERSIFICATION

Figure 11.1 illustrates the point we've been discussing. What we have plotted is the standard deviation of the return versus the number of stocks in the portfolio. Notice in Figure 11.1 that the benefit in terms of risk reduction from adding securities drops off as we add more and more. By the time we have 10 securities, most of the diversification effect is already realized, and by the time we get to 30 or so, there is very little remaining benefit.

The diversification benefit does depend on the time period over which returns and variances are calculated. For example, the data in Table 11.7 precede 1987. Scholars recently revisited diversification benefits by looking at stock returns and variances from 1986 to 1997 and found that 50 stocks are needed to build a highly diversified portfolio in this time

FIGURE 11.1 | Portfolio Diversification

WHY A BROAD MIX HELPS IN LONG TERM

Stock-market diversification is sold as a short-term sedative for antsy investors. But it's also your best bet for ensuring decent long-run returns. In recent columns, I've written a lot about diversification. There's a good reason for that: If this 2001 bear market has anything to teach us, it is the value of spreading your stock-market bets widely. Over the past year, the hardest-hit investors have been those who pooh-poohed diversification and loaded up on technology stocks, only to see their portfolios decimated by NASDAQ's implosion. Clearly, these folks would have fared far better with a broader array of stocks. But diversification is more than just a defense against short-run market gyrations. To understand why, consider the performance of large, small, and foreign stocks over the past 30 years.

At first blush, the results seem to encourage investors to shun diversification and instead stick with the big blue-chip stocks they know and love. After all, over the 30 years, large, small, and foreign stocks generated almost exactly the same average annual total return. According to Chicago researchers Ibbotson Associates, Standard & Poor's 500-stock index of large-company stocks was up an average 13.2% a year, smaller U.S. companies gained 14.7%, and Morgan Stanley's Europe, Australasia, and Far East index climbed 13.1%. In other words, if all you owned was a smattering of blue-chip stocks, you should have done just fine over the past 30 years.

But the raw data don't tell the whole story. Here's why:

Tenacity Tested: Suppose that in 1970 you settled on a portfolio consisting exclusively of large U.S.

stocks. Would you have hung onto that portfolio through the entire 30 years? I doubt it. For starters, you had to sit tight through the unnerving stock-market declines of 1973–74, 1976–78, 1980–82, 1987, and 1990. That would have been tough with an all-stock portfolio. But even if you had an unflinching determination to stick with stocks, you would have been constantly second-guessing your commitment to blue-chip companies. For instance, in the 1970s, you would have been tempted to swap into small companies and foreign shares, both of which outpaced U.S. large-company stocks. In the 1980s, foreign markets again outstripped U.S. large companies. Indeed, it was only in the 1990s that these blue-chip stocks reigned supreme.

Out of Time: Planning on sticking with U.S. large-company stocks for the next three decades? Circumstances may intervene. Maybe you will be forced to liquidate your stock portfolio early because you get divorced, lose your job, or get hit with hefty medical bills. Alternatively, maybe your time horizon isn't quite as long as you imagine. For instance, you might be looking at a 30-year retirement. But if you are living off your portfolio, you will probably have to sell many of your stocks before the 30 years are up.

In that case, you will definitely want to be globally diversified, because that will provide vital portfolio protection over this shorter period. For proof, check out the accompanying table. It takes the past 30 years, picks out the roughest 5, 10, 15, and 20-year stretches for large-company stocks, and then shows how other investments fared.

period. The point is that investors should be thinking in terms of 30 to 50 individual stocks when they are building a diversified portfolio.

Figure 11.1 illustrates two key points. First, some of the riskiness associated with individual assets can be eliminated by forming portfolios. The process of spreading an investment across assets (and thereby forming a portfolio) is called *diversification*. The **principle of diversification** tells us that spreading an investment across many assets will eliminate some of the risk. Not surprisingly, risks that can be eliminated by diversification are called "diversifiable" risks.

The second point is equally important. There is a minimum level of risk that cannot be eliminated by simply diversifying. This minimum level is labeled "nondiversifiable risk" in

principle of diversification

Spreading an investment across a number of assets will eliminate some, but not all, of the risk.

"In each of these bad periods, small stocks and international stocks did better," notes William Reichenstein, an investments professor at Baylor University. "There's a lot to be said for a portfolio that includes a little bit of everything."

On Target: Diversification won't just limit your losses during rough markets. When it's combined with regular rebalancing, it can also boost returns. When you rebalance, you set targets for what percentage of your portfolio is in different investments. Then, every so often, you re-jigger your portfolio to get back to these targets. If you invest in two market sectors, "a rebalanced portfolio may actually do better than the two assets on their own, because rebalancing forces you to buy low and sell high," says William Bernstein, an investment adviser in North Bend, Ore., and author of "The Intelligent Asset Allocator." "Rebalancing is the only form of market timing that works."

Suppose you held a portfolio that was one-third large stocks, one-third small stocks, and one-third foreign stocks. At the end of each year, you rebalanced to get back to these portfolio targets. Result? According to Ibbotson, over the past 30 years, your portfolio would have gained 14.2% a year before taxes and trading costs, compared with 13.7% if you had never rebalanced. You are most likely to get this performance bonus when you rebalance among different stock-market sectors, which should have roughly comparable long-run returns. But sometimes, you can also bolster returns by rebalancing between stocks and bonds. Consider, for instance, the 10 years through December 1981. Over that stretch, large stocks struggled, climbing just 6.5% a year, but they still outpaced intermediate government bonds, which returned 5.8%. But an annually rebalanced mix of 50% stocks and 50% bonds did even better, gaining 6.6% a year, Mr. Reichenstein calculates.

Source: Jonathan Clements, *The Wall Street Journal*, April 3, 2001. © 2001 Dow Jones & Company, Inc. All Rights Reserved Worldwide.

Hiding Places: How various investments fared during the roughest patches for large-company stocks over the past 30 years					
		Worst			30 Years
	5 Years*	10 Years*	15 Years*	20 Years*	(through Dec. 2000)
Large companies	−0.2%	+6.5%	+9.9%	+11.2%	+13.2%
Small companies	+10.8	+17.3	+16.2	+13.3	+14.7
Foreign stocks	+2.6	+10.6	+15.6	+15.4	+13.1
Intermediate bonds	+6.4	+5.8	+9.2	+9.1	+8.5
Inflation	+7.9	+8.6	+6.9	+6.3	+5.0

Note: The results shown are annual averages and include reinvested dividends.

*Through year-end 1977, 1981, 1987, and 1990, respectively.

Source: Ibbotson Associates.

Figure 11.1. Taken together, these two points are another important lesson from financial market history: Diversification reduces risk, but only up to a point. Put another way, some risk is diversifiable and some is not.

CHECK THIS

11.3a What happens to the standard deviation of return for a portfolio if we increase the number of securities in the portfolio?

11.3b What is the principle of diversification?

11.4 Correlation and Diversification

We've seen that diversification is important. What we haven't discussed is how to get the most out of diversification. For example, in our previous section, we investigated what happens if we simply spread our money evenly across randomly chosen stocks. We saw that significant risk reduction resulted from this strategy, but you might wonder whether even larger gains could be achieved by a more sophisticated approach. As we begin to examine that question here, the answer is yes.

WHY DIVERSIFICATION WORKS

correlation

The tendency of the returns on two assets to move together.

Why diversification reduces portfolio risk as measured by the portfolio standard deviation is important and worth exploring in some detail. The key concept is **correlation**, which is the extent to which the returns on two assets move together. If the returns on two assets tend to move up and down together, we say they are *positively* correlated. If they tend to move in opposite directions, we say they are *negatively* correlated. If there is no particular relationship between the two assets, we say they are *uncorrelated.*

Measure portfolio diversification using Instant X-ray at www.morningstar.com (use the search feature)

The *correlation coefficient,* which we use to measure correlation, ranges from -1 to $+1$, and we will denote the correlation between the returns on two assets, say A and B, as $\text{Corr}(R_A, R_B)$. The Greek letter ρ (rho) is often used to designate correlation as well. A correlation of $+1$ indicates that the two assets have a *perfect* positive correlation. For example, suppose that whatever return Asset A realizes, either up or down, Asset B does the same thing by exactly twice as much. In this case, they are perfectly correlated because the movement on one is completely predictable from the movement on the other. Notice, however, that perfect correlation does not necessarily mean they move by the same amount.

A zero correlation means that the two assets are uncorrelated. If we know that one asset is up, then we have no idea what the other one is likely to do; there simply is no relation between them. Perfect negative correlation [$\text{Corr}(R_A, R_B) = -1$] indicates that they always move in opposite directions. Figure 11.2 illustrates the three benchmark cases of perfect positive, perfect negative, and zero correlation.

FIGURE 11.2	Correlations

Perfect positive correlation
Corr $(R_A, R_B) = +1$

Returns

Both the return on Security A and the return on Security B are higher than average at the same time. Both the return on Security A and the return on Security B are lower than average at the same time.

Perfect negative correlation
Corr $(R_A, R_B) = -1$

Returns

Security A has a higher-than-average return when Security B has a lower-than-average return, and vice versa.

Zero correlation
Corr $(R_A, R_B) = 0$

Returns

The return on Security A is completely unrelated to the return on Security B.

TABLE 11.8 | Annual Returns on Stocks A and B

Year	Stock A	Stock B	Portfolio AB
2001	10%	15%	12.5%
2002	30	−10	10
2003	−10	25	7.5
2004	5	20	12.5
2005	10	15	12.5
Average returns	9	13	11
Standard deviations	14.3	13.5	2.2

Diversification works because security returns are generally not perfectly correlated. We will be more precise about the impact of correlation on portfolio risk in just a moment. For now, it is useful to simply think about combining two assets into a portfolio. If the two assets are highly positively correlated (the correlation is near +1), then they have a strong tendency to move up and down together. As a result, they offer limited diversification benefit. For example, two stocks from the same industry, say, General Motors and Ford, will tend to be relatively highly correlated because the companies are in essentially the same business, and a portfolio of two such stocks is not likely to be very diversified.

In contrast, if the two assets are negatively correlated, then they tend to move in opposite directions; whenever one zigs, the other tends to zag. In such a case, the diversification benefit will be substantial because variation in the return on one asset tends to be offset by variation in the opposite direction from the other. In fact, if two assets have a perfect negative correlation [$\text{Corr}(R_A, R_B) = -1$], then it is possible to combine them such that all risk is eliminated. Looking back at our example involving Jpod and Starcents in which we were able to eliminate all of the risk, what we now see is that they must be perfectly negatively correlated.

To further illustrate the impact of diversification on portfolio risk, suppose we observed the actual annual returns on two stocks, A and B, for the years 2001–2005. We summarize these returns in Table 11.8. In addition to actual returns on stocks A and B, we also calculated the returns on an equally weighted portfolio of A and B in Table 11.8. We label this portfolio as AB. In 2001, for example, Stock A returned 10 percent and Stock B returned 15 percent. Because Portfolio AB is half invested in each, its return for the year was:

$$1/2 \times 10\% + 1/2 \times 15\% = 12.5\%$$

The returns for the other years are calculated similarly.

At the bottom of Table 11.8, we calculated the average returns and standard deviations on the two stocks and the equally weighted portfolio. These averages and standard deviations are calculated just as they were in Chapter 1 (check a couple just to refresh your memory). The impact of diversification is apparent. The two stocks have standard deviations in the 13 percent to 14 percent per year range, but the portfolio's volatility is only 2.2 percent. In fact, if we compare the portfolio to Stock A, it has a higher return (11 percent vs. 9 percent) and much less risk.

Figure 11.3 illustrates in more detail what is occurring with our example. Here we have three bar graphs showing the year-by-year returns on Stocks A and B and Portfolio AB. Examining the graphs, we see that in 2002, for example, Stock A earned 30 percent while Stock B lost 10 percent. The following year, Stock B earned 25 percent, while A lost

FIGURE 11.3   Impact of Diversification

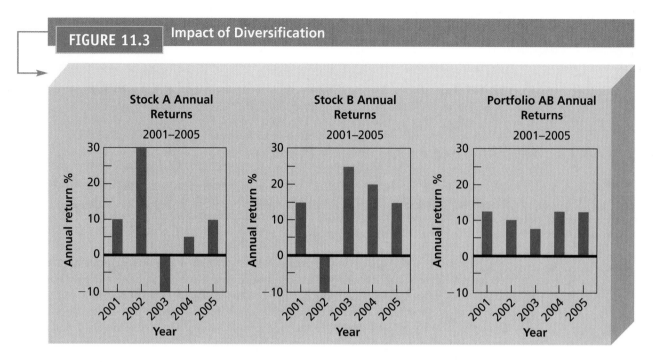

10 percent. These ups and downs tend to cancel out in our portfolio, however, with the result that there is much less variation in return from year to year. In other words, the correlation between the returns on stocks A and B is relatively low.

Calculating the correlation between stocks A and B is not difficult, but it would require us to digress a bit. Instead, we will explain the needed calculation in the next chapter, where we build on the principles developed here.

CALCULATING PORTFOLIO RISK

We've seen that correlation is an important determinant of portfolio risk. To further pursue this issue, we need to know how to calculate portfolio variances directly. For a portfolio of two assets, A and B, the variance of the return on the portfolio, σ_P^2, is given by Equation 11.3:

$$\sigma_P^2 = x_A^2 \sigma_A^2 + x_B^2 \sigma_B^2 + 2x_A x_B \sigma_A \sigma_B \text{Corr}(R_A, R_B) \qquad (11.3)$$

In this equation, x_A and x_B are the percentages invested in assets A and B. Notice that $x_A + x_B = 1$. (Why?)

For a portfolio of three assets, the variance of the return on the portfolio, σ_P^2, is given by Equation 11.4:

$$\sigma_P^2 = x_A^2 \sigma_A^2 + x_B^2 \sigma_B^2 + x_C^2 \sigma_C^2 + 2x_A x_B \sigma_A \sigma_B \text{Corr}(R_A, R_B) \qquad (11.4)$$
$$+ 2x_A x_C \sigma_A \sigma_C \text{Corr}(R_A, R_C) + 2x_B x_C \sigma_B \sigma_C \text{Corr}(R_B, R_C)$$

Note that six terms appear in Equation 11.4. There is a term involving the squared weight and the variance of the return for each of the three assets (A, B, and C) as well as a *cross-term* for each pair of assets. The cross-term involves pairs of weights, pairs of standard deviations of returns for each asset, and the correlation between the returns of the asset pair. If you had a portfolio of six assets, you would have an equation with 21 terms. (Can you write this equation?) If you had a portfolio of 50 assets, the equation for the variance of this portfolio would have 1,275 terms! Let's return to Equation 11.3.

Equation 11.3 looks a little involved, but its use is straightforward. For example, suppose Stock A has a standard deviation of 40 percent per year and Stock B has a standard deviation of 60 percent per year. The correlation between them is .15. If you put half your money in each, what is your portfolio standard deviation?

To answer, we just plug the numbers into Equation 11.3. Note that x_A and x_B are each equal to .50, while σ_A and σ_B are .40 and .60, respectively. Taking $\mathrm{Corr}(R_A, R_B) = .15$, we have:

$$\sigma_P^2 = .50^2 \times .40^2 + .50^2 \times .60^2 + 2 \times .50 \times .50 \times .40 \times .60 \times .15$$
$$= .25 \times .16 + .25 \times .36 + .018$$
$$= .148$$

Thus, the portfolio variance is .148. As always, variances are not easy to interpret since they are based on squared returns, so we calculate the standard deviation by taking the square root:

$$\sigma_P = \sqrt{.148} = .3847 = 38.47\%$$

Once again, we see the impact of diversification. This portfolio has a standard deviation of 38.47 percent, which is less than either of the standard deviations on the two assets that are in the portfolio.

EXAMPLE 11.5 | **Portfolio Variance and Standard Deviation**

In the example we just examined, Stock A has a standard deviation of 40 percent per year and Stock B has a standard deviation of 60 percent per year. Suppose now that the correlation between them is .35. Also suppose you put one-fourth of your money in Stock A. What is your portfolio standard deviation?

If you put 1/4 (or .25) in Stock A, you must have 3/4 (or .75) in Stock B, so $x_A = .25$ and $x_B = .75$. Making use of our portfolio variance equation (11.3), we have:

$$\sigma_P^2 = .25^2 \times .40^2 + .75^2 \times .60^2 + 2 \times .25 \times .75 \times .40 \times .60 \times .35$$
$$= .0625 \times .16 + .5625 \times .36 + .0315$$
$$= .244$$

Thus the portfolio variance is .244. Taking the square root, we get:

$$\sigma_P = \sqrt{.244} = .49396 \approx 49\%$$

This portfolio has a standard deviation of 49 percent, which is between the individual standard deviations. This shows that a portfolio's standard deviation isn't necessarily less than the individual standard deviations.

THE IMPORTANCE OF ASSET ALLOCATION, PART 1

asset allocation
How an investor spreads portfolio dollars among assets.

To illustrate why correlation and **asset allocation** are important, practical, real-world considerations, suppose that as a very conservative, risk-averse investor, you decide to invest all of your money in a bond mutual fund. Based on your analysis, you think this fund has an expected return of 6 percent with a standard deviation of 10 percent per year. A stock fund is available, however, with an expected return of 12 percent, but the standard deviation of 15 percent is too high for your taste. Also, the correlation between the returns on the two funds is about .10.

Is the decision to invest 100 percent in the bond fund a wise one, even for a very risk-averse investor? The answer is no; in fact, it is a bad decision for any investor. To see why,

TABLE 11.9   Risk and Return with Stocks and Bonds

Portfolio Weights		Expected Return	Standard Deviation (Risk)
Stocks	Bonds		
1.00	.00	12.00%	15.00%
.95	.05	11.70	14.31
.90	.10	11.40	13.64
.85	.15	11.10	12.99
.80	.20	10.80	12.36
.75	.25	10.50	11.77
.70	.30	10.20	11.20
.65	.35	9.90	10.68
.60	.40	9.60	10.21
.55	.45	9.30	9.78
.50	.50	9.00	9.42
.45	.55	8.70	9.12
.40	.60	8.40	8.90
.35	.65	8.10	8.75
.30	.70	7.80	8.69
.25	.75	7.50	8.71
.20	.80	7.20	8.82
.15	.85	6.90	9.01
.10	.90	6.60	9.27
.05	.95	6.30	9.60
.00	1.00	6.00	10.00

Table 11.9 shows expected returns and standard deviations available from different combinations of the two mutual funds. In constructing the table, we begin with 100 percent in the stock fund and work our way down to 100 percent in the bond fund by reducing the percentage in the stock fund in increments of .05. These calculations are all done just like our examples just above; you should check some (or all) of them for practice.

Beginning on the first row in Table 11.9, we have 100 percent in the stock fund, so our expected return is 12 percent, and our standard deviation is 15 percent. As we begin to move out of the stock fund and into the bond fund, we are not surprised to see both the expected return and the standard deviation decline. However, what might be surprising to you is the fact that the standard deviation falls only so far and then begins to rise again. In other words, beyond a point, adding more of the lower risk bond fund actually *increases* your risk!

The best way to see what is going on is to plot the various combinations of expected returns and standard deviations calculated in Table 11.9 as we do in Figure 11.4. We simply placed the standard deviations from Table 11.9 on the horizontal axis and the corresponding expected returns on the vertical axis.

Examining the plot in Figure 11.4, we see that the various combinations of risk and return available all fall on a smooth curve (in fact, for the geometrically inclined, it's a hyperbola). This curve is called an **investment opportunity set** because it shows the possible combinations of risk and return available from portfolios of these two assets. One important thing to notice is that, as we have shown, there is a portfolio that has the smallest standard deviation (or variance—same thing) of all. It is labeled "minimum variance portfolio" in Figure 11.4. What are (approximately) its expected return and standard deviation?

investment opportunity set
Collection of possible risk–return combinations available from portfolios of individual assets.

FIGURE 11.4

Risk and Return with Stocks and Bonds

Now we see clearly why a 100 percent bonds strategy is a poor one. With a 10 percent standard deviation, the bond fund offers an expected return of 6 percent. However, Table 11.9 shows us that a combination of about 60 percent stocks and 40 percent bonds has almost the same standard deviation, but a return of about 9.6 percent. Comparing 9.6 percent to 6 percent, we see that this portfolio has a return that is fully 60 percent greater ($6\% \times 1.6 = 9.6\%$) with the same risk. Our conclusion? Asset allocation matters.

Going back to Figure 11.4, notice that any portfolio that plots below the minimum variance portfolio is a poor choice because, no matter which one you pick, there is another portfolio with the same risk and a much better return. In the jargon of finance, we say that these undesirable portfolios are *dominated* and/or *inefficient.* Either way, we mean that given their level of risk, the expected return is inadequate compared to some other portfolio of equivalent risk. A portfolio that offers the highest return for its level of risk is said to be an **efficient portfolio**. In Figure 11.4, the minimum variance portfolio and all portfolios that plot above it are therefore efficient.

WWW

Review modern portfolio theory at
www.moneychimp.com

efficient portfolio
A portfolio that offers the highest return for its level of risk.

EXAMPLE 11.6   More Portfolio Variance and Standard Deviation

Looking at Table 11.9, suppose you put 57.627 percent in the stock fund. What is your expected return? Your standard deviation? How does this compare with the bond fund?

If you put 57.627 percent in stocks, you must have 42.373 percent in bonds, so $x_A = .57627$ and $x_B = .42373$. From Table 11.9, you can see that the standard deviation for stocks and bonds is 15% and 10%, respectively. Also, the correlation between stocks and bonds is .10. Making use of our portfolio variance equation (11.3), we have:

$$\sigma_P^2 = .57627^2 \times .15^2 + .42373^2 \times .10^2 + 2 \times .57627 \times .42373 \times .15 \times .10 \times .10$$

$$= .332 \times .0225 + .180 \times .01 + .0007325$$

$$= .01$$

Thus, the portfolio variance is .01, so the standard deviation is .1, or 10 percent. Check that the expected return is 9.46 percent. Compared to the bond fund, the standard deviation is now identical, but the expected return is almost 350 basis points higher.

MORE ON CORRELATION AND THE RISK-RETURN TRADE-OFF

Given the expected returns and standard deviations on the two assets, the shape of the investment opportunity set in Figure 11.4 depends on the correlation. The lower the correlation, the more bowed to the left the investment opportunity set will be. To illustrate, Figure 11.5 shows the investment opportunity for correlations of -1, 0, and $+1$ for two stocks, A and B. Notice that Stock A has an expected return of 12 percent and a standard deviation of 15 percent, while Stock B has an expected return of 6 percent and a standard deviation of 10 percent. These are the same expected returns and standard deviations we used to build Figure 11.4, and the calculations are all done the same way; just the correlations are different. Notice also that we use the symbol ρ to stand for the correlation coefficient.

In Figure 11.5, when the correlation is $+1$, the investment opportunity set is a straight line connecting the two stocks, so, as expected, there is little or no diversification benefit. As the correlation declines to zero, the bend to the left becomes pronounced. For correlations between $+1$ and zero, there would simply be a less pronounced bend.

Finally, as the correlation becomes negative, the bend becomes quite pronounced, and the investment opportunity set actually becomes two straight-line segments when the correlation hits -1. Notice that the minimum variance portfolio has a *zero* variance in this case.

It is sometimes desirable to be able to calculate the percentage investments needed to create the minimum variance portfolio. We will just state the result here, but a problem at the end of the chapter asks you to show that the weight on Asset A in the minimum variance portfolio, x_A^*, is:

$$x_A^* = \frac{\sigma_B^2 - \sigma_A \sigma_B \text{Corr}(R_A, R_B)}{\sigma_A^2 + \sigma_B^2 - 2\sigma_A \sigma_B \text{Corr}(R_A, R_B)} \tag{11.5}$$

In Equation 11.5, we will take Asset A to be the one with the larger standard deviation. If the standard deviations happened to be the same, then Asset A could be either.

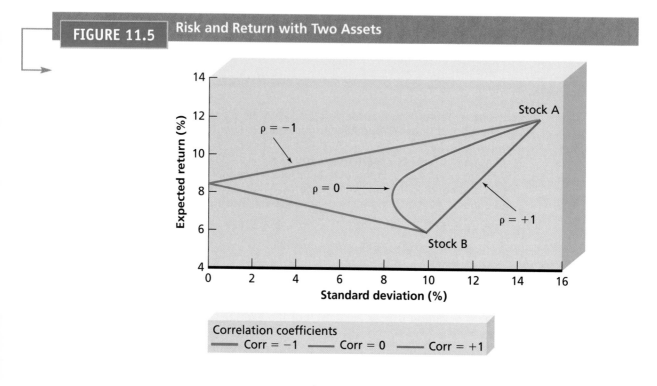

FIGURE 11.5   **Risk and Return with Two Assets**

EXAMPLE 11.7

Finding the Minimum Variance Portfolio

Looking back at Table 11.9, what combination of the stock fund and the bond fund has the lowest possible standard deviation? What is the minimum possible standard deviation?

Recalling that the standard deviations for the stock fund and bond fund were .15 and .10, respectively, and noting that the correlation was .1, we have:

$$x_A^* = \frac{.10^2 - .15 \times .10 \times .10}{.15^2 + .10^2 - 2 \times .15 \times .10 \times .10}$$

$$= .288136$$

$$\approx 28.8\%$$

Thus, the minimum variance portfolio has 28.8 percent in stocks and the balance, 71.2 percent, in bonds. Plugging these into our formula for portfolio variance, we have:

$$\sigma_P^2 = .288^2 \times .15^2 + .712^2 \times .10^2 + 2 \times .288 \times .712 \times .15 \times .10 \times .10$$

$$= .007551$$

The standard deviation is the square root of .007551, about 8.7 percent. Notice that this is where the minimum occurs in Figure 11.5.

CHECK THIS

11.4a Fundamentally, why does diversification work?

11.4b If two stocks have positive correlation, what does this mean?

11.4c What is an efficient portfolio?

11.5 The Markowitz Efficient Frontier

In the previous section, we looked closely at the risk-return possibilities available when we consider combining two risky assets. Now we are left with an obvious question: What happens when we consider combining three or more risky assets? As we will see, at least on a conceptual level, the answer turns out to be a straightforward extension of our previous examples that use two risky assets.

THE IMPORTANCE OF ASSET ALLOCATION, PART 2

As you saw in Equation 11.4, the formula to compute a portfolio variance with three assets is a bit cumbersome. Indeed, the amount of calculation increases greatly as the number of assets in the portfolio grows. The calculations are not difficult, but using a computer is highly recommended for portfolios consisting of more than three assets!

We can, however, illustrate the importance of asset allocation using only three assets. How? Well, a mutual fund that holds a broadly diversified portfolio of securities counts as only one asset. So, with three mutual funds that hold diversified portfolios, we can construct a diversified portfolio with these three assets. Suppose we invest in three index funds—one that represents U.S. stocks, one that represents U.S. bonds, and one that represents foreign stocks. Then we can see how the allocation among these three diversified

FIGURE 11.6 Markowitz Efficient Portfolio

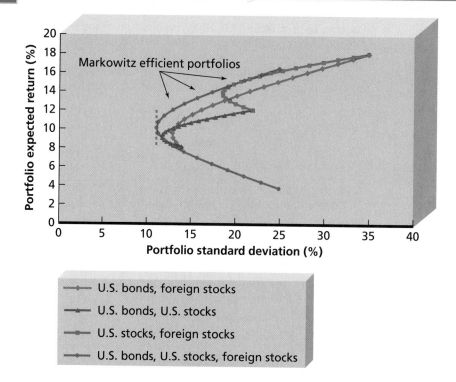

portfolios matters. (Our Get Real box at the end of the chapter presents a more detailed discussion of mutual funds and diversification.)

Figure 11.6 shows the result of calculating the expected returns and portfolio standard deviations when there are three assets. To illustrate the importance of asset allocation, we calculated expected returns and standard deviations from portfolios composed of three key investment types: U.S. stocks, foreign (non-U.S.) stocks, and U.S. bonds. These asset classes *are not* highly correlated in general; therefore, we assume a zero correlation in all cases. When we assume that all correlations are zero, the return to this portfolio is still:

$$R_P = x_F R_F + x_S R_S + x_B R_B \qquad (11.6)$$

But when all correlations are zero, the variance of the portfolio becomes:

$$\sigma_P^2 = x_F^2 \sigma_F^2 + x_S^2 \sigma_S^2 + x_B^2 \sigma_B^2 \qquad (11.7)$$

Suppose the expected returns and standard deviations are as follows:

	Expected Returns	Standard Deviations
Foreign stocks, *F*	18%	35%
U.S. stocks, *S*	12	22
U.S. bonds, *B*	8	14

We can now compute risk-return combinations as we did in our two-asset case. We create tables similar to Table 11.9, and then we can plot the risk-return combinations.

In Figure 11.6, each point plotted is a possible risk-return combination. Comparing the result with our two-asset case in Figure 11.4, we see that now not only do some assets plot below the minimum variance portfolio on a smooth curve, but we have portfolios plotting

Several Web sites allow you to perform a Markowitz-type analysis. Here is an example from www.finportfolio.com. This portfolio has four stocks, Citigroup (C), General Electric (GE), Intel (INTC), and Wal-Mart (WMT). It also has two mutual funds, the AIM Aggressive Growth Fund (AAGFX) and the Vanguard

Total International Stock Index Fund (VGTSX). The column labeled "Current" shows our current portfolio. The column labeled "Optimal" shows a portfolio with the same risk but with a much better return. The graph shows the Markowitz efficient frontier and illustrates how inefficient our portfolio is.

Efficient Frontier

Volatility=24.34%, Return=29.3%

	Current	Optimal
Return	24.34%	29.30%
Volatility	24.34%	24.34%
Sharpe	0.78	0.99
☐ C	16.50%	23.67%
■ GE	17.23%	16.48%
☐ INTC	5.35%	4.75%
☐ WMT	19.87%	26.59%
■ AAGFX	24.24%	.00%
■ VGTSX	16.81%	28.51%

Degree of optimization - current portfolio : 83%

The reason our portfolio is 83 percent optimized is that the return of 24.34 percent is 83 percent of the potential return of 29.30 percent. The entry labeled "Sharpe" is a common measure of the risk-return trade-off. We will discuss it in a later chapter.

Markowitz efficient frontier

The set of portfolios with the maximum return for a given standard deviation.

inside as well. Only combinations that plot on the upper left-hand boundary are efficient; all the rest are inefficient. This upper left-hand boundary is called the **Markowitz efficient frontier**, and it represents the set of risky portfolios with the maximum return for a given standard deviation.

Figure 11.6 makes it clear that asset allocation matters. For example, a portfolio of 100 percent U.S. stocks is highly inefficient. For the same standard deviation, there is a portfolio with an expected return almost 400 basis points, or 4 percent, higher. Or, for the same expected return, there is a portfolio with about half as much risk! Our nearby *Work the Web* box shows you how an efficient frontier can be created online.

The analysis in this section can be extended to any number of assets or asset classes. In principle, it is possible to compute efficient frontiers using thousands of assets. As a practical matter, however, this analysis is most widely used with a relatively small number of asset classes. For example, most investment banks maintain so-called model portfolios. These are simply recommended asset allocation strategies typically involving three to six asset categories.

WWW

Check out the online journal at
www.efficientfrontier. com

A primary reason that the Markowitz analysis is not usually extended to large collections of individual assets has to do with data requirements. The inputs into the analysis are (1) expected returns on all assets; (2) standard deviations on all assets; and (3) correlations between every pair of assets. Moreover, these inputs have to be measured with some precision, or we just end up with a garbage-in, garbage-out (GIGO) system.

Suppose we just look at 2,000 NYSE stocks. We need 2,000 expected returns and standard deviations. This is already a problem since returns on individual stocks cannot be predicted with precision at all. To make matters worse, however, we need to know the correlation between every *pair* of stocks. With 2,000 stocks, there are $2{,}000 \times 1{,}999/2 = 1{,}999{,}000$, or almost 2 million unique pairs![3] Also, as with expected returns, correlations between individual stocks are very difficult to predict accurately. We will return to this issue in our next chapter, where we show that there may be an extremely elegant way around the problem.

CHECK THIS

11.5a What is the Markowitz efficient frontier?

11.5b Why is Markowitz portfolio analysis most commonly used to make asset allocation decisions?

11.6   Summary and Conclusions

In this chapter, we covered the basics of diversification and portfolio risk and return. From this material we saw that:

1. A portfolio's expected return is a simple weighted combination of the expected returns on the assets in the portfolio, but the standard deviation on a portfolio is not.

2. Diversification is a very important consideration. The principle of diversification tells us that spreading an investment across many assets can reduce some, but not all, of the risk. Based on U.S. stock market history, for example, about 60 percent of the risk associated with owning individual stocks can be eliminated by naive diversification.

3. Diversification works because asset returns are not perfectly correlated. All else the same, the lower the correlation, the greater is the gain from diversification.

4. When we consider the possible combinations of risk and return available from portfolios of assets, we find that some are inefficient (or dominated), meaning that they offer too little return for their risk.

5. Finally, for any group of assets, there is a set that is efficient. That set is known as the Markowitz efficient frontier.

The most important thing to carry away from this chapter is an understanding of diversification and why it works. Once you understand this, then the importance of asset allocation follows immediately. Our story is not complete, however, because we have not considered one important asset class: riskless assets. This will be the first task in our next chapter.

---

[3]With 2,000 stocks, there are $2{,}000^2 = 4{,}000{,}000$ possible pairs. Of these, 2,000 involve pairing a stock with itself. Further, we recognize that the correlation between A and B is the same as the correlation between B and A, so we only need to actually calculate half of the remaining 3,998,000 correlations.

This chapter explained diversification, a very important consideration for real-world investors and money managers. The chapter also explored the famous Markowitz efficient portfolio concept, which shows how (and why) asset allocation affects portfolio risk and return.

Building a diversified portfolio is not a trivial task. Of course, as we discussed many chapters ago, mutual funds provide one way for investors to build diversified portfolios, but there are some significant caveats concerning mutual funds as a diversification tool. First of all, investors sometimes assume a fund is diversified simply because it holds a relatively large number of stocks. However, with the exception of some index funds, most mutual funds will reflect a particular style of investing, either explicitly, as stated in the fund's objective, or implicitly, as favored by the fund manager. For example, in the mid- to late-1990s, stocks as a whole did very well, but mutual funds that concentrated on smaller stocks generally did not do well at all.

It is tempting to buy a number of mutual funds to ensure broad diversification, but even this may not work. Within a given fund family, the same manager may actually be responsible for multiple funds. In addition, managers within a large fund family frequently have similar views about the market and individual companies.

Thinking just about stocks for the moment, what does an investor need to consider to build a well-diversified portfolio? At a minimum, such a portfolio probably needs to be diversified across industries, with no undue concentrations in particular sectors of the economy; it needs to be diversified by company size (small, midcap, and large), and it needs to be diversified across "growth" (i.e., high-P/E) and "value" (low-P/E) stocks. Perhaps the most controversial diversification issue concerns international diversification. The correlation between international stock exchanges is surprisingly low, suggesting large benefits from diversifying globally.

Perhaps the most disconcerting fact about diversification is that it leads to the following paradox: A well-diversified portfolio will always be invested in something that does not do well! Put differently, such a portfolio will almost always have both winners and losers. In many ways, that's the whole idea. Even so, it requires a lot of financial discipline to stay diversified when some portion of your portfolio seems to be doing poorly. The payoff is that, over the long run, a well-diversified portfolio should provide much steadier returns and be much less prone to abrupt changes in value.

Key Terms

Chapter Review Problems and Self-Test ____ ■

Use the following table of states of the economy and stock returns to answer the review problems:

State of Economy	Probability of State of Economy	Security Returns If State Occurs	
		Roten	Bradley
Bust	.40	−10%	30%
Boom	.60	40	10
	1.00		

1. **Expected Returns**   Calculate the expected returns for Roten and Bradley.
2. **Standard Deviations**   Calculate the standard deviations for Roten and Bradley.
3. **Portfolio Expected Returns**   Calculate the expected return on a portfolio of 50 percent Roten and 50 percent Bradley.
4. **Portfolio Volatility**   Calculate the volatility of a portfolio of 50 percent Roten and 50 percent Bradley.

Answers to Self-Test Problems

1. We calculate the expected return as follows:

		Roten		Bradley	
(1) State of Economy	(2) Probability of State of Economy	(3) Return If State Occurs	(4) Product (2) × (3)	(5) Return If State Occurs	(6) Product (2) × (5)
Bust	.40	−10%	−.04	30%	.12
Boom	.60	40	.24	10	.06
			$E(R) = 20\%$		$E(R) = 18\%$

2. We calculate the standard deviation as follows:

(1) State of Economy	(2) Probability of State of Economy	(3) Return Deviation from Expected Return	(4) Squared Return Deviation	(5) Product (2) × (4)
Roten				
Bust	.40	−.30	.09	.036
Boom	.60	.20	.04	.024
				$\sigma^2 = .06$
Bradley				
Bust	.40	.12	.0144	.00576
Boom	.60	−.08	.0064	.00384
				$\sigma^2 = .0096$

Taking square roots, the standard deviations are 24.495 percent and 9.798 percent.

3. We calculate the expected return on a portfolio of 50 percent Roten and 50 percent Bradley as follows:

(1) State of Economy	(2) Probability of State of Economy	(3) Portfolio Return If State Occurs	(4) Product (2) × (3)
Bust	.40	10%	.04
Boom	.60	25	.15
			$E(R_P) = 19\%$

4. We calculate the volatility of a portfolio of 50 percent Roten and 50 percent Bradley as follows:

(1) State of Economy	(2) Probability of State of Economy	(3) Portfolio Return If State Occurs	(4) Squared Deviation from Expected Return	(5) Product (2) × (4)
Bust	.40	.10	.0081	.00324
Boom	.60	.25	.0036	.00216
				$\sigma_P^2 = .00540$
				$\sigma_P = 7.3485\%$

Test Your Investment Quotient

1. **Diversification**   Starcents has an expected return of 25 percent and Jpod has an expected return of 20 percent. What is the likely investment decision for a risk-averse investor?

   a. Invest all funds in Starcents.
   b. Invest all funds in Jpod.
   c. Do not invest any funds in Starcents and Jpod.
   d. Invest funds partly in Starcents and partly in Jpod.

2. **Return Standard Deviation**   Starcents experiences returns of 5 percent or 45 percent, each with an equal probability. What is the return standard deviation for Starcents?

   a. 30 percent
   b. 25 percent
   c. 20 percent
   d. 10 percent

3. **Return Standard Deviation**   Jpod experiences returns of 0 percent, 25 percent, or 50 percent, each with a one-third probability. What is the approximate return standard deviation for Jpod?

   a. 30 percent
   b. 25 percent
   c. 20 percent
   d. 10 percent

4. **Expected Return**   An analyst estimates that a stock has the following return probabilities and returns depending on the state of the economy:

State of Economy	Probability	Return
Good	.1	15%
Normal	.6	13
Poor	.3	7

What is the expected return of the stock?

a. 7.8 percent
b. 11.4 percent
c. 11.7 percent
d. 13.0 percent

5. **Risk Aversion**   Which of the following statements best reflects the importance of the asset allocation decision to the investment process? The asset allocation decision

a. Helps the investor decide on realistic investment goals.
b. Identifies the specific securities to include in a portfolio.
c. Determines most of the portfolio's returns and volatility over time.
d. Creates a standard by which to establish the appropriate investment time horizon.

6. **Efficient Frontier**   The Markowitz efficient frontier is best described as the set of portfolios that has

a. The minimum risk for every level of return.
b. Proportionally equal units of risk and return.
c. The maximum excess rate of return for every given level of risk.
d. The highest return for each level of beta used on the capital asset pricing model.

7. **Diversification**   An investor is considering adding another investment to a portfolio. To achieve the maximum diversification benefits, the investor should add an investment that has a correlation coefficient with the existing portfolio closest to

a. −1.0
b. −.5
c. .0
d. +1.0

8. **Risk Premium**   Starcents has an expected return of 25 percent, Jpod has an expected return of 20 percent, and the risk-free rate is 5 percent. You invest half your funds in Starcents and the other half in Jpod. What is the risk premium for your portfolio?

a. 20 percent
b. 17.5 percent
c. 15 percent
d. 12.5 percent

9. **Return Standard Deviation**   Both Starcents and Jpod have the same return standard deviation of 20 percent, and Starcents and Jpod returns have zero correlation. You invest half your funds in Starcents and the other half in Jpod. What is the return standard deviation for your portfolio?

a. 20 percent
b. 14.14 percent
c. 10 percent
d. 0 percent

10. **Return Standard Deviation**   Both Starcents and Jpod have the same return standard deviation of 20 percent, and Starcents and Jpod returns have a correlation of +1. You invest half your funds in Starcents and the other half in Jpod. What is the return standard deviation for your portfolio?

a. 20 percent
b. 14.14 percent
c. 10 percent
d. 0 percent

11. **Return Standard Deviation**   Both Starcents and Jpod have the same return standard deviation of 20 percent, and Starcents and Jpod returns have a correlation of −1. You invest half your funds in Starcents and the other half in Jpod. What is the return standard deviation for your portfolio?

a. 20 percent
b. 14.14 percent
c. 10 percent
d. 0 percent

12. **Minimum Variance Portfolio**   Both Starcents and Jpod have the same return standard deviation of 20 percent, and Starcents and Jpod returns have zero correlation. What is the minimum attainable return variance for a portfolio of Starcents and Jpod?

  a. 20 percent
  b. 14.14 percent
  c. 10 percent
  d. 0 percent

13. **Minimum Variance Portfolio**   Both Starcents and Jpod have the same return standard deviation of 20 percent, and Starcents and Jpod returns have a correlation of −1. What is the minimum attainable return variance for a portfolio of Starcents and Jpod?

  a. 20 percent
  b. 14.14 percent
  c. 10 percent
  d. 0 percent

14. **Minimum Variance Portfolio**   Stocks A, B, and C each have the same expected return and standard deviation. The following shows the correlations between returns on these stocks:

	Stock A	Stock B	Stock C
Stock A	+1.0		
Stock B	+0.9	+1.0	
Stock C	+0.1	−0.4	+1.0

Given these correlations, which of the following portfolios constructed from these stocks would have the lowest risk?

  a. One equally invested in stocks A and B.
  b. One equally invested in stocks A and C.
  c. One equally invested in stocks B and C.
  d. One totally invested in stock C.

15. **Markowitz Efficient Frontier**   Which of the following portfolios cannot lie on the efficient frontier as described by Markowitz?

	Portfolio	Expected Return	Standard Deviation
a.	W	9%	21%
b.	X	5	7
c.	Y	15	36
d.	Z	12	15

Concept Questions _____

1. **Diversification and Market History**   Based on market history, what is the average annual standard deviation of return for a single, randomly chosen stock? What is the average annual standard deviation for an equally weighted portfolio of many stocks?

2. **Interpreting Correlations**   If the returns on two stocks are highly correlated, what does this mean? If they have no correlation? If they are negatively correlated?

3. **Efficient Portfolios**   What is an efficient portfolio?

4. **Expected Returns**   True or false: If two stocks have the same expected return of 12 percent, then any portfolio of the two stocks will also have an expected return of 12 percent.

5. **Portfolio Volatility**   True or false: If two stocks have the same standard deviation of 45 percent, then any portfolio of the two stocks will also have a standard deviation of 45 percent.

6. **Diversification** You are an investment adviser and a client makes the following statement: I do not want a diversified portfolio since I will never get the highest possible return. How do you respond to your client?

7. **Investment Opportunity Set** You have a portfolio created from two assets. As you add more of the lower risk asset to your portfolio, the risk of your portfolio increases. What do you know about your current portfolio?

8. **Minimum Variance Portfolio** Why is the minimum variance portfolio important in regard to the Markowitz efficient frontier?

9. **Markowitz Efficient Frontier** True or false: It is impossible for a single asset to lie on the Markowitz efficient frontier.

10. **Portfolio Variance** Suppose two assets have zero correlation and the same standard deviation. What is true about the minimum variance portfolio?

Questions and Problems _____

Core Questions

1. **Expected Returns** Use the following information on states of the economy and stock returns to calculate the expected return for Dingaling Telephone:

State of Economy	Probability of State of Economy	Security Return If State Occurs
Recession	.20	−10%
Normal	.60	14
Boom	.20	27

2. **Standard Deviations** Using the information in the previous question, calculate the standard deviation of returns.

3. **Expected Returns and Deviations** Repeat Questions 1 and 2 assuming that all three states are equally likely.

Use the following information on states of the economy and stock returns to answer Questions 4–7:

State of Economy	Probability of State of Economy	Security Returns If State Occurs	
		Roll	Ross
Bust	.40	−10%	21%
Boom	.60	28	8

4. **Expected Returns** Calculate the expected returns for Roll and Ross by filling in the following table (verify your answer by expressing returns as percentages as well as decimals):

		Roll		Ross	
(1) State of Economy	(2) Probability of State of Economy	(3) Return If State Occurs	(4) Product (2) × (3)	(5) Return If State Occurs	(6) Product (2) × (5)
Bust					
Boom					

5. **Standard Deviations** Calculate the standard deviations for Roll and Ross by filling in the following table (verify your answer using returns expressed in percentages as well as decimals):

(1) State of Economy	(2) Probability of State of Economy	(3) Return Deviation from Expected Return	(4) Squared Return Deviation	(5) Product (2) × (4)
Roll				
Bust				
Boom				
Ross				
Bust				
Boom				

6. **Portfolio Expected Returns** Calculate the expected return on a portfolio of 40 percent Roll and 60 percent Ross by filling in the following table:

(1) State of Economy	(2) Probability of State of Economy	(3) Portfolio Return If State Occurs	(4) Product (2) × (3)
Bust			
Boom			

7. **Portfolio Volatility** Calculate the volatility of a portfolio of 70 percent Roll and 30 percent Ross by filling in the following table:

(1) State of Economy	(2) Probability of State of Economy	(3) Portfolio Return If State Occurs	(4) Squared Deviation from Expected Return	(5) Product (2) × (4)
Bust				
Boom				
$\sigma_p^2 =$				
$\sigma_p =$				

8. **Calculating Returns and Standard Deviations** Based on the following information, calculate the expected return and standard deviation for the two stocks.

State of Economy	Probability of State of Economy	Rate of Return If State Occurs	
		Stock A	Stock B
Recession	.15	.04	−.20
Normal	.70	.09	.13
Boom	.15	.12	.33

9. Returns and Standard Deviations   Consider the following information:

State of Economy	Probability of State of Economy	Rate of Return If State Occurs		
		Stock A	Stock B	Stock C
Boom	.20	.30	.45	.33
Good	.40	.12	.10	.15
Poor	.30	.01	−.15	−.05
Bust	.10	−.06	−.30	−.09

  a. Your portfolio is invested 25 percent each in A and C, and 50 percent in B. What is the expected return of the portfolio?

  b. What is the variance of this portfolio? The standard deviation?

10. Portfolio Returns and Volatilities   Fill in the missing information in the following table. Assume that Portfolio AB is 30 percent invested in Stock A.

	Annual Returns		
Year	Stock A	Stock B	Portfolio AB
2001	18%	50%	
2002	40	−30	
2003	−15	45	
2004	20	2	
2005	4	20	
Average returns			
Standard deviations			

Intermediate Questions

11. Portfolio Returns and Volatilities   Given the following information, calculate the expected return and standard deviation for a portfolio that has 20 percent invested in Stock A, 35 percent in Stock B, and the balance in Stock C.

State of Economy	Probability of State of Economy	Returns		
		Stock A	Stock B	Stock C
Boom	.70	15%	18%	20%
Bust	.30	10	0	−10

12. Portfolio Variance   Use the following information to calculate the expected return and standard deviation of a portfolio that is 40 percent invested in 3 Doors, Inc., and 60 percent invested in Down Co.:

	3 Doors, Inc.	Down Co.
Expected return, $E(R)$	15%	10%
Standard deviation, σ	50	38
Correlation		.15

13. More Portfolio Variance   In the previous question, what is the standard deviation if the correlation is +1? 0? −1? As the correlation declines from +1 to −1 here, what do you see happening to portfolio volatility? Why?

14. **Minimum Variance Portfolio**   In Problem 12, what are the expected return and standard deviation on the minimum variance portfolio?

15. **Asset Allocation**   Fill in the missing information assuming a correlation of .15.

Portfolio Weights			
Stocks	Bonds	Expected Return	Standard Deviation
1.00		12%	21%
.80			
.60			
.40			
.20			
.00		6%	9%

16. **Minimum Variance Portfolio**   Consider two stocks, Stock D with an expected return of 13 percent and a standard deviation of 54 percent and Stock I, an international company, with an expected return of 16 percent and a standard deviation of 78 percent. The correlation between the two stocks is $-.10$. What is the weight of each stock in the minimum variance portfolio?

17. **Minimum Variance Portfolio**   What are the expected return and standard deviation of the minimum variance portfolio in the previous problem?

18. **Minimum Variance Portfolio**   Asset K has an expected return of 15 percent and a standard deviation of 53 percent. Asset L has an expected return of 6 percent and a standard deviation of 10 percent. The correlation between the assets is .02. What are the expected return and standard deviation of the minimum variance portfolio?

19. **Minimum Variance Portfolio**   The stock of Bruin, Inc., has an expected return of 17 percent and a standard deviation of 43 percent. The stock of Wildcat Co. has an expected return of 15 percent and a standard deviation of 52 percent. The correlation between the two stocks is .25. Is it possible for there to be a minimum variance portfolio since the highest-return stock has the lowest standard deviation? If so, calculate the expected return and standard deviation of the minimum variance portfolio. Graph the investment opportunity set for these two stocks.

20. **Portfolio Variance**   You have a three-stock portfolio. Stock A has an expected return of 12 percent and a standard deviation of 41 percent, Stock B has an expected return of 16 percent and a standard deviation of 58 percent, and Stock C has an expected return of 13 percent and a standard deviation of 48 percent. The correlation between Stocks A and B is .30, between Stocks A and C is .20, and between Stocks B and C is .05. Your portfolio consists of 30 percent Stock A, 50 percent Stock B, and 20 percent Stock C. Calculate the expected return and standard deviation of your portfolio. The formula for calculating the variance of a three-stock portfolio is:

$$\sigma_P^2 = x_A^2 \sigma_A^2 + x_B^2 \sigma_B^2 + x_C^2 \sigma_C^2 + 2x_A x_B \sigma_A \sigma_B \text{Corr}(R_A, R_B)$$
$$+ 2x_A x_C \sigma_A \sigma_C \text{Corr}(R_A, R_C) + 2x_B x_C \sigma_B \sigma_C \text{Corr}(R_B, R_C)$$

21. **Minimum Variance Portfolio**   You are going to invest in Asset J and Asset S. Asset J has an expected return of 15 percent and a standard deviation of 58 percent. Asset S has an expected return of 9 percent and a standard deviation of 24 percent. The correlation between the two assets is .60. What are the standard deviation and expected return of the minimum variance portfolio? What is going on here?

22. **Portfolio Variance**   Suppose two assets have perfect positive correlation. Show that the standard deviation on a portfolio of the two assets is simply:

$$\sigma_P = x_A \times \sigma_A + x_B \times \sigma_B$$

(*Hint*: Look at the expression for the variance of a two-asset portfolio. If the correlation is $+1$, the expression is a perfect square.)

23. **Portfolio Variance**   Suppose two assets have perfect negative correlation. Show that the standard deviation on a portfolio of the two assets is simply:

$$\sigma_P = \pm(x_A \times \sigma_A - x_B \times \sigma_B)$$

(*Hint*: See previous problem.)

24. **Portfolio Variance**   Using the result in Problem 23, show that whenever two assets have perfect negative correlation it is possible to find a portfolio with a zero standard deviation. What are the portfolio weights? (*Hint*: Let x be the percentage in the first asset and $(1 - x)$ be the percentage in the second. Set the standard deviation to zero and solve for x.)

25. **Portfolio Variance**   Derive our expression in the chapter for the portfolio weight in the minimum variance portfolio. (Danger! Calculus required!) (*Hint*: Let x be the percentage in the first asset and $(1 - x)$ the percentage in the second. Take the derivative with respect to x, and set it to zero. Solve for x.)

CHAPTER 12

Return, Risk, and the Security Market Line

"To win, you have to risk loss."

–Franz Klammer

An important insight of modern financial theory is that some investment risks yield an expected reward, while other risks do not. Essentially, risks that can be eliminated by diversification do not yield an expected reward, and risks that cannot be eliminated by diversification do yield an expected reward. Thus, financial markets are somewhat fussy regarding what risks are rewarded and what risks are not. ■

Chapter 1 presented some important lessons from capital market history. The most noteworthy, perhaps, is that there is a reward, on average, for bearing risk. We called this reward a *risk premium*. The second lesson is that this risk premium is positively correlated with an investment's risk.

In this chapter, we return to an examination of the reward for bearing risk. Specifically, we have two tasks to accomplish. First, we have to define risk more precisely and then discuss how to measure it. Second, once we have a better understanding of just what we mean by "risk," we will go on to quantify the relation between risk and return in financial markets.

When we examine the risks associated with individual assets, we find there are two types of risk: systematic and unsystematic. This distinction is crucial because, as we will see, systematic risk affects almost all assets in the economy, at least to some degree, whereas unsystematic risk affects at most only a small number of assets. This observation allows us to say a great deal about the risks and returns on individual assets. In particular, it is the basis for a famous relationship between risk and return called the *security market line,* or

SML. To develop the SML, we introduce the equally famous beta coefficient, one of the centerpieces of modern finance. Beta and the SML are key concepts because they supply us with at least part of the answer to the question of how to go about determining the expected return on a risky investment.

12.1 Announcements, Surprises, and Expected Returns

In our previous chapter, we discussed how to construct portfolios and evaluate their returns. We now begin to describe more carefully the risks and returns associated with individual securities. Thus far, we have measured volatility by looking at the difference between the actual return on an asset or portfolio, R, and the expected return, $E(R)$. We now look at why those deviations exist.

EXPECTED AND UNEXPECTED RETURNS

To begin, consider the return on the stock of a hypothetical company called Flyers. What will determine this stock's return in, say, the coming year?

The return on any stock traded in a financial market is composed of two parts. First, the normal, or expected, return from the stock is the part of the return that investors predict or expect. This return depends on the information investors have about the stock, and it is based on the market's understanding today of the important factors that will influence the stock in the coming year.

The second part of the return on the stock is the uncertain, or risky, part. This is the portion that comes from unexpected information revealed during the year. A list of all possible sources of such information would be endless, but here are a few basic examples:

News about Flyers's product research.

Government figures released on gross domestic product.

The latest news about exchange rates.

The news that Flyers's sales figures are higher than expected.

A sudden, unexpected drop in interest rates.

Based on this discussion, one way to express the return on Flyers stock in the coming year would be:

$$\text{Total return} - \text{Expected return} = \text{Unexpected return} \tag{12.1}$$

or

$$R - E(R) = U$$

where R stands for the actual total return in the year, $E(R)$ stands for the expected part of the return, and U stands for the unexpected part of the return. What this says is that the actual return, R, differs from the expected return, $E(R)$, because of surprises that occur during the year. In any given year, the unexpected return will be positive or negative, but, through time, the average value of U will be zero. This simply means that, on average, the actual return equals the expected return.

ANNOUNCEMENTS AND NEWS

We need to be careful when we talk about the effect of news items on stock returns. For example, suppose Flyers's business is such that the company prospers when gross domestic product (GDP) grows at a relatively high rate and suffers when GDP is relatively stagnant. In this case, in deciding what return to expect this year from owning stock in Flyers, investors either implicitly or explicitly must think about what GDP is likely to be for the coming year.

When the government actually announces GDP figures for the year, what will happen to the value of Flyers stock? Obviously, the answer depends on what figure is released. More to the point, however, the impact depends on how much of that figure actually represents new information.

At the beginning of the year, market participants will have some idea or forecast of what the yearly GDP figure will be. To the extent that shareholders have predicted GDP, that prediction will already be factored into the expected part of the return on the stock, $E(R)$. On the other hand, if the announced GDP is a surprise, then the effect will be part of U, the unanticipated portion of the return.

As an example, suppose shareholders in the market had forecast that the GDP increase this year would be .5 percent. If the actual announcement this year is exactly .5 percent, the same as the forecast, then the shareholders don't really learn anything, and the announcement isn't news. There will be no impact on the stock price as a result. This is like receiving redundant confirmation about something that you suspected all along; it reveals nothing new.

To give a more concrete example, Nabisco once announced it was taking a massive $300 million charge against earnings for the second quarter in a sweeping restructuring plan. The company also announced plans to cut its workforce sharply by 7.8 percent, eliminate some package sizes and small brands, and relocate some of its operations. This all seems like bad news, but the stock price didn't even budge. Why? Because it was already fully expected that Nabisco would take such actions, and the stock price already reflected the bad news.

A common way of saying that an announcement isn't news is to say that the market has already discounted the announcement. The use of the word "discount" here is different from the use of the term in computing present values, but the spirit is the same. When we discount a dollar to be received in the future, we say it is worth less to us today because of the time value of money. When an announcement or a news item is discounted into a stock price, we say that its impact is already a part of the stock price because the market already knew about it.

Going back to Flyers, suppose the government announces that the actual GDP increase during the year has been 1.5 percent. Now shareholders have learned something, namely, that the increase is 1 percentage point higher than they had forecast. This difference between the actual result and the forecast, 1 percentage point in this example, is sometimes called the *innovation* or the *surprise*.

This distinction explains why what seems to be bad news can actually be good news. For example, Gymboree, a retailer of children's apparel, had a 3 percent decline in same-store sales for a particular month, yet its stock price shot up 13 percent on the news. In the retail business, same-store sales, which are sales by existing stores in operation at least a year, are a crucial barometer, so why was this decline good news? The reason was that analysts had been expecting significantly sharper declines, so the situation was not as bad as previously thought.

A key fact to keep in mind about news and price changes is that news about the future is what matters. For example, America Online (AOL) once announced third-quarter earnings that exceeded Wall Street's expectations. That seems like good news, but America Online's stock price promptly dropped 10 percent. The reason was that America Online also announced a new discount subscriber plan, which analysts took as an indication that future revenues would be growing more slowly. Similarly, shortly thereafter, Microsoft reported a 50 percent jump in profits, exceeding projections. That seems like *really*

Visit the earnings calendar at www.individualinvestor. com

good news, but Microsoft's stock price proceeded to decline sharply. Why? Because Microsoft warned that its phenomenal growth could not be sustained indefinitely, so its 50 percent increase in current earnings was not such a good predictor of future earnings growth.

WWW

See recent earnings surprises at earnings.nasdaq.com

To summarize, an announcement can be broken into two parts, the anticipated, or expected, part plus the surprise, or innovation:

$$\text{Announcement} = \text{Expected part} + \text{Surprise} \qquad (12.2)$$

The expected part of any announcement is the part of the information that the market uses to form the expectation, $E(R)$, of the return on the stock. The surprise is the news that influences the unanticipated return on the stock, U.

Our discussion of market efficiency in a previous chapter bears on this discussion. We are assuming that relevant information known today is already reflected in the expected return. This is identical to saying that the current price reflects relevant publicly available information. We are thus implicitly assuming that markets are at least reasonably efficient in the semistrong-form sense. Henceforth, when we speak of news, we will mean the surprise part of an announcement and not the portion that the market had expected and therefore already discounted.

EXAMPLE 12.1 | **In the News**

Suppose Intel were to announce that earnings for the quarter just ending were up by 40 percent relative to a year ago. Do you expect that the stock price would rise or fall on the announcement?

The answer is that you can't really tell. Suppose the market was expecting a 60 percent increase. In this case, the 40 percent increase would be a negative surprise, and we would expect the stock price to fall. On the other hand, if the market was expecting only a 20 percent increase, there would be a positive surprise, and we would expect the stock to rise on the news.

CHECK THIS

12.1a   What are the two basic parts of a return on common stock?

12.1b   Under what conditions will an announcement have no effect on common stock prices?

12.2 Risk: Systematic and Unsystematic

It is important to distinguish between expected and unexpected returns because the unanticipated part of the return, that portion resulting from surprises, is the significant risk of any investment. After all, if we always receive exactly what we expect, then the investment is perfectly predictable and, by definition, risk-free. In other words, the risk of owning an asset comes from surprises—unanticipated events.

There are important differences, though, among various sources of risk. Look back at our previous list of news stories. Some of these stories are directed specifically at Flyers, and some are more general. Which of the news items are of specific importance to Flyers?

Announcements about interest rates or GDP are clearly important for nearly all companies, whereas the news about Flyers's president, its research, or its sales is of specific interest to Flyers investors only. We distinguish between these two types of events, because, as we will see, they have very different implications.

SYSTEMATIC AND UNSYSTEMATIC RISK

systematic risk
Risk that influences a large number of assets. Also called *market risk*.

unsystematic risk
Risk that influences a single company or a small group of companies. Also called *unique* or *asset-specific risk*.

The first type of surprise, the one that affects most assets, we label **systematic risk**. A systematic risk is one that influences a large number of assets, each to a greater or lesser extent. Because systematic risks have marketwide effects, they are sometimes called *market risks*.

The second type of surprise we call **unsystematic risk**. An unsystematic risk is one that affects a single asset, or possibly a small group of assets. Because these risks are unique to individual companies or assets, they are sometimes called *unique* or *asset-specific risks*. We use these terms interchangeably.

As we have seen, uncertainties about general economic conditions, such as GDP, interest rates, or inflation, are examples of systematic risks. These conditions affect nearly all companies to some degree. An unanticipated increase, or surprise, in inflation, for example, affects wages and the costs of supplies that companies buy; it affects the value of the assets that companies own; and it affects the prices at which companies sell their products. Forces such as these, to which all companies are susceptible, are the essence of systematic risk.

In contrast, the announcement of an oil strike by a particular company will primarily affect that company and, perhaps, a few others (such as primary competitors and suppliers). It is unlikely to have much of an effect on the world oil market, however, or on the affairs of companies not in the oil business, so this is an unsystematic event.

SYSTEMATIC AND UNSYSTEMATIC COMPONENTS OF RETURN

Analyze risk at
www.portfolioscience.com

The distinction between a systematic risk and an unsystematic risk is never really as exact as we would like it to be. Even the most narrow and peculiar bit of news about a company ripples through the economy. This is true because every enterprise, no matter how tiny, is a part of the economy. It's like the proverb of a kingdom that was lost because one horse lost a horseshoe nail. This is mostly hairsplitting, however. Some risks are clearly much more general than others.

The distinction between the two types of risk allows us to break down the surprise portion, U, of the return on the Flyers stock into two parts. Earlier, we had the actual return broken down into its expected and surprise components: $R - E(R) = U$. We now recognize that the total surprise component for Flyers, U, has a systematic and an unsystematic component, so:

$$R - E(R) = \text{Systematic portion} + \text{Unsystematic portion} \tag{12.3}$$

Because it is traditional, we will use the Greek letter epsilon ϵ to stand for the unsystematic portion. Because systematic risks are often called "market" risks, we use the letter m to stand for the systematic part of the surprise. With these symbols, we can rewrite the formula for the total return:

$$R - E(R) = U = m + \epsilon \tag{12.4}$$

The important thing about the way we have broken down the total surprise, U, is that the unsystematic portion, ϵ, is unique to Flyers. For this reason, it is unrelated to the unsystematic portion of return on most other assets. To see why this is important, we need to return to the subject of portfolio risk.

EXAMPLE 12.2 | **Systematic versus Unsystematic Events**

Suppose Intel were to unexpectedly announce that its latest computer chip contains a significant flaw in its floating point unit that left it unable to handle numbers bigger than a couple of gigatrillion (meaning that, among other things, the chip cannot calculate Intel's quarterly profits). Is this a systematic or unsystematic event?

Obviously, this event is for the most part unsystematic. However, it would also benefit Intel's competitors to some degree and, at least potentially, harm some users of Intel products such as personal computer makers. Thus, as with most unsystematic events, there is some spillover, but the effect is mostly confined to a relatively small number of companies.

CHECK THIS

12.2a   What are the two basic types of risk?

12.2b   What is the distinction between the two types of risk?

12.3 Diversification, Systematic Risk, and Unsystematic Risk

In the previous chapter, we introduced the principle of diversification. What we saw was that some of the risk associated with individual assets can be diversified away and some cannot. We are left with an obvious question: Why is this so? It turns out that the answer hinges on the distinction between systematic and unsystematic risk.

DIVERSIFICATION AND UNSYSTEMATIC RISK

By definition, an unsystematic risk is one that is particular to a single asset or, at most, a small group of assets. For example, if the asset under consideration is stock in a single company, such things as successful new products and innovative cost savings will tend to increase the value of the stock. Unanticipated lawsuits, industrial accidents, strikes, and similar events will tend to decrease future cash flows and thereby reduce share value.

Here is the important observation: If we hold only a single stock, then the value of our investment will fluctuate because of company-specific events. If we hold a large portfolio, on the other hand, some of the stocks in the portfolio will go up in value because of positive company-specific events, and some will go down in value because of negative events.

The net effect on the overall value of the portfolio will be relatively small, however, because these effects will tend to cancel each other out.

Now we see why some of the variability associated with individual assets is eliminated by diversification. When we combine assets into portfolios, the unique, or unsystematic, events—both positive and negative—tend to "wash out" once we have more than just a few assets. This is an important point that bears repeating:

> Unsystematic risk is essentially eliminated by diversification, so a portfolio with many assets has almost no unsystematic risk.

In fact, the terms *diversifiable risk* and *unsystematic risk* are often used interchangeably.

DIVERSIFICATION AND SYSTEMATIC RISK

We've seen that unsystematic risk can be eliminated by diversification. What about systematic risk? Can it also be eliminated by diversification? The answer is no because, by definition, a systematic risk affects almost all assets. As a result, no matter how many assets we put into a portfolio, systematic risk doesn't go away. Thus, for obvious reasons, the terms *systematic risk* and *nondiversifiable risk* are used interchangeably.

Because we have introduced so many different terms, it is useful to summarize our discussion before moving on. What we have seen is that the total risk of an investment can be written as:

$$\text{Total risk} = \text{Systematic risk} + \text{Unsystematic risk} \qquad (12.5)$$

Systematic risk is also called *nondiversifiable risk* or *market risk.* Unsystematic risk is also called *diversifiable risk, unique risk,* or *asset-specific risk.* Most important, for a well-diversified portfolio, unsystematic risk is negligible. For such a portfolio, essentially all risk is systematic.

CHECK THIS

12.3a   Why is some risk diversifiable? Why is some risk not diversifiable?

12.3b   Why can't systematic risk be diversified away?

12.4   Systematic Risk and Beta

We now begin to address another question: What determines the size of the risk premium on a risky asset? Put another way, why do some assets have a larger risk premium than other assets? The answer, as we discuss next, is also based on the distinction between systematic and unsystematic risk.

THE SYSTEMATIC RISK PRINCIPLE

Thus far, we've seen that the total risk associated with an asset can be decomposed into two components: systematic and unsystematic risk. We have also seen that unsystematic risk can be essentially eliminated by diversification. The systematic risk present in an asset, on the other hand, cannot be eliminated by diversification.

Based on our study of capital market history in Chapter 1, we know that there is a reward, on average, for bearing risk. However, we now need to be more precise about what we mean by risk. The **systematic risk principle** states that the reward for bearing risk depends only on the systematic risk of an investment.

The underlying rationale for this principle is straightforward: Because unsystematic risk can be eliminated at virtually no cost (by diversifying), there is no reward for bearing it. In other words, the market does not reward risks that are borne unnecessarily.

The systematic risk principle has a remarkable and very important implication:

The expected return on an asset depends only on its systematic risk.

There is an obvious corollary to this principle: No matter how much total risk an asset has, only the systematic portion is relevant in determining the expected return (and the risk premium) on that asset.

MEASURING SYSTEMATIC RISK

Because systematic risk is the crucial determinant of an asset's expected return, we need some way of measuring the level of systematic risk for different investments. The specific measure we will use is called the **beta coefficient**, designated by the Greek letter β. A beta coefficient, or just beta for short, tells us how much systematic risk a particular asset has relative to an average asset. By definition, an average asset has a beta of 1.0 relative to itself. An asset with a beta of .50, therefore, has half as much systematic risk as an average asset. Likewise, an asset with a beta of 2.0 has twice as much systematic risk.

Table 12.1 presents the estimated beta coefficients for the stocks of some well-known companies. (Note that *Value Line* rounds betas to the nearest .05.) The range of betas in Table 12.1 is typical for stocks of large U.S. corporations. Betas outside this range occur, however, as you can see in our nearby *Work the Web*.

The important thing to remember is that the expected return, and thus the risk premium, on an asset depends only on its systematic risk. Because assets with larger betas have greater systematic risks, they will have greater expected returns. Thus, from Table 12.1, an investor who buys stock in ExxonMobil, with a beta of .80, should expect to earn less and lose less, on average, than an investor who buys stock in General Motors, with a beta of about 1.25.

TABLE 12.1	Beta Coefficients

| Company | Beta, β | |
	Value Line	Standard and Poor's
ExxonMobil	0.80	0.40
IBM	1.05	1.58
Starbucks	0.80	0.46
Wal-Mart	0.90	0.67
General Motors	1.25	1.18
Microsoft	1.15	1.65
Harley-Davidson	1.10	1.06
eBay	1.45	1.75
Nordstrom	1.20	1.67

Sources: *Value Line* Investment Survey and *S&P Stock Reports.*

Suppose you want to find the beta for a company like US Airways Group (LCC). One way is to go to the Web. We went to finance.yahoo.com, looked up US Airways Group, and followed the "Key Statistics" link. This is part of what we found:

Fiscal Year		Stock Price History	
Fiscal Year Ends:	31-Dec	Beta:	3.385
Most Recent Quarter (mrq):	30-Jun-05	52-Week Change[3]:	N/A
		S&P500 52-Week Change[3]:	6.01%
Profitability		52-Week High (28-Oct-05)[3]:	23.90
Profit Margin (ttm):	-1.99%	52-Week Low (29-Sep-05)[3]:	20.10
Operating Margin (ttm):	-0.48%	50-Day Moving Average[3]:	21.94
Management Effectiveness		200-Day Moving Average[3]:	21.94
Return on Assets (ttm):	-0.47%	**Share Statistics**	
Return on Equity (ttm):	-46.38%	Average Volume (3 month)[3]:	1,031,550
Income Statement		Average Volume (10 day)[3]:	809,912
Revenue (ttm):	2.55B	Shares Outstanding:	36.10M
Revenue Per Share (ttm):	70.738	Float:	33.97M
Qtrly Revenue Growth (yoy):	20.00%	% Held by Insiders[4]:	21.46%
Gross Profit (ttm):	2.35B	% Held by Institutions[4]:	2.20%
EBITDA (ttm):	124.77M	Shares Short (as of 11-Oct-05)[3]:	5.93M
Net Income Avl to Common (ttm):	-50.64M	Short Ratio (as of 11-Oct-05)[3]:	3.7
Diluted EPS (ttm):	-1.13	Short % of Float (as of 11-Oct-05)[3]:	177.60%
Qtrly Earnings Growth (yoy):	30.50%	Shares Short (prior month)[3]:	0

The reported beta for US Airways is about 3.39, which means that US Airways has about 3.4 times the systematic risk of a typical stock. You would expect that the company is very risky, and, looking at the other numbers, we agree. US Airways's return on assets is −.47 percent and its profit margin is −1.99 percent. What's even more amazing is that the company's return on equity is −46.38 percent! To make matters worse, at the time this beta estimate was reported US Airways Group was in bankruptcy hearings. Overall, US Airways seems to be a good candidate for a high beta.

One cautionary note is in order: Not all betas are created equal. For example, in Table 12.1, *Value Line*, a widely used source of betas, reports a beta for Nordstrom of 1.20. At the same time, however, another widely used source, *S&P Stock Reports*, puts Nordstrom's beta at 1.67, substantially larger. The difference results from the different procedures used to calculate beta coefficients. We will have more to say on this subject when we explain how betas are calculated in a later section. Our nearby *Work the Web* box shows one way to find betas online.

EXAMPLE 12.3 **Total Risk versus Beta**

Consider the following information on two securities. Which has greater total risk? Which has greater systematic risk? Greater unsystematic risk? Which asset will have a higher risk premium?

	Standard Deviation	Beta
Security A	40%	.50
Security B	20	1.50

From our discussion in this section, Security A has greater total risk, but it has substantially less systematic risk. Because total risk is the sum of systematic and unsystematic risk, Security A must have greater unsystematic risk. Finally, from the systematic risk principle, Security B will have a higher risk premium and a greater expected return, despite the fact that it has less total risk.

PORTFOLIO BETAS

Earlier, we saw that the riskiness of a portfolio has no simple relation to the risks of the assets in the portfolio. By contrast, a portfolio beta can be calculated just like a portfolio expected return. For example, looking again at Table 12.1, suppose you put half of your money in IBM and half in eBay. Using *Value Line* betas, what would the beta of this combination be? Because IBM has a beta of 1.05 and eBay has a beta of 1.45, the portfolio's beta, β_p, would be:

$$\beta_p = .50 \times \beta_{IBM} + .50 \times \beta_{eBay}$$
$$= .50 \times 1.05 + .50 \times 1.45$$
$$= 1.25$$

In general, if we had a large number of assets in a portfolio, we would multiply each asset's beta by its portfolio weight and then add the results to get the portfolio's beta.

EXAMPLE 12.4 **Portfolio Betas**

Suppose we have the following information:

Security	Amount Invested	Expected Return	Beta
Stock A	$1,000	8%	.80
Stock B	2,000	12	.95
Stock C	3,000	15	1.10
Stock D	4,000	18	1.40

What is the expected return on this portfolio? What is the beta of this portfolio? Does this portfolio have more or less systematic risk than an average asset?

To answer, we first have to calculate the portfolio weights. Notice that the total amount invested is $10,000. Of this, $1,000/$10,000 = 10% is invested in Stock A.

(continued)

Similarly, 20 percent is invested in Stock B, 30 percent is invested in Stock C, and 40 percent is invested in Stock D. The expected return, $E(R_P)$, is thus:

$$E(R_p) = .10 \times E(R_A) + .20 \times E(R_B) + .30 \times E(R_C) + .40 \times E(R_D)$$
$$= .10 \times 8\% + .20 \times 12\% + .30 \times 15\% + .40 \times 18\%$$
$$= 14.9\%$$

Similarly, the portfolio beta, β_p, is:

$$\beta_p = .10 \times \beta_A + .20 \times \beta_B + .30 \times \beta_C + .40 \times \beta_D$$
$$= .10 \times .80 + .20 \times .95 + .30 \times 1.10 + .40 \times 1.40$$
$$= 1.16$$

This portfolio thus has an expected return of 14.9 percent and a beta of 1.16. Because the beta is larger than 1, this portfolio has greater systematic risk than an average asset.

CHECK THIS

12.4a   What is the systematic risk principle?

12.4b   What does a beta coefficient measure?

12.4c   How do you calculate a portfolio beta?

12.4d   True or false: The expected return on a risky asset depends on that asset's total risk. Explain.

12.5   The Security Market Line

We're now in a position to see how risk is rewarded in the marketplace. To begin, suppose that Asset A has an expected return of $E(R_A) = 16\%$ and a beta of $\beta_A = 1.6$. Further suppose that the risk-free rate is $R_f = 4\%$. Notice that a risk-free asset, by definition, has no systematic risk (or unsystematic risk), so a risk-free asset has a beta of zero.

BETA AND THE RISK PREMIUM

Consider a portfolio made up of Asset A and a risk-free asset. We can calculate some different possible portfolio expected returns and betas by varying the percentages invested in these two assets. For example, if 25 percent of the portfolio is invested in Asset A, then the expected return is:

$$E(R_p) = .25 \times E(R_A) + (1 - .25) \times R_f$$
$$= .25 \times 16\% + .75 \times 4\%$$
$$= 7\%$$

Similarly, the beta on the portfolio, β_p, would be:

$$\beta_p = .25 \times \beta_A + (1 - .25) \times 0$$
$$= .25 \times 1.6$$
$$= .40$$

Notice that, because the weights have to add up to 1, the percentage invested in the risk-free asset is equal to 1 minus the percentage invested in Asset A.

WWW

For more information on risk management visit
www.fenews.com

One thing that you might wonder about is whether the percentage invested in Asset A can exceed 100 percent. The answer is yes. This can happen if the investor borrows at the risk-free rate and invests the proceeds in stocks. For example, suppose an investor has $100 and borrows an additional $50 at 4 percent, the risk-free rate. The total investment in Asset A would be $150, or 150 percent of the investor's wealth. The expected return in this case would be:

$$E(R_p) = 1.50 \times E(R_A) + (1 - 1.50) \times R_f$$
$$= 1.50 \times 16\% - .50 \times 4\%$$
$$= 22\%$$

The beta on the portfolio would be:

$$\beta_p = 1.50 \times \beta_A + (1 - 1.50) \times 0$$
$$= 1.50 \times 1.6$$
$$= 2.4$$

We can calculate some other possibilities, as follows:

Percentage of Portfolio in Asset A	Portfolio Expected Return	Portfolio Beta
0%	4%	.0
25	7	.4
50	10	.8
75	13	1.2
100	16	1.6
125	19	2.0
150	22	2.4

In Figure 12.1A, we plot these portfolio expected returns against portfolio betas. Notice that all the combinations fall on a straight line.

THE REWARD-TO-RISK RATIO

What is the slope of the straight line in Figure 12.1A? As always, the slope of a straight line is equal to the rise over the run. In this case, as we move out of the risk-free asset into Asset A, the expected return goes from 4 percent to 16 percent, a rise of 12 percent. At the same time, the beta increases from zero to 1.6, a run of 1.6. The slope of the line is thus $12\%/1.6 = 7.5\%$.

Notice that the slope of our line is just the risk premium on Asset A, $E(R_A) - R_f$, divided by Asset A's beta, β_A:

$$\text{Slope} = \frac{E(R_A) - R_f}{\beta_A}$$
$$= \frac{16\% - 4\%}{1.6}$$
$$= 7.50\%$$

What this tells us is that Asset A offers a *reward-to-risk* ratio of 7.5 percent.[1] In other words, Asset A has a risk premium of 7.50 percent per "unit" of systematic risk.

[1]This ratio is sometimes called the *Treynor index,* after one of its originators.

FIGURE 12.1

Betas and Portfolio Returns

A. Portfolio expected returns and betas for Asset A

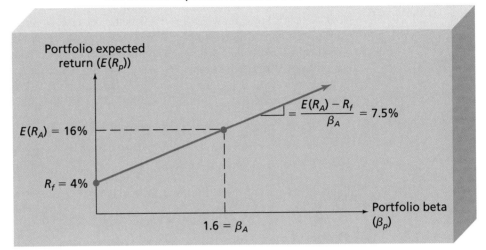

B. Portfolio expected returns and betas for Asset B

C. Portfolio expected returns and betas for both assets

THE BASIC ARGUMENT

Now suppose we consider a second asset, Asset B. This asset has a beta of 1.2 and an expected return of 12 percent. Which investment is better, Asset A or Asset B? You might think that we really cannot say—some investors might prefer A; some investors might prefer B. Actually, however, we can say: A is better because, as we will demonstrate, B offers inadequate compensation for its level of systematic risk, at least relative to A.

To begin, we calculate different combinations of expected returns and betas for portfolios of Asset B and a risk-free asset, just as we did for Asset A. For example, if we put 25 percent in Asset B and the remaining 75 percent in the risk-free asset, the portfolio's expected return will be:

$$E(R_p) = .25 \times E(R_B) + (1 - .25) \times R_f$$
$$= .25 \times 12\% + .75 \times 4\%$$
$$= 6\%$$

Similarly, the beta on the portfolio, β_p, would be:

$$\beta_p = .25 \times \beta_B + (1 - .25) \times 0$$
$$= .25 \times 1.2$$
$$= .30$$

Some other possibilities are as follows:

Percentage of Portfolio in Asset B	Portfolio Expected Return	Portfolio Beta
0%	4%	.0
25	6	.3
50	8	.6
75	10	.9
100	12	1.2
125	14	1.5
150	16	1.8

When we plot these combinations of portfolio expected returns and portfolio betas in Figure 12.1B, we get a straight line, just as we did for Asset A.

The key thing to notice is that when we compare the results for Assets A and B, as in Figure 12.1C, the line describing the combinations of expected returns and betas for Asset A is higher than the one for Asset B. What this tells us is that for any given level of systematic risk (as measured by beta), some combination of Asset A and the risk-free asset always offers a larger return. This is why we were able to state that Asset A is a better investment than Asset B.

Another way of seeing that Asset A offers a superior return for its level of risk is to note that the slope of our line for Asset B is:

$$\text{Slope} = \frac{E(R_B) - R_f}{\beta_B}$$
$$= \frac{12\% - 4\%}{1.2}$$
$$= 6.67\%$$

Thus, Asset B has a reward-to-risk ratio of 6.67 percent, which is less than the 7.5 percent offered by Asset A.

THE FUNDAMENTAL RESULT

The situation we described for Assets A and B could not persist in a well-organized, active market because investors would be attracted to Asset A and away from Asset B. As a result, Asset A's price would rise and Asset B's price would fall. Because prices and expected returns move in opposite directions, A's expected return would decline and B's would rise.

This buying and selling would continue until the two assets plotted on exactly the same line, which means they would offer the same reward for bearing risk. In other words, in an active, competitive market, we must have the situation that:

$$\frac{E(R_A) - R_f}{\beta_A} = \frac{E(R_B) - R_f}{\beta_B} \qquad (12.6)$$

This is the fundamental relation between risk and return.

Our basic argument can be extended to more than just two assets. In fact, no matter how many assets we had, we would always reach the same conclusion:

The reward-to-risk ratio must be the same for all assets in a competitive financial market.

This result is really not too surprising. What it says is that, for example, if one asset has twice as much systematic risk as another asset, its risk premium will simply be twice as large.

EXAMPLE 12.5 | **Using Reward-to-Risk Ratios**

Suppose we see that the reward-to-risk ratio for all assets equals 7.2. If the risk-free rate is 4 percent, what is the required return for an arbitrary asset i, with (1) beta equal 1? (2) beta equal 0?

To answer question (1), write down the reward-to-risk equation, and set it equal to 7.2. Because we know the risk-free rate and the beta of the asset, we can easily solve for the expected return of the asset:

$$\frac{E(R_i) - R_f}{\beta_i} = 7.2$$

$$\frac{E(R_i) - 4.0}{1} = 7.2$$

Therefore, $E(R_i) = 11.2$ percent.

Question (2) is a bit trickier. We cannot use the approach of (1) directly, because we would have to divide by zero. But let's think. Beta is the measure of risk in the reward-to-risk equation. If the portfolio has zero risk, its expected return should not reflect a premium for carrying risk. Therefore, the answer is 4 percent, the rate of return on the risk-free asset.

Because all assets in the market must have the same reward-to-risk ratio, they all must plot on the same line. This argument is illustrated in Figure 12.2, where the subscript i on the return R_i and beta β_i indexes Assets A, B, C, and D. As shown, Assets A and B plot directly on the line and thus have the same reward-to-risk ratio.

If an asset plotted above the line, such as C in Figure 12.2, its reward-to-risk ratio is too high because its expected return is too high. An expected return has two inputs: the expected price and the price today. The expected return is calculated as $E(R) = [E(P) - P_{today}]/P_{today}$, or $[E(P)/P_{today}] - 1$. To *lower* the expected return for Asset C, its price today must *increase* until the reward-to-risk ratio for Asset C plots exactly on the line. Similarly,

FIGURE 12.2   Expected Returns and Systematic Risk

The fundamental relationship between beta and expected return is that all assets must have the same reward-to-risk ratio, $[E(R_i) - R_f]/\beta_i$. This means that they would all plot on the same straight line. Assets A and B are examples of this behavior. Asset C's expected return is too high; Asset D's is too low.

if an asset is plotted below the line, such as D in Figure 12.2, its reward-to-risk ratio is too low because its expected return is too low. To *increase* the expected return for Asset D, its price today must *fall* until the reward-to-risk ratio for Asset D also plots exactly on the line.

The arguments we have presented apply to active, competitive, well-functioning markets. Active financial markets, such as the NYSE, best meet these criteria. Other markets, such as real asset markets, may or may not. For this reason, these concepts are most useful in examining active financial markets.

EXAMPLE 12.6   Buy Low, Sell High

A security is said to be *overvalued* relative to another security if its price today is too high given its expected return and risk. Suppose you observe the following:

Security	Beta	Expected Return
Melan Co.	1.3	14%
Choly Co.	.8	10
Baby Co.	1.0	11.5

The risk-free rate is currently 6 percent. Is one of the securities overvalued relative to the others?

To answer, we compute the reward-to-risk ratios. For Melan, this ratio is (14% − 6%)/1.3 = 6.15%; for Choly, this ratio is 5 percent; and for Baby, it is 5.5 percent. What we conclude is that Choly offers an insufficient expected return for its level of risk, at least relative to Melan and Baby. Because its expected return is too low, its price is too high. In other words, Choly is overvalued relative to Melan and Baby, and we would expect to see its price fall relative to Melan and Baby. Notice that we could also say Melan and Baby are *undervalued* relative to Choly. What can you say about the relative pricing of Melan and Baby?

THE SECURITY MARKET LINE

The line that results when we plot expected returns and beta coefficients is obviously of some importance, so it's time we gave it a name. This line, which we use to describe the relationship between systematic risk and expected return in financial markets, is usually called the **security market line (SML)**, and it is one of the most important concepts in modern finance.

security market line (SML)

Graphical representation of the linear relationship between systematic risk and expected return in financial markets.

MARKET PORTFOLIOS We will find it very useful to know the equation of the SML. Although there are many different ways we could write it, we will discuss the most frequently seen version. Suppose we consider a portfolio made up of all of the assets in the market. Such a portfolio is called a *market portfolio*, and we will express the expected return on this market portfolio as $E(R_M)$.

Because all the assets in the market must plot on the SML, so must a market portfolio made up of those assets. To determine where it plots on the SML, we need to know the beta of the market portfolio, β_M. Because this portfolio is representative of all of the assets in the market, it must have average systematic risk. In other words, it has a beta of 1. We could therefore express the slope of the SML as:

$$\text{SML slope} = \frac{E(R_M) - R_f}{\beta_M} = \frac{E(R_M) - R_f}{1} = E(R_M) - R_f$$

market risk premium

The risk premium on a market portfolio, i.e., a portfolio made of all assets in the market.

The term $E(R_M) - R_f$ is often called the **market risk premium** because it is the risk premium on a market portfolio.

THE CAPITAL ASSET PRICING MODEL To finish up, if we let $E(R_i)$ and β_i stand for the expected return and beta, respectively, on any asset in the market, then we know that the asset must plot on the SML. As a result, we know that its reward-to-risk ratio is the same as that of the overall market:

$$\frac{E(R_i) - R_f}{\beta_i} = E(R_M) - R_f$$

If we rearrange this, then we can write the equation for the SML as:

$$E(R_i) = R_f + [E(R_M) - R_f] \times \beta_i \qquad (12.7)$$

EXAMPLE 12.7 | **Risk and Return**

Suppose the risk-free rate is 4 percent, the market risk premium is 8.6 percent, and a particular stock has a beta of 1.3. Based on the CAPM, what is the expected return on this stock? What would the expected return be if the beta were to double?

With a beta of 1.3, the risk premium for the stock is $1.3 \times 8.6\%$, or 11.18 percent. The risk-free rate is 4 percent, so the expected return is 15.18 percent. If the beta were to double to 2.6, the risk premium would double to 22.36 percent, so the expected return would be 26.36 percent.

FIGURE 12.3   Security Market Line (SML)

The slope of the security market line is equal to the market risk premium, i.e., the reward for bearing an average amount of systematic risk. The equation describing the SML can be written as:

$$E(R_i) = R_f + [E(R_M) - R_f] \times \beta_i$$

which is the capital asset pricing model (CAPM).

capital asset pricing model (CAPM)

A theory of risk and return for securities in a competitive capital market.

Equation (12.7) is the famous **capital asset pricing model (CAPM)**.[2] What the CAPM shows is that the expected return for an asset depends on three things:

1. *The pure time value of money.* As measured by the risk-free rate, R_f, this is the reward for merely waiting for your money, without taking any risk.

2. *The reward for bearing systematic risk.* As measured by the market risk premium, $E(R_M) - R_f$, this component is the reward the market offers for bearing an average amount of systematic risk.

3. *The amount of systematic risk.* As measured by β_i, this is the amount of systematic risk present in a particular asset relative to that in an average asset.

There's a CAPM calculator (if you really need it!) at
www.moneychimp.com

By the way, the CAPM works for portfolios of assets just as it does for individual assets. In an earlier section, we saw how to calculate a portfolio's beta in the CAPM equation.

Figure 12.3 summarizes our discussion of the SML and the CAPM. As before, we plot expected return against beta. Now we recognize that, based on the CAPM, the slope of the SML is equal to the market risk premium, $E(R_M) - R_f$.

This concludes our presentation of concepts related to the risk-return trade-off. Table 12.2 summarizes the various concepts in the order in which we discussed them.

---

[2]Our discussion of the CAPM is actually closely related to the more recent development, arbitrage pricing theory (APT). The theory underlying the CAPM is more complex than we have indicated here, and it has implications beyond the scope of this discussion. As we present it here, the CAPM has essentially identical implications to those of the APT, so we don't distinguish between them.

TABLE 12.2 Risk and Return Summary

1. **Total risk.** The *total risk* of an investment is measured by the variance or, more commonly, the standard deviation of its return.

2. **Total return.** The *total return* on an investment has two components: the expected return and the unexpected return. The unexpected return comes about because of unanticipated events. The risk from investing stems from the possibility of an unanticipated event.

3. **Systematic and unsystematic risks.** *Systematic risks* (also called *market risks*) are unanticipated events that affect almost all assets to some degree because the effects are economywide. *Unsystematic risks* are unanticipated events that affect single assets or small groups of assets. Unsystematic risks are also called *unique* or *asset-specific risks*.

4. **The effect of diversification.** Some, but not all, of the risk associated with a risky investment can be eliminated by diversification. The reason is that unsystematic risks, which are unique to individual assets, tend to wash out in a large portfolio, but systematic risks, which affect all of the assets in a portfolio to some extent, do not.

5. **The systematic risk principle and beta.** Because unsystematic risk can be freely eliminated by diversification, the *systematic risk principle* states that the reward for bearing risk depends only on the level of systematic risk. The level of systematic risk in a particular asset, relative to the average, is given by the *beta* of that asset.

6. **The reward-to-risk ratio and the security market line.** The *reward-to-risk ratio* for Asset i is the ratio of its risk premium, $E(R_i) - R_f$, to its beta, β_i.

$$\frac{E(R_i) - R_f}{\beta_i}$$

In a well-functioning market, this ratio is the same for every asset. As a result, when asset expected returns are plotted against asset betas, all assets plot on the same straight line, called the *security market line* (SML).

7. **The capital asset pricing model.** From the SML, the expected return on Asset i can be written:

$$E(R_i) = R_f + [E(R_M) - R_f] \times \beta_i$$

This is the *capital asset pricing model* (CAPM). The expected return on a risky asset thus has three components. The first is the pure time value of money (R_f); the second is the market risk premium, $E(R_M) - R_f$; and the third is the beta for the asset (β_i).

CHECK THIS

12.5a   What is the fundamental relationship between risk and return in active markets?

12.5b   What is the security market line (SML)? Why must all assets plot directly on it in a well-functioning market?

12.5c   What is the capital asset pricing model (CAPM)? What does it tell us about the required return on a risky investment?

12.6   More on Beta

In our last several sections, we discussed the basic economic principles of risk and return. We found that the expected return on a security depends on its systematic risk, which is measured using the security's beta coefficient, β. In this final section, we examine beta in more detail. We first illustrate more closely what it is that beta measures. We then show how betas can be estimated for individual securities, and we discuss why it is that different sources report different betas for the same security.

A CLOSER LOOK AT BETA

Going back to the beginning of the chapter, we discussed how the actual return on a security, R, could be written as follows:

$$R - E(R) = m + \epsilon \qquad (12.8)$$

Recall that in Equation 12.8, m stands for the systematic or marketwide portion of the unexpected return. Based on our discussion of the CAPM, we can now be a little more precise about this component.

Specifically, the systematic portion of an unexpected return depends on two things. First, it depends on the size of the systematic effect. We will measure this as $R_M - E(R_M)$, which is simply the difference between the actual return on the overall market and the expected return. Second, as we have discussed, some securities have greater systematic risk than others, and we measure this risk using beta. Putting it together, we have:

$$m = [R_M - E(R_M)] \times \beta \qquad (12.9)$$

In other words, the marketwide, or systematic, portion of the return on a security depends on both the size of the marketwide surprise, $R_M - E(R_M)$, and the sensitivity of the security to such surprises, β.

Now, if we combine Equations 12.8 and 12.9, we have:

$$R - E(R) = m + \epsilon \qquad (12.10)$$
$$= [R_M - E(R_M)] \times \beta + \epsilon$$

Equation 12.10 gives us some additional insight into beta by telling us why some securities have higher betas than others. A high-beta security is simply one that is relatively sensitive to overall market movements, whereas a low-beta security is one that is relatively insensitive. In other words, the systematic risk of a security is just a reflection of its sensitivity to overall market movements.

A hypothetical example is useful for illustrating the main point of Equation 12.10. Suppose a particular security has a beta of 1.2, the risk-free rate is 5 percent, and the expected return on the market is 12 percent. From the CAPM, we know that the expected return on the security is:

$$E(R) = R_f + [E(R_M) - R_f] \times \beta$$
$$= .05 + (.12 - .05) \times 1.2$$
$$= .134$$

Thus, the expected return on this security is 13.4 percent. However, we know that in any year the actual return on this security will be more or less than 13.4 percent because of unanticipated systematic and unsystematic events.

Columns 1 and 2 of Table 12.3 list the actual returns on our security, R, for a five-year period along with the actual returns for the market as a whole, R_M, for the same period.

TABLE 12.3	Decomposition of Total Returns into Systematic and Unsystematic Portions

| Year | Actual Returns | | Unexpected Returns | | Systematic Portion | Unsystematic Portion (ϵ) |
	R	R_M	$R - E(R)$	$R_M - E(R_M)$	$[R_M - E(R_M)] \times \beta$	$[R - E(R)] - [R_M - E(R_M)] \times \beta$
2001	20%	15%	6.6%	3%	3.6%	3%
2002	−24.6	−3	−38	−15	−18	−20
2003	23	10	9.6	−2	−2.4	12
2004	36.8	24	23.4	12	14.4	9
2005	3.4	7	−10	−5	−6	−4

Given these actual returns and the expected returns on the security (13.4 percent) and the market as a whole (12 percent), we can calculate the unexpected returns on the security, $R - E(R)$, along with the unexpected return on the market as a whole, $R_M - E(R_M)$. The results are shown in columns 3 and 4 of Table 12.3.

Next we decompose the unexpected returns on the security—that is, we break them down into their systematic and unsystematic components in columns 5 and 6. From Equation 12.9, we calculate the systematic portion of the unexpected return by taking the security's beta, 1.2, and multiplying it by the market's unexpected return:

$$\text{Systematic portion} = m = [R_M - E(R_M)] \times \beta$$

Finally, we calculate the unsystematic portion by subtracting the systematic portion from the total unexpected return:

$$\text{Unsystematic portion} = \epsilon = [R - E(R)] - [R_M - E(R_M)] \times \beta$$

Notice that the unsystematic portion is essentially whatever is left over after we account for the systematic portion. For this reason, it is sometimes called the "residual" portion of the unexpected return.

Figure 12.4 illustrates the main points of this discussion by plotting the unexpected returns on the security in Table 12.3 against the unexpected return on the market as a whole. These are the individual points in the graph, each labeled with its year. We also plot the systematic portions of the unexpected returns in Table 12.3 and connect them with a straight line. Notice that the slope of the straight line is equal to 1.2, the beta of the security. As indicated, the distance from the straight line to an individual point is the unsystematic portion of the return, ϵ, for a particular year.

WHERE DO BETAS COME FROM?

As our discussion to this point shows, beta is a useful concept. It allows us to estimate the expected return on a security, it tells how sensitive a security's return is to unexpected market events, and it lets us separate out the systematic and unsystematic portions of a security's return. In our example just above, we were given that the beta was 1.2, so the required calculations were all pretty straightforward. Suppose, however, that we didn't have the beta ahead of time. In this case, we would have to estimate it.

FIGURE 12.4 **Unexpected Returns and Beta**

A security's beta is a measure of how sensitive the security's return is to overall market movements. That sensitivity depends on two things: (1) how closely correlated the security's return is with the overall market's return and (2) how volatile the security is relative to the market. Specifically, going back to our previous chapter, let $Corr(R_i, R_M)$ stand for the correlation between the return on a particular security i and the overall market. As before, let σ_i and σ_M be the standard deviations on the security and the market, respectively. Given these numbers, the beta for the security, β_i, is simply:

$$\beta_i = Corr(R_i, R_M) \times \sigma_i / \sigma_M \qquad (12.11)$$

In other words, the beta is equal to the correlation multiplied by the ratio of the standard deviations.

From previous chapters, we know how to calculate the standard deviations in Equation 12.11. However, we have not yet discussed how to calculate correlations. This is our final task for this chapter. The simplest way to proceed is to construct a worksheet like Table 12.4.

The first six columns of Table 12.4 are familiar from Chapter 1. The first two contain five years of returns on a particular security and the overall market. We add these up and divide by 5 to get the average returns of 10 percent and 12 percent for the security and the market, respectively, as shown in the table. In the third and fourth columns we calculate the return deviations by taking each individual return and subtracting out the average return. In columns 5 and 6 we square these return deviations. To calculate the variances, we total these squared deviations and divide by $5 - 1 = 4$. We calculate the standard deviations by taking the square root of the variances, and we find that the standard deviations for the security and the market are 18.87 percent and 15.03 percent, respectively.

Now we come to the part that's new. In the last column of Table 12.4, we have calculated the *product* of the return deviations by simply multiplying columns 3 and 4. When we total these products and divide by $5 - 1 = 4$, the result is called the **covariance**.

covariance
A measure of the tendency of two things to move or vary together.

Covariance, as the name suggests, is a measure of the tendency of two things to vary together. If the covariance is positive, then the tendency is to move in the same direction, and vice versa for a negative covariance. A zero covariance means there is no particular

TABLE 12.4	Calculating Beta

| Year | Returns | | Return Deviations | | Squared Deviations | | Product of Deviations |
	Security (1)	Market (2)	Security (3)	Market (4)	Security (5)	Market (6)	(7)
2001	.10	.08	.00	−.04	.0000	.0016	.0000
2002	−.08	−.12	−.18	−.24	.0324	.0576	.0432
2003	−.04	.16	−.14	.04	.0196	.0016	−.0056
2004	.40	.26	.30	.14	.0900	.0196	.0420
2005	.12	.22	.02	.10	.0004	.0100	.0020
Totals	.50	.60	0	0	.1424	.0904	.0816

	Average Returns	Variances	Standard Deviations
Security	.50/5 = .10 = 10%	.1424/4 = .0356	$\sqrt{.0356} = .1887 = 18.87\%$
Market	.60/5 = .12 = 12%	.0904/4 = .0226	$\sqrt{.0226} = .1503 = 15.03\%$

Covariance $= Cov(R_i, R_M) = .0816/4 = .0204$
Correlation $= Corr(R_i, R_M) = .0204/(.1887 \times .1503) = .72$
Beta $= \beta = .72 \times (.1887/.1503) = .9039 \approx .9$

SPREADSHEET ANALYSIS

	A	B	C	D	E	F	G	H
1								
2			Using a Spreadsheet to Calculate Beta					
3								
4	To illustrate how to calculate betas, correlations, and covariances using a spreadsheet,							
5	we have entered the information from Table 12.4 into the spreadsheet below. Here, we							
6	use Excel functions to do all the calculations.							
7								
8				Returns				
9				Security	Market			
10			2001	10%	8%	Note: The Excel Format is		
11			2002	−8%	−12%	set to percent, but the		
12			2003	−4%	16%	numbers are entered as		
13			2004	40%	26%	decimals.		
14			2005	12%	22%			
15								
16			Average:	10%	12%	(Using the =AVERAGE function)		
17			Std. Dev.:	18.87%	15.03%	(Using the =STDEV function)		
18			Correlation:	0.72		=CORREL(D10:D14,E10:E14)		
19								
20			Beta:	0.90				
21								
22	Excel also has a covariance function, =COVAR, but we do not use it because it divides							
23	by n instead of n-1. Verify that you get a Beta of about 0.72 if you use the COVAR							
24	function divided by the variance of the Market Returns (Use the Excel function, =VAR).							
25								
26	Question 1: How would you correct the covariance calculation?							
27	Question 2: What happens when you use =SLOPE, an Excel function?							
28								

relation. For our security in Table 12.4, the covariance is +.0204, so the security tends to move in the same direction as the market.

A problem with covariances is that, like variances, the actual numbers are hard to interpret (the sign, of course, is not). For example, our covariance is .0204, but, just from this number, we can't really say if the security has a strong tendency to move with the market or only a weak one. To fix this problem, we divide the covariance by the product of the two standard deviations. The result is the correlation coefficient, introduced in the previous chapter.

From Table 12.4, the correlation between our security and the overall market is .72. Recalling that correlations range from −1 to +1, this .72 tells us that the security has a fairly strong tendency to move with the overall market, but that tendency is not perfect.

Now, we have reached our goal of calculating the beta coefficient. As shown in the last row of Table 12.4, from Equation 12.11, we have:

$$\beta_i = \text{Corr}(R_i, R_M) \times \sigma_i / \sigma_M$$
$$= .72 \times (.1887/.1503)$$
$$= .90$$

We find that this security has a beta of .9, so it has slightly less than average systematic risk. As our nearby *Spreadsheet Analysis* box shows, these calculations can be done easily with a spreadsheet.

WHY DO BETAS DIFFER?

Finally, we consider why different sources report different betas. The important thing to remember is that betas are estimated from actual data. Different sources estimate differently, possibly using different data. We discuss some of the key differences next.

First, there are two issues concerning data. Betas can be calculated using daily, weekly, monthly, quarterly, or annual returns. In principle, it does not matter which is chosen, but with real data, different estimates will result. Second, betas can be estimated over relatively short periods such as a few weeks or over long periods of 5 to 10 years (or even more).

The trade-off here is not hard to understand. Betas obtained from high-frequency returns, such as daily returns, are less reliable than those obtained from less frequent returns, such as monthly returns. This argues for using monthly or longer returns. On the other hand, any time we estimate something, we would like to have a large number of recent observations. This argues for using weekly or daily returns. There is no ideal balance; the most common choices are three to five years of monthly data or a single year of weekly data. The betas we get from a year of weekly data are more current in the sense that they reflect only the previous year, but they tend to be less stable than those obtained from longer periods.

Another issue has to do with choice of a market index. All along, we have discussed the return on the "overall market," but we have not been very precise about how to measure this. By far the most common choice is to use the S&P 500 stock market index to measure the overall market, but this is not the only alternative. Different sources use different indexes to capture the overall market, and different indexes will lead to different beta estimates.

You might wonder whether some index is the "correct" one. The answer is yes, but a problem comes up. In principle, in the CAPM, when we speak of the overall market, what we really mean is the market for *every* risky asset of every type. In other words, what we would need is an index that included all the stocks, bonds, real estate, precious metals, and everything else in the entire world (not just the United States). Obviously, no such index exists, so instead we must choose some smaller index to proxy for this much larger one.

Last, a few sources (including *Value Line,* one source for Table 12.1) calculate betas the way we described in Table 12.4, but then they go on to adjust them for statistical reasons. The nature of the adjustment goes beyond our discussion, but such adjustments are another reason why betas differ across sources.

12.7 Extending CAPM

The previous two sections introduced you to the famous capital asset pricing model, or CAPM for short. For investors, the CAPM has a stunning implication: What you earn, through time, on your portfolio depends only on the level of systematic risk you bear. The corollary is equally striking: As a diversified investor, you do not need to be concerned with the total risk or volatility of any individual asset in your portfolio—it is simply irrelevant.

Of course, we should note that the CAPM is a theory, and, as with any theory, whether it is correct is a question for the data. So does the CAPM work or not? Put more directly, does expected return depend on beta, and beta alone, or do other factors come into play? There is no more hotly debated question in all of finance.

In this section, we first present a short history of attempts to test the CAPM. Then we discuss one of the most important extensions of the CAPM, the so-called Fama-French three-factor model.

A (VERY) BRIEF HISTORY OF TESTING CAPM

The CAPM was introduced in the mid-1960s (but, perhaps surprisingly, tests of this model began to appear only in the early 1970s). When researchers test the CAPM, they essentially look to see whether average returns are linearly related to beta. That is, they want to know if asset returns and beta line up as shown in Figure 12.3. The earliest tests of the CAPM suggested that return and risk (as measured by beta) showed a reasonable relationship. However, the relationship was not so strong that financial researchers were content to move on and test other theories.

SMALL CAP VALUE MAY NO LONGER BE A VALUE

Good things come in small packages. Just ask investors in small-cap value stocks.

Value stocks in the Russell 2000 Index, a benchmark for small stocks, have done twice as well as the Standard & Poor's 500 has over the last 24 months.

And over the past decade small-cap value stocks are up an eye-popping 168%, easily outpacing the S&P's 103% advance and the Russell 2000 Growth index's mere 44% gain.

So, not surprisingly, some small value stocks are starting to look pricey.

The Russell 2000, whose median market cap is about $576 million, fetches 23.4 times earnings estimates for the next four quarters. That's far richer than the S&P 500's 15.5 times forward earnings, according to Thomson Financial/Baseline.

That's why some money managers advise taking profits in the priciest value small caps and replacing them with shares of larger companies.

"We think it would be a good idea for investors to sell some of their small cap-stocks," says Ned Notzon, chairman of the asset allocation committee at T. Rowe Price Associates.

Small caps (which typically have a market capitalization of $1 billion or less) can be great long-term investments, even though their returns can fluctuate much more than shares of large, well-known companies.

For the last 78 years, small caps have generated compound annual returns of 12.7%, compared with 10.4% for large caps, according to Ibbotson Associates. Historically, small-cap value stocks do best—they've risen nearly 15% compared with the 9.6% returns for small-cap growth.

Value stocks typically have stable earnings growth and lower price-to-book and price-to-earnings ratios.

Growth stocks tend to have higher growth rates and valuations.

The question is, how long can the current run for small caps last?

Small-cap stocks outperformed others for nearly a decade during the bull market that began in 1974, says Roger Ibbotson, chief executive officer of the Chicago research firm Ibbotson Associates.

But in the fourth year of the two most recent bull markets (which is where we are in the current one), small caps have underperformed big-cap stocks, according to Sam Stovall, chief investment strategist at S&P.

"I would not be optimistic about small caps in 2006," Ibbotson says. "The run has got to be about over, even though momentum is working for the seventh year in a row."

Barry James, a portfolio manager at James Investment Research near Dayton, Ohio, recommends that investors cut their allocations for small caps to 10 to 15% of their portfolios, from 25%.

He's looking for small caps in the technology sector to hold up well, however, and expects smaller energy stocks to resist a broader market decline, even if oil prices drop.

Arthur Nunes, at IMS Capital, says that in the past 20 years, mid-cap stocks—those whose market capitalization is between $1 billion and $5 billion—have been silent winners, offering 15.2% returns with a lower risk than small caps.

Ultimately, investors who have profited by thinking small over the last few years may now need to look at the bigger picture.

Source: Dimitra Defotis, *Barron's Online*, October 11, 2005.

To summarize years of testing, the relationship between returns and beta appeared to vary depending on the time period that was studied. Over some periods, the relationship was strong. In others, it was apparent but not strong. In others, it was seemingly nonexistent. Over the years, researchers refined their techniques to measure betas. In addition, the question was raised whether researchers could calculate betas at all. The basic argument was that betas could not be calculated relative to the overall market portfolio because we cannot observe the true market portfolio. Nonetheless, despite this insightful critique, researchers continue to test CAPM and debate the findings of CAPM research to this day.

Despite the debate between CAPM critics and CAPM champions, some important ideas have emerged. Few researchers question these general principles:

- Investing has two dimensions: risk and return.
- It is inappropriate to look at the risk of an individual security. What is appropriate is how the individual security contributes to the risk of a diversified portfolio.
- Risk can be decomposed into systematic risk and nonsystematic risk.
- Investors will be compensated only for taking systematic risk.

THE FAMA-FRENCH THREE-FACTOR MODEL

To illustrate some aspects of the debate surrounding CAPM, we now briefly explore the Fama-French three-factor model, which gets its name from its creators, Gene Fama and Ken French. Table 12.5 illustrates an important finding from years of research into stock market returns. As shown, two groups of stocks have tended to do noticeably better than the market as a whole: (1) stocks with a small-market capitalization (small-cap stocks) and (2) stocks that have a higher than average ratio of book (or accounting) value to market value of equity (so-called value stocks).

Table 12.5 is formed as follows. First, for each year of historical data, a large set of stocks are ranked on the basis of their market cap, or size. The smallest 20 percent of the stocks are placed into the market cap quintile number 1, the next smallest 20 percent are placed into market cap quintile number 2, and so on. Then, the same set of stocks are ranked on the basis of their book/market (B/M) ratio. The smallest 20 percent are placed into B/M quintile number 1, the next smallest 20 percent are placed into B/M quintile number 2, and so on.

Let's look at the cell with an average annual return of 8.42 percent. This number is calculated as follows. After the sorting described above, we put stocks into portfolios according to both of their quintile scores, for a total of 25 (= 5 × 5) portfolios. So, for example, the stocks with both the smallest cap and the lowest B/M end up in the quintile 1–1 portfolio. As shown in Table 12.5, over the time period 1926 to 2004, the average annual return for stocks in the quintile 1–1 portfolio is 8.42 percent.

Three things should jump out at you in Table 12.5. Notice that the cell 1-5, which contains stocks with the smallest cap and highest B/M, has had the highest returns. Looking down each column, you can see that in three columns the highest return belongs to the smallest cap quintile (this happens in columns 3, 4, and 5). Looking across each row, you can see that in every row, the highest return belongs to the highest B/M quintile.

Based on further analysis of these data, Professors Fama and French concluded that differences in beta were not sufficient to explain the differences in returns in Table 12.5. They therefore argue that two additional factors beyond beta must be considered to understand differences in expected returns on stocks, namely, market cap and B/M. Thus, their model of stock returns has a total of three factors. Whether these extra factors are truly sources of systematic risk is a subject of ongoing debate.

WWW

You can download lots of data behind the Fama-French model at http://mba.tuck.dartmouth.edu/pages/faculty/ken.french/

TABLE 12.5	Average Annual Percentage Returns from 25 Portfolios Formed on Size (Cap) and Book to Market, 1926–2004				
Quintile	1 (Lowest B/M)	2	3	4	5 (Highest B/M)
1 (smallest cap)	8.42	14.34	18.09	22.06	22.95
2	11.57	16.20	18.06	19.02	19.76
3	12.99	15.83	16.48	17.27	18.47
4	12.44	13.57	15.64	16.51	17.75
5 (largest cap)	11.64	11.32	12.84	13.29	14.92

Source: Author calculations using data from the Web site of Ken French.

12.8   Summary and Conclusions

This chapter has covered the essentials of risk and return. Along the way, we have introduced a number of definitions and concepts. The most important of these is the security market line, or SML. The SML is important because it tells us the reward offered in financial markets for bearing risk.

Because we have covered quite a bit of ground, it's useful to summarize the basic economic logic underlying the SML as follows:

1. Based on capital market history, there is a reward for bearing risk. This reward is the risk premium on an asset.

2. The total risk associated with an asset has two parts: systematic risk and unsystematic risk. Unsystematic risk can be freely eliminated by diversification (this is the principle of diversification), so only systematic risk is rewarded. As a result, the risk premium on an asset is determined by its systematic risk. This is the systematic risk principle.

3. An asset's systematic risk, relative to the average, can be measured by its beta coefficient, β_i. The risk premium on an asset is then given by the market risk premium multiplied by the asset's beta coefficient, $[E(R_M) - R_f] \times \beta_i$.

4. The expected return on an asset, $E(R_i)$, is equal to the risk-free rate, R_f, plus the asset's risk premium:

$$E(R_i) = R_f + [E(R_M) - R_f] \times \beta_i$$

This is the equation of the SML, and it is often called the capital asset pricing model (CAPM).

Toward the end of the chapter, we showed how betas are calculated and we discussed some of the main reasons different sources report different beta coefficients. We closed the chapter by presenting a discussion of the Fama-French three-factor model, an important extension to the basic CAPM.

GET REAL

An immediate implication of the CAPM is that you, as an investor, need to be aware of the level of systematic risk you are carrying. Look up the betas of the stocks you hold in your simulated brokerage account and compute your portfolio's systematic risk. Is it bigger or smaller than 1.0? More important, is the portfolio's beta consistent with your desired level of portfolio risk?

Betas are particularly useful for understanding mutual fund risk and return. Since most mutual funds are at least somewhat diversified (the exceptions being sector funds and other specialized funds), they have relatively little unsystematic risk, and their betas can be measured with some precision. Look at the funds you own and learn their betas (www.morningstar.com is a good source). Are the risk levels what you intended? As you study mutual fund risk, you will find some other measures exist, most of which are closely related to the measures discussed in this chapter. Take a few minutes to understand these as well.

Does expected return depend on beta, and beta alone, or do other factors come into play? There is no more hotly debated question in all of finance, and the research that exists to date is inconclusive. (Some researchers would dispute this!) At a minimum, beta appears to be a useful measure of market-related volatility, that is, risk. Whether beta is a useful measure of expected return (much less a comprehensive one) awaits more research. Lots more research.

Key Terms

Chapter Review Problems and Self-Test

1. **Risk and Return**   Suppose you observe the following situation:

Security	Beta	Expected Return
Sanders	1.8	22.00%
Janicek	1.6	20.44

   If the risk-free rate is 7 percent, are these two stocks correctly priced relative to each other? What must the risk-free rate be if they are correctly priced?

2. **CAPM**   Suppose the risk-free rate is 8 percent. The expected return on the market is 16 percent. If a particular stock has a beta of .7, what is its expected return based on the CAPM? If another stock has an expected return of 24 percent, what must its beta be?

Answers to Self-Test Problems

1. If we compute the reward-to-risk ratios, we get $(22\% - 7\%)/1.8 = 8.33\%$ for Sanders versus 8.4% for Janicek. Relative to Sanders, Janicek's expected return is too high, so its price is too low.

   If they are correctly priced, then they must offer the same reward-to-risk ratio. The risk-free rate would have to be such that:

$$\frac{22\% - R_f}{1.8} = \frac{20.44\% - R_f}{1.6}$$

   With a little algebra, we find that the risk-free rate must be 8 percent:

$$22\% - R_f = (20.44\% - R_f)(1.8/1.6)$$
$$22\% - 20.44\% \times 1.125 = R_f - R_f \times 1.125$$
$$R_f = 8\%$$

2. Because the expected return on the market is 16 percent, the market risk premium is $16\% - 8\% = 8\%$ (the risk-free rate is also 8 percent). The first stock has a beta of .7, so its expected return is $8\% + 8\% \times .7 = 13.6\%$.

   For the second stock, notice that the risk premium is $24\% - 8\% = 16\%$. Because this is twice as large as the market risk premium, the beta must be exactly equal to 2. We can verify this using the CAPM:

$$E(R_i) = R_f + [E(R_M) - R_f] \times \beta_i$$
$$24\% = 8\% + (16\% - 8\%) \times \beta_i$$
$$\beta_i = 16\%/8\% = 2.0$$

Test Your Investment Quotient

1. **Portfolio Return**   According to the CAPM, what is the rate of return of a portfolio with a beta of 1?
   a. Between R_M and R_f
   b. The risk-free rate, R_f
   c. Beta $\times (R_M - R_f)$
   d. The return on the market, R_M

2. **Stock Return** The return on a stock is said to have which two of the following basic parts?

   a. An expected return and an unexpected return.
   b. A measurable return and an unmeasurable return.
   c. A predicted return and a forecast return.
   d. A total return and a partial return.

3. **News Components** A news announcement about a stock is said to have which two of the following parts?

   a. An expected part and a surprise.
   b. Public information and private information.
   c. Financial information and product information.
   d. A good part and a bad part.

4. **News Effects** A company announces that its earnings have increased 50 percent over the previous year, which matches analysts' expectations. What is the likely effect on the stock price?

   a. The stock price will increase.
   b. The stock price will decrease.
   c. The stock price will rise and then fall after an overreaction.
   d. The stock price will not be affected.

5. **News Effects** A company announces that its earnings have decreased 25 percent from the previous year, but analysts expected a small increase. What is the likely effect on the stock price?

   a. The stock price will increase.
   b. The stock price will decrease.
   c. The stock price will rise and then fall after an overreaction.
   d. The stock price will not be affected.

6. **News Effects** A company announces that its earnings have increased 25 percent from the previous year, but analysts actually expected a 50 percent increase. What is the likely effect on the stock price?

   a. The stock price will increase.
   b. The stock price will decrease.
   c. The stock price will rise and then fall after an overreaction.
   d. The stock price will not be affected.

7. **News Effects** A company announces that its earnings have decreased 50 percent from the previous year, but analysts only expected a 25 percent decrease. What is the likely effect on the stock price?

   a. The stock price will increase.
   b. The stock price will decrease.
   c. The stock price will rise and then fall after an overreaction.
   d. The stock price will not be affected.

8. **Security Risk** The systematic risk of a security is also called its

   a. Perceived risk
   b. Unique or asset-specific risk
   c. Market risk
   d. Fundamental risk

9. **Security Risk** Which type of risk is essentially eliminated by diversification?

   a. Perceived risk
   b. Market risk
   c. Systematic risk
   d. Unsystematic risk

10. **Security Risk** The systematic risk principle states that

    a. Systematic risk doesn't matter to investors.
    b. Systematic risk can be essentially eliminated by diversification.
    c. The reward for bearing risk is independent of the systematic risk of an investment.
    d. The reward for bearing risk depends only on the systematic risk of an investment.

11. **Security Risk** The systematic risk principle has an important implication, which is

    a. Systematic risk is preferred to unsystematic risk.
    b. Systematic risk is the only risk that can be reduced by diversification.
    c. The expected return on an asset is independent of its systematic risk.
    d. The expected return on an asset depends only on its systematic risk.

12. **CAPM** A financial market's security market line (SML) describes

    a. The relationship between systematic risk and expected returns.
    b. The relationship between unsystematic risk and expected returns.
    c. The relationship between systematic risk and unexpected returns.
    d. The relationship between unsystematic risk and unexpected returns.

13. **Risk Aversion** Which of the following is not an implication of risk aversion for the investment process?

    a. The security market line is upward sloping.
    b. The promised yield on AAA-rated bonds is higher than on A-rated bonds.
    c. Investors expect a positive relationship between expected return and risk.
    d. Investors prefer portfolios that lie on the efficient frontier to other portfolios with equal rates of return.

14. **Unsystematic Risk** In the context of capital market theory, unsystematic risk

    a. Is described as unique risk.
    b. Refers to nondiversifiable risk.
    c. Remains in the market portfolio.
    d. Refers to the variability in all risk assets caused by macroeconomic factors and other aggregate market-related variables.

15. **Security Market Line** Which of the following statements about the security market line (SML) is false?

    a. Properly valued assets plot exactly on the SML.
    b. The SML leads all investors to invest in the same portfolio of risky assets.
    c. The SML provides a benchmark for evaluating expected investment performance.
    d. The SML is a graphic representation of the relationship between expected return and beta.

Concept Questions

1. **Diversifiable Risk** In broad terms, why is some risk diversifiable? Why are some risks nondiversifiable? Does it follow that an investor can control the level of unsystematic risk in a portfolio, but not the level of systematic risk?

2. **Announcements and Prices** Suppose the government announces that, based on a just-completed survey, the growth rate in the economy is likely to be 2 percent in the coming year, compared to 5 percent for the year just completed. Will security prices increase, decrease, or stay the same following this announcement? Does it make any difference whether the 2 percent figure was anticipated by the market? Explain.

3. **Announcements and Risk** Classify the following events as mostly systematic or mostly unsystematic. Is the distinction clear in every case?

    a. Short-term interest rates increase unexpectedly.
    b. The interest rate a company pays on its short-term debt borrowing is increased by its bank.
    c. Oil prices unexpectedly decline.
    d. An oil tanker ruptures, creating a large oil spill.
    e. A manufacturer loses a multi-million-dollar product liability suit.
    f. A Supreme Court decision substantially broadens producer liability for injuries suffered by product users.

4. **Announcements and Risk**   Indicate whether the following events might cause stocks in general to change price, and whether they might cause Big Widget Corp.'s stock to change price.

   a. The government announces that inflation unexpectedly jumped by 2 percent last month.
   b. Big Widget's quarterly earnings report, just issued, generally fell in line with analysts' expectations.
   c. The government reports that economic growth last year was at 3 percent, which generally agreed with most economists' forecasts.
   d. The directors of Big Widget die in a plane crash.
   e. Congress approves changes to the tax code that will increase the top marginal corporate tax rate. The legislation had been debated for the previous six months.

5. **Diversification and Risk**   True or false: The most important characteristic in determining the expected return of a well-diversified portfolio is the variances of the individual assets in the portfolio. Explain.

6. **Announcements**   As indicated by examples in this chapter, earnings announcements by companies are closely followed by, and frequently result in, share price revisions. Two issues should come to mind. First, earnings announcements concern past periods. If the market values stocks based on expectations of the future, why are numbers summarizing past performance relevant? Second, these announcements concern accounting earnings. Such earnings may have little to do with cash flow, so, again, why are they relevant?

7. **Beta**   Is it possible that a risky asset could have a beta of zero? Explain. Based on the CAPM, what is the expected return on such an asset? Is it possible that a risky asset could have a negative beta? What does the CAPM predict about the expected return on such an asset? Can you give an explanation for your answer?

8. **Relative Valuation**   Suppose you identify a situation in which one security is overvalued relative to another. How would you go about exploiting this opportunity? Does it matter if the two securities are both overvalued relative to some third security? Are your profits certain in this case?

9. **Reward-to-Risk Ratio**   Explain what it means for all assets to have the same reward-to-risk ratio. How can you increase your return if this holds true? Why would we expect that all assets have the same reward-to-risk ratio in liquid, well-functioning markets?

10. **Systematic versus Firm-Specific Risk**   Dudley Trudy, CFA, recently met with one of his clients. Trudy typically invests in a master list of 30 securities drawn from several industries. After the meeting concluded, the client made the following statement: "I trust your stock-picking ability and believe that you should invest my funds in your five best ideas. Why invest in 30 companies when you obviously have stronger opinions on a few of them?" Trudy plans to respond to his client within the context of Modern Portfolio Theory.

    a. Contrast the concept of systematic and firm-specific risk and give one example of each.
    b. Critique the client's suggestion. Discuss the impact of the systematic risk and firm-specific risk on portfolio risk as the number of securities in a portfolio is increased.

Questions and Problems

Core Questions

1. **Stock Betas**   A stock has an expected return of 13.6 percent, the risk-free rate is 4 percent, and the market risk premium is 7.5 percent. What must the beta of this stock be?

2. **Market Returns**   A stock has an expected return of 12 percent, its beta is .85, and the risk-free rate is 5 percent. What must the expected return on the market be?

3. **Risk-Free Rates**   A stock has an expected return of 11 percent, a beta of .70, and the expected return on the market is 13 percent. What must the risk-free rate be?

4. **Market Risk Premium**   A stock has a beta of 1.3 and an expected return of 16 percent. If the risk-free rate is 5.5 percent, what is the market risk premium?

5. **Portfolio Betas**   You own a stock portfolio invested 15 percent in Stock Q, 20 percent in Stock R, 25 percent in Stock S, and 40 percent in Stock T. The betas for these four stocks are 1.2, .6, 1.5, and .9, respectively. What is the portfolio beta?

6. **Portfolio Betas**   You own 200 shares of Stock A at a price of $60 per share, 300 shares of Stock B at $85 per share, and 100 shares of Stock C at $25 per share. The betas for the stocks are 1.2, .9, and 1.6, respectively. What is the beta of your portfolio?

7. **Stock Betas**   You own a portfolio equally invested in a risk-free asset and two stocks. If one of the stocks has a beta of 1.2, and the total portfolio is exactly as risky as the market, what must the beta be for the other stock in your portfolio?

8. **Expected Returns**   A stock has a beta of 1.15, the expected return on the market is 12 percent, and the risk-free rate is 5.8 percent. What must the expected return on this stock be?

9. **CAPM and Stock Price**   A share of stock sells for $48 today. The beta of the stock is 1.2, and the expected return on the market is 11 percent. The stock is expected to pay a dividend of $1.10 in one year. If the risk-free rate is 4.5 percent, what will the share price be in one year?

10. **Portfolio Weights**   A stock has a beta of 1.1 and an expected return of 15 percent. A risk-free asset currently earns 6 percent.

   a. What is the expected return on a portfolio that is equally invested in the two assets?
   b. If a portfolio of the two assets has a beta of .5, what are the portfolio weights?
   c. If a portfolio of the two assets has an expected return of 12 percent, what is its beta?
   d. If a portfolio of the two assets has a beta of 1.80, what are the portfolio weights? How do you interpret the weights for the two assets in this case? Explain.

Intermediate
Questions

11. **Portfolio Risk and Return**   Asset W has an expected return of 15 percent and a beta of 1.2. If the risk-free rate is 7 percent, complete the following table for portfolios of Asset W and a risk-free asset. Illustrate the relationship between portfolio expected return and portfolio beta by plotting the expected returns against the betas. What is the slope of the line that results?

Percentage of Portfolio in Asset W	Portfolio Expected Return	Portfolio Beta
0%		
25		
50		
75		
100		
125		
150		

12. **Relative Valuation**   Stock Y has a beta of 1.5 and an expected return of 18 percent. Stock Z has a beta of .80 and an expected return of 11 percent. If the risk-free rate is 6 percent and the market risk premium is 7 percent, are these stocks correctly priced?

13. **Relative Valuation**   In the previous problem, what would the risk-free rate have to be for the two stocks to be correctly priced relative to each other?

14. **CAPM**   Using the CAPM, show that the ratio of the risk premiums on two assets is equal to the ratio of their betas.

15. **Relative Valuation**   Suppose you observe the following situation:

Security	Beta	Expected Return
Oxy Co.	1.10	16%
More-On Co.	.75	12

Assume these securities are correctly priced. Based on the CAPM, what is the expected return on the market? What is the risk-free rate?

16. **Calculating Beta**   Show that another way to calculate beta is to take the covariance between the security and the market and divide by the variance of the market's return.

17. **Calculating Beta**   Fill in the following table, supplying all the missing information. Use this information to calculate the security's beta.

Year	Returns		Return Deviations		Squared Deviations		Product of Deviations
	Security	Market	Security	Market	Security	Market	
2001	12%	6%					
2002	−9	−12					
2003	−6	0					
2004	30	−4					
2005	18	30					
Totals	45	20					

18. **Analyzing a Portfolio**   You have $100,000 to invest in a portfolio containing Stock X, Stock Y, and a risk-free asset. You must invest all of your money. Your goal is to create a portfolio that has an expected return of 15 percent and that has only 90 percent of the risk of the overall market. If X has an expected return of 19 percent and a beta of 1.5, Y has an expected return of 12.2 percent and a beta of 1.1, and the risk-free rate is 6 percent, how much money will you invest in Stock Y? How do you interpret your answer?

19. **Systematic versus Unsystematic Risk**   Consider the following information on Stocks I and II:

State of Economy	Probability of State of Economy	Rate of Return If State Occurs	
		Stock I	Stock II
Recession	.25	.04	−.20
Normal	.50	.21	.11
Irrational exuberance	.25	.16	.34

The market risk premium is 8 percent, and the risk-free rate is 5 percent. Which stock has the most systematic risk? Which one has the most unsystematic risk? Which stock is "riskier"? Explain.

20. **Systematic and Unsystematic Risk**   The beta for a certain stock is 1.20, the risk-free rate is 6 percent, and the expected return on the market is 13 percent. Complete the following table to decompose the stock's return into the systematic return and the unsystematic return.

Year	Actual Returns		Unexpected Returns		Systematic Portion	Unsystematic Portion (ϵ)
	R	R_M	$R - E(R)$	$R_M - E(R_M)$	$[R_M - E(R_M)] \times \beta$	$[R - E(R)] - [R_M - E(R_M)] \times \beta$
2001	26%	19%				
2002	12	8				
2003	−21	−13				
2004	−3	4				
2005	38	22				

CFA PROBLEMS

21. **CAPM** John Wilson, a portfolio manager, is evaluating the expected performance of two common stocks, Furhman Labs, Inc., and Garten Testing, Inc. The risk-free rate is 5 percent, the expected return on the market is 11.5 percent, and the betas of the two stocks are 1.5 and .8, respectively. Wilson's own forecasts of the returns on the two stocks are 13.25 percent for Furhman Labs and 11.25 percent for Garten. Calculate the required return for each stock. Is each stock undervalued, fairly valued, or overvalued?

Use the following information for the next four questions: Abigail Grace has a $900,000 fully diversified portfolio. She subsequently inherits ABC Company common stock worth $100,000. Her financial adviser provided her with the forecasted information below:

	Monthly Expected Returns	Expected Standard Deviation of Monthly Returns
Original portfolio	.67%	2.37%
ABC Company	1.25	2.95

The expected correlation coefficient of ABC stock returns and the original portfolio is .40. The inheritance changes her overall portfolio and she is deciding whether to keep the ABC stock.

22. **Portfolio Return and Standard Deviation** Assuming Grace keeps the ABC stock, calculate the expected return of the new portfolio, the covariance of ABC stock with the original portfolio, and the expected standard deviation of the new portfolio.

23. **Portfolio Return and Standard Deviation** If Grace sells the ABC stock, she will invest the proceeds in risk-free government securities yielding .42 percent monthly. Calculate the expected return of the new portfolio, the covariance of the government security returns with the original portfolio, and the expected standard deviation of the new portfolio.

24. **Beta** Determine whether the beta of Grace's new portfolio, which includes the government securities, will be higher or lower than the beta of her original portfolio. Justify your response with one reason. No calculations are necessary.

25. **Diversification** Based on a conversation with her husband, Grace is considering selling the $100,000 of ABC stock and acquiring $100,000 of XYZ Company common stock instead. XYZ stock has the same expected return and standard deviation as ABC stock. Her husband comments, "It doesn't matter whether you keep all of the ABC stock or replace it with $100,000 of the XYZ stock." Are her husband's comments correct or incorrect? Justify your response.

Spreadsheet Problem

26. **Calculating Correlation** You are given the following information concerning a stock and the market:

	Returns	
Year	Market	Stock
2000	34%	49%
2001	27	24
2002	11	6
2003	19	10
2004	−12	−25
2005	8	3

Calculate the average return and standard deviation for the market and the stock. Next, calculate the correlation between the stock and the market. Use a spreadsheet to calculate your answers.

S&P Problems

www.mhhe.com/edumarketinsight

Note: These problems can be calculated manually, but a spreadsheet program such as Excel is recommended for use in calculations.

1. **Return Correlations**   Go to the "Excel Analytics" link for Kellogg (K) and Delta Airlines (DAL) and download the monthly adjusted stock prices. Copy the monthly returns for each stock into a new spreadsheet. Calculate the correlation between the two stock returns. Would you expect a higher or lower correlation if you had chosen American Airlines instead of Kellogg? What is the standard deviation of a portfolio 75 percent invested in K and 25 percent in DAL? What about a portfolio equally invested in the two stocks? What about a portfolio 25 percent in K and 75 percent in DAL?

2. **Beta**   Go to the "Excel Analytics" link for Harley-Davidson (HD) and download the monthly adjusted stock prices. Copy the monthly returns for Harley-Davidson and the monthly S&P 500 returns into a new spreadsheet. Calculate the beta of Harley-Davidson for the entire period of data available. Now download the monthly stock prices for Emerson Electric (EMR) and calculate the beta for this company. Are the betas similar? Would you have expected the beta of Harley-Davidson to be higher or lower than the beta for Emerson Electric? Why?

What's on the Web

1. **Expected Return**   You want to find the expected return for Home Depot using CAPM. First you need the risk-free rate. Go to www.bloomberg.com and find the current interest rate for three-month Treasury bills. Use the average large-company stock risk premium from Chapter 1 as the market risk premium. Next, go to finance.yahoo.com, enter the ticker symbol HD for Home Depot, and find the beta for Home Depot. What is the expected return for Home Depot using CAPM? What assumptions have you made to arrive at this number?

2. **Portfolio Beta**   You have decided to invest in an equally weighted portfolio consisting of American Express, Procter & Gamble, Johnson and Johnson, and United Technologies and need to find the beta of your portfolio. Go to finance.yahoo.com and find the beta for each of the companies. What is the beta for your portfolio?

3. **Beta**   Which stock has the highest and lowest beta? Go to finance.yahoo.com and find the stock screener. Enter 0 as the maximum beta and enter search. How many stocks currently have a beta less than 0? Which stock has the lowest beta? Go back to the stock screener and enter 3 as the minimum value. How many stocks have a beta greater than 3? What about 4? Which stock has the highest beta?

4. **Security Market Line**   Go to finance.yahoo.com and enter the ticker symbol GE for General Electric. Find the beta for this company and the target stock price in one year. Using the current share price and the target stock price, compute the expected return for this stock. Don't forget to include the expected dividend payments over the next year. Now go to www.bloomberg.com and find the current interest rate for three-month Treasury bills. Using this information, calculate the expected return of the market using the reward-to-risk ratio. Does this number make sense? Why or why not?

CHAPTER 13

Performance Evaluation and Risk Management

"It is not the return on my investment that I am concerned about; it is the return of my investment!"

–Will Rogers

"The stock market will fluctuate!"

–J. P. Morgan

Humorist Will Rogers expressed concern about "the return *of* [his] investment." Famed financier J. P. Morgan, when asked by a reporter what he thought the stock market would do, replied, "The stock market will fluctuate!" Both Will Rogers and J. P. Morgan understood a basic fact of investing—investors holding risky assets worry: How well are my investments doing? How much money am I making (or losing)? and What are my chances of incurring a significant loss? ∎

This chapter examines methods to deal with two related problems faced by investors in risky assets. These are (1) evaluating risk-adjusted investment performance and (2) assessing and managing the risks involved with specific investment strategies. Both subjects have come up previously in our text, but we have deferred a detailed discussion of them until now.

We first consider the problem of performance evaluation. Specifically, suppose we have investment returns data for several portfolios covering a recent period, and we wish to evaluate how well these portfolios have performed relative to other portfolios or some investment benchmark. The need for this form of scrutiny arises in a number of situations, including:

- An investor planning to choose a mutual fund wants to first compare the investment performance of several dozen candidate funds.
- A pension fund administrator wants to select a money manager and thus needs to compare the investment performance of a group of money managers.
- An employer wants to compare the performance of several investment companies before selecting one for inclusion in her company-sponsored 401(k) retirement plan.

In the first section of this chapter, we examine several useful evaluation measures of portfolio performance and discuss how they might be applied to these and similar situations.

In the second part of the chapter, we discuss the important problem of risk management from the perspective of an investor or money manager concerned with the possibility of a large loss. Specifically, we examine methods to assess the probabilities and magnitudes of losses we might expect to experience during a set future time period. These risk assessment techniques are commonly employed in a number of situations, including:

- A New York Stock Exchange specialist wants to know how much of a loss is possible with a 5 percent probability during the coming day's trading from the specialist firm's inventory.
- The foreign currency manager of a commercial bank wants to know how much of a loss is possible with a 2 percent probability on the bank's foreign currency portfolio during the coming week.
- A futures exchange clearinghouse wants to know how much margin funds should be deposited by exchange members to cover extreme losses that might occur with a "once in a century" probability.

Methods used to assess risk in these and similar scenarios fall into the category commonly referred to as "Value-at-Risk." Value-at-Risk techniques are widely applied by commercial banks, securities firms, and other financial institutions to assess and understand the risk exposure of portfolios under their management.

13.1 Performance Evaluation

performance evaluation
The assessment of how well a money manager achieves a balance between high returns and acceptable risks.

Investors have a natural (and very rational) interest in how well particular investments have done. This is true whether the investor manages his or her own portfolio or has money managed by a professional. Concern with investment performance motivates the topic of **performance evaluation**. In general terms, performance evaluation focuses on assessing how well a money manager achieves high returns balanced with acceptable risks.

Going back to our discussion of efficient markets in an earlier chapter, we raised the question of risk-adjusted performance and whether anyone can consistently earn an "excess" return, thereby "beating the market." The standard example is an evaluation of investment performance achieved by the manager of a mutual fund. Such a performance evaluation is more than an academic exercise, because its purpose is to help investors decide whether they would entrust investment funds with the fund manager. Our goal here is to introduce you to the primary tools used to make this assessment.

PERFORMANCE EVALUATION MEASURES

A variety of measures are used to evaluate investment performance. Here, we examine three of the best-known and most popular measures: the Sharpe ratio, the Treynor ratio, and

raw return

States the total percentage return on an investment with no adjustment for risk or comparison to any benchmark.

Jensen's alpha. But before we do so, let us first briefly discuss a naive measure of performance evaluation—the **raw return** on a portfolio.

The raw return on an investment portfolio, here denoted by R_p, is simply the total percentage return on the portfolio with no adjustment for risk or comparison to any benchmark. Calculating percentage returns was discussed in Chapter 1. The fact that a raw portfolio return does not reflect any consideration of risk suggests that its usefulness is limited when making investment decisions. After all, risk is important to almost every investor.

THE SHARPE RATIO

Sharpe ratio

Measures investment performance as the ratio of portfolio risk premium over portfolio return standard deviation.

A basic measure of investment performance that includes an adjustment for risk is the Sharpe ratio, originally proposed by Nobel laureate William F. Sharpe. The **Sharpe ratio** is computed as a portfolio's risk premium divided by the standard deviation of the portfolio's return:

$$\text{Sharpe ratio} = \frac{R_p - R_f}{\sigma_p} \tag{13.1}$$

In this case, the portfolio risk premium is the raw portfolio return less a risk-free return, that is, $R_p - R_f$, which we know is the basic reward for bearing risk. The return standard deviation, σ_p, is a measure of risk, which we have discussed in previous chapters.

WWW

Visit Professor Sharpe at www.stanford.edu/~wfsharpe

More precisely, return standard deviation is a measure of the *total* risk (as opposed to systematic risk) for a security or a portfolio. Thus, the Sharpe ratio is a reward-to-risk ratio that focuses on total risk. Because total risk is used to make the adjustment, the Sharpe ratio is probably most appropriate for evaluating relatively diversified portfolios.

EXAMPLE 13.1 — **Look Sharpe**

Over a recent three-year period, the average annual return on a portfolio was 20 percent, and the annual return standard deviation for the portfolio was 25 percent. During the same period, the average return on 90-day Treasury bills was 5 percent. What is the Sharpe ratio for this portfolio during this three-year period? Referring to the equation above, we calculate:

$$\text{Sharpe ratio} = \frac{.20 - .05}{.25} = .6$$

This indicates that the Sharpe ratio of portfolio excess return to total risk is .6.

THE TREYNOR RATIO

Treynor ratio

Measures investment performance as the ratio of portfolio risk premium over portfolio beta.

Another standard measure of investment performance that includes an adjustment for systematic risk is the Treynor ratio (or index), originally suggested by Jack L. Treynor. The **Treynor ratio** is computed as a portfolio's risk premium divided by the portfolio's beta coefficient:

$$\text{Treynor ratio} = \frac{R_p - R_f}{\beta_p} \tag{13.2}$$

As with the Sharpe ratio, the Treynor ratio is a reward-to-risk ratio. The key difference is that the Treynor ratio looks at systematic risk only, not total risk.

EXAMPLE 13.2 **The Treynor Ratio**

Over a three-year period, the average return on a portfolio was 20 percent, and the beta for the portfolio was 1.25. During the same period, the average return on 90-day Treasury bills was 5 percent. What is the Treynor ratio for this portfolio during this period?

Referring to the Treynor ratio equation above, we calculate:

$$\text{Treynor ratio} = \frac{.20 - .05}{1.25} = .12$$

This reveals that the Treynor ratio of portfolio excess return to portfolio beta is .12.

You may recall that we saw the Treynor ratio in a previous chapter. There we said that in an active, competitive market, a strong argument can be made that all assets (and portfolios of those assets) should have the same Treynor ratio, that is, the same reward-to-risk ratio, where "risk" refers to systematic risk. To the extent that they don't, then there is evidence that at least some portfolios have earned excess returns.

JENSEN'S ALPHA

Jensen's alpha
Measures investment performance as the raw portfolio return less the return predicted by the capital asset pricing model.

A third common measure of investment performance that draws on capital asset pricing theory for its formulation is Jensen's alpha, proposed by Michael C. Jensen. **Jensen's alpha** is computed as the raw portfolio return less the expected portfolio return predicted by the capital asset pricing model (CAPM).

Recall from a previous chapter that, according to the CAPM, a portfolio expected return, $E(R_p)$, can be written as:

$$E(R_p) = R_f + [E(R_M) - R_f] \times \beta_p \qquad (13.3)$$

To compute Jensen's alpha, we compare the actual return, R_p, to the predicted return. The difference is the alpha, denoted α_p:

$$\alpha_p = R_p - E(R_p) \qquad (13.4)$$
$$= R_p - \{R_f + [E(R_M) - R_f] \times \beta_p\}$$

Jensen's alpha is easy to understand. It is simply the excess return above or below the security market line, and, in this sense, it can be interpreted as a measure of by how much the portfolio "beat the market." This interpretation is illustrated in Figure 13.1, which shows a portfolio with a positive (A), zero (B), and negative (C) alpha, respectively. As shown, a positive alpha is a good thing because the portfolio has a relatively high return given its level of systematic risk.

EXAMPLE 13.3 **Jensen's Alpha**

Over a three-year period, the average annual return on a portfolio was 20 percent, and the beta for the portfolio was 1.25. During the same period, the average annual return on 90-day Treasury bills was 5 percent, and the average return on the market portfolio was 15 percent. What is Jensen's alpha for this portfolio during this period?

Referring to the Jensen-alpha equation above, we calculate:

$$.20 - [.05 + (.15 - .05)1.25] = .025$$

This shows that the portfolio had an alpha measure of portfolio excess return of 2.5 percent.

FIGURE 13.1   Jensen's Alpha

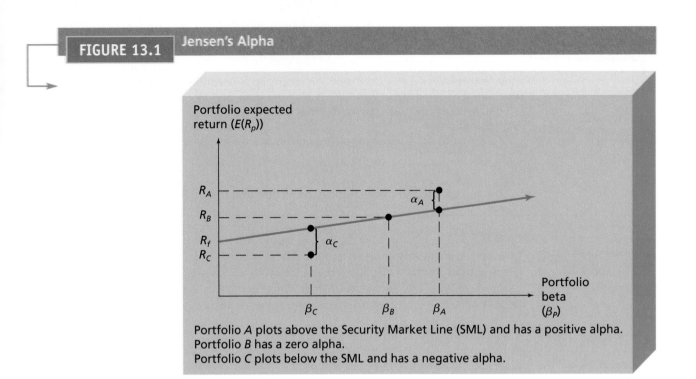

Portfolio A plots above the Security Market Line (SML) and has a positive alpha.
Portfolio B has a zero alpha.
Portfolio C plots below the SML and has a negative alpha.

CHECK THIS

13.1a   What is the Sharpe ratio of portfolio performance?

13.1b   What is the Treynor ratio of portfolio performance?

13.1c   What is Jensen's alpha?

13.1d   Why can Jensen's alpha be interpreted as measuring by how much an investment portfolio beat the market?

13.2 Comparing Performance Measures

Table 13.1 presents investment performance data for three risky portfolios, A, B, and C, along with return data for the market portfolio and a risk-free portfolio, denoted by M and F, respectively. Based on the performance data in Table 13.1, Table 13.2 provides computed performance measures for portfolios A, B, C, and a market portfolio, M. The market portfolio is a benchmark of investment performance. Often the familiar S&P 500 index is the adopted proxy for the market portfolio.

As shown in Table 13.2, the Sharpe ratio ranks the three risky portfolios in the ascending order of performance A, B, and C. By contrast, the Treynor ratio ranks these three risky portfolios in the reversed order of performance C, B, and A. Jensen's alpha yields another portfolio ranking altogether, with the ascending order of performance C, A, and B.

The example above illustrates that the three performance measures can yield substantially different performance rankings. The fact that each of the three performance measures

TABLE 13.1	Investment Performance Data			
Portfolio	R_p	σ_p	β_p	
A	12%	40%	.5	
B	15%	30%	.75	
C	20%	22%	1.4	
M	15%	15%	1	
F	5%	0%	0	

TABLE 13.2	Portfolio Performance Measurement		
Portfolio	Sharpe Ratio	Treynor Ratio	Jensen's Alpha
A	.175	.14	2%
B	.333	.133	2.5%
C	.682	.107	1%
M	.667	.10	0%

can produce such different results leaves us with the burning question: "Which performance measure should we use to evaluate portfolio performance?"

Well, the simple answer is: "it depends." If you wish to select a performance measure to evaluate an entire portfolio held by an investor, then the Sharpe ratio is appropriate. But if you wish to choose a performance measure to individually evaluate securities or portfolios for possible inclusion in a broader (or "master") portfolio, then either the Treynor ratio or Jensen's alpha is appropriate.

In broader terms, all three measures have strengths and weaknesses. Jensen's alpha is, as we have seen, easy to interpret. Comparing Jensen's alpha and the Treynor ratio, we see that they are really very similar. The only difference is that the Treynor ratio standardizes everything, including any excess return, relative to beta. If you were to take Jensen's alpha and divide it by beta, then you would have a Jensen-Treynor alpha, which measures excess return relative to beta.

A common weakness of the Jensen and Treynor measures is that both require a beta estimate. As we discussed in our last chapter, betas from different sources can differ substantially, and, as a result, what appears to be a positive alpha might just be due to a mismeasured beta.

The Sharpe ratio has the advantage that no beta is necessary, and standard deviations can be calculated unambiguously. The drawback is that total risk is frequently not what really matters. However, for a relatively well-diversified portfolio, most of the risk is systematic, so there's not much difference between total risk and systematic risk. For this reason, for doing things like evaluating mutual funds, the Sharpe ratio is probably the most frequently used. Furthermore, if a mutual fund is not very diversified, then its standard deviation would be larger, resulting in a smaller Sharpe ratio. Thus, the Sharpe ratio, in effect, penalizes a portfolio for being undiversified.

To see how these performance measures are used in practice, have a look at our nearby *Work the Web* box, which shows some actual numbers for a mutual fund.

The various performance measures we've discussed are frequently used to evaluate mutual funds, or, more accurately, mutual fund managers. For example, the information below concerns the Fidelity Low-Priced Stock Fund, which is a small-cap value fund. We obtained the numbers from www.morningstar.com by entering the fund's ticker symbol (FLPSX) and following the "Risk Measures" link. By the way, you'll see the abbreviation "MPT" in this context quite a bit. MPT is an acronym for "Modern Portfolio Theory," which is the general label for things related to Markowitz-type portfolio analysis and the CAPM.

For this fund, the beta is .97, so the degree of market risk is about average. The fund's alpha is 7.47 percent, a relatively high number. The fund's standard deviation is 12.44 percent. The mean reported, 24.85 percent, is the geometric return of the fund over the past three years. The Sharpe ratio for the fund is 1.72. Of course we can't judge this value in isolation, but at least we know it is positive. Other measures of risk are reported here, but they are specific to Morningstar. To learn more, visit the Web site.

Fidelity Low-Priced Stock FLPSX   See Fund Family Data ▸▸   Fidelity

Volatility Measurements	Trailing 3-Yr through 09-30-05	*Trailing 5-Yr through 09-30-05		
Standard Deviation	12.44	Sharpe Ratio	1.72
Mean	24.85	Bear Market Decile Rank*	1

Modern Portfolio Theory Statistics		Trailing 3-Yr through 09-30-05
	Standard Index S&P 500	**Best Fit Index** Wil 4500
R-Squared	74	93
Beta	0.97	0.92
Alpha	7.47	1.95

EXAMPLE 13.4   Picking Portfolios

Suppose you are restricted to investing all of your money in only a single portfolio from among the choices A, B, and C presented in Table 13.1. Which portfolio should you choose?

Because you can select only a single portfolio, the Sharpe-ratio measure of portfolio performance should be used. Referring to Table 13.2, we see that portfolio C has the highest Sharpe ratio of excess return per unit of total risk. Therefore, portfolio C should be chosen.

EXAMPLE 13.5   Picking Portfolios Again

Suppose you are considering whether portfolios A, B, and C presented in Table 13.1 should be included in a master portfolio. Should you select one, two, or all three portfolios for inclusion in your master portfolio?

(continued)

Since you are selecting portfolios for inclusion in a master portfolio, either the Treynor ratio or Jensen's alpha should be used. Suppose you decide to consider any portfolio that outperforms the market portfolio *M*, based on either the Treynor ratio or Jensen's alpha. Referring to Table 13.2, we see that all three portfolios have Treynor ratios and Jensen's alphas greater than the market portfolio. Therefore, you should decide to include all three portfolios in your master portfolio.

CHECK THIS

13.2a Explain the difference between systematic risk measured by beta and total risk measured by standard deviation. When are they essentially the same?

13.2b Alter the returns data in Table 13.1 so that portfolios *A*, *B*, and *C* all have a raw return of 15 percent. Which among these three portfolios then have a Treynor ratio or Jensen's alpha greater than that of the market portfolio *M*?

SHARPE-OPTIMAL PORTFOLIOS

In this section, we show how to obtain a funds allocation with the highest possible Sharpe ratio. Such a portfolio is said to be "Sharpe optimal." The method is closely related to the procedure of obtaining a Markowitz efficient frontier discussed in a previous chapter. This is no surprise, as both methods are used to achieve an optimal balance of risk and return for investment portfolios.

To illustrate the connection, have a look at Figure 13.2. This figure shows the investment opportunity set of risk-return possibilities for a portfolio of two assets, a stock fund and a bond fund. Now the question is: "Of all of these possible portfolios, which one is Sharpe optimal?" To find out, consider the portfolio labeled *A* in the figure. Notice that we have drawn a straight line from the risk-free rate running through this point.

FIGURE 13.2 The Sharpe-Optimal Portfolio

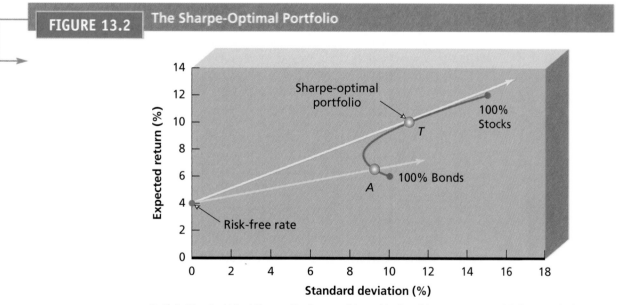

Portfolio *T* has the highest Sharpe ratio of any possible combination of these two assets, so it is Sharpe optimal.

What is the slope of this straight line? As always, the slope of a straight line is the "rise over the run." In this case, the return rises from the risk-free rate, R_f, to the expected return on portfolio A, so the rise is $E(R_A) - R_f$. At the same time, risk moves from zero for a risk-free asset up to the standard deviation on portfolio A, so the run is $\sigma_A - 0 = \sigma_A$. Thus, the slope is $[E(R_A) - R_f]/\sigma_A$, which is just the Sharpe ratio for portfolio A.

So, the slope of a straight line drawn from the risk-free rate to a portfolio in Figure 13.2 tells us the Sharpe ratio for that portfolio. This is always the case, even if there are many assets, not just two. The problem of finding the Sharpe-optimal portfolio thus boils down to finding the line with the steepest slope. Looking again at Figure 13.2, we quickly figure out that the line with the steepest slope is always going to be the one that just touches (i.e., is tangent to) the investment opportunity set. We have labeled this portfolio T (for tangent).

We now have an interesting and important result. The Markowitz efficient frontier tells us which portfolios are efficient, but it does not tell us which of the efficient portfolios is the best. What Figure 13.2 shows is that, of those efficient portfolios, one is the very best, at least in the sense of being Sharpe optimal.

To illustrate how to find the Sharpe optimal portfolio, recall from Chapter 11 that the returns of the stock and bond funds are 12 percent and 6 percent. The standard deviations are 15 percent and 10 percent, respectively, and the correlation is .10. From our discussion in Chapter 11, we know that the expected return on a portfolio of two assets is given by:

$$E(R_p) = x_S E(R_S) + x_B E(R_B)$$

where x_S and x_B are the percentages invested in the stock and bond fund, respectively. Also from Chapter 11, the variance on a portfolio of these two assets is:

$$\sigma_P^2 = x_S^2 \sigma_S^2 + x_B^2 \sigma_B^2 + 2x_S x_B \sigma_S \sigma_B \text{Corr}(R_S, R_B)$$

Putting it all together, the Sharpe ratio for our two-asset portfolio looks like this:

$$\frac{E(R_p) - R_f}{\sigma_p} = \frac{x_S E(R_S) + x_B E(R_B) - R_f}{\sqrt{x_S^2 \sigma_S^2 + x_B^2 \sigma_B^2 + 2x_S x_B \sigma_S \sigma_B \text{Corr}(R_S, R_B)}} \qquad (13.5)$$

Our task is to find the values of x_S and x_B that make this ratio as large as possible. This looks like a tough job, but, as our nearby *Spreadsheet Analysis* box shows, it can be done relatively easily. As shown there, assuming a risk-free interest rate of 4 percent, the highest possible Sharpe ratio is .553 based on a 70–30 mix between stocks and bonds.

You can use the Solver tool to solve for the weights that maximize the Sharpe ratio. In the nearby *Spreadsheet Analysis,* we did just that. Once the formulas are entered for the portfolio return, standard deviation, and Sharpe ratio, we can solve for the portfolio weights that give us the highest possible Sharpe ratio. We do not have to worry about the weight in bonds because the weight in bonds is simply equal to one minus the weight in stocks. You can see in the *Spreadsheet Analysis* that we ask Solver to change the portfolio weight in stock so that the maximum Sharpe ratio is obtained. Note that we also required that the weights in stocks and bonds both be equal to or greater than zero. If any of the returns, standard deviations, or correlations are changed, the Solver tool must be rerun.

CHECK THIS

13.2c   What is a Sharpe-optimal portfolio?

13.2d   Among the many Markowitz efficient portfolios, which one is Sharpe optimal?

	A	B	C	D	E	F	G	H
1								
2		Optimal Sharpe Ratio with Two Risky Assets, Stocks and Bonds						
3								
4		Expected Returns:						
5		Stocks =	0.12					
6		Bonds =	0.06			Portfolio Return, E(Rp) =		0.102
7								
8		Risk-Free Rate =	0.04			Portfolio Standard Deviation, SD(Rp) =		0.112
9								
10		Standard Deviations:					Sharpe Ratio =	0.553
11		Stocks =	0.15					
12		Bonds =	0.10					
13						Portfolio Weights to Maximize Sharpe Ratio:		
14		Correlation between					Stocks =	0.7000
15		Stocks and Bonds =	0.10				Bonds =	0.3000
16							(= 1 − H15)	
17								
18	Formulas for Portfolio Return, Portfolio Standard Deviation, and Sharpe Ratio:							
19								
20	E(Rp) =	H14*C5+H15*C6						
21								
22	SD(Rp) =	SQRT(H14*H14*C11*C11+H15*H15*C12*C12+2*H14*H15*C15*C11*C12)						
23								
24	Sharpe Ratio = (E(Rp) - RF) / SD(Rp) = (H6-C8)/H8							
25								
26	Using SOLVER® to compute portfolio weights that maximize the Sharpe Ratio:							

Solver Parameters

Set Target Cell: H10

Equal To: ⦿ Max ○ Min ○ Value of: 0

By Changing Cells:
H14

Subject to the Constraints:
H14 >= 0
H15 >= 0

Solve
Close
Guess
Options
Add
Change
Delete
Reset All
Help

13.3 Investment Risk Management

investment risk management
Concerns a money manager's control over investment risks, usually with respect to potential short-run losses.

In the first part of this chapter, we discussed performance evaluation within a framework of optimizing the trade-off between risk and return for an investment portfolio. In the remainder of this chapter, we examine **investment risk management** within the framework of a money manager's concern over potential losses for an investment portfolio within a specific time horizon. We focus on what is known as the Value-at-Risk approach. However, risk can be viewed in many different ways, and, for some alternative viewpoints, we suggest reading the nearby *Investment Updates* box.

SHARPE POINT: RISK GAUGE IS MISUSED

William F. Sharpe was probably the biggest expert in the room when economists from around the world gathered in Sonoma, Calif., to hash out a pressing problem in July: How to gauge hedge-fund risk.

About 40 years ago, Dr. Sharpe, now a retired professor from Stanford University, created a simple calculation for measuring the return that investors should expect for the level of volatility they are accepting. The so-called Sharpe Ratio became a cornerstone of modern finance, as investors used it to help select money managers and mutual funds. But at the Sonoma meeting, the use of the ratio was criticized by many prominent academics—including Dr. Sharpe himself.

The ratio is commonly used—"misused," Dr. Sharpe says—for promotional purposes by hedge funds. "That is very disturbing," says the 71-year-old Dr. Sharpe. Hedge funds often use complex strategies that are vulnerable to surprise events and elude any simple formula for measuring risk. "Past average experience may be a terrible predictor of future performance," Dr. Sharpe says.

"This is becoming more of a problem because there is a movement to offer retail versions of hedge funds," says Andrew Lo, a Massachusetts Institute of Technology finance professor and a partner in the AlphaSimplex Group, a hedge fund that manages $350 million. "The typical retail investor might very well be misled by amazing looking Sharpe Ratios."

"Hedge funds can manipulate the ratio to misrepresent their performance," adds Dr. Sharpe, a founder of Financial Engines, a Palo Alto, Calif., investment adviser and manager. In a recent study, Dr. Lo found that the annual Sharpe Ratio for hedge funds can be overstated by as much as 65%. "You can legitimately generate very attractive Sharpe Ratios and still, in time, lose money," he says. "People should not take the Sharpe Ratio at face value."

Even if it isn't manipulated, Dr. Sharpe says, it doesn't foreshadow hedge-fund woes because "no number can." The formula can't predict such troubles as the inability to sell off investments quickly if they start to head south, nor can it account for extreme unexpected events. Long-Term Capital Management, a huge hedge fund in Connecticut, had a glowing Sharpe Ratio before it abruptly collapsed in 1998 when Russia devalued its currency and defaulted on debt.

In Hong Kong, the government bars hedge funds from opening unless they can prove they aren't going to fail—and yet there is no adequate measure, says Sally Wong, executive director of the Hong Kong Investment Funds Association. Her problem with the Sharpe Ratio is that it assumes that a fund's returns will remain even over time. "Many hedge-fund strategies have greater downside events," Ms. Wong says. She favors another measure, the Sortino Ratio. That is similar to the Sharpe Ratio, but instead of using the standard deviation as the denominator, it uses downside deviation—the amount a portfolio strays from its average downturns—to distinguish between "good" and "bad" volatility.

But even the namesake of that ratio is troubled by its use for evaluating hedge funds. "I think it's used too much because it makes hedge funds look good," says Frank Sortino, who developed the ratio 20 years ago and is director of the Pension Research Institute in San Francisco. "It's misleading to say the least," he adds. "I hate that they're using my name."

Dr. Sharpe feels similarly. "I never named it the Sharpe Ratio," he says of his formula. "I called it the Reward-to-Variability ratio."

Source: Ianthe Jeanne Dugan, *The Wall Street Journal*, August 31, 2005.

Value-at-Risk (VaR)
Assesses risk by stating the probability of a loss a portfolio might experience within a fixed time horizon with a specified probability.

VALUE-AT-RISK

An important goal of this chapter is to learn how to assess portfolio risk using **Value-at-Risk**. In essence, the Value-at-Risk (usually abbreviated VaR) method involves evaluating the probability of a significant loss. The basic approach we describe here is widely used by many different financial institutions.

You agree with J. P. Morgan that the stock market will fluctuate and have become concerned with how these fluctuations might affect your stock portfolio. Having read about the VaR method for measuring investment risk, you decide to apply it to your portfolio.

Suppose you believe that there is a 5 percent chance of a return of –18 percent or worse in the coming week. Mathematically, this risk assessment can be stated as:

$$Prob(R_p \leq -18\%) = 5\%$$

Taken together, this −18 percent or worse expected loss and 5 percent probability form a VaR "statistic" for your stock portfolio.

---

normal distribution
A statistical model for assessing probabilities related to many phenomena, including security returns.

The VaR measure of investment risk is closely related to something we discussed way back in Chapter 1. There we said that if the returns on an investment follow a **normal distribution**, then we can state the probability that a portfolio's return will be within a certain range. Since a normal distribution is completely specified by its mean and standard deviation, these are all that we need to state this probability.

For example, suppose you own an S&P 500 index fund. What is the probability of a return of −7 percent or worse in a particular year? As we saw in Chapter 1, since 1925, the return on the S&P 500 index has averaged 13 percent per year with a standard deviation of about 20 percent per year. A return of −7 percent is exactly one standard deviation below the average (.13 − .20 = −.07). We know from Chapter 1 (and basic statistics) that the odds of being within one standard deviation are about 2/3, or .67. Being *within* one standard deviation of the mean of .13 means being *between* .13 plus .20 and .13 minus .20, i.e., between −.07 and +.33.

If the odds of being within this range are 2/3, then the odds of being *outside* this range are about 1/3. Finally, if we are outside this range, then half of the time we'll be above this range and half of the time we'll be below. Half of 1/3 is 1/6, so we'll experience a return of −.07 or worse 1/6, or about 17 percent, of the time.

Learn all about VaR at
www.gloriamundi.org

Putting it together, if you own an S&P 500 index fund, this risk assessment can be stated:

$$Prob(R_p \leq -.07) = 17\%$$

Your VaR statistic is thus a return of −.07 or worse with a probability of 17 percent. By the way, here is an important note: When we say a loss of −.07 or worse, we mean that, *one year from now*, your portfolio value is down by 7 percent or more.

CHECK THIS

13.3a What is the probability of realizing a portfolio return one or more standard deviations below the expected mean return?

13.3b What is the probability of realizing a portfolio return two or more standard deviations below the expected mean return?

13.3c Your portfolio has a mean return of 15 percent and a return standard deviation of 25 percent. What portfolio return is two standard deviations below the mean?

HOW TO PLAY THE GAME OF RISK WHEN INVESTING YOUR MONEY

If we want our portfolios to go up, we need to spend a little time looking down. Take too much risk with our investments, and we could end up selling in a panic at the worst possible time. Take too little risk, and we will likely clock unnecessarily low returns. So how do we settle on the right amount of risk? Here are some thoughts on this messy notion:

Looking for Danger

High risk is meant to lead to high returns. But what do we mean by "high risk"? If we bet all our money on a couple of hot stocks, we are undoubtedly taking a ton of risk. But there is every chance we will lose our shirts. Instead, when academics talk about risk getting rewarded, they are referring to market risk. When investing in stocks, we can eliminate the risk of owning any one stock by spreading our money across a fistful of different companies. But even if we do that, we will still take a hit if the broad market declines. This market risk, which we can't diversify away, is the risk we get rewarded for taking.

What does this mean for our portfolios? If we want higher long-run returns, we need to take more market risk, by keeping less in conservative investments and more in stocks. But to be confident of getting our reward, we need to ensure that our stock portfolios are well diversified. This diversification has the added advantage of bolstering our tenacity. Have shares just tumbled 20%? If all we own are a couple of stocks, we will no doubt fret over whether our shares will ever bounce back. But if we own a broadly diversified portfolio, we will have greater confidence that our stocks should eventually generate decent gains.

Looking Up

To gauge risk, investment experts have traditionally looked at an investment's volatility, as reflected in statistical measures such as standard deviation and beta. Standard deviation is a gauge of how far an investment's results have strayed from its average performance, while beta measures an investment's price gyrations relative to a broad market index.

But investors often dismiss such statistical measures, complaining that they aren't bothered when volatility works to their advantage and generates big gains. Instead, what they care about is losses, and it is these losses that risk measures should seek to capture. But in fact, upside volatility is a great measure of downside risk. Consider technology stocks. Their dismal performance in the recent bear market was foretold by their equally astonishing rise during the late 1990s bull market.

Looking Out

When measuring risk, some experts don't just look at volatility. They also consider longer-run performance. For instance, if we hold stocks for 20 years, we are unlikely to lose money and we will almost

---

13.4 More on Computing Value-at-Risk

In this section we extend our discussion of computing VaR. Our goal is mainly to examine how to evaluate horizons that are shorter or longer than one year. The easiest way to do this is to take our earlier example concerning the S&P 500 and extend it a bit.

Once again, suppose you own an S&P 500 index fund. What is the probability of a loss of 30 percent or more over the next *two* years? To answer, we need to know the average two-year return and the average two-year return standard deviation. Getting the average two-year return is easy enough; we just have to double the one-year average. So, the two-year average return is $2 \times .13 = .26$, or 26 percent.

certainly outpace bonds. That has led some commentators to argue that stocks are less risky than bonds. But this is nonsense. If we look out far enough, the highest-returning investments will always appear to be the least risky. Indeed, I fear such foolishness could lead folks to bet far too much on stocks.

"Over a long enough period, risk and return become the same thing," says William Bernstein, author of "The Intelligent Asset Allocator" and an investment adviser in North Bend, Ore. "The reason stocks have seemed so low risk is because the returns have been so high. But the high returns may not be true going forward." Moreover, not everybody has a 20-year time horizon, and not many investors can ignore short-term market turmoil. "People feel risk in their gut in the short term and in their brain in the long term," Mr. Bernstein says. "Unfortunately, they react to their gut."

Looking Pale

How much risk can each of us stomach? Mutual-fund companies and investment advisers have questionnaires that try to help folks figure out whether they are aggressive or conservative investors. But often, people later discover that their risk tolerance is far higher or lower. What to do? Eleanor Blayney, a financial planner in McLean, Va., says investors should spend time studying their own investment history. "The best indicator of risk tolerance is past behavior," she argues. In particular, Ms. Blayney likes to ask clients what they believe their best and worst investment decisions were. She says aggressive investors tend to fret about missing out on gains, while conservative investors tend to dwell on their losses.

Looking for Safety

Even if we set out to take a lot of risk, we often gravitate toward investments we perceive to be safe. For instance, we may choose to invest a hefty amount in the stock market. But when it comes to picking individual stocks, we often select companies we view as safe. Indeed, if we didn't think a stock was a pretty safe bet, we probably wouldn't have the courage to buy.

Result? We tend to invest in widely admired corporations or those shares that have lately performed well. Meanwhile, we shy away from companies that have had financial problems or have suffered steep share-price declines, even though studies suggest that these tarnished companies often generate market-beating gains. "People will accept that risk gets rewarded if they are forced to listen to the finance-professor spiel," says Hersh Shefrin, a finance professor at Santa Clara University in California. "They will accept the notion intellectually. But emotionally, they associate good stocks with safe stocks."

Source: Jonathan Clements, *The Wall Street Journal*, February 2, 2002. © 2002 Dow Jones & Company, Inc. All Rights Reserved Worldwide.

WWW

Learn about the risk management profession at
www.garp.com

The two-year standard deviation is a little trickier. The two-year *variance* is just double the one-year variance. In our case, the one-year variance is $.20^2 = .04$, and the two-year variance is thus .08. As always, to get the two-year standard deviation, we take the square root of this, which is .28, or 28 percent. The main thing to notice is that the two-year standard deviation is not just double the one-year number. In fact, if you look at it, the two-year number is equal to the one-year number multiplied by the square root of 2, or 1.414.

Now we can answer our question. A two-year loss of 30 percent is equal to the two-year average return of 26 percent less two standard deviations: $.26 - 2 \times .28 = -.30$. From Chapter 1, we know that the odds of being within two standard deviations are 95 percent, so the odds of being outside this range are 5 percent. The odds of being on the bad side (the loss side) are half that, namely, 2.5 percent.

EXAMPLE 13.7

VaR Risk Statistic

The Ned Kelley Hedge Fund focuses on investing in bank and transportation companies in Australia with above-average risk. The average annual return is 15 percent with an annual return standard deviation of 50 percent. What loss level can we expect over a two-year investment horizon with a probability of .17?

We assume a two-year expected return of 30 percent. The one-year variance is $.50^2 = .25$, so the two-year variance is .50. Taking the square root, we get a two-year standard deviation of .7071, or 70.71 percent. A loss probability of .17 corresponds to one standard deviation below the mean, so the answer to our question is $.30 - .7071 = -.4071$, a substantial loss. We can write this succinctly as:

$$Prob(R_p \leq -40.71\%) = 17\%$$

Notice that there is a 17 percent chance of a 40.71 percent loss or worse over the next two years.

EXAMPLE 13.8

VaR Risk Statistic

Going back to the Ned Kelley Hedge Fund in our previous example, what loss level might we expect over six months with a probability of .17?

The six-month expected return is half of 15 percent, or 7.5 percent. The six-month standard deviation is $.5 \times \sqrt{1/2} = .3536$. So the answer to our question is $.075 - .3536 = -.2786$. Again, we can write this succinctly as:

$$Prob(R_p \leq -27.86\%) = 17\%$$

Thus there is a 17 percent chance of a 27.86 percent loss or worse over the next six months.

EXAMPLE 13.9

A One-in-Twenty Loss

For the Ned Kelley Hedge Fund specified in our previous examples, what is the expected loss for the coming year with a probability of 5 percent?

In this case, with an annual return mean of 15 percent and an annual return standard deviation of 50 percent, set $T = 1$ for a one-year time horizon and calculate this VaR statistic:

$$Prob[R_{p,1} \leq E(R_p) \times 1 - 1.645\sigma_p \times \sqrt{1}] = Prob(R_{p,1} \leq 15\% - 1.645 \times 50\%)$$
$$= Prob(R_{p,1} \leq -67.25\%) = 5\%$$

Thus we can expect a loss of 67.25 percent or worse over the next year with a 5 percent probability.

A One-in-a-Hundred Loss

For the Ned Kelley Hedge Fund specified in our previous examples, what is the expected loss for the coming month with a 1 percent probability?

Setting $T = 1/12$ for a one-month time horizon, we calculate this VaR statistic:

$$Prob[R_{p,T} \leq E(R_p) \times 1/12 - 2.326\sigma_p \times \sqrt{1/12}]$$
$$= Prob(R_{p,T} \leq 1.25\% - 2.326 \times 50\% \times .2887)$$
$$= Prob(R_{p,T} \leq -32.32\%) = 1\%$$

Thus we can expect a loss of 32.32 percent or more with a 1 percent probability over the next month.

In general, if we let T stand for the number of years, then the expected return on a portfolio over T years, $E(R_{p,T})$ can be written as:

$$E(R_{p,T}) = E(R_p) \times T \qquad (13.6)$$

Similarly, the standard deviation can be written as:

$$\sigma_{p,T} = \sigma_p \times \sqrt{T} \qquad (13.7)$$

If the time period is less than a year, the T is just a fraction of a year.

When you do a VaR analysis, you have to pick the time horizon and loss level probability. You can pick any probability you want, of course, but the most common are 1, 2.5, and 5 percent. We know that 2.5 percent, which is half of 5 percent, corresponds to two standard deviations (actually 1.96 to be more precise) below the expected return. To get the 1 percent and 5 percent numbers, you would need to find an ordinary "z" table to tell you the number of standard deviations. We'll save you the trouble. The 1 percent level is 2.326 standard deviations below the average, and the 5 percent level is 1.645 "sigmas" below.

Wrapping up our discussion, the VaR statistics for these three levels can be summarized as follows:

$$Prob(R_{p,T} \leq E(R_p) \times T - 2.326 \times \sigma_p\sqrt{T}) = 1\% \qquad (13.8)$$
$$Prob(R_{p,T} \leq E(R_p) \times T - 1.96 \times \sigma_p\sqrt{T}) = 2.5\%$$
$$Prob(R_{p,T} \leq E(R_p) \times T - 1.645 \times \sigma_p\sqrt{T}) = 5\%$$

Notice that if T, the number of years, is equal to 1, the 1 percent level corresponds to once in a century. Similarly, 5 percent is once every 20 years, and 2.5 percent is once every 40 years.

As an application of Value-at-Risk, consider the problem of determining VaR statistics for a Sharpe-optimal stock and bond portfolio. As with any VaR problem for a portfolio, remember that the key to the problem is to first determine the expected return and standard deviation for the portfolio. From our discussion in Chapter 11 and earlier in this chapter, we know that the expected return and standard deviation of a stock and bond portfolio are specified by these two equations:

$$E(R_P) = x_S E(R_S) + x_B E(R_B)$$

$$\sigma_P = \sqrt{x_S^2\sigma_S^2 + x_B^2\sigma_B^2 + 2x_S x_B \sigma_S \sigma_B \text{Corr}(R_S, R_B)}$$

Thus the problem of calculating VaR statistics for a Sharpe-optimal portfolio is the same for any portfolio once the appropriate portfolio weights are determined.

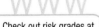

Check out risk grades at
www.riskmetrics.com

EXAMPLE 13.11   **VaR for a Sharpe-Optimal Portfolio**

Suppose you have the following expected return and risk information for stocks and bonds that will be used to form a Sharpe-optimal portfolio. Calculate VaR risk statistics for a one-year investment horizon.

$$E(R_S) = .12; \quad \sigma_S = .15; \quad E(R_B) = .06; \quad \sigma_B = .10; \quad Corr(R_S, R_B) = .10; \quad R_F = .04$$

In the case of just two risky assets, stocks and bonds, the formulas for the portfolio weights for the optimal Sharpe portfolio are:

$$x_S = \frac{\sigma_B^2 \times [E(R_S) - R_F] - Corr(R_S, R_B) \times \sigma_S \times \sigma_B \times [E(R_B) - R_F]}{\sigma_B^2 \times [E(R_S) - R_F] + \sigma_S^2 \times [E(R_B) - R_F] - [E(R_S) + E(R_B) - 2 \times R_F] \times Corr(R_S, R_B) \times \sigma_S \times \sigma_B}$$

and

$$x_B = 1 - x_S$$

Inserting the expected return and risk information into these formulas yields these optimal Sharpe portfolio weights for stocks and bonds:

$$x_S = \frac{.10^2 \times [.12 - .04] - .10 \times .15 \times .10 \times [.06 - .04]}{.10^2 \times [.12 - .04] + .15^2 \times [.06 - .04] - [.12 + .06 - 2 \times .04] \times .10 \times .15 \times .10} = .70$$

and

$$x_B = 1 - x_S = 1 - .70 = .30$$

With these results, we now have all the information needed to calculate the expected return and standard deviation for the Sharpe-optimal portfolio:

$$E(R_p) = x_S E(R_S) + x_B E(R_B)$$
$$= .70 \times .12 + .30 \times .06$$
$$= .102, \text{ or } 10.2\%$$

$$\sigma_p = \sqrt{x_S^2 \sigma_S^2 + x_B^2 \sigma_B^2 + 2 x_S x_B \sigma_S \sigma_B Corr(R_S, R_B)}$$
$$= \sqrt{.70^2 \times .15^2 + .30^2 \times .10^2 + 2 \times .70 \times .30 \times .15 \times .10 \times .10}$$
$$= .112, \text{ or } 11.2\%$$

Thus, with a one-year investment horizon, you can obtain the following VaR statistics for 5 percent and 1 percent probabilities:

$$5\% \, VaR = Prob[R_p \leq E(R_p) - 1.645\sigma_p] = Prob[R_p \leq 10.2\% - 1.645 \times 11.2\%]$$
$$= Prob[R_p \leq -8.22\%]$$

$$1\% \, VaR = Prob[R_p \leq E(R_p) - 2.326\sigma_p] = Prob[R_p \leq 10.2\% - 2.326 \times 11.2\%]$$
$$= Prob[R_p \leq -15.85\%]$$

These calculations indicate that over the next year, we can expect a loss of 8.22 percent or more with a 5 percent probability and a loss of 15.85 percent with a 1 percent probability.

13.4a Your portfolio allocates 40 percent of funds to ABC stock and 60 percent to XYZ stock. ABC has a return mean and standard deviation of 15 percent and 20 percent, respectively. XYZ stock has a return mean and standard deviation of 25 percent and 30 percent, respectively. What is the portfolio return standard deviation if the return correlation between ABC and XYZ stocks is zero?

13.4b Based on your answer to the previous question, what is the smallest expected loss for your portfolio in the coming year with a probability of 1 percent? What is the smallest expected loss for your portfolio in the coming month with a probability of 5 percent?

13.5 Summary and Conclusions

In this chapter, we covered the related topics of performance measurement and risk management. Our goal with performance measurement is essentially to rank investments based on their risk-adjusted returns. We introduced and discussed the three most common tools used to do this: the Sharpe ratio, the Treynor ratio, and Jensen's alpha. As we saw, each has a somewhat different interpretation and which one is the most suitable depends on the specific question.

We then moved over to the issue of risk management by introducing you to the popular and widely used "Value-at-Risk," or VaR, approach. Here the goal is usually to assess the probability of a large loss within a fixed time frame. Investors use this tool both to better understand the risks of their existing portfolios and to assess the risks of potential investments.

GET REAL

This chapter covered the essentials of performance evaluation and investment risk management. With thousands of mutual funds and investment companies competing for performance while trying to control risk, these topics are especially important. If you wish to learn more about these subjects, a good place to start is the Internet.

Some useful and informative Web sites on investment performance analysis are Performance Analysis (www.andreassteiner.net/performanceanalysis), an informative Web site on investment performance analysis; Professor William F. Sharpe (www.stanford.edu/~wfsharpe), Web site of the Nobel laureate who created the Sharpe ratio; and FinPlan (www.finplan.com), a financial planning Web site with a useful section on investment performance analysis. You can also consult www.garp.com, which is the Web site of the Global Association of Risk Professionals (GARP), an independent organization of financial risk management practitioners and researchers.

Because financial institutions generally prefer that their risk profiles be kept private, a large part of the world of financial risk management is hidden from public view. Nevertheless, the field of risk management is large and growing. If you want to know more about this fascinating subject, some interesting Web sites that provide a wealth of information are Gloria Mundi (www.gloriamundi.org), a site that tells you all about Value-at-Risk; Risk Metrics (www.riskmetrics.com), a leading risk management consultancy group; Margrabe (www.margrabe.com), the Web site of a professional risk management consultant; and E-Risks (www.erisks.com), a general resource site for risk management.

Key Terms ────────────────────────────────────

investment risk management 433
Jensen's alpha 427
normal distribution 435
performance evaluation 425

raw return 426
Sharpe ratio 426
Treynor ratio 426
Value-at-Risk (VaR) 434

Chapter Review Problems and Self-Test ─────

1. **Performance Measures**   Compute Sharpe ratios, Treynor ratios, and Jensen's alphas for portfolios A, B, and C based on the following returns data, where M and F stand for the market portfolio and risk-free rate, respectively:

Portfolio	R_p	σ_p	β_p
A	10%	30%	0.75
B	15%	25%	1.00
C	20%	40%	1.50
M	15%	15%	1.00
F	5%	0%	0.00

2. **Value-at-Risk (VaR)**   A portfolio manager believes her $100 million stock portfolio will have a 10 percent return standard deviation during the coming week and that her portfolio's returns are normally distributed. What is the probability of her losing $10 million or more? What is the dollar loss expected with a 5 percent probability? What is the dollar loss expected with a 1 percent probability?

Answers to Self-Test Problems

1. Using Equations 13.1, 13.2, 13.3 yields these performance measurement values:

Portfolio	Sharpe Ratio	Treynor Ratio	Jensen's Alpha
A	.167	.0667	−2.5%
B	.400	.10	0%
C	.375	.10	0%
M	.667	.10	0%

2. Because a mean is not given but the time horizon is only one week, we can simply assume a mean of zero. Thus the probability of a $10 million or greater loss is the probability of a loss of one or more return standard deviations, which for a normal distribution is 15.87 percent. For a normal distribution, a realization 1.645 or more standard deviations below the mean occurs with a 5 percent probability, yielding a potential loss of at least 1.645 × $10 million = $16.45 million. For a normal distribution, a realization 2.326 or more standard deviations below the mean occurs with a 1 percent probability, yielding a potential loss of at least 2.326 × $10 million = $23.26 million.

Test Your Investment Quotient

CFA®
PROBLEMS

1. **Beta and Standard Deviation**   Beta and standard deviation differ as risk measures in that beta measures
   a. Only unsystematic risk, whereas standard deviation measures total risk.
   b. Only systematic risk, whereas standard deviation measures total risk.
   c. Both systematic and unsystematic risk, whereas standard deviation measures only unsystematic risk.
   d. Both systematic and unsystematic risk, whereas standard deviation measures only systematic risk.

   Answer Questions 2 through 8 based on the following information.

	Risk and Return Data		
Portfolio	Average Return	Standard Deviation	Beta
P	17%	20%	1.1
Q	24%	18%	2.1
R	11%	10%	0.5
S	16%	14%	1.5
S&P 500	14%	12%	1.0

A pension fund administrator wants to evaluate the performance of four portfolio managers. Each manager invests only in U.S. common stocks. During the most recent five-year period, the average annual total return on the S&P 500 was 14 percent, and the average annual rate on Treasury bills was 8 percent. The table above shows risk and return measures for each portfolio.

CFA®
PROBLEMS

2. **Treynor Ratio**   The Treynor portfolio performance measure for Portfolio P is
   a. 8.18
   b. 7.62
   c. 6.00
   d. 5.33

CFA®
PROBLEMS

3. **Sharpe Ratio**   The Sharpe portfolio performance measure for Portfolio Q is
   a. .45
   b. .89
   c. .30
   d. .57

4. **Jensen's Alpha**   The Jensen's alpha portfolio performance measure for Portfolio R is
   a. 2.4 percent
   b. 3.4 percent
   c. 0 percent
   d. −1 percent

5. **Treynor Ratio**   Which portfolio has the highest Treynor ratio?
   a. P
   b. Q
   c. R
   d. S

6. **Sharpe Ratio**   Which portfolio has the highest Sharpe ratio?
   a. P
   b. Q
   c. R
   d. S

7. **Jensen's Alpha**   Which portfolio has the highest Jensen's alpha?

   a. *P*
   b. *Q*
   c. *R*
   d. *S*

8. **Sharpe Ratio**   Assuming uncorrelated returns, the Sharpe ratio for a master portfolio with equal allocations to Portfolio *S* and Portfolio *Q* is

   a. .71
   b. 1.4
   c. .95
   d. 1.05

9. **Normal Distribution**   Given a data series that is normally distributed with a mean of 100 and a standard deviation of 10, about 95 percent of the numbers in the series will fall within

   a. 60 to 140
   b. 70 to 130
   c. 80 to 120
   d. 90 to 110

10. **Normal Distribution**   Given a data series that is normally distributed with a mean of 100 and a standard deviation of 10, about 99 percent of the numbers in the series will fall within

    a. 60 to 140
    b. 80 to 120
    c. 70 to 130
    d. 90 to 110

11. **Normal Distribution**   A normal distribution is completely specified by its

    a. Mean and correlation
    b. Variance and correlation
    c. Variance and standard deviation
    d. Mean and standard deviation

12. **Standard Normal Distribution**   A normal random variable is transformed into a standard normal random variable by

    a. Subtracting its mean and dividing by its standard deviation.
    b. Adding its mean and dividing by its standard deviation.
    c. Subtracting its mean and dividing by its variance.
    d. Adding its mean and multiplying by its standard deviation.

13. **Standard Normal Distribution**   The probability that a standard normal random variable is either less than −1 or greater than +1 is

    a. 2 percent
    b. 5 percent
    c. 10 percent
    d. 31.74 percent

14. **Standard Normal Distribution**   The probability that a standard normal random variable is either less than −1.96 or greater than +1.96 is approximately

    a. 2 percent
    b. 5 percent
    c. 10 percent
    d. 31.74 percent

15. **Value-at-Risk (VaR)**   The Value-at-Risk statistic for an investment portfolio states

    a. The probability of an investment loss.
    b. The value of the risky portion of an investment portfolio.
    c. The smallest investment loss expected with a specified probability.
    d. The largest investment loss expected with a specified probability.

Concept Questions ————————————————————— ■

1. **Performance Evaluation Ratios** Explain the difference between the Sharpe ratio and the Treynor ratio.

2. **Performance Evaluation Measures** What is a common weakness of Jensen's alpha and the Treynor ratio?

3. **Jensen's Alpha** Explain the relationship between Jensen's alpha and the security market line (SML) of the capital asset pricing model (CAPM).

4. **Sharpe Ratio** What is one advantage and one disadvantage of the Sharpe ratio?

5. **Normal Distribution** Which two parameters completely specify a normal distribution?

6. **Optimal Sharpe Ratio** What is meant by a Sharpe-optimal portfolio?

7. **Optimal Sharpe Ratio** What is the relationship between the Markowitz efficient frontier and the optimal Sharpe ratio?

8. **Value-at-Risk (VaR) Statistic** Explain the meaning of a Value-at-Risk statistic in terms of a smallest expected loss and the probability of such a loss.

9. **Value-at-Risk (VaR) Statistic** The largest expected loss for a portfolio is –20 percent with a probability of 95 percent. Relate this statement to the Value-at-Risk statistic.

10. **Normal Probabilities** The probability that a normal random variable X is less than x is equal to 50 percent, i.e., $Pr(X < x)$. What is this value of x?

Questions and Problems ————————————————————— ■

Core Questions

1. **Standard Deviation** You find a particular stock has an annual standard deviation of 54 percent. What is the standard deviation for a two-month period?

2. **Standard Deviation** A portfolio has an annual variance of .0607. What is the standard deviation over a two-month period?

3. **Standard Deviation** You find the monthly standard deviation of a stock is 16.18 percent. What is the annual standard deviation of the stock?

4. **Standard Deviation** The weekly standard deviation of a stock is 7.48 percent. What is the monthly standard deviation? The annual standard deviation?

5. **Performance Evaluation** You are given the following information concerning three portfolios, the market portfolio, and the risk-free asset:

Portfolio	R_p	σ_p	β_p
X	18%	39%	1.3
Y	15	26	1.2
Z	8	17	.8
Market	12	21	1.0
Risk-free	5	0	.0

What is the Sharpe ratio, Treynor ratio, and Jensen's alpha for each portfolio?

6. **Normal Probabilities** What is the probability that a normal random variable is less than one standard deviation below its mean?

7. **Normal Probabilities** What are the probabilities that a normal random variable is less than n standard deviations below its mean for values of n equal to 1.645, 1.96, 2.326?

8. **Normal Probabilities** The probabilities that a normal random variable X is less than various values of x are 5 percent, 2.5 percent, and 1 percent. What are these values of x?

9. **Value-at-Risk (VaR) Statistic**   Raybrooks Co. stock has an annual return mean and standard deviation of 13 percent and 25 percent, respectively. What is the smallest expected loss in the coming year with a probability of 5 percent?

10. **Value-at-Risk (VaR) Statistic**   Joi, Inc., stock has an annual return mean and standard deviation of 16 percent and 33 percent, respectively. What is the smallest expected loss in the coming month with a probability of 2.5 percent?

11. **Value-at-Risk (VaR) Statistic**   Your portfolio allocates equal funds to the Raybrooks Co. and Joi, Inc., stocks referred to in the previous two questions. The return correlation between Raybrooks Co. and Joi, Inc., is zero. What is the smallest expected loss for your portfolio in the coming month with a probability of 2.5 percent?

12. **Value-at-Risk (VaR) Statistic**   The stock of Metallica Bearings has an average annual return of 15 percent and a standard deviation of 47 percent. What is the smallest expected loss in the next year with a probability of 1 percent?

13. **Value-at-Risk (VaR) Statistic**   Osbourne, Inc., stock has an annual mean return of 18 percent and a standard deviation of 58 percent. What is the smallest expected loss in the next week with a probability of 2.5 percent?

14. **Value-at-Risk (VaR) Statistic**   Your portfolio is equally weighted between Metallica Bearings and Osbourne, Inc., stocks in the previous two questions. The return correlation between the two stocks is zero. What is the smallest expected loss on your portfolio in the next month with a probability of 5 percent?

15. **Sharpe Ratio**   What is the formula for the Sharpe ratio for a stock and bond portfolio with a zero correlation between stock and bond returns?

16. **Sharpe Ratio**   What is the formula for the Sharpe ratio for an equally weighted portfolio of stocks and bonds?

17. **Sharpe Ratio**   What is the formula for the Sharpe ratio for a portfolio of stocks and bonds with equal expected returns, i.e., $E(R_S) = E(R_B)$, and a zero return correlation?

18. **Value-at-Risk (VaR) Statistic**   A stock has an annual return of 14 percent and a standard deviation of 63 percent. What is the smallest expected loss over the next year with a probability of 1 percent? Does this number make sense?

19. **Value-at-Risk (VaR) Statistic**   For the stock in the previous problem, what is the smallest expected gain over the next year with a probability of 1 percent? Does this number make sense? What does this tell you about stock return distributions?

20. **Value-at-Risk (VaR) Statistic**   Tyler Trucks stock has an annual return mean and standard deviation of 12 percent and 41 percent, respectively. Michael Moped Manufacturing stock has an annual return mean and standard deviation of 17 percent and 62 percent, respectively. Your portfolio allocates equal funds to Tyler Trucks stock and Michael Moped Manufacturing stock. The return correlation between Tyler Trucks and Michael Moped Manufacturing is .5. What is the smallest expected loss for your portfolio in the coming month with a probability of 5 percent?

21. **Value-at-Risk (VaR) Statistic**   Using the same return means and standard deviations as in the previous question for Tyler Trucks and Michael Moped Manufacturing stocks, but assuming a return correlation of $-.5$, what is the smallest expected loss for your portfolio in the coming month with a probability of 5 percent?

22. **Value-at-Risk (VaR) Statistic**   Your portfolio allocates equal amounts to three stocks. All three stocks have the same mean annual return of 16 percent. Annual return standard deviations for these three stocks are 40 percent, 50 percent, and 60 percent. The return correlations among all three stocks are zero. What is the smallest expected loss for your portfolio in the coming year with a probability of 1 percent?

23. **Value-at-Risk (VaR) Statistic**   Using the same return means and standard deviations as in the previous question for the three stocks, but assuming a correlation of .2 among returns for all three stocks, what is the smallest expected loss for your portfolio in the coming year with a probability of 1 percent?

Intermediate
Questions

24. **Optimal Sharpe Portfolio Value-at-Risk** You are constructing a portfolio of two assets, Asset A and Asset B. The expected returns of the assets are 12 percent and 16 percent, respectively. The standard deviations of the assets are 34 percent and 59 percent, respectively. The correlation between the two assets is .20 and the risk-free rate is 5 percent. What is the optimal Sharpe ratio in a portfolio of the two assets? What is the smallest expected loss for this portfolio over the coming year with a probability of 2.5 percent?

Spreadsheet Problem

25. **Optimal Sharpe Ratio** You are constructing a portfolio of two assets. Asset A has an expected return of 10 percent and a standard deviation of 21 percent. Asset B has an expected return of 15 percent and a standard deviation of 62 percent. The correlation between the two assets is .30 and the risk-free rate is 4 percent. What is the weight of each asset in the portfolio of the two assets that has the largest possible Sharpe ratio?

STANDARD &POOR'S

S&P Problem

Note: This problem can be done manually, but a spreadsheet program such as Excel is recommended for use in calculations.

1. **Performance Evaluation** Go to the "Excel Analytics" link for Pepsico (PEP) and download the monthly adjusted stock prices. Copy the monthly returns for Pepsico and the monthly S&P 500 returns into a new spreadsheet. Calculate the Sharpe ratio, Jensen's alpha, and the Treynor ratio for this company. Assume a risk-free rate of 5 percent.

What's on the Web

1. **Morningstar Ratings** Go to www.morningstar.com and find out how to interpret the "Bear Market Decile Rank." While you are at the Web site, also learn more about the best-fit index numbers. What do the best-fit index numbers mean?

2. **Morningstar Risk** Go to www.morningstar.com and find out how Morningstar calculates the "Morningstar Rating" category. What percentage of funds are rated as Below Average by Morningstar? What percentage are rated Average?

3. **Modified VaR** Go to www.alternativesoft.com and learn about modified VaR proposed at the Web site. Why would you want to use a modified VaR?

4. **VaR Data** You can calculate your own VaR statistics by downloading recent security price data off the Web. Go to finance.yahoo.com and enter the ticker symbol ^SPX (don't forget the caret when entering ticker symbols for stock indexes). Now click on the link for "Historical Prices." There you will see that you can get daily, weekly, or monthly price data for any period desired by setting the beginning and ending dates as indicated under "Historical Prices." You can also download the price data into a spreadsheet. Go to the bottom of the page and click on the link "Download To Spreadsheet." With the downloaded price data, you will need to calculate returns and then return averages and standard deviations. Using these, calculate the VaR statistics for your data as discussed and illustrated in this chapter.

CHAPTER 14

Futures Contracts

"There are two times in a man's life when he should not speculate: when he can't afford it and when he can."

–Mark Twain

"When you bet on a sure thing—hedge!"

–Robert Half

Futures contracts can be used for speculation or for risk management. For would-be speculators, Mark Twain's advice is well worth considering. In addition to their risk dimension, trading in futures contracts adds a time dimension to commodity markets. A futures contract separates the date of the agreement—when a delivery price is specified—from the date when delivery and payment actually occur. Both buyers and sellers can manage risk effectively when these dates are separated. This fundamental feature of futures contracts is one of the reasons that futures contracts have withstood the test of time. ■

This chapter covers modern-day futures contracts. The first sections discuss the basics of futures contracts and how their prices are quoted in the financial press. From there, we move into a general discussion of how futures contracts are used and the relationship between current cash prices and futures prices.

14.1 Futures Contracts Basics

forward contract
Agreement between a buyer and a seller, who both commit to a transaction at a future date at a price set by negotiation today.

By definition, a **forward contract** is a formal agreement between a buyer and a seller who both commit to a commodity transaction at a future date at a price set by negotiation today. The genius of forward contracting is that it allows a producer to sell a product to a willing buyer before it is actually produced. By setting a price today, both buyer and seller remove price uncertainty as a source of risk. With less risk, buyers and sellers mutually benefit and commerce is stimulated. This principle has been understood and practiced for centuries.

futures contract
Contract between a seller and a buyer specifying a commodity or financial instrument to be delivered and price paid at contract maturity. Futures contracts are managed through an organized futures exchange.

Futures contracts represent a step beyond forward contracts. Futures contracts and forward contracts accomplish the same economic task, which is to specify a price today for future delivery. This specified price is called the **futures price**. However, while a forward contract can be struck between any two parties, futures contracts are managed through an organized futures exchange. Sponsorship through a futures exchange is a major distinction between a futures contract and a forward contract.

MODERN HISTORY OF FUTURES TRADING

futures price
Price negotiated by buyer and seller at which the underlying commodity or financial instrument will be delivered and paid for to fulfill the obligations of a futures contract.

The oldest organized futures exchange in the United States is the Chicago Board of Trade (CBOT). The CBOT was established in 1848 and grew with the westward expansion of American ranching and agriculture. Today, the CBOT is the largest, most active futures exchange in the world. Other early American futures exchanges still with us today include the MidAmerica Commodity Exchange (founded in 1868), New York Cotton Exchange (1870), New York Mercantile Exchange (1872), Chicago Mercantile Exchange (1874), New York Coffee Exchange (1882), and the Kansas City Board of Trade (1882).

For more than 100 years, American futures exchanges devoted their activities exclusively to commodity futures. However, a revolution began in the 1970s with the introduction of financial futures. Unlike commodity futures, which call for delivery of a physical commodity, financial futures require delivery of a financial instrument. The first financial futures were foreign currency contracts introduced in 1972 at the International Monetary Market (IMM), a division of the Chicago Mercantile Exchange (CME).

Next came interest rate futures, introduced at the Chicago Board of Trade in 1975. An interest rate futures contract specifies delivery of a fixed-income security. For example, an interest rate futures contract may specify a U.S. Treasury bill, note, or bond as the underlying instrument. Finally, stock index futures were introduced in 1982 at the Kansas City Board of Trade (KBT), the Chicago Mercantile Exchange, and the New York Futures Exchange (NYFE). A stock index futures contract specifies a particular stock market index as its underlying instrument.

Financial futures have been so successful that they now constitute the bulk of all futures trading. This success is largely attributed to the fact that financial futures have become an indispensable tool for financial risk management by corporations and portfolio managers. As we will see, futures contracts can be used to reduce risk through hedging strategies or to increase risk through speculative strategies. In this chapter, we discuss futures contracts generally, but, since this text deals with financial markets, we will ultimately focus on financial futures.

Visit these futures exchange Web sites:
www.cbot.com
www.nymex.com
www.cme.com
www.kcbt.com
www.nybot.com

FUTURES CONTRACT FEATURES

Futures contracts are a type of derivative security because the value of the contract is derived from the value of an underlying instrument. For example, the value of a futures contract to buy or sell gold is derived from the market price of gold. However, because a futures contract represents a zero-sum game between a buyer and a seller, the net value of a futures contract is always zero. That is, any gain realized by the buyer is exactly equal to a loss realized by the seller, and vice versa.

Futures are contracts and, in practice, exchange-traded futures contracts are standardized to facilitate convenience in trading and price reporting. Standardized futures contracts have a set contract size specified according to the particular underlying instrument. For example, a standard gold futures contract specifies a contract size of 100 troy ounces. This means that a single gold futures contract obligates the seller to deliver 100 troy ounces of gold to the buyer at contract maturity. In turn, the contract also obligates the buyer to accept the gold delivery and pay the negotiated futures price for the delivered gold.

To properly understand a futures contract, we must know the specific terms of the contract. In general, futures contracts must stipulate at least the following five contract terms:

1. The identity of the underlying commodity or financial instrument.
2. The futures contract size.
3. The futures maturity date, also called the expiration date.
4. The delivery or settlement procedure.
5. The futures price.

First, a futures contract requires that the underlying commodity or financial instrument be clearly identified. This is stating the obvious, but it is important that the obvious is clearly understood in financial transactions.

Second, the size of the contract must be specified. As stated earlier, the standard contract size for gold futures is 100 troy ounces. For U.S. Treasury note and bond futures, the standard contract size is $100,000 in par value notes or bonds, respectively.

The third contract term that must be stated is the maturity date. Contract maturity is the date on which the seller is obligated to make delivery and the buyer is obligated to make payment.

Fourth, the delivery process must be specified. For commodity futures, delivery normally entails sending a warehouse receipt for the appropriate quantity of the underlying commodity. After delivery, the buyer pays warehouse storage costs until the commodity is sold or otherwise disposed.

Finally, the futures price must be mutually agreed on by the buyer and seller. The futures price is quite important, since it is the price that the buyer will pay and the seller will receive for delivery at contract maturity.

For financial futures, delivery is often accomplished by a transfer of registered ownership. For example, ownership of U.S. Treasury bill, note, and bond issues is registered at the Federal Reserve in computerized book-entry form. Futures delivery is accomplished by a notification to the Fed to make a change of registered ownership.

Other financial futures feature cash settlement, which means that the buyer and seller simply settle up in cash with no actual delivery. We discuss cash settlement in more detail when we discuss stock index futures. The important thing to remember for now is that delivery procedures are selected for convenience and low cost. Specific delivery procedures are set by the futures exchange and may change slightly from time to time.

FUTURES PRICES

For futures markets information for many more contracts, visit www.wsf.com/free

The largest volume of futures trading in the United States takes place at the Chicago Board of Trade, which accounts for about half of all domestic futures trading. However, futures trading is also quite active at other futures exchanges. Current futures prices for contracts traded at the major futures exchanges are reported each day in *The Wall Street Journal*. Our

One problem with futures quotes from newspapers is that the prices are from the previous trading day. If you need quotes from today, one of the best places to find current quotes is the exchange Web site. We wanted to find current prices for the Dow Jones Industrial Average (DJIA) futures, so we went to www.cbot.com, the Chicago Board of Trade, where DJIA futures are traded. Here is what we found:

DJIA Futures ($10) Futures (DJ)

Delayed 10 minute data as of November 16, 2005 16:00 CST   Want Real-Time Quotes? CBOT Advantage FREE Trial!

| Quotes | Settlement | Daily Vol | Time & Sales | Volatility | Hist Data |

Open Auction | Electronic | Live Book | Real-Time Quotes

Exp	Last 1 Last 2	Net Chg	Open	High	Low	Close	Settle	Prev Settle	Hi/Lo Limit
05Dec 田 Ω	10706 15:15 10705 15:15	-13	10718 10720 7:21	10737 8:32	10675 13:37	10707 10705 15:15	10706	10719	11756 9656
06Mar 田 Ω	10756 15:16	-13	10773 7:53	10775 7:58	10734 13:37	10756 15:16	10756	10769	11806 9706
06Jun 田 Ω	10793 15:16	-13				10793 15:16	10793	10806	11843 9743
06Dec 田 Ω	10856 15:16	-13				10856 15:16	10856	10869	11906 9806
					Table generated November 16, 2005 16:00 CST 田 = Chart Ω = Option				

The Web site reports information on four different futures contracts on the Dow Jones Industrial Average. Most of the information is self-explanatory. The major difference among these futures contracts is when they expire. As you can see, one contract expires in December 2005 and three others expire in different months of 2006.

nearby *Work the Web* box shows how to get prices online, and Figure 14.1 reproduces a portion of the daily "Futures Prices" report of *The Wall Street Journal.*

In this section of the *Journal,* the information is divided into sections according to categories of the underlying commodities or financial instruments. For example, the section "Agricultural Futures" lists futures price information for wheat, oats, soybeans, live cattle, live hogs, coffee, sugar and cocoa, among others. The section "Metal & Petroleum Futures" reports price information for copper, gold, and petroleum products. There are separate sections for financial futures, which include "Interest Rate," "Currency," and "Index" categories.

Each section states the contract name, futures exchange, and contract size, along with price information for various contract maturities. For example, under "Metal & Petroleum Futures" we find the Copper contract traded at the Commodities Exchange (CMX), i.e., the COMEX (which is a division of the New York Mercantile Exchange). The standard contract size for copper is 25,000 pounds per contract. The futures price is quoted in cents per pound.

FIGURE 14.1 Futures Prices

THE WALL STREET JOURNAL.

FUTURES

Tuesday, December 13, 2005

Agriculture Futures

	OPEN	HIGH	LOW	SETTLE	CHG	LIFETIME HIGH	LIFETIME LOW	OPEN INT
Corn (CBT)-5,000 bu.; cents per bu.								
Dec	195.00	195.50	191.00	195.50	1.25	288.50	185.75	3,413
Mr06	207.00	209.00	204.25	208.75	1.00	276.50	199.50	471,834
Oats (CBT)-5,000 bu.; cents per bu.								
Dec	220.00	220.75	220.00	220.50	3.00	220.75	141.25	61
Mr06	205.00	206.00	201.75	205.00	...	206.00	146.50	9,224
Soybeans (CBT)-5,000 bu.; cents per bu.								
Jan	582.25	598.00	579.00	597.50	13.50	777.00	526.00	109,732
Mar	591.00	609.00	588.50	608.25	13.75	760.00	529.00	96,863
Soybean Meal (CBT)-100 tons; $ per ton.†								
Dec	188.50	196.00	188.00	196.00	7.50	244.80	159.20	1,184
Ja06	188.00	195.00	185.90	194.30	6.30	241.00	161.00	37,221
Soybean Oil (CBT)-60,000 lbs.; cents per lb.								
Dec	20.85	20.95	20.70	20.90	.03	26.94	19.50	308
Mr06	21.36	21.58	21.17	21.40	.03	26.45	19.70	70,068
Rough Rice (CBT)-2,000 cwt.; cents per cwt.								
Jan	784.00	785.00	772.00	782.00	-3.50	810.00	670.00	3,989
Mar	813.00	813.00	800.00	808.50	-4.00	823.00	690.00	3,757
Wheat (CBT)-5,000 bu.; cents per bu.								
Dec	300.00	304.00	298.00	304.00	4.50	406.00	292.50	479
Mr06	314.50	319.00	310.50	318.50	3.75	393.00	307.00	224,724
Wheat (KC)-5,000 bu.; cents per bu.								
Dec	355.00	355.00	351.50	353.00	2.00	392.50	321.00	181
Mr06	360.00	362.50	354.00	360.00	-.25	394.00	331.50	69,368
Wheat (MPLS)-5,000 bu.; cents per bu.								
Dec	366.50	369.00	361.00	367.00	7.00	410.00	332.00	42
Mr06	370.00	372.00	366.50	370.50	.50	399.00	340.75	21,651
Cattle-Feeder (CME)-50,000 lbs.; cents per lb.								
Jan	114.975	115.250	114.425	114.825	.650	117.900	95.800	15,666
Mar	113.600	114.500	113.600	114.325	.825	116.100	96.000	8,757
Cattle-Live (CME)-40,000 lbs.; cents per lb.								
Dec	93.500	93.825	92.700	93.725	1.250	94.450	80.200	15,670
Fb06	95.600	96.675	95.500	96.250	1.050	96.950	82.100	118,603
Hogs-Lean (CME)-40,000 lbs.; cents per lb.								
Dec	62.350	62.550	62.250	62.375	.250	65.650	51.000	6,519
Fb06	66.375	67.100	65.750	66.575	.725	68.300	55.100	75,154
Pork Bellies (CME)-40,000 lbs.; cents per lb.								
Feb	84.600	85.600	84.100	84.200	-1.400	98.400	74.500	1,345
Mar	84.850	85.200	83.975	83.975	-.825	98.000	75.000	145
Lumber (CME)-110,000 bd. ft.; $ per 1,000 bd. ft.								
Jan	323.20	327.30	322.70	323.80	-3.20	359.50	276.00	2,682
Mar	336.00	342.40	336.00	339.50	-3.30	361.10	288.00	1,843
Milk (CME)-200,000 lbs.; cents per lb.								
Dec	13.37	13.44	13.37	13.42	.04	13.65	12.00	2,149
Ja06	12.96	13.04	12.96	13.00	.04	13.30	11.90	2,105
Cocoa (NYBOT)-10 metric tons; $ per ton.								
Dec	1,476	1,487	1,487	1,485	1	1,887	1,315	366
Mr06	1,480	1,497	1,475	1,480	1	1,890	1,344	55,880
Coffee (NYBOT)-37,500 lbs.; cents per lb.								
Dec	96.50	96.15	95.25	95.40	-1.05	147.00	79.00	71
Mr06	100.45	101.20	98.00	98.30	-1.40	148.75	82.60	61,106
Sugar-World (NYBOT)-112,000 lbs.; cents per lb.								
Mar	13.63	13.90	13.63	13.81	-.15	14.06	6.61	298,011
May	13.69	13.93	13.69	13.87	-.08	14.05	7.65	78,829
Sugar-Domestic (NYBOT)-112,000 lbs.; cents per lb.								
Mar	21.20	21.50	21.20	21.40	.17	22.04	20.40	3,207
July	21.40	21.85	21.40	21.83	.36	22.00	20.88	3,539
Cotton (NYBOT)-50,000 lbs.; cents per lb.								
Mar	53.30	53.75	53.30	53.69	.28	69.00	48.30	79,800
May	53.95	54.38	53.95	54.27	.27	61.20	49.25	13,679
Orange Juice (NYBOT)-15,000 lbs.; cents per lb.								
Jan	129.60	130.80	128.50	130.40	-.20	130.80	81.50	21,133
Mar	131.50	132.60	130.50	132.45	-.05	133.00	87.25	11,591

Metal & Petroleum Futures

	OPEN	HIGH	LOW	SETTLE	CHG	LIFETIME HIGH	LIFETIME LOW	OPEN INT
Copper-High (CMX)-25,000 lbs.; cents per lb.								
Dec	216.20	219.90	215.30	217.30	1.75	219.90	99.00	5,363
Mr06	199.00	203.60	198.65	202.65	4.05	204.60	98.00	74,649
Gold (CMX)-100 troy oz.; $ per troy oz.								
Dec	528.40	530.70	519.50	521.00	-7.40	538.50	298.40	1,919
Fb06	530.60	533.00	522.90	524.10	-7.40	544.50	415.00	249,199
Apr	534.40	536.10	527.00	528.40	-7.40	548.40	418.00	12,068
June	538.40	541.00	531.00	532.80	-7.50	551.80	312.00	20,310
Dec	552.50	554.00	544.50	546.40	-7.60	565.60	338.00	10,717
Dc07	580.00	580.00	575.50	573.70	-7.80	592.50	368.00	7,111

Platinum (NYM)-50 troy oz.; $ per troy oz.

	OPEN	HIGH	LOW	SETTLE	CHG	LIFETIME HIGH	LIFETIME LOW	OPEN INT
Jan	1018.80	1018.80	984.00	995.90	-22.20	1026.00	870.00	11,093
Apr	1012.00	1012.00	990.00	1000.70	-22.10	1030.00	815.00	1,734

Silver (CMX)-5,000 troy oz.; cnts per troy oz.

Dec	875.0	877.5	848.0	849.7	-29.5	917.0	447.0	1,236
Mr06	891.0	895.0	851.5	858.5	-29.7	934.5	662.5	105,114

Crude Oil, Light Sweet (NYM)-1,000 bbls.; $ per bbl.

Jan	61.29	61.90	60.76	61.37	0.07	71.68	25.25	145,304
Feb	62.01	62.85	61.67	62.31	0.05	-71.87	25.85	169,368
Mar	62.80	63.45	62.25	62.89	0.03	71.11	25.54	80,167
June	64.00	64.00	63.19	63.69	-0.03	70.30	23.75	46,284
Dec	64.04	64.68	64.04	64.35	-0.13	68.79	19.10	52,824
Dc07	63.45	63.83	63.45	63.46	-0.22	66.35	19.50	50,696

Heating Oil No. 2 (NYM)-42,000 gal.; $ per gal.

Jan	1.7725	1.8425	1.7626	1.8365	.0640	2.2200	.9730	53,191
Feb	1.8230	1.8825	1.8106	1.8705	.0553	2.2250	1.0350	55,026

Gasoline-NY Unleaded (NYM)-42,000 gal.; $ per gal.

Jan	1.6474	1.6620	1.6290	1.6459	-.0009	2.0200	1.3260	46,841
Feb	1.6949	1.7085	1.6800	1.6958	-.0011	2.0000	1.3620	36,001

Natural Gas (NYM)-10,000 MMBtu.; $ per MMBtu.

Jan	14.900	15.780	14.851	15.378	.537	15.780	4.020	63,905
Feb	14.954	15.780	14.920	15.427	.514	15.780	3.850	59,199
Mar	14.815	15.550	14.800	15.287	.483	15.550	3.781	72,395
Apr	11.320	11.650	11.240	11.487	.233	11.680	3.786	38,275
May	10.915	11.154	10.855	11.037	.163	11.266	3.571	27,403
Oct	11.001	11.185	11.001	11.117	.133	11.390	3.732	27,082

Interest Rate Futures

	OPEN	HIGH	LOW	SETTLE	CHG	LIFETIME HIGH	LIFETIME LOW	OPEN INT
Treasury Bonds (CBT)-$100,000; pts 32nds of 100%								
Dec	112-01	112-12	111-30	112-04	3	119-07	106-08	25,520
Mr06	111-23	112-05	111-21	111-28	3	118-19	110-01	516,783
Treasury Notes (CBT)-$100,000; pts 32nds of 100%								
Dec	108-160	108-250	108-155	108-200	4.5	113-205	106-260	99,745
Mr06	108-075	108-190	108-070	108-125	4.5	112-300	106-220	1,611,879
5 Yr. Treasury Notes (CBT)-$100,000; pts 32nds of 100%								
Dec	106-005	106-045	105-310	106-010	3.0	108-295	105-115	25,322
Mr06	105-245	106-025	105-235	105-275	3.0	108-240	105-060	1,118,799
2 Yr. Treasury Notes (CBT)-$200,000; pts 32nds of 100%								
Dec	102-197	102-202	102-190	102-200	7	103-280	102-097	31,763
Mr06	102-155	102-187	102-145	102-165	1.0	102-272	102-100	321,036
30 Day Federal Funds (CBT)-$5,000,000; 100 - daily avg.								
Dec	95.840	95.840	95.835	95.840	...	96.955	95.830	90,282
Fb06	95.525	95.530	95.520	95.530	...	96.290	95.500	123,646

	OPEN	HIGH	LOW	SETTLE	CHG	YIELD	CHG	OPEN INT
1 Month Libor (CME)-$3,000,000; pts of 100%								
Dec	95.6250	95.6250	95.6200	95.6200	...	4.3800	...	18,611
Ja06	95.5050	95.5125	95.5000	95.5025	-.0025	4.4975	.0025	10,338
Eurodollar (CME)-$1,000,000; pts of 100%								
Dec	95.4950	95.4975	95.4900	95.4925	-.0025	4.5075	.0025	1,114,476
Mr06	95.2150	95.2800	95.1950	95.2200	...	4.7800	...	1,165,170
June	95.0950	95.1900	95.0900	95.1300	.0350	4.8700	-.0350	1,327,539
Dec	95.1200	95.2100	95.1200	95.1600	.0350	4.8400	-.0350	1,093,585

Currency Futures

	OPEN	HIGH	LOW	SETTLE	CHG	LIFETIME HIGH	LIFETIME LOW	OPEN INT
Japanese Yen (CME)-¥12,500,000; $ per 100¥								
Dec	.8355	.8365	.8307	.8342	-.0013	1.0084	.8252	132,895
Mr06	.8442	.8453	.8395	.8429	-.0013	.9660	.8338	85,668
Canadian Dollar (CME)-CAD 100,000; $ per CAD								
Dec	.8692	.8710	.8668	.8696	.0010	.8710	.7480	62,682
Mr06	.8713	.8729	.8690	.8718	.0010	.8729	.7927	75,707
British Pound (CME)-£62,500; $ per £								
Dec	1.7754	1.7782	1.7653	1.7695	-.0062	1.9090	1.7046	59,282
Mr06	1.7759	1.7780	1.7651	1.7692	-.0062	1.8550	1.7050	50,218
Swiss Franc (CME)-CHF 125,000; $ per CHF								
Dec	.7758	.7777	.7717	.7737	-.0012	.8922	.7548	56,612
Mr06	.7822	.7839	.7778	.7799	-.0012	.8888	.7610	53,669
Australian Dollar (CME)-AUD 100,000; $ per AUD								
Dec	.7556	.7568	.7525	.7543	-.0006	.7835	.6664	51,686
Mr06	.7543	.7549	.7506	.7524	-.0006	.7675	.6920	27,901
Mexican Peso (CME)-MXN 500,000; $ per 10MXN								
Dec	.93800	.94175	.93400	.93950	-.00075	.96025	.82400	44,845
Mr06	.93100	.93500	.92600	.93175	-.00075	.95150	.81300	63,680
Euro (CME)-€125,000; $ per €								
Dec	1.1957	1.1992	1.1910	1.1957	.0005	1.3740	1.1661	135,566
Mr06	1.2015	1.2047	1.1966	1.2013	.0005	1.3789	1.1719	54,687

Index Futures

	OPEN	HIGH	LOW	SETTLE	CHG	LIFETIME HIGH	LIFETIME LOW	OPEN INT
DJ Industrial Average (CBT)-$10 x index								
Dec	10775	10872	10757	10838	64	11066	10037	31,413
Mr06	10827	10932	10810	10892	65	11029	10257	25,433
Mini DJ Industrial Average (CBT)-$5 x index								
Dec	10776	10877	10758	10838	64	10987	10060	77,356
Mr06	10826	10932	10810	10892	65	11036	10238	31,709
S&P 500 Index (CME)-$250 x index								
Dec	1260.20	1273.00	1259.10	1268.90	7.80	1274.50	1071.50	242,675
Mr06	1269.60	1281.30	1267.20	1277.10	7.90	1282.80	1075.50	491,647
Mini S&P 500 Index (CME)-$50 x index								
Dec	1261.25	1273.25	1259.25	1269.00	8.00	1274.50	1171.75	735,914
Mr06	1269.50	1281.50	1267.25	1277.00	7.75	1282.50	1179.00	751,490
Nasdaq 100 (CME)-$100 x index								
Dec	1698.50	1712.00	1695.00	1706.50	6.50	1719.50	1430.50	41,825
Mr06	1717.50	1731.00	1711.00	1724.00	7.00	1734.50	1523.50	37,042
Mini Nasdaq 100 (CME)-$20 x index								
Dec	1700.0	1713.5	1694.5	1706.5	6.5	1719.0	1486.0	282,304
Mr06	1717.5	1731.0	1713.5	1724.0	7.0	1745.0	1539.0	187,497
Russell 1000 (NYBOT)-$500 x index								
Dec	686.00	686.15	686.00	690.30	4.00	692.15	636.70	16,882
Mr06	690.75	695.75	690.50	695.00	4.10	695.75	684.00	81,497
U.S. Dollar Index (NYBOT)-$1,000 x index								
Dec	90.32	90.57	90.14	90.34	.03	92.53	81.20	14,516
Mr06	89.98	90.37	89.82	90.06	.03	92.20	86.00	20,103

Electricity Price Indexes

Explanatory Notes
Figures represent weighted average price of electricity traded at the indicated hubs. All indexes quoted in dollars per megawatt hour; volumes in megawatt hours. **Firm:** Electricity that meets the minimum criteria of being Financially Firm and backed by liquidating damages. **Non Firm:** Electricity subject to interruption at any time. **On Peak:** 16-hour period of heavy demand. **Off Peak:** Eighthour period of light demand. **r:** Revised. **n.q.:** No quote. **s:** Surveyed data. **n.a.:** One-day lag for non-firm, not available for others. **For questions and additional hubs from Dow Jones please call 609-520-4663.**

Tuesday, December 13, 2005

DJ COB California-Oregon and Nevada-Oregon Borders

	DEC 13	DEC 12	DEC 11	DEC 10
FIRM				
On Peak	132.02	134.00	n.q.	136.72
Volume	5,664	6,992	n.q.	7,728
Off Peak	105.58	109.48	n.q.	107.33
Volume	936	2,096	n.q.	2,664
NON FIRM				
On Peak	n.a.	s107.20	n.a.	s109.38
Volume	n.a.	0	n.a.	0
Off Peak	n.a.	s87.58	s98.53	s85.86
Volume	n.a.	0	0	0

In Figure 14.1, locate the gold and wheat contracts. Where are they traded? What are the contract sizes for the gold and wheat contracts and how are their futures prices specified?

The gold contract trades on the CMX, the COMEX Division of the New York Mercantile Exchange. One gold contract calls for delivery of 100 troy ounces. The gold futures price is quoted in dollars per ounce.

Wheat contracts are traded on the Chicago Board of Trade (CBT), the Kansas City Board of Trade (KC), and the Minneapolis Grain Exchange (MPLS). One wheat contract calls for delivery of 5,000 bushels of wheat, and wheat futures prices are quoted in cents per bushel. Why do you think there are different wheat prices at these exchanges? Isn't wheat wheat?

For futures prices and price charts, visit these Web sites:
futures.tradingcharts.com
www.barchart.com

The reporting format for each futures contract is similar. For example, the first column of a price listing gives the contract delivery/maturity month. For each maturity month, the next five columns report futures prices observed during the previous day at the opening of trading ("Open"), the highest intraday price ("High"), the lowest intraday price ("Low"), the price at close of trading ("Settle"), and the change in the settle price from the previous day ("Chg").

The next two columns ("Lifetime," "High" and "Low") report the highest and lowest prices for each maturity observed over the previous year. Finally, the last column reports open interest for each contract maturity, which is the number of contracts outstanding at the end of that day's trading.

By now, we see that four of the contract terms for futures contracts are stated in the futures prices listing. These are:

1. The identity of the underlying commodity or financial instrument.

2. The futures contract size.

3. The futures maturity date.

4. The futures price.

Exact contract terms for the delivery process are available from the appropriate futures exchange on request.

In Figure 14.1, locate the soybean contract with the greatest open interest. Explain the information provided.

The soybean (or just "bean") contract with the greatest open interest is specified by the contract maturity with the greatest number of contracts outstanding, so the January 2006 contract is the one we seek. One contract calls for delivery of 5,000 bushels of beans (a bushel, of course, is four pecks and weighs about 60 pounds). The closing price for delivery at maturity is quoted in cents per bushel. Because there are 5,000 bushels in a single contract, the total contract value is the quoted price per bushel of 597.50 cents times 5,000, or $29,875 for the January contract.

GARISH JACKETS ADD TO CLAMOR OF CHICAGO PITS

For the inhabitants of Chicago's futures and options trading pits, dressing for success means throwing good taste to the wind.

Take James Oliff, a trader in the Chicago Mercantile Exchange's newly opened Mexican peso futures pit. Daily, he dons a multicolored jacket bedecked with cacti and sombreros, in keeping, he says, with the "theme" of the product he trades.

Twisting and turning to display his gaudy garb, the veteran currency options trader explains: "I wanted a jacket that would be easy to pick out in the crowd. Runners get orders to me more quickly, and clerks find me faster when I'm trying to do trades."

It's important to have what veterans of the mayhem describe as "pit presence" to make money in the crowded and noisy trading pits of the Merc and the Chicago Board of Trade. That elusive quality, they say, involves such stratagems as finding the best spot in the pit from which to communicate with clerks and other traders, maintaining good posture and using a loud, well-projected voice and forceful hand signals to attract attention.

Increasingly, in places such as the CBOT's bond pit, where hundreds of people cram into a space only slightly larger than a tennis court, garb is being used to grab attention. Hence the insatiable demand for magenta, lime-green, and silver-lamé jackets, featuring designs that run the gamut from the Mighty Morphin Power Rangers to bucolic farmhouses and sunflowers.

"I'd come in buck naked if I could," says Thomas Burke, a trader in the CBOT's overpopulated bond-futures pit. "As it is, the more obnoxious the jacket, the better. The louder it is, the more I can rest my voice and let my jacket draw the attention."

Chicago's exchanges quietly tolerate the proliferation of the garish trading jackets. Dress codes ban jeans and still require members to wear shirts with collars and don ties (although some of these may be little more than strings, having been worn daily for more than a decade). The rules also say that trading jackets must have sleeves that come below the elbow and contain pockets into which the traders stuff their trading cards and other documents. But during the past decade, traders say, exchange efforts to regulate the color and design of the jackets, or gently encourage their wearers to opt for something in quiet good taste, have been dropped as an exercise in futility.

Robert Pierce, who trades corn options at the CBOT, says the old brown jackets made him look like

---

To get an idea of the magnitude of financial futures trading, take a look at the first entry under "Interest Rate Futures" in Figure 14.1, the CBT Treasury bond contract. One contract calls for the delivery of $100,000 in par value bonds. The total open interest in these contracts often exceeds half a million contracts. Thus, the total face value represented by these contracts is close to half a *trillion* dollars.

Who does all this trading? The orders originate from money managers around the world and are sent to the various exchanges' trading floors for execution. On the floor, the orders are executed by professional traders who are quite aggressive at getting the best prices. On the floor and off, futures traders can be recognized by their colorful jackets. As *The Wall Street Journal* article in the nearby *Investment Updates* box reports, these garish jackets add a touch of clamor to the trading pits. In the next section we will discuss how and why futures contracts are used for speculation and hedging.

a UPS delivery man. "When someone gave me a UPS cap on the floor one day as a joke, I decided it was time for a change of style," he says. The switch, to a comparatively tasteful multicolored geometric pattern, has the added advantage of disguising pen and pencil marks, adds his wife, Cathy.

Dawn Guera, a former clerk at the CBOT, has spun the traders' need to stand out in the crowd into a four-year-old business designing and manufacturing custom trading jackets. Traders wander into her storefront operation next door to the CBOT to choose from dozens of fabrics with designs ranging from a subdued Harvard University crest on a crimson background to a slinky leopard skin pattern or turquoise frogs cavorting on a neon-pink background.

"Everyone has their own hobbies and interests and wants the jackets to reflect that," she explains, pointing to fabrics with designs of dice and cards aimed at traders willing to acknowledge their addiction to gambling in the markets. "It's like a vanity license plate."

And, at $50 a pop, traders are willing, even eager, to order multiple jackets, Ms. Guera says, especially since many believe that washing or dry cleaning a "lucky" jacket will launder out the luck in it. Some, like the CBOT's Gilbert Leistner, take a seasonal approach to jackets: in summer and fall he wears a brightly colored turquoise and aquamarine jacket decorated with tropical fish, but switches to a Southwestern theme come Thanksgiving.

"It's my version of going south for the winter," he says, adding he's contemplating donning something in gold lamé for New Year's celebrations.

Ms. Guera, a former sportswear designer in New York, says traders have a long way to go before they'll pull themselves off the worst-dressed lists. To be sure, some of the early emphasis on flashiness is easing a bit, she says, and demands for fluorescent geometric patterns are giving way to a new trend favoring subtler paisley-type patterns with lapels, cuffs, and pockets in a contrasting, solid color.

"I think it would be great if we could really push the fashion envelope here and remove the collar and cuffs from the jackets, or even persuade the exchanges to let traders wear vests instead," she says. "I'm looking for a way of making this whole trading process more artistic and creative."

Source: Suzanne McGee, *The Wall Street Journal*, July 31, 1995. Reprinted by permission of Dow Jones & Company, Inc., via Copyright Clearance Center, Inc. © 1995 Dow Jones & Company, Inc. All Rights Reserved Worldwide.

CHECK THIS

14.1a What is a forward contract?

14.1b What is a futures contract, and why is it different from a forward contract?

14.1c What is a futures price?

14.2 Why Futures?

Futures contracts can be used for speculation or for hedging. Certainly, hedging is the major economic purpose for the existence of futures markets. However, a viable futures market cannot exist without participation by both hedgers and speculators. Hedgers transfer price risk to speculators, and speculators absorb price risk. Hedging and speculating are complementary activities. We next discuss speculating with futures; then we discuss hedging with futures.

SPECULATING WITH FUTURES

Suppose you are thinking about speculating on commodity prices because you believe you can accurately forecast future prices most of the time. The most convenient way to speculate is with futures contracts. If you believe that the price of gold will go up, then you can speculate on this belief by buying gold futures. Alternatively, if you think gold will fall in price, you can speculate by selling gold futures. To be more precise, you think that the current futures price is either too high or too low relative to what gold prices will be in the future.

Buying futures is often referred to as "going long," or establishing a **long position**. Selling futures is often called "going short," or establishing a **short position**. A **speculator** accepts price risk in order to bet on the direction of prices by going long or short.

To illustrate the basics of speculating, suppose you believe the price of gold will go up. In particular, suppose the current futures price for delivery in three months is $400 per ounce. You think that gold will be selling for more than that three months from now, so you go long 100 three-month gold contracts. Each gold contract represents 100 troy ounces, so 100 contracts represent 10,000 ounces of gold with a total contract value of $10,000 \times \$400 = \$4,000,000$. In futures jargon, this is a $4 million long gold position.

Now, suppose your belief turns out to be correct, and, at contract maturity, the market price of gold is $420 per ounce. From your long futures position, you accept delivery of 10,000 troy ounces of gold at $400 per ounce and immediately sell the gold at the market price of $420 per ounce. Your profit is $20 per ounce, or $10,000 \times \$20 = \$200,000$, less applicable commissions.

Of course, if your belief turned out wrong and gold fell in price, you would lose money because you must still buy the 10,000 troy ounces at $400 per ounce to fulfill your futures contract obligation. Thus, if gold fell to, say, $390 per ounce, you would lose $10 per ounce, or $10,000 \times \$10 = \$100,000$ (plus applicable commissions). As this example suggests, futures speculation is risky, but it is potentially rewarding if you can accurately forecast the direction of future commodity price movements.

As another example of commodity speculation, suppose an analysis of weather patterns has convinced you that the coming winter months will be warmer than usual, and that this will cause heating oil prices to fall as unsold inventories accumulate. You can speculate on this belief by selling heating oil futures.

The standard contract size for heating oil is 42,000 gallons. Suppose you go short 10 contracts at a futures price of 155 cents per gallon. This represents a short position with a total contract value of $10 \times 42,000 \times \$1.55 = \$651,000$.

If, at contract maturity, the price of heating oil is, say, $1.50 per gallon, you could buy 420,000 gallons for delivery to fulfill your futures commitment. Your profit would be 5 cents per gallon, or $10 \times 42,000 \times \$.05 = \$21,000$, less applicable commissions. Of course, if heating oil prices rise by 5 cents per gallon, you would lose $21,000 (plus applicable commissions) instead. Again, speculation is risky but rewarding if you can accurately forecast the weather.

WWW

To learn more about futures, visit www.usafutures.com

long position

In futures jargon, refers to the contract buyer. A long position profits from a futures price increase.

short position

In futures jargon, refers to the seller. A short position profits from a futures price decrease.

speculator

Trader who accepts price risk by going long or short to bet on the future direction of prices.

EXAMPLE 14.3 | **What Would Juan Valdez Do?**

After an analysis of political currents in Central and South America, you conclude that future coffee prices will be lower than currently indicated by futures prices. Would you go long or short? Analyze the impact of a swing in coffee prices of 10 cents per pound in either direction if you have a 10-contract position, where each contract calls for delivery of 37,500 pounds of coffee.

(continued)

You would go short since you expect prices to decline. You are short 10 contracts, so you must deliver 10 × 37,500 = 375,000 pounds of coffee. If coffee prices fall to 10 cents below your originally contracted futures price, then you make 10 cents per pound, or $37,500. Of course, if you're wrong and prices are 10 cents higher, you lose $37,500.

HEDGING WITH FUTURES

Many businesses face price risk when their activities require them to hold a working inventory. For example, suppose you own a regional gasoline distributorship and must keep a large operating inventory of gasoline on hand, say, 5 million gallons. In futures jargon, this gasoline inventory represents a long position in the underlying commodity.

If gasoline prices go up, your inventory goes up in value; but if gasoline prices fall, your inventory value goes down. Your risk is not trivial, since even a 5-cent fluctuation in the gallon price of gasoline will cause your inventory to change in value by $250,000. Because you are in the business of distributing gasoline, and not speculating on gasoline prices, you would like to remove this price risk from your business operations. Acting as a **hedger**, you seek to transfer price risk by taking a futures position opposite to an existing position in the underlying commodity or financial instrument. In this case, the value of your gasoline inventory can be protected by selling gasoline futures contracts.

Gasoline futures are traded on the New York Mercantile Exchange (NYM), and the standard contract size for gasoline futures is 42,000 gallons per contract. Because you wish to hedge 5 million gallons, you need to sell 5,000,000 / 42,000 = 119 gasoline contracts. With this hedge in place, any change in the value of your long inventory position is canceled by an approximately equal but opposite change in value of your short futures position. Because you are using this short position for hedging purposes, it is called a **short hedge**.

By hedging, you have greatly reduced or even eliminated the possibility of a loss from a decline in the price of gasoline. However, you have also eliminated the possibility of a gain from a price increase. This is an important point. If gasoline prices rise, you would have a substantial loss on your futures position, offsetting the gain on your inventory. Overall, you are long in the underlying commodity because you own it; you offset the risk in your long position in the underlying commodity with a short position in futures.

Of course, your business activities may also include distributing other petroleum products like heating oil and natural gas. Futures contracts are also available for these petroleum products, and therefore they may be used for inventory hedging purposes too.

hedger
Trader who seeks to transfer price risk by taking a futures position opposite to an existing position in the underlying commodity or financial instrument.

short hedge
Sale of futures to offset potential losses from falling prices.

EXAMPLE 14.4	Short Hedging

Suppose you have an inventory of 1.2 million pounds of soybean oil. Describe how you would hedge this position.

Because you are long in the underlying commodity, bean oil, you need to go short in futures (i.e., sell). A single bean oil contract calls for delivery of 60,000 pounds of bean oil. To hedge your position, you need to sell 1.2 million / 60,000 = 20 futures contracts.

long hedge
Purchase of futures to offset potential losses from rising prices.

The opposite of a short hedge is a **long hedge**. In this case, you do not own the underlying commodity, but you need to acquire it in the future. You can lock in the price you will pay in the future by buying, or going long in, futures contracts. In effect, you are "short" the underlying commodity because you must buy it in the future. Taking a long futures position today offsets the risk of paying a higher price for the underlying commodity in the future.

You need to buy 600,000 pounds of orange juice in three months. How can you hedge the price risk associated with this future purchase? What price will you effectively lock in? One orange juice contract calls for delivery of 15,000 pounds of juice concentrate.

You are effectively "short" orange juice because you don't currently own it but plan to buy it later. To offset the risk of higher orange juice prices when you actually buy it, you need to go long in futures. You should buy 600,000/15,000 = 40 contracts. The price you lock in is the original futures price.

Suppose your company will receive payment of £10 million in six months, which will then be converted to U.S. dollars. What is the standard futures contract size for British pounds? Describe how you could use futures contracts to lock in an exchange rate from British pounds to U.S. dollars for your planned receipt of £10 million, including how many contracts are required.

Your company will be receiving £10 million, so you are effectively long pounds. To hedge, you need to short (sell) futures contracts. Put differently, you will want to exchange pounds for dollars. By selling a futures contract, you obligate yourself to deliver the underlying commodity, in this case currency, in exchange for payment in dollars. One British pound contract calls for delivery of £62,500. You will therefore sell £10 million / £62,500 = 160 contracts.

CHECK THIS

14.2a   What is a long position in futures? A short position?

14.2b   For a speculator, when is a long position appropriate and when is a short position appropriate?

14.2c   What is a long hedge? A short hedge?

14.2d   For a hedger, when is a long hedge appropriate and when is a short hedge appropriate?

14.3   Futures Trading Accounts

A futures exchange, like a stock exchange, allows only exchange members to trade on the exchange. Exchange members may be firms or individuals trading for their own accounts, or they may be brokerage firms handling trades for customers. Some firms conduct both trading and brokerage operations on the exchange. In this section, we discuss the mechanics of a futures trading account as it pertains to a customer with a trading account at a brokerage firm.

WWW

For a list of online
futures brokers visit the
Commodities & Futures
section of Investor
Links at
www.investorlinks.com

futures margin
Deposit of funds in a fu-
tures trading account dedicated to covering potential
losses from an outstanding
futures position.

initial margin
Amount required when a
futures contract is first
bought or sold. Initial margin varies with the type
and size of a contract, but
it is the same for long and
short futures positions.

marking-to-market
In futures trading ac-
counts, the process
whereby gains and losses
on outstanding futures positions are recognized on
a daily basis.

**maintenance
margin**
The minimum margin level
required in a futures trading account at all times.

margin call
Notification to increase
the margin level in a trading account.

reverse trade
A trade that closes out a
previously established
futures position by taking
the opposite position.

The biggest customer trading accounts are those of corporations that use futures to manage their business risks and money managers who hedge or speculate with clients' funds.
Many individual investors also have futures trading accounts of their own, although speculation by individual investors is not recommended without a full understanding of all risks
involved. Whether a futures trading account is large or small, the mechanics of account
trading are essentially the same.

There are several essential things to know about futures trading accounts. The first thing
is that margin is required. In this way, futures accounts resemble the stock margin accounts
we discussed in a previous chapter; however, the specifics are quite different. **Futures
margin** is a deposit of funds in a futures trading account dedicated to covering potential
losses from an outstanding futures position. An **initial margin** is required when a futures
position is first established. The amount varies according to contract type and size, but margin requirements for futures contracts usually range between 2 percent and 5 percent of
total contract value. Initial margin is the same for both long and short futures positions.

The second thing to know about a futures trading account is that contract values in outstanding futures positions are marked to market on a daily basis. **Marking-to-market** is a
process whereby gains and losses on outstanding futures positions are recognized at the
end of each trading day.

For example, suppose one morning you call your broker and instruct her to go long five
U.S. Treasury bond contracts for your account. A few minutes later, she calls back to confirm order execution at a futures price of 110. Because the Treasury bond contract size is
$100,000 par value, contract value is 110% × $100,000 = $110,000 per contract. Thus, the
total position value for your order is $550,000, for which your broker requires $25,000 initial margin. In addition, your broker requires that at least $20,000 in **maintenance margin**
be present at all times. The necessary margin funds are immediately wired from a bank account to your futures account.

Now, at the end of trading that day Treasury bond futures close at a price of 108.
Overnight, all accounts are marked to market. Your Treasury bond futures position is
marked to $108,000 per contract, or $540,000 total position value, representing a loss of
$10,000. This loss is deducted from your initial margin to leave only $15,000 of margin
funds in your account.

Because the maintenance margin level on your account is $20,000, your broker will
issue a **margin call** on your account. Essentially, your broker will notify you that you must
immediately restore your margin level to the initial margin level of $25,000, or else she will
close out your Treasury bond futures position at whatever trading price is available at the
exchange.

This example illustrates what happens when a futures trading account is marked to market and the resulting margin funds fall below the maintenance margin level. The alternative, and more pleasant, experience occurs when a futures price moves in your favor, and
the marking-to-market process adds funds to your account. In this case, marking-to-market
gains can be withdrawn from your account so long as remaining margin funds are not less
than the initial margin level.

The third thing to know about a futures trading account is that a futures position can be
closed out at any time; you do not have to hold a contract until maturity. A futures position
is closed out by simply instructing your broker to close out your position. To actually close
out a position, your broker will enter a **reverse trade** for your account.

A reverse trade works like this: Suppose you are currently short five Treasury bond contracts, and you instruct your broker to close out the position. Your broker responds by going
long five Treasury bond contracts for your account. In this case, going long five contracts
is a reverse trade because it cancels exactly your previous five-contract short position. At
the end of the day in which you make your reverse trade, your account will be marked to

market at the futures price realized by the reverse trade. From then on, your position is closed out, and no more gains or losses will be realized.

This example illustrates that closing out a futures position is no more difficult than initially entering into a position. There are two basic reasons to close out a futures position before contract maturity. The first is to capture a current gain or loss, without realizing further price risk. The second is to avoid the delivery requirement that comes from holding a futures contract until it matures. In fact, over 98 percent of all futures contracts are closed out before contract maturity, which indicates that less than 2 percent of all futures contracts result in delivery of the underlying commodity or financial instrument.

Before closing this section, let's briefly list the three essential things to know about a futures trading account as discussed above:

1. Margin is required.
2. Futures accounts are marked to market daily.
3. A futures position can be closed out any time by a reverse trade.

Understanding the items in this list is important to anyone planning to use a futures trading account.

CHECK THIS

14.3a What are the three essential things you should know about a futures trading account?

14.3b What is meant by initial margin for a futures position? What is meant by maintenance margin for a futures position?

14.3c Explain the process of marking-to-market a futures trading account. What is a margin call, and when is one issued?

14.3d How is a futures position closed out by a reverse trade? What proportion of all futures positions are closed out by reverse trades rather than by delivery at contract maturity?

14.4 Cash Prices versus Futures Prices

We now turn to the relationship between today's price of some commodity or financial instrument and its futures price. We begin by examining current cash prices.

CASH PRICES

cash price
Price of a commodity or financial instrument for current delivery. Also called the *spot price*.

cash market
Market in which commodities or financial instruments are traded for immediate delivery. Also called the *spot market*.

The **cash price** of a commodity or financial instrument is the price quoted for current delivery. The cash price is also called the *spot price,* as in "on the spot." In futures jargon, terms like "spot gold" or "cash wheat" are used to refer to commodities being sold for current delivery in what is called the **cash market** or the *spot market*.

Figure 14.2 reproduces the "Cash Prices" column of *The Wall Street Journal*, published the same day as the "Futures Prices" column seen in Figure 14.1. The column is divided into sections according to commodity categories. For example, the first section, "Grains and Feeds," lists spot price information for wheat, corn, soybeans, and similar crops. Other commodity sections include "Foods," "Fats and Oils," "Precious Metals," and "Metals." Each section gives commodity names along with cash market prices for the last two days of trading and one year earlier.

FIGURE 14.2 | Commodity Cash Prices

Cash Prices

December 13, 2005

Grains and Feeds	LO/HI RANGE TUE	TUE	MON	YEAR AGO
Barley, top-quality Mpls., bu	u2.8	sp	2.75	2.5
Bran, wheat middlings, KC ton	u76	81	76.5	63
Corn, No. 2 yel. Cent. Ill. bu	bpu1.895	sp	1.885	1.86
Corn Gluten Feed, Midwest, ton	uw48	60	53.5	55
Cottonseed Meal, ton	uw165	sp	155	120
Hominy Feed, Cent. Ill. ton	uw50	60	53	49
Meat-Bonemeal, 50% pro Ill. ton	uw152	157.5	157.5	177.5
Oats, No. 2 milling, Mpls., bu	u2.28	2.3	2.2275	1.81
Sorghum, (Milo) No. 2 Gulf cwt	u4.35	4.44	4.38	4.17
Soybean Meal, Cent. Ill., rail, ton 48%	u196	202	193	166.7
Soybeans, No. 1 yel Cent. Ill., bu	bpu5.84	sp	5.71	5.43
Wheat, Spring 14%-pro Mpls bu.	u4.805	4.955	4.9675	4.755
Wheat, No. 2 sft red, St.Lou. bu	bpu3.075	sp	3.035	3.395
Wheat, hard, KC bu	4.355	sp	4.3575	4.25
Wheat, No. 1 sft wht, del Port Ore	u3.44	sp	3.41	3.96

Foods

	TUE	TUE	MON	YEAR AGO
Beef, Carcass Equiv. Index Value, choice 1-3,600-900 lbs.	u144.89	sp	144.05	129.7
Beef, Carcass Equiv. Index Value, select 1-3,600-900 lbs.	u133.62	sp	133.5	123.09
Broilers, Dressed "A" lb.	ux.7019	sp	.7019	.6756
Broilers, 12-Cty Comp Wtd Av	uw.6442	sp	.6442	.6748
Butter, AA, Chgo., lb.	u1.37	sp	1.37	1.55
Cheddar Cheese, barrels, Chgo lb.	n139.75	sp	139	139.75
Cheddar Cheese, blocks, Chgo lb.	n143.5	sp	143.5	142.25
Milk, Non-fat Dry, Chgo	96.25	sp	96.25	86
Cocoa, Ivory Coast, $metric ton	z	sp	1,686	1,833
Coffee, Brazilian, Comp.	n.9702	sp	.9395	z
Coffee, Colombian, NY lb.	n1.0703	sp	1.0392	z
Eggs, Lge white, Chgo doz.	u.61	.7	.655	.725
Flour, hard winter KC cwt	11.3	sp	11.3	11.3
Hams, 17-20 lbs, Mid-US lb fob	u.82	sp	z	.79
Hogs, Iowa-S.Minn. avg. cwt.	u59.93	sp	61.44	68.41
Hogs, Sioux Falls, SD avg cwt	u44	45	45.5	47
Pork Bellies, 12-14 lbs Mid-US lb	u.75	sp	z	.91
Pork Loins, 13-19 lbs, Mid-US lb	u.96	1.04	1	1.125
Steers, Tex.-Okla. ch avg cwt	z	sp	91	83.96
Steers, Feeder, Okl Cty, av cwt	u123.38	sp	122.125	111.94
Sugar, cane, raw, world, lb. fob	14.97	sp	15.08	10.02

Fats and Oils

	TUE	TUE	MON	YEAR AGO
Corn Oil, crd wet/dry mill	u-s25.5	26.5	26	27.25
Grease, choice white, Chgo lb.	n.17	sp	a.17	.16625
Lard, Chgo lb.	u.1725	sp	.1725	.26
Soybean Oil, crd, Central Ill. Lb.	u.2055	.2105	.2077	.21535
Tallow, bleachable, Chgo lb.	n.165	sp	.165	.1675
Tallow, edible, Chgo lb.	u.19	sp	.19	.175

	TUE	MON	YEAR AGO
Fibers and Textiles			
Burlap, 10 oz 40-in NY yd	nw.4375	.4375	.4125
Cotton, 1 1/16 str lw-md Mphs lb	.5119	.5116	.4138
Wool, 64s Staple, Terr. Del. Lb.	uw1.4	1.4	2.15
Miscellaneous			
Hides, hvy native steers lb., fob	u78.5-80.5	77.5-80.5	82

Precious Metals

Gold, troy oz.	TUE	MON	YEAR AGO
Engelhard indus bullion	524.04	538.06	438.49
Engelhard fabric prods	563.34	578.42	471.38
Handy & Harman base price	522.50	536.50	437.10

Complete futures prices and futures options data can be found at wsj.com/free

	TUE	WED	YEAR AGO
Handy & Harman fabric price	564.30	579.42	472.07
London fixing AM 522.80 PM	522.50	536.50	437.10
Krugerrand, whol	ae526.80	533.70	442.25
Maple Leaf, troy oz.	ae542.67	549.85	458.06
American Eagle, troy oz.	ae542.67	549.85	458.06
Platinum, (Free Mkt.)	995.00	1004.00	833.00
Platinum, indust (Engelhard)	998.00	1019.00	833.00
Platinum, fabrc prd (Engelhard)	1098.00	1119.00	933.00
Palladium, indust (Engelhard)	274.00	295.00	190.00
Palladium, fabrc prd (Engelhard)	374.00	395.00	290.00
Silver, troy oz.			
Engelhard indust bullion	8.580	9.170	6.770
Engelhard fabric prods	10.296	11.004	7.989
Handy & Harman base price	8.500	9.110	6.755
Handy & Harman fabric price	10.200	10.932	7.971
London Fixing (in pounds)			
Spot (U.S. equiv. $8.7400)	4.9447	5.2296	3.5106
Coins, whol $1,000 face val	a6,053	6,214	4,845

Metals

	TUE	WED	YEAR AGO
Aluminum Comex lb.	1.037	1.022	0.874
Antimony, RN Spot, $/lb.	d1.85-87	1.85-87	1.38
Copper, high gr lb., Cmx sp price	2.173	2.1555	1.444
Lead, RN NA Solder, cts./lb.	d75.218	75.218	64.663
St. Steel Scrap, US, $/gross ton	d1245	1245	1550
Tin, RN NA Solder, cts./lb.	d457.811	459.344	567.134
Zinc, RN NA Dealer, cts./lb.	d86.031	87.097	55.459

a-Asked. b-Bid. bp-Country elevator bids to producers. c-Corrected. d-Ryan's Notes h-Reuters. e-Manfra, Tordella & Brookes, Inc. n-Nominal. na-Not available. r-Rail bids. s-high price = asked, low price = bid. u-U.S. Dept. of Agriculture. w-weekly price. x-Less than truckloads. z-Not quoted. xx-f.o.b tankcars. sp-Single price.

Oil Prices

December 13, 2005

CRUDE GRADES	TUE	MON	YR AGO
Offshore-d			
European "spot" or free market prices			
Forties	59.65	58.22	38.35
Brent	58.85	57.42	37.25
Bonny lt.	59.55	58.12	36.15
Urals-Medit.	55.85	54.27	32.45
Domestic-f			
Spot market			
W. Tex. Int Cush (5550-6082) (Jan)	61.38	61.31	41.83
W. Tex.sour, Midl (5048-5543)	56.08	56.01	38.08
LA sweet St.James (5675-6050)	61.78	61.51	41.83
Al. No. Slope Pacific Del.	59.22	c59.15	35.09

Open-Market crude oil values in Northwest Europe around 17:50 GMT in dlrs per barrel, for main loading ports in country of origin for prompt loading, except as indicated.

Refined Products

	TUE	WED	YEAR AGO
Fuel Oil, No. 2 NY gal.	1.7740	1.7098	1.2733
Diesel Fuel, 0.05 S. NY harbor low sulfur	1.8003	1.7338	1.3033
Gasoline, unlded, premium NY gal. non-oxygenated	1.7734	1.7743	1.0905
Gasoline, unlded, premium NY gal. Oxygenated	1.7822	1.7843	1.0855
Gasoline, unlded, reg. NY gal. non-oxygenated	1.6547	1.6468	1.0568
Gasoline, unlded, reg. NY gal. Oxygenated	1.6209	1.6168	1.0568
Gasoline, CARBOB, reg. LA gal.	m1.6550	1.5750	1.1700
Propane, non-tet, Mont Belviue, Texas, gal.	1.1488	1.0850	.7450
Propane, wet-tet, Mont Belvieu, Texas, gal.	1.1475	1.0863	.7625
Butane, normal, Mont Belvieu, Texas, gal.	1.3675	1.3238	.9050

Raw Products

	TUE	WED	YEAR AGO
Natural gas Henry Hub, $ per mmbtu	15.410	14.800	6.840

a-Asked. b-Bid. c-Corrected. d-As of 11 a.m. ET in Northwest Europe. f-As of 4 p.m. ET. Refiners' posted buying prices are in parentheses. m-Midday price. na-Not available. z-Not quoted. n-Nominal. r-Revised. Source: Dow Jones Energy Service

CASH-FUTURES ARBITRAGE

Intuitively, you might think that the cash price of a commodity is closely related to its futures price. If you do, then your intuition is quite correct. In fact, your intuition is backed up by strong economic argument and more than a century of experience observing the simultaneous operation of cash and futures markets.

As a routine matter, cash and futures prices are closely watched by market profession-als. To understand why, suppose you notice that spot gold is trading for $400 per ounce while the two-month futures price is $450 per ounce. Do you see a profit opportunity?

You should, because buying spot gold today at $400 per ounce while simultaneously selling gold futures at $450 per ounce locks in a $50 per ounce profit. True, gold has stor-age costs (you have to put it somewhere), and a spot gold purchase ties up capital that could be earning interest. However, these costs are small relative to the $50 per ounce gross profit, which is $50 / $400 = 12.5% per two months, or about 100 percent per year (with compounding). Furthermore, this profit is risk-free! Alas, in reality, such easy profit oppor-tunities are the stuff of dreams.

Earning risk-free profits from an unusual difference between cash and futures prices is called **cash-futures arbitrage**. In a competitive market, cash-futures arbitrage has very slim profit margins. In fact, the profit margins are almost imperceptible when they exist at all.

Comparing cash prices for commodities in Figure 14.2 with their corresponding futures prices reported in Figure 14.1, you will find that cash prices and futures prices are seldom equal. In futures jargon, the difference between a cash price and a futures price is called **basis**.[1]

For commodities with storage costs, the cash price is usually less than the futures price. This is referred to as a **carrying-charge market**. Sometimes, however, the cash price is greater than the futures price, and this is referred to as an **inverted market**. We can sum-marize this discussion of carrying-charge markets, inverted markets, and basis as follows:

Carrying-charge market: Basis = Cash price − Futures price < 0   (14.1)
Inverted market: Basis = Cash price − Futures price > 0

A variety of factors can lead to an economically justifiable difference between a com-modity's cash price and its futures price, including availability of storage facilities, trans-portation costs, and seasonal price fluctuations. However, the primary determinants of the cash-futures basis are storage costs and interest costs. Storage cost is the cost of holding the commodity in a storage facility, and interest cost refers to interest income forgone on funds used to buy and hold the commodity.

If a futures price rises far enough above a cash price to more than cover storage costs and interest expense, commodity traders will undertake cash-futures arbitrage by buying in the cash market and selling in the futures market. This drives down the futures price and drives up the cash price until the basis is restored to an economically justifiable level.

Similarly, if a futures price falls far enough relative to a cash price, traders will under-take cash-futures arbitrage by short selling in the cash market and buying in the futures market. This drives down the cash price and drives up the futures price until an economi-cally justifiable basis is restored. In both cases, arbitrage ensures that the basis is kept at an economically appropriate level.

SPOT-FUTURES PARITY

We can be slightly more precise in illustrating the relationship between spot and futures prices for financial futures. Consider the example of futures contracts for shares of stock in a single company. One place such futures contracts are traded in the United States is OneChicago, a joint venture of the major Chicago exchanges. Single-stock futures con-tracts have a standard contract size of 100 shares of the underlying stock, but futures prices are quoted on a per-share basis.

Suppose we are examining a particular single-stock futures contract that calls for deliv-ery of 100 shares of stock in one year. The current (i.e., cash or spot) stock price is $50 per

cash-futures arbitrage
Strategy for earning risk-free profits from an unusual difference between cash and futures prices.

basis
The difference between the cash price and the futures price for a com-modity, i.e., basis = cash price − futures price.

carrying-charge market
The case where the fu-tures price is greater than the cash price; i.e., the basis is negative.

inverted market
The case where the fu-tures price is less than the cash price; i.e., the basis is positive.

For more information on single-stock futures trading visit www.onechicago.com and the Futures Source Web site at www.futuresource.com

[1]The official Commodity Trading Manual of the Chicago Board of Trade defines basis as the difference between the cash and the futures price, i.e., basis = cash price − futures price. We will be consistent with the CBOT definition. For nonagricultural futures, however, the basis is nearly always defined as the futures price minus the cash price.

share, and the stock does not pay dividends. Also, 12-month T-bills are yielding 6 percent. What should the futures price be? To answer, notice that you can buy 100 shares of stock for $50 per share, or $5,000 total. You can eliminate all of the risk associated with this purchase by selling one futures contract. The net effect of this transaction is that you have created a risk-free asset. Because the risk-free rate is 6 percent, your investment must have a future value of $5,000 × 1.06 = $5,300. In other words, the futures price should be $53 per share.

Suppose the futures price is, in fact, $52 per share. What would you do? To make money, you would short 100 shares of stock at $50 per share and invest the $5,000 proceeds at 6 percent.[2] Simultaneously, you would buy one futures contract.

At the end of the year, you would have $5,300. You would use $5,200 to buy the stock to fulfill your obligation on the futures contract and then return the stock to close out the short position. You pocket $100. This is just another example of cash-futures arbitrage.

More generally, if we let F be the futures price, S be the spot price, and r be the risk-free rate, then our example illustrates that:

$$F = S(1 + r) \qquad (14.2)$$

spot-futures parity
The relationship between spot prices and futures prices that holds in the absence of arbitrage opportunities.

In other words, the futures price is simply the future value of the spot price, calculated at the risk-free rate. This is the famous **spot-futures parity** condition. This condition must hold in the absence of cash-futures arbitrage opportunities.

More generally, if r is the risk-free rate per period, and the futures contract matures in T periods, then the spot-futures parity condition is:

$$F_T = S(1 + r)^T \qquad (14.3)$$

Notice that T could be a fraction of one period. For example, if we have the risk-free rate per year, but the futures contract matures in six months, T would be 1/2.

EXAMPLE 14.7 | **Parity Check**

A non–dividend-paying stock has a current price of $12 per share. The risk-free rate is 4 percent per year. If a futures contract on the stock matures in three months, what should the futures price be?
From our spot-futures parity condition, we have:

$$F_T = S(1 + r)^T$$
$$= \$12(1.04)^{1/4}$$
$$= \$12.12$$

The futures price should be $12.12. Notice that r and T are expressed in years for this example. Therefore, we set $r = .04$ and $T = 1/4$.

MORE ON SPOT-FUTURES PARITY

In our spot-futures parity example just above, we assumed that the underlying financial instrument (the stock) had no cash flows (no dividends). If there are dividends (for a stock future) or coupon payments (for a bond future), then we need to modify our spot-futures parity condition.

---

[2]For the sake of simplicity, we ignore the fact that individual investors do not earn interest on the proceeds from a short sale, and we assume the stock does not pay dividends.

For a stock, we let D stand for the dividend, and we assume that the dividend is paid in one period, at or near the end of the futures contract's life. In this case, the spot-futures parity condition becomes:

$$F = S(1+r) - D \qquad (14.4)$$

Notice that we have simply subtracted the amount of the dividend from the future value of the stock price. The reason is that if you buy the futures contract, you will not receive the dividend, but the dividend payment will reduce the stock price.

An alternative, and very useful, way of writing the dividend-adjusted spot-futures parity result in Equation 14.4 is to define d as the dividend yield on the stock. Recall that the dividend yield is just the upcoming dividend divided by the current price. In our current notation, this is just $d = D/S$. With this in mind, we can write the dividend-adjusted parity result as:

$$\begin{aligned} F &= S(1+r) - D(S/S) \qquad (14.5) \\ &= S(1+r) - S(D/S) \\ &= S(1+r) - Sd \\ &= S(1+r-d) \end{aligned}$$

Finally, as above, if there is something other than a single period involved, we would write:

$$F_T = S(1+r-d)^T \qquad (14.6)$$

where T is the number of periods (or fraction of a period), and r is the interest rate per period.

For example, suppose there is a futures contract on a stock with a current price of \$80. The futures contract matures in six months. The risk-free rate is 7 percent per year, and the stock has an annual dividend yield of 3 percent. What should the futures price be?

Plugging in the values to our dividend-adjusted parity equation, we have:

$$\begin{aligned} F_T &= S(1+r-d)^T \\ &= \$80(1 + .07 - .03)^{1/2} \\ &= \$81.58 \end{aligned}$$

Notice that we set T equal to 1/2 because the contract matures in six months.

CHECK THIS

14.4a What is the spot price for a commodity?

14.4b With regard to futures contracts, what is the basis?

14.4c What is an inverted market?

14.4d What is the spot-futures parity condition?

14.5 Stock Index Futures

There are a number of futures contracts on stock market indexes. Because these contracts are particularly important, we devote this entire section to them. We first describe the contracts and then discuss some trading and hedging strategies involving their use.

BASICS OF STOCK INDEX FUTURES

Locate the section labeled "Index Futures" in Figure 14.1. Here we see various stock index futures contracts. The third contract listed, on the S&P 500 index, is the most important.

With this contract, actual delivery would be very difficult or impossible because the seller of the contract would have to buy all 500 stocks in exactly the right proportions to deliver. Clearly, this is not practical, so this contract features cash settlement.

To understand how stock index futures work, suppose you bought one S&P 500 contract at a futures price of 1,250. The contract size is $250 times the level of the index. What this means is that, at maturity, the buyer of the contract will pay the seller $250 times the difference between the futures price of 1,250 and the level of the S&P 500 index at contract maturity.

For example, suppose that at maturity the S&P had actually fallen to 1,220. In this case, the buyer of the contract must pay $250 × (1,250 − 1,220) = $7,500 to the seller of the contract. In effect, the buyer of the contract has agreed to purchase 250 "units" of the index at a price of $1,250 per unit. If the index is below 1,250, the buyer will lose money. If the index is above that, then the seller will lose money.

For information on stock index futures visit the CBOT Web site at www.cbot.com

---

EXAMPLE 14.8   Index Futures

Suppose you are convinced that the Dow stocks are going to skyrocket in value. Consequently, you buy 20 DJIA futures contracts maturing in six months at a price of 10,500. Suppose that the Dow Jones index is at 10,920 when the contracts mature. How much will you make or lose?

The futures price is 10,500, and the contract size is $10 times the level of the index. At maturity, if the index is at 10,920, you make $10 × (10,920 − 10,500) = $4,200 per contract. With 20 contracts, your total profit is $84,000.

INDEX ARBITRAGE

index arbitrage
Strategy of monitoring the futures price on a stock index and the level of the underlying index to exploit deviations from parity.

The spot-futures parity relation we developed above is the basis for a common trading strategy known as **index arbitrage**. Index arbitrage refers to monitoring the futures price on a stock index along with the level of the underlying index. The trader looks for violations of parity and trades as appropriate.

For example, suppose the S&P 500 futures price for delivery in one year is 1,540. The current level is 1,500. The dividend yield on the S&P is projected to be 3 percent per year, and the risk-free rate is 5 percent. Is there a trading opportunity here?

From our dividend-adjusted parity equation (14.6), the futures price should be:

$$F_T = S(1 + r - d)^T$$
$$= 1,500(1 + .05 - .03)^1$$
$$= 1,530$$

Thus, based on our parity calculation, the futures price is too high. We want to buy low, sell high, so we buy the index and simultaneously sell the futures contract.

program trading
Computer-assisted monitoring of relative prices of financial assets; it sometimes includes computer submission of buy and sell orders to exploit perceived arbitrage opportunities.

Index arbitrage is often implemented as a **program trading** strategy. While this term covers a lot of ground, it generally refers to the monitoring of relative prices by computer to more quickly spot opportunities. In some cases it includes submitting the needed buy and sell orders using a computer to speed up the process.

Whether a computer is used in program trading is not really the issue; instead, a program trading strategy is any coordinated, systematic procedure for exploiting (or trying to exploit) violations of parity or other arbitrage opportunities. Such a procedure is a trading "program" in the sense that whenever certain conditions exist, certain trades are made. Thus, the process is sufficiently mechanical that it can be automated, at least in principle.

Technically, the NYSE defines program trading as the simultaneous purchase or sale of at least 15 different stocks with a total value of $1 million or more. Program trading can account for up to half the total trading volume on the NYSE, and about 10 percent of all program trading involves stock-index arbitrage.

There was another phenomenon often associated with index arbitrage and, more generally, futures and options trading. S&P 500 futures contracts have four expiration months per year, and they expire on the third Friday of those months. On these same four Fridays, options on the S&P index and various individual stock options also expired. These Fridays were dubbed the "triple witching hour" because all three types of contracts expired, sometimes leading to unusual price behavior.

In particular, on triple witching hour Fridays, all positions must be liquidated, or "unwound." To the extent that large-scale index arbitrage and other program trading has taken place, enormous buying or selling sometimes occurs late in the day on such Fridays, as positions are closed out. Large price swings and, more generally, increased volatility are often seen. To curtail this problem, the exchanges have adopted rules regarding the size of a position that can be carried to expiration. In addition, options on the S&P 500 index now expire on Friday morning.

www

For information on program trading, visit www.programtrading .com

HEDGING STOCK MARKET RISK WITH FUTURES

We earlier discussed hedging using futures contracts in the context of a business protecting the value of its inventory. We now discuss some hedging strategies available to portfolio managers based on financial futures. Essentially, an investment portfolio is an inventory of securities, and financial futures can be used to reduce the risk of holding a securities portfolio.

We consider the specific problem of an equity portfolio manager wishing to protect the value of a stock portfolio from the risk of an adverse movement of the overall stock market. Here, the portfolio manager wishes to establish a short hedge position to reduce risk and must determine the number of futures contracts required to properly hedge a portfolio.

In this hedging example, you are responsible for managing a broadly diversified stock portfolio with a current value of $160 million. Analysis of market conditions leads you to believe that the stock market is unusually susceptible to a price decline during the next few months. Of course, nothing is certain regarding stock market fluctuations, but still you are sufficiently concerned to believe that action is required.

A fundamental problem exists for you, however, in that no futures contract exactly matches your particular portfolio. As a result, you decide to protect your stock portfolio from a fall in value caused by a falling stock market using stock index futures. This is an example of a **cross-hedge**, where a futures contract on a related, but not identical, commodity or financial instrument is used to hedge a particular spot position.

Thus, to hedge your portfolio, you wish to establish a short hedge using stock index futures. To do this, you need to know how many index futures contracts are required to form an effective hedge. Three basic inputs are needed to calculate the number of stock index futures contracts required to hedge a stock portfolio:

cross-hedge

Hedging a particular spot position with futures contracts on a related, but not identical, commodity or financial instrument.

1. The current value of your stock portfolio.
2. The beta of your stock portfolio.
3. The contract value of the index futures contract used for hedging.

Based on previous chapters, you are familiar with the concept of beta as a measure of market risk for a stock portfolio. Essentially, beta measures portfolio risk relative to the overall stock market. We will assume that you have maintained a beta of 1.25 for your $160 million stock portfolio.

You believe that the market (and your portfolio) will fall in value over the next three months and you decide to eliminate market risk from your portfolio. That is, you would like to convert your risky portfolio with a beta of 1.25 to a riskless portfolio with a beta of zero. Because you hold a stock portfolio, you know that you will need to establish a short hedge using futures contracts. You decide to use futures contracts on the S&P 500 index, because this is the index you used to calculate the beta for your portfolio.

From *The Wall Street Journal,* you find that the S&P 500 futures price for contracts that mature in three months is currently 1,280. Because the contract size for the S&P 500 futures is 250 times the index level, the current value of a single S&P 500 index futures contract is $250 \times 1,280 = \$320,000$.

You now have all the information you need to calculate the number of S&P 500 index futures contracts needed to hedge your $160 million stock portfolio. The number of stock index futures contracts needed to convert the beta of your portfolio from 1.25 to zero is determined by the following formula:

$$\text{Number of contracts} = (\beta_D - \beta_P) \times \frac{V_P}{V_F} \qquad (14.7)$$

where: β_D = Desired beta of the stock portfolio
β_P = Current beta of the stock portfolio
V_P = Value of the stock portfolio
V_F = Value of one stock index futures contract

For your particular hedging problem, $\beta_D = 0$, $\beta_P = 1.25$, $V_P = \$160$ million, and $V_F = \$320,000$, thereby yielding this calculation:

$$\text{Number of contracts} = (0 - 1.25) \times \frac{160,000,000}{320,000} = -625$$

Thus, you can establish an effective short hedge by going short 625 S&P 500 index futures contracts. This short hedge will protect your stock portfolio against the risk of a general fall in the stock market during the remaining three-month life of the futures contract.

Equation 14.7 reinforces the notion that you want to go short futures contracts to lower the beta of your portfolio. The negative number of contracts is a reminder that you are trying to shed risk, which calls for a short position in the S&P 500 index futures market.

You can see that Equation 14.7 can also be used to change the beta of your portfolio to any level you want. However, any level other than zero is not considered a hedge, because your portfolio will still retain some systematic risk.

EXAMPLE 14.9 **Hedging with Stock Index Futures**

How many stock index futures contracts are required to hedge a $250 million stock portfolio, assuming a portfolio beta of .75 and an S&P 500 index futures level of 1,500?

Using Equation 14.7 and the knowledge that a true hedge reduces the portfolio beta to zero, we have:

$$\text{Number of contracts} = (0 - .75) \times \frac{250,000,000}{375,000} = -500$$

Therefore, you need to short 500 stock index futures contracts to hedge this $250 million portfolio. In this example, note that the value of one futures contract is given by $250 \times 1,500 = \$375,000$.

HEDGING INTEREST RATE RISK WITH FUTURES

Having discussed hedging a stock portfolio, we now turn to hedging a bond portfolio. As we will see, the bond portfolio hedging problem is similar to the stock portfolio hedging problem. Once again, we will be cross-hedging, but this time using futures contracts on U.S. Treasury notes. Here, our goal is to protect the bond portfolio against changing interest rates.

In this example, you are responsible for managing a bond portfolio with a current value of $100 million. Recently, rising interest rates have caused your portfolio to fall in value slightly, and you are concerned that interest rates may continue to trend upward for the next several months. You decide to establish a short hedge based on 10-year Treasury note futures.

The formula for the number of U.S. Treasury note futures contracts needed to hedge a bond portfolio is:

$$\text{Number of contracts} = \frac{D_P \times V_P}{D_F \times V_F} \tag{14.8}$$

where: D_p = Duration of the bond portfolio
V_P = Value of the bond portfolio
D_F = Duration of the futures contract
V_F = Value of a single futures contract

We already know the value of the bond portfolio, which is $100 million. Also, suppose that the duration of the portfolio is given as eight years. Next, we must calculate the duration of the futures contract and the value of the futures contract.

As a useful rule of thumb, the duration of an interest rate futures contract is equal to the duration of the underlying instrument plus the time remaining until contract maturity:

$$D_F = D_U + M_F \tag{14.9}$$

where: D_F = Duration of the futures contract
D_U = Duration of the underlying instrument
M_F = Time remaining until contract maturity

For simplicity, let us suppose that the duration of the underlying U.S. Treasury note is 6 1/2 years and the futures contract has a maturity of 1/2 year, yielding a futures contract duration of 7 years.

The value of a single futures contract is the current futures price times the futures contract size. The standard contract size for U.S. Treasury note futures contracts is $100,000 par value. Now suppose that the futures price is 98, or 98 percent of par value. This yields a futures contract value of $100,000 \times .98 = $98,000.

You now have all inputs required to calculate the number of futures contracts needed to hedge your bond portfolio. The number of U.S. Treasury note futures contracts needed to hedge the bond portfolio is calculated as follows:

$$\text{Number of contracts} = \frac{8 \times \$100,000,000}{7 \times \$98,000} = 1,166$$

Thus, you can establish an effective short hedge by going short 1,166 futures contracts for 10-year U.S. Treasury notes. This short hedge will protect your bond portfolio against the risk of a general rise in interest rates during the life of the futures contracts.

EXAMPLE 14.10   **Hedging with U.S. Treasury Note Futures**

How many futures contracts are required to hedge a $250 million bond portfolio with a portfolio duration of 5 years using 10-year U.S. Treasury note futures with a duration of 7.5 years and a futures price of 105?

Using the formula for the number of contracts, we have:

$$\text{Number of contracts} = \frac{5 \times \$250,000,000}{7.5 \times \$105,000} = 1,587$$

You therefore need to sell 1,587 contracts to hedge this $250 million portfolio.

FUTURES CONTRACT DELIVERY OPTIONS

cheapest-to-deliver option
Seller's option to deliver the cheapest instrument when a futures contract allows several instruments for delivery. For example, U.S. Treasury note futures allow delivery of any Treasury note with a maturity between 6 1/2 and 10 years.

Many futures contracts have a delivery option, whereby the seller can choose among several different "grades" of the underlying commodity or instrument when fulfilling delivery requirements. Naturally, we expect the seller to deliver the cheapest among available options. In futures jargon, this is called the **cheapest-to-deliver option**. The cheapest-to-deliver option is an example of a broader feature of many futures contracts, known as a "quality" option. Of course, futures buyers know about the delivery option, and therefore the futures prices reflect the value of the cheapest-to-deliver instrument.

As a specific example of a cheapest-to-deliver option, the 10-year Treasury note contract allows delivery of *any* Treasury note with a maturity between 6 1/2 and 10 years. This complicates the bond portfolio hedging problem. For the portfolio manager trying to hedge a bond portfolio with U.S. Treasury note futures, the cheapest-to-deliver feature means that a note can be hedged only based on an assumption about which note will actually be delivered. Furthermore, through time the cheapest-to-deliver note may vary, and, consequently, the hedge will have to be monitored regularly to make sure that it correctly reflects the note issue that is most likely to be delivered. Fortunately, because this is a common problem, many commercial advisory services provide this information to portfolio managers and other investors.

CHECK THIS

14.5a   What is a cross-hedge?

14.5b   What are the three basic inputs required to calculate the number of stock index futures contracts needed to hedge an equity portfolio?

14.5c   What are the basic inputs required to calculate the number of U.S. Treasury note futures contracts needed to hedge a bond portfolio?

14.5d   What is the cheapest-to-deliver option?

14.6   Summary and Conclusions

This chapter surveyed the basics of futures contracts. In it, we saw that:

1. A forward contract is an agreement between a buyer and a seller for a future commodity transaction at a price set today. Futures contracts are a step beyond forward contracts. Futures contracts and forward contracts accomplish the same task, but a

This chapter covered the essentials of what many consider to be a complex subject, futures contracts. We hope you realize that futures contracts per se are not complicated at all; in fact, they are, for the most part, quite simple. This doesn't mean that they're for everybody, of course. Because of the tremendous leverage possible, very large gains and losses can (and do) occur with great speed.

To experience some of the gains and losses from outright speculation, you should buy and sell a variety of contracts in a simulated brokerage account such as Stock-Trak. Be sure to go both long and short and pick a few of each major type of contract.

The Internet offers a rich source for more information on trading futures. Probably the best place to begin is by visiting the Web sites of the major futures exchanges: the Chicago Board of Trade (www.cbot.com), the Chicago Mercantile Exchange (www.cme.com), the New York Mercantile Exchange (www.nymex.com), and the Kansas City Board of Trade (www.kcbt.com). You might also visit the Web sites of some major international futures exchanges: the London International Financial Futures Exchange (www.liffe.com), Sydney Futures Exchange (www.sfe.com.au), Tokyo International Financial Futures Exchange (www.tfx.co.jp/en), and the Singapore Exchange (www.ses.com.sg). The reference section of Numa's Web site (www.numa.com) maintains an extensive list of the world's futures exchanges.

For information on futures markets regulation, the federal agency charged with regulating U.S. futures markets is the Commodities Futures Trading Commission (www.cftc.gov). The professional organization charged with self-regulation is the National Futures Association (www.nfa.futures.org). General information on futures markets and trading can be found at the Futures Industry Association (www.futuresindustry.org).

Useful Web sites on trading futures are Futures Trading (www.futures-trading.org), Commodity Traders Club (www.ctcn.com), Daily Futures (www.dailyfutures.com), and Trading Markets (www.tradingmarkets.com). For a very large list of links to anything and everything related to futures, visit the commodities and futures section of Investor Links (www.investorlinks.com).

forward contract can be struck between any two parties, while standardized futures contracts are managed through organized futures exchanges.

2. Commodity futures call for delivery of a physical commodity. Financial futures require delivery of a financial instrument or, in some cases, cash. Futures contracts are a type of derivative security, because the value of the contract is derived from the value of an underlying instrument.

3. Hedging is the major economic reason for the existence of futures markets. However, a viable futures market requires participation by both hedgers and speculators. Hedgers transfer price risk to speculators, and speculators absorb price risk. Hedging and speculating are thus complementary activities.

4. Futures trading accounts have three essential features: margin is required, futures accounts are marked to market daily, and a futures position can be closed out any time by a reverse trade.

5. The cash price of a commodity or financial instrument is the price quoted for current delivery. The cash price is also called the spot price.

6. The difference between a cash price and a futures price is called basis. For commodities with storage costs, the cash price is usually less than the futures price. This is referred to as a carrying-charge market. Sometimes the cash price is greater than the futures price, and this case is referred to as an inverted market.

7. There is a simple relationship between cash and futures prices known as spot-futures parity. Violations of parity give rise to arbitrage opportunities, including index arbitrage, which involves stock index futures.

8. Cross-hedging refers to using futures contracts on a related commodity or instrument to hedge a particular spot position. Stock index futures, for example, can be used to hedge an equities portfolio against general declines in stock prices, and U.S. Treasury note futures can be used to hedge a bond portfolio.

Key Terms

basis 462
carrying-charge market 462
cash-futures arbitrage 462
cash market 460
cash price 460
cheapest-to-deliver option 469
cross-hedge 466
forward contract 449
futures contract 449
futures margin 459
futures price 449
hedger 457
index arbitrage 465

initial margin 459
inverted market 462
long hedge 457
long position 456
maintenance margin 459
margin call 459
marking-to-market 459
program trading 465
reverse trade 459
short hedge 457
short position 456
speculator 456
spot-futures parity 463

Chapter Review Problems and Self-Test

1. **Futures Gains and Losses**   Suppose you purchase 10 orange juice contracts today at the settle price of $1 per pound. How much do these 10 contracts cost you? If the settle price is lower tomorrow by 2 cents per pound, how much do you make or lose? The contract size is 15,000 pounds.

2. **Spot-Futures Parity**   There is a futures contract on a stock, which is currently selling at $200 per share. The contract matures in two months; the risk-free rate is 5 percent annually. The current dividend yield on the stock is 0 percent. What does the parity relationship imply the futures price should be?

Answers to Self-Test Problems

1. If you go long (purchase) 10 contracts, you pay nothing today (you will be required to post margin, but a futures contract is an agreement to exchange cash for goods later, not today). If the settle price drops by 2 cents per pound, you lose 15,000 pounds (the contract size) × $.02 = $300 per contract. With 10 contracts, you lose $3,000.

2. The spot-futures parity condition is:

$$F_T = S(1 + r - d)^T$$

where S is the spot price, r is the risk-free rate, d is the dividend yield, F is the futures price, and T is the time to expiration measured in years.

Plugging in the numbers we have, with zero for the dividend yield and 1/6 for the number of years (2 months out of 12), gets us:

$$F_{1/6} = \$200(1 + .05)^{1/6} = \$201.63$$

Test Your Investment Quotient

1. **Futures Exchanges** Which of the following is the oldest and currently the most active futures exchange in the United States?
   a. Kansas City Board of Trade (KBOT)
   b. Chicago Mercantile Exchange (CME)
   c. New York Mercantile Exchange (NYMX)
   d. Chicago Board of Trade (CBOT)

2. **Futures Exchanges** The first financial futures contracts, introduced in 1972, were
   a. Currency futures at the CME
   b. Interest rate futures at the CBOT
   c. Stock index futures at the KBOT
   d. Wheat futures at the CBOT

3. **Futures Exchanges** Which of the following futures exchanges trades futures contracts on common stocks?
   a. OneBoston
   b. OneChicago
   c. FutureRama
   d. Niffe-Quorum

4. **Futures versus Forward Contracts** Which of the following statements is true regarding the distinction between futures contracts and forward contracts?
   a. Futures contracts are exchange-traded, whereas forward contracts are OTC-traded.
   b. All else equal, forward prices are higher than futures prices.
   c. Forward contracts are created from baskets of futures contracts.
   d. Futures contracts are cash-settled at maturity, whereas forward contracts result in delivery.

5. **Futures versus Forward Contracts** In which of the following ways do futures contracts differ from forward contracts?
   I. Futures contracts are standardized.
   II. For futures, performance of each party is guaranteed by a clearinghouse.
   III. Futures contracts require a daily settling of any gains or losses.
      a. I and II only
      b. I and III only
      c. II and III only
      d. I, II, and III

6. **Futures Contracts** The open interest on a futures contract at any given time is the total number of outstanding
   a. Contracts
   b. Unhedged positions
   c. Clearinghouse positions
   d. Long and short positions

7. **Futures Margin** Initial margin for a futures contract is usually
   a. Regulated by the Federal Reserve.
   b. Less than 2 percent of contract value.
   c. In the range between 2 percent and 5 percent of contract value.
   d. In the range between 5 percent and 15 percent of contract value.

8. **Futures Margin**   In futures trading, the minimum level to which an equity position may fall before requiring additional margin is *most accurately* termed the

   a. Initial margin
   b. Variation margin
   c. Cash flow margin
   d. Maintenance margin

9. **Futures Margin**   A silver futures contract requires the seller to deliver 5,000 troy ounces of silver. An investor sells one July silver futures contract at a price of $8 per ounce, posting a $2,025 initial margin. If the required maintenance margin is $1,500, the price per ounce at which the investor would first receive a maintenance margin call is closest to

   a. $5.92
   b. $7.89
   c. $8.11
   d. $10.80

10. **Futures Margin**   Which of the following statements is false about futures account margin?

   a. Initial margin is higher than maintenance margin.
   b. A margin call results when account margin falls below maintenance margin.
   c. Marking-to-market of account margin occurs daily.
   d. A margin call results when account margin falls below initial margin.

11. **Futures Contracts**   Which of the following contract terms changes daily during the life of a futures contract?

   a. Futures price
   b. Futures contract size
   c. Futures maturity date
   d. Underlying commodity

12. **Futures Trading Accounts**   Which of the following is perhaps the least essential thing to know about a futures trading account?

   a. Margin is required.
   b. Futures accounts are marked-to-market daily.
   c. A futures position can be closed by a reverse trade.
   d. A commission is charged for each trade.

13. **Futures Delivery**   On the maturity date, stock index futures contracts require delivery of

   a. Common stock
   b. Common stock plus accrued dividends
   c. Treasury bills
   d. Cash

14. **Futures Delivery**   On the maturity date, Treasury note futures contracts require delivery of

   a. Treasury notes plus accrued coupons over the life of the futures contract
   b. Treasury notes
   c. Treasury bills
   d. Cash

15. **Spot-Futures Parity**   A Treasury bond futures contract has a quoted price of 100. The underlying bond has a coupon rate of 7 percent, and the current market interest rate is 7 percent. Spot-futures parity then implies a cash bond price of

   a. 93
   b. 100
   c. 107
   d. 114

16. **Spot-Futures Parity**   A stock index futures contract maturing in one year has a currently traded price of $1,000. The cash index has a dividend yield of 2 percent, and the interest rate is 5 percent. Spot-futures parity then implies a cash index level of

    a. $933.33
    b. $970.87
    c. $1,071
    d. $1,029

17. **Spot-Futures Parity**   A stock index futures contract matures in one year. The cash index currently has a level of $1,000 with a dividend yield of 2 percent. If the interest rate is 5 percent, then spot-futures parity implies a futures price of

    a. $943.40
    b. $970.87
    c. $1,060
    d. $1,030

18. **Futures Hedging**   You manage a $100 million stock portfolio with a beta of .8. Given a contract size of $100,000 for a stock index futures contract, how many contracts are needed to hedge your portfolio?

    a. 8
    b. 80
    c. 800
    d. 8,000

19. **Futures Hedging**   You manage a $100 million bond portfolio with a duration of 9 years. You wish to hedge this portfolio against interest rate risk using T-bond futures with a contract size of $100,000 and a duration of 12 years. How many contracts are required?

    a. 750
    b. 1,000
    c. 133
    d. 1,333

20. **Futures Hedging**   Which of the following is not an input needed to calculate the number of stock index futures contracts required to hedge a stock portfolio?

    a. The value of the stock portfolio.
    b. The beta of the stock portfolio.
    c. The contract value of the index futures contract.
    d. The initial margin required for each futures contract.

Concept Questions

1. **Understanding Futures Quotations**   Using Figure 14.1, answer the following questions:
    a. How many exchanges trade wheat futures contracts?
    b. If you have a position in 10 gold futures, what quantity of gold underlies your position?
    c. If you are short 20 oat futures contracts and you opt to make delivery, what quantity of oats must you supply?
    d. Which maturity of the unleaded gasoline contract has the largest open interest? Which one has the smallest open interest?

2. **Hedging with Futures**   Kellogg's uses large quantities of corn in its breakfast cereal operations. Suppose the near-term weather forecast for the corn-producing states is droughtlike conditions, so corn prices are expected to rise. To hedge its costs, Kellogg's decides to use the Chicago Board of Trade corn futures contracts. Should the company be a short hedger or a long hedger in corn futures?

3. **Hedging with Futures**   Suppose one of Fidelity's mutual funds closely mimics the S&P 500 index. The fund has done very well during the year, and, in November, the fund manager

wants to lock in the gains he has made using stock index futures. Should he take a long or short position in S&P 500 index futures?

4. **Hedging with Futures**   A mutual fund that predominantly holds long-term Treasury bonds plans on liquidating the portfolio in three months. However, the fund manager is concerned that interest rates may rise from current levels and wants to hedge the price risk of the portfolio. Should she buy or sell Treasury bond futures contracts?

5. **Hedging with Futures**   An American electronics firm imports its completed circuit boards from Japan. The company signed a contract today to pay for the boards in Japanese yen upon delivery in four months; the price per board in yen was fixed in the contract. Should the importer buy or sell Japanese yen futures contracts?

6. **Hedging with Futures**   Jed Clampett just dug another oil well, and, as usual, it's a gusher. Jed estimates that, in two months, he'll have 2 million barrels of crude oil to bring to market. However, Jed would like to lock in the value of this oil at today's prices, since the oil market has been skyrocketing recently. Should Jed buy or sell crude oil futures contracts?

7. **Hedging with Futures**   The town of South Park is planning a bond issue in six months and Kenny, the town treasurer, is worried that interest rates may rise, thereby reducing the value of the bond issue. Should Kenny buy or sell Treasury bond futures contracts to hedge the impending bond issue?

8. **Futures Markets**   Is it true that a futures contract represents a zero-sum game, meaning that the only way for a buyer to win is for a seller to lose, and vice versa?

9. **Program Trading**   Program traders closely monitor relative futures and cash market prices, but program trades are not actually made on a fully mechanical basis. What are some of the complications that might make program trading using, for example, the S&P 500 contract more difficult than the spot-futures parity formula indicates?

10. **Short Selling**   What are the similarities and differences in short selling a futures contract and short selling a stock? How do the cash flows differ?

Questions and Problems

Core Questions

1. **Understanding Futures Quotations**   Using Figure 14.1, answer the following questions:
   a. What was the settle price for March 2006 coffee futures on this date? What is the total dollar value of this contract at the close of trading for the day?
   b. What was the settle price for CBT December 2005 Treasury bond futures on this date? If you held 10 contracts, what is the total dollar value of your futures position?
   c. Suppose you held an open position of 25 March 2006 DJ Industrial Average futures on this day. What is the change in the total dollar value of your position for this day's trading? If you held a long position, would this represent a profit or a loss to you?
   d. Suppose you are short 10 January 2006 soybean oil futures contracts. Would you have made a profit or a loss on this day?

2. **Futures Profits and Losses**   You are long 20 March 2006 soybean futures contracts. Calculate your dollar profit or loss from this trading day using Figure 14.1.

3. **Futures Profits and Losses**   You are short 15 December 2005 corn futures contracts. Calculate your dollar profit or loss from this trading day using Figure 14.1.

4. **Futures Profits and Losses**   You are short 30 March 2006 five-year Treasury note futures contracts. Calculate your profit or loss from this trading day using Figure 14.1.

5. **Open Interest**   Referring to Figure 14.1, what is the total open interest on the December 2005 Japanese yen contract? Does it represent long positions, short positions, or both? Based on the settle price on the contract, what is the dollar value of the open interest?

6. **Spot-Futures Parity**   A non-dividend-paying stock is currently priced at $64.87. The risk-free rate is 5 percent, and a futures contract on the stock matures in four months. What price should the futures be?

7. **Spot-Futures Parity** A non-dividend-paying stock has a futures contract with a price of $87.62 and a maturity of three months. If the risk-free rate is 4.5 percent, what is the price of the stock?

8. **Spot-Futures Parity** A non-dividend-paying stock has a current share price of $32.17 and a futures price of $33.53. If the maturity of the futures contract is eight months, what is the risk-free rate?

9. **Spot-Futures Parity** A stock has a current share price of $74.13 and a dividend yield of 1.5 percent. If the risk-free rate is 5.4 percent, what is the futures price if the maturity is four months?

10. **Spot-Futures Parity** A stock futures contract is priced at $61.57. The stock has a dividend yield of 1.25 percent, and the risk-free rate is 6.1 percent. If the futures contract matures in six months, what is the current stock price?

Intermediate Questions

11. **Margin Call** Suppose the initial margin on heating oil futures is $1,500, the maintenance margin is $1,250 per contract, and you establish a long position of 10 contracts today, where each contract represents 42,000 gallons. Tomorrow, the contract settles down .02 from the previous day's price. Are you subject to a margin call? What is the maximum price decline on the contract that you can sustain without getting a margin call?

12. **Marking-to-Market** You are long 10 gold futures contracts, established at an initial settle price of $480 per ounce, where each contract represents 100 ounces. Your initial margin to establish the position is $1,000 per contract, and the maintenance margin is $750 per contract. Over the subsequent four trading days, gold settles at $473, $479, $482, and $486, respectively. Compute the balance in your margin account at the end of each of the four trading days, and compute your total profit or loss at the end of the trading period. Assume that a margin call requires you to fund your account back to the initial margin requirement.

13. **Marking-to-Market** You are short 25 gasoline futures contracts, established at an initial settle price of 1.52 per gallon, where each contract represents 42,000 gallons. Your initial margin to establish the position is $6,075 per contract, and the maintenance margin is $4,500 per contract. Over the subsequent four trading days, oil settles at $1.46, $1.55, $1.59, and $1.62, respectively. Compute the balance in your margin account at the end of each of the four trading days, and compute your total profit or loss at the end of the trading period. Assume that a margin call requires you to fund your account back to the initial margin requirement.

14. **Futures Profits** You went long 20 March 2006 crude oil futures contracts at a price of 58.75. Looking back at Figure 14.1, if you closed your position at the settle price on this day, what was your profit?

15. **Futures Profits** You shorted 15 March 2006 British pound futures contracts at the lifetime high of the contract. Looking back at Figure 14.1, if you closed your position at the settle price on this day, what was your profit?

16. **Index Arbitrage** Suppose the CAC-40 index (a widely followed index of French stock prices) is currently at 4,512, the expected dividend yield on the index is 2 percent per year, and the risk-free rate in France is 7 percent annually. If CAC-40 futures contracts that expire in six months are currently trading at 4,640, what program trading strategy would you recommend?

17. **Cross-Hedging** You have been assigned to implement a three-month hedge for a stock mutual fund portfolio that primarily invests in medium-sized companies. The mutual fund has a beta of 1.15 measured relative to the S&P Midcap 400, and the net asset value of the fund is $300 million. Should you be long or short in the Midcap 400 futures contracts? Assuming the Midcap 400 index is at 740 and its futures contract size is 500 times the index, determine the appropriate number of contracts to use in designing your cross-hedge strategy.

18. **Spot-Futures Parity** Suppose the 180-day S&P 500 futures price is 1,253.80, while the cash price is 1,231.21. What is the *implied difference* between the risk-free interest rate and the dividend yield on the S&P 500?

19. **Spot-Futures Parity** Suppose the 180-day S&P 500 futures price is 1,274.19, while the cash price is 1,243.71. What is the *implied dividend yield* on the S&P 500 if the risk-free interest rate is 7 percent?

20. **Hedging Interest Rate Risk**   Suppose you want to hedge a $900 million bond portfolio with a duration of 5.1 years using 10-year Treasury note futures with a duration of 8.5 years, a futures price of 103, and 3 months to expiration. The multiplier on Treasury note futures is $100,000. How many contracts do you buy or sell?

21. **Hedging Interest Rate Risk**   Suppose you want to hedge a $400 million bond portfolio with a duration of 11.2 years using 10-year Treasury note futures with a duration of 8 years, a futures price of 102, and 85 days to expiration. The multiplier on Treasury note futures is $100,000. How many contracts do you buy or sell?

22. **Futures Arbitrage**   A non-dividend-paying stock is currently priced at $87.12 per share. A futures contract maturing in five months has a price of $88.38 and the risk-free rate is 4 percent. Describe how you could make an arbitrage profit from this situation. How much could you make on a per-share basis?

23. **Futures Arbitrage**   A stock is currently priced at $80.34 and the futures on the stock that expire in six months have a price of $82.76. The risk-free rate is 7 percent, and the stock is not expected to pay a dividend. Is there an arbitrage opportunity here? How would you exploit it? What is the arbitrage opportunity per share of stock?

24. **Futures Arbitrage**   Joan Tam, CFA, believes she has identified an arbitrage opportunity as indicated by the information given below:

Spot price for commodity:	$120
Futures price for commodity expiring in one year:	$125
Interest rate for one year:	8%

    a. Describe the transactions necessary to take advantage of this specific arbitrage opportunity.
    b. Calculate the arbitrage profit.
    c. Describe two market imperfections that could limit Tam's ability to implement this arbitrage strategy.

25. **Futures Arbitrage**   Donna Doni, CFA, wants to explore inefficiencies in the futures market. The TOBEC stock index has a spot value of 185 now. TOBEC futures are settled in cash and underlying contract values are determined by multiplying $100 times the index value. The current annual risk-free interest rate is 6 percent.

    a. Calculate the theoretical price of the futures contract expiring six months from now, using the cost-of-carry model.
    b. The total (round-trip) transaction cost for trading a futures contract is $15. Calculate the lower bound for the price of the futures contract expiring six months from now.

What's on the Web? _____

1. **One Chicago**   Go to www.onechicago.com. How many single-stock futures and narrow-based indexes are traded at One Chicago? What is the contract size of a single-stock future? What is the minimum tick size, contract month, and contract expiration? What is the margin requirement?

2. **Spot-Futures Parity**   Go to www.onechicago.com and find the futures quotes for eBay. Now go to finance.yahoo.com and find the current stock price for eBay. What is the implied risk-free rate using these prices? Does each different maturity give you the same interest rate? Why or why not?

3. **Contract Specifications**   You want to find the contract specifications for futures contracts. Go to the Chicago Board of Trade at www.cbot.com and find the contract specifications for corn, rough rice, butter, and lean hogs. What are the contract sizes for each of these contracts?

4. **New York Board of Trade**   Go to the New York Board of Trade Web site at www.nybot.com. What contracts are traded on the New York Board of Trade? What does FCOJ stand for? What are the trading months for FCOJ futures contracts? What are the position limits for FCOJ futures contracts? What is the last trading day of the expiration month for FCOJ futures? What

are the trading months and last trading day for FCOJ options contracts? What is the FCOJ Differential contract?

5. **Hedging with Futures** You are working for a company that processes beef and will take delivery of 720,000 pounds of cattle in August. You would like to lock in your costs today because you are concerned about an increase in cattle prices. Go to the Chicago Mercantile Exchange (CME) at www.cme.com and find the contract size for live cattle. How many futures contracts will you need to hedge your exposure? Will you go long or short on these contracts? Now find the most recent price quote for live cattle futures on the CME Web site. What price are you effectively locking in if you traded at the last price? Suppose cattle prices increase 5 percent before the expiration. What is your profit or loss on the futures position? What if the price decreases by 5 percent? Explain how your futures position has eliminated your exposure to price risk in the live cattle market.

Stock-Trak Exercises

STOCK|TRAK

GLOBAL PORTFOLIO SIMULATIONS

To access the Stock-Trak Exercise for this chapter, please visit the book Web site at www.mhhe.com/jm4e and choose the corresponding chapter.

CHAPTER 15

Stock Options

"I have no objection to the granting of options. Companies should use whatever form of compensation best motivates employees— whether this be cash bonuses, trips to Hawaii, restricted stock grants or stock options."

–Warren Buffett

Options have fascinated investors for centuries. The option concept is simple. Instead of buying stock shares today, you buy an option to buy the stock at a later date at a price specified in the option contract. You are not obligated to exercise the option, but if doing so benefits you, of course you will. Moreover, the most you can lose is the original price of the option, which is normally only a fraction of the stock price. Sounds good, doesn't it? ∎

Options on common stocks have traded in financial markets for about as long as common stocks have. However, it was not until 1973, when the Chicago Board Options Exchange was established, that options trading became a large and important part of the financial landscape. Since then, the success of options trading has been phenomenal.

Much of the success of options trading is attributable to the tremendous flexibility that options offer investors in designing investment strategies. For example, options can be used to reduce risk through hedging strategies or to increase risk through speculative strategies. As a result, when properly understood and applied, options are appealing both to conservative investors and to aggressive speculators.

In this chapter, we discuss options generally, but our primary focus is on options on individual common stocks. However, later in the chapter we also discuss options on stock market indexes, which are options on portfolios of common stocks. We begin by reviewing some of the ideas we touched on in an earlier chapter, where we very briefly discussed options.

15.1   Options on Common Stocks

OPTION BASICS

derivative security
Security whose value is derived from the value of another security. Options are a type of derivative security.

As we have discussed, options on common stock are a type of **derivative security** because the value of a stock option is "derived" from the value of the underlying common stock. For example, the value of an option to buy or sell IBM stock is derived from the value of IBM stock. However, the relationship between the value of a particular stock option and the value of the underlying stock depends on the specific type of option.

Recall that there are two basic option types: **call options** and **put options**. Call options are options to buy, and put options are options to sell. Thus, a call option on IBM stock is an option to buy IBM shares, and a put option on IBM stock is an option to sell IBM shares. More specifically, a call option on common stock grants the holder the right, but not the obligation, to buy the underlying stock at a given **strike price** before the option expiration date. Similarly, a put option on common stock grants the holder the right, but not the obligation, to sell the underlying stock at a given strike price before the option expiration date. The strike price, also called the *exercise price,* is the price at which stock shares are bought or sold to fulfill the obligations of the option contract.

call option
Grants the holder the right, but not the obligation, to buy the underlying at a given strike price.

put option
Grants the holder the right, but not the obligation, to sell the underlying at a given strike price.

Options are contracts, and, in practice, option contracts are standardized to facilitate convenience in trading and price reporting. Standardized stock options have a contract size of 100 shares of common stock per option contract. This means that a single call option contract involves an option to buy 100 shares of stock. Likewise, a single put option contract involves an option to sell 100 shares of stock.

strike price
Price specified in an option contract that the holder pays to buy shares (in the case of call options) or receives to sell shares (in the case of put options) if the option is exercised. Also called the *exercise price.*

Because options are contracts, an understanding of stock options requires that we know the specific contract terms. In general, options on common stock must stipulate at least the following six contract terms:

1. The identity of the underlying stock.

2. The strike price, also called the striking or exercise price.

3. The option contract size.

4. The option expiration date, also called the option maturity.

5. The option exercise style.

6. The delivery or settlement procedure.

First, a stock option contract requires that the specific stock issue be clearly identified. While this may seem to be stating the obvious, in financial transactions it is important that the "obvious" is in fact clearly and unambiguously understood by all concerned parties.

Second, the strike price, also called the exercise price, must be stipulated. The strike price is quite important, since the strike price is the price that an option holder will pay (in the case of a call option) or receive (in the case of a put option) if the option is exercised.

Third, the size of the contract must be specified. As stated earlier, the standard contract size for stock options is 100 stock shares per option.

American option
An option that can be exercised any time before expiration.

The fourth contract term that must be stated is the option expiration date. An option cannot be exercised after its expiration date. If an option is unexercised and its expiration date has passed, the option becomes worthless.

European option
An option that can be exercised only at expiration.

Fifth, the option's exercise style determines when the option can be exercised. There are two basic exercise styles: American and European. **American options** can be exercised any time before option expiration, but **European options** can be exercised only at expiration. Options on individual stocks are normally American style, and stock index options are usually European style.

Finally, in the event that a stock option is exercised, the settlement process must be stipulated. For stock options, standard settlement requires delivery of the underlying stock shares several business days after a notice of exercise is made by the option holder.

Stock options are traded in financial markets in a manner similar to the way that common stocks are traded. For example, there are organized options exchanges, and there are over-the-counter (OTC) options markets. The largest volume of stock options trading in the United States takes place at the Chicago Board Options Exchange (CBOE). However, stock options are also actively traded at the Philadelphia Stock Exchange (PHLX), the New York Stock Exchange (NYSE), the American Stock Exchange (AMEX), and the Pacific Stock Exchange (PSE). Like a stock exchange, or, for that matter, any securities exchange, an options exchange is a marketplace where buy and sell orders from customers are matched up with each other.

WWW

Visit these option exchanges:
www.cboe.com
www.amex.com
www.phlx.com
www.nyse.com
www.pacificex.com

OPTION PRICE QUOTES

Closing prices for stock options traded at the major options exchanges are reported each day in the free online version of *The Wall Street Journal,* www.wsj.com/free. Figure 15.1 reproduces a page from the "Listed Options" report available in the Free Markets Data section of the Web site.

FIGURE 15.1 Listed Options Quotations

LISTED OPTIONS QUOTATIONS
Friday, January 6, 2006

OPTION/STRIKE		EXP	-CALL-		-PUT-	
			VOL	LAST	VOL	LAST
Wachovia	55	Feb	2,356	.87	...	...
WalMart	45	Jan	1,715	1.15	2,842	0.25
45.88	45	Feb	605	1.75	3,409	0.75
45.88	45	Mar	880	2.25	915	1.10
45.88	47.50	Jan	3,075	.10	400	1.70
45.88	47.50	Feb	7,224	.65	2,229	2.05
45.88	47.50	Mar	2,295	.95	299	2.40
45.88	50	Feb	58	.15	1,402	4.50
Walgrn	42.50	Jul	...	...	4,269	1.90
43.37	45	Jul	51	2.20	5,026	3.10
WA Mutl	45	Jan	6,927	1.05	795	0.70
45.35	45	Feb	2,072	1.55	65	1.50
45.35	45	Apr	3,438	2.45	3,257	2.15
45.35	47.50	Apr	5,847	1.35	3	3.80
WellPoint	80	Jan	1,598	.75	18	1.80
78.93	80	Feb	2,420	2.25	23	3
WellsFrgo	55	Apr	16	8.87	20,050	0.30
63.36	55	Jul	6	9.20	913	0.65
63.36	60	Apr	20	4.30	19,300	0.85
63.36	60	Jul	26	5.10	1,223	1.35
Wendy	55	Jan	5,721	1.05	3,748	0.40
WSilver g	12.50	Mar	1,010	1.25	2,000	1
WillmsCos	25	Jan	3,942	.20	16	1.20
Wyeth	45	Jan	1,532	2.85	27	0.10
WynnRes	55	Jan	1,563	.85	263	1.75
XM SatRad	27.50	Jan	1,703	1.16	333	0.60
27.95	30	Jan	1,000	.20	231	2.20
Xilinx	27.50	Jan	1,377	1.90	447	0.25
Yahoo	37.50	Jan	1,088	5.90	4,454	0.20
43.21	40	Jan	4,402	3.65	9,398	0.50
43.21	40	Feb	1,046	4.10	3,696	0.80
43.21	42.50	Jan	11,017	1.95	6,771	1.20
43.21	45	Jan	13,986	.80	2,127	2.50
43.21	45	Feb	5,797	1.36	1,824	3
43.21	47.50	Jan	1,182	.30	181	4.40

Source: Reprinted from *The Wall Street Journal,* January 6, 2006, www.wsj.com/free. © 2006 Dow Jones & Company, Inc. All Rights Reserved Worldwide.

For each underlying stock with options listed in Figure 15.1, in the first column under a stock name is simply the stock's closing price. The second column states strike prices of the various options available for each stock. Notice that the range of available strike prices for stock options typically brackets a current stock price.

The third column states the expiration month of each available option contract. By convention, standardized stock options expire on the Saturday following the third Friday of their expiration month. Because of this convention, the exact date on which an option expires can be known exactly by referring to a calendar to identify the third Friday of its expiration month.

These first three contract terms—the identity of the underlying stock, the strike price, and the expiration month—will not change during the life of the option. However, because the price of a stock option depends in part on the price of the underlying stock, the price of an option changes as the stock price changes.

Option prices are reported in columns 5 and 7 of Figure 15.1. Column 5 gives call option prices, and column 7 gives put option prices. Option prices are stated on a per-share basis, but the actual price of an option contract is 100 times the per-share price. This is because each option contract represents an option on 100 shares of stock. Fractional contracts for, say, 50 shares, are not normally available.

In Figure 15.1, trading volume for each contract is reported in columns 4 and 6. Column 4 states the number of call option contracts traded for each available strike-maturity combination, while column 6 states the number of put option contracts traded for each strike-maturity combination.

Useful online sources for option prices include the Chicago Board Options Exchange (quote.cboe.com) and Yahoo! Finance (finance.yahoo.com). The nearby *Work the Web* exhibit contains an **option chain** for Walt Disney Co. (DIS) stock options. The small box reports the time and price for the last trade in Disney stock, along with the change in price from the previous day and the trading volume for the current day. The large box contains the Disney option chain, with separate sections for call options and put options and with a strike price column dividing the two sections.

The first column of each section (labeled "Symbol") lists ticker symbols for specific option contracts. The tickers for Disney options have five letters identifying the contract. The sixth letter (X) is just used by Yahoo! to indicate an option ticker. The first three letters are DIS, which is the ticker symbol for Disney stock. For the next two letters, the first letter specifies the expiration month and whether the option is a call or a put, while the second letter identifies the strike price. Option tickers are discussed in more detail below.

The second column ("Last") reports the option price for the last trade. The third column ("Chg") states the change in price from the previous day's last trade, where a zero indicates either no change in price or no trade that day. The next two columns ("Bid" and "Ask") contain representative bid and ask price quotes from dealers. Finally, the sixth column ("Vol") reports trading volume as the number of contracts traded that day, and the seventh column ("Open Int") states open interest as the total number of contracts outstanding.

option chain

A list of available option contracts and their prices for a particular security arrayed by strike price and maturity.

CHECK THIS

15.1a   What is a call option? What is a put option?

15.1b   What are the six basic contract terms that an options contract must specify?

15.1c   What is an option chain?

Here is a stock quote and an option chain for Walt Disney Co. (DIS) from Yahoo! Finance (finance.yahoo.com).

WALT DISNEY-DISNEY C (NYSE:DIS) Delayed quote data [Edit]

Last Trade:	**24.85**	Day's Range:	24.72 - 24.92
Trade Time:	11:37AM ET	52wk Range:	22.89 - 29.99
Change:	↑ 0.11 (0.44%)	Volume:	2,022,100
Prev Close:	24.74	Avg Vol (3m):	8,227,530
Open:	24.85	Market Cap:	47.80B
Bid:	N/A	P/E (ttm):	20.32
Ask:	N/A	EPS (ttm):	1.22
1y Target Est:	31.45	Div & Yield:	0.27 (1.10%)

DIS 9-Jan 11:37am (C)Yahoo!
24.95 24.90 24.85 24.80 24.75 24.70
10am 12pm 2pm 4pm
1d 5d 3m 6m 1y 2y 5y max

Annual Report for DIS

View By Expiration: **Jan 06** | Feb 06 | Apr 06 | Jul 06 | Jan 07 | Jan 08

CALL OPTIONS — Expire at close Fri, Jan 20, 2006

Strike	Symbol	Last	Chg	Bid	Ask	Vol	Open Int
10.00	DISAB.X	**15.00**	0.00	14.80	15.00	2	8
12.50	DISAT.X	**13.00**	0.00	12.30	12.50	1,552	22
15.00	DISAC.X	**9.50**	0.00	9.80	10.00	5	52
17.50	DISAW.X	**7.20**	↑ 0.60	7.30	7.50	3	76
20.00	DISAD.X	**4.80**	0.00	4.80	5.00	60	1,402
22.50	DISAX.X	**2.35**	0.00	2.40	2.45	5	4,045
25.00	DISAE.X	**0.30**	↑ 0.05	0.30	0.35	980	59,221
27.50	DISAY.X	**0.05**	0.00	N/A	0.05	10	13,192
30.00	DISAF.X	**0.05**	0.00	N/A	0.05	8	56,653
35.00	DISAG.X	**0.05**	0.00	N/A	0.05	100	11,196
40.00	DISAH.X	**0.05**	0.00	N/A	0.05	9	2,539

PUT OPTIONS — Expire at close Fri, Jan 20, 2006

Strike	Symbol	Last	Chg	Bid	Ask	Vol	Open Int
10.00	DISMB.X	**0.00**	0.00	N/A	0.05	0	1,583
12.50	DISMT.X	**0.00**	0.00	N/A	0.05	0	53
15.00	DISMC.X	**0.05**	0.00	N/A	0.05	2	2,246
17.50	DISMW.X	**0.05**	0.00	N/A	0.05	85	13,064
20.00	DISMD.X	**0.05**	0.00	N/A	0.10	250	7,344
22.50	DISMX.X	**0.05**	0.00	N/A	0.05	157	18,449
25.00	DISME.X	**0.40**	↓ 0.10	0.40	0.45	169	45,496
27.50	DISMY.X	**3.00**	0.00	2.60	2.70	10	1,200
30.00	DISMF.X	**5.20**	0.00	5.00	5.20	14	6,071
35.00	DISMG.X	**10.30**	0.00	10.00	10.20	26	16

Highlighted options are in-the-money.

STOCK OPTION TICKER SYMBOLS

To trade stock options, it is useful to know something about option ticker symbols. The ticker symbol for a stock option identifies not only the underlying stock, but also the option type, the expiration date, and the strike price. A stock option ticker symbol has two parts. The first part contains a three-letter symbol for the underlying stock. The second part contains a two-letter symbol specifying the option type—put or call, the expiration month, and the strike price. For example, consider Coca-Cola call options with a $50 strike price with a March expiration. The ticker symbol is KO-CJ. The first part is KO, the ticker symbol for Coca-Cola stock. The second part is CJ, where C indicates a March call option and J indicates a $50 strike price. As another example, consider Disney put options with a $35 strike price and a September expiration. The ticker symbol is DIS-UG. The first part is DIS, the ticker symbol for Disney stock. The second part is UG, where U indicates a September put option and G indicates a $35 strike price.

TABLE 15.1 — Stock Option Ticker Symbol and Strike Price Codes

Expiration Month	Calls	Puts
January	A	M
February	B	N
March	C	O
April	D	P
May	E	Q
June	F	R
July	G	S
August	H	T
September	I	U
October	J	V
November	K	W
December	L	X

Strike		Strike	
5	A	70	N
10	B	75	O
15	C	80	P
20	D	85	Q
25	E	90	R
30	F	95	S
35	G	100	T
40	H	7.5	U
45	I	12.5	V
50	J	17.5	W
55	K	22.5	X
60	L	27.5	Y
65	M	32.5	Z

Table 15.1 specifies the letters used to indicate option type, expiration month, and strike price. Notice that the 12 letters A–L denote the 12 expiration months January through December for call options. Similarly, the 12 letters M–X represent the 12 expiration months for put options. The 20 letters A–T represent strike prices from 5 through 100 in five-dollar increments. The six letters U–Z are reserved for the six strikes, 7.5, 12.5, 17.5, 22.5, 27.5, and 32.5, respectively. For strikes greater than 100, the letters repeat themselves. For example, the letter A represents strikes of 5, 105, 205, and so on.

Options exchanges use special option ticker symbols for NASDAQ stocks, which have four or more letters in their stock ticker symbols. For example, the ticker symbol for Microsoft stock is MSFT, which becomes MSQ for Microsoft stock options. So a Microsoft October call option with a $25 strike price has the ticker symbol MSQ-JE. Similarly, the ticker symbol for Sun Microsystems is SUNW, which becomes SUQ for Sun stock options and a November put option with a $5 strike price has the ticker symbol SUQ-WA. Many brokers insulate their customers from this inconvenience and accept full NASDAQ stock tickers for option orders. So, for example, an order to buy MSQ-JE options would be accepted as MSFT-JE by most brokers. Also, options for many securities have more complicated option ticker symbols for which it is necessary to refer to an official list of ticker symbols maintained by the options exchanges. If you are interested in seeing such a complete list, go to the CBOE Web site (www.cboe.com).

WWW

For information on option ticker symbols, see
www.cboe.com
www.schaeffersresearch
.com
www.optionsxpress.com

CHECK THIS

15.1d What are the option types, expiration months, and strike prices for the following Alcoa (AA) options: AA-FF, AA-RF, AA-HK, and AA-TL?

15.1e What are the two-letter extensions for the following options: January 80 calls, July 25 puts, April 12.5 calls, and October 27.5 puts?

15.2 The Options Clearing Corporation

Suppose that you ordered a new car through a local dealer and paid a $2,000 deposit. Further suppose that two weeks later you receive a letter informing you that your dealer had entered bankruptcy. No doubt, you would be quite upset at the prospect of losing your $2,000 deposit.

Now consider a similar situation where you pay $2,000 for several call options through a broker. On the day before expiration you tell your broker to exercise the options, since they would produce, say, a $5,000 payoff. Then, a few days later, your broker tells you that the call writer entered bankruptcy proceedings and that your $2,000 call premium and $5,000 payoff were lost. No doubt, this would also be quite upsetting. However, if your options were traded through a registered options exchange, the integrity of your options investment would be guaranteed by the **Options Clearing Corporation (OCC)**.

The Options Clearing Corporation is the clearing agency for all options exchanges in the United States. Both the exchanges and the clearing agency are subject to regulation by the Securities and Exchange Commission (SEC). Most options investors are unaware of the OCC because only member firms of an options exchange deal directly with it. However, in fact, all option contracts traded on U.S. options exchanges are originally issued, guaranteed, and cleared by the OCC. Brokerage firms merely act as intermediaries between investors and the OCC.

To better understand the function of the OCC, let us examine a hypothetical order to buy options. In this example, assume that you instruct your broker to buy, say, 10 August 100 put options on IBM. For simplicity, let us also assume that your broker works for a member firm of the CBOE and therefore can relay your order directly to the CBOE.

When the order arrives at the CBOE, it is directed to one of several dealers for IBM options. The CBOE dealer accepts the order by taking the position of a writer for the 10 put contracts. The order is then transferred to the OCC. Once the OCC verifies that there are matching orders from a buyer and a writer, for a small fee it takes over the dealer's position as the writer for your 10 August 100 puts.

By assuming the writer's obligation, the clearing corporation guarantees that the terms of your put contracts will be fulfilled if you later decide to exercise the options. From the CBOE dealer's perspective, the clearing corporation becomes the buyer of the 10 August 100 puts. As such, the CBOE dealer becomes obligated to the clearing corporation as the writer of 10 August 100 put options.

In this way, all dealer default risk is transferred to the clearing corporation. Ultimately, the OCC ensures the performance of all options traded on all registered options exchanges in the United States. Without the OCC, these options exchanges could not function nearly as efficiently as they do in practice.

Options Clearing Corporation (OCC)
Private agency that guarantees that the terms of an option contract will be fulfilled if the option is exercised; issues and clears all option contracts traded on U.S. exchanges.

Visit the OCC at
www.optionsclearing
.com

15.3 Why Options?

As a stock market investor, a basic question you might ask is: "Why buy stock options instead of shares of stock directly?" Good question! To answer it properly, we need to compare the possible outcomes from two investment strategies. The first investment strategy entails simply buying stock. The second strategy involves buying a call option that allows the holder to buy stock any time before option expiration.

For example, suppose you buy 100 shares of IBM stock at a price of $90 per share, representing an investment of $9,000. Afterwards, three things could happen: the stock price could go up, go down, or remain the same. If the stock price goes up, you make money; if it goes down, you lose money. Of course, if the stock price remains the same, you break even.

For more information on options education, see www.optionscentral.com

Now, consider the alternative strategy of buying a call option with a strike price of $90 expiring in three months at a per-share price of $5. This corresponds to a contract price of $500 since the standard option contract size is 100 shares. The first thing to notice about this strategy is that you have invested only $500, and therefore the most that you can lose is only $500.

To compare the two investment strategies just described, let's examine three possible cases for IBM's stock price at the close of trading on the third Friday of the option's expiration month. In case 1, the stock price goes up to $100. In case 2, the stock price goes down to $80. In case 3, the stock price remains the same at $90.

Case 1: If the stock price goes up to $100, and you originally bought 100 shares at $90 per share, then your profit is $100 \times (\$100 - \$90) = \$1,000$. As a percentage of your original investment amount of $9,000, this represents a return on investment of $\$1,000/\$9,000 = 11.11\%$.

Alternatively, if you originally bought the call option, you can exercise the option and buy 100 shares at the strike price of $90 and sell the stock at the $100 market price. After accounting for the original cost of the option contract, your profit is $100 \times (\$100 - \$90) - \$500 = \$500$. As a percentage of your original investment of $500, this represents a return on investment of $\$500/\$500 = 100\%$.

Case 2: If the stock price goes down to $80, and you originally bought 100 shares at $90 per share, then your loss is $100 \times (\$80 - \$90) = -\$1,000$. As a percentage of your original investment, this represents a return of $-\$1,000/\$9,000 = -11.11\%$.

If instead you originally bought the call option, exercising the option would not pay, and it would expire worthless. You would then realize a total loss of your $500 investment, and your return is -100 percent.

Case 3: If the stock price remains the same at $90, and you bought 100 shares, you break even, and your return is zero percent.

However, if you bought the call option, exercising the option would not pay, and it would expire worthless. Once again, you would lose your entire $500 investment.

As these three cases illustrate, the outcomes of the two investment strategies differ significantly, depending on subsequent stock price changes. Whether one strategy is preferred over another is a matter for each individual investor to decide. What is important is the fact that options offer an alternative means of formulating investment strategies.

EXAMPLE 15.1	Stock Returns

Suppose you bought 100 shares of stock at $50 per share. If the stock price goes up to $60 per share, what is the percentage return on your investment? If, instead, the stock price falls to $40 per share, what is the percentage return on your investment?

If the stock goes to $60 per share, you make $\$10/\$50 = 20\%$. If it falls to $40, you lose $\$10/\$50 = 20\%$.

Call Option Returns

In Example 15.1 just above, suppose that you bought one call option contract for $200. The strike price is $50. If the stock price is $60 just before the option expires, should you exercise the option? If you exercise the option, what is the percentage return on your investment? If you don't exercise the option, what is the percentage return on your investment?

If the stock price is $60, you should definitely exercise. If you do, you will make $10 per share, or $1,000, from exercising. Once we deduct the $200 original cost of the option, your net profit is $800. Your percentage return is $800/$200 = 400%. If you don't exercise, you lose your entire $200 investment, so your loss is 100 percent.

More Call Option Returns

In Example 15.2, if the stock price is $40 just before the option expires, should you exercise the option? If you exercise the option, what is the percentage return on your investment? If you don't exercise the option, what is the percentage return on your investment?

If the stock price is $40, you shouldn't exercise since, by exercising, you will be paying $50 per share. If you did exercise, you would lose $10 per share, or $1,000, plus the $200 cost of the option, or $1,200 total. This would amount to a $1,200/$200 = 600% loss! If you don't exercise, you lose the $200 you invested, for a loss of 100 percent.

Of course, we can also calculate percentage gains and losses from a put option purchase. Here we make money if the stock price declines. So, suppose you buy a put option with a strike price of $20 for $.50. If you exercise your put when the stock price is $18, what is your percentage gain?

You make $2 per share since you are selling at $20 when the stock is worth $18. Your put contract cost $50, so your net profit is $200 − $50 = $150. As a percentage of your original $50 investment, you made $150/$50 = 300%.

CHECK THIS

15.3a   If you buy 100 shares of stock at $10 and sell out at $12, what is your percentage return?

15.3b   If you buy one call contract with a strike of $10 for $100 and exercise it when the stock is selling for $12, what is your percentage return?

15.4   Option "Moneyness"

in-the-money option
An option that would yield a positive payoff if exercised.

To understand option payoffs and profits, we need to know two important terms related to option value: **in-the-money options** and **out-of-the-money options**. Essentially, an in-the-money option is one that would yield a positive payoff if exercised immediately and an out-of-the-money option is one that would not yield a positive payoff if exercised.

EXAMPLE 15.4   In-the-Money Call Option

IBM stock is currently $55 per share. Let's look at a call option to buy IBM stock at $50 ($50 is the strike price). The stock price is greater than the strike price. If the call option were exercised immediately, there would be a positive payoff of $5 = $55 − $50. Because the option has a positive payoff if it is exercised immediately, this option is known as an in-the-money option.

EXAMPLE 15.5   Out-of-the-Money Call Option

IBM stock is currently $55 per share. Let's look at a call option to buy IBM stock at $60 ($60 is the strike price). Because the stock price is less than the strike price, immediate exercise would not benefit the option holder. Because option exercise would not yield a positive payoff, this option is called an out-of-the-money option.

EXAMPLE 15.6   In-the-Money Put Option

GE stock is selling at $33. Let's look at a put option to sell GE at a price of $40 per share ($40 is the strike price). Notice that the stock price is less than the strike price. If the put option were exercised immediately, it would yield a payoff of $7 = $40 − $33. Because the option has a positive payoff if exercised immediately, it is known as an in-the-money option.

EXAMPLE 15.7   Out-of-the-Money Put Option

GE stock is selling at $33. Let's look at a put option to sell GE at a price of $30 per share ($30 is the strike price). Because the stock price is greater than the strike price, immediate exercise would not benefit the option holder. Because option exercise would not yield a positive payoff, this option is called an out-of-the-money option.

out-of-the-money option
An option that would not yield a positive payoff if exercised.

If this all seems a little complicated, simply remember that if the stock price, S, is greater than the strike price, K, a call option is said to be "in the money" and a put option is said to be "out of the money." Likewise, if the current stock price is less than the strike price, a call option is "out of the money" and a put option is "in the money." The chart immediately below summarizes the relationship between the stock price and the strike price for in-the-money and out-of-the-money options.

	In the Money	Out of the Money
Call option	$S > K$	$S < K$
Put option	$S < K$	$S > K$

CHECK THIS

15.4a All else equal, would an in-the-money option or an out-of-the-money option have a higher price? Why?

15.4b Does an out-of-the-money option ever have value? Why?

15.5 Option Payoffs and Profits

Options are appealing because they offer investors a wide variety of investment strategies. In fact, there is essentially no limit to the number of different investment strategies available using options. However, fortunately for us, only a small number of basic strategies are available, and more complicated strategies are built from these. We discuss the payoffs from these basic strategies here and in the next section.

OPTION WRITING

Thus far, we have discussed options from the standpoint of the buyer only. However, options are contracts, and every contract must link at least two parties. The two parties to an option contract are the buyer and the seller. The seller of an option is called the "writer," and the act of selling an option is referred to as **option writing**.

option writing
Taking the seller's side of an option contract.

By buying an option you buy the right, but not the obligation, to exercise the option before the option's expiration date. By selling or writing an option, you take the seller's side of the option contract. As a result, option writing involves receiving the option price and, in exchange, assuming the obligation to satisfy the buyer's exercise rights if the option is exercised.

call writer
One who has the obligation to sell stock at the option's strike price if the option is exercised.

For example, a **call writer** is obligated to sell stock at the option's strike price if the buyer decides to exercise the call option. Similarly, a **put writer** is obligated to buy stock at the option's strike price if the buyer decides to exercise the put option.

put writer
One who has the obligation to buy stock at the option's strike price if the option is exercised.

OPTION PAYOFFS

It is useful to think about option investment strategies in terms of their initial cash flows and terminal cash flows. The initial cash flow of an option is the price of the option, also called the option *premium*. To the option buyer, the option price (or premium) is a cash outflow. To the option writer, the option price (or premium) is a cash inflow. The terminal cash flow of an option is the option's payoff that could be realized from the exercise privilege. To the option buyer, a payoff entails a cash inflow. To the writer, a payoff entails a cash outflow.

To learn more on options, see
www.numa.com
www.optionscentral.com
www.optionsxpress.com

For example, suppose the current price of IBM stock is $80 per share. You buy a call option on IBM with a strike price of $80. The premium is $4 per share. Thus, the initial cash flow is −$400 for you and +$400 for the option writer. What are the terminal cash flows for you and the option writer if IBM has a price of $90 when the option expires? What are the terminal cash flows if IBM has a price of $70 when the option expires?

If IBM is at $90, then you experience a cash inflow of $10 per share, whereas the writer experiences an outflow of $10 per share. If IBM is at $70, you both have a zero cash flow when the option expires because it is worthless. Notice that in both cases the buyer and the seller have the same cash flows, just with opposite signs. This shows that options are a "zero-sum game," meaning that any gains to the buyer must come at the expense of the seller and vice versa.

PAYOFF DIAGRAMS

When investors buy options, the price that they are willing to pay depends on their assessment of the likely payoffs (cash inflows) from the exercise privilege. Likewise, when investors write options, an acceptable selling price depends on their assessment of the likely payoffs (cash outflows) resulting from the buyers' exercise privilege. Given this, a general understanding of option payoffs is critical for understanding how option prices are determined.

A payoff diagram is a very useful graphical device for understanding option payoffs. The payoffs from buying a call option and the payoffs from writing a call option are seen in the payoff diagram in Figure 15.2. The vertical axis of Figure 15.2 measures option payoffs, and the horizontal axis measures the possible stock prices on the option expiration date. These examples assume that the call option has a strike price of $50 and that the option will be exercised only on its expiration date.

In Figure 15.2, notice that the call option payoffs are zero for all stock prices below the $50 strike price. This is because the call option holder will not exercise the option to buy stock at the $50 strike price when the stock is available in the stock market at a lower price. In this case, the option expires worthless.

In contrast, if the stock price is higher than the $50 strike price, the call option payoff is equal to the difference between the market price of the stock and the strike price of the option. For example, if the stock price is $60, the call option payoff is equal to $10, which is the difference between the $60 stock price and the $50 strike price. This payoff is a cash inflow to the buyer, because the option buyer can buy the stock at the $50 strike price and sell the stock at the $60 market price. However, this payoff is a cash outflow to the writer, because the option writer must sell the stock at the $50 strike price when the stock's market price is $60.

Putting it all together, the distinctive "hockey-stick" shape of the call option payoffs shows that the payoff is zero if the stock price is below the strike price. Above the strike price, however, the buyer of the call option gains $1 for every $1 increase in the stock price. Of

FIGURE 15.2 Call Option Payoffs

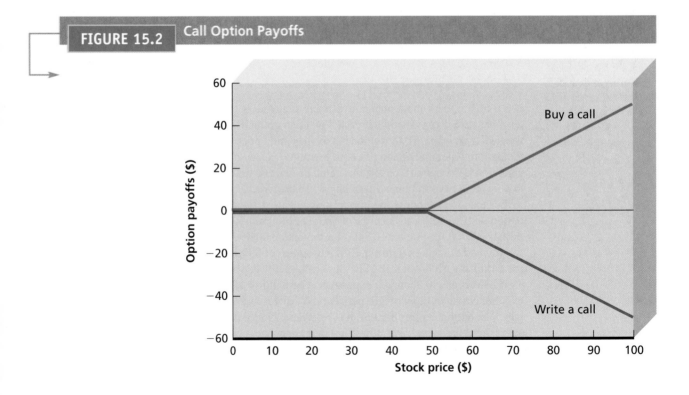

FIGURE 15.3 Put Option Payoffs

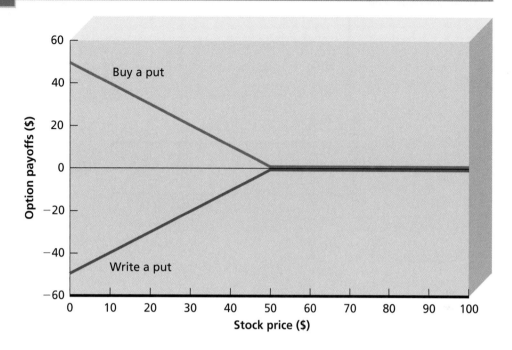

course, as shown, the call option writer loses $1 for every $1 increase in the stock price above the strike price.

Figure 15.3 is an example of a payoff diagram illustrating the payoffs from buying a put option and from writing a put option. As with our call option payoffs, the vertical axis measures option payoffs, and the horizontal axis measures the possible stock prices on the option expiration date. Once again, these examples assume that the put has a strike price of $50, and that the option will be exercised only on its expiration date.

In Figure 15.3, the put option payoffs are zero for all stock prices above the $50 strike price. This is because a put option holder will not exercise the option to sell stock at the $50 strike price when the stock can be sold in the stock market at a higher price. In this case, the option expires worthless.

In contrast, if the stock price is lower than the $50 strike price, the put option payoff is equal to the difference between the market price of the stock and the strike price of the option. For example, if the stock price is $40, the put option payoff is equal to $10, which is the difference between the $40 stock price and the $50 strike price. This payoff is a cash inflow to the buyer, because the option buyer can buy the stock at the $40 market price and sell the stock at the $50 strike price. However, this payoff is a cash outflow to the writer, because the option writer must buy the stock at the $50 strike price when the stock's market price is $40.

Our payoff diagrams illustrate an important difference between the maximum possible gains and losses for puts and calls. Notice that if you buy a call option, there is no upper limit to your potential profit because there is no upper limit to the stock price. However, with a put option, the most you can make is the strike price. In other words, the best thing that can happen to you if you buy a put is for the stock price to go to zero. Of course, whether you buy a put or a call, your potential loss is limited to the option premium you pay.

Similarly, as shown in Figure 15.2, if you write a call, there is no limit to your possible loss, but your potential gain is limited to the option premium you receive. As shown in

FIGURE 15.4   Call Option Profits

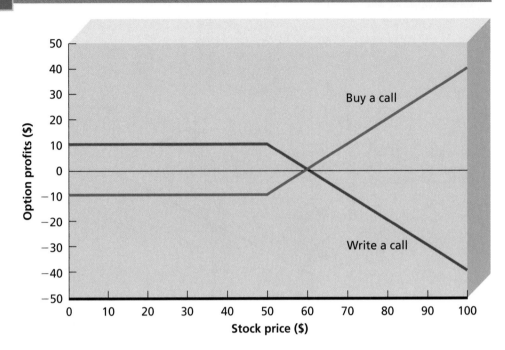

Figure 15.3, if you write a put, both your gain and loss are limited, although the potential loss could be substantial.

OPTION PROFITS

For even more on options, see
www.investorlinks.com

Between them, Figures 15.2 and 15.3 tell us essentially everything we need to know about the payoffs from the four basic strategies involving options, buying and writing puts and calls. However, these figures give the payoffs at expiration only and so do not consider the original cash inflow or outflow. Option profit diagrams are an extension of payoff diagrams that do take into account the initial cash flow.

As we have seen, the profit from an option strategy is the difference between the option's terminal cash flow (the option payoff) and the option's initial cash flow (the option price, or premium). An option profit diagram simply adjusts option payoffs for the original price of the option. This means that the option premium is subtracted from the payoffs from buying options and added to payoffs from writing options.

To illustrate, Figures 15.4 and 15.5 are profit diagrams corresponding to the four basic investment strategies for options. In each diagram, the vertical axis measures option profits, and the horizontal axis measures possible stock prices. Each profit diagram assumes that the option's strike price is $50 and that the put and call option prices are both $10. Notice that in each case the characteristic hockey-stick shape is maintained; the "stick" is just shifted up or down.

CHECK THIS

15.5a   What is option writing?

15.5b   What are the payoffs from writing call options?

15.5c   What are the payoffs from writing put options?

FIGURE 15.5 Put Option Profits

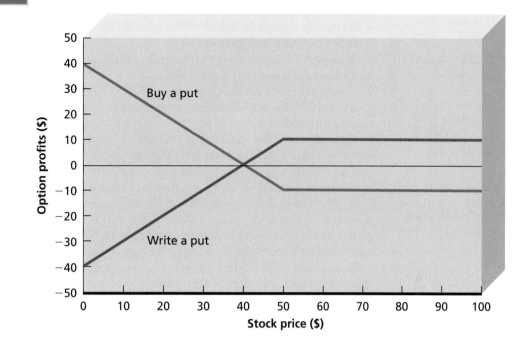

15.6 Option Strategies

Thus far, we have considered the payoffs and profits from buying and writing individual calls and puts. In this section, we consider what happens when we start to combine puts, calls, and shares of stock. There are numerous combinations that we could examine, but we will stick to just a few of the most basic and most important strategies.

THE PROTECTIVE PUT STRATEGY

Suppose you own a share of TelMex (Teléfonos de México) stock, currently worth $50. Suppose you additionally purchase a put option with a strike price of $50 for $2. What is the net effect of this purchase?

For ideas on option trading strategies, see www.commodityworld. com

To answer, we can compare what happens if TelMex stock stays at or above $50 to what happens if it drops below $50. If TelMex stays at or above $50, your put will expire worthless since you would choose not to exercise it. You would be out the $2 purchase price. However, if TelMex falls below $50, you would exercise your put, and the put writer would pay you $50 for your stock. No matter how far below $50 the price falls, you are guaranteed that you will receive $50 for your stock.

Thus, by purchasing a put option, you have protected yourself against a price decline. In the jargon of Wall Street, you have paid $2 to eliminate the "downside risk." For this reason, a strategy of buying a put option on a stock you already own is called a **protective put** strategy.

protective put
Strategy of buying a put option on a stock already owned. This protects against a decline in value.

Notice that this use of a put option *reduces* the overall risk faced by an investor, so it is a conservative strategy. This is a good example of how options, or any derivative asset, can be used to decrease risk rather than increase it. Stated differently, options can be used to hedge as well as speculate, so they do not inherently increase risk.

Buying a put option on an asset you own is just like buying term insurance. When you buy car insurance, for example, you are effectively buying a put option on your car. If, because of an accident or theft, your car's value declines, you "exercise" your option, and the insurance company essentially pays for the decline in value.

THE COVERED CALL STRATEGY

WWW

For more on covered calls,
see
www.writecall.com
www.giscor.com

Another conservative option strategy is to write call options on stock you already own. For example, again suppose you own some TelMex stock currently selling at $50. Now, instead of buying a put, consider selling a call option for, say, $2, with an exercise price of $55. What is the effect of this transaction?

To answer, we can compare what happens if TelMex stays below $55 (the exercise price on the option you sold) to what happens if it rises above $55. If TelMex stays below $55, the option will expire worthless, and you pocket the $2 premium you received. If the stock rises above $55, the option will be exercised against you, and you will deliver the stock in exchange for $55.

Thus, when you sell a call option on stock you already own, you keep the option premium no matter what. The worst thing that can happen to you is that you will have to sell your stock at the exercise price. Since you already own the stock, you are said to be "covered," and this strategy is known as a **covered call** strategy.

covered call

Strategy of selling a call option on stock already owned.

In our covered call strategy example, the stock is currently selling for $50. Since the strike price on the option is $55, the net effect of the strategy is to give up the possibility of a profit greater than $5 on the stock in exchange for the certain option premium of $2. This decreases the uncertainty surrounding the return on the investment and therefore decreases its risk.

In the jargon of Wall Street, a covered call exchanges "upside" potential for current income. In contrast, a strategy of selling call options on stock you do not own is a "naked" call strategy and, as we saw earlier, has unlimited potential losses. Thus, selling call options is either quite risky or else acts to reduce risk, depending on whether you are covered or naked. This is important to understand.

STRADDLES

Suppose a share of stock is currently selling at $50. You think the price is going to make a major move, but you are uncertain about the direction. What could you do? One answer is buy a call *and* buy a put, both with a $50 exercise price. That way, if the stock goes up sharply, your call will pay off; if it goes down sharply, your put will pay off. This is an example of a long **straddle**.

straddle

Buying or selling both a call and a put with the same exercise price. Buying is a *long straddle*; selling is a *short straddle*.

This is called a "straddle" because you have, in effect, straddled the current $50 stock price. It is a long straddle because you bought both options. If you thought the stock price was *not* going to move in either direction, you might sell a put and a call, thereby generating some income. As long as the stock price stays at $50, both options would expire worthless. This is an example of a short straddle.

There are many other strategies, with colorful names such as strips, strangles, collars, and spreads, but we need to move on. In our next section, we discuss some upper and lower bounds on option values. For some interesting discussions of option strategies, see our nearby *Investment Updates* box.

EXAMPLE 15.8	Option Strategies

You own a share of stock worth $80. Suppose you sell a call option with a strike price of $80 and also buy a put with a strike of $80. What is the net effect of these transactions on the risk of owning the stock?

Notice that what you have done is combine a protective put and a covered call strategy. To see the effect of doing this, suppose that, at option expiration, the stock is selling for more than $80. In this case, the put is worthless. The call will be exercised against you, and you will receive $80 for your stock. If the stock is selling for less than $80, the call is worthless. You would exercise your put and sell the stock for $80. In other words, the net effect is that you have guaranteed that you will exchange the stock for $80 no matter what happens, so you have created a riskless asset!

SOME STOCK-OPTION STRATEGIES WIN A GUARDED ENDORSEMENT

Let's start with a concession: Maybe options aren't totally devoid of merit.

I don't like exchange-traded stock options. They are complicated. They are often used for mindless speculation. And the odds are unattractive. For every winner, there is a loser. In fact, after trading costs, investors collectively end up out of pocket. Still, I did manage to find two options strategies that almost pass muster. Options come in two flavors: puts and calls. By buying a put, you acquire the right to sell stock at a fixed price. Similarly, by purchasing a call, you acquire the right to buy stock at a set price.

But these rights don't come cheap. You have to pay a premium to the sellers of these options. Indeed, many folks sell puts and calls as a way of generating extra investment income. But that strategy can backfire if the stock involved has a big move. Sellers of call options may miss out on big gains by the underlying shares, while sellers of puts can be forced to pay a lofty price for a now-battered stock.

Sound confusing? To get a better handle on what is involved, consider these two strategies that may appeal to certain investors.

Easing Out

Suppose you have 1,000 shares of Microsoft that you bought for a pittance. You know you ought to diversify, but you are reluctant to sell because of the resulting tax bill. Options could ease the pain of selling. The idea is to write call options against your Microsoft position. Let's say you sold July calls, with a $75 strike price, somewhat above the current $68.47 share price. By writing the calls, you agree to sell your Microsoft shares for $75 any time between now and the options' expiration date. In return, you will receive $4,200 in option premiums, which will help to offset the tax bill, should your stock get called away.

"The problem is the downside," says Eric Seff, a financial planner in Mamaroneck, N.Y. What if your Microsoft shares plunge? Mr. Seff says the option premiums you collected probably wouldn't compensate for your losses. To guard against a big decline in Microsoft's shares, you could combine the sale of call options with the purchase of Microsoft puts. That would give you downside protection. But the premium you pay for the puts will likely wipe out the income you earned by selling the calls.

What to do? Maybe you should forget the puts and instead sell calls with a strike price very close to today's share price. For instance, you could sell Microsoft calls with a strike price of $70, just above the current stock price. That way, you will earn some extra income, while being almost certain that the options you sold will be exercised and thus your Microsoft stock will get called away. Or maybe you should just dump the shares. "If you know you should get out of the stock, then get out of the stock and forget the options," advises Minneapolis financial planner Ross Levin. "The taxes may hurt. But that's the price of good investment choices you made in the past."

Looking Down

What if a bear market hits when you are retired? If you are already a few years into retirement, you are probably in fine shape, thanks to the cushion created by earlier investment gains. But if you have just retired, you could find yourself in deep trouble, as your portfolio is rapidly depleted through a combination of tumbling stock prices and your own withdrawals.

To protect yourself during the critical first few years of retirement, you might buy put options, says Moshe Milevsky, a finance professor at York University in Toronto and author of "The Probability of Fortune." Suppose you bought puts on the Standard & Poor's 500-stock index that expire in December and that will limit your losses during the next year to 8%. This insurance will currently cost you about 5% of your stock portfolio's value. Sounds like a heap of change? To pay for this downside protection, you could sell call options. But those calls will limit your potential gain. To earn enough to pay for the puts, you would probably have to write calls that cap your stock-market earnings during the next year at 8%.

That would be a big mistake if your first year of retirement turns out to be a gangbuster year for stocks. "If you are worried about the upside, sell a call at a higher strike price and finance part of the put out of your own pocket," Prof. Milevsky suggests. Because these calls with a higher strike price won't generate as big a premium, protecting against a one-year market decline of greater than 8% might cost you 3% or 4% of your stock portfolio's value. For antsy investors, that might be money well spent. But I would rather keep the cash and take my chances.

Source: Jonathan Clements, *The Wall Street Journal*, January 15, 2002. © 2002 Dow Jones & Company, Inc. All Rights Reserved Worldwide.

CHECK THIS

15.6a What is a protective put strategy? A covered call strategy?

15.6b What is a short straddle? When might it be appropriate?

15.7 Option Prices, Intrinsic Values, and Arbitrage

The range of values that an option price can attain in competitive options markets is strictly limited. We will have much to say about the determinants of an option's value in the next chapter. Here we touch on the subject by discussing some basic boundaries for the price of an option.

THE UPPER BOUND FOR A CALL OPTION PRICE

What is the most a call option could sell for? To answer, suppose we have a call option on a share of stock. The current stock price is $60. Without more information, we can't say a lot about the price of the call option, but we do know one thing: The price of the option must be less than $60!

If you think about it, the right to buy a share of stock cannot be worth more than the share itself. To illustrate, suppose the call option was actually selling for $65 when the stock was selling at $60. What would you do?

What you would do is get very rich, very fast. You would sell call options at $65 and buy stock at $60. You pocket the $5 difference. The worst thing that can happen to you is that the options are exercised and you receive the exercise price. In this case, you could make an enormous amount of money at no risk.

This is an example of a true *arbitrage* opportunity. An arbitrage is an opportunity that (1) requires no net investment on your part, (2) has no possibility of loss, and (3) has the potential for a gain. The case of a call option selling for more than its underlying asset is a particularly juicy arbitrage because it puts money in your pocket today, and later either leaves you with the stock you acquired at no cost or else leaves you with the exercise price on the option. Very nice, indeed! But too good to be true.

THE UPPER BOUND FOR A PUT OPTION PRICE

We've seen that a call option cannot sell for more than the underlying stock. How about a put option? To answer, suppose again that the stock price is $60. If a put sells for $65, is there an arbitrage opportunity?

It may look a little odd, but, without more information, we can't tell if there is an arbitrage or not. To see this, suppose the exercise price on the put option is $1,000. The right to sell a share of stock for $1,000 when its current worth is only $60 is obviously valuable, and it is obviously worth more than $65.

As this example suggests, the upper bound on a put option's price depends on the strike price. To illustrate, suppose we have a put option with an exercise price of $50 and a price of $60. What would you do?

This situation is an arbitrage opportunity. You would simply sell a put for $60 and deposit the proceeds in the bank. The worst thing that could happen to you is that you would have to buy the stock for $50 a share, leaving you with the stock, $10 per share in cash (the difference between the $60 you received and the $50 you paid for the stock), and interest on the proceeds. So you would either end up with stock that cost you nothing to acquire plus some cash and interest or, if the option expires worthless, you would keep the entire $60 (and interest). We therefore conclude that a put option must sell for less than its strike price.

THE LOWER BOUNDS ON OPTION PRICES

Having established the most a call or put could sell for, we now want to know what is the least they could sell for. We observe that an option cannot have a negative value, since, by definition, an option can simply be discarded.

intrinsic value
The payoff that an option holder receives assuming the underlying stock price remains unchanged from its current value.

To further address this question, it is useful to define what is known as the **intrinsic value** of an option. The intrinsic value of an option is the payoff that an option holder receives if the underlying stock price does not change from its current value. Equivalently, it is what the option would be worth if it were expiring immediately.

For example, suppose a certain call option contract specifies a strike price of $50, and the underlying stock price for the option is currently $45. Suppose the option was about to expire. With the stock price at $45 and the strike at $50, this option would have no value. Thus, this call option's intrinsic value is zero.

Alternatively, suppose the underlying stock price is currently $55. If the option was about to expire, it would be exercised, yielding a payoff of $5. This $5, which is simply the difference between the $55 stock price and the $50 strike price, is the call option's intrinsic value.

As another example of intrinsic value, suppose a put option has a strike price of $50, and the current stock price is $55. If the put were about to expire, it would be worthless. In this case, the put option's intrinsic value is zero.

Alternatively, suppose the underlying stock price was $45. The put option would be exercised, yielding a payoff of $5, which is the difference between the $50 strike price and the $45 stock price. In this case, the put option's intrinsic value is $5.

Based on our examples, the intrinsic value of a call option and a put option can be written as follows, where S is the current stock price and K is the option's strike price. The term "*max*" is a shorthand notation for maximum.

$$\text{Call option intrinsic value} = max\,[0, \ S - K] \qquad (15.1)$$

$$\text{Put option intrinsic value} = max\,[0, \ K - S]$$

This notation simply means that the intrinsic value of a call option is equal to $S - K$ or zero, whichever is bigger. Similarly, the intrinsic value of a put option is equal to $K - S$ or zero, whichever is bigger.

An option with a positive intrinsic value is said to be "in the money," and an option with a zero intrinsic value is said to be "out of the money" or "out the money." If the stock price and the strike price are essentially equal, the option is said to be "at the money." Thus, a call option is in the money when the stock price is greater than the strike price, and a put option is in the money when the stock price is less than the strike price.

Having defined an option's intrinsic value, we now ask: Is it possible for an option to sell for less than its intrinsic value? The answer is no. To see this, suppose the current stock price is $S = \$60$, and a call option with a strike price of $K = \$50$ has a price of $C = \$5$. Clearly, this call option is in the money, and the $5 call price is less than the option's intrinsic value of $S - K = \$10$.

If you are actually presented with these stock and option prices, you have an arbitrage opportunity to obtain a riskless arbitrage profit by following a simple three-step strategy. First, buy the call option at its price of $C = \$5$. Second, immediately exercise the call option and buy the stock from the call writer at the strike price of $K = \$50$. At this point, you have acquired the stock for $55, which is the sum of the call price plus the strike price.

As a third and final step, simply sell the stock at the current market price of $S = \$60$. Because you acquired the stock for $55 and sold the stock for $60, you have earned an arbitrage profit of $5. Clearly, if such an opportunity continued to exist, you would repeat these three steps over and over until you became bored with making easy money (as if that could ever happen!). But realistically, such easy arbitrage opportunities do not exist, and it therefore follows that a call option's price is never less than its intrinsic value.

A similar arbitrage argument applies to put options. For example, suppose a current stock price is $S = \$40$, and a put option with a strike price of $K = \$50$ has a price of $P = \$5$. This $5 put price is less than the option's intrinsic value of $K - S = \$10$. To exploit this opportunity, you first buy the put option at its price of $P = \$5$, and then buy the stock at its current price of $S = \$40$. At this point, you have acquired the stock for $45, which is the sum of the put price plus the stock price. Now you immediately exercise the put option, thereby selling the stock to the option writer at the strike price of $S = \$50$. Because you acquired the stock for $45 and sold the stock for $50, you have earned an arbitrage profit of $5. Again, you would not realistically expect such an easy arbitrage opportunity to exist, and therefore we conclude that a put option's price is never less than its intrinsic value.

Our conclusion that call option and put option prices are never less than their intrinsic values can be stated as follows, where the mathematical symbol "$\geq$" means "greater than or equal to":

$$\text{Call option price} \geq max\,[0,\ S - K] \qquad\qquad (15.2)$$
$$\text{Put option price} \geq max\,[0,\ K - S]$$

In plain English, these equations simply state that an option's price is never less than the intrinsic value of the option.

Note this important caveat concerning our lower bounds on option values. If you pick up *The Wall Street Journal*, it is relatively easy to find cases in which an option appears to be selling for less than its intrinsic value, at least by a small amount. However, if you tried to actually exploit the apparent arbitrage, you would find that the prices in the *Journal* are not the ones you could actually trade at! There are a variety of reasons for this, but, at a minimum, keep in mind that the prices you see for the stock and the option are probably not synchronous, so the two prices may never have existed at the same moment in time.

CHECK THIS

15.7a   What is the most a call option could be worth? The least?

15.7b   What is the most a put option could be worth? The least?

15.7c   What is an out-of-the-money put option?

15.8   Employee Stock Options

employee stock option (ESO)
An option granted to an employee by a company giving the employee the right to buy shares of stock in the company at a fixed price for a fixed time.

In this section, we take a brief look at **employee stock options**, or **ESOs**. An ESO is, in essence, a call option that a firm gives to its employees, giving them the right to buy shares of stock in the company. The practice of granting options to employees has become widespread. It is almost universal for upper management, but some companies, like The Gap and Starbucks, have granted options to almost every employee. Thus, an understanding of ESOs is important. Why? Because you may very soon be an ESO holder!

ESO FEATURES

Because ESOs are basically call options, we have already covered most of the important aspects. However, ESOs have a few features that make them different from regular stock options. The details differ from company to company, but a typical ESO has a 10-year life, which is much longer than most ordinary options. Unlike traded options, ESOs cannot be sold. They also have what is known as a "vesting" period. Often, for up to three years or so, an ESO cannot be exercised and also must be forfeited if an employee leaves the company. After this period, the options "vest," which means they can be exercised. Sometimes employees who resign with vested options are given a limited time to exercise their options.

Why are ESOs granted? There are basically two reasons. First, the owners of a corporation (the shareholders) face the basic problem of aligning shareholder and management interests and providing incentives for employees to focus on corporate goals. ESOs are a powerful motivator because, as we have seen, the payoffs on options can be very large. High-level executives in particular stand to gain enormous wealth if they are successful in creating value for stockholders.

The second reason some companies rely heavily on ESOs is that an ESO has no immediate, upfront, out-of-pocket cost to the corporation. In smaller, possibly cash-strapped, companies, ESOs are simply a substitute for ordinary wages. Employees are willing to accept them instead of cash, hoping for big payoffs in the future. In fact, ESOs are a major recruiting tool, allowing businesses to attract talent that they otherwise could not afford.

ESO REPRICING

ESOs are almost always "at the money" when they are issued, meaning that the stock price is equal to the strike price. Notice that, in this case, the intrinsic value is zero, so there is no value from immediate exercise. Of course, even though the intrinsic value is zero, an ESO is still quite valuable because of, among other things, its very long life.

If the stock falls significantly after an ESO is granted, then the option is said to be "underwater." On occasion, a company will decide to lower the strike price on underwater options. Such options are said to be "restruck" or "repriced."

The practice of repricing ESOs is very controversial. Companies that do it argue that once an ESO becomes deeply out of the money, it loses its incentive value because employees recognize there is only a small chance that the option will finish in the money. In fact, employees may leave and join other companies where they receive a fresh options grant.

Critics of repricing point out that a lowered strike price is, in essence, a reward for failing. They also point out that if employees know that options will be repriced, then much of the incentive effect is lost. Today, many companies award options on a regular basis, perhaps annually or even quarterly. That way, an employee will always have at least some options that are near the money even if others are underwater. Also, regular grants ensure that employees always have unvested options, which gives them an added incentive to stay with their current employer rather than forfeit the potentially valuable options.

CHECK THIS

15.8a   What are the key differences between a traded stock option and an ESO?

15.8b   What is ESO repricing? Why is it controversial?

ESOs AT THE GAP, INC.

The Gap, Inc., is a large, well-known company whose stock trades under the ticker symbol GPS (GAP is the ticker symbol for Great Atlantic & Pacific Tea Co., which you probably know as A&P). The Gap grants employee stock options that are fairly standard. This description of The Gap's ESOs is taken from its annual report:

> Under our stock option plans, options to purchase common stock are granted to officers, directors, eligible employees and consultants at exercise prices equal to the fair market value of the stock at the date of grant. Stock options generally expire 10 years from the grant date, three months after termination, or one year after the date of retirement or death, if earlier. Stock options generally vest over a four-year period, with shares becoming exercisable in equal annual installments of 25 percent.

The GAP's ESOs are not European-style options because they vest in equal increments over a four-year period. By "vest," we mean the holders can exercise these options. If you were granted options on 500 shares of GPS stock, you could exercise options on 125 shares one year after the grant date, another 125 shares two years after the grant date, another 125 shares three years after the grant date, and the last 125 shares four years after the grant date. Of course, you wouldn't have to exercise your options this quickly. As long as you stay with the company you could wait 10 years to exercise your options just before they expire.

CHECK THIS

15.8c If you terminate your employment at The Gap, Inc., how long do you have to decide whether you will exercise your employee stock options?

15.9 Put-Call Parity

put-call parity
Theorem asserting a certain parity relationship between call and put prices for European-style options with the same strike price and expiration date.

Put-call parity is perhaps the most fundamental relationship between two option prices. **Put-call parity** states that the difference between a call option price and a put option price for European-style options with the same strike price and expiration date is equal to the difference between the underlying stock price and the discounted strike price. The put-call parity relationship is algebraically represented as:

$$C - P = S - K/(1 + r)^T \qquad (15.3)$$

where the variables are defined as follows:

C = Call option price	P = Put option price
S = Current stock price	K = Option strike price
r = Risk-free interest rate	T = Time remaining until option expiration

The logic behind put-call parity is based on the fundamental principle of finance stating that two securities with the same riskless payoff on the same future date must have the same price. To illustrate how this principle is applied to demonstrate put-call parity, suppose we form a portfolio of risky securities by following these three steps:

1. Buy 100 shares of Microsoft stock (MSFT).

2. Write one Microsoft call option contract.

3. Buy one Microsoft put option contract.

For information on trading options, see
www.ino.com

Both Microsoft options have the same strike price and expiration date. We assume that these options are European style and, therefore, cannot be exercised before the last day prior to their expiration date.

TABLE 15.2   **Put-Call Parity**

Expiration Date Stock Price	Expiration Date Payoffs	
	$S_T > K$	$S_T < K$
Buy stock	S_T	S_T
Write one call option	$-(S_T - K)$	0
Buy one put option	0	$(K - S_T)$
Total portfolio expiration date payoff	K	K

Table 15.2 states the payoffs to each of these three securities based on the expiration date stock price, denoted by S_T. For example, if the expiration date stock price is greater than the strike price, that is, $S_T > K$, then the put option expires worthless and the call option requires a payment from writer to buyer of $(S_T - K)$. Alternatively, if the stock price is less than the strike price, that is, $S_T < K$, the call option expires worthless and the put option yields a payment from writer to buyer of $(K - S_T)$.

In Table 15.2, notice that no matter whether the expiration date stock price is greater or less than the strike price, the payoff to the portfolio is always equal to the strike price. This means that the portfolio has a risk-free payoff at option expiration equal to the strike price. Since the portfolio is risk-free, the cost of acquiring this portfolio today should be no different from the cost of acquiring any other risk-free investment with the same payoff on the same date. One such riskless investment is a U.S. Treasury bill.

The cost of a U.S. Treasury bill paying K dollars at option expiration is the discounted strike price $K/(1 + r)^T$, where r is the risk-free interest rate and T is the time remaining until option expiration. By the fundamental principle of finance stating that two riskless investments with the same payoff on the same date must have the same price, it follows that this cost is also equal to the cost of acquiring the stock and options portfolio. Because this portfolio is formed by (1) buying the stock, (2) writing a call option, and (3) buying a put option, its cost is the sum of the stock price plus the put price, less the call price. Setting this portfolio cost equal to the discounted strike price yields this equation:

$$S + P - C = K/(1 + r)^T$$

By a simple rearrangement of terms we obtain the originally stated put-call parity equation, thereby validating our put-call parity argument:

$$C - P = S - K/(1 + r)^T$$

The put-call parity argument stated above assumes that the underlying stock paid no dividends before option expiration. If the stock does pay a dividend before option expiration, then the put-call parity equation is adjusted as follows, where *Div* represents the *present value* of any dividend paid before option expiration.

$$C - P = S - Div - K/(1 + r)^T \tag{15.4}$$

The logic behind this adjustment is the fact that a dividend payment reduces the value of the stock, since company assets are reduced by the amount of the dividend payment. When the dividend payment occurs before option expiration, investors adjust the effective stock price determining option payoffs to be made after the dividend payment. This adjustment reduces the value of the call option and increases the value of the put option.

WWW

To learn more about trading options, see www.optionetics.com

EXAMPLE 15.9 **Implied Put Option Prices**

A current stock price is $50, and a call option with a strike price of $55 maturing in two months has a price of $8. The stock will pay a $1 dividend in one month. If the risk-free interest rate is 6 percent, what is the price implied by put-call parity for a put option with the same strike price and maturity?

Rearranging the put-call parity equation yields the following price for a put option:

$$P = C - S + Div + K/(1 + r)^T$$
$$\$13.44 = \$8 - \$50 + \$1/(1.06)^{1/2} + \$55/(1.06)^{2/12}$$

CHECK THIS

15.9a The argument supporting put-call parity is based on the fundamental principle of finance that two securities with the same riskless payoff on the same future date must have the same price. Restate the demonstration of put-call parity based on this fundamental principle. (*Hint*: Start by recalling and explaining the contents of Table 15.1.)

15.9b Exchange-traded options on individual stock issues are American style, and, therefore, put-call parity does not hold exactly for these options. In the "Listed Options Quotations" page of *The Wall Street Journal*, compare the differences between selected call and put option prices with the differences between stock prices and discounted strike prices. How closely does put-call parity appear to hold for these American-style options?

15.10 Stock Index Options

Following the tremendous success of stock options trading on the Chicago Board Options Exchange, the exchange looked for other new financial products to offer to investors and portfolio managers. In 1982, the CBOE created stock index options, which, at the time, represented a new type of option contract.

INDEX OPTIONS: FEATURES AND SETTLEMENT

stock index option
An option on a stock market index. The most popular stock index options are options on the S&P 100 index, S&P 500 index, and Dow Jones Industrials index.

A **stock index option** is an option on a stock market index. The first stock index options were contracts on the Standard & Poor's index of the 100 largest companies in terms of market capitalization. This index is often simply called the "S&P 100." S&P 100 index options trade under the ticker symbol OEX, and S&P 100 index options are referred to as "OEX options." The second stock index options introduced by the CBOE were contracts on the Standard & Poor's index of 500 companies, the "S&P 500." S&P 500 index options trade under the ticker symbol SPX and are referred to as "SPX options." In 1997, the CBOE introduced options on the Dow Jones Industrial Average (DJIA), which trade under the ticker symbol DJX.

Besides the different underlying indexes, the major difference between SPX, DJX, and OEX contracts is that OEX options are American style, whereas SPX and DJX options are European style. As we noted earlier, American-style options can be exercised any time

**cash-settled
option**

An option contract settled
by a cash payment from
the option writer to the
option holder when the
option is exercised.

before expiration, whereas European-style options can be exercised only on the last day before option expiration.

Before stock index options could be introduced, one very important detail that had to be worked out was what to do when an index option is exercised. Exchange officials saw that settlement by delivery was obviously impractical because of the number of stocks comprising an index. Instead, a cash settlement procedure was adopted for index options. For this reason, all stock index options are **cash-settled options**. With cash settlement, when a stock index option is exercised, the option writer pays a cash amount to the option buyer based on the difference between the exercise date index level and the option's strike price. For example, suppose you had purchased an SPX call option with a strike price of $1,520, and the S&P 500 index was $1,540 on the day of exercise. The difference between the index level and the strike price is $1,540 − $1,520 = $20. Because the contract size for SPX options is 100 times the S&P 500 index, the option writer must pay 100 × $20 = $2,000 to the option holder exercising the option.

In the example above, the contract size for SPX options was stated to be 100 times the S&P 500 index. In fact, the contract size for almost all standardized stock index options is 100 times the underlying index. Thus, the actual price of a stock index option is 100 times the price stated on an index level basis. There are only a few exceptions to this rule. For example, the CBOE offers so-called Reduced Value index options with a contract size that is one-tenth the size of standard index options. Reduced Value index options are appealing to some individual investors, but they represent only a minuscule share of all index options trading.

INDEX OPTION PRICE QUOTES

Options are now available for a wide variety of stock market indexes. Each business day, *The Wall Street Journal* provides a summary of the previous day's activity in stock index options. Figure 15.6, "Index Options Trading," excerpts this summary.

The most prominent component of this column is the box entitled "Underlying Indexes," which contains information on the more than 35 major stock market indexes for which index options are now available. In the first column of this box, the name of each index and (in parentheses) its ticker symbol are listed. Columns 2, 3, 4, and 5 report the corresponding high, low, close, and net change values, respectively, for each stock market index from the previous day's trading. For each stock index, the columns labeled "YTD Net Chg" and "YTD % Chg" report the index level value change and percentage value change, respectively, since the beginning of the current year.

Outside the indexes box, index options trading data are reported separately for each options exchange and index. Figure 15.6 contains information for options on several indexes. The first column of data for each index reports contract expiration months, and the second column reports strike prices. The letters next to each strike price denote whether the option is a call or a put. The third column reports trading volume measured as the number of contracts traded during the previous day's trading. The fourth column, labeled "Last," reports the contract price for the last trade of the previous day, and the fifth column, labeled "Net Chg," reports the price change from the last price on the previous trading day. Finally, the sixth column, labeled "Open Int," lists the total number of contracts outstanding.

At the bottom of each index options listing, total call volume and open interest are reported, followed by put volume and open interest. Trading volume is measured by the number of contracts traded on a given day. Open interest is measured by the total number of contracts outstanding on a given day.

The majority of trading in stock index options is conducted on the Chicago Board Options Exchange. Figure 15.6 provides OEX and SPX information. Notice the large number of strike prices available for these contracts. Also notice the large open interest on the SPX.

FIGURE 15.6 | Index Options Trading

Source: Reprinted by permission of *The Wall Street Journal*, November 30, 2005, via Copyright Clearance Center, Inc. © 2005, Dow Jones & Company, Inc. All Rights Reserved Worldwide.

INDEX OPTIONS TRADING

Tuesday, November 29, 2005

Volume, last, net change and open interest for all contracts with volume of at least 50. Volume figures are unofficial. Open interest reflects previous trading day. p-Put c-Call. The totals for call and put volume are midday figures

Underlying Indexes

	HIGH	LOW	CLOSE	NET CHG	YTD NET CHG	YTD % CHG
DJ Indus (DJX)	109.60	108.88	108.88	-0.03	1.05	1.0
DJ Trans (DTX)	416.19	412.09	412.99	0.81	33.18	8.7
DJ Util (DUX)	406.54	402.17	403.57	1.60	68.62	20.5
S&P 100 (OEX)	582.94	578.84	578.84	-0.29	3.55	0.6
S&P 500 (SPX)	1266.18	1257.46	1257.48	0.02	45.56	3.8
CB-Tech (TXX)	647.62	638.41	638.43	-3.86	25.84	4.2
CB-Mexico (MEX)	130.51	129.02	129.07	-0.89	24.78	23.8
M5 Multintl (NFT)	678.42	673.49	673.50	-1.11	13.30	2.0
GSTI Comp (GTC)	198.50	196.24	196.24	-0.70	6.38	3.4
Nasdaq 100 (NDX)	1697.58	1676.76	1676.84	-7.55	55.72	3.4
NYSE (NYA)	7733.77	7687.42	7692.99	5.57	442.93	6.1
Russell 2000 (RUT)	678.06	671.50	673.69	2.19	22.12	3.4
Lps S&P 100 (OEX)	116.59	115.77	115.77	-0.06	0.71	0.6
Lps S&P 500 (SPX)	126.62	125.75	125.75	...	4.56	3.8
Volatility (VIX)	11.96	11.61	11.89	0.05	-1.40	-10.5
S&P Midcap (MID)	738.15	730.76	733.66	2.90	70.35	10.6
Major Mkt (XMI)	1108.06	1100.71	1101.30	0.59	-38.99	-3.4
Eurotop 100 (AEUR)	270.31	268.66	269.21	0.55	42.69	18.8
HK Fltg (HKO)	299.51	299.51	299.51	-1.37	16.64	5.9
IW Internet (IIX)	178.84	175.61	175.62	-2.02	1.88	1.1
AM-Mexico (MXY)	162.95	161.39	161.55	-0.79	35.30	28.0
Institut'l-A.M. (XII)	619.62	614.52	614.53	-1.44	14.20	2.4
Japan (JPN)			158.99	-0.55	38.51	32.0
MS Cyclical (CYC)	780.16	771.74	776.99	5.25	-7.11	-0.9
MS Consumr (CMR)	595.74	592.31	592.52	0.21	1.73	0.3
MS Hi Tech (MSH)	535.83	528.52	528.57	-3.31	20.90	4.1
MS Internet (MOX)	15.26	14.93	14.98	-0.21	0.14	0.9
Pharmaceutical (DRG)	310.63	307.62	307.67	-1.05	-8.95	-2.8
Biotech (BTK)	676.05	668.04	668.47	-3.06	124.22	22.8
Gold/Silver (XAU)	118.09	116.65	117.46	-0.82	18.11	18.2
Utility Index (UTY)	431.99	428.04	428.48	0.99	54.87	14.7
Value Line (VAY)	1916.82	1900.86	1904.19	3.33	110.00	6.1
Bank (BKX)	105.96	105.23	105.32	-0.14	1.21	1.2
Semicond (SOXX)	484.14	475.51	475.78	-2.98	42.47	9.8
Street.com (DOT)	214.10	211.11	211.18	-1.22	2.87	1.4
Oil Service (OSX)	177.19	173.09	174.47	0.11	50.53	40.8
PSE Tech (PSE)	846.24	837.96	837.97	-1.43	58.91	7.6

CHICAGO

DJ INDUS AVG(DJX)

STRIKE	VOL	LAST	NET CHG	OPEN INT
Dec 100 c	50	9.30	0.20	19,072
Dec 101 c	119	8.30	1.20	3,215
Mar 102 p	140	0.80	-0.50	75
Mar 103 p	120	0.90	...	4,513
Jan 105 c	100	5	0.10	6,026
Dec 106 c	140	3.30	0.10	27,809
Jan 106 p	119	0.65	-0.10	3,085
Dec 108 p	231	0.60	...	15,985
Dec 109 c	215	0.95	-0.10	5,857
Dec 109 p	587	0.90	...	6,818
Jan 109 c	61	1.85	0.05	5,274
Jan 109 p	79	1.40	-0.15	1,386
Jan 110 c	91	1.30	-0.05	5,369
Jan 110 p	135	1.80	-0.15	2,204
Feb 110 p	50	2.30	-0.30	2,103
Dec 112 c	59	0.10	...	21,216
Feb 116 p	325	6.40	...	402
Mar 116 c	50	0.50	...	3,275
Feb 120 p	100	10.40	...	...
Call Vol. 8,576			**Open Int.**..364,564	
Put Vol. 8,874			**Open Int.**..342,887	

NASDAQ-100(NDX)

STRIKE	VOL	LAST	NET CHG	OPEN INT
Jan 1450 p	465	1.85	0.05	1,490
Dec 1500 p	70	0.80	0.20	33,193
Jan 1500 p	80	3.20	0.45	1,760
Dec 1525 p	239	0.70	-0.05	13,031
Jan 1525 p	368	4.10	0.40	2,645
Dec 1550 p	382	1.05	0.05	31,996
Jan 1550 p	206	5	-0.10	2,657
Feb 1550 p	115	10.70	0.90	86
Jan 1575 p	136	7.20	0.30	2,328
Dec 1585 p	143	1.70	0.20	18,828
Dec 1590 p	110	2.20	0.45	1,209
Dec 1600 p	584	2.60	0.60	13,137
Jan 1600 p	208	10.80	1.30	3,712
Jan 1625 p	57	14.70	1.40	2,419
Dec 1650 p	634	9	1.70	14,015
Jan 1650 p	455	21.60	2.30	953
Dec 1660 p	215	11.10	1.70	786
Dec 1675 c	517	22.50	-5.70	10,338
Jan 1675 c	531	43.70	-3.20	960
Jan 1675 p	791	27.80	0.90	521
Dec 1700 p	432	31.10	7.10	2,596
Jan 1700 c	161	30	-1.80	2,759
Mar 1700 c	50	59	-8.00	2,028
Mar 1700 p	75	54.50	1.50	208
Dec 1725 c	877	4.80	-1.50	6,563
Dec 1725 p	71	48.10	8.00	487
Jan 1725 c	134	18.60	-4.10	1,617
Dec 1740 c	358	2.80	-0.70	10,524
Dec 1750 c	361	1.65	-0.55	8,636
Jan 1750 c	542	11	-2.90	4,312
Dec 1775 c	291	0.65	-0.35	8,052
Jan 1775 c	114	6	-1.60	1,912
Dec 1800 c	58	0.30	-0.05	14,953
Jan 1800 c	248	3.50	-0.90	974
Mar 1800 c	80	17.60	-2.20	969
Dec 1825 c	140	0.25	0.05	11,191
Jan 1850 c	177	1.05	-0.15	157
Jan 1900 c	90	0.35	-0.05	67
Call Vol. 2,396			**Open Int.**..300,190	
Put Vol. 5,000			**Open Int.**..387,520	

S & P 100(OEX)

STRIKE	VOL	LAST	NET CHG	OPEN INT
Jan 520 p	127	0.50	-0.05	1,919
Jan 530 p	520	0.75	...	1,772
Dec 535 c	97	0.20	-0.05	5,654
Dec 540 p	339	0.20	-0.10	13,498
Dec 545 p	807	0.30	-0.05	3,934
Jan 545 p	130	1.35	-0.15	433
Dec 550 p	890	0.40	-0.05	8,364
Jan 550 p	70	1.60	-0.30	1,863
Dec 555 p	591	0.60	-0.05	5,659
Jan. 555 p	130	2.40	0.05	251
Dec 560 c	295	22	0.30	4,950
Jan 560 c	194	25.20	0.30	1,110
Mar 560 c	73	7.50	0.50	1,921
Dec 565 c	61	16.60	-0.20	2,499
Dec 565 p	796	1.15	-0.05	6,490
Dec 570 c	817	11.80	-0.80	5,664
Dec 575 c	462	8.20	-0.30	7,226
Jan 575 c	253	13.60	0.30	125
Jan 575 p	159	6.50	-0.20	496
Dec 580 c	178	9.50	-0.10	4,372
Dec 580 p	157	8.40	0.10	576
Feb 580 p	54	11.10	0.30	16
Dec 585 p	371	8	0.30	2,190
Dec 590 p	269	11.90	-0.50	124
Jan 600 c	336	1.80	...	4,714
Jan 605 c	57	1	0.10	1,653
Feb 610 c	56	1.70	-0.50	350
Dec 620 c	201	0.05	...	4,108
Feb 620 c	120	0.65	0.15	7
Mar 620 c	264	2.05	0.05	865
Call Vol. 22,080			**Open Int.**..118,222	
Put Vol. 24,429			**Open Int.**..183,966	

S & P 500(SPX)

STRIKE	VOL	LAST	NET CHG	OPEN INT
Mar 800 p	82	0.10	...	19,155
Mar 1000 p	79	0.95	...	12,020
Dec 1075 p	300	0.15	-0.15	58,917
Mar 1125 p	525	5	0.30	25,060
Dec 1135 c	186	0.35	-0.05	27,021
Jan 1140 p	71	1.50	0.10	4,385
Jan 1150 p	79	1.75	-0.10	12,070
Dec 1160 p	188	0.40	-0.10	28,442
Jan 1165 p	185	2.50	0.10	3,589
Dec 1175 p	932	0.65	-0.10	128,957
Mar 1175 c	100	9.30	0.30	30,351
Dec 1190 p	212	0.80	-0.20	37,388
Dec 1195 c	71	0.95	-0.10	20,781
Dec 1205 c	209	63.50	1.80	15,931
Jan 1205 p	110	5.50	...	133
Dec 1210 p	7,317	1.60	-0.20	29,877
Dec 1215 p	484	1.80	-0.30	18,932
Dec 1220 c	414	45.80	3.60	30,116
Jan 1220 p	813	7.80	-0.10	2,876
Dec 1225 c	196	38	0.20	121,697
Jan 1225 c	102	52.80	4.80	14,842
Mar 1225 c	303	64	-1.00	22,793
Dec 1230 c	506	35	-0.20	22,926
Jan 1230 p	740	9	-0.50	3,932
Dec 1240 c	60	24.70	-0.30	33,205
Jan 1240 p	73	12	-1.10	5,061
Dec 1245 c	115	22.20	-0.40	28,861
Dec 1245 p	166	6.50	0.10	17,211
Jan 1245 c	258	13.50	0.50	3,362
Feb 1245 p	60	17.50	2.00	4
Dec 1250 c	753	35.80	-4.30	1,299
Mar 1250 c	558	45	1.60	35,487
Dec 1255 c	969	13.80	-1.70	19,101
Dec 1255 p	840	9.30	-0.10	15,378
Dec 1260 c	6,225	11	-1.00	20,060
Dec 1260 p	7,853	11	-1.00	16,893
Jan 1260 c	230	22	-0.30	5,632
Jan 1265 c	405	20.10	0.60	3,476
Jan 1265 p	445	20.10	...	1,509
Dec 1270 p	663	16	-1.30	15,831
Jan 1270 p	401	20.80	-1.70	1,568
Dec 1275 c	6,432	4.60	-0.40	74,724
Dec 1275 p	475	19.80	-0.90	10,035
Jan 1275 p	59	24.10	-0.60	7,013
Mar 1275 c	181	28.20	-0.80	39,513
Dec 1280 p	51	22	1.20	1,201
Jan 1280 c	165	11.80	-0.70	8,481
Jan 1280 p	60	27.70	-1.50	18
Dec 1295 c	96	0.95	-0.35	4,205
Dec 1300 p	70	36.30	-4.30	8,725
Feb 1300 p	564	11.30	-0.20	1,866
Dec 1305 c	469	4.05	-0.25	15,144
Feb 1305 c	50	10.30	-0.30	33
Dec 1310 c	179	0.50	-0.20	70,189
Dec 1325 c	227	0.15	-0.10	193,479
Feb 1325 c	142	5	-0.50	1,311
Mar 1325 c	376	9.40	-0.20	32,539
Jan 1335 c	919	1	-0.20	193
Dec 1350 c	200	0.05	-0.25	50,343
Mar 1350 c	131	5.50	1.20	24,084
Call Vol. 67,511			**Open Int.**2,290,926	
Put Vol. 222,467			**Open Int.**3,712,998	

WSJ.com *Complete listed options quotations can be found at* **wsj.com/free**

Suppose you bought 10 July 990 SPX call contracts at a quoted price of $5. How much did you pay in total? At option expiration, suppose the S&P 500 is at 1000. What would you receive?

The price per SPX contract is 100 times the quoted price. Because you bought 10 contracts, you paid a total of $5 \times 100 \times 10 = \$5,000$. If, at expiration, the S&P 500 is at 1000, you would receive $\$100 \times (1000 - 990) = \$1,000$ per contract, or $10,000 in all. This $10,000 would be paid to you in cash, because index options feature cash settlement.

CHECK THIS

15.10a In addition to the underlying asset, what is the major difference between any ordinary stock option and a stock index option?

15.10b In addition to the underlying index, what is the major difference between the OEX and SPX option contracts?

15.11 Summary and Conclusions

In 1973, organized stock options trading began when the Chicago Board Options Exchange (CBOE) was established. Since then, options trading has grown enormously. In this chapter, we examined a number of concepts and issues surrounding stock options. We saw that:

1. Options on common stock are derivative securities because the value of a stock option is derived from the value of the underlying common stock. There are two basic types of options: call options and put options. Call options are options to buy, and put options are options to sell.

2. Options are contracts. Standardized stock options represent a contract size of 100 shares of common stock per option contract. We saw how standardized option prices are quoted in the financial press.

3. The Options Clearing Corporation (OCC) is the clearing agency for all options exchanges in the United States. It guarantees that the terms of an option contract will be fulfilled if the option is exercised.

4. Various strategies exist with options, ranging from buying and selling individual puts and calls to combination strategies involving calls, puts, and the underlying stock. There are many common strategies, including protective puts and covered calls.

5. Option prices have boundaries enforced by arbitrage. A call option cannot sell for more than the underlying asset, and a put option cannot sell for more than the strike price on the option.

6. An option's intrinsic value is a lower bound for an option's price. The intrinsic value of an option is the payoff that an option holder receives if the underlying stock price does not change from its current value.

7. An employee stock option (ESO) is an option granted by a firm to an employee. Such options provide an incentive for employees to work to increase the firm's stock price.

8. Put-call parity states that the difference between a call price and a put price for European-style options with the same strike price and expiration date is equal to the difference between the dividend-adjusted stock price and the discounted strike price.

9. A stock index option is an option on a stock market index such as the S&P 500. All stock index options use a cash settlement procedure when they are exercised. With a cash settlement procedure, when a stock index option is exercised, the option writer pays a cash amount to the option buyer.

GET REAL

This chapter added to your understanding of put and call options by covering the rights, obligations, and potential gains and losses involved in trading options. How should you put this information to work? You need to buy and sell options to experience the gains and losses that options can provide. So, with a simulated brokerage account (such as Stock-Trak), you should first execute each of the basic option transactions: buy a call, sell a call, buy a put, and sell a put.

For help getting started, you can find an enormous amount of information about options on the Internet. Useful places to start are the options exchanges: Chicago Board Options Exchange (www.cboe.com), American Stock Exchange (www.amex.com), Pacific Stock Exchange (www.pacificex.com), and Philadelphia Stock Exchange (www.phlx.com). Excellent Web sites devoted to options education are the Options Industry Council (www.optionscentral.com) and the Options Clearing Corporation (www.optionsclearing.com). You might also look at the options section of Trading Markets (www.tradingmarkets.com) or Investor Links (www.investorlinks.com).

For information on option trading strategies, try entering the strategy name into an Internet search engine. For example, enter the search phrases "covered calls" or "protective puts" for online information about those strategies. For more general information, try the search phrase "options trading strategies" to find sites like Commodity World (www.commodityworld.com). For a sales pitch on writing covered calls, check out Write Call (www.writecall.com).

If you're having trouble understanding options ticker symbols, don't feel alone because almost everyone has trouble at first. For help on the net, try the search phrases "option symbols" or "options symbols" to find sites like www.optionscentral.com. Of course, the options exchanges listed above also provide complete information on the option ticker symbols they use.

Key Terms

American option 480
call option 480
call writer 489
cash-settled option 503
covered call 494
derivative security 480
employee stock option (ESO) 498
European option 480
in-the-money option 487
intrinsic value 497
option chain 482

Options Clearing Corporation (OCC) 485
option writing 489
out-of-the-money option 488
protective put 493
put-call parity 500
put option 480
put writer 489
straddle 494
strike price 480
stock index option 502

Chapter Review Problems and Self-Test ___ ■

1. **Call Option Payoffs**   You purchase 25 call contracts on Blue Ox stock. The strike price is $22, and the premium is $1. If the stock is selling for $24 per share at expiration, what are your call options worth? What is your net profit? What if the stock were selling for $23? $22?

2. **Stock versus Options**   Stock in Bunyan Brewery is currently priced at $20 per share. A call option with a $20 strike and 60 days to maturity is quoted at $2. Compare the percentage gains and losses from a $2,000 investment in the stock versus the option in 60 days for stock prices of $26, $20, and $18.

3. **Put-Call Parity**   A call option sells for $8. It has a strike price of $80 and six months until expiration. If the underlying stock sells for $60 per share, what is the price of a put option with an $80 strike price and six months until expiration? The risk-free interest rate is 6 percent per year.

Answers to Self-Test Problems

1. Blue Ox stock is selling for $24. You own 25 contracts, each of which gives you the right to buy 100 shares at $22. Your options are thus worth $2 per share on 2,500 shares, or $5,000. The option premium was $1, so you paid $100 per contract, or $2,500 total. Your net profit is $2,500. If the stock is selling for $23, your options are worth $2,500, so your net profit is exactly zero. If the stock is selling for $22, your options are worthless, and you lose the entire $2,500 you paid.

2. Bunyan stock costs $20 per share, so if you invest $2,000, you'll get 100 shares. The option premium is $2, so an option contract costs $200. If you invest $2,000, you'll get $2,000/$200 = 10 contracts. If the stock is selling for $26 in 60 days, your profit on the stock is $6 per share, or $600 total. The percentage gain is $600/$2,000 = 30%.

   In this case, your options are worth $6 per share, or $600 per contract. You have 10 contracts, so your options are worth $6,000 in all. Since you paid $2,000 for the 10 contracts, your profit is $4,000. Your percentage gain is a whopping $4,000/$2,000 = 200%.

   If the stock is selling for $20, your profit is $0 on the stock, so your percentage return is 0 percent. Your options are worthless (why?), so the percentage loss is −100 percent. If the stock is selling for $18, verify that your percentage loss on the stock is −10 percent and your loss on the options is again −100 percent.

3. Using the put-call parity formula, we have:

$$C - P = S - K/(1+r)^T$$

Rearranging to solve for P, the put price, and plugging in the other numbers gets us:

$$P = C - S + K/(1+r)^T$$
$$= \$8 - \$60 + 80/(1.06)^{1/2}$$
$$= 25.70$$

Test Your Investment Quotient ___ ■

1. **Option Contracts**   Which of the following is not specified by a stock option contract?
   a. The underlying stock's price.
   b. The size of the contract.
   c. Exercise style—European or American.
   d. Contract settlement procedure—cash or delivery.

2. **Option Contracts** A July 50 call option contract for SOS stock is identified by which ticker symbol?

a. SOS-JG
b. SOS-JS
c. SOS-GJ
d. SOS-SJ

3. **Option Contracts** An April 40 put option contract for SOS stock is identified by which ticker symbol?

a. SOS-HD
b. SOS-HP
c. SOS-DH
d. SOS-PH

4. **Option Payoffs** All of the following statements about the value of a call option at expiration are true, except that the:

a. Short position in the same call option can result in a loss if the stock price exceeds the exercise price.
b. Value of the long position equals zero or the stock price minus the exercise price, whichever is higher.
c. Value of the long position equals zero or the exercise price minus the stock price, whichever is higher.
d. Short position in the same call option has a zero value for all stock prices equal to or less than the exercise price.

5. **Option Strategies** Which of the following stock option strategies has the greatest potential for large losses?

a. Writing a covered call
b. Writing a covered put
c. Writing a naked call
d. Writing a naked put

6. **Option Strategies** Which statement does not describe an at-the-money protective put position (comprised of owning the stock and the put)?

a. Protects against loss at any stock price below the strike price of the put.
b. Has limited profit potential when the stock price rises.
c. Returns any increase in the stock's value, dollar for dollar, less the cost of the put.
d. Provides a pattern of returns similar to a stop-loss order at the current stock price.

7. **Put-Call Parity** Which of the following is not included in the put-call parity condition?

a. Price of the underlying stock.
b. Strike price of the underlying call and put option contracts.
c. Expiration dates of the underlying call and put option contracts.
d. Volatility of the underlying stock.

8. **Put-Call Parity** According to the put-call parity condition, a risk-free portfolio can be created by buying 100 shares of stock and

a. Writing one call option contract and buying one put option contract.
b. Buying one call option contract and writing one put option contract.
c. Buying one call option contract and buying one put option contract.
d. Writing one call option contract and writing one put option contract.

9. **Option Strategies** Investor A uses options for defensive and income reasons. Investor B uses options as an aggressive investment strategy. What is an appropriate use of options for Investors A and B, respectively?

a. Writing covered calls / buying puts on stock not owned.
b. Buying out-of-the-money calls / buying puts on stock owned.
c. Writing naked calls / buying in-the-money calls.
d. Selling puts on stock owned / buying puts on stock not owned.

10. **Option Strategies** Which one of the following option combinations best describes a straddle? Buy both a call and a put on the same stock with

   a. Different exercise prices and the same expiration date.
   b. The same exercise price and different expiration dates.
   c. The same exercise price and the same expiration date.
   d. Different exercise prices and different expiration dates.

11. **Option Strategies** Which of the following strategies is the riskiest options transaction if the underlying stock price is expected to increase substantially?

   a. Writing a naked call option.
   b. Writing a naked put option.
   c. Buying a call option.
   d. Buying a put option.

12. **Option Gains and Losses** You create a "strap" by buying two calls and one put on ABC stock, all with a strike price of $45. The calls cost $5 each, and the put costs $4. If you close your position when ABC stock is priced at $55, what is your per-share gain or loss?

   a. $4 loss
   b. $6 gain
   c. $10 gain
   d. $20 gain

13. **Option Gains and Losses** A put on XYZ stock with a strike price of $40 is priced at $2.00 per share, while a call with a strike price of $40 is priced at $3.50. What is the maximum per-share loss to the writer of the uncovered put and the maximum per-share gain to the writer of the uncovered call?

	Maximum Loss to Put Writer	Maximum Gain to Call Writer
a.	$38.00	$ 3.50
b.	$38.00	$36.50
c.	$40.00	$ 3.50
d.	$40.00	$40.00

14. **Option Pricing** If a stock is selling for $25, the exercise price of a put option on that stock is $20, and the time to expiration of the option is 90 days, what are the minimum and maximum prices for the put today?

   a. $0 and $5
   b. $0 and $20
   c. $5 and $20
   d. $5 and $25

15. **Option Strategies** Which of the following strategies is most suitable for an investor wishing to eliminate "downside" risk from a long position in stock?

   a. A long straddle position.
   b. A short straddle position.
   c. Writing a covered call option.
   d. Buying a protective put option.

16. **Covered Calls** The current price of an asset is $75. A three-month, at-the-money American call option on the asset has a current value of $5. At what value of the asset will a covered call writer break even at expiration?

   a. $70
   b. $75
   c. $80
   d. $85

17. Option Strategies The current price of an asset is $100. An out-of-the-money American put option with an exercise price of $90 is purchased along with the asset. If the breakeven point for this hedge is at an asset price of $114 at expiration, then the value of the American put at the time of purchase must have been

a. $0
b. $4
c. $10
d. $14

18. Option Strategies The following diagram shows the value of a put option at expiration:

Ignoring transaction costs, which of the following statements about the value of the put option at expiration is true?

a. The value of the short position in the put is $4 if the stock price is $76.
b. The value of the long position in the put is − $4 if the stock price is $76.
c. The long put has value when the stock price is below the $80 exercise price.
d. The value of the short position in the put is zero for stock prices equaling or exceeding $76.

19. Options Tickers A letter indicating an exchange is sometimes added to an options ticker. Which of the following correctly matches these letters with their exchanges?

a. X–PSX, A–AMEX, C–CBOE, P–PHLX
b. X–NYSE, A–AMEX, C–CBOT, P–PSE
c. X–PSX, A–AMEX, C–CBOT, P–PHLX
d. X–PHLX, A–AMEX, C–CBOE, P–PSE

20. Options Tickers Which of the following is not a legitimate option ticker?

a. DIS-JF
b. DIS-VL
c. DIS-ZG
d. DIS-PH

Concept Questions _____

1. Basic Properties of Options What is a call option? A put option? Under what circumstances might you want to buy each? Which one has greater potential profit? Why?

2. Calls versus Puts Complete the following sentence for each of these investors:

a. A buyer of call options
b. A buyer of put options
c. A seller (writer) of call options
d. A seller (writer) of put options

The (buyer/seller) of a (put/call) option (pays/receives) money for the (right/obligation) to (buy/sell) a specified asset at a fixed price for a fixed length of time.

3. **Option Breakeven** In general, if you buy a call option, what stock price is needed for you to break even on the transaction ignoring taxes and commissions? If you buy a put option?

4. **Protective Puts** Buying a put option on a stock you own is sometimes called "stock price insurance." Why?

5. **Defining Intrinsic Value** What is the intrinsic value of a call option? How do we interpret this value?

6. **Defining Intrinsic Value** What is the intrinsic value of a put option? How do we interpret this value?

7. **Arbitrage and Options** You notice that shares of stock in the Patel Corporation are going for $50 per share. Call options with an exercise price of $35 per share are selling for $10. What's wrong here? Describe how you could take advantage of this mispricing if the option expires today.

Use the following options quotations to answer questions 8 through 11:

Option & N.Y. Close	Strike Price	Expiration	Calls		Puts	
			Vol.	Last	Vol.	Last
Milson						
59	55	Mar	98	3.50	66	1.06
59	55	Apr	54	6.25	40	1.94
59	55	Jul	25	8.63	17	3.63
59	55	Oct	10	10.25	5	3.25

8. **Interpreting Options Quotes** How many options contracts on Milson stock were traded with an expiration date of July? How many underlying shares of stock do these options contracts represent?

9. **Interpreting Options Quotes** Are the call options in the money? What is the intrinsic value of a Milson Corp. call option?

10. **Interpreting Options Quotes** Are the put options in the money? What is the intrinsic value of a Milson Corp. put option?

11. **Interpreting Options Quotes** Two of the options are clearly mispriced. Which ones? At a minimum, what should the mispriced options sell for? Explain how you could profit from the mispricing in each case.

12. **Option Strategies** Recall the options strategies of a protective put and covered call discussed in the text. Suppose you have sold short some shares of stock. Discuss analogous option strategies and how you would implement them. (*Hint*: They're called protective calls and covered puts.)

13. **Put-Call Parity** A put and a call option have the same maturity and strike price. If both are at the money, which is worth more? Prove your answer and then provide an intuitive explanation.

14. **Put-Call Parity** A put and a call option have the same maturity and strike price. If they also have the same price, which one is in the money?

15. **Put-Call Parity** One thing the put-call parity equation tells us is that given any three of a stock, a call, a put, and a T-bill, the fourth can be synthesized or replicated using the other three. For example, how can we replicate a share of stock using a put, a call, and a T-bill?

Questions and Problems

Core Questions

1. **Call Option Payoffs** Suppose you purchase eight call contracts on Macron Technology stock. The strike price is $80, and the premium is $3. If, at expiration, the stock is selling for $88 per share, what are your call options worth? What is your net profit?

2. **Put Option Payoffs** Suppose you purchase five put contracts on Testaburger Co. The strike price is $45, and the premium is $3. If, at expiration, the stock is selling for $38 per share, what are your put options worth? What is your net profit?

3. **Stock versus Options** Stock in Cheezy-Poofs Manufacturing is currently priced at $80 per share. A call option with an $80 strike and 90 days to maturity is quoted at $3. Compare the percentage gains and losses from a $12,000 investment in the stock versus the option in 90 days for stock prices of $70, $80, and $90.

Use the following options quotations to answer questions 4 through 7:

Option & N.Y. Close	Strike Price	Expiration	Calls		Puts	
			Vol.	Last	Vol.	Last
Hendreeks						
75	70	July	72	5.80	50	.65
75	70	Aug	41	6.70	29	1.20
75	70	Oct	16	7.90	10	2.70
75	70	Jan	8	9.50	2	3.90

4. **Calculating Option Payoffs** Suppose you buy 50 August 70 call option contracts. How much will you pay, ignoring commissions?

5. **Calculating Option Payoffs** In Problem 4, suppose that Hendreeks stock is selling for $84 per share on the expiration date. How much is your options investment worth? What if the terminal stock price is $75?

6. **Calculating Option Payoffs** Suppose you buy 30 January 70 put option contracts. What is your maximum gain? On the expiration date, Hendreeks is selling for $63 per share. How much is your options investment worth? What is your net gain?

7. **Calculating Option Payoffs** In Problem 6, suppose you write 30 of the January 70 put contracts. What is your net gain or loss if Hendreeks is selling for $55 at expiration? For $100? What is the break-even price, that is, the terminal stock price that results in a zero profit?

8. **Put-Call Parity** A call option is currently selling for $6. It has a strike price of $65 and six months to maturity. What is the price of a put option with a $65 strike price and six months to maturity? The current stock price is $61, and the risk-free interest rate is 5 percent.

9. **Put-Call Parity** A call option currently sells for $8. It has a strike price of $80 and six months to maturity. A put with the same strike and expiration date sells for $4. If the risk-free interest rate is 4 percent, what is the current stock price?

10. **Put-Call Parity** A put option with a strike price of $75 sells for $8.90. The option expires in two months, and the current stock price is $78. If the risk-free interest rate is 5 percent, what is the price of a call option with the same strike price?

Intermediate Questions

11. **Put-Call Parity** A call option is currently selling for $9.40. It has a strike price of $55 and five months to maturity. The current stock price is $58, and the risk-free rate is 5 percent. The stock has a dividend yield of 2 percent. What is the price of a put option with the same exercise price?

12. **Put-Call Parity** A call option is currently selling for $3.80. It has a strike price of $70 and three months to maturity. A put option with the same strike price sells for $7.10. The risk-free rate is 6 percent, and the stock has a dividend yield of 3 percent. What is the current stock price?

13. **Put-Call Parity**   A put option is currently selling for $6.20. It has a strike price of $80 and seven months to maturity. The current stock price is $83. The risk-free rate is 5 percent, and the stock has a dividend yield of 2 percent. What is the price of a call option with the same strike price?

14. **Call Option Writing**   Suppose you write 20 call option contracts with a $50 strike. The premium is $3.50. Evaluate your potential gains and losses at option expiration for stock prices of $40, $50, and $60.

15. **Put Option Writing**   Suppose you write 15 put option contracts with a $35 strike. The premium is $2.40. Evaluate your potential gains and losses at option expiration for stock prices of $25, $35, and $45.

16. **Index Options**   Suppose you buy one SPX call option contract with a strike of 1300. At maturity, the S&P 500 index is at 1340. What is your net gain or loss if the premium you paid was $21?

17. **Option Strategies**   You write a put with a strike price of $70 on stock that you have shorted at $70 (this is a "covered put"). What are the expiration date profits to this position for stock prices of $60, $65, $70, $75, and $80 if the put premium is $3.50?

18. **Option Strategies**   You buy a call with a strike price of $70 on stock that you have shorted at $70 (this is a "protective call"). What are the expiration date profits to this position for stock prices of $60, $65, $70, $75, and $80 if the call premium is $5.20?

19. **Option Strategies**   You simultaneously write a covered put and buy a protective call, both with strike prices of $70, on stock that you have shorted at $70. What are the expiration date payoffs to this position for stock prices of $60, $65, $70, $75, and $80?

20. **Option Strategies**   You simultaneously write a put and buy a call, both with strike prices of $70, naked, i.e., without any position in the underlying stock. What are the expiration date payoffs to this position for stock prices of $60, $65, $70, $75, and $80?

21. **Option Strategies**   You buy a straddle, which means you purchase a put and a call with the same strike price. The put price is $2.10 and the call price is $4.60. Assume the strike price is $75. What are the expiration date profits to this position for stock prices of $65, $70, $75, $80, and $85? What are the expiration date profits for these same stock prices? What are the break-even stock prices?

22. **Index Option Positions**   Suppose you buy one SPX call option with a strike of 1300 and write one SPX call option with a strike of 1350. What are the payoffs at maturity to this position for S&P 500 index levels of 1250, 1300, 1350, 1400, and 1450?

23. **Index Option Positions**   Suppose you buy one SPX put option with a strike of 1300 and write one SPX put option with a strike of 1350. What are the payoffs at maturity to this position for S&P 500 index levels of 1200, 1250, 1300, 1350, and 1400?

24. **Index Option Positions**   Suppose you buy one SPX call option with a strike of 1300 and write one SPX put option with a strike of 1300. What are the payoffs at maturity to this position for S&P 500 index levels of 1200, 1250, 1300, 1350, and 1400?

25. **Index Option Positions**   Suppose you buy one each SPX call options with strikes of 1200 and 1400 and write two SPX call options with a strike of 1300. What are the payoffs at maturity to this position for S&P 500 index levels of 1100, 1150, 1200, 1250, 1300, 1350, and 1400?

What's on the Web

1. **Option Prices**   You want to find the option prices for Intel (INTC). Go to finance.yahoo.com and find the option price quotes for Intel. What is the option premium and strike price for the highest and lowest strike price options that are nearest to expiring? What are the option premium and strike price for the highest and lowest strike price options expiring next month?

2. **Option Symbol Construction**   What is the option symbol for a call option on Cisco Systems (CSCO) with a strike price of $25 that expires in July? Go to www.cboe.com, and find the links for the option ticker symbol construction. Find the basic ticker symbol for Cisco Systems

options, the codes for the expiration month, and strike price. Use these codes to construct the call option ticker symbol. Now construct the ticker symbol for a put option with the same strike price and expiration.

3. **Option Expiration**   Go to www.cboe.com, and find the expiration calendar for options traded on the CBOE. What day do equity options expire in the current month? What day do they expire next month?

4. **LEAPS**   Go to www.cboe.com and find the link for LEAPS. What are LEAPS? What are the two types of LEAPS? What are the benefits of equity LEAPS? What are the benefits of index LEAPS?

5. **FLEX Options**   Go to www.cboe.com and find the link for "FLEX Options." What is a FLEX option? When do FLEX options expire? What is the minimum size of a FLEX option?

Stock-Trak Exercises

STOCK|TRAK
GLOBAL PORTFOLIO SIMULATIONS

To access the Stock-Trak Exercise for this chapter, please visit the book Web site at www.mhhe.com/jm4e and choose the corresponding chapter.

CHAPTER 16

Option Valuation

"I have compared the results of observation with those of theory . . . to show that the market, unwittingly, obeys a law which governs it, the law of probability."

–Louis Bachelier

Just what is an option worth? Actually, this is one of the more difficult questions in finance. Option valuation is an esoteric area of finance since it often involves complex mathematics. Fortunately, just like most options professionals, you can learn quite a bit about option valuation with only modest mathematical tools. But no matter how far you might wish to delve into this topic, you must begin with the Black-Scholes-Merton option pricing model. This model is the core from which all other option pricing models trace their ancestry. ■

The previous chapter introduced the basics of stock options. From an economic standpoint, perhaps the most important subject was the expiration date payoffs of stock options. Bear in mind that when investors buy options today, they are buying risky future payoffs. Likewise, when investors write options today, they become obligated to make risky future payments. In a competitive financial marketplace, option prices observed each day are collectively agreed on by buyers and writers assessing the likelihood of all possible future payoffs and payments. Option prices are set accordingly.

In this chapter, we discuss stock option prices. This discussion begins with the Black-Scholes-Merton option pricing model, which is widely regarded by finance professionals as the premier model of stock option valuation.

TWO U.S. ECONOMISTS WIN THE NOBEL PRIZE FOR WORK ON OPTIONS

Two economists with close ties to Wall Street, Robert C. Merton and Myron S. Scholes, won the Nobel Memorial Prize in Economic Science for path-breaking work that helped spawn the $148 billion stock-options industry.

The Nobel economics prize is given to innovators whose work breaks new ground and sires whole bodies of economic research. But this year, the prize committee chose laureates not only with distinguished academic records, but also with especially pragmatic bents, to split the $1 million award. Prof. Merton, 53 years old, teaches at Harvard Business School, while Prof. Scholes, 56, has emeritus status from the Stanford Graduate School of Business.

In the early 1970s, Prof. Scholes, with the late mathematician Fischer Black, invented an insightful method of pricing options and warrants at a time when most investors and traders still relied on educated guesses to determine the value of various stock-market products. Prof. Merton later demonstrated the broad applicability of the Black-Scholes options-pricing formula, paving the way for the incredible growth of markets in options and other derivatives.

"Thousands of traders and investors now use this formula every day to value stock options in markets throughout the world," the Royal Swedish Academy of Sciences said yesterday.

The Black-Scholes Formula

In their paper, Black and Scholes obtained exact formulas for pricing options.

$$C = SN(d) - Ke^{-rT}N(d - \sigma\sqrt{T})$$

According to the formula, the value of the call option C is given by the difference between the expected share value (the first term on the right-hand-side of the equation) and the expected cost (the second term) if the option is exercised at maturity.

The Black-Scholes option-pricing model "is really the classic example of an academic innovation that has been adopted widely in practice," said Gregg Jarrell, professor of economics at the University of Rochester's William E. Simon Business School and former chief economist at the Securities and Exchange Commission. "It is one of the most elegant and precise models that any of us has ever seen."

Options allow investors to trade the future rights to buy or sell assets—such as stocks—at a set price. An investor who holds 100 shares of International Business Machines Corp. stock today, for example, might buy an option that grants the right to sell 100 IBM shares at a fixed price in three months'

16.1 The Black-Scholes-Merton Option Pricing Model

Option pricing theory made a great leap forward in the early 1970s with the development of the Black-Scholes option pricing model by Fischer Black and Myron Scholes. Recognizing the important theoretical contributions by Robert Merton, many finance professionals knowledgeable in the history of option pricing theory refer to an extended version of the model as the Black-Scholes-Merton option pricing model. In 1997, Myron Scholes and Robert Merton were awarded the Nobel Prize in Economics for their pioneering work in option pricing theory. Unfortunately, Fischer Black had died two years earlier and so did not share the Nobel Prize, which cannot be awarded posthumously. The nearby *Investment Updates* box presents *The Wall Street Journal* story of the Nobel Prize award.

time. The investor is therefore partially protected against a fall in the stock price during the life of the option.

Until the Black-Scholes model gained acceptance, the great minds of economics and finance were unable to develop a method of putting an accurate price on those options. The problem was how to evaluate the risk associated with options, when the underlying stock price changes from moment to moment. The risk of an option depends on the price of the stock underlying the option.

That breakthrough allowed the economists to create a pricing formula that included the stock price, the agreed sale or "strike" price of the option, the stock's volatility, the risk-free interest rate offered with a secure bond, and the time until the option's expiration. They published their work in 1973, the same year the Chicago Board Options Exchange turned the scattered world of options trading into a more formal market.

Prof. Merton himself forged a formal theoretical framework for the Black-Scholes formula, and extended the analysis to other derivative products—financial instruments in which the value of the security depends on the value of another indicator, such as mortgage, interest, or exchange rates. More broadly, his work allowed economists and financial professionals to view a wide variety of commonly traded financial instruments—such as corporate bonds—as derivatives and to price them using the ideas first expounded by Dr. Black and Prof. Scholes. "For the most part, the thing was conceived entirely in theory," said Prof. Merton.

The practical implications soon became apparent, however, as market participants flocked to the Black-Scholes-Merton approach to determine how much options are worth. "It's just a terrific yardstick for investors to help make that judgment," said Bill Kehoe, vice president and manager of the options marketing group at Merrill Lynch & Co., and an options trader since 1961.

Options markets have grown astronomically in the quarter century since the formula reached trading floors around the country. The value of U.S. exchange-traded options in 1995 was $118 billion. Last year, it surged to $148 billion, and in the first nine months of 1997, the figure hit $155 billion. More than 100,000 options series are now available. "Even now, we calculate the value of options world-wide using the Black-Scholes formula," said Yair Orgler, chairman of the Tel Aviv Stock Exchange.

Source: Michael M. Phillips, *The Wall Street Journal*, October 15, 1997. Reprinted by permission of Dow Jones & Company, Inc., via Copyright Clearance Center, Inc. © 1997 Dow Jones & Company, Inc. All Rights Reserved Worldwide

The Black-Scholes-Merton option pricing model states the value of a European stock option as a function of these six input factors:

1. The current price of the underlying stock.
2. The dividend yield of the underlying stock.
3. The strike price specified in the option contract.
4. The risk-free interest rate over the life of the option contract.
5. The time remaining until the option contract expires.
6. The price volatility of the underlying stock.

To learn more about the Black-Scholes-Merton formula, see www.jeresearch.com

The six inputs are algebraically defined as follows:

S = Current stock price

y = Stock dividend yield

K = Option strike price

The CBOE has a free options calculator that will do most of the calculations in this chapter at www.cboe.com

r = Risk-free interest rate

T = Time remaining until option expiration

σ = Sigma, representing stock price volatility

In terms of these six inputs, the Black-Scholes-Merton formula for the price of a European call option on a single share of common stock is:

$$C = Se^{-yT}N(d_1) - Ke^{-rT}N(d_2) \qquad (16.1)$$

The Black-Scholes-Merton formula for the price of a European put option on a share of common stock is:

$$P = Ke^{-rT}N(-d_2) - Se^{-yT}N(-d_1) \qquad (16.2)$$

In these call and put option formulas, the numbers d_1 and d_2 are calculated as:

expiry
A shortened way of saying "time to maturity."

$$d_1 = \frac{\ln(S/K) + (r - y + \sigma^2/2)T}{\sigma\sqrt{T}} \quad \text{and} \quad d_2 = d_1 - \sigma\sqrt{T}$$

For many links to option-related topics, see www.numa.com

In the formulas above, call and put option prices are algebraically represented by C and P, respectively. In addition to the six input factors S, K, r, y, T, and σ, the following three mathematical functions are used in the call and put option pricing formulas:

1. e^x, or $exp(x)$, denoting the natural exponent of the value of x.

2. $ln(x)$, denoting the natural logarithm of the value of x.

3. $N(x)$, denoting the standard normal probability of the value of x.

EXAMPLE 16.1 Computing Black-Scholes-Merton Option Prices

Calculate call and put option prices, given the following inputs to the Black-Scholes-Merton option pricing formula.

Stock price	$S = \$50$
Dividend yield	$y = 2\%$
Strike price	$K = \$45$
Time to maturity	$T = 3$ months
Stock volatility	$\sigma = 25\%$
Interest rate	$r = 6\%$

Referring to Equations 16.1 and 16.2, first we compute values for d_1 and d_2:

$$d_1 = \frac{\ln(50/45) + (.06 - .02 + .25^2/2).25}{.25\sqrt{.25}}$$

$$= \frac{.10536 + .07125 \times .25}{.125}$$

$$= .98538$$

$$d_2 = d_1 - .25\sqrt{.25}$$

$$= .86038$$

The following standard normal probabilities are provided:

$N(d_1) = N(.98538) = .83778 \qquad N(-d_1) = 1 - N(d_1) = .16222$

$N(d_2) = N(.86038) = .80521 \qquad N(-d_2) = 1 - N(d_2) = .19479$

(continued)

We can now calculate the price of the call option as:

$$C = \$50 \times e^{-.02 \times .25} \times .83778 - \$45 \times e^{-.06 \times .25} \times .80521$$
$$= \$50 \times .99501 \times .83778 - \$45 \times .98511 \times .80521$$
$$= \$5.985$$

and the price of the put option as:

$$P = \$45 \times e^{-.06 \times .25} \times .19479 - \$50 \times e^{-.02 \times .25} \times .16222$$
$$= \$45 \times .98511 \times .19479 - \$50 \times .99501 \times .16222$$
$$= \$.565$$

Exact standard normal probabilities provided in this example are obtained from Excel using the function NORMSDIST(x). A detailed example of how to use an Excel spreadsheet to calculate Black-Scholes-Merton option prices is shown in a *Spreadsheet Analysis* box later in this chapter.

EXAMPLE 16.2 | **Using a Web-Based Option Calculator**

The purpose of Example 16.1 was to show you that the Black-Scholes-Merton formula is not hard to use—even if at first it looks imposing. If you are in a hurry to price an option or if you simply want to verify the price of an option that you have calculated, a number of option calculators are available on the Web. Let's check our previous answers by using the option calculator we found at www.DerivativesModels.com:

Solve For	Price
	European Call
Asset	50
Strike	45
Volatility	25
Rate	6
Dividend	2
Expiry	.25
Price	5.98514
Delta	0.8336
Gamma	0.03909
Vega	6.13278

www.DerivativesModels.com

Solve For	Price
	European Put
Asset	50
Strike	45
Volatility	25
Rate	6
Dividend	2
Expiry	.25
Price	0.56455
Delta	-0.16141
Gamma	0.03909
Vega	6.13278

www.DerivativesModels.com

As you can see, our answers in Example 16.1 check out (except for small rounding differences). You might be wondering about the word "expiry." **Expiry** is a shortened way of saying "time to option contract maturity" or "time to maturity" for any contract. You might also be wondering what delta, gamma, and vega represent. We discuss these terms later in the chapter.

CHECK THIS

16.1a Consider the following inputs to the Black-Scholes-Merton option pricing model.

$$S = \$65 \qquad y = 0\%$$
$$K = \$60 \qquad r = 5\%$$
$$T = .25 \text{ years} \qquad \sigma = 25\%$$

These input values yield a call option price of $6.78 and a put option price of $1.03.

Verify these prices from your own calculations.

16.2 Valuing Employee Stock Options

Visit the Coca-Cola
Web site at
www.coca-cola.com
for more investor
information

An interesting application of the Black-Scholes-Merton option pricing formula is the valuation of employee stock options, which we discussed in our previous chapter. Companies issuing stock options to employees must report estimates of their value in financial statements. The Black-Scholes-Merton formula is widely used for this purpose. For example, in December 2002, the Coca-Cola Company granted employee stock options to several executives representing over a half million shares of Coke stock. The options had a stated term of 15 years, but, to allow for the fact that employee stock options are often exercised before maturity, Coca-Cola used two time horizon assumptions to value the options: the longest possible term of 15 years and an expected term of 6 years. The company then adjusted their interest rate, dividend yield, and volatility assumptions to each of these terms.

The different input values assumed and the resulting Black-Scholes option values are summarized in Table 16.1. Notice that Coca-Cola assumed a higher volatility and dividend yield, but a lower riskless interest rate for the six-year time horizon assumption. This seems reasonable given that stock market volatility was high and interest rates were low in 2002 compared to recent experience. A *Wall Street Journal* article discussing the valuation of these Coke options is contained in the nearby *Investment Updates* box.

TABLE 16.1	Coca-Cola Employee Stock Options

Inputs	Input Value Assumptions	
Stock price	$44.55	$44.55
Exercise price	$44.655	$44.655
Time horizon	15 years	6 years
Volatility	25.53%	30.20%
Risk-free interest rate	5.65%	3.40%
Dividend yield	1.59%	1.70%
Black-Scholes-Merton option value	$19.92	$13.06

COKE PLAN FOR OPTION VALUING FIZZLES OUT AFTER FEW MONTHS: NEWS DASHES HOPES FOR ALTERNATIVE TO BLACK-SCHOLES EXPENSING MODELS

Coca-Cola Co.'s novel plan for valuing its employee stock-option compensation has fizzled out.

The world's biggest soft-drink company made a splash in July by announcing it would begin recognizing stock-option compensation as an expense on its financial statements. But it wasn't just Coke's decision to expense that piqued market interest. Even more noteworthy was the unique valuation method it planned to use, at Coke director Warren Buffett's urging. Instead of using Wall Street's much maligned, but widely used, Black-Scholes mathematical models, Coke said it would solicit quotations from two independent financial institutions to buy and sell Coke shares under the identical terms of the options to be expensed. Coke then would average the quotations to determine the value of the options.

So much for that plan.

Coke now concedes it won't work and that it will use Black-Scholes after all, notwithstanding the method's drawbacks. The disclosure almost certainly will disappoint investors who favor mandatory expensing of option-based compensation, but had been hoping for a feasible alternative to the subjective results often produced by Black-Scholes models.

It also signals that Black-Scholes, like it or not, may remain the norm even should the Financial Accounting Standards Board follow through with its plans to unveil a proposal this year mandating that public companies treat stock-option compensation as an expense.

Coke executives Thursday said they had no choice but to abandon the Buffett-backed plan. They said the company eventually concluded that current accounting standards wouldn't allow the new approach and instead require companies to perform their own value calculations.

In any event, the disclosure in Coke's proxy shows that dealer quotes wouldn't have yielded any different results than a Black-Scholes calculation. Coke says it determined the value of the options through Black-Scholes calculations—and only then obtained independent market quotes from two dealers "to ensure the best market-based assumptions were used." And, as it turned out, "our Black-Scholes value was not materially different from the independent quotes," Coke's proxy says. Coke declined to name the two financial institutions.

Because the dealer quotes were so similar, "you can assume they use Black-Scholes too," says Gary Fayard, Coke's chief financial officer. Asked if an alternative to Black-Scholes is needed, Mr. Fayard says, "I think it's something that business and the accounting profession need to work on and evaluate."

Given the lack of any meaningful difference, some accounting specialists say future efforts to seek market quotations for employee options likely will be pointless. "All they did was go to the expense of getting quotes from two independent parties who may have used the Black-Scholes model themselves," says Jack Ciesielski, publisher of the Analyst's Accounting Observer newsletter in Baltimore. "The whole affair winds up being an exercise in circularity."

While expensing options remains voluntary, all public companies are required to disclose what the effect on their earnings would be if they did expense options. Most such disclosures rely on variants of the model published in the 1970s by economists Fischer Black and Myron Scholes.

Like almost all valuation models, Black-Scholes hinges on lots of assumptions. For instance, option-pricing models typically require projections of the underlying security's future volatility, as well as the option's expected life. Those aren't easy to project with any precision. Even small changes in assumptions can make crucial differences in results and, consequently, a company's reported expenses. What's more, the Black-Scholes model wasn't designed to value options that, like the kind companies grant to employees, aren't freely transferable.

For example, SEC proxy rules required Coke to assume the options' time horizon would be the full life of the options' terms, or 15 years. That drove Coke to assume relatively lower volatility, given the lengthy time horizon. Using those assumptions, Coke calculated that the value of its options was $19.92 a share. However, accounting rules required Coke to use the options' "expected life" when calculating the time horizon. Coke assumed six years. That reduced the options' value, though the effect was partly offset by Coke's assumptions that volatility would be higher, given the shorter time span. The result: Under that Black-Scholes calculation, the value was $13.06 a share.

Source: Jonathan Weil and Betsy McKay, *The Wall Street Journal*, March 7, 2003. © 2003 Dow Jones & Company, Inc. All Rights Reserved Worldwide.

CHECK THIS

16.2a Go to finance.yahoo.com, check the current price of Coca-Cola stock under the ticker symbol KO, and compare it to the stock price on the employee stock option grant data given in Table 16.1.

16.2b Recalculate the Black-Scholes option value for the Coca-Cola employee stock options based on the current stock price for Coke shares.

16.3 Varying the Option Price Input Values

An important goal of this chapter is to provide an understanding of how option prices change as a result of varying each of the six input values. Table 16.2 summarizes the sign effects of the six inputs on call and put option prices. A plus sign indicates a positive effect, and a minus sign indicates a negative effect. Where the magnitude of the input impact has a commonly used name, this is stated in the rightmost column.

The two most important inputs determining stock option prices are the stock price and the strike price. However, the other input factors are also important determinants of option value. We next discuss each input factor separately.

VARYING THE UNDERLYING STOCK PRICE

Certainly, the price of the underlying stock is one of the most important determinants of the price of a stock option. As the stock price increases, the call option price increases and the put option price decreases. This is not surprising, since a call option grants the right to buy stock shares and a put option grants the right to sell stock shares at a fixed strike price. Consequently, a higher stock price at option expiration increases the payoff of a call option. Likewise, a lower stock price at option expiration increases the payoff of a put option.

For a given set of input values, the relationship between call and put option prices and an underlying stock price is illustrated in Figure 16.1. In Figure 16.1, stock prices are measured on the horizontal axis and option prices are measured on the vertical axis. Notice that the graph lines describing relationships between call and put option prices and the underlying stock price have a convex (bowed) shape. Convexity is a fundamental characteristic of the relationship between option prices and stock prices.

TABLE 16.2   Six Inputs Affecting Option Prices

	Sign of Input Effect		
Input	Call	Put	Common Name
Underlying stock price (S)	+	−	Delta
Strike price of the option contract (K)	−	+	
Time remaining until option expiration (T)	+	+	Theta
Volatility of the underlying stock price (σ)	+	+	Vega
Risk-free interest rate (r)	+	−	Rho
Dividend yield of the underlying stock (y)	−	+	

FIGURE 16.1 Put and Call Option Prices

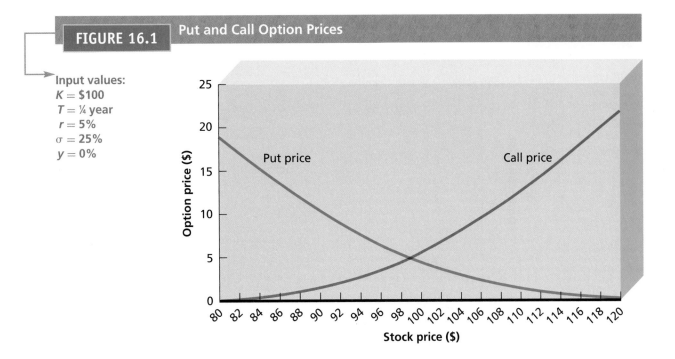

Input values:
K = $100
T = ¼ year
r = 5%
σ = 25%
y = 0%

VARYING THE OPTION'S STRIKE PRICE

As the strike price increases, the call price decreases and the put price increases. This is reasonable, since a higher strike price means that we must pay a higher price when we exercise a call option to buy the underlying stock, thereby reducing the call option's value. Similarly, a higher strike price means that we will receive a higher price when we exercise a put option to sell the underlying stock, thereby increasing the put option's value. Of course, this logic works in reverse also; as the strike price decreases, the call price increases and the put price decreases.

VARYING THE TIME REMAINING UNTIL OPTION EXPIRATION

Time remaining until option expiration is an important determinant of option value. As time remaining until option expiration lengthens, both call and put option prices normally increase. This is expected, since a longer time remaining until option expiration allows more time for the stock price to move away from a strike price and increase the option's payoff, thereby making the option more valuable. The relationship between call and put option prices and time remaining until option expiration is illustrated in Figure 16.2, where time remaining until option expiration is measured on the horizontal axis and option prices are measured on the vertical axis.

VARYING THE VOLATILITY OF THE STOCK PRICE

Stock price volatility (sigma, σ) plays an important role in determining option value. As stock price volatility increases, both call and put option prices increase. This is as expected, since the more volatile the stock price, the greater is the likelihood that the stock price will move farther away from a strike price and increase the option's payoff, thereby making the option more valuable. The relationship between call and put option prices and stock price volatility is graphed in Figure 16.3, where volatility is measured on the horizontal axis and option prices are measured on the vertical axis.

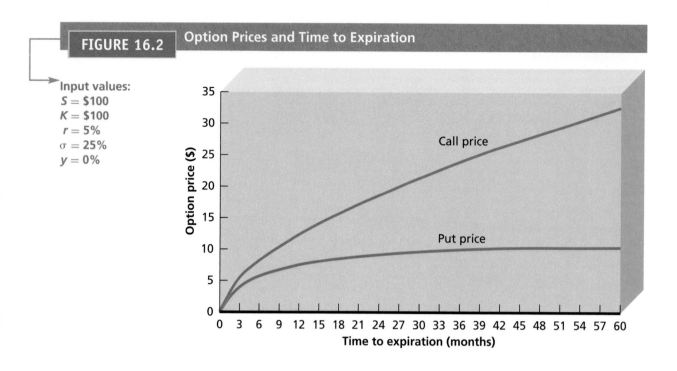

FIGURE 16.2 Option Prices and Time to Expiration

Input values:
$S = \$100$
$K = \$100$
$r = 5\%$
$\sigma = 25\%$
$y = 0\%$

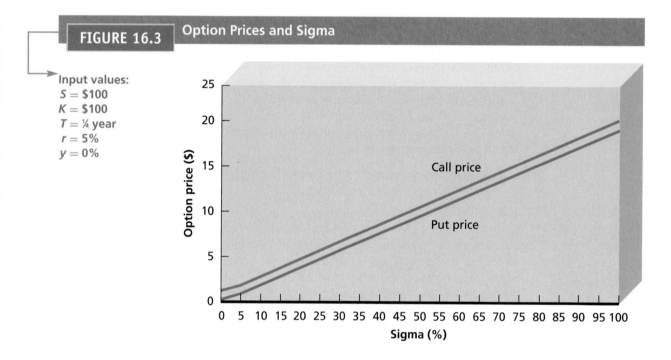

FIGURE 16.3 Option Prices and Sigma

Input values:
$S = \$100$
$K = \$100$
$T = \frac{1}{4}$ year
$r = 5\%$
$y = 0\%$

VARYING THE INTEREST RATE

Although seemingly not as important as the other inputs, the interest rate still noticeably affects option values. As the interest rate increases, the call price increases and the put price decreases. This is explained by the time value of money. A higher interest rate implies a greater discount, which lowers the present value of the strike price that we pay when we

FIGURE 16.4   Option Prices and Interest Rates

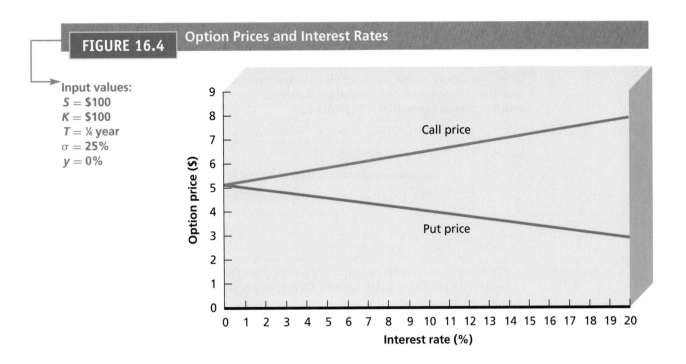

Input values:
$S = \$100$
$K = \$100$
$T = ¼$ year
$\sigma = 25\%$
$y = 0\%$

exercise a call option or receive when we exercise a put option. Figure 16.4 graphs the re-lationship between call and put option prices and interest rates, where the interest rate is measured on the horizontal axis and option prices are measured on the vertical axis.

VARYING THE DIVIDEND YIELD

A stock's dividend yield has an important effect on option values. As the dividend yield in-creases, the call price decreases and the put price increases. This follows from the fact that when a company pays a dividend, its assets are reduced by the amount of the dividend, causing a like decrease in the price of the stock. Then, as the stock price decreases, the call price decreases and the put price increases.

16.4 Measuring the Impact of Input Changes on Option Prices

Investment professionals using options in their investment strategies have standard meth-ods to state the impact of changes in input values on option prices. The two inputs that most affect stock option prices over a short period, say, a few days, are the stock price and the stock price volatility. The approximate impact of a stock price change on an option price is stated by the option's **delta**. In the Black-Scholes-Merton option pricing model, expres-sions for call and put option deltas are stated as follows, where the mathematical functions e^x and $N(x)$ are as previously defined:

delta
Measure of the dollar impact of a change in the underlying stock price on the value of a stock option. Delta is positive for a call option and negative for a put option.

$$\text{Call option delta} = e^{-yT} N(d_1) > 0$$
$$\text{Put option delta} = -e^{-yT} N(-d_1) < 0$$

As shown above, a call option delta is always positive and a put option delta is always negative. This can be seen in Table 16.2, where + indicates a positive effect for a call option and − indicates a negative effect for a put option resulting from an increase in the underlying stock price.

EXAMPLE 16.3 | **Computing Call and Put Option Deltas**

Given the inputs to the Black-Scholes-Merton option pricing formula provided in Example 16.1, calculate call and put option deltas. The necessary values for d_1, $N(d_1)$, and $N(-d_1)$ were provided in Example 16.1.

$$N(d_1) = N(.98538) = .83778 \qquad N(-d_1) = 1 - N(d_1) = .16222$$

Deltas are then calculated as:

$$\textit{Call option delta} = .99501 \times .83778 = .83360$$
$$\textit{Put option delta} = -.99501 \times .16222 = -.16141$$

eta

Measure of the percentage impact of a change in the underlying stock price on the value of a stock option. Eta is positive for a call option and negative for a put option.

The approximate percentage impact of a stock price change on an option price is stated by the option's **eta**. In the Black-Scholes-Merton option pricing model, expressions for call and put option etas are stated as follows, where the mathematical functions e^x and $N(x)$ are as previously defined:

$$\textit{Call option eta} = \quad e^{-yT} N(d_1) S/C \quad > 1$$
$$\textit{Put option eta} = -e^{-yT} N(-d_1) S/P < -1$$

In the Black-Scholes-Merton option pricing model, a call option eta is greater than $+1$ and a put option eta is less than -1.

EXAMPLE 16.4 | **Computing Call and Put Option Etas**

Given the inputs to the Black-Scholes-Merton option pricing formula provided in Example 16.1, calculate call and put option etas.

As shown above, option etas are simply option deltas multiplied by the stock price and divided by the option price. Thus, in this example, they are calculated from values provided above as follows:

$$\textit{Call option eta} = .83360 \times 50/5.985 = 6.964$$
$$\textit{Put option eta} = -.16141 \times 50/.565 = -14.284$$

vega

Measure of the impact of a change in stock price volatility on the value of a stock option. Vega is positive for both a call option and a put option.

The approximate impact of a volatility change on an option's price is measured by the option's **vega**.[1] In the Black-Scholes-Merton option pricing model, vega is the same for call and put options and is stated as follows, where the mathematical function $n(x)$ represents a standard normal density.

$$Vega = S e^{-yT} n(d_1) \sqrt{T} > 0$$

Vega is always positive. Again, this can be seen in Table 16.2, where + indicates a positive effect on price for both a call option and a put option from a volatility increase.

---

[1] Those of you who are scholars of the Greek language recognize that "vega" is not a Greek letter like the other option sensitivity measures. (It is a star in the constellation Lyra.) Alas, the term *vega* has entered the options professionals' vocabulary and is in widespread use.

Computing Call and Put Option Vegas

Given the inputs to the Black-Scholes-Merton option pricing formula provided in Example 16.1, calculate call and put option vegas.

The vega for a call option is the same as the vega for a put option. Computing vega requires calculation of the standard normal density value for d_1. This is calculated as shown here.

$$n(d_1) = \frac{e^{-d_1^2/2}}{\sqrt{2\pi}} = \frac{e^{-.98538^2/2}}{\sqrt{6.28318}} = .245508$$

Substituting appropriate values into the vega formula yields this vega value:

$$\textit{Vega} = 50 \times .99501 \times .245508 \times \sqrt{.25} = 6.107$$

Refer to the nearby *Spreadsheet Analysis* box for examples of calculating Black-Scholes-Merton call and put option prices as well as deltas, etas, and vega using a spreadsheet. Note that rounding errors result in a slightly different value for the put option eta.[2]

INTERPRETING OPTION DELTAS

Interpreting the meaning of an option delta is relatively straightforward. Delta measures the impact of a change in the stock price on an option price, where a $1 change in the stock price causes an option price to change by approximately delta dollars. For example, using the input values stated immediately below, we obtain a call option price (rounded) of $5.99 and a put option price of $.56. These yield a call option delta of +.83 and a put option delta of −.16.

$$S = \$50 \qquad y = 2\%$$
$$K = \$45 \qquad r = 6\%$$
$$T = .25 \qquad \sigma = 25\%$$

If we change the stock price from $50 to $51, we get a call option price of $6.84 and a put option price of $.42. Thus, a +$1 stock price change increased the call option price by $.85 and decreased the put option price by $.14. These price changes are close to, but not exactly equal to, the call option delta value of +.83 and put option delta value of −.16.

INTERPRETING OPTION ETAS

Eta measures the percentage impact of a change in the stock price on an option price, where a 1 percent change in the stock price causes an option price to change by approximately eta percent. For example, the input values stated above yield a call option price of $5.99, and a put option price of $.56, a call option eta of 6.96, and a put option eta of −14.28. If the stock price changes by 1 percent from $50 to $50.50, we get a call option price of $6.41 and a put option price of $.49. Thus, a 1 percent stock price change increased the call option price by 7.01 percent and decreased the put option price by 12.50 percent. These percentage price changes are close to the call option eta value of +6.96 and put option eta value of −14.28.

INTERPRETING OPTION VEGAS

Interpreting the meaning of an option vega is also straightforward. Vega measures the impact of a change in stock price volatility on an option price, where a 1 percent change in sigma changes an option price by approximately the amount of .01 times vega. For example,

[2]The careful reader will note that the value for vega also differs slightly from the value in Example 16.2.

SPREADSHEET ANALYSIS

	A	B	C	D	E	F	G
1							
2			Calculating Black-Scholes-Merton Option Prices				
3							
4	XYZ stock has a price of $50 and an annual return volatility of 25 percent. The riskless						
5	interest rate is 6 percent and the stock pays a 2 percent dividend yield. Calculate						
6	call and put option prices with a strike price of $45 and a 3-month time to expiration.						
7							
8	Stock =	50		d1 =	0.9854	N(d1) =	0.8378
9	Strike =	45				N(-d1) =	0.1622
10	Volatility =	0.25		d2 =	0.8604	N(d2) =	0.8052
11	Yield =	0.02				N(-d2) =	0.1948
12	Time =	0.25				exp(-Yield x Time) =	0.9950
13	Rate =	0.06				exp(-Rate x Time) =	0.9851
14							
15	Call Price =	Stock x exp(-Yield x Time) x N(d1)					
16		-Strike x exp(-Rate x Time) x N(d2) =			5.985		
17							
18	Put Price =	Strike x exp(-Rate x Time) x N(-d2)					
19		-Stock x exp(-Yield x Time) x N(-d1) =			0.565		
20							
21	Formula entered in E8 is =(LN(B8/B9)+(B13-B11+0.5*B10^2)*B12)/(B10*SQRT(B12))						
22	Formula entered in E10 is =E8-B10*SQRT(B12)						
23	Formulas entered in G8 and G9 are =NORMSDIST(E8) and =NORMSDIST(-E8)						
24	Formulas entered in G10 and G11 are =NORMSDIST(E10) and =NORMSDIST(-E10)						
25							
26							
27			Calculating Black-Scholes-Merton Greeks				
28							
29	Call Delta =	exp(-Yield x Time) x N(d1) =					0.8336
30	Put Delta =	-exp(-Yield x Time) x N(-d1) =					−0.1614
31	Call Eta =	Call Delta x Stock/Call Price =					6.9639
32	Put Eta =	Put Delta x Stock/Put Price =					−14.2952
33	Gamma =	(exp(-(d1^2/2))/sqrt(2*Pi)) /					
34		(exp(-Yield x Time) x Stock x Volatility x sqrt(Time)) =					0.0395
35	Vega =	(exp(-(d1^2/2))/sqrt(2 x Pi)) x					
36		exp(-Yield x Time) x Stock x sqrt(Time) =					6.1071
37							
38	Notes: Gamma and Vega are the same for calls and puts using the Black-Scholes-Merton						
39	model. Also, we use the Excel function =PI() in the calculations. (Pi = 3.141592....)						
40							
41							

using the same input values stated earlier we obtain call and put option prices of $5.99 and $.56, respectively. We also get an option vega of +6.1. If we change the stock price volatility to $\sigma = 26\%$, we then get call and put option prices of $6.05 and $.63. This +1 percent stock price volatility change increased call and put option prices by $.06 and $.07, respectively, as predicted by vega.

INTERPRETING AN OPTION'S GAMMA, THETA, AND RHO

In addition to delta, eta, and vega, options professionals commonly use three other measures of option price sensitivity to input changes: gamma, theta, and rho.

gamma
Measure of delta
sensitivity to a stock
price change.

Gamma measures delta sensitivity to a stock price change, where a one-dollar stock price change causes delta to change by approximately the amount gamma. In the Black-Scholes-Merton option pricing model, gammas are the same for call and put options.

theta
Measure of the impact on
an option price from a
change in time remaining
until option expiration.

Theta measures option price sensitivity to a change in time remaining until option expiration, where a given change in option maturity causes the option price to change by approximately the amount theta. A common convention is to calibrate theta so that it measures an option price change due to a one-week change in option maturity.

rho
Measure of option price
sensitivity to a change in
the interest rate.

Rho measures option price sensitivity to a change in the interest rate, where a 1 percent interest rate change causes the option price to change by approximately the amount rho. Rho is positive for a call option and negative for a put option.

16.5 Implied Standard Deviations

The Black-Scholes-Merton stock option pricing model is based on six inputs: a stock price, a strike price, an interest rate, a dividend yield, the time remaining until option expiration, and the stock price volatility. Of these six factors, only the stock price volatility is not directly observable and must be estimated somehow. A popular method to estimate stock price volatility is to use an implied value from an option price. A stock price volatility estimated from an option price is called an **implied standard deviation** or **implied volatility**, often abbreviated as **ISD** or **IVOL**, respectively. Implied volatility and implied standard deviation are two terms for the same thing.

**implied standard
deviation (ISD)**
An estimate of stock price
volatility obtained from an
option price.

**implied volatility
(IVOL)**
Another term for implied
standard deviation.

Calculating an implied volatility requires that all input factors have known values, except sigma, and that a call or put option price be known. For example, consider the following option price input values, absent a value for sigma.

$$S = \$50 \qquad y = 2\%$$
$$K = \$45 \qquad r = 6\%$$
$$T = .25$$

Suppose we also have a call price of $C = \$5.99$. Based on this call price, what is the implied volatility? In other words, in combination with the input values stated above, what sigma value yields a call price of $C = \$5.99$? The answer comes from Example 16.1, which shows that a sigma value of .25, or 25 percent, yields a call option price of $5.99.

Now suppose we wish to know what volatility value is implied by a call price of $C = \$7$. To obtain this implied volatility value, we must find the value for sigma that yields this call price. By trial and error, you can try various sigma values until a call option price of $7 is obtained. This occurs with a sigma value of 39.22 percent, which is the implied standard deviation (ISD) corresponding to a call option price of $7.

EXAMPLE 16.6 | **Computing Implied Volatility**

Options professionals compute implied volatilities using special computer programs. The formula immediately below provides a useful alternative to compute implied volatility when you do not have a special computer program. This formula yields accurate implied volatility values as long as the stock price is not too far from the strike price of the option contract.

$$\sigma \approx \frac{\sqrt{2\pi/T}}{Y + X} \left[C - \frac{Y - X}{2} + \sqrt{\left(C - \frac{Y - X}{2}\right)^2 - \frac{(Y - X)^2}{\pi}} \right]$$

(continued)

In this formula,

$$Y = Se^{-yT} \quad \text{and} \quad X = Ke^{-rT}$$

As an example calculation, substitute the following input values into the above formula:

$S = \$50 \qquad y = 2\%$

$K = \$45 \qquad r = 6\%$

$T = .25 \qquad C = \$7$

The result yields this implied standard deviation value:

$$\frac{\sqrt{6.2832/.25}}{49.75 + 44.33}\left[7 - \frac{49.75 - 44.33}{2} + \sqrt{\left(7 - \frac{49.75 - 44.33}{2}\right)^2 - \frac{(49.75 - 44.33)^2}{3.1416}}\right]$$

$$= .3889 = 38.89\%$$

This is quite close to the exact implied standard deviation of 39.22 percent obtained using a special computer program.

WWW

For applications of implied volatility, see www.ivolatility.com

You can easily obtain an estimate of stock price volatility for almost any stock with option prices reported in *The Wall Street Journal*. For example, suppose you wish to obtain an estimate of stock price volatility for Microsoft common stock. Because Microsoft stock trades on NASDAQ under the ticker MSFT, stock price and dividend yield information are obtained from the "NASDAQ National Market Issues" pages. Microsoft options information is obtained from www.wsj.com/free. Interest rate information is obtained from the "Treasury Bonds, Notes and Bills" column.

The following information was obtained for Microsoft common stock and Microsoft options from *The Wall Street Journal,* and www.wsj.com/free:

Stock price = \$89   Dividend yield = 0%

Strike price = \$90   Interest rate = 5.5%

Time until contract expiration = 73 days

Call price = \$8.25

Substituting these input values into the formula from Example 16.6 yields this implied volatility for Microsoft:

$$\frac{\sqrt{6.2832/.2}}{89 + 89.0154}\left[8.25 - \frac{89 - 89.0154}{2} + \sqrt{\left(8.25 - \frac{89 - 89.0154}{2}\right)^2 - \frac{(89 - 89.0154)^2}{3.1416}}\right]$$

$$= .52 = 52\%$$

This is quite close to the exact implied standard deviation of 52.12 percent obtained using a special computer program. Our nearby *Work the Web* box shows how to get ISDs the easy way.

VIX, VXO, VXN

Volatility indexes for the S&P 500, S&P 100, and NASDAQ 100 stock indexes, respectively, based on stock index options.

CBOE IMPLIED VOLATILITIES FOR STOCK INDEXES

The Chicago Board Options Exchange (CBOE) publishes three implied volatility indexes: the S&P 500 Volatility Index (**VIX**), the S&P 100 Volatility Index (**VXO**), and the NASDAQ 100 Volatility Index (**VXN**). These are three of the most popular measures of investor expectations of future stock market volatility. They are based on options traded on

From our discussion of implied standard deviations (ISDs), you know that solving for an ISD when you know the option price is a tedious calculation. Fortunately, most option calculators will do the work for you. Suppose you have a call option with a strike price of $85 that matures in 48 days. The stock currently sells for $88.42, the option sells for $8.65, and the interest rate is 5.2 percent per year, compounded continuously. What is the ISD? To find out, we went to the options calculator at www.numa.com. After entering all this information, here is what we got:

Implied volatility for european call option

| INPUT DATA | Share Price: 88.420 | Strike Price: 85.000 | Maturity(yrs): 0.132 |
| | Dividend Yld: 0 | Interest Rate: 5.20 | Option Price: 8.650 |

| OUTPUT | Implied Volatility = 51.77 |
| | Intrinsic Value: 3.420 | Time Value: 5.230 |

Notice the calculator changes the days to maturity to 0.132, which is 48/365 of a year. Based on the input data, the underlying stock has an ISD of 51.77 percent per year.

three major stock market indexes: the S&P 500, the S&P 100, and the NASDAQ 100. The ticker symbols for these three volatility indexes and the underlying stock indexes are summarized as follows:

Volatility Index Ticker	Stock Index	Stock Index Ticker
VIX	S&P 500	SPX
VXO	S&P 100	OEX
VXN	NASDAQ 100	NDX

Current levels for these volatility indexes are available at the CBOE Web site (www.cboe.com). You can also check them at Yahoo! Finance (finance.yahoo.com), along with the levels of their underlying stock indexes, using their ticker symbols. Note that the ticker symbols for these indexes do not correspond to traded securities and so must be preceded by a caret sign, that is, ^VIX, ^VXO, and ^VXN.

The VIX, VXO, and VXN implied volatility indexes are reported as annualized standard deviations. These volatility indexes provide investors with current estimates of expected market volatility in the month ahead. Figures 16.5A, 16.5B, and 16.5C plot VIX, VXO, and VXN volatility indexes along with their corresponding historical volatilities for the S&P 500, S&P 100, and NASDAQ 100 indexes, respectively, over the period 1995 through 2004. Notice the generally rising volatility levels until 2002, when volatility began falling back to levels observed in the mid-1990s.

FIGURE 16.5A VIX versus S&P 500 Index Realized Volatility

VIX implied volatility — Realized volatility

FIGURE 16.5B VXO versus S&P 100 Realized Volatility

VXO implied volatility — Realized volatility

FIGURE 16.5C

VXN versus NASDAQ 100 Index Realized Volatility

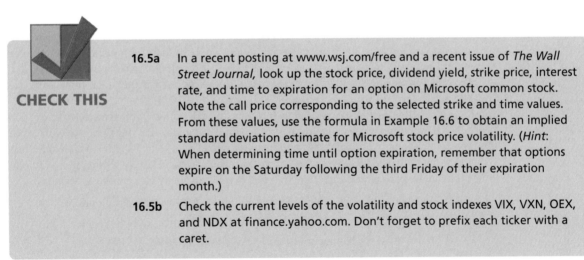

CHECK THIS

16.5a In a recent posting at www.wsj.com/free and a recent issue of *The Wall Street Journal,* look up the stock price, dividend yield, strike price, interest rate, and time to expiration for an option on Microsoft common stock. Note the call price corresponding to the selected strike and time values. From these values, use the formula in Example 16.6 to obtain an implied standard deviation estimate for Microsoft stock price volatility. (*Hint*: When determining time until option expiration, remember that options expire on the Saturday following the third Friday of their expiration month.)

16.5b Check the current levels of the volatility and stock indexes VIX, VXN, OEX, and NDX at finance.yahoo.com. Don't forget to prefix each ticker with a caret.

16.6 Hedging Stock with Stock Options

Options provide investors with the opportunity to protect themselves against losses. Taking advantage of this opportunity is known as hedging.

Suppose you own 1,000 shares of XYZ stock, the stock we analyzed in the *Spreadsheet Analysis* earlier in the chapter. From the assumptions used in the *Spreadsheet Analysis,* we calculated prices and deltas for call and put options. If we had used all the same assumptions but used a stock price of $49 instead of $50, we would get a different set of prices and deltas for call and put options. Table 16.3 provides a convenient summary (notice we have rounded the option prices to two decimal places). In Table 16.3, all option prices use these

TABLE 16.3 Using the Black-Scholes-Merton Option Model for Hedging

XYZ Stock Price	Call Price	Call Delta	Put Price	Put Delta
$50	$5.99	0.8336	$0.56	−0.1614
$49	$5.17	0.7910	$0.75	−0.2040
Change in option price:	$−0.81		$0.19	

inputs: a Strike of $45, Volatility of 25%, Dividend Yield of 2%, Risk-Free Rate of 6%, and three months to maturity.

Further suppose that you want to protect yourself against declines in XYZ stock price. That is, you want to hedge: you want to have a portfolio that does not change in value if the stock price changes. Thus, you want changes in your portfolio value from stock price changes to be equal to changes in the value of your portfolio due to options.

$$\text{Change in stock price} \times \text{Shares} = \text{Change in option price} \times \text{Number of options} \quad (16.3)$$

From earlier in the chapter, we know that the delta of an option is a prediction of how the option price will change when the stock price changes. So we can rewrite Equation 16.3 as:

$$\text{Change in stock price} \times \text{Shares} = \text{Option delta} \times \text{Number of options} \quad (16.4)$$

HEDGING USING CALL OPTIONS—THE PREDICTION

As shown in Table 16.2, stock prices and call option prices are directly related. When the stock price increases, so do prices of call options on these shares. From Table 16.3, the call option delta is .8336 when XYZ stock price is $50. The call option delta is a prediction that the call option price will increase (decrease) by about $.83 if the stock price increases (decreases) by $1.00.

So, to hedge declines in XYZ share prices using call options, you need to write, or short sell, call options to protect against a price decline. But notice that if the price of XYZ stock fell by $1.00 and you had 1,000 options, you would gain only $833.60. This would partially, but not fully, offset your loss of $1,000. You can do better by writing more options. Fortunately, you can use Equation 16.4 to tell you how many call options to write:

$$\text{Change in stock price} \times \text{Shares} = \text{Option delta} \times \text{Number of options}$$
$$-1 \times 1,000 = .8336 \times \text{Number of options}$$
$$\text{Number of options} = -1,000/.8336 = -1,199.62$$

The minus sign confirms that you should write, or sell, call options. Because traded call options have 100 options per contract, you would need to write:

$$1,199.62/100 \approx 12$$

call option contracts to create a hedge using call options with a strike of $45.

HEDGING USING CALL OPTIONS—THE RESULTS

Suppose you write 12 call option contracts at a price of $5.99 per option, or $599 per contract. Further, just as you feared, XYZ stock fell in value by $1.00, so you suffered a $1,000 loss in the value of your shares. But what happened to the value of the call options you wrote? At the new XYZ stock price of $49, each call option is now worth $5.17, a decrease of $.81 for each call, or $81 per contract. Because you wrote 12 call option contracts, your call option gain was $972.

Your gain in the call options nearly offsets your loss of $1,000 in XYZ shares. Why isn't it exact? You can see from Table 16.3 that delta also fell when the stock price fell. This means that you did not sell quite enough options. But because options contracts consist of 100 shares, you really did about as well as you could in this case.

HEDGING USING PUT OPTIONS—THE PREDICTION

As shown in Table 16.2, stock prices and put option prices are inversely related. When the stock price increases, put option prices on these shares decrease. From Table 16.3, the put option delta is −.1614 when the stock price is $50. The put option delta is a prediction that the put option price will decrease (increase) by about $.16 if the stock price increases (decreases) by $1.00.

This means that you want to purchase put options to profit from their price increase if the stock price decreases. But notice that if the price of XYZ stock fell by $1.00 and if you had 1,000 put options, you would gain only $161.40. This is insignificant when compared to your $1,000 loss in XYZ shares. You will have to purchase more put options if you are going to have a better hedge. Fortunately, Equation 16.4 also tells you how many put options to purchase:

$$\text{Change in stock price} \times \text{Shares} = \text{Option delta} \times \text{Number of options}$$
$$-1 \times 1,000 = -.1614 \times \text{Number of options}$$
$$\text{Number of options} = -1,000/-.1614 = 6,195.79$$

Because this number is positive, this confirms that you want to purchase put options. Because traded put options have 100 options per contract, you would need to purchase:

$$6,195.79/100 \approx 62$$

put option contracts to create a hedge using put options with a strike of $45.

HEDGING USING PUT OPTIONS—THE RESULTS

Suppose you purchase 62 put option contracts at a price of $.56 per option, or $56 per contract. Again, as you feared, XYZ stock fell in value by $1.00, so you suffered a $1,000 loss in the value of your shares. But what happened to the value of the put options? At the new XYZ stock price of $49, each put option is now worth $.75, an increase of $.19 for each put option, or $19 per contract. Because you purchased 62 put option contracts, your put option gain was $1,178.

Your gain in the put options more than offsets your loss of $1,000 in XYZ shares. Why isn't it exact? You can see from Table 16.3 that the put delta also fell when the stock price fell (but it increased in absolute value). This means that you purchased too many put options. If you had purchased 52 or 53 put option contracts, you would have offset your share loss more closely. How would you have known the 52 or 53 put options make a better hedge than 62 options?

By constructing a table similar to Table 16.3 in advance, you would know that these put options increase in value by $.19 when the stock falls in value by $1. Therefore, each put option contract increases by about $19. Dividing $1,000 by $19 yields 52.63, telling us that 52 or 53 put contracts will provide a good hedge.

CHECK THIS

16.6a What happens to call and put prices when the price of the underlying stock changes?

16.6b What is the goal of a hedger who uses options?

16.7 Hedging a Stock Portfolio with Stock Index Options

Hedging is a common use of stock options among portfolio managers. In particular, many institutional money managers make some use of stock index options to hedge the equity portfolios they manage. In this section, we examine how an equity portfolio manager might hedge a diversified stock portfolio using stock index options.

To begin, suppose that you manage a $10 million diversified portfolio of large-company stocks and that you maintain a portfolio beta of 1 for this portfolio. With a beta of 1, changes in the value of your portfolio closely follow changes in the Standard & Poor's 500 index. Therefore, you decide to use options on the S&P 500 index as a hedging vehicle. S&P 500 index options trade on the Chicago Board Options Exchange (CBOE) under the ticker symbol SPX. SPX option prices are reported daily in the "Index Options Trading" column of *The Wall Street Journal*. Each SPX option has a contract value of 100 times the current level of the S&P 500 index.

WWW

For stock option reports, see www.aantix.com

SPX options are a convenient hedging vehicle for an equity portfolio manager because they are European style and because they settle in cash at expiration. For example, suppose you hold one SPX call option with a strike price of 1500 and at option expiration, the S&P 500 index stands at 1507. In this case, your cash payoff is 100 times the difference between the index level and the strike price, or $100 \times (\$1507 - 1500) = \$700$. Of course, if the expiration date index level falls below the strike price, your SPX call option expires worthless.

Hedging a stock portfolio with index options requires first calculating the number of option contracts needed to form an effective hedge. While you can use either put options or call options to construct an effective hedge, we assume that you decide to use call options to hedge your $10 million equity portfolio. Using stock index call options to hedge an equity portfolio involves writing a certain number of option contracts. In general, the number of stock index option contracts needed to hedge an equity portfolio is stated by the equation:

$$\text{Number of option contracts} = \frac{\text{Portfolio beta} \times \text{Portfolio value}}{\text{Option delta} \times \text{Option contract value}} \quad (16.5)$$

In your particular case, you have a portfolio beta of 1 and a portfolio value of $10 million. You now need to calculate an option delta and option contract value.

The option contract value for an SPX option is simply 100 times the current level of the S&P 500 index. Checking the "Index Options Trading" column in *The Wall Street Journal* you see that the S&P 500 index has a value of 1508, which means that each SPX option has a current contract value of $150,800.

To calculate an option delta, you must decide which particular contract to use. You decide to use options with an October expiration and a strike price of 1500, that is, the October 1500 SPX contract. From the "Index Options Trading" column, you find that the price for these options is 64⅝, or 64.625. Options expire on the Saturday following the third Friday of their expiration month. Counting days on your calendar yields a time remaining until option expiration of 73 days. The interest rate on Treasury bills maturing closest to option expiration is 6 percent. The dividend yield on the S&P 500 index is not normally reported in *The Wall Street Journal*. Fortunately, the S&P 500 trades in the form of depository shares on the American Stock Exchange (AMEX) under the ticker SPY. SPY shares represent a claim on a portfolio designed to match the S&P 500 as closely as possible. By looking up information on SPY shares on the Internet, you find that the dividend yield is 1.5 percent.

With the information now collected, you use the input values $S = 1508.80$, $K = 1500$, $T = .2$, $r = 6\%$, and $y = 1.5\%$ and option price $C = 64.625$ to get an implied volatility of 20 percent. This represents a current estimate of S&P 500 index volatility. Using this sigma value of 20 percent then yields a call option delta of .579. You now have sufficient

INVESTMENT UPDATES

MONEY MANAGERS USE OPTIONS TO HEDGE PORTFOLIOS

Traders and money managers began using options to hedge their portfolios yesterday after spending the past week ignoring defensive strategies to speculate on earnings and stock price movements.

The turning point came late in the morning when the Standard & Poor's 500 index slid below 1140. This wiped out many S&P 500 index futures positions and market professionals responded by buying S&P 500 index options to protect their portfolios from the market's volatility.

This hedging activity marked a change in the approach they have taken to the market. Many professionals recently stopped hedging their portfolios because the stock market has quickly corrected in the past. They spent money for hedges they ultimately didn't need.

"A lot of people were completely unhedged when the decline began," said Leon Gross, Salomon Smith Barney's options strategist. He noted that the S&P 500 index's rise to 1186 from 1086 took six weeks, while it dropped 50 points in only four days.

The fear in the options market spiked higher as the S&P index fell along with the Dow Jones Industrial Average.

The option market's fear gauge, the Chicago Board Options Exchange Volatility Index, rose 1.72, or 7.5%, to 24.66. "This is an indication that people are getting nervous and paying for puts," Mr. Gross said.

Options prices reflected this discomfort, which made hedging portfolios even more expensive than normal. For more aggressive traders, such as hedge funds, high options prices created opportunities to short sell puts and sectors.

The NASDAQ index of the 100 largest nonfinancial stocks was a popular way to short the technology sector. Other traders sold put options because they think the fear is overdone and they'll be able to buy the contracts back for less money.

Source: Steven M. Sears, *The Wall Street Journal*, July 29, 1998. Reprinted by permission of Dow Jones & Company, Inc., via Copyright Clearance Center, Inc. © 1998 Dow Jones & Company, Inc. All Rights Reserved Worldwide.

---

information to calculate the number of option contracts needed to effectively hedge your equity portfolio. By using Equation 16.5, we can calculate the number of October 1500 SPX options that you should write to form an effective hedge.

$$\frac{1.0 \times \$10,000,000}{.579 \times \$150,800} \approx 115 \text{ contracts}$$

Furthermore, by writing 115 October 1500 call options, you receive $115 \times 100 \times 64.625 = \$743,187.50$.

To assess the effectiveness of this hedge, suppose the S&P 500 index and your stock portfolio both immediately fall in value by 1 percent. This is a loss of $100,000 on your stock portfolio. After the S&P 500 index falls by 1 percent, its level is 1493.71, which then yields a call option price of $C = 56.21$. Now, if you were to buy back the 115 contracts, you would pay $115 \times 100 \times 56.21 = \$646,415$. Since you originally received $743,187.50 for the options, this represents a gain of $\$743,187.50 - \$646,415 = \$96,772.50$, which cancels most of the $100,000 loss on your equity portfolio. In fact, your final net loss is only $3,227.50, which is a small fraction of the loss that would have been realized with an unhedged portfolio.

To maintain an effective hedge over time, you will need to rebalance your options hedge on, say, a weekly basis. Rebalancing simply requires calculating anew the number of option contracts needed to hedge your equity portfolio, and then buying or selling options in the amount necessary to maintain an effective hedge. The nearby *Investment Updates* box contains a brief *Wall Street Journal* report on hedging strategies using stock index options.

EXAMPLE 16.7	The Option Hedge Ratio for a Stock Portfolio

You are managing a $15 million stock portfolio with a beta of 1.1 which you decide to hedge by buying index put options with a contract value of $125,000 per contract and a delta of .4. How many option contracts are required?

Plugging our information into Equation 16.5 yields this calculation:

$$\frac{1.1 \times \$15,000,000}{.4 \times \$125,000} = 330 \text{ contracts}$$

Thus, you would need to buy 330 put option contracts. (Note that this formula uses the absolute value of the put delta.)

CHECK THIS

16.7a In the hedging example above, suppose instead that your equity portfolio had a beta of 1.5. What number of SPX call options would be required to form an effective hedge?

16.7b Alternatively, suppose that your equity portfolio had a beta of .5. What number of SPX call options would then be required to form an effective hedge?

16.8 Summary and Conclusions

In this chapter, we examined stock option prices. Many important aspects of option pricing were covered, including the following:

1. The Black-Scholes-Merton option pricing formula states that the value of a stock option is a function of the current stock price, the stock dividend yield, option strike price, risk-free interest rate, time remaining until option expiration, and the stock price volatility.

2. The two most important determinants of the price of a stock option are the price of the underlying stock and the strike price of the option. As the stock price increases, call prices increase and put prices decrease. Conversely, as the strike price increases, call prices decrease and put prices increase.

3. Time remaining until option expiration is an important determinant of option value. As time remaining until option expiration lengthens, both call and put option prices normally increase. Stock price volatility also plays an important role in determining option value. As stock price volatility increases, both call and put option prices increase.

4. Although less important, the interest rate can noticeably affect option values. As the interest rate increases, call prices increase and put prices decrease. A stock's dividend yield also affects option values. As the dividend yield increases, call prices decrease and put prices increase.

5. The two input factors that most affect stock option prices over a short period, say, a few days, are the stock price and the stock price volatility. The impact of a stock price change on an option price is measured by the option's delta. The impact of a volatility change on an option's price is measured by the option's vega.

6. A call option delta is always positive, and a put option delta is always negative. Delta measures the impact of a stock price change on an option price, where a

one-dollar change in the stock price causes an option price to change by approximately delta dollars.

7. Vega measures the impact of a change in stock price volatility (sigma, σ) on an option price, where a 1 percent change in volatility changes an option price by approximately the amount vega.

8. Of the six input factors to the Black-Scholes-Merton option pricing model, only the stock price volatility is not directly observable and must be estimated somehow. A stock price volatility estimated from an option price is called an implied volatility or an implied standard deviation, which are two terms for the same thing.

9. Options on the underlying stock can be used by investors to protect themselves from declines in shares that they own. Option deltas can be used to calculate the number of options needed to hedge shares that are owned. Investors can write call options or purchase put options to provide protection from decreases in share prices.

10. Options on the S&P 500 index are a convenient hedging vehicle for an equity portfolio because they are European style and because they settle for cash at option expiration. Hedging a stock portfolio with index options requires calculating the number of option contracts needed to form an effective hedge.

11. To maintain an effective hedge over time, you should rebalance the options hedge on a regular basis. Rebalancing requires recalculating the number of option contracts needed to hedge an equity portfolio and then buying or selling options in the amount necessary to maintain an effective hedge.

GET REAL

This chapter began by introducing you to the Nobel-Prize-winning Black-Scholes-Merton option pricing formula. We saw that the formula and its associated concepts are fairly complex, but, despite that complexity, the formula is very widely used by traders and money managers. You can find out more about the Black-Scholes-Merton option pricing model on the Internet. Enter "Black-Scholes-Merton" into an Internet search engine for links to hundreds of Web sites, like J&E Research (www.jeresearch.com).

To put into practice some real-world uses for the concepts we discussed, you should gather options trading information off the Web and then use the information to trade options through Stock-Trak. Some suggested Web sites are the Web Center for Futures and Options (www.ino.com), NUMA Derivatives (www.numa.com), Optionetics (www.optionetics.com), PM Publishing (www.pmpublishing.com), and Antix Stock Option Report (www.aantix.com). Of course, don't forget the most extensive Web site for options at the Chicago Board Options Exchange (www.cboe.com).

Another important use for option pricing theory is to gain some insight into stock market volatility. Recall that in Chapter 1 we discussed the probabilities associated with returns equal to the average plus or minus a particular number of standard deviations. Implied standard deviations (ISDs) provide a means of broadening this analysis to anything with traded options. Try calculating a few ISDs for both stock index options and some high-flying technology stocks. You can learn a lot about implied volatilities and how they are used by options professionals on the Internet. Enter the search phrases "implied volatility" or "implied standard deviation" into your favorite Internet search engine for links to dozens of Web sites, like IVolatility (www.ivolatility.com).

Key Terms

delta 525
eta 526
expiry 518
gamma 529
implied standard deviation (ISD) 529

implied volatility (IVOL) 529
rho 529
theta 529
vega 526
VIX, VXO, VXN 530

Chapter Review Problems and Self-Test

1. **Black-Scholes Formula**   What is the value of a call option if the underlying stock price is $100, the strike price is $90, the underlying stock volatility is 40 percent, and the risk-free rate is 4 percent? Assume the option has 60 days to expiration.

2. **Black-Scholes Formula**   What is the value of a put option using the assumptions from the previous problem?

Answers to Self-Test Problems

1. We will use these input values to calculate the price of the call option.

   S = current stock price = $100
   K = option strike price = $90
   r = risk-free interest rate = .04
   σ = stock volatility = .40
   T = time to expiration = 60 days

   We first compute values for d_1 and d_2.

   $$d_1 = \frac{\ln(100/90) + (.04 + .4^2/2) \times 60/365}{.4\sqrt{60/365}}$$

   $$= \frac{.10536 + .12 \times .16438}{.16218}$$

   $$= .77130$$

   $$d_2 = d_1 - .16218$$

   $$= .60912$$

   The following standard normal probabilities are given:

   $$N(d_1) = N(.7713) = .77973 \qquad N(d_2) = N(.60912) = .72878$$

   We can now calculate the price of the call option as:

   $$C = \$100 \times .77973 - \$90 \times e^{-.04 \times 60/365} \times .72878$$

   $$= \$100 \times .77973 - \$90 \times .99345 \times .72878$$

   $$= \$12.81$$

2. Since we already know the values for d_1 and d_2, we can solve for $N(-d_1)$ and $N(-d_2)$ as follows:

   $$N(-d_1) = 1 - N(d_1) = 1 - .77973 = .22027$$

   $$N(-d_2) = 1 - N(d_2) = 1 - .72878 = .27122$$

   We can now calculate the price of the put option as:

   $$P = \$90 \times e^{-.04 \times 60/365} \times .27122 - \$100 \times .22027$$

   $$= \$90 \times .99345 \times .27122 - \$100 \times .22027$$

   $$= \$2.22$$

Alternatively, using put-call parity from the previous chapter:

$$P = C + Ke^{-rT} - S$$
$$= \$12.81 + \$90 \times e^{-.05 \times 90/365} - \$100$$
$$= \$12.81 + \$90 \times .99345 - \$100$$
$$= \$2.22$$

Test Your Investment Quotient

1. **Black-Scholes-Merton Model** The only variable in the Black-Scholes-Merton option pricing model that cannot be directly observed is the
   a. Stock price volatility
   b. Dividend yield
   c. Stock price
   d. Risk-free rate

2. **Delta** You purchase a call option with a delta of .34. If the stock price decreases by $2.00, the price of the option will
   a. Increase by $.34
   b. Decrease by $.34
   c. Increase by $.68
   d. Decrease by $.68

3. **Black-Scholes-Merton Model** In the Black-Scholes-Merton option pricing model, the value of an option contract is a function of six inputs. Which of the following is not one of these inputs?
   a. The price of the underlying stock.
   b. The strike price of the option contract.
   c. The expected return on the underlying stock.
   d. The time remaining until option expiration.

4. **Black-Scholes Formula** In the Black-Scholes option valuation formula, an increase in a stock's volatility
   a. Increases the associated call option value.
   b. Decreases the associated put option value.
   c. Increases or decreases the option value, depending on the level of interest rates.
   d. Does not change either the put or call option value because put-call parity holds.

5. **Option Prices** Which of the following variables influence the value of options?
   I. Level of interest rates
   II. Time to expiration of the option
   III. Dividend yield of underlying stock
   IV. Stock price volatility

   a. I and IV only
   b. II and III only
   c. I, III, and IV only
   d. I, II, III, and IV

6. **Option Prices** Which of the following factors does not influence the market price of options on a common stock?
   a. Expected return on the underlying stock.
   b. Volatility of the underlying stock.
   c. Relationship between the strike price of the options and the market price of the underlying stock.
   d. Option's expiration date.

CFA® PROBLEMS

7. **Option Prices**   Which one of the following will increase the value of a call option?
   a. An increase in interest rates.
   b. A decrease in time to expiration of the call.
   c. A decrease in the volatility of the underlying stock.
   d. An increase in the dividend rate of the underlying stock.

CFA® PROBLEMS

8. **Option Prices**   Which one of the following would tend to result in a high value of a call option?
   a. Interest rates are low.
   b. The variability of the underlying stock is high.
   c. There is little time remaining until the option expires.
   d. The exercise price is high relative to the stock price.

9. **Option Price Factors**   Which of the following incorrectly states the signs of the impact of an increase in the indicated input factor on call and put option prices?

	Call	Put
a. Risk-free interest rate.	+	−
b. Underlying stock price.	+	−
c. Dividend yield of the underlying stock.	−	+
d. Volatility of the underlying stock price.	+	−

10. **Option Price Factors**   Which of the following incorrectly states the signs of the impact of an increase in the indicated input factor on call and put option prices?

	Call	Put
a. Strike price of the option contract.	+	−
b. Time remaining until option expiration.	+	+
c. Underlying stock price.	+	−
d. Volatility of the underlying stock price.	+	+

11. **Option Price Sensitivities**   Which of the following measures the impact of a change in the underlying stock price on the option price?
   a. Vega
   b. Rho
   c. Delta
   d. Theta

12. **Option Price Sensitivities**   Which of the following measures the impact of a change in the time remaining until option contract expiration on the option price?
   a. Vega
   b. Rho
   c. Delta
   d. Theta

13. **Option Price Sensitivities**   Which of the following measures the impact of a change in the underlying stock's price volatility on the option price?
   a. Vega
   b. Rho
   c. Delta
   d. Theta

14. **Option Price Sensitivities**   Which of the following measures the impact of a change in the risk-free interest rate on the option price?
   a. Vega
   b. Rho
   c. Delta
   d. Theta

15. **Hedging with Options**   You wish to hedge a $5 million stock portfolio with a portfolio beta equal to 1. The hedging index call option has a delta equal to .5 and a contract value equal to $100,000. Which of the following hedging transactions is required to hedge the stock portfolio?

   a. Write 200 index call option contracts.
   b. Write 100 index call option contracts.
   c. Buy 200 index call option contracts.
   d. Buy 100 index call option contracts.

16. **Hedging with Options**   You wish to hedge a $10 million stock portfolio with a portfolio beta equal to 1. The hedging index put option has a delta equal to .5 and a contract value of $200,000. Which of the following hedging transactions is required to hedge the stock portfolio?

   a. Write 200 put option contracts.
   b. Write 100 put option contracts.
   c. Buy 200 put option contracts.
   d. Buy 100 put option contracts.

17. **Implied Volatility**   Which of the following provides the best economic interpretation of implied volatility for an underlying stock?

   a. Implied volatility predicts the stock's future volatility.
   b. Implied volatility states the stock's historical volatility.
   c. Implied volatility is unrelated to the underlying stock.
   d. Implied volatility is an accurate measure of interest rate risk.

18. **Implied Volatility**   Two call options on the same underlying stock with the same expiration dates have strike prices of $40 and $60 and yield implied volatilities of 45 percent and 35 percent, respectively. The stock price is $50. This means that

   a. The underlying stock has two different volatilities.
   b. Both options are incorrectly priced.
   c. The volatility skew has a negative slope.
   d. The underlying stock will soon pay a dividend.

19. **Implied Volatility**   With respect to call options with three months to expiration on a particular underlying stock, in-the-money implied volatilities are higher than out-of-the-money implied volatilities. This means that

   a. The volatility skew is shifting.
   b. The volatility skew is flat.
   c. The volatility skew has a negative slope.
   d. The volatility skew has a positive slope.

20. **Implied Volatility**   The implied volatility for an at-the-money call option suddenly jumps from 25 percent to 50 percent. This most likely means that

   a. The underlying stock has just paid a dividend.
   b. The volatility jump is temporary.
   c. The option has a short time to expiration.
   d. An unforeseen event has increased the risk of the underlying stock.

Concept Questions

1. **Option Prices**   What are the six factors that determine an option's price?

2. **Options and Expiration Dates**   What is the impact of lengthening the time to expiration on an option's value? Explain.

3. **Options and Stock Price Volatility**   What is the impact of an increase in the volatility of the underlying stock on an option's value? Explain.

4. **Options and Dividend Yields**   How do dividend yields affect option prices? Explain.

5. **Options and Interest Rates**   How do interest rates affect option prices? Explain.

6. **Time Value** What is the time value of a call option? Of a put option? What happens to the time value of a call option as the maturity increases? What about a put option?

7. **Delta** What does an option's delta tell us? Suppose a call option with a delta of .60 sells for $5.00. If the stock price rises by $1, what will happen to the call's value?

8. **Eta** What is the difference between an option's delta and its eta? Suppose a call option has an eta of 10. If the underlying stock rises from $100 to $104, what will be the impact on the option's price?

9. **Vega** What does an option's vega tell us? Suppose a put option with a vega of .80 sells for $15.00. If the underlying volatility rises from 40 to 41 percent, what will happen to the put's value?

10. **Rho** What does an option's rho measure? Suppose a call option with a rho of .14 sells for $10.00. If the interest rate rises from 4 to 5 percent, what will happen to the call value?

Questions and Problems

Core Questions

1. **Call Option Prices** What is the value of a call option if the underlying stock price is $108, the strike price is $105, the underlying stock volatility is 62 percent, and the risk-free rate is 4 percent? Assume the option has 270 days to expiration.

2. **Call Option Prices** What is the value of a call option if the underlying stock price is $47, the strike price is $50, the underlying stock volatility is 50 percent, and the risk-free rate is 4 percent? Assume the option has 60 days to expiration and the underlying stock has a dividend yield of 2 percent.

3. **Call Option Prices** What is the value of a call option if the underlying stock price is $81, the strike price is $75, the underlying stock volatility is 60 percent, and the risk-free rate is 5 percent? Assume the option has 45 days to expiration.

4. **Call Option Prices** A stock is currently priced at $87 and has an annual standard deviation of 43 percent. The dividend yield of the stock is 2 percent, and the risk-free rate is 6 percent. What is the value of a call option on the stock with a strike price of $95 and 45 days to expiration?

5. **Call Option Prices** The stock of Nugents Nougats currently sells for $44 and has an annual standard deviation of 45 percent. The stock has a dividend yield of 1.5 percent, and the risk-free rate is 7 percent. What is the value of a call option on the stock with a strike price of $40 and 65 days to expiration?

6. **Put Option Prices** The stock of Lead Zeppelin, a metal manufacturer, currently sells for $86 and has an annual standard deviation of 67 percent. The risk-free rate is 6 percent. What is the value of a put option with a strike price of $85 and 29 days to expiration?

7. **Put Option Prices** What is the value of a put option if the underlying stock price is $75, the strike price is $80, the underlying stock volatility is 47 percent, the dividend yield of the stock is 2 percent, and the risk-free rate is 5 percent? Assume the option has 120 days to expiration.

8. **Put Option Prices** A stock with an annual standard deviation of 60 percent currently sells for $104. The dividend yield of the stock is 1.2 percent, and the risk-free rate is 6 percent. What is the value of a put option with a strike price of $115 and 150 days to expiration?

9. **Hedging with Options** You are managing a pension fund with a value of $200 million and a beta of 1.15. You are concerned about a market decline and wish to hedge the portfolio. You have decided to use SPX calls. How many contracts do you need if the delta of the call option is .55 and the S&P index is currently at 1180?

10. **Hedging with Options** Suppose you have a stock market portfolio with a beta of .95 that is currently worth $300 million. You wish to hedge against a decline using index options. Describe how you might do so with puts and calls. Suppose you decide to use SPX calls. Calculate the number of contracts needed if the contract you pick has a delta of .50, and the S&P 500 index is at 1100.

11. **Black-Scholes-Merton Model**   A call option matures in six months. The underlying stock price is $90, and the stock's return has a standard deviation of 20 percent per year. The risk-free rate is 4 percent per year, compounded continuously. If the exercise price is $0, what is the price of the call option?

12. **Black-Scholes-Merton Model**   A call option has an exercise price of $90 and matures in six months. The current stock price is $95, and the risk-free rate is 5 percent per year, compounded continuously. What is the price of the call if the standard deviation of the stock is 0 percent per year?

13. **Black-Scholes-Merton Model**   A stock is currently priced at $40. A call option with an expiration of one year has an exercise price of $50. The risk-free rate is 12 percent per year, compounded continuously, and the standard deviation of the stock's return is infinitely large. What is the price of the call option?

14. **ISDs**   A call option has a price of $7.25. The underlying stock price, strike price, and dividend yield are $108, $115, and 2 percent, respectively. The option has 100 days to expiration, and the risk-free interest rate is 6 percent. What is the implied volatility?

15. **ISDs**   A put option has a price of $12.10. The underlying stock price, strike price, and dividend yield are $92, $100, and 2 percent, respectively. The option has 75 days to expiration, and the risk-free interest rate is 6 percent. What is the implied volatility?

16. **Calculating the Greeks**   Calculate the price and the following "greeks" for a call and a put option with 60 days to expiration: delta, eta, and vega. The stock price is $82, the strike price is $90, the volatility is 50 percent, the dividend yield is 1.5 percent, and the risk-free interest rate is 5 percent.

17. **Employee Stock Options**   In its 10-K dated January 28, 2005, Dell, Inc., had outstanding employee stock options (ESOs) representing over 365 million shares of its stock. Dell accountants estimated the value of these options using the Black-Scholes-Merton formula and the following assumptions:

    S = current stock price = $41.06

    K = option strike price = $29.70

    r = risk-free interest rate = .0289

    σ = stock volatility = .36

    T = time to expiration = 3.8 years

    What was the estimated value of these employee stock options per share of stock?

18. **Employee Stock Options**   Suppose you hold Dell employee stock options (ESOs) representing options to buy 10,000 shares of Dell stock. You wish to hedge your position by buying put options with three-month expirations and a $45 strike price. How many put option contracts are required? Use the same assumptions specified in the previous problem. (Note that such a trade may not be permitted by the covenants of many ESO plans. If the trade were permitted, it could be considered unethical.)

19. **Employee Stock Options**   Immediately after establishing your put options hedge, volatility for Dell stock suddenly jumps to 45 percent. This changes the number of put options required to hedge your Dell employee stock options (ESOs). How many put option contracts are now required? (Except for the new volatility, use the same assumptions specified in the previous problem.)

20. **Employee Stock Options**   Suppose the put option in the previous problem has a price of $6. What is the implied volatility? (Use the same assumptions specified in the previous problems.)

    Use the following information for the next three problems: Donna Donie, CFA, has a client who believes the common stock price of TRT Materials (currently $58 per share) could move substantially in either direction in reaction to an expected court decision involving the company. The client currently owns no TRT shares, but asks Donie for advice about implementing a strangle strategy to capitalize on the possible stock price movement. Donie gathers the TRT option pricing data shown below. *Note*: A long strangle is similar to a long straddle but involves purchasing a put option at K_1 and purchasing a call option at K_2 where $K_1 < K_2$.

	Call Option	Put Option
Price	$ 5	$ 4
Strike price	$60	$55
Time to expiration	90 days	90 days

21. **Strangles**   Should Donie choose a long strangle strategy or a short strangle strategy to achieve the client's objective? Justify your recommendation with one reason.

22. **Strangle Payoff**   For the appropriate strategy in the previous problem, calculate at expiration the maximum possible loss per share, the maximum possible gain per share, and the break-even stock price(s).

23. **Delta**   The delta of the call option in the previous problems is .625, and TRT stock does not pay any dividends. Calculate the approximate change in price for the call option if TRT's stock price immediately increases to $59.

24. **Black-Scholes-Merton Model**   A stock has a price of $78 and an annual return volatility of 55 percent. The risk-free rate is 3.8 percent, and the stock pays a 1.3 percent dividend yield. Using a computer spreadsheet program, calculate the call and put option prices with a strike price of $75 and a 65-day expiration.

25. **Greeks**   Using the information in the previous problem, construct a second spreadsheet that calculates the delta for the put and call, the eta for the put and call, and the vega.

What's on the Web? _____

1. **Black-Scholes**   Go to www.cfo.com and find the options pricing calculator. There is a call and a put option on a stock that expire in 30 days. The strike price is $55 and the current stock price is $58.70. The standard deviation of the stock is 45 percent per year, and the risk-free rate is 4.8 percent per year, compounded continuously. What is the price of the call and the put? What are the delta, gamma, theta, and vega of the call and the put?

2. **Black-Scholes**   Go to www.cboe.com and find the options pricing calculator. A stock is currently priced at $98 per share and has a standard deviation of 58 percent per year. Options are available with an exercise price of $95, and the risk-free rate of interest is 5.2 percent per year, compounded continuously. What is the price of the call and the put that expire next month? What are the delta, gamma, seven-day theta, vega, and rho of the call and the put? How do you interpret these numbers? How do your answers change for an exercise price of $100?

3. **Implied Standard Deviation**   Go to www.numa.com and find the options pricing calculator. You purchased a call option for $11.50 that matures in 55 days. The strike price is $95 and the underlying stock has a price of $99.50. If the risk-free rate is 5.4 percent, compounded continuously, what is the implied standard deviation of the stock? Using this implied standard deviation, what is the price of a put option with the same characteristics?

4. **Black-Scholes with Dividends**   Recalculate the first two problems assuming a dividend yield of 2 percent per year. How does this change your answers?

CHAPTER 17

Projecting Cash Flow and Earnings

"Financial statements are like fine perfume; to be sniffed, but never swallowed."

–Abraham Briloff

Cash flow is a company's lifeblood, and, for a healthy company, the primary source of cash flow is earnings. Security analysts strive to make accurate predictions about future cash flow and earnings because an analyst who predicts these well has a head start in forecasting future stock performance. ∎

Like any security analyst, we must examine financial statements to make cash flow and earnings projections. The quality of our financial statement analysis depends on accurate and timely financial statements. Generally, firms issue financial statements that provide a fair and accurate summary of the firm's financial health. You should know, however, that firms do have some discretion in reporting financial information. In rare cases, firms issue inaccurate, or even fraudulent, financial statements. Therefore, Abraham Briloff offers sound advice when he advocates a careful viewing of financial statements.

In a previous chapter, we examined some important concepts of stock analysis and valuation. Many of these concepts depend on either cash flow or earnings forecasts. In this chapter, we probe more deeply into the topic of stock valuation through an analysis of financial statements. In particular, we focus on cash flow and earnings forecasting. In this chapter, you will become acquainted with the financial accounting concepts necessary to understand basic financial statements and to make forecasts of cash flow and earnings. You may not become an expert analyst—this requires experience. But you will have a solid grasp of the fundamentals, which is a really good start.

Most investors have a difficult time reading the financial statements that are directly issued by firms. These investors rely on secondary sources of financial information. Bear in mind, however, that no one is paid well just for reading secondary sources of financial information.

By studying this chapter, you are taking an important step toward becoming "financial-statement literate" (a good course in financial accounting is also very helpful). Ultimately, you learn how to read financial statements by reading financial statements! You know that your golf or tennis game improves with practice. Your financial statement reading skills also improve with practice. If you have an aptitude for it, financial statement analysis is a skill worth mastering. Good analysts are paid well because they provide good analyses. Who knows? Perhaps you, too, will become a financial analyst.

17.1 Sources of Financial Information

Review Regulation FD at the SEC Web site
www.sec.gov

Good financial analysis begins with good financial information. An excellent primary source of financial information about any company is its annual report to stockholders. Most companies expend considerable resources preparing and distributing annual reports. In addition to their stockholders, companies also make annual reports available to anyone requesting a copy. A convenient way to request copies of annual reports from several companies simultaneously is to use the annual reports service provided by *The Wall Street Journal*. If you open the *Journal* to its daily stock price reports, you will see a shamrock symbol (♣) next to entries for many individual stocks. The shamrock indicates that the company will send annual reports to readers who request them through *The Wall Street Journal*. Requests can be submitted by telephone or by fax.

The Internet is a convenient source of financial information about many companies. For example, the New York Stock Exchange Web site (www.nyse.com) provides a directory of Web sites for companies whose stock trades on the exchange. The content of company Web sites varies greatly, but many provide recent quarterly or annual financial reports.

In addition to company annual reports, a wealth of primary financial information is available to investors through the Securities and Exchange Commission. The SEC requires corporations with publicly traded securities to prepare and submit financial statements on a regular basis. When received, these documents are made available for immediate public access through the SEC's Electronic Data Gathering and Retrieval (EDGAR) archives. The **EDGAR** archives are accessible free of charge through the Internet (www.sec.gov) and are an excellent source of timely financial information.

The most important EDGAR document is the annual **10K** report, often simply called the "10K." Companies are required to submit an EDGAR-compatible 10K file to the SEC at the end of each fiscal year. They are also required to file quarterly updates, called 10Qs. The **10Q** is a mini-10K filed each quarter, except when the 10K is filed. Every 10K and 10Q report contains three important financial statements: a balance sheet, an income statement, and a cash flow statement. You must be familiar with these three financial statements to analyze company earnings and cash flow.

The Securities and Exchange Commission's **Regulation FD (Fair Disclosure)** stipulates that when a company discloses **material nonpublic information** to security analysts and stockholders who may trade on the basis of the information, it must also make a simultaneous disclosure of that information to the general public. Most companies satisfy Regulation FD by distributing important announcements via e-mail alerts. To receive these e-mail alerts automatically, you can simply register for the service at the company's Web site. You can usually find the registration page in the investor relations section of the company's Web site.

EDGAR
Electronic archive of company filings with the SEC.

10K
Annual company report filed with the SEC.

10Q
Quarterly updates of 10K reports filed with the SEC.

Regulation FD (Fair Disclosure)
Requires companies making a public disclosure of material nonpublic information to do so fairly without preferential recipients.

material nonpublic information
Any information that could reasonably be expected to affect the price of a security.

17.2 Financial Statements

Financial statements reveal the hard facts about a company's operating and financial performance. This is why the SEC requires timely dissemination of financial statements to the public. It's also why security analysts spend considerable time poring over a firm's financial statements before making an investment recommendation. A firm's balance sheet, income statement, and cash flow statement are essential reading for security analysts. Each of these interrelated statements offers a distinct perspective. The **balance sheet** provides a snapshot view of a company's assets and liabilities on a particular date. The **income statement** measures operating performance over an accounting period, usually a quarter or a year, and summarizes company revenues and expenses. The **cash flow statement** reports how cash was generated and where it was used over the accounting period. Understanding the format and contents of these three financial statements is a prerequisite for understanding earnings and cash flow analysis.

We begin by considering the basic structure and general format of financial statements through a descriptive analysis of the balance sheet, income statement, and cash flow statement of a hypothetical intergalactic company—the Borg Corporation.

balance sheet
Accounting statement that provides a snapshot view of a company's assets and liabilities on a particular date.

income statement
Summary statement of a firm's revenues and expenses over a specific accounting period, usually a quarter or a year.

cash flow statement
Analysis of a firm's sources and uses of cash over the accounting period, summarizing operating, investing, and financing cash flows.

WWW
Look at the Research/
Tools section at
www.thestreet.com

THE BALANCE SHEET

Table 17.1 presents year-end 2535 and 2536 balance sheets for Borg Corporation. The format of these balance sheets is typical of those contained in company annual reports distributed to stockholders and company 10K filings with the SEC. You will see quickly the accounting practice of specifying subtraction with parentheses and calculating subtotals with underlines. For example, Borg's 2536 fixed assets section is reproduced below, with the left numerical column following standard accounting notation and the right numerical column following standard arithmetic notation:

Fixed Assets	Accounting Style	Numeric Style
Plant facilities	$35,000	$35,000
Production equipment	20,000	+20,000
Administrative facilities	15,000	+15,000
Distribution facilities	10,000	+10,000
Accumulated depreciation	(20,000)	−20,000
Total fixed assets	$60,000	= $60,000

In the accounting style column, locate the row labeled "Total fixed assets." The single underline indicates this number will be used in another sum. Referring to Table 17.1, notice that total fixed assets is a subtotal used to calculate total assets, which is indicated by a double underline. With these conventions in mind, let us look over these sample balance sheets and try to become familiar with their format and contents.

The Borg Corporation balance sheet has four major **asset** categories: current assets, fixed assets, goodwill, and other assets. Current assets are cash or items that will be converted to cash or be used within a year. For example, inventory will be sold, accounts receivable will be collected, and materials and supplies will be used within a year. Cash is, of course, the quintessential current asset. Fixed assets have an expected life longer than one year and are used in normal business operations. Fixed assets may be tangible or intangible. Property, plant, and equipment are the most common tangible fixed assets. The Borg

asset
Anything a company owns that has value.

TABLE 17.1   **Borg Corporation** Balance Sheets, 2536 and 2535

	Year 2536	Year 2535
Current assets		
Cash	$ 2,000	$ 1,480
Accounts receivable	6,200	6,200
Prepaid expenses	1,500	1,500
Materials and supplies	1,300	1,300
Inventory	9,000	9,000
Total current assets	$20,000	$19,480
Fixed assets		
Plant facilities	$35,000	$35,000
Production equipment	20,000	20,000
Administrative facilities	15,000	15,000
Distribution facilities	10,000	
Accumulated depreciation	(20,000)	(17,000)
Total fixed assets	$60,000	$53,000
Goodwill	$ 5,000	
Other assets	3,000	3,000
Total assets	$88,000	$75,480
Current liabilities		
Short-term debt	$10,000	$10,000
Accounts payable	5,000	5,000
Total current liabilities	$15,000	$15,000
Long-term debt	$30,000	$20,000
Other liabilities	3,000	3,000
Total liabilities	$48,000	$38,000
Shareholder equity		
Paid-in capital	$10,000	$10,000
Retained earnings	30,000	27,480
Total shareholder equity	$40,000	$37,480
Total liabilities and equity	$88,000	$75,480
Shares outstanding	2,000	2,000
Year-end stock price	$40	$36

Corporation has no intangible fixed assets. However, rights, patents, and licenses are examples of intangible assets. Except for land, all fixed assets normally depreciate in value over time. Goodwill measures the premium paid over market value to acquire an asset. Other assets includes miscellaneous items not readily fitting into any of the other asset categories.

liability
A firm's financial obligation.

The Borg balance sheet has three major **liability** categories: current liabilities, long-term debt, and other liabilities. Current liabilities normally require payment or other action within a one-year period. These include accounts payable and short-term debt. Long-term debt includes notes, bonds, or other loans with a maturity longer than one year. Other liabilities include miscellaneous items not belonging to any other liability category.

TABLE 17.2 Borg Corporation Condensed 2536 Balance Sheet

Cash	$ 2,000	Current liabilities	$15,000
Operating assets	18,000	Long-term debt	30,000
Fixed assets	60,000	Other liabilities	3,000
Goodwill and Other assets	8,000	Shareholder equity	40,000
Total assets	$88,000	Total liabilities and equity	$88,000

equity
An ownership interest in the company.

Shareholder **equity** is the difference between total assets and total liabilities. It includes paid-in capital, which is the amount received by the company from issuing common stock, and retained earnings, which represents accumulated income not paid out as dividends but instead used to finance company growth.

The fundamental accounting equation for balance sheets states that assets are equal to liabilities plus equity:

$$\text{Assets} = \text{Liabilities} + \text{Equity} \tag{17.1}$$

This equation says that the balance sheet must always "balance" because the left side must always equal the right side. If an imbalance occurs when a balance sheet is created, then an accounting error has been made and needs to be corrected.

Financial analysts often find it useful to condense a balance sheet down to its principal categories. This has the desirable effect of simplifying further analysis while still revealing the basic structure of the company's assets and liabilities. How much a balance sheet can be condensed and still be useful is a subjective judgment of the analyst. When making this decision, recall Albert Einstein's famous dictum: "Simplify as much as possible, but no more."

Table 17.2 is a condensed version of Borg's 2536 balance sheet that still preserves its basic structure. Notice that the current assets rows are reduced to two components, cash and operating assets. We separate cash from operating assets for a good reason.

Later, we show that the net cash increase from the cash flow statement is used to adjust cash on the balance sheet. This adjustment is more clearly illustrated by first separating current assets into cash and operating assets.

CHECK THIS

17.2a What are some examples of current assets?

17.2b What are some examples of fixed assets?

17.2c What are some examples of current liabilities?

17.2d Which accounts in Table 17.1 show changes between 2535 and 2536 balance sheets?

THE INCOME STATEMENT

income
The difference between a company's revenues and expenses, used to pay dividends to stockholders or kept as retained earnings within the company to finance future growth.

Table 17.3 is a condensed income statement for Borg Corporation. This income statement reports revenues and expenses for the corporation over a one-year accounting period. Examine it carefully and be sure you are familiar with its top-down structure.

The income statement begins with net sales, from which cost of goods sold (COGS) is subtracted to yield gross profit. Cost of goods sold represents direct costs of production and sales, that is, costs that vary directly with the level of production and sales. Next, depreciation and operating expenses are subtracted from gross profit to yield operating **income**. Operating expenses are indirect costs of administration and marketing. That is,

TABLE 17.3   Borg Corporation Income Statement, Year 2536

	Year 2536
Net sales	$110,000
Cost of goods sold	(89,000)
Gross profit	$21,000
Depreciation	(3,000)
Other operating expenses	(10,000)
Operating income	$ 8,000
Interest expense	(2,000)
Pretax income	$ 6,000
Income taxes	(2,400)
Net income	$ 3,600
Dividends	(1,080)
Retained earnings	$ 2,520

these costs do not vary directly with production and sales. Subtracting interest expense on debt from operating income yields pretax income. Finally, subtracting income taxes from pretax income yields net income. Net income is often referred to as the "bottom line" because it is normally the last line of the income statement. In this example, however, we have added dividends and retained earnings information (items that often appear in a separate financial statement). To avoid a separate statement, we show here that Borg Corporation paid dividends during the year. The sum of dividends and retained earnings is equal to net income:

$$\text{Net income} = \text{Dividends} + \text{Retained earnings} \qquad (17.2)$$

In Table 17.3, note that we assume a 40 percent tax rate.

CHECK THIS

17.2e   What is cost of goods sold (COGS)?

17.2f   What is the difference between gross profit and operating income?

17.2g   What is the difference between net income and pretax income?

17.2h   What is meant by retained earnings?

THE CASH FLOW STATEMENT

cash flow
Income realized in cash form.

noncash items
Income and expense items not realized in cash form.

The cash flow statement reports where a company generated cash and where cash was used over a specific accounting period. The cash flow statement assigns all cash flows to one of three categories: operating cash flows, investment cash flows, or financing cash flows.

Table 17.4 is a condensed cash flow statement for Borg Corporation. The cash flow statement begins with net income, which is the principal accounting measure of earnings for a corporation. However, net income and **cash flow** are not the same and often deviate greatly from each other. A primary reason why net income differs from cash flow is that net income contains **noncash items**. For example, depreciation is a noncash expense that must

TABLE 17.4 | **Borg Corporation** Condensed 2536 Cash Flow Statement

	Year 2536
Net income	$ 3,600
Depreciation	3,000
Operating cash flow	$ 6,600
Investment cash flow[a]	(15,000)
Financing cash flow[b]	8,920
Net cash increase	$ 520

[a]December 31, 2536, purchase of distribution facilities from Klingon Enterprises for $15,000 (including $5,000 goodwill).

[b]Issue of $10,000 par value 5 percent coupon bonds, less a $1,080 dividend payout.

operating cash flow

Cash generated by a firm's normal business operations.

investment cash flow

Cash flow resulting from purchases and sales of fixed assets and investments.

financing cash flow

Cash flow originating from the issuance or repurchase of securities and the payment of dividends.

be added to net income when calculating cash flow. Adjusting net income for noncash items yields **operating cash flow**.

Operating cash flow is the first of three cash flow categories reported in the cash flow statement. The second and third categories are investment cash flow and financing cash flow. **Investment cash flow** (or "investing" cash flow) includes any purchases or sales of fixed assets and investments. For example, Borg's purchase of Klingon Enterprises distribution facilities reported in footnote "a" is an investment cash flow. **Financing cash flow** includes any funds raised by issuing securities or expended by a repurchase of outstanding securities. In this example, Borg's $10,000 debt issue and $1,080 dividend payout reported in footnote "b" are examples of financing cash flows.

Standard accounting practice specifies that dividend payments to stockholders are financing cash flows, whereas interest payments to bondholders are operating cash flows. One reason is that dividend payments are discretionary, while interest payments are mandatory. Also, dividend payouts are not tax deductible, but interest payments are.

The sum of operating cash flow, investment cash flow, and financing cash flow yields the net change in the firm's cash. This change is the "bottom line" of the cash flow statement and reveals how much cash flowed into or out of the company's cash account during an accounting period. In this case, $520 of cash flowed into Borg Corporation (you can also see this change in cash by comparing the cash columns in Table 17.1).

CHECK THIS

17.2i What is the difference between net income and operating cash flow?

17.2j What are some noncash items used to calculate operating cash flow?

17.2k What is the difference between an investment cash flow and a financing cash flow?

17.2l What is meant by net increase in cash?

17.2m Can you explain why a cash item like interest expense does not appear on the cash flow statement?

PERFORMANCE RATIOS AND PRICE RATIOS

Annual reports and 10Ks normally contain various items of supplemental information about the company. For example, certain profitability ratios may be reported to assist interpretation of the company's operating efficiency. For Borg Corporation, some standard profitability ratios for 2536 are calculated immediately below:

Ratio	Formula	Calculation
Gross margin	$\dfrac{\text{Gross profit}}{\text{Net sales}}$	$\dfrac{\$21{,}000}{\$110{,}000} = 19.09\%$
Operating margin	$\dfrac{\text{Operating income}}{\text{Net sales}}$	$\dfrac{\$8{,}000}{\$110{,}000} = 7.27\%$
Return on assets (ROA)	$\dfrac{\text{Net income}}{\text{Total assets}}$	$\dfrac{\$3{,}600}{\$88{,}000} = 4.09\%$
Return on equity (ROE)	$\dfrac{\text{Net income}}{\text{Shareholder equity}}$	$\dfrac{\$3{,}600}{\$40{,}000} = 9.00\%$

return on assets (ROA)

Net income stated as a percentage of total assets.

return on equity (ROE)

Net income stated as a percentage of shareholder equity.

Notice that **return on assets (ROA)** and **return on equity (ROE)** are calculated using current year-end values for total assets and shareholder equity. It could be argued that prior-year values should be used for these calculations. However, the use of current year-end values is more common.

Annual reports and 10Ks may also report per-share calculations of book value, earnings, and operating cash flow, respectively. Per-share calculations require the number of common stock shares outstanding. Borg's balance sheet reports 2,000 shares of common stock outstanding. Thus, for Borg Corporation, these per-share values are calculated as follows:

Check out the security analysis sections at www.uoutperform.com

Ratio	Formula	Calculation
Book value per share (BVPS)	$\dfrac{\text{Shareholder equity}}{\text{Shares outstanding}}$	$\dfrac{\$40{,}000}{2{,}000} = \$20.00$
Earnings per share (EPS)	$\dfrac{\text{Net income}}{\text{Shares outstanding}}$	$\dfrac{\$3{,}600}{2{,}000} = \$1.80$
Cash flow per share (CFPS)	$\dfrac{\text{Operating cash flow}}{\text{Shares outstanding}}$	$\dfrac{\$6{,}600}{2{,}000} = \$3.30$

Notice that cash flow per share (CFPS) is calculated using operating cash flow—*not* the bottom line on the cash flow statement (see Table 17.4). Most of the time when you hear the term "cash flow," it refers to operating cash flow.

Recall that in a previous chapter, we made extensive use of price ratios to analyze stock values. Using per-share values calculated immediately above, and Borg's year-end stock price of $40 per share, we get the following price ratios:

Ratio	Formula	Calculation
Price-book (P/B)	$\dfrac{\text{Stock price}}{\text{BVPS}}$	$\dfrac{\$40}{\$20} = 2.00$
Price-earnings (P/E)	$\dfrac{\text{Stock price}}{\text{EPS}}$	$\dfrac{\$40}{\$1.80} = 22.22$
Price-cash flow (P/CF)	$\dfrac{\text{Stock price}}{\text{CFPS}}$	$\dfrac{\$40}{\$3.30} = 12.12$

We use these price ratios later when assessing the potential impact of a sales campaign on Borg Corporation's future stock price. Our nearby *Work the Web* box shows another use for price ratios.

One of the more common uses of financial ratios is stock screening. Stock screening is the process of selecting stocks based on specific criteria. A popular method used by the legendary investor Warren Buffett, among others, is searching for value stocks that have high growth potential. A value stock has relatively low price ratios. However, low price ratios can also be an indication of low future growth potential, so we also want to determine if these stocks have future growth possibilities. We went to finance.yahoo.com and used the stock screener we found there. We used the preset screen named "large, growing, and cheap." This screen looks for stocks with a market cap greater than $5 billion; estimated EPS growth greater than 20 percent; P/E less than 20; and P/S less than 1.3. Here is what we found:

Yahoo! Finance Screener 2.0.6

File   Edit   View   Export   Tools   Help

New Screen   Open Screen ▾   Save Screen   Email Screen

Screen: large,growing,and cheap

Criteria	Conditions	Values
Market Cap	>=	5b
Earnings Growth Est Thi...	>=	20
P/E	<=	20
P/S	<=	1.3

Return Top   5   matches

Run Screen

Result showing top 5 matches (out of 51)

View Table | View Histogram

Ticker	Company Name	Mkt Cap	Earning...	P/E	P/S	Last T..
XOM	EXXON MOBIL CP	375.786B	33	12.733	0.398	59.6
TOT	TOTAL S.A.	159.722B	48.4	13.939	1.005	128.5
INTC	INTEL CP	145.135B	24.1	18.221	1.163	23.82
CVX	CHEVRON CORP	127.122B	25.2	9.707	0.779	61
COP	CONOCOPHILLIPS	88.529B	53.5	8.365	0.63	63.6

▸ **Quick Comparsion**   Enter Symbol(s):

Using stock screening as an investment tool is not really this simple. What we have done here is narrowed the universe of stocks to a few stocks that meet our criteria. It is now up to us to further examine the companies to determine if they are actually good investments. In other words, stock screening is not the end of the investment process—it simply narrows the field of candidates.

CHECK THIS

17.2n What is the difference between gross margin and operating margin?

17.2o What is the difference between return on assets and return on equity?

17.2p What is the difference between earnings per share and cash flow per share?

17.2q How is cash flow per share calculated?

17.3 Financial Statement Forecasting

In December 2536, Borg publicly announces the completion of an acquisition of some distribution outlets from Klingon Enterprises, LLC. The stated purpose of the acquisition was to expand sales. Complementing the acquisition, Borg also announces plans for a marketing campaign to increase next year's net sales to a targeted $137,500.

As a Borg analyst, you must examine the potential impact of these actions. You immediately contact Borg management to inquire about the details of the acquisition and the marketing campaign. Armed with this additional information, you decide to construct **pro forma financial statements** for Borg Corporation for the year 2537.

pro forma financial statements
Statements prepared using certain assumptions about future income, cash flow, and other items. Pro forma literally means according to prescribed form.

THE PERCENTAGE OF SALES APPROACH

A simple model to construct pro forma financial statements is one in which every item increases at the same rate as sales. This may be a reasonable assumption for some financial statement items. For others, such as long-term debt, it probably is not, because the amount of long-term debt is something set by company management. Therefore, long-term debt levels do not necessarily relate directly to the level of sales.

A more sophisticated model builds on the basic idea of separating the income statement and balance sheet items into two groups: those that do vary directly with sales and those that do not. Given a sales forecast, calculating how much financing the firm will need to support the predicted sales level is easy. This quick and practical model is known as the **percentage of sales approach**. You have decided to use this approach to generate pro forma financial statements for Borg Corporation for the year 2537.

percentage of sales approach
A financial planning method in which some accounts vary with the level of predicted sales.

THE PRO FORMA INCOME STATEMENT

The Borg Corporation announced projected sales for the year 2537 of $137,500—an increase of 25 percent over 2536. We use the 2536 Borg Corporation income statement and several assumptions to generate the pro forma income statement. From Table 17.3, we see that in the year 2536, the ratio of total costs to net sales was about 94.55 percent (actually 94.5454 percent). We assume the ratio of total costs to sales will be 94.55 percent in the year 2537 also.

Table 17.5 is our pro forma income statement for the Borg Corporation for 2537. To generate Table 17.5, we assume that the ratio of cost of goods sold to net sales will be the same in 2537 as it was in 2536 (80.91 percent).

We see in Table 17.4 that depreciation in the year 2536 was $3,000. Accountants grapple with various methods to produce depreciation schedules. Here, as a practical matter, we simply apply the percentage of sales approach. Depreciation expense as a percentage of sales in 2536 was $3,000/$110,000 ≈ 2.7272 percent. For the year 2537, we estimate depreciation expense to be ($3,000/$110,000) × $137,500 = $3,750. (Note that we multiplied the actual ratio in 2536 to estimated sales in the year 2537.)

TABLE 17.5 **Borg Corporation** Pro Forma Income Statement, Year 2537

	Year 2536	Year 2537
Net sales	$110,000	$137,500
Cost of goods sold	(89,000)	(111,250)
Gross profit	$ 21,000	$ 26,250
Depreciation	(3,000)	(3,750)
Other operating expenses	(10,000)	(12,500)
Operating income	$ 8,000	$ 10,000
Interest expense	(2,000)	(2,500)
Pretax income	$ 6,000	$ 7,500
Income taxes	(2,400)	(3,000)
Net income	$ 3,600	$ 4,500
Dividends	(1,080)	(1,350)
Retained earnings	$ 2,520	$ 3,150
Profit margin	3.27%	3.27%
Total costs/Net sales	94.55%	94.55%

The Borg Corporation financed the purchase of the distribution outlets with 5 percent coupon bonds, which represent long-term debt. To estimate the 2537 interest expense, we assume that the Borg Corporation pays 4 percent simple interest on its short-term debt and 8 percent on its existing long-term debt. Given these assumptions, the 2536 interest expense of $2,000 was split $400 ($10,000 × .04) for short-term debt and $1,600 ($20,000 × .08) for long-term debt. Therefore, the additional $10,000 in long-term debt added at the end of 2536 will increase interest expense on long-term debt to $2,100 ($20,000 × .08 + $10,000 × .05). Adding an assumed $400 for interest on short-term debt, the total interest expense in the year 2537 will be $2,500.

Finally, recall that we assume that the ratio of total costs to net sales will be the same in 2537 as it was in 2536 (about 94.55 percent). To achieve this, we assume that the other operating expenses account is our "plug" and if we set this account to $12,500, we maintain the desired ratio of 94.55 percent.

The effect of assuming that total costs are a constant percentage of sales is to assume that the profit margin (net income/net sales) is constant. To check this, notice that in Table 17.5 Borg Corporation's profit margin was $3,600/$110,000 = 3.27 percent in 2536 and $4,500/$137,500 = 3.27 percent projected for 2537. In this calculation, a tax rate of 40 percent is assumed for both years.

Next, we need to project the dividend payment. The decision of how much of net income will be paid in dividends is a decision that rests with the management of the Borg Corporation. However, two dividend payment schemes are reasonable: one where the *dollar* payout is the same from year to year, and one where the *percentage* payout is the same from year to year.

We will assume that Borg management has a policy of paying a dividend that is a constant percentage of net income. For 2536, the dividend payout ratio was $1,080/$3,600 = 30 percent. We can also calculate the ratio of the addition to retained earnings to net income, which is $2,520/$3,600 = 70 percent for 2536. This ratio is called the *retention ratio* or *plowback ratio,* and it is equal to one minus the dividend payout ratio. The term "plowback ratio" is logical because if net income is not paid out to the shareholders, it must be retained by the company. Assuming the payout ratio is constant, the projected dividends are $4,500 × .30 = $1,350. Thus, the addition to retained earnings is $3,150.

THE PRO FORMA BALANCE SHEET

To generate a pro forma balance sheet, we start with the balance sheet for 2536 shown in Table 17.1. On this balance sheet, we assume that some of the items vary directly with sales and others do not. For the items that do vary with sales, we express each as a percentage of sales for the year just completed, year 2536. When an item does not vary directly with sales, we write "n/a" for "not applicable." For example, on the asset side, inventory is equal to about 8.2 percent of sales in 2536. We assume that this percentage also applies to 2537, so for each $1 increase in sales, inventory will increase by $.082.

The ratio of total assets to sales for 2536 is $88,000/$110,000 = .80, or 80 percent. The ratio of total assets to sales is sometimes called the **capital intensity ratio**. This ratio tells us the amount of assets needed to generate $1 in sales. So the higher this ratio, the more capital intensive is the firm. For the Borg Corporation, $.80 in assets was needed to generate $1 in sales in 2536. If we assume that capital intensity ratio is constant, total assets of $110,000 will be needed to generate sales of $137,500 in 2537.

On the liability side of the balance sheet, we have assumed that only accounts payable vary with sales. The reason is that we expect Borg to place more orders with its suppliers as sales increase, so payables will change directly with sales. Short-term debt, on the other hand, represents bank borrowing. This account is not likely to vary directly with sales. Therefore, we write n/a in the "Percent of Sales" column for short-term debt in Table 17.6. Similarly, we write n/a for long-term debt because long-term debt will not vary directly with sales. The same is true for other liabilities and the paid-in capital account.

Retained earnings, however, will change with an increase in sales, but the increase in retained earnings will not be a simple percentage of sales. Instead, we must calculate the change in retained earnings based on our projected net income and dividends, which come from our pro forma income statement.

We can now construct a partial pro forma balance sheet for the Borg Corporation, as shown in Table 17.6. We construct the column labeled 2537 by using the percentage of sales wherever possible to calculate projected amounts. For example, inventory in 2537 is projected to be ($9,000/$110,000) × $137,500 = $11,250. More generally, the ratio of total fixed assets to sales was about 54.5 percent in 2536. For 2537 total fixed assets is projected to be ($60,000/$110,000) × $137,500 = $75,000. This amount represents an increase of $15,000 from the total fixed assets in 2536.

For the items that do not vary directly with sales, note that we initially assume no change and simply write in the existing amounts. You can see the application of this method in the column labeled 2537 in Table 17.6. Notice that the change in retained earnings is projected to be $3,150—which is the amount shown in Table 17.5.

Inspecting the partial pro forma balance sheet for the Borg Corporation, we see that total assets are projected to increase by $22,000 in 2537. However, without additional financing, liabilities and equity will increase by only $4,400, leaving a shortfall, or imbalance, of $22,000 − $4,400 = $17,600. In Table 17.6, to be safe, we have calculated this $17,600 shortfall in two ways: as the difference between total assets ($110,000) and total liabilities and equity ($92,400) and as the difference between the change in total assets ($22,000) and the change in total assets and liabilities ($4,400). We have labeled the shortfall amount as *external financing needed (EFN)*.

SCENARIO ONE

The creation of a pro forma income statement and a pro forma balance sheet points out a potentially serious problem with Borg Corporation's projected sales increase of 25 percent—it isn't going to happen unless Borg Corporation can somehow raise $17,600 in new

capital intensity ratio

A firm's total assets divided by its sales, or the amount of assets needed to generate $1 in sales.

TABLE 17.6   **Borg Corporation** Partial Pro Forma Balance Sheet, Year 2537

	2536	Approximate Percent of Sales	2537	Change
Current assets				
Cash	$ 2,000	1.8%	$ 2,500	$ 500
Accounts receivable	6,200	5.6	7,750	1,550
Prepaid expenses	1,500	1.4	1,875	375
Materials and supplies	1,300	1.2	1,625	325
Inventory	9,000	8.2	11,250	2,250
Total current assets	$20,000	18.2	$ 25,000	$ 5,000
Total fixed assets	$60,000	54.5	$ 75,000	$15,000
Other assets	$8,000	7.3	$ 10,000	$ 2,000
Total assets	$88,000	80.0	$110,000	$22,000
Current liabilities				
Short-term debt	$10,000	n/a	$ 10,000	$ 0
Accounts payable	5,000	4.5	6,250	1,250
Total current liabilities	$15,000		$ 16,250	$ 1,250
Long-term debt	$30,000	n/a	$ 30,000	$ 0
Other liabilities	3,000	n/a	3,000	0
Total liabilities	$48,000		$ 49,250	$ 1,250
Shareholder equity				
Paid-in capital	$10,000	n/a	$ 10,000	$ 0
Retained earnings	30,000	n/a	33,150	3,150
Total shareholder equity	$40,000		$ 43,150	$ 3,150
Total liabilities and equity	$88,000		$ 92,400	$ 4,400
External financing needed:			$ 17,600	$17,600
Through short-term debt:				$ 2,500
Through long-term debt:				$15,100

financing. For analysts working for the Borg Corporation, this is a good example of how the planning process can point out problems and potential conflicts. For example, if the Borg Corporation had a goal of not raising new financing, then an increase in sales of 25 percent is not possible.

If we take the need for $17,600 in new financing as given, we know that the Borg Corporation has three possible sources: short-term debt, long-term debt, and new equity. The choice of the exact combination of the three sources of financing is a decision that the management of the Borg Corporation must make. For illustration, however, we will choose one of the many possible combinations.

Suppose the Borg Corporation decides to borrow the needed funds, some via short-term debt and some via long-term debt. In Table 17.6, you can see that current assets increased by $5,000, but short-term debt increased only by $1,250 (the increase in accounts payable). If the Borg Corporation wanted to keep the ratio between current assets and current liabilities constant, it should borrow $2,500 in short-term debt. In 2536, the ratio between total current assets and total current liabilities was 4 to 3, or 1.3333 ($20,000/$15,000). In 2537, total current assets are $25,000, which means total current liabilities should be $18,750, or $2,500 more than the amount shown in Table 17.6.

TABLE 17.7

Borg Corporation Pro Forma Balance Sheet, Year 2537

	2536	Approximate Percent of Sales	2537	Change
Current assets				
Cash	$ 2,000	1.8%	$ 2,500	$ 500
Accounts receivable	6,200	5.6	7,750	1,550
Prepaid expenses	1,500	1.4	1,875	375
Materials and supplies	1,300	1.2	1,625	325
Inventory	9,000	8.2	11,250	2,250
Total current assets	$20,000	18.2	$ 25,000	$ 5,000
Total fixed assets	$60,000	54.5	$ 75,000	$15,000
Other assets	$ 8,000	7.3	$ 10,000	$ 2,000
Total assets	$88,000	80.0	$110,000	$22,000
Current liabilities				
Short-term debt	$10,000	n/a	$12,500	$ 2,500
Accounts payable	5,000	4.5	6,250	1,250
Total current liabilities	$15,000		$18,750	$ 3,750
Long-term debt	$30,000	n/a	$45,100	$15,100
Other liabilities	3,000	n/a	3,000	0
Total liabilities	$48,000	n/a	$66,850	$18,850
Shareholder equity				
Paid-in capital	$10,000	n/a	$10,000	$ 0
Retained earnings	30,000	n/a	33,150	3,150
Total shareholder equity	$40,000		$43,150	$ 3,150
Total liabilities and equity	$88,000		$110,000	$22,000
External financing needed (EFN):			$ 0	$ 0

If Borg borrows $2,500 in short-term debt, this leaves $15,100 to be raised by issuing additional long-term debt. These financing amounts are shown at the bottom of Table 17.6. Table 17.7 shows a completed pro forma balance sheet given this assumed financing decision.

We have used a combination of short-term debt and long-term debt to solve the financing problem for the Borg Corporation. It is extremely important for us to emphasize that this is only one possible strategy—and it might not even be the best strategy for the Borg Corporation. As analysts, we could (and should) investigate many other scenarios. For example, we would have to ask how the increased debt load would affect future earnings of the company.

SCENARIO TWO

The assumption that assets are a fixed percentage of sales is convenient, but it may not be suitable in many cases. In particular, we made a hidden assumption when we constructed pro forma financial statements for the Borg Corporation: We assumed that the Borg Corporation was using its fixed assets at 100 percent of capacity, because any increase in sales led to an increase in fixed assets. For most businesses, there would be some slack, or excess capacity, and production could be increased by, perhaps, running an extra shift or utilizing spare equipment.

TABLE 17.8 · **Borg Corporation** Pro Forma Balance Sheet, Year 2537

	2536	Percent of Sales	2537	Change
Current assets				
Cash	$ 2,000	1.8%	$ 2,500	$ 500
Accounts receivable	6,200	5.6	7,750	1,550
Prepaid expenses	1,500	1.4	1,875	375
Materials and supplies	1,300	1.2	1,625	325
Inventory	9,000	8.2	11,250	2,250
Total current assets	$20,000	18.2	$25,000	$5,000
Total fixed assets	$60,000	n/a	$60,000	$ 0
Other assets	$8,000	7.3	$10,000	$2,000
Total assets	$88,000		$95,000	$7,000
Current liabilities				
Short-term debt	$10,000	n/a	$12,600	$2,600
Accounts payable	5,000	4.5	6,250	1,250
Total current liabilities	$15,000		$18,850	$3,850
Long-term debt	$30,000	n/a	$30,000	$ 0
Other liabilities	3,000	n/a	3,000	0
Total liabilities	$48,000	n/a	$51,850	$3,850
Shareholder equity				
Paid-in capital	$10,000	n/a	$10,000	$ 0
Retained earnings	30,000	n/a	33,150	3,150
Total shareholder equity	$40,000		$43,150	$3,150
Total liabilities and equity	$88,000		$95,000	$7,000

If we assume that the Borg Corporation is running at 75 percent of capacity, then the need for external funds will be quite different. When we say "75 percent of capacity," we mean that the current sales level is 75 percent of the full-capacity sales level:

$$\text{Current sales} = \$110,000 = .75 \times \text{Full-capacity sales}$$
$$\text{Full-capacity sales} = \$110,000 / .75 = \$146,667$$

This calculation tells us that sales could increase by one-third, from $110,000 to $146,667, before any new fixed assets would be needed.

In Scenario One, we assumed that adding $15,000 in net fixed assets would be necessary. In our current scenario, no spending on fixed assets is needed, because sales are projected to rise only to $137,500, which is substantially less than the $146,667 full-capacity sales level. As a result, our Scenario One estimate of $17,600 in external funds needed is too high. In fact, an argument could be made in Scenario Two that the level of external funds needed is $2,600.

To begin, you can see in Table 17.8 that we have now written n/a next to the total fixed assets account and we have written in a value of $60,000 (the same as for the year 2536). When there is no change assumed for the total fixed assets account, the total assets account increases by $7,000. On the liability side of the balance sheet as shown in Table 17.5, a sales level of $137,500 generates an increase of $3,150 in retained earnings. In addition, this sales level means that the accounts payable account will increase by $1,250. The difference between the increase in total assets and the increase in total liabilities and equity would be $2,600 without any external financing ($7,000 − $3,150 − $1,250). In Table 17.8, a completed year 2537 pro forma balance sheet, we see that this is the amount that the short-term debt account has increased. That is, we have assumed that the Borg Corporation will use only short-term debt as its EFN source. You will note, however, that this assumption means that the ratio between total current assets and total current liabilities will decrease (slightly).

CHECK THIS

17.3a What is the basic idea behind the percentage of sales approach?

17.3b Unless it is modified, what does the percentage of sales approach assume about fixed asset capacity usage?

PROJECTED PROFITABILITY AND PRICE RATIOS

In addition to preparing pro forma financial statements, you also decide to calculate projected profitability ratios and per-share values under the new sales forecast. These are reported immediately below and compared with their original year-end values.

	Year 2536	Year 2537
Gross margin	19.09%	19.09%
Operating margin	7.27%	7.27%
Return on assets (ROA)	4.09%	4.09%/4.74%
Return on equity (ROE)	9.00%	10.43%
Book value per share (BVPS)	$20	$21.57
Earnings per share (EPS)	$ 1.80	$ 2.25
Cash flow per share (CFPS)	$ 3.30	$ 4.25

Note that two ROA numbers are provided for 2537. The first is from Scenario One, where we assume Borg is already running at 100 percent capacity. The second is from Scenario Two, where we assume Borg is running at 75 percent capacity.

One common method of analysis is to calculate projected stock prices under the new sales scenario using prior-period price ratios and projected per-share values from pro forma financial statements. For Borg Corporation, you decide to take your previously calculated year-end 2536 price ratios and multiply each ratio by its corresponding pro forma per-share value. The results of these projected stock price calculations (rounded) are shown immediately below.

$$P/B \times BVPS = 2 \times \$21.57 = \$43.14$$
$$P/E \times EPS = 22.22 \times \$2.25 = \$50.00$$
$$P/CF \times CFPS = 12.12 \times \$4.25 = \$51.51$$

Which projected stock price is correct? Well, it clearly depends on which sales level is realized and which price ratio the financial markets will actually use to value Borg Corporation's stock. This is where experience and breadth of knowledge count immensely. Of course, no one can make perfectly accurate predictions, but the analyst's job is to expertly assess the situation and make an investment recommendation supported by reasonable facts and investigation. But some analysts are better than others. Like professional baseball players, professional stock analysts with better batting averages can do very well financially.

17.4 Starbucks Corporation Case Study

After carefully reading the analysis of Borg Corporation, you should have a reasonably clear picture of how earnings and cash flow analyses might proceed using pro forma financial statements. To further illustrate the use of pro forma financial statements in earnings and cash flow analysis, this section presents an analysis based on the 2005 financial statements for Starbucks Corporation. Using data for a real company provides a real challenge.

This section begins with a review of the 2005 financial statements for Starbucks. We then proceed to analyze the effects on earnings and cash flow that might result from two sales projection scenarios. The analysis is similar to that for Borg Corporation, with a few important differences. Note that amounts shown are in thousands of dollars (except for earnings per share).

WWW

Visit Starbucks
Web site at
www.starbucks.com

Table 17.9 is the 2005 condensed balance sheet for Starbucks. This balance sheet shows that at fiscal year-end 2005 (October 2, 2005), Starbucks had $3,514 million of total assets and $2,090 million of shareholder equity. In Table 17.10, which is the 2005 condensed income statement for Starbucks, the bottom line reveals that Starbucks earned $494.5 million in net income from $6,369 million in net sales.

From these values, we calculate Starbucks return on assets (ROA) as 14.1 percent and return on equity (ROE) as 23.7 percent. Also, after its most recent 2:1 stock split (on October 24, 2005), Starbucks Corporation had 815.4 million shares outstanding. Therefore, earnings per share in 2005 were $.61. Based on a fiscal year-end 2005 stock price of $25.20, the price-book ratio for Starbucks was 9.83, and the price-earnings ratio was 41.31.

Starbucks stock price gradually increased in value before the company filed its annual financial information with the SEC on December 16, 2005. At the close of trading on December 19, 2005, Starbucks's price was $30.65. At this time, the price-book ratio for Starbucks was 11.96, and the price-earnings ratio was 50.25.

	2005	2004
Current assets		
Cash and cash equivalents	$ 173,809	$ 145,053
Short-term investments	133,227	507,956
Accounts receivable	190,762	140,226
Inventory	546,299	422,663
Prepaid expenses	94,429	71,347
Deferred income taxes	70,808	63,650
Total current assets	$1,209,334	$1,350,895
Fixed assets		
Long-term investments	$ 261,936	$ 302,919
Property, plant and equipment, net	1,842,019	1,551,416
Other assets	72,893	85,561
Total fixed assets	$2,176,848	$1,939,896
Goodwill	$ 92,474	$ 68,950
Other intangible assets	35,409	26,800
Total assets	$3,514,065	$3,386,541
Current liabilities		
Accounts payable	$ 220,975	$ 199,346
Accrued expenses	728,273	546,178
Short-term debt	277,748	735
Total current liabilities	$1,226,996	$ 746,259
Long-term debt	$ 2,870	$ 3,618
Other long-term liabilities	193,565	166,453
Total liabilities	$1,423,431	$ 916,330
Shareholder equity		
Paid-in capital	$ 151,275	$1,025,319
Retained earnings	1,939,359	1,444,892
Total shareholder equity	$2,090,634	$2,470,211
Total liabilities and equity	$3,514,065	$3,386,541

PRO FORMA INCOME STATEMENT

To construct a 2006 pro forma income statement for Starbucks, we will use forecasted sales and the percentage of sales approach, just as we did for the Borg Corporation. As shown in the nearby *Work the Web* box, we visited finance.yahoo.com and entered the ticker symbol for Starbucks, SBUX.

Clicking on the "Analyst Estimates" link, we saw that the highest estimate for Starbucks 2006 sales was $7.9 billion, or an increase of about 24 percent from Starbucks's 2005 sales level. The low estimate was $7.46 billion, but we arbitrarily shaved that to $7.2 billion (to be very conservative relative to these estimates), which is still an increase of about

Calculating company growth rates can involve detailed research, and a major part of a stock analyst's job is to provide estimates of growth rates. One place to find earnings and sales growth rates on the Web is Yahoo! Finance at finance.yahoo.com. We pulled up a quote for Starbucks (SBUX) and followed the "Analyst Estimates" link. Below, you will see an abbreviated look at the results.

Earnings Est	Current Qtr Dec-05	Next Qtr Mar-06	Current Year Sep-06	Next Year Sep-07
Avg. Estimate	0.19	0.13	0.65	0.81
No. of Analysts	16	16	17	10
Low Estimate	0.18	0.12	0.64	0.78
High Estimate	0.21	0.14	0.68	0.86
Year Ago EPS	0.18	0.12	0.61	0.65

Revenue Est	Current Qtr Dec-05	Next Qtr Mar-06	Current Year Sep-06	Next Year Sep-07
Avg. Estimate	1.93B	1.83B	7.68B	9.08B
No. of Analysts	13	13	16	9
Low Estimate	1.89B	1.78B	7.46B	8.65B
High Estimate	1.97B	1.88B	7.90B	9.44B
Year Ago Sales	1.59B	1.52B	N/A	7.68B
Sales Growth (year/est)	21.4%	20.8%	N/A	18.3%

You can see that analysts expect sales and earnings growth to continue at brisk rates.

Growth Est	SBUX	Industry	Sector	S&P 500
Current Qtr.	5.6%	24.1%	14.1%	12.3%
Next Qtr.	8.3%	19.6%	13.6%	12.0%
This Year	6.6%	19.0%	27.6%	13.2%
Next Year	24.6%	21.1%	18.5%	13.1%
Past 5 Years (per annum)	N/A	N/A	N/A	N/A
Next 5 Years (per annum)	22.0%	13.58%	13.71%	10.50%
Price/Earnings (avg. for comparison categories)	41.3	24.16	23.22	16.67
PEG Ratio (avg. for comparison categories)	1.88	1.78	1.69	1.59

Analysts also are required to provide price targets for companies that they are following.

PRICE TARGET SUMMARY	
Mean Target:	34.17
Median Target:	35.00
High Target:	40.00
Low Target:	25.00
No. of Brokers:	12

Data provided by Thomson/First Call

	2005	2004
Total revenue	$6,369,300	$5,294,247
Cost of revenue	(2,605,212)	(2,191,440)
Gross profit	$3,764,088	$3,102,807
Operating and general expenses	$2,165,911	$1,790,168
Depreciation expense	340,169	289,182
General and administrative expenses	357,114	304,293
Other expenses	197,024	171,648
Total operating expenses	$3,060,218	$2,555,291
Operating income	$703,870	$547,516
Interest and other income	$92,574	$73,211
Earnings before interest and taxes (EBIT)	$796,444	$620,727
Income tax expense	301,977	231,754
Net income	$494,467	$388,973
Earnings per share	$0.61	$0.47
Shares outstanding (000's)	815,417	822,930

13 percent over sales in 2005. Analysts forecast earnings growth for Starbucks to be 22 percent. For our pro forma income statement for 2006, we will assume earnings growth levels of 24 percent and 13 percent.

Table 17.11 is our pro forma income statement for Starbucks for 2006. We have included 2005 for comparison. For both the high and low estimate for sales, we have assumed that gross margin, operating margin, interest income as a percentage of sales, and the income tax rate will be the same in 2006 as they were in 2005. This has the net effect of assuming that the profit margin will remain the same, about 7.8 percent.

We assume that Starbucks will not declare any dividends in 2006 and assume that Starbucks will not issue or repurchase shares. Therefore, all net income will flow to retained earnings, and shares outstanding will remain at 815.4 million. Combined, these assumptions and the two sales forecasts result in earnings per share of $.75 using the high sales estimate and $.69 per share with the low sales estimate.

PRO FORMA BALANCE SHEET

Table 17.12 contains partial pro forma balance sheets for Starbucks for 2006 using the percentage of sales approach we discussed earlier in the chapter. Again, we included the actual 2005 balance sheet for comparison. Notice that we assumed that all asset accounts will increase with sales. However, an argument could be made that short-term and long-term

STARBUCKS BREWS UP SUCCESSFUL FORMULA FOR GROWTH—BUT SOME BELIEVE STOCK IS OVERPRICED

As one of the country's great growth-stock stories, Starbucks continues to generate earnings above the market average, an extraordinary streak that has taken place every quarter since the company went public in 1992, said Ashley Reed Woodruff, restaurant analyst at Bear Stearns.

Looking at Starbucks' fiscal 2006, which began Oct. 3, Wall Street analysts expect the company's earnings to grow 20 percent to 24 percent, and revenue to rise roughly 20 percent, to about $7.6 billion, according to Thomson Financial.

Growth is something Starbucks knows, and knows well. Starbucks shares are up 27 percent since the end of August. But the stock isn't cheap. Based on forward 12-month earnings, Starbucks' price-to-earnings multiple is around 40, well above the market's average of 15.5.

Because Starbucks has historically traded at a 120 percent premium to the market, its current valuation is a bit pricey for Jim Margard, chief investment officer at Rainier Investment Management. "We're looking for growth at a reasonable price, and right now, though they're doing extremely well executing their business plan, we struggle with paying that premium," he said.

Then again, the company's profit is growing at a clip well above the market's long-term earnings-per-share rate of 7 percent to 9 percent, said Woodruff. And that's the main reason she encourages investors to buy the stock. "The debate on Starbucks is always, do they deserve that historical multiple around 40? And we think it does," she said. "The P/E is high, but they're growing at 20 to 25 percent. If the multiple stays the same, and we think it will, you should see shares also rise 20 to 25 percent."

Woodruff said stock-pickers should expect to pay extra for consistency. Rather than growing in sharp bursts and then falling backward, Starbucks has maintained same-store sales growth in the 7 percent to 9 percent range for years, she said.

By all estimates, Starbucks remains an extraordinary growth company, buyer of 2.2 percent of the world's coffee. Locally owned coffeehouses be warned: Over its next fiscal year, Starbucks plans to open 1,300 new U.S. locations—stores, kiosks, and licensed venues such as those in airports and hotels—and another 500 internationally.

David Klaskin, manager of the Pioneer Oak Ridge Large Cap Growth Fund, agrees Starbucks is first rate. But he, too, isn't so sure its shares are a good buy. To compare Starbucks with other stocks, Klaskin uses the so-called PEG valuation. To calculate it, take a company's 12-month forward-price-to-earnings multiple and divide that by its annual earnings growth rate. The lower the figure, the more affordable the shares. Currently, the market's average is 1.5.

Using a 20 percent to 21 percent annual growth rate, Klaskin calculates Starbucks' PEG multiple at 2.2. "That's not a great risk-reward," he said, adding that world coffee prices could rise and same-store sales growth could slow.

Source: Leon Lazaroff, *Chicago Tribune*, December 18, 2005. Copyright © 2005, Chicago Tribune.

---

investment levels will reflect decisions that will be made by senior management at Starbucks. Nevertheless, we will stick with our assumption. We assumed that only two liability accounts will vary with sales, accounts payable, and accrued expenses. In both cases, this assumption is reasonable.

Looking at the partial pro forma balance sheet using the high sales estimate, we see that the EFN is only about $5 million. That is, we estimate that the amount of external financing needed to increase Starbucks sales by 24 percent is insignificant (keep in mind that Starbucks has $3.5 billion in assets, so $5 million is a rounding error).

	2005	2006 (High Est.)	2006 (Low Est.)
Net sales	$6,369,300	$7,900,000	$7,200,000
Cost of revenue	(2,605,212)	(3,231,100)	(2,944,800)
Gross profit	$3,764,088	$4,668,900	$4,255,200
Operating expenses	(3,060,218)	(3,795,950)	(3,459,600)
Operating income	$703,870	$872,950	$795,600
Interest and other income	92,574	114,550	104,400
Taxable income	$796,444	$987,500	$900,000
Taxes (37.9%)	(301,977)	(374,263)	(341,100)
Net income	$494,467	$613,238	$558,900
Dividends	0	0	0
Retained earnings	$494,467	$613,238	$558,900
Gross margin	59.1%	59.1%	59.1%
Operating margin	11.1%	11.1%	11.1%
Interest income/Net sales	1.5%	1.5%	1.5%
Income tax rate	37.9%	37.9%	37.9%
Profit margin	7.8%	7.8%	7.8%
Earnings per share	$0.61	$0.75	$0.69
Shares outstanding (000's)	815,417	815,417	815,417

Looking at the partial pro forma balance sheet using the low sales estimate, we get quite a different scenario. Here, the external financing needed is a negative $222 million. How does this happen, and what does it mean? In this scenario, assets will grow by about $98 million less than the amount added to retained earnings (i.e., net income). In addition, current liabilities increase by about $124 million. This means that under the low-growth scenario (a sales increase of only 13 percent), Starbucks becomes quite the "cash cow." That is, the existing profit margin Starbucks enjoys is such that considerable future growth can be financed out of sales. At a lower projected sales growth level, less cash is needed to finance this growth, so "excess" cash accumulates.

Under the low-growth scenario, we estimate that Starbucks will generate about $222 million in additional, or "excess," cash. Senior management at Starbucks could use this additional cash in many ways. In terms of investments, Starbucks could purchase other companies, look for new ways to expand the company, or buy back its own shares in the open market. Management at Starbucks could simply let this cash accumulate while looking for places to spend it. They could even, if they choose, decide to declare a cash dividend and distribute some cash to shareholders.

At this point, we can generate a pro forma balance sheet that actually balances, depending on what sales forecast we use. Using the high sales forecast, we assume that management at Starbucks simply uses short-term borrowing for their external financing requirement. Using the low sales forecast, we assume that management puts the excess cash generated into the cash and cash equivalent accounts. Table 17.13 contains these pro forma balance sheets.

	2005	Percent of Sales	2006 (High Est.)	Change	2006 (Low Est.)	Change
Current assets						
Cash and cash equivalents	$ 173,809	2.7%	$ 213,300	$ 39,491	$ 194,400	$ 20,591
Short-term investments	133,227	2.1	165,900	32,673	151,200	17,973
Accounts receivable	190,762	3.0	237,000	46,238	216,000	25,238
Inventory	546,299	8.6	679,400	133,101	619,200	72,901
Prepaid expenses	94,429	1.5	118,500	24,071	108,000	13,571
Deferred income taxes	70,808	1.1	86,900	16,092	79,200	8,392
Total current assets	$1,209,334		$1,501,000	$291,666	$1,368,000	$158,666
Fixed assets						
Long-term investment	$ 261,936	4.1%	$ 323,900	$ 61,964	$ 295,200	$ 33,264
Property plant and equipment net	1,842,019	28.9	2,283,100	441,081	2,080,800	238,781
Other assets	72,893	1.1	86,900	14,007	79,200	6,307
Total fixed assets	$2,176,848		$2,693,900	$517,052	$2,455,200	$278,352
Goodwill	$ 92,474	1.5%	$ 118,500	$ 26,026	$ 108,000	$ 15,526
Other intangible assets	35,409	0.6	47,400	11,991	43,200	7,791
Total assets	$3,514,065		$4,360,800	$846,735	$3,974,400	$460,335
Current liabilities						
Accounts payable	$ 220,975	3.5%	$ 276,500	$ 55,525	$ 252,000	$ 31,025
Accrued expenses	728,273	11.4	900,600	172,327	820,800	92,527
Short-term debt	277,748	n/a	277,748	0	277,748	0
Total current liabilities	$1,226,996		$1,454,848	$227,852	$1,350,548	$123,552
Long-term debt	$ 2,870	n/a	$ 2,870	$ 0	$ 2,870	$ 0
Other long-term liabilities	193,565	n/a	193,565	0	193,565	0
Total liabilities	$1,423,431		$1,651,283	$227,852	$1,546,983	$123,552
Shareholder equity						
Paid-in capital	$ 151,275	n/a	$ 151,275	$ 0	$ 151,275	$ 0
Retained earnings	1,939,359	n/a	2,552,597	613,238	2,498,259	558,900
Total shareholder equity	$2,090,634		$2,703,872	$613,238	$2,649,534	$558,900
Total liabilities and equity	$3,514,065		$4,355,155	$841,090	$4,196,517	$682,452
External financing needed (EFN):			$5,646	$5,646	($222,117)	($222,117)

CHECK THIS

17.4a Use the high sales estimate and data in Table 17.12 to determine the level of external financing needed if short-term and long-term investments were held at their 2005 levels.

17.4b Using the high sales estimate and data in Table 17.12, do you think it is more likely that Starbucks will use short-term or long-term debt if external financing needed was $5,646,000? What financial data support your answer?

TABLE 17.13 **Starbucks Corporation** Pro Forma Balance Sheet, 2006 ($ in 000's)

	2005	Percent of Sales	2006 (High Est.)	Change	2006 (Low Est.)	Change
Current assets						
Cash and cash equivalents	$ 173,809	2.7%	$ 213,300	$ 39,491	$ 416,517	$242,708
Short-term investments	133,227	2.1	165,900	32,673	151,200	17,973
Accounts receivable	190,762	3.0	237,000	46,238	216,000	25,238
Inventory	546,299	8.6	679,400	133,101	619,200	72,901
Prepaid expenses	94,429	1.5	118,500	24,071	108,000	13,571
Deferred income taxes	70,808	1.1	86,900	16,092	79,200	8,392
Total current assets	$1,209,334	19.0	$1,501,000	$291,666	$1,590,117	$380,783
Fixed assets						
Long-term investments	$ 261,936	4.1%	$ 323,900	$ 61,964	$ 295,200	$ 33,264
Net property, plant, and equipment	1,842,019	28.9	2,283,100	441,081	2,080,800	238,781
Other assets	72,893	1.1	86,900	14,007	79,200	6,307
Total fixed assets	$2,176,848	34.2	$2,693,900	$517,052	$2,455,200	$278,352
Goodwill	$ 92,474	1.5%	$ 118,500	$ 26,026	$ 108,000	$ 15,526
Other intangible assets	35,409	0.6	47,400	11,991	43,200	7,791
Total assets	$3,514,065	55.2	$4,360,800	$846,735	$4,196,517	$682,452
Current liabilities						
Accounts payable	$ 220,975	3.5%	$ 276,500	$ 55,525	$ 252,000	$ 31,025
Accrued expenses	728,273	11.4	900,600	172,327	820,800	92,527
Short-term debt	277,748	n/a	283,394	5,646	277,748	0
Total current liabilities	$1,226,996		$1,460,494	$233,498	$1,350,548	$123,552
Long-term debt	$ 2,870	n/a	$ 2,870	$ 0	$ 2,870	$ 0
Other long-term liabilities	193,565	n/a	193,565	0	193,565	0
Total liabilities	$1,423,431		$1,656,929	$233,498	$1,546,983	$123,552
Shareholder equity						
Paid-in capital	$ 151,275	n/a	$ 151,275	$ 0	$ 151,275	$ 0
Retained earnings	1,939,359	n/a	2,552,597	613,238	2,498,259	558,900
Total shareholder equity	$2,090,634		$2,703,872	$613,238	$2,649,534	$558,900
Total liabilities and equity	$3,514,065		$4,360,800	$846,735	$4,196,517	$682,452

VALUING STARBUCKS USING RATIO ANALYSIS

We now turn our attention to valuing Starbucks using ratio analysis and the pro forma income statement and balance sheets that we generated. Immediately below, we report actual and projected profitability and per-share values for 2005 and 2006.

Starbucks Corporation	2005	2006 (High Sales Forecast)	2006 (Low Sales Forecast)
Gross margin	59.1%	59.1%	59.1%
Operating margin	11.1%	11.1%	11.1%
Return on assets (ROA)	14.1%	14.1%	13.3%
Return on equity (ROE)	23.7%	22.7%	21.1%
Earnings per share (EPS)	$0.61	$0.75	$0.69
Book value per share (BVPS)	$2.56	$3.32	$3.25

For Starbucks, taking the 2005 price ratios and multiplying each ratio by its corresponding projected 2006 per-share value results in the following stock price calculations:

				2006 (High Sales Forecast)	2006 (Low Sales Forecast)
Using Fiscal Year-End Stock Price of $25.20					
P/E ratio	41.31		P/E × EPS	$30.98	$28.50
P/B ratio	9.83		P/B × BVPS	$32.64	$31.95
Using SEC Reporting Date Stock Price of $30.65					
P/E ratio	50.25		P/E × EPS	$37.69	$34.67
P/B ratio	11.96		P/B × BVPS	$39.71	$38.87

Using ratio analysis, we generate Starbucks prices that range from $28.50 to $39.71. When our price range is compared to the price range in the nearby *Work the Web* box, we see that our estimated price levels for Starbucks are within the price ranges ($25–$40) forecast by actual analysts.

Looking across sales forecasts, you can see that the prices we generate for Starbucks do not differ greatly. Interestingly, our projected Starbucks stock prices are more sensitive to the values picked for the price/earnings (P/E) ratio and price/book (P/B) ratio than they are to the value of the sales forecast picked.

VALUING STARBUCKS USING A TWO-STAGE RESIDUAL INCOME MODEL

In a previous chapter, we introduced the residual income model (RIM), which is an appropriate valuation model to use when you are trying to value the shares of a company, like Starbucks, that does not pay dividends. The version of RIM that we introduced earlier in the text incorporated the assumption that earnings would grow at a constant rate forever. However, for a fast-growing company like Starbucks, this is not a reasonable assumption. Eventually, the growth rate in earnings for Starbucks must decrease.

Fortunately, the RIM can be modified to reflect the assumption that earnings will grow at rate g_1 for T periods and then grow at rate g_2 forever thereafter. The RIM in this case is:

$$P_0 = BVPS_0 + \frac{EPS_0(1 + g_1) - BVPS_0 \times k}{k - g_1}\left[1 - \left(\frac{1 + g_1}{1 + k}\right)^T\right]$$

$$+ \frac{EPS_0(1 + g_1)^T(1 + g_2) - BVPS_0(1 + k)^T k}{(k - g_2)/(1 + k)^T}$$

(17.3)

In Equation 17.3, we need values for earnings per share, EPS_0, and book value per share, $BVPS_0$, as of time 0 (2005 in this case). We can pluck these values, $.61 and $2.56, respectively, from data provided previously. However, we need earnings growth rates for the two periods, and an appropriate discount rate.

From the nearby *Work the Web* box, we can see that analysts collectively think that Starbucks will be able to grow earnings at 22 percent for the next five years. After that, we will assume that Starbucks will be able to grow earnings *forever* at 5 percent. Even though this is quite a dropoff from 22 percent, it is still significantly higher than the long-term real growth rate of the U.S. economy, which is 3 percent. Therefore, in Equation 17.3, $g_1 = .22$ and $g_2 = .05$.

We calculate an initial discount rate using the capital asset pricing model (CAPM). If we use a risk-free rate of 3.1 percent, a market risk premium of 9 percent, and a Starbucks beta of .80 (from *ValueLine*), the discount rate, k, is $3.1 + .80 \times 9.0 = 10.3\%$.

Using these inputs into Equation 17.3, we obtain this value for Starbucks:

$$P_0 = \$2.56 + \frac{\$.61 \times 1.22 - \$2.56 \times .103}{.103 - .22}\left[1 - \left(\frac{1.22}{1.103}\right)^5\right]$$

$$+ \frac{\dfrac{\$.61 \times (1.22)^5 \times 1.05 - \$2.56 \times (1.103)^5 \times .103}{.103 - .05}}{(1.103)^5}$$

$$= \$2.56 + \$2.69 + \$40.07 = \$45.32$$

This estimate is about 50 percent higher than the Starbucks stock price of $30.65, which was observed at the time Starbucks filed its financial information with the SEC. As any good analyst would, we now vary our inputs to see how sensitive the estimated price is to changes in these inputs. Even though we could change the growth rates, we will not. Instead, we will vary the discount rate and the length of time that Starbucks will exhibit an earnings growth rate of 22 percent.

We generate a set of additional discount rates by varying the beta for Starbucks. Beginning with the value of .80, we increase and decrease beta twice by .10, while keeping the risk-free rate and the market risk premium the same as before. We suspect that the estimate of the length of time that Starbucks will grow earnings at the robust rate of 22 percent could be too long. But we are not really sure, so we vary this length of time from three to five years. We then recalculate a price for Starbucks using each of these combinations. The results appear immediately below.

Beta	Discount Rate	Length of Time Starbucks Grows Earnings at 22%		
		3 Years	4 Years	5 Years
0.60	8.5	$36.51	$49.14	$65.98
0.70	9.4	29.34	39.72	53.68
0.80	10.3	24.50	33.33	45.32
0.90	11.2	20.97	28.64	39.16
1.00	12.1	18.25	25.01	34.36

This sensitivity analysis indicates that both the discount rate and the length of time that Starbucks grows its earnings by 22 percent are important in estimating a value for Starbucks. We highlight six values above that are in line with the Starbucks prices we generated with our ratio analysis and observed in our nearby *Work the Web* box. For an analyst, performing various "what-if" scenarios concerning input values that are used in valuation formulas is good practice.

VALUING STARBUCKS: WHAT DOES THE MARKET SAY?

As with many publicly traded companies, analysts often offer conflicting opinions concerning the future growth prospects of Starbucks and its current value. You can read opinions about Starbucks in our preceding *Investment Updates* box. If you are a believer in the efficient markets hypothesis, the easiest way to value Starbucks is to look at what its shares are selling for in the open market. After all, the market price for Starbucks shares is the result of the collective assessment from thousands of analysts and investors. If, however, you believe that you are an above-average prognosticator for futures sales and earnings growth for Starbucks, you can use the methods discussed in this chapter to assist you in your personal investing decisions concerning Starbucks and other companies.

The methods presented in this chapter are intended to help you become a better financial analyst. Calibrating these methods using a publicly traded company is a useful way to get familiar with how inputs and assumptions affect the resulting valuation. These methods could be valuable to you if you are an internal analyst. For example, suppose you are asked to calculate whether the company you work for needs more financing to meet its expected sales growth levels. You can use the percentage of sales approach when you perform this task.

The methods in this chapter are especially useful if you are trying to value a nontraded company after you are given its financial data. Someday, you might find yourself working on calculating a per-share tender offer in a hostile takeover attempt. In any case, we are confident that this chapter will help you become more "financial statement–literate" and help you develop as a financial analyst.

17.5 Summary and Conclusions

This chapter focuses on earnings and cash flow analysis using financial statement information. Several important aspects of financial statements and their use were covered. These are summarized as follows:

1. A primary source of financial information is a company's annual report. In addition, the annual 10K report and the quarterly 10Q updates filed with the SEC are available from the EDGAR archives.

2. Three financial statements are essential reading for securities analysts: the balance sheet, the income statement, and the cash flow statement.

3. The balance sheet has three sections: assets, which are used to generate earnings; liabilities, which are financial obligations; and equity, representing ownership claims. A fundamental accounting identity for balance sheets states that assets are equal to liabilities plus equity:

$$\text{Assets} = \text{Liabilities} + \text{Equity}$$

4. The balance sheet has four major asset categories: current assets, fixed assets, investments, and other assets.

5. The balance sheet has three major liability categories: current liabilities, long-term debt, and other liabilities.

6. The income statement reports revenues and expenses. Income is used to pay dividends or is retained to finance future growth. Net income is the "bottom line" for a company.

7. The cash flow statement reports how cash was generated and where it was used. The cash flow statement assigns all cash flows to one of three categories: operating cash flow, investment cash flow, or financing cash flow. The sum of operating cash flow, investment cash flow, and financing cash flow yields the net cash increase.

8. Profitability ratios based on financial statement information are often reported to assist in the interpretation of a company's operating efficiency. Some standard profitability ratios are calculated as follows:

$$\text{Gross margin} = \frac{\text{Gross profit}}{\text{Net sales}}$$

$$\text{Operating margin} = \frac{\text{Operating income}}{\text{Net sales}}$$

$$\text{Return on assets (ROA)} = \frac{\text{Net income}}{\text{Total assets}}$$

$$\text{Return on equity (ROE)} = \frac{\text{Net income}}{\text{Shareholder equity}}$$

9. Annual reports and 10Ks may also report per-share calculations of book value, earnings, and operating cash flow, respectively. These per-share values are calculated as follows:

$$\text{Book value per share (BVPS)} = \frac{\text{Shareholder equity}}{\text{Shares outstanding}}$$

$$\text{Earnings per share (EPS)} = \frac{\text{Net income}}{\text{Shares outstanding}}$$

$$\text{Cash flow per share (CFPS)} = \frac{\text{Operating cash flow}}{\text{Shares outstanding}}$$

Dividing the common stock price by the preceding per-share values, we get the following price ratios:

$$\text{Price-book ratio (P/B)} = \frac{\text{Stock price}}{\text{BVPS}}$$

$$\text{Price-earnings ratio (P/E)} = \frac{\text{Stock price}}{\text{EPS}}$$

$$\text{Price-cash flow ratio (P/CF)} = \frac{\text{Stock price}}{\text{CFPS}}$$

10. One common method of analysis is to calculate projected stock prices using prior-period price ratios and projected per-share values from pro forma financial statements. These projected stock prices are calculated as follows:

$$\text{P/B} \times \text{BVPS} = \text{Projected price based on pro forma book value}$$

$$\text{P/E} \times \text{EPS} = \text{Projected price based on pro forma earnings}$$

$$\text{P/CF} \times \text{CFPS} = \text{Projected price based on pro forma cash flow}$$

This chapter delves deeper into earnings and cash flow concepts, which are two of the most important tools of fundamental analysis. It focuses on using financial statement information to develop pro forma numbers to use in stock valuation. How should you, as an investor or investment manager, get started putting this information to work? The answer is that you need to get your fingers dirty! Dig into the financial statements of a few companies and develop your own pro forma financial statements.

Excellent sources for financial statement information are the SEC Edgar database (www.sec.gov) and Free EDGAR (www.freeedgar.com). Other useful online sources are Report Gallery (www.reportgallery.com), Annual Report Service (www.annualreportservice.com), and Free Annual Reports (www.prars.com). Other useful Internet sites for company analysis are Global Reports (www.global-reports.com) and Corporate Information (www.corporateinformation.com).

A good place to start is to download the most recent financial reports for Starbucks from SEC Edgar (www.sec.gov) or the Starbucks company Web site (www.starbucks.com). Then try your hand at developing pro forma financial statements for Starbucks similar to the ones developed in this chapter.

A next step is to pick a company you are interested in and examine its financial statements. As you read a company's financial statements, an important exercise is to try to understand what each number really represents. Why is it there? Is it a cash or market value? Or is it just an accounting number (like depreciation)? Once you are familiar with a company's current financial statements, try to develop pro forma statements for various sales scenarios as was done in this chapter. You really can learn a lot by doing this.

Key Terms

Chapter Review Problems and Self-Test

1. **Margin Calculations** Use the following income statement for Paul Bunyan Lumber Co. to calculate gross and operating margins.

www.mhhe.com/jm4e

Paul Bunyan Lumber 2006 Income Statement

Net sales	$8,000
Cost of goods sold	(6,400)
Gross profit	$1,600
Operating expenses	(400)
Operating income	$1,200
Other income	80
Net interest expense	(120)
Pretax income	$1,160
Income tax	(464)
Net income	$ 696
Earnings per share	$3.48
Recent share price	$76.56

2. **Return Calculations** Use the following balance sheet for Paul Bunyan Lumber Co. along with the income statement in the previous question to calculate return on assets and return on equity.

Paul Bunyan Lumber 2006 Balance Sheet

Cash and cash equivalents	$ 400
Operating assets	400
Property, plant, and equipment	3,160
Other assets	216
Total assets	$4,176
Current liabilities	$ 720
Long-term debt	612
Other liabilities	60
Total liabilities	$1,392
Paid-in capital	$ 600
Retained earnings	2,184
Total shareholder equity	$2,784
Total liabilities and equity	$4,176

3. **Pro Forma Income Statements** Prepare a pro forma income statement for Paul Bunyan Lumber Co. assuming a 5 percent increase in sales. Based only on the pro forma income statement, what is the projected stock price? (*Hint:* What is the price-earnings ratio?)

Answers to Self-Test Problems

1. Gross margin is $1,600/$8,000 = 20%
   Operating margin is $1,200/$8,000 = 15%

2. Return on assets is $696/$4,176 = 16.67%
   Return on equity is $696/$2,784 = 25%

3. With 5 percent sales growth, sales will rise to $8,400 from $8,000. The pro forma income statement follows. A constant gross margin is assumed, implying that cost of goods sold will also rise by 5 percent. A constant tax rate of 40 percent is used. Items in italics are carried over unchanged.

Paul Bunyan Lumber Pro Forma 2007 Income Statement	
Net sales	$8,400
Cost of goods sold	(6,720)
Gross profit	$1,680
Operating expenses	(400)
Operating income	$1,280
Other income	80
Net interest expense	(120)
Pretax income	$1,240
Income tax	(496)
Net income	$744
Earnings per share	$3.72

To get a projected stock price, notice that the 2006 price-earnings ratio was $76.56/$3.48 = 22. Using this ratio as a benchmark, the pro forma earnings of $3.72 imply a stock price of 22 × $3.72 = $81.84.

Test Your Investment Quotient

1. Balance Sheet Assets White Company assets as of December 31, 2005:

Cash and cash equivalents	$ 150
Operating assets	$1,190
Property, plant, and equipment	$1,460
Total assets	$2,800

White Co. experienced the following events in 2006:

Old equipment that cost $120 and that was fully depreciated was scrapped

Depreciation expense was $125

Cash payments for new equipment were $200

Based on the information above, what was White Co.'s net amount of property, plant, and equipment at the end of 2006?

 a. $1,415
 b. $1,535
 c. $1,655
 d. $1,660

2. Cash Flow Cash flow per share is calculated as

 a. Net cash flow/Shares outstanding.
 b. Operating cash flow/Shares outstanding.
 c. Investing cash flow/Shares outstanding.
 d. Financing cash flow/Shares outstanding.

3. Cash Flow Which of the following is not an adjustment to net income used to obtain operating cash flow?

 a. Changes in operating assets
 b. Changes in current liabilities
 c. Loss on sale of assets
 d. Dividends paid

4. **Cash Flow**   The difference between net income and operating cash flow is at least partially accounted for by which of the following items?

   a. Retained earnings
   b. Cash and cash equivalents
   c. Depreciation
   d. Dividends paid

5. **Financial Ratios**   Which of the following profitability ratios is incorrect?

   a. Gross margin = Gross profit/Cost of goods sold
   b. Operating margin = Operating income/Net sales
   c. Return on assets = Net income/Total assets
   d. Return on equity = Net income/Shareholder equity

6. **Financial Ratios**   Which of the following per-share ratios is incorrect?

   a. Book value per share = Total assets/Shares outstanding
   b. Earnings per share = Net income/Shares outstanding
   c. Cash flow per share = Operating cash flow/Shares outstanding
   d. Dividends per share = Dividends paid/Shares outstanding

7. **Dividend Payment**   A dividend payment has which of the following effects on the balance sheet?

   a. An increase in shares outstanding
   b. A decrease in shareholder equity
   c. A decrease in paid-in capital
   d. An increase in retained earnings

8. **Sales Growth**   A particular firm is operating at less than full capacity. If sales are expected to grow at only a modest rate next year, which of the following is true?

   a. Assets will likely increase faster than sales in the short-term future.
   b. Dividends should be reduced to conserve cash.
   c. No further financial planning should be performed until the sales growth rate increases.
   d. External financing will likely not be needed next year.

9. **Capacity Usage**   Which of the following is true regarding the full-capacity sales level of a firm?

   a. A firm that is operating at less than full capacity will never need external financing.
   b. For a firm that is operating at less than full capacity, fixed assets will typically increase at the same rate as sales.
   c. A firm with excess capacity has the room to expand without increasing its investment in fixed assets.
   d. Only firms operating at full capacity can grow rapidly.

Use the following raw data to answer the next four questions:

Net income:	$16
Depreciation/amortization:	$4
Repurchase of outstanding common stock:	$10
Issuance of new debt:	$18
Sale of property:	$12
Purchase of equipment:	$14
Dividend payments:	$4

10. **Cash Flow Analysis**   Operating cash flow is

    a. $20
    b. $16
    c. $12
    d. $30

11. **Cash Flow Analysis**   Investing cash flow is

    a. $2
    b. $(2)
    c. $12
    d. $(12)

12. **Cash Flow Analysis**   Financing cash flow is

 a. $8
 b. $(8)
 c. $4
 d. $(4)

13. **Cash Flow Analysis**   Net cash increase is

 a. $18
 b. $20
 c. $22
 d. $24

Use the following financial data to answer the next three questions:

Cash payments for interest:	$(12)
Retirement of common stock:	$(32)
Cash payments to merchandise suppliers:	$(85)
Purchase of land:	$(8)
Sale of equipment:	$30
Payments of dividends:	$(37)
Cash payment for salaries:	$(35)
Cash collection from customers:	$260
Purchase of equipment:	$(40)

14. **Cash Flow Analysis**   Cash flows from operating activities are

 a. $91
 b. $128
 c. $140
 d. $175

15. **Cash Flow Analysis**   Cash flows from investing activities are

 a. $(67)
 b. $(48)
 c. $(18)
 d. $(10)

16. **Cash Flow Analysis**   Cash flows from financing activities are

 a. $(81)
 b. $(69)
 c. $(49)
 d. $(37)

17. **Cash Flow Analysis**   A firm has net sales of $3,000, cash expenses (including taxes) of $1,400, and depreciation of $500. If accounts receivable increase over the period by $400, cash flow from operations equals

 a. $1,200
 b. $1,600
 c. $1,700
 d. $2,100

18 **Cash Flow Analysis**   A firm using straight-line depreciation reports gross investment in fixed assets of $80 million, accumulated depreciation of $45 million, and annual depreciation expense of $5 million. The approximate average age of fixed assets is

 a. 7 years
 b. 9 years
 c. 15 years
 d. 16 years

19. **Preferred Dividends**   What proportion of preferred stock dividends received by a corporation is normally exempt from federal income taxation?

 a. 25–35 percent
 b. 50–60 percent

    c. 70–80 percent

    d. 90–100 percent

20. **Price Ratios**   All else the same, which of the following ratios is unaffected by an increase in depreciation?

    a. Price-earnings (P/E)

    b. Price-book (P/B)

    c. Price-cash flow (P/CF)

    d. Price-sales (P/S)

Concept Questions

1. **10K and 10Q**   What are the 10K and 10Q reports? Who are they filed by? What do they contain? Who are they filed with? What is the easiest way to retrieve one?

2. **Sales Forecast**   Why do you think most long-term financial planning begins with sales forecasts? Put differently, why are future sales the key input?

3. **Current Events**   What makes current assets and liabilities "current"? Are operating assets "current"?

4. **Income and EPS**   What is the relationship between net income and earnings per share (EPS)?

5. **Noncash Items**   Why do we say depreciation is a "noncash item"?

6. **Cash Flow**   What are the three sections on a standard cash flow statement?

7. **Operating Cash Flow**   In the context of the standard cash flow statement, what is operating cash flow?

8. **Comparing ROE and ROA**   Both ROA and ROE measure profitability. Which one is more useful for comparing two companies? Why?

9. **Retained Earnings**   What is the difference between the "retained earnings" number on the income statement and the balance sheet?

10. **Gross!**   What is the difference between gross margin and operating margin? What do they tell us? Generally speaking, are larger or smaller values better?

11. **More Gross**   Which is larger, gross margin or operating margin? Can either be negative? Can both?

12. **Dividends and Taxes**   Are dividends paid a tax-deductible expense to the paying company? Suppose a company receives dividends from another. How are these taxed?

13. **Cash Flow**   The bottom line on a standard cash flow statement is calculated how? What exactly does it represent?

14. **Retained Earnings**   Take a look at the balance sheet for Starbucks (Table 17.12). On it, retained earnings are about $1.9 billion. How do you interpret this amount? Does it mean that Starbucks has $1.9 billion in cash available to spend?

15. **Price Ratios**   Peninsular Research has a client who has inquired about the valuation method best suited for comparison of companies in an industry that has the following characteristics:

    Principal competitors within the industry are located in the United States, France, Japan, and Brazil.

    The industry is currently operating at a cyclical low, with many firms reporting losses.

    The industry is subject to rapid technological change.

    John Jones, CFA, recommends that the client consider the price-earnings ratio, price-book value ratio, and price-sales ratio. Determine which one of the three valuation ratios is most appropriate for comparing companies in this industry. Support your answer with two reasons that make that ratio superior to either of the other two ratios.

Questions and Problems

1. **Income Statements** Given the following information for Smashville, Inc., construct an income statement for the year:

Cost of goods sold:	$135,000
Investment income:	$2,100
Net sales:	$234,000
Operating expense:	$53,000
Interest expense:	$4,600
Dividends:	$5,800
Tax rate:	35%

   What are retained earnings for the year?

2. **Balance Sheets** Given the following information for Smashville, Inc., construct a balance sheet:

Current liabilities:	$29,000
Cash:	$26,000
Long-term debt:	$87,000
Other assets:	$27,000
Fixed assets:	$125,000
Other liabilities:	$9,000
Investments:	$26,000
Operating assets:	$69,000

3. **Performance Ratios** Given the information in the previous two problems, calculate the gross margin, the operating margin, return on assets, and return on equity for Smashville, Inc.

4. **Per-Share Ratios** During the year, Smashville, Inc., had 12,000 shares of stock outstanding and depreciation expense of $13,000. Calculate the book value per share, earnings per share, and cash flow per share.

5. **Price Ratios** At the end of the year, Smashville stock sold for $48 per share. Calculate the price-book ratio, price-earnings ratio, and the price-cash flow ratio.

6. **Calculating EFN** The most recent financial statements for Bradley, Inc., are shown here (assuming no income taxes):

Income Statement		Balance Sheet			
Sales	$4,400	Assets	$13,400	Debt	$ 9,100
Costs	(2,685)			Equity	4,300
Net income	$1,715	Total	$13,400	Total	$13,400

   Assets and costs are proportional to sales. Debt and equity are not. No dividends are paid. Next year's sales are projected to be $5,192. What is the external financing needed?

7. **Operating Cash Flow** Weston Corporation had earnings per share of $2.14, depreciation expense of $265,000, and 180,000 shares outstanding. What was the operating cash flow per share? If the share price was $34, what was the price-cash flow ratio?

8. **Earnings per Share** Alphonse Inc. has a return on equity of 20 percent, 35,000 shares of stock outstanding, and a net income of $65,000. What are earnings per share?

9. **Addition to Retained Earnings** Lemon Co. has net income of $125,000 and 30,000 shares of stock. If the company pays a dividend of $1.60, what are the additions to retained earnings?

10. **Cash Flow Statement** Given the following information for Hetrich, Inc., calculate the operating cash flow, investment cash flow, financing cash flow, and net cash flow:

Net income:	$128
Depreciation:	45
Issuance of new stock:	12

Repurchase of debt:	15
Sale of property:	16
Purchase of equipment:	50
Dividend payments:	8
Interest payments:	34

11. EFN The most recent financial statements for Martin, Inc., are shown here:

Income Statement			Balance Sheet			
Sales	$19,200	Assets	$93,000	Debt	$20,400
Costs	(15,550)			Equity	72,600
Taxable income	$ 3,650	Total	$93,000	Total	$93,000
Taxes (34%)	(1,241)				
Net income	$ 2,409				

Assets and costs are proportional to sales. Debt and equity are not. A dividend of $963.60 was paid, and Martin wishes to maintain a constant payout ratio. Next year's sales are projected to be $23,040. What is the external financing needed?

Intermediate Questions

Use the following financial statement information to answer the next five questions. Amounts are in thousands of dollars (except number of shares and price per share):

Kiwi Fruit Company Balance Sheet	
Cash and cash equivalents	$ 440
Operating assets	530
Property, plant, and equipment	2,200
Other assets	90
Total assets	$3,260
Current liabilities	$ 450
Long-term debt	1,260
Other liabilities	120
Total liabilities	$1,830
Paid-in capital	$ 340
Retained earnings	1,090
Total shareholder equity	$1,430
Total liabilities and equity	$3,260

Kiwi Fruit Company Income Statement	
Net sales	$7,000
Cost of goods sold	(5,300)
Gross profit	$1,700
Operating expenses	(825)
Operating income	$ 875
Other income	140
Net interest expense	(200)
Pretax income	$ 815
Income tax	(260)
Net income	$ 555
Earnings per share	$ 1.39
Shares outstanding	400,000
Recent price	$ 18

Kiwi Fruit Company Cash Flow Statement	
Net income	$ 555
Depreciation and amortization	205
Changes in operating assets	(145)
Changes in current liabilities	(110)
Operating cash flow	$ 505
Net additions to properties	345
Changes in other assets	(210)
Investing cash flow	$ 135
Issuance/redemption of long-term debt	(300)
Dividends paid	(120)
Financing cash flow	$ (420)
Net cash increase	$ 220

12. **Calculating Margins**   Calculate the gross and operating margins for Kiwi Fruit.

13. **Calculating Profitability Measures**   Calculate ROA and ROE for Kiwi Fruit and interpret these ratios.

14. **Calculating Per-Share Measures**   Calculate the price-book, price-earnings, and price-cash flow ratios for Kiwi Fruit.

15. **Pro Forma Financial Statements**   Following the examples in the chapter, prepare a pro forma income statement, balance sheet, and cash flow statement for Kiwi Fruit assuming a 10 percent increase in sales.

16. **Projected Share Prices**   Based on the previous two questions, what is the projected stock price assuming a 10 percent increase in sales?

17. **Full-Capacity Sales**   Thorpe Mfg., Inc., is currently operating at only 85 percent of fixed asset capacity. Current sales are $510,000. How fast can sales grow before any new fixed assets are needed?

18. **Fixed Assets and Capacity Usage**   For the company in the previous problem, suppose fixed assets are $415,000 and sales are projected to grow to $680,000. How much in new fixed assets are required to support this growth in sales?

19. **Calculating EFN**   The most recent financial statements for Moose Tours, Inc., follow. Sales for 2007 are projected to grow by 20 percent. Interest expense will remain constant; the tax rate and the dividend payout rate will also remain constant. Costs, other expenses, current assets, and accounts payable increase spontaneously with sales. If the firm is operating at full capacity and no new debt or equity is issued, what is the external financing needed to support the 20 percent growth rate in sales?

MOOSE TOURS, INC. 2006 Income Statement		
Sales		$905,000
Costs		(710,000)
Other expenses		(12,000)
Earnings before interest and taxes		$183,000
Interest paid		(19,700)
Taxable income		163,300
Taxes (35%)		(57,155)
Net income		$106,145
Dividends	$ 42,458	
Addition to retained earnings	63,687	

MOOSE TOURS, INC.			
Balance Sheet as of December 31, 2006			
Assets		**Liabilities and Owners' Equity**	
Current assets		Current liabilities	
Cash	$ 25,000	Accounts payable	$ 65,000
Accounts receivable	43,000	Notes payable	9,000
Inventory	76,000	Total	$ 74,000
Total	$144,000	Long-term debt	$156,000
Fixed assets		Owners' equity	
Net plant and		Common stock and paid-in surplus	$21,000
equipment	$364,000	Retained earnings	257,000
		Total	$278,000
Total assets	$508,000	Total liabilities and owners' equity	$508,000

20. **Capacity Usage and Growth**   In the previous problem, suppose the firm was operating at only 80 percent capacity in 2006. What is EFN now?

S&P Problems

www.mhhe.com/edumarketinsight

1. **Company Performance**   Under the "S&P Stock Reports" for American Eagle Outfitters (AOES), download the Stock Report and Industry Outlook. What is the outlook for the industry? What is the outlook for the company? What are the factors mentioned in the Stock Report that affect the future outlook for American Eagle Outfitters?

2. **Cash Flow Statement**   Under the "Excel Analytics" link, download the Cash Flow Statement for Barnes & Noble (BKS). Using the most recent cash flow statement, explain the various cash flows for Barnes & Noble. Make sure you note whether each item is an inflow or an outflow.

3. **Cash Flow Statement**   Look up the information for Apple Computer (APPL). Under "Excel Analytics," you will find the annual income statements, balance sheets, and cash flow statements. Although we covered the basics of the cash flow statement in this chapter, you can see that Apple's cash flow statement is much more detailed. For the most recent year, use the income statement and balance sheets to reproduce the cash flow statement provided. Confirm the numbers provided on the cash flow statement where possible.

What's on the Web?

1. **Ratio Analysis**   Go to www.investor.reuters.com and enter the ticker symbol PFE for Pfizer. Look under the "Ratio Comparison" link to find ratios for Pfizer, the industry, the sector, and the S&P 500. Discuss Pfizer's performance using the following ratios: gross margin, operating margin, return on assets, return on equity, book value per share, earnings per share, cash flow per share, price-book, price-earnings, and price-cash flow.

2. **Ratio Calculation**   Under the Investor Center at Du Pont's Web site (www.dupont.com) you will find financial statements for the company. Using the most recent 10K form, calculate the following ratios for Du Pont over the three years reported: gross margin, operating margin, return on assets, return on equity, book value per share, earnings per share, cash flow per

share, price-book, price-earnings, and price-cash flow. How have these ratios changed over this period?

3. **Cash Flow Statement** You can find financial statements for 3M in the company's Annual Report located in the Investor Relations section of the company's Web site, www.mmm.com. Locate the Statement of Cash Flows in the Annual Report. How have the items changed over the years? Explain 3M's most recent cash flow statement in words.

Stock-Trak Exercises

STOCK|TRAK
GLOBAL PORTFOLIO SIMULATIONS

To access the Stock-Trak Exercise for this chapter, please visit the book Web site at www.mhhe.com/jm4e and choose the corresponding chapter.

CHAPTER 18

Corporate Bonds

"If you want to know the value of money, go and borrow some."
–Benjamin Franklin

A corporation issues bonds intending to meet all obligations of interest and repayment of principal. Investors buy bonds believing the corporation intends to fulfill its debt obligation in a timely manner. Although defaults can and do occur, the market for corporate bonds exists only because corporations are able to convince investors of their original intent to avoid default. Reaching this state of trust is not a trivial process, and it normally requires elaborate contractual arrangements. ■

Almost all corporations issue notes and bonds to raise money to finance investment projects. Indeed, for many corporations, the value of notes and bonds outstanding can exceed the value of common stock shares outstanding. Nevertheless, most investors do not think of corporate bonds when they think about investing. This is because corporate bonds represent specialized investment instruments that are usually bought by financial institutions like insurance companies and pension funds. For professional money managers at these institutions, a knowledge of corporate bonds is absolutely essential. This chapter introduces you to the specialized knowledge that these money managers possess.

18.1 Corporate Bond Basics

Corporate bonds represent the debt of a corporation owed to its bondholders. More specifically, a corporate bond is a security issued by a corporation that represents a promise to pay to its bondholders a fixed sum of money at a future maturity date, along with periodic payments of interest. The fixed sum paid at maturity is the bond's *principal,* also called its par or face value. The periodic interest payments are called *coupons.*

From an investor's point of view, corporate bonds represent an investment distinct from common stock. The three most fundamental differences are these:

1. Common stock represents an ownership claim on the corporation, whereas bonds represent a creditor's claim on the corporation.

2. Promised cash flows—that is, coupons and principal—to be paid to bondholders are stated in advance when the bond is issued. By contrast, the amount and timing of dividends paid to common stockholders may change at any time.

3. Most corporate bonds are issued as callable bonds, which means that the bond issuer has the right to buy back outstanding bonds before the maturity date of the bond issue. When a bond issue is called, coupon payments stop and the bondholders are forced to surrender their bonds to the issuer in exchange for the cash payment of a specified call price. By contrast, common stock is almost never callable.

The corporate bond market is large, with several trillion dollars of corporate bonds outstanding in the United States. The sheer size of the corporate bond market prompts an important inquiry: Who owns corporate bonds and why? The answer is that most corporate bond investors belong to only a few distinct categories. The single largest group of corporate bond investors is life insurance companies, which hold about a third of all outstanding corporate bonds. Remaining ownership shares are roughly equally balanced among individual investors, pension funds, banks, and foreign investors.

The pattern of corporate bond ownership is largely explained by the fact that corporate bonds provide a source of predictable cash flows. While individual bonds occasionally default on their promised cash payments, large institutional investors can diversify away most default risk by including a large number of different bond issues in their portfolios. For this reason, life insurance companies and pension funds find that corporate bonds are a natural investment vehicle to provide for future payments of retirement and death benefits, since both the timing and amount of these benefit payments can be matched with bond cash flows. These institutions can eliminate much of their financial risk by matching the timing of cash flows received from a bond portfolio to the timing of cash flows needed to make benefit payments—a strategy called cash flow matching. For this reason, life insurance companies and pension funds together own more than half of all outstanding corporate bonds. For similar reasons, individual investors might own corporate bonds as a source of steady cash income. However, since individual investors cannot easily diversify default risk, they should normally invest only in bonds with higher credit quality.

Every corporate bond issue has a specific set of issue terms associated with it. The issue terms associated with any particular bond can range from a relatively simple arrangement, where the bond is little more than an IOU of the corporation, to a complex contract specifying in great detail what the issuer can and cannot do with respect to its obligations to bondholders. Bonds issued with a standard, relatively simple set of features are popularly called **plain vanilla bonds** or "bullet" bonds.

As an illustration of a plain vanilla corporate debt issue, Table 18.1 summarizes the issue terms for a note issue by Software Iz Us. Referring to Table 18.1, we see that the Software Iz Us notes were issued in December 2005 and mature five years later in

For more information on corporate bonds visit www.investinginbonds.com

plain vanilla bonds
Bonds issued with a relatively standard set of features. Also known as *bullet bonds.*

TABLE 18.1　Software Iz Us Five-Year Note Issue

Issue amount	$20 million	Note issue total face value is $20 million
Issue date	12/15/2005	Notes offered to the public in December 2005
Maturity date	12/31/2010	Remaining principal due December 31, 2010
Face value	$1,000	Face value denomination is $1,000 per note
Coupon interest	$100 per annum	Annual coupons are $100 per note
Coupon dates	6/30, 12/31	Coupons are paid semiannually
Offering price	100	Offer price is 100 percent of face value
Yield to maturity	10%	Based on stated offer price
Call provision	Not callable	Notes may not be paid off before maturity
Security	None	Notes are unsecured
Rating	Not rated	Privately placed note issue

December 2010. Each individual note has a face value denomination of $1,000. Since the total issue amount is $20 million, the entire issue contains 20,000 notes. Each note pays a $100 annual coupon, which is equal to 10 percent of its face value. The annual coupon is split between two semiannual $50 payments made each June and December. Based on the original offer price of 100, which means 100 percent of the $1,000 face value, the notes have a yield to maturity of 10 percent. The notes are not callable, which means that the debt may not be paid off before maturity.

unsecured debt
Bonds, notes, or other debt issued with no specific collateral pledged as security for the bond issue.

The Software Iz Us notes are **unsecured debt**, which means that no specific collateral has been pledged as security for the notes. In the event that the issuer defaults on its promised payments, the noteholders may take legal action to acquire sufficient assets of the company to settle their claims as creditors.

When issued, the Software Iz Us notes were not reviewed by a rating agency like Moody's or Standard & Poor's. Thus, the notes are unrated. If the notes were to be assigned a credit rating, they would probably be rated as "junk grade." The term "junk," commonly used for high-risk debt issues, is unduly pejorative. After all, your company must repay the debt. However, the high-risk character of the software industry portends an above-average probability that your company may have difficulty paying off the debt in a timely manner.

Reflecting their below-average credit quality, the Software Iz Us notes were not issued to the general public. Instead, the notes were privately placed with two insurance companies. Such private placements are common among relatively small debt issues. Private placements will be discussed in greater detail later in this chapter.

18.2 Types of Corporate Bonds

debentures
Unsecured bonds issued by a corporation.

Debentures are the most frequently issued type of corporate bond. Debenture bonds represent an unsecured debt of a corporation. Debenture bondholders have a legal claim as general creditors of the corporation. In the event of a default by the issuing corporation, the bondholders' claim extends to all corporate assets. However, they may have to share this claim with other creditors who have an equal legal claim or yield to creditors with a higher legal claim.

mortgage bond
Debt secured with a property lien.

In addition to debentures, there are three other basic types of corporate bonds: mortgage bonds, collateral trust bonds, and equipment trust certificates. **Mortgage bonds** represent debt issued with a lien on specific property, usually real estate, pledged as security for the bonds. A mortgage lien gives bondholders the legal right to foreclose on property pledged by the issuer to satisfy an unpaid debt obligation. However, in actual practice, foreclosure and sale of mortgaged property following a default may not be the most desirable strategy for bondholders. Instead, it is common for a corporation in financial distress to reorganize itself and negotiate a new debt contract with bondholders. In these negotiations, a mortgage lien can be an important bargaining tool for the trustee representing the bondholders.

collateral trust bond
Debt secured with financial collateral.

Collateral trust bonds are characterized by a pledge of financial assets as security for the bond issue. Collateral trust bonds are commonly issued by holding companies, which may pledge the stocks, bonds, or other securities issued by their subsidiaries as collateral for their own bond issue. The legal arrangement for pledging collateral securities is similar to that for a mortgage lien. In the event of an issuer's default on contractual obligations to bondholders, the bondholders have a legal right to foreclose on collateralized securities in the amount necessary to settle an outstanding debt obligation.

equipment trust certificate
Shares in a trust with income from a lease contract.

Equipment trust certificates represent debt issued by a trustee to purchase heavy industrial equipment that is leased and used by railroads, airlines, and other companies with a demand for heavy equipment. Under this financial arrangement, investors purchase equipment trust certificates, and the proceeds from this sale are used to purchase equipment. Formal ownership of the equipment remains with a trustee appointed to represent the certificate holders. The trustee then leases the equipment to a company. In return, the company promises to make a series of scheduled lease payments over a specified leasing period. The trustee collects the lease payments and distributes all revenues, less expenses, as dividends to the certificate holders. These distributions are conventionally called dividends because they are generated as income from a trust. The lease arrangement usually ends after a specified number of years when the leasing company makes a final lease payment and may take possession of the used equipment. From the certificate holders' point of view, this financial arrangement is superior to a mortgage lien since they actually own the equipment during the leasing period. Thus, if the leasing corporation defaults, the equipment can be sold without the effort and expense of a formal foreclosure process. Since the underlying equipment for this type of financing is typically built according to an industry standard, the equipment can usually be quickly sold or leased to another company in the same line of business.

Figure 18.1 is a *Wall Street Journal* bond announcement for an aircraft equipment trust for Northwest Airlines. Notice that the $243 million issue is split into two parts: $177 million of senior notes paying 8.26 percent interest and $66 million of subordinated notes paying 9.36 percent interest. The senior notes have a first claim on the aircraft in the event of a default by the airline, while the subordinated notes have a secondary claim. In the event of a default, investment losses for the trust will primarily be absorbed by the subordinated noteholders. For this reason, the subordinated notes are riskier and, therefore, pay a higher interest rate. Of course, if no default actually occurs, it would turn out that the subordinated notes were actually a better investment. However, there is no way of knowing this in advance.

WWW

Visit the Northwest Airlines Web site at
www.nwa.com

CHECK THIS

18.2a Given that a bond issue is one of the four basic types discussed in this section, how would the specific bond type affect the credit quality of the bond?

18.2b Why might some bond types be more or less risky with respect to the risk of default?

18.2c Given that a default has occurred, why might the trustee's job of representing the financial interests of the bondholders be easier for some bond types than for others?

y

FIGURE 18.1 Equipment Trust Notes Issue

These securities have not been registered under the Securities Act of 1933 and may not be offered or sold in the United States or to U.S. persons except in accordance with the resale restrictions applicable thereto. These securities having been previously sold, this announcement appears as a matter of record only.

$243,000,000

NWA Trust No. 1

$177,000,000 8.26% Class A Senior Aircraft Notes

$66,000,000 9.36% Class B Subordinated Aircraft Notes

NORTHWEST A I R L I N E S

The 8.26% Class A Senior Aircraft Notes and the 9.36% Class B Subordinated Aircraft Notes are secured by, among other things, a security interest in certain aircraft sold by Northwest Airlines, Inc. ("Northwest") to an owner trust for a purchase price of $443 million and the lease relating to such Aircraft, including the right to receive amounts payable by Northwest under such lease. The Noteholders also have the benefit of a liquidity facility, initially provided by General Electric Capital Corporation, to support certain payments of interest on the Notes.

Lehman Brothers   BT Securities Corporation

18.3 Bond Indentures

A bond indenture is a formal written agreement between the corporation and the bondholders. It is an important legal document that spells out in detail the mutual rights and obligations of the corporation and the bondholders with respect to the bond issue. Indenture contracts are often quite long, sometimes several hundred pages, and make for very tedious reading. In fact, very few bond investors ever read the original indenture, but instead might refer to an **indenture summary** provided in the **prospectus** that was circulated when the bond issue was originally sold to the public. Alternatively, a summary of the most important features of an indenture is published by debt rating agencies.

The Trust Indenture Act of 1939 requires that any bond issue subject to regulation by the Securities and Exchange Commission (SEC), which includes most corporate bond and note issues sold to the general public, must have a trustee appointed to represent the interests of the bondholders. Also, all responsibilities of a duly appointed trustee must be specified in detail in the indenture. Some corporations maintain a blanket or open-ended indenture that applies to all currently outstanding bonds and any new bonds that are issued, while other corporations write a new indenture contract for each new bond issue sold to the public.

Descriptions of the most important provisions frequently specified in a bond indenture agreement are presented next.

BOND SENIORITY PROVISIONS

A corporation may have several different bond issues outstanding; these issues normally can be differentiated according to the seniority of their claims on the firm's assets. Seniority usually is specified in the indenture contract.

Consider a corporation with two outstanding bond issues: (1) a mortgage bond issue with certain real estate assets pledged as security and (2) a debenture bond issue with no specific assets pledged as security. In this case, the mortgage bond issue has a senior claim on the pledged assets but no specific claim on other corporate assets. The debenture bond has a claim on all corporate assets not specifically pledged as security for the mortgage bond, but it would have only a residual claim on assets pledged as security for the mortgage bond issue. This residual claim would apply only after all obligations to the mortgage bondholders have been satisfied.

As another example, suppose a corporation has two outstanding debenture issues. In this case, seniority is normally assigned to the bonds first issued by the corporation. The bonds issued earliest have a senior claim on the pledged assets and are called **senior debentures**. The bonds issued later have a junior or subordinate claim and are called **subordinated debentures**.

The seniority of an existing debt issue is usually protected by a **negative pledge clause** in the bond indenture. A negative pledge clause prohibits a new issue of debt with seniority over a currently outstanding issue. However, it may allow a new debt issue to share equally in the seniority of an existing issue. A negative pledge clause is part of the indenture agreement of most senior debenture bonds.

CALL PROVISIONS

Most corporate bond issues have a call provision allowing the issuer to buy back all or part of its outstanding bonds at a specified call price sometime before the bonds mature. The most frequent motive for a corporation to call outstanding bonds is to take advantage of a general fall in market interest rates. Lower interest rates allow the corporation to replace currently outstanding high-coupon bonds with a new issue of bonds paying lower coupons. Replacing existing bonds with new bonds is called **bond refunding**.

indenture summary
Description of the contractual terms of a new bond issue included in a bond's prospectus.

prospectus
Document prepared as part of a security offering detailing information about a company's financial position, its operations, and investment plans.

WWW

The Trust Indenture Act of 1939 is available at the SEC Web site
www.sec.gov

senior debentures
Bonds that have a higher claim on the firm's assets than other bonds.

subordinated debentures
Bonds that have a claim on the firm's assets after those with a higher claim have been satisfied.

negative pledge clause
Bond indenture provision that prohibits new debt from being issued with seniority over an existing issue.

bond refunding
Process of calling an outstanding bond issue and refinancing it with a new bond issue.

TRADITIONAL FIXED-PRICE CALL PROVISIONS There are two major types of call provisions, traditional *fixed-price* and *make-whole*. From an investor's point of view, a fixed-price call provision has a distinct disadvantage. For example, suppose an investor is currently holding bonds paying 10 percent coupons. Further suppose that, after a fall in market interest rates, the corporation is able to issue new bonds that only pay 8 percent coupons. By calling existing 10 percent coupon bonds, the issuer forces bondholders to surrender their bonds in exchange for the fixed call price. But this happens at a time when the bondholders can reinvest funds only at lower interest rates. If instead the bonds were noncallable, the bondholders would continue to receive the original 10 percent coupons. For this reason, callable bonds are less attractive to investors than noncallable bonds. Consequently, a callable bond will sell at a lower price than a comparable noncallable bond.

Despite their lower prices, corporations generally prefer to issue fixed-price callable bonds. However, to reduce the price gap between callable and noncallable bonds, issuers typically allow the indenture contract to specify certain restrictions on their ability to call an outstanding bond issue. Three features are commonly used to restrict an issuer's call privilege:

1. Callable bonds usually have a *deferred call provision* which provides a *call protection period* during which a bond issue cannot be called. For example, a bond may be call-protected for a period of five years after its issue date.

2. A call price often includes a *call premium* over par value. A standard arrangement stipulates a call premium equal to one-year's coupon payments for a call occurring at the earliest possible call date. Over time, the call premium is gradually reduced until it is eliminated entirely. After some future date, the bonds become callable at par value.

3. Some indentures specifically prohibit an issuer from calling outstanding bonds for the purpose of refunding at a lower coupon rate but still allow a call for other reasons. This *refunding provision* prevents the corporation from calling an outstanding bond issue solely as a response to falling market interest rates. However, the corporation can still pay off its bond debt ahead of schedule by using funds acquired from, say, earnings, or funds obtained from the sale of newly issued common stock.

After a bond's call protection period has elapsed, a rational investor would be unwilling to pay much more than the call price for the bond since the issuer might call the bond at any time and pay only the call price for the bond. Consequently, a bond's call price serves as an effective ceiling on its market price. It is important for bond investors to understand how the existence of a price ceiling for callable bonds alters the standard price-yield relationship for bonds.

The relationship between interest rates and prices for comparable callable and noncallable bonds is illustrated in Figure 18.2. In this example, the vertical axis measures bond prices, and the horizontal axis measures bond yields. In this two-bond example, both bonds pay an 8 percent coupon and are alike in all respects except that one of the bonds is callable any time at par value.

As shown, the noncallable bond has the standard *convex price-yield relationship*, where the price-yield curve is bowed toward the origin. When the price-yield curve is bowed to the origin this is called *positive convexity*. In contrast, the fixed-price callable bond has a convex or bowed price-yield relationship in the region of high yields, but is bowed away from the origin in the region of low yields. This is called *negative convexity*. The important lesson here is that no matter how low market interest rates might fall, the maximum price of an unprotected fixed-price callable bond is generally bounded above by its call price.

FIGURE 18.2	Noncallable Bonds and Fixed-Price Callable Bonds

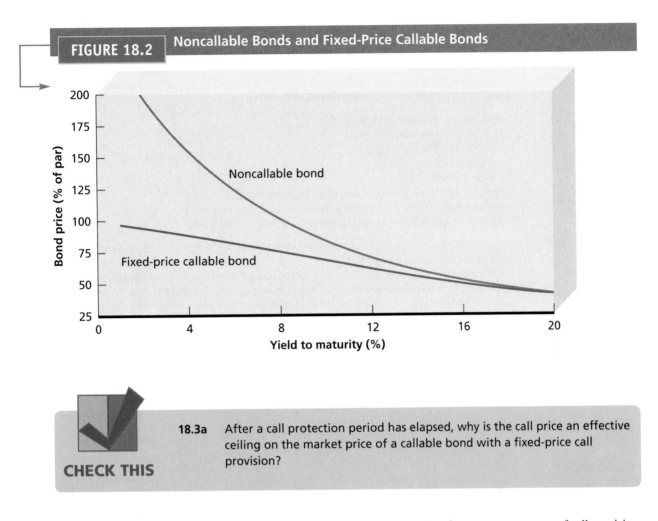

CHECK THIS

18.3a After a call protection period has elapsed, why is the call price an effective ceiling on the market price of a callable bond with a fixed-price call provision?

MAKE-WHOLE CALL PROVISION In just the last few years, a new type of call provision, a "make-whole" call, has become common in the corporate bond market. If a callable bond has a make-whole call provision, bondholders receive approximately what the bond is worth if the bond is called. This call provision gets its name because the bondholder does not suffer a loss in the event of a call; that is, the bondholder is "made whole" when the bond is called.

Like a fixed-price call provision, a make-whole call provision allows the borrower to pay off the remaining debt early. Unlike a fixed-price call provision, however, a make-whole call provision requires the borrower to make a lump-sum payment representing the present value of all payments that will not be made because of the call. The discount rate used to calculate the present value is usually equal to the yield on a comparable maturity U.S. Treasury security plus a fixed, prespecified *make-whole premium.*

Because the yield of a comparable U.S. Treasury security changes over time, the call price paid to bondholders changes over time. As interest rates decrease, the make-whole call price increases because the discount rate used to calculate the present value decreases. As interest rates increase, the make-whole call price decreases. In addition, make-whole call provisions typically specify that the minimum amount received by a bondholder is the par value of the bond.

As interest rates decline, even in the region of low yields, the price of bonds with a make-whole call provision will increase. That is, these bonds exhibit the standard *convex price-yield relationship* in all yield regions. In contrast, recall that bond prices with a fixed-price call provision exhibit *negative convexity* in the region of low yields.

EXAMPLE 18.1

Calculating the Make-Whole Call Premium

On October 29, 2005, *The Wall Street Journal* reported that Tanger Properties, LP, issued $250 million of notes with the following terms:

Settlement: November 4, 2005
Maturity: November 15, 2015
Coupon: 6.15%
Price: 99.635
Yield: 6.199%
Spread: 160 basis points above U.S. Treasury Notes
Make-whole call at 25 basis points above U.S. Treasury notes
Ratings: Baa3 (Moody's), triple-B-minus (Standard & Poor's)

If these notes were to be called immediately, what price would Tanger Properties have to pay to its note holders?

To calculate the make-whole call premium of these notes, we need to add 25 basis points to the yield on comparable maturity U.S. Treasury notes. To do this, we can subtract the 160 basis point spread from the yield of the note to get the comparable Treasury yield and then add the make-whole premium: 6.199% − 1.60% + .25% = 4.849%. Discounting the remaining cash flows of the note at 4.849 percent, we get a make-whole call price of about $110.24, or about $10.60 more than the current price of the notes, which is $99.635. You can verify this price using Excel. Using the information above, enter =PRICE("11/4/2005","11/15/2015", 0.0615,0.04849,100,2) into an Excel cell, and you will get a price of $110.236.

CHECK THIS

18.3b   Suppose you hold a bond with a make-whole call provision. The coupon rate on this bond is 6.15 percent. At what yield to maturity will this bond sell for par?

PUT PROVISIONS

put bonds

Bonds that can be sold back to the issuer at a prespecified price on any of a sequence of prespecified dates. Also called *extendible bonds*.

A bond issue with a put provision grants bondholders the right to sell their bonds back to the issuer at a special *put price*, normally set at par value. These so-called **put bonds** are "putable" on each of a series of designated *put dates*. These are often scheduled to occur annually but sometimes occur at more frequent intervals. At each put date, the bondholder decides whether to sell the bond back to the issuer or continue to hold the bond until the next put date. For this reason, put bonds are often called *extendible bonds* because the bondholder has the option of extending the maturity of the bond at each put date.

Notice that by granting bondholders an option to sell their bonds back to the corporation at par value, the put feature provides an effective floor on the market price of the bond. Thus, the put feature offers protection to bondholders from rising interest rates and the associated fall in bond prices.

A put feature also helps protect bondholders from acts of the corporation that might cause a deterioration of the bond's credit quality. However, this protection is not granted without a cost to bond investors, since a putable bond will command a higher market price than a comparable nonputable bond.

CHECK THIS

18.3c Using Figure 18.2 as a guide, what would the price-yield relationship look like for a noncallable bond putable at par value?

18.3d Under what conditions would a put feature not yield an effective floor for the market price of a put bond? (*Hint*: Think about default risk.)

BOND-TO-STOCK CONVERSION PROVISIONS

Some bonds have a valuable bond-to-stock conversion feature. These bonds are called convertible bonds. **Convertible bonds** grant bondholders the right to exchange each bond for a designated number of common stock shares of the issuing firm. To avoid confusion in a discussion of convertible bonds, it is important to understand some basic terminology.

convertible bonds
Bonds that holders can exchange for common stock according to a prespecified conversion ratio.

1. The number of common stock shares acquired in exchange for each converted bond is called the *conversion ratio*:

   Conversion ratio = Number of stock shares acquired by conversion

2. The par value of a convertible bond divided by its conversion ratio is called the bond's *conversion price*:

   $$\text{Conversion price} = \frac{\text{Bond par value}}{\text{Conversion ratio}}$$

3. The market price per share of common stock acquired by conversion times the bond's conversion ratio is called the bond's *conversion value*:

   Conversion value = Price per share of stock × Conversion ratio

For example, suppose a convertible bond with a par value of $1,000 can be converted into 20 shares of the issuing firm's common stock. In this case, the conversion price is $1,000/20 = $50. Continuing this example, suppose the firm's common stock has a market price of $40 per share; then the conversion value of a single bond is 20 × $40 = $800.

Figure 18.3 is *The Wall Street Journal* announcement of an issue of convertible subordinated notes by Advanced Micro Devices (AMD). The notes pay a 6 percent coupon rate and mature in 2005. The conversion price for this note issue is $37 per share, which implies a conversion ratio of 27.027 shares of common stock for each $1,000 face value note.

From an investor's perspective, the conversion privilege of convertible bonds has the distinct advantage that bondholders can receive a share of any increase in common stock value. However, the conversion option has a price. A corporation can sell convertible bonds at par value with a coupon rate substantially less than the coupon rate of comparable nonconvertible bonds. This forgone coupon interest represents the price of the bond's conversion option.

When convertible bonds are originally issued, their conversion ratio is customarily set to yield a conversion value of 10 percent to 20 percent less than par value. For example, suppose the common stock of a company has a price of $30 per share and the company issues convertible bonds with a par value of $1,000 per bond. To set the original conversion value at $900 per bond, the company would set a conversion ratio of 30 stock shares per bond. Thereafter, the conversion ratio is fixed, but each bond's conversion value becomes linked to the firm's stock price, which may rise or fall in value. The price of a convertible

WWW

Find out more about convertible bonds at
www.convertbond.com

FIGURE 18.3   Convertible Notes Issue

This announcement is neither an offer to sell, nor a solicitation of an offer to buy, any of these securities.
The offer is made only by the Prospectus and related Prospectus Supplement.

$517,500,000

AMD

Advanced Micro Devices, Inc.

6% Convertible Subordinated Notes due 2005

The 6% Convertible Subordinated Notes due 2005 (the "Notes") will be convertible at the option of the holder into shares of common stock, par value $.01 per share (the "Common Stock"), of Advanced Micro Devices, Inc. (the "Company") at any time at or prior to maturity, unless previously redeemed or repurchased, at a conversion price of $37.00 per share (equivalent to a conversion rate of 27.027 shares per $1,000 principal amount of Notes), subject to adjustment in certain events.

Price 100%

Copies of the Prospectus and related Prospectus Supplement may be obtained in any State from such of the undersigned as may legally offer these securities in compliance with the securities laws of such State.

Donaldson, Lufkin & Jenrette
Securities Corporation

Salomon Smith Barney

bond reflects the conversion value of the bond. In general, the higher the conversion value the higher is the bond price, and vice versa.

Investing in convertible bonds is more complicated than owning nonconvertible bonds, because the conversion privilege presents convertible bondholders with an important timing decision. When is the best time to exercise a bond's conversion option and exchange the bond for shares of common stock? The answer is that investors should normally postpone conversion as long as possible, because while they hold the bonds they continue to receive coupon payments. After converting to common stock, they lose all subsequent coupons. In general, unless the total dividend payments on stock acquired by conversion are somewhat greater than the forgone bond coupon payments, investors should hold on to their convertible bonds to continue to receive coupon payments.

The rational decision of convertible bondholders to postpone conversion as long as possible is limited, however, since convertible bonds are almost always callable. Firms customarily call outstanding convertible bonds when their conversion value has risen by 10 percent to 15 percent above bond par value, although there are many exceptions to this rule. When a convertible bond issue is called by the issuer, bondholders are forced to make an immediate decision whether to convert to common stock shares or accept a cash payment of the call price. Fortunately, the decision is simple—convertible bondholders should choose whichever is more valuable, the call price or the conversion value.

Visit the AMD
Web site at
www.amd.com

CHECK THIS

18.3e Describe the conversion decision that convertible bondholders must make when the bonds mature.

GRAPHICAL ANALYSIS OF CONVERTIBLE BOND PRICES

The price of a convertible bond is closely linked to the value of the underlying common stock shares that can be acquired by conversion. A higher stock price implies a higher bond price, and, conversely, a lower stock price yields a lower bond price.

The relationship between the price of a convertible bond and the price of the firm's common stock is depicted in Figure 18.4. In this example, the convertible bond's price is measured on the vertical axis, and the stock price is measured along the horizontal axis. The straight, upward-sloping line is the bond's conversion value; the slope of the line is the conversion ratio. The horizontal line represents the price of a comparable nonconvertible bond with the same coupon rate, maturity, and credit quality.

in-the-money bond
A convertible bond whose conversion value is greater than its call price.

intrinsic bond value
The price below which a convertible bond cannot fall, equal to the value of a comparable nonconvertible bond. Also called *investment value*.

A convertible bond is said to be an **in-the-money bond** when its conversion value is greater than its call price. If an in-the-money convertible bond is called, rational bondholders will convert their bonds into common stock. When the conversion value is less than the call price, a convertible bond is said to be *out of the money*. If an out-of-the-money bond is called, rational bondholders will accept the call price and forgo the conversion option. In practice, however, convertible bonds are seldom called when they are out of the money.

The curved line in Figure 18.4 shows the relationship between a convertible bond's price and the underlying stock price. As shown, there are two lower bounds on the value of a convertible bond. First, a convertible bond's price can never fall below its **intrinsic bond value**, also commonly called its *investment value* or *straight bond value*. This value is what the

FIGURE 18.4 | Convertible Bond Prices

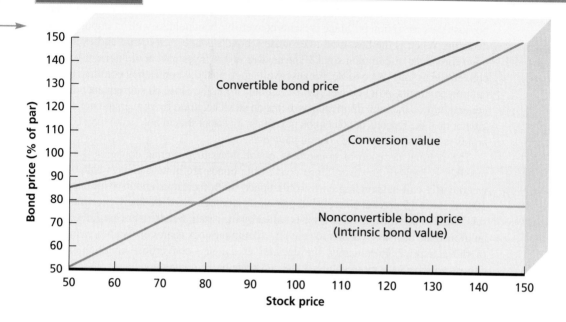

bond would be worth if it were not convertible, but otherwise identical in terms of coupon, maturity, and credit quality. Second, a convertible bond can never sell for less than its *conversion value* because, if it did, investors could simply buy the bond and convert, thereby realizing an immediate, riskless profit.

Thus, the *floor value* of a convertible bond is its intrinsic bond value or its conversion value, whichever is larger. As shown in Figure 18.4, however, a convertible bond will generally sell for more than this floor value. This extra is the amount that investors are willing to pay for the right, but not the obligation, to convert the bond at a future date at a potentially much higher stock price.

An interesting variation of a bond-to-stock conversion feature occurs when the company issuing the bonds is different from the company whose stock is acquired by the conversion. In this case, the bonds are called **exchangeable bonds**. Figure 18.5 presents a *Wall Street Journal* announcement of an issue of exchangeable subordinated debentures by the McKesson Corporation. These debentures are exchangeable for common stock shares of Armor All Products Corporation. McKesson is a retail distributor, and Armor All markets consumer chemical products. Exchangeable bonds, while not unusual, are less common than convertible bonds.

exchangeable bonds

Bonds that can be converted into common stock shares of a company other than the issuer's.

CHECK THIS

18.3f For nonconvertible bonds, the call price is a ceiling on the market price of the bond. Why might the call price not be an effective ceiling on the price of a convertible bond?

FIGURE 18.5 Exchangeable Debentures Issue

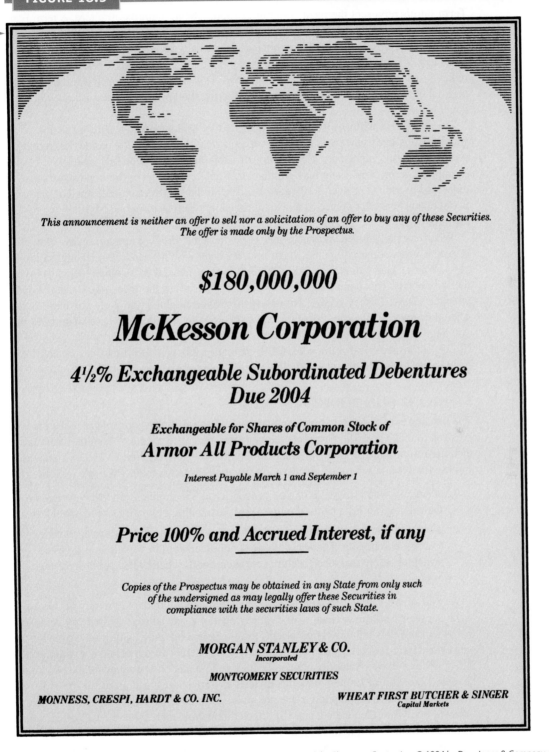

This announcement is neither an offer to sell nor a solicitation of an offer to buy any of these Securities.
The offer is made only by the Prospectus.

$180,000,000

McKesson Corporation

4½% Exchangeable Subordinated Debentures Due 2004

Exchangeable for Shares of Common Stock of
Armor All Products Corporation

Interest Payable March 1 and September 1

Price 100% and Accrued Interest, if any

Copies of the Prospectus may be obtained in any State from only such
of the undersigned as may legally offer these Securities in
compliance with the securities laws of such State.

MORGAN STANLEY & CO.
Incorporated

MONTGOMERY SECURITIES

MONNESS, CRESPI, HARDT & CO. INC.   **WHEAT FIRST BUTCHER & SINGER**
Capital Markets

BOND MATURITY AND PRINCIPAL PAYMENT PROVISIONS

term bonds
Bonds issued with a single maturity date.

Term bonds represent the most common corporate bond maturity structure. A term bond issue has a single maturity date. On this date, all outstanding bond principal must be paid off. The indenture contract for a term bond issue normally stipulates the creation of a *sinking fund,* that is, an account established to repay bondholders through a series of fractional redemptions before the bond reaches maturity. Thus, at maturity, only a fraction of the original bond issue will still be outstanding. Sinking fund provisions are discussed in more detail later.

serial bonds
Bonds issued with a regular sequence of maturity dates.

An alternative maturity structure is provided by **serial bonds**, where a fraction of an entire bond issue is scheduled to mature in each year over a specified period. Essentially, a serial bond issue represents a collection of subissues with sequential maturities. As an example, a serial bond issue may stipulate that one-tenth of an entire bond issue must be redeemed in each year over a 10-year period, with the last fraction redeemed at maturity. Serial bonds generally do not have a call provision, whereas term bonds usually do have a call provision.

When originally issued, most corporate bonds have maturities of 30 years or less. However, in recent years some companies have issued bonds with 40- and 50-year maturities. In 1993, Walt Disney Company made headlines in the financial press when it sold 100-year maturity bonds. This bond issue became popularly known as the "Sleeping Beauty" bonds, after the classic Disney movie. However, the prince might arrive early for these bonds since they are callable after 30 years. Nevertheless, this was the first time since 1954 that 100-year bonds were sold by any borrower in the United States. Only days later, however, Coca-Cola issued $150 million of 100-year maturity bonds. Both the Disney and Coke bond issues locked in the unusually low interest rates prevailing in 1993.

SINKING FUND PROVISIONS

sinking fund
An account used to provide for scheduled redemptions of outstanding bonds.

The indentures of most term bonds include a **sinking fund** provision that requires the corporation to make periodic payments into a trustee-managed account. Account reserves are then used to provide for scheduled redemptions of outstanding bonds. The existence of a sinking fund is an important consideration for bond investors mainly for two reasons:

1. A sinking fund provides a degree of security to bondholders, since payments into the sinking fund can be used only to pay outstanding obligations to bondholders.

2. A sinking fund provision requires fractional bond issue redemptions according to a preset schedule. Therefore, some bondholders will be repaid their invested principal before the stated maturity for their bonds whether they want repayment or not.

As part of a *scheduled sinking fund redemption,* some bondholders may be forced to surrender their bonds in exchange for cash payment of a special *sinking fund call price.* For this reason, not all bondholders may be able to hold their bonds until maturity, even though the entire bond issue has not been called according to a general call provision. For example, the indenture for a 25-year maturity bond issue may require that one-twentieth of the bond issue be retired annually, beginning immediately after an initial 5-year call protection period.

Typically, when a redemption is due, the sinking fund trustee will select bonds by lottery. Selected bonds are then called, and the affected bondholders receive the call price, which for sinking fund redemptions is usually par value. However, the issuer normally has a valuable option to buy back the required number of bonds in the open market and deliver them to the sinking fund trustee instead of delivering the cash required for a par value redemption. Issuers naturally prefer to exercise this option when bonds can be repurchased in the open market at less than par value.

INVESTMENT UPDATES

KATRINA CLAIMS COULD LEAVE HOLDERS OF A "CAT BOND" WITH MAJOR LOSSES

As Hurricane Katrina approached the Gulf Coast, those anxiously following the storm included big investors around the globe. They are owners of $5.3 billion of "catastrophe bonds" that insurers issued in recent years to help pay claims from natural disasters.

Now, it appears holders of one such "cat bond" may be out of pocket by almost $200 million, while most of the other investors have avoided such losses.

The bond in question: a special-purpose vehicle called Kamp Re. Under the terms of the $190 million bond, issued in August, investors lose their money if Zurich Financial Services, the big Swiss insurance company, pays insurance claims of more than $1 billion on any hurricane or earthquake in the United States within five years. Zurich's total losses from Katrina, which hit New Orleans and the Gulf Coast on Aug. 29, are estimated at almost $2 billion, according to the company.

Several people in the market said the Kamp Re bonds are being quoted at zero value in anticipation that investors have been wiped out. The bonds were sold in a private placement to institutional investors, like most cat bonds. If the Kamp Re bondholders lose all of their investment, it would be the first cat-bond issue to totally call in investors' funds, though some have cost investors modest chunks of their principal in past years. The event could lead investors to demand more protection, such as higher trigger points and interest payments, some market participants said.

Catastrophe bonds, or "cat bonds" for short, were launched in the 1990s by financial wizards on Wall Street and elsewhere to provide insurance companies an alternative to steeply priced reinsurance. In short, reinsurance is coverage insurers buy to spread the risk of losses from policies they sell to individuals and companies.

Here is how cat bonds generally work: Insurance companies sell bonds to investors and agree to pay them an annual interest rate, typically three to five percentage points above the benchmark London interbank offered rate, or Libor. At current rates, the cost would be about 7% to 9%. The money raised is placed in a trust fund.

If a natural catastrophe strikes of sufficient magnitude—measured by wind speed, earthquake force, or, as in the Kamp Re instance, insured losses—the issuer gets to keep the cash to help pay its policyholders' claims. The bonds typically have a three-year maturity but often are rolled over.

Buyers of cat bonds are mostly sophisticated investors like hedge funds, pension funds, and banks, which see them as an opportunity to diversify their investment portfolios. Since they first appeared, the global insurance industry has issued $13.41 billion of natural-catastrophe bonds. The largest single issuer is Swiss Re, also based in Zurich, which has more than $1 billion in catastrophe bonds outstanding.

Katrina, to be sure, was a big deal: U.S. risk-management firm ISO estimated Tuesday that total private-sector insurance claims would amount to $34.4 billion, making it the costliest natural disaster in history.

Source: Charles Fleming, *The Wall Street Journal*, October 6, 2005. Reprinted by permission of Dow Jones & Company, Inc., via Copyright Clearance Center, Inc. © 2005 Dow Jones & Company, Inc. All Rights Reserved Worldwide.

18.3g For bond investors, what are some of the advantages and disadvantages of a sinking fund provision?

CHECK THIS

COUPON PAYMENT PROVISIONS

Coupon rates are stated on an annual basis. For example, an 8 percent coupon rate indicates that the issuer promises to pay 8 percent of a bond's face value to the bondholder each year. However, splitting an annual coupon into two semiannual payments is an almost universal practice in the United States. An exact schedule of coupon payment dates is specified in the bond indenture when the bonds are originally issued.

If a company suspends payment of coupon interest, it is said to be in default. Default is a serious matter. In general, bondholders have an unconditional right to the timely payment of interest and principal. They also have a right to bring legal action to enforce such payments. Upon suspension of coupon payments, the bondholders could, for example, demand an acceleration of principal repayment along with all past-due interest. However, a corporation in financial distress has a right to seek protection in bankruptcy court from inflexible demands by bondholders. As a practical matter, it is often in the best interests of both the bondholders and the corporation to negotiate a new debt contract. Indeed, bankruptcy courts normally encourage a settlement that minimizes any intervention on their part.

18.4 Protective Covenants

protective covenants

Restrictions in a bond indenture designed to protect bondholders.

In addition to the provisions already discussed, a bond indenture is likely to contain a number of **protective covenants**. These agreements are designed to protect bondholders by restricting the actions of a corporation that might cause a deterioration in the credit quality of a bond issue. Protective covenants can be classified into two types: negative covenants and positive, or affirmative, covenants.

A *negative covenant* is a "thou shalt not" for the corporation. Here are some examples of negative covenants that might be found in an indenture agreement:

1. The firm cannot pay dividends to stockholders in excess of what is allowed by a formula based on the firm's earnings.

2. The firm cannot issue new bonds that are senior to currently outstanding bonds. Also, the amount of a new bond issue cannot exceed an amount specified by a formula based on the firm's net worth.

3. The firm cannot refund an existing bond issue with new bonds paying a lower coupon rate than the currently outstanding bond issue it would replace.

4. The firm cannot buy bonds issued by other companies, nor can it guarantee the debt of any other company.

A *positive covenant* is a "thou shalt." It specifies things that a corporation must do, or conditions that it must abide by. Here are some common examples of positive covenants:

1. Proceeds from the sale of assets must be used either to acquire other assets of equal value or to redeem outstanding bonds.

2. In the event of a merger, acquisition, or spinoff, the firm must give bondholders the right to redeem their bonds at par value.

3. The firm must maintain the good condition of all assets pledged as security for an outstanding bond issue.

4. The firm must periodically supply audited financial information to bondholders.

CHECK THIS

18.4a Why would a corporation voluntarily include protective covenants in its bond indenture contract?

18.5 Event Risk

event risk
The possibility that the issuing corporation will experience a significant change in its bond credit quality.

Protective covenants in a bond indenture help shield bondholders from event risk. **Event risk** is broadly defined as the possibility that some structural or financial change to the corporation will cause a significant deterioration in the credit quality of a bond issue, thereby causing the affected bonds to lose substantial market value.

A classic example of event risk, and what could happen to bondholders without adequate covenant protection, is provided by an incident involving Marriott Corporation, best known for its chain of hotels and resorts. In October 1992, Marriott announced its intention to spin off part of the company. The spinoff, called Host Marriott, would acquire most of the parent company's debt and its poorly performing real estate holdings. The parent, Marriott International, would be left relatively debt-free with possession of most of the better performing properties, including its hotel management division.

Visit Marriott and Host Marriott Web sites at
www.marriott.com
and
www.hostmarriott.com

On the announcement date, the affected Marriott bonds fell in value by about 30 percent, reflecting severe concern about the impact of the spinoff on the credit quality of the bonds. On the same day, Marriott stock rose in value by about 30 percent, reflecting a large wealth transfer from bondholders to stockholders. A subsequent bondholder legal challenge was unsuccessful. Standard & Poor's later announced that it was formally revising its credit ratings on Marriott bonds to recognize the impact of the spinoff. (Credit ratings are discussed in detail in a later section.) Debt remaining with Marriott International would have an investment-grade rating, while bonds assigned to Host Marriott would have junk bond status. *The Wall Street Journal* report covering the story is reproduced in the nearby *Investment Updates* box.

CHECK THIS

18.5a What are some possible protective covenants that would have protected Marriott bondholders from the adverse impact of the spinoff described here?

18.6 Bonds without Indentures

private placement
A new bond issue sold to one or more parties in private transactions not available to the public.

The Trust Indenture Act of 1939 does not require an indenture when a bond issue is not sold to the general public. For example, the bonds may be sold only to one or more financial institutions in what is called a **private placement**. Private placements are exempt from registration requirements with the SEC. Nevertheless, even privately placed debt issues often have a formal indenture contract.

MARRIOTT TO SPLIT, MAKING 2 FIRMS

Marriott Corp. shareholders approved a plan to split the company into a real-estate concern, with most of Marriott's debt, and a high-growth hotel-management company.

The split, approved by 85% of the shares voted, was the main issue at Marriott's annual meeting Friday. Under the plan, which is expected to take effect in September, stockholders will receive a share of Marriott International, Inc., the hotel-management operation, for each Marriott share they own. Then Marriott Corp. will be renamed Host Marriott Corp., an entity that will operate the real-estate side of the business.

The plan stunned bondholders when it was announced in October. They argued that the financial support of their debt was being undermined, and a suit by some of the bondholders is still pending.

Marriott shares have risen 60% since the plan's announcement. In New York Stock Exchange trading Friday, Marriott closed at $27.785, up 12.5 cents. The stock has traded as low as $15.50 in the past year.

The Marriott family controls more than 25% of the 100.8 million shares outstanding as of Jan. 1.

Marriott's directors set a distribution date for the split dividend of Sept. 10 for shares of record Sept. 1.

J. W. Marriott, 61 years old and currently chairman and president of the company, will be chairman, president, and chief executive officer of Marriott International, while his brother, Richard E. Marriott, 54, will be chairman of Host Marriott. Richard Marriott is currently vice chairman and executive vice president of the company.

In addition to the bondholders' lawsuit seeking to block the reorganization, Marriott had faced a suit by holders of preferred stock. Marriott said that the holders have agreed to dismiss their case and convert their preferred shares into common stock.

The suit by the group of bondholders, representing about a dozen institutional investors, is still pending, however. Under the reorganization plan, holders of about $1.5 billion in Marriott bonds would have the option to swap their notes for new notes of a unit of the new real-estate entity. The company will retain $2.1 billion of Marriott's $3 billion long-term debt and will own 139 hotels and other real-estate assets.

Larry Kill, attorney for the bondholders, said the suit would proceed despite the shareholder vote. "This was a very unfair transaction," he said.

As a separate company, Host Marriott would have had about $1.2 billion in sales in 1992, according to the company's estimates. Marriott International, Inc., the new hotel concern, will operate more than 760 hotels through Marriott's four hotel-management units and related management services. Marriott International would have had $7.8 billion in sales last year, the company estimates.

In 1992, Marriott had net income of $85 million, or 64 cents a share, on sales of $8.72 billion. It had about $3 billion in long-term debt as of Jan. 1.

Moody's Investors Service, Inc., downgraded its ratings on the senior unsecured debt of Marriott Corp., affecting about $2.3 billion in debt, to Ba-2 from single-B-2. Moody's said the bond-exchange plan will leave a Host Marriott unit highly leveraged "with modest debt protection." Moody's said it expects only gradual improvement in operating earnings, given the sluggish economy and glut of hotel rooms. Moody's said, however, that the Host Marriott unit will be well-positioned for increased earnings when the recovery hits full speed.

When a corporation issues debt without an indenture, it makes an unconditional promise to pay interest and principal according to a simple debt contract. Debt issued without an indenture is basically a simple IOU of the corporation. Bond analysts sometimes reserve the designation "bonds" to mean corporate debt subject to an indenture and refer to corporate debt not subject to an indenture as "notes." However, bonds and notes are more commonly distinguished on the basis of maturity, where bonds designate relatively long maturities, say, 10 years or longer, and notes designate maturities less than 10 years. Both definitions overlap since most long-term debt is issued subject to an indenture, and most privately placed short-term debt is issued as a simple IOU. In between, however, privately placed intermediate-maturity debt may or may not be issued subject to an indenture and therefore might be referred to as either a bond or a note regardless of the existence of an indenture. As in any profession, the jargon of investments is sometimes ambiguous.

18.7 Preferred Stock

preferred stock
A security with a claim to dividend payments that is senior to common stock.

Preferred stock has some of the features of both bonds and common stock. Preferred stockholders have a claim to dividend payments that is senior to the claim of common stockholders—hence the term "preferred stock." However, their claim is subordinate to the claims of bondholders and other creditors. A typical preferred stock issue has the following basic characteristics:

1. Preferred stockholders do not normally participate with common stockholders in the election of a board of directors. However, a few preferred stock issues do grant voting rights to their holders.

2. Preferred stockholders are promised a stream of fixed dividend payments. Thus, preferred dividends resemble bond coupons.

3. Preferred stock normally has no specified maturity, but it is often callable by the issuer.

4. Management can suspend payment of preferred dividends without setting off a bankruptcy process, but only after suspending payment of all common stock dividends.

5. If preferred dividends have been suspended, all unpaid preferred dividends normally become a cumulative debt that must be paid in full before the corporation can resume any payment of common stock dividends. Preferred stock with this feature is termed *cumulative preferred.*

6. Some preferred stock issues have a conversion feature similar to convertible bonds. These are called *convertible preferred stock.*

All else equal, preferred stock normally pays a lower interest rate to investors than do corporate bonds. This is because, when most investors buy preferred stock, the dividends received are taxed at the same rate as bond interest payments. However, if a business corporation buys preferred stock, it can usually exclude at least 70 percent of the preferred dividends from income taxation. As a result, most preferred stock is owned by corporations that can take advantage of the preferential tax treatment of preferred dividends. However, companies that issue ordinary preferred stock must treat preferred dividends the same as common stock dividends for tax purposes and, therefore, cannot deduct preferred dividends from their taxable income.

CHECK THIS

18.7a From the perspective of common stockholders and management, what are some of the advantages of issuing preferred stock instead of bonds or new shares of common stock?

18.8 Adjustable-Rate Bonds and Adjustable-Rate Preferred Stock

adjustable-rate bonds
Securities that pay coupons that change according to a prespecified rule. Also called *floating-rate bonds* or simply *floaters*.

Many bond, note, and preferred stock issues allow the issuer to adjust the annual coupon according to a rule or formula based on current market interest rates. These securities are called **adjustable-rate bonds**; they are also sometimes called *floating-rate bonds* or *floaters*.

For example, a typical adjustment rule might specify that the coupon rate be reset annually to be equal to the current rate on 180-day maturity U.S. Treasury bills plus 2 percent. Alternatively, a more flexible rule might specify that the coupon rate on a bond issue cannot be set below 105 percent of the yield to maturity of newly issued five-year Treasury notes. Thus, if five-year Treasury notes have recently been sold to yield 6 percent, the minimum allowable coupon rate is $1.05 \times 6\% = 6.3\%$.

Adjustable-rate bonds and notes are often putable at par value. For this reason, an issuer may set a coupon rate above an allowable minimum to discourage bondholders from selling their bonds back to the corporation.

CHECK THIS

18.8a How does an adjustable coupon rate feature affect the interest rate risk of a bond?

18.8b How might bondholders respond if the coupon rate on an adjustable-rate putable bond was set below market interest rates?

18.9 Corporate Bond Credit Ratings

credit rating
An assessment of the credit quality of a bond issue based on the issuer's financial condition.

When a corporation sells a new bond issue to investors, it usually subscribes to several bond rating agencies for a credit evaluation of the bond issue. Each contracted rating agency then provides a **credit rating**—an assessment of the credit quality of the bond issue based on the issuer's financial condition. Rating agencies charge a fee for this service. As part of the contractual arrangement between the bond issuer and the rating agency, the issuer agrees to allow a continuing review of its credit rating even if the rating deteriorates. Without a credit rating a new bond issue would be very difficult to sell to the public, which is why almost all bond issues originally sold to the general public have a credit rating assigned at the time of issuance. Also, most public bond issues have ratings assigned by several rating agencies.

Established rating agencies in the United States include Duff and Phelps, Inc. (D&P); Fitch Investors Service (Fitch); McCarthy, Crisanti and Maffei (MCM); Moody's Investors Service (Moody's); and Standard & Poor's Corporation (S&P). Of these, the two best known rating agencies are Moody's and Standard & Poor's. These companies publish regularly updated credit ratings for thousands of domestic and international bond issues.

It is important to realize that corporate bond ratings are assigned to particular bond issues and not to the issuer of those bonds. For example, a senior bond issue is likely to have a higher credit rating than a subordinated issue even if both are issued by the same corporation. Similarly, a corporation with two bond issues outstanding may have a higher credit rating assigned to one issue because that issue has stronger covenant protection specified in the bond's indenture contract.

Visit these rating agency Web sites: Duff & Phelps at
www.dufflic.com
Fitch at
www.fitchibca.com
Moody's at
www.moodys.com
S&P at
www.standardandpoors.
com

| TABLE 18.2 | Corporate Bond Credit Rating Symbols |

Moody's	Rating Agency Duff and Phelps	Standard & Poor's	Credit Rating Description
	Investment-Grade Bond Ratings		
Aaa	1	AAA	Highest credit rating, maximum safety
Aa1	2	AA+	
Aa2	3	AA	High credit quality, investment-grade bonds
Aa3	4	AA−	
A1	5	A+	
A2	6	A	Upper-medium quality, investment-grade bonds
A3	7	A−	
Baa1	8	BBB+	
Baa2	9	BBB	Lower-medium quality, investment-grade bonds
Baa3	10	BBB−	
	Speculative-Grade Bond Ratings		
Ba1	11	BB+	Low credit quality, speculative-grade bonds
Ba2	12	BB	
Ba3	13	BB−	
B1	14	B+	Very low credit quality, speculative-grade bonds
B2	15	B	
B3	16	B−	
	Extremely Speculative-Grade Bond Ratings		
Caa	17	CCC+	Extremely low credit standing, high-risk bonds
		CCC	
		CCC−	
Ca		CC	Extremely speculative
C		C	
		D	Bonds in default

Seniority and covenant protection are not the only things affecting bond ratings. Bond rating agencies consider a number of factors before assigning a credit rating, including an appraisal of the financial strength of the issuer, the caliber of the issuer's management, and the issuer's position in an industry as well as the industry's position in the economy. In general, a bond rating is intended to be a comparative indicator of overall credit quality for a particular bond issue. However, the rating in itself is not a recommendation to buy or sell a bond.

Table 18.2 summarizes corporate bond rating symbols and definitions used by Moody's (first column), Duff and Phelps (second column), and Standard & Poor's (third column). As shown, bond credit ratings fall into three broad categories: investment-grade, speculative-grade, and extremely speculative-grade.

WHY BOND RATINGS ARE IMPORTANT

Bond credit ratings assigned by independent rating agencies are quite important to bond market participants. Only a few institutional investors have the resources and expertise necessary to properly evaluate a bond's credit quality on their own. Bond ratings provide investors with reliable, professional evaluations of bond issues at a reasonable cost. This information is indispensable for assessing the economic value of a bond.

Chapter 18 ■ Corporate Bonds **607**

prudent investment guidelines
Restrictions on investment portfolios stipulating that securities purchased must meet a certain level of safety.

Furthermore, many financial institutions have **prudent investment guidelines** stipulating that only securities with a certain level of investment safety may be included in their portfolios. For example, bond investments for many pension funds are limited to investment-grade bonds rated at least Baa by Moody's or at least BBB by Standard & Poor's. Bond ratings provide a convenient measure to monitor implementation of these guidelines.

Individual investors investing in bonds also find published bond ratings useful. Individual investors generally do not have the ability to diversify as extensively as do large institutions. With limited diversification opportunities, an individual should invest only in bonds with higher credit ratings.

CHECK THIS

18.9a Does a low credit rating necessarily imply that a bond is a bad investment?

18.9b What factors besides the credit rating might be important in deciding whether a particular bond is a worthwhile investment?

18.10 Junk Bonds

high-yield bonds
Bonds with a speculative credit rating that is offset by a yield premium offered to compensate for higher credit risk. Also called *junk bonds*.

Bonds with a speculative or low grade rating—that is, those rated Ba or lower by Moody's or BB or lower by Standard & Poor's—are commonly called **high-yield bonds**, or, more colorfully, *junk bonds*. The designation "junk" is somewhat misleading and often unduly pejorative, since junk bonds *have* economic value. Junk bonds simply represent debt with a higher than average credit risk. To put the term in perspective, one should realize that most consumer debt and small business debt represents higher than average credit risk. Yet it is generally considered desirable from an economic and social perspective that credit be available to consumers and small businesses.

Junk bonds that were originally issued with an investment-grade credit rating that subsequently fell to speculative grade because of unforeseen economic events are called *fallen angels*. Another type, *original-issue junk,* is defined as bonds originally issued with a speculative-grade rating.

Junk bonds are attractive investments for many institutional investors with well-diversified portfolios. The logic of junk bond investing revolves around the possibility that the *yield premium* for junk bonds might be high enough to justify accepting the higher default rates of junk bonds. As an example of this logic, consider the following back-of-the-envelope calculations.

Suppose that the average yield on junk bonds is 10 percent when U.S. Treasury bonds yield 7 percent. In this case, the yield premium of junk bonds over default-free Treasury bonds is 3 percent. Further suppose that an investor expects about 4 percent of all outstanding junk bonds to default each year, and experience suggests that when junk bonds default bondholders on average receive 50 cents for each dollar of bond face value. Based on these rough assumptions, diversified junk bond investors expect to lose 2 percent (.04 × .50) of their portfolio value each year through defaults. But with a junk bond yield premium of 3 percent, the junk bond portfolio is expected to outperform U.S. Treasury bonds by 1 percent per year. It is true that a junk bond portfolio is much more expensive to manage than a Treasury bond portfolio. However, for a $1 billion bond portfolio, a junk bond

One important reason you need the credit rating for a bond is the yield spread. The yield spread is the extra return, in the form of an increased yield to maturity, that investors receive for buying a bond with a lower credit rating. Because of the credit risk, investors demand a risk premium for investing in lower rated bonds. You can create a yield curve for bonds with different credit ratings. We went to finance.yahoo.com and looked up the yields for U.S. Treasuries and corporate bonds. Here is what we found:

U.S. Treasury Bonds				
Maturity	Yield	Yesterday	Last Week	Last Month
3 Month	3.82	3.82	3.79	3.61
6 Month	4.09	4.13	4.09	3.94
2 Year	4.38	4.45	4.47	4.26
3 Year	4.40	4.47	4.51	4.30
5 Year	4.41	4.49	4.55	4.35
10 Year	4.46	4.55	4.64	4.49
30 Year	4.66	4.74	4.83	4.71

Corporate Bonds				
Maturity	Yield	Yesterday	Last Week	Last Month
2yr AA	4.53	4.57	4.58	4.36
2yr A	4.57	4.63	4.65	4.41
5yr AAA	4.71	4.73	4.74	4.52
5yr AA	4.73	4.77	4.84	4.62
5yr A	4.82	4.88	4.90	4.66
10yr AAA	5.24	5.23	5.19	4.95
10yr AA	5.07	5.13	5.17	5.00
10yr A	5.15	5.20	5.25	5.07
20yr AAA	5.56	5.53	5.46	5.30
20yr AA	5.76	5.80	5.77	5.63
20yr A	5.89	5.81	5.86	5.66

If you calculate the yield spread for a five-year AAA credit–rated corporate bond, you should find it is 30 basis points (4.71% − 4.41%). Similarly, the yield spread for a five-year A credit–rated corporate bond is 41 basis points (4.82% − 4.41%). Although these yield spreads look small, remember they are for highly rated corporate bonds. A yield spread on junk bonds exceeding 10 percent is not uncommon.

yield premium of 1 percent represents $10 million of additional interest income per year. Our nearby *Work the Web* box has more on credit ratings and yield spreads.

Of course, actual default rates could turn out to be much different than expected. History suggests that the major determinant of aggregate bond default rates is the state of economic activity. During an expansionary economic period, bond default rates are usually low. But in a recession, default rates can rise dramatically. For this reason, the investment performance of a junk bond portfolio largely depends on the health of the economy.

Prices and yields of selected junk bonds are published regularly in *The Wall Street Journal* in its "High-Yield Bonds" report. A sample report is displayed in Figure 18.6. We discuss the data in Figure 18.6 in more detail in our next section. For an interesting discussion on investing in junk bonds, see the nearby *Investment Updates* box.

STOCK INVESTORS COULD STAND A LITTLE "JUNK" IN THEIR DIETS

Hungry for healthy stock-market returns? Here's an intriguing suggestion: Buy junk bonds. Like stocks, junk (or "high yield") bonds have had a rough time lately. Mutual funds that invest in junk bonds tumbled an average 8.1% last year and shed an additional 1.8% in this year's first 10 months, according to Chicago researcher Morningstar Inc.

Stocks, of course, have suffered even more. Still, I believe there is a decent chance that high-yield bonds, those risky securities issued by heavily indebted companies, could outpace stocks in the years ahead. As I have argued in many columns this year, expected stock-market returns remain modest, despite the 30% decline in share prices. The outlook seems especially grim for blue-chip U.S. shares, which continue to sport nosebleed share-price-to-earnings multiples and skimpy dividend yields.

By contrast, junk bonds today offer lush 13% yields. Don't believe junk-bond prices will rebound soon? As they say on Wall Street, you are getting paid to wait. "One of the reasons investors may gravitate in this direction is, in part, because they don't see a lot of upside in stocks," says Martin Fridson, chief high-yield strategist at Merrill Lynch & Co. "They might say, 'Ordinarily, I'm not that excited

about bonds, but that 12% or 13% looks pretty attractive right now.'"

Today's 13% yield is some nine percentage points higher than the yield on 10-year Treasury notes. How unusual is that? Put it this way: The spread between junk and Treasury yields was only slightly wider during the economic turmoil of 1990–91. That was the last time that junk bonds got really pummeled, and many investors still remember the pain. In the late 1980s, unscrupulous securities salesmen hawked junk-bond funds as higher-yielding certificates of deposit.

That fantasy was shredded in late 1989 and 1990, as junk-bond issuers struggled with an overdose of debt and a slowing economy. Junk-bond funds proved anything but safe, as their rich yields failed to compensate for shrinking fund-share prices. But for those who hung tough, the story had a happy ending. After getting hammered in 1990, both junk bonds and stocks came roaring back in 1991. In fact, in 1991, junk-bond funds soared an average 37.1%, rivaling the performance of diversified U.S.-stock funds. Naysayers might dismiss the parallels, noting that the economy is likely to deteriorate further in 2002, triggering a rash of defaults among junk-bond

FIGURE 18.6	Junk Bond Trading

High-Yield Bonds
Tuesday, January 3, 2006

Ten most active fixed-coupon high-yield, or "junk", corporate bonds

COMPANY (TICKER)	COUPON	MATURITY	LAST PRICE	LAST YIELD	*EST SPREAD	UST†	EST VOL (000's)
Ford Motor Credit Co (F)	7.000	Oct 01, 2013	86.250	9.551	518	10	120,757
Dana Corp (DCN)	6.500	Mar 01, 2009	82.500	13.488	915	3	97,448
General Motors Corp (GM)	8.375	Jul 15, 2033	67.500	12.623	807	30	87,977
Ford Motor Credit Co (F)	7.375	Oct 28, 2009	89.500	10.801	650	3	78,943
Ford Motor Credit Co (F)	7.375	Feb 01, 2011	88.250	10.414	611	5	76,837
Pilgrims Pride Corp (PPC)	9.625	Sep 15, 2011	106.250	7.088	277	5	67,190
Ford Motor Co (F)	7.450	Jul 16, 2031	68.625	11.194	664	30	65,349
General Motors Acceptance Corp (GM)	8.000	Nov 01, 2031	98.250	8.162	361	30	64,532
Adelphia Communications Corp (ADELQ)	10.250	Jun 15, 2011	61.500	23.273	1897	5	60,250
Ford Motor Credit Co (F)	7.250	Oct 25, 2011	87.060	10.259	596	5	58,437

Volume represents total volume for the market; price/yield data are for trades of $100,000 and greater. * Estimated spreads, in basis points (100 basis points is one percentage point), over the 2, 3, 5, 10 or 30-year hot run Treasury note/bond. 2-year: 4.250 11/07; 3-year: 4.375 11/08; 5-year: 4.375 12/10; 10-year: 4.500 11/15; 30-year: 5.375 02/31. †Comparable U.S. Treasury issue.

Source: MarketAxess Corporate BondTicker

issuers. But that won't necessarily mean lousy junk-bond returns, says Ken Gregory, president of Litman/Gregory, a money manager in Orinda, Calif.

For instance, 1991 was a terrible year for junk-bond defaults, and yet the bonds posted fabulous gains. "Like every other financial asset, high-yield bonds discount the future," Mr. Gregory notes. "There are a lot of defaults forecasted for next year, but that's not inconsistent with high returns." In 1990–91, junk bonds and stocks seemed to move in lockstep, first losing money together and then rebounding together. But junk bonds could do well in the next few years, even if stocks don't. Mr. Gregory reckons that the worst-case scenario for junk bonds is "a zero return over the next 12 months," as slumping junk-bond prices and defaults wipe out the entire gain from the 13% yield. "I think the downside in stocks is a lot greater than that," Mr. Gregory says. "It's hard to argue that the stock market is at bargain levels. Over the next five years, I see annual returns of maybe 3% on the low side and 9% on the high side."

By contrast, junk bonds seem to offer far higher potential gains. Historically, junk-bond investors have lost 2% a year to defaults. Even if you subtract two percentage points from today's 13% yield, that still leaves investors collecting 11%. And returns could be much higher, if junk-bond prices bounce back. If you are intrigued by junk bonds, consider no-load funds such as Fidelity Capital & Income, Northeast Investors Trust, T. Rowe Price High-Yield, Strong High-Yield Bond, and Vanguard High-Yield Corporate. According to Morningstar, all have expenses below 1%, managers with better-than-average five-year records, and investment minimums of $3,000 and below. Because junk funds are so tax inefficient, they are best held in a retirement account, unless you plan to spend the income.

Here's an added consideration: Don't buy a fund that has done too well this year. Again, cast your mind back to 1990–91. The 50% of funds that held up best in 1990 went on to gain an average 32.8% in 1991. But the funds that got hit hardest in 1990 did even better in 1991, climbing 42.1%. That suggests the best funds to own may be those that have made little or no money this year. "If you look just at the funds that have done best this year, you're limiting yourself to the higher-quality high-yield funds," Mr. Gregory says. "We would rather look at funds that we consider pure plays."

Source: Jonathan Clements, *The Wall Street Journal*, November 13, 2001. © 2001 Dow Jones & Company, Inc. All Rights Reserved Worldwide.

CHECK THIS

18.10a Can junk bond default risk be completely diversified away by large institutional bond investors?

18.10b From an investor's perspective, is there any importance in distinguishing between fallen angels and original-issue junk?

18.11 Bond Market Trading

Consistent with the need to hold bonds for predictable cash flows, most corporate bond investors buy and hold bonds until they mature. However, many investors need to liquidate some bonds before they mature, and others wish to purchase outstanding bonds originally issued by a particular corporation several years earlier. For these and many other reasons, the existence of an active secondary market for corporate bonds is important for most bond investors. Fortunately, an active secondary market with a substantial volume of bond trading does exist to satisfy most of the liquidity needs of investors.

Almost as many different bond issues are listed on the New York Stock Exchange (NYSE) as there are different common stock issues. These NYSE-traded bond issues represent the most actively traded bonds of large corporations. However, there are many more thousands of different corporate debt issues outstanding. Most of these debt issues trade in the over-the-counter (OTC) market. In fact, it is estimated that less than 1 percent of all corporate bond trading actually takes place on the New York Stock Exchange. While some bond trading activity occurs on the American Stock Exchange and other regional exchanges, corporate bond trading is characteristically an OTC activity.

Before mid-2002, the OTC corporate bond market had limited transparency, meaning that, unlike stocks, relatively little information was available on trading. This lack of transparency made it difficult for bond investors to get accurate, up-to-date prices. However, at the request of the Securities and Exchange Commission (SEC), recently adopted rules require reporting of corporate bond trades through what is known as the Trade Reporting and Compliance Engine (TRACE), and transparency has dramatically improved. As this is written, transaction prices are now reported on more than 4,000 bonds, amounting to approximately 75 percent of investment-grade market volume. More bonds will be added over time.

WWW

Learn more about TRACE at
www.nasd.com
See TRACE data at
www.nasdbondinfo.com

CHECK THIS

18.11a All else equal, is an actively traded bond more or less risky as an investment than a thinly traded bond? (*Hint*: Is liquidity a good or a bad thing for a bond?)

18.11b Why might a current yield for a convertible bond be uninformative for the purpose of making a comparison between two or more bonds?

18.12 Summary and Conclusions

This chapter covers the important topic of corporate bonds, a major source of capital used by corporations. In this chapter we saw that:

1. A corporate bond represents a corporation's promise to pay bondholders a fixed sum of money at maturity, along with periodic payments of interest. The sum paid at maturity is the bond's principal, and the periodic interest payments are coupons. Most bonds pay fixed coupons, but some pay floating coupon rates adjusted regularly according to prevailing market interest rates.

2. Corporate bonds are usually callable, which means that the issuer has the right to buy back outstanding bonds before maturity. When a bond issue is called, bondholders surrender their bonds in exchange for a prespecified call price.

3. The largest category of corporate bond investors is life insurance companies, which own about a third of all outstanding corporate bonds. Remaining ownership shares are roughly equally distributed among individual investors, pension funds, banks, and foreign investors.

4. Debentures are the most common type of corporate bond. Debenture bonds represent the unsecured debt of a corporation. Mortgage bonds represent debt issued with a

lien on specific property pledged as security for the bonds. Collateral trust bonds are characterized by a pledge of financial assets as security for a bond issue. Equipment trust certificates are issued according to a lease form of financing, where investors purchase equipment trust certificates and the proceeds from this sale are used to purchase equipment that is leased to a corporation.

5. A bond indenture is a formal agreement between the corporation and bondholders that spells out the legal rights and obligations of both parties with respect to a bond issue. An indenture typically specifies the seniority of a bond issue, along with any call provisions, put provisions, bond-to-stock conversion provisions, and sinking fund provisions.

6. When a corporation sells a new bond issue to the public, it usually has a credit rating assigned by several independent bond rating agencies. Without a credit rating, a new bond issue would be difficult to sell, which is why almost all bond issues sold to the public have credit ratings assigned.

7. Bonds with a speculative or lower grade rating, commonly called high-yield bonds, or junk bonds, represent corporate debt with higher than average credit risk. Credit ratings for junk bonds are frequently revised to reflect changing financial conditions.

8. The existence of an active secondary market for corporate bonds is important to most bond investors. The greatest total volume of bond trading occurs in the OTC market.

GET REAL

This chapter explored the world of corporate bonds, an important category of investments for institutions, such as pension funds and life insurance companies, and also for individuals. This category also includes convertible bonds and preferred stock. How should you put this information to work?

Now that you understand the most important features of corporate bonds, you need to buy several different issues to experience the real-world gains and losses that come with managing a bond portfolio. So, with a simulated brokerage account (such as Stock-Trak), try putting roughly equal dollar amounts into three or four different corporate bond issues. Be sure to include some junk bonds in your selections. Check the credit ratings of the bond issues you have selected at a site such as Bonds Online (www.bondsonline.com).

You can find out more information about corporate bonds at the many Web sites now specializing in bonds, including Investing In Bonds (www.investinginbonds.com), Bond Markets (www.bondmarkets.com), and Convertible Bonds (www.convertbond.com). The Web sites of bond rating agencies such as Moody's (www.moodys.com), Standard & Poor's (www.standardandpoors.com), Duff & Phelps (www.dufflllc.com), and Fitch (www.fitchibca.com) are also quite informative.

As you monitor the prices of your bonds, notice how interest rates influence their prices. You may also notice that for bonds with lower credit ratings, the stock price of the issuing company is an important influence. Why do you think this is so?

Of course, with the convertible issues the bond price will definitely be influenced by the underlying stock value, but the impact depends on the specific conversion features of the bond, including whether the bond is in the money or not.

Key Terms

Chapter Review Problems and Self-Test

1. **Callable Bonds**   A particular bond matures in 30 years. It is callable in 10 years at 110. The call price is then cut by 1 percent of par each year until the call price reaches par. If the bond is called in 12 years, how much will you receive? Assume a $1,000 face value.

2. **Convertible Bonds**   A convertible bond features a conversion ratio of 50. What is the conversion price? If the stock sells for $30 per share, what is the conversion value?

3. **Convertible Bonds**   A convertible bond has an 8 percent coupon, paid semiannually, and will mature in 15 years. If the bond were not convertible, it would be priced to yield 9 percent. The conversion ratio on the bond is 40, and the stock is currently selling for $24 per share. What is the minimum value of this bond?

Answers to Self-Test Problems

1. The call price will be $110\% - 2 \times 1\% = 108\%$ of face value, or $1,080.

2. The conversion price is face value divided by the conversion ratio, $1,000/50 = $20. The conversion value is what the bond is worth on a converted basis, $50 \times $30 = $1,500.

3. The minimum value is the larger of the conversion value and the intrinsic bond value. The conversion value is $40 \times $24 = $960. To calculate the intrinsic bond value, note that we have a face value of $1,000 (by assumption), a semiannual coupon of $40, an annual yield of 9 percent (4.5 percent per half-year), and 15 years to maturity (30 half-years). Using the standard bond pricing formula from an earlier chapter, the bond's price (be sure to verify this) if it were not convertible is $918.56. This convertible bond thus will sell for more than $960.

Test Your Investment Quotient

1. **Trust Certificates**   An airline elects to finance the purchase of some new airplanes using equipment trust certificates. Under the legal arrangement associated with such certificates, the airplanes are pledged as collateral, but which other factor applies?

   a. The airline still has legal title to the planes.
   b. Legal title to the planes resides with the manufacturer.
   c. The airline does not get legal title to the planes until the manufacturer is paid off.
   d. Legal title to the planes resides with a third party who then leases the planes to the airline.

2. **Callable Bonds**   What does the call feature of a bond mean?

   a. Investor can call for payment on demand.
   b. Investor can only call if the firm defaults on an interest payment.
   c. Issuer can call the bond issue prior to the maturity date.
   d. Issuer can call the issue during the first three years.

3. **Callable Bonds**   Who benefits from a call provision on a corporate bond?

   a. The issuer
   b. The bondholders
   c. The trustee
   d. The government regulators

4. **Callable Bonds**   Which of the following describes a bond with a call feature?

   a. It is attractive, because the immediate receipt of principal plus premium produces a high return.
   b. It is more likely to be called when interest rates are high, because the interest savings will be greater.
   c. It would usually have a higher yield than a similar noncallable bond.
   d. It generally has a higher credit rating than a similar noncallable bond.

5. **Callable Bonds**   Which of the following is not a component of call risk for a bond investor?

   a. The cash flow pattern for the bond is not known with certainty.
   b. When the issuer calls a bond, the investor is exposed to reinvestment risk.
   c. The value of a callable bond drops when expected interest rate volatility decreases.
   d. The capital appreciation potential of a callable bond is lower than a noncallable bond.

6. **Callable Bonds**   Two bonds are identical, except one is callable and the other is noncallable. Compared to the noncallable bond, the callable bond has

   a. Negative convexity and a lower price.
   b. Negative convexity and a higher price.
   c. Positive convexity and a lower price.
   d. Positive convexity and a higher price.

7. **Convexity**   What does positive convexity on a bond imply?

   a. The direction of change in yield is directly related to the change in price.
   b. Prices increase at a faster rate as yields drop than they decrease as yields rise.
   c. Price changes are the same for both increases and decreases in yields.
   d. Prices increase and decrease at a faster rate than the change in yield.

8. **Convexity**   A bond with negative convexity is best described as having a price-yield relationship displaying

   a. Positive convexity at high yields and negative convexity at low yields.
   b. Negative convexity at high yields and positive convexity at low yields.
   c. Negative convexity at low and high yields and positive at medium yields.
   d. Positive convexity at low and high yields and negative at medium yields.

9. **Convexity and Duration**   Which of the following *most accurately* measures interest rate sensitivity for bonds with embedded options?

   a. Convexity
   b. Effective duration
   c. Modified duration
   d. Macaulay duration

10. **Convexity and Duration**   Which of the following most accurately measures interest rate sensitivity for bonds *without* embedded options?

   a. Convexity
   b. Effective duration
   c. Modified duration
   d. Macaulay duration

www.mhhe.com/jm4e

11. Indentures   Which of the following is not a responsibility of a corporate trustee with regard to a bond's trust indenture?

a. Checking compliance
b. Authenticating the bonds issued
c. Negotiating the terms
d. Declaring defaults

12. Refundings   The refunding provision of an indenture allows bonds to be retired unless

a. They are replaced with a new issue having a lower interest cost.
b. The remaining time to maturity is less than five years.
c. The stated time period in the indenture has not passed.
d. The stated time period in the indenture has passed.

13. Debentures   Holders of unsecured debentures with a negative pledge clause can claim which of the following assurances?

a. No additional secured debt will be issued in the future.
b. If any secured debt is issued in the future, the unsecured debentures must be redeemed at par.
c. The debentures will be secured, but to a lesser degree than any secured debt issued in the future.
d. The debentures will be secured at least equally with any secured debt issued in the future.

14. Credit Risk   An "original issue junk" bond is *best* described as a bond issued

a. Below investment grade.
b. At an original issue discount.
c. As investment grade, but declined to speculative grade.
d. As below investment grade, but upgraded to speculative grade.

15. Credit Risk   A "fallen angel" bond is *best* described as a bond issued

a. Below investment grade.
b. At an original issue discount.
c. As investment grade, but declined to speculative grade.
d. As a secured bond, but the collateral value declined below par value.

16. Preferred Stock   Nonconvertible preferred stock has which of the following in comparison to common stock?

a. Preferential claim on a company's earnings.
b. A predetermined dividend rate.
c. Preferential voting rights.
d. All of the above.

17. Preferred Stock   A preferred stock that is entitled to dividends in arrears is known as

a. Convertible
b. Cumulative
c. Extendible
d. Participating

18. Preferred Stock   Why does a firm's preferred stock often sell at yields below its bonds?

a. Preferred stock generally carries a higher agency rating.
b. Owners of preferred stock have a prior claim on the firm's earnings.
c. Owners of preferred stock have a prior claim on the firm's assets in a liquidation.
d. Corporations owning stock may exclude from income taxes most of the dividend income they receive.

19. Convertible Bonds   Which one of the following statements about convertible bonds is true?

a. The longer the call protection on a convertible, the less the security is worth.
b. The more volatile the underlying stock, the greater the value of the conversion feature.
c. The smaller the spread between the dividend yield on the stock and the yield to maturity on the bond, the more the convertible is worth.
d. The collateral that is used to secure a convertible bond is one reason convertibles are more attractive than the underlying common stocks.

20. Convertible Bonds Which one of the following statements about convertible bonds is false?

   a. The yield on the convertible will typically be higher than the yield on the underlying common stock.

   b. The convertible bond will likely participate in a major upward movement in the price of the underlying common stock.

   c. Convertible bonds are typically secured by specific assets of the issuing company.

   d. A convertible bond can be valued as a straight bond with an attached option.

21. Convertible Bonds Consider the possible advantages of convertible bonds for investors:

   I. The conversion feature enables the convertible to participate in major upward moves in the price of the underlying common stock.

   II. The bonds are typically secured by specific assets of the issuing company.

   III. Investors may redeem their bonds at the stated conversion price any time during the life of the issue.

   IV. The yield on the convertible will almost always be higher than the yield on the underlying common stock.

Which are true?

   a. I and II only

   b. II and III only

   c. I and III only

   d. I and IV only

22. Convertible Bonds A convertible bond sells at $1,000 par with a conversion ratio of 40 and an accompanying stock price of $20 per share. The conversion price and conversion value are, respectively,

   a. $20 and $1,000

   b. $20 and $800

   c. $25 and $1,000

   d. $25 and $800

23. Convertible Bonds A convertible bond sells at $1,000 par with a conversion ratio of 25 and conversion value of $800. What is the price of the underlying stock?

   a. $12

   b. $48

   c. $40

   d. $32

24. Convertible Bonds A convertible bond has a par value of $1,000 and a conversion ratio of 20. The price of the underlying stock is $40. What is the conversion value?

   a. $20

   b. $800

   c. $1,000

   d. $25

25. International Bonds A U.S. investor who buys Japanese bonds will most likely maximize his return if interest rates

   a. Fall and the dollar weakens relative to the yen.

   b. Fall and the dollar strengthens relative to the yen.

   c. Rise and the dollar weakens relative to the yen.

   d. Rise and the dollar strengthens relative to the yen.

Concept Questions

1. Bond Types What are the four main types of corporate bonds?

2. Bond Features What is a bond refunding? Is it the same thing as a call?

3. Callable Bonds With regard to the call feature, what are call protection and the call premium? What typically happens to the call premium through time?

www.mhhe.com/jm4e

4. **Put Bonds** What is a put bond? Is the put feature desirable from the investor's perspective? The issuer's?

5. **Bond Yields** What is the impact on a bond's coupon rate from
   a. A call feature?
   b. A put feature?

6. **Exchangeable Bonds** What is the difference between an exchangeable bond and a convertible bond?

7. **Event Risk** What is event risk? In addition to protective covenants, which bond feature do you think best reduces or eliminates such risk?

8. **Floaters** From the bondholder's perspective, what are the potential advantages and disadvantages of floating coupons?

9. **Effective Duration** Why is effective duration a more accurate measure of interest rate risk for bonds with embedded options?

10. **Embedded Options** What are some examples of embedded options in bonds? How do they affect the price of a bond?

11. **Junk Bonds** Explain the difference between an original issue junk bond and a fallen angel bond.

12. **Put Bonds** What is the difference between put bonds and extendible bonds?

13. **Callable Bonds** All else the same, callable bonds have less interest rate sensitivity than non-callable bonds. Why? Is this a good thing?

14. **Callable Bonds** Two callable bonds are essentially identical, except that one has a refunding provision while the other has no refunding provision. Which bond is more likely to be called by the issuer? Why?

15. **Inverse Floaters** An "inverse floater" is a bond with a coupon that is adjusted down when interest rates rise and up when rates fall. What is the impact of the floating coupon on the bond's price volatility?

Questions and Problems

Core Questions

1. **Conversion Price** A convertible bond has a $1,000 face value and a conversion ratio of 35. What is the conversion price?

2. **Conversion Price** A convertible bond has a conversion ratio of 18 and a par value of $1,000. What is the conversion price?

3. **Conversion Ratio** A company just sold a convertible bond at par value of $1,000. If the conversion price is $42, what is the conversion ratio?

4. **Conversion Value** A convertible bond has a $1,000 face value and a conversion ratio of 45. If the stock price is $26, what is the conversion value?

5. **Conversion Value** A convertible bond has a conversion ratio of 20 and a par value of $1,000. If the stock is currently priced at $47, what is the conversion value?

6. **Conversion Ratio** You find a convertible bond outstanding with a conversion value of $896. The stock is currently priced at $32. What is the conversion ratio of the bond?

7. **Callable Bonds** A bond matures in 25 years, but is callable in 10 years at 112. The call premium decreases by 2 percent of par per year. If the bond is called in 13 years, how much will you receive?

8. **Call Premium** You own a bond with an 8 percent coupon rate and a yield to call of 8.65 percent. The bond currently sells for $1,029.07. If the bond is callable in five years, what is the call premium of the bond?

9. **Convertible Bonds** A convertible bond has a 9 percent coupon, paid semiannually, and will mature in 10 years. If the bond were not convertible, it would be priced to yield 10 percent. The conversion ratio on the bond is 20, and the stock is currently selling for $53 per share. What is the minimum value of this bond?

10. **Convertible Bonds** You own a convertible bond with a conversion ratio of 30. The stock is currently selling for $38 per share. The issuer of the bond has announced a call; the call price is 110. What are your options here? What should you do?

Intermediate Questions

11. **Convertible Bonds** There is a 30-year bond with a 10 percent coupon and a 7 percent yield to maturity. The bond is callable in 10 years at par value. What is the Macaulay duration of the bond assuming it is not called? What is the Macaulay duration if the bond is called? Which number is more relevant?

Use the following information to answer the next two questions: Rajiv Singh, a bond analyst, is analyzing a convertible bond. The characteristics of the bond are given below.

Convertible Bond Characteristics	
Par value	$1,000
Annual coupon rate (annual pay)	6.5%
Conversion ratio	22
Market price	105% of par
Straight value	99% of par
Underlying Stock Characteristics	
Current market price	$40 per share
Annual cash dividend	$1.20 per share

12. **Convertible Bonds** Compute the bond's conversion value and market conversion price.

13. **Convertible Bonds** Determine whether the value of a callable convertible bond will increase, decrease, or remain unchanged if there is an increase in stock price volatility. What if there is an increase in interest rate volatility? Justify each of your responses.

Use the following information to answer the next two questions: Rich McDonald, CFA, is evaluating his investment alternatives in Ytel Incorporated by analyzing a Ytel convertible bond and Ytel common equity. Characteristics of the two securities are as follows:

Characteristic	Convertible Bond	Common Equity
Par value	$1,000	
Coupon (annual payment)	4%	
Current market price	$980	$35 per share
Straight bond value	$925	
Conversion ratio	25	
Conversion option	At any time	
Dividend		$0
Expected market price in one year	$1,125	$45 per share

14. **Convertible Bonds** Calculate the following:

a. The current market conversion price for the Ytel convertible bond.
b. The expected one-year rate of return for the Ytel convertible bond.
c. The expected one-year rate of return for the Ytel common equity.

15. **Convertible Bonds** One year has passed and Ytel's common equity price has increased to $51 per share. Also, over the year, the interest rate on Ytel's nonconvertible bonds of the same maturity has increased, while credit spreads remained unchanged. Name the two components of the convertible bond's value. Indicate whether the value of each component should increase, stay the same, or decrease in response to the increase on Ytel's common equity and the increase in interest rates.

What's on the Web

1. **Bond Quotes**   Go to www.nasdbondinfo.com and find the corporate bond search. Enter "Ford Motor" for Ford Motor Company in Issue box and search for Ford bonds. How many bonds are listed for sale? What are the different credit ratings for these bonds? What is the yield to maturity for the longest maturity bond? What is its price?

2. **Credit Spreads**   What are the current credit spreads? Go to finance.yahoo.com and find the U.S. Treasury yields and the corporate bond yields. Calculate the yield spreads for AAA, AA, and A credit–rated bonds for 2-, 5-, and 10-year bonds. Are the yield spreads linear? In other words, does the yield spread increase by the same number of basis points for each decline in credit rating? Why or why not? Why are the yield spreads higher for longer term bonds?

3. **Historical Credit Spreads**   The Federal Reserve Bank of St. Louis has files with historical interest rates on its Web site at www.stls.frb.org. Go to the site and find the monthly Moody's Seasoned Aaa Corporate Bond Yield and the monthly Moody's Seasoned Baa Corporate Bond Yield. You can calculate a credit spread as the difference between these two returns. When was the largest credit spread? The smallest? What factors do you think led to the large credit spreads and the small credit spreads?

4. **Bond Terminology**   Go to www.investinginbonds.com and find the definitions for the following terms: bond resolution, cap, collar, defeasance, extraordinary redemption, overcollateralization, and refunding.

Stock-Trak Exercises

To access the Stock-Trak Exercise for this chapter, please visit the book Web site at www.mhhe.com/jm4e and choose the corresponding chapter.

CHAPTER 19

Government Bonds

"Blessed are the young, for they shall inherit the national debt."

–Herbert Hoover

U.S. Treasury bonds are among the safest investments available because they are secured by the considerable resources of the federal government. Many bonds issued by federal government agencies, and by state and local municipal governments, are also nearly free of default risk. Consequently, government bonds are generally excellent vehicles for conservative investment strategies seeking predictable investment results. ■

The largest and most important debt market is that for debt issued by the U.S. government. This market is truly global in character since a large share of federal debt is sold to foreign investors, and it thereby sets the tone for debt markets around the world. In contrast, the market for debt issued by states and municipalities is almost exclusively a domestic market since almost all U.S. municipal securities are owned by U.S. investors. These two broad categories make up the government bond market. In this chapter, we examine securities issued by federal, state, and local governments, which represent a combined value of many trillions of dollars.

19.1 Government Bond Basics

The U.S. federal government is the largest single borrower in the world. In 2005, the public debt of the U.S. government exceeded $4 trillion. Responsibility for managing outstanding government debt belongs to the U.S. Treasury, which acts as the financial agent of the federal government.

The U.S. Treasury finances government debt by issuing marketable securities and nonmarketable securities. Most of the gross public debt is financed by the sale of marketable securities at regularly scheduled Treasury auctions. Marketable securities include Treasury bills, Treasury notes, and Treasury bonds, often simply called T-bills, T-notes, and T-bonds, respectively. Outstanding marketable securities trade among investors in a large, active financial market called the Treasury market. Nonmarketable securities include U.S. Savings Bonds, Government Account Series, and State and Local Government Series. Many individuals are familiar with U.S. Savings Bonds since they are sold only to individual investors. Government Account Series are issued to federal government agencies and trust funds, in particular, the Social Security Administration trust fund. State and Local Government Series are purchased by municipal governments.

Treasury security ownership is registered with the U.S. Treasury. When an investor sells a U.S. Treasury security to another investor, registered ownership is officially transferred by notifying the U.S. Treasury of the transaction. However, only marketable securities allow registered ownership to be transferred. Nonmarketable securities do not allow a change of registered ownership and therefore cannot be traded among investors. For example, a U.S. Savings Bond is a nonmarketable security. If an investor wishes to sell a U.S. Savings Bond, it must be redeemed by the U.S. Treasury. This is normally a simple procedure. For example, most banks handle the purchase and sale of U.S. Savings Bonds for their customers.

Another large market for government debt is the market for municipal government debt. There are more than 80,000 state and local governments in the United States, most of which have issued outstanding debt obligations. In a typical year, well over 10,000 new municipal debt issues are brought to market. Total municipal debt outstanding in the United States is estimated to be over $2 trillion. Of this total, individual investors hold about half, either through direct purchase or indirectly through mutual funds. The remainder is split about equally between holdings of property and casualty insurance companies and commercial banks.

The value of the outstanding U.S. federal government debt can be found at www.publicdebt.treas.gov

Visit www.investinginbonds.com for more information on U.S. Treasury securities

19.2 U.S. Treasury Bills, Notes, Bonds, and STRIPS

face value
The value of a bill, note, or bond at its maturity when a payment of principal is made. Also called *redemption value*.

discount basis
Method of selling a Treasury bill at a discount from face value.

imputed interest
The interest paid on a Treasury bill determined by the size of its discount from face value.

Treasury bills are short-term obligations that mature in six months or less. They are originally issued with maturities of 4, 13, or 26 weeks. A T-bill entitles its owner to receive a single payment at the bill's maturity, called the bill's **face value** or *redemption value*. The smallest denomination T-bill has a face value of $1,000. T-bills are sold on a **discount basis**, where a price is set at a discount from face value. For example, if a $10,000 bill is sold for $9,500, then it is sold at a discount of $500, or 5 percent. The discount represents the **imputed interest** on the bill.

Treasury notes are medium-term obligations with original maturities of 10 years or less, but more than 1 year. They are normally issued with original maturities of 2, 5, or 10 years, and they have face value denominations as small as $1,000. Besides a payment of face value at maturity, T-notes also pay semiannual coupons.

Treasury bonds are long-term obligations with much longer original-issue maturities. Since 1985, the Treasury has only issued T-bonds with a maturity of 30 years in its regular bond offerings. Like T-notes, T-bonds pay their face value at maturity, pay semiannual coupons, and have face value denominations as small as $1,000.

The coupon rate for T-notes and T-bonds is set according to interest rates prevailing at the time of issuance. For example, if the prevailing interest rate for a Treasury note of a certain maturity is 5 percent, then the coupon rate—that is, the annual coupon as a percentage of par value—for a new issue with that maturity is set at or near 5 percent. Thus, a $10,000 par value T-note paying a 5 percent coupon would pay two $250 coupons each year. Coupon payments normally begin six months after issuance and continue to be paid every six months until the last coupon is paid along with the face value at maturity. Once set, the coupon rate remains constant throughout the life of a U.S. Treasury note or bond.

Treasury STRIPS are derived from Treasury notes originally issued with maturities of 10 years and from Treasury bonds issued with 30-year maturities. Since 1985, the U.S. Treasury has sponsored the **STRIPS** program, an acronym for *Separate Trading of Registered Interest and Principal of Securities.* This program allows brokers to divide Treasury bonds and notes into *coupon strips* and *principal strips*, thereby allowing investors to buy and sell the strips of their choice. Principal strips represent face-value payments, and coupon strips represent coupon payments. For example, a 30-year maturity T-bond can be separated into 61 strips, representing 60 semiannual coupon payments and a single face value payment. Under the Treasury STRIPS program, each of these strips can be separately registered to different owners.

The terms "STRIPS" and "strips" can sometimes cause confusion. The acronym STRIPS is used when speaking specifically about the Treasury STRIPS program. However, the term *strips* now popularly refers to any separate part of a note or bond issue broken down into its component parts. In this generic form, the term strips is acceptable.

Since each strip created under the STRIPS program represents a single future payment, STRIPS securities effectively become **zero coupon bonds** and are commonly called *zeroes.* The unique characteristics of Treasury zeroes make them an interesting investment choice.

The yield to maturity of a zero coupon bond is the interest rate that an investor will receive if the bond is held until it matures. Table 19.1 lists bond prices for zero coupon bonds with a face value of $10,000, maturities of 5, 10, 20, and 30 years, and yields from 3 percent to 15 percent. As shown, a $10,000 face-value zero coupon bond with a term to maturity of 20 years and an 8 percent yield has a price of $2,082.89.

STRIPS
Treasury program allowing investors to buy individual coupon and principal payments from a whole Treasury note or bond. Acronym for *Separate Trading of Registered Interest and Principal of Securities.*

zero coupon bond
A note or bond paying a single cash flow at maturity. Also called *zeroes.*

WWW
Visit the U.S. Treasury at
www.ustreas.gov

EXAMPLE 19.1 | **Calculating a STRIPS Price**

What is the price of a STRIPS maturing in 20 years with a face value of $10,000 and a yield to maturity of 7 percent?

The STRIPS price is calculated as the present value of a single cash flow as follows:

$$\text{STRIPS price} = \frac{\$10,000}{(1 + 0.07/2)^{40}}$$

$$= \$2,525.72$$

You can also calculate a STRIPS price using a built-in spreadsheet function. For example, the nearby *Spreadsheet Analysis* box contains this STRIPS price calculation using an Excel spreadsheet.

TABLE 19.1 Zero Coupon Bond Prices, $10,000 Face Value

Yield to Maturity	Bond Maturity			
	5 Years	10 Years	20 Years	30 Years
3.0%	$8,616.67	$7,424.70	$5,512.62	$4,092.96
3.5	8,407.29	7,068.25	4,996.01	3,531.30
4.0	8,203.48	6,729.71	4,528.90	3,047.82
4.5	8,005.10	6,408.16	4,106.46	2,631.49
5.0	7,811.98	6,102.71	3,724.31	2,272.84
5.5	7,623.98	5,812.51	3,378.52	1,963.77
6.0	7,440.94	5,536.76	3,065.57	1,697.33
6.5	7,262.72	5,274.71	2,782.26	1,467.56
7.0	7,089.19	5,025.66	2,525.72	1,269.34
7.5	6,920.20	4,788.92	2,293.38	1,098.28
8.0	6,755.64	4,563.87	2,082.89	950.60
8.5	6,595.37	4,349.89	1,892.16	823.07
9.0	6,439.28	4,146.43	1,719.29	712.89
9.5	6,287.23	3,952.93	1,562.57	617.67
10.0	6,139.13	3,768.89	1,420.46	535.36
10.5	5,994.86	3,593.83	1,291.56	464.17
11.0	5,854.31	3,427.29	1,174.63	402.58
11.5	5,717.37	3,268.83	1,068.53	349.28
12.0	5,583.95	3,118.05	972.22	303.14
12.5	5,453.94	2,974.55	884.79	263.19
13.0	5,327.26	2,837.97	805.41	228.57
13.5	5,203.81	2,707.96	733.31	198.58
14.0	5,083.49	2,584.19	667.80	172.57
14.5	4,966.23	2,466.35	608.29	150.02
15.0	4,851.94	2,354.13	554.19	130.46

EXAMPLE 19.2 Calculating a STRIPS Yield

What is the yield to maturity of a STRIPS maturing in 10 years with a face value of $10,000 and a price of $5,500?

The STRIPS yield is calculated as a yield to maturity of a single cash flow as follows:

$$\text{STRIPS yield} = 2 \times \left[\left(\frac{\$10,000}{\$5,500} \right)^{1/20} - 1 \right]$$

$$= 6.07\%$$

The nearby *Spreadsheet Analysis* box contains an example of this STRIPS yield calculation using an Excel spreadsheet.

Figure 19.1 graphs prices of zero coupon bonds with a face value of $10,000. The vertical axis measures bond prices, and the horizontal axis measures bond maturities. Bond prices for yields of 4, 8, and 12 percent are illustrated.

	A	B	C	D	E	F	G
1							
2			Calculating the Price of a Zero Coupon STRIPS				
3							
4	A STRIPS traded on March 30, 2006, matures in 20 years on March 30, 2026.						
5	Assuming a 7 percent yield to maturity, what is the STRIPS price?						
6	Hint: Use the Excel function PRICE with the coupon rate set to zero.						
7							
8		$25.2572	=PRICE("3/30/2006","3/30/2026",0,0.07,100,2,3)				
9							
10	For a bond with a $10,000 face value, multiply the price by 100 to get $2,525.72.						
11							
12			Calculating the Yield to Maturity of a STRIPS				
13							
14	A STRIPS traded on March 30, 2006, matures in 10 years on March 30, 2016.						
15	The STRIPS price is $55. What is its yield to maturity?						
16	Hint: Use the Excel function YIELD with the coupon rate set to zero.						
17							
18		6.07%	=YIELD("3/30/2006","3/30/2016",0,55,100,2,3)				
19							
20							

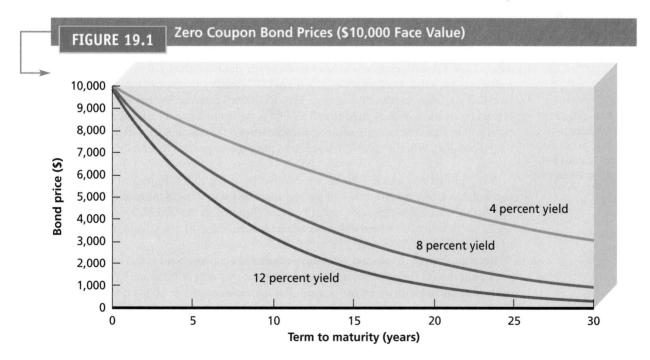

FIGURE 19.1   Zero Coupon Bond Prices ($10,000 Face Value)

4 percent yield

8 percent yield

12 percent yield

Bond price ($)

Term to maturity (years)

19.2a What are some possible reasons why individual investors might prefer to buy Treasury STRIPS rather than common stocks?

19.2b What are some possible reasons why individual investors might prefer to buy individual Treasury STRIPS rather than whole T-notes or T-bonds?

19.2c For zero coupon bonds with the same face value and yield to maturity, is the price of a zero with a 15-year maturity larger or smaller than the average price of two zeroes with maturities of 10 years and 20 years? Why?

TREASURY BOND AND NOTE PRICES

Figure 19.2 displays a partial *Wall Street Journal* listing of prices and other relevant information for Treasury securities. Notice that Treasury notes and bonds are listed together, but there are separate sections for Treasury bills and Treasury STRIPS. The sections for Treasury bills and STRIPS were discussed in detail in a previous chapter. We discuss the section for Treasury notes and bonds next.

Treasury bond and note price quotes are stated on a percentage of par basis where, for example, a price of 102 equals par value plus 2 percent. Fractions of a percent are stated in thirty-seconds. Thus a price stated as 102:28 is actually equal to $102 + 28/32$, or 102.875. To illustrate, the first column in the section for notes and bonds in Figure 19.2 states the annual coupon rate. The next two columns report maturity in month–year format. Dealer bid and asked price quotes come next, followed by changes in ask quotes from the previous day. The last column gives the yield to maturity implied by an asked price quote. The letter *n* next to various maturity dates indicates a T-note. The absence of the letter *n* indicates a T-bond.

About a dozen of the T-bonds in Figure 19.2 have a fixed-price call provision. If a particular issue is callable, the Treasury has the right to buy it back at face value, but only during the last five years of its life. For example, locate the bond maturing in May 2011. Although it is not indicated, this issue became callable in 2006. Because the May 11 bond pays a 13.875 percent coupon, but has a much lower yield to maturity, this bond has a price well above par value. On January 13, 2006, the U.S. Treasury announced that this bond will be called at its earliest possible call date, May 15, 2006. Therefore, the reported asked yield is actually a yield to call. A **yield to call (YTC)** is the interest rate for a bond assuming the bond will be called at its earliest possible call date and the bondholder will hold the bond until it is called. When a callable T-bond has a price above par, the reported yield is a yield to call.

yield to call (YTC)
The interest rate on a bond that assumes the bond will be called at its earliest possible call date.

You can find out which T-bonds are callable by going to the Bureau of Public Debt (www.publicdebt.treas.gov) and looking at the monthly statement of the public debt. You'll see that the callable issues have maturity dates clustered in the 2009–2015 range. Since 1985, the Treasury has issued only noncallable bonds. Thus, all listed bonds with a maturity of 2015 or later are noncallable.

Because Treasury bonds and notes pay semiannual coupons, bond yields are stated on a semiannual basis. The relationship between the price of a note or bond and its yield to maturity was discussed in an earlier chapter. For convenience, the bond price formula from that chapter is restated here:

$$\text{Bond price} = \frac{\text{Annual coupon}}{YTM} \times \left[1 - \frac{1}{(1 + YTM/2)^{2M}} \right] + \frac{\text{Face value}}{(1 + YTM/2)^{2M}}$$

FIGURE 19.2 — U.S. Treasury Securities

Treasury Bonds, Notes and Bills
January 12, 2006

Explanatory Notes

Representative Over-the-Counter quotation based on transactions of $1 million or more. Treasury bond, note and bill quotes are as of mid-afternoon. Colons in bid-and-asked quotes represent 32nds; 101:01 means 101 1/32. Net changes in 32nds. n-Treasury note. I-Inflation-Indexed issue. Treasury bill quotes in hundredths, quoted on terms of a rate of discount. Days to maturity calculated from settlement date. All yields are to maturity and based on the asked quote. Latest 13-week and 26-week bills are boldfaced. For bonds callable prior to maturity, yields are computed to the earliest call date for issues quoted above par and to the maturity date for issues quoted below par. *When issued.
Source: eSpeed/Cantor Fitzgerald

U.S. Treasury strips as of 3 p.m. Eastern time, also based on transactions of $1 million or more. Colons in bid and asked quotes represent 32nds; 99:01 means 99 1/32. Net changes in 32nds. Yields calculated on the asked quotation. ci-stripped coupon interest. bp-Treasury bond, stripped principal. np-Treasury note, stripped principal. For bonds callable prior to maturity, yields are computed to the earliest call date for issues quoted above par and to the maturity date for issues below par.
Source: Bear, Stearns & Co. via Street Software Technology Inc.

Source: Reprinted with permission from *The Wall Street Journal*, via Copyright Clearance Center, January 13, 2006. © 2006 Dow Jones & Company, Inc. All Rights Reserved Worldwide.

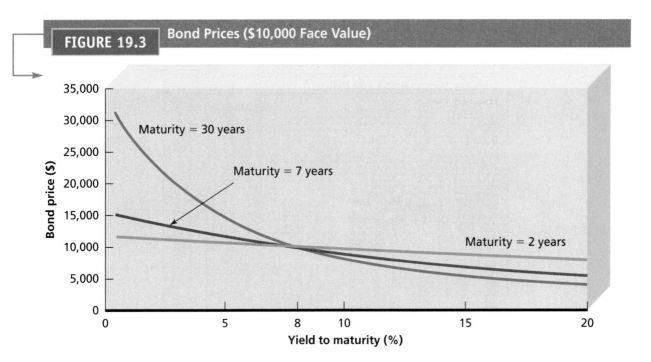

FIGURE 19.3 Bond Prices ($10,000 Face Value)

Figure 19.3 illustrates the relationship between the price of a bond and its yield to maturity for 2-year, 7-year, and 30-year terms to maturity. Notice that each bond has a price of 100 when its yield is 8 percent. This indicates that each bond has an 8 percent coupon rate, because when a bond's coupon rate is equal to its yield to maturity, its price is equal to its par value.

bid-ask spread
The difference between a dealer's ask price and bid price.

The difference between a dealer's asked and bid prices is called the **bid-ask spread**. The bid-ask spread measures the dealer's gross profit from a single round-trip transaction of buying a security at the bid price and then selling it at the asked price.

CHECK THIS

19.2d What would Figure 19.3 look like if the three bonds all had coupon rates of 6 percent? What about 10 percent?

19.2e In Figure 19.2, which Treasury issues have the narrowest spreads? Why do you think this is so?

19.2f Examine the spreads between bid and asked prices for Treasury notes and bonds listed in a recent *Wall Street Journal*.

TREASURY INFLATION–PROTECTED SECURITIES

In recent years, the U.S. Treasury has issued securities that guarantee a fixed rate of return in excess of realized inflation rates. These inflation-indexed Treasury securities, commonly called TIPS, pay a fixed coupon rate on their current principal and adjust their principal semiannually according to the most recent inflation rate.

For example, suppose an inflation-indexed note is issued with a coupon rate of 3.5 percent and an initial principal of $1,000. Six months later, the note will pay a coupon of $1,000 × 3.5%/2 = $17.50. Assuming 2 percent inflation over the six months since issuance, the note's principal is then increased to $1,000 × 102% = $1,020. Six months later, the note pays $1,020 × 3.5%/2 = $17.85, and its principal is again adjusted to compensate for recent inflation.

Price and yield information for inflation-indexed Treasury securities is reported in *The Wall Street Journal* in the same section with other Treasury securities, as shown in Figure 19.2. Locating the listing for inflation-indexed Treasury securities in Figure 19.2, we see that the first and second columns report the fixed coupon rate and maturity, respectively. The third and fourth columns report current bid/ask prices and the price change from the previous trading day. Prices for inflation-indexed securities are reported as a percentage of current accrued principal. The fifth and sixth columns list an inflation-adjusted yield to maturity and current accrued principal reflecting all cumulative inflation adjustments.

For investors wanting long-term protection against inflation along with the safety of U.S. Treasury bonds, inflation-indexed Treasury securities are perhaps the perfect investment. The nearby *Investment Updates* box further discusses the attractive features of inflation-indexed Treasury securities.

19.3 U.S. Treasury Auctions

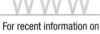

For recent information on Treasury auctions visit www.publicdebt. treas.gov

The Federal Reserve Bank conducts regularly scheduled auctions for Treasury securities. At each Treasury auction, the Federal Reserve accepts sealed bids of two types: competitive bids and noncompetitive bids. Competitive bids for T-bills specify a bid price and a bid quantity. The bid price is what the bidder is willing to pay, and the bid quantity is the face value amount that the bidder will purchase if the bid is accepted. Noncompetitive bids specify only a bid quantity since the price charged to noncompetitive bidders will be determined by the results of the competitive auction process. Individual investors can submit noncompetitive bids, but only Treasury securities dealers can submit competitive bids.

stop-out bid
The lowest competitive bid in a U.S. Treasury auction that is accepted.

At the close of bidding, all sealed bids are forwarded to the U.S. Treasury for processing. As a first step, all noncompetitive bids are accepted automatically and are subtracted from the total issue amount. Then a **stop-out bid** is determined; this is the price at which all competitive bids are sufficient to finance the remaining issue amount. Competitive bids at or above the stop-out bid are accepted, and bids below the stop-out bid are rejected.

Since 1998, all U.S. Treasury auctions have been single-price auctions in which all accepted competitive bids pay the stop-out bid. The stop-out bid is also the price paid by noncompetitive bidders. For example, suppose an auction for T-bills with $20 billion of face value receives $28 billion of competitive bids and $4 billion of noncompetitive bids. Noncompetitive bids are automatically accepted, leaving $16 billion for competitive bidders. Now suppose the stop-out bid for this $16 billion amount is $9,700 for a $10,000 face-value T-bill. Accepted competitive bidders and all noncompetitive bidders pay this price of $9,700.

The process is similar for T-bond and T-note issues, except that bids are made on a yield basis, where competitive bids state yields instead of prices. A coupon rate for the entire issue is then set according to the average competitive-bid yield.

INVESTMENT UPDATES

"INFLATION-LINKED TREASURYS HOLD SURPRISING APPEAL"

Inflation-indexed treasury bonds don't quite rival the Swiss Army Knife. But it's amazing what you can do with them. Need income? Worried about stocks? Want a place to park some cash? Inflation bonds can come in handy. Here's how:

RISING INCOME: Each year, the value of inflation bonds is stepped up along with consumer prices. Investors also collect interest based on this ever-rising principal value. Those twin attributes make the bonds an intriguing investment for retirees.

Suppose you invested $1,000 in inflation bonds at the current yield of 3.8%. If consumer prices rose 2.5% over the next year, your principal would climb to $1,025 and you would earn interest equal to 3.8% of this growing sum. Thus, if you spent the interest but didn't cash in any bonds, you would enjoy a rising stream of income, while keeping your principal's spending power intact.

Retirees should still keep some money in stocks, so they have a shot at even higher returns. After all, many folks won't have a big enough portfolio to live off inflation bonds' 3.8% yield. Still, inflation bonds are a good choice for at least part of your portfolio. "The long-run total return may not be as high as it is from stocks," says Ken Volpert, co-manager of Vanguard Inflation Protected Securities Fund, a no-load fund with $120 million in assets. "But you have greater certainty that the rise in your income and your principal will be in line with inflation."

INFLATION INSURANCE: Need protection against rising consumer prices? Inflation bonds may be just the ticket. Suppose you are going to retire next year, and you plan to buy an annuity at that point. If you buy inflation bonds now, you have protected yourself against a short-term spike in inflation.

Alternatively, suppose you sold your house and won't buy another for a few years. Maybe you are taking a job overseas or planning to rent while you look for the perfect spot to retire. If you plunked your home equity into inflation bonds and earned 3.8 percentage points a year more than inflation, you should have a good shot at keeping pace with real-estate prices.

PORTFOLIO PROTECTION: If inflation takes off or the economy tumbles into recession, stocks will get whacked. Want to cushion that blow? Traditionally, stock investors have added a dollop of regular bonds to their portfolios. That works well in a recession, when interest rates tend to fall, driving up the price of regular bonds, whose fixed-interest payouts now seem more attractive. But when inflation takes off, interest rates climb. Result: Both stocks and regular bonds get crushed.

That is where inflation bonds come in. They won't do as well as regular bonds in a recession. But during periods of rising consumer prices, inflation bonds will sparkle, thus helping to offset your stock-market losses.

PARKING PLACE: Because inflation bonds don't perform as erratically as regular bonds, they can be a good place to stash your emergency money. You never know when you will need this emergency money. Maybe you will have to call on your reserve next month—or maybe the money will sit untouched for the next decade. Because your time horizon is uncertain, you want the money to be readily available, but you also want it to earn healthy returns. Inflation bonds look good on both counts. Mr. Volpert figures your chances of losing money in any given year are slim. "You might even have better downside protection than you would with a short-term bond fund," he says.

Source: Jonathan Clements, *The Wall Street Journal*, December 12, 2000. Reprinted by permission of Dow Jones & Company, Inc., via Copyright Clearance Center, Inc. © 2000 Dow Jones & Company, Inc. All Rights Reserved Worldwide.

CHECK THIS

19.3a The Federal Reserve announces an offering of Treasury bills with a face value amount of $25 billion. The response is $5 billion of noncompetitive bids, along with the following competitive bids:

(continued)

Bidder	Price Bid	Quantity Bid
A	$9,500	$5 billion
B	9,550	5 billion
C	9,600	5 billion
D	9,650	5 billion
E	9,700	5 billion

In a single-price auction, which bids are accepted and what prices are paid by each bidder? How much money is raised by the entire offering?

19.4 U.S. Savings Bonds

The U.S. Treasury offers an interesting investment opportunity for individual (U.S.) investors in the form of savings bonds. Two types of saving bonds are currently available, Series EE and Series I. (Other types exist, but they are no longer available or can be obtained only by converting from one type to another.)

SERIES EE SAVINGS BONDS

WWW

For the latest on savings bonds visit

www.savingsbonds .com

or the savings bond section of

www.publicdebt. treas.gov

Series EE bonds are available in face value denominations ranging from $25 to $10,000, but the original issue price of a Series EE bond is always set at exactly half its face value. Thus, Series EE bonds are sold to resemble zero coupon securities. However, individuals purchasing Series EE bonds receive monthly interest accruals. This interest is paid as an accrual to the redemption value of the bond, where the current redemption value is the original price of the bond plus all prior accrued interest.

Savings bonds purchased after May 1, 2005, pay a fixed rate of interest. Rates for new issues are set each May 1 and November 1, with each new rate effective for all bonds issued during the following six months. Interest accrues monthly and is compounded semiannually. Savings bonds must be held at least one year and a three-month interest penalty is applied to bonds held less than five years. However, the bond's value is guaranteed to double if it is held until its original 20-year maturity. For example, suppose a $10,000 face-value savings bond pays 3 percent interest. Compounding semiannually for 20 years yields a value of $9,070, which is less than a doubling of its original issue price of $5,000. If you hold the bond until maturity, you are guaranteed to receive its face value of $10,000. This works out to an effective interest rate of about 3.496 percent.

SERIES I SAVINGS BONDS

Series I bonds are designed for investors seeking to earn a guaranteed real rate of return. Series I bonds are an accrual-type security with interest added to the bond monthly and paid when the bond is redeemed. Series I bonds are available in face value denominations ranging from $50 to $10,000 and are sold at face value (i.e., investors pay $100 for a $100 Series I bond).

Series I bonds earn interest for up to 30 years. The interest rate on these bonds comes from two rates: a fixed rate of return (which is constant for the life of the bond) and a variable semiannual inflation rate. Interest on Series I bonds accrues monthly and is compounded semiannually.

Fixed rates for new Series I bonds are announced each May and November. The fixed rate of return announced in May of a given year is the fixed rate of return over the entire life of the I bond purchased between May 1 and October 31 of that year. Likewise, the fixed rate of return announced in November of a given year applies to the entire life of an I bond purchased between November 1 and April 30 of the following year.

The semiannual inflation rate is also announced each May and November. The semiannual inflation rate is based on changes in the Consumer Price Index for all Urban consumers (CPI-U). The inflation rate reflects a three-month lag. That is, the semiannual inflation rate announced in May is a measure of inflation over the preceding October through March; the inflation rate announced in November is a measure of inflation over the preceding April through September.

Investors can redeem Series I bonds after 12 months. At redemption, investors receive their original investment plus interest earned. However, an investor who redeems a Series I bond within the first five years of purchase incurs a three-month earnings penalty. For example, if you redeem a Series I bond after 24 months, you will get 21 months of earnings.

CHECK THIS

19.4a What are the differences between Series EE savings bonds and Series I savings bonds?

19.4b Compare the methods by which interest is paid for Series EE savings bonds and Series I bonds. Which method would be preferred if inflation decreased? Which would be preferred if inflation increased?

19.4c Compare the methods by which interest is paid for Series EE savings bonds and Series I inflation-indexed Treasury securities.

19.5 Federal Government Agency Securities

Visit
www.investinginbonds
.com
for more information
on agency securities

Most U.S. government agencies consolidate their borrowing through the Federal Financing Bank, which obtains funds directly from the U.S. Treasury. However, several federal agencies are authorized to issue securities directly to the public. For example, the Resolution Trust Funding Corporation, the World Bank, and the Tennessee Valley Authority issue notes and bonds directly to investors. Bonds issued by U.S. government agencies share an almost equal credit quality with U.S. Treasury issues. Although most agency debt does not carry an explicit guarantee of the U.S. government, a federal agency on the verge of default would probably receive government support to ensure timely payment of interest and principal on outstanding debt. This perception is supported by historical experience and the political reality that Congress would likely feel compelled to rescue an agency that it created if it became financially distressed.

What makes government agency notes and bonds attractive to many investors is that they offer higher yields than comparable U.S. Treasury securities. However, the market for agency debt is less active than the market for U.S. Treasury debt, and therefore the spread between dealers' bid and asked prices is greater for agency issues than for Treasury issues. For example, Figure 19.4 presents dealer price quotes for agency issues as reported in *The Wall Street Journal.* The listing format is the same as for Treasury notes and bonds described previously, except that callable bonds are indicated by an asterisk with only the maturity date shown.

If you compare bid and asked dealer price quotes for agency bonds listed in Figure 19.4 with similar Treasury bonds listed in Figure 19.2, you will find that agency bonds have a higher bid-ask spread than Treasury bonds. The reason for the higher bid-ask spread is that agency bond trading volume is much lower than Treasury bond trading volume. To

FIGURE 19.4   Agency Securities

Government Agency & Similar Issues

Over-the-Counter mid-afternoon quotations based on large transactions, usually $1 million or more. Colons in bid and asked quotes represent 32nds; 101:01 means 101 1/32.

All, yields are calculated to maturity, and based on the asked quote.
*Callable issue, maturity date shown. For issues callable prior to maturity, yields are computed to the earliest call date for issues quoted above par, or 100, and to the maturity date for issues below par.

Source: Bear, Stearns & Co. via Street Software Technology Inc.

Fannie Mae Issues

RATE	MAT	BID	ASKED	YLD
5.50	2-06	100:03	100:04	4.14
2.13	4-06	99:11	99:12	4.54
5.50	5-06	100:08	100:09	4.49
2.25	5-06	99:06	99:07	4.61
5.25	6-06	100:07	100:08	4.61
2.50	6-06	99:02	99:03	4.67
1.75	6-06	98:24	98:25	4.68
2.75	8-06	98:28	98:29	4.69
4.38	10-06	99:23	99:24	4.70
2.63	11-06	98:08	98:10	4.72
4.75	1-07	100:00	100:01	4.70
5.00	1-07	100:13	100:14	4.54
2.38	2-07	97:21	97:22	4.59
7.13	3-07	102:25	102:26	4.62
5.25	4-07	100:22	100:23	4.65
4.25	7-07	99:13	99:14	4.64
6.63	10-07	103:10	103:11	4.62
3.25	11-07	97:19	97:20	4.62
3.13	12-07	97:09	97:10	4.60
3.25	1-08	97:12	97:13	4.61
3.50	1-08	97:21	97:22	4.71
5.75	2-08	102:06	102:07	4.62
6.00	5-08	102:31	103:00	4.62
2.88	5-08	96:06	96:07	4.59
2.50	6-08	95:04	95:05	4.64
3.25	8-08	96:22	96:23	4.61
4.00	9-08	98:03	98:04	4.77
3.75	9-08	97:25	97:26	4.63
3.38	12-08	96:17	96:18	4.64
5.25	1-09	101:22	101:23	4.63
3.25	2-09	96:00	96:01	4.64
3.13	3-09*	95:12	95:13	4.69
4.25	5-09	98:24	98:25	4.65
6.38	6-09	105:08	105:09	4.68
6.63	9-09	106:14	106:15	4.68
7.25	1-10	109:07	109:08	4.69
3.88	2-10	97:01	97:02	4.67
7.13	6-10	109:18	109:19	4.70
6.63	11-10	108:04	108:05	4.72
6.25	2-11	105:22	105:23	4.95
5.50	3-11	103:15	103:16	4.73
6.00	5-11	105:26	105:27	4.75
5.38	11-11	103:04	103:05	4.75
6.13	3-12	107:07	107:08	4.75
5.25	8-12	101:04	101:05	5.04
4.38	9-12	97:31	98:00	4.72
4.75	2-13*	99:02	99:03	4.90
4.63	5-13	97:11	97:12	5.06
4.38	7-13*	96:14	96:15	4.94
4.63	10-13	98:29	98:30	4.79
5.13	1-14	100:08	100:09	5.08
4.13	4-14	95:17	95:18	4.78
6.25	5-29	117:14	117:17	4.97
7.13	1-30	130:00	130:03	4.97
7.25	5-30	131:30	132:01	4.97
6.63	11-30	123:15	123:18	4.96

Freddie Mac

RATE	MAT	BID	ASKED	YLD
1.88	2-06	99:24	99:25	4.46
2.38	4-06	99:13	99:14	4.53
5.50	7-06	100:12	100:13	4.65
2.75	8-06	98:27	98:28	4.69
2.88	12-06	98:11	98:12	4.71
2.38	2-07	97:18	97:19	4.66
4.88	3-07	100:08	100:09	4.63
3.50	9-07	98:07	98:08	4.60
3.25	2-08	97:03	97:04	4.68
2.75	3-08	96:05	96:06	4.61
5.75	4-08	102:14	102:15	4.58
3.63	9-08	97:15	97:17	4.62
5.13	10-08	101:07	101:08	4.63
5.75	3-09	103:07	103:08	4.64
3.38	4-09	96:22	96:23	4.47
4.25	7-09	98:20	98:21	4.67
6.63	9-09	106:14	106:15	4.68
7.00	3-10	108:20	108:21	4.69
6.88	9-10	109:00	109:01	4.70
4.13	2-11*	97:03	97:04	4.76
5.63	3-11	104:02	104:03	4.72
5.88	3-11	104:06	104:07	4.94
6.00	6-11	105:29	105:30	4.74
6.38	8-11*	100:16	100:17	5.36
5.50	9-11	103:21	103:22	4.75
5.75	1-12	105:05	105:06	4.75
6.25	3-12*	101:09	101:10	5.05
5.13	7-12	102:00	102:01	4.76
5.25	11-12*	98:21	98:22	5.48
4.50	1-13	98:14	98:15	4.76
4.38	3-13	97:21	97:22	4.76
4.00	6-13*	94:19	94:20	4.87
4.50	7-13	98:08	98:09	4.77
4.88	11-13	100:17	100:18	4.79
4.50	1-14	98:04	98:05	4.78
5.00	1-14*	98:18	98:19	5.22
6.75	9-29	124:16	124:19	4.97
6.75	3-31	125:15	125:18	4.96
6.25	7-32	119:06	119:09	4.94

Federal Farm Credit Bank

RATE	MAT	BID	ASKED	YLD
2.50	3-06	99:20	99:21	4.39
2.25	9-06	98:14	98:15	4.73
2.38	10-06	98:11	98:12	4.72
3.00	4-08*	96:19	96:20	4.59

Federal Home Loan Bank

RATE	MAT	BID	ASKED	YLD
2.00	2-06	99:24	99:25	4.44

RATE	MAT	BID	ASKED	YLD
5.13	3-06	100:03	100:04	4.15
2.50	3-06	99:20	99:21	4.39
5.38	5-06	100:07	100:08	4.56
2.25	5-06	99:06	99:07	4.61
1.88	6-06	98:25	98:26	4.70
2.88	9-06	98:25	98:26	4.71
4.88	11-06	100:04	100:05	4.69
1.88	1-07	97:11	97:12	4.58
5.38	2-07	100:24	100:25	4.62
2.75	3-08	96:04	96:05	4.63
2.63	7-08	95:11	95:12	4.60
5.80	9-08	102:27	102:28	4.62
3.63	11-08	97:13	97:14	4.60
6.00	5-11	105:22	105:23	4.77
5.63	11-11	104:05	104:06	4.80
5.75	5-12	105:16	105:17	4.73
4.50	11-12	98:19	98:20	4.74
6.13	4-18	94:18	94:19	4.75
4.50	9-13	98:07	98:08	4.77
5.25	6-14	103:05	103:06	4.79

GNMA Mtge. Issues

RATE	MAT	BID	ASKED	YLD
4.00	30Yr	91:26	91:27	...
4.50	30Yr	96:12	96:13	...
5.00	30Yr	99:00	99:01	...
5.50	30Yr	100:28	100:29	...
6.00	30Yr	102:24	102:25	...
6.50	30Yr	104:21	104:22	...
7.00	30Yr	105:02	105:03	...
7.50	30Yr	105:06	105:07	...
8.00	30Yr	106:16	106:17	...

Tennessee Valley Authority

RATE	MAT	BID	ASKED	YLD
5.38	11-08	102:01	102:02	4.59
5.63	1-11	103:18	103:19	4.81
6.00	3-13	107:12	107:13	4.77
4.75	8-13	99:24	99:25	4.79
6.25	12-17	111:21	111:23	4.94
6.75	11-25	121:29	122:00	4.99
7.13	5-30	130:16	130:19	4.95

Source: Reprinted with permission from *The Wall Street Journal*, January, 13, 2006, via Copyright Clearance Center, Inc. © 2006 Dow Jones & Company, Inc. All Rights Reserved Worldwide.

compensate for the lower volume, dealers charge higher spreads. Thus, trading agency bonds is costlier than trading Treasury bonds. Consequently, agency bonds are usually purchased by institutional investors planning to hold the bonds until they mature. Another reason for the higher yields on agency bonds compared to Treasury bonds is that interest income from agency bonds is subject to state and local taxation, whereas Treasury interest payments are subject only to federal taxation.

CHECK THIS

19.5a   In Figure 19.4, what does the asterisk indicate?

19.5b   Examine spreads between bid and asked prices for government agency notes and bonds listed in a recent *Wall Street Journal*. What is the typical bid-ask spread?

19.6   Municipal Bonds

Municipal notes and bonds are intermediate- to long-term interest-bearing obligations of state and local governments or agencies of those governments. The defining characteristic of municipal notes and bonds, often called "munis," is that coupon interest is usually

INVESTMENT UPDATES

NOT ALL TAX-FREE MUNI BONDS ARE REALLY EXEMPT FROM TAX

For safety-conscious investors looking for tax-free income, this is a good time to consider municipal bonds. Just be careful: Not all tax-free bonds are really tax-free. Even tax experts agree the $1.7 trillion market for state and local government bonds can be surprisingly tricky. Municipal bonds come in many different shades and flavors. The Bond Market Association, a trade group that represents securities firms and banks that buy, sell, and trade bonds (www.bondmarkets.com), estimates there are more than 50,000 state and local entities that issue "munis," and there are more than two million separate bond issues outstanding. So never purchase a muni without carefully investigating the bond's tax status with your broker or financial advisor. This subject can get so tricky that I recommend you ask the same question of more than one expert. I speak from experience here: I covered the credit markets for *The Wall Street Journal* for nearly a decade and found many myths and misconceptions about this area. Here are just a few tax considerations to keep in mind when you're shopping for munis:

State and Local Taxes. Muni-bond income isn't always exempt from state and local taxes. The general rule of thumb is that bonds issued by the state you live in, or municipalities of that state, pay tax-free interest. But if you live in a state with an income tax and you buy out-of-state bonds, the interest typically would be taxable in your home state.

For example, I live in New York City. If I buy a New York City or New York State bond, I typically wouldn't owe any federal, state, or local taxes on the interest. Those bonds are, as bond peddlers like to call them, "triple tax-free." But if I buy an out-of-state bond, such as one issued by California, the interest income would be fully taxable in New York. That's why many investors in high-tax areas such as New York City favor bonds issued within their home state. Or they may buy shares of mutual funds that specialize in bonds only from a single state. Just don't be a slave to this strategy. Sometimes, investors can do better by buying out-of-state bonds, even though it means having to pay their home state's tax.

Unfortunately, you also can't assume that all in-state bonds will be free from your state tax. That can depend on what state you call home, says Alexandra Lebenthal, president of Lebenthal & Co., a New York–based firm specializing in municipal bonds. Check this not only with your broker but also with your state tax department. The Federation of Tax Administrators in Washington, D.C., has a Web site that includes links to state tax departments.

Intangible Property. Naturally, you don't have to worry about such state income-tax considerations if you're from a state with no income tax, such as Florida or Texas. But Floridians have another taxing issue to consider: The state has an "intangible personal

Visit
www.investinginbonds
.com
for more about
municipal bonds

exempt from federal income tax. Consequently, the market for municipal debt is commonly called the *tax-exempt market*. Most of the 50 states also have an income tax, but their tax treatment of municipal debt interest varies. Only a few states exempt coupon interest on out-of-state municipal bonds from in-state income tax, but most states do allow in-state municipal debt interest an exemption from in-state income tax. In any case, state income tax rates are normally much lower than federal income tax rates, and state taxes can be used as an itemized deduction from federal taxable income. Consequently, state taxes are usually a secondary consideration for municipal bond investors.

The federal income tax exemption makes municipal bonds attractive to investors in the highest income tax brackets. This includes many individual investors, commercial banks, and property and casualty insurance companies—precisely those investors who actually hold almost all municipal debt. However, yields on municipal debt are less than on corporate debt with similar features and credit quality. This eliminates much, but not all, of the advantage of the tax exemption. Therefore, tax-exempt investors, including pension funds property" tax, an annual tax based on the market value of stock holdings and other "intangible" personal property. Some types of investments, such as bonds issued by the state of Florida, aren't subject to this tax. To find out what other investments are exempt from this tax, see the Web site of the Florida Department of Revenue.

Alternative Minimum Tax. Lawmakers created the AMT decades ago to prevent high-income people from escaping all federal income taxes through a combination of tax credits, deductions, and other items. But since the tax wasn't adjusted for inflation, it's now hitting rapidly growing numbers of Americans. Unfortunately, some types of bonds pay interest that is considered income when you're calculating the AMT.

Investinginbonds.com, another Web site run by the Bond Market Association, offers a helpful primer on muni-bond income and the AMT. (Click on "Taxation of Municipals" in the left-hand navigation bar and then scroll way down to the "Alternative Minimum Tax" section.) If you're subject to this tax and you're on the phone with an eager bond salesman, be sure to ask if a bond you're considering is an "AMT bond."

Social Security. One of the biggest surprises for many elderly investors is that buying munis can affect how much, if any, of their Social Security benefits are taxable. The law says that you have to include tax-exempt bond income when you're doing the number-crunching. The Investinginbonds.com Web site also has more information on this subject—in fact, you'll find it right below the section mentioned above on the AMT. So if you're receiving Social Security income, be sure to have a tax professional evaluate your situation before purchasing muni bonds.

Taxable Munis. A taxable muni is just what it sounds like: It's a muni bond where the interest "is not excluded from the gross income of its owners for federal income tax purposes," says Lynnette K. Hotchkiss, senior vice president and associate general counsel of the Bond Market Association. She says some munis are taxable because they were issued "for purposes that the federal government deems not to provide a significant benefit to the public at large," such as certain types of economic-development projects that solely benefit a corporation.

Capital Gains and Losses. There also may be capital-gains tax considerations. If you sell a muni bond—or a muni-bond fund—for more than you paid for it, capital gains taxes may have to be considered.

While this isn't a comprehensive list, it's a reminder that buying munis can be much trickier than it may seem at first glance.

Source: Tom Herman, *The Wall Street Journal*, May 21, 2002. © 2002 Dow Jones & Company, Inc. All Rights Reserved Worldwide.

and retirement accounts of individuals, nonprofit institutions, and some life insurance companies, normally do not invest in municipal bonds. Instead, they prefer to invest in higher-yielding corporate bonds. For some more interesting details on the tax status of various municipal bonds, see the nearby *Investment Updates* box.

Municipal bonds are typically less complicated investments than corporate bonds. However, while municipal debt often carries a high credit rating, **default risk** does exist. Thus, investing in municipal debt requires more care than investing in U.S. Treasury securities.

To illustrate some standard features of a municipal bond issue, Table 19.2 summarizes the issue terms for a hypothetical bond issued by the city of Bedford Falls. We see that the bonds were issued in December 1999 and mature 30 years later in December 2029. Each bond has a face value denomination of $5,000 and pays an annual coupon equal to 6 percent of face value. The annual coupon is split between two semiannual payments each June and December. Based on the original offer price of 100, or 100 percent of par value, the

default risk

The risk that a bond issuer will cease making scheduled payments of coupons or principal or both.

TABLE 19.2 City of Bedford Falls General Obligation Bonds

Issue amount	$50 million	Bond issue represents a total face value amount of $50 million
Issue date	12/15/99	Bonds were offered to the public on December 15, 1999
Maturity date	12/31/29	All remaining principal must be paid at maturity on December 31, 2029
Par value	$5,000	Each bond has a face value of $5,000
Coupon rate	6%	Annual coupons of $300 per bond
Coupon dates	12/31, 6/30	Semiannual coupons of $150
Offering price	100	Offer price is 100% of par value
Yield to maturity	6%	Based on stated offer price
Call provision	Callable after 12/31/09	Bonds are call-protected for 10 years
Call price	100	Bonds are callable at par value
Trustee	Potters Bank of Bedford Falls	The trustee is appointed to represent the bondholders and administer the sinking fund
Sinking fund	$2.5 million annual par redemptions after 12/31/09	City must redeem at par value $2.5 million of the bond issue each year beginning in 2010

bonds have a yield to maturity of 6 percent. The Bedford Falls bonds are call-protected for 10 years, until January 2009. Thereafter, the bonds are callable any time at par value.

general obligation bonds (GOs)
Bonds issued by a municipality that are secured by the full faith and credit of the issuer.

The Bedford Falls bonds are **general obligation bonds (GOs)**, which means that the bonds are secured by the full faith and credit of the city of Bedford Falls. "Full faith and credit" means the power of the municipality to collect taxes. The trustee for the bond issue is the Potters Bank of Bedford Falls. A trustee is appointed to represent the financial interests of bondholders and administer the sinking fund for the bond issue. A sinking fund requires a bond issuer to redeem for cash a fraction of an outstanding bond issue on a periodic basis. The sinking fund in this example requires that, beginning 10 years after issuance, the city must redeem at par value $2.5 million of the bond issue each year. At each annual redemption, a fraction of the bond issue is called and the affected bondholders receive the par value call price.

MUNICIPAL BOND FEATURES

Municipal bonds are typically callable, pay semiannual coupons, and often have a par value denomination of $5,000. Municipal bond prices are stated as a percentage of par value. Thus, a price of 102 indicates that a bond with a par value of $5,000 has a price of $5,100. By convention, however, municipal bond dealers commonly use yield quotes rather than price quotes in their trading procedures. For example, a dealer might quote a bid-yield of 6.25 percent for a 5 percent coupon bond with seven years to maturity, indicating a willingness to buy at a price determined by that yield. The actual dollar bid price in this example is $4,649.99, as shown in the following bond price calculation:

Check out municipal bonds at
www.municipalbonds.com

$$\frac{\$250}{.0625} \times \left[1 - \frac{1}{(1.03125)^{14}} \right] + \frac{\$5,000}{(1.03125)^{14}} = \$4,649.99$$

Because many thousands of different municipal bond issues are outstanding, only a few large issues trade with sufficient frequency to justify having their prices reported in the financial press. A *Wall Street Journal* listing of some actively traded municipal bonds is

FIGURE 19.5 Municipal Securities

Tax-Exempt Bonds

Representative prices for several active tax-exempt revenue and refunding bonds, based on institutional trades, but may not reflect actual transactions. Yield is to maturity. n-new.
Source: The Bond Buyer/Standard & Poor's Securities Evaluations. All rights reserved.

ISSUE	COUPON	MAT	PRICE	CHG	BID YLD	ISSUE	COUPON	MAT	PRICE	CHG	BID YLD
Brevard Co Hlth Facs FL	5.000	04-01-34	100.469	+.159	4.94	Metro Washington Arpt DC	5.000	10-01-34	102.047	+.143	4.71
Burlington KS env Sr 2005	4.650	09-01-35	99.580	+.317	4.68	MetropolitanTransAthNY	5.000	11-15-31	103.685	+.118	4.38
CA Hlth Facs Fin Auth	5.000	11-15-27	102.099	+.158	4.73	MetroTrans AthNY tran	5.000	11-15-35	103.372	+.240	4.57
CA Stewde Cmm Dev	5.000	11-15-43	100.767	+.155	4.90	Miami-DadeCoFLAviaRvSr05	5.000	10-01-38	101.609	+.155	4.79
CA Stwde Cmm Ath hlth	5.000	03-01-35	100.723	+.146	4.90	NC Cap Facs Fin Agcy rev	5.000	10-01-41	103.815	+.238	4.51
Chicago IL gen arpt 3d	5.000	01-01-33	103.573	+.242	4.55	NYC GOs Ser Fiscal 2006 E	4.500	08-01-35	96.650	+.463	4.71
Chicago IL gen arpt 3d	5.000	01-01-29	104.225	+.163	4.48	NYC Muni Wtr Fin Auth	4.500	06-15-28	100.226	+.153	4.47
ChicagoIL genarpt 3rdref	5.250	01-01-34	103.217	+.133	4.76	NYS Dorm Auth rev Ser 06	5.000	07-01-31	105.677	+.171	4.33
Chrltte-Mcklnbrg Hosp NC	5.000	01-15-45	100.866	+.145	4.88	NYS Dorm Auth state inc	5.000	03-15-35	103.795	+.228	4.49
Chula Vista CA indl rev bds	5.000	12-01-27	101.428	+.180	4.84	Prto Rco Eltrc Pwr Auth	5.000	07-01-35	104.762	+.235	4.39
DallasFtWorthTX JointRv0	5.000	11-01-32	102.099	+.130	4.83	Puerto Rico Muni Fin Agy	5.000	08-01-30	105.274	+.159	4.33
Downtown Phoenix Htl Cp	5.000	07-01-36	103.898	+.243	4.51	Puerto Rico pub impr GO	5.000	07-01-34	100.685	+.138	4.90
Empire State Dev NY bds	5.000	11-15-35	104.501	+.242	4.44	Sacramento Co Sanit Dist	5.000	12-01-35	104.519	+.298	4.39
Gainesville FL util sys rev	5.000	10-01-35	104.697	+.160	4.41	Sales Tx Asset Rec Corp NY	5.000	10-15-32	104.908	+.147	4.33
Indianapls Pub Imp Bnd Bk	4.750	01-01-33	99.097	+.298	4.81	Sales Tx Asset Rec Corp NY	5:000	10-15-29	105.206	+.147	4.29
LA Dpt Wtr/Pwr CA pwr	5.000	07-01-35	104.762	+.314	4.39	SaltRiver Prj Agri Imprv	4.750	01-01-32	101.122	+.118	4.56
LA Dpt Wtr/Pwr CA pwr	5.000	07-01-31	104.762	+.156	4.39	SaltRiver Prj Agri Imprv	5.000	01-01-31	103.870	+.120	4.36
LA Dpt Wtr/Pwr CA pwr	5.000	07-01-40	103.976	+.390	4.48	San Antonio TX wtr sys	5.000	05-15-36	103.619	+.231	4.52
Lehigh ColndDevAth PA	4.700	09-01-29	101.195	+.149	4.54	Univ of CA Regents ltd pro	4.750	05-15-38	100.404	+.205	4.69
Mass HEFA rev bds	5.000	07-15-35	105.256	+.238	4.33	Univ of CA Regents ltd pro	5.000	05-15-33	104.075	+.141	4.42

seen in Figure 19.5. The listing reports the name of the issuer, the coupon rate and maturity of the issue, the most recent bid price quote and the change from an earlier price quote, and a yield to maturity based on a dealer's bid yield. Our nearby *Work the Web* box provides more information on municipal bond prices and liquidity.

call provision
Feature of a municipal bond issue that specifies when the bonds may be called by the issuer and the call price that must be paid.

A **call provision** is a standard feature of most municipal bond issues. A call provision allows an issuer to retire outstanding bonds before they mature, usually to refund with new bonds after a fall in market interest rates. When the bond is called, each bondholder receives the bond's call price in exchange for the bond. However, two bond features often limit an issuer's call privilege. First, callable municipal bonds usually offer a period of call protection following their original issue date. Since a bond issue is not callable during this period, the earliest possible call date is the end of the call protection period. Second, a call price is often specified with a call premium. A call premium is the difference between a bond's call price and its par value. A common arrangement is to specify a call premium equal to one year's coupons for a call occurring at the earliest possible call date. This is then followed by a schedule of call premium reductions, until about 5 to 10 years before maturity, when the call premium is eliminated entirely. Thereafter, the bond issue is callable any time at par value.

serial bonds
Bonds issued with maturity dates scheduled at intervals, so that a fraction of the bond issue matures in each year of a multiple-year period.

Municipal bonds are commonly issued with a serial maturity structure, hence the term **serial bonds**. In a serial bond issue, a fraction of the total issue amount is scheduled to mature in each year over a multiple-year period. As an example, a serial bond issue may contain bonds that mature in each year over a 5-year period, with the first group maturing 11 years after the original issue date and the last group maturing 15 years after issuance. The purpose of a serial maturity structure is to spread out the principal repayment, thereby avoiding a lump-sum repayment at a single maturity date.

term bonds
Bonds from an issue with a single maturity date.

When an entire bond issue matures on a single date, the bonds are called **term bonds**. Term bonds normally have a sinking fund provision. A sinking fund is a trustee-managed account to which the issuer makes regular payments. Account reserves are dedicated to

As we mentioned earlier in this chapter, municipal bonds are less liquid than Treasury securities and often have higher bid-ask spreads. So how high can the spreads go? We went to www.municipalbonds.com to find out. Below you see part of what we found for the second quarter of 2004.

2004/Q2 Worst Bid/Offer Spreads

Here is the 2004/Q2 list of the one hundred worst Municipal Bond market spreads between the lowest bid and the highest offer. Because this study measures spreads, it is limited to Municipal Bonds that traded twice or more in one day.

Date	CUSIP	Municipal Bond Name / Description	Coupon	Maturity	Bid Side Customer Sold to Dealer (Lowest / Highest)	Offer Side Customer Purchase from Dealer (Lowest / Highest)	Spread	# of Trades	Volume (000)
05/13/2004	014393-DC-3	ALDINE TEX INDPT SCH DIST SER A	5.125	02/15/2012	65.000 / 75.000	104.775 / 105.575	40.575	4	210
06/29/2004	104373-EE-1	BRADFORD PA AREA SCH DIST	2.100	10/01/2007	97.092 / 97.092	132.710 / 132.710	35.618	3	75
06/01/2004	718904-AD-7	PHOENIX ARIZ INDL DEV AUTH SINGLE FAMILY MTG REV CAP APPRECIATION		12/01/2014	60.944 / 60.944	92.904 / 92.904	31.960	2	45
05/12/2004	235035-AH-5	DALLAS-FORT WORTH TEX INTL ARPT FAC IMPT CORP REV AMERICAN AIRLINES INC	7.250	11/01/2030	67.000 / 68.000	64.060 / 98.625	31.625	39	2860
04/28/2004	047870-DG-2	ATLANTA GA WTR & WASTEWTR REV SER A-PREREFUNDED	5.000	11/01/2038	109.194 / 110.064	111.057 / 140.079	30.885	6	380

This table shows some alarming news for municipal bond investors. As you can see, the biggest bid-ask spread in the table is for an independent school district bond in Aldine, Texas. Assuming trades occurred at the bid and ask (offer) prices posted, the lowest price received by a customer on this day was 65.00 and the highest price paid by a customer was 105.575. Assuming a $5,000 par value, this means one customer sold this bond for $3,250 and another paid about $5,279 for the same bond. These prices represent a whopping difference of about $2,029. In addition, look at the difference between the lowest (65.00) and highest (75.00) bids for this bond. If these prices are posted simultaneously, they represent a $500 difference in the price that an investor can sell this bond, assuming a $5,000 par value.

redeeming a fraction of the bond issue on each of a series of scheduled redemption dates. Each redemption usually proceeds by lottery, where randomly selected bonds are called and the affected bondholders receive the sinking fund call price. Alternatively, scheduled redemptions can be implemented by purchasing bonds from investors at current market prices. This latter option is usually selected by the issuer when the bonds are selling at a discount from par value. The motive for a sinking fund provision is similar to that for a serial maturity structure; it provides a means for the issuer to avoid a lump-sum principal repayment at a single maturity date.

put bonds
Bonds that can be sold back to the issuer.

Some municipal bonds are putable, and these are called **put bonds**. The holder of a put bond, also called a *tender offer bond*, has the option of selling the bond back to the issuer, normally at par value. Some put bonds can be tendered any time, whereas others can be tendered only on regularly scheduled dates. Weekly, monthly, quarterly, semiannual, and annual put date schedules are all used. Notice that with a put bond, maturity is effectively the choice of the bondholder. This feature protects bondholders from rising interest rates and the associated fall in bond prices. However, a putable bond will have a higher price than a comparable nonputable bond. The price differential simply reflects the value of the put option to sell back the bonds.

While most municipal bonds maintain a constant coupon rate (hence the term fixed-rate bonds), interest rate risk has induced many municipalities to issue **variable-rate notes**, often called *floaters*. For these debt issues, the coupon rate is adjusted periodically according to an index-based rule. For example, at each adjustment the coupon rate may be set at 60 percent of the prevailing rate on 91-day maturity U.S. Treasury bills. A variable-rate note may also be putable, in which case it is called a *variable-rate demand obligation*, often abbreviated to VRDO. A stipulation attached to most VRDOs allows the issuer to convert an entire variable-rate issue to a fixed-rate issue following a specified conversion procedure. Essentially, the issuer notifies each VRDO holder of the intent to convert the outstanding VRDO issue to a fixed-rate issue on a specific future date. In response, VRDO holders have the option of tendering their VRDOs for cash, or they can accept conversion of their VRDOs into fixed-rate bonds.

TYPES OF MUNICIPAL BONDS

There are two basic types of municipal bonds: revenue bonds and general obligation bonds, often referred to as GOs. General obligation bonds are issued by all levels of municipal governments, including states, counties, cities, towns, school districts, and water districts. They are secured by the general taxing powers of the municipalities issuing the bonds. For state governments and large city governments, tax revenue is collected from a diverse base of income taxes on corporations and individuals, sales taxes, and property taxes. In contrast, tax revenues for smaller municipalities are largely derived from property taxes, although sales taxes have become increasingly important. Because of their large, diverse tax bases, general obligation bonds issued by states and large cities are often called *unlimited tax bonds* or *full faith and credit bonds*.

However, some general obligation bonds are called *limited tax bonds*. The distinction between limited and unlimited tax bonds arises when a constitutional limit or other statutory limit is placed on the power of a municipality to assess taxes. For example, an amendment to the California state constitution, popularly known as Proposition 13 when it was enacted, placed rigid limits on the ability of California municipalities to assess taxes on real estate.

Revenue bonds constitute the bulk of all outstanding municipal bonds. **Revenue bonds** are bonds secured by proceeds collected from the projects they finance. Thus, the credit quality of a revenue bond issue is largely determined by the ability of a project to generate revenue. A few examples of the many different kinds of projects financed by revenue bonds are listed below.

Airport and seaport bonds: Used to finance development of airport and seaport facilities. Secured by user fees and lease revenues.

College dormitory bonds: Used to finance construction and renovation of dormitory facilities. Secured by rental fees.

Industrial development bonds: Used to finance development of projects ranging from factories to shopping centers. Secured by rental and leasing fees.

Multifamily housing bonds: Used to finance construction of housing projects for senior citizens or low-income families. Secured by rental fees.

Highway and road gas tax bonds: Used to finance highway construction. May be secured by specific toll revenues or general gas tax revenues.

Student loan bonds: Used to purchase higher education guaranteed student loans. Secured by loan repayments and federal guarantees.

hybrid bonds

Municipal bonds secured by project revenues with some form of general obligation credit guarantees.

Many municipal bonds possess aspects of both general obligation and revenue bonds; these are called **hybrid bonds**. Typically, a hybrid is a revenue bond secured by project-specific cash flows, but with additional credit guarantees. A common form of hybrid is the *moral obligation bond*. This is a state-issued revenue bond with provisions for obtaining general revenues when project-specific resources are inadequate. Usually, extra funds can be obtained only with approval of a state legislature, which is said to be "morally obligated" to assist a financially distressed state-sponsored project. However, a moral obligation is not a guarantee, and the likelihood of state assistance varies. Municipal bond credit analysts consider each state's history of assistance, as well as current state financial conditions, when evaluating the credit-quality enhancement of the moral obligation. In general, experienced municipal bond investors agree that a state will first service its own general obligation debt before providing service assistance to moral obligation debt. This is typically evidenced by the higher yields on moral obligation debt compared to general obligation debt.

Since 1983, all newly issued municipal bonds have had to be registered—that is, with the identity of all bondholders registered with the issuer. With registered bonds, the issuer sends coupon interest and principal payments only to the registered owner of a bond. Additionally, it is now standard practice for registered bonds to be issued in book entry form; bondholders are not issued printed bond certificates, but instead receive notification that their ownership is officially registered. The actual registration record is maintained by the issuer in computer files. This contrasts with the now defunct practice (in the United States) of issuing bearer bonds, where coupon interest and principal were paid to anyone presenting the bond certificates.

MUNICIPAL BOND CREDIT RATINGS

Check out these rating agency Web sites:
Moody's at
www.moodys.com
Fitch at
www.fitchibca.com
S&P at
www.standardandpoors.com

Municipal bond credit rating agencies provide investors with an assessment of the credit quality of individual bond issues. As part of the issuance and credit rating process, the rating agency is paid a fee to assign a credit rating to a new bond issue, to periodically reevaluate the issue, and to make these ratings available to the public. The three largest municipal bond credit rating agencies are Moody's Investors Service, Standard & Poor's Corporation, and Fitch Investors Service. Among them, they rate thousands of new issues each year. Table 19.3 compares and briefly describes the credit rating codes assigned by these three agencies.

The highest credit rating that can be awarded is "triple-A," which indicates that interest and principal are exceptionally secure because of the financial strength of the issuer. Notice that "triple-A" and "double-A" ratings are denoted as AAA and AA, respectively, by Standard & Poor's and Fitch, but as Aaa and Aa, respectively, by Moody's. Also notice that "triple-B" and "double-B" ratings—that is, BBB and BB, respectively—by Standard & Poor's and Fitch correspond to "B-double-a" and "B-single-a" ratings—Baa and Ba, respectively—by Moody's. The same pattern holds for C ratings.

The highest four credit ratings, BBB or Baa and above, designate investment-grade bonds. As a matter of policy, many financial institutions will invest only in investment-grade bonds. Lower rankings indicate successively diminishing levels of credit quality. Ratings of BB or Ba and below designate speculative-grade bonds. Individual investors should probably avoid speculative-grade bonds. A rating of C or below indicates that actual or probable default makes the bond issue unsuitable for most investors.

Visit Web sites of these municipal bond insurers:
www.mbia.com
www.ambac.com

It is not unusual for the ratings assigned to a particular bond issue to differ slightly across credit rating agencies. For example, a bond issue may be rated AA by Standard & Poor's, Aa by Moody's, but only A by Fitch. When this occurs, it usually reflects a difference in credit rating methods rather than a disagreement regarding basic facts. For example, Moody's may focus on the budgetary status of the issuer when assigning a credit

TABLE 19.3   Municipal Bond Credit Ratings

Rating Agency			
Standard & Poor's	Moody's	Fitch	Credit Rating Description
Investment-Grade Bond Ratings			
AAA	Aaa	AAA	Highest credit quality
AA	Aa	AA	High credit quality
A	A	A	Good credit quality
BBB	Baa	BBB	Satisfactory credit quality
Speculative-Grade Bond Ratings			
BB	Ba	BB	Speculative credit quality
B	B	B	Highly speculative quality
CCC	Caa	CCC	Poor credit quality
CC	Ca	CC	Probable default
Extremely Speculative-Grade Bond Ratings			
C	C	C	Imminent default
D		DDD	In default
		DD, D	

rating, while Standard & Poor's may emphasize the economic environment of the issuer. Remember that Standard & Poor's, Moody's, and Fitch are competitors in the bond rating business, and, like competitors in any industry, they try to differentiate their products.

MUNICIPAL BOND INSURANCE

insured municipal bonds

Bonds secured by an insurance policy that guarantees bond interest and principal payments should the issuer default.

In the last two decades, it has become increasingly common for municipalities to obtain bond insurance for new bond issues. **Insured municipal bonds**, besides being secured by the issuer's resources, are also backed by an insurance policy written by a commercial insurance company. The policy provides for prompt payment of coupon interest and principal to municipal bondholders in the event of a default by the issuer. The cost of the insurance policy is paid by the issuer at the time of issuance. The policy cannot be canceled while any bonds are outstanding. With bond insurance, the credit quality of the bond issue is determined by the financial strength of the insurance company, not the municipality alone. Credit rating agencies are certainly aware of this fact. Consequently, a bond issue with insurance can obtain a higher credit rating than would be possible without insurance, and therefore sell at a higher price.

Municipal bond insurance companies manage default risk in three ways. First, they insure bond issues only from municipalities that have a good credit rating on their own. Second, municipal bond insurers diversify default risk by writing insurance policies for municipalities spread across a wide geographic area. Third, and perhaps most important, to compete in the municipal bond insurance business, insurers must maintain substantial investment portfolios as a source of financial reserves. Without sizable reserves, a company's insurance policies are not credible and municipalities will avoid purchasing insurance from them. The ability of municipal bond insurance companies to maintain triple-A credit ratings for the municipal bonds they insure was severely tested during the 2005 hurricane season (see *The Wall Street Journal* article in the nearby *Investments Updates* box).

INVESTMENT UPDATES

MUNIS HAVE WEATHERED STORMS BEFORE

Financial markets have been resilient in the wake of Hurricane Katrina, but a question mark hangs over one market that has traditionally been considered among the safest: municipal bonds.

Though states and municipalities in the Gulf face potential financial hardships, the risk for muni investors flows largely from what Katrina's aftermath could do to the companies whose business it is to stand behind municipal-bond issuers. Four big bond-insurance companies—MBIA Inc.'s MBIA Insurance Corp., Ambac Financial Group Inc.'s Ambac Assurance Corp., FGIC Corp.'s Financial Guaranty Insurance Co., and Financial Security Assurance Inc.—guarantee payments on about 80% of the $2 trillion in muni bonds outstanding. (Financial Security is a unit of French-Belgian financial services firm Dexia.)

Bonds issued by governments in Louisiana, Mississippi, and Alabama comprise less than 1% of the entire muni market, but if hurricane-related claims put pressure on the bond insurers' triple-A credit ratings, they could in turn affect the ratings and potentially the prices of tens of thousands of insured bonds across the country—bonds owned mostly by individual investors, either directly or through mutual funds.

"The more global issue is the effect on the bond insurers," says Judy Wesalo Temel, director of credit research at Samson Capital Advisors, an investment-management firm that focuses on muni bonds. "The triple-A rating is key."

It is still early to guess how bad the financial damage will be, and states, cities, and other entities that sell tax-free muni bonds almost never renege on their debts, even after major natural disasters. Most bond-market professionals think the insurers will be fine, and might actually benefit from the opportunity to demonstrate the value of their service by stepping in to meet missed payments. "If we get through this OK, it will justify the bond-insurance

industry," says Gary Pollack, head of fixed income at Deutsche Bank Private Wealth Management.

Katrina, however, has wrought more damage than any of its predecessors, wiping out or damaging many of the parks, housing projects, and other public works built with muni-bond money as well as the ports and other businesses that generate money to make payments on the bonds. Ratings firms Moody's and Standard & Poor's have put about $9.5 billion in affected bonds on watch for a potential downgrade. S&P issued a report saying that "more severe downgrades" or "actual long-term default by multiple issuers" could threaten bond insurers' triple-A ratings.

"The history has been that we have not seen material, if any, defaults," says Richard Smith, credit analyst at S&P. "Unfortunately, this hurricane is different than what we've experienced before. So I'm not sure that I would count on that history." Fitch Ratings has said it doesn't expect hurricane-related losses to affect its ratings of the bond insurers.

So far, the insurers say they have paid out more than $2 million to cover missed bond payments in the affected areas.

Most bond-market professionals tend to agree that the area's credit will ultimately rebound as federal money pours in and New Orleans rebuilds. "In the long run New Orleans is not a city that's just going to go away," says Peter Coffin, president of Breckinridge Capital, an asset-management firm that specializes in municipal bonds. "At this point the view is that they'll rebuild, and that through that rebuilding and with some assistance they'll manage."

Source: Mark Whitehouses, *The Wall Street Journal*, September 13, 2005. Reprinted by permission of Dow Jones & Company, Inc., via Copyright Clearance Center, Inc. © 2005 Dow Jones & Company, Inc. All Rights Reserved Worldwide.

19.7 Equivalent Taxable Yield

Consider an individual investor who must decide whether to invest in a corporate bond paying annual coupon interest of 8 percent or a municipal bond paying annual coupon interest of 5 percent. Both bonds are new issues with a triple-A credit rating, both bonds sell at par value, and the investor plans to hold the bonds until they mature. Since both bonds are purchased at par value, their coupon rates are equal to their originally stated yields to maturity. For the municipal bond this is a tax-exempt yield, and for the corporate bond this is a taxable yield.

Clearly, if the investment was for a tax-exempt retirement account, corporate debt is preferred since the coupon interest is higher and tax effects are not a consideration. But if the investment is not tax-exempt, the decision should be made on an aftertax basis. Essentially, the investor must decide which investment provides the highest return after accounting for income tax on corporate debt interest. This is done by comparing the tax-exempt yield of 5 percent on municipal bonds with an equivalent taxable yield. An equivalent taxable yield depends on the investor's marginal tax rate and is computed as follows:

$$\text{Equivalent taxable yield} = \frac{\text{Tax-exempt yield}}{1 - \text{Marginal tax rate}}$$

For example, suppose the investor is in a 35 percent marginal tax bracket. Then a tax-exempt yield of 5 percent is shown to correspond to an equivalent taxable yield of 7.69 percent as follows:

$$\text{Equivalent taxable yield} = \frac{5\%}{1 - .35} = 7.69\%$$

In this case, the investor would prefer the taxable yield of 8 percent on the corporate bond to the equivalent taxable yield of 7.69 percent on the municipal bond.

Alternatively, the investor could compare the aftertax yield on the corporate bond with the tax-exempt yield on the municipal bond. An aftertax yield is computed as follows:

$$\text{Aftertax yield} = \text{Taxable yield} \times (1 - \text{Marginal tax rate})$$

To change the example, suppose that the investor is in a 40 percent marginal tax bracket. This results in an aftertax yield of 4.8 percent, as shown below.

$$\text{Aftertax yield} = 8\% \times (1 - .40) = 4.8\%$$

In this case, the tax-exempt yield of 5 percent on the municipal bond is preferred to the aftertax yield of 4.8 percent on the corporate bond.

Another approach is to compute the critical marginal tax rate that would leave an investor indifferent between a given tax-exempt yield on a municipal bond and a given taxable yield on a corporate bond. A critical marginal tax rate is found as follows:

$$\text{Critical marginal tax rate} = 1 - \frac{\text{Tax-exempt yield}}{\text{Taxable yield}}$$

For the example considered here, the critical marginal tax rate is 37.5 percent, determined as follows:

$$\text{Critical marginal tax rate} = 1 - \frac{5\%}{8\%} = 37.5\%$$

Investors with a marginal tax rate higher than the critical marginal rate would prefer the municipal bond, whereas investors in a lower tax bracket would prefer the corporate bond.

CHECK THIS

19.7a   An investor with a marginal tax rate of 30 percent is interested in a tax-exempt bond with a yield of 6 percent. What is the equivalent taxable yield of this bond?

19.7b   A taxable bond has a yield of 10 percent, and a tax-exempt bond has a yield of 7 percent. What is the critical marginal tax rate for these two bonds?

19.8 Taxable Municipal Bonds

private activity bonds

Taxable municipal bonds used to finance facilities used by private businesses.

The Tax Reform Act of 1986 imposed notable restrictions on the types of municipal bonds that qualify for federal tax exemption of interest payments. In particular, the 1986 act expanded the definition of **private activity bonds**. Private activity bonds include any municipal security where 10 percent or more of the issue finances facilities used by private entities and is secured by payments from private entities.

Interest on private activity bonds is tax-exempt only if the bond issue falls into a so-called qualified category. Qualified private activity bonds that still enjoy a tax-exempt interest privilege include public airport bonds, multifamily housing bonds, nonvehicular mass commuting bonds, and various other project bonds. The major types of private activity bonds that do not qualify for tax-exempt interest are those used to finance sports stadiums, convention facilities, parking facilities, and industrial parks. However, these taxable private activity bonds may still enjoy exemption from state and local income tax. In any case, as a result of the 1986 act and the continuing need to finance private activity projects, new issues of taxable municipal revenue bonds are frequently sold with yields similar to corporate bond yields.

19.9 Summary and Conclusions

This chapter covers the topic of government bonds, including U.S. Treasury bonds, notes, and bills, and state, city, county, and local municipal bonds. In the chapter, we saw that:

1. The U.S. federal government is the largest single borrower in the world, with well over $4 trillion of publicly held debt. Responsibility for managing this debt belongs to the U.S. Treasury, which issues Treasury bills, notes, and bonds at regular auctions to finance government debt.

2. Treasury bills are short-term obligations that are sold on a discount basis. Treasury notes are medium-term obligations that pay fixed semiannual coupons as well as payment of face value at maturity. Treasury bonds are long-term obligations that pay their face value at maturity and pay fixed semiannual coupons.

3. The U.S. Treasury sponsors the STRIPS program, where Treasury bonds and notes are broken down into principal strips, which represent face value payments, and coupon strips, which represent individual coupon payments. Since each strip created under the STRIPS program represents a single future payment, strips effectively become zero coupon bonds.

4. Several federal agencies are authorized to issue securities directly to the public. Bonds issued by U.S. government agencies have a credit quality almost identical to U.S. Treasury issues, but agency notes and bonds are attractive to many investors because they offer higher yields than comparable U.S. Treasury securities. However, the market for agency debt is less active than the market for U.S. Treasury debt and investors are potentially subject to state income taxes on agency debt interest, while U.S. Treasury debt interest is not subject to state taxes.

5. Another large market for government debt is the market for municipal government debt. Total municipal debt outstanding currently exceeds $2 trillion, divided among most of the more than 80,000 state and local governments in the United States. Individual investors hold about half this debt, while the remainder is roughly split equally between holdings of property and casualty insurance companies and commercial banks.

6. Municipal notes and bonds are intermediate- to long-term interest-bearing obligations of state and local governments or agencies of those governments. Municipal debt is commonly called the tax-exempt market because the coupon interest is usually exempt from federal income tax, which makes municipal bonds attractive to investors in the highest income tax brackets. However, yields on municipal debt are less than yields on corporate debt with similar features and credit quality, thus eliminating much of the advantage of the tax exemption.

7. Most municipal bonds pay a constant coupon rate, but some municipal notes pay variable coupon rates that change according to prevailing market interest rates. Also, a call provision is a standard feature of most municipal bond issues. A call provision allows an issuer to retire outstanding bonds before they mature. When the bond is called, each bondholder receives the bond's call price in exchange for returning the bond to the issuer.

8. There are two basic types of municipal bonds: revenue bonds and general obligation bonds. Revenue bonds, which constitute the bulk of all outstanding municipal bonds, are secured by proceeds collected from the projects they finance. General obligation bonds, which are issued by all levels of municipal governments, are secured by the general taxing powers of the municipalities issuing the bonds.

9. As part of the process for issuing municipal bonds to the public, a rating agency is paid a fee to assign a credit rating to a new bond issue. In the last two decades, it has become increasingly common for municipalities to obtain bond insurance for new bond issues through an insurance policy written by a commercial insurance company. With bond insurance, the credit quality of the bond issue is determined by the financial strength of the insurance company, not the municipality alone.

GET REAL

This chapter covered government bonds, a large and important securities market. How should you put your knowledge to work? Begin by purchasing (in a simulated brokerage account like Stock-Trak) the various types of government securities that are available for trading out there. Observe how their prices and yields change over time.

You should also learn more about buying Treasury securities. A great place to start is the Bureau of Public Debt Web site (www.publicdebt.treas.gov). There you can examine and download the forms needed to bid in the regular auctions. You can also obtain current Treasury auction information, including forthcoming auctions and the results of previous auctions. You can also read about the *Treasury Direct* program, which is probably the best way of purchasing Treasury issues for individual investors. But if you prefer U.S. Savings Bonds, then check out the Web site that tells you all you need to know about them (www.savingsbonds.gov).

You will probably find that you cannot trade municipal bonds through a simulated brokerage account. The reason is that the market for municipals is so thin that getting timely price information for a particular issue isn't possible. In practice, municipal bonds are best suited for buy-and-hold investors who buy the bonds when originally issued and hold them until maturity. You can now buy municipal bonds online through a number of brokers. Try, for example, First Miami (www.firstmiami.com) or Lebenthal Investments (www.lebenthal.com). Also take a look at Muni Auction (www.muniauction.com).

Key Terms

Chapter Review Problems and Self-Test

1. **Treasury Yields**   A callable Treasury bond's price is 140:25. It has a coupon rate of 10 percent, makes semiannual payments, and matures in 21 years. What yield would be reported in the financial press?

2. **Equivalent Yields**   A particular investor faces a 40 percent tax rate. If a AA-rated municipal bond yields 4 percent, what must a similar taxable issue yield for the investor to be impartial to them?

Answers to Self-Test Problems

1. First, note that this is a callable issue selling above par, so the yield to call will be reported. All callable Treasury bonds are callable at face value five years before they mature. Thus, to calculate the yield to call, all we have to do is pretend that the bond has 16 years to maturity instead of 21. We therefore have a bond with a price of 140.78125 (after converting from thirty-seconds), a coupon of 10 percent paid semiannually, and a maturity of 16 years (or 32 periods). Verify, using the standard bond formula from an earlier chapter, that the semiannual yield to call is 3 percent, so the reported yield would be 6 percent.

2. The equivalent taxable yield is the municipal yield "grossed up" by one minus the tax rate:

$$\frac{4\%}{1 - .40} = 6.67\%$$

Test Your Investment Quotient

1. **Zero Coupon Bonds**   What is the yield to maturity (YTM) on a zero coupon bond?
   a. The interest rate realized if the bond is held to maturity.
   b. The interest rate realized when the bond is sold.
   c. The coupon yield for an equivalent coupon bond.
   d. A fixed rate when the bond is issued.

2. **Treasury Notes**   The coupon rate for a Treasury note is set
   a. The same for all Treasury note issues.
   b. By a formula based on the size of the Treasury note issue.
   c. According to prevailing interest rates at time of issuance.
   d. According to the supply and demand for money.

3. **Treasury Notes and Bonds**   U.S. Treasury notes and bonds have face value denominations as small as
   a. $1,000
   b. $5,000

    c. $10,000
    d. $25,000

4. **Treasury Bonds**   What is the dollar value of a U.S. Treasury bond quoted at 92:24?

    a. $922.75
    b. $922.40
    c. $927.50
    d. Indeterminable

5. **Treasury Bonds**   The following are quotes for a U.S. Treasury bond:

Bid	Asked
102:02	102:05

If the face value of the bond is $1,000, the price an investor should pay for the bond is *closest* to

    a. $1,020.63
    b. $1,021.56
    c. $1,025.00
    d. $1,026.25

6. **Treasury Bonds**   A trader purchases $5 million face value of Treasury bonds at 95:16 and then later sells the bonds at 95:24. What is the round-trip gain on these transactions?

    a. $1,250
    b. $12,500
    c. $4,000
    d. $40,000

7. **Treasury STRIPS**   When originally issued, a 10-year maturity Treasury note can be stripped into how many separate components?

    a. 10
    b. 11
    c. 20
    d. 21

8. **Treasury Bills**   Treasury bills are sold on a discount basis, meaning that the difference between their issued price and their redemption value is

    a. The same for all T-bill issues.
    b. The imputed interest on the T-bill.
    c. Never less than the issued price.
    d. The bond equivalent yield for the T-bill.

9. **Treasury Auctions**   Which of the following statements about single-price Treasury auctions is false?

    a. Competitive bidders pay the stop-out bid.
    b. Noncompetitive bidders pay the stop-out bid plus a small premium.
    c. Noncompetitive bidders pay the stop-out bid.
    d. All of the above are true.

10. **Treasury Dealers**   When trading U.S. Treasury securities, Treasury dealers

    a. Buy at the bid price and sell at the asked price.
    b. Sell at the bid price and buy at the asked price.
    c. Buy at the stop-out bid price and sell at the market price.
    d. Sell at the stop-out bid price and buy at the market price.

11. **Savings Bonds**   A Series EE Savings Bond with a face value of $1,000 is originally sold for

    a. $1,000.
    b. $500.
    c. A price based on the recent inflation rate.
    d. 90 percent of the price of a recently issued five-year T-note.

12. **Savings Bonds**   Series EE savings bonds are guaranteed to double in price if they are held for

   a. 10 years
   b. 5 years
   c. 15 years
   d. 20 years

13. **Savings Bonds**   A Series I savings bond with a face value of $1,000 is originally sold at a price of

   a. $1,000.
   b. $500.
   c. A price based on the recent inflation rate.
   d. 90 percent of the price of a recently issued five-year T-note.

14. **Savings Bonds**   The interest rate on Series I savings bonds is reset every six months as

   a. 90 percent of the rate on newly issued five-year T-notes.
   b. 90 percent of the rate on newly issued five-year T-notes plus the recent inflation rate.
   c. A fixed rate plus the recent inflation rate.
   d. An adjustable rate plus the recent inflation rate.

15. **Agency Bonds**   Which statement applies to a bond issued by an agency of the U.S. government?

   a. It is exempt from the federal income tax on interest.
   b. It becomes a direct obligation of the U.S. Treasury in case of default.
   c. It is secured by assets held by the agency.
   d. None of the above.

16. **Agency Bonds**   Which is true for bonds issued by all agencies of the U.S. government?

   a. They become direct obligations of the U.S. Treasury.
   b. They are secured bonds backed by government holdings.
   c. They are exempt from federal income tax.
   d. None of the above.

17. **Agency Bonds**   Which of the following investors is most likely to invest in agency bonds?

   a. High-income individual with a need for liquidity.
   b. High-income individual living in a triple income tax municipality.
   c. Commercial bank.
   d. Life insurance company.

18. **Municipal Bonds**   Which of the following constitutes the bulk of all outstanding municipal bonds?

   a. Revenue bonds
   b. General obligation bonds
   c. Moral obligation bonds
   d. Private activity bonds

19. **Municipal Bonds**   Which of the following investors is most likely to invest in locally issued municipal bonds?

   a. High-income individual with a need for liquidity.
   b. High-income individual living in a triple income tax municipality.
   c. Commercial bank.
   d. Life insurance company.

20. **Revenue Bonds**   A revenue bond is distinguished from a general obligation bond in that revenue bonds have which of the following characteristics?

   a. They are issued by counties, special districts, cities, towns, and state-controlled authorities, whereas general obligation bonds are issued only by the states themselves.
   b. They are typically secured by limited taxing power, whereas general obligation bonds are secured by unlimited taxing power.

    c. They are issued to finance specific projects and are secured by the revenues of the project being financed.

    d. They have first claim to any revenue increase of the issuing tax authority.

21. **Insured Municipal Bonds** Which of the following is not a method used by municipal bond insurers to manage default risk?

    a. Only insure bonds from municipalities with a good credit rating.

    b. Diversify default risk by writing insurance policies for municipalities spread across a wide geographic area.

    c. Maintain substantial investment portfolios as a source of financial reserves.

    d. All of the above are used to manage default risk.

22. **Insured Municipal Bonds** Which one of the following generally is not true of an insured municipal bond?

    a. The price on an insured bond is higher than that on an otherwise identical uninsured bond.

    b. The insurance can be canceled in the event the issuer fails to maintain predetermined quality standards.

    c. The insurance premium is a one-time payment made at the time of issuance.

    d. The insurance company is obligated to make all defaulted principal and/or interest payments in a prompt and timely fashion.

23. **Taxable Equivalent Yield** A municipal bond carries a coupon of 6 3/4 percent and is trading at par. To a taxpayer in the 34 percent tax bracket, what would the taxable equivalent yield of this bond be?

    a. 4.5 percent

    b. 10.2 percent

    c. 13.4 percent

    d. 19.9 percent

24. **Taxable Equivalent Yield** A 20-year municipal bond is currently priced at par to yield 5.53 percent. For a taxpayer in the 33 percent tax bracket, what equivalent taxable yield would this bond offer?

    a. 8.25 percent

    b. 10.75 percent

    c. 11.40 percent

    d. None of the above

25. **Taxable Equivalent Yield** The coupon rate on a tax-exempt bond is 5.6 percent, and the coupon rate on a taxable bond is 8 percent. Both bonds sell at par. At what tax bracket (marginal tax rate) would an investor show no preference between the two bonds?

    a. 30.0 percent

    b. 39.6 percent

    c. 41.7 percent

    d. 42.9 percent

Concept Questions

1. **Bills versus Bonds** What are the key differences between T-bills and T-bonds?

2. **Notes versus Bonds** What are the key differences between T-notes and T-bonds?

3. **Zeroes** What two Treasury securities are zeroes?

4. **Spreads** What are typical spreads for T-notes and T-bonds? Why do you think they differ from issue to issue?

5. **Agencies versus Treasuries** From an investor's standpoint, what are the key differences between Treasury and agency issues?

6. **Municipals versus Treasuries** From an investor's standpoint, what are the main differences between Treasury and municipal issues?

7. **Serial Bonds**   What are serial bonds? What purpose does this structure serve?

8. **VRNs**   In the context of the muni market, what are variable-rate notes? What is likely true about their risks compared to those of ordinary issues?

9. **Revenues versus General Obligation Munis**   What is the difference between a revenue bond and a general obligation bond?

10. **Private Activity Munis**   What is a private activity muni? What type of investor would be interested in it?

11. **Treasury versus Municipal Bonds**   Treasury and municipal yields are often compared to calculate critical tax rates. What concerns might you have about such a comparison? What do you think is true about the calculated tax rate?

12. **Callable Treasury Bonds**   For a callable Treasury bond selling above par, is it necessarily true that the yield to call will be less than the yield to maturity? Why or why not?

13. **Callable Agency Issues**   For a callable agency bond selling above par, is it necessarily true that the yield to call will be less than the yield to maturity? Why or why not?

14. **Treasury versus Municipal Bonds**   Why might the yield to maturity on, say, a BBB-rated municipal bond with moderate default risk actually be less than that of a U.S. Treasury bond with no default risk?

15. **Treasury versus Municipal Bonds**   In a recent issue of *The Wall Street Journal*, compare the yields on U.S. Treasury bonds with the yields on municipal bonds. Why might these yield spreads depend on the state of the economy?

Questions and Problems _____

Core Questions

1. **STRIPS Price**   What is the price of a STRIPS with a maturity of 20 years, a face value of $10,000, and a yield to maturity of 7.5 percent?

2. **STRIPS YTM**   A STRIPS with 16 years until maturity and a face value of $10,000 is trading for $2,912. What is the yield to maturity?

3. **Treasury Auctions**   The Federal Reserve announces an offering of Treasury bills with a face value of $40 billion. Noncompetitive bids are made for $8 billion, along with the following competitive bids:

Bidder	Price Bid	Quantity Bid
A	$9,250	$13 billion
B	9,300	9 billion
C	9,320	9 billion
D	9,350	7 billion
E	9,400	6 billion
F	9,410	5 billion

In a single-price auction, which bids are accepted and what prices are paid by each bidder? How much money is raised by the entire offering?

4. **Municipal Bonds**   A municipal bond with a coupon rate of 4.9 percent has a yield to maturity of 5.6 percent. If the bond has 10 years to maturity, what is the price of the bond?

5. **Yield to Maturity**   A municipal bond with a coupon rate of 5.2 percent sells for $5,380 and has seven years until maturity. What is the yield to maturity of the bond?

6. **Yield to Maturity**   A municipal bond has 18 years until maturity and sells for $5,820. If the coupon rate on the bond is 5.70 percent, what is the yield to maturity?

7. **Yield to Call**   Assume the bond in the previous problem can be called in eight years. What is the yield to call if the call price is 103 percent of par?

8. **Aftertax Yield**   A municipal bond has a yield to maturity of 5.9 percent. What corporate bond yield would make an investor in the 38 percent tax bracket indifferent between the two bonds, all else the same?

9. **Tax Equivalent Yields**   A taxable corporate issue yields 8.5 percent. For an investor in a 31 percent tax bracket, what is the equivalent aftertax yield?

10. **Tax Rates**   A taxable issue yields 9.6 percent, and a similar municipal issue yields 6.1 percent. What is the critical marginal tax rate?

Intermediate Questions

11. **Treasury Prices**   A Treasury bill has a bid yield of 4.76 and an asked yield of 4.73. The bill matures in 160 days. What is the least you could pay to acquire a bill? (Note: You may need to review material from an earlier chapter for the relevant formula.)

12. **Treasury Prices**   At what price could you sell the Treasury bill referred to in the previous question? What is the dollar spread for this bill? (Note: You may need to review material from an earlier chapter for the relevant formula.)

13. **Treasury Prices**   A Treasury issue is quoted at 112:09 bid and 112:12 ask. What is the least you could pay to acquire a bond?

14. **Treasury Prices**   A noncallable Treasury bond has a quoted yield of 5.86 percent. It has a 6.5 percent coupon and 12 years to maturity. What is its dollar price assuming a $1,000 par value? What is its quoted price?

15. **Treasury Yields**   A Treasury bond with the longest maturity (30 years) has an asked price quoted at 101:15. The coupon rate is 6.1 percent, paid semiannually. What is the yield to maturity of this bond?

16. **Treasury Yields**   In a recent *Wall Street Journal*, locate the Treasury bond with the longest maturity (the so-called bellwether bond). Verify that, given the ask price, the reported yield is correct.

17. **Yield to Call**   A Treasury bond maturing in November 2014 and callable in November 2009 has a quoted price of 126:06 and a coupon rate of 11.75 percent. Assuming the bond matures in exactly 8 years, what is the yield to call?

18. **Callable Treasury Bonds**   In a recent *Wall Street Journal*, examine the yields on Treasury bonds maturing in 2014 and 2015. Why do you think the yields for the issues maturing in 2014 are so different?

Spreadsheet Problems

19. **Zero Price**   A STRIPS traded on May 1, 2006, matures in 23 years on May 1, 2029. Assuming a 6.5 percent yield to maturity, what is the STRIPS price?

20. **Zero YTM**   A STRIPS traded on July 1, 2006, matures in 18 years on July 1, 2024. The quoted STRIPS price is 37. What is its yield to maturity?

What's on the Web? _____

1. **Treasury Auctions**   Go to www.publicdebt.treas.gov and find the next Treasury auctions scheduled. When are the auctions scheduled? What instruments will be offered at these auctions?

2. **Treasury Auctions**   Go to www.publicdebt.treas.gov and find the recently completed Treasury auctions for bills and notes. When did the auctions occur? What were the yields for each bill and note sold at these auctions?

3. **Municipal Bond Spreads**   Go to www.municipalbonds.com. What was the highest bid-side spread for the most recent quarter? What was the highest offer-side spread over this same period? What were the dollar amounts of these spreads?

4. **Municipal Bond Prices**   Go to www.municipalbonds.com and find the municipal bonds traded yesterday for your state. What was the most active bond in terms of the number of trades? Which bond traded the highest dollar amount? How many bonds had a spread of more than one point in trading yesterday?

5. **Savings Bonds** In this chapter, we discussed U.S. Series EE savings bonds. There are also Series HH savings bonds. These two bonds are different in several respects. Go to www.publicdebt.treas.gov and find out how the Series HH bonds work. What are the differences in these two types of savings bonds?

Stock-Trak Exercises

STOCK|TRAK

GLOBAL PORTFOLIO SIMULATIONS

To access the Stock-Trak Exercise for this chapter, please visit the book Web site at www.mhhe.com/jm4e and choose the corresponding chapter.

CHAPTER 20

Mortgage-Backed Securities

"I had been putting what little money I had in Ocean Frontage, for the sole reason that there was only so much of it and no more, and that they wasn't making any more."

–Will Rogers

Will Rogers wryly advised buying real estate because "they wasn't making any more." Almost all real estate purchases are financed by mortgages. Indeed, most of us become familiar with mortgages by financing the purchase of a home. But did you ever stop to think about what happens to a mortgage after it is originated? Today, they are usually pooled to create mortgage-backed securities. The basic concept is simple. Collect a portfolio of mortgages into a mortgage pool. Then issue securities with pro rata claims on mortgage pool cash flows. These mortgage-backed securities are attractive to investors because they represent a claim on a diversified portfolio of mortgages and, therefore, are considerably less risky than individual mortgage contracts. ∎

Mortgage financing makes home ownership possible for almost everyone. With mortgage financing, a home buyer makes only a down payment and borrows the remaining cost of a home with a mortgage loan. The mortgage loan is obtained from a mortgage originator, usually a local bank or other mortgage broker. Describing this financial transaction, we can say that a home buyer *issues* a mortgage and an originator *writes* a mortgage. A mortgage loan distinguishes itself from other loan contracts by a pledge of real estate as collateral for the loan. In this chapter, we carefully examine the investment characteristics of mortgage pools.

20.1 A Brief History of Mortgage-Backed Securities

Traditionally, savings banks and savings and loans (S&Ls) wrote most home mortgages and then held the mortgages in their portfolios of interest-earning assets. This changed radically during the 1970s and 1980s when market interest rates ascended to their highest levels in American history. Entering this financially turbulent period, savings banks and S&Ls held large portfolios of mortgages written at low pre-1970s interest rates. These portfolios were financed from customers' savings deposits. When market interest rates climbed to near 20 percent levels in the early 1980s, customers flocked to withdraw funds from their savings deposits to invest in money market funds that paid higher interest rates. As a result, savings institutions were often forced to sell mortgages at depressed prices to satisfy the onslaught of deposit withdrawals. For this, and other reasons, the ultimate result was the collapse of many savings institutions.

Today, home buyers still commonly turn to local banks for mortgage financing, but few mortgages are actually held by the banks that originate them. After writing a mortgage, an originator usually sells the mortgage to a mortgage repackager who accumulates them into mortgage pools. To finance the creation of a mortgage pool, the mortgage repackager issues mortgage-backed bonds, where each bond claims a pro rata share of all cash flows derived from mortgages in the pool. A pro rata share allocation pays cash flows in proportion to a bond's face value. Essentially, each mortgage pool is set up as a trust fund, and a servicing agent for the pool collects all mortgage payments. The servicing agent then passes these cash flows through to bondholders. For this reason, mortgage-backed bonds are often called **mortgage passthroughs**, or simply *pass-throughs*. However, all securities representing claims on mortgage pools are generically called **mortgage-backed securities (MBSs)**. The primary collateral for all mortgage-backed securities is the underlying pool of mortgages.

The transformation from mortgages to mortgage-backed securities is called **mortgage securitization**. More than $3 trillion of mortgages have been securitized in mortgage pools. This represents tremendous growth in the mortgage securitization business, since in the early 1980s less than $1 billion of home mortgages were securitized in pools. Yet despite the multi-trillion-dollar size of the mortgage-backed securities market, the risks involved with these investments are often misunderstood even by experienced investors.

mortgage passthroughs
Bonds representing a claim on the cash flows of an underlying mortgage pool passed through to bondholders.

mortgage-backed securities (MBSs)
Securities whose investment returns are based on a pool of mortgages.

mortgage securitization
The creation of mortgage-backed securities from a pool of mortgages.

20.2 Fixed-Rate Mortgages

fixed-rate mortgage
Loan that specifies constant monthly payments at a fixed interest rate over the life of the mortgage.

Understanding mortgage-backed securities begins with an understanding of the mortgages from which they are created. Most home mortgages are 15-year or 30-year maturity **fixed-rate mortgages** requiring constant monthly payments. As an example of a fixed-rate mortgage, consider a 30-year mortgage representing a loan of $100,000 financed at an annual interest rate of 8 percent. This translates into a monthly interest rate of 8 percent/12 months = .67%, and it requires a series of 360 monthly payments. The size of the monthly payment is determined by the requirement that the present value of all monthly payments, based on the financing rate specified in the mortgage contract, be equal to the original loan amount of $100,000. Mathematically, the constant monthly payment for a $100,000 mortgage is calculated using the following formula:

$$\text{Monthly payment} = \frac{\text{Mortgage amount} \times r/12}{1 - \dfrac{1}{(1 + r/12)^{T \times 12}}} \qquad (20.1)$$

where: r = Annual mortgage financing rate

$r/12$ = Monthly mortgage financing rate

T = Mortgage term in years

$T \times 12$ = Mortgage term in months

In the example of a $100,000, thirty-year mortgage financed at 8 percent, the monthly payment is $733.76. This amount is calculated as follows:

$$\text{Monthly payment} = \frac{\$100,000 \times .08/12}{1 - \dfrac{1}{(1 + .08/12)^{360}}}$$

$$= \$733.76$$

EXAMPLE 20.1 | **Calculating Monthly Mortgage Payments**

What is the monthly payment for a 15-year, $100,000 mortgage loan financed at 8 percent interest?

A 15-year mortgage specifies 180 monthly payments. Using the monthly payment formula we get a monthly payment of $955.65 as follows:

$$\text{Monthly payment} = \frac{\$100,000 \times 0.08/12}{1 - \dfrac{1}{(1 + 0.08/12)^{180}}}$$

$$= \$955.65$$

If you wish to calculate mortgage payments for other interest rates, maturities, and loan amounts, we suggest using a built-in spreadsheet function. For example, the nearby *Spreadsheet Analysis* box contains an example mortgage payment calculation using an Excel spreadsheet.

CHECK THIS

20.2a The most popular fixed-rate mortgages among home buyers are those with 15-year and 30-year maturities. What might be some of the comparative advantages and disadvantages of these two mortgage maturities?

20.2b Suppose you were to finance a home purchase using a fixed-rate mortgage. Would you prefer a 15-year or 30-year maturity mortgage? Why?

Monthly mortgage payments are sensitive to the interest rate stipulated in the mortgage contract. Table 20.1 provides a schedule of monthly payments required for 5-year, 10-year, 15-year, 20-year, and 30-year mortgages based on annual interest rates ranging from 5 percent to 15 percent in increments of .5 percent. Notice that monthly payments required for a $100,000, thirty-year mortgage financed at 5 percent are only $536.82, while monthly payments for the same mortgage financed at 15 percent are $1,264.44.

mortgage principal
The amount of a mortgage loan outstanding, which is the amount required to pay off the mortgage.

FIXED-RATE MORTGAGE AMORTIZATION

Each monthly mortgage payment has two separate components. The first component represents payment of interest on outstanding **mortgage principal**. Outstanding mortgage principal is also called a mortgage's *remaining balance* or *remaining principal*. It is the amount required to pay off a mortgage before it matures. The second component represents a

INVESTMENT UPDATES

MANAGE YOUR HOME LIKE AN INVESTMENT

Smart investing begins at home. Many folks diligently nurture their portfolios of stocks, bonds, and mutual funds. Got a mortgage on your house? You should manage your home loan with the same sort of investment savvy. Planning to refinance? Considering extra principal payments? Here's how to make smarter decisions when handling your mortgage:

Reducing Your Rate

Imagine you bought your house seven years ago. At the time, you borrowed $200,000 through a 30-year mortgage with a fixed 7% rate, resulting in a monthly mortgage payment of $1,331. Now, a loan officer at the local bank says that, for $2,500 in fees, you could refinance and get a new 30-year loan at 6%.

At first blush, that might seem appealing. Your seven years of mortgage payments has left you with a loan balance of $182,295. If you refinanced that sum at 6% over 30 years, your monthly payment would drop to $1,093.

A sweet deal? It isn't quite as sweet as it seems. Think about it: You are replacing what's now a 23-year loan with a 30-year loan. Even if your mortgage rate stayed the same, your monthly payment would still drop, because you are now paying back the sum borrowed over an additional seven years.

Instead, to make a fair comparison, you have to compare your current 23-year, 7% loan with a new 23-year, 6% loan. To that end, try playing with mortgage calculators at sites like www.bankrate.com,

www.hsh.com, www.mortgage-x.com, and www.realestateabc.com.

If you compare the two 23-year loans, you'll find you could save $111 a month by refinancing. Divide that $111 into the $2,500 in fees. Result: Refinancing makes sense, provided you stay in your current house for just over 22 months. Your local bank won't actually offer you a 23-year loan. Instead, you might opt for, say, a 20-year loan. But taking that shorter loan could be a smart move, says Michael Maloon, a financial planner in San Ramon, Calif.

"If people are refinancing and going back to a 30-year mortgage, they're crazy," he contends. "If you do that and you end up with an extra couple of hundred dollars a month in discretionary income, you will get used to spending that amount. Now, you need even more to retire," because you are accustomed to a higher standard of living. Instead, Mr. Maloon argues that folks who refinance should look to shorten the length of their loans, with a view to getting their mortgages paid off before they retire. "To win in the refi game, you want to lower the rate, lower your payments and pay off your mortgage sooner," he says. "I don't know how you retire if you still have a mortgage."

Paying Down Principal

To get your mortgage paid off by the time you retire, you might also want to make extra principal payments. By adding $100 or $200 to each monthly

pay-down, or *amortization,* of mortgage principal. The relative amounts of each component change throughout the life of a mortgage. For example, a 30-year, $100,000 mortgage financed at 8 percent requires 360 monthly payments of $733.76. The first monthly payment consists of a $666.67 payment of interest and a $67.10 pay-down of principal. The first month's interest payment, representing one month's interest on a mortgage balance of $100,000, is calculated as:

$$\$100,000 \times .08/12 = \$666.67$$

After this payment of interest, the remainder of the first monthly payment, that is, $733.76 − $666.67 = $67.10 (there's a small rounding error), is used to amortize outstanding mortgage principal. Thus, after the first monthly payment, outstanding principal is reduced to $100,000 − $67.10 = $99,932.90.

The second monthly payment includes a $666.22 payment of interest calculated as:

$$\$99,932.90 \times .08/12 = \$666.22$$

mortgage check, you could save yourself thousands of dollars in interest and pay off your loan years earlier.

Sound attractive? To figure out whether this is the right strategy for you, consider not only the interest rate on your mortgage, but also your tax situation and what else you might do with the money. Let's say you have a mortgage with a 6.5% interest rate. That 6.5% is the interest expense you avoid by making extra principal payments and thus that is the effective pretax rate of return you earn. You should be able to do better than that 6.5% by buying stocks or bonds within a retirement account or by purchasing stocks in a taxable account.

But what if you have maxed out on your retirement accounts and you already own plenty of stocks? What if the alternative is to buy bonds or certificates of deposit within your taxable account? In that case, making extra principal payments could be a smart strategy. Suppose you are choosing between paying down your 6.5% mortgage and buying a corporate bond for your taxable account that yields 5.5%. If your mortgage interest is tax-deductible and you are in the 27% federal income-tax bracket, the after-tax return from paying down your mortgage is 4.75%. But the after-tax return on the corporate bond would be even lower. After paying federal income taxes on the bond's 5.5% yield, you would be left with just 4.02%.

In fact, paying down your mortgage may garner you an even higher return. Imagine you are married and you file a joint tax return. In 2003, you and your spouse are entitled to a standard deduction of $7,950. But let's assume you don't take the standard deduction. Instead, you itemize your deductions by filing Schedule A along with your federal tax return. This year, you expect to have itemized deductions of $10,000, consisting of $5,000 in mortgage interest and another $5,000 in property taxes, charitable gifts, and state income taxes. Because your total of $10,000 in itemized deductions is greater than your $7,950 standard deduction, you save taxes by itemizing.

Even so, the tax benefit you get from your mortgage interest is still fairly modest. Indeed, I would argue that just $2,050 of your mortgage interest is truly tax-deductible. The reason: If you had $2,050 less in annual mortgage interest, you would take the standard deduction instead and thus you wouldn't get any tax benefit from your mortgage. Nonetheless, the after-tax return from adding an extra $100 to your mortgage check would still be 4.75%. How come? The interest you avoid by making extra principal payments is interest you could have deducted. Eventually, however, as you pay down your mortgage and thereby reduce the amount of interest you incur each year, your itemized deductions will fall below $7,950 and you will take the standard deduction instead. At that point, the after-tax return from making extra principal payments jumps to the full 6.5%.

Source: Jonathan Clements, *The Wall Street Journal*, April 27, 2003.
© 2003 Dow Jones & Company, Inc. All Rights Reserved Worldwide.

The remainder of the second monthly payment, that is, $733.76 − $666.22 = $67.54, is used to reduce mortgage principal to $99,932.91 − $67.54 = $99,865.37.

This process continues throughout the life of the mortgage. The interest payment component gradually declines, and the payment of principal component gradually increases. Finally, the last monthly payment is divided into a $4.86 payment of interest and a final $728.91 pay-down of mortgage principal. The process of paying down mortgage principal over the life of a mortgage is called **mortgage amortization**.

mortgage amortization

The process of paying down mortgage principal over the life of the mortgage.

Mortgage amortization is described by an amortization schedule. An amortization schedule states the remaining principal owed on a mortgage at any point in time and also states the scheduled principal payment and interest payment in any month. Amortization schedules for 15-year and 30-year, $100,000 mortgages financed at a fixed-rate of 8 percent are listed in Table 20.2. The payment month is given in the left-hand column. Then, for each maturity, the first column reports remaining mortgage principal immediately after a monthly payment is made. Columns 2 and 3 for each maturity list the principal payment and the interest payment scheduled for each monthly payment. Notice that immediately after the

SPREADSHEET ANALYSIS

	A	B	C	D	E	F	G
1							
2		Monthly Payments for a 30-Year Mortgage					
3							
4	A 30-year mortgage specifies an annual interest rate of 8 percent						
5	and a loan amount of $100,000. What are the monthly payments?						
6	Hint: Use the Excel function PMT.						
7							
8		-$733.76	=PMT(0.08/12,360,100000,0,0)				
9							
10		Monthly interest is 8%/12 = 0.667%					
11		Number of monthly payments is 12 x 30 = 360.					
12		Initial principal is $100,000.					
13		First zero indicates complete repayment after last monthly payment.					
14		Second zero indicates end-of-month payments.					
15							
16	For a 15-year mortgage, we get a bigger monthly payment.						
17							
18		-$955.65	=PMT(0.08/12,180,100000,0,0)				
19							
20							

TABLE 20.1 $100,000 Mortgage Loan Monthly Payments

	Mortgage Maturity				
Interest Rate	30-Year	20-Year	15-Year	10-Year	5-Year
5.0%	$ 536.82	$ 659.96	$ 790.79	$1,060.66	$1,887.12
5.5	567.79	687.89	817.08	1,085.26	1,910.12
6.0	599.55	716.43	843.86	1,110.21	1,933.28
6.5	632.07	745.57	871.11	1,135.48	1,956.61
7.0	665.30	775.30	898.83	1,161.08	1,980.12
7.5	699.21	805.59	927.01	1,187.02	2,003.79
8.0	733.76	836.44	955.65	1,213.28	2,027.64
8.5	768.91	867.82	984.74	1,239.86	2,051.65
9.0	804.62	899.73	1,014.27	1,266.76	2,075.84
9.5	840.85	932.13	1,044.22	1,293.98	2,100.19
10.0	877.57	965.02	1,074.61	1,321.51	2,124.70
10.5	914.74	998.38	1,105.40	1,349.35	2,149.39
11.0	952.32	1,032.19	1,136.60	1,377.50	2,174.24
11.5	990.29	1,066.43	1,168.19	1,405.95	2,199.26
12.0	1,028.61	1,101.09	1,200.17	1,434.71	2,224.44
12.5	1,067.26	1,136.14	1,232.52	1,463.76	2,249.79
13.0	1,106.20	1,171.58	1,265.24	1,493.11	2,275.31
13.5	1,145.41	1,207.37	1,298.32	1,522.74	2,300.98
14.0	1,184.87	1,243.52	1,331.74	1,552.66	2,326.83
14.5	1,224.56	1,280.00	1,365.50	1,582.87	2,352.83
15.0	1,264.44	1,316.79	1,399.59	1,613.35	2,378.99

30-Year Mortgage $733.76 Monthly Payment				15-Year Mortgage $955.65 Monthly Payment			
Payment Month	Remaining Principal	Principal Reduction	Interest Payment	Payment Month	Remaining Principal	Principal Reduction	Interest Payment
1	$99,932.90	$ 67.10	$666.67	1	$99,711.01	$288.99	$666.67
12	99,164.64	72.19	661.58	12	96,402.15	310.90	644.75
24	98,259.94	78.18	655.59	24	92,505.69	336.70	618.95
36	97,280.15	84.67	649.10	36	88,285.81	364.65	591.00
48	96,219.04	91.69	642.07	48	83,715.70	394.91	560.74
60	95,069.86	99.30	634.46	60	78,766.26	427.69	527.96
72	93,825.29	107.55	626.22	72	73,406.02	463.19	492.46
84	92,477.43	116.47	617.29	84	67,600.89	501.64	454.02
96	91,017.70	126.14	607.63	96	61,313.93	543.27	412.38
108	89,436.81	136.61	597.16	108	54,505.16	588.36	367.29
120	87,724.70	147.95	585.82	120	47,131.26	637.20	318.46
132	85,870.50	160.23	573.54	132	39,145.34	690.08	265.57
144	83,862.39	173.53	560.24	144	30,496.58	747.36	208.29
156	81,687.61	187.93	545.84	156	21,129.99	809.39	146.26
168	79,332.33	203.53	530.24	168	10,985.97	876.57	79.08
180	76,781.56	220.42	513.35	180	0.00	949.32	6.33
192	74,019.08	238.71	495.05				
204	71,027.31	258.53	475.24				
216	67,787.23	279.98	453.78				
228	64,278.22	303.22	430.54				
240	60,477.96	328.39	405.38				
252	56,362.29	355.65	378.12				
264	51,905.02	385.16	348.60				
276	47,077.79	417.13	316.63				
288	41,849.91	451.75	282.01				
300	36,188.12	489.25	244.52				
312	30,056.40	529.86	203.91				
324	23,415.75	573.83	159.93				
336	16,223.93	621.46	112.30				
348	8,435.20	673.04	60.72				
360	0.00	728.91	4.86				

180th monthly payment for a 30-year, $100,000 mortgage, $76,781.56 of mortgage principal is still outstanding. Notice also that as late as the 252nd monthly payment, the interest payment component of $378.12 still exceeds the principal payment component of $355.65.

EXAMPLE 20.2   Mortgage Amortization

After five years of payments on a mortgage loan financed at 8 percent, what are the remaining balance and interest and principal reduction components of the monthly payment?

For the 30-year mortgage, referring to Table 20.1 we see that the monthly payment is $733.76. Referring to the 60th monthly payment in Table 20.2, we find that

(continued)

the remaining balance on the mortgage is $95,069.86. Principal reduction for this payment is $99.30, and the interest payment is $634.46.

For the 15-year mortgage, the monthly payment is $955.65 and, after the 60th monthly payment, the remaining balance is $78,766.26, principal reduction is $427.69, and the interest payment is $527.96.

If you wish to calculate interest and principal reduction components for other interest rates, maturities, and loan amounts, we suggest using built-in spreadsheet functions. A nearby *Spreadsheet Analysis* box contains an example calculation of interest and principal reduction components for a mortgage using an Excel spreadsheet. Another *Spreadsheet Analysis* box contains an example calculation of the remaining balance on a mortgage.

The amortization process for a 30-year, $100,000 mortgage financed at 8 percent interest is illustrated graphically in Figure 20.1. Figure 20.1A graphs the outstanding mortgage principal over the life of the mortgage. Figure 20.1B graphs the rising principal payment component and the falling interest payment component of the mortgage.

FIGURE 20.1 Mortgage Principal and Payment Components for a $100,000 30-Year Mortgage with an 8 Percent Interest Rate

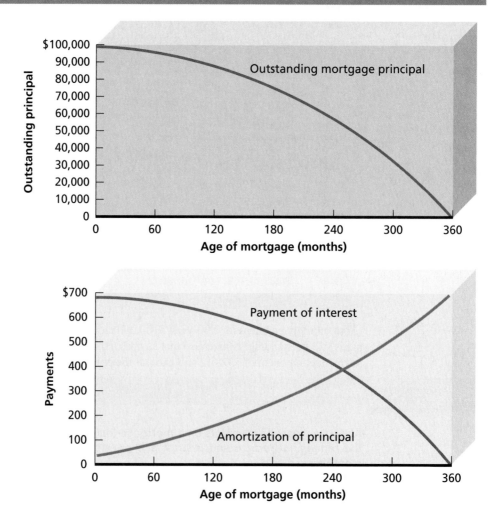

	A	B	C	D	E	F	G
1							
2		Amortization Schedule for a 30-Year Mortgage					
3							
4	A 30-year mortgage specifies an annual interest rate of 8 percent						
5	and a loan amount of $100,000. What are the monthly interest and principal payments?						
6	Hint: Use the Excel functions IPMT and PPMT.						
7							
8	After 10 years, i.e., for the 120th payment interest and principal payments are:						
9							
10		-$585.82	=IPMT(0.08/12,120,360,100000,0)				
11							
12		-$147.95	=PPMT(0.08/12,120,360,100000,0)				
13							
14							
15	After 20 years, i.e., for the 240th payment interest and principal payments are:						
16							
17		-$405.38	=IPMT(0.08/12,240,360,100000,0)				
18							
19		-$328.39	=PPMT(0.08/12,240,360,100000,0)				
20							
21							

	A	B	C	D	E	F	G
1							
2		Remaining Balance for a 30-Year Mortgage					
3							
4	A 30-year mortgage specifies an annual interest rate of 8 percent						
5	and a loan amount of $100,000. What is the remaining balance?						
6	Hint: Use the Excel function CUMPRINC.						
7							
8	After 8 years and 4 months, the remaining balance is the present value of payment						
9	number 101 through payment number 360.						
10							
11		−$90,504.68	=CUMPRINC(0.08/12,360,100000,101,360,0)				
12							
13	After 16 years and 8 months, the remaining balance is the present value of payment						
14	number 201 through payment number 360.						
15							
16		−$72,051.18	=CUMPRINC(0.08/12,360,100000,201,360,0)				
17							
18							

FIXED-RATE MORTGAGE PREPAYMENT AND REFINANCING

mortgage prepayment
Paying off all or part of outstanding mortgage principal ahead of its amortization schedule.

A mortgage borrower has the right to pay off an outstanding mortgage at any time. This right is similar to the call feature on corporate bonds, whereby the issuer can buy back outstanding bonds at a prespecified call price. Paying off a mortgage ahead of its amortization schedule is called **mortgage prepayment**.

Prepayment can be motivated by a variety of factors. A homeowner may pay off a mortgage in order to sell the property when a family moves because of, say, new employment or retirement. After the death of a spouse, a surviving family member may pay off a mortgage with an insurance benefit. These are examples of mortgage prepayment for personal reasons. However, mortgage prepayments often occur for a purely financial reason: an existing mortgage loan may be refinanced at a lower interest rate when a lower rate becomes available.

Consider a 30-year, $100,000 fixed-rate 8 percent mortgage with a monthly payment of $733.76. Suppose that, 10 years into the mortgage, market interest rates have fallen, and the financing rate on new 20-year mortgages is 6.5 percent. After 10 years (120 months), the remaining balance for the original $100,000 mortgage is $87,724.70. The monthly payment on a new 20-year, $90,000 fixed-rate 6.5 percent mortgage is $671.02, which is $62.74 less than the $733.76 monthly payment on the old 8 percent mortgage with 20 years of payments remaining. Thus, a homeowner could profit by prepaying the original 8 percent mortgage and refinancing with a new 20-year, 6.5 percent mortgage. Monthly payments would be lower by $62.75, and the $2,275.30 difference between the new $90,000 mortgage balance and the old $87,724.70 mortgage balance would defray any refinancing costs.

As this example suggests, during periods of falling interest rates, mortgage refinancings are an important reason for mortgage prepayments. The nearby *Investment Updates* box presents a *Wall Street Journal* article discussing the merits of mortgage refinancing.

The possibility of prepayment and refinancing is an advantage to mortgage borrowers but a disadvantage to mortgage investors. For example, consider investors who supply funds to write mortgages at a financing rate of 8 percent. Suppose that mortgage interest rates later fall to 6.5 percent, and, consequently, homeowners rush to prepay their 8 percent mortgages so as to refinance at 6.5 percent. Mortgage investors recover their outstanding investment principal from the prepayments, but the rate of return that they can realize on a new investment is reduced because mortgages can now be written only at the new 6.5 percent financing rate. The possibility that falling interest rates will set off a wave of mortgage refinancings is an ever-present risk that mortgage investors must face.

20.3 Government National Mortgage Association

Government National Mortgage Association (GNMA)
Government agency charged with promoting liquidity in the home mortgage market.

fully modified mortgage pool
Mortgage pool that guarantees timely payment of interest and principal.

prepayment risk
Uncertainty faced by mortgage investors regarding early payment of mortgage principal and interest.

In 1968, Congress established the **Government National Mortgage Association (GNMA)**, colloquially called "Ginnie Mae," as a government agency within the Department of Housing and Urban Development (HUD). GNMA was charged with the mission of promoting liquidity in the secondary market for home mortgages. Liquidity is the ability of investors to buy and sell securities quickly at competitive market prices. Essentially, mortgages repackaged into mortgage pools are a more liquid investment product than the original unpooled mortgages. GNMA has successfully sponsored the repackaging of several trillion dollars of mortgages into hundreds of thousands of mortgage-backed securities pools.

GNMA mortgage pools are based on mortgages issued under programs administered by the Federal Housing Administration (FHA), the Veteran's Administration (VA), and the Farmer's Home Administration (FmHA). Mortgages in GNMA pools are said to be **fully modified** because GNMA guarantees bondholders full and timely payment of both principal and interest even in the event of default of the underlying mortgages. The GNMA guarantee augments guarantees already provided by the FHA, VA, and FmHA. Since GNMA, FHA, VA, and FmHA are all agencies of the federal government, GNMA mortgage passthroughs are free of default risk. But while investors in GNMA passthroughs do not face default risk, they still face **prepayment risk**.

GNMA operates in cooperation with private underwriters certified by GNMA to create mortgage pools. The underwriters originate or otherwise acquire the mortgages to form a pool. After verifying that the mortgages comply with GNMA requirements, GNMA authorizes the underwriter to issue mortgage-backed securities with a GNMA guarantee.

As a simplified example of how a GNMA pool operates, consider a hypothetical GNMA fully modified mortgage pool containing only a single mortgage. After obtaining approval from GNMA, the pool has a GNMA guarantee and is called a *GNMA bond*. The underwriter then sells the bond, and the buyer is entitled to receive all mortgage payments, less servicing and guarantee fees. If a mortgage payment occurs ahead of schedule, the early payment is passed through to the GNMA bondholder. If a payment is late, GNMA makes a timely payment to the bondholder. If any mortgage principal is prepaid, the early payment is passed through to the bondholder. If a default occurs, GNMA settles with the bondholder by making full payment of remaining mortgage principal. In effect, to a GNMA bondholder, mortgage default is the same thing as a prepayment.

When originally issued, the minimum denomination of a GNMA mortgage-backed bond is $25,000 with subsequent increments of $5,000. The minimum size for a GNMA mortgage pool is $1 million, although it could be much larger. Thus, for example, a GNMA mortgage pool might conceivably represent only 40 bonds with an initial bond principal of $25,000 par value per bond. However, initial bond principal only specifies a bond's share of mortgage pool principal. Over time, mortgage-backed bond principal declines because of scheduled mortgage amortization and mortgage prepayments.

GNMA CLONES

While GNMA is perhaps the best-known guarantor of mortgage-backed securities, two government-sponsored enterprises (GSEs) are also significant mortgage repackaging sponsors. These are the **Federal Home Loan Mortgage Corporation (FHLMC)**, colloquially called "Freddie Mac," and the **Federal National Mortgage Association (FNMA)**, called "Fannie Mae." FHLMC was chartered by Congress in 1970 to increase mortgage credit availability for residential housing. It was originally owned by the Federal Home Loan Banks operated under direction of the U.S. Treasury. But in 1989, FHLMC was allowed to become a private corporation with an issue of common stock. Freddie Mac stock trades on the New York Stock Exchange under the ticker symbol FRE.

The Federal National Mortgage Association was originally created in 1938 as a government-owned corporation of the United States. Thirty years later, FNMA was split into two government corporations: GNMA and FNMA. Soon after, in 1970, FNMA was allowed to become a private corporation and has since grown to become one of the major financial corporations in the United States. Fannie Mae stock trades on the New York Stock Exchange under the ticker symbol FNM.

Like GNMA, both FHLMC and FNMA operate with qualified underwriters who accumulate mortgages into pools financed by an issue of bonds that entitle bondholders to cash flows generated by mortgages in the pools, less the standard servicing and guarantee fees. However, the guarantees on FHLMC and FNMA passthroughs are not exactly the same as for GNMA passthroughs. Essentially, FHLMC and FNMA are only government-sponsored enterprises, whereas GNMA is a government agency. Congress may be less willing to rescue a financially strapped GSE.

Before June 1990, FHLMC guaranteed timely payment of interest but only *eventual* payment of principal on its mortgage-backed bonds. However, beginning in June 1990, FHLMC began its Gold program whereby it guaranteed timely payment of both interest and principal. Therefore, FHLMC Gold mortgage-backed bonds are fully modified passthrough securities. FNMA guarantees timely payment of both interest and principal on its mortgage-backed bonds, and, therefore, these are also fully modified passthrough securities. But since FHLMC and FNMA are only GSEs, their fully modified passthroughs do not carry the same default protection as GNMA fully modified passthroughs.

Visit the GNMA and HUD
Web sites at
www.ginniemae.gov
www.hud.gov

Federal Home Loan Mortgage Corporation (FHLMC) and **Federal National Mortgage Association (FNMA)**
Government-sponsored enterprises charged with promoting liquidity in the home mortgage market.

Check out the FNMA and
FHLMC Web sites at
www.fanniemae.com
www.freddiemac.com

CHECK THIS

20.3a Look up prices for Freddie Mac (FHLMC) and Fannie Mae (FNMA) common stock under their ticker symbols FRE and FNM in *The Wall Street Journal*.

20.4 Public Securities Association Mortgage Prepayment Model

prepayment rate
The probability that a mortgage will be prepaid during a given year.

Mortgage prepayments are typically described by stating a **prepayment rate**, which is the probability that a mortgage will be prepaid in a given year. The greater the prepayment rate for a mortgage pool, the faster the mortgage pool principal is paid off, and the more rapid is the decline of bond principal for bonds supported by the underlying mortgage pool. Historical experience shows that prepayment rates can vary substantially from year to year depending on mortgage type and various economic and demographic factors.

Conventional industry practice states prepayment rates using a prepayment model specified by the Public Securities Association (PSA). According to this model, prepayment rates are stated as a percentage of a PSA benchmark. The PSA benchmark specifies an annual prepayment rate of .2 percent in month 1 of a mortgage, .4 percent in month 2, then .6 percent in month 3, and so on. The annual prepayment rate continues to rise by .2 percent per month until reaching an annual prepayment rate of 6 percent in month 30 of a mortgage. Thereafter, the benchmark prepayment rate remains constant at 6 percent per year. This PSA benchmark represents a mortgage prepayment schedule called 100 PSA, which means 100 percent of the PSA benchmark. Deviations from the 100 PSA benchmark are stated as a percentage of the benchmark. For example, 200 PSA means 200 percent of the 100 PSA benchmark, and it doubles all prepayment rates relative to the benchmark. Similarly, 50 PSA means 50 percent of the 100 PSA benchmark, halving all prepayment rates relative to the benchmark. Prepayment rate schedules illustrating 50 PSA, 100 PSA, and 200 PSA are graphically presented in Figure 20.2.

Visit the Public Securities Association at
www.bondmarkets.com

seasoned mortgages
Mortgages over 30 months old.

Based on historical experience, the PSA prepayment model makes an important distinction between **seasoned mortgages** and **unseasoned mortgages**. In the PSA model, unseasoned mortgages are those less than 30 months old with rising prepayment rates. Seasoned mortgages are those over 30 months old with constant prepayment rates.

unseasoned mortgages
Mortgages less than 30 months old.

Prepayment rates in the PSA model are stated as **conditional prepayment rates (CPRs)**, since they are conditional on the age of mortgages in a pool. For example, the CPR for a seasoned 100 PSA mortgage is 6 percent, which represents a 6 percent probability of mortgage prepayment in a given year. By convention, the probability of prepayment in a given month is stated as a *single monthly mortality (SMM)*. SMM is calculated using a CPR as follows:

conditional prepayment rate (CPR)
The prepayment rate for a mortgage pool conditional on the age of the mortgages in the pool.

$$SMM = 1 - (1 - CPR)^{1/12} \qquad (20.2)$$

For example, the SMM corresponding to a seasoned 100 PSA mortgage with a 6 percent CPR is .5143 percent, which is calculated as:

$$SMM = 1 - (1 - .06)^{1/12}$$
$$= .5143\%$$

As another example, the SMM corresponding to an unseasoned 100 PSA mortgage in month 20 of the mortgage with a 4 percent CPR is .3396 percent, which is calculated as:

$$SMM = 1 - (1 - .04)^{1/12} = .3396\%$$

average life
Average time for a mortgage in a pool to be paid off.

Some mortgages in a pool are prepaid earlier than average, some are prepaid later than average, and some are not prepaid at all. The **average life** of a mortgage in a pool is the

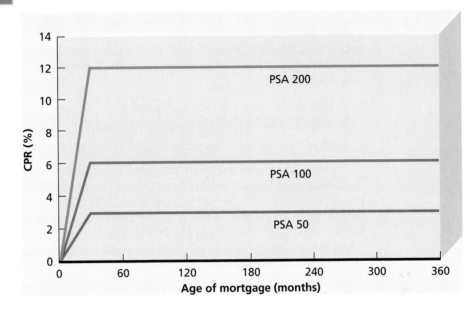

average time for a single mortgage in a pool to be paid off, either by prepayment or by making scheduled payments until maturity. Because prepayment shortens the life of a mortgage, the average life of a mortgage is usually much less than a mortgage's stated maturity. We can calculate a mortgage's projected average life by assuming a particular prepayment schedule. For example, the average life of a mortgage in a pool of 30-year mortgages, assuming several PSA prepayment schedules, is stated immediately below.

Prepayment Schedule	Average Mortgage Life (years)
50 PSA	20.40
100 PSA	14.68
200 PSA	8.87
400 PSA	4.88

Notice that an average life ranges from slightly less than 5 years for 400 PSA prepayments to slightly more than 20 years for 50 PSA prepayments.[1]

Bear in mind that these are expected averages given a particular prepayment schedule. Since prepayments are somewhat unpredictable, the average life of a mortgage in any specific pool is likely to deviate somewhat from an expected average.

CHECK THIS

20.4a Referring to Figure 20.2, what are the CPRs for seasoned 50 PSA, 200 PSA, and 400 PSA mortgages?

20.4b Referring to Figure 20.2, what is the CPR for an unseasoned 200 PSA mortgage in month 20 of the mortgage?

20.4c Referring to Figure 20.2, what is the CPR for an unseasoned 400 PSA mortgage in month 20 of the mortgage?

[1]Formulas used to calculate average mortgage life are complicated and depend on the assumed prepayment model. For this reason, average life formulas are omitted here.

20.5 Cash Flow Analysis of GNMA Fully Modified Mortgage Pools

Each month, GNMA mortgage-backed bond investors receive pro rata shares of cash flows derived from fully modified mortgage pools. Each monthly cash flow has three distinct components:

1. Payment of interest on outstanding mortgage principal.
2. Scheduled amortization of mortgage principal.
3. Mortgage principal prepayments.

As a sample GNMA mortgage pool, consider a $10 million pool of 30-year, 8 percent mortgages financed by the sale of 100 bonds at a par value price of $100,000 per bond. For simplicity, we ignore servicing and guarantee fees. The decline in bond principal for these GNMA bonds is graphed in Figure 20.3A for the cases of prepayment rates following 50 PSA, 100 PSA, 200 PSA, and 400 PSA schedules. In Figure 20.3A, notice that 50 PSA prepayments yield a nearly straight-line amortization of bond principal. Also notice that for the extreme case of 400 PSA prepayments, over 90 percent of bond principal is amortized within 10 years of mortgage pool origination.

Monthly cash flows for these GNMA bonds are graphed in Figure 20.3B for the cases of 50 PSA, 100 PSA, 200 PSA, and 400 PSA prepayment schedules. In Figure 20.3B, notice the sharp spike in monthly cash flows associated with 400 PSA prepayments at about month 30. Lesser PSA prepayment rates blunt the spike and level the cash flows.

As shown in Figures 20.3A and 20.3B, prepayments significantly affect the cash flow characteristics of GNMA bonds. However, these illustrations assume that prepayment schedules remain unchanged over the life of a mortgage pool. This can be unrealistic, since prepayment rates often change from those originally forecast. For example, sharply falling interest rates could easily cause a jump in prepayment rates from 100 PSA to 400 PSA. Since large interest rate movements are unpredictable, future prepayment rates can also be unpredictable. Consequently, GNMA mortgage-backed bond investors face substantial cash flow uncertainty. This makes GNMA bonds an unsuitable investment for many investors, especially relatively unsophisticated investors unaware of the risks involved. Nevertheless, GNMA bonds offer higher yields than U.S. Treasury bonds, which makes them attractive to professional fixed-income portfolio managers.

CHECK THIS

20.5a GNMA bond investors face significant cash flow uncertainty. Why might cash flow uncertainty be a problem for many portfolio managers?

20.5b Why might cash flow uncertainty be less of a problem for investors with a very long-term investment horizon?

MACAULAY DURATIONS FOR GNMA MORTGAGE-BACKED BONDS

Macaulay duration
A measure of interest rate risk for fixed-income securities.

For mortgage pool investors, prepayment risk is important because it complicates the effects of interest rate risk. With falling interest rates, prepayments speed up and the average life of mortgages in a pool shortens. Similarly, with rising interest rates, prepayments slow down and average mortgage life lengthens. Recall from a previous chapter that interest rate risk for a bond is often measured by **Macaulay duration**. However, Macaulay duration

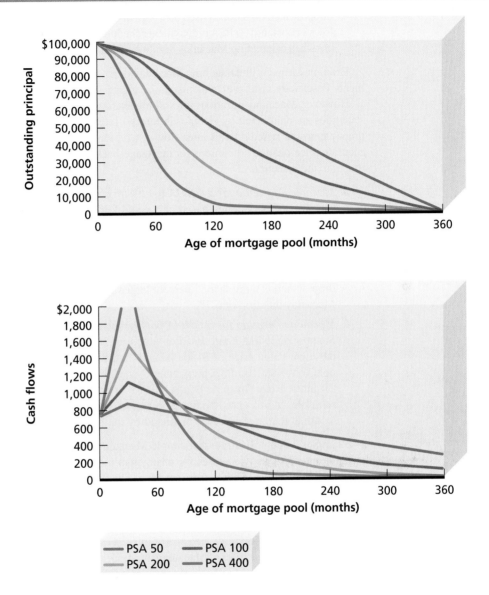

assumes a fixed schedule of cash flow payments. But the schedule of cash flow payments for mortgage-backed bonds is not fixed because it is affected by mortgage prepayments, which in turn are affected by interest rates. For this reason, Macaulay duration is a deficient measure of interest rate risk for mortgage-backed bonds. The following examples illustrate the deficiency of Macaulay duration when it is unrealistically assumed that interest rates do not affect mortgage prepayment rates.[2]

1. *Macaulay duration for a GNMA bond with zero prepayments.* Suppose a GNMA bond is based on a pool of 30-year, 8 percent fixed-rate mortgages. Assuming an

[2]The Macaulay duration formula for a mortgage is not presented here since, as our discussion suggests, its usage is not recommended.

8 percent interest rate, their price is equal to their initial par value of $100,000. The Macaulay duration for these bonds is 9.56 years.

2. *Macaulay duration for a GNMA bond with a constant 100 PSA prepayment schedule.* Suppose a GNMA bond based on a pool of 30-year, 8 percent fixed-rate mortgages follows a constant 100 PSA prepayment schedule. Accounting for this prepayment schedule when calculating Macaulay duration, we obtain a Macaulay duration of 6.77 years.

Examples 1 and 2 illustrate how Macaulay duration can be affected by mortgage prepayments. Essentially, faster prepayments cause earlier cash flows and shorten Macaulay durations.

However, Macaulay durations are still misleading because they assume that prepayment schedules are unaffected by changes in interest rates. When falling interest rates speed up prepayments, or rising interest rates slow down prepayments, Macaulay durations yield inaccurate price-change predictions for mortgage-backed securities. The following examples illustrate the inaccuracy.

3. *Macaulay duration for a GNMA bond with changing PSA prepayment schedules.* Suppose a GNMA bond based on a pool of 30-year, 8 percent fixed-rate mortgages has a par value price of $100,000 and that, with no change in interest rates, the pool follows a 100 PSA prepayment schedule. Further suppose that when the market interest rate for these bonds rises to 9 percent, prepayments fall to a 50 PSA schedule. In this case, the price of the bond falls to $92,644, representing a 7.36 percent price drop, which is more than .5 percent larger than the drop predicted by the bond's Macaulay duration of 6.77.

4. *Macaulay duration for a GNMA bond with changing PSA prepayment schedules.* Suppose a GNMA bond based on a pool of 30-year, 8 percent fixed-rate mortgages has a par value price of $100,000 and that, with no change in interest rates, the pool follows a 100 PSA prepayment schedule. Further suppose that when the market interest rate for these bonds falls to 7 percent, prepayments rise to a 200 PSA schedule. In this case, the bond price rises to $105,486, which is over 1.2 percent less than the price increase predicted by the bond's Macaulay duration of 6.77.

Examples 3 and 4 illustrate that simple Macaulay durations overpredict price increases and underpredict price decreases for changes in mortgage-backed bond prices caused by changing interest rates. These errors are caused by the fact that Macaulay duration does not account for prepayment rates changing in response to interest rate changes. The severity of these errors depends on how strongly interest rates affect prepayment rates. Historical experience indicates that interest rates significantly affect prepayment rates and that Macaulay duration is a very conservative measure of interest rate risk for mortgage-backed securities.

effective duration for MBS

Duration measure that accounts for how mortgage prepayments are affected by changes in interest rates.

To correct the deficiencies of Macaulay duration, a method often used in practice to assess interest rate risk for mortgage-backed securities is to first develop projections regarding mortgage prepayments. Projecting prepayments for mortgages requires analyzing both economic and demographic variables. In particular, it is necessary to estimate how prepayment rates will respond to changes in interest rates. A duration model that accounts for these factors is called **effective duration**. In practice, effective duration is used to calculate predicted prices for mortgage-backed securities based on hypothetical interest rate and prepayment scenarios.

CHECK THIS

20.5c   Why is it important for portfolio managers to know by how much a change in interest rates will affect mortgage prepayments?

20.5d   Why is it important for portfolio managers to know by how much a change in interest rates will affect mortgage-backed bond prices?

20.6 Collateralized Mortgage Obligations

collateralized mortgage obligations (CMOs)
Securities created by splitting mortgage pool cash flows according to specific allocation rules.

When a mortgage pool is created, cash flows from the pool are often carved up and distributed according to various allocation rules. Mortgage-backed securities representing specific rules for allocating mortgage cash flows are called **collateralized mortgage obligations (CMOs)**. Indeed, a CMO is defined by the rule that created it. Like all mortgage passthroughs, primary collateral for CMOs are the mortgages in the underlying pool. This is true no matter how the rules for cash flow distribution are actually specified.

The three best-known types of CMO structures using specific rules to carve up mortgage pool cash flows are (1) interest-only strips (IOs) and principal-only strips (POs), (2) sequential CMOs, and (3) protected amortization class securities (PACs). Each of these CMO structures is discussed immediately below. Before beginning, however, we retell an old Wall Street joke that pertains to CMOs: Question: "How many investment bankers does it take to *sell* a lightbulb?" Answer: "401; one to hit it with a hammer, and 400 to sell off the pieces."

The moral of the story is that mortgage-backed securities can be repackaged in many ways, and the resulting products are often quite complex. Even the basic types we consider here are significantly more complicated than the basic fixed-income instruments we considered in earlier chapters. Consequently, we do not go into great detail regarding the underlying calculations for CMOs. Instead, we examine only the basic properties of the most commonly encountered CMOs.

INTEREST-ONLY AND PRINCIPAL-ONLY MORTGAGE STRIPS

interest-only strips (IOs)
Securities that pay only the interest cash flows to investors.

principal-only strips (POs)
Securities that pay only the principal cash flows to investors.

Perhaps the simplest rule for carving up mortgage pool cash flows is to separate payments of principal from payments of interest. Mortgage-backed securities paying only the interest component of mortgage pool cash flows are called **interest-only strips**, or simply **IOs**. Mortgage-backed securities paying only the principal component of mortgage pool cash flows are called **principal-only strips**, or simply **POs**. Mortgage strips are more complicated than straight mortgage passthroughs. In particular, IO strips and PO strips behave quite differently in response to changes in prepayment rates and interest rates.

Let us begin an examination of mortgage strips by considering a $100,000 par value GNMA bond that has been stripped into a separate IO bond and a PO bond. The whole GNMA bond receives a pro rata share of all cash flows from a pool of 30-year, 8 percent mortgages. From the whole bond cash flow, the IO bond receives the interest component, and the PO bond receives the principal component. The sum of IO and PO cash flows reproduces the whole bond cash flow.

Assuming various PSA prepayment schedules, cash flows to IO strips are illustrated in Figure 20.4A, and cash flows to PO strips are illustrated in Figure 20.4B. Holding the interest rate constant at 8 percent, IO and PO strip values for various PSA prepayment schedules are listed immediately below:

Prepayment Schedule	IO Strip Value	PO Strip Value
50 PSA	$63,102.80	$36,897.20
100 PSA	53,726.50	46,273.50
200 PSA	41,366.24	58,633.76
400 PSA	28,764.16	71,235.84

Notice that total bond value is $100,000 for all prepayment schedules because the interest rate is unchanged from its original 8 percent value. Nevertheless, even with no change in interest rates, faster prepayments imply *lower* IO strip values and *higher* PO strip values, and vice versa.

FIGURE 20.4 Cash Flows for $100,000 Par Value 30-Year, 8 Percent Bonds

IO Strip

PO Strip

— PSA 50 — PSA 100
— PSA 200 — PSA 400

There is a simple reason why PO strip value rises with faster prepayment rates. Essentially, the only cash flow uncertainty facing PO strip holders is the timing of PO cash flows, not the total amount of cash flows. No matter what prepayment schedule applies, total cash flows paid to PO strip holders over the life of the pool will be equal to the initial principal of $100,000. Therefore, PO strip value increases as principal is paid earlier to PO strip holders because of the time value of money.

In contrast, IO strip holders face considerable uncertainty regarding the total amount of IO cash flows that they will receive. Faster prepayments reduce principal more rapidly, thereby reducing interest payments since interest is paid only on outstanding principal. The best that IO strip holders could hope for is that no mortgages are prepaid, which would maximize total interest payments. Prepayments reduce total interest payments. Indeed, in the extreme case, where all mortgages in a pool are prepaid, IO cash flows stop completely.

The effects of changing interest rates compounded by changing prepayment rates are illustrated by considering IO and PO strips from a $100,000 par value GNMA bond based on a pool of 30-year, 8 percent mortgages. First, suppose that an interest rate of 8 percent yields a 100 PSA prepayment schedule. Also suppose that a lower interest rate of 7 percent yields 200 PSA prepayments, and a higher interest rate of 9 percent yields 50 PSA prepayments. The resulting whole bond values and separate IO and PO strip values for these combinations of interest rates and prepayment rates are listed immediately below:

Interest Rate	Prepayments	IO Strip Value	PO Strip Value	Whole Bond Value
9%	50 PSA	$59,124.79	$35,519.47	$ 94,644.26
8	100 PSA	53,726.50	46,273.50	100,000.00
7	200 PSA	43,319.62	62,166.78	105,486.40

When the interest rate increases from 8 percent to 9 percent, total bond value falls by $5,355.74. This results from the PO strip price *falling* by $10,754.03 and the IO strip price *increasing* by $5,398.29. When the interest rate decreases from 8 percent to 7 percent, total bond value rises by $5,486.40. This results from the PO strip price *increasing* by $15,893.28 and the IO strip price *falling* by $10,406.88. Thus, PO strip values change in the same direction as the whole bond value, but the PO price change is larger. Notice that the IO strip price changes in the opposite direction of the whole bond and PO strip price change.

CHECK THIS

20.6a Suppose a $100,000 mortgage financed at 9 percent (.75 percent monthly) is paid off in the first month after issuance. In this case, what are the cash flows to an IO strip and a PO strip from this mortgage?

SEQUENTIAL COLLATERALIZED MORTGAGE OBLIGATIONS

sequential CMOs
Securities created by splitting a mortgage pool into a number of slices, called tranches.

One problem with investing in mortgage-backed bonds is the limited range of maturities available. An early method developed to deal with this problem is the creation of **sequential CMOs**. Sequential CMOs carve a mortgage pool into a number of tranches. *Tranche*, the French word for slice, is a commonly used financial term to describe the division of a whole into various parts. Sequential CMOs are defined by rules that distribute mortgage pool cash flows to sequential tranches. While almost any number of tranches are possible, a basic sequential CMO structure might have four tranches: A-tranche, B-tranche, C-tranche, and Z-tranche. Each tranche is entitled to a share of mortgage pool principal and interest on that share of principal.

As a hypothetical sequential CMO structure, suppose a 30-year, 8 percent GNMA bond initially represents $100,000 of mortgage principal. Cash flows to this whole bond are then carved up according to a sequential CMO structure with A-, B-, C-, and Z-tranches. The A-, B-, and C-tranches initially represent $30,000 of mortgage principal each. The Z-tranche initially represents $10,000 of principal. The sum of all four tranches reproduces the original whole bond principal of $100,000. The cash flows from the whole bond are passed through to each tranche according to the following rules:

Rule 1: Mortgage principal payments. All payments of mortgage principal, including scheduled amortization and prepayments, are first paid to the A-tranche. When all A-tranche principal is paid off, subsequent payments of mortgage principal are then paid to the B-tranche. After all B-tranche principal is paid off, all principal payments are then paid to the C-tranche. Finally, when all C-tranche principal is paid off, all principal payments go to the Z-tranche.

Rule 2: Interest payments. All tranches receive interest payments in proportion to the amount of outstanding principal in each tranche. Interest on A-, B-, and C-tranche principal is passed through immediately to A-, B-, and C-tranches. Interest on Z-tranche principal is paid to the A-tranche as cash in exchange for the transfer of an equal amount of principal from the A-tranche to the Z-tranche. After A-tranche principal is fully paid, interest on Z-tranche principal is paid to the B-tranche in exchange for an equal amount of principal from the B-tranche to the Z-tranche. This process continues sequentially through each tranche.

For example, the first month's cash flows from a single whole bond are allocated as follows. Scheduled mortgage payments yield a whole bond cash flow of $733.76, which is divided between $67.10 principal amortization and $666.67 payment of interest. All scheduled principal amortization is paid to the A-tranche, and A-tranche principal is reduced by a like amount. Since outstanding principal was *initially* equal to $30,000 for the A-, B-, and C-tranche bonds, each of these tranches receives an interest payment of $30,000 × .08/12 = $200. In addition, the Z-tranche interest payment of $10,000 × .08/12 = $66.67 is paid to the A-tranche in cash in exchange for transferring $66.67 of principal to the Z-tranche. In summary, A-tranche principal is reduced by $67.10 + $66.67 = $133.77 plus any prepayments, and Z-tranche principal is increased by $66.67.

Remaining principal amounts for A-, B-, C-, and Z-tranches, assuming 100 PSA prepayments, are graphed in Figure 20.5A. Corresponding cash flows for the A-, B-, C-, and Z-tranches, assuming 100 PSA prepayments, are graphed in Figure 20.5B.

CHECK THIS

20.6b Figures 20.5A and 20.5B assume a 100 PSA prepayment schedule. How would these figures change for a 200 PSA prepayment schedule or a 50 PSA prepayment schedule?

20.6c While A-, B-, and C-tranche principal is being paid down, Z-tranche interest is used to acquire principal for the Z-tranche. What is the growth rate of Z-tranche principal during this period?

protected amortization class bond (PAC)
Mortgage-backed security that takes priority for scheduled payments of principal.

PAC support bond
Mortgage-backed security that has subordinate priority for scheduled payments of principal. Also called *PAC companion bond.*

PROTECTED AMORTIZATION CLASS BONDS

Another popular security used to alleviate the problem of cash flow uncertainty when investing in mortgage-backed bonds is a **protected amortization class (PAC) bond**, or simply **PAC**. Like all CMOs, PAC bonds are defined by specific rules that carve up cash flows from a mortgage pool. Essentially, a PAC bond carves out a slice of a mortgage pool's cash flows according to a rule that gives PAC bondholders first priority entitlement to promised PAC cash flows. Consequently, PAC cash flows are predictable so long as mortgage pool prepayments remain within a predetermined band. PAC bonds are attractive to investors who require a high degree of cash flow certainty from their investments.

After PAC bondholders receive their promised cash flows, residual cash flows from the mortgage pool are paid to non-PAC bonds, often referred to as **PAC support bonds** or *PAC companion bonds.* In effect, almost all cash flow uncertainty is concentrated in the non-PAC bonds. The non-PAC bond supports the PAC bond and serves the same purpose as a

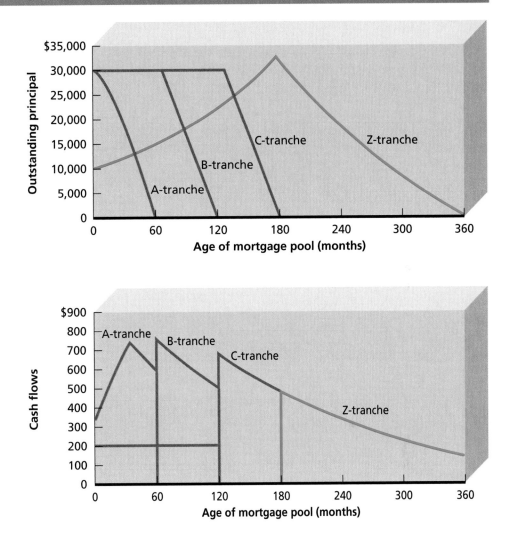

FIGURE 20.5 Sequential CMO Principal and Cash Flows for a $100,000 Par Value GNMA Bond

Z-tranche bond in a sequential CMO structure. For this reason, a non-PAC bond is sometimes called a PAC Z-tranche.

Creation of a PAC bond entails three steps. First, we must specify two PSA prepayment schedules that form the upper and lower prepayment bounds of a PAC bond. These bounds define a **PAC collar**. For example, suppose we create a single PAC bond from a new $100,000 par value GNMA bond based on a pool of 30-year fixed-rate mortgages. The PAC collar specifies a 100 PSA prepayment schedule as a lower bound and a 300 PSA prepayment schedule as an upper bound. Cash flows to the PAC bond are said to enjoy protected amortization so long as mortgage pool prepayments remain within this 100–300 PSA collar.

Our second step in creating a PAC bond is to calculate principal-only (PO) cash flows from our 30-year, $100,000 par value GNMA bond, assuming 100 PSA and 300 PSA prepayment schedules. These PO cash flows, which include both scheduled amortization and

PAC collar
Range defined by upper and lower prepayment schedules of a PAC bond.

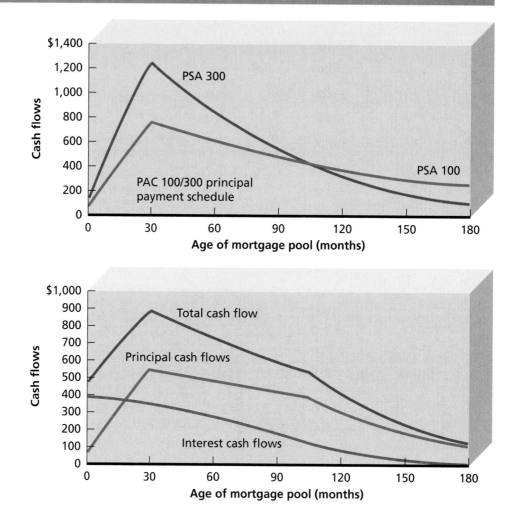

prepayments, are plotted in Figure 20.6A. In Figure 20.6A, notice that principal-only cash flows for 100 PSA and 300 PSA prepayment schedules intersect in month 103. Before the 103rd month, 300 PSA PO cash flows are greater. After that month, 100 PSA PO cash flows are greater. PAC bond cash flows are specified by the 100 PSA schedule before month 103 and the 300 PSA schedule after month 103. Because the PAC bond is specified by 100 PSA and 300 PSA prepayment schedules, it is called a PAC 100/300 bond.

Our third step is to specify the cash flows to be paid to PAC bondholders on a priority basis. PAC bondholders receive payments of principal according to the PAC collar's lower PSA prepayment schedule. For the PAC 100/300 bond in this example, principal payments are made according to the 100 PSA prepayment schedule until month 103, when the schedule switches to the 300 PSA prepayment schedule. The sum of all scheduled principal to be paid to PAC 100/300 bondholders represents total initial PAC bond principal. In addition to payment of principal, a PAC bondholder also receives payment of interest on outstanding PAC principal. For example, if the mortgage pool financing rate is 9 percent, the PAC bondholder receives an interest payment of .75 percent per month of outstanding PAC principal.

Total monthly cash flows paid to the PAC bond, including payments of principal and interest, are graphed in Figure 20.6B. As shown, total cash flow reaches a maximum in month 30, thereafter gradually declining. So long as mortgage pool prepayments remain within the 100/300 PSA prepayment collar, PAC bondholders will receive these cash flows exactly as originally specified.

PAC collars are usually sufficiently wide so that actual prepayments move outside the collar only infrequently. In the event that prepayments move outside a collar far enough to interfere with promised PAC cash flows, PAC bonds normally specify the following two contingency rules:

PAC contingency rule 1. When actual prepayments fall below a PAC collar's lower bound, there could be insufficient cash flow to satisfy a PAC bond's promised cash flow schedule. In this case, the PAC bond receives all available cash flow, and any shortfall is carried forward and paid on a first-priority basis from future cash flows. Non-PAC bonds receive no cash flows until all cumulative shortfalls to PAC bonds are paid off.

PAC contingency rule 2. When actual prepayments rise above a PAC collar's upper bound, it is possible that all outstanding principal for the non-PAC support bonds is paid off before the PAC bond. When all non-PAC principal is paid off, the PAC cash flow schedule is abandoned and all mortgage pool cash flows are paid to PAC bondholders.

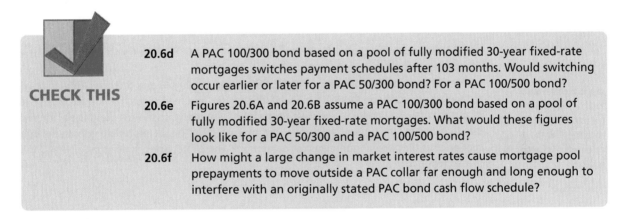

CHECK THIS

20.6d   A PAC 100/300 bond based on a pool of fully modified 30-year fixed-rate mortgages switches payment schedules after 103 months. Would switching occur earlier or later for a PAC 50/300 bond? For a PAC 100/500 bond?

20.6e   Figures 20.6A and 20.6B assume a PAC 100/300 bond based on a pool of fully modified 30-year fixed-rate mortgages. What would these figures look like for a PAC 50/300 and a PAC 100/500 bond?

20.6f   How might a large change in market interest rates cause mortgage pool prepayments to move outside a PAC collar far enough and long enough to interfere with an originally stated PAC bond cash flow schedule?

20.7   Yields for Mortgage-Backed Securities and Collateralized Mortgage Obligations

Yields for mortgage-backed securities (MBSs) and collateralized mortgage obligations (CMOs) for representative GNMA, FHLMC, and FNMA mortgage pools are published daily in *The Wall Street Journal*. Figure 20.7 is a sample listing. The first column lists the type of mortgage pool. For example, the first mortgage pool type is 30-year FMAC (i.e., Freddie Mac) Gold paying 5.5 percent interest on outstanding principal. The second mortgage pool type is 30-year FMAC Gold paying 6.0 percent interest on outstanding principal. Column 2 reports the price (in 32nds of a point) for the MBS. The third column is the change in the price from the previous day. The fourth column shows the estimated average life of the mortgages in the underlying pool. The fifth column gives the spread (in basis points) between the yield to maturity on the MBS and the yield on a U.S. Treasury note or

FIGURE 20.7   MBS Yields

Mortgage-Backed Securities

Indicative, not guaranteed; from Bear Stearns Cos./Street Pricing Service

RATE		PRICE (FEB) (PTS-32DS)	PRICE CHANGE (32DS)	AVG LIFE (YEARS)	SPRD TO AVG LIFE (YEARS)	SPREAD CHANGE (BPS)	PSA (PREPAY SPEED)	YIELD TO MAT*
30-year								
FMAC GOLD	5.5%	99-10	+08	7.8	130	−2	188	5.65
FMAC GOLD	6.0%	101-06	+08	5.6	143	−2	277	5.74
FMAC GOLD	6.5%	102-19	+05	4.2	144	−3	345	5.74
FNMA	5.5%	99-08	+08	7.6	129	−1	197	5.63
FNMA	6.0%	101-04	+08	5.1	138	−3	323	5.69
FNMA	6.5%	102-22	+05	4.1	134	−3	360	5.65
GNMA **	5.5%	100-26	+07	7.2	103	−1	201	5.37
GNMA **	6.0%	102-18	+08	5.8	112	−2	239	5.44
GNMA **	6.5%	104-14	+05	4.2	90	−5	329	5.21
15-year								
FMAC GOLD	5.0%	99-07	+09	5.5	87	−2	181	5.18
FNMA	5.0%	99-05	+09	5.5	85	−2	184	5.16
GNMA **	5.0%	99-30	+09	5.3	71	−2	182	5.02

*Extrapolated from benchmarks based on projections from Bear Stearns prepayment model, assuming interest rates remain unchanged. ** Government guaranteed.

Collateralized Mortgage Obligations

Spread of CMO yields above U.S. Treasury securities of comparable maturity, in basis points (100 basis points = 1 percentage point of interest)

MAT	SPREAD	CHG FROM PREV DAY
Sequentials		
2-year	100	...
5-year	125	...
7-year	127	...
10-year	132	...
20-year	116	...
PACS		
2-year	75	...
5-year	110	...
7-year	111	...
10-year	117	...
20-year	106	...

Source: *The Wall Street Journal,* January 4, 2006. Reprinted by permission of Dow Jones & Company, Inc., via Copyright Clearance Center, Inc. © 2006 Dow Jones & Company. All Rights Reserved Worldwide.

bond with a maturity similar to the average life of the MBS. Column 6 shows the change in this spread from the previous day.

cash flow yield
Yield to maturity for a mortgage-backed security conditional on an assumed prepayment pattern.

Finally, column 7 shows the assumed PSA prepayment rate and the last column shows the yield to maturity on the MBS calculated using the assumed prepayment rate. This yield to maturity is also known as the **cash flow yield**. Essentially, cash flow yield is the interest rate that equates the present value of all future cash flows on the mortgage pool to the current price of the pool, assuming a particular prepayment rate. Spread information on CMOs is also reported.

20.8   Summary and Conclusions

This chapter discusses the large and growing market for mortgage-backed securities. Many aspects of this market were covered, including the following items.

1. Most Americans finance their homes with mortgages. The buyer makes a down payment and borrows the remaining cost with a mortgage loan. Mortgages are often repackaged into mortgage-backed securities through a process called mortgage securitization. Currently, about half of all mortgages in the United States have been securitized, yet the risks involved in these investments are often misunderstood.

2. Most home mortgages are 15- or 30-year fixed-rate mortgages requiring constant monthly payments. The present value of all monthly payments is equal to the original amount of the mortgage loan. Each monthly payment has two components: payment of interest on outstanding mortgage principal and a scheduled pay-down of mortgage principal. The relative amounts of each component change throughout the

life of a mortgage. The interest payment component gradually declines, and the pay-down of principal component gradually increases.

3. A mortgage borrower has the right to pay off a mortgage early, which is called mortgage prepayment. Borrowers frequently prepay to refinance an existing mortgage at a lower interest rate. Prepayment and refinancing, advantages to mortgage borrowers, are disadvantages to mortgage investors. Thus, mortgage investors face prepayment risk.

4. In 1968, Congress established the Government National Mortgage Association (GNMA) as a government agency charged with promoting liquidity in the secondary market for home mortgages. GNMA is the largest single guarantor of mortgage-backed securities. Two government-sponsored enterprises (GSEs) are also significant mortgage repackaging sponsors: the Federal Home Loan Mortgage Corporation (FHLMC) and the Federal National Mortgage Association (FNMA).

5. Each month, GNMA, FHLMC, and FNMA mortgage-backed bond investors receive cash flows derived from fully modified mortgage pools. Each monthly cash flow has three distinct components: payment of interest on outstanding mortgage principal, scheduled amortization of mortgage principal, and mortgage principal prepayments.

6. Mortgage prepayments are stated as a prepayment rate. The greater the prepayment rate, the faster mortgage pool principal is paid off. Prepayment rates can vary substantially from year to year, depending on mortgage type and various economic and demographic factors. Conventional industry practice states prepayment rates using a prepayment model specified by the Public Securities Association (PSA). This model states prepayment rates as a percentage of a PSA benchmark, which represents an annual prepayment rate of 6 percent for seasoned mortgages, and is called 100 PSA. Deviations from the 100 PSA benchmark are stated as a percentage of the benchmark.

7. Prepayment risk complicates the effects of interest rate risk. Interest rate risk for a bond is related to its effective maturity as measured by Macaulay duration. However, Macaulay duration assumes a fixed schedule of cash flow payments. But the schedule of cash flow payments for mortgage-backed bonds is not fixed because it is affected by mortgage prepayments, which in turn are affected by interest rates. For this reason, Macaulay duration is a deficient measure of interest rate risk for mortgage-backed bonds.

8. Cash flows from mortgage pools are often carved up and distributed according to various rules. Mortgage-backed securities representing specific rules for allocating mortgage cash flows are called collateralized mortgage obligations (CMOs). The three best known types of CMO structures using specific rules to carve up mortgage pool cash flows are interest-only (IO) and principal-only (PO) strips, sequential CMOs, and protected amortization class securities (PACs).

9. Cash flow yields for mortgage-backed securities (MBSs) and collateralized mortgage obligations (CMOs) for GNMA, FHLMC, and FNMA mortgage pools are published daily in *The Wall Street Journal.* Cash flow yield for a mortgage-backed security corresponds to the yield to maturity for an ordinary bond. Essentially, cash flow yield is the interest rate that discounts all future expected cash flows from a mortgage pool to be equal to the price of the mortgage pool.

This chapter covered one of the more complex investments available, mortgage-backed securities (MBSs). Ironically, these investments are fairly complicated, but unlike most exotic instruments, the basic types of MBSs are very suitable for ordinary individual investors. In fact, GNMAs and similar investments are frequently recommended, and rightly so, for even very conservative investors.

However, as a practical matter, directly buying into mortgage pools is not practical for most individual investors. It is also probably unwise, because not all pools are equally risky in terms of prepayments, and analysis of individual pools is best left to experts. Instead, most investors in MBSs end up in mutual funds specializing in these instruments, and most of the major mutual fund families have such funds.

If you are interested in learning more about these investments, the Internet contains a large amount of information. The first places to visit are the Web sites for GNMA (www.ginniemae.gov), FNMA (www.fanniemae.com), and FHLMC (www.freddiemac.com). For much information on the home mortgage business, along with current mortgage rates across the country, try Mortgage Mag (www.mortgagemag.com). Some informative sites with good-to-excellent sections on mortgage-backed securities include Investing in Bonds (www.investinginbonds.com) and Bond Markets (www.bondmarkets.com). If you are thinking about a research project and need some data on mortgage-backed securities, look at what's available at Financial Data Services (www.dataonfindata.com).

Key Terms

Chapter Review Problems and Self-Test

1. **Mortgage Payments** What are the monthly payments on a 30-year, $150,000 mortgage if the mortgage rate is 6 percent? What portion of the first payment is interest? Principal?

2. **Mortgage Prepayments** Consider a 15-year, $210,000 mortgage with a 7 percent interest rate. After 10 years, the borrower (the mortgage issuer) pays it off. How much will the lender receive?

Answers to Self-Test Problems

1. This is a standard time value of money calculation in which we need to find an annuity-type payment. The present value is $150,000. The interest rate is .06/12 = .005, or .5 percent, per month. There is a total of 360 payments. Using the formula from the text, we have:

$$\text{Monthly payment} = \frac{\text{Mortgage amount} \times r/12}{1 - \dfrac{1}{(1 + r/12)^{T \times 12}}}$$

Plugging in $r = .06$ and $T = 30$, we get a payment of $899.33. The interest portion for a month is equal to the mortgage balance at the beginning of the month ($150,000 in this case) multiplied by the interest rate per month (.5 percent), or $150,000 × .005 = $750. The remaining portion of the payment, $899.33 − $750 = $149.33, goes to reduce the principal balance.

2. We first need to know the monthly payment. Here, the original balance is $210,000, the rate is 7 percent, and the original life is 15 years. Plugging in the numbers using the formula just above, check that we get a monthly payment of $1,887.54. From here, there are two ways to go. One is relatively easy; the other is relatively tedious. The tedious way would be to construct an amortization table for the mortgage and then locate the balance in the table. However, we need only a single balance, so there is a much faster way. After 10 years, we can treat this mortgage as though it were a five-year mortgage with payments of $1,887.54 and an interest rate of 7 percent. We can then solve for the mortgage balance using the same formula:

$$\text{Monthly payment} = \frac{\text{Mortgage balance} \times .07/12}{1 - \dfrac{1}{(1 + .07/12)^{5 \times 12}}} = \$1,887.54$$

Solving for the mortgage balance gets us $95,324.50.

Test Your Investments Quotient

1. **Fixed-Rate Mortgages**   Which of the following statements about fixed-rate mortgages is false?

   a. 15-year mortgages have higher monthly payments than 30-year mortgages.
   b. Scheduled monthly payments are constant over the life of the mortgage.
   c. Actual monthly payments may vary over the life of the mortgage.
   d. Actual monthly payments are never more than scheduled monthly payments.

2. **Fixed-Rate Mortgages**   The interest component of a monthly payment for a fixed-rate mortgage is

   a. Highest during the first year of the mortgage.
   b. Highest during the middle year of the mortgage.
   c. Highest during the last year of the mortgage.
   d. Constant throughout the life of the mortgage.

3. **Fixed-Rate Mortgages**   The principal reduction component of a monthly payment for a fixed-rate mortgage is

   a. Highest during the first year of the mortgage.
   b. Highest during the middle year of the mortgage.
   c. Highest during the last year of the mortgage.
   d. Constant throughout the life of the mortgage.

4. **Fixed-Rate Mortgages**   The remaining balance on a 30-year, $100,000 mortgage loan financed at 8 percent after the 180th payment is (no calculation necessary)

   a. $100,000
   b. $50,000
   c. $76,782
   d. $23,219

5. **Fixed-Rate Mortgages**   Which of the following mortgages has the lowest monthly payment (no calculation necessary)?

   a. 30-year, 8 percent
   b. 30-year, 10 percent
   c. 15-year, 8 percent
   d. 15-year, 10 percent

6. **Fixed-Rate Mortgages**   Which of the following mortgages will pay the smallest total interest over the life of the mortgage (no calculation necessary)?

   a. 30-year, 8 percent
   b. 30-year, 10 percent
   c. 15-year, 8 percent
   d. 15-year, 10 percent

7. **Fixed-Rate Mortgages**   Which of the following mortgages will have the largest remaining balance after 180 monthly payments (no calculation necessary)?

   a. 30-year, 8 percent
   b. 30-year, 10 percent
   c. 15-year, 8 percent
   d. 15-year, 10 percent

8. **GNMA Bonds**   Mortgages in GNMA pools are said to be fully modified because GNMA guarantees bondholders which of the following?

   a. A minimum rate of return on their investment.
   b. A modified schedule of cash flows over the life of the pool.
   c. Full and timely payment of both principal and interest in the event of default.
   d. Eventual payment of both principal and interest in the event of default.

9. **GNMA Bonds**   Which of the following is not a source of risk for GNMA mortgage pool investors?

   a. Prepayment risk
   b. Default risk
   c. Interest rate risk
   d. Reinvestment risk

10. **GNMA Bonds**   Which one of the following sets of features most accurately describes a GNMA mortgage passthrough security?

	Average Life	Payment Frequency	Credit Risk
a.	Predictable	Monthly	High
b.	Predictable	Semiannual	Low
c.	Unpredictable	Monthly	Low
d.	Unpredictable	Semiannual	Low

11. **GNMA Bonds**   In contrast to original-issue U.S. Treasury securities, original-issue GNMA passthrough securities

   a. Provide quarterly payments to the investor.
   b. Have a limited availability of maturities.
   c. Are often issued in zero coupon form.
   d. Have interest payments.

12. **GNMA Bonds**   Which of the following should a bond portfolio manager purchase if the manager is looking for mortgage-backed securities that would perform best during a period of rising interest rates?

   a. A 12 percent GNMA with an average life of 5.6 years.
   b. An 8 percent GNMA with an average life of 6.0 years.
   c. A 10 percent GNMA with an average life of 8.5 years.
   d. A 6 percent GNMA with an average life of 9.0 years.

CFA® PROBLEMS

13. **GNMA Bonds**   Why will the effective yield on a GNMA bond be higher than that of a U.S. Treasury bond with the same quoted yield to maturity? Because

   a. GNMA yields are figured on a 360-day basis.
   b. GNMAs carry higher coupons.
   c. GNMAs have longer compounding periods.
   d. GNMA interest is paid monthly.

14. **Mortgage-Backed Bonds**   If a mortgage-backed bond is issued as a fully modified passthrough security, it means that

   a. Bondholders will receive full and timely payment of principal and interest even if underlying mortgage payments are not made.
   b. The bond has been structured to include both conforming and nonconforming loans.
   c. The interest rates on the underlying mortgages have been altered so that they equal the weighted-average coupon on the bond.
   d. The security carries a balloon payment to ensure that the bond is fully amortized in a set time frame (12 to 15 years).

15. **Prepayments**   Projecting prepayments for mortgage passthrough securities

   a. Requires only a projection of changes in the level of interest rates.
   b. Requires analyzing both economic and demographic variables.
   c. Is not necessary to determine a cash flow yield.
   d. Is not necessary to determine duration.

16. **Prepayments**   A bond analyst at Omnipotent Bank (OB) notices that the prepayment experience on his holdings of high-coupon GNMA issues has been moving sharply higher. What does this indicate?

   a. Interest rates are falling.
   b. The loans comprising OB's pools have been experiencing lower default rates.
   c. The pools held by OB are older issues.
   d. All of the above.

17. **Mortgage-Backed Bonds**   Which of the following statements about mortgage passthrough securities is (are) correct?

   I. Passthroughs offer better call protection than most corporates and Treasuries.
   II. Interest and principal payments are made on a monthly basis.
   III. It is common practice to use the weighted-average maturity on a passthrough in place of its duration.
   IV. Passthroughs are relatively immune from reinvestment risk.

   a. I and III only
   b. II and III only
   c. II only
   d. IV only

18. **Mortgage-Backed Bonds**   Which of the following are advantages of mortgage-backed securities (MBSs)?

   I. MBS yields are above those of similarly rated corporate and U.S. Treasury bonds.
   II. MBSs have high-quality ratings, usually AAA, with some backed by the full faith and credit of the U.S. government.
   III. MBSs have no call provision, thus protecting the investor from having to make a reinvestment decision before maturity.

   a. I and II only
   b. II and III only
   c. I and III only
   d. I, II, and III

19. **Mortgage-Backed Bonds**   Which of the following are characteristics that would make mortgage-backed securities (MBSs) inappropriate for less sophisticated, conservative investors?

   I. The maturity of MBSs is quite variable and difficult to determine.

II. Due to their convexity, the realized total return on MBSs is often more dependent on interest rate levels than other bonds of similar maturity.

III. Due to a possible unfamiliarity with prepayment concepts, investors may not be able to evaluate the true yield on MBS issues.

IV. Many MBS issues are not quoted widely and are difficult to monitor.

a. I, II, and III only
b. I, III, and IV only
c. II and IV only
d. I, II, III, and IV

20. **Collateralized Mortgage Obligations**   For a given mortgage pool, which of the following CMOs based on that pool is the riskiest investment?

a. 100/300 PAC bond
b. A-tranche sequential CMO
c. Interest-only (IO) strip
d. Principal-only (PO) strip

21. **Collateralized Mortgage Obligations**   For a given mortgage pool, which of the following CMOs based on that pool is most likely to increase in price when market interest rates increase?

a. 100/300 PAC bond
b. A-tranche sequential CMO
c. Interest-only (IO) strip
d. Principal-only (PO) strip

22. **MBS Duration**   Higher prepayments have what impact on the effective duration of a mortgage passthrough security?

a. Decrease effective duration for all maturity mortgages.
b. Increase effective duration for all maturity mortgages.
c. Increase (decrease) effective duration for short (long) maturity mortgages.
d. Increase (decrease) effective duration for long (short) maturity mortgages.

23. **MBS Duration**   Which of the following *most accurately* measures interest rate sensitivity for mortgage passthrough securities with prepayment risk?

a. Static duration
b. Effective duration
c. Modified duration
d. Macaulay duration

24. **CMO Duration**   Which of the following *most accurately* measures interest rate sensitivity for collateralized mortgage obligations?

a. Static duration
b. Effective duration
c. Modified duration
d. Macaulay duration

25. **MBS Duration**   The most important difference between effective duration and Macaulay duration for a mortgage passthrough security is that

a. Macaulay duration is easier to calculate.
b. Effective duration is easier to calculate.
c. Macaulay duration accounts for prepayment sensitivity.
d. Effective duration accounts for prepayment sensitivity.

Concept Questions _____

1. **Mortgage Securitization**   How does mortgage securitization benefit borrowers?

2. **Mortgage Securitization**   How does mortgage securitization benefit mortgage originators?

3. **Mortgage Payments**   All else the same, will the payments be higher on a 15-year mortgage or a 30-year mortgage? Why?

4. **Ginnie, Freddie, and Fannie**   From an investor's point of view, what is the difference between mortgage pools backed by GNMA, FNMA, and FHLMC?

5. **Mortgage Pools**   What does it mean for a mortgage pool to be fully modified?

6. **Prepayments**   What are some of the reasons that mortgages are paid off early? Under what circumstances are mortgage prepayments likely to rise sharply? Explain.

7. **Prepayments**   Explain why the right to prepay a mortgage is similar to the call feature contained in most corporate bonds.

8. **Prepayments**   Evaluate the following argument: "Prepayment is not a risk to mortgage investors because prepayment actually means that the investor is paid both in full and ahead of schedule." Is the statement always true or false?

9. **Prepayments**   Mortgage pools also suffer from defaults. Explain how defaults are handled in a fully modified mortgage pool. In the case of a fully modified mortgage pool, explain why defaults appear as prepayments to the mortgage pool investor.

10. **CMOs**   What is a collateralized mortgage obligation? Why do they exist? What are three popular types?

11. **IO and PO Strips**   What are IO and PO strips? Assuming interest rates never change, which is riskier?

12. **IO and PO Strips**   Which has greater interest rate risk, an IO or a PO strip?

13. **Sequential CMOs**   Consider a single whole bond sequential CMO. It has two tranches, an A-tranche and a Z-tranche. Explain how the payments are allocated to the two tranches. Which tranche is riskier?

14. **PACs**   Explain in general terms how a protected amortization class CMO works.

15. **Duration and MBSs**   Why is Macaulay duration an inadequate measure of interest rate risk for an MBS? Why is effective duration a better measure of interest rate risk for an MBS?

Questions and Problems

Core Questions

1. **Mortgage Payments**   What is the monthly payment on a 30-year fixed-rate mortgage if the original balance is $190,000 and the rate is 6.8 percent?

2. **Mortgage Balances**   If a mortgage has monthly payments of $1,060, a life of 30 years, and a rate of 7.2 percent per year, what is the mortgage amount?

3. **Mortgage Payments**   A homeowner takes out a $230,000, 30-year fixed-rate mortgage at a rate of 6.9 percent. What are the monthly mortgage payments?

4. **Mortgage Balance**   You have decided to buy a house. You can get a mortgage rate of 7.1 percent, and you want your payments to be $1,250 or less. How much can you borrow on a 30-year fixed-rate mortgage?

5. **SMM**   What is the single monthly mortality assuming the conditional prepayment rate is 4 percent?

6. **CPR**   What is the conditional prepayment rate if the single monthly mortality is .583 percent?

7. **IO and PO Values**   A $100,000 GNMA passthrough bond issue has a value of $96,483. The value of the interest-only payments is $37,155. What is the value of the principal-only payment?

8. **Mortgage Interest**   A 30-year, $220,000 mortgage has a rate of 7.3 percent. What are the interest and principal portions in the first payment? In the second?

9. **Mortgage Balances**   A homeowner takes a 25-year fixed-rate mortgage for $225,000 at 8.1 percent. After seven years, the homeowner sells the house and pays off the remaining principal. How much is the principal payment?

10. **Mortgage Balances**   Consider a 30-year, $300,000 mortgage with a 7.4 percent interest rate. After six years, the borrower (the mortgage issuer) pays it off. How much will the lender receive?

Intermediate Questions

11. **Prepayments**   Consider a 30-year, $190,000 mortgage with a rate of 8 percent. Nine years into the mortgage, rates have fallen to 6 percent. What would be the monthly saving to a homeowner from refinancing the outstanding mortgage balance at the lower rate?

12. **Prepayments**   Consider a 25-year, $180,000 mortgage with a rate of 8.5 percent. Eight years into the mortgage, rates have fallen to 7 percent. What would be the monthly saving to a homeowner from refinancing the outstanding mortgage balance at the lower rate?

13. **Prepayments**   Consider a 30-year, $215,000 mortgage with a rate of 6.85 percent. Five years into the mortgage, rates have fallen to 6.24 percent. Suppose the transaction cost of obtaining a new mortgage is $2,500. Should the homeowner refinance at the lower rate?

14. **Mortgage Prepayments**   A homeowner took out a 30-year, fixed-rate mortgage of $195,000. The mortgage was taken out six years ago at a rate of 7.82 percent. If the homeowner refinances, the charges will be $3,500. What is the highest interest rate at which it would be beneficial to refinance the mortgage?

15. **Mortgage Prepayments**   A homeowner took out a 30-year fixed-rate mortgage of $170,000. The mortgage was taken out 22 years ago at a rate of 8.15 percent. If the homeowner refinances, the charges will be $3,000. What is the highest interest rate at which it would be beneficial to refinance the mortgage?

16. **CPRs**   What are the conditional prepayment rates for seasoned 50 PSA, 200 PSA, and 400 PSA mortgages if the 100 PSA benchmark is 5 percent per year? How do you interpret these numbers?

17. **SMMs**   In the previous question, what is the single monthly mortality for seasoned 50 PSA, 200 PSA, and 400 PSA mortgages? How do you interpret these numbers?

Spreadsheet Problems

18. **Mortgage Payments**   A 30-year mortgage has an annual interest rate of 7.18 percent and a loan amount of $180,000. What are the monthly mortgage payments?

19. **Mortgage Amortization**   A 30-year mortgage has an annual interest rate of 6.84 percent and a loan amount of $250,000. What are the interest and principal for the 120th payment?

20. **Mortgage Balance**   A 30-year mortgage has an annual interest rate of 7.42 percent and a loan amount of $200,000. What is the remaining balance at the 180th payment?

What's on the Web?

1. **FICC**   Go to www.ficc.com. What is the role of the FICC? What par value of mortgage-backed securities was cleared in each of the last three months?

2. **Fannie Mae**   Go to the mortgage-backed security section at www.fanniemae.com. What were the longest term bonds recently issued by Fannie Mae? What are the coupon rates? What are the coupon rates on the shortest term bonds issued?

3. **SMBS**   Go to the mortgage-backed security section at www.fanniemae.com. Find the SMBS section. What is an SMBS? How do they work? Is an SMBS a suitable investment for most investors?

Appendix A

Answers to Test Your Investment Quotient Questions

Chapter 1

1-1	b (*Source:* 1994 Level I CFA Study Guide © 1994)
1-2	b (*Source:* 2001 Level I CFA Practice Exam © 2001)
1-3	c (*Source:* 2001 Level I CFA Practice Exam © 2001)
1-4	b (*Source:* 2001 Level I CFA Practice Exam © 2001)
1-5	b (*Source:* 2003 Level I CFA Practice Exam © 2003)
1-6	c (*Source:* 1994 Level I CFA Study Guide © 1994)
1-7	d
1-8	a
1-9	a
1-10	d
1-11	d
1-12	d
1-13	d
1-14	a (*Source:* 2003 Level I CFA Practice Exam © 2003)
1-15	b (*Source:* 2001 Level I CFA Practice Exam © 2001)

Chapter 2

2-1	a (*Source:* 2003 Level I CFA Practice Exam © 2003)
2-2	c (*Source:* 2003 Level I CFA Practice Exam © 2003)
2-3	c
2-4	c
2-5	b
2-6	b
2-7	b
2-8	a
2-9	c
2-10	b
2-11	a
2-12	a
2-13	c
2-14	c
2-15	d

Chapter 3

3-1	d
3-2	a
3-3	c
3-4	a
3-5	c
3-6	b
3-7	c
3-8	c
3-9	c
3-10	c (*Source:* 2003 Level I CFA Practice Exam © 2003)

Chapter 4

4-1	c (*Source:* 2001 Level I CFA Practice Exam © 2001)
4-2	b
4-3	d
4-4	d
4-5	d
4-6	d
4-7	a
4-8	b
4-9	a
4-10	c
4-11	b
4-12	d
4-13	a
4-14	a
4-15	d

Chapter 5

5-1	a (*Source:* 1986 Level I CFA Study Guide © 1986)
5-2	b (*Source:* 1986 Level I CFA Study Guide © 1986)
5-3	c
5-4	c (*Source:* 2003 Level I CFA Practice Exam © 2003)
5-5	a (*Source:* 2003 Level I CFA Practice Exam © 2003)
5-6	b (*Source:* 1991 Level I CFA Study Guide © 1991)
5-7	c (*Source:* 1991 Level I CFA Study Guide © 1991)
5-8	a (*Source:* 1991 Level I CFA Study Guide © 1991)
5-9	a (*Source:* 1991 Level I CFA Study Guide © 1991)
5-10	b (*Source:* 1990 Level I CFA Study Guide © 1990)
5-11	c (*Source:* 1990 Level I CFA Study Guide © 1990)
5-12	b
5-13	c
5-14	d
5-15	c

Chapter 6

6-1	c
6-2	a (*Source:* 1994 Level I CFA Study Guide © 1994)
6-3	a (*Source:* 1998 Level I CFA Practice Exam © 1998)
6-4	b (*Source:* 1994 Level I CFA Study Guide © 1994)
6-5	b (*Source:* 1994 Level I CFA Study Guide © 1994)
6-6	c (*Source:* 1994 Level I CFA Study Guide © 1994)
6-7	d (*Source:* 1994 Level I CFA Study Guide © 1994)
6-8	c (*Source:* 1998 Level I CFA Study Guide © 1998)
6-9	c (*Source:* 1994 Level I CFA Study Guide © 1994)
6-10	a (*Source:* 1991 Level I CFA Study Guide © 1991)

6-11 a (*Source:* 1994 Level I CFA Study Guide © 1994)
6-12 d
6-13 d
6-14 c
6-15 c (*Source:* 1998 Level I CFA Study Guide © 1998)
6-16 c (*Source:* 2001 Level I CFA Practice Exam © 2001)
6-17 c (*Source:* 2001 Level I CFA Practice Exam © 2001)
6-18 a
6-19 a
6-20 b

Chapter 7

7-1 d (*Source:* 2003 Level I CFA Practice Exam © 2003)
7-2 c (*Source:* 2001 Level I CFA Practice Exam © 2001)
7-3 d
7-4 d
7-5 c
7-6 a
7-7 a
7-8 d
7-9 c
7-10 d
7-11 c
7-12 d
7-13 b
7-14 d
7-15 d

Chapter 8

8-1 d (*Source:* 1994 Level I CFA Practice Exam © 1994)
8-2 c
8-3 d
8-4 b
8-5 a
8-6 b
8-7 c
8-8 a
8-9 d
8-10 b
8-11 c
8-12 b
8-13 c
8-14 b
8-15 d

Chapter 9

9-1 b
9-2 a
9-3 a
9-4 d
9-5 d (*Source:* 1988 Level I CFA Study Guide © 1988)
9-6 b
9-7 a
9-8 c
9-9 c (*Source:* 1991 Level I CFA Study Guide © 1991)
9-10 b (*Source:* 2001 Level I CFA Practice Exam © 2001)
9-11 a (*Source:* 2001 Level I CFA Practice Exam © 2001)
9-12 a
9-13 d (*Source:* 1993 Level I CFA Study Guide © 1993)
9-14 a (*Source:* 1988 Level I CFA Study Guide © 1988)

9-15 b (*Source:* 1989 Level I CFA Study Guide © 1989)
9-16 a (*Source:* 1992 Level I CFA Study Guide © 1992)
9-17 b
9-18 c
9-19 d (*Source:* 1994 Level I CFA Study Guide © 1994)
9-20 d (*Source:* 1998 Level I CFA Practice Exam © 1998)

Chapter 10

10-1 b (*Source:* 1993 Level I CFA Study Guide © 1993)
10-2 c (*Source:* 1989 Level I CFA Study Guide © 1989)
10-3 d (*Source:* 1992 Level I CFA Study Guide © 1992)
10-4 a
10-5 a
10-6 b (*Source:* 1991 Level I CFA Study Guide © 1991)
10-7 a (*Source:* 1991 Level I CFA Study Guide © 1991)
10-8 a (*Source:* 1998 Level I CFA Practice Exam © 1998)
10-9 b (*Source:* 1992 Level I CFA Study Guide © 1992)
10-10 c (*Source:* 1992 Level I CFA Study Guide © 1992)
10-11 a (*Source:* 1994 Level I CFA Study Guide © 1994)
10-12 a
10-13 c (*Source:* 1988 Level I CFA Study Guide © 1988)
10-14 c (*Source:* 1990 Level I CFA Study Guide © 1990)
10-15 c (*Source:* 1992 Level I CFA Study Guide © 1992)
10-16 a (*Source:* 1991 Level I CFA Study Guide © 1991)
10-17 a (*Source:* 1992 Level I CFA Study Guide © 1992)
10-18 b (*Source:* 1992 Level I CFA Study Guide © 1992)
10-19 a (*Source:* 1992 Level I CFA Study Guide © 1992)
10-20 d (*Source:* 2003 Level I CFA Practice Exam © 2003)
10-21 b
10-22 a
10-23 c
10-24 c (*Source:* 2003 Level I CFA Practice Exam © 2003)
10-25 c (*Source:* 2003 Level I CFA Practice Exam © 2003)

Chapter 11

11-1 d
11-2 c
11-3 c
11-4 b (*Source:* 1994 Level I CFA Study Guide © 1994)
11-5 c (*Source:* 2003 Level I CFA Practice Exam © 2003)
11-6 a (*Source:* 2003 Level I CFA Practice Exam © 2003)
11-7 a (*Source:* 2003 Level I CFA Practice Exam © 2003)
11-8 b
11-9 b
11-10 a
11-11 d
11-12 b
11-13 d
11-14 c (*Source:* 1994 Level I CFA Study Guide © 1994)
11-15 a (*Source:* 1994 Level I CFA Study Guide © 1994)

Chapter 12

12-1 d (*Source:* 1994 Level I CFA Study Guide © 1994)
12-2 a
12-3 a
12-4 d
12-5 b
12-6 b
12-7 b
12-8 c

12-9 d
12-10 d
12-11 d
12-12 a
12-13 b (*Source:* 2003 Level I CFA Practice Exam © 2003)
12-14 a (*Source:* 2003 Level I CFA Practice Exam © 2003)
12-15 b (*Source:* 2003 Level I CFA Practice Exam © 2003)

Chapter 13

13-1 b (*Source:* 1994 Level I CFA Study Guide © 1994)
13-2 a (*Source:* 1994 Level I CFA Study Guide © 1994)
13-3 b (*Source:* 1994 Level I CFA Study Guide © 1994)
13-4 c
13-5 a
13-6 b
13-7 b
13-8 d
13-9 c (*Source:* 1994 Level I CFA Study Guide © 1994)
13-10 c
13-11 d
13-12 a
13-13 d
13-14 b
13-15 c

Chapter 14

14-1 d
14-2 a
14-3 b
14-4 a
14-5 d (*Source:* 1993 Level I CFA Study Guide © 1993)
14-6 a (*Source:* 1999 Level I CFA Practice Exam © 1999)
14-7 c
14-8 d (*Source:* 2003 Level I CFA Practice Exam © 2003)
14-9 c (*Source:* 2003 Level I CFA Practice Exam © 2003)
14-10 d
14-11 a
14-12 d
14-13 d (*Source:* 1993 Level I CFA Study Guide © 1993)
14-14 b
14-15 b
14-16 b
14-17 d
14-18 c
14-19 a
14-20 d

Chapter 15

15-1 a
15-2 c
15-3 d
15-4 c (*Source:* 2003 Level I CFA Practice Exam © 2003)
15-5 c
15-6 b (*Source:* 1992 Level I CFA Study Guide © 1992)
15-7 d
15-8 a
15-9 a (*Source:* 1990 Level I CFA Study Guide © 1990)
15-10 c (*Source:* 1994 Level I CFA Study Guide © 1994)
15-11 a
15-12 b (*Source:* 1993 Level I CFA Study Guide © 1993)

15-13 a (*Source:* 1993 Level I CFA Study Guide © 1993)
15-14 b (*Source:* 1991 Level I CFA Study Guide © 1991)
15-15 d
15-16 a (*Source:* 2003 Level I CFA Practice Exam © 2003)
15-17 d (*Source:* 2003 Level I CFA Practice Exam © 2003)
15-18 c (*Source:* 2003 Level I CFA Practice Exam © 2003)
15-19 d
15-20 c

Chapter 16

16-1 a
16-2 d
16-3 c
16-4 a (*Source:* 1992 Level I CFA Study Guide © 1992)
16-5 d (*Source:* 1990 Level I CFA Study Guide © 1990)
16-6 a (*Source:* 1989 Level I CFA Study Guide © 1989)
16-7 a (*Source:* 1993 Level I CFA Study Guide © 1993)
16-8 b (*Source:* 1998 Level I CFA Study Guide © 1998)
16-9 d
16-10 a
16-11 c
16-12 d
16-13 a
16-14 b
16-15 b

Chapter 17

17-1 b (*Source:* 1999 Level I CFA Practice Exam © 1999)
17-2 b
17-3 d
17-4 c
17-5 a
17-6 a
17-7 b
17-8 d
17-9 c
17-10 a
17-11 b
17-12 c
17-13 c
17-14 b (*Source:* 1994 Level I CFA Study Guide © 1994)
17-15 c (*Source:* 1994 Level I CFA Study Guide © 1994)
17-16 b (*Source:* 1994 Level I CFA Study Guide © 1994)
17-17 a (*Source:* 1994 Level I CFA Study Guide © 1994)
17-18 b (*Source:* 1994 Level I CFA Study Guide © 1994)
17-19 c
17-20 d

Chapter 18

18-1 d (*Source:* 1990 Level I CFA Study Guide © 1990)
18-2 c (*Source:* 1988 Level I CFA Study Guide © 1988)
18-3 a (*Source:* 1989 Level I CFA Study Guide © 1989)
18-4 c (*Source:* 1990 Level I CFA Study Guide © 1990)
18-5 c (*Source:* 1998 Level I CFA Practice Exam © 1998)
18-6 a
18-7 b (*Source:* 1991 Level I CFA Study Guide © 1991)
18-8 a
18-9 b (*Source:* 2003 Level I CFA Practice Exam © 2003)
18-10 b
18-11 c (*Source:* 1992 Level I CFA Study Guide © 1992)

18-12 a (*Source:* 1989 Level I CFA Study Guide © 1989)
18-13 d (*Source:* 1990 Level I CFA Study Guide © 1990)
18-14 a
18-15 c (*Source:* 1998 Level I CFA Practice Exam © 1998)
18-16 b (*Source:* 1990 Level I CFA Study Guide © 1990)
18-17 b (*Source:* 1988 Level I CFA Study Guide © 1988)
18-18 d (*Source:* 1994 Level I CFA Study Guide © 1994)
18-19 b (*Source:* 1991 Level I CFA Study Guide © 1991)
18-20 c (*Source:* 1993 Level I CFA Study Guide © 1993)
18-21 c (*Source:* 1991 Level I CFA Study Guide © 1991)
18-22 d (*Source:* 1994 Level I CFA Study Guide © 1994)
18-23 d
18-24 b
18-25 a (*Source:* 2003 Level I CFA Practice Exam © 2003)

Chapter 19

19-1 a
19-2 c
19-3 a
19-4 c (*Source:* 1990 Level I CFA Study Guide © 1990)
19-5 b (*Source:* 1998 Level I CFA Practice Exam © 1998)
19-6 b
19-7 d
19-8 b
19-9 b
19-10 a
19-11 b
19-12 a
19-13 a
19-14 c
19-15 d (*Source:* 1992 Level I CFA Study Guide © 1992)
19-16 d (*Source:* 1989 Level I CFA Study Guide © 1989)
19-17 d
19-18 a

19-19 b
19-20 c (*Source:* 1990 Level I CFA Study Guide © 1990)
19-21 d
19-22 b (*Source:* 1991 Level I CFA Study Guide © 1991)
19-23 b (*Source:* 1992 Level I CFA Study Guide © 1992)
19-24 a (*Source:* 1991 Level I CFA Study Guide © 1991)
19-25 a (*Source:* 1994 Level I CFA Study Guide © 1994)

Chapter 20

20-1 d
20-2 a
20-3 c
20-4 c
20-5 a
20-6 c
20-7 b
20-8 c
20-9 b
20-10 c (*Source:* 1988 Level I CFA Study Guide © 1988)
20-11 b (*Source:* 1988 Level I CFA Study Guide © 1988)
20-12 a (*Source:* 1989 Level I CFA Study Guide © 1989)
20-13 d (*Source:* 1991 Level I CFA Study Guide © 1991)
20-14 a (*Source:* 1991 Level I CFA Study Guide © 1991)
20-15 b (*Source:* 1990 Level I CFA Study Guide © 1990)
20-16 a (*Source:* 1989 Level I CFA Study Guide © 1989)
20-17 c (*Source:* 1991 Level I CFA Study Guide © 1991)
20-18 a (*Source:* 1991 Level I CFA Study Guide © 1991)
20-19 d (*Source:* 1989 Level I CFA Study Guide © 1989)
20-20 c
20-21 c
20-22 a
20-23 b
20-24 b
20-25 d

Appendix B

Answers to Selected Questions and Problems

Chapter 1

1-1 $920
1-5 Jurassic average return = 7.40%
Stonehenge average return = 8.20%
1-9 Arithmetic average = 11.17%
Geometric average = 9.50%
1-13 Probability of doubling = 0.62%
Probability of tripling = 0.0000017%
1-17 Small company stocks = 12.15%
Long-term government bonds = 5.45%
Treasury bills = 3.79%
Inflation = 3.05%

Chapter 2

2-1 313.25 shares
2-5 $23,636.36
2-9 Critical stock price = $64.62
Account equity = $19,380
2-13 $49.29
2-17 $1,916.68
2-21 −30.90%
2-25 Effective annual return = 27.44%

Chapter 3

3-1 Closing price = $22.82
Round lots = 2,855
3-5 Next payment = $16,800
Payments at maturity = $416,800
3-9 Current yield = 6.10%
Treasury yield = 4.36%
3-13 $33,675
3-20 107.36%

Chapter 4

4-1 $34.62
4-5 $26.33
4-9 $17.46; −12.54%
4-13 2.74%
4-18 $7,380
4-21 5.73%
4-25 $103,500

Chapter 5

5-1 2.22892
5-5 14.18%

5-9 4.10843
5-13 0.334896

Chapter 6

6-1 $43.02
6-5 $374.63
6-9 $2.16; $2.36
6-13 $60.25
6-17 $17.77
6-22 $29.19
6-25 16.42 times
6-29 $87.31
6-33 ROE = 11.87%
$g = 8.31\%$

Chapter 7

None

Chapter 8

8-2 0.822; 0.947; 1.035; 1.001; 0.771
8-6 0.5200; 0.5333; 0.4733; 0.5467; 0.5800
8-15 0.7241; 1.0230; 0.9356; 0.8310

Chapter 9

9-1 68:28
9-5 7.90%
9-9 $997,112.50
9-13 BEY = 6.555%
Discount yield = 6.329%
9-17 5-year STRIP = 74:26
$f_{1,5} = 5.976\%$
2-year STRIP = 88:26
$f_{2,3} = 6.112\%$
9-21 $f_{1,1} = 6.51\%$
$f_{1,2} = 7.16\%$
$f_{1,3} = 7.84\%$

Chapter 10

10-1 $1,068.34
10-5 9.68%
10-9 10.48%
10-13 11.06%
10-19 10.71%
10-21 YTM = 8.07%
Realized yield = 3.20%

10-25 $0.769

10-29 Macaulay duration = 11.844
Modified duration = 11.443

10-33 6.65%

Chapter 11

11-1 11.80%

11-5 Roll = 18.62%
Ross = 6.37%

11-9 *a.* 7.93%
b. 0.03419; 18.49%

11-17 Standard deviation = 39.93%
Expected return = 14.13%

11-20 Standard deviation = 37.06%
Expected return = 14.20%

Chapter 12

12-1 1.28

12-5 1.035

12-9 $52.80

12-13 3.00%

12-17 1.27

12-23 Expected return = 0.645%
Standard deviation = 2.13%

Chapter 13

13-1 22.05%

13-4 Monthly standard deviation = 14.96%
Annual standard deviation = 53.94%

13-9 −28.12%

13-13 −15.42%

13-18 −132.56%

13-21 −11.76%

Chapter 14

14-1 *a.* $35,775
b. $1,121,250
c. $16,250
d. −$180

14-5 $13,857,626,125

14-9 $75.08

14-13 Day 1: $214,875
Day 2: $120,375
Day 3: $151,875
Day 4: $120,375
Profit = −$105,000

14-17 923.43

14-21 5334.9

14-25 *a.* 190.55
b. 190.40

Chapter 15

15-1 $4,000

15-5 $70,000; $25,000

15-9 $82.42

15-13 $10.54

15-16 $1,900

Chapter 16

16-1 $25.23

16-5 $5.81

16-9 3,544

16-13 $40

16-17 $18.12

16-20 45.92%

Chapter 17

17-1 $19,745

17-5 P/B = 3.89 times
P/E = 22.55 times
P/CF = 14.94 times

17-9 $97,000

17-13 P/B = 5.03 times
P/E = 12.97 times
P/CF = 9.47 times

17-17 Maximum sales growth = 17.65%

Chapter 18

18-1 $28.57

18-5 $940

18-8 $84

18-12 Conversion value = $880
Conversion price = $47.73

Chapter 19

19-1 $2,293.38

19-5 3.95%

19-9 5.87%

19-13 $1,123.75

19-17 2.62%

Chapter 20

20-1 $1,238.66

20-5 0.34%

20-9 $198,805.34

20-13 $60.68

20-17 50 PSA: 0.2108%
200 PSA: 0.8742%
400 PSA: 1.8423%

Name Index

Page numbers followed by n indicate notes.

Equation Index

Page numbers followed by n indicate notes.

A

Abnormal return, 213
Actual return, 408
Aftertax yield, 643
Announcement, 392
Arithmetic average dividend growth
rate, 169
Arms, 263–264
Assets, 551

B

Bank discount basis, 289
Basis, 462
Beta, 399–400, 402, 408, 410, 411
Black-Scholes-Merton option pricing,
518–519
Blume's formula, 26
Bond duration, 337–338
Bond equivalent yield, 291
Bond hedging with futures, 468
Bond price, 321–322, 330,
336, 626
Book value per share, 554

C

Callable bond price, 330
Call option delta, 525–526
Call option eta, 526
Call option intrinsic value, 497
Call option price, 498,
518–519
Capital asset pricing model,
405–406
Capital gains yield, 4
Carrying-charge market, 462
Cash flow per share, 554
Clean surplus relationship, 179
Compounding, 284
Constant growth rate model, 166
Constant perpetual growth model, 167, 179
Conversion price, 595
Conversion ratio, 595
Conversion value, 595
Coupon rate, 320
Critical marginal tax rate, 643
Critical price, 46
Current yield, 321

D

Discount basis, 289
Discounting, 284
Discount rate, 177
Dividend-adjusted spot-futures
parity, 464
Dividend discount model, 165
Dividend yield, 4
Dollar value of an 01, 340
Duration of futures contracts, 468

E

Earnings per share, 554
Earnings yield, 180
Effective annual rate, 293
Effective annual return, 46
Equivalent taxable yield, 643
Expected return, 399–400, 402, 408, 439

F

Forward rate, 306–307
Futures price, 463
Future value, 301
Future value of money, 284

G

Geometric average dividend growth
rate, 169
Geometric average return, 24
Gross margin, 554

H

Hedging with futures, 467, 468
Hedging with stock index options, 536
Hedging with stock options, 534–535
Historical variance, 19

I

Implied volatility, 529–530
Index divisor, 153
Interest rate futures contracts, 468
Inverted market, 462

J

Jensen's alpha, 427

M

Macaulay duration, 335
Market sentiment index, 259
Minimum variance portfolio, 374–375
Modified duration, 336
Mortgage monthly payment, 654–655
Moving averages, 267–268

N

Net income, 552
Nominal interest rates, 309, 311

O

Operating margin, 554
Option intrinsic value, 497
Option price, 498, 502, 518–519

P

Par value bond duration, 337
Percentage change in bond
price, 336
Portfolio betas, 398–399
Portfolio expected return, 361–362, 427,
432, 439
Portfolio return, 363, 376
Portfolio risk, 370–371
Portfolio variance, 362–363, 370–371,
376, 432
Present value, 301
Present value of money, 284
Price-book ratio, 184, 554
Price-cash flow ratio, 181, 554
Price-earnings ratio, 180, 554
Price-sales ratio, 184
Put-call parity, 500–501
Put option delta, 525–526
Put option eta, 526
Put option intrinsic value, 497
Put option price, 498, 502,
518–519

R

Real interest rate, 302
Residual income model, 178–179, 571–572
Return on assets, 554
Return on equity, 170, 554
Reward-to-risk ratio, 400, 402
Risk and return, 403
Risk premium, 358

S

Security market line, 405
Sharpe optimal portfolio, 432, 440
Sharpe ratio, 426
Single monthly mortality, 664
SML slope, 405
Spot-futures parity, 463–464
Standard deviation, 19, 359, 363, 371, 439

Stock index futures, 467
Stock index options, 536
Stock options, 534–535
Straight bond prices, 321–322
STRIPS price, 301, 623
STRIPS yield, 301
STRIPS yield to maturity, 624
Surprise, 390, 393
Sustainable growth rate, 170
Systematic risk, 408–409

T

T-bill price, 292
Time value of money, 284
Total percent return, 4
Total return, 393, 408
Total risk, 395
Treynor index, 400n

Treynor ratio, 426
Trin, 263–264
Two-stage dividend growth model, 173–174

U

Unexpected return, 390, 393
Unsystematic risk, 408–409

V

Variance, 19, 359, 370–371
VaR statistics, 439
Vega, 526–527

Y

Yield to maturity, 624
Yield value of a 32nd, 340

Subject Index

Page numbers followed by n indicate notes; by f, figures; by t, tables.

A

AAII (American Association of Individual Investors), 193
Abnormal returns, 213–214
Account equity, 42, 51
Accrued interest, 326
Adjustable-rate bonds, 606, 639
Adjustable-rate preferred stock, 606
Advance/decline line, 263
Advanced Micro Devices, 595–596
Advisory accounts, 48
After-tax returns, 61
Agency securities, 632–633; *see also* *specific agency*
AIM Aggressive Growth Fund, 377
AllianceBernstein Investment Research and Management, 255
AllianceBernstein Wealth Appreciation Strategies Fund, 255
Alliance Capital Management, 254
Alpha, 427–428
AlphaSimplex Group, 434
Alternative investments, 82
Ambac Assurance Corporation, 642
Ambac Financial Group Inc., 642
American Association of Individual Investors (AAII), 193
American Electric Power, 140, 167–168, 171
American Express, 140, 174
American Funds, 121
American options, 88, 480, 502–503
American Stock Exchange (AMEX), 138, 481, 536, 612
America Online (AOL), 391
AMEX (American Stock Exchange), 138, 481, 536, 612
Amex Internet Index, 233–234
Amortization, 655–661
Analyst's Accounting Observer (Ciesielski), 521
Announcements and news, 211–213, 228, 390–392
Annualized returns, 46–48
Annual percentage rate (APR), 293–295
Annual reports, 103, 548, 553–554
Appaloosa Management, 182
Apple Computer, 148
APR (annual percentage rate), 293–295
APT (arbitrage pricing theory), 406n
Arbitrage
    cash-futures, 461–462

definition, 496
index, 465–466
limits to, 256–259
market efficiency and, 207–208
option, 496–498
Arbitrage pricing theory (APT), 406n
Arbitration, 41
Arcelor, 182
Arithmetic average dividend growth rate, 168–170
Arithmetic average return, 24, 26–27
Armor All Products Corporation, 598
Artisan Funds, 120
Asian crash, 232–233
Ask price, 138
Asset allocation
    bond funds and, 371–372, 432
    correlation and, 371–373
    definition, 371
    investor objectives and, 62–63, 81–82, 334
    Markowitz efficient frontier and, 375–378
    rebalancing, 81–82, 367
Asset allocation funds, 113
Asset management accounts, 49
Assets, 60, 61, 549–550
Asset-specific risk, 393, 395
Association for Investment Management and Research, 193
At-the-money, 497
AT&T, 136
AT&T Wireless, 136
Availability bias, 255
Average life, 664–665
Average returns, 12–17, 23–27

B

Back-end load, 104
Balanced funds, 113
Balance sheets, 549–551, 558, 566–570
Banc of America Specialist, Inc., 140
BancOne, 255
Bank discount basis, 288–289
Bank discount yields, 288, 291–292
Banker's acceptances, 287
Banks
    CDs, 74, 286–287
    FDIC insurance, 40, 109
    money market deposit accounts, 109
    money market interest rates, 285–288
Barings Bank, 247–248
Base-year values, 153–154

Basis, 462
Basis points, 76, 288, 340
Baylor University, 367
Bearer bonds, 640
Bear markets, 17, 259–260
Bear Stearns, 567
"Beating the market," 207, 427
Behavioral finance
    about, 244–245
    definition, 245
    limits to arbitrage, 256–259
    overconfidence, 249–250
    prospect theory, 245–249
    randomness and chance events, 250–256
    sentiment-based risk, 256
Bell curve, 20
Bellwether rate, 285
Berkshire, 218
Berkshire Hathaway Inc., 219
Best effort, 135
Beta coefficient
    calculating, 410–412
    definition, 396
    discount rates and, 177
    Fama-French three-factor model, 414
    portfolio, 398–399
    portfolio returns and, 401
    returns and, 408–409
    risk premium and, 399–400
    source of, 409–412
    systematic risk and, 395–399
Bid-ask spread, 628, 638
Bid price, 138, 629
Bid rates, 286
Big Board; *see* New York Stock Exchange
Black Monday, 230
Black-Scholes-Merton option pricing model
    about, 516–520
    Coca-Cola employee options pricing, 520–521
    computing, 517–519, 527–528
    dividend yield, 525
    interest rate, 524–525
    measuring changes to variables
        delta, 525–526, 527
        eta, 526, 527
        gamma, 528–529
        rho, 528–529
        theta, 528–529
        vega, 526–528
    stock price, 522–523, 525–526

695

Black-Scholes-Merton option pricing
model—*Cont.*
  stock price volatility, 523–524, 526–527,
    529–530
  strike price, 523
  time remaining to expiration, 523–524
Black Tuesday, 230
Block trades, 264
Bloomberg, 298
Blue chip stocks, 117n
Blume's formula, 26
BNP Paribas, 296
Bollinger bands, 268, 269
Bond(s); *see also subsequent bond entries*
  asset allocation and, 82
  basics, 320–321
  in bear markets, 17
  common stocks compared, 587
  dedicated portfolios, 342, 344–346
  definitions, 604–605
  Federal Reserve and, 296–297, 305
  hedging with futures, 468–469
  markets and trading, 611–612
  NYSE-listed, 612
  as unsecured debt, 588
Bond equivalent yields, 291–295
Bond features
  basis points, 76, 288, 340
  call provisions, 329–331, 591–594, 637
  conversion to stock, 79, 595–597
  coupon, 74–75, 299, 587, 602, 623
  current yield, 75, 320–321
  event risk, 603
  fixed-income, 74
  interest; *see* Coupon
  intermediate-term, 17, 21
  leap year equivalent yields, 292
  maturity, 332, 335–340, 600
  par, 323, 587
  principal payments, 587, 600
  protective covenants, 602–603
  put features, 594–595, 638–639
  reinvestment risk, 342–343
  relationships among yield measures,
    325–326
  seniority, 589, 591
  sinking funds, 600–601
Bond funds, 110–113, 371–372, 432
Bond indenture provisions
  bonds without indentures, 603–605
  bond-to-stock conversion, 595–599
  call features, 591–594
  coupon payments, 602
  maturity and principal payments, 600
  put features, 594–595
  seniority, 591
  sinking funds, 600–601
Bond Market Association, 634–635
Bond prices; *see also* Yield to maturity
  accrued interest and, 326
  clean, 326
  convertible bonds, 597–599
  corporate bonds, 75–77

dirty, 326
duration, 335–340
immunization, 344–346
interest rate risk and, 331–332, 340–341
Malkiel's theorems, 332–335
premium and discount bonds, 323–325
price-yield curve, 592–593
reinvestment rate risk and, 345
risk measures based on duration,
  340–341
straight bonds, 321–323
Treasury bonds, 327, 626–628
yield to call, 329–331, 626
Bond refunding, 591, 592
Bond types; *see also* Corporate bonds;
    Government bonds; Municipal bonds
  adjustable-rate, 606
  bearer, 640
  bullet, 587
  catastrophe, 601
  collateral trust, 589
  convertible, 79, 595–599
  debentures, 588, 591
  equipment trust certificates, 589
  exchangeable, 598–599
  general obligation, 299, 636, 639
  government, 6–9, 11, 13–14, 25
  high-yield, 297, 588, 608–611
  hybrid, 640
  indentureless, 603–605
  junk, 297, 588, 608–611
  limited tax, 639
  long-term, 6–9, 11, 13–15, 21, 25
  moral obligation, 640
  mortgage, 588–589
  100-year maturity, 600
  par, 323–325
  plain vanilla, 587
  private activity, 644
  registered, 640
  revenue, 299, 639
  serial, 600, 637
  straight, 320, 321–323
  tax-exempt, 297–299
  term, 600, 637–638
  unlimited tax, 639
  variable-rate, 639
  Yankee, 297
  zero coupon, 299–302, 623–625
Book-to-market ratio, 184, 414
Book value per share (BVPS), 554
Boston Stock Exchange (BSE), 138
Break-even, 247
Breckinridge Capital, 642
Brokerage accounts
  advisory accounts, 48
  arbitration clauses, 41
  asset management accounts, 49
  cash accounts, 41
  discretionary accounts, 49
  futures trading accounts, 458–460
  getting started, 39–41
  margin; *see* Margin accounts

mutual funds as alternative to, 49
street name registration, 48
wrap accounts, 49
Brokers
  choosing, 39–40
  commissions, 39–40
  customer relations, 40–41
  dealers and, 138
  "house" margin requirements, 43
  online, 40
  services provided by, 39–40
BSE (Boston Stock Exchange), 138
Bubbles, 229, 232–234
Buffett-Falk & Co., 218
Bullet bonds, 587
Bull markets, 259–260
Bureau of Public Debt, 626
Buttonwood Tree Agreement, 134
Buying securities; *see* Brokerage
    accounts; Brokers
BVPS (book value per share), 554

C

Callable at par, 329
Callable bonds, 329–331, 591–594
Call money rate, 41, 286
Call options; *see also* Options; Option
    valuation
  about, 88–91, 480
  arbitrage, 497–498
  Black-Scholes-Merton pricing model,
    518–519
  covered calls, 494
  delta, 525–526, 527
  employee stock options, 498–500
  eta, 526, 527
  gamma, 528–529
  hedging stock with, 534–535
  in-the-money, 488, 497
  intrinsic value of, 497–498
  out-of-the-money, 488, 497
  payoffs, 489–492
  pricing, 496–498
  profits, 492
  put-call parity, 500–502
  rho, 528–529
  stocks versus options, 486–487
  theta, 528–529
  vega, 526–528
  writing, 489, 491
Call premium, 592, 637
Call price, 329
Call protection period, 329–330,
    592, 637
Call provisions, 329–331, 591–594, 637
Call writer, 489
Capital appreciation funds, 110
Capital asset pricing model (CAPM), 177,
    405–406, 412–414
Capital gains and losses, 2–3
Capital gains yield, 4
Capital intensity ratio, 558

Portfolios
    beta coefficients and, 398–399
    dedicated, 342, 344–346
    definition, 360
    diversification and asset allocation in,
        360–364
    efficient, 373
    expected returns, 361–362
    hedging with futures, 466–469
    hedging with stock index options,
        536–538
    inefficient, 373
    market, 405
    rebalancing, 81–82, 367
    Sharpe-optimal, 431–433
    variance, 362–364, 370–371, 372–373
Portfolio weights, 360–361
Positive convexity, 592
Positive correlation, 368–369
Positive covenants, 602
POs (principal-only strips), 669–671
Preferred habitat theory, 308
Preferred stocks, 78–81, 605–606
Premium bonds, 323–326
Prepayment
    GNMA mortgage default and,
        662–663
    Macaulay duration deficiency,
        666–668
    mortgage, 656–657, 661–662
    PSA model, 664–665
    refinancing and, 656–657, 661–662
Prepayment rate, 664
Prepayment risk, 662, 666–668
Present value, 301
Pretax income, 552
Price-book ratio, 184, 554
Price-cash flow (P/CF) ratio, 181–184, 554
Price channels, 265–266
Price-earnings (P/E) ratio, 180–181,
    228, 554
Price quotes; see Wall Street Journal
Price ratio analysis
    applications of, 184–186
    McGraw-Hill Company case study,
        190–191
    price-book ratio, 184
    price-cash flow ratios, 181–184
    price-earnings ratios, 180–181
    price-sales ratios, 184
    using, 190–191
Price ratios
    performance ratios and, 553–556
    projected profitability and, 562–563
    Starbucks Corporation case study,
        570–571
    of value stocks, 555
Price risk, 344
Price-sales ratio, 184
Price-weighted indexes, 151–153
Primary assets, 84
Primary market, 135–136
Prime rate, 285

Primitive assets, 84
Principal, 587, 600
Principal-only strips (POs), 669–671
Principal strips, 623
Principle of diversification, 366
Private activity bonds, 644
Private placements, 603–605
The Probability of Fortune
    (Milevsky), 495
Proceeds from sale, 51
Pro forma balance sheets, 558, 566–570
Pro forma financial statements, 556
Pro forma income statements, 556–558,
    564–566
Program trading, 231, 465–466
Projected risk premium, 358
Promised yield, 321, 331–332
Prospect theory, 245–249
Prospectuses, 103, 105, 136, 591
Protected amortization class (PAC) bonds,
    672–675
Protective covenants, 602–603
Protective put strategy, 493
Prudent investment guidelines, 608
PSA (Public Securities Association),
    664–665
PSE (Pacific Stock Exchange), 138
Public Securities Association (PSA)
        mortgage prepayment model,
        664–665
Pure discount securities, 288
Put bonds, 594–595, 638–639
Put-call parity, 500–502
Put dates, 594
Put options; see also Options; Option
        valuation
    about, 88–91, 480
    arbitrage, 498
    Black-Scholes-Merton pricing model,
        518–519
    delta, 525–526, 527
    eta, 526, 527
    gains and losses, 487
    gamma, 528–529
    hedging stock with, 535
    in-the-money, 488, 497
    intrinsic value of, 497–498
    out-of-the-money, 488, 497
    payoffs, 491–492
    pricing, 496–498
    profits, 492–493
    protective put strategy, 493
    put-call parity, 500–502
    rho, 528–529
    theta, 528–529
    vega, 526–528
    writing, 489, 492
Put price, 594
Put writer, 489

R

Rainier Investment Management, 567
Randomness, 250–256
Random walk, 211
Rate of return, 4
Rating agencies, 606
Ratios
    book-to-market, 184, 414
    capital intensity, 558
    conversion, 595
    market-book, 184, 414
    payout, 170
    performance, 553–556
    plowback, 557
    price-book, 184, 554
    price-cash flow, 181–184, 554
    price-earnings, 180–181, 228, 554
    price-sales, 184
    retention, 170, 557
    reward-to-risk, 400–404
    Sharpe, 426, 434
    Sortino, 434
    Treynor, 426–427
Raw return, 426
Real interest rates, 302–303
Realized returns, 357
Realized yield, 331–332
Recency bias, 254–255
Redemption value, 622
Red herrings, 136
Reduced Value index options, 503
Refunding provisions, 591, 592
Registered bonds, 640
Regret aversion, 248
Regulation FD (Fair Disclosure), 548
Reinvestment rate risk, 342–345
REITs, 16–17
Relative strength, 264
Relevant information problem, 217
Representativeness heuristic, 251
Residual income, 178
Residual income model (RIM), 178–180,
    189–190, 571–573
Resistance levels, 261
Resolution Trust Funding Corporation, 632
Retained earnings, 170, 551, 552
Retention ratio, 170, 557
Retirement plans, 61, 100, 125
Return on assets (ROA), 554
Return on equity (ROE), 554
Returns; see also Risk and return
    abnormal, 213–214
    after-tax, 61
    annualized, 46–48
    average, 12–17, 24–27
    correlation of, 368–370
    dollar, 2–4, 22
    effective annual, 46–48
    excess, 207
    expected; see Expected returns
    historical; see Historical returns
    holding periods and, 46–48

Q

percentage, 4–6, 22
portfolio, 400–401
professional money managers, 62
raw, 426
realized, 357
total, 408
uncorrelated, 368
unexpected, 390, 392, 409
Revenue bonds, 299, 639
Reversal patterns, 265
Reverse trades, 459–460
Reward-to-risk ratio, 400–404
Rho, 528–529
RIM (residual income model), 178–180,
    189–190, 571–573
Risk; *see also* Diversification; Hedging
asset-specific, 393, 395
common stocks, 78
default, 74, 77, 310–311, 635, 641
diversifiable, 366, 395
event, 603
firm-specific, 256
fixed-income securities, 74, 76–77
growth mutual funds, 110
interest rate, 309–310, 331–335,
    340–341, 468–469
liquidity, 310–311
market, 393, 395, 466–467
market efficiency versus, 217
money market instruments, 74
mutual fund performance and, 119
noise trader, 256
nondiversifiable, 366, 395
portfolio, 364–367, 369–370, 370–371
preferred stocks, 78
prepayment, 662, 666–668
price, 344
reinvestment rate, 342–345
reward and, 15–16, 22, 27–29, 59–60
reward-to-risk ratio, 400–404
sentiment-based, 256
short selling, 55
small-company stocks, 8–9
systematic; *see* Systematic risk
total, 395, 398, 407
unique, 393, 395
unsystematic, 392–395, 409
Risk-adjustment problem, 217
Risk and return
about, 389–390
announcements and news, 390–392
beta, 395–399
correlation, 374–375
diversification, 394–395
expected and unexpected returns, 390
investor risk tolerance, 59–60
large-company stocks, 28
potential reward and, 22
return, 374–375
for risky assets, 15–16
security market line, 399–406
small-company stocks, 28
systematic risk, 392–399

tradeoffs, 27–28, 374–375
unsystematic risk, 392–395
Risk-averse behavior, 245
Risk-averse investors, 59–60
Risk-free rate, 15, 27–28
Risk management; *see* Investment
    risk management
Risk premium
beta and, 399–400
calculating, 358
definition, 15, 389
risk-return tradeoff, 27–28, 177
Risk-taking behavior, 245
Risk tolerance, 56–60
ROA (return on assets), 554
ROE (return on equity), 554
Roth IRAs (Individual Retirement
    Accounts), 61
Round lots, 80
Royal Dutch/Shell price ratio example,
    257–258
Royal Swedish Academy of Sciences, 516
Russell 1000 Index, 112
Russell 2000 Index, 413

S

Safety First pension fund example, 342–346
Sales charge, 104
Salomon Smith Barney, 537
Samson Capital Advisors, 642
Santa Clara University, 437
Savings bonds, 622, 631–632
Scheduled sinking fund redemption, 600
Schwab 1000 Fund, 112
Seasoned mortgages, 664
SEC; *see* Securities and Exchange Commission
Secondary market, 135–138
Sector funds, 111
Securities and Exchange Commission (SEC)
bond regulation by, 591, 612
Coca-Cola ESO valuation rules, 521
EDGAR archives, 548
financial information from, 548
hedge funds regulation, 124
illegal trading activities monitoring,
    215–216
IPO regulation by, 136
options regulation by, 485
Regulation FD, 548
12b-1 fees, 104
uptick rule suspension by, 144n
Securities Exchange Act of 1934, 43
Security analysis, 63, 164; *see also* Common
    stock valuation
Security Investors Protection Corporation
    (SIPC), 40
Security market line (SML)
beta and risk premium, 399–400
capital asset pricing model, 405–406
definition, 389–390, 405
market portfolios, 405
reward-to-risk ratio, 400–404

Security selection, 63
Security types
classifying, 73
derivatives, 84–87
    futures contracts, 84–87
    option contracts, 88–91
equities, 78–81
    common stock, 78, 79–81, 91
    preferred stock, 78–81
interest-bearing assets, 73–77
    fixed-income securities, 74–77
    money market instruments, 74
primary assets, 84
Self-attribution bias, 255
Selling securities; *see* Brokerage accounts;
    Brokers
Semistrong-form efficient markets, 209
Senior debentures, 589, 591
Sentiment-based risk, 256
Separate Trading of Registered Interest and
    Principal of Securities; *see* STRIPS
Sequential CMOs, 671–673
Serial bonds, 600, 637
Series EE savings bonds, 631
Series I savings bonds, 631–632
ShareBuilder Securities Corporation, 125
Shareholder equity, 551
Sharpe-optimal portfolios, 431–433, 440
Sharpe ratio, 426, 434
Short hedge, 457
Short interest, 53–55
Short positions, 49, 51, 456
Short-sale orders, 144
Short sales, 49–55, 144, 271
Short-term bond funds, 112
Short-term mutual funds, 107–109
Sigma, 523–524, 526–527, 529–530
Simple interest rates, 293
Simple moving averages, 267
Single-country funds, 111
Single monthly mortality (SMM), 664
Single-price auctions, 629
Single-state municipal bond funds,
    113, 634
Single-stock futures contracts, 462–463
Sinking fund, 600–601, 636–638
Sinking fund call price, 600
SIPC (Security Investors Protection
    Corporation), 40
"Sleeping Beauty" bonds, 600
Small-company funds, 110
Small-company stocks
average returns, 12–17
in bear markets, 17
geometric versus arithmetic average
    returns, 25
growth stocks, 22–23
historical record, 6–8, 10f, 366–367,
    413, 414
market capitalization, 7, 110
return variability for, 21
risk-return tradeoff, 28
total returns (1926–2005), 10f

With the purchase of a New Book*

You Can Access the Real Financial Data that the Experts Use!

*If you purchased a used book, see other side for access information.

This card entitles the purchaser of a new textbook to a semester of access to the Educational Version of Standard & Poor's Market Insight®, a rich online resource featuring hundreds of the most often researched companies in the Market Insight database.

For 1,000 companies, this website provides you:

- Access to six years' worth of fundamental financial data from the renowned Standard & Poor's COMPUSTAT® database
- 12 Excel Analytics Reports, including balance sheets, income statements, ratio reports and cash flow statements; adjusted prices reports, and profitability; forecasted values and monthly valuation data reports
- Access to Financial Highlights Reports including key ratios
- S & P Stock Reports that offer fundamental, quantitative and technical analysis
- EDGAR reports updated throughout the day
- Industry Surveys, written by S & P's Equity analysts
- News feeds (updated hourly) for companies and industries.

STANDARD &POOR'S

McGraw-Hill Irwin

See other side for your unique site ID access code.

Welcome to the Educational Version of Market Insight!

www.mhhe.com/edumarketinsight

Check out your textbook's website for details on how this special offer enhances the value of your purchase!

1. To get started, use your web browser to go to **www.mhhe.com/edumarketinsight**

2. Enter your site ID exactly as it appears below.

3. You may be prompted to enter the site ID for future use—please keep this card.

Your site ID is:

> ra2a8a25

STANDARD &POOR'S

ISBN: 978-0-07-325739-6
MHID: 0-07-325739-7

Mc Graw Hill McGraw-Hill Irwin

---

*If you purchased a used book, this site ID may have expired. For new password purchase, please go to www.mhhe.com/edumarketinsight. Password activation is good for a 6 month duration.

Instructor Support to Fit All of Your Course Needs

By accessing the Online Learning Center (OLC), you can view everything your students see, plus the following password-protected support items:

- Instructor's Manual and PowerPoints
- Solutions Manual
- Excel Template Solutions
- Video clips & suggested video exercises to go along with each clip
- Teaching Notes to accompany *Investments Online*

The following support materials are located on the Instructor's Resource CD-ROM:

- Instructor's Manual
- Solutions Manual
- Test Bank/Computerized Test Bank
- Instructor's PowerPoints

S&P

A free (with each new text purchased) exclusive partnership through McGraw-Hill/Irwin and the Institutional Market Services division of Standard & Poor's allows you and your students to access this rich online database. Containing six years of fundamental financial data for over 1,000 companies, your students can use this database to research and help answer the corresponding end-of-chapter S&P problems. For more details and to register, please see the bound-in card inside the front cover of this text or visit **www.mhhe.com/edumarketinsight**.